VII Java

36 Introduction to Java   963

37 Developing Java Applets   981

About the Authors

Eric Ladd (eric@rockcreekweb.com) is the owner and chief developer for Rock Creek Web Solutions, a Web-based applications development firm in Arlington, Virginia. In addition to his development work, he is a member of the Interactive Multimedia and Web Development faculty at the George Washington University in Washington, DC. Eric has worked on nearly a dozen titles for Que, including (with his co-author, Jim O'Donnell) *Platinum Edition Using HTML 4, Java 1.1, and JavaScript 1.2, Second Edition, Special Edition Using Microsoft Internet Explorer 4*, and *Using HTML 4*.

Eric earned two degrees in mathematics from Rensselaer Polytechnic Institute in Troy, New York, where he also taught fun subjects such as differential equations and complex variables for several years.

Outside of work and writing, Eric enjoys hitting the gym, biking, country dancing, and being dragged around the Metro DC area by his Boxer Zack.

Jim O'Donnell was born on October 17, 1963, in Pittsburgh, Pennsylvania (you may forward birthday greetings to odonnj@rpi.edu). After a number of unproductive years, he went to Rensselaer Polytechnic Institute, where he spent 11 years earning three degrees, graduating for the third (and final) time in 1992. Currently, he works as an aerospace engineer, building satellites in metropolitan Washington, DC.

Jim has been working as an author and technical editor for Macmillan Computer Publishing for four years, contributing to over 30 books, and lead-authoring (with Eric Ladd) five. When Jim isn't writing or researching for Macmillan, he can often be found on IRC (under the nick of JOD or HockeyJOD); you can also visit The House of JOD at http://www.rpi.edu/~odonnj. When he isn't on the computer, Jim likes to run, play ice hockey, read, collect comic books and PEZ dispensers, and play the second-best board game ever, Axis & Allies.

Contributing Author Bios

Michael Morgan (michmor@regent.edu) is founder and president of DSE, Inc., a full-service Web presence provider and software development shop. The DSE team has developed software for such companies as Intelect, Magnavox, DuPont, the American Biorobotics Company and Satellite Systems Corporation, as well as for the government of Iceland and the Royal Saudi Air Force. DSE's Web sites are noted for their effectiveness—one of the company's sites generated sales of more than $100,000 within 30 days of being announced.

During academic year 1989-1990, Mike was invited by retired Navy Admiral Ron Hays to serve as the first Fellow of the Pacific International Center for High Technology Research (PICHTR) in Honolulu. PICHTR is a spin-off of the University of Hawaii and bridges the gap between academic research and industrial applications. Mike directed the first technology transfer initiatives at PICHTR and helped PICHTR win its first industrial contract. Mike assisted Admiral Hayes in presenting PICHTR and its mission to the Hawaii research community, the Hawaii legislature, and Hawaii's representatives to Congress.

Mike is a frequent speaker at seminars on information technology and has taught computer science and software engineering at Chaminade University (the University of Honolulu) and in the graduate program of Hawaii Pacific University. He has given seminars for the IEEE, National Seminars, the University of Hawaii, Purdue University, and Notre Dame.

He holds a Master of Science in Systems Management from the Florida Institute of Technology and a Bachelor of Science in Mathematics from Wheaton College, where he concentrated his studies on computer science. He has taken numerous graduate courses in computer science through the National Technological University. Mike is currently a student in the doctoral program at the Center for Leadership Studies at Regent University, where he is exploring the relationship between software processes and organizational theory.

Mike can usually be found in his office at DSE, drinking Diet Pepsi and writing Java. He lives in Virginia Beach with his wife, Jean, and their six children.

Melissa Niles is a Web programmer and consultant for ITM Services (`http://www.itm.com/`). Although she specializes in Web/database access, she has worked for companies around the world, building Web- and Internet-based client/server applications. She can be reached at `mniles@itm.com`.

Dedication

For my sister, Brenda—Eric Ladd

For my little sister, Christine, who always has a smile. Well, almost always…—Jim O'Donnell

Acknowledgments

A tome like this does not write itself. It is the result of the orchestrated efforts of many, all of whom deserve recognition. Eric and Jim would like to thank the entire staff at Que that helped with this book. Special thanks go to Jeff Taylor for getting us started and to Tim Ryan and Jon Steever for seeing us through the rest of the process. Also, we would like to thank the cadre of contributing authors and technical editors, without whom this book would be woefully incomplete. Finally, we want to express a special note of thanks to Doshia Stewart, who got the whole thing started, and to Jane Brownlow, for helping to make our time spent working with Que a pleasant experience.

Eric is indebted to many people who provided support and encouragement over the course of the project. Special thanks to Dad, Brenda, Bob Leidich, Tara Bridgman, Mike Crow, John Guzman, Gordon Vivace, Chad Cipiti, Phil Attey, Carolyn McHale, Michelle Keen, Ryan Miller, August Jackson, and Randy Bowers. Also, an extra special tip of the hat to Carol Greco, Emily Stollar, and Frank Kolencik, who helped me through the stressful process of closing on my first home while the writing process was beginning.

Jim would like to thank his family and friends for their support while he worked on this book. He would like to especially thank his roommates, Richard and Darby, the Weekly Poker Crew, Brian, Doug, Stuart, Richard, David, Philippe, and Chris, and his teammates on the DC Nationals. Finally, an extra special thank you goes to Anthony Smith, Jim's "Marine Corps Marathon Road Crew"… Thanks for being there, Anthony, I couldn't do it without you!

Tell Us What You Think!

As the reader of this book, *you* are our most important critic and commentator. We value your opinion and want to know what we're doing right, what we could do better, what areas you'd like to see us publish in, and any other words of wisdom you're willing to pass our way.

As the Executive Editor for the Java team at Macmillan Computer Publishing, I welcome your comments. You can fax, email, or write me directly to let me know what you did or didn't like about this book—as well as what we can do to make our books stronger.

Please note that I won't have time to help you with technical problems related to the topic of this book, and that due to the high volume of mail I receive, I might not be able to reply to every message.

When you write, please be sure to include this book's title and author as well as your name and phone or fax number. I will carefully review your comments and share them with the author and editors who worked on the book.

Fax: 317-817-7070

Email: java@mcp.com

Mail: Tim Ryan, Executive Editor
         Java Team
         Macmillan Computer Publishing
         201 West 103rd Street
         Indianapolis, IN 46290 USA

Introduction

The Hypertext Markup Language (HTML) and the World Wide Web altered the face of the Internet and of personal computing forever. At one time regarded as the province of universities and government organizations, the Internet has grown to touch more and more lives every day. In addition, the multimedia content that can be provided via HTML and other Web technologies such as JavaScript, Java, XML, CGI, and others makes the Web an exciting place to be.

Through the efforts of standards organizations such as the World Wide Web Consortium, and those of companies such as Netscape, Microsoft, Macromedia, and Sun Microsystems, HTML and the other languages and technologies used to present information over the Web have continued to develop and evolve. The number of possibilities for providing information content over the Web is astounding, and it's growing every day.

That is where *Platinum Edition, Using HTML 4, XML, and Java 1.2* steps in to help. This book is the single source you need to quickly get up to speed and greatly enhance your skill and productivity in providing information on the World Wide Web.

Note: In December 1998, Sun released Java 2 Platform. The actual name of the JDK that you download, however, is JDK 1.2, so we have elected to refer to the latest version of Java as JDK 1.2 throughout this book.

How to Use This Book

This book was designed and written from the ground up with two important purposes:

- First, *Platinum Edition Using HTML 4, XML, and Java 1.2* makes it easy for you to find the most effective means to accomplish any task or present almost any kind of information on the Web.

- Second, this book covers the major Web technologies—not only HTML, XML, and Java, but also JavaScript, Microsoft's VBScript scripting language, CGI, and both Microsoft and Netscape's implementations of Dynamic HTML—in a depth and breadth that you won't find anywhere else. It also includes a CD-ROM filled with Web software, helpful documentation, and code from the examples in this book.

With these goals in mind, how do you use this book?

If you are familiar with HTML and with setting up Web pages and Web sites, you may be able to skim through the first couple of chapters to see what some of the issues in page and site design are, and you can glance through the basic HTML elements discussed in the first two or three parts. Even if you are familiar with HTML, some information in those parts may be new to you, especially some of the new HTML 4.0 information. You can then read the advanced sections on HTML, as well as the sections on other Web technologies, such as JavaScript and Java, XML, CGI, and Dynamic HTML, to determine which of those elements you want to include in your Web pages.

Platinum Edition, Using HTML 4, XML, and Java 1.2 was written with the experienced HTML programmer in mind. Your experience may be limited to a simple Web home page you threw together, or you may be designing and programming professional Web sites. Either way, you will find comprehensive coverage of HTML and other Web technologies. Throughout the book, techniques are described for creating quality, effective Web pages and Web sites.

How This Book Is Organized

Part I: Design

Chapter 1, "Web Site Design," discusses the issues concerned with how to establish a consistent look-and-feel and how to organize your Web pages so that they come together to form a coherent whole.

Chapter 2, "Web Page Design," gives you an overview of some of the issues that need to be considered when designing and laying out your Web pages.

Part II: HTML and Graphics

Chapter 3, "HTML 4.0 Tag Reference," gives you a quick reference to all the HTML 4.0 tags in a format that is easy to understand and use.

Chapter 4, "Imagemaps," shows how graphics can be used as imagemaps—graphic navigation aids formatted to enable the user to link to other URLs by clicking sections of the graphic. The chapter discusses both server-side and client-side imagemaps.

Chapter 5, "Advanced Graphics," talks about the basic HTML tags used to include graphics in an HTML document and discusses the graphics formats and display options supported. The chapter also discusses some of the many uses of graphics.

Chapter 6, "Tables," discusses the use of HTML tables, both to present data and information in a tabular format and also to achieve great control of the relative placement and alignment of HTML text, images, and other objects.

Chapter 7, "Frames," shows you how to split the Web browser window into frames and how to use each to display a different HTML document. Some of the potential uses of frames are also shown and discussed.

Chapter 8, "Forms," discusses HTML forms—the primary way that user input and interactivity are currently supported in Web pages.

Chapter 9, "Style Sheets," takes a look at a recommended and increasingly popular formatting option available in HTML: Cascading Style Sheets. Style sheets are a way of setting up a custom document template that gives the Web page author a great deal more control over how Web pages will look to those viewing the pages.

Chapter 10, "Microsoft FrontPage Components," discusses the additional capabilities you can add to your Web pages by using Microsoft's FrontPage components (formerly known as Web bots) and a Web server with the FrontPage Extensions installed.

Part III: XML

Chapter 11, "Introduction to XML," introduces you to XML—a new markup language that has the potential to provide increased capabilities for formatting information for the Web, the Internet, and beyond.

Chapter 12, "Anatomy of an XML Document," takes you through the different parts of an XML document and gives you a feel for the purpose of the parts.

Chapter 13, "Creating XML Documents," goes into greater depth in the creation of XML content and gives you some simple examples of what you can achieve using XML.

Chapter 14, "Creating XML Document Type Definitions," discusses the syntax of an XML Document Type Definition (DTD), which enables you to define your own tags for marking up XML content.

Chapter 15, "XML Characters, Notations, and Entities," describes the XML notions of characters, notations, and entities and shows you how you can use them to make it easier to create XML documents.

Chapter 16, "XML DTD and Document Validation," shows you how to use some of the existing XML software tools to validate your XML documents and DTDs.

Chapter 17, "CDF and Active Desktop Components," describes Microsoft's Channel Definition Format standard and its relation to XML. This standard enables you to configure an HTML document or other Web browser object to become a live, dynamic component right on a user's desktop.

Part IV: JavaScript

Chapter 18, "Introduction to JavaScripting," discusses Netscape's JavaScript Web browser scripting language and shows some of the uses to which you can put it in a Web page.

Chapter 19, "The Web Browser Object Model," discusses the object model included with Netscape Navigator and Microsoft Internet Explorer. That object model enables you to use scripting languages to interact with HTML documents.

Chapter 20, "Manipulating Windows and Frames with JavaScript," shows you how to use JavaScript to create and use Web browser windows, dynamically generate HTML documents, and manipulate and cross-communicate between multiple windows and frames.

Chapter 21, "Using JavaScript to Create Smart Forms," shows you how you can use JavaScript to pre-process information entered into HTML forms and thus ensure that only valid data is submitted to the Web server.

Chapter 22, "Cookies and State Maintenance," shows you how to interface with and manipulate Web browser cookies with JavaScript. This enables you to remember information from one page to another in a Web site and across multiple visits to a Web site from a single user.

Chapter 23, "Using JavaScript to Control Web Browser Objects," shows you how you can use Netscape's LiveConnect and Microsoft's ActiveX technologies to access and manipulate Java applets, plug-in content, ActiveX Controls, and other objects through JavaScript.

Part V: Dynamic HTML

Chapter 24, "Introduction to Dynamic HTML," introduces you to the Dynamic HTML implementations of Netscape and Microsoft—two very different ways of adding increased animation and interactivity to Web pages.

Chapter 25, "Advanced Netscape Dynamic HTML," goes into greater depth to show you more of Netscape's version of Dynamic HTML, centered around Netscape's use of manipulating style sheet attributes, the nonstandard <LAYER> tag, and Netscape's downloadable font technology.

Chapter 26, "Advanced Microsoft Dynamic HTML," explores the set of Web technologies that Microsoft has dubbed Dynamic HTML, including extensions to Microsoft's Web Browser Object Model and the use of ActiveX Controls and other Web browser objects to implement new capabilities to Microsoft's Web browser.

Chapter 27, "Cross-Browser Dynamic HTML," discusses techniques to create Dynamic HTML Web pages that can be successfully viewed using either Netscape Navigator or Microsoft Internet Explorer.

Part VI: CGI and Server-Side Processing

Chapter 28, "Programming CGI Scripts," describes the basics of the Common Gateway Interface (CGI) and how you can use programs, scripts, and processes that can be run on the Web server with Web browsers.

Chapter 29, "Custom Database Query Scripts," discusses database processing that can be done at the server to provide an interactive user interface over the Internet between someone using a Web browser and a central store of information.

Chapter 30, "Web Database Tools," discusses some of the tools and utilities you can use to set up databases for access over the Web.

Chapter 31, "Indexing and Adding an Online Search Engine," goes through the steps and software necessary to add an online search engine to your Web site that will give your users quick and ready access to anything on your site.

Chapter 32, "Server-Side Includes," explains server-side includes (SSI)—what they are, how they are used, and some sample applications that show them in action.

Chapter 33, "Active Server Pages and VBScript," discusses the Active Server Pages component of Microsoft's Internet Information Server Web server, and how you can use it to dynamically configure and tailor the output of your Web site according to the capabilities of your clients. It also discusses Microsoft's VBScript scripting language, which can be used with the ASP technology.

Chapter 34, "Using ColdFusion," covers Allaire's ColdFusion, a development tool for writing Web-based applications that communicate with server-side, ODBC-compliant databases.

Chapter 35, "Server-Side Security Issues," discusses in much greater depth the security issues involved with running and using server-side processing. The discussion also examines what to do with bad data and how to help ensure the safety of your server against malevolent attacks.

Part VII: Java

Chapter 36, "Introduction to Java," gives you an overview of the latest on Java and the technologies that support it. It includes a discussion of all the new features in Java 1.2, as well as security and performance enhancements.

Chapter 37, "Developing Java Applets," discusses the basics of designing, writing, and debugging Java applets by using a variety of software development tools.

Chapter 38, "User Input and Interactivity with Java," examines how you can use Java applets to add another way of soliciting user input and adding interactivity between Web pages and users.

Chapter 39, "Graphics and Animation," shows some of the graphics capabilities of Java and how you can use Java to create both static and dynamic images within a Web page.

Chapter 40, "Network Programming," explains how you can use Java sockets to interface Java applets with other sources of data and information anywhere on the Internet.

Chapter 41, "Security," explains some of the special security issues related to writing, providing, and running Java applets over the Web.

Appendixes

Appendix A, "JavaScript 1.2 Language Reference," provides a reference to the properties, functions, and statements included in the JavaScript language.

Appendix B, "What's on the CD-ROM," describes the software, utilities, code, and documentation available on the CD-ROM that accompanies this book.

Special Features in the Book

Que has more than a decade of experience in writing and developing the most successful computer books available. With that experience, we've learned what special features help readers most. Look for the following special features throughout the book to enhance your learning experience:

Notes

Notes present interesting or useful information that isn't necessarily essential to the discussion. This secondary track of information enhances your understanding of Windows, but you can safely skip Notes and not be in danger of missing crucial information. Notes look like the following:

N O T E Microsoft Internet Explorer 4 supports the inline display of Windows Bitmap (.BMP) graphics in addition to GIFs and JPEGs. ■

Tips

Tips present advice on quick or often overlooked procedures. These include shortcuts that save you time. A Tip looks like the following:

 Using an asterisk (*) as the value of your ALT attribute gives users with nongraphical browsers a bulletlike character in front of each list item.

Cautions

Cautions serve to warn you about potential problems that a procedure may cause, about unexpected results and mistakes to avoid. Cautions look like the following:

> **CAUTION**
>
> Don't let an animation run indefinitely. An animation that's running constantly can be a distraction from the rest of the content on your page.

Troubleshooting

No matter how carefully you follow the steps in the book, you eventually come across something that just doesn't work the way you think it should. Troubleshooting sections anticipate these common errors or hidden pitfalls and present solutions. A Troubleshooting section looks like the following:

TROUBLESHOOTING

A small, hyperlinked line appeared at the bottom right of my linked images. How do I get rid of it?

Your problem most likely stems from HTML code such as the following:

```
<A HREF="author.html">
<IMG SRC="ericzack.jpg" WIDTH=300 HEIGHT=400 ALT="Eric and Zack">
</A>
```

By having a carriage return after the <IMG> tag but before the </A> tag, you often get an extraneous line at the bottom-right corner of the linked image (see Figure 5.10). By placing the </A> tag immediately after the <IMG> tag

```
<A HREF="author.html">
<IMG SRC="ericzack.jpg" WIDTH=300 HEIGHT=400 ALT="Eric and Zack"></A>
```

it should take care of that annoying little line.

On the Web References

Throughout this book, you will find On the Web references that point you to World Wide Web addresses where you can find additional information about topics. On the Web references look like the following:

ON THE WEB

`http://hoohoo.ncsa.uiuc.edu/`   This site is the home of the NCSA Web server, providing complete documentation that will help you configure the NCSA server.

Cross References

Throughout the book, you will see references to other sections, chapters, and pages in the book. These cross references point you to related topics and discussion in other parts of the book. Cross references look like the following:

▶ **See** "Web Browser Object Model," **p. 461**.

Other Features

In addition to the previous special features, several conventions are used in this book to make it easier to read and understand.

Shortcut Key Combinations   In this book, shortcut key combinations are joined with plus signs. Ctrl+V, for example, means hold down the Ctrl key while you press the V key.

Typefaces   This book also has the following typeface enhancements to indicate special text, as shown in the following table:

Typeface	Description
italic	Italic is used to indicate new terms.
`computer type`	This typeface is used for onscreen messages, commands, and code. It is also used to indicate text you type and locators in the online world.
`computer italic type`	This typeface is used to indicate placeholders in code and commands.

Design

Web Site Design

by Eric Ladd

In this chapter

The Many Facets of Web Design

Designing Web sites is both a complex and rewarding activity. Hours of careful thought are needed at the planning stage. You need to take the time to think about who will be reading your pages—how they see and understand information, what types of computers they use, what browser software they have, and how fast their connections are. After you have profiled your audience, you must then consider the message you want to communicate via the Web site and how best to convey that message to your target audience. Finally, you need to consider the possibilities and limitations of Web publishing to determine how you will actually create the site. Web site design is a struggle among these competing forces. As a designer, you must decide how you will meet the requirements of each one.

This chapter and the following chapter give you some things to think about during the planning stages both for entire sites and for individual pages. After you have a good handle on site and page planning, you will be ready to move on to later chapters. These later chapters introduce you to Hypertext Markup Language (HTML), the document description language used to author Web pages. With knowledge of HTML and intelligent design, you can create sites that are accessible to the broadest audience possible and that effectively communicate what you have to say.

Know Your Audience

Web site design should be driven by audience considerations. It doesn't matter how powerful a server you have, how skilled a Java programmer you are, or how flashy your graphics are if your message is lost on the end user. If you gain just one concept from this chapter, let it be that you keep your audience uppermost in your mind during the design process.

Audience characteristics can fall into many categories. Because most sites have to be designed to provide maximum audience appeal, this chapter looks at two broad, yet important, categories:

- How will users move through the information? A Web site is different from a single Web page in that a user can visit many major sections within a site. By developing an awareness of how people think about the information you're presenting, you can design a structure that is intuitive and that harnesses the natural associations your audience members are likely to make.

- What technologies do your users have? The primary reason that many sites avoid the high-end stuff, such as Java applets or ActiveX controls, is because end users don't have a machine, a browser, or a connection to support them. With all the diversity in Web-surfing technology, you should take some time to learn about the tools your audience is using. This enables you to create a more accessible design.

How Will Users Move Through the Information?

You can't know how all your users think, but you can usually make some valid generalizations that can guide you during the design process. As you assess different cognitive characteristics of your audience, think about how you can use those characteristics to achieve the following design objectives:

- Make use of association. Association is a mental process in which one concept is paired with another. People in general are prone to making certain associations, whereas other associations may be particular to a specific user group. Identify whatever associations between informational items you think your audience will make. After you identify the associations, you can express them on your site through the use of hypertext links. A *hypertext link* is highlighted text on a page that, when clicked by the user, instructs the browser to load a new document. Presumably, the new document is related to the hypertext link that the user clicked to load it.

- Make use of consistency. A consistent approach to the many aspects of your site—look and feel, navigation, presentation of information, and so on—reduces the amount of mental effort the user must make to get around. Introduce your approaches to these things as early as you can and carry it through the entire site. Borders makes consistent use of graphics, navigation bars, and its Quick Search box to produce an easy-to-use shopping interface (see Figure 1.1).

FIGURE 1.1

Consistent use of graphics, navigation options, and content structure helps visitors get around your site.

Graphics

Quick Search box

Navigation bar

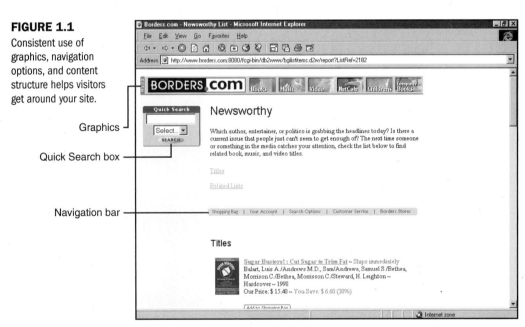

- Make use of context. Provide users with a context to which they can relate. Make sure they can get to all the important sections of your site from any other section (see Figure 1.2). This is critical because you can never predict on which page a user will enter your site. If you provide context only on the home page, users entering the site at a subordinate page will be unaware of the available options.

FIGURE 1.2

Jakob Nielsen's useit.com site has a colored bar across the top of every page that shows where you are in the site hierarchy and provides links to other parts of the site.

Site hierarchy indicator

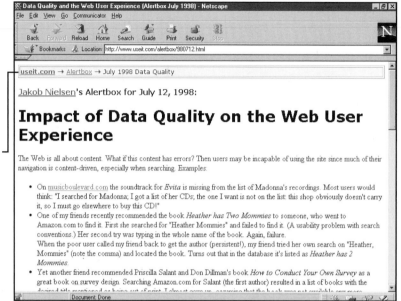

What Technologies Do Your Users Have?

The equipment your audience has access to is another key characteristic you must assess. Thankfully, HTML is platform independent, and so the type of machines your audience is using should be largely irrelevant. As long as your audience can run some type of browser program, they should be able to view your pages.

Other technology concerns influence design decisions, as well. These include

* Monitor—Because the Web is largely a visual medium, it helps to know for which monitors you are designing. If you are not certain, it is still best to design to a lower-end standard: a 14-inch monitor, set at 640×480, with the standard 256-color Windows palette. Remember that not everyone has the sophisticated monitors that many designers have, although more and more users tend to have monitors set at 800×600 pixel resolution.

N O T E Lynda Weinman explains the notion of the "browser safe" color palette on her Web site at http://www.lynda.com/hex.html. The palette comprises colors that will be rendered the same way on Macintosh and Windows platforms, so you'll have an assurance that all users will see the exact same thing.

* Browser software—Netscape Navigator and Microsoft Internet Explorer support all the latest extensions to HTML, but not every browser does. Some browsers, such as Lynx, are text only, which means users won't be able to see your graphics. Additionally, a good number of your users will be visiting your site from America Online (AOL), Compu-Serve, Prodigy, or some other online service. Each service's browser has its own

quirks that you must consider when designing; AOL's browser could not process the HTML table tags for the longest time, for example, so AOL users missed out on some attractive layouts that used tables.

Visually impaired users may be using Braille or speech-based browsers, which means that all your visible content will be lost on them unless you provide text alternatives for graphics, Java applets, and other embedded content. The World Wide Web Consortium has expanded the accessibility of many HTML constructs for users with speech-based browsers. Many HTML 4 additions for the form tags, for example, were driven by the need for forms to be more usable by the blind or visually impaired.

Remember that if you design to a higher-end graphical browser, you need to make alternative content available to people using less capable browsers as well.

- Helper applications and plug-ins—Even though many of today's browsers are incredibly powerful, they can't do it all alone. Audio clips, video clips, multimedia content, and some image formats require the use of a separate viewer program (a helper application) or a program that works with the browser to display content inline (a plug-in). Before you load up your site with these elements, make sure your audience has (or at least has access to) the additional software needed to view them.

 T I P The home page of many sites provides a notice that informs users of combinations of browser software and plug-ins the site is best viewed with (see Figure 1.3). Many of these notices also include links to pages where you can download the software. This is a helpful service that can maximize a user's experience when he or she visits your site.

- Connection speed—Some designers put together pages on a local drive and browse the pages right on the same machine. Other designers may port finished pages to a server and view them over a high-speed connection. Neither type of designer will appreciate the exasperation of having to wait for a page to download over a 14.4Kbps modem. Consider the types of connections your users will have and design appropriately. This may compel you to scale back on multimedia content and perhaps even some graphics content as well. Another way you can show respect for those with slower connections is to make available versions of your pages that are largely text, with minimal or no graphics.

N O T E More and more Web page authoring programs come with tools that estimate how long it will take a given page to download. The FrontPage 98 Editor, for example, displays an estimated download time over a 28.8Kbps connection for whatever page you are editing. This time displays near the bottom right of the Editor window along the status bar.

Allaire's HomeSite includes a Document Weight function that computes estimated download times for 14.4Kbps, 28.8Kbps, and 57.6Kbps connections.

FIGURE 1.3

Coca-Cola's site tells users which browsers and plug-ins will enhance their visit and gives them the option to visit different versions of the site, depending on which technology they have.

List of browsers and plug-ins

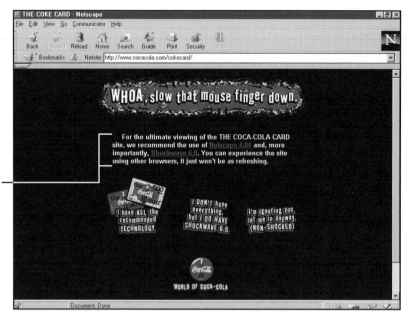

 T I P   Set up separate links to large multimedia items and indicate the file size somewhere close to the link (see Figure 1.4). This enables users to decide whether they want to download the file.

FIGURE 1.4

DOWNLOAD.COM always lets you know how big the file is that you're about to download.

Size of downloadable file

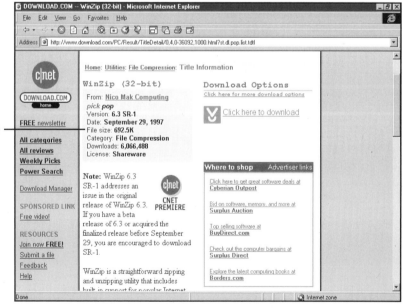

Considering Your Own Objectives

It is possible to spend so much time assessing audience factors that you can forget your reasons for wanting to create a Web site. User considerations are of paramount importance, but during the design process, you should not lose sight of your own motivations.

When planning your site, you should compose a mission statement, requirements document, or list of objectives that articulates why you want to create a Web site. This statement or list is another factor that should contribute to the site's design.

Use your mission statement or objective list to ground yourself during the design process. Keep checking your design against your reasons for designing the site in the first place. By balancing end-user considerations with your own objectives, you will produce a site that has broad appeal and that helps you attain your communications goals.

 T I P Post your mission statement, requirements summary, or objective list in a public place on a whiteboard or on newsprint so that you and your design team (if you have one) can always be reminded of why you're doing what you're doing.

Structuring Information

Audience characteristics and your own objectives for creating a site are the human factors that go into Web-site design. As you begin to focus on the site itself, you will discover that two other factors are vying for a visitor's attention: the information you're presenting and the graphics look of the site. Just as you had to strike a balance between audience characteristics and your objectives, you need to do the same for these site-related factors.

Two approaches for structuring content have emerged during the Web's short history: the drill-down structure (also known as the layered structure) and the flat structure.

The Drill-Down Structure

Most early Web sites made use of the drill-down structure. A *drill-down structure* means that the information in the site is layered several levels beneath the home page of the site, and users must drill down through those layers to see it. The idea is much like having to navigate down through several folders and subfolders to find a desired file in Windows 98 or Macintosh (or down through several directories and subdirectories to find a desired file in DOS or in a UNIX system). Yahoo! uses this structure on its site (see Figure 1.5). The drilling down occurs as you move from general to specific topics.

N O T E One advantage of the drill-down approach for site administrators is that they can interpret the number of levels a visitor drills down through as a measure of the visitor's interest in the site's content. ■

FIGURE 1.5
You drill down through several more general topics as you key in on a specific topic on Yahoo!'s site.

Drill-down structure (each segment represents a deeper layer)

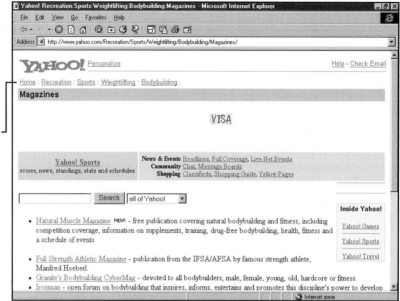

The drill-down approach provided a systematic way to structure content on early sites, but users quickly grew tired of plowing through so many levels to get the information they wanted and then navigating back up through the levels to move on to another part of the site. User feedback about so much layering led designers to consider different techniques. The flat structure emerged from these deliberations.

The Flat Structure

The flat structure isn't so much a structure of its own as it is a lessening of the drill-down approach. Every site will probably have one or two levels of drill down (from the home page to any subordinate page, for example), but you can seek to minimize the number of layers so that fewer barriers exist between users and the information they want. Two ways to do this are

■ Limit the number of subdirectories you use. You are more likely to end up with a drill-down structure if you use a lot of subdirectories (or subfolders) on your server to store and organize your HTML documents. Try to keep your documents up as close to the root level as you can.

 T I P   Draw out a map of your site hierarchy in outline form and try to identify places where you can reduce the number of information layers.

■ Increase navigation options. Give users access to as much as possible on every page. Figure 1.6 shows the AltaVista home page, which makes available a list of links to all major areas of the site.

Part

I

Ch

1

FIGURE 1.6
Providing several
navigation options
helps visitors to avoid
having to drill through
several layers to get the
information they want.

Multiple navigation
options support a
flatter structure

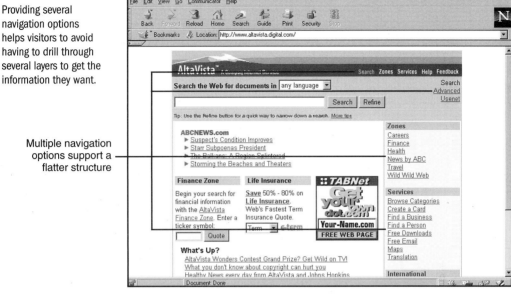

Developing a Look

A sharp graphical look is important to your site as well. Often it is the graphics that hook visitors and influence them to stop and read your content. Additionally, a consistent look provides a unique identity for the site.

The general rule you should remember when you develop a look and feel is that it should enhance the delivery of your message without overpowering it. A well-done look and feel initially draws in users and then fades into the background as the users move around within the site. If you throw in too much glitz, you run the risk of detracting from what you really want to get across.

The next four sections share some other design ideologies to keep in mind as you develop a look and feel for your site.

Less Is Often More

The fact that browsers can display images does not justify heaping a whole bunch of them on to all your pages to create a high-impact look. Don't forget that some users have text-only browsers, and others have slow connections. These people will not have the ability or the patience to view a site that relies heavily on a lot of graphics for its look.

Try to keep the number of graphics you use to a minimum. Graphics for logos and navigation are almost essential, but beyond that, give careful consideration to the images you put in your pages. Make sure they add value to the site by enhancing the presentation of your content.

After you decide on a set of images to use, continue to use the same images throughout the site. This helps promote a consistent look. Additionally, after the images are stored in users' caches, users spend less time waiting for pages to download.

Backgrounds

A good background should stay exactly there—in the background. If a background is so obtrusive that it interferes with presentation of content in the foreground, you are less likely to get your point across.

Many sites these days have gone to a plain white background. Although this may seem rather ordinary, it supports a clean and professional look that many users appreciate, and it keeps download times to a minimum (see Figure 1.7).

FIGURE 1.7
Lucent Technologies portrays a highly professional image, thanks, in part, to a clean, white page background.

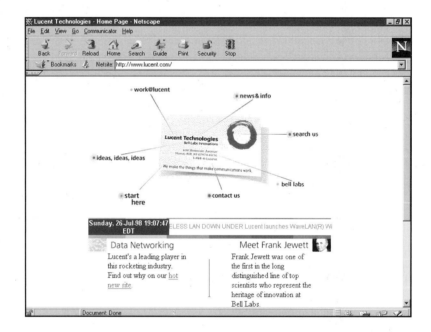

HTML supports the use of other colors as backgrounds. If you choose a color other than white, you need to make sure that sufficient contrast exists between the background color and all elements in the foreground. If you change the background color to black, for example, you also need to change the color of your body text. If you don't, you will have black text on a black background and your content will be invisible!

You can also use images in the background (see Figure 1.8). Background images are read in and tiled to fill the entire browser window. Again, the critical thing is that the background image does not intrude on the content in the foreground. Additionally, you want to design your image so that it tiles seamlessly. Being able to see the boundaries where the tiling occurs can distract users from the information you want them to see.

TIP You can use a background color and background image simultaneously on your pages; the color you use, however, should be the same as the dominant color in the image. The background color will be rendered immediately by the browser, and then the background image will be placed and tiled after the image is read in. This way, if a delay occurs in downloading the image, you still have a colored background that approximates the color scheme of the image. After the image has transferred, its appearance onscreen should not be too distracting because of the close match between it and the background color.

FIGURE 1.8

George Washington University's Center for Career Education uses a page background with a "GW" monogram in the upper left.

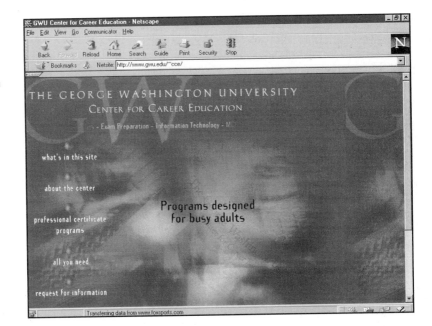

Color Choices

HTML provides control over other page colors, too. Controlling background and body text color was mentioned in the preceding section. You can control the color of three types of hypertext links as well: unvisited, visited, and active (a link is active only for the instant that the user clicks it). Colors for all three types should be chosen so that they provide good contrast with the background color or image. Beyond that, it is a good visitor service to color visited links a different color from unvisited links because this provides a visual cue to users as to where they have been in the site.

TIP Hypertext link colors are a nice way to work in your company's color scheme if you're designing for a corporate site. Painting link colors in this way subtly promotes corporate identity throughout the site.

Iconography: Is It Intuitive?

Many designers choose to represent major sections of a site with *icons*, small images that are meant to convey what type of content is found in each section. Yahoo!'s main site uses icons for the navigation bar at the top of the home page (see Figure 1.9).

The critical test that icons must pass is the intuitiveness test. Because you are using a small image to communicate a possibly complicated idea, you need to make sure that users can make a quick association between the image and the idea. The best way to do this is to test the icons with potential users. Get some people together who know nothing about the site you're designing and show them your icons. As they see each icon, ask them to write down what Web site information or functionality might be associated with it. After you have gathered their responses, share the icons with them again, this time giving the significance of each icon. Ask for their feedback on whether they think the icon truly represents what you want it to. By combining user responses from the first viewing with feedback from the second viewing, you should be able to make a good assessment of how intuitive your icons are.

FIGURE 1.9
Icons should almost immediately suggest the nature of the content they link to.

Icons ——

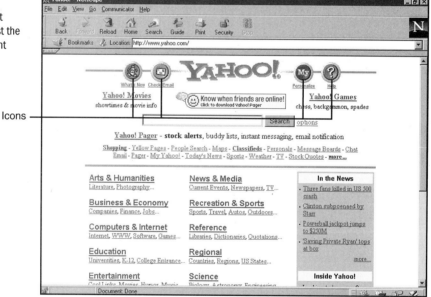

Using Prepackaged Graphical Themes

Just because you may not have a dedicated graphic artist to help you come up with a visual identity, you are not necessarily resigned to having a bland site. Many ready-to-use sets of images are available that you can download and use freely in your design.

Perhaps the easiest set of prepackaged themes to use comes as part of the FrontPage Editor. You can choose from one of seven themes, previewing them all in the Themes dialog box (see Figure 1.10). Each theme includes banner, background, button, bullet, horizontal rule, and navigation images, as well as specs to set up heading and body text styles.

If you do have a little graphics expertise yourself, it would be a simple matter to import any of the graphics in the theme into a capable graphics program, such as Photoshop or Paint Shop Pro, and customize them for your site. You might, for example, add your company's name to the banner image so that it is always visible to the reader.

If you are having trouble coming up with a look and feel for your site, feel free to look at and experiment with a prepackaged theme from FrontPage or any other source. They are an easy way to put an attractive face on your site with a minimal amount of effort.

FIGURE 1.10
The FrontPage Editor comes with dozens of different built-in graphical themes that you can preview and use.

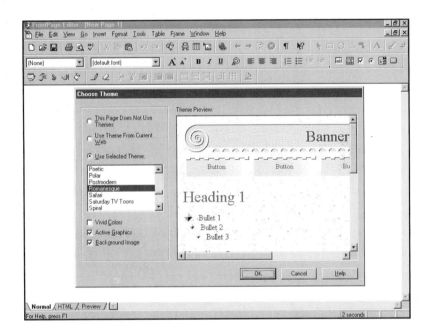

Desirable Site Elements

Expectation is another powerful mental process that you can harness. Anticipating and meeting users' expectations will impress them and make it more likely that they will come back to your site.

Over time, Web users have come to rely on certain functionality being present on most Web sites. The next several sections catalog these features so that you can consider building them into the design for your site.

Tables of Contents

A site-wide table of contents lays out everything available on the site—usually as hypertext links so that users can click and go wherever they want. Depending on the size of your site, it may take some time to compile and code a comprehensive table of contents. Remember, however, that users will appreciate the quick access to all parts of your site.

TIP Microsoft's FrontPage comes with a Table of Contents component that you can use to automatically generate and update a table of contents for your site (see Figure 1.11).

FIGURE 1.11

Microsoft FrontPage can automatically generate and maintain a site-wide table of contents, such as the one shown here.

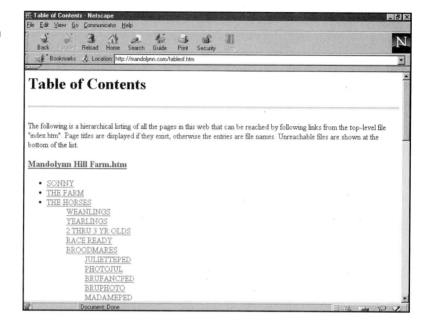

Search Engines

Indexing your site to make it searchable is a great way to make any part of your site available without a lot of drill down. Figure 1.12 shows the MCI home page, which includes a Search field at the bottom right. Many such pages are as simple as the one input field you see in the figure.

Outfitting your site with a search engine may be easier than you think. Some search-engine programs, such as ICE, are publicly available and fairly painless to install. Major server programs, such as Netscape Enterprise Server and Microsoft's Internet Information Server, are coming bundled with search-engine software.

▶ For more information on search engines, **see** "Indexing and Adding an Online Search Engine," **p. 747**.

Navigation Tools

▶ To learn more about setting up site navigation, **see** "Desirable Page Elements," **p. 45**.

Comprehensive navigation options should be available to users on every page. At the very least, you need to provide links to every major content section of your site (see Figure 1.13). Additionally, you should think about providing links to important functional areas of the site, such as the Table of Contents and the search engine discussed in the previous sections.

FIGURE 1.12

Making your site searchable spares users hours of effort trying to find the information they need.

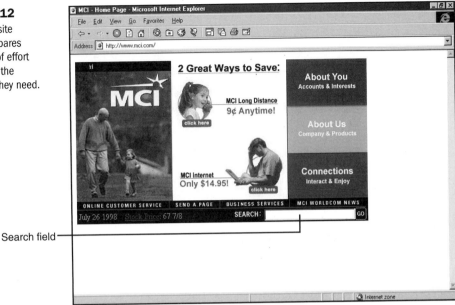

Search field —

FIGURE 1.13

DIGEX provides links to all major portions of its Web Site Management site and also provides links within the content area you're currently viewing.

Navigation options —

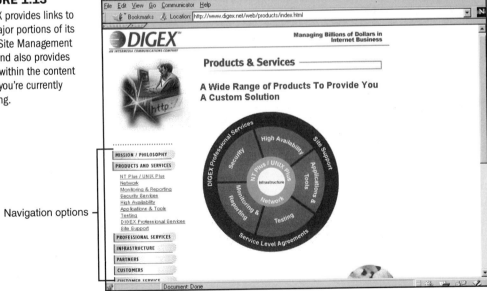

What's New

People who visit your site frequently will appreciate a What's New section so that they can quickly find out what has changed since their last visit (see Figure 1.14). This spares them having to go through the whole site to discover new content.

You can maintain your What's New section manually, or you can have it generated on-the-fly by your Web server by using publicly available common gateway interface (CGI) scripts. These scripts check the files on your site for their last changed dates and display a list of files that have been altered within a specified period of time. The pages generated by these scripts don't tend to be very descriptive, so it is best to maintain your What's New section manually if you have the resources.

N O T E Make sure you include a date with each item on your What's New page so that visitors know just how new the information is. ■

T I P You can also use software such as NetMind's URL Minder to dispatch an email to visitors when something on your site changes.

FIGURE 1.14

The Federal Deposit Insurance Corporation (FDIC) maintains a What's New page to keep visitors apprised of recently added content.

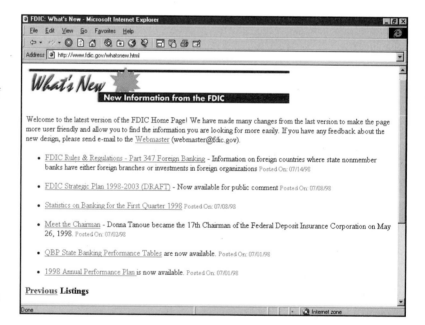

Guest Books

Sign in, please! Guest books provide a record of visitors to the site. Signing the guest book is almost always voluntary, but links to the guest book page from the home page encourage visitors to sign.

▷ To learn how to create an HTML form, **see** "Forms," **p. 233**.

A guest book uses HTML forms to gather information about the visitor and then archives the information on the server (see Figure 1.15). Try to keep your guest book form short. Users who are willing to sign may change their minds if they see that they have to fill out an extensive form.

TIP You can use name and address information from your guest book to compile a mailing list for targeted marketing campaigns for your business.

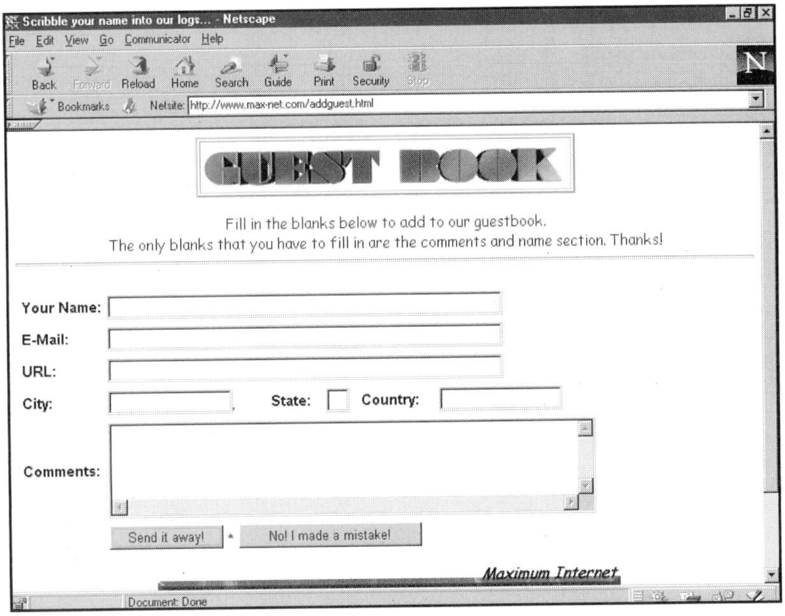

FIGURE 1.15

Canada's Maximum Internet encourages site visitors to leave name and address information.

Feedback Mechanism

▷ **See** "Desirable Page Elements," **p. 45**, for more information on ways to collect visitor feedback.

You should always be gathering feedback on your site so that you can build on it and improve it. Putting a feedback mechanism on your site is a great way to collect opinions from people as they visit.

Feedback mechanisms can take two forms. A simple way to support user feedback is to place an email hypertext link on your pages. By clicking the link, users open a mail window in their browsers where they can compose and send a feedback message to you.

The second approach is to create an HTML form that asks specific questions (see Figure 1.16). This requires a bit more effort than setting up an email link, but it does provide the advantage of gathering responses to a standard set of questions.

FIGURE 1.16
Visitors to international
telecommunications
giant Global One's site
can offer feedback by
filling out an online
form.

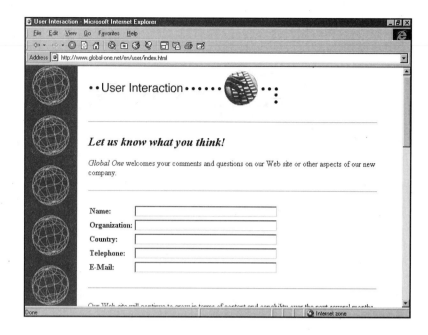

Mailing Lists

A mailing list gateway enables users to subscribe to mailing lists that will keep them up to date on changes to the site or on some other topic of interest. Figure 1.17 shows USEIT.COM'S link that users can follow to sign up for a mailing list that notifies them when new articles are posted.

FIGURE 1.17
Mailing lists are a great
way to keep previous
visitors apprised of new
content.

Mailing list sign-up link—

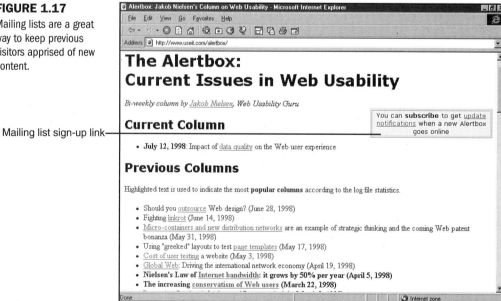

Threaded Discussion Groups

Threaded discussion groups are very much like having Usenet newsgroups right on your site. Users can participate in discussions about the site or about topics relevant to content on the site by posting their ideas and opinions or by responding to posts by others.

If you are unsure as to how you can set threaded discussion on your site, you can check out some solutions available from various software vendors. Allaire produces a product called Allaire Forums to support browser-based threaded discussions (see Figure 1.18). By using Forums' ColdFusion engine, users can read and post to any of a number of related groups.

FIGURE 1.18

The ColdFusion Advisor site enables developers to ask each other questions through a threaded discussion forum.

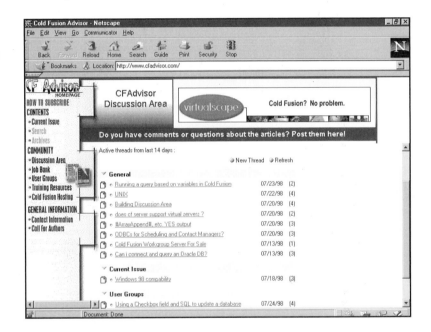

Chat Channels

Chat channels enable users to interact in real-time. Some sites support a general chat channel where users can discuss the site or topics that relate to site content. Another application of chat channels is to provide a question-and-answer session with a subject-matter expert or celebrity.

T I P Most chat servers have a feature that enables you to record a chat session. Reviewing the transcripts of a chat is a terrific way to gather feedback and other ideas for improving your site.

Multimedia Content

As browsers become better able to display multimedia content inline, you will see more and more of it on Web sites. The biggest impediment continues to be bandwidth. Most multimedia files are quite large and may take several minutes to download.

You have many options when it comes to providing multimedia content, including

- Audio
- Video
- Macromedia Director movies

Most multimedia files require a helper application or plug-in to view them, so be sure to notify users about what viewer programs they need to download before they get to pages with multimedia content.

Audio clips are especially popular on music sites, where they enable a visitor to preview parts of an album before buying. Audio files come in several formats, including .wav, .au, and .aiff for sound bytes and .mid for music.

Streamed audio is different from other audio formats in that the sound is played as information is received by the browser, rather than after the entire file is downloaded. Progressive Network's RealAudio (.ra or .ram) is the leading streamed audio format. You can learn more about RealAudio by directing your browser to `http://www.realaudio.com/`.

Computer video files also come in several formats. The most popular are MPEG (.mpg), QuickTime from Apple (.qt or .mov), and Video for Windows from Microsoft (.avi, short for Audio Video Interleave). Computer video files are also huge, usually on the order of 1MB or more of information for a video clip that lasts only a few seconds. Combine this with limited bandwidth and you can see why Web video hasn't attained the prominence of other multimedia forms.

Nonetheless, progress is being made on the Web video front. Streaming can enable video to be displayed as it is received, although this technique is still in a formative stage. Microsoft made a bold move by making ActiveMovie technology available for Internet Explorer 4. ActiveMovie eliminates the need for video helper applications by enabling Internet Explorer to display MPEG, QuickTime, and Video for Windows files inline. Additionally, Real Video by Progressive Networks provides support for streaming video content.

Macromedia Director is an authoring tool for composing multimedia presentations or movies. A movie draws on text, graphics, audio, and video information to create interactive applications that can be run on Macintosh and Windows platforms or that can be delivered over the Internet (see Figure 1.19).

Director movies are viewed in a browser using Shockwave, a plug-in freely available from Macromedia. Because Director movie files are typically quite large, Macromedia also provides a utility called AfterBurner, which compresses the movie file and optimizes it for transfer over the Internet.

FIGURE 1.19

Comedy Central animates one of its "South Park" characters using Macromedia's Shockwave.

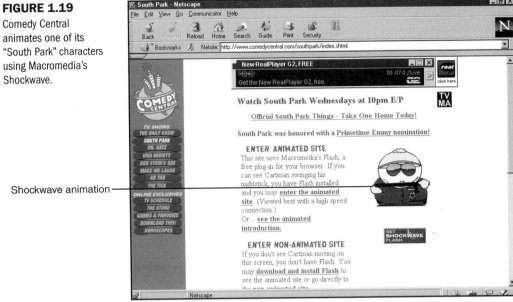

Shockwave animation

Testing Your Design

After you have completed your design work and have a first cut of your site developed, you should consider testing the design and looking for ways to improve it before final roll-out. The following three sections give you some different tests to try.

Pilot the Site

Taking the site for a test drive with some potential users is a great way to gather ideas for making it better. To do this, round up some people who have some degree of Web-surfing experience, but who have not seen the site. Turn them loose on the site and encourage them to look for things that they would change. You can even give them a feedback form to fill out with a standard set of questions and an open-ended question for other thoughts they may have.

 TIP   If you do pilot your site with a group of users, watch them as they do it! You'll be amazed at what you can learn from facial expressions and body language.

Try It with Different Browsers

As you developed the site, you probably used only one browser. After you are finished, you owe it to your audience to view the site in other browsers, including at least one non-graphical browser. Record any corrections needed, then go back to your HTML files and look for ways to address the problems you find.

T I P   As an extension to trying out your site with different browsers, you can also change your monitor's resolution so that you can see what your site looks like at 640×480, 800×600, and 1024×768 pixels.

Try It at Different Connection Speeds

To accomplish this one, you may have to send people home to sign on. It is, however, well worth the effort. Have them check the pages on the site and time how long it takes for each to download. One general rule suggests that it should not take more than 15 seconds for each page to download. Identify pages that take longer than this and look for ways to scale back the amount of information.

Trends in Web Site Design

When the Web was growing at its fastest rate, new, high-end technologies were being thrown at content providers and users at an alarming rate—so fast, in fact, that few people took the time to think about whether they were really appropriate. Instead, many technologies were used just for the sake of using them. Frequently, the result was disastrous—lengthy download times, unusable pages, and annoyed users. In the late 1990s, the Web community has demonstrated a move that could be seen as "getting back to basics," in which the high-end stuff is rarely, if ever, used. This chapter closes with a look at this and some of the other site design trends that will carry us into the new millennium.

Server-Side Processing

When Java was released, it was touted as the panacea for Web programming. Several years later, though, Java has not panned out as the "end-all" language for Web-based data processing. Part of the problem was that users were just too impatient to wait for Java applets to load. Security was also a concern as programmers discovered security "holes" in Java that could put a user's machine at risk.

A similar thing has happened with ActiveX technologies. ActiveX controls also take time to download, and they have had their share of security issues. Additionally, only Microsoft Internet Explorer has native support for ActiveX controls, so users with other browsers would either miss out on ActiveX technology or have to find a plug-in that enables their browser to work with an ActiveX control.

The common thread in both the Java and ActiveX stories is that they tried to be *client-side* technologies in the face of users wanting short download times and a secure environment. After it was clear that neither technology was really delivering on those counts, the fervor over them subsided. It's true that both are still around, but they are by no means the hot technologies that make the Web interactive.

Rather than shift the burden of interactivity to the browser, support for interactive sites is now being refocused on the server. Indeed, server-side Java is becoming more and more prevalent, and Microsoft's Internet Information Server (IIS) can easily work with server-side ActiveX controls. In addition, many "middleware" technologies, such as Allaire's ColdFusion and Microsoft's Active Server Pages, are available on the server side to make it a fairly simple matter to develop Web-enabled database applications. All these server-side technologies return HTML to a browser, enabling fast downloads and the security of knowing that no executable files are being placed on a user's machine.

As time goes on, look for more and more processing to occur on the server side of the HTTP coin. Client-side processing will likely be limited to scripts written in JavaScript or VBScript to perform tasks such as form validation or to support other client-side technologies such as Dynamic HTML.

Respecting an International Audience

Site designers and content developers often forget about the "World" in "World Wide Web." As the Internet expands to more and more of the globe, you need to be aware that your visitors can be coming from anywhere on Earth, not only from your own city, state, or country.

You can demonstrate sensitivity to an international audience in several ways:

- Use the HTML tags that specify the meaning of your content and let the various international versions of browsers handle the language-specific nuances of rendering that content. You can use the <Q> tag, for example, to mark up a quotation. Then a Spanish-language browser would know to offset the content with << and >>, rather than with quotation marks.

- Use the LANG attribute available for many HTML tags to specify a language context for a piece of content or for an entire document.

- Use iconography that is not culture specific.

- If you specify dates and times, make sure you note the time zone and/or a reference city so users can deduce when things happened or are going to happen in their time zones.

- Check your server access logs to see what kinds of hits you're getting from countries other than your own. If you're detecting a number of hits from Portugal, you might go so far as to have key content translated into Portuguese so that visitors from Portugal can read your content in their native language.

You should also test your site with an international audience as well. This can be fairly easy if you work in a corporation with offices around the globe. In that case, just call around and line up some volunteers from each office to walk through the site and offer their feedback.

Respecting a Disabled Audience

HTML 4 went a long way toward increasing the accessibility of information published on the Web for users who use browsers that are not screen based. Visually impaired users, for example, might use a browser that renders to Braille or even synthesized speech.

Perhaps the best way to make your pages accessible to non-visual browsers is to make judicious use of the HTML tags and attributes that support the rendering of non-visual content. These include

- The heading tags (`<H1>`–`<H6>`), which define a hierarchical structure in your document.

- The `ALT` attribute to specify a text-based alternative for an image, applet, or other embedded object.

- The `<LABEL>`, `<FIELDSET>`, and `<LEGEND>` tags, which make it possible to create Web forms that are more accessible to users. Marking up the prompting text in front of a form field, for example, will enable a speech-based browser to use that text to prompt a user for input.

In addition to using accessible HTML, you can also make use of style sheets that enhance accessibility. You can use relative sizing in your style sheets, for example, rather than absolute sizing, so that a user who has set the base font size to a larger value to enhance readability won't have the size reset to an absolute value by your style sheet.

The Cascading Style Sheet level 2 specification also provides support for assigning style information to sound information delivered by an audio browser. You can use these style sheet properties to control volume, pitch, and position of the voice the user hears. By creating the illusion of different people delivering the information, you can simulate a conversation or assign one person to a class of information so that the user comes to associate a specific voice with a specific kind of content.

Finally, the new Java 1.2 standard includes several accessibility hooks that are useful for developing content for the disabled.

▶ For more information on writing Java applets for maximum accessibility, **see** "User Input and Interactivity with Java," **p. 1025**.

Web Page Design

by Eric Ladd

In this chapter

Page Design Follows Site Design

Many of the issues that go into designing a Web site also go into the design of a single Web page, but some page design considerations are unique. Ideally, page design should follow site design; and when you get ready to start a page, you should already have a good sense of what the page needs to accomplish, given its place in your site design.

A book this size could be written about all the issues that go into the design of quality Web pages. This chapter summarizes only the major concepts and elements of a good design. By looking at the work of others and doing design yourself, you will build up your own good design sense and the skills you need to implement a first-rate Web site.

 TIP Check out the Usenet comp.infosystems.www.authoring newsgroups to learn about design concepts, approaches, and philosophies used by other Web designers around the world.

Know Your Audience

The cardinal rule for Web site design is also the cardinal rule for page design. Knowing your audience and designing to that audience requires you to gather as much information about them as possible, including

- Equipment configuration (hardware, software, and Internet connection)
- Learning characteristics (how to best present information so that they understand it)
- Motivations for surfing the Web (business, professional, personal, entertainment, or educational reasons)
- Demographic factors (age, amount of education, geographic location, language)
- Cultural characteristics (any other factors that could influence how they read a page)

You need to gather all this information before you start designing pages. As with all things, finding out as much as you can beforehand will save you a whole lot of headaches later.

In addition to gathering as many user characteristics as you can, you should keep in mind the following two things that are common to all users:

- They are visiting your pages because they are interested in the information you have put there.
- They are using some type of Web browser to visit your site.

Knowledge of these two factors provides a good basis for beginning your Web page design. The next two sections investigate some of the specifics of each.

N O T E   Unless you have the luxury of developing for a homogeneous group of people, you will probably have to design your pages to be accessible to the broadest audience possible. In the absence of proper information about your audience, designing for maximum readability is the best rule.

Corporate Intranets: Designing for a Homogenous Group

If you are working on an intranet page for your company, one thing you can typically take advantage of is a common platform. Many companies that put up intranets get a site license for their browser of choice. After you know that everyone is using the same browser, you can design to that browser's level of performance. If your intranet users are using Netscape Navigator 4, for example, you can design pages with frames, client-side imagemaps, Java applets, and the <LAYER> tag (a Netscape extension to standard HTML). If everyone is using Internet Explorer 4, however, you could use one of the Microsoft proprietary tags such as <MARQUEE>. Additionally, everyone is most likely running the software on the same platform with the same connection speed, so you can design to those parameters as well.

Another advantage you can harness in a corporate intranet design situation is a common culture. Most firms have a way of doing things that can be captured on the intranet pages. This gives the pages a context to which all your users can relate.

Some cautions go along with intranet design, though. First, you should make your intranet site sufficiently different from your external Web site so that employees can quickly tell the difference between the two. Additionally, because intranets tend to support people in their work, your intranet design should be as task oriented as possible. Many firms make the mistake of using their internal organizational structure as a basis for their intranet information design, but this doesn't provide the best service to the intranet users.

Designing for an audience whose members are more or less the same is a luxury that few people get to experience. If you find yourself in this situation, be sure to make full use of the characteristics common to your users.

Choosing Information

When you choose information for a page and choose how you are going to format that information, you should think about how you can minimize the effort the reader has to make to understand your message. If a page has relevant content that is presented in a well-organized layout, readers are much more likely to get something out of it than if the page is crammed with a lot of extraneous information and is displayed in a cluttered way.

When choosing what information to put on a page, keep the following two—often competing— parameters in mind:

- What information does the page need to get across to accomplish your communication objectives?
- What information is your audience genuinely interested in reading?

The first point in the preceding list presupposes that you have good and proper reasons for wanting to post content on the Web in the first place. Assuming that you have key communication objectives you want to reach, distill the messages that support those objectives down to their bare essence. Dressing up your messages with frivolous content or burying them in irrelevant information means the reader has to make a greater effort to extract them. This reduces the likelihood that your readers will come away with the messages you want them to receive.

N O T E   If you haven't formulated what goals you hope to achieve by creating Web pages, go back
to the drawing board and write some down. Your set of goals should be one of the driving
forces behind your decisions about what qualifies as appropriate content. ▩

On the other side of the coin is the information in which the audience is interested. A visitor to
your Web page also has specific objectives in mind. In a perfect world, your audience visits
your pages because they want to read the messages you want to convey. When visitors leave
your Web page and understand your message, both of you have satisfied your objectives.

Of course, the objectives of a Web page author and a Web page reader are not always conver-
gent. In these cases, you may need to include content on your pages that attracts the audience
you want. You have to achieve a fine balance, however. You must include enough content to get
people to your page, but not so much that it obscures the message you want to get across.

Presenting the Information

After you have selected the information to go on a page, you then need to think about how you
want to display it. The rule to keep in mind here is that users rarely *read* an entire page. Usability studies (such as those by Jakob Nielsen, formerly of Sun Microsystems and author of the
Alertbox column at `www.useit.com`) have demonstrated that most users simply *scan* a Web
page. Knowing this, you have to take steps to make key information stand out prominently so
that a person scanning the page can come away with the messages you wanted to convey.

Between standard HTML and extended HTML (browser-specific HTML instructions that are
not part of the standard), many ways to place content on a page permit creativity, good organization, and scanability. These include

- ▩ Paragraphs—You probably learned back in grade school that every paragraph should
  speak to a unique idea. The same holds true for Web page paragraphs; you can use them
  to convey an important concept. Figure 2.1 shows a page from the *Washington Post*'s Web
  site. Notice how paragraphs are kept short and to-the-point.

T I P   When writing your paragraphs (or entire Web documents for that matter), be sure to present your main
point first and then fill in the details. This way, users scanning the paragraph will get the gist of your
point right away and can read on if they want more details.

- ▩ Lists—HTML includes extensive support for lists. Placing items in a bulleted or ordered
  list makes for a readable and easy-to-understand presentation of information. Ordered
  lists are also useful for conveying a sequential relationship among the list items. A
  definition list provides a means of presenting a term, followed by its definition.
  Figures 2.2 and 2.3 illustrate some of the layouts possible with HTML lists.
- ▩ Images—Graphics content is one of the forces that has made the Web so popular, and
  users almost always expect graphics on a Web page. Clever use of images can communicate your message to those who visit your pages (see Figure 2.4). Images can also be
  used as page backgrounds, hyperlink anchors, and as site navigation aids. Just be careful

not to overload your page with images to the point that users won't wait for it to download.

FIGURE 2.1

Each paragraph should put forward one major point that supports your communications goals.

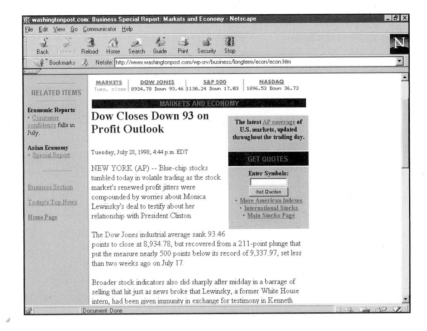

FIGURE 2.2

Web-site hosting provider DIGEX outlines the advantages of its services in highly readable bulleted lists.

Bulleted list ──

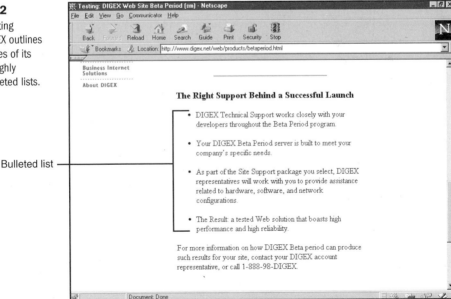

FIGURE 2.3

Numbered lists are useful for labeling clauses in a document or for outlining a procedure.

Numbered list ——

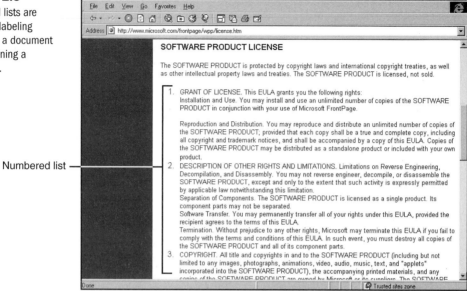

FIGURE 2.4

USA Today uses a combination of graphics and pictures to add flavor to its Web pages.

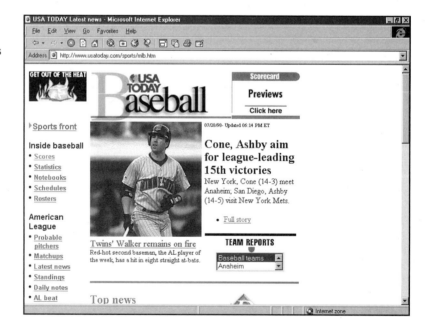

Font styles—You can make key words and phrases stand out from regular text by using one of HTML's many font formats. Text can be rendered in bold, in italic, or in a fixed-width font such as Courier (see Figure 2.5). Additionally, you can use other HTML instructions to change the size, color, and typeface of text. Now that they are standard, HTML style sheets provide even greater flexibility for page authors applying style information to their pages.

CAUTION

Don't overdo it with multiple typefaces on a page. Too many fonts can be distracting. Try to limit yourself to two—one serif and one sans serif.

▶ For more information, **see** "Style Sheets," **p. 261**.

Part

I

Ch

2

FIGURE 2.5

US Airways lists flights in a fixed-width font, and other information on the page is in a proportional, serifed font.

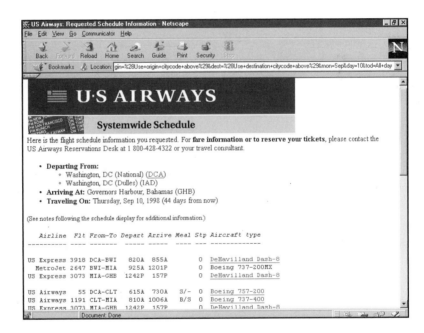

Tables—HTML tables enable you to put information into an easy-to-read, tabular form (see Figure 2.6). Tables also permit very precise alignment control inside their component cells; many resourceful HTML authors have made creative use of this feature to produce onscreen layouts that could not be achieved any other way (see Figure 2.7).

 When presenting tabular data, make sure your column heads are clearly labeled. The HTML <TH> tag will automatically make your column heads centered and bold.

▶ **See** "Tables," **p. 183**.

FIGURE 2.6

Yahoo!'s job listings are presented in table form for increased readability.

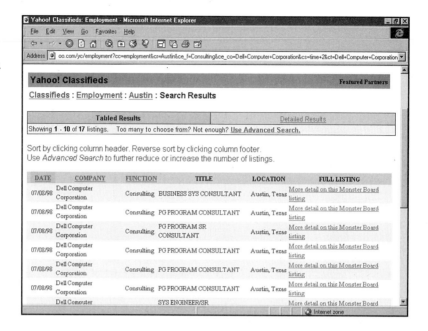

FIGURE 2.7

The complex page layout on CNN's site would not be possible without HTML tables.

■ Frames—When you split a browser window into two or more regions, the individual regions are called *frames*. Each frame is capable of displaying its own document, and so you can have multiple pages onscreen simultaneously. Figure 2.8 shows a Web page that makes effective use of frames by keeping search options available in the frame at the bottom of the page while presenting search results in the upper frame.

> **CAUTION**
>
> Frames tend to take away from the usability of your site. For example, it may become hard to bookmark a specific page in a framed layout. If you do use frames, make sure that you keep the layout as simple as possible and test your layout with users before rolling out the site.

▷ **See** "Frames," **p. 211**.

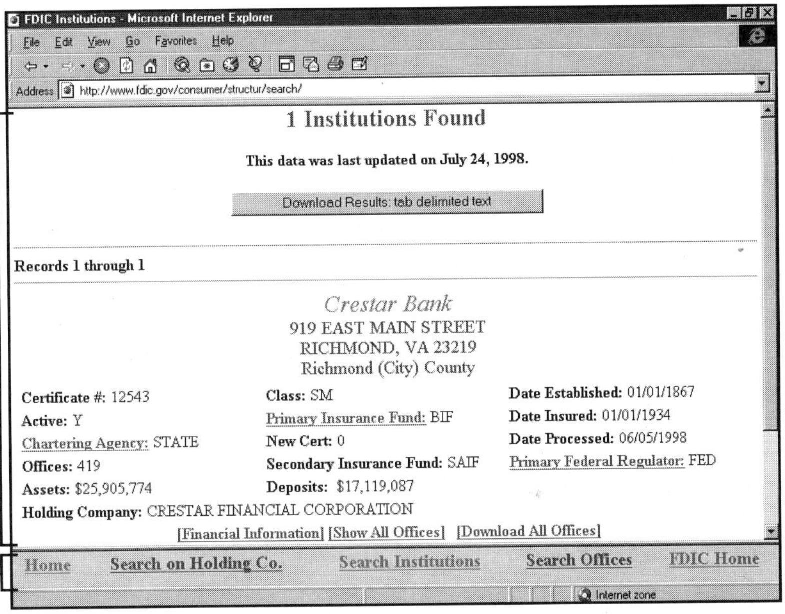

FIGURE 2.8
You can target the output from a search to a new frame, enabling search options to continue being displayed.

Results frame —

Search options frame —

The page elements noted in the preceding list give you a design palette with which to work. It is up to you to decide which elements best communicate your message in a way that is clear to your audience.

HTML Standards and Browser Compatibility

The current HTML standard is HTML 4, which incorporates most of the page elements discussed in the previous list. Even the frame tags are part of HTML 4 spec, including the concept of "floating frames" as proposed by Microsoft.

> **N O T E** Floating frames are frames that you can place on a page just as you would an image. ▪

Most mainstream browsers are already in compliance with the HTML 4 tags that create paragraphs, lists, and font effects, as well as those that place images, tables, and frames on a page. If you discover that some of your audience will be using a browser that is not HTML 4 compliant, you should research which tags the browser does not support and make sure you don't use those tags in your page design unless you can provide some kind of alternative way to view the content. Fortunately, a couple of approaches provide alternatives. The next two sections discuss these approaches.

N O T E Not all browsers are up to speed on some of the HTML tags that support enhanced usability for persons with disabilities. If you're marking up content with sensitivity to a disabled audience, make sure you test your code to see which browsers support the tags you're using.

Alternative HTML

One of the great features of HTML is that it enables you to provide alternative content if your primary content is not viewable. The HTML instruction that places an image on a page, for example, also supports the display of a text-based alternative to the image for users with text-only browsers, for users who have turned off image loading on their graphical browsers, or for users who use non-visual browsers. As you read the chapters on HTML in this book, make note of the ways you can provide alternative content on your pages. Using these techniques will also help to maximize your audience.

Alternative HTML Pages

Sometimes users cannot view an entire page. One case of this is a framed page. Although most users will probably be using a browser that can process frames, you still need to be sensitive to "frames-challenged" browsers. You can do this by creating non-frames versions of your framed pages. Many sites that use frames provide links to pages that contain the same information but don't use frames (see Figure 2.9).

Alternatives to Scripts

Scripts are like images in that a user may have a browser that does not support a scripting language, or the user may have turned off the browser's ability to parse and execute scripts. For these reasons, you should be sure to include alternative content in the event that your scripts can't run on a user's browser.

Fortunately, HTML 4 makes this a fairly simple matter with the <NOSCRIPT> and </NOSCRIPT> tags. Any content you place between these tags will be rendered by a script-capable browser when it is unable to run a script. Browsers that don't support any scripting languages will ignore the <SCRIPT> and <NOSCRIPT> tags and simply render what you have placed between the <NOSCRIPT> and </NOSCRIPT> tags. Thus, no matter what kind of browser a user has, your <NOSCRIPT> content will be displayed when it is appropriate.

FIGURE 2.9
The city of Sunnyvale, California, offers both framed and non-framed versions of its pages.

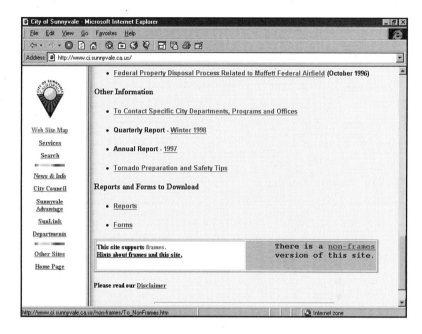

N O T E To keep your script code hidden from browsers that don't support a scripting language, you should enclose the code in an HTML comment tag. This way, the raw code won't be displayed on the browser screen. ■

Desirable Page Elements

As users traverse the Web, they become accustomed to seeing certain items on pages. They come to rely on these items being present to enhance their Web browsing experience. This section looks at a few common page elements that are also good end-user services.

Last Updated Date

▶ To learn how to automate your last updated dates, **see** "Microsoft FrontPage Components," **p. 281**.

Everyone craves fresh content, so it makes sense to have some kind of "freshness dating" on your pages. A last-updated date tells visitors how recently the information on a page has changed (see Figure 2.10). Assuming they remember the last time they visited your page, regular visitors can use the last-updated date to decide whether any new content exists that they need to check out.

 T I P Server-side includes are another good way to have the server automatically stamp your pages with last-updated dates. See Chapter 32, "Server-Side Includes," for more information.

CAUTION

Having a last-updated date can create image problems for you if you don't keep refreshing your pages. Users will be unimpressed if they see a last-updated date of six months ago!

FIGURE 2.10

Investors in the New York Stock Exchange want the most up-to-date information possible, so it's important to include date information on each page.

Last updated information ─┘

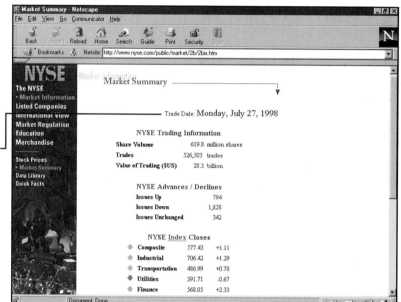

Contact Information

User feedback is important to your efforts to maintain and improve your pages. Many Web pages have contact information at the bottom, typically the email address of the Webmaster or the page author. Others take you to a separate HTML page to collect feedback (see Figure 2.11). These email addresses are often hyperlinked so that users can click them and compose a feedback message.

N O T E It is better to include your email address right in the hyperlink so that visitors can just click to send mail. That way, if someone is seeing a printout of the page only, she still knows where to send the feedback.

Navigation Tools

It frustrates users when they get that "you can't get there from here" feeling. To avoid the Web equivalent of this, it is imperative that you place navigation tools on your pages. Depending on where users are, they will have different expectations about which navigation tools should be available.

FIGURE 2.11

You can contact the Peace Corps through a link at the bottom of its Web page.

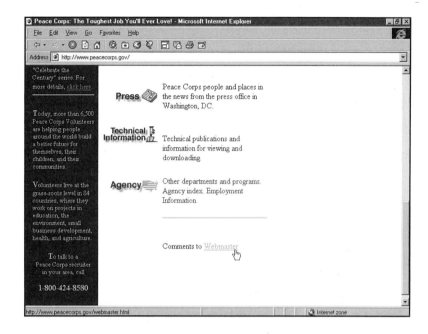

A visitor hitting the home page of a site will most likely be looking for some type of clickable image or imagemap that can take her to the major subsections of the site (see Figure 2.12). A home page that is well designed will also include a set of hypertext links that duplicate the links on the imagemap. This enables people with text-only browsers, or people with image loading turned off, to navigate from the home page as well.

FIGURE 2.12

An imagemap on Motorola's home page links you to all major parts of the site.

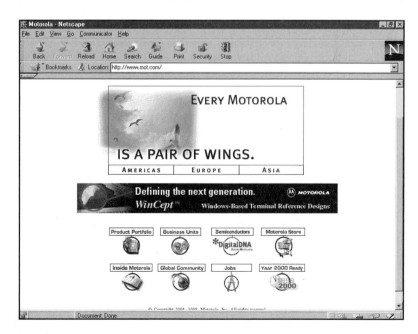

When on an inside page of a site, users typically look for navigation bars either at the top or bottom of the page (see Figure 2.13). Some pages have navigation bars at both the top and bottom so that the user has the option of using the closest one. In other cases, a page will have a set of links across the top of the page that point to the major areas of the site, and another set along the bottom of the page pointing to functional areas.

 TIP Try to keep your navigation links as close to the top of the page as you can. This enhances usability by eliminating the need for the user to scroll to find your links.

FIGURE 2.13
American Airlines provides links to major content and support areas of its site at the top of each page.

Navigation bar ⏤

Counters

Some people think counters, which are graphical displays of the number of people who have visited a page (see Figure 2.14), are annoying. Counters can be annoying if they are used in a grandstanding or self-indulgent way. They can be a useful service, however, if they are built into pages in an unobtrusive way. Counters are helpful to

- Users, who can get a sense of how many other people are interested in the content on the page.

- Page authors, who can better track the traffic on their pages.

▶ To learn how to add a counter to one of your pages, **see** "Microsoft FrontPage Components," **p. 281** or "Custom Database Query Scripts," **p. 721**.

You can go about placing a counter on a page in two ways. One approach involves programming the counter yourself. This is a fairly straightforward thing to do, but it does require that your Web page server supports Common Gateway Interface (CGI) programs. If you want to avoid programming altogether, you can drop the FrontPage Hit Counter Component onto your page and let it do all the work for you.

FIGURE 2.14

Carol Greco, a Northern Virginia realtor, keeps a count of how many potential buyers and sellers have visited her page.

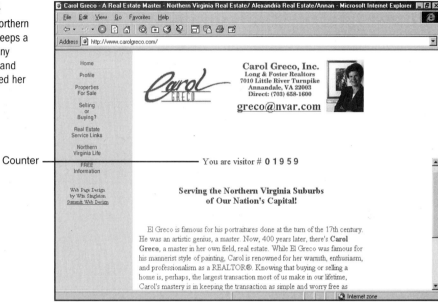

If you don't have CGI support on your server, you can use one of the online counter services. Figure 2.15 shows you the counter service at http://www.pagecount.com/. The service won't cost you anything, but Pagecount will place an advertising graphic on your page along with the hit count.

CAUTION

When you use an online counter service, the images that make up the counter display have to be transferred from your host service. This can delay page loading and make visitors to your Web pages impatient.

Also, don't put a counter on every page you create. Usually a counter on the home page of a site is sufficient. If you need information on subordinate pages of your site, use an HTTP access log analysis tool such as WebTrends to gather the information you require.

Breaking Up Long Pages

You should avoid placing too much content on a single page. You read earlier in this chapter that users typically scan a page rather than read it, so most of the content you pack onto a long page will be lost on them. On top of that, forcing users to scroll through large amounts of text serves only to annoy them. If you have a lot of content, you should try to think of ways to divide it over several pages so that users can read it in smaller, more digestible chunks.

FIGURE 2.15

Pagecount is an online service that provides page counters to sites otherwise unable to implement them.

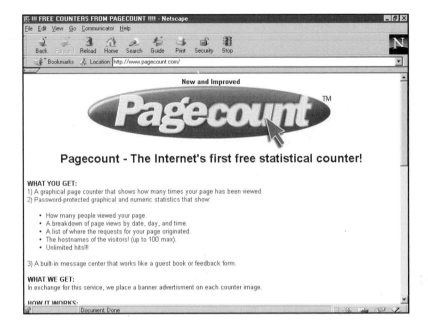

Sometimes long pages are unavoidable. For those instances, you can make use of some of the graphics elements techniques, discussed in the following section, to make reading long pages less of an effort for your audience.

Graphics Elements

Graphics elements are a terrific way to break up a sea of text. Graphics give users' eyes a break from line after line of content. Intelligent placement of the graphics can also create interesting and attractive layouts.

With the HTML you will learn in this book, you will be able to use the following three effective graphics elements:

- Horizontal rules
- Images
- Pull quotes

Horizontal Rules   A *horizontal rule* is a simple horizontal line across the width of a page (see Figure 2.16). Simple proves very effective in this case because a horizontal rule can break a long page into smaller sections and give the readers' eyes a reprieve from an abundance of text.

Images   Images can break up a lot of text, and they are particularly effective when text wraps around them (see Figure 2.17). HTML 4 includes instructions for placing "floating images" that permit text wrapping.

FIGURE 2.16
The CIA offsets its site's warning notice with horizontal rules above and below the notice.

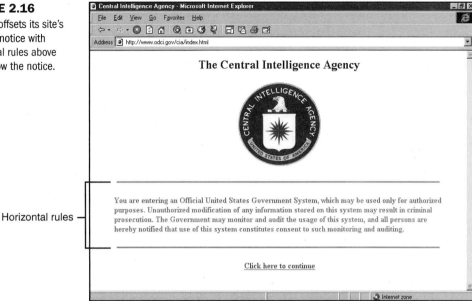

Horizontal rules —

FIGURE 2.17
General Electric uses floating images in each of the three columns of text on its home page.

Pull Quotes   A *pull quote* is a key phrase or sentence from a manuscript that is repeated in larger, bold text. Pull quotes provide you with a doubly powerful page element: They break up big blocks of text and they reiterate important points (see Figure 2.18).

FIGURE 2.18

Pull quotes taken from favorable reviews are popular features on product information pages.

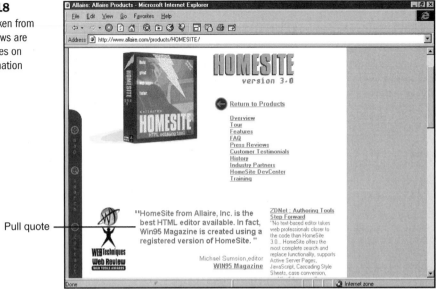

Pull quote ──────

It is easy to make a pull quote by using HTML tables. You can do this by floating a table in the middle of your document's text and placing a large, formatted excerpt from the text in the table. It is also a good idea to have the table borders turned off and to use horizontal lines above and below the excerpted text.

Table of Contents

If a page is really long, you should make the extra effort to set up a small table of contents at the top of the page (see Figure 2.19). By clicking entries in the table of contents, users can jump right to the section of the document they are interested in and not have to scroll through the document to find it. To make it easy for users to get back to the table of contents, you should include a link back to the top of the page at the end of each major section.

Text Effects

You can make critical points stand out on long pages by marking them up in boldface or with color. This way, even if users are scanning the long page, the highlighted text will jump right off the page at them (see Figure 2.20).

N O T E When marking up text you want rendered in boldface, it is best to use the <STRONG> tag rather than the <B> tag. This enables non-visual browsers to understand that the content is to be strongly emphasized and to render the content in a way that lets the users know that the content is important.

FIGURE 2.19

Long documents placed on a single page should have a table of contents at the top to assist the reader in navigating the document.

Document table of contents

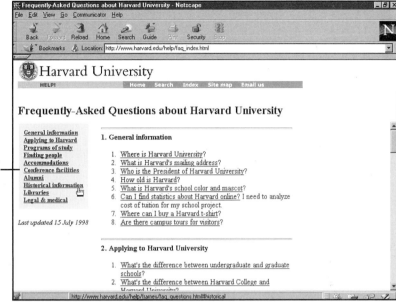

FIGURE 2.20

Usability expert Jakob Nielsen practices what he preaches by employing bold text to make key points stand out on a page.

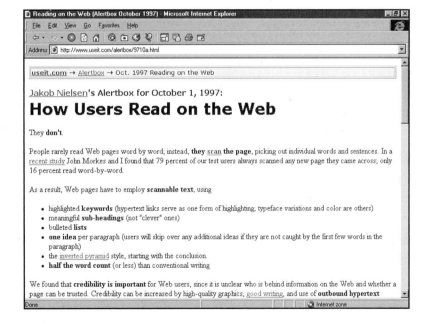

HTML and Graphics

HTML 4.0 Tag Reference

by Eric Ladd

In this chapter

Reference Scope

This chapter is unique in the book because it is written to serve as a reference for all the tags included in the HTML 4.0 recommendation, as published by the World Wide Web Consortium (W3C). It is a one-stop catalog of each tag, including the tag's attributes, syntax, and examples of uses. By necessity, the chapter covers a large amount of information, but you'll soon come to appreciate the value of having all the relevant facts about all HTML tags—together with tips on how to use them—right at your fingertips.

N O T E   This chapter covers only the tags included in the recommended HTML 4.0 Document Type Definition (DTD), as published by the World Wide Web Consortium in April 1998. Browser-specific extensions to HTML 4.0 are beyond the scope of this chapter, but may be covered elsewhere in the book. The <LAYER> tag introduced by Netscape Communications Corporation, for example, is discussed in detail in Chapter 24, "Introduction to Dynamic HTML," and Chapter 25, "Advanced Netscape Dynamic HTML."

For the most up-to-date status of HTML 4.0, consult http://www.w3.org/TR/PR-html40/, where you will find links to the most current version of the standard and the version just prior to that.

How This Chapter Is Organized

Because of the vast coverage of the chapter, the information presented has been carefully structured to make it as easy as possible for you to look up the tags you need. At the highest level, the chapter is organized into major sections that cover a group of related tags. The major sections and the tags they cover include

- Document structure tags (see p. **62**): <HTML>, <HEAD>, <BASE>, <ISINDEX>, <META>, <LINK>, <SCRIPT>, <STYLE>, <TITLE>, <BDO>, and <BODY>.
- Formatting tags (see p. **72**): <B>, <BASEFONT>, <BIG>, <FONT>, <I>, <S>, <STRIKE>, <SMALL>, <SUB>, <SUP>, <TT>, <U>, <ABBR>, <ACRONYM>, <ADDRESS>, <CITE>, <CODE>, <DEL>, <DFN>, <EM>, <INS>, <KBD>, <Q>, <SAMP>, <STRONG>, <VAR>, <BLOCKQUOTE>, <BR>, <CENTER>, <DIV>, <HR>, <H1>-<H6>, <P>, <PRE>, and <SPAN>.
- List tags (see p. **95**): <LI>, <DIR>, <DL>, <DT>, <DD>, <MENU>, <OL>, and </UL>.
- Hyperlink tags: <A>.
- Image and imagemap tags (see p. **104**): <IMG>, <MAP>, and <AREA>.
- Table tags (see p. **109**): <TABLE>, <CAPTION>, <THEAD>, <TFOOT>, <TBODY>, <COLGROUP>, <COL>, <TR>, <TD>, and <TH>.
- Form tags (see p. **119**): <FORM>, <INPUT>, <SELECT>, <OPTION>, <OPTGROUP>, <TEXTAREA>, <BUTTON>, <LABEL>, <FIELDSET>, and <LEGEND>.
- Frame tags (see p. **129**): <FRAMESET>, <FRAME>, <NOFRAMES>, and <IFRAME>.
- Executable content tags (see p. **133**): <APPLET>, <PARAM>, and <OBJECT>.

T I P In some cases, tags covered in this chapter get a more thorough treatment in a later chapter of the book. Look for cross-references to point you to this expanded coverage.

Within a given section, several tags are discussed in detail. Specifically, you'll find the following information about each tag:

- The tag's keyword—For example, the `<INPUT>` tag's keyword is `INPUT`.

- What kind of tag it is—Every HTML tag is either a *container tag* or a *standalone tag*. A container tag is one that activates an effect and that has a companion tag that discontinues the effect. For example, `<I>` is a container tag that, together with its companion closing tag `</I>`, causes all text found between them to be rendered in italic. The `<I>` tag turns on the italic effect and the `</I>` tag turns it off.

  A standalone tag is one that does not have a companion tag. For example, the `<IMG>` tag simply places an image on a page. `<IMG>` has no effect that was turned on and needs to be turned off, so no closing tag is needed.

N O T E Standalone tags are sometimes called *empty tags*. ■

- The tag's function—A description of the effect or page element that the tag controls.

- The tag's syntax—HTML is derived from the Standard Generalized Markup Language (SGML) by applying SGML constructs according to a certain set of rules. These rules define a tag's syntax.

- The tag's attributes—An attribute modifies how a tag's effect is applied. Some tags take no attributes, and others may be able to take several. Additionally, attributes can sometimes take on only one of a set number of values. In these cases, the possible values of the attribute are listed along with the attribute. Use of some attributes may be required (such as the `SRC` attribute for the `<IMG>` tag), and use of others may be optional. A tag's required attributes, if any, are noted in each attribute discussion.

- Example usage—You can learn more about how a tag is used by looking over the sample code given in the tag description.

- Related tags—Some tags work in conjunction with others to produce an effect. In these cases, you'll find a listing of the other HTML tags related to the one being described. Often, you'll find that the related tags are discussed in the same section.

Within a section, tags are listed alphabetically by keyword, unless they need to be used in a certain order, in which case, they are presented in the order that they are typically used.

Global Attributes

Although most tag attributes tend to be unique to the tag, some are almost universal and usable with any tag. Table 3.1 summarizes these attributes, showing which tags do take the attributes and how each attribute is used.

Table 3.1 Global HTML Attributes

Attribute	Purpose	Used With
CLASS	Space-separated list of classes of the tag	All tags but `<BASE>`, `<BASEFONT>`, `<HEAD>`, `<HTML>`, `<META>`, `<PARAM>`, `<SCRIPT>`, `<STYLE>`, and `<TITLE>`.
DIR	Direction for weak or neutral text	All tags but `<APPLET>`, `<BASE>`, `<BASEFONT>`, `<BDO>`, ` `, `<FRAME>`, `<FRAMESET>`, `<HR>`, `<IFRAME>`, `<PARAM>`, and `<SCRIPT>`.
ID	Unique, document-wide identifier	All tags but `<BASE>`, `<HEAD>`, `<HTML>`, `<META>`, `<SCRIPT>`, `<STYLE>`, and `<TITLE>`.
LANG	Specifies document language context	All tags but `<APPLET>`, `<BASE>`, `<BASEFONT>`, ` `, `<FRAME>`, `<FRAMESET>`, `<HR>`, `<IFRAME>`, `<PARAM>`, and `<SCRIPT>`.
STYLE	Binds style information to the tag	All tags but `<BASE>`, `<BASEFONT>`, `<HEAD>`, `<HTML>`, `<META>`, `<PARAM>`, `<SCRIPT>`, `<STYLE>`, and `<TITLE>`.
TITLE	Advisory title	All tags but `<BASE>`, `<BASEFONT>`, `<HEAD>`, `<HTML>`, `<META>`, `<PARAM>`, `<SCRIPT>`, `<STYLE>`, and `<TITLE>`.

The global attribute you'll probably use most often is the STYLE attribute, which is used to assign style information to a tag. To color a level 2 heading red, for example, you could use the HTML:

```
<H2 STYLE="color: red">Red Heading</H2>
```

The ID attribute is also useful when you need to have a unique identifier for a tag. This situation comes into play when you write scripts to support dynamic HTML documents because you frequently want to change the properties of some marked-up text. To do this, you need to be able to address the tag that marks up the text via JavaScript, JScript, or VBScript, and the best way to do that is to give the tag a unique name. Then it becomes fairly simple to address the tag via the browser's object model.

▶ **See** "Introduction to Dynamic HTML," **p. 581**.

LANG can be helpful in situations where you are marking up content in multiple languages. The value of LANG gives browsers a "heads-up" as to what language is being used. LANG is usually set equal to a two-character language code that denotes the language being used. For example, "fr" denotes French; "de" denotes German, and so on. In cases where variants on a language exist, you'll see expanded language codes, such as "en-US" for English spoken in the United States or "en-Br" for English spoken in Britain.

DIR refers to the directionality—left-to-right or right-to-left—of text when it cannot otherwise be deduced from the context of the document. DIR can take on values of LTR (left-to-right) or RTL (right-to-left).

The TITLE attribute enables you to specify descriptive text to associate with the tag. This information may be helpful to nonvisual browsers, such as those that generate speech or Braille output.

Finally, the CLASS attribute enables you to create different classes of the same tag. For example, you might have:

```
<A HREF="xrefs.html" CLASS="cross-reference"> ... </A>
<A HREF="defns.html" CLASS="definition"> ... </A>
<A HREF="biblio.html" CLASS="bibliography"> ... </A>
```

This creates three classes of the <A> tag. After these classes are established, you can reference them elsewhere in your document. One popular application of this is in a style sheet:

```
A.cross-reference {color: navy}
A.definition {color: yellow}
A.bibliography {color: fuschia}
```

The style information above would color cross-reference links navy blue, definition links yellow, and bibliography links fuschia.

Event Handlers

The HTML 4.0 recommendation also allows for several event handlers that can be used to trigger the execution of script code embedded in an HTML document. Each event handler is tied to a specific event that can occur during a person's use of a browser. When a user submits a form, for example, you can capture that event and launch a field validation script using the onsubmit event handler:

```
<FORM ACTION="register.cgi" METHOD="POST" onsubmit="validate();">
```

▶ For the specifics on writing scripts for your HTML documents, **see** "Introduction to JavaScripting," **p. 439** or "Active Server Pages and VBScript," **p. 835**.

Thus, when a user clicks the Submit button, the scripted function named "validate" fires and checks the data the user is submitting for appropriate formatting, content, or other validation checks.

Table 3.2 details the event handlers available under HTML 4.0. Most can be used within any HTML element, but a few are limited to specific elements. These special cases are noted in the table.

Part
II

Ch
3

Table 3.2   HTML 4.0 Event Handlers

Event Handler	Triggered when...
onload	A document or frameset is loaded; only allowed in the \<BODY\> and \<FRAMESET\> elements
onunload	A document or frameset is unloaded; only allowed in the \<BODY\> and \<FRAMESET\> elements
onclick	The mouse button is clicked once
ondblclick	The mouse button is clicked twice
onmousedown	The mouse button is depressed
onmouseup	The mouse button is released
onmouseover	The mouse pointer is over a page element
onmousemove	The mouse pointer is moved while over a page element
onmouseout	The mouse pointer is moved off a page element
onfocus	A form field receives focus by tabbing to it or by clicking it with the mouse pointer; only allowed in the \<INPUT\>, \<SELECT\>, \<TEXTAREA\>, \<LABEL\>, and \<BUTTON\> elements
onblur	A form field loses focus by tabbing out of it or by clicking a different field with the mouse pointer; only allowed in the \<INPUT\>, \<SELECT\>, \<TEXTAREA\>, \<LABEL\>, and \<BUTTON\> elements
onkeypress	A key is pressed and released over a page element
onkeydown	A key is pressed over a page element
onkeyup	A key is released over a page element
onsubmit	A form is submitted; only allowed in the \<FORM\> tag
onreset	A form is reset; only allowed in the \<FORM\> tag
onselect	A user selects some text in a text field; only allowed in the \<INPUT\> and \<TEXTAREA\> elements
onchange	A form field loses focus and its value has changed since gaining focus; only allowed in the \<INPUT\>, \<TEXTAREA\>, and \<SELECT\> elements

Document Structure Tags

Every HTML document has three major components: the HTML declaration, the head, and the body. The document structure tags are those that define each component.

<HTML>

Type:

Container

Function:

Declares the document to be an HTML document. All document content and supporting HTML code goes between the <HTML> and </HTML> tags.

Syntax:

```
<HTML> ... </HTML>
```

Attributes:

Technically speaking, the <HTML> tag can take the VERSION attribute, but this has been deprecated in favor of version information being specified in the <!DOCTYPE> tag (see "Related Tags" below).

Example:

```
<HTML>
... all content and HTML code goes here ...
</HTML>
```

Related Tags:

Although the <HTML> tag is typically the first tag in a document, it is sometimes preceded by a <!DOCTYPE> tag that specifies what level of HTML conformance the document displays. A document conforming to the HTML 4.0 standard might have a <!DOCTYPE> tag that reads:

```
<!DOCTYPE HTML PUBLIC "-//W3C//DTD HTML 4.0//EN">
```

Technically, <!DOCTYPE> is an SGML tag, not an HTML tag, so it is acceptable for it to be outside the <HTML> and </HTML> tags.

<HEAD>

Type:

Container

Function:

Contains the tags that compose the document head.

Syntax:

```
<HEAD> ... </HEAD>
```

Attributes:

<HEAD> can take the PROFILE attribute, which gets set equal to a space-separated list of URLs that point to meta data profiles for the document.

Example:

```
<HTML>
<HEAD PROFILE="http://www.server.com/profiles/">
... tags making up the document head go here ...
</HEAD>
... all other content and HTML code goes here ...
</HTML>
```

Related Tags:

A number of tags can be placed between the <HEAD> and </HEAD> tags, including <BASE>, <ISINDEX>, <LINK>, <META>, <SCRIPT>, <STYLE>, and <TITLE>. Each of these is described next.

<BASE>

Type:

Standalone

Function:

Declares global reference values for the HREF and TARGET attributes. The reference or base HREF value is used as a basis for computing all relative URL references. The base TARGET name is used to identify the frame into which all linked documents should be loaded.

Syntax:

```
<BASE HREF="base_url">
```

or

```
<BASE TARGET="frame_name">
```

Attributes:

The <BASE> tag takes either the HREF or the TARGET attribute. A given <BASE> tag can contain only one of these, so if you need to specify a base URL and a base target frame, you need to have two <BASE> tags in the head of your document. These two attributes work as follows:

- HREF—Specifies the reference URL that is used to help compute relative URLs. If the BASE HREF URL is http://www.myserver.com/sports/hockey/skates.html and you use the relative URL pucks.html elsewhere in the document, for example, the relative URL will really point to http://www.myserver.com/sports/hockey/pucks.html.

- TARGET—Specifies the default frame name to which all links are targeted.

N O T E When used in a <BASE> tag, HREF is typically set to the URL of the document.

Example:

```
<HEAD>
<BASE HREF="http://www.myserver.com/index.html">
```

```
<BASE TARGET="bigframe">
...
</HEAD>
```

This code sets the document's base URL to `http://www.myserver.com/index.html` and the base frame for targeting hyperlinks to the frame named `"bigframe"`.

<ISINDEX>

Type:

Standalone

Function:

Produces a single-line input field used to collect query information.

Syntax:

```
<ISINDEX PROMPT="Please enter the value to search for.">
```

Attributes:

The PROMPT attribute specifies what text should appear before the input field. In the absence of a PROMPT attribute, the text will read `"This is a searchable index. Enter search criteria:"`

Example:

```
<HEAD>
<ISINDEX PROMPT="Enter the last name of the employee you want to search for:">
...
</HEAD>
```

N O T E   <ISINDEX> was used in the early days when the <FORM> tags had yet to come onto the scene. The W3C has deprecated the <ISINDEX> tag, meaning that it discourages its use in favor of using the <FORM> tags and it expects to drop the tag from the standard in the future.

<META>

Type:

Standalone

Function:

Defines document meta-information, such as keywords, expiration date, author, page generation software used, and many other document-specific items. It also supports the notion of *client pull*—a dynamic document technique in which the browser loads a new document after a specified delay.

Syntax:

```
<META HTTP-EQUIV="header" CONTENT="value">
```

Part

II

Ch

3

or

```
<META NAME="name" CONTENT="value">
```

Attributes:

The <META> tag takes the following attributes:

- ▣ HTTP-EQUIV—Specifies a type of HTTP header to be sent with the document. The value of the header is given by the CONTENT attribute. The two most commonly used values of HTTP-EQUIV are REFRESH, which refreshes the page after a specified delay, and EXPIRES, which gives the date after which content in the document is not considered to be reliable.

- ▣ NAME—Set equal to the name of the document meta-variable you want to specify. The value of the variable is given in the CONTENT attribute. Typical values for NAME include AUTHOR, KEYWORDS, GENERATOR, and DESCRIPTION. The KEYWORDS value is particularly useful for specifying words you would like a search engine's indexing program to associate with the page.

- ▣ SCHEME—Provides information on how to interpret the meta-variable. For example, with the following <META> tag:

  ```
  <META SCHEME="9-digit-ZipCode" NAME="zip" CONTENT="02134-1078">
  ```

  a browser may not know how to interpret "02134-1078" without information from the SCHEME attribute.

- ▣ CONTENT—Specifies either the HTTP header or the value of the meta-variable.

Example:

```
<HEAD>
<!-- The first <META> tag instructs the browser to load a new page after 5
seconds. -->
<!-- This is useful for creating a splash screen effect. -->
<META HTTP-EQUIV="Refresh" CONTENT="5; URL=http://www.myserver.com/index2.html">
<!-- The remaining <META> tags specify author and keyword information. -->
<META NAME="AUTHOR" CONTENT="Eric Ladd">
<META NAME="KEYWORDS" CONTENT="Main page, welcome, neat stuff">
...
</HEAD>
```

<LINK>

Type:

Standalone

Function:

Denotes the linking relationship between two files.

Syntax:

```
<LINK HREF="url_of_linked_file" TITLE="title" REL="forward_relationship"
REV="reverse_relationship">
```

Attributes:

The `<LINK>` tag takes the following attributes:

- `CHARSET`—Denotes which character encoding scheme to use.
- `HREF`—Set equal to the URL of the file to which you're making the linking reference.
- `HREFLANG`—Specifies the language code for the linked file.
- `MEDIA`—Provides the intended display destination for the linked document. The default value of `MEDIA` is "screen."
- `TARGET`—Specifies which frame to target.
- `TITLE`—Gives the link a descriptive title.
- `REL`—Specifies the relationship of the linked file to the current file.
- `REV`—Specifies how the current file relates to the linked file.

Table 3.3 shows some possible values for `REL` and `REV` and what these values mean.

Table 3.3   Possible Values for the *REL* and *REV* Attributes

Value	Meaning
Copyright	Web site's copyright page
Glossary	Glossary of terms for a site
Help	Site help page
Home	Site home page
Index	Site index page
Made	Mail to URL pointing to the email address of the page author
Next	Page that logically follows the current page
Previous	Page that precedes the current page
Stylesheet	File containing style information for the page
TOC	Site table of contents
Up	Page that is above the current page in a site's hierarchy

N O T E   Because so many types of linked files exist, it is permissible to have more than one `<LINK>` tag in a document. ▪

Example:

```
<HEAD>
<LINK HREF="/style/styles.css" REL="Stylesheet">
<LINK HREF="/index.html" REL="Home">
```

Part

II

Ch

3

```
<LINK HREF="/help.html" REL="Help">
<LINK HREF="back_one.html" REV="Previous">
...
</HEAD>
```

<SCRIPT>

Type:

Container

Function:

Contains script code referenced in the body of the document.

Syntax:

```
<SCRIPT LANGUAGE="scripting_language">
... script code goes here ...
</SCRIPT>
```

Attributes:

The <SCRIPT> tag can take the following attributes:

- ▓ CHARSET—Denotes which character encoding scheme to use.

- ▓ DEFER—Specifying the DEFER attribute tells the browser that the script does not generate any document content. This enables the browser to continue parsing and rendering the document without having to execute the script.

- ▓ LANGUAGE—Set equal to the scripting language used to write the script. LANGUAGE is being deprecated in favor of using the TYPE attribute.

- ▓ SRC—Specifies the URL of a file containing the script code, if not contained between the <SCRIPT> and </SCRIPT> tags.

- ▓ TYPE—Set equal to the MIME type of the script code, usually text/javascript or text/vbscript. When specifying a specific version of a scripting language, you can set TYPE equal to a value that includes version information as well (for example, TYPE="text/javascript1.1"). TYPE is a required attribute under HTML 4.0.

```
<SCRIPT LANGUAGE="VBScript">
<!--
Sub ScriptEx
document.write("<HR>")
document.write("<H1 ALIGN=CENTER>Thank you for your submission!</H1>")
document.write("<HR>")
-->
</SCRIPT>
```

N O T E Script code is often placed between <!-- and --> tags so that browsers that can't process scripts will treat the code as a comment. ▓

Related Tags:

You can use the <NOSCRIPT> tag to specify what a browser should do if it is unable to execute a script contained in the <SCRIPT> and </SCRIPT> tags.

<NOSCRIPT>

Type:

Container

Function:

Provides alternate content to use if a script cannot be executed. A browser might not be able to execute a script because the user has turned scripting off or because it does not know the scripting language used to write the script.

Syntax:

```
<NOSCRIPT>
... alternative to script code goes here ...
</NOSCRIPT>
```

Attributes:

None.

Example:

```
<SCRIPT LANGUAGE="VBScript">
   document.write("Hello, World!");
</SCRIPT>
<NOSCRIPT>
   You either have scripting turned off or your browser does not
   understand VBScript.
</NOSCRIPT>
```

<STYLE>

Type:

Container

Function:

Specifies style information for the document.

Syntax:

```
<STYLE TYPE="mime_type" MEDIA="media_type" TITLE="title">
... style information goes here ...
</HTML>
```

Attributes:

The <STYLE> tag takes the following three attributes:

- MEDIA—Specifies what media types the styles are to be used for (visual browser, speech-based browser, Braille browser, and so on).

- TITLE—Gives the style information a descriptive title.

- TYPE—Set equal to the Internet content type for the style language. You will most likely say TYPE="text/css1" to denote the use of the style language put forward in the Cascading Style Sheets, Level 1 specification. TYPE is a required attribute of the <STYLE> tag.

Example:

```
<STYLE TYPE="text/css1">
<!--
   BODY {font: 10 pt Palatino; color: silver margin-left: 0.25 in}
   H1 {font: 18 pt Palatino; font-weight: bold}
   H2 {font: 16 pt Palatino; font-weight: bold}
   P {font: 12 pt Arial; line-height: 14 pt; text-indent: 0.25 in}
-->
</STYLE>
```

N O T E   Style information is usually contained between <!-- and --> tags so that browsers that cannot process it will treat the style information as a comment. ▪

<TITLE>

Type:

Container

Function:

Gives a descriptive title to a document. Use of the <TITLE> tag is required by the HTML 4.0 DTD for many good reasons. Titles show up in browser window title bars and in bookmark and history listings. In each of these cases, you provide an important reader service when you specify a title because otherwise the browser will display just the document's URL. Additionally, Web search engines, such as Yahoo! and AltaVista, frequently look for title information when they index a document.

Syntax:

```
<TITLE> ... document title goes here ... </TITLE>
```

Attributes:

None.

Example:

```
<TITLE>
The Advantages of a Corporate Web Site
</TITLE>
```

T I P   Try to keep titles to 40 characters or fewer so that browsers can display them completely.

<BDO>

Type:

Container

Function:

When mixing languages in an HTML document, it sometimes becomes necessary to be sensitive to the direction in which the language is read (left-to-right versus right-to-left). When languages that have mixed directions are used in a document, an approach called the *bidirectional algorithm* is used to ensure proper presentation of the content. In cases where you want to override the bidirectional algorithm for a block of text, you can enclose that text in the <BDO> and </BDO> tags.

Syntax:

```
<BDO DIR="LTR¦RTL"> ... directional text goes here ... </BDO>
```

Attributes:

The <BDO> tag takes the DIR attribute, which can be set to LTR to specify left-to-right directionality or to RTL to specify right-to-left directionality.

Example:

```
<BODY LANG="he" ...> <!-- Hebrew language context - RTL directionality>
... <BDO DIR="LTR">Here's some English text.</BDO> ...
...
</BODY>
```

<BODY>

Type:

Container

Function:

Contains all content and tags that compose the document body.

Syntax:

```
<BODY BGCOLOR="background_color" BACKGROUND="background_image"
   LINK="unvisited_link_color" ALINK="active_link_color"
   VLINK="visited_link_color" TEXT="text_color">
... document body goes here ...
</BODY>
```

Attributes:

The <BODY> tag takes the following attributes, which focus on global background and coloring properties. Each color-related attribute can be set equal to one of the 16 reserved color names (BLACK, WHITE, AQUA, SILVER, GRAY, MAROON, RED, PURPLE, FUSCHIA, GREEN, LIME, OLIVE, YELLOW, NAVY, BLUE, and TEAL) or to an RGB hexadecimal triplet.

- ■ ALINK—Set equal to the color you want to paint active links (a link is active in the instant that the user clicks it).

- ■ BACKGROUND—Set equal to the URL of an image to use in the document background. The image will be horizontally and vertically tiled if it is not large enough to fill the entire browser screen.

- ■ BGCOLOR—Set equal to the color you want to paint the document's background.

- ■ LINK—Set equal to the color you want to paint unvisited links. (A link is unvisited if a user has yet to click it.)

- ■ TEXT—Set equal to the color you want to paint the body text of the document.

- ■ VLINK—Set equal to the color you want to paint visited links. (A link is visited if a user has already clicked it.)

N O T E   All the attributes listed have been deprecated in favor of using style sheet characteristics to specify the same information. ■

Example:

```
<BODY BGCOLOR="white" TEXT="#FF0088" LINK="#DD0F00" VLINK="#00FF9A">
... all document body content and HTML code goes here ...
</BODY>
```

Related Tags:

Dozens of tags are allowed between the <BODY> and </BODY> tags. In fact, with the exception of some of the frame-related tags, any tag in the rest of the chapter can be placed between <BODY> and </BODY>.

By putting together what you've learned in this section, you can come up with a generic HTML document template such as the following:

```
<HTML>
<HEAD>
<TITLE>Document Template</TITLE>
... <META>, <BASE>, <LINK>, <SCRIPT>, <STYLE>, <ISINDEX> tags ...
</HEAD>
<BODY>
... document body content and tags ...
</BODY>
</HTML>
```

When creating a new document, you can use this code to get started, and then fill in tags and other information according to your needs.

Formatting Tags

HTML provides a host of tags that you can use to change how text is displayed on a browser screen. After all, 12-point Times Roman gets a little tiring after a while, and it's nice to give a reader an occasional break from a sea of ordinary text.

You can apply formatting instructions at two levels within a document. The first is at the text level, which means you are marking up at least a single character, but often much more than that. The second is at the paragraph or block level, which means you are formatting a specific logical chunk of the document. This section looks at both types of markup, starting with text-level formatting.

Text-Level Formatting

Text-level formatting can occur in one of two ways. An HTML tag that formats text can make changes to the font properties of the text (*font formatting* or *physical styles*), or it can describe how the text is being used in the context of the document (*phrase formatting* or *logical styles*). The next two sections introduce you to the tags used for each type of formatting.

Font Formatting

<B>

Type:

Container

Function:

Contains text to be rendered in boldface (see Figure 3.1).

Syntax:

```
<B> ... bold text goes here ... </B>
```

FIGURE 3.1

Boldface text stands out from the plain text around it, drawing the reader's attention to it.

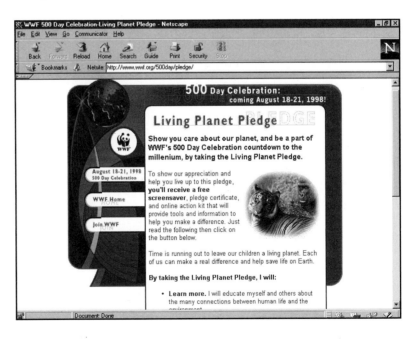

Attributes:

None.

Example:

`<B>First Name:</B> <INPUT TYPE="TEXT" NAME="fname">`

<BASEFONT>

Type:

Standalone

Function:

Sets base size, color, and typeface properties for the body text font. The `<BASEFONT>` tag and all its attributes have been deprecated in favor of using style sheets.

Syntax:

`<BASEFONT SIZE="size" COLOR="color" FACE="list_of_typefaces">`

Attributes:

`<FONT>` can take any combination of the following attributes:

- `COLOR`—Set to any of the 16 reserved, English-language color names or an RGB hexa-decimal triplet. The default font color is black.
- `FACE`—Set to a list of typefaces that the browser should use to render the text. The browser will use the first face in the list if that face is available. If not, it will work through the rest of the list and use the first face it finds available.
- `SIZE`—Set equal to an integer value between 1 and 7. This number is mapped to a font size in points by the browser, according to the user's preferences. The default `SIZE` value is 3.

Example:

`<BASEFONT SIZE=5 COLOR="navy" FACE="Arial,Helvetica,Times">`

Related Tags:

The `<FONT>` tag is typically used if you need to modify any of the base font properties specified in the `<BASEFONT>` tag. The `<FONT>` tag has been deprecated as well.

<BIG>

Type:

Container

Function:

Contains text to be rendered in a font size bigger than the default font size (see Figure 3.2).

FIGURE 3.2

Using the <BIG> tag increases the point size that text is rendered in.

Drop caps done with the <BIG> tag

Syntax:

```
<BIG> ... big text goes here ... </BIG>
```

Attributes:

None.

Example:

```
<BIG>D</BIG>rop <BIG>C</BIG>aps are a nice onscreen effect.
```

Related Tags:

The <SMALL> tag has the opposite effect (see later in this chapter).

<FONT>

Type:

Container

Function:

Contains text whose font properties are to be modified. Like most tags that specify presentation information, <FONT> has been deprecated by the W3C.

Syntax:

```
<FONT SIZE="size" COLOR="color" FACE="list of typefaces">
... text with modified font properties ...
</FONT>
```

Attributes:

Note that the <FONT> tag has the same attributes as the <BASEFONT> tag. <FONT> is used to change font properties from the base values provided in the <BASEFONT> tag or from their default values. SIZE can be set to a value between 1 and 7, or it can be set equal to how much larger or smaller you want the font size to go (-1 for one size smaller, +3 for three sizes larger, and so forth). COLOR and FACE work exactly as they did for the <BASEFONT> tag.

Example:

```
<FONT SIZE=+1 COLOR="red">Warning! Warning!</FONT> Danger, Will Robinson!
```

Related Tags:

<FONT> changes properties specified in the <BASEFONT> tag.

<I>

Type:

Container

Function:

Contains text to be rendered in italic (see Figure 3.3).

Syntax:

```
<I> ... italicized text goes here ... </I>
```

FIGURE 3.3

Italicized text can be used to denote emphasis or the title of something.

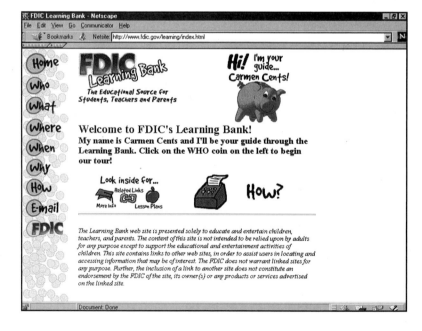

Attributes:

None.

Example:

```
I just bought the Beatles' <I>Abbey Road</I> on CD.
```

<S>, <STRIKE>

Type:

Container

Function:

Contains text to be marked with a strikethrough character. Both the `<s>` tags have been deprecated by the W3C. You should use style sheets to render strikethrough text instead.

Syntax:

```
<S> ... strikethrough text goes here ... </S>
```

or

```
<STRIKE> ... strikethrough text goes here ... </STRIKE>
```

Attributes:

None.

Example:

```
Content that has been struck from the record will be denoted as
follows: <S>removed content</S>.
```

<SMALL>

Type:

Container

Function:

Contains text to be rendered in a font size smaller than the default font size.

Syntax:

```
<SMALL> ... smaller text goes here ... </SMALL>
```

Attributes:

None.

Example:

```
<SMALL>"Sssssssshhh!"</SMALL>, he whispered in a tiny voice.
```

Related Tags:

The `<BIG>` tag has the opposite effect (see the `<BIG>` tag section earlier in the chapter).

Part

II

Ch

3

<SUB>

Type:

Container

Function:

Contains text to be a subscript to the text that precedes it.

Syntax:

```
<SUB> ... subscript text goes here ... </SUB>
```

Attributes:

None.

Example:

```
a<SUB>1</SUB>, a<SUB>2</SUB>, and a<SUB>3</SUB> are the coefficients of
 the variables x, y, and z.
```

<SUP>

Type:

Container

Function:

Contains text to be rendered as a superscript to the text that precedes it (see Figure 3.4).

FIGURE 3.4
Superscripts are useful for indicating trademark or copyright information.

Superscript —

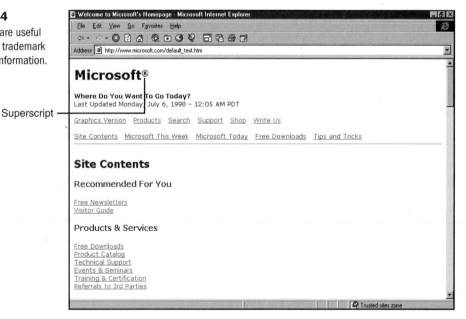

Syntax:

```
<SUP> ... superscript text goes here ... </SUP>
```

Attributes:

None.

Example:

```
x<SUP>2</SUP> + y<SUP>2</SUP> = 1 defines the unit circle.
```

<TT>

Type:

Container

Function:

Contains text to be rendered in a fixed-width font. Typically, this font is Courier or some kind of typewriter font (see Figure 3.5).

FIGURE 3.5
Typewriter text is good for displaying computer-related content or for varying the fonts used in the document.

Typewriter text —

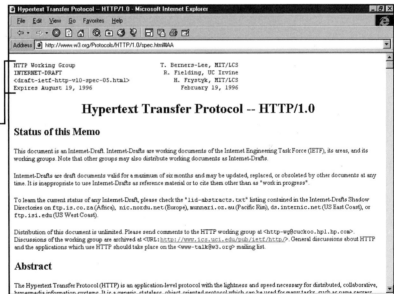

Syntax:

```
<TT> ... text to be in fixed-width font goes here ... <TT>
```

Attributes:

None.

Example:

```
The computer will then display the <TT>Login:</TT> prompt.
```

<U>

Type:

Container

Function:

Contains text to be rendered with an underline. The <U> tag has been deprecated by the W3C. If you need to underline text, you can do so using style sheets. However, keep in mind that a user might confuse your underlined text with hypertext and try to click it. Also, in keeping with general typesetting rules, if you italicize for form or style, you should not underline.

Syntax:

```
<U> ... text to be underlined ... </U>
```

Attributes:

None.

Example:

```
All first-year medical students purchase <U>Gray's Anatomy</U>.
```

Phrase Formatting Recall that phrase formatting indicates the *meaning* of the text it marks up and not necessarily how the text will be rendered on the browser screen. Nevertheless, text marked with a phrase formatting tag will typically have some kind of special rendering to set it apart from unmarked text.

<ABBR>

Type:

Container

Function:

Contains text that is an abbreviation of something. This is useful information for browsers that are not vision-based because it enables them to treat the abbreviation differently. A speech-based browser, for example, could know to look in an abbreviation table for pronunciation if you marked up "Dr." with the <ABBR> tag. That way, it could say the word "doctor" rather than making the "dr" sound you would get by pronouncing the "d" and the "r" together.

Syntax:

```
<ABBR> ... acronym goes here ... </ABBR>
```

Attributes:

None.

Example:

```
She got her doctorate (<ABBR>PhD</ABBR>) from the University of Virginia.
```

<ACRONYM>

Type:

Container

Function:

Contains text that specifies an acronym. This tag is also useful for nonvisual browsers. The tag might tell a speech-based browser to pronounce the letters in the acronym one at a time, for example, rather than trying to pronounce the acronym as a word.

Syntax:

```
<ACRONYM> ... acronym goes here ... </ACRONYM>
```

Attributes:

None.

Example:

```
Practical Extraction and Reporting Language <ACRONYM>(PERL)</ACRONYM> is
a popular CGI scripting language.
```

<ADDRESS>

Type:

Container

Function:

Contains either a postal or an electronic mail address. Text marked with this tag is typically rendered in italic (see Figure 3.6).

Syntax:

```
<ADDRESS> ... address goes here ... </ADDRESS>
```

Attributes:

None.

Example:

```
If you have any comments, please send them to
<ADDRESS>webmaster@your-isp.com</ADDRESS>.
```

<CITE>

Type:

Container

Part II Ch 3

FIGURE 3.6

Marking up address information provides a logical marker for programs processing the document and a visual marker for those reading the document.

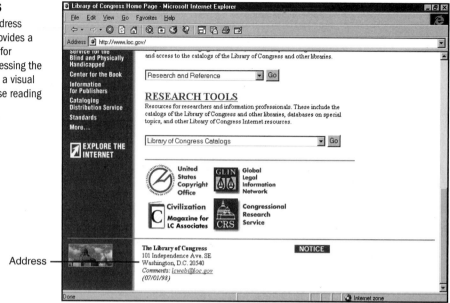

Address

Function:

Contains the name of a source from which a passage is cited. The source's name is typically rendered in italic.

Syntax:

```
<CITE> ... citation source goes here ... </CITE>
```

Attributes:

None.

Example:

```
According to the <CITE>HTML 4.0 Recommendation</CITE>, the <FONT> tag
has been deprecated.
```

<CODE>

Type:

Container

Function:

Contains chunks of computer language code. Browsers commonly display text marked with the <CODE> tag in a fixed-width font such as Courier.

Syntax:

```
<CODE> ... code fragment goes here ... </CODE>
```

Attributes:

None.

Example:

```
<CODE>
document.location.href = 'index.html';
return TRUE;
</CODE>
```

<DEL>

Type:

Container

Function:

Contains text that has been deleted from the document. The tag is intended mainly for documents with multiple authors and/or editors who would want to see all the content in an original draft, even though it may have been deleted by a reviewer.

N O T E The idea of logically marking up deleted text is similar to the idea of using revision marks in Microsoft Word. When revision marks are turned on, you can see the deleted text even though it is technically no longer part of the document. ▨

Syntax:

```
<DEL CITE="url" DATETIME="YYYYMMDDThh:mm:ss"> ... deleted text goes here
... </DEL>
```

Attributes:

`<DEL>` can take two attributes:

- ▨ `CITE`—Provides the URL of a document that explains why the deletion was necessary.
- ▨ `DATETIME`—Puts a "timestamp" on the deletion.

Example:

```
She just got a big<DEL>, huge</DEL> raise.
```

In this example, the use of the word "huge" is redundant, so an astute copy editor would delete it.

Related Tags:

The `<INS>` tag has a similar function for inserted text.

\<DFN>

Type:

Container

Function:

Denotes the defining instance of a term. Internet Explorer will display text tagged with \<DFN> in italic, whereas Netscape Navigator will not use any special formatting.

Syntax:

```
<DFN> ... term being introduced goes here ... </DFN>
```

Attributes:

None.

Example:

```
Freud proposed the idea of a <DFN>catharsis</DFN> - a release
of psychic tension.
```

\<EM>

Type:

Container

Function:

Contains text to be emphasized. Most browsers render emphasized text in italic.

Syntax:

```
<EM> ... emphasized text goes here ... </EM>
```

Attributes:

None.

Example:

```
Please do <EM>not</EM> disturb the dog.
```

\<INS>

Type:

Container

Function:

Contains text that has been inserted into the document after its original draft.

Syntax:

```
<INS> ... inserted text goes here ... </INS>
```

Attributes:

Like <DEL>, <INS> can take two attributes:

- ■ CITE—Provides the URL of a document that explains why the insertion was necessary.
- ■ DATETIME—Puts a "timestamp" on the insertion.

Example:

```
The New World was discovered by <DEL>Magellan</DEL>
<INS>Columbus</INS> in 1492.
```

> **N O T E** Note how <DEL> and <INS> are used together to strike some text and then to insert a correction in its place. ■

Related Tags:

The <DEL> tag logically represents deleted text.

<KBD>

Type:

Container

Function:

Contains text that represents keyboard input. Browsers typically render such text in a fixed-width font.

Syntax:

```
<KBD> ... keyboard input goes here ... </KBD>
```

Attributes:

None.

Example:

```
To begin, type <KBD>go</KBD> and press Enter.
```

<Q>

Type:

Container

Function:

Contains a direct quotation to be displayed inline.

Syntax:

```
<Q CITE="URL_of_cited_document"> ... quotation goes here ... </Q>
```

Attributes:

If you're quoting from an online source, you can set the CITE attribute equal to the source's URL. Also, you may wish to consider using the LANG attribute because quotes are denoted with different characters in many languages.

Related Tags:

The <BLOCKQUOTE> tag can also be used to denote quoted text, but block quotes are displayed with increased right and left indents and are not in line with the rest of the body text.

<SAMP>

Type:

Container

Function:

Contains text that represents the literal output from a program. Such output is sometimes referred to as *sample text*. Most browsers will render sample text in a fixed-width font.

Syntax:

```
<SAMP> ... program output goes here ... </SAMP>
```

Attributes:

None.

Example:

```
A common first exercise in a programming course is to write a program
to produce the message <SAMP>Hello World</SAMP>.
```

<STRONG>

Type:

Container

Function:

Contains text to be strongly emphasized. Browsers typically render strongly emphasized text in boldface (see Figure 3.7).

Syntax:

```
<STRONG> ... strongly emphasized text goes here ... </STRONG>
```

Attributes:

None.

Example:

```
<STRONG>STOP!</STRONG> Do not proceed any further.  Contact your system
administrator.
```

FIGURE 3.7
The <STRONG> tag is useful for marking up recommendations with extra emphasis.

STRONG text —

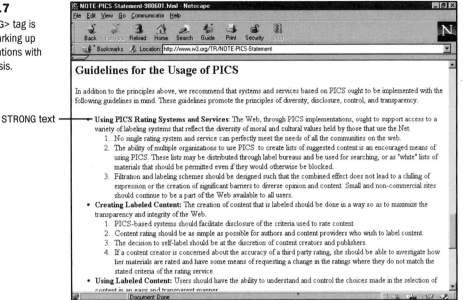

<VAR>

Type:

Container

Function:

Denotes a variable from a computer program. Variables are typically rendered in a fixed-width font.

Syntax:

```
<VAR> ... program variable goes here ... </VAR>
```

Attributes:

None.

Example:

```
The <VAR>RecordCount</VAR> variable is set to the number of records
that the query retrieved.
```

Block-Level Formatting Tags

Block-level formatting tags are usually applied to larger content than the text-level formatting tags. As such, the block-level tags define major sections of a document, such as paragraphs, headings, abstracts, chapters, and so on. The tags profiled in this section are the ones to turn to when you want to define the block-level elements in a document you're authoring.

<BLOCKQUOTE>

Type:

Container

Function:

Contains quoted text that is to be displayed indented from regular body text (see Figure 3.8).

FIGURE 3.8

Blockquotes are used to offset longer quoted passages.

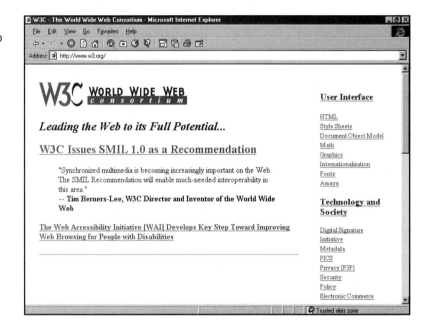

Syntax:

```
<BLOCKQUOTE CITE="URL_of_cited_document"> ... quoted text goes here ...
</BLOCKQUOTE>
```

Attributes:

If you're quoting from an online source, you can set the CITE attribute equal to the source's URL.

Example:

```
Fans of Schoolhouse Rock will always be able to recite the preamble
of the United States Constitution:
<BLOCKQUOTE>
We, the people, in order to form a more perfect Union ...
</BLOCKQUOTE>
```

Related Tags:

The <Q> tag is used to denote quoted text that is to be displayed in line with the body text.

*
*

Type:

Standalone

Function:

Inserts a line break in the document. Carriage returns in the HTML code do not translate to line breaks on the browser screen, so authors often need to insert the breaks themselves. The <BR> tag is indispensable when rendering text with frequent line breaks, such as addresses or poetry. Unlike the <P> tag or the heading tags, <BR> adds no additional vertical space after the break.

Syntax:

```
<BR CLEAR="LEFT¦RIGHT¦ALL">
```

Attributes:

The CLEAR attribute tells which margin to break to when breaking beyond a floating page element, such as an image (see Figure 3.9). Setting CLEAR="LEFT" breaks to the first line in the left margin free of the floating object. CLEAR="RIGHT" breaks to the first clear right margin, and CLEAR="ALL" breaks to the first line in which both the left and right margins are clear.

FIGURE 3.9

The <BR> tag can break to the next line or to the next line that is free of floating objects such as images or tables.

 with CLEAR attribute so that next image is on the line below.

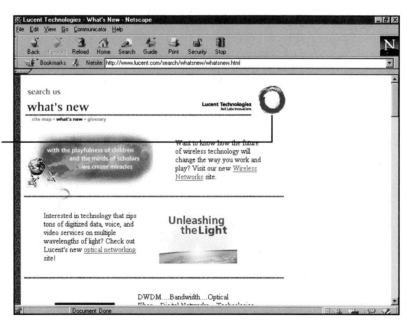

Example:

```
First Name: <INPUT TYPE="TEXT" NAME="fname"><BR>
Last Name: <INPUT TYPE="TEXT" NAME="lname"><BR>
Telephone: <INPUT TYPE="TEXT" NAME="phone"><BR>
Email: <INPUT TYPE="TEXT" NAME="email">
```

<CENTER>

Type:

Container

Function:

Centers all text and other page components it contains.

Syntax:

```
<CENTER> ... centered page components go here ... </CENTER>
```

Attributes:

None.

Example:

```
<CENTER>
<I>A Midsummer Night's Dream</I><BR>
by William Shakespeare
</CENTER>
```

N O T E   The W3C has deprecated the <CENTER> tag in favor of using the <DIV
ALIGN="CENTER"> tag (see the following tag) or style sheets for centering. ■

<DIV>

Type:

Container

Function:

Defines a section or division of a document that requires a special alignment.

Syntax:

```
<DIV ALIGN="LEFT¦RIGHT¦CENTER¦JUSTIFY">
...
</DIV>
```

Attributes:

The ALIGN attribute controls how text contained between the <DIV> and </DIV> tags is aligned. You can set ALIGN equal to LEFT, RIGHT, CENTER, or JUSTIFY, depending on the kind of alignment you need.

Example:

```
<DIV ALIGN="RIGHT">
Everything in this section is right-justified.  Hard to read, isn't it?
...
</DIV>
```

<HR>

Type:

Standalone

Function:

Places a horizontal line on the page (see Figure 3.10).

FIGURE 3.10

Horizontal rules are a great way to break up a page and give the readers' eyes a rest.

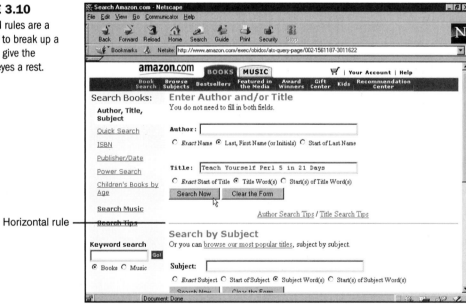

Horizontal rule ——

Syntax:

```
<HR ALIGN="alignment" NOSHADE SIZE="thickness"
WIDTH="pixels_or_percentage_of_screen">
```

Attributes:

The unmodified <HR> tag places a line, 1 pixel thick, across the page. The line will have a shading effect to give the illusion of being three-dimensional. You can change how the default line is displayed by using combinations of the following attributes:

■ ALIGN—You can set ALIGN equal to LEFT, RIGHT, or CENTER to change how the horizontal line is aligned on the page. Note that this matters only when you've changed the width of the line to be something less than the browser screen width. The default value of ALIGN is CENTER.

■ NOSHADE—Placing the NOSHADE attribute in an <HR> tag suppresses the shading effect and yields a solid line.

■ SIZE—SIZE controls the thickness of the line. You set SIZE equal to the number of pixels in thickness you'd like the line to be.

■ WIDTH—A line's WIDTH can be specified in one of two ways. You can set it equal to a number of pixels, or you can set it equal to a percentage of the user's browser screen width (or table cell, if you're placing a line inside a cell). Because you can't know the screen resolution settings of every user, you should use the percentage approach whenever possible.

All the attributes of the <HR> tag have been deprecated in favor of using style sheets to control horizontal rule properties.

Example:

```
<HR NOSHADE WIDTH=80% SIZE=4>
<DIV ALIGN="CENTER">Return to the Home Page</DIV>
<HR NOSHADE WIDTH=80% SIZE=4>
```

<H1>-<H6>

Type:

Container

Function:

Establishes a hierarchy of document heading levels. Level 1 has the largest font size. Increasing through the levels causes the font size to decrease. All headings are rendered in boldface and have a little extra line spacing built in above and below them (see Figure 3.11).

N O T E Although the headings' tags are meant to be used in a strictly hierarchical fashion, many authors use them out of sequence to achieve the formatting effects they want. ■

Syntax:

```
<Hn ALIGN="LEFT¦RIGHT¦CENTER¦JUSTIFY"> ... Level n heading ... </Hn>
```

where n = 1, 2, 3, 4, 5, or 6.

Attributes:

The ALIGN attribute controls how the heading is aligned on the page. You can set a heading's alignment to values of LEFT, RIGHT, CENTER, or JUSTIFY. The default alignment is LEFT.

FIGURE 3.11
Headings are rendered in boldface and are usually in a type size different from the body text.

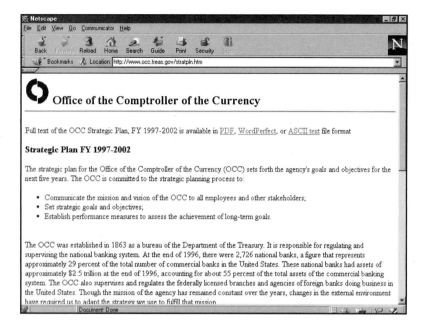

Example:

```
<H1 ALIGN="CENTER">Table of Contents</H1>
<H2>Chapter 1 - Introduction</H2>
...
<H2>Chapter 2- Prior Research</H2>
...
```

<P>

Type:

Container

Function:

Denotes a paragraph. Most browsers ignore the use of multiple <P> tags to increase the amount of vertical space in a document.

Syntax:

```
<P ALIGN="LEFT¦RIGHT¦CENTER¦JUSTIFY">
paragraph text
</P>
```

Attributes:

The ALIGN attribute controls how text in the paragraph is aligned. You can set ALIGN to LEFT (the default), RIGHT, CENTER, or JUSTIFY.

Example:

```
<P ALIGN="CENTER"><H1>Welcome!</H1></P>
```

N O T E Although most browsers can parse standalone <P> tags without errors, the HTML 4.0
recommendation discourages the use of empty <P> tags. ▪

<PRE>

Type:

Container

Function:

Denotes text to be treated as preformatted. Browsers render preformatted text in a fixed-width
font. Whitespace characters, such as spaces, tabs, and carriage returns, found between the
<PRE> and </PRE> tags are not ignored. This makes preformatted text a viable option for pre-
senting tables of information.

Syntax:

```
<PRE WIDTH="width_of_widest_line">
... preformatted text goes here ...
</PRE>
```

Attributes:

The <PRE> tag's WIDTH attribute is set to the number of characters in the widest line of the
preformatted text block. This information helps some browsers choose the font size for displaying the text. Use of the WIDTH attribute has been deprecated in HTML 4.0.

Example:

```
<PRE WIDTH=34>
Catalog No.  Item         Price
AZ-1390      Polo Shirt   $29.99
FT-0081      Sweater      $52.99
CL-9334      Belt         $16.99
</PRE>
```

<SPAN>

Type:

Container

Function:

Generic container tag for defining a document block. One popular use is for applying style
information.

Syntax:

```
<SPAN STYLE="style information" ALIGN="LEFT¦RIGHT¦CENTER¦JUSTIFY">
range of text over which style is to be applied
</SPAN>
```

Attributes:

If you're assigning style information, you can set the STYLE attribute to a sequence of as many characteristic: value pairs as you need to specify the style information you're applying. Valid style characteristics are those put forward in the Cascading Style Sheets Level 2 specification.

The ALIGN attribute can take on the customary values of LEFT, RIGHT, CENTER, and JUSTIFY.

Example:

```
<SPAN STYLE="font-weight: bold; color: red; text-indent: 0.25 in">
Here is some bold, red, text that's indented by one quarter of an inch.
</SPAN>
```

List Tags

Technically, HTML lists are a form of block-level formatting, but because lists are such a useful way of presenting content, the list tags merit their own section in the chapter.

HTML 4.0 continues to support five types of lists, although tags for two of the five have been deprecated. Using the tags in this section, you can create the following types of lists:

- Definition lists
- Directory lists (deprecated)
- Menu lists (deprecated)
- Ordered (numbered) lists
- Unordered (bulleted) lists

Most HTML lists make use of the list item tag, <LI>, so this tag is covered first, followed by the tags you use to create each type of list.

<LI>

Type:

Container

Function:

Denotes an item in a list.

Syntax:

```
<LI TYPE="list_type" START="start_value"> ... list item goes here ... </LI>
```

Attributes:

The <LI> tag can take four attributes:

- COMPACT—Instructs the browser to render the list item in as small a space as possible.
- START—(Ordered lists only) You can change the starting value of the numbering sequence from the default of 1 to any other value you choose.
- TYPE—(Ordered and unordered lists) You can modify the numbering scheme in an ordered list or the bullet character in an unordered list by setting TYPE to one of the list types available. Ordered list types include 1 (Arabic numerals), A (uppercase alphabet), a (lowercase alphabet), I (uppercase Roman numerals), and i (lowercase Roman numerals). The unordered list types include DISC (solid circular bullet), SQUARE (solid square bullet), and CIRCLE (open circular bullet).
- VALUE—Sets the numbering value of the list item.

All the attributes listed above have been deprecated.

N O T E Even if you are not using an Arabic numeral numbering scheme, you should still set START equal to a numeric value. Browsers know to map the START value to any numbering scheme you've specified in a TYPE attribute. For example, the code:

```
<LI TYPE="a" START="4">
```

will produce an ordered list beginning with the lowercase letter d. ▨

Example:

```
<LI>Cookie Dough</LI>
<LI>Rocky Road</LI>
<LI>Mint Chocolate Chip</LI>
```

Related Tags:

The <LI> tag is always used in conjunction with one of the other HTML list tags: <DIR>, <MENU>, <OL>, and <UL>.

N O T E Even though the <LI> tag is technically a container tag, most people use it as a standalone tag, and most browsers are able to interpret standalone <LI> tags correctly. ▨

<DIR>

Type:

Container

Function:

Creates a directory listing. Items in a directory list are bulleted and generally short—usually not more than 20 characters in length. Originally, directory lists were intended for rendering narrow columns of information, such as indexes or telephone directory listings.

The <DIR> tag has been deprecated by the W3C. You should use an unordered list (<UL>) instead.

Syntax:

```
<DIR COMPACT>
<LI>List item 1</LI>
<LI>List item 2</LI>
...
</DIR>
```

Attributes:

The optional COMPACT attribute instructs a browser to reduce the spacing between list items so that the list is rendered in the smallest amount of vertical space possible.

Example:

```
<DIR>
<LI>Mary Garrison, x521</LI>
<LI>Tom Hinkle, x629</LI>
<LI>Pat Joseph, x772</LI>
</DIR>
```

Related Tags:

List items in a directory list are specified with the <LI> tag.

<DL>

Type:

Container

Function:

Denotes a definition list (see Figure 3.12).

Syntax:

```
<DL COMPACT>
 ... terms and definitions go here ...
</DL>
```

Attributes:

The COMPACT attribute is optional and enables you to compress the list into the smallest vertical space possible on the browser screen.

Example:

```
<DL>
<DT>Browser</DT>
<DD>A program that allow a user to view World Wide Web pages</DD>
<DT>Server</DT>
<DD>A program that fields requests for web pages</DD>
</DL>
```

FIGURE 3.12

Definition lists have a term/definition structure similar to a glossary at the back of a book.

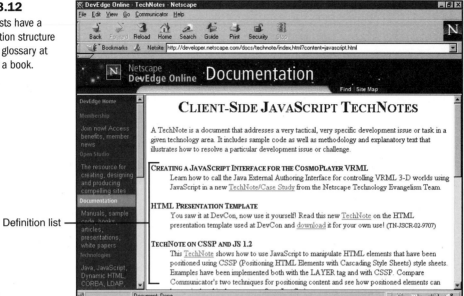

Definition list

Related Tags:

Terms in a definition list are specified with the <DT> tag, and their definitions are specified with the <DD> tag.

<DT>

Type:

Container

Function:

Contains a term to be defined in a definition list.

NOTE Some browsers will automatically render a definition list term in boldface.

Syntax:

```
<DT> ... term being defined goes here ... </DT>
```

Attributes:

None.

Example:

```
<DL>
<DT>Creatine</DT>
<DD>A nutritional supplement that promotes muscle development</DD>
...
</DL>
```

Related Tags:

Use of the <DT> tag makes sense only in the context of a definition list (between the <DL> and </DL> tags). The <DD> tag is used to give the term's definition.

<DD>

Type:

Container

Function:

Contains a term's definition. The definition is typically indented from the term, making it easier for the reader to see the term-definition structure of the list.

Syntax:

```
<DD> ... term definition goes here ... </DD>
```

Attributes:

None.

Example:

```
<DL>
<DT>HTML</DT>
<DD>A document description language used to author Web pages</DD>
...
</DL>
```

Related Tags:

The <DD> tag should be used only when contained by <DL> and </DL> tags. A term, specified by a <DT> tag, should precede each definition.

<MENU>

Type:

Container

Function:

Creates a menu listing. Menu list items are typically short—usually not more than 20 characters in length— and are arranged in a single column. Most browsers render a menu list in the same way they render a bulleted list.

The use of menu lists has been deprecated by the W3C. You should use the unordered list tag (<UL>) instead.

Syntax:

```
<MENU COMPACT>
<LI>Menu list item 1</LI>
<LI>Menu list item 2</LI>
...
</MENU>
```

Attributes:

The optional COMPACT attribute is used to reduce vertical spacing between list items.

Example:

```
<MENU COMPACT>
<LI>Enter a Purchase Order</LI>
<LI>Payroll Functions</LI>
<LI>Generate invoices</LI>
</MENU>
```

Related Tags:

List items in a menu listing are specified with the <LI> tag.

<OL>

Type:

Container

Function:

Creates an ordered or numbered list (see Figure 3.13).

Syntax:

```
<OL TYPE="1¦A¦a¦I¦i" START="start_value" COMPACT>
<LI>List item 1</LI>
<LI>List item 2</LI>
...
</OL>
```

Attributes:

The <OL> tag can take the following attributes:

- COMPACT—Instructs the browser to reduce vertical spacing between list items.
- START—You can change to a position other than the first position in the ordering scheme by using the START attribute. For example, setting START to 3 with TYPE set equal to I produces a list that begins numbering with III (3 in uppercase Roman numerals).

FIGURE 3.13
Ordered and unordered lists are commonly used on Web pages today.

Ordered list (TYPE=A)

Ordered list (TYPE=1)

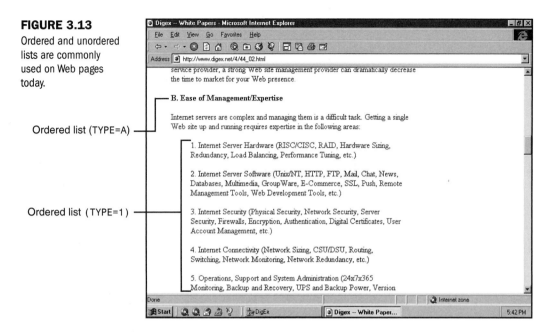

■ TYPE—Controls the numbering scheme used when rendering the list. The default value of 1 indicates the use of Arabic numerals, but you can also choose from uppercase letters (A), lowercase letters (a), uppercase Roman numerals (I), or lowercase Roman numerals (i).

All the attributes of the <OL> tag have been deprecated.

Example:

```
Book Outline
<OL TYPE="A">
<LI>HTML</LI>
<LI>XML</LI>
<LI>Dynamic HTML</LI>
<LI>Java</LI>
<LI>JavaScript</LI>
</OL>
```

Related Tags:

List items in an ordered list are specified with the <LI> tag.

<UL>

Type:

Container

Function:

Creates an unordered or bulleted list.

Syntax:

```
<UL TYPE="DISC¦SQUARE¦CIRCLE" COMPACT>
<LI>List item 1</LI>
<LI>List item 2</LI>
...
</UL>
```

Attributes:

The <UL> tag can take the following attributes:

- COMPACT—Reduces the vertical spacing between list items.
- TYPE—Enables you to specify which bullet character to use when rendering the list. This can be helpful when nesting bulleted lists because browsers have a default progression of bulleted characters that they use. You can override the browser's choice of bulleted characters in the nested lists by using TYPE.

The attributes listed above have been deprecated in HTML 4.0.

Example:

```
Web Browsers
<UL TYPE="SQUARE">
<LI>Netscape Navigator</LI>
<LI>Microsoft Internet Explorer</LI>
<LI>NCSA Mosaic</LI>
</UL>
```

Related Tags:

List items in an unordered list are specified with the <LI> tag.

Hyperlink Tags

The capability of linking Web resources is what makes the Web so fascinating. By following links, you can be looking up job opportunities one moment and then be reading up on the latest mixed drink recipes the next! Linking between documents is accomplished with the one simple tag described in this section.

<A>

Type:

Container

Function:

The <A> tag can do one of two things, depending on which attributes you use. Used with the HREF attribute, the <A> tag sets up a hyperlink from whatever content is found between the <A>

and </A> tags and the document at the URL specified by HREF (see Figure 3.14). When you use the <A> tag with the NAME attribute, you set up a named anchor within a document that can be targeted by other hyperlinks. This helps make navigating a large document easier because you can set up anchors at the start of major sections and then place a set of links at the top of the document that points to the anchors at the beginning of each section.

FIGURE 3.14

Hypertext linking between documents puts the "Web" in World Wide Web.

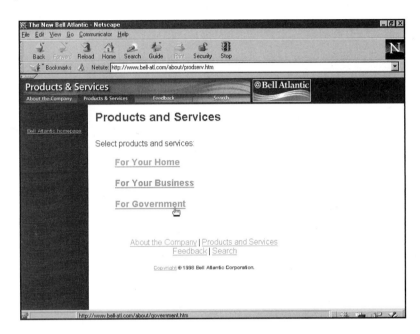

N O T E Hypertext links are typically colored and underlined. A linked graphic will be rendered with a colored border. If you don't want a border around your linked image, be sure to specify BORDER=0 in the <IMG> tag you use to place the image.

Syntax:

```
<!-- Setting up a hyperlink -->
<A HREF="URL_of_linked_document" TARGET="frame_name"
   REL="forward_link_type" REV="reverse_link_type"
   ACCESSKEY="key_letter" TABINDEX="tab_order_position">
... hyperlinked element goes here ...
</A>
```

or

```
<!-- Setting up a named anchor -->
<A NAME="anchor_name">
... text to act as named anchor ...
</A>
```

Attributes:

The <A> tag can take a host of attributes, including

- ACCESSKEY—An access key is a shortcut key a reader can use to activate the hyperlink. If you set the access key to the letter "C", for example, Windows users can press Alt+C on their keyboards to activate the link.
- CHARSET—Denotes what character encoding to use for the linked document.
- HREF—Gives the URL of the Web resource to which the hyperlink should point.
- HREFLANG—Denotes the language context of the linked resource.
- NAME—Specifies the name of the anchor being set up.
- REL—Describes the nature of the forward link (see Table 3.3 for possible values).
- REV—Describes the nature of the reverse link (see Table 3.3 for possible values).
- TABINDEX—Specifies the link's position in the document's tabbing order.
- TARGET—Tells the browser into which frame the linked document should be loaded.
- TYPE—Specifies the MIME type of the linked resource.

Examples:

The following code sets up a simple hyperlink:

```
You can learn more about our
<A HREF="prodserv.html TARGET="main" ACCESSKEY="P">
products and services</A> as well.
```

To follow the link, a user can click the hypertext products and services or press Alt+P (on a Windows machine) or Cmd+P (on a Macintosh).

This code establishes a named anchor within a document:

```
...
<A NAME="toc">
<H1>Table of Contents</H1>
</A>
...
```

With the anchor set up, you can point a hyperlink to it by using code such as this:

```
<A HREF="index.html#toc">Back to the Table of Contents</A>
```

Image and Imagemap Tags

Without images, the Web would just be another version of Gopher. Web graphics give pages powerful visual appeal and often add significantly to the messages that authors are trying to convey.

Placing an image on a page is as simple as using the HTML <IMG> tag. In its most basic form, the <IMG> tag needs only one attribute to do its job. However, <IMG> supports as many as 10 attributes that you can use to modify how the image is presented.

▶ **See** "Advanced Graphics," **p. 155**.

<IMG>

Type:

Standalone

Function:

Places an inline image into a document (see Figure 3.15).

FIGURE 3.15
Pictures, logos, and other graphical effects are placed into a document using the <IMG> tag.

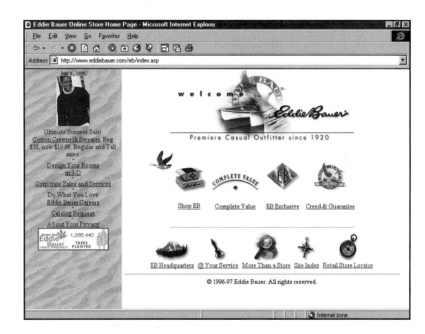

Syntax:

```
<IMG SRC="URL_of_image_file"
  WIDTH="width_in_pixels" HEIGHT="height_in_pixels"
  ALT="text_description" BORDER="thickness_in_pixels"
  ALIGN="TOP¦MIDDLE¦BOTTOM¦LEFT¦RIGHT"
  HSPACE="horizontal_spacing_in_pixels"
  VSAPCE="vertical_spacing_in_pixels"
  LONGDESC="URL_of_long_description"
  ISMAP USEMAP="map_name">
```

Attributes:

As you can see from the tag's syntax, <IMG> can take several attributes (each attribute is described in detail in this section):

- SRC—Specifies the URL of the file containing the image.
- WIDTH and HEIGHT—Gives the width and height of the image in pixels. Specifying this information in the tag means that the browser can allot space for the image and then continue laying out the page while the image file loads.

- ALT—A text-based description of the image content. Using ALT is an important courtesy to users with nonvisual browsers or with image loading turned off.

- BORDER—Controls the thickness of the border around an image. An image has no border by default. However, a hyperlinked image will be rendered with a colored border. If you don't want the border to appear around your image, you need to set BORDER=0.

- ALIGN—Controls how text flows around the image. TOP, MIDDLE, and BOTTOM alignment aligns text following the image with the top, middle, or bottom of the image, respectively. However, after the text reaches the end of the current line, it will break to a position *below* the image. If you want text to wrap around the entire image, you need to use the LEFT or RIGHT values of the ALIGN attribute to float the image in the left or right margin. Text will wrap smoothly around a floated image.

- HSPACE and VSPACE—Controls the amount of whitespace left around the image. HSPACE is set to the number of whitespace pixels to use on the left and right sides of the image. VSPACE controls the number of whitespace pixels remaining above and below the image.

- LONGDESC—Points to a resource that contains a longer description of the image's content.

- ISMAP—Identifies the image as being used as part of a server-side imagemap.

- USEMAP—Set equal to the name of the client-side imagemap to be used with the image.

Example:

```
<IMG SRC="/images/logo.gif" WIDTH=600 HEIGHT=120
  ALT="Welcome to XYZ Corporation" USEMAP="#main"
  VSPACE=10>
```

One popular use of images is to set up *imagemaps*—clickable images that take users to different URLs, depending on where they click. Imagemaps are popular page elements on many sites because they provide users with an easy-to-use graphical interface for navigating the site (see Figure 3.16).

Imagemaps come in two flavors: server-side and client-side. When a user clicks a server-side imagemap, the coordinates of the click are sent to the server, where a program processes them to determine which URL the browser should load. To accomplish this, the server needs to have access to a file containing information about which regions on the image are clickable and with which URLs those regions should be paired.

With client-side imagemaps, the client (browser) processes the coordinates of the user's click, rather than passing them to the server for processing. This is a more efficient approach because it reduces the computational load on the server and eliminates the opening and closing of additional HTTP connections. For the browser to be able to process a user's click, it has to have access to the same information about the clickable regions and their associated URLs as the server does when processing a server-side imagemap. The method of choice for getting this information to the client is to pass it in an HTML file—usually the file that contains the document with the imagemap, although it does not necessarily have to be this way. HTML 4.0 supports two tags that enable you to store imagemap data in your HTML files: <MAP> and <AREA>. A discussion of these tags rounds out the coverage in this section.

▶ **See** "Imagemaps," **p. 137**.

FIGURE 3.16
Imagemaps are
commonly used as
navigation interfaces
and are usually
accompanied by an
equivalent set of
hypertext links.

Imagemap —

<MAP>

Type:

Container

Function:

Contains HTML tags that define the clickable regions (hot regions) of an imagemap.

Syntax:

```
<MAP NAME="map_name">
... hot region definitions go here ...
</MAP>
```

Attributes:

The NAME attribute gives the map information a unique name so it can be referenced by the USEMAP attribute in the <IMG> tag that places the imagemap graphic.

Example:

```
<MAP NAME="navigation">
<AREA SHAPE="RECT" COORDS="23,47,58,68" HREF="search.html">
<AREA SHAPE="CIRCLE" COORDS="120,246,150,246" HREF="about.html">
...
</MAP>
```

With the imagemap data defined by the map named navigation, you would reference the map in an <IMG> tag as follows:

Part
II

Ch
3

```
<IMG SRC="navigation.gif" USEMAP="#navigation">
```

If the map were stored in a file different from the document's HTML file, you would reference it this way:

```
<IMG SRC="navigation.gif" USEMAP="maps.html#navigation">
```

Related Tags:

The <AREA> tag is used to define the individual hot regions in the imagemap. The named map is referenced by the USEMAP attribute of the <IMG> tag.

<AREA>

Type:

Standalone

Function:

Defines a hot region in a client-side imagemap.

Syntax:

```
<AREA SHAPE="RECT¦CIRCLE¦POLY¦DEFAULT" COORDS="coordinate_list"
  HREF="URL_of_linked_document" TARGET="frame_name"
  ALT="text_alternative" TABINDEX="tab_order_position" NOHREF
  ACCESSKEY="key_letter">
```

Attributes:

The <AREA> tag takes a number of attributes, including

- ACCESSKEY—Defines a shortcut key combination that the user can press to activate the hot region (see the attribute listing for the <A> tag for more details).

- ALT—Provides a text alternative for the hot region in the event that the image does not load or the user has image loading turned off. ALT text is also used by spoken-word browsers for the visually impaired.

- COORDS—Specifies the coordinates that define the hot region. Coordinates are given as a list of numbers, separated by commas. No coordinates are needed when specifying a DEFAULT region.

- HREF—Set equal to the URL of the document to associate with the hot region.

- NOHREF—Using the NOHREF attribute in an <AREA> tag essentially deactivates the hot region by having it point to nothing.

- SHAPE—Specifies the shape of the hot region being defined. Possible values of SHAPE include RECT for rectangles, CIRCLE for circles, POLY for polygons, and DEFAULT for any point on the image not part of another hot region.

- TABINDEX—Defines the hot region's position in the tabbing order of the page.

- TARGET—Specifies into which frame to load the linked document.

N O T E Each type of hot region has a specific number of coordinate points that you need to specify to completely define the hot region. A rectangular region is defined by the coordinates of the upper-left and lower-right corners, a circular region by the coordinates of the center point and a point along the edge of the region, and a polygonal region by the coordinates of the polygon's vertices.

Example:

```
<MAP NAME="main">
<AREA SHAPE="POLY" COORDS="35,80,168,99,92,145" HREF="profile.html">
<AREA SHAPE="CIRCLE" COORDS="288,306,288,334" HREF="feedback.html">
<AREA SHAPE="DEFAULT" HREF="index.html">
</MAP>
```

Related Tags:

<AREA> tags are allowable only between <MAP> and </MAP> tags.

Table Tags

HTML table tags are not only a great way to present information, but a useful layout tool as well (see Figure 3.17). HTML 4.0 expands the table tags in several important ways:

- Support for rendering parts of the frame around a table, rather than "all or nothing."
- Control over which boundaries to draw between cells.
- Table header, body, and footer sections can be defined as separate entities.

FIGURE 3.17

Tables make complex page layouts possible because of the very fine alignment control you have within the table.

This section looks at all the table-related tags and their many attributes.

▶ **See** "Tables," **p. 183**.

<TABLE>

Type:

Container

Function:

Contains all HTML tags that compose a table.

Syntax:

```
<TABLE ALIGN="LEFT¦CENTER¦RIGHT" BORDER="thickness_in_pixels"
  BGCOLOR="color" WIDTH="pixels_or_percentage_of_browser_width"
  COLS="number_of_columns" CELLPADDING="pixels" CELLSPACING="pixels"
  FRAME="outer_border_rendering" RULES="inner_border_rendering"
  SUMMARY="description_of_table_contents_and_structure">
...
</TABLE>
```

Attributes:

The <TABLE> tag can take the following attributes to modify how the table is presented:

▪ ALIGN—Controls how the table is aligned on the page. Possible values are LEFT, CENTER, and RIGHT. Tables that are left- or right-aligned will float in the margin, and text can wrap around them. The ALIGN attribute of the <TABLE> tag has been deprecated.

▪ BORDER—Specifies the thickness of the table border in pixels.

▪ BGCOLOR—Set equal to the background color to use in the cells of the table.

▪ CELLPADDING—Controls the amount of whitespace between the contents of a cell and the edge of the cell.

▪ CELLSPACING—Specifies how many pixels of space to leave between individual cells.

▪ COLS—Set equal to the number of columns in the table. Knowing this value enables the browser to compose the table faster.

▪ FRAME—Controls which parts of the table's outer border are rendered. FRAME can take on the values shown in Table 3.4.

Table 3.4   Values of the *FRAME* Attribute of the *<TABLE>* Tag

Value	Purpose
ABOVE	Displays a border on the top of a table frame
BELOW	Displays a border at the bottom of a table frame
BORDER	Displays a border on all four sides of a table frame
BOX	Same as BORDER

Value	Purpose
HSIDES	Displays a border on the left and right sides of a table frame
LHS	Displays a border on the left side of a table frame
RHS	Displays a border on the right side of a table frame
VSIDES	Displays a border at the top and bottom of a table frame
VOID	Suppresses the display of all table frame borders

■ RULES—Controls which parts of the table's inner borders are displayed. RULES can be set equal to one of the values shown in Table 3.5.

Table 3.5   Values of the *RULES* Attribute of the *<TABLE>* Tag

Value	Purpose
ALL	Displays a border between all rows and columns
COLS	Displays a border between all columns
GROUPS	Displays a border between all logical groups (as defined by the <THEAD>, <TBODY>, <TFOOT>, and <COLGROUP> tags)
NONE	Suppresses all inner borders
ROWS	Displays a border between all table rows

■ SUMMARY—Provides a synopsis of what's in the table and how the table is structured.

■ WIDTH—Specifies the width of the table in pixels or as a percentage of the browser screen width.

Example:

```
<TABLE BORDER=2 CELLPADDING=4 FRAME=BORDER RULES=ALL ALIGN=CENTER>
...
</TABLE>
```

Related Tags:

The <TABLE> and </TABLE> tags form the container for all the other table-related tags. The many tags you can use between <TABLE> and </TABLE> include <CAPTION>, <THEAD>, <TFOOT>, <TBODY>, <COLGROUP>, <COL>, <TR>, <TH>, and <TD>.

<CAPTION>

Type:

Container

Function:

Specifies a caption for a table.

Syntax:

```
<CAPTION ALIGN="TOP¦BOTTOM¦LEFT¦RIGHT">
... caption text goes here ...
</CAPTION>
```

Attributes:

The ALIGN attribute gives you fine control over how the caption is placed. Setting ALIGN to TOP or BOTTOM places the caption above or below the table, respectively. Using LEFT or RIGHT floats the caption in the left or right margin. The ALIGN attribute has been deprecated in HTML 4.0.

Example:

```
<CAPTION ALIGN="BOTTOM">
Table 1 - Return on Investment
</CAPTION>
```

<THEAD>

Type:

Container

Function:

Defines the header section of a table. Being able to define the header separately enables the browser to duplicate the header when breaking the table across multiple pages.

Syntax:

```
<THEAD ALIGN="LEFT¦CENTER¦RIGHT¦JUSTIFY¦CHAR"
 VALIGN="TOP¦MIDDLE¦BOTTOM¦BASELINE" CHAR="alignment_character"
 CHAROFF="alignment_character_offset">
... rows that comprise the header ...
</THEAD>
```

Attributes:

The <THEAD> tag can take the following four attributes:

- ALIGN—Controls the horizontal alignment within the cells of the table header. ALIGN can take on values of LEFT, RIGHT, CENTER, JUSTIFY, or CHAR. CHAR is used to align cells by a common character.

- CHAR—Specifies the alignment character for when ALIGN="CHAR" is used.

- CHAROFF—Prescribes the offset distance from the alignment character.

- VALIGN—Controls the vertical alignment in the header cells. VALIGN can take on values of TOP, MIDDLE, BOTTOM, or BASELINE.

Example:

```
<THEAD ALIGN="CENTER" VALIGN="BASELINE">
<TR>
<TH>ID #</TH>
<TH>Property</TH>
<TH>Tax Assessment</TH>
...
</TR>
</THEAD>
```

Related Tags:

The rows of the table header are built with <TR>, <TH>, and <TD> tags. Each table header must comprise at least one row.

<TFOOT>

Type:

Container

Function:

Defines the footer section of the table.

Syntax:

```
<TFOOT ALIGN="LEFT¦CENTER¦RIGHT¦JUSTIFY¦CHAR"
 VALIGN="TOP¦MIDDLE¦BOTTOM¦BASELINE" CHAR="alignment_character"
 CHAROFF="alignment_character_offset">
...
</TFOOT>
```

Attributes:

<TFOOT> can take the same ALIGN and VALIGN attributes as the <THEAD> tag:

- ALIGN—Controls the horizontal alignment within the cells of the table footer. ALIGN can take on values of LEFT, RIGHT, CENTER, JUSTIFY, or CHAR.

- CHAR—Specifies the alignment character for when ALIGN="CHAR" is used.

- CHAROFF—Prescribes the offset distance from the alignment character.

- VALIGN—Controls the vertical alignment in the footer cells. VALIGN can take on values of TOP, MIDDLE, BOTTOM, or BASELINE.

Example:

```
<TFOOT ALIGN="JUSTIFY" VALIGN="TOP">
<TR>
<TD>&copy; 1998 - Macmillan Computer Publishing USA</TD>
...
</TR>
</TFOOT>
```

Related Tags:

You specify the rows and cells in the table footer by using the `<TR>`, `<TH>`, and `<TD>` tags. A table footer must be made up of at least one row.

<TBODY>

Type:

Container

Function:

Defines the body section of the table.

Syntax:

```
<TBODY ALIGN="LEFT¦CENTER¦RIGHT¦JUSTIFY¦CHAR"
 VALIGN="TOP¦MIDDLE¦BOTTOM¦BASELINE" CHAR="alignment_character"
 CHAROFF="alignment_character_offset">
...
</TBODY>
```

Attributes:

`<TBODY>` can take the following attributes:

- ▓ `ALIGN`—Controls the horizontal alignment within the cells of the table body. `ALIGN` can take on values of `LEFT`, `RIGHT`, `CENTER`, `JUSTIFY`, and `CHAR`.
- ▓ `CHAR`—Specifies the alignment character for when `ALIGN="CHAR"` is used.
- ▓ `CHAROFF`—Prescribes the offset distance from the alignment character.
- ▓ `VALIGN`—Controls the vertical alignment in the body cells. `VALIGN` can take on values of `TOP`, `MIDDLE`, `BOTTOM`, or `BASELINE`.

Example:

```
<TBODY ALIGN="LEFT" VALIGN="BASELINE">
<TR>
<TD>Red Storm Rising</TD>
<TD>1500 pages (paperback)</TD>
<TD>$9.95</TD>
...
</TR>
</TBODY>
```

Related Tags:

You specify the rows and cells in the table body by using the `<TR>`, `<TH>`, and `<TD>` tags. A table body section must contain at least one row.

<COLGROUP>

Type:

Container

Function:

Groups a set of columns so that properties may be assigned to all columns in the group rather than to each one individually.

Syntax:

```
<COLGROUP SPAN="number_of_columns" WIDTH="width_of_column_group"
  ALIGN="LEFT¦RIGHT¦CENTER¦JUSTIFY¦CHAR"
  VALIGN="TOP¦MIDDLE¦BOTTOM¦BASELINE"
  CHAR="alignment_character" CHAROFF="alignment character_offset">
...
</COLGROUP>
```

The `<COLGROUP>` and `</COLGROUP>` tags have no content or code between them if the properties put forward in the `<COLGROUP>` tag are to apply to each column in the group. You can also use the `<COL>` tag between `<COLGROUP>` and `</COLGROUP>` to specify column properties for a sub-group of the larger group.

Attributes:

`<COLGROUP>` can take the following attributes:

- `ALIGN`—Controls the horizontal alignment within the column group. `ALIGN` can take on values of LEFT, RIGHT, CENTER, JUSTIFY, or CHAR.
- `CHAR`—Specifies the alignment character for when `ALIGN="CHAR"` is used.
- `CHAROFF`—Prescribes the offset distance from the alignment character.
- `SPAN`—Tells the browser how many columns are in the group.
- `VALIGN`—Controls the vertical alignment in the column group. `VALIGN` can take on values of TOP, MIDDLE, BOTTOM, or BASELINE.
- `WIDTH`—Specifies how wide (in pixels or in terms of relative width) the enclosed columns should be.

Example:

```
<COLGROUP SPAN=3 ALIGN="CENTER" VALIGN="TOP">
</COLGROUP>
<TR>
<TD>Column 1 - center/top alignment</TD>
<TD>Column 2 - center/top alignment</TD>
<TD>Column 3 - center/top alignment</TD>
<TD>Column 4 - default alignment</TD>
</TR>
</TFOOT>
```

Related Tags:

The `<COL>` tag can be used between the `<COLGROUP>` and `</COLGROUP>` tags to refine column properties for a subset of the column group.

Part

II

Ch

3

<COL>

Type:

Standalone

Function:

Specifies properties for a column or columns within a group.

Syntax:

```
<COL SPAN="number_of_columns" WIDTH="width_of_column_subgroup"
 ALIGN="LEFT¦RIGHT¦CENTER¦JUSTIFY"
 VALIGN="TOP¦MIDDLE¦BOTTOM¦BASELINE"
 CHAR="alignment_character" CHAROFF="alignment_character_offset">
```

Attributes:

<COL> can take the following attributes:

- ALIGN—Controls the horizontal alignment within the column cells. ALIGN can take on values of LEFT, RIGHT, CENTER, JUSTIFY, or CHAR.

- CHAR—Specifies the alignment character for when ALIGN="CHAR" is used.

- CHAROFF—Prescribes the offset distance from the alignment character.

- SPAN—Tells the browser how many columns to which to apply the property.

- VALIGN—Controls the vertical alignment in the column cells. VALIGN can take on values of TOP, MIDDLE, BOTTOM, or BASELINE.

- WIDTH—Specifies the width (in pixels or in terms of relative width) of the column or column group.

Example:

```
<TABLE BORDER=1>
<COLGROUP>
    <COL ALIGN=CENTER>
    <COL ALIGN=RIGHT>
</COLGROUP>
<COLGROUP>
    <COL ALIGN=CENTER SPAN=2>
</COLGROUP>
<TBODY>
    <TR>
        <TD>First column in first group, center aligned</TD>
        <TD>Second column in first group, right aligned</TD>
        <TD>First column in second group, center aligned</TD>
        <TD>Second column in second group, center aligned</TD>
    </TR>
</TBODY>
</TABLE>
```

<TR>

Type:

Container

Function:

Defines a row of a table, table header, table footer, or table body.

Syntax:

```
<TR ALIGN="LEFT¦RIGHT¦CENTER¦JUSTIFY¦CHAR"
  VALIGN="TOP¦MIDDLE¦BOTTOM¦BASELINE">
...
</TR>
```

Attributes specified in a <TR> tag apply only to the row that the tag is defining and will override any default values.

Attributes:

The <TR> tag can take the following attributes:

- ALIGN—Controls the horizontal alignment within the cells in the row. ALIGN can take on values of LEFT, RIGHT, CENTER, JUSTIFY, or CHAR.
- CHAR—Specifies the alignment character for when ALIGN="CHAR" is used.
- CHAROFF—Prescribes the offset distance from the alignment character.
- VALIGN—Controls the vertical alignment of the cells in the row. VALIGN can take on values of TOP, MIDDLE, BOTTOM, or BASELINE.

Example:

```
<TR BGCOLOR="white" VALIGN="TOP">
<TD>Phone</TD>
<TD>Extension</TD>
<TD>Fax</TD>
...
</TR>
```

Related Tags:

Cells in a row are defined using the <TD> or <TH> tags.

<TD>, <TH>

Type:

Container

Function:

Defines a cell in a table. <TH> creates a header cell whose contents will be rendered in boldface and with a centered horizontal alignment. <TD> creates a regular data cell whose contents are aligned flush left and in a normal font weight. Vertical alignment for both types of cells is MIDDLE by default.

Syntax:

```
<TD ALIGN="LEFT¦RIGHT¦CENTER¦JUSTIFY¦CHAR"
 VALIGN="TOP¦MIDDLE¦BOTTOM¦BASELINE"
 CHAR="alignment_character" CHAROFF="alignment_character_offset"
 NOWRAP ROWSPAN="number_of_rows"
 COLSPAN="number_of_columns"
 ABBR="header_cell_abbreviation" AXIS="list_of_category_names"
 HEADERS="list_of_ID headers" SCOPE="ROW¦COL¦ROWGROUP¦COLGROUP">
```

or

```
<TH ALIGN="LEFT¦RIGHT¦CENTER¦JUSTIFY¦CHAR"
 VALIGN="TOP¦MIDDLE¦BOTTOM¦BASELINE"
 CHAR="alignment_character" CHAROFF="alignment_character_offset"
 NOWRAP ROWSPAN="number_of_rows"
 COLSPAN="number_of_columns"
 ABBR="cell_abbreviation" AXIS="list_of_category_names"
 HEADERS="list_of_ID headers" SCOPE="ROW¦COL¦ROWGROUP¦COLGROUP">
```

Attributes:

Both the <TH> and <TD> tags can take the following attributes:

- ABBR—Specifies an abbreviation form of a cell's contents.
- ALIGN—Controls the horizontal alignment within the cell. ALIGN can take on values of LEFT, RIGHT, CENTER, JUSTIFY, or CHAR.
- AXIS—Used to group cells into logical categories.
- CHAR—Specifies the alignment character for when ALIGN="CHAR" is used.
- CHAROFF—Prescribes the offset distance from the alignment character.
- COLSPAN—Specifies the number of columns the cell should occupy.
- HEADERS—Provides a list of IDs of cells that provide header information for the current cell.
- NOWRAP—Suppresses text wrapping within the cell.
- ROWSPAN—Specifies the number of rows the cell should occupy.
- SCOPE—A simpler form of the AXIS attribute, SCOPE lets you group cells into rows, columns, row groups, or column groups, instead of arbitrarily named logical groups.
- VALIGN—Controls the vertical alignment of the cell. VALIGN can take on values of TOP, MIDDLE, BOTTOM, or BASELINE.

Example:

```
<TR VALIGN="BOTTOM">
<TH>Column 1 - center/bottom alignment</TH>
<TD VALIGN="MIDDLE">Column 2 - left/middle alignment</TD>
<TD ALIGN="JUSTIFY">Column 3 - justify/bottom alignment</TD>
<TD COLSPAN=2>Columns 4 and 5 - left/bottom alignment</TD>
</TR>
```

Form Tags

HTML forms are a Web surfer's gateway to interactive content. Forms collect information from a user, and then a script or program on a Web server uses the information to compose a custom response to the form submission.

For all the form controls that are available to you as a document author, you need to know surprisingly few tags to produce them. These tags, together with some new tags introduced in the HTML 4.0 recommendation that improve form accessibility for the disabled, are covered in this section.

▶ **See** "Forms," **p. 233**.

<FORM>

Type:

Container

Function:

Contains the text and tags that compose an HTML form (see Figure 3.18).

FIGURE 3.18
HTML forms gather user input and send that information to a server for processing.

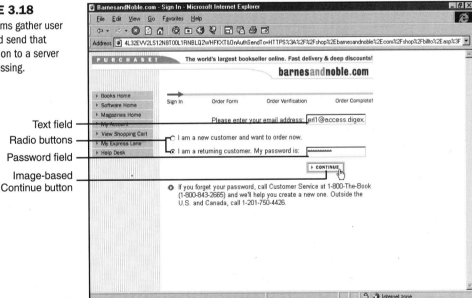

Syntax:

```
<FORM ACTION="URL_of_processing_script" METHOD="GET¦POST"
  TARGET="frame_name" ENCTYPE="MIME_type_of_file_to_upload"
  ACCEPT-CHARSET="acceptable_character_sets"
```

```
         ACCEPT="acceptable_MIME_types">
...
</FORM>
```

The <FORM> tag and its attributes are sometimes referred to as the *form header*.

Attributes:

The <FORM> tag takes the following attributes:

- ACCEPT—Specifies a list of acceptable content types (MIME types) that a server processing the form can handle correctly.
- ACCEPT-CHARSET—Set equal to a list of character sets that the form's processing script can handle.
- ACTION—Set equal to the URL of the script or program that will process the form data. ACTION is a required attribute of the <FORM> tag.
- ENCTYPE—Used when you're expecting a file upload as part of the form data submission and is set equal to the expected MIME type of the file.
- METHOD—Refers to the HTTP method used to send the form data to the server. The default METHOD is GET, which appends the data to the end of the processing script URL. If you set METHOD="POST", the form data will be sent to the server in a separate HTTP transaction.
- TARGET—Enables you to target the response from the processing script or program to a specific frame.

Example:

```
<FORM ACTION="/shopping_cart.cfm" METHOD="POST" TARGET="response">
...
</FORM>
```

Related Tags:

The following tags are valid only when used between the <FORM> and </FORM> tags: <INPUT>, <SELECT>, <OPTION>, <OPTGROUP>, <TEXTAREA>, <BUTTON>, <LABEL>, <FIELDSET>, and <LEGEND>. Each of these tags is described in this section.

<INPUT>

Type:

Standalone

Function:

Places one of the following form controls:

- Text, password, or hidden fields
- Check boxes
- Radio buttons

- File upload fields
- Image-based buttons
- Scripted buttons
- Submit and reset buttons

Syntax:

```
<!-- Text and password fields -->
<INPUT TYPE="TEXT¦PASSWORD" NAME="field_name" VALUE="default_value"
  SIZE="field_size" MAXLENGTH="maximum_input_length"
  DISABLED READONLY>
```

or

```
<!-- Hidden field -->
<INPUT TYPE="HIDDEN" NAME="field_name" VALUE="field_value">
```

or

```
<!-- Checkbox -->
<INPUT TYPE="CHECKBOX" NAME="field_name" VALUE="field_value"
  CHECKED DISABLED>
```

or

```
<!-- Radio button -->
<INPUT TYPE="RADIO" NAME="field_name" VALUE="field_value"
  CHECKED DISABLED>
```

or

```
<!-- File upload -->
<INPUT TYPE="FILE" NAME="field_name" VALUE="default_value"
  ACCEPT="acceptable_MIME_types" DISABLED>
```

or

```
<!-- Image-based button -->
<INPUT TYPE="IMAGE" SRC="URL_of_image_file" ALT="text_description"
  ALIGN="TOP¦MIDDLE¦BOTTOM¦LEFT¦RIGHT" USEMAP="map_name" DISABLED>
```

or

```
<!-- Scripted button -->
<INPUT TYPE="BUTTON" VALUE="button_label" onclick="script_name"
  DISABLED>
```

or

```
<!-- Submit/reset button -->
<INPUT TYPE="SUBMIT¦RESET" VALUE="button_label" DISABLED>
```

Attributes:

The <INPUT> tag is easily the most versatile of all the HTML tags. It has a large number of attributes, although not all are applicable in every situation. The following list examines each

Part

II

Ch

3

variant of the <INPUT> tag (which corresponds to changing values of the TYPE attribute) and notes what each applicable attribute does in that situation.

- Text and password fields (TYPE="TEXT¦PASSWORD")—The NAME attribute gives the input field a unique name so it can be identified by the processing script. The VALUE attribute is appropriate for a text field when you want to prepopulate the field with a default value. LENGTH is set equal to the number of characters wide the input field should be onscreen. MAXLENGTH sets an upper limit on how many characters long the input from the field can be. The DISABLED attribute deactivates the field, and READONLY leaves the field active while disallowing the user from typing any new input into it.

- Hidden fields (TYPE="HIDDEN")—NAME and VALUE specify the name of the field and the value to pass to the server.

- Check box (TYPE="CHECKBOX")—NAME gives the check box field a unique name, and VALUE is set equal to the value you want passed to the server if the box is checked. Including CHECKED makes the box preselected, and DISABLED disables the check box altogether.

- Radio buttons (TYPE="RADIO")—NAME gives a name to the entire set of radio buttons. All buttons can have the same NAME because their corresponding VALUEs have to be mutually exclusive options. The CHECKED attribute preselects a radio button and DISABLED shuts down the radio button.

- File upload (TYPE="FILE")—NAME gives the field a unique name, and VALUE is set to the default value of the field (presumably a filename). The ACCEPT attribute provides a set of acceptable MIME types for upload. Specifying the DISABLED attribute deactivates the field.

- Image-based button (TYPE="IMAGE")—The SRC attribute tells the browser where it can find the image file for the button. ALT provides a text-based alternative to the image should the image file not be available. You can use ALIGN to control how the image is aligned on the page. USEMAP is set equal to a client-side imagemap name, enabling you to take different actions depending on where the user clicks. Using the DISABLED attribute shuts off the button.

- Scripted button (TYPE="BUTTON")—Whatever you specify for the VALUE attribute will be the text that appears on the face of the button. The onclick attribute is set equal to the name of the script that is to execute when the button is clicked. If you specify the DISABLED attribute, the scripted button will be deactivated.

- Submit and reset buttons (TYPE="SUBMIT¦RESET")—The VALUE attribute specifies what text to place on the button. If DISABLED, the submit or reset button will be turned off.

Additionally, you can use the following attributes with the <INPUT> tag:

- ACCESSKEY—Defines a shortcut key combination that the user can press to give focus to the input field (see the attribute listing for the <A> tag for more details).

- TABINDEX—Defines the input field's position in the tabbing order of the page.

Example:

```
<FORM ACTION="/cgi-bin/submit_it.pl">
Login Name: <INPUT TYPE="TEXT" NAME="login" SIZE=12>
Password: <INPUT TYPE="PASSWORD" NAME="passwd" SIZE=12>
<INPUT TYPE="HIDDEN" NAME="browser" VALUE="IE4">
Sex: <INPUT TYPE="RADIO" NAME="sex" VALUE="F">Female
     <INPUT TYPE="RADIO" NAME="sex" VALUE="M">Male
<INPUT TYPE="BUTTON" VALUE="Check data" onclick="validate()">
<INPUT TYPE="SUBMIT" VALUE="Login">
<INPUT TYPE="RESET" VALUE="Clear">
</FORM>
```

<SELECT>

Type:

Container

Function:

Sets up a list of choices from which a user can select one or many.

Syntax:

```
<SELECT NAME="field_name" SIZE="visible_rows" MULTIPLE DISABLED
 ACCESSKEY="shortcut_key_letter" TABINDEX="tab_position">
...
</SELECT>
```

Attributes:

You can use the following attributes with the <SELECT> tag:

- ACCESSKEY—Defines a shortcut key combination that the user can press to give focus to the select field (see the attribute listing for the <A> tag for more details).
- DISABLED—Deactivates the field.
- MULTIPLE—Enables the user to choose more than one of the options by holding down the Ctrl key and clicking.
- NAME—Gives the field a unique name so it can be identified by the processing script.
- SIZE—Set equal to the number of options that should be visible on the screen.
- TABINDEX—Defines the select field's position in the tabbing order of the page.

N O T E If you set SIZE=1 and don't specify MULTIPLE, the field will be displayed as a drop-down list. Otherwise, the field appears as a scrollable list of options.

Example:

```
<SELECT NAME="size" SIZE=4>
<OPTION>Small</OPTION>
<OPTION>Medium</OPTION>
<OPTION>Large</OPTION>
```

```
<OPTION>X-Large</OPTION>
...
</SELECT>
```

Related Tags:

Individual options in the list are specified using the <OPTION> tag. You can also use the <OPTGROUP> tag to place options into logical groups.

<OPTION>

Type:

Container

Function:

Defines an option in a <SELECT> field listing.

Syntax:

```
<OPTION VALUE="option_value" SELECTED DISABLED LABEL="label_text">
... option text ...
</OPTION>
```

Attributes:

The <OPTION> tag takes the following attributes:

- DISABLED—Makes the option unavailable.
- LABEL—Provides a short label for the menu option. If specified, this label is used in place of the option text itself.
- SELECTED—Preselects an option.
- VALUE—Specifies a value to pass to the browser if the option is selected. If no VALUE is given, the browser will pass the option text to the server for processing.

Example:

```
<SELECT NAME="state" SIZE=5>
<OPTION VALUE="AL">Alabama</OPTION>
<OPTION VALUE="NM" SELECTED>New Mexico</OPTION>
<OPTION VALUE="OK">Oklahoma</OPTION>
...
</SELECT>
```

Related Tags:

The <OPTION> tag is valid only between the <SELECT> and </SELECT> tags. You can place options into logical groups by using the <OPTGROUP> tag.

<OPTGROUP>

Type:

Container

Function:

Defines a logical group of select list options.

Syntax:

```
<OPTGROUP LABEL="label_text" DISABLED>
<OPTION> ... </OPTION>
<OPTION> ... </OPTION>
<OPTION> ... </OPTION>
...
</OPTGROUP>
```

Attributes:

<OPTGROUP> can take two attributes:

  ▓ DISABLED—Disables the options in the group.

  ▓ LABEL—Specifies a label for the option group.

Example:

```
<OPTGROUP LABEL="months">
<OPTION VALUE="Jan">January</OPTION>
<OPTION VALUE="Feb">February</OPTION>
<OPTION VALUE="Mar">March</OPTION>
...
</OPTION>
```

Related Tags:

The <OPTGROUP> tag should be used only inside the <SELECT> and </SELECT> tags. The only tag allowable inside the <OPTGROUP> and </OPTGROUP> tags is the <OPTION> tag.

<TEXTAREA>

Type:

Container

Function:

Sets up a multiple-line text input window.

Syntax:

```
<TEXTAREA NAME="field_name" ROWS="number_of_rows"
  COLS="number_of_columns" DISABLED READONLY
  ACCESSKEY="shortcut_key_letter" TABINDEX="tab_position">
... default text to appear in window ...
</TR>
```

Attributes:

The <TEXTAREA> tag can take the following attributes:

- ACCESSKEY—Defines a shortcut key combination that the user can press to give focus to the text input window (see the attribute listing for the <A> tag for more details).

- COLS—Set equal to the number of columns wide the text window should be.

- DISABLED—Deactivates the text window.

- NAME—Assigns a unique name to the input window so that the processing program can identify it.

- READONLY—Leaves the window active, but the user will not be able to change the default text that is displayed.

- ROWS—Set equal to the number of rows high the text window should be.

- TABINDEX—Defines the text window's position in the tabbing order of the page.

Example:

```
<TEXTAREA NAME="feedback" ROWS=10 COLS=40>
We appreciate your comments!  Please delete this
text and type in your feedback.
</TEXTAREA>
```

<BUTTON>

Type:

Container

Function:

Places a button on the form. This type of button is different from the one rendered by <INPUT> because it has improved presentation features, such as three-dimensional rendering and up/down movement when clicked.

Syntax:

```
<BUTTON TYPE="SUBMIT¦RESET¦BUTTON" NAME="button_name" VALUE="button_value"
  DISABLED ACCESSKEY="shortcut_key_letter" TABINDEX="tab_position">
... text for button face or <IMG> tag ...
</BUTTON>
```

If text is placed between the <BUTTON> and </BUTTON> tags, that text will appear on the face of the button. If an <IMG> tag is placed between <BUTTON> and </BUTTON>, the image will be used as the button.

Attributes:

You can use the following attributes with the <BUTTON> tag:

- ACCESSKEY—Defines a shortcut key combination that the user can press to click the button (see the attribute listing for the <A> tag for more details).

- DISABLED—Disables the button.

- NAME—Gives the button a unique name.

- TABINDEX—Defines the button's position in the tabbing order of the page.
- TYPE—Set to SUBMIT, RESET, or BUTTON, depending on the type of button you're defining. TYPE="BUTTON" is typically used for defining a scripted button.
- VALUE—Specifies what is passed to the server when the button is clicked.

Example:

```
<BUTTON NAME="validate" VALUE="form_validation" onClick="validate();">
Click here to validate your input.
</BUTTON>
```

<LABEL>

Type:

Container

Function:

Denotes a form field label. Labels are typically text next to the field that prompts the user for the type of input expected. This works fine for text-based browsers, but it makes forms inaccessible for users who are visually impaired and who use speech-based or Braille browsers. Marking field labels with the <LABEL> tag makes it possible to prompt these users for the necessary input.

Syntax:

```
<LABEL FOR="field_ID" ACCESSKEY="shortcut_key_letter">
... label text goes here ...
</LABEL>
```

Attributes:

The <LABEL> tag takes the following attributes:

- ACCESSKEY—Defines a shortcut key combination that the user can press to give focus to the label (see the attribute listing for the <A> tag for more details).
- FOR—Set equal to the value of the ID attribute for the field that goes with the label.

Example:

```
<LABEL FOR="PW" ACCESSKEY="P">Enter your password:</LABEL>
<INPUT TYPE="PASSWORD" ID="PW" NAME="passwd">
```

Related Tags:

<LABEL> is typically used with the <INPUT>, <SELECT>, or <TEXTAREA> tags.

<FIELDSET>

Type:

Container

Part

II

Ch

3

Function:

Groups related form input fields.

Syntax:

```
<FIELDSET>
... related input fields ...
</FIELDSET>
```

Attributes:

None.

Example:

```
<FIELDSET>
Login: <INPUT TYPE="TEXT" NAME="login">
Password: <INPUT TYPE="PASSWORD" NAME="passwd">
</FIELDSET>
```

Related Tags:

The <LEGEND> tag can be used to give a field grouping a specific name.

<LEGEND>

Type:

Container

Function:

Names a group of related form fields.

Syntax:

```
<LEGEND ALIGN="LEFT¦RIGHT¦TOP¦BOTTOM" ACCESSKEY="shortcut_key_letter">
... legend text goes here ...
</LEGEND>
```

Attributes:

The <LEGEND> tag has two attributes:

- ■ ACCESSKEY—Defines a shortcut key combination that the user can press to give focus to the legend (see the attribute listing for the <A> tag for more details).
- ■ ALIGN—Controls how the legend text is horizontally aligned with respect to the group of fields and can be set equal to LEFT, RIGHT, TOP, or BOTTOM. ALIGN has been deprecated in favor of using style sheet information to align a legend.

Example:

```
<FIELDSET>
<LEGEND ALIGN="TOP">User Login Information</LEGEND>
Login: <INPUT TYPE="TEXT" NAME="login">
```

```
Password: <INPUT TYPE="PASSWORD" NAME="passwd">
</FIELDSET>
```

Related Tags:

`<LEGEND>` gives a name to a set of fields grouped together by the `<FIELDSET>` tag.

Frame Tags

Framed layouts are ones in which the browser window is broken into multiple regions called *frames*. Each frame can contain a distinct HTML document, enabling you to display several documents at once, rather than just one (see Figure 3.19).

FIGURE 3.19

Frames enable you to keep key page elements (such as navigation) on the screen all the time, while other parts of the page change.

Navigation frame —

Content frame —

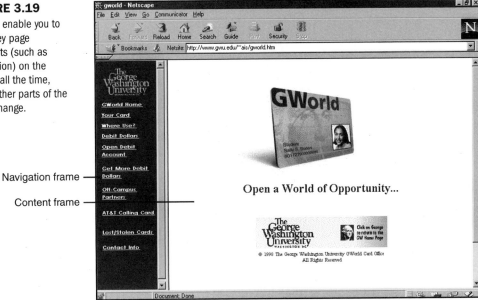

You need to know only a few tags to set up a framed page. These tags are covered in this section.

▶ **See** "Frames," **p. 211**.

<FRAMESET>

Type:

Container

Function:

Divides the browser window into frames.

Syntax:

```
<FRAMESET ROWS="list_of_row_sizes" COLS="list_of_column_sizes">
...
</FRAMESET>
```

Attributes:

<FRAMESET> can take the ROWS or COLS attribute, but not both at the same time. ROWS specifies how the browser screen should be broken up into multiple rows. ROWS is set equal to a list of values that describe the size of each row. The number of items in the list determines how many rows there will be. The values in the list determine the size of each row. Sizes can be in pixels, percentages of screen depth, or relative to the amount of available space. COLS works the same way, except it will divide the screen into columns.

N O T E If you try to use ROWS and COLS in the same <FRAMESET> tag, a browser will typically use the first attribute it finds and ignore the second. ▓

Example:

```
<!-- Divide the screen into four rows: 125 pixels, 30% of screen,
     88 pixels, and whatever is left over. -->
<FRAMESET ROWS="125,30%,88,*">
...
</FRAMESET>
```

Related Tags:

<FRAMESET> only breaks up the screen into multiple regions. You need to use the <FRAME> tag to populate each frame with content. Also, you can use the <NOFRAMES> tag to specify alternative content for browsers that cannot process frames.

N O T E <FRAMESET> tags may be nested to create even more complex layouts. ▓

<FRAME>

Type:

Standalone

Function:

Places content into a frame.

Syntax:

```
<FRAME SRC="URL_of_document" NAME="frame_name" FRAMEBORDER="0¦1"
  MARGINWIDTH="width_in_pixels" MARGINHEIGHT="height_in_pixels"
  NORESIZE SCROLLING="YES¦NO¦AUTO" LONGDESC="URL_of_description">
```

Attributes:

The <FRAME> tag can take several attributes:

- FRAMEBORDER—Setting FRAMEBORDER to 1 turns on the frame's borders; setting it to 0 turns them off.
- LONGDESC—Set equal to the URL of a resource that contains a more detailed description of the frame's content.
- MARGINHEIGHT—Specifies the size (in pixels) of the top margin of the frame.
- MARGINWIDTH—Specifies the size (in pixels) of the left margin of the frame.
- NAME—Gives the frame a unique name so it can be targeted by other tags (such as <A>, <FORM>, and <AREA>).
- NORESIZE—Suppresses the user's ability to drag and drop a frame border in a new location.
- SCROLLING—Controls the presence of scrollbars on the frame. Setting SCROLLING to YES makes the browser always put scrollbars on the frame, setting it to NO suppresses the scrollbars, and setting it to the default of AUTO enables the browser to decide whether the scrollbars are needed.
- SRC—Tells the browser the URL of the HTML file to load into the frame. SRC is a required attribute of the <FRAME> tag.

Example:

```
<FRAMESET COLS="25%,75%"> <!-- Make 2 columnar frames -->
   <!-- Populate frame #1 -->
   <FRAME SRC="leftframe.html" NORESIZE NAME="left" FRAMEBORDER=0>
   <!-- Populate frame #2 -->
   <FRAME SRC="rightframe.html" NORESIZE NAME="right" FRAMEBORDER=0>
...
</FRAMESET>
```

Related Tags:

The <FRAME> tag is valid only between the <FRAMESET> and </FRAMESET> tags.

<NOFRAMES>

Type:

Container

Function:

Provides an alternative layout for browsers that cannot process frames.

Syntax:

```
<NOFRAMES>
... non-frames content goes here ...
</NOFRAMES>
```

Part
II

Ch
3

Attributes:

None.

Example:

```
<FRAMESET COLS="25%,75%"> <!-- Make 2 columnar frames -->
    <!-- Populate frame #1 -->
    <FRAME SRC="leftframe.html" NORESIZE NAME="left" FRAMEBORDER=0>
    <!-- Populate frame #2 -->
    <FRAME SRC="rightframe.html" NORESIZE NAME="right" FRAMEBORDER=0>
<NOFRAMES>
Your browser cannot process frames.  Please visit the
<A HREF="/noframes/index.html">non-frames version</A>
of our site.
</NOFRAMES>
</FRAMESET>
```

Related Tags:

<NOFRAMES> is valid only between the <FRAMESET> and </FRAMESET> tags. Your <NOFRAMES> content should be specified before any nested <FRAMESET> tags.

<IFRAME>

Type:

Container

Function:

Places a floating frame on a page. *Floating frames* are best described as "frames that you can place like images."

Syntax:

```
<IFRAME SRC="URL_of_document" NAME="frame_name" FRAMEBORDER="0¦1"
  WIDTH="frame_width_in_pixels_or_percentage"
  HEIGHT="frame_height_in_pixels_or_percentage"
  MARGINWIDTH="margin_width_in_pixels"
  MARGINHEIGHT="margin_height_in_pixels"
  SCROLLING="YES¦NO¦AUTO" ALIGN="TOP¦MIDDLE¦BOTTOM¦LEFT¦RIGHT"
  LONGDESC="URL_of_description">
... text or image alternative to the floating frame ...
</IFRAME>
```

Attributes:

The <IFRAME> tag can take the following attributes:

- ALIGN—Controls how the floating frame is aligned, and can be set to TOP, MIDDLE, BOTTOM, LEFT, or RIGHT. TOP, MIDDLE, and BOTTOM alignments make text appear next to the frame, starting at the top, middle, or bottom of the frame. Setting ALIGN to LEFT or RIGHT floats the frame in the left or right margin and enables text to wrap around it.

- FRAMEBORDER—Setting FRAMEBORDER to 1 turns on the floating frame's borders; setting it to 0 turns them off.
- HEIGHT—Specifies the height of the floating frame in pixels.
- LONGDESC—Set equal to the URL of a resource that contains more detail about the contents of the floating frame.
- MARGINHEIGHT—Specifies the size (in pixels) of the top margin of the floating frame.
- MARGINWIDTH—Specifies the size (in pixels) of the left margin of the floating frame.
- NAME—Gives the floating frame a unique name so it can be targeted by other tags (such as <A>, <FORM>, and <AREA>).
- SCROLLING—Controls the presence of scrollbars on the floating frame. Setting SCROLLING to YES makes the browser always put scrollbars on the floating frame, setting it to NO suppresses the scrollbars, and setting it to the default of AUTO enables the browser to decide whether the scrollbars are needed.
- SRC—Tells the browser the URL of the HTML file to load into the floating frame. SRC is a required attribute of the <IFRAME> tag.
- WIDTH—Specifies the width of the floating frame in pixels.

Example:

```
<IFRAME SRC= "float_content.html " WIDTH= "50% " HEIGHT= "50% " ALIGN="RIGHT"
  SCROLLING= "NO " NAME= "floater " FRAMEBORDER=1>
Your browser does not support floating frames. :(
</IFRAME>
```

Executable Content Tags

One of the ways in which Web pages have become more dynamic is through their support of executable content, such as Java applets and ActiveX controls. These page elements are downloaded to the browser and run in its memory space to produce dynamic content on the browser screen.

HTML 4.0 supports two ways for placing executable content: the <APPLET> tag for Java applets and the <OBJECT> tag for other executable objects. These tags, along with the supporting <PARAM> tag, are profiled in this section.

<APPLET>

Type:

Container

Function:

Places a Java applet on a page. The <APPLET> tag has been deprecated in favor of using the more generic <OBJECT> tag to place applets.

Part
II

Ch
3

Syntax:

```
<APPLET WIDTH= "width_in_pixels " HEIGHT= "height_in_pixels "
  CODEBASE= "base_URL_for_applet " CODE= "applet_class file "
  OBJECT= "serialized_applet_file " NAME= "applet_name "
  ARCHIVE= "archive_list " ALT= "text_alternative "
  ALIGN= "TOP¦MIDDLE¦BOTTOM¦LEFT¦RIGHT "
  HSPACE= "pixels " VSPACE= "pixels ">
...
</APPLET>
```

Attributes:

As the following list demonstrates, many of the <APPLET> tag's attributes are the same as those for the <IMG> tag:

- ALIGN—Positions adjacent text at the TOP, MIDDLE, or BOTTOM of the applet window, or you can float the window in the LEFT or RIGHT margin.

- ALT—Provides a text-based alternative to the applet.

- ARCHIVE—Set equal to a comma-delimited list of archive locations.

- CODE—Specifies the class file.

- CODEBASE—Set equal to the URL of the code.

- HEIGHT—Specifies the height of the applet window in pixels. HEIGHT is a required attribute of the <APPLET> tag.

- HSPACE—Controls the amount of whitespace (in pixels) to the left and right of the applet window.

- NAME—Gives the applet a unique name so that it can be referenced by other Java applets.

- OBJECT—Provides the name of a serialized applet file.

- VSPACE—Controls the amount of whitespace (in pixels) above and below the applet window.

- WIDTH—Specifies the width of the applet window in pixels. WIDTH is a required attribute of the <APPLET> tag.

N O T E   Either the CODE or the OBJECT attribute must be used in an <APPLET> tag. If they are both used and they each specify a different class name, the browser should return an error message. ▨

Example:

```
<APPLET WIDTH=250 HEIGHT=200 CODE= "marquee.class " NAME= "marquee "
  ALT= "Scrolling text marquee applet " ALIGN= "RIGHT "
  HSPACE=5 VSPACE=12>
  <PARAM NAME= "message " VALUE= "Hello World! ">
...
</APPLET>
```

Related Tags:

Parameters are passed to a Java applet using the <PARAM> tag.

<PARAM>

Type:

Standalone

Function:

Passes a parameter to a Java applet (<APPLET>) or other executable object (<OBJECT>).

Syntax:

```
<PARAM ID= "unique_identifier " NAME= "parameter_name "
 VALUE= "parameter_value " VALUETYPE= "DATA¦REF¦OBJECT "
 TYPE= "expected_content_type ">
```

Attributes:

The <PARAM> tag can take the following attributes:

- ID—Assigns a unique identifying name to the parameter.
- NAME—Provides the name of the parameter.
- TYPE—Tells the browser what the parameter's Internet media (MIME) type is.
- VALUE—Specifies the value of the parameter.
- VALUETYPE—Provides more detail about the nature of the VALUE being passed and can be set to DATA, REF, or OBJECT.

Example:

```
<APPLET WIDTH=300 HEIGHT=224 CODE= "test.class ALT= "Test applet "
   ALIGN= "TOP " NAME= "test " >
   <PARAM ID= "P1 " NAME= "tolerance " VALUE= "0.001 " VALUETYPE= "DATA ">
   <PARAM ID= "P2" NAME= "pi " VALUE= "3.14159 " VALUETYPE= "DATA ">
...
</APPLET>
```

Related Tags:

<PARAM> tags can be used only between the <APPLET> and </APPLET> tags or between the <OBJECT> and </OBJECT> tags.

<OBJECT>

Type:

Container

Function:

Places an executable object on a page.

Syntax:

```
<OBJECT CLASSID= "implementation_info " CODEBASE= "URL_of_object "
   CODETYPE= "MIME_type " DATA= "URL_to_data " TYPE= "data_MIME_type "
   ARCHIVE= "list_of_archives " USEMAP= "map_name " TABINDEX= "tab_position "
```

Part

II

Ch

3

```
      STANDBY= "message_while_loading " DECLARE
      ALIGN= "TEXTTOP¦MIDDLE¦TEXTMIDDLE¦BASELINE¦TEXTBOTTOM¦LEFT¦CENTER¦RIGHT "
      WIDTH= "width_in_pixels_or_percentage " NAME= "object_name "
      HEIGHT= "height_in_pixels_or_percentage "
      HSPACE= "pixels " VSPACE= "pixels " BORDER= "pixels ">
  ...
  </OBJECT>
```

Attributes:

The <OBJECT> tag has an exhausting list of attributes, but many of them are the same as those for the <IMG> tag, so they are fairly easy to understand:

- ALIGN—Controls how content adjacent to the object area is aligned. Note that this ALIGN attribute has many more possible values than ALIGN attributes for other tags.

- WIDTH and HEIGHT—Specifies the dimensions of the object area as a number of pixels or as a percentage of available space.

- BORDER—Set equal to the number of pixels that the border thickness should be.

- HSPACE and VSPACE—Controls the amount of whitespace around the object area.

Additionally, <OBJECT> can take these attributes:

- ARCHIVE—Set equal to a comma-delimited list of archive locations.

- CLASSID—Identifies which implementation or release of the object you're using.

- CODEBASE—Set equal to the URL of the object.

- CODETYPE—Describes the code's MIME type.

- DATA—Set equal to list of URLs where data for the object can be found.

- DECLARE—Instructs the browser to declare, but not instantiate, a flag for the object.

- STANDBY—Enables you to display a message to the user while the object is loading.

- TYPE—Specifies the MIME type of the data passed to the object.

- USEMAP—Points to client-side map data, if imagemaps are used.

Example:

```
<OBJECT WIDTH=100% HEIGHT=100 CODETYPE= "application/x-oleobject "
  CLASSID= "CLSID: 1A4DA620-6217-11CF-BE62-0080C72EDD2D "
  CODEBASE= "http://activex.microsoft.com/controls/iexplorer/marquee.ocx "
  HSPACE=5 VSPACE=10 ALIGN=MIDDLE BORDER=0>
  <PARAM NAME= "image " VALUE= "greeting.gif ">
  <PARAM NAME= "speed " VALUE= "7 ">
  <PARAM NAME= "repeat " VALUE= "1 ">
...
</OBJECT>
```

Related Tags:

Parameters passed to the object are given by the <PARAM> tag. ●

## CHAPTER 4

Imagemaps

by Eric Ladd

In this chapter

What Are Imagemaps?

If you use a graphical browser, you have probably noticed that many major Web sites have a large clickable image on their main page. These images are different from your run-of-the-mill hyperlinked graphic in that your browser loads a different document, depending on where you click. The image is somehow "multilinked" and can take you to a number of places. Such a multilinked image is called an *imagemap*.

The challenge in preparing an imagemap is defining which parts of the image are linked to which URLs. Linked regions in an imagemap are called *hot regions*, and each hot region is associated with the URL of the document that is to be loaded when the hot region is clicked. After you decide the hot regions and their associated URLs, you need to determine whether the Web server or the Web client will make the "decision" about which document to load, based on the user's click. This choice is the difference between server-side and client-side imagemaps. Either approach is easy to implement after you know how to define the hot regions.

This chapter walks you through the necessary steps for creating both client-side and server-side imagemaps and introduces you to some software programs that make the task of defining hot regions much less tedious.

Client-Side Imagemaps

Client-side imagemaps are a great idea because they permit faster imagemap processing and enhance the portability of your HTML documents. Client-side imagemaps involve sending the map data to the client as part of an HTML file rather than having the client contact the server each time the map data is needed. This process may add slightly to the transfer time of the HTML file, but the resultant increased efficiency is well worth it.

The movement toward client-side imagemaps has been fueled by the promise of a number of advantages, including the following:

- Immediate processing—After the browser has the map file information, it can process a user's click immediately instead of connecting to the server and waiting for a response.

- Offline viewing of Web pages—If you're looking at a site from a hard drive or a CD-ROM drive, no server is available to do any imagemap computations. Client-side imagemaps enable imagemaps to be used when you're looking at pages offline.

- No special configurations based on server program—Client-side imagemaps are always implemented the same way. You don't need to format the map data differently, depending on whether a server expects CERN or NCSA imagemaps, because no server is involved.

Previously, the only disadvantage of using client-side imagemaps was that it wasn't standard HTML and, therefore, not implemented by all browsers. Now that client-side imagemaps have been adopted as part of the HTML 4.0 recommendation, you would be hard pressed to find a graphical browser that does not support them.

Creating a client-side image map involves three steps:

1. Create the graphic that you want to make into an imagemap.

2. Define the hot regions for the graphic and place that information between the <MAP> and </MAP> tags in your HTML document.

3. Use the <IMG> tag to insert the graphic for the imagemap and link it to the hot region information you defined in the <MAP> section.

Defining a Map

A client-side imagemap is defined using HTML tags and attributes, usually right in the HTML file that contains the document with the imagemap. The map data is stored between the <MAP> and </MAP> container tags. The <MAP> tag has the mandatory attribute NAME, which is used to give the imagemap data a unique identifier that can be used when referencing the data.

Inside the <MAP> and </MAP> tags, hot regions are defined by standalone <AREA> tags—one <AREA> tag for each hot region. The <AREA> tag takes the attributes shown in Table 4.1.

Table 4.1   Attributes of the <AREA> Tag

Attribute	Purpose
ACCESSKEY	Designates a shortcut key for the region
ALT	Provides a text-based alternative to the hot region
COORDS	Lists the coordinates of points needed to define the hot region
HREF	Supplies the URL to be associated with the hot region
NOHREF	Specifies that no URL is associated with the hot region
SHAPE	Set equal to the keyword (rect, circle, poly, and default) that specifies the shape of the hot region
TABINDEX	Specifies the region's position in the page's tabbing order
TARGET	Identifies the frame where the linked document should be rendered

Part

II

Ch

4

N O T E The SHAPE attribute can take on values of rect, circle, poly, and default. The point keyword is not supported in HTML 4.0.

These regions, as their names suggest, refer to the geometric shape of the hot region. Their defining coordinates are determined as pixel points relative to the upper-left corner of the imagemap graphic, which is taken to have coordinates 0,0 (see Figure 4.1).

N O T E One important difference with client-side imagemaps is that when you specify a circular hot region, you need only give the coordinates of the center point and the radius of the circle.

To set up a circular hot region, for example, you would use code such as the following:

```
<MAP NAME="circle">
<AREA SHAPE="circle" COORDS="123,89,49"
HREF="http://www.server.com/circle.html" ALT="Circle Link">
</MAP>
```

The preceding HTML sets up a map named *circle* that has one hot region. Note that the numbers in the list of coordinates for the COORDS attribute are all separated by commas, and the URL in the HREF attribute is fully qualified. Note also that the coordinates list comprises the coordinates of the center point followed by a single number that represents the radius of the circle.

The <AREA> tag can also take a NOHREF attribute, which tells the browser to do nothing if the user clicks the hot region. Any part of the image that is not defined as a hot region is taken to be a NOHREF region—if users click outside a hot region, they don't go anywhere by default. This approach saves you from setting up an <AREA SHAPE="DEFAULT" NOHREF> tag for all your maps.

N O T E You can have as many <AREA> tags as you like. If the hot regions defined by two <AREA> tags overlap, the <AREA> tag listed first has precedence. ▓

Setting Up the Imagemap

After the imagemap data is set up in HTML form, you need to set up the imagemap itself. To do this, you use the <IMG> tag along with the USEMAP attribute. USEMAP tells the browser that the image to be used is a client-side imagemap. It is set equal to the name of the map that contains the appropriate map data. For the client-side imagemap defined previously, the setup would look like this:

```
<IMG SRC="images/mainpage.gif" USEMAP="#circle">
```

The pound sign (#) before the map name indicates that the map data is found in the same HTML file. If the map data is in another file called maps.html (which is perfectly okay), your <IMG> tag would look like the following:

```
<IMG SRC="images/mainpage.gif"
USEMAP="http://www.server.com/maps.html#circle">
```

T I P If you have standard navigation imagemaps on your site, you should consider storing the map data for them in a single HTML file for easier maintenance.

N O T E Although the HTML 4.0 recommendation says that the USEMAP attribute can be set to any valid URL, some browsers do not support the ability to reference another file when looking for map information. In these cases, you can still maintain the map information in a single file and read it into your HTML files as needed, using a Server-Side Include (SSI). This way, you can still make changes in the map information in one place and the changes will propagate throughout your site.

To learn more about SSIs, consult Chapter 32, "Server-Side Includes." ▓

Example: A Main Page Imagemap

Figure 4.1 shows an image to be used as an imagemap on the main page of a small corporate site. The coordinates to define the hot regions in the image are given in Table 4.2.

Table 4.2 Coordinates and URLs for Main Page Imagemap Example

Shape	Coordinates	URL
Rectangle	(166,255),(368,382)	http://www.server.com/info.html
Circle	(160,151),(160,224)	http://www.server.com/index.html
Polygon	(308,86), (378,109), (421,52), (421,122), (491,149), (420,169), (419,245), (377,185), (306,205), (349,148)	http://www.server.com/new.html

FIGURE 4.1

An imagemap on a home page typically provides navigation links to all major areas of a site.

Upper-left corner of image has coordinates 0,0

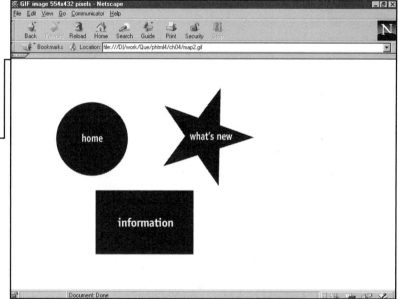

To set up the map information to make the image in Figure 4.1 a client-side imagemap, you could use the following HTML:

```
<MAP NAME="mainpage">
<AREA SHAPE="rect" COORDS="166,255,368,382"
HREF="http://www.server.com/info.html" ALT="Site Map">
<AREA SHAPE="circle" COORDS="160,151,73"
HREF="http://www.server.com/index.html" ALT="Search">
<AREA SHAPE="polygon"
```

```
COORDS="308,86,378,109,421,52,421,122,491,149,420,169,
419,245,377,185,306,205,349,148"
HREF="http://www.yourserver.com/whatsnew.html" ALT="What's New">
</MAP>
```

Then, to set up the imagemap, you would use the following if the map information were in the same file:

```
<IMG SRC="images/map2.gif" USEMAP="#mainpage">
```

If the map information were stored in the file `maps.html`, you would modify the preceding `<IMG>` tag to read as follows:

```
<IMG SRC="images/map2.gif" USEMAP="http://www.server.com/maps.html#mainpage">
```

Example: A Navigation Imagemap

Another common use of imagemaps is for navigation bars at the top or bottom of a Web page. Figure 4.2 shows a typical navigation graphic with the hot regions defined by the information in Table 4.3.

Table 4.3 Coordinates and URLs for Navigation Imagemap Example

Shape	Coordinates	URL
Rectangle	(1,1),(112,36)	http://www.server.com/index.html
Rectangle	(113,1),(224,36)	http://www.server.com/new.html
Rectangle	(225,1),(335,36)	http://www.server.com/info.html
Rectangle	(336,1),(447,36)	http://www.server.com/search/index.html
Rectangle	(448,1),(560,36)	http://www.server.com/contact.html

To use the image in Figure 4.2 as a client-side imagemap, you first need to set up the map information in an HTML file:

```
<MAP NAME="navigate">
<AREA SHAPE="rect" COORDS="1,1,112,36"
 HREF="http://www.server.com/index.html" ALT="Home Page">
<AREA SHAPE="rect" COORDS="113,1,224,36"
 HREF="http://www.server.com/new.html" ALT="What's New">
<AREA SHAPE="rect" COORDS="225,1,335,36"
 HREF="http://www.server.com/info.html" ALT="Information">
<AREA SHAPE="rect" COORDS="336,1,447,36"
 HREF="http://www.server.com/search/index.html" ALT="Search">
<AREA SHAPE="rect" COORDS="448,1,560,36"
 HREF="http://www.server.com/contact.html" ALT="Contact Us">
</MAP>
```

With the map data in place, you can reference it with the `<IMG>` tag if the map data is in the same HTML file:

```
<IMG SRC="images/navigate2.gif" USEMAP="#navigate">
```

FIGURE 4.2

A footer graphic frequently supports navigation options from each page in a site.

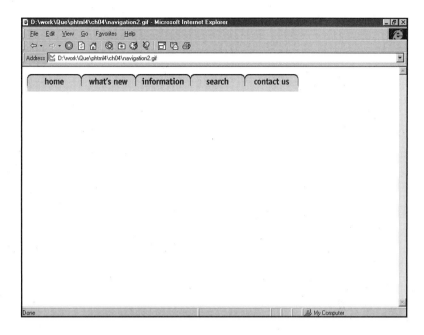

Because the same navigation maps are often used on several pages on a site, you might want to put the map data in a single map file and reference the file each time you need the map:

```
<IMG SRC="images/navigate2.gif" USEMAP="maps.html#navigate">
```

As noted earlier, this is an efficient way to manage imagemaps common to many pages.

Server-Side Imagemaps

A server-side imagemap is one in which the server determines which document should be loaded, based on where the user clicked the imagemap. To make this determination, the server needs the following information:

- The coordinates of the user's click—This information is passed to the server by the client program.

- A program that takes the click coordinates as input and provides a URL as output—Most servers have a routine built in that handles this task.

- Access to the information that defines the hot regions and their associated URLs—This information is critical to the processing program that checks the hot regions to see whether the user's click corresponds to a URL. When the program finds a match, it returns the URL paired with the clicked hot region. The file on the server that contains this information is called the *map file*.

Additionally, you need two other "ingredients" to complete a server-side imagemap:

- An image—An imagemap is like any other graphic in that you need to have a GIF or a JPEG file that contains the image.

- Proper setup in your HTML file—When you place the imagemap graphic, you use the <IMG> tag with a special attribute to alert the browser that the image is to be used as a server-side imagemap.

As an HTML author, you need to be most concerned about two of the items just listed: the map file and the setup in the HTML file. The next two sections discuss these aspects of creating an imagemap.

Preparing the Map File

The map file is a text file that contains information about the hot regions of a specific imagemap graphic. Therefore, a separate map file is necessary for each imagemap graphic you want to use. The definition specifies the type of hot region as a rectangle, circle, polygon, or point.

The following list identifies basic imagemap shape keywords and their required coordinates:

- rect—Indicates that the hot region is a rectangle. The coordinates required for this type of shape are the upper-left and lower-right pixels in the rectangle. The active region is the area within the rectangle.

- circle—Indicates that the hot region is circular. Coordinates required for using a circle are the center-point pixel and one edge-point pixel (a pixel on the circle itself). The active region is the area within the circle.

- poly—Indicates that the hot region is a polygon. To specify the polygon, you need to provide a list of coordinates for all the polygon's vertices. A polygonal region can have as many as 100 vertices. The active region is the area within the polygon.

- point—Indicates that the region is a point on the image. A point coordinate is one specific pixel measured from the upper-left corner of the imagemap graphic. A point is considered active if the click occurs closest to that point on the graphic, yet not within another active region.

- default—A catch-all that defines all areas of an imagemap graphic that are not specified by any other active region.

 An imagemap definition file should, whenever possible, be configured with a default HTML link. The default link takes the user to an area that isn't designated as being an active link. This URL should provide the user with feedback or helpful information about using that particular imagemap.

CAUTION

An imagemap definition file should never contain both a point and a default region. If point regions are defined and a user does not click a hot region, the server sends the user to the URL associated with the closest point region and the default URL will never be used.

Following each type of region in the imagemap definition file is the URL that is returned to the user when a click within that area is recorded. Active regions in the definition file are read from the first line down. If two regions overlap in their coordinates, the imagemap program uses the first region it encounters in the file.

> **CAUTION**
>
> URLs in map files should always be absolute or fully qualified URLs—that is, the URL should specify a protocol, a server name, and a filename (including the directory path to the file).

N O T E You can use the pound sign (#) to comment on a line in the imagemap definition file. Any line beginning with a pound sign is ignored by the imagemap program. Comments are useful for adding information, such as the date of creation, the physical path to the imagemap graphic, or specific comments about the server configuration.

Two primary types of map file configurations exist: one for the original CERN-style imagemaps and one for the NCSA server's implementation of imagemaps. Both use the same types of hot regions and the same coordinates to define each type. However, the formatting of this information in each map file is different. Therefore, you should check with the system administrator about the particular imagemap setup of the server you are using.

N O T E Most major HTTP servers today use the NCSA map format. This includes Netscape Enterprise Server and Windows 98/NT–based servers, such as Microsoft Internet Information Server (IIS) or Microsoft Peer Web Services (PWS).

CERN Map File Format   Lines in a CERN-style map file have the following form:

```
region_type coordinates URL
```

The coordinates must be in parentheses, and the x and y coordinates must be separated by a comma. The CERN format also doesn't allow for comments about hot regions. A sample CERN-style hot region definition might look like the following:

```
circle (123,89) (146,132) http://www.server.com/circle.html
```

NSCA Map File Format   NCSA developed a slightly different format from CERN's for map file information. Their format is as follows:

```
region_type URL coordinates
```

The coordinates don't have to be in parentheses, but they do have to be separated by commas. The equivalent of the map data line presented previously in NCSA format is as follows:

```
circle http://www.server/circle.html 123,89,146,132
```

Setting Up the Imagemap

Because of the differences in imagemap processing programs on different servers, you can use two techniques for setting up imagemaps.

Part

II

Ch

4

Pointing Directly at the Processing Scripting The first approach, most commonly used with NCSA and CERN servers, involves a direct call to the imagemap processing program on the server. The HREF attribute is set equal to the URL to the imagemap processing script followed by a slash (/) and the name of the map defined in the server's imagemap.conf file. In the following example, the name of the map is mainpage. The actual graphic is then included with the <IMG> tag. The <IMG> tag also includes the ISMAP attribute, indicating that the image placed by the tag is to be a server-side imagemap. Using this approach, your imagemap link might look like this:

```
<A HREF="/cgi-bin/imagemap/mainpage">
<IMG SRC="images/mainpage.gif" ISMAP></A>
```

For this example to work, the imagemap.conf file must also include a line pointing to a map file for the imagemap mainpage. That line might look like the following:

```
mainpage : /maps/mainpage.map
```

Entries in the imagemap.conf file enable the imagemap program to find the map files you create. You need a similar entry in the imagemap.conf file for each imagemap you want the server to process.

Pointing Directly at the Map File Linking to the imagemap script on the server is somewhat easier under Netscape and Microsoft HTTP servers. For this program, you just use the following line with an NCSA-style map file:

```
<A HREF="/maps/mainpage.map">
<IMG SRC="images/mainpage.gif" ISMAP></A>
```

These servers don't require the imagemap.conf file, so you can "eliminate the middleman" and point directly to the map file. When the server detects a call for a map file, it automatically invokes the imagemap processing program.

Example: A Main Page Imagemap

You use the following code to set up the image you saw in Figure 4.1 in a CERN-style map file:

```
rect (166,255) (368,382) http://www.server.com/info.html
circle (160,151) (160,224) http://www.server.com/index.html
poly (308,86) (378,109) (421,52) (421,122) (491,149) (420,169) (419,245)
(377,185) (306,205) (349,148) http://www.server.com/new.html
```

For a server that works with the NCSA map file format, you use this:

```
rect http://www.server.com/info.html 166,255 368,382
circle http://www.server.com/index.html 160,151 160,224
poly http://www.server.com/new.html 308,86 378,109 421,52 421,122
491,149 420,169 419,245 377,185 306,205 349,148
```

With a map file set up in one style or another, you then set up the imagemap with this code:

```
<A HREF="http://www.server.com/cgi-bin/imagemap/mainpage">
<IMG SRC="images/map2.gif" ISMAP ...></A>
```

The preceding code is for servers that use an imagemap.conf file or with this:

```
<A HREF="http://www.server.com/maps/mainpage.map">
<IMG SRC="images/map2.gif" ISMAP ...></A>
```

This code is for servers that automatically go to the map file.

N O T E If you are using a server with an `imagemap.conf` file, you also need a line in that file matching the name "mainpage" with the map file `mainpage.map`:

```
mainpage : /maps/mainpage.map
```

Example: A Navigation Imagemap

The CERN format map file for the image you saw in Figure 4.2 would look like the following:

```
rect (1,1) (112,36) http://www.server.com/index.html
rect (113,1) (224,36) http://www.server.com/new.html
rect (225,1) (335,36) http://www.server.com/info.html
rect (336,1) (447,36) http://www.server.com/search/index.html
rect (448,1) (560,36) http://www.server.com/contact.html
```

If you are preparing a map file in NCSA format, use the following:

```
rect http://www.server.com/index.html 1,1 112,36
rect http://www.server.com/new.html 113,1 224,36
rect http://www.server.com/info.html 225,1 335,36
rect http://www.server.com/search/index.html 336,1 447,36
rect http://www.server.com/contact.html 448,1 560,36
```

After your map file is done in the appropriate format, you set up the imagemap with

```
<A HREF="http://www.server.com/cgi-bin/imagemap/navigate">
<IMG SRC="images/navigation2.gif" ISMAP ...></A>
```

or with

```
<A HREF="http://www.server.com/maps/navigate.map">
<IMG SRC="images/navigation.gif" ISMAP ...></A>
```

depending on whether the server uses an `imagemap.conf` file.

Part
II

Ch
4

Using Server-Side and Client-Side Imagemaps Together

Client-side imagemaps are a great idea because they permit faster imagemap processing and enhance the portability of your HTML documents. Unfortunately, you can't be certain all graphical browsers are compliant with the HTML 4.0 recommendation and support the client-side imagemap approach just described. To be on the safe side, you can combine server-side and client-side imagemaps, essentially implementing both at the same time, to ensure your imagemaps are accessible to the broadest possible audience.

To combine a server-side imagemap with a client-side imagemap for the main page example discussed earlier, you can modify the earlier HTML as follows:

```
<A HREF="http://www.server/maps/mainpage.map">
<IMG SRC="images/map2.gif" USEMAP="#mainpage" ISMAP></A>
```

Flanking the `<IMG>` tag with `<A>` and `</A>` tags makes it point to the `mainpage.map` file on the server. You need to include the `ISMAP` attribute in the `<IMG>` tag to let the browser know that the image is linked as a server-side imagemap as well.

N O T E   You can link NCSA- and CERN-style server-side imagemaps to client-side imagemaps by having the `HREF` in the `<A>` tag point to the imagemap script instead of pointing directly to the map file. ▪

Providing a Text Alternative to an Imagemap

When you use an imagemap—in particular, a server-side imagemap—it is important to provide a text-based alternative to users who have a text-only browser, who have image loading turned off, or who are using a nonvisual browser. These users won't be able to view your image, so the entire imagemap will be lost on them if a text-based alternative is not supplied.

Additionally, not all Web robots can follow the links set up in a server-side imagemap. By providing a text-based set of links that replicate the links in the imagemap, you give the robots a way to better index your pages.

N O T E   Text-based alternatives are less critical for client-side imagemaps because of the `ALT` attribute of the `<AREA>` tag. You are still free to include such alternatives, however, if you are willing to make the effort. ▪

Most sites place their text-based alternatives to an imagemap just below the imagemap graphic. Usually the links are in a smaller font size and are separated by vertical bars or some such separator character (see Figure 4.3).

Imagemap Tools

Whether you are creating a server-side or client-side imagemap, it can be cumbersome determining and typing in all the coordinates of all the points needed to define hot regions. Luckily, programs are available to help you through this process. They enable you to load your imagemap image, trace out the hot regions right onscreen, and then write the appropriate map file or HTML file to implement the imagemap. The following sections describe two of these programs: Mapedit and Microsoft's FrontPage.

Mapedit

Mapedit 2.31 is a shareware imagemap tool produced by Boutell.Com, Inc. This version of Mapedit supports client-side images and targeting of individual frames when you use an imagemap within a framed document.

FIGURE 4.3

Duplicating imagemap links with hypertext links makes it possible for users with text-only browsers to navigate your site.

Image links —

Hypertext links —

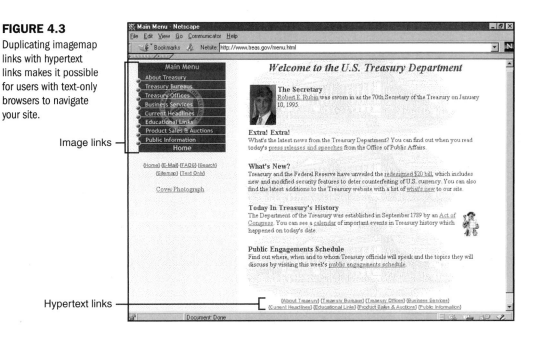

Using Mapedit is easy. From the File menu, choose Open HTML Document to begin. In the dialog box that appears, you won't see a choice between doing a server-side and a client-side imagemap. Rather, you first tell Mapedit which HTML file contains the image for which you're building the imagemap. Next, tell Mapedit which file contains the imagemap image. When you click OK, the image file is loaded into the Mapedit window, and you're ready to start defining hot regions.

You can choose Rectangle, Circle, or Polygon tools from the Mapedit Tools menu or from the toolbar just below the menus. Each tool enables you to trace out a hot region shaped like the name of the tool. To use the Rectangle tool, point your mouse to the upper-left corner of the rectangular hot region and click the left mouse button. Then move your mouse pointer to the lower-right corner of the region. As you do so, a black rectangular outline is dragged along with the pointer, eventually opening up to enclose your hot region (see Figure 4.4).

With the mouse pointer pointing at the lower-right corner, left-click the mouse again. When you do, you see a dialog box like the one shown in Figure 4.5. Type the URL associated with the hot region you are defining into the dialog box, along with any comments you want to include, and click OK. Mapedit puts this information into the file it is building and is then ready to define another hot region or to save the file and exit.

Mapedit's Circle and Polygon tools work similarly. With the Circle tool, you place your mouse pointer at the center of the circular region (which is sometimes difficult to estimate!) and left-click. Then move the pointer to a point on the circle and left-click again to define the region and call up the dialog box. To use the Polygon tool, just left-click the vertices of the polygon in ‍ sequence. When you hit the last unique vertex (that is, the next vertex in the sequence is the first one you clicked), right-click instead to define the region and reveal the dialog box.

FIGURE 4.4

Mapedit's hot region tracing tools are easy to use.

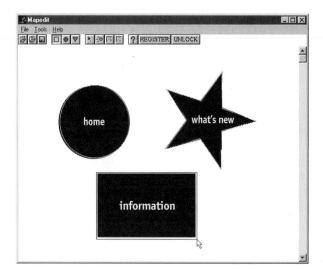

FIGURE 4.5

After your hot region is defined, Mapedit prompts you for the URL to associate with it.

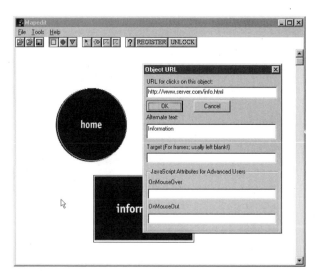

 T I P If you are unhappy with how your trace is coming out, just press the Esc key to erase your trace and start over.

Other Mapedit Tool menu options enable you to move an entire hot region (Move), add points (Add Points), or remove points (Remove Points) from a polygon and test the imagemap file as it currently stands. The Edit Default URL option, under the File menu, enables you to specify a default URL to go to if a user clicks somewhere other than a hot region. Mapedit's test mode (choose Tools, Test+Edit) presents the imagemap graphic to you and enables you to click it. If you click a hot region, the URL dialog box opens and displays the URL associated with the region you clicked.

The most recent version of Mapedit for Windows 95 and Windows NT places a heavy emphasis on creating client-side imagemaps, but you can still use Mapedit to create server-side maps as well. Under the File menu, you'll now find Import Old Server Map and Export Old Server Map options that read in or write out a map file, respectively.

N O T E   Mapedit is available for all Windows platforms, Macintosh, and many kinds of UNIX. You can find Mapedit on the CD-ROM that comes with this book. After a 30-day evaluation period, you must license Mapedit at a cost of $25. Site licenses are also available. Educational and nonprofit users do not have to pay for a license, but should register their copies of Mapedit. For more information, visit http://www.boutell.com/. ▧

Microsoft FrontPage

The FrontPage Editor comes with an Image toolbar that activates whenever you select an image. In addition to basic image operations such as cropping, rotating, and changing contrast, buttons on the Image toolbar can also help you set up hot regions in an imagemap. The imagemap-related buttons are the first five you see on the left end of the toolbar (see Figure 4.6).

▶ **See** "How FrontPage Handles Imagemaps," **p. 300.**

Part

II

Ch

4

FIGURE 4.6
FrontPage's Image toolbar includes buttons for setting up imagemaps.

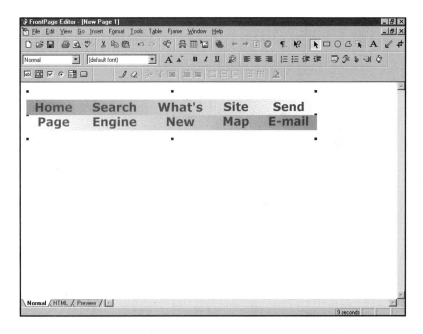

An important thing to note about FrontPage's imagemap handling is that, by default, it is done using a preprogrammed page object called a *bot*. When you look at the code FrontPage generates to support an imagemap, you will see something like this:

```
<!--webbot bot="ImageMap"
polygon=" (201,163) (237,139) (303,148) (329,180) (310,208) pageone.htm"
 rectangle=" (228,309) (278, 397)  pagetwo.htm"
circle=" (281,83) 60  pagethree.htm" src="map.gif"
alt="map.gif (18273 bytes)" align="right" width="600" height="380" -->
```

This is a call to the FrontPage Imagemap bot—a piece of executable code that resides on a FrontPage-compliant Web server. If you're not using a FrontPage-compliant server, this code won't do you or your visitors any good. Fortunately, you can instruct FrontPage to write client-side imagemap code instead by performing these steps:

1. In the FrontPage Explorer, choose Tools, Web Settings; then click the Advanced tab.

2. Make sure the Generate Client-Side Imagemaps option near the top of the dialog box is checked.

3. Select the Netscape option from the Style drop-down list.

4. Click OK.

This tells FrontPage that it should not use the Imagemap bot, and the code you find in your HTML files should be consistent with the HTML standard for client-side imagemaps.

After you have loaded an imagemap graphic, you can select the Rectangle, Circle, or Polygon tool by clicking its button on the toolbar. When using the Rectangle tool, click the upper-left corner of the rectangular hot region and then click the lower-right corner. As you move from upper left to lower right, a rectangular trace will be dragged across the hot region. After you click the lower right, you will see the Create Hyperlink dialog box shown in Figure 4.7. Here you can enter the URL to be associated with the hot region.

FIGURE 4.7
You can enter a URL for a hot region or link to a page available in the open FrontPage Web.

The FrontPage Circle tool works much the same as Mapedit's—click at the center of the circle, move the mouse pointer to a point on the edge of the circle, and then release the mouse button to open the dialog box you saw in Figure 4.7. To use the FrontPage Polygon tool, click the first vertex of the polygon, followed by each of the other vertices, until you hit the last one. Then click again on the first vertex and the URL box will appear.

If you are dissatisfied with how a trace is coming out, switch to the Select tool (the first button on the Image toolbar), select the trace, and then press the Delete key.

Live Image

Live Image is an easy-to-use imagemapping tool for Windows 95 and Windows NT. If you have used a program called Map This! in the past, Live Image may seem very familiar. Indeed, Live Image is an enhanced version of Map This!, but the enhancements come (literally) with a price. A single-user license for Live Image will set you back $29.95.

Figure 4.8 shows the Live Image interface. The large area on the right side of the window is where the imagemap graphic loads. On the left is a listing of the hot regions you have defined. You can drag the separator bar between the two sides to a new position, if you want to change the size of either.

FIGURE 4.8

Live Image enables you to see both the imagemap graphic and your hot regions simultaneously.

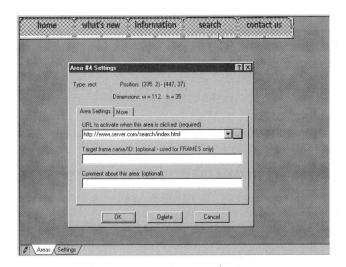

Part

II

Ch

4

Live Image's interface is very intuitive, particularly those buttons you use to create hot regions. Just click the button corresponding to the shape of the hot region you want to define, and then trace the hot region with your mouse. When you finish, you will see a dialog box like the one in Figure 4.8 prompting you for a URL, a target frame, and any comments you want to associate with the region. Note also that hot regions are shaded on the graphic.

You also receive a lot of extras in Live Image that you don't receive in other imagemap programs. In addition to being able to zoom in and out on the graphic, for example, you can also set up a grid over the image to assist you with very precise hot region traces. You can control the fineness of the grid, and you can even have points in your hot region trace snap to the grid.

Live Image enables you to test an imagemap in two ways. The first is through a "simulated browser" built into Live Image. When you test this way, you move your mouse pointer over the imagemap graphic and you will see URLs show up at the bottom of the screen as you pass over a hot region. The second way is to load the HTML file that Live Image produces into a actual browser and test it there.

Some of the other distinguishing features of Live Image include the following:

- A URL Checker that tests the URLs you associate with your hot regions to make sure they are valid
- Support for morphing one type of hot region into another
- The ability to work with more advanced types of files, such as ColdFusion templates, Active Server Page files, and Cascading Style Sheets
- JavaScript support for mouse-related events (onMouseOver and onMouseOut)
- Sample imagemaps and extensive help files
- A Settings tab where you can specify a map's name, author, default URL, and other information

Although you do have to pay a small amount of money for Live Image, you get quite a lot in return. You can learn more about Live Image by visiting http://www.mediatec.com/. ●

## CHAPTER 5

Advanced Graphics

by Eric Ladd

Sorting Through the Graphic Possibilities

It is unlikely that the Web would be so popular if it didn't support graphical content. Graphics give Web pages visual appeal that keeps users surfing for hours. Graphics are also essential for people designing and posting Web pages because graphics often convey a message more powerfully than text alone.

Placing an image on a Web page is a relatively easy matter— you need only one HTML tag. This tag also has many attributes that give you a good bit of control over how your graphics are presented.

Intelligent use of images requires planning, so you need to think about what idea you want to put forward, how to best represent the idea graphically, and what format is most appropriate for the graphic. The thought you put into your graphic content should be at least as much as you put into textual content—perhaps even more so because a reader gets a sense of an image just by quickly looking at it, whereas reading and comprehending text-based information requires more time. And making a Web graphic requires more than just creating the illustration. You need to consider the appropriateness of one of the many special effects that are possible with the available graphics file formats: GIF, JPG, and PNG. For GIFs, this means asking yourself the following questions:

- Should the GIF be transparent?
- Should it be interlaced?
- Should it be animated?

When considering JPEGs, you can ask

- How much should the JPEG be compressed?
- Should it be a progressive JPEG (analogous to an interlaced GIF)?

Additionally, you need to think about color, depth, textures, filters, drop shadows, embossing, and all the other possible visual effects. Through everything, you also need to keep the size of your graphics files as small as possible so that they don't take too long to download. How can you balance all these constraints?

This chapter helps you to answer these questions so that your graphics content is as effective as it can be; it starts with an in-depth discussion of the `<IMG>` tag and how this simple tag brings great variety to the way images are presented. Then the discussion examines the two major Web graphics storage formats and the merits and drawbacks of each. Finally, the chapter focuses on many of the Web graphics effects previously noted, on why you might want to use each one, and how to create them with readily available software (including some software on the CD-ROM that comes with this book). Mastering the content of this chapter will not necessarily make you a first-rate digital-media design guru, but it will give you an awareness of what is possible in the realm of Web graphics.

Layout Considerations when Using the *<IMG>* Tag

After you have an image stored and ready to be posted on the Web, you need to use the HTML <IMG> tag to place the image on a page. <IMG> is a standalone tag that takes the attributes shown in Table 5.1. According to the HTML 4.0 standard, only SRC is mandatory. You will quickly find, however, that you want to use many of the attributes.

Table 5.1   Attributes of the *<IMG>* Tag

Attribute	Purpose
ALT	Supplies a text-based alternative for the image
ALIGN	Controls alignment of text following the image
BORDER	Specifies the size of the border to place around the image
HEIGHT	Specifies the height of the image in pixels
HSPACE	Controls the amount of whitespace to the left and right of the image
ISMAP	Denotes an image to be used as part of a server-side imagemap
LONGDESC	Provides the URL of a link to a longer description of the image's content
SRC	Specifies the URL of the file where the image is stored
USEMAP	Specifies a client-side imagemap to use with the image
VSPACE	Controls the amount of whitespace above and below the image
WIDTH	Specifies the width of the image in pixels

The Basics

Even though the SRC attribute is the only attribute technically required in an <IMG> tag, you should get into the habit of considering three others as mandatory:

- HEIGHT and WIDTH—By providing image HEIGHT and WIDTH information, you speed up the page layout process and enable users to see pages faster. A browser uses the HEIGHT and WIDTH values in the <IMG> tag to reserve a space for the image, and it actually places the image after it has finished downloading. Without these two attributes, the browser has to download the entire image, compute its size, place it on the page, and then continue laying out the rest of the page. If a page has a lot of graphical content, leaving off HEIGHT and WIDTH can seriously delay presentation of the page and annoy visitors.

- ALT—Don't forget that some users don't have graphical or vision-based browsers and can't see your images at all. For these users, you should provide a text alternative to your image with the ALT attribute. Also, because Web robots can't parse images, they often use the ALT description in an <IMG> tag to index the image.

Part

II

Ch

5

Your basic `<IMG>` tag, then, should look like the following:

```
<IMG SRC="URL_of_image_file" WIDTH=width_in_pixels
HEIGHT=height_in_pixels ALT="alternative_text_description">
```

Most sites make conscientious use of these attributes in each `<IMG>` tag. Figure 5.1, for example, shows the banner graphic on the World Wide Web Consortium's main page along with the corresponding HTML source code in Listing 5.1.

FIGURE 5.1

The banner graphic on the W3C home page is set up with `WIDTH`, `HEIGHT`, and `ALT` attributes. These attributes produce the box labeled "W3C" that you see in the upper left.

Text alternative specified by the ALT attribute

Space for image defined by WIDTH and HEIGHT attributes

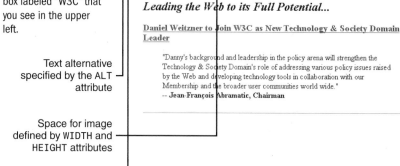

Listing 5.1 _<IMG>_ Tag from the W3C Home Page

```
<TD COLSPAN="4">.
<H1><IMG ALT="W3C" HEIGHT=48 WIDTH=307 SRC="Icons/WWW/w3c_main"></H1>
<H2><I>Leading the Web to its Full Potential...</I></H2>
...
</TD>
```

N O T E You can also use the HEIGHT and WIDTH attributes to scale the size of your images on some browsers. If you have an image that is 420 pixels wide by 220 pixels high, for example, its dimensions can be halved with the use of the following tag:

```
<IMG SRC="graphic.gif" WIDTH=210 HEIGHT=110 ALT="Reduced image">
```

Similarly, you could scale the image size up by using a WIDTH greater than 420 and a HEIGHT greater than 220.

Although this is one way to modify the size of images, it is probably not the best way because browsers don't always do the best job at resizing. Additionally, this does not change the download time because the file size is still the same.

Your best bet is to use a program such as Photoshop or LView Pro to resize the graphic before placing it on your Web page. Not only are these programs better suited to resize an image, they also enable you to preserve the aspect ratio (ratio of width to height) during the resize. ▪

Adding a Border

The BORDER attribute gives you a simple way to instruct the browser to place a border around an image. BORDER is set equal to the number of pixels wide you want the border to be. Figure 5.2 shows an image with a seven-pixel-wide border. The default border is no border.

FIGURE 5.2

Borders look good when placed on photos; they give the picture the appearance of being framed.

Adding Space Around Your Image

Whitespace around an image is called *gutter space* or *runaround*. Putting a little extra space around an image is a good way to give it some breathing room on the page and make it stand out better.

Runaround is controlled by the HSPACE and VSPACE attributes. Each is set to the number of pixels of extra space to leave to the right and left of an image (HSPACE) or above and below an image (VSPACE). Figures 5.3 and 5.4 show some images with varying amounts of HSPACE and VSPACE. In each figure, all images have either extra HSPACE (see Figure 5.3) or extra VSPACE (see Figure 5.4) around them.

N O T E   HSPACE and VSPACE don't have to be used independently of each other. In fact, they are often used together. The following code would leave 10 pixels of space all the way around the image, for example:

```
<IMG SRC="picture.jpg" HSPACE=10 VSPACE=10 ...>
```
▪

CAUTION

You cannot increase space on only one side of an image. Remember that HSPACE adds space to both the left and the right of an image and VSPACE adds space both above and below the image.

FIGURE 5.3

HSPACE controls the distance between an image and page elements to the right and left of the image.

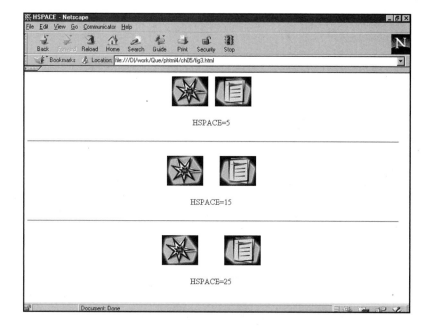

FIGURE 5.4

VSPACE can open up room above and below an image.

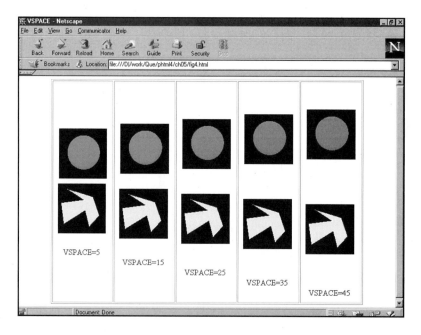

The *ALIGN* Attribute and Floating Images

The ALIGN attribute of the <IMG> tag can take on one of the five values summarized in Table 5.2. TOP, MIDDLE, and BOTTOM refer to how text should be aligned following the image. LEFT and RIGHT create floating images in either the left or right margin.

Table 5.2   Values of the *ALIGN* Attribute in the *<IMG>* Tag

Value	Purpose
TOP	Aligns the top of subsequent text with the top of the image
MIDDLE	Aligns the baseline (the line on which the text appears to sit) of subsequent text with the middle of the image
BOTTOM	Aligns the baseline of subsequent text with the bottom of the image
LEFT	Floats the image in the left margin and enables text to wrap around the right side of the image
RIGHT	Floats the image in the right margin and enables text to wrap around the left side of the image

Figure 5.5 shows text aligned with TOP, MIDDLE, and BOTTOM (the default alignment). One important thing to note with TOP and MIDDLE alignments is that once the text reaches a point where it needs to break, it breaks at a point below the image and leaves some whitespace between the lines of text.

FIGURE 5.5

Of TOP, MIDDLE, and BOTTOM alignments, only BOTTOM enables text to properly wrap around an image.

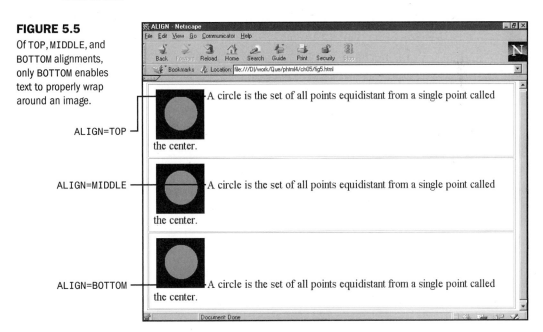

Values of LEFT and RIGHT for the ALIGN attribute were adopted as part of the HTML 3.2 standard to allow for floating images that permit text to wrap around them. Figure 5.6 shows an image floating in the left margin with text wrapping around it to the right.

FIGURE 5.6

Floating images sit in one margin and enable text to wrap around them.

Floating image ——

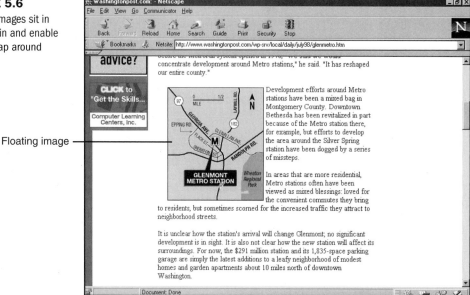

Floating images opened the door to many creative and interesting layouts. It is even possible to overlap images by floating one in the left margin and one in the right margin.

The advent of floating images created a need for a way to break to the first left or right margin that is clear of a floating image. To satisfy this need, the CLEAR attribute was added to the <BR> tag. Setting CLEAR to LEFT breaks to the first instance of a left margin that is clear of floating images. CLEAR=RIGHT does the same thing, except it breaks to the first right margin. You can clear both margins by setting CLEAR=ALL.

ISMAP and USEMAP

Imagemaps are clickable images that load different pages depending on where you click the image. They are frequently found on the main page of a site, where they typically serve as a navigational tool to the major sections of the site.

▶ **See** "Imagemaps," **p. 137.**

The ISMAP attribute of the <IMG> tag is a standalone attribute that tells the browser that the image is to be used as part of a server-side imagemap.

The USEMAP attribute of the <IMG> tag is set equal to the name of a client-side imagemap. With client-side imagemaps, map information is named and sent directly to the browser. Setting USEMAP equal to a map name instructs the browser to use the map information associated with that name.

LONGDESC

The LONGDESC attribute was added to HTML 4.0 as a way of making image content more accessible to users with nonvisual browsers. You set LONGDESC equal to the URL of a document that can provide a longer description of the image's content than you would otherwise put in an ALT attribute. A speech- or Braille-based browser could then access the URL and furnish a description of the image to the user.

Images as Hyperlink Anchors

As explained in Chapter 3, "HTML 4.0 Tag Reference," the <A> container tag is used to create hypertext anchors. By clicking the hypertext, you instruct your browser to load the resource at the URL specified in the HREF attribute of the <A> tag.

No law says that hyperlink anchors can only be text. You will often find images serving as anchors, as well. By linking images to other Web pages, you create a button-like effect—the user clicks the button and the browser loads a new page, submits a form, or performs some other action. You can even rig a linked image with JavaScript to submit a form:

```
<IMG SRC="..." onClick="document.form_name.submit();">
```

To use a graphic as a hyperlink anchor, put the <IMG> tag that places the graphic between <A> and </A> tags:

```
<A HREF="button.html">
<IMG SRC="images/button.gif" ALT="Push button"></A>
```

This results in the linked image shown in Figure 5.7. Notice that the image has a border even though no BORDER attribute was specified. Hyperlinked images automatically receive a border colored with the same colors that you set up for hypertext links using the LINK, VLINK, and ALINK attributes of the <BODY> tag.

Borders around hyperlinked images are usually distracting, especially if the image is a transparent GIF. Notice in Figure 5.7 how the border shows the extent of the otherwise transparent bounding box around the image. To eliminate the border, include BORDER=0 inside the <IMG> tag.

TROUBLESHOOTING

A small, hyperlinked line is present at the bottom right of my linked images. How do I get rid of it?

Your problem most likely stems from HTML code such as the following:

```
<A HREF="pickupday.html">
<IMG SRC="ea1.jpg" WIDTH=300 HEIGHT=400 ALT="Eric and Anthony">
</A>
```

By having a carriage return after the <IMG> tag but before the </A> tag, you often get an extraneous line at the bottom-right corner of the linked image (see Figure 5.8). By placing the </A> tag immediately after the <IMG> tag, you can take care of that annoying little line.

```
<A HREF="pickupday.html">
<IMG SRC="ea1.jpg" WIDTH=300 HEIGHT=400 ALT="Eric and Anthony"></A>
```

Part
II

Ch
5

FIGURE 5.7

A hyperlinked image will automatically receive a border unless you specify BORDER=0.

Hyperlinked transparent GIF with border

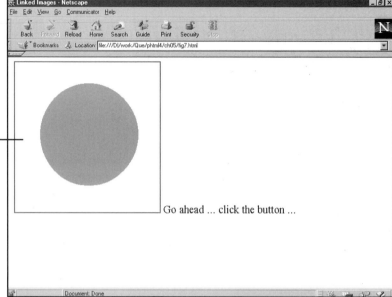

FIGURE 5.8

Browsers don't always ignore carriage returns, as evidenced by the extraneous line at the bottom right of this linked image.

Extraneous hyperlink line

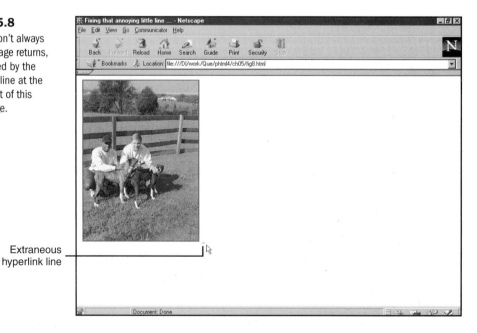

Images as Bullet Characters

Some people opt to create their own bullet characters for bulleted lists instead of using the characters that browsers provide. To do this, you need to place the bullet graphic with an <IMG> tag and follow it with a list item:

```
<IMG SRC="bullet.gif" WIDTH=12 HEIGHT=12 ALT="*">HTML 4.0<BR>
<IMG SRC="bullet.gif" WIDTH=12 HEIGHT=12 ALT="*">XML 1.0<BR>
<IMG SRC="bullet.gif" WIDTH=12 HEIGHT=12 ALT="*">Java 1.2<BR>
<IMG SRC="bullet.gif" WIDTH=12 HEIGHT=12 ALT="*">JavaScript 1.3<BR>
```

 TIP Using an asterisk (*) as the value of your ALT attribute gives users with nongraphical browsers a bullet-like character in front of each list item.

Several things should be noted about this HTML:

- You must have a separate <IMG> tag for each bullet.
- You may need to experiment with the ALIGN attribute to find the best alignment between bullets and list items.
- You have to place line breaks manually with a <BR> tag at the end of each list item.

Usually, this is enough to deter many page authors from using their own bullet characters. If you are still determined to use custom bullets, however, you need to be aware of one more alignment issue: If a list item is long enough to break to a new line, the next line starts below the bullet graphic; it is not indented from it (see Figure 5.9). This detracts from the nicely indented presentation that users expect from a bulleted list.

One way to avoid this problem is to make list items short enough to fit on one line. If that isn't possible, you should consider setting up your list with custom bullets in an HTML table. By placing the bullet image in its own cell and the list item text in the adjacent cell in the same table row, you can control both alignment and line breaking.

▶ **See** "Tables," **p. 183.**

Images as Horizontal Rules

Some sites also use a custom graphic in place of a horizontal rule (see Figure 5.10). This is a nice way to subtly reinforce a site's graphic theme.

Alignment problems are less of an issue with a custom rule, but you should keep a couple of rules in mind:

- Assume a screen width of 640 pixels and keep your rule sized accordingly. Don't let the rule's width exceed 640 pixels.
- The default alignment for a rule placed with the <HR> tag is centered. You can replicate this effect for your custom rule by placing the <IMG> tag for the rule graphic between <DIV ALIGN=CENTER> and </DIV> tags.

Part
II

Ch
5

■ Use a row of about 70 dashes for your ALT text in the <IMG> tag so that text-only users can get a rule effect as well.

FIGURE 5.9

If you are using a custom bullet graphic, you will also be responsible for things such as text wrapping and alignment.

Custom bullet graphic

Text does not indent properly on its own

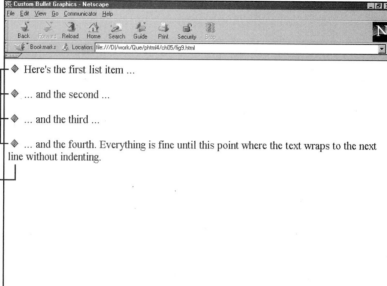

FIGURE 5.10

The White House's Web site uses a red, white, and blue image for horizontal lines, instead of using the <HR> tag.

Custom rule graphic

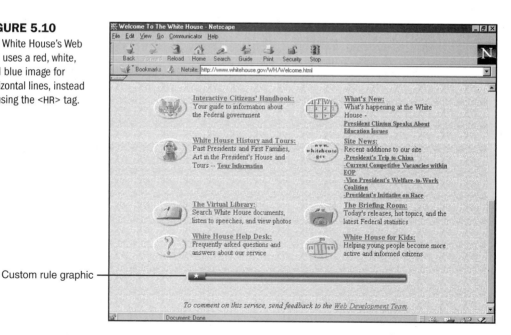

Graphic Storage Formats

Technically, Web graphics can be stored in any format, but only two formats display inline on all of today's popular graphical browsers: GIF and JPEG. A third format, PNG, is gaining ground, and you should expect to see full inline support for PNG graphics soon. Other graphics formats have to be displayed by a helper application, which is launched by the browser when it detects a format it can't display.

N O T E Microsoft Internet Explorer 4 supports the inline display of Windows Bitmap (.BMP) graphics in addition to GIFs and JPEGs. ■

GIF

Graphics Interchange Format (GIF) was originally developed for users of CompuServe as a standard for storing image files. The GIF standards have undergone a couple of revisions since their inception. The current standard is GIF89a.

Graphics stored in GIF are limited to 256 colors. Because full-color photos require many more colors to look sharp, you shouldn't store full-color photos as GIFs. GIF is best used with line art, logos, and icons. If you do store a full-color photo as a GIF, its palette is reduced to just 256 colors, and the photo will not look as good on your Web page.

In spite of a limited number of colors, the GIF89a standard supports the following three Web page effects:

- Interlacing—In an interlaced GIF image, nonadjacent parts of the image are stored together. As a browser reads in an interlaced GIF, the image appears to fade in over several passes. This is useful because the user can get a sense of what the entire image looks like without having to wait for the whole thing to load.

- Transparency—In a transparent GIF, one of the colors is designated as transparent, enabling the background of the document to show through. Figure 5.11 illustrates a transparent and nontransparent GIF. Notice in the nontransparent GIF that the bounding box around the circle is visible. By specifying the color of the bounding box to be transparent, the background color shows through, and the circle appears to be sitting on the background.

    Transparent GIFs are very popular, and many of the graphics programs available today support the creation of transparent GIFs. On the PC, LView Pro is one program that creates transparent GIFs. PhotoGIF is a plug-in to Photoshop that enables you to create both transparent and interlaced GIFs. Jasc's Paint Shop Pro is a reasonably priced graphics program that supports transparent GIFs. You can even use Microsoft FrontPage (or its companion program, Microsoft Image Composer) to create transparent GIFs from existing images.

- Animation—Animated GIFs are created by storing in one file the sequence of images used to produce the animation. A browser that fully supports the GIF89a standard is designed to present the images in the file one after the other to produce the animation. The programs that enable you to store the multiple images in the GIF file also enable you to specify how much delay should occur before beginning the animation and how many times the animation should repeat. Web designers are making widespread use of animated GIFs because they are much easier to implement than server push or even Java animations (see Figure 5.12). A server-push animation requires a CGI program to send the individual images down an open HTTP connection.

FIGURE 5.11

The background color in a transparent GIF takes on the page's background color to make objects in the image appear to sit right on the page.

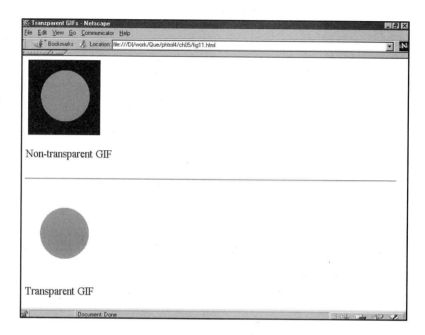

FIGURE 5.12

Gateway animates the computer screen on its site with the faces of several users.

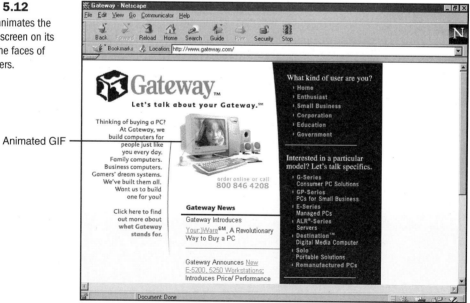

JPEG

Joint Picture Experts Group (JPEG) refers to a set of formats that support full-color images and stores them in a compressed form. JPEG is a 24-bit storage format that allows for 2^{24} or 16,777,216 colors! With that much color data, it is easy to see why some form of compression is necessary. Typically, you can control the degree of compression at the time you create the JPEG file. Keep in mind that the more you compress the image, the more you reduce the image's sharpness.

Although JPEG is great for full-color images, it does not permit some of the nice effects that GIF does. Transparency is not possible with JPEG images because the compression tends to make small mathematical changes to the image data. With the exception of a server-push approach, animation is not yet possible with JPEGs. An analogy to interlaced GIFs exists, how-ever. The progressive JPEG (p-JPEG) format has recently emerged, which gives the effect of an image fading in the same as an interlaced GIF would.

PNG

The GIF Format began to fall out of favor with the Internet community when, in 1990, Unisys and CompuServe announced their intention to collect royalties for use of the format. The ratio-nale behind this announcement was that GIF was developed by CompuServe and used a com-pression technique developed by Unisys, so the two companies were entitled to compensation. Most of the rest of the world did not share this philosophy, however, and, as part of the fallout, the Portable Network Graphics (PNG, pronounced *ping*) working group was formed and began drafting a proposal for this new, open format. In October 1996, the World Wide Web Consor-tium accepted the proposed PNG standard as a recommendation.

The PNG format is able to support the two major effects that originally made GIFs so popular: transparency and interlacing. In fact, PNG is an improvement over GIF in that it implements these effects in a more flexible way. Specifically, for transparency, PNG provides for an *alpha channel* that supports up to 254 levels of partial transparency—in contrast to the GIFs ap-proach, which supports only two levels: totally transparent or totally opaque. For interlacing, PNG employs a seven-pass, two-dimensional interlacing scheme that presents initial image data eight times faster than one-dimensional GIF interlacing.

NOTE PNG is also an improvement over GIF when it comes to compression. Compression ratios are typically 5% to 25% higher, with no data loss. ▦

PNG offers broad support for many kinds of images, including

- ▦ True color images—Prior to PNG, your only option for true color (24-bit color) was to use the JPEG format.
- ▦ 8-bit palette images—PNG, like GIF, supports images that are composed of 8-bit color palettes. PNG can also support 1-, 2-, and 4-bit palettes as well, so you can reduce the color depth (and hence the file size) of a PNG graphic if you don't have too many colors.
- ▦ Grayscale images—PNG allows for 1-, 2-, 4-, 8-, and 16-bit grayscale images.

Part II

Ch 5

One thing that PNG does not support, however, is animation. Recall that for animated GIFs, the many images that compose the animation are stored together in one file. PNG was developed as a single-image file format, so no way exists for it to support animation.

N O T E A proposal is under development for a format called MNG that will support storage of multiple images and, therefore, animation. ■

Browser and image software support for PNG was a little tentative for the first year, but then Microsoft took the step of making PNG the native format for its Office97 suite of products and announced its intention to provide inline support for PNG graphics in release 4 of its Internet Explorer browser. Since then, many other companies have followed suit, and PNG is now supported by the following software:

- Netscape Navigator 4.0 and later
- CorelDRAW 7.0 and later
- Macromedia Free Hand Graphics Studio 7.0 and later
- Microsoft Image Composer 1.5 and later
- SoftQuad HoTMetaL 3.0 and later
- Adobe Illustrator 7.0 and later
- Adobe Photoshop 4.0 and later
- Jasc, Inc. Paint Shop Pro 3.01 and later

Thus, it is possible for you to start creating PNG graphics for your Web pages now, and visitors using the most recent releases of Netscape or Microsoft browsers will be able to view them. Alternatively, you can convert your existing GIF and JPEG graphics to PNG using one of the more PNG-compliant conversion tools such as Adobe File Utilities, DeBabelizer Pro (Windows), or DeBabelizer ToolBox (Macintosh).

N O T E For the latest about PNG, including documentation of the standard, sample images, and a list of PNG-compliant software, consult the PNG home page at `http://www.cdrom.com/pub/png/png.html`. ■

Choosing a Format

The question of which format to use is often a daunting one for beginning designers. Fortunately, some ways are available to focus your thinking as you make this choice:

- Do you need to create a transparency effect? If so, you have your choice of either GIF or PNG.
- Do you need to produce an animation? Unless you want to code a server push animation, it is easier to place animations on your pages by using animated GIFs.
- Is your graphic a full-color image? Full-color images, particularly photographs of things in nature, are best stored in JPEG or PNG formats so that you can harness their support for more than 16 million colors.

- Does your graphic have any sharp color changes or boundaries? Some graphics change quickly from one color to another, rather than fading gradually over a continuum of colors. Because of the mathematics behind the compression algorithm, JPEGs don't cope well with sudden color changes. Use GIF or PNG to handle images such as these.

- Do you need a fade-in effect? This isn't too much of a discriminator because GIF, JPEG, and PNG all support some type of fade-in effect—interlacing for GIF and PNG, and p-JPEG for JPEG.

Using the Browser-Safe Color Palette

Lynda Weinman, a popular author on the topics of Web graphics and color, has advanced the idea of a *browser-safe palette*—a set of colors rendered the same way by *any* browser on *any* platform. Netscape Navigator and Microsoft Internet Explorer both use the same default 256-color palette when rendering Web pages, but because of slight differences between the PC and the Macintosh, 40 of these colors can appear differently, depending on the platform. If you remove these 40 colors from the default palette, the remaining 216 colors compose a palette that should appear the same regardless of a user's hardware or software.

The browser-safe color palette is freely available from `http://www.lynda.com/hex.html`, ordered both by hue and by RGB color values. You are welcome to download the palette and use it to make your GIF images and other colored page elements as browser friendly as possible. Macintosh users can check out PANTONE's ColorWeb color selection application at `http://www.pantone.com/catalog/colorwebss.html`.

Creating Transparent GIFs

When you make a transparent GIF, you designate one color in the image's palette to be the transparent color. Pixels painted with the transparent color enable the background color to show through. Figure 5.11 showed you transparent and nontransparent versions of the same image.

This technique is useful in getting rid of the bounding box that typically surrounds a graphic. When you compose an image in a graphics program, the workspace is almost always rectangular. Your image goes inside this rectangular region (the bounding box), and invariably some amount of space exists between the image and the edges of the box. By choosing the color of the excess space pixels to be transparent, you make them disappear on the browser screen. This is what happened in Figure 5.11. The bounding box pixels in the image using the transparency option were the ones designated as transparent, so they enabled the white background to show through and give the effect of the circle sitting right on top of the Web page.

 TIP Think twice before putting a border around a transparent GIF because it will outline the bounding box and ruin the transparency effect.

Many popular graphic programs support transparent GIFs. One such program that you will find on the CD-ROM with this book is LView Pro. LView Pro is a terrific shareware program that is well worth the $40 you will pay for the license.

Creating a transparent GIF in LView Pro involves the following two simple steps:

1. Designating a color as the background color
2. Instructing LView Pro to note the background color as the transparent color when saving the file

Figure 5.13 shows the LView Pro interface. On the right side of the screen, you will find the Color Selection dialog bar. Along the top of the bar, three rectangles display, from left to right, the foreground color, the background color, and the transparent color. To change the transparent color, move your mouse pointer to the color in the color palette (at the bottom of the dialog bar) that you want to be the new transparent color; press the Alt key and click either mouse button. You should see the color in the third rectangle at the top change to the color you selected.

Color Selection dialog bar

FIGURE 5.13

LView Pro gives you access to an image's entire color palette, enabling you to choose one color as the background color.

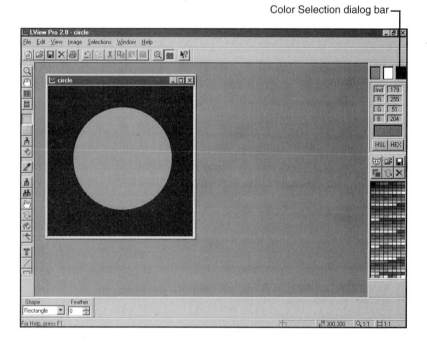

With the background color set, all you need to do is tell LView Pro to make that color transparent in the GIF file. You do this by choosing File, Preferences, Graphics File Formats, and clicking the GIF tab. Checking Save Transparent Color Information (GIF89a Only) ensures that LView Pro will designate your chosen background color as transparent (see Figure 5.14).

FIGURE 5.14

Instructing LView Pro to save transparent color information means that pixels painted with the background color will be designated as transparent.

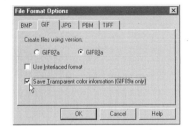

Making a Transparent PNG

Creating a transparent PNG is a fairly simple matter when you're using Microsoft's Image Composer. To make a transparent PNG, follow these steps:

1. Choose File, Save As to open the Save As dialog box (see Figure 5.15)

2. From the Save as Type drop-down list, choose the Portable Network Graphics format.

3. Make sure the Color Format selection is set to True Color.

4. Choose the Keep Transparency box if you want to save the image with its alpha channel (this allows for the multiple levels of transparency). Otherwise, click the Transparent Color box and choose a color to act as the transparent color (just as you would with a transparent GIF image).

5. Click the Save button to save the transparent PNG.

FIGURE 5.15

When doing a transparent PNG in Image Composer, you can choose multilevel or single color transparency.

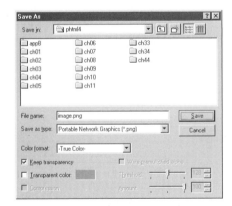

Why Aren't There Transparent JPEGs?

Transparency is only supported in the GIF format. A JPEG image cannot use a transparency effect because the algorithm used to compress a JPEG file is lossy. This means that during decompression, some pixels are not painted with the exact same color they had before the compression. These color changes are so small that they are usually imperceptible to the human eye, although you may be able to detect color differences after several cycles of compression and decompression. However, a

continues

continued

computer can detect the difference and therein lies the demise of the transparent JPEG. To understand further, consider the following example:

You scan in a photograph of a field of flowers and you want to save it as a JPEG. The JPEG format supports over 16.7 million colors. Suppose that you choose color number 3,826,742 as the transparent color and save the file. During the compression and subsequent decompression, some data loss occurs in the file. As a result of the loss, a pixel originally painted with color number 3,826,742 is now colored with color number 3,826,740. The pixel was supposed to be transparent, but because its color number was changed by the compression, it will not be. The pixel will be painted with color number 3,826,740 and not let the background show through.

The reverse situation can happen as well. Suppose a pixel originally colored with color number 3,826,745 ends up being painted with color number 3,826,742. This is the transparent color, so the pixel will adopt the background color rather than color number 3,826,745, as originally intended.

As long as JPEG continues to be a lossy format, it will be impossible to use transparency with them. If you have to use a transparent graphic, you must use a GIF.

Making an Image Fade In

Even when image files are made as small as possible, it can still take a while for them to download. Initially, browsers had to load and process the entire file before it began to present the image onscreen. This meant users had to sit there staring at a blank screen for minutes at a time. Because Web-user attention spans are short, people would often give up in frustration and move on to another page instead of waiting for an image to finish downloading.

Since those early days, two approaches to reducing user frustration have emerged. Both involve having an image "fade in" as the image data is read by the browser. The user sees a blurry, incomplete image at first, but then the image quality improves as more data is read in. The key thing for users is that they immediately see an approximation to the finished image on their screens. This keeps them engaged and makes it less likely that they will move on to another page.

The two approaches to fading an image on to a page are actually variations on the same idea, modified for different storage formats. In each case, the image data is not stored in top-to-bottom order. Instead, the image data is reordered so that adjacent rows of pixel information are no longer stored contiguously in the file. As the browser reads down the file, it places the rows of noncontiguous data up on the screen. The result is an incomplete image that fills itself in as the rest of the image data is read. A GIF stored in this way is called an interlaced GIF. The same idea applied to a JPEG file yields a progressive JPEG or p-JPEG.

 T I P A different kind of fade-in effect is to have a black-and-white version of an image load first, followed by the full-color version. You can accomplish this by using the LOWSRC attribute of the <IMG> tag. LOWSRC is set equal to the URL of the black-and-white image file. This file loads and is rendered more quickly because it is generally much smaller than its full-color equivalent (less color information to store means a smaller file size). The full-color version is then rendered in place of the LOWSRC image after it is read in. This gives the appearance of the black-and-white image being "painted" with color.

Making Interlaced GIFs

Creating an interlaced GIF is a simple matter with LView Pro. To instruct LView Pro to save a GIF in interlaced form, select File, Preferences, Graphics File Formats, and then click the GIF tab (refer to Figure 5.14). Checking the Use Interlaced Format box will do the trick. To deactivate saving in the interlaced format, just uncheck the box.

Progressive JPEGs

P-JPEGs are relatively new, but LView Pro is current enough to have the capability to help you make them. To activate saving in a progressive JPEG format, choose File, Preferences, Graphics File Formats, and then click the JPG tab. Check the Use Progressive JPEG Compression Format box, and you're ready to go (see Figure 5.16).

> **N O T E** The two-dimensional interlacing scheme used in PNG graphics is implemented automatically when you save the file as a PNG.

FIGURE 5.16
LView Pro saves a JPEG in p-JPEG format if you instruct it to do so.

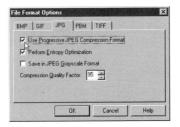

Part
II

Ch
5

Creating Animated GIFs

One of the biggest crazes to hit the Web in the past year is doing animations with animated GIFs instead of relying on a dynamic document technique such as server push or client pull. The irony is that animated GIFs have been around since 1989—at least in theory. The GIF89a standard has always supported multiple images stored in the same GIF file, but, until recently, no one caught on that you can do Web animations this way.

It is surprising that this development didn't happen sooner, given that GIF animations are so much easier to implement than server-push animations. A server-push animation requires a server that is CGI-capable, a program to pipe the individual frames of the animation down an open HTTP connection, and a browser that can handle the experimental MIME type used. All you need for a GIF animation is a program to help you set up the GIF file and a browser that is completely compliant with the GIF89a standard. That you don't need any CGI programming is a relief to those publishing on a server that either does not have CGI or that restricts CGI access to certain users.

One program that will help you build animated GIFs is the Microsoft GIF Animator that comes with Image Composer. Figure 5.17 shows the GIF Animator program window with an animated GIF file loaded. The individual frames of the animation are displayed on the left, and you change animation parameters on the tabs on the right.

FIGURE 5.17

Microsoft's GIF Animator enables you to create animated GIFs with a minimum of hassle.

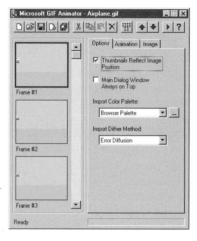

On the GIF Animator's Option tab, you'll see check boxes for specifying whether the thumbnails should reflect image position and whether the GIF Animator program window should always be displayed at the top of your desktop. Additionally, you can choose color palettes and dithering techniques for your animation.

On the Animation tab (see Figure 5.18), you can specify the size of the animation, how many frames compose the animation, and whether the animation should loop. If you do choose to loop the animation, you can designate a number of times for the animation to repeat, or you can enable it to repeat indefinitely.

CAUTION

Don't let an animation run indefinitely. An animation that is going constantly can be a distraction from the rest of the content on your page.

Finally, the Image tab enables you to designate properties for each frame in the animation. You can set the height and width, how long the frame should be displayed, how to undraw the frame, and which color to use as the transparent color (see Figure 5.19).

N O T E   FrontPage also provides support for animation of page elements. You can make images or text fly on to the page from any part of the browser screen, thanks to the Java applets resident in the FrontPage Editor. ▪

FIGURE 5.18
Properties specific to the animation are set on the GIF Animator Animation tab.

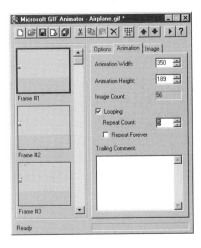

FIGURE 5.19
GIF Animator enables you to control properties of each individual frame in the animation as well.

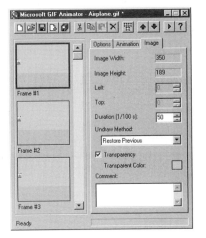

Part
II

Ch
5

Using Image Effects That Create Depth

Although a computer screen is inherently two-dimensional, Web graphic artists try not to let that get them down. They draw on a variety of techniques that give Web pages the illusion of depth. Creating these effects usually involves the use of a higher-end graphics program, such as Paint Shop Pro or Photoshop. These are well worth the time and expense, however, because they give Web pages a richness that is hard to beat.

Light Sources

Photoshop enables you to apply three types of light sources in any of 10 styles to an image from the Lighting Effects dialog box shown in Figure 5.20. You call up the dialog box by choosing Filter, Render, and then selecting Lighting Effects from the Render pop-up menu.

FIGURE 5.20

Let there be light—on your Web pages, that is. Light sources give images a sense of depth and reality.

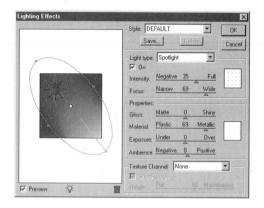

The cardinal rule to remember when lighting the images on your pages is to illuminate each object with the same light source at the same position. Think of it as the sun shining on your page. Only one sun is in the sky, and all the objects on the page are getting light from it simultaneously. If you light different objects with different light sources at different positions, the lighting will seem counterintuitive to those who view the page. You should try to make the lighting seem as natural as possible so that the page is more inviting.

Drop Shadows

Placing drop shadows behind page elements is a great way to make them appear elevated from the page (see Figure 5.21). An easy way to make a drop shadow is to make a copy of the page element, paint it black, and drop it in behind and to one side of the element being shadowed. If you are using Photoshop, you can achieve increased realism by copying the page element to a subordinate layer, painting it black, expanding it by several pixels, blurring it a few times, and positioning it as desired.

> **CAUTION**
>
> Make sure that the location of your drop shadows is consistent with your light sources.

Embossing

Embossing a graphic element makes it appear to be raised and gives it a more textured appearance (see Figure 5.22). Photoshop has a built-in embossing filter that you can use by selecting Filters, Stylize, and then selecting Emboss from the Stylize pop-up menu.

Ray Tracing

Ray tracing is a technique for making two-dimensional images look three-dimensional. You can usually tell a ray-traced image by its distinct use of perspective (objects get smaller as they move away from you).

To create your own ray-traced images, you need a special program. Windows users can check out Caligari Truespace; Strata Vision is a good program for the Macintosh. For more information on other ray-tracing software, consult `http://www.yahoo.com/Computers_and_Internet/Graphics/Ray_Tracing/`.

FIGURE 5.21
Combinations of light and shadow make an image appear to be floating over the page.

Drop shadows

FIGURE 5.22
Embossing highlights the edges of an object, making it appear raised.

Embossed image

Part

II

Ch

5

Keeping File Sizes Small

One of the greatest courtesies you can extend to your users is to keep your graphics files small. Invariably, it is the graphics that take the longest time to download. By keeping the file sizes small, you minimize the time that users spend waiting to see your pages. Your typical 30K to 50K graphics file may load in a few seconds over a T1 connection, but it may take several minutes for users dialing up with a 28.8Kbps or 14.4Kbps connection.

You can enlist a number of techniques to help keep your file sizes small:

- Making the image dimensions as small as possible
- Using thumbnail versions of images
- Saving GIFs with natural color gradients as JPEGs or PNGs
- Increasing the amount of JPEG compression
- Using fewer bits per pixel to store the image
- Adjusting image contrast
- Suppressing dithering

Each technique is discussed briefly over the next several sections.

Resizing the Image

Larger images take up more disk space—it is as simple as that. The reason for this is straight-forward: More pixels are present in a larger image, so more color information must be stored.

The height and width of your graphics should be no larger than they have to be. By keeping the onscreen dimensions of your images small, you contribute to a smaller overall file size.

 TIP   If you resize an image in a graphics program to make it smaller, be sure to keep the aspect ratio (ratio of width to height) the same. This prevents the image from looking stretched or squashed.

Using Thumbnails

Thumbnails are small versions of an image—usually a photograph. By placing a thumbnail of an image on a page, you reduce file size by using an image that has a smaller width and height than the original.

Thumbnails are usually set up so that users can click them to see the full image. If you do this, you should include the size (in kilobytes) of the file that contains the full image so that users can make an informed decision about downloading it.

> **CAUTION**
>
> Recall that you can resize an image by reducing the WIDTH and HEIGHT attributes in the <IMG> tag. However, this does not save on download time, and browsers generally don't do the best job of resizing the image.

Storing GIFs as JPEGs or PNGs

JPEGs are created with a very efficient (albeit lossy) compression scheme. The compression works best on images with a lot of natural color gradation. This is why JPEG is the format of choice for color photos placed on the Web.

If you have a GIF with a lot of color gradation, you can experiment with saving as a JPEG to see whether you can compress the file size further. It may not always work, but it is worth a try. You don't have to worry about color loss either because JPEG can accommodate millions of colors to GIF's 256 colors.

Conversely, if you have an image with large blocks of contiguous color, you are better off storing it as a GIF because GIF's compression scheme is geared toward exploiting adjacent pixels painted the same color.

If you're concerned about loss of image quality with the JPEG format, consider converting your GIFs to PNG. PNG compression is more efficient than GIF compression, and PNG is not a lossy format.

Increasing the JPEG Compression Ratio

JPEG compression often achieves impressive compression ratios (on the order of 50:1) with very little loss in image quality. You can crank the ratio higher to make your file size smaller, but the image will not look as good when it is decompressed and decoded. A highly compressed JPEG will take slightly longer to decompress, as well.

Reducing Color Depth

GIFs and PNGs can use a palette of up to 256 colors. This corresponds to eight bits per pixel (2^8 equals 256). But what if you don't need that many colors? Sometimes GIFs and PNGs use just two or three colors. That small amount of color information can be stored in much less than eight bits per pixel. It would seem as though some of that storage space could be recovered, resulting in a smaller file size.

It turns out that you can reduce the number of bits per pixel used to store color information. This is called reducing the image's color depth. Lowering the color depth is a great way to reduce file size because you can often cut the amount of space you are using in half or better.

Suppose, for example, that you have a GIF that uses six distinct colors. The number six is between four (2^2) and eight (2^3), so you would need three bits per pixel to describe the color information. (Two bits per pixel only supports the first four colors, so you have to go to the next highest exponent.) By reducing the color depth from eight bits per pixel to three bits, you realize a savings of over 60%!

LView Pro gives you an easy way to reduce your color depth. By choosing Image, Color Depth, you get the dialog box you see in Figure 5.23. A true color image is one that uses 24-bit color (for example, a JPEG); the color depth for these images cannot be changed. Palette-based images are ones that draw their colors from a palette of no more than 256 colors. For palette images, LView Pro enables you to choose 256 colors (eight bits per pixel), a palette with a custom number of colors, or a predefined palette read in from a file.

FIGURE 5.23

Reducing a GIF's color depth can greatly reduce the amount of space needed to store the image.

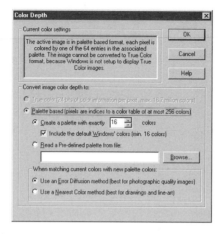

Adjusting Contrast

Contrast in an image refers to the brightness of objects relative to one another. Making changes to the contrast in your image generally affects the size of the resulting image file. If your file is still too big, tweaking the contrast may be a way to bring it down more.

One way to change contrast in your images is to adjust the Gamma correction. Increasing the Gamma correction into positive values tends to brighten the entire image and reduce overall file size because there are fewer colors to store. Conversely, negative Gamma correction values darken an image and increase its file size. You can change the Gamma correction in LView Pro by selecting Image, Color Adjustment, Pre-defined, and then selecting Gamma Correction from the list of available image parameters.

No Dithering

Dithering makes an image appear to have more colors in its palette than it actually does. This is accomplished by combining colors in the existing palette to produce colors that are not in the palette. Dithering can be helpful with GIF images with a lot of subtle color gradations. Otherwise, for images with just a few solid colors, you probably won't want to use dithering.

One thing to be aware of when using dithering is that it tends to increase file size because fewer pixels in a row have the same color. The compression scheme used with GIF files exploits adjacent pixels that have the same color. When fewer same-colored pixels exist, the compression can't make the file as small.

> **CAUTION**
>
> Dithering can also create an unattractive graininess in your images. If you enable dithering, be sure to look at your image before you put it on the Web to make sure that the dithering does not detract from it.

Tables

by Eric Ladd

Introduction to HTML Tables and Their Structure

This chapter introduces you to tables as they have been written into the HTML 4.0 recommendation. Although tables are intended for the display of columnar data, you'll find, as you progress through this chapter, that tables are much more than that—they are a bona fide page design tool as well.

To understand the basic table tags better, it helps to take a moment to consider how HTML tables are structured. The fundamental building blocks of an HTML table are *cells*, which can contain a *data element* of the table or a *heading* for a column of data. Related cells are logically grouped in a *row* of the table. The rows, in turn, combine to make up the entire table.

If you can keep this breakdown in mind as you read the next few sections, the syntax of the table tags will make much more sense to you (see "Table Sections and Column Properties," later in this chapter). Remember

- Cells are the basic units of a table; they can contain data elements or column headers.
- Cells are grouped into rows.
- Rows are grouped together to produce an entire table.

N O T E   HTML 4.0 provides support for the treatment of table columns as well as rows. That means you can treat a column or columns of a table as a logical unit. This is particularly useful when you want to apply formatting instructions to an entire column or columns of data.

The Table Tags

Before delving into the more advanced uses of tables, it's instructive to look at a table used for the purpose tables are intended: to display columns of data. The next three sections present the tags you need to create a simple table for this purpose.

All table-related tags occur between the <TABLE> and </TABLE> container tags. Any table-related tags occurring outside of these tags will be ignored.

A good habit you should get into immediately is to put the </TABLE> tag into your HTML file when you put the <TABLE> tag in. If you don't have a </TABLE> tag and you go to a browser to preview your work, the browser won't render the table. Browsers read through all the code to produce a table before rendering it. It has to do this to compute how much space it needs for the table and, after the amount of space is known and allocated, the browser goes back and fills in the cells. Without a </TABLE> tag, a browser can't know that it has hit the end of a table and, therefore, won't render any of it.

N O T E   If you're using an HTML-editing program that enables you to compose a table onscreen, you won't have to worry about the <TABLE> and </TABLE> tags or any other table-related tag. The program will write the code to produce the table for you.

Additionally, most tag-based HTML editors can automatically insert a </TABLE> tag when you insert a <TABLE> tag. Make sure that this feature is turned on if you're using a tag-based editing tool.

Creating a Table Row

Tables are made up of rows, so you need to know how to define a row. The `<TR>` and `</TR>` tags are used to contain the HTML tags that define the individual cells. You can place as many `<TR>` and `</TR>` tag pairs as you need inside a table, each pair accounting for one row.

So far, then, the code for a basic HTML table with m rows looks like

```
<TABLE>
    <TR> ... </TR>    <!-- Row 1 -->
    <TR> ... </TR>    <!-- Row 2 -->
    ...
    <TR> ... </TR>    <!-- Row m -->
</TABLE>
```

 TIP Indenting your table code helps you keep better track of individual cells and rows.

Creating a Table Cell

Table cells come in two varieties: header cells for headers that appear over a column of data and data cells for the individual entries in the table.

A table header cell is defined with the `<TH>` and `</TH>` tag pair. The contents of a table header cell are automatically centered and appear in boldface, so typically, you don't need to format them further.

In a standard table, headers usually compose the first row so that each column in the table has some type of heading over it. If the basic table you're developing has n columns of data, the HTML for the table would look like

```
<TABLE>
    <TR>      <!-- Row 1 -->
        <TH>Header 1</TH>
        <TH>Header 2</TH>
        ...
        <TH>Header n</TH>
    </TR>
    <TR> ... </TR>    <!-- Row 2 -->
    ...
    <TR> ... </TR>    <!-- Row m -->
</TABLE>
```

Data cells are defined by the `<TD>` tag. Text in data cells is left justified by default. Any special formatting, such as boldface or italic, has to be done by including the appropriate formatting tags inside the `<TD>` and `</TD>` pairs.

If data cells make up the rest of the basic table you're constructing, you'll have the template shown in Listing 6.1:

Listing 6.1   A Basic Table Template

```
<TABLE>
    <TR>     <!-- Row 1 -->
        <TH>Header 1</TH>
        <TH>Header 2</TH>
        ...
        <TH>Header n</TH>
    </TR>
    <TR>     <!-- Row 2 -->
        <TD>Data element 1</TD>
        <TD>Data element 2</TD>
        ...
        <TD>Data element n</TD>
    </TR>
    ...
    <TR>     <!-- Row m -->
        <TD>Data element 1</TD>
        <TD>Data element 2</TD>
        ...
        <TD>Data element n</TD>
    </TR>
</TABLE>
```

The HTML above makes for a nice template that you can use whenever you're starting a table. By filling in the headers and data elements with some genuine information, you can produce a table like the one providing some details from a real estate search shown in Figure 6.1.

```
<TABLE>
    <TR>     <!-- Row 1 -->
        <TH>ID #</TH>
        <TH>Address</TH>
        <TH>Bedrooms/Bathrooms</TH>
        <TH>Heat/AC</TH>
        <TH>Selling Price</TH>
    </TR>
    <TR>     <!-- Row 2 -->
        <TD>AR-1897-3</TD>
        <TD>1850 North Quincy Street</TD>
        <TD>4 BR, 2 BA</TD>
        <TD>Gas/Central Air</TD>
        <TD>$248,000</TD>
    </TR>
    <TR>     <!-- Row 3 -->
        <TD>AR-9854-22</TD>
        <TD>4614 22nd Street North</TD>
        <TD>3 BR, 2.5 BA</TD>
        <TD>Oil/Central Air</TD>
        <TD>$237,000</TD>
    </TR>
    <TR>     <!-- Row 4 -->
        <TD>AR-5634-7</TD>
        <TD>1022 Glebe Road</TD>
        <TD>5 BR, 2.5 BA</TD>
```

```
        <TD>Electric/Central Air</TD>
        <TD>$358,000</TD>
    </TR>
</TABLE>
```

FIGURE 6.1
Results from database searches are typically presented in table form to improve readability.

Header cells
Data cells

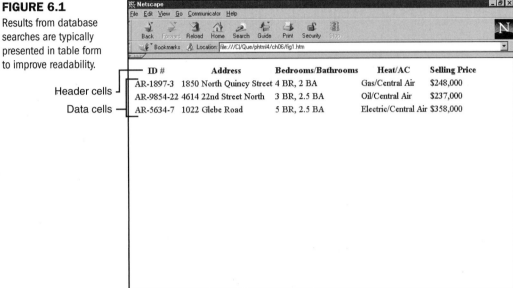

N O T E   If the contents of a table cell are too wide to fit across the cell, a browser will break the contents onto multiple lines. If you want the content of a cell to be placed on one line with no breaking, include the NOWRAP attribute in the <TD> or <TH> tag that defines the cell. ▪

Alignment

The beauty of HTML tables is the precise control you have over the alignment of content in individual cells and over the table itself. You can specify two types of alignment:

Part
II

Ch

6

- ▪ Horizontal alignment—The alignment of an element across the width of something, such as the alignment of a header across the width of a cell, for example, or the alignment of a table across the width of the page. Horizontal alignment is controlled by the ALIGN attribute. You can set ALIGN equal to LEFT, CENTER, or RIGHT.

- ▪ Vertical alignment—The alignment of an element between the top and bottom of a cell. Vertical alignment of cell contents is controlled by setting the VALIGN attribute to TOP, MIDDLE, or BOTTOM.

N O T E   You cannot specify vertical alignment for an entire table because, unlike the page width, a page's length isn't fixed. ▪

Aligning the Entire Table

You can use the ALIGN attribute in the <TABLE> tag to specify how the table should be aligned relative to the browser window. Setting ALIGN to LEFT or RIGHT floats the table in the left or right margin, respectively. Floating tables behave much like floating images in that you can wrap text around them. This is how you produce a page element such as the author byline you see in Figure 6.2.

FIGURE 6.2

This article on the ESPN SportsZone site uses a floating table to create an author byline that even includes a photo.

Floating table ───

Using the CENTER value of ALIGN centers the table in the browser window, although not all browsers support this. If you can't center a table this way, you can enclose the HTML that produces the table between the <CENTER> and </CENTER> tags. This should become unnecessary, however, as browsers come into compliance with the HTML 4.0 recommendation.

N O T E   The ALIGN attribute of the <TABLE> tag has been deprecated in the HTML 4.0 recommendation from the W3C, which means that its use is discouraged. This was done to encourage document authors to use style information to specify how the table should be aligned on a page. ■

Alignment Within a Row

If you want the vertical or the horizontal alignment to be the same for every cell in a given row, you can use the VALIGN and ALIGN attributes in the row's <TR> tag. Any alignment specified in a <TR> tag will override all default cell alignments.

NOTE The default vertical alignment for both header and data cells is MIDDLE. The default horizontal alignment depends on the type of cell: Header cells have a CENTER alignment and data cells have a LEFT alignment. ▨

Alignment Within a Cell

HTML 4.0 permits alignment control all the way down to the cell level. You can prescribe vertical or horizontal alignments in both header and data cells by using the VALIGN or ALIGN attributes in <TD> tags. Any alignment specified at the cell level overrides any default alignments and any alignments specified in a <TR> tag.

Setting alignments in individual cells represents the finest level of control of table alignment. In theory, you can manually specify vertical and horizontal alignments in every single cell of your tables if you need to. Unfortunately, it's easy to get lost among all those VALIGN and ALIGN attributes, especially when it comes to deciding which will take precedence. If you have trouble mastering table alignment, remember the following hierarchy:

- Alignments specified in <TD> or <TH> tags override all other alignments but apply only to the cell being defined.
- Alignments specified in a <TR> tag override default alignments and apply to all cells in a row, unless overridden by an alignment specification in a <TD> or </TH> tag.
- In the absence of alignment specifications in <TR>, <TD>, or <TH> tags, default alignments are used.

Controlling Other Table Attributes

In addition to tweaking alignments, you have a say in other aspects of the tables you create. These include

- Content summary
- Background color
- Captions
- Width of the table
- Borders
- Spacing within and between cells

The next six sections walk you through each of these table features and discuss the HTML tags and attributes you need to know to produce them.

Content Summary

Each revision to the HTML standard has shown increasing support for specialized browsers, such as those that are Braille based or speech based. Using these improvements makes your content more accessible to visually-impaired users with text-based or speech-based browsers,

Part

II

Ch

6

and you should look for opportunities to work these new tags and attributes into your HTML documents whenever possible.

HTML 4.0 provides for a SUMMARY attribute of the <TABLE> tag. SUMMARY is set equal to a text string that summarizes the table's content, purpose, and structure. Non-visual browsers can use this information to better communicate the content of your table to their users.

In the real estate listing table in Figure 6.1, the <TABLE> tag might be modified to include a summary such as

```
<TABLE SUMMARY="Real estate listings matching your search criteria,
columns include ID number, address, number of bedrooms, number of
bathrooms, and selling price">
```

Background Color

An easy way to add some contrast to your table to make it stand out from the rest of the content on a page is to give the table a background color different from the document's background color. By adding the BGCOLOR attribute to the <TABLE> tag, you can color the table background with an English-language color name or any RGB hexadecimal triplet, the same as you would specify the document's background color in the <BODY> tag.

 Determining a desired color's RGB hexadecimal code is one of the more tedious tasks in Web page authoring. Fortunately, many people have made color resources available on the Web that enable you to choose a color and have the RGB hexadecimal code returned to you. For a wide selection of such sites, point your browser to www.yahoo.com/Arts/Design_Arts/Graphic_Design/ Web_Page_Design_and_Layout/Color_Information/.

Also, most HTML authoring programs provide some kind of color selection support. Typically, you can choose a color from a palette presented by the program, and the corresponding RGB hexadecimal code is inserted for you.

Many browsers also support the use of BGCOLOR in the <TR>, <TD>, and <TH> tags, enabling you to present rows and cells in different colors. One effective use of this technique is to paint the top row of the table (presumably the row containing the column headers) with one background color and the remaining rows with a different color. This further distinguishes the items in the top row as column heads. You can make rows of data stand out by alternating a white and gray background color as well (see Figure 6.3).

Adding a Caption

To put a caption on your table, enclose the caption text between the <CAPTION> and </CAPTION> tags. Captions appear centered over the table and the text may be broken to match the table's width (see Figure 6.4). You can also use physical style tags to mark up your caption text. The HTML to produce Figure 6.4 follows:

```
<TABLE>
   <CAPTION><B>Homes for Sale Matching Your Preferences</B></CAPTION>
<TR>    <!-- Row 1 -->
      <TH>ID #</TH>
```

```
    <TH>Address</TH>
    <TH>Bedrooms/Bathrooms</TH>
    <TH>Heat/AC</TH>
    <TH>Selling Price</TH>
</TR>
<TR>    <!-- Row 2 -->
    <TD>AR-1897-3</TD>
    <TD>1850 North Quincy Street</TD>
    <TD>4 BR, 2 BA</TD>
    <TD>Gas/Central Air</TD>
    <TD>$248,000</TD>
</TR>
<TR>    <!-- Row 3 -->
    <TD>AR-9854-22</TD>
    <TD>4614 22nd Street North</TD>
    <TD>3 BR, 2.5 BA</TD>
    <TD>Oil/Central Air</TD>
    <TD>$237,000</TD>
</TR>
<TR>    <!-- Row 4 -->
    <TD>AR-5634-7</TD>
    <TD>1022 Glebe Road</TD>
    <TD>5 BR, 2.5 BA</TD>
    <TD>Electric/Central Air</TD>
    <TD>$358,000</TD>
</TR>
</TABLE>
```

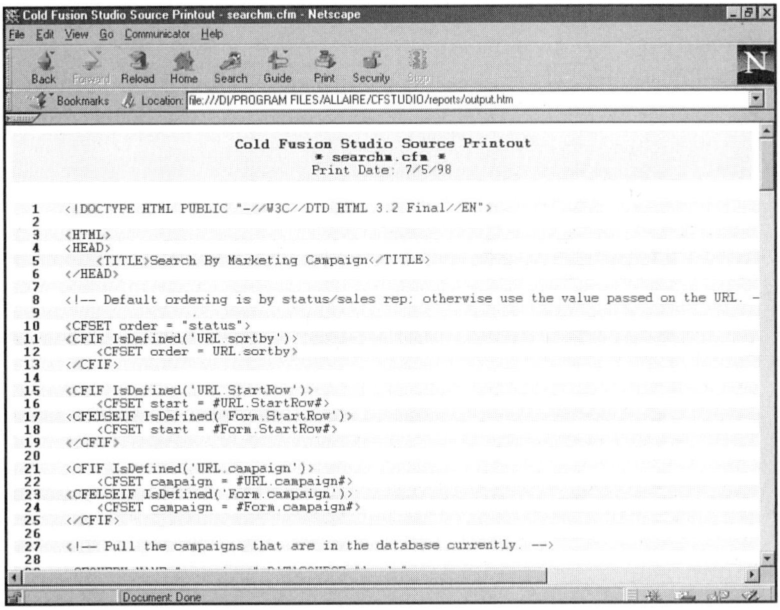

FIGURE 6.3

Alternating background colors makes individual rows easier to read, particularly when several rows of information are present, as in this code listing.

If you prefer your caption below the table, you can include the ALIGN=BOTTOM attribute in the <CAPTION> tag. You can also left-justify or right-justify your caption by setting ALIGN equal to LEFT or RIGHT, respectively.

FIGURE 6.4

Captions put the contents of your table into context for the reader.

Caption ⎯

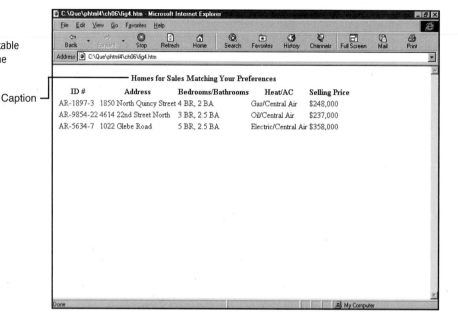

 T I P Put your caption immediately after the `<TABLE>` tag or immediately before the `</TABLE>` tag to prevent your caption from unintentionally becoming part of a table row or cell.

Setting the Width

The WIDTH attribute of the `<TABLE>` tag enables you to specify how wide the table should be in the browser window. You can set WIDTH to a specific number of pixels or to a percentage of the available screen width.

WIDTH is often used to force a table to occupy the entire width of the browser window. If we change the `<TABLE>` tag in the HTML code in the previous section to

```
<TABLE WIDTH=100%>
```

the table is rendered as shown in Figure 6.5. The information is centered in the columns for easier readability. When you compare the table in Figure 6.5 to the one in Figure 6.4, you can see how using the full screen width can enhance the readability of the table.

 T I P Because you can't know how every user has set his or her screen width, you should set WIDTH equal to a percentage whenever possible. The only exception to this is if the table has to be a certain number of pixels wide to accommodate an image in one of the cells or to achieve a certain layout effect.

Some browsers, such as Netscape Navigator 4 and Internet Explorer 4, support the use of the WIDTH attribute in a `<TD>` or `<TH>` tag to control the width of individual columns. The use of WIDTH (as well as HEIGHT) as an attribute of these tags has been deprecated in HTML 4.0, so you should expect to control the size of table cells and headers with style sheets sometime in the near future.

FIGURE 6.5

You have control over how much of the browser screen width a table occupies thanks to the WIDTH attribute.

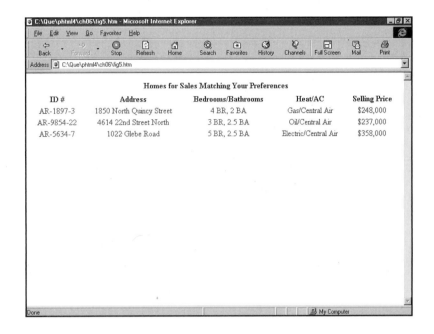

Adding a Border

You can place a border around your table by using the BORDER attribute of the <TABLE> tag. BORDER is set to the number of pixels wide you want the border to be. A version of our real estate search table with a 4-pixel border is shown in Figure 6.6. The modified <TABLE> tag that accomplishes this effect is

```
<TABLE WIDTH=100% BORDER=4>
```

You can also set BORDER equal to zero. This means that no border will be used and the browser should give back any space it has reserved to put in a border. This is an especially good approach to use when you're using a table to position page elements because it enables you to place the elements right up against one another without any one- or two-pixel gutters between them.

Spacing Within a Cell

The distance between the content of a cell and the boundaries of the cell is called *cell padding*. The CELLPADDING attribute of the <TABLE> tag enables you to control the amount of cell padding used in your tables. Typically, Web page authors increase the cell padding from its default value of 1 to put a little extra whitespace between the contents and the edges of a cell (compare the two tables shown in Figure 6.7). This gives the whole table a bit more room to breathe. The <TABLE> tags used to produce the tables in Figure 6.7 are

Part
II

Ch
6

```
<TABLE WIDTH=100% BORDER=2 CELLPADDING=6>
...
</TABLE>
<TABLE WIDTH=100% BORDER=2 CELLPADDING=12>
...
</TABLE>
```

FIGURE 6.6

Table borders create a visual boundary between cells and frequently make your tables easier to read.

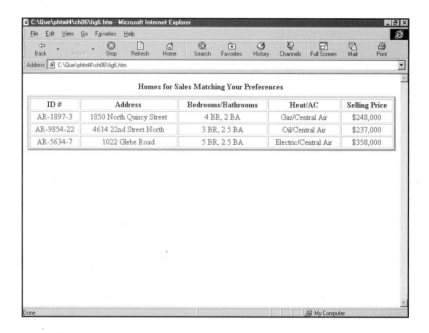

FIGURE 6.7

Increasing cell padding makes your tables appear less cluttered.

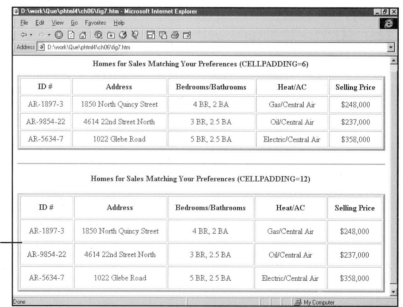

Spacing Between Cells

You also have control over the amount of space between cells. By increasing the value of the CELLSPACING attribute of the <TABLE> tag, you can open up a table even further (see Figure 6.8). Notice that the size of the border used between the cells increases as you increase the cell spacing. The <TABLE> tag used in Figure 6.8 is

```
<TABLE WIDTH=100% BORDER=2 CELLSPACING=8>
```

FIGURE 6.8

Increasing the amount of space between cells can give the illusion of your border being thicker than it really is.

Increased cell spacing ——

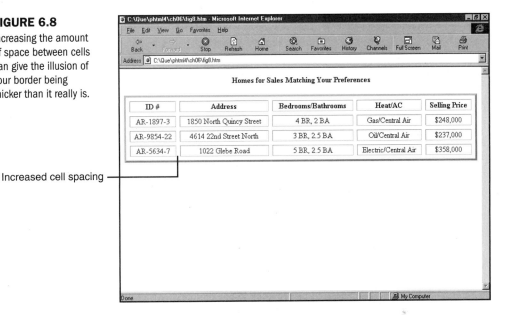

Spanning Multiple Rows or Columns

By default, a cell occupies or *spans* one row and one column. For most tables, this is sufficient. When you start to use tables for layout purposes, though, you'll encounter instances where you want a cell to span more than one row or column. HTML 4.0 supports attributes of the <TH> and <TD> tags that permit this effect.

Part

II

Ch

6

Using the *COLSPAN* Attribute

The COLSPAN attribute inside of a <TH> or <TD> tag instructs the browser to make the cell defined by the tag take up more than one column. You set COLSPAN equal to the number of columns the cell is to occupy.

COLSPAN is useful when one row of the table is forcing the table to be a certain number of columns wide, and the content in other rows can be accommodated in a smaller number of columns. Figure 6.9 shows a table that makes good use of the COLSPAN attribute. In the figure, the author used the COLSPAN attribute to get the page header (navigation links, sidewalk.com logo, and the date) to occupy three columns of the table.

FIGURE 6.9

Forcing a cell to occupy more than one column is helpful in creating more readable page layouts.

Navigation menu spans the three columns

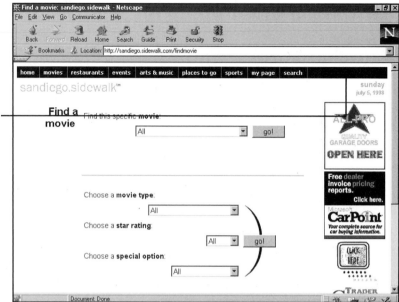

Using the *ROWSPAN* Attribute

ROWSPAN works in much the same way as COLSPAN, except that it enables a cell to take up more than one row. Figure 6.10 shows the international links sections of the Netscape NetCenter page. The "Professional Connections" link is in a single cell that spans eight rows (ROWSPAN=8) of the table. The HTML code to place the link might look like

```
<TABLE>
<TR>
<TD> ... contents of first cell ... </TD>
<TD> ... contents of second cell ... </TD>
<TD ROWSPAN=8><A HREF="prfcon.html">Professional Connections ...</A></TD>
</TR>
...
</TABLE>
```

What Elements Can Be Placed in a Table Cell?

HTML tables were developed with the intent of presenting columns of information, but that information does not necessarily have to be text based. You can place many types of page elements in a given table cell:

■ Text—Text is the most obvious thing to put in a table cell, but don't forget that you can format the text with physical and logical styles, heading styles, list formatting, line and paragraph breaks, and hypertext anchor formatting.

FIGURE 6.10

Table elements can occupy more than one row of the table when you use the ROWSPAN attribute.

These links span the five rows to the left

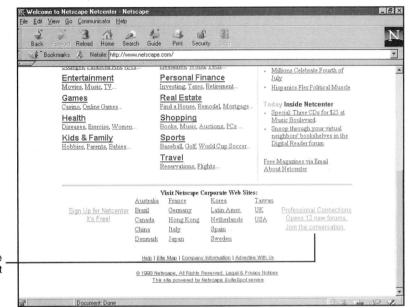

■ Images—You can place an image in a table cell by enclosing an `<IMG>` tag between the `<TD>` and `</TD>` tags that define the cell. This is useful for designing page layout with tables because you aren't constrained only to text.

■ Blank space—Sometimes it's useful to put a blank cell in a table. You can accomplish this by putting nothing between the cell's defining tags (`<TD></TD>`) or by placing a nonbreaking space between the tags (`<TD> </TD>`). Use of the nonbreaking space is preferable because, if you have borders turned on, a cell with a nonbreaking space picks up a border, but a cell created with `<TD></TD>` may not.

■ Form fields—The ability to place form fields inside of a table cell is very important, especially when you consider that the prompting text in front of form fields are of varying lengths. By putting prompting text and form fields in a table, you can align them all and make the form much more readable.

■ Other tables—You can embed one table inside of another, although this can induce quite a headache for many people! Previously, only Netscape Navigator and Microsoft Internet Explorer supported tables within tables; but now that it is part of the HTML 4.0 standard, other browsers should support it as they come into compliance with the new standard.

Part

II

Ch

6

T I P If you plan to embed a table within a table, it's helpful to do a pencil-and-paper sketch first. The sketch should help you code the tables more efficiently.

Table Sections and Column Properties

The W3C has added several table-related tags to the HTML 4.0 recommendation that enables you to split tables into logical sections and to control alignment properties of rows or columns of data.

Table Sections

The <THEAD>, <TBODY>, and <TFOOT> container tags denote the start of a table header, body, and footer, respectively. By explicitly distinguishing the different parts of your table, you can control your row and column attributes. The separation of the table header and footer also makes it easier for the browser to render and print tables that are broken across several pages. Additionally, it makes it simple to set up a static header or footer in frames at the top and bottom of a browser screen and to place the body of the table in a scrollable frame between the header and footer frame.

<THEAD> contains the rows that compose the table header and <TFOOT> contains the rows that compose the footer. In the absence of <THEAD> and <TFOOT> tags, the <TBODY> tag becomes optional. You can use multiple <TBODY> tags in long tables to make smaller, more manageable chunks. All three tags can take both the ALIGN and VALIGN attributes to control horizontal and vertical alignment within the sections they define.

N O T E All three tags are only valid between the <TABLE> and </TABLE> tags. ▮

A typical table created with these tags might look like this:

```
<TABLE>
    <THEAD>
        <TR>
            . . .
        </TR>
    </THEAD>
    <TBODY>
        <TR>
            . . .
        </TR>
        <TR>
            . . .
        </TR>
        . . .
        <TR>
            . . .
        </TR>
    </TBODY>
    <TFOOT>
        <TR>
            . . .
        </TR>
    </TFOOT>
</TABLE>
```

Used in conjunction with the column grouping tags discussed in the next section, the table section tags are an ideal way to control how different properties are applied to different parts of a table.

Setting Column Properties

The <TR> tag supports attributes that enable you to specify all sorts of properties for an entire row of a table. In particular, you get very good control over both horizontal and vertical alignment with the ALIGN and VALIGN attributes. HTML 4.0 takes this a step further by making it possible to apply horizontal alignment properties to columns of data as well.

You have two options when applying alignment properties to columns. The <COLGROUP> tag is appropriate when applying properties over several columns. It takes the attributes ALIGN, which can be set to LEFT, CENTER, or RIGHT; VALIGN, which can be set to TOP, MIDDLE, BOTTOM, or BASELINE; WIDTH, which is set equal to the desired width of the group; and SPAN, which is set to the number of consecutive columns to which the properties apply.

```
<TABLE BORDER=1>
    <COLGROUP ALIGN=LEFT SPAN=4>
    <COLGROUP ALIGN=RIGHT SPAN=2>
    <COLGROUP ALIGN=CENTER>
    <TBODY>
        <TR>
            <TD>First column group, left horizontal alignment</TD>
            <TD>First column group, left horizontal alignment</TD>
            <TD>First column group, left horizontal alignment</TD>
            <TD>First column group, left horizontal alignment</TD>
            <TD>Second column group, right horizontal alignment</TD>
            <TD>Second column group, right horizontal alignment</TD>
            <TD>Third column group, center horizontal alignment</TD>
        </TR>
    </TBODY>
</TABLE>
```

The seven columns are split into three groups. The first four columns have left-aligned table entries, the fifth and sixth columns have entries horizontally aligned along the right, and the last column has centered entries (see Figure 6.11).

If columns in a group are to have differing properties, you can use <COLGROUP> to set up the group, and then specify the individual properties with the <COL> tag. <COL> takes the same attributes as <COLGROUP>, but these attributes only apply to a subset of the columns in a group. For example, the HTML splits the five columns of the table into two groups:

Part

II

Ch

6

FIGURE 6.11

Grouping columns enables you to assign common alignment properties to a number of columns simultaneously.

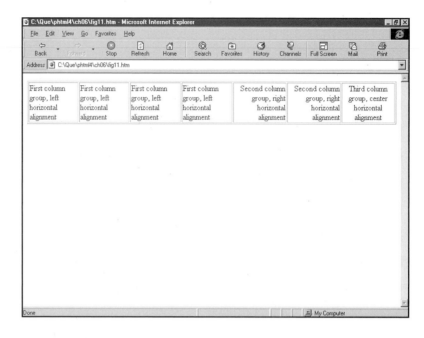

```
<TABLE BORDER=1 CELLPADDING=16>
    <COLGROUP>
        <COL ALIGN=CENTER>
        <COL ALIGN=RIGHT>
        <COL ALIGN=LEFT>
    </COLGROUP>
    <COLGROUP>
        <COL ALIGN=RIGHT SPAN=2>
    </COLGROUP>
    <TBODY>
        <TR>
            <TD>First column in first group, center horizontal alignment</TD>
            <TD>Second column in first group, right horizontal alignment</TD>
            <TD>Third column in first group, left horizontal alignment</TD>
            <TD>First column in second group, right horizontal alignment</TD>
            <TD>Second column in second group, right horizontal alignment</TD>
        </TR>
    </TBODY>
</TABLE>
```

The first group's columns use center, right, and left horizontal alignments, whereas both columns in the second group use only right horizontal alignment (see Figure 6.12).

Other Attributes of the *<TABLE>* Tag

Because of the new support for dividing tables into logical sections and the grouping of columns, the W3C has introduced some new attributes for the <TABLE> tag that enable you to control inner and outer borders of a table. Inner borders are controlled by the RULES attribute. You can think of inner borders as the dividing lines between certain components of the table. RULES can take on the values shown in Table 6.1.

FIGURE 6.12

You can also group columns and still assign alignment parameters on an individual basis.

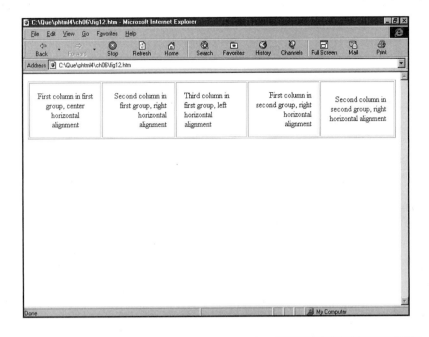

Table 6.1 Values of the *RULES* Attribute of the *<TABLE>* Tag

Value	Purpose
ALL	Display a border between all rows and columns
COLS	Display a border between all columns
GROUPS	Display a border between all logical groups (as defined by the <THEAD>, <TBODY>, <TFOOT>, and <COLGROUP> tags)
NONE	Suppress all inner borders
ROWS	Display a border between all table rows

The FRAME attribute controls which sides of the outer borders are displayed. In the context of tables, FRAME refers to the outer perimeter of the entire table and not frames such as those discussed in Chapter 7, "Frames." FRAME can take on the values summarized in Table 6.2.

Table 6.2 Values of the *FRAME* Attribute of the *<TABLE>* Tag

Value	Purpose
ABOVE	Displays a border on the top of a table frame
BELOW	Displays a border at the bottom of a table frame
BORDER	Displays a border on all four sides of a table frame

continues

Part II

Ch 6

Table 6.2 Continued	
BOX	Same as BORDER
HSIDES	Displays a border on the left and right sides of a table frame
LHS	Displays a border on the left side of a table frame
RHS	Displays a border on the right side of a table frame
VSIDES	Displays a border at the top and bottom of a table frame
VOID	Suppresses the display of all table frame borders

Tables as a Design Tool

Although tables were developed for presenting columnar data, they have evolved to the point where they can do much more. Three primary driving forces are behind the rise of tables as a design tool:

- You aren't restricted to only putting text in table cells.
- You can make a cell occupy more than one row or column.
- You get incredibly fine control over the alignment of content in individual cells.

Creating a Complex Layout

The ABCNEWS.com page is a complex combination of embedded tables (see Figure 6.13). The navigation images you see down the right side are contained in the rightmost cell of the overall table that creates the structure for the page.

Aligning Images of Different Sizes

Figure 6.14 shows MCI's and Continental Airlines' joint promotion for frequent flyer miles. Note that image of the MCI Calling Card and the image containing the text next to it are of different heights. Because each image is of a slightly different size, it was necessary to place each in its own table cell and then use the VALIGN attribute to make them line up along their baselines.

Aligning Form Fields

The checkout page on Cdnow.com's Web site would be a mess if it weren't for the different form fields placed in table cells (see Figure 6.15). The prompting text in front of the fields (Address Line 1, Address Line 2, City, State, and so on) are of varying lengths. If the fields started right after each word, none of them would line up. By placing both the prompting text and the form fields in common table rows, the alignment is perfect.

FIGURE 6.13

Sites such as ABCNEWS.com typically use tables to create a columnar look for the layout.

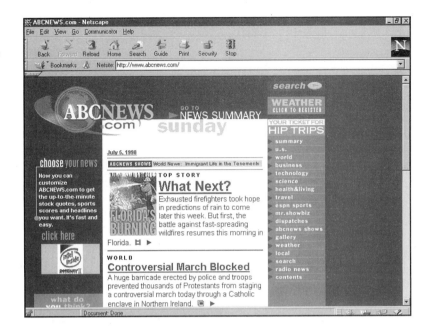

FIGURE 6.14

Different image sizes can make a page look unaligned. By placing images in a table and using alignment attributes, everything lines up cleanly.

Image #1

Image #2 (larger than Image #1)

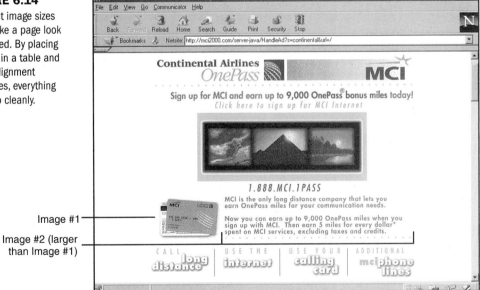

FIGURE 6.15

Using a table to align form fields is an essential part of making a form readable and usable.

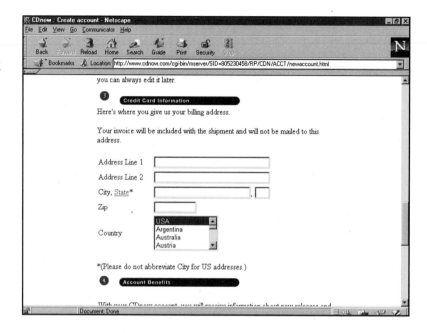

Creating Tables with Web Page Authoring Tools

The table tags have vexed some content developers from the beginning because it is hard for some folks to keep track of all their <TR>, <TH>, and <TD> tags. It didn't take long for many popular document authoring tools to provide support for the creation and modification of HTML tables—particularly WYSIWYG support that spares a developer from seeing any table tags at all. This chapter closes with a look at how four authoring tools can help you create tables.

Microsoft FrontPage 98

The FrontPage Editor gives you extensive table support from the moment you start a table. In particular, you can create a new table in three ways:

- Choose Table, Draw Table to activate the Table Drawing tool. This enables you to draw the boundaries of your table and then draw the lines to form the rows and columns (see Figure 6.16).

- Choose Table, Insert Table to launch a dialog box that prompts you for basic table information, such as the number of rows and columns, width, border size, alignment, cell padding, and cell spacing. After these parameters are collected, FrontPage creates the shell of the table for you.

- Click the Insert Table button on the toolbar. This reveals a 4-row-by-5-column grid that you can drag your mouse pointer over to specify the dimensions of your table. After you have the proper size selected, simply release your mouse button and FrontPage will place the empty table on the page.

FIGURE 6.16

FrontPage's Drawing tool enables you to sketch out your table directly on the screen.

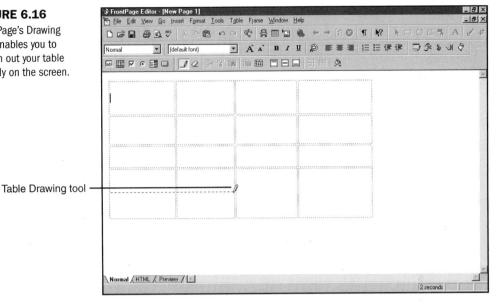

Table Drawing tool

The end product of any of the previous actions is a blank table waiting to have content placed in the cells. If you place text into the cells, you can simply type it in. You can also place images, horizontal rules, blank space, and other tables in individual cells in much the same way as you would on the full-sized page.

FrontPage's extensive Table menu also helps you with many table-related tasks that are cumbersome to create otherwise. You can choose to insert a caption, cell, row, or column into an existing table, for example—something that can be tedious to do if you were working with the raw HTML code. The Table menu can also assist with

- Cell operations—You can choose to delete or merge a set of cells or to split one cell into multiple cells.

- Selection operations—It's often a tricky thing to select a particular cell, row, or column within a table. The Select options on the Table menu make it a simple matter. To select a column, for example, you can place the cursor in a cell that occupies the column you want to select; then choose Table, Select Column. You can select the contents of the entire table this way as well.

- Even distribution—When you draw a table by hand, you might not get your rows or columns to be the same size. To even things out, you can select the rows or columns and choose one of the distribute evenly Table menu options to make each row or column the same size.

- Text/Table conversion—Switching between plain text and table format is a breeze with FrontPage's options that enable you to convert between the two.

- Properties—You can call up Properties dialog boxes for your table's caption, a selected cell, or for the entire table (see Figure 6.17).

Part
II

Ch
6

FIGURE 6.17

Global table properties are easy to change, as are those for individual cells.

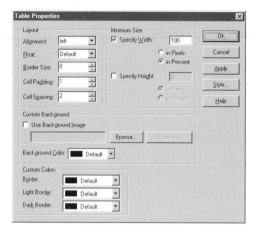

 TIP Many of the options on the Table menu are also replicated on the FrontPage Table toolbar. If you don't see the toolbar, choose View, Table Toolbar to activate it.

Netscape Composer

Netscape's integrated Web document authoring tool Composer checks in with a fair amount of table support as well. By clicking the Table button on the Composer toolbar or by choosing Insert, Table, Table, you get the table kickoff dialog box shown in Figure 6.18. Here you can specify all the parameters that Composer needs to set up a new table. After you click OK, Composer will place a blank table on the page according to your specs. After the blank table is in place, you're free to fill in the individual cells with whatever content you choose.

FIGURE 6.18

Netscape Composer prompts you for any global table attributes you want to specify when first setting up a table.

Should you need to insert or delete any cells, rows, or columns, Composer can help you. You can find the insert options under the Insert menu. Choosing Insert, Table reveals a set of items that you can insert. Similarly, you can choose Edit, Delete Table to see a list of table components that you can remove.

Like the FrontPage Editor, Composer gives you access to cell, row, or table properties, but all the property settings are lumped into one dialog box. To call up the properties, right-click a cell in the table and choose Table Properties from the pop-up menu that appears. Figure 6.19 shows you the result of this action. Note that tabs exist in the dialog box for table, row, and cell level properties.

FIGURE 6.19

Need to tweak your table? Netscape Composer enables you to do it all from one place.

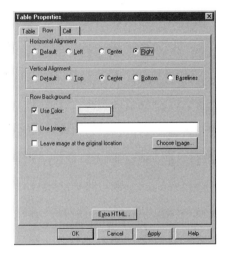

Allaire HomeSite

Allaire's HomeSite HTML editor gives you a number of ways to work with tables. Probably the fastest way to start is to use the Quick Table button at the end of the Tables toolbar. Clicking this button reveals a 12-row-by-6-column grid that you can drag your mouse pointer over to choose the size of your table. After you select the appropriate size, HomeSite writes in the necessary HTML tags to support the table.

N O T E The Quick Table option only produces the HTML tags to create the structure of the table. It's up to you to go back through the code and place content in the table. ■

Your other option for starting is to use the Table Wizard, which you can activate by clicking the Table Wizard button on the Tables toolbar or by pressing Ctrl+Shift+T. The wizard is composed of two dialog boxes, the first of which is shown in Figure 6.20. From this dialog box, you can set up the number of rows and columns your table should have, as well as any special row or column spanning. Clicking the Next button takes you to the second dialog box where you can set other table, row, and cell parameters. When you're done, you can click the Finish button

Part

II

Ch

6

and HomeSite will write the necessary table tags into your document. Then all you need to do is fill in the contents of the individual cells.

FIGURE 6.20

The HomeSite Table Wizard is a visual tool for establishing the structure of a table.

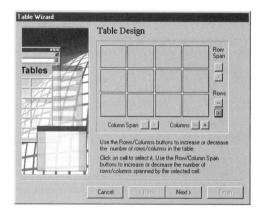

To change properties for an individual cell, place your cursor in the cell you want to change and switch to the Cell Properties tab in the Wizard dialog box. There you can adjust the cell's width, height, alignment values, text wrapping properties, and spanning values.

If you're the kind who likes to get down into the guts of things and work with HTML tags, you'll want to make use of the buttons on the HomeSite Tables toolbar. The buttons with a blue bar across the top of them place table-related tags (<TABLE>, <TR>, <TH>, and <TD>) by means of a dialog box that prompts you for an attribute that should go into the opening tag. The buttons to the right of those that don't have a blue bar place the tag pair in the document and leave it to you to fill in any needed attributes. You can use these buttons to place <TABLE>, <TR>, <TD>, <TH>, and <CAPTION> tag pairs.

Adobe PageMill

You can easily create tables with PageMill's intuitive table support. To begin, click the Insert Table tool on the toolbar shown in Figure 6.21. After you click the tool, you can specify the number of desired rows and columns in the ensuing dialog box. Alternatively, you can click the Insert Table tool and drag the mouse—either vertically or horizontally—the proper distance to denote the number of desired rows and columns.

You can resize tables in PageMill by selecting a table and dragging the tab on the right side or at the bottom to resize it. The number of rows and columns will remain the same, but their widths and heights will remain proportional to the size of the table.

As you work on tables in PageMill, the program's interface will adapt to provide you with helpful tools. When you select cells in your tables, for example, the PageMill toolbar will change to include buttons that do the following:

- Join or divide cells
- Delete or insert columns
- Delete or insert rows

FIGURE 6.21

PageMill offers several tools with which you can modify your HTML tables.

Insert Table tool —

Drag to create table of desired size —

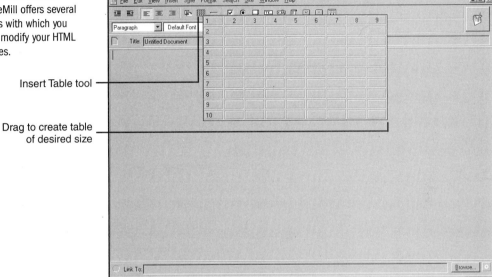

You can manipulate the look of your table through the PageMill Attributes Inspector. The Inspector is a utility that enables you to specify the attributes for objects (tables, graphics, and so on), forms, frames, and pages, with each attribute set arranged on a different tab. To access the Inspector, press F8 or select Show Inspector from the View menu.

 TIP Leaving the width field blank in the Inspector instructs PageMill to size the table just wide enough to accommodate the contents of the table cells.

The Inspector enables you to place a caption at the bottom or on top of the tables, as seen in Figure 6.22. You can also specify the table border, cell spacing, and cell padding.

The Inspector will also enable you to modify the contents of a table cell. Simply select the cell to be modified, and the Inspector displays the cell attributes. Once again, you can specify the table width using the width parameter on the Object tab. With the Inspector, you can set certain cells as header cells and suppress word-wrapping as well. Finally, using the Inspector, you can specify the vertical and horizontal alignment of the cell contents.

Part

II

Ch

6

FIGURE 6.22

The Inspector enables you to modify some of the attributes of your table.

Frames

by Eric Ladd

In this chapter

Introduction to Frames

Netscape introduced the idea of frames when it released Netscape Navigator 2.0. At the same time, Netscape proposed frames to the World Wide Web Consortium (W3C) for inclusion in the HTML 3.0 standard. When the HTML 3.2 draft was released, frames were not part of the standard, but W3C indicated it was still considering other proposals that were put forward for HTML 3.0. When it released the HTML 4.0 specification, the W3C included the frame tags as proposed by Netscape, along with a few new twists that Microsoft and other W3C members threw in.

Since their introduction, frames have evolved much like tables. Initially, a number of browsers implemented both tables and frames, even though they were not part of the HTML standard. Frames are part of the HTML 4.0 recommendation now, however, so you can feel more comfortable about using frame-related tags. Used wisely, frames can provide users with an improved interface and a better experience with your site. However, some developers do not use frames wisely, and that has resulted in an outcry from people who try to promote usable Web pages. If you hear dissent about frames these days, it is most likely related to these usability issues and not to frames being non-standard HTML.

This chapter introduces you to the basics of frames and how you can make intelligent use of frames on your site. Before jumping into how to create framed documents, it's helpful to take a moment to get a feel for what they are, what they do, and what browsers render them correctly.

The main idea behind a framed document is that you can split the browser window into two or more regions called *frames*. After this is done, you can load separate HTML documents into each frame and enable users to see different pages simultaneously (see Figure 7.1). Each frame can have its own scrollbars if the document is too big to fit in the allocated space.

FIGURE 7.1

You can present multiple Web documents simultaneously using frames.

Navigation frame —

Content frame —

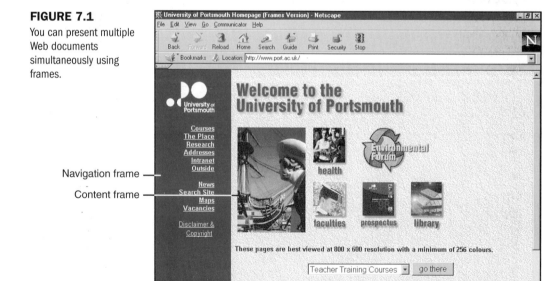

Additionally, you can resize a frame with your mouse. To resize a frame, follow these steps:

1. Place your mouse pointer over the border of the frame you want to resize.

2. Click and hold down the left mouse button.

3. Drag the border to its new position and release the mouse button (see Figure 7.2).

FIGURE 7.2
Unless the content author has specified otherwise, users are free to resize frames to their liking.

Moveable frame border

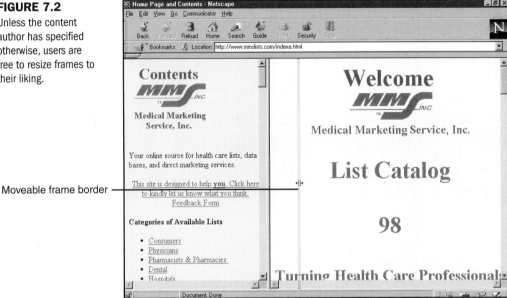

After the border is moved to its new position, the browser repaints any affected frames according to the new distribution of screen real estate.

N O T E   In some instances, a document author might include a command in the frame setup that prevents users from resizing the framed layout. You should do this only if it is absolutely essential that your layout be maintained exactly as you specified. This is occasionally the case when you have an image in a frame and you want the entire image showing at all times. ■

Applications

Like any page element, frames should not be used just because they're cool. Your decision to use frames should be based on the needs and characteristics of your audience and how effective frames will be in communicating your messages.

Frames lend themselves well to applications in which you want one set of content to remain on the browser screen while another set of content changes. This is easily accomplished by splitting the browser window into two frames: one for static content and one for changing content. Items typically found in static content frames include

Part

II

Ch

7

- Navigation tools
- Tables of contents
- Banners and logos
- Search interface forms

Users interact with the static content (click a hypertext link, enter search criteria into a form, and so on), and the result of their action appears in the changing content frame.

Another useful application for frames is for documents that are heavy on definitions or footnotes. You can display the main document in a large frame and have a glossary or bibliography file displayed in a secondary frame. A user could then click key terms or footnote indicators in the large frame to cause the appropriate glossary entry or footnote to appear in the secondary frame.

Setting Up a Frames Document

After you've made the decision to use frames on your site, you need to know the HTML tags that make it possible. The next several sections show you how to create framed pages and how to provide alternatives for those who can't view frames.

 TIP A good first step, especially for intricately framed layouts, is to draw a pencil-and-paper sketch of how you want the framed page to look. In addition to helping you think about how to create the most efficient layout, your sketch also helps you determine how to order your <FRAMESET> tags, if you have more than one.

The *<FRAMESET>* Tag

The first step in creating a framed document is to split the browser screen into the frames you want to use. You accomplish this with an HTML file that uses the <FRAMESET> and </FRAMESET> container tags instead of the <BODY> and </BODY> tags. <FRAMESET> and </FRAMESET> are not just container tags. Attributes of the <FRAMESET> tag are instrumental in defining the frame regions.

Each <FRAMESET> tag needs one of two attributes: ROWS, to divide the screen into multiple rows, or COLS, to divide the screen into multiple columns. ROWS and COLS are set equal to a list of values that instructs a browser how big to make each row or column. The values can be a number of pixels, a percentage of a browser window's dimensions, or an asterisk (*), which acts as a wildcard character and tells the browser to use whatever space it has left. The following HTML, for example:

```
<FRAMESET ROWS="40%,20%,20%,5%,15%">
...
</FRAMESET>
```

breaks the browser window into five rows (see Figure 7.3). The first row has a height equal to 40% of the browser screen height; the second and third rows each have a height equal to 20% of the browser screen; the fourth row has a height equal to 5% of the screen; and the fifth row has a height equal to 15% of the screen. Similarly, the following HTML:

```
<FRAMESET COLS="135,75,4*,*">
...
</FRAMESET>
```

splits the window into four columns (see Figure 7.4). The first column is 135 pixels wide; the second is 75 pixels wide; and the remaining space is divided between the third and fourth columns, with the third column four times as wide (4*) as the fourth (*).

CAUTION

Don't put a ROWS and a COLS attribute in the same <FRAMESET> tag. Frames-capable browsers can do only one at a time. Normally, these browsers will act on the first attribute they encounter.

The <FRAMESET> tag can also take two script-related attributes: onload and onunload. These event handlers execute the script code you assign to them when the framed layout is loaded and unloaded, respectively.

T I P Netscape Navigator and Microsoft Internet Explorer still recognize the FRAMEBORDER attribute of the <FRAMESET> tag, which you can use to set the thickness of the border between frames. You can even set FRAMEBORDER to zero so that frames appear seamless (no visible boundaries between frames so that the layout looks continuous). The HTML 4.0 recommendation calls for FRAMEBORDER to be an attribute of the <FRAME> tag discussed later in the chapter.

FIGURE 7.3

The <FRAMESET> tag enables you to break the browser screen into any number of rows...

Browser screen split into five rows

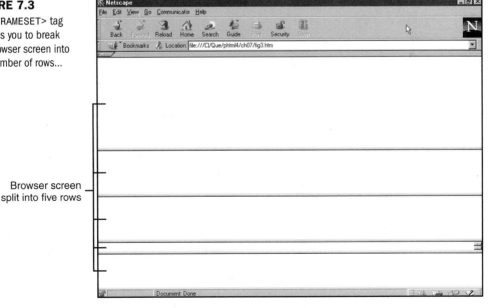

Part
II

Ch
7

FIGURE 7.4

...or into any number of columns. You have control over how big each row or column will be.

Browser screen split into four columns

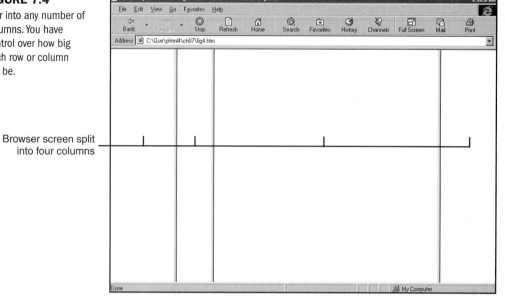

Nesting <FRAMESET> Tags to Achieve Complex Layouts

To produce really interesting layouts, you can nest <FRAMESET> and </FRAMESET> tags. Suppose you want to split the browser window into eight equal regions. You can first split the screen into four equal rows with the following HTML:

```
<FRAMESET ROWS="25%,25%,25%,25%">
...
</FRAMESET>
```

This produces the screen shown in Figure 7.5.

Next, you need to divide each row in half. To do this, you need a <FRAMESET> tag for each row that splits the row into two equal columns. The HTML

```
<FRAMESET COLS="50%,50%">
...
</FRAMESET>
```

does the trick. Nesting these tags in the HTML at the beginning of this section produces the following:

```
<FRAMESET ROWS="25%,25%,25%,25%">
    <FRAMESET COLS="50%,50%"> <!-- Split Row 1 into two columns -->
        ...
    </FRAMESET>
    <FRAMESET COLS="50%,50%"> <!-- Split Row 2 into two columns -->
        ...
    </FRAMESET>
    <FRAMESET COLS="50%,50%"> <!-- Split Row 2 into two columns -->
        ...
```

FIGURE 7.5

The first step in producing a complex framed layout is to split the browser screen into rows or columns.

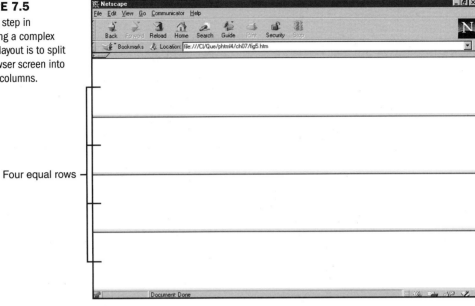

Four equal rows

```
    </FRAMESET>
    <FRAMESET COLS="50%,50%"> <!-- Split Row 4 into two columns -->
        ...
    </FRAMESET>

</FRAMESET>
```

The HTML above completes the task of splitting the window into eight equal regions. The resulting screen is shown in Figure 7.6.

 Not sure whether to do a <FRAMESET> with ROWS or COLS first? Take a look at your sketch of the browser window. If you have unbroken horizontal lines that go from one edge of the window to the other, do your ROWS first. If you have unbroken vertical lines that go from the top of the window to the bottom, do your COLS first.

Of course, you're not limited to making regions that are all the same size. Suppose you want an 108-pixel-wide table of contents frame to appear down the left side of the browser window, and on the right side, you need a 92-pixel row for a logo; the balance of the right side is for changing content. In this case, you could use the HTML

```
<FRAMESET COLS="108,*">  <!-- Split screen into two columns. -->
        ...             <!-- Placeholder for table of contents. -->
<FRAMESET ROWS="92,*">  <!-- Split column 2 into two rows. -->
        ...     <!-- Placeholder for logo. -->
        ...     <!-- Placeholder for changing content frame. -->
    </FRAMESET>
</FRAMESET>
```

Part

II

Ch

7

FIGURE 7.6
You further divide the initial rows or columns to produce the final layout.

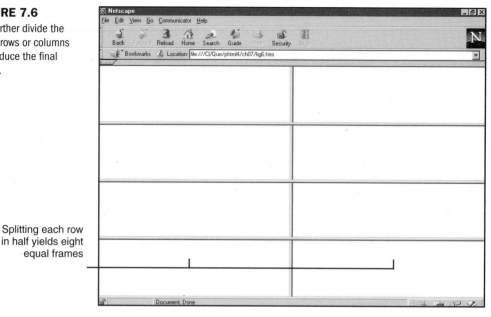

Splitting each row in half yields eight equal frames

The ellipses you see in the preceding code are placeholders for the tags that place the content into the frames that the <FRAMESET> tags create. You put a document in each using the <FRAME> tag discussed in the next section.

Placing Content in Frames with the *<FRAME>* Tag

Using <FRAMESET> tags is only the beginning of creating a framed page. After the browser window is split into regions, you need to fill each region with content. The keys to doing this are the <FRAME> tag and its many attributes.

With your frames all set up, you're ready to place content in each frame with the <FRAME> tag. The most important attribute of the <FRAME> tag is SRC, which tells the browser the URL of the document you want to load into the frame. The <FRAME> tag can also take the attributes summarized in Table 7.1. If you use the NAME attribute, the name you give the frame must begin with an alphanumeric character.

Table 7.1   Attributes of the *<FRAME>* Tag

Attribute	Purpose
FRAMEBORDER=1 ¦ 0	Turns frame borders on or off
MARGINHEIGHT=n	Specifies the amount of whitespace (in pixels) to be left at the top and bottom of the frame
MARGINWIDTH=n	Specifies the amount of whitespace (in pixels) to be left along the sides of the frame

Attribute	Purpose
LONGDESC="url"	Provides the URL of a document that gives a more detailed description of what's in the frame; useful for nonvisual browsers
NAME="name"	Gives the frame a unique name so it can be targeted by other documents
NORESIZE	Disables the user's ability to resize the frame
SCROLLING=YES¦NO¦AUTO	Controls the appearance of horizontal and vertical scrollbars in the frame
SRC="url"	Specifies the URL of the document to load into the frame

To place content in each of the regions you created at the end of the previous section, you can use the following HTML:

```
<FRAMESET COLS="108,*">  <!-- Split screen into two columns. -->
   <FRAME SRC="toc.html">   <!-- Placeholder for table of contents. -->
   <FRAMESET ROWS="92,*">  <!-- Split column 2 into two rows. -->
      <FRAME SRC="logo.html">    <!-- Placeholder for logo. -->
      <FRAME SRC="content.html"> <!-- Placeholder for changing content -->
   </FRAMESET>
</FRAMESET>
```

The resulting screen appears in Figure 7.7.

Certainly, the SRC attribute in a <FRAME> tag is essential. Otherwise the browser would not know where to look for the content that is to go into the frame.

FIGURE 7.7
Each frame in your layout should have a corresponding <FRAME> tag that populates it with content or a <FRAMESET> tag that subdivides it further.

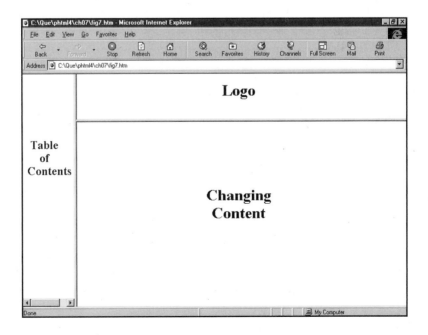

Part
II

Ch

7

You'll probably find that you frequently use the other attributes as well. In particular, MARGINWIDTH and MARGINHEIGHT enable you to set up left and right (MARGINWIDTH) and top and bottom (MARGINHEIGHT) margins within each frame. Putting a little whitespace around the content in each frame enhances readability, especially when you have FRAMEBORDER set to zero.

The NORESIZE and SCROLLING attributes are handy when you want to modify the user-controlled aspects of a frame. Recall that a user can change the size of a frame by clicking a border of a frame and dragging it to a new position. NORESIZE is a Boolean attribute that, when present in a <FRAME> tag, suppresses the user's ability to change the size of the frame. You might want to do this if it is imperative that the size of a frame not change so that it can always accommodate a key piece of content. SCROLLING can be set to YES if you always want horizontal and vertical scrollbars on the frame, and to NO if you never want scrollbars. The default value of SCROLLING is AUTO, in which the browser places scrollbars on the frame if they're needed and leaves them off if they're not needed.

> **CAUTION**
>
> Be careful about setting SCROLLING to NO. You should do this only if you are absolutely sure that all the content in a frame will always be visible. Otherwise, users might find themselves in a situation where content runs off the side or bottom of a frame, and they have no way to scroll around to see it.

Targeting Named Frames

Probably the trickiest thing about frames is getting content to appear where you want it to appear. This is where naming the frames you create becomes critical. By naming the changing content frame "main," you can then use the TARGET attribute in all your <A> tags to direct all hyperlinked documents to be loaded into that frame:

```
<FRAMESET COLS="108,*">  <!-- Split screen into two columns. -->
   <FRAME SRC="toc.html">
   <FRAMESET ROWS="92,*">  <!-- Split column 2 into two rows. -->
      <FRAME SRC="logo.html">
      <FRAME SRC="content.html" NAME="main">
   </FRAMESET>
</FRAMESET>
```

With frames set up by the preceding code, an example link in the file "toc.html" might look like this:

```
<A HREF="orderform.html" TARGET="main">Order Now!</A>
```

The TARGET attribute tells the browser that the file orderform.html should be loaded into the frame named *main* (the changing content frame) whenever a user clicks the hypertext Order Now! in the table of contents frame.

If all the links in toc.html target the frame named *main*, you can use the <BASE> tag in the head of the document to set a value for TARGET that applies to all links:

```
<HEAD>
<TITLE>Table of Contents</TITLE>
<BASE TARGET="main">
</HEAD>
```

With this `<BASE>` tag in place, every hyperlink targets the changing content window named *main*.

Netscape set aside some reserved frame names when it introduced the frame-related tags. These special target names include

- `_blank` Targets a new blank window that is not named.
- `_self` Targets the frame where the hyperlink is found.
- `_parent` Targets the parent `<FRAMESET>` of the frame where the hyperlink is found. This defaults to behaving like `_self` if no parent document exists.
- `_top` Targets the full window before any frames are introduced. This creates a good way to jump out of a nested sequence of framed documents.

CAUTION

When using the reserved frame names, make sure that the character following the underscore character is lowercase. Otherwise, you are likely to see targeting behavior that you don't expect.

Although the TARGET attribute is useful for targeting the effects of hyperlinks, you can use it in other HTML tags as well. Placing the TARGET attribute in a `<FORM>` tag instructs the browser to target the response from the form submission to the specified frame. This enables you to set up a search form in one frame and have the search results appear in a separate frame.

Another tag that takes the TARGET attribute is the `<AREA>` tag, which is used to define a hot region in a client-side imagemap. This permits the document associated with a hot region to be loaded into the frame of your choice.

Finally, you can also use the TARGET attribute with the `<LINK>` tag. `<LINK>` is used to establish links to files that provide supporting information to a browser on how to render a file. You can link a style sheet to a page for example, using the `<LINK>` tag.

Respecting the Frames-Challenged Browsers

If you create a document with frames, people who are using a browser other than Netscape Navigator 4.0 or Microsoft Internet Explorer 4.0 might not be able to see the content you want them to see because their browsers don't understand the `<FRAMESET>`, `</FRAMESET>`, and `<FRAME>` tags. As a courtesy to users with frames-challenged browsers, you can place alternative HTML code between the `<NOFRAMES>` and `</NOFRAMES>` container tags. Any HTML between these two tags is understood and rendered by other browsers. A frames-capable browser, on the other hand, ignores anything between these tags and works just with the frame-related HTML.

Part
II

Ch
7

N O T E You should also consider providing <NOFRAMES> content for browsers running on screens with a 640×480 monitor. Frames are difficult to use at that resolution. ▪

Some users have a browser that can render frames, but the users dislike framed documents. For this portion of your audience, you should consider having a non-frames version of all your pages available (see Figure 7.8). This way, users who like frames can stick with them, and those who don't like frames have a way to view the same content without being burdened with an uncomfortable interface.

T I P When making framed versions of existing pages, don't discard your non-frames content. Very often, you can use the non-frames HTML documents as the alternative content found between the <NOFRAMES> and </NOFRAMES> tags.

CAUTION

The <NOFRAMES> and </NOFRAMES> tags must occur after the initial <FRAMESET> tag, but before any nested <FRAMESET> tags.

FIGURE 7.8

Providing a non-frames version of your framed content is an important user courtesy.

Link to non-frames version

Creating Floating Frames

Microsoft introduced the concept of a floating frame with Internet Explorer 3. You can think of a floating frame as a smaller browser window that you can open in your main browser window—much like the picture-in-a-picture feature that comes with many television sets. The same as with regular frames, you can load any HTML document you want into a floating frame. The primary difference is that floating frames can be placed anywhere on a page that you can place an image. In fact, you'll find the HTML syntax for placing floating frames to be similar to that for placing an image.

You place a floating frame on a page by using the `<IFRAME>` and `</IFRAME>` tags. A browser that can do floating frames ignores anything between these two tags, enabling you to place an alternative to the floating frame (most likely text or an image) on the page as well. This way, browsers that don't know how to render floating frames can ignore the `<IFRAME>` and `</IFRAME>` tags and act on what is found between them. The `<IFRAME>` tag can take the attributes summarized in Table 7.2.

Table 7.2   Attributes of the *<IFRAME>* Tag

Attribute	Purpose
`ALIGN=LEFT¦RIGHT`	Floats the floating frame in the left or right margin
`FRAMEBORDER=0¦1`	Controls the presence of the beveled border around the floating frame
`HEIGHT=pixels¦percent`	Specifies the height of the floating frame
`LONGDESC="url"`	Provides the URL of a document that gives a more detailed description of what's in the floating frame; useful for non-visual browsers
`NAME="frame_name"`	Gives the floating frame a unique name so it can be targeted by hyperlinks
`SCROLLING=YES¦NO¦AUTO`	Controls the presence of scrollbars on the floating frame
`SRC="url"`	Specifies the URL of the document to load into the floating frame
`WIDTH=pixels¦percent`	Specifies the width of the floating frame

The `<IFRAME>` tag has three required attributes: `WIDTH`, `HEIGHT`, and `SRC`. `WIDTH` and `HEIGHT` specify the width and height of the floating frame in pixels or as a percentage of the browser screen's width and height. `SRC` tells the browser the URL of the document to load into the floating frame. Thus, your basic floating frame HTML looks like this:

```
<IFRAME WIDTH=250 HEIGHT=112 SRC="http://www.server.com/floating.html">
Text or image-based alternative to the floating frame
</IFRAME>
```

In addition to the three required attributes, the `<IFRAME>` tag takes several other attributes that give you good control over the floating frame's appearance. These include

- FRAMEBORDER—By setting `FRAMEBORDER=1`, you place a beveled border around the floating frame. This gives the frame the appearance of being slightly recessed on the page. If you prefer a more seamless look (as in Figure 7.9), you can use the `FRAMEBORDER` attribute in the `<IFRAME>` tag. Setting `FRAMEBORDER=0` eliminates the beveled border.

Part

II

Ch

7

FIGURE 7.9

Floating frames enable you to place a new document right in the middle of the main document. The quote you see on this page is actually randomly selected from within a floating frame.

Floating frame

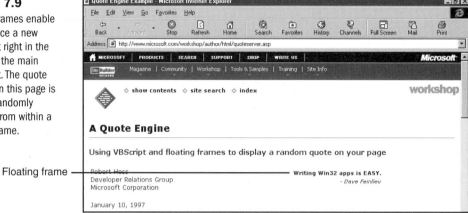

- ![] SCROLLING—A browser that can render floating frames puts a scrollbar on the floating frame if the document it contains exceeds the dimensions of the frame. You can suppress the scrollbars by specifying SCROLLING=NO in the <IFRAME> tag. If you always want scrollbars present, you can set SCROLLING equal to YES.

- ![] LONGDESC—Speech- and Braille-based browsers can use the URL specified by the LONGDESC attribute to get more information about what's being presented in the floating frame.

- ![] ALIGN—You can float the floating frame in the left or right margins by specifying ALIGN=LEFT or ALIGN=RIGHT. Any text following the floated frame wraps around it to the right or left, respectively. You can use the <BR> tag with the appropriate CLEAR attribute to break to the first line clear of floated frames.

- ![] NAME—Naming a floating frame enables you to target it with the TARGET attribute in an <A> tag. Thus, you can set up links to documents and have them appear in the floating frame.

N O T E Early incarnations of the <IFRAME> tag took the HSPACE and VSPACE attributes. If your floating frame needs some clear space around it, the HSPACE and VSPACE attributes of the <IFRAME> tag work the same as they do for the <IMG> tag: HSPACE adds clear space to the left and right of the floating frame, and VSPACE adds clear space above and below. HSPACE and VSPACE values are in pixels.

The HTML 4.0 recommendation does not include these attributes for the <IFRAME> tag, so if you use them, be aware that you are using nonstandard HTML. ![]

Using Hidden Frames

A technique that has emerged recently involves the use of hidden frames. Hidden frames are frames that have no size and, therefore, are not visible to a user. You might set up a hidden frame with code such as

```
<FRAMESET ROWS="30%,70%,*">
   <FRAME SRC="frame1.html" NAME="frame1">
   <FRAME SRC="frame2.html" NAME="frame2">
   <FRAME SRC="frame3.html" NAME="hidden_frame">
</FRAMESET>
```

This creates a frameset with three rows. The first row has a height equal to 30% of the browser window height, the second row a height equal to 70% of the browser screen, and the third row a height of whatever is left over. However, because the entire browser window height is consumed by the first two rows, the third row has a height of zero and is hidden from view.

You may be asking: if a frame can't be seen, what good is it? The answer is that it is good for behind-the-scenes kinds of activity such as JavaScripting. When Netscape released its NetHelp online help package with Navigator 4, it used JavaScript tucked away in hidden frames to control aspects of the NetHelp interface such as the processing stack, activity tracking, and error handling. JavaScript code for all these functions is read into a hidden frame named SystemFrame, and a NetHelp application is able to make calls to this frame to invoke script code when needed.

Another use of hidden frames is in applications developed in ColdFusion or Active Server Pages. With either technology, an HTML document is dynamically generated and returned to the browser. Occasionally, it is appropriate to build a hidden frame into the HTML document that contains state information that cannot be stored as a cookie or on the server.

▶ **See** "Active Server Pages and VBScript," **p. 835.**

▶ **See** "Using ColdFusion," **p. 879.**

Developing Framed Layouts in an HTML Editor

When the frame tags first came on the scene, many content developers were challenged by their complexity. Things were made worse by having to do all the code by hand and without the luxury of any kind of WYSIWYG preview capability. Fortunately, most top-notch content development programs now include some support for authoring framed documents. This chapter closes with a look at three such programs.

Microsoft FrontPage 98

The FrontPage 98 Editor has its own Frames menu from which you can initiate just about any frames-related task. To get started with a framed layout, choose Frames, New Frames Page to call up the dialog box you see in Figure 7.10. Here you find a list of 10 preconfigured framed layouts that FrontPage can set up for you automatically.

N O T E You can access this same list of available framed layouts by choosing File, New, and then clicking the Frames tab. ▪

As you highlight the different selections, you see a preview of how each breaks up the browser screen. After you find the one you want, click OK and the framed layout is loaded into the Editor. Figure 7.11 shows the Header, Footer and Contents layout.

Part

II

Ch

7

FIGURE 7.10

The FrontPage Editor can set up <FRAMESET> tags for 10 framed layouts.

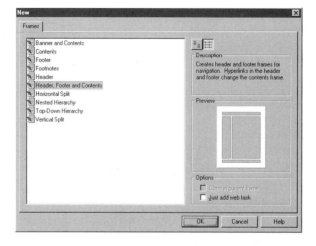

FIGURE 7.11

A selected frame layout gets loaded into the FrontPage Editor, where you can work on each frame individually.

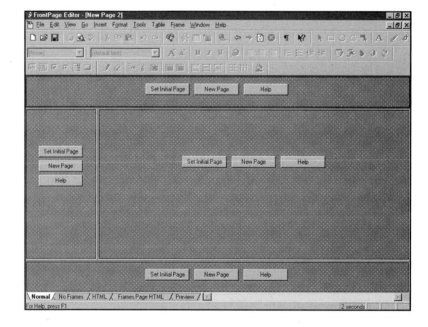

Note in Figure 7.11 that each frame initially has three buttons in it. The Set Initial Page button enables you to assign an existing document to that frame. Clicking the button enables you to browse to find the file. The New Page button clears out the frame and enables you to work the same as you would in the full FrontPage Editor window. You click this button if you have not yet prepared any content for the frame.

Another thing to notice is how the tabs near the bottom of the Editor window change. When you are working with a framed layout, you get two extra tabs: No Frames, to show you what your framed document will look like on a browser that doesn't support frames, and Frames Page HTML, which contains all the <FRAMESET> tags that make the layout possible.

After you have a framed layout in place, you can start using the other options found under the Frames menu. The Split Frame option enables you to subdivide your selected frame (denoted by a blue outline) into two equal rows or columns. Choosing Delete Frame eliminates the selected frame and reduces the framed layout to whatever frames are left after the deletion. The Set Initial Page option repeats the functionality of the button bearing the same label. If you prefer to create the content for a frame in a full-sized window, you can choose the Open Page in a New Window option. The Save Page and Save Page As options enable you to save the content you've developed for a frame.

The last two options in the Frames menu enable you to alter properties of either the entire framed layout or one of the frames within the layout. Choosing the Frames Page Properties option opens the dialog box shown in Figure 7.12 where you can specify attributes of the whole layout, such as whether to display borders, how much spacing to use between frames, what kinds of margins to use, what to use as a background, and how to title the layout.

FIGURE 7.12

Because the framed layout is created by an HTML document, you can alter many of the same properties for the layout as you can for any document.

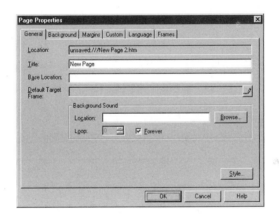

The Frame Properties option launches the dialog box shown in Figure 7.13. Here you can modify the attributes of the select frame, including whether the frame can be resized, whether it should have scrollbars, what its height and width should be, what margins should be used inside the frame, and what the frame's initial page should be. A Frames Page button opens the Frames Page Properties dialog box you saw in Figure 7.12.

Allaire HomeSite

Allaire's HomeSite tends to be focused on creating an HTML document at the source code level, enabling you to work directly with the HTML tags. HomeSite provides good support for creating a framed layout, including a wizard that walks you through the set up of the layout and then writes out the appropriate HTML tags that reproduce the layout on a browser screen.

Part
II

Ch
7

FIGURE 7.13

Each frame in the layout has its own set of properties that you can tweak as needed.

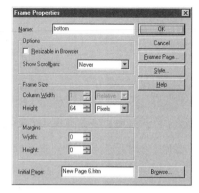

Most of HomeSite's frames support resides on the Frames toolbar, which is found on the Frames tab of the HomeSite SpeedBar (see Figure 7.14). The various buttons on the bar provide different levels of support, and you are free to choose whichever ones are best suited to your authoring preferences.

FIGURE 7.14

The HomeSite Frames toolbar gives you access to a Frame Wizard, dialog boxes that collect frame tag attributes, or just the frame tags themselves.

Frame Wizard button (leftmost button on Frames toolbar)

Frames toolbar

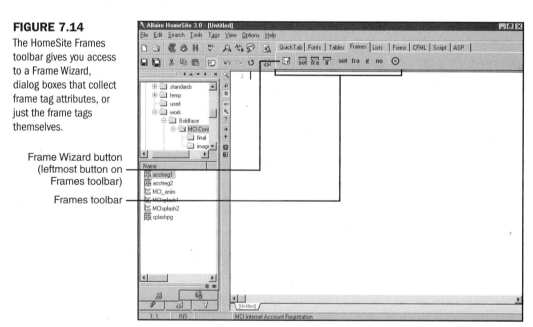

The leftmost button on the toolbar launches the HomeSite Frame Wizard. Like most wizards, the Frame Wizard takes you through a sequence of dialog boxes wherein you specify how you want your framed layout to be set up. After the wizard has all the information it needs, it writes the <FRAMESET> tags that create your desired layout. When you fire up the wizard, you're first asked if you want to split the screen into rows or columns. With this information collected, the wizard gives you a preview of what your layout will look like (see Figure 7.15). In the same dialog box where you see the preview, you can also establish the properties of each of the individual frames, including its name, source document URL, margin width and height, whether scrollbars should be present, and whether the user should be able to resize the frame.

 T I P You can also invoke the Frame Wizard by selecting File, New, and then selecting the Frame Wizard document.

FIGURE 7.15

HomeSite's Frame Wizard is more flexible than the preset frames configurations you get with FrontPage.

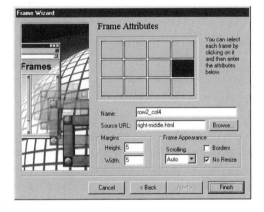

After you set the parameters for each of the frames in your layout, click the Finish button to instruct HomeSite to create the <FRAMESET> and <FRAME> tags that will support the layout. HomeSite writes this code right into the main editing window.

N O T E After you set up the <FRAMESET> and <FRAME> tags, you still need to create the files that will populate each frame. ■

The Frame Wizard is HomeSite's most automated form of frames support. Just to the right of the Frame Wizard button are three other buttons that open dialog boxes for setting up <FRAMESET>, <FRAME>, and <IFRAME> tags, respectively. If you're the type of author who likes placing your own tags, but you don't mind a little help setting up the attributes, then you'll make use of these buttons. As Figure 7.16 shows, you can specify every attribute of the <IFRAME> tag from the dialog box and then click Apply to write the entire tag into your document.

The remaining five buttons on the toolbar place a tag in the document, after which it falls to you to go back and add in any attributes you need. The first four buttons place the <FRAMESET>, <FRAME>, <IFRAME>, and <NOFRAMES> tags, respectively, including closing tags where appropriate. The rightmost button on the toolbar adds a <BASE> tag to your document with the TARGET attribute so you can set up global targeting within the document.

Adobe PageMill

Frames are simple to construct using PageMill; the necessary frameset and HTML source code are transparently generated while you construct the frames using drag-and-drop techniques.

Part

II

Ch

7

FIGURE 7.16

Other buttons on the Frames toolbar are more tag focused, enabling you to set up an entire tag in one step.

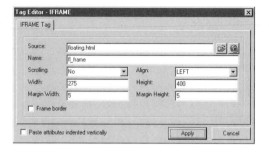

To build a framed document in PageMill, start with a blank page. Hold down the Ctrl key while dragging from one of the window margins. You'll notice that, in effect, you drag a border across the page. You can create horizontal or vertical frame elements in this manner.

TIP Holding the Ctrl key while moving borders enables you to create new frames. Dragging the borders without holding the Ctrl key simply moves the borders.

When you create frames in PageMill, several files are actually constructed. The base document, which starts out as a blank page, contains the frameset. This file describes the names of the different frames, as well as their sizes and other attributes. The HTML code used to populate the different frames named in your frameset is stored in various other files. Opening the frameset file in PageMill launches the entire suite of frames. In contrast, opening the HTML source code for one of the frames merely brings up the frame contents in an isolated PageMill window.

You can select frames in your PageMill document by clicking their contents. When selected, the frame borders are highlighted. You save the content in a single frame by selecting it and saving it individually. If you resize any of the frames, you are prompted to save the frameset. PageMill arbitrarily assigns names to the individual frames; when saving the frame HTML, PageMill creates filenames with the frame name appended with an HTML suffix.

TIP PageMill enables you to individually save frames, to save the frameset, or, most usefully, to save the entire set of frames. Located under the File menu you will see the Frameset, Save Everything command, which saves the individual frame HTML as well as the frameset in the proper files.

To modify your frames, you might want to use the utility called the PageMill Attributes Inspector. As described in the last chapter, the Inspector enables you to specify the attributes for objects (tables, graphics, and so on), forms, frames, and pages, with each attribute set arranged on a different tab. To access the Inspector, press F8 or select Show Inspector from the View menu. The Frame tab is one of four major tabs available in the Attributes Inspector.

As depicted in Figure 7.17, the Frame tab enables you to modify attributes of the individual frames. Simply select one of the frames in the frameset and activate the Inspector.

FIGURE 7.17

It's easy to modify a series of frames using the PageMill Inspector.

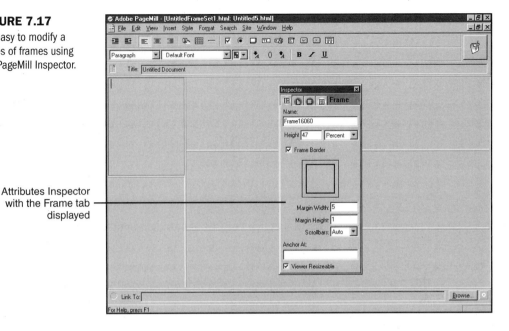

Attributes Inspector with the Frame tab displayed

Notice that you can change the names of the different frames to something that is perhaps more meaningful than the name Assigned by PageMill. This can help you to keep better track of the nature of the content in each frame. Furthermore, the width of the frame can be changed or expressed using different bases; you can express the frame width as

■ A percentage of the browser window width

■ A set number of pixels

■ Relative to other frames in the frameset

Notice in Figure 7.17 that you can also set the height and width of the frame margins. Furthermore, you can specify whether the frames will contain margins and if the user will have the ability to manually resize the frame.

Naturally, you want to set up hypertext links between your different frame documents. This is accomplished by assigning targets to the links described in different frames. PageMill has a special function that aids in assigning targets to your individual URLs.

Triple-click a link to select it; then right-click the link after it's selected. A box appears that gives you a variety of choices from which you can send pages corresponding to the link. You can do the following:

■ Open the link in the default frame

■ Open the link in a new window

■ Open the link in the parent window

Part

II

Ch

7

- Open the link in the same frame
- Open the link in the same window

You might notice a map at the bottom of the pop-up box that mimics the structure of the open frameset document. You can also drag the mouse pointer over to one of the representative frames in the pop-up image to denote a target frame for a given link. ●

## CHAPTER 8

Forms

by Eric Ladd

In this chapter

Overview: Forms and CGI

As the Web becomes more interactive, the need for interface components to gather data from users is greater than ever. Fortunately, this need was anticipated in earlier versions of HTML and resulted in the introduction of the form tags. *Forms* are the visible or front-end portion of interactive pages. Users enter information into form fields or controls—user interface elements that are similar to those found on Windows and Macintosh operating systems—and click a button to submit the data. The browser then packages the data, opens an HTTP connection, and sends the data to a server. Things then move to the transparent or back-end part of the process.

Web servers are programs that know how to distribute Web pages. They are not programmed to process data from every possible form, so the best they can do is hand off the form data to a program that does know what to do with it. This handoff occurs with the help of the *Common Gateway Interface* or *CGI*—a set of standards by which servers communicate with external programs.

The program that processes the form data is called a *CGI script* or a *CGI program*. The script or program performs manipulations of the data and composes a response—typically an HTML page. The response page is handed back to the server (via CGI), which in turn passes it along to the browser that initiated the request.

▶ To learn more about CGI programming, **see** "Programming CGI Scripts," **p. 689**.

Forms and CGI are opposite sides of the same coin. Both are essential to creating interactive pages, but it is the forms side of the coin that the user sees. This chapter examines how to create Web forms and gives an overview of some of the behind-the-scenes activity that has to occur to produce the custom pages, electronic commerce sites, and other dynamic functionality that Web users have come to love.

N O T E When a CGI script or program composes an HTML page, it is said to be generating HTML *on-the-fly*. The capability to generate pages on-the-fly is what makes custom responses to database and forms submission possible. ▨

Creating Forms

HTML's form support is simple and complete. A handful of HTML tags create the most popular elements of modern graphical interfaces, including text windows, check boxes and radio buttons, pull-down menus, and push buttons.

Composing HTML forms might sound like a complex task, but you need to master surprisingly few tags to do it. All form-related tags occur between the <FORM> and </FORM> container tags. If you have more than one form in an HTML document, the closing </FORM> tag is essential for distinguishing between the multiple forms.

TIP Adding a </FORM> tag immediately after creating a <FORM> tag is a good practice; then you can go back to fill in the contents. Following this procedure helps you avoid leaving off the closing tag after you finish. Many of today's popular HTML editing programs take care of placing the </FORM> tag for you, so be sure to check to see if the editor you're using does this.

Each HTML form has three main components: the form header, one or more named input fields, and one or more action buttons.

The *<FORM>* Tag

The form header and the <FORM> tag are actually one and the same. The <FORM> tag takes the six attributes shown in Table 8.1. The ACTION attribute is required in every <FORM> tag.

Table 8.1 Attributes of the *<FORM>* Tag

Attribute	Purpose
ACCEPT	Specifies a list of MIME types that the server will process correctly
ACCEPT-CHARSET	Provides a list of character sets that are acceptable to the server
ACTION	Specifies the URL of the processing script
ENCTYPE	Supplies the MIME type of a file used as form input
METHOD=GET¦POST	Tells the browser how it should send the form data to the server
TARGET	Gives the name of the frame where the response from the form submission is to appear

ACTION is set equal to the URL of the processing script so that the browser knows where to send the form data after it is entered. Without it, the browser has no idea where the form data should go. A full ACTION URL has the following form:

```
protocol://server/path/script_file
```

You can also use a relative URL if you are calling a script on the same server.

METHOD specifies the HTTP method to use when passing the data to the script and can be set to values of GET or POST. When you're using the GET method, the browser appends the form data to the end of the URL of the processing script. The POST method sends the form data to the server in a separate HTTP transaction.

METHOD is not a mandatory attribute of the <FORM> tag. In the absence of a specified method, the browser uses the GET method.

CAUTION

Some servers might have operating environment limitations that prevent them from processing a URL that exceeds a certain number of characters—typically one kilobyte of data. This limitation can be a problem when you're using the GET method to pass a large amount of form data. Because the GET method appends the data to the end of the processing script URL, you run a greater risk of passing a URL that's too big for the server to handle. If URL size limitations are a concern on your server, you should use the POST method to pass form data.

The ENCTYPE attribute was introduced by Netscape for the purpose of providing a file name to be uploaded as form input. You set ENCTYPE equal to the MIME type expected for the file being uploaded. ENCTYPE does not create the input field for the filename; rather, it gives the browser a cue as to what kind of file it is sending. When prompting for a file to upload, you need to use an <INPUT> tag with TYPE set equal to FILE.

As an example of these three <FORM> tag attributes, examine the following HTML:

```
<FORM ACTION="logo_upload.cgi" METHOD=POST ENCTYPE="image/gif">
Please enter the name of the GIF file containing your logo:
<INPUT TYPE="FILE" NAME="logo">
<INPUT TYPE="SUBMIT" VALUE="Upload">
</FORM>
```

The form header of this short form instructs the server to process the form data using the program named logo_upload.cgi. Form data is passed using the POST method, and the expected type of file being submitted is a GIF file.

New <FORM> tag attributes in HTML 4.0 include TARGET, which is used to direct the response from the processing script to a particular frame; ACCEPT, which denotes the MIME types of files that the server processing the form can handle correctly (this is useful when a user is submitting a set of files to the server because you can then check to make sure that all the submitted files are of an acceptable MIME type); and ACCEPT-CHARSET, which specifies the character sets the server understands. Incorporating these attributes, the code above might look like this:

```
<FORM ACTION="logo_upload.cgi" METHOD=POST ENCTYPE="image/gif"
  ACCEPT="image/gif,image/jpeg" TARGET="main"
  ACCEPT-CHARSET="EUC-JP">
Please enter the name of the GIF file containing your logo:
<INPUT TYPE="FILE" NAME="logo">
<INPUT TYPE="SUBMIT" VALUE="Upload">
</FORM>
```

The EUC-JP value for the ACCEPT-CHARSET attribute suggests the use of a Japanese character set to the server that processes the form.

The <FORM> tag can also take two event handlers—onSubmit and onReset. This gives you the capability to execute some script code when the form is submitted or reset, respectively. If you write a JavaScript function that validates the data a user enters into a form, for example, you could invoke the script using an event handler as follows:

```
<FORM ACTION="upload_logo.cgi" onSubmit="validateform()">
```

▶ To learn more about using JavaScript to validate form input, **see** "Using JavaScript to Create Smart Forms," **p. 513**.

Named Input Fields

The named input fields typically compose the bulk of a form. The fields appear as standard GUI controls, such as text boxes, check boxes, radio buttons, and menus. You assign each field a unique name that eventually becomes the variable name used in the processing script.

TIP If you are not coding your own processing scripts, be sure to sit down with your programmer to agree on variable names. The names used in the form should exactly match those used in coding the script.

You can use different GUI controls to enter information into forms. The controls for named input fields appear in Table 8.2.

Table 8.2   Types of Named Input Fields

Field Type	HTML Tag(s)
text box	`<INPUT TYPE="TEXT">`
password box	`<INPUT TYPE="PASSWORD">`
check box	`<INPUT TYPE="CHECKBOX">`
radio button	`<INPUT TYPE="RADIO">`
hidden field	`<INPUT TYPE="HIDDEN">`
file	`<INPUT TYPE="FILE">`
text window	`<TEXTAREA>...</TEXTAREA>`
menu	`<SELECT>...<OPTION>...</SELECT>`

The *<INPUT>* Tag

You might notice in Table 8.2 that the `<INPUT>` tag handles the majority of named input fields. `<INPUT>` is a standalone tag that, thanks to the many values of its TYPE attribute, can place most of the fields you need on your forms. `<INPUT>` also takes other attributes depending on which TYPE is in use. These additional attributes are covered for each type, as appropriate, over the next several sections.

N O T E   The `<INPUT>` tag and other tags that produce named input fields create only the fields themselves. You, as the form designer, must include some descriptive text next to each field so that users know what information to enter. You might also need to use line breaks (`<BR>`), paragraph breaks (`<P>`), and nonbreaking space (` `) to create the spacing you want between form fields. ▪

TIP Because browsers ignore whitespace, lining up the left edges of text input boxes on multiple lines is difficult because the text to the left of the boxes is of different lengths. In this instance, HTML tables are invaluable. By setting up the text labels and input fields as cells in the same row of an HTML table, you can produce a nicely formatted form. To learn more about forms using table conventions, consult Chapter 6, "Tables."

Text and Password Fields   Text and password fields are simple data entry fields. The only difference between them is that text typed into a password field appears onscreen as asterisks (*).

> **CAUTION**
>
> Using a password field protects users' passwords from the people looking over their shoulders, but it does not protect the password as it travels over the Internet. To protect password data as it moves from browser to server, you need to use some type of encryption (usually by *Secure Sockets Layer,* or *SSL,* on the Web server) or a similar security measure. Authentication of both the server and client by using signed digital certificates are two other steps you can take to keep Internet transactions secure.

A text or password field is produced by the HTML (attributes in square brackets are optional):

```
<INPUT TYPE="{TEXT|PASSWORD}" NAME="Name" [VALUE="default_text"]
[SIZE="width"] [MAXLENGTH="max_width"]>
```

The NAME attribute is mandatory because it provides a unique identifier for the data entered into the field.

The optional VALUE attribute enables you to place some default text in the field, rather than have it initially appear blank. This capability is useful if a majority of users will enter a certain text string into the field. In such cases, you can use VALUE to put the text into the field, thereby saving most users the effort of typing it.

The optional SIZE attribute gives you control over how many characters wide the field should be. The default SIZE is typically about 20 characters, although this number can vary from browser to browser. MAXLENGTH is also optional and enables you to specify the maximum number of characters that can be entered into the field.

Figure 8.1 shows a form on Crestar Bank's Internet Banking site used to prompt for a Customer Number and PIN (password). Notice how password text appears as asterisks. The corresponding HTML is shown in Listing 8.1.

Listing 8.1   HTML Code to Produce Text and Password Fields

```
<DIV ALIGN=left>
<IMG SRC="images/drop_p.gif" WIDTH=18 HEIGHT=28 BORDER=0 HSPACE=0
VSPACE=0 ALIGN="BOTTOM">lease enter your Customer Number
<BR>and Personal Identification Number (PIN).</DIV>
<P><BR><P><BR><P>
Customer Number:
<INPUT TYPE="text" NAME="cin" SIZE="12" MAXLENGTH="9" VALUE="">
```

```
<BR>
Pin:
<INPUT TYPE="password" NAME="pin" SIZE="12" MAXLENGTH="4" VALUE=">
<P>
```

FIGURE 8.1

Text and password fields are frequently used together to produce a login interface.

Text field ——

Password field ——

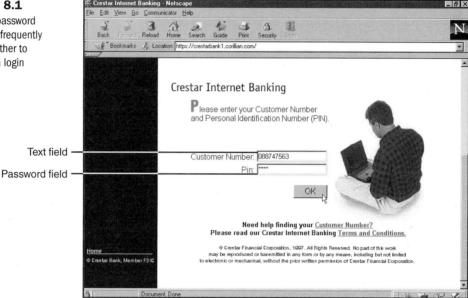

Check Boxes   Check boxes are used to provide users with several choices from which they can select as many of the choices as they want. An <INPUT> tag that is used to produce a check box option has the following syntax:

```
<INPUT TYPE="CHECKBOX" NAME="Name" VALUE="Value" [CHECKED]>
```

Each check box option is created by its own <INPUT> tag and must have its own unique NAME. If you give multiple check box options the same NAME, the script has no way to determine which choices the user actually made.

The VALUE attribute specifies which data is sent to the server if the corresponding check box is chosen. This information is transparent to the user. The optional CHECKED attribute preselects a commonly selected check box when the form is rendered on the browser screen.

Figure 8.2 shows the Flight Wizard on Microsoft's Expedia travel site. When searching for flights, you can choose to look for flights with no change penalties, flights with no advance purchase requirement, direct flights, or any combination of these by putting checks in the appropriate check boxes. The HTML that produces the check boxes is shown in Listing 8.2.

N O T E   If they are selected, check box options show up in the form data sent to the server. Options that are not selected do not appear. ■

FIGURE 8.2

Users can choose as
many check box options
as they prefer.

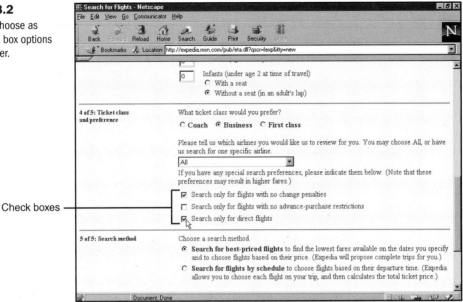

Check boxes

Listing 8.2 HTML Code to Produce Check Boxes

```
<TABLE BORDER=0>
<TR>
    <TD HEIGHT=3> </TD>
</TR>
<TR>
    <TD VALIGN=TOP><INPUT TYPE=CHECKBOX NAME=tktp VALUE=1 ></TD>
    <TD VALIGN=TOP>Search only for flights with no change penalties</TD>
</TR>
<TR>
    <TD VALIGN=TOP ><INPUT TYPE=CHECKBOX NAME=tktr VALUE=1 ></TD>
    <TD VALIGN=TOP>Search only for flights with no advance-purchase
    restrictions</TD>
</TR>
<TR>
    <TD VALIGN=TOP ><INPUT TYPE=CHECKBOX NAME=tktc VALUE=1 ></TD>
    <TD VALIGN=TOP>Search only for direct flights</TD>
</TR>
</TABLE>
```

Radio Buttons Radio buttons are used to present users with a set of choices from which they can choose only one. When you set up options with a radio button format, you should make sure that the options are mutually exclusive so that a user doesn't try to select more than one.

The HTML code used to produce a set of three radio button options is as follows:

```
<FORM ...>
<INPUT TYPE="RADIO" NAME="Name" VALUE="VALUE1" [CHECKED]>Option 1<P>
```

```
<INPUT TYPE="RADIO" NAME="Name" VALUE="VALUE2">Option 2<P>
<INPUT TYPE="RADIO" NAME="Name" VALUE="VALUE3">Option 3<P>
...
</FORM>
```

The VALUE and CHECKED attributes work the same as they do for check boxes, although you should have only one preselected radio button option. A fundamental difference with a set of radio button options is that they all have the same NAME. This is permissible because the user can select only one of the options.

A new user of the Netscape/AOL Instant Messenger Service would need to select a privacy radio button value as shown in Figure 8.3; the corresponding HTML is in Listing 8.3.

FIGURE 8.3

Users can choose only one of a set of radio button options.

Radio buttons

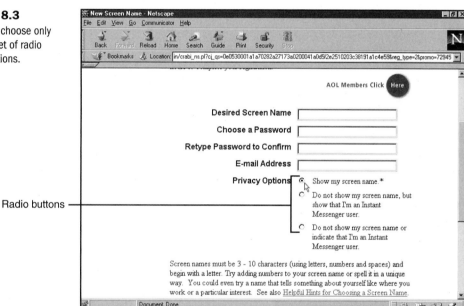

Listing 8.3   HTML Code to Produce Radio Buttons

```
<TR VALIGN="top" ALIGN="left">
  <TD ALIGN="right">
    <B><FONT FACE="Arial,Helvetica">Privacy Options</FONT></B>
  </TD>
  <TD>
    <INPUT TYPE="radio" NAME="privacy" VALUE=1 CHECKED >
  </TD>
  <TD>
    Show my screen name.*
  </TD>
<TR VALIGN="top" ALIGN="left">
  <TD></TD>
  <TD>
```

continues

Listing 8.3 Continued

```
    <INPUT TYPE="radio" NAME="privacy" VALUE=2>
  </TD>
  <TD>
    Do not show my screen name, but show that
    <FONT COLOR="#000000">I'm an Instant Messenger user.</FONT>
  </TD>
</TR>
<TR VALIGN="top" ALIGN="left">
  <TD></TD>
  <TD>
    <INPUT TYPE="radio" NAME="privacy" VALUE=3>
  </TD>
  <TD>
    Do not show my screen name or indicate
    <FONT COLOR="#000000">that I'm an Instant Messenger user.</FONT>
  </TD>
</TR>
```

N O T E   Just as with check boxes, values for radio button fields are not sent to the server if no option is selected. ▪

Hidden Fields   Technically, hidden fields are not meant for data input. You can send information to the server about a form without displaying that information anywhere on the form itself. The general format for including hidden fields is as follows:

```
<INPUT TYPE="HIDDEN" NAME="name" VALUE="value">
```

One possible use of hidden fields is to enable a single general script to process data from different forms. The script needs to know which form is sending the data, and a hidden field can provide this information without requiring anything on the part of the user.

Because HTTP is a stateless protocol (information from the user's session is not tracked), it is not possible for the input from one form to be carried forward to another. Thus, another application of hidden fields is doing just that. This enables you to split up a long form into several smaller forms and still keep all the user's input in one place by passing it from one form to the next in the sequence. Suppose, for example, that in the first of a sequence of several forms, you collect a visitor's name and mailing address. That information is passed to the script that processes the form. Because part of what this script has to do is build the next form in the sequence, it would be an easy matter to have the script include in the next form hidden fields that carry the name and address information forward.

N O T E   Because hidden fields are transparent to users, it doesn't matter where you put them in your HTML code. Just make sure they occur between the <FORM> and </FORM> tags that define the form that contains the hidden fields. ▪

Hidden fields are integral in the development of ColdFusion and Active Server Page applications. Look for examples of hidden field usage as you read Chapter 33, "Active Server Pages and VBScript," and Chapter 34, "Using ColdFusion."

Files   You can upload an entire file to a server by using a form. The first step is to include the ENCTYPE attribute in the <FORM> tag. To enter a filename in a field, the user needs the <INPUT> tag with TYPE set equal to FILE:

```
<FORM ACTION="upload.cgi" ENCTYPE="application/x-www-form-urlencoded">
What file would you like to submit: <INPUT TYPE="FILE" NAME="upload_file">
...
</FORM>
```

Being able to send an entire file is useful when submitting a document produced by another program—for example, an Excel spreadsheet, a résumé in Word format, or a compiled executable file.

N O T E   You can also use the ACCEPT attribute when you have an <INPUT> field of type FILE to specify the MIME types of files that are acceptable for upload.

N O T E   File upload fields are usually accompanied by a Browse button that enables users to browse to the file that they want to upload. The Browse button is supplied by the browser, and you don't need to do anything special to place the button there.

CAUTION

Depending on the user's browser version and operating system, it's possible for the name of the file that gets copied to the Web server to not match the name of the source file. That is, a user could submit budget.xls from her machine and the file copied onto the server might have some other name. Be sure to test your applications that use file upload fields to verify that the naming stays consistent.

Multiple Line Text Windows

Text and password boxes are used for simple, one-line input fields. You can create multiline text windows that function in much the same way by using the <TEXTAREA> and </TEXTAREA> container tags. The HTML syntax for a text window is as follows:

```
<TEXTAREA NAME="Name" [ROWS="rows"] [COLS="columns"]>
Default_window_text
</TEXTAREA>
```

The NAME attribute gives the text window a unique identifier, the same as it does with the variations on the <INPUT> tag. The optional ROWS and COLS attributes enable you to specify the dimensions of the text window as it appears on the browser screen. The default number of rows and columns varies by browser.

The text that appears between the <TEXTAREA> and </TEXTAREA> tags shows up in the input window by default. To type in something else, users need to delete the default text and enter their text.

Multiline text windows are ideal for entry of long pieces of text, such as feedback comments or email messages (see the Concert Feedback page in Figure 8.4 and corresponding code in Listing 8.4). Some corporate sites on the Web that collect information on potential employees might ask you to copy and paste your entire résumé into multiline text windows!

FIGURE 8.4

A multiline text window is ideal for gathering free-response text, such as comments or feedback.

Multiline text window

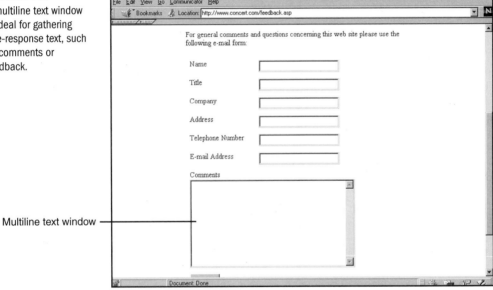

Listing 8.4 HTML Code to Produce a Multiline Text Window

```
<TR valign="top">
<TD colspan=2>Comments<BR>
<TEXTAREA name="comments" cols="40" rows="10"></TEXTAREA>
</TD>
</TR>
```

A useful attribute of the <TEXTAREA> tag that is supported by Netscape Navigator 4 and Internet Explorer 4 is WRAP. WRAP is a Boolean attribute that, when present, instructs the browser to wrap text within the input window rather than to let it scroll horizontally. Users will appreciate your use of this attribute because it spares them from having to remember to press the Enter key each time they want to move to a new line in the text window.

Menus

The final technique for creating a named input field is to use the `<SELECT>` and `</SELECT>` container tags to produce pull-down or scrollable option menus (see Figure 8.5 and Listing 8.5). The HTML code used to create a general menu is as follows:

```
<FORM ...>
<SELECT NAME="Name" [SIZE="size"] [MULTIPLE]>
<OPTION [SELECTED]>Option 1</OPTION>
<OPTION [SELECTED]>Option 2</OPTION>
<OPTION [SELECTED]>Option 3</OPTION>
...
<OPTION [SELECTED]>Option n</OPTION>
</SELECT>
....
</FORM>
```

In the `<SELECT>` tag, the NAME attribute again gives the input field a unique identifier. The optional SIZE attribute enables you to specify how many options should be displayed when the menu renders on the browser screen. If you have more options than you have space to display them, you can access them either by using a pull-down window or by scrolling through the window with scroll bars. The default SIZE is 1. If you want to let users choose more than one menu option, include the MULTIPLE attribute. When MULTIPLE is specified, users can choose multiple options by holding down the Ctrl key and clicking the options they want.

N O T E If you specify the MULTIPLE attribute and SIZE=1, a one-line scrollable list box displays instead of a drop-down list box. This box appears because you can select only one item (not multiple items) in a drop-down list box. ▪

FIGURE 8.5

Job seekers on www.careerbuilder.com can choose their geographic area and their field of expertise from menus created with the `<SELECT>` tag.

Scrollable list menus

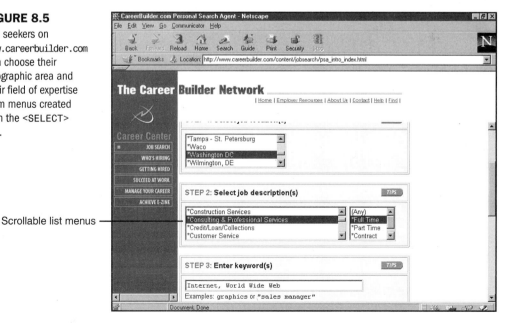

Listing 8.5 HTML Code to Produce a Menu

```
<SELECT MULTIPLE SIZE=4 NAME="nsLO">
<OPTION>(Any)
<OPTION>*Albany - Schenectady-Troy
<OPTION>*Albuquerque
<OPTION>*Anchorage
<OPTION>*Atlanta
<OPTION>*Austin
...
<OPTION>*Waco
<OPTION>*Washington DC
<OPTION>*Wilmington, DE
...
</SELECT>
```

Each option in the menu is specified inside of its own <OPTION> container tag. If you want an option to be preselected, include the SELECT attribute in the appropriate <OPTION> tag. The value passed to the server is the menu item that follows the <OPTION> tag unless you supply an alternative using the VALUE attribute. For example:

```
<FORM ...>
<SELECT NAME="STATE" MULTIPLE>
<OPTION VALUE="NY">New York</OPTION>
<OPTION VALUE="DC">Washington, DC</OPTION>
<OPTION VALUE="FL">Florida</OPTION>
...
</SELECT>
...
</FORM>
```

In the preceding menu, the user clicks a state name, but it is the state's two-letter abbreviation that passes to the server.

NOTE If multiple menu options are selected, all the values are passed to the server using the name specified by the NAME attribute in the <SELECT> tag. This means that multiple "copies" of that variable have to be created—one for each value selected.

In the code above, for example, a user might choose the states of New York and Florida. In that case, you would have two copies of the form field STATE—one set equal to "NY" and the other set equal to "FL," and both would be passed on to the server. This means your processing script has to be ready to handle multiple instances of a variable if they appear. ■

One other tag related to the <SELECT> tag is <OPTGROUP>. <OPTGROUP> and its companion closing tag </OPTGROUP> enable you to create logical groups of menu options. You specify the name to associate with the option group by using the LABEL attribute of the <OPTGROUP> tag.

Grouping-related menu options can be invaluable in a long list of options where it may be difficult for the user to keep track of them all. Consider, for example, the following list of Web server configuration options:

```
<SELECT NAME="server_options" MULTIPLE>
<OPTION>Windows NT 4.0
<OPTION>Solaris 2.6
<OPTION>Netscape Enterprise Server
<OPTION>Apache
<OPTION>Microsoft IIS
<OPTION>Firewall server
<OPTION>Pre-production test server
<OPTION>Emergency backup server
</SELECT>
```

Many options are in the list, but they are something of a mixed bag—a collection of operating systems, HTTP servers, and other support computers. You can use the <OPTGROUP> tag to logically group these options into a more intelligible list:

```
<SELECT NAME="server_options" MULTIPLE>
<OPTGROUP LABEL="Operating Systems">
    <OPTION>Windows NT 4.0
    <OPTION>Solaris 2.6
</OPTGROUP>
<OPTGROUP LABEL="HTTP Servers">
    <OPTION>Netscape Enterprise Server
    <OPTION>Apache
    <OPTION>Microsoft IIS
</OPTGROUP>
<OPTGROUP LABEL="Other Servers">
    <OPTION>Firewall server
    <OPTION>Pre-production test server
    <OPTION>Emergency backup server
</OPTGROUP>
</SELECT>
```

Although it is not required of browsers, one presentation possibility for menus that use logically grouped options is to present a cascading menu—although as of this writing, no major browsers have implemented this approach. When users first see the menu, they see only the names of the option groups. Then, by moving their mouse pointer over one of the option group names, they can reveal the individual options under that group. You can see an example of this behavior in the way a browser handles bookmarks. Bookmarks that are grouped into subfolders are presented via cascading menus (see Figure 8.6).

FIGURE 8.6

Logically grouped menu options may someday be available via cascading menus, like Netscape Navigator bookmarks are.

Logically grouped menu options

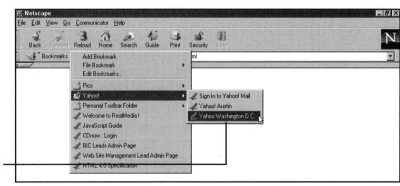

Action Buttons

The handy <INPUT> tag provides an easy way of creating the form action buttons you see in many of the preceding figures. Action buttons can be of two types: Submit and Reset. Clicking a Submit button instructs the browser to package the form data and send it to the server. Clicking a Reset button clears out any data entered into the form and sets all the named input fields back to their default values.

Regular Submit and Reset Buttons Any form you compose should have a Submit button so that users can submit the data they enter. The one exception to this rule is a form containing only one input field. For such a form, pressing Enter automatically submits the data. Reset buttons are technically not necessary but are usually provided as a user courtesy.

TIP Even though you technically don't need to include a Submit button on a single-field form, you should do so as a guide for users who are less experienced with Web forms.

TIP If you want to get fancy, you can leave the Submit button off and use the JavaScript `submit()` method to submit the form. See Chapter 21 for more details.

To create Submit or Reset buttons, use the <INPUT> tags as follows:

```
<INPUT TYPE="SUBMIT" VALUE="Submit Data">
<INPUT TYPE="RESET" VALUE="Clear Data">
```

Use the VALUE attribute to specify the text that appears on the button. You should set VALUE to a text string that concisely describes the function of the button. If VALUE is not specified, the button text is "Submit" for Submit buttons and "Reset" for Reset buttons.

Using Images as Submit Buttons You can create a custom image to be a Submit button for your forms, and you can set up the image so that clicking it instructs the browser to submit the form data (see Figure 8.7). To do this, you set TYPE equal to IMAGE in your <INPUT> tag, and you provide the URL of the image you want to use with the SRC attribute:

```
<INPUT TYPE="IMAGE" SRC="images/submit_button.gif">
```

You can also use the ALIGN attribute in this variation of the <INPUT> tag to control how text appears next to the image (TOP, MIDDLE, or BOTTOM), or to float the image in the left or right margin (LEFT or RIGHT).

Imagemapped Submit Buttons

A future possibility for image-based Submit buttons is to include the USEMAP attribute so that clicking different parts of the image would cause different instructions to be sent to the server. The various instructions would be set up using the <AREA> tag, the same as you set up different URLs in a client-side imagemap. Some details about how the browser would gather and pass the coordinates of the click still need to be ironed out, however, before this becomes standard. Until then, the USEMAP attribute has been reserved for use with the <INPUT TYPE="IMAGE"> tag just for this purpose.

FIGURE 8.7

Images make a
refreshing change from
the standard "gray box"
Submit and Reset
buttons.

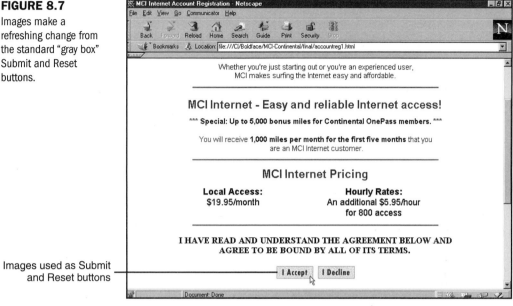

Images used as Submit
and Reset buttons

Listing 8.6   HTML Code to Produce an Image-Based Submit Button

```
<TABLE>
<TR>
  <TD>
    <FORM ACTION="accountreg2.html" METHOD="POST">
    <INPUT TYPE="IMAGE" SRC="accept.gif" ALT="I Accept" BORDER=0>
    </FORM>
</TD>
  <TD>
    <FORM ACTION="index.html" METHOD="POST">
    <INPUT TYPE="IMAGE" SRC="decline.gif" ALT="I Decline" BORDER=0>
    </FORM>
  </TD>
</TR>
</TABLE>
```

Scripted Buttons   A new variant on action buttons in HTML 4.0 is the *scripted button*—one
that executes a client-side script when clicked. To create a scripted button, you still use the
<INPUT> tag, but with TYPE set equal to BUTTON. The VALUE attribute still specifies what text
should appear on the face of the button.

By default, a button created in this way has no behavior associated with it. To make the button
do something when clicked, you need to include the onclick event handler. You set onclick
equal to a name of a script that has presumably been set up using the <SCRIPT> tag earlier in
the document. Thus, the code to produce a fully defined scripted button might look like this:

```
<INPUT TYPE="BUTTON" VALUE="Check data" onclick="check_data()">
```

Set up in this way, the button sends an instruction to the browser to execute the script check_data whenever it is clicked.

▶ To learn more about JavaScript-enabled forms, **see** "Using JavaScript to Create Smart Forms," **p. 513**.

The <BUTTON> Tag   The <BUTTON> tag was introduced with HTML 4.0 to allow for action buttons with better presentation features. The first thing to note about the <BUTTON> tag is that it is a container tag, which means a companion </BUTTON> tag must also be used. What goes between the <BUTTON> and </BUTTON> tags has everything to do with how the button looks onscreen. If only text is between the tags, that text appears on the face of the button. If an <IMG> tag is between them, the image is used as the button.

<BUTTON> takes the TYPE attribute, which can be set to SUBMIT, RESET, or BUTTON. Each of these options produces a button very similar to the ones you get by using the <INPUT> tag with the same TYPE values, but subtle differences exist in how the buttons appear onscreen. This is particularly so in the case of image-based buttons, which are rendered three-dimensionally (with a drop shadow) and which move down when clicked and then up when released.

<BUTTON> can take the NAME and VALUE attributes as well. You need to assign a name to a button when it is a Submit button in a set of more than one. The VALUE attribute is what gets passed to the server when the button is clicked.

Labeling Input Fields

It was noted earlier in the chapter that it is up to you as a form author to include prompting text in front of your form fields to suggest to a user how he or she should fill in the field. The HTML 4.0 <LABEL> tag formalizes the relationship between the prompting text (the label) and the form field it is paired with. <LABEL> takes the FOR attribute, where FOR is set equal to the ID attribute value of the associated form field. In the example

```
<LABEL FOR="Zip">Enter your 9-digit ZIP code: </LABEL>
<INPUT TYPE="TEXT" NAME="ZIP" ID="Zip">
```

the prompting text "Enter your 9-digit ZIP code:" composes the label. Note how the label is associated with the subsequent field with the matching FOR and ID attributes.

How a label is rendered varies from browser to browser, so you should continue to place labels and their associated form fields in tables for proper alignment. Thus, the preceding example is better done as

```
<FORM ...>
<TABLE>
<TR>
<TD><LABEL FOR="Zip">Enter your 9-digit ZIP code: </LABEL></TD>
<TD><INPUT TYPE="TEXT" NAME="ZIP" ID="Zip"></TD>
</TR>
</TABLE>
...
</FORM>
```

N O T E You can also implicitly associate a label with a form field by placing the tag that created the field between the <LABEL> and </LABEL> tags. Done this way, the form field in the previous example looks like this:

`<LABEL>Enter your 9-digit ZIP code: <INPUT TYPE="TEXT" NAME="ZIP"></LABEL>`

Although this might reduce how much you have to type, it's worth noting that this approach precludes you from putting your labels and form fields in their own table cells.

Although labels might not seem to do much for you, they're important to include for visually impaired users who use a speech-based browser. In this case, the browser knows to treat the label as prompting text for a form field, and it instructs the user accordingly.

Additionally, you can associate an *access key* with your form field label by using the ACCESSKEY attribute. ACCESSKEY is set equal to a single letter from the user's keyboard. After it is set up, users can use the ACCESSKEY keystroke to go directly to the associated form field (an action called *giving focus* to the field) and fill it in. Expanding the previous password example to include an access key yields the following:

```
<FORM ...>
<TABLE>
<TR>
<TD><LABEL FOR="Zip" ACCESSKEY="Z">Enter your 9-digit <U>Z</U>IP code: </LABEL>
</TD>
<TD><INPUT TYPE="TEXT" NAME="ZIP" ID="Zip"></TD>
</TR>
</TABLE>
...
</FORM>
```

The ACCESSKEY attribute in the <LABEL> tag associates the letter Z with the form field label. Thus, whenever Windows users type Alt+Z or Macintosh users type Cmd+Z, they give focus to the Password field, which means that the cursor moves there and enables the user to type in a zip code.

T I P If you assign an ACCESSKEY to a form field label, be sure you make the key known to your users. In the preceding example, the letter Z in Zip code was put between <U> and </U> tags so that it would appear underlined. This is consistent with the way Windows programs label their access keys (for example, the underlined F in the File menu means you can press Alt+F to activate the menu).

T I P You can use the ACCESSKEY attribute with the <A> tag as well. This way, users can jump to a linked document by pressing the access key rather than by clicking the link.

Grouping Related Fields

Two other tags that were added to the HTML 4.0 form tags in recognition of nonvisual browsers are the <FIELDSET> and <LEGEND> tags. <FIELDSET> enables you to group related form fields together in a logical group, and <LEGEND> enables you to assign descriptive text to the group of fields. Neither of these might seem necessary on a standard visual browser, but for a visually impaired user with a speech-based browser, these extra features make a form much more usable.

N O T E One advantage of using <FIELDSET> grouping on a visual browser is that it facilitates tabbing through the form field. After the browser knows about a group of fields, it can tab you through the fields in sequence. ▪

<FIELDSET> does not have any attributes, but it does have a companion closing </FIELDSET> tag. To create a logical grouping of fields, you place the tags that create the fields between <FIELDSET> and </FIELDSET>.

Each logical <FIELDSET> grouping can have a <LEGEND> tag associated with it. The text between <LEGEND> and </LEGEND> is what captions the grouping, and you can use the ALIGN attribute in the <LEGEND> tag to align the legend text with respect to the grouped fields. Possible values for ALIGN in this case are TOP, BOTTOM, LEFT, and RIGHT.

N O T E Aligning the legend text produces an effect only on visual browsers. ▪

<LEGEND> can also take the ACCESSKEY attribute so that you can set up an access key for the form field grouping.

As an example of how <FIELDSET> and <LEGEND> work together, consider the following example:

```
<FORM ...>
<FIELDSET>
<LEGEND ALIGN="LEFT">Shipping Address</LEGEND>
<TABLE>
<TR>
<TD COLSPAN=2>Address:</TD>
<TD COLSPAN=4><INPUT TYPE="TEXT" NAME="SH_ADDR"></TD>
</TR>
<TR>
<TD>City:</TD>
<TD><INPUT TYPE="TEXT" NAME="SH_CITY"></TD>
<TD>State:</TD>
<TD><INPUT TYPE="TEXT" NAME="SH_STATE"></TD>
<TD>Zip:</TD>
<TD><INPUT TYPE="TEXT" NAME="SH_ZIP"></TD>
</TR>
</TABLE>
</FIELDSET>
<FIELDSET>
<LEGEND ALIGN="LEFT">Billing Address</LEGEND>
<TABLE>
<TR>
<TD COLSPAN=2>Address:</TD>
```

```
<TD COLSPAN=4><INPUT TYPE="TEXT" NAME="BL_ADDR"></TD>
</TR>
<TR>
<TD>City:</TD>
<TD><INPUT TYPE="TEXT" NAME="BL_CITY"></TD>
<TD>State:</TD>
<TD><INPUT TYPE="TEXT" NAME="BL_STATE"></TD>
<TD>Zip:</TD>
<TD><INPUT TYPE="TEXT" NAME="BL_ZIP"></TD>
</TR>
</TABLE>
</FIELDSET>
...
</FORM>
```

In the preceding code, the form fields are grouped into two logical groups: shipping address fields and billing address fields. On a visual browser, the legend text Shipping Address and Billing Address appears above each logical grouping.

Disabled and Read-Only Fields

Many of the HTML 4.0 form tags accept attributes that render the fields they produce as disabled—meaning the field is grayed out—or as read-only, which means that the text appearing in the field by default cannot be changed. The DISABLED attribute takes care of disabling a field and can be used with the following tags:

- <INPUT>
- <LABEL>
- <SELECT>
- <OPTION>
- <TEXTAREA>
- <BUTTON>

You might want to disable an option in a drop-down list, for example, if you know from other information gathered from the user that the option was inappropriate to present.

N O T E Disabled form fields are skipped over as a user tabs through the form. Also, any values assigned to a disabled field are not passed to the server when the form is submitted.

The READONLY attribute works only for the <INPUT> tag with TYPE set to TEXT or PASSWORD and the <TEXTAREA> tag because these are the only tags that can be prepopulated with text. In these cases, the text is presented only for the user's information, not so that it can be changed.

N O T E Read-only form fields are included when a user tabs through a form, and values assigned to these fields are passed to the server upon form submission.

Form Field Event Handlers

The W3C has also added a number of scripting event handlers to work with many of the form tags to facilitate the execution of script code while a user fills out a form. These event handlers include

- `onfocus`
- `onblur`
- `onselect`
- `onchange`

Two of the most widely usable event handlers are `onfocus` and `onblur`. Recall that a field receives focus when you've tabbed to it or clicked it to make it active. At the moment a field receives focus, you can choose to execute a script by setting the `onfocus` attribute of the corresponding form field tag equal to the name of a script defined in the document.

When you tab out of a form field that has focus, the field is said to blur. You can execute a script when a blur event occurs by setting `onblur` equal to the name of the script you want to run.

`onfocus` and `onblur` can be used with the following HTML form tags:

- `<BUTTON>`
- `<INPUT>`
- `<LABEL>`
- `<SELECT>`
- `<TEXTAREA>`

Additionally, the `<INPUT>`, `<SELECT>`, and `<TEXTAREA>` tags can take the `onselect` and `onchange` event handlers that launch scripts when the field is selected or changed, respectively.

All these form event handlers are useful for invoking JavaScript functions that validate the data in the form field. Chapter 21 introduces you to the scripting techniques you can employ to perform the validation tests.

Passing Form Data

After a user enters form data and clicks a Submit button, the browser does two things. First, it packages the form data into a single string, a process called encoding. Then it sends the encoded string to the server by either the GET or POST HTTP method. The next two sections close out the chapter by providing details on each of these steps.

URL Encoding

When a user clicks the Submit button on a form, the browser gathers all the data and strings it together in NAME=VALUE pairs, each separated by an ampersand (&) character. This process is called *encoding*. It is done to package the data into one string that is sent to the server.

Consider the following HTML code:

```
<FORM ACTION="http://www.server.com/cgi-bin/process_it.cgi" METHOD="POST">
    Favorite color: <INPUT TYPE="TEXT" NAME="Color">
    Favorite movie: <INPUT TYPE="TEXT" NAME="Movie">
    <INPUT TYPE="SUBMIT">
</FORM>
```

If a user's favorite color is blue and his favorite movie is *Titanic*, his browser creates the following data string and sends it to the CGI script:

```
Color=blue&Movie=Titanic
```

If the GET method is used instead of POST, the same string is appended to the URL of the processing script, producing the following encoded URL:

```
http://www.server.com/cgi-bin/process_it.cgi?Color=blue&Movie=Titanic
```

A question mark (?) separates the script URL from the encoded data string.

Storing Encoded URLs

As you learned in the previous discussion of URL encoding, packaging form data into a single text string follows a few simple formatting rules. Consequently, you can fake a script into believing that it is receiving form data without using a form. To do so, you simply send the URL that would be constructed if a form were used. This approach can be useful if you frequently run a script with the same data set.

Suppose, for example, you frequently search the Web index Yahoo! for new documents related to XML. If you are interested in checking for new documents several times a day, you could fill out the Yahoo! search query each time. A more efficient way, however, is to store the query URL as a bookmark. Each time you select that item from your bookmarks, a new query generates as if you had filled out the form. The stored URL looks like the following:

```
http://search.yahoo.com/bin/search?p=XML
```

Further encoding occurs with data that is more complex than a single word. Such encoding replaces spaces with the plus character and translates any other possibly troublesome character (control characters, the ampersand and equal sign, some punctuation, and so on) to a percent sign, followed by its hexadecimal equivalent. Thus, the following string:

```
I love HTML!
```

becomes:

```
I+love+HTML%21
```

HTTP Methods

You have two ways to read the form data submitted to a CGI script, depending on the method the form used. The type of method the form used—either GET or POST—is stored in an environment variable called REQUEST_METHOD and, based on that, the data should be read in one of the following ways:

- If the data is sent by the GET method, the input stream is stored in an environment variable called QUERY_STRING. As noted previously, this input stream usually is limited to about one kilobyte of data. This is why GET is losing popularity to the more flexible POST.

- If the data is submitted by the POST method, the input string waits on the server's input device, with the available number of bytes stored in the environment variable CONTENT_LENGTH. POST accepts data of any length, up into the megabytes, although it is not yet very common for form submissions to be that large.

Creating Forms with Authoring Tools

Composing HTML forms is another one of those daunting tasks that faced early content developers. Trying to keep all your <INPUT> tags and their NAMEs straight in your head can often get frustrating. And now that the form tags are expanding and becoming increasingly complex, it's more important than ever to have access to an authoring tool that can assist you with the task of creating a form. This section looks at the forms support you get from Microsoft FrontPage 98, Allaire HomeSite, and Adobe PageMill.

FrontPage 98

The FrontPage Editor helps you compose forms in a couple of ways. The most obvious is the Form Toolbar, which contains buttons for placing single-line text fields, multiline text boxes, check boxes, radio buttons, drop-down menus, and action buttons. When you click any of these, the desired control appears on the page, along with Submit and Reset buttons (if you haven't started a form yet). The form is contained by a box with a dashed rule, and any other controls you place in the box are part of that form (see Figure 8.8).

FIGURE 8.8

Forms in FrontPage are delineated from the rest of the document by a dashed line.

Form field placed by Toolbar button

Submit and Reset buttons are added automatically

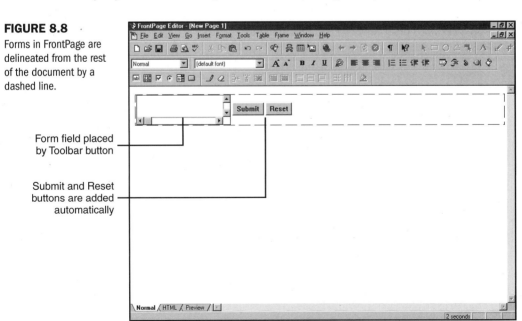

After you have at least one form field on a page, you can access different properties menus to specify the field's details. In particular, right-clicking a form control and then selecting Form Field Properties opens a properties dialog box for that control where you can type in the values for the attributes in the tag that creates the control. Additionally, you can choose Form Properties to specify attributes of the <FORM> tag, or you can choose Form Field Validation to set up some script code behind the form to do basic error-checking on the user's input (see Figure 8.9).

FIGURE 8.9

Each form control has a Properties box where you can specify values for attributes of the corresponding HTML tag.

The other way FrontPage can assist you with form composition is through the Insert, Form Field option. Choosing this option reveals a pop-up list of available form fields, including a few that aren't on the Forms Toolbar, such as Image and Label. After you select a field, FrontPage places the field on the page, and you can modify its properties in the same way you would for a field placed by using the toolbar.

Allaire HomeSite

Like FrontPage, Allaire's HomeSite also has a Forms Toolbar with buttons that place the most popular form controls. The Form button lives at the left end of the toolbar and is used to set up the <FORM> and </FORM> tags for the form. As the dialog box in Figure 8.10 shows, you can set up the form's ACTION, METHOD, ENCTYPE, and TARGET attributes all in one shot.

FIGURE 8.10

The Form tab on the HomeSite toolbar has buttons that enable you to set up the form as well as individual form controls.

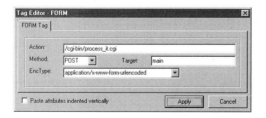

The other buttons in the toolbar call up a dialog box with appropriate fields that enable you to specify the attributes of the tag you're setting up. Figure 8.11 shows the dialog box you get when placing a text field. Note how the dialog box has fields corresponding to the NAME, VALUE, SIZE, and MAXLENGTH attributes of the <INPUT> tag.

N O T E   HomeSite's Forms Toolbar does not include a button for password fields.

FIGURE 8.11

HomeSite provides a tabbed dialog box that enables you to configure every type of form control.

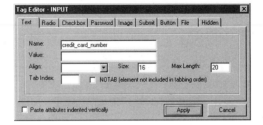

Adobe PageMill

Like the preceding products, forms are easily created in PageMill with the toolbar buttons shown in Figure 8.12.

FIGURE 8.12

You use the form-related toolbar buttons together with the Attribute Inspector to create forms in PageMill.

Form-related toolbar buttons

Attributes Inspector with Object tab displayed

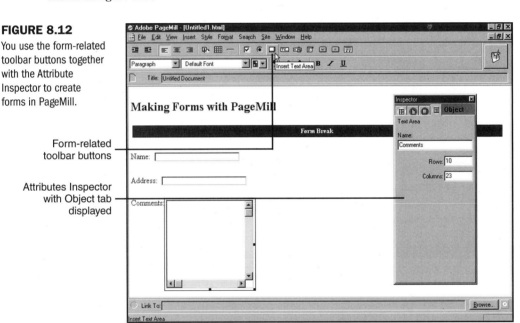

Creating forms with PageMill is simple. Click any of the toolbar buttons shown in Figure 8.12 to create a form element. For check boxes and radio buttons, enter the accompanying text by clicking to the right of the elements. Elements such as text areas, buttons, and pop-up menus can be selected and resized.

You can edit your form elements using the PageMill Attributes Inspector. As described in previous chapters, the Attributes Inspector is a utility that enables you to specify the attributes for objects (such as tables, graphics, and forms), as well as frames, pages, and so on. Each attribute set is arranged on a different tab. To access the Inspector, select Show Inspector from the View menu. The Object tab is one of the four major tabs available in the Attributes

Inspector. The versatility of the Inspector becomes apparent when you're using forms. Select a form while the Inspector is active and you'll see the form's attributes displayed in the Object tab, as shown in Figure 8.12. Notice that the attributes change as you click different form elements. Because these different elements have different attributes, you can modify them individually with the Inspector. ●

## CHAPTER 9

Style Sheets

by Eric Ladd

In this chapter

What Are Style Sheets?

Two forces compete in Web page authoring: content and presentation. When HTML was first released, the tags were largely focused on content, and they descriptively defined the various parts of a document: a heading, a paragraph, a list, and so on. Over time, instructions were added to help with presentation issues at the font level. These instructions included tags for boldface, italic, and typewriter styles.

Then, as graphical browsers became standard equipment, a greatly increased focus on presentation began. In particular, Netscape introduced proprietary extensions to HTML that only its browser could render properly. These extensions generally produced attractive effects on pages, and users began using Netscape en masse. Not to be left out, Microsoft began producing its own browser—Internet Explorer—and with it, its own proprietary HTML extensions. Content authors, who could only watch the new tags emerge, were frequently left confused and frustrated because it was hard to tell which browser to write for and how long it would be before the next new set of bells and whistles became available.

As designers push for more control over page attributes, such as indentation and line spacing, the evolution of HTML stands at a fork in the road. One path leads to the continued introduction of proprietary tags by the people making the browsers—a path that will lead HTML into even muddier waters. The other path leads to an explicit separation of content and presentation by introducing style sheets—documents that provide specifications for how content should look onscreen. By separating these two otherwise competing forces, HTML is free to evolve as a language that describes document content and will be less susceptible to seemingly endless extensions by browser software companies.

The W3C's first stab at separating content and presentation was the Cascading Style Sheets, level 1 (CSS1) specification—a formal statement on how to specify style information. In May 1998, the W3C released Cascading Style Sheets, level 2 (CSS2) as a published recommendation, so you should adhere to that standard when preparing style sheets

---

Changes from CSS1 to CSS2

If you've developed style sheets that are valid under the CSS1 standard, you'll be happy to learn that those style sheets are valid under CSS2 as well. The biggest changes on moving from CSS1 to CSS2 were in the areas of

- Accessibility—CSS2 provides support for aural style sheets to be used when marking up content for speech- and sound-based browsers. Aural style-sheet properties give you control over volume, speech quality, pauses, cues, mixing of sounds, and spatial variations of sound (for example, differences that help you to determine where different voices are coming from in a room).

- Internationalization—The Web's user community is distributed throughout the world, and as more and more users emerge, it becomes important to support languages other than English. Specifically, CSS2 provides for differences in list numbering and quotation marks and for bidirectional text (for languages that are read right-to-left and not left-to-right).

The new features introduced in these areas have essentially no impact on style properties introduced in CSS1, so that's why your CSS1 style sheets are also valid under CSS2.

Some subtle differences between CSS1 and CSS2 are worth noting, however. New features to CSS2 include

- Properties that can take an inherit value, which says that an element should inherit the property from its parent element.
- Style sheets for different media types (aural, print, Braille, projection, and so on); they are controlled by using the @import rule (which imports a style sheet from a given URL) or the @media rule.
- A text-shadow property for doing drop-shadows behind text.
- Support for paged media, which enables you to present a document in discrete pages rather than as a single, continuous page. Pagination is controlled by the @page rule.
- An expanded font selection algorithm that allows for downloadable fonts.
- Fixed positioning, which enables you to place an element in the browser window and not have it move from that position when the page is scrolled. This is similar to the idea of a "watermarked" background image that does not move when the page is scrolled, except the fixed-positioned content is presumably in the foreground of the document.
- The capability to specify clipping regions, overflow, visibility, and minimum and maximum widths and heights in the visual formatting model.

Before you look at the different ways to build style information into your pages, it will be helpful to review some of the basics behind the concept of a style sheet.

Style sheets are collections of style information that are applied to plain text. Style information includes font attributes such as type size, special effects (bold, italic, underline), color, and alignment. Style sheets also provide broader formatting instructions by specifying values for quantities such as line spacing and left and right margins.

Style sheets are not really a new concept; word processing programs such as Microsoft Word have been making use of user-defined style for a number of years. Figure 9.1 shows a Word style definition in the Style dialog box. Notice how the style accounts for many of the presentation attributes previously mentioned.

FIGURE 9.1

Word processors enable users to store content presentation attributes together as a style.

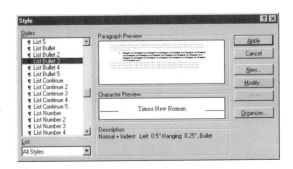

Part II Ch 9

Why Style Sheets Are Valuable

Simply put, style sheets separate content and presentation. Apart from freeing up HTML to develop as a content description language, it gives Web page designers precise control over how their content appears onscreen. Other benefits of style sheets include

- Central repositories of style information—If you use a standard set of styles on all your pages, you can store the corresponding style information in one file. This way, if you have to edit the style information, you have to make the change in only one place instead of in every file.

- Little-to-no new HTML to learn—With style information stored in style sheets, virtually no new HTML tags should be needed for the purposes of formatting. This promises to reduce the confusion that often arises out of browser-specific extensions to HTML.

- Consistent rendering of content—Browsers vary slightly in how they render content, especially the logical text styles (emphasized text (<EM>), keyboard input (<KBD>), and so on). By assigning specific style information to logical style tags, Web page authors can be assured that their content will look the same on every browser.

Different Approaches to Style Sheets

The W3C is advocating the Cascading Style Sheet proposal for implementing style sheets. *Cascading* refers to a certain set of rules that browsers use, in cascading order, to determine how to use the style information. Such a set of rules is useful in the event of conflicting style information because the rules would give the browser a way to determine which style is given precedence.

The CSS2 recommendation supports three ways of including style information in a document. These approaches include

- Linked styles—Style information is read from a separate file that is specified in the <LINK> tag.

- Embedded styles—Style information is defined in the document head using the <STYLE> and </STYLE> tags.

- Inline styles—Style information is placed inside an HTML tag and applies to all content between that tag and its companion closing tag. You can left-indent an entire paragraph one-half inch, for example, by using the <P STYLE="margin-left: .5 in"> tag to start the paragraph. If the content to which you want to apply style information isn't conveniently grouped by a set of container tags, you can also use the <SPAN> and </SPAN> tags to do the same job.

Using Multiple Approaches

You aren't limited to using only one of the described style sheet approaches. You can use all three simultaneously if needed. One case in which you may want to do this is on an intranet site where you have the following:

■ Global styles—Certain styles used on every page are best stored in a single style sheet file and linked to each page with the <LINK> tag. This might apply to styles mandated as a corporate standard, such as the use of a plain white background and a single typeface.

■ Subsection styles—Intranet sites typically have many subdivisions, each with its own look and feel. To support a subdivision's look, you can store styles between the <STYLE> and </STYLE> tags in the head of each document in the subdivision. The subdivisions might represent different business units within the corporation, or it can just be a set of related documents, such as product specs or white papers.

■ Page-specific styles—If you need to make a small deviation from your chosen global or subsection styles, you can use an inline style to make the change where you want it. You might use a page-specific style if a page in one of your subdivisions has particular presentation requirements. A key passage in a white paper, for example, might be highlighted by rendering it in bold and in color.

Part

II

Ch

9

However, you shouldn't use all three approaches in the same document just for the sake of doing it. You should seek to optimize your use of style sheets by choosing the approach or combination of approaches that enables you to apply the styles you want, where you want them, without a lot of unnecessary code.

Remember style precedence when using multiple approaches. The idea behind a Cascading Style Sheet is that browsers apply a set of rules in cascading order to determine which style information takes precedence. You need to be aware of these rules so that you do not produce unintended style effects on your pages. In general, you'll be fine if you remember the following:

■ Inline styles override both linked style sheets and style information stored in the document head with the <STYLE> tag.

■ Styles defined in the document head override linked style sheets.

■ Linked style sheets override browser defaults.

Keeping these rules in mind will make troubleshooting your style sheet setup much easier.

N O T E One important point for content authors to remember is that users can develop style sheets of their own. CSS2 supports the "!important" keyword in the specification of any property, which enables the user's style sheet to override the specification in the author's style sheet. ■

Linking to Style Information in a Separate File

One important thing to realize is that you don't have to store your style sheet information inside each of your HTML documents. If you anticipate applying the same styles across several HTML pages, it is much more efficient for you to store the style information in one place and have each HTML document linked to it. This makes it much easier to change the formatting of all your pages by changing the style sheet instead of changing every page.

Setting Up the Style Information

To set up a linked style sheet, you first need to create the file with the style information. This takes the form of a plain-text file with style information entries. Each entry starts with an HTML tag, followed by a list of presentation attributes to associate with the rendering of the effect of that tag. Some sample lines in a style sheet file might look like

```
BODY {font: 12 pt New Baskerville; color: navy; margin-left: 0.25in}
H1 {font 18 pt Arial; color: red}
H2 {font 16 pt Arial; color: CC3366}
```

The first line sets the body text to 12-point New Baskerville type rendered in navy blue with a one-quarter inch left margin. The second line redefines the level 1 heading to 18-point Arial type rendered in red, and the third line sets the level 2 heading to 16-point Arial type, rendered in the color represented by the hexadecimal triplet "CC3366."

N O T E   When setting colors in your style sheet file, you can use one of the 16 English-language color names or an RGB hexadecimal triplet to describe the color. The acceptable English-language color names are

- AQUA
- BLACK
- BLUE
- FUCHSIA
- GRAY
- GREEN
- LIME
- MAROON
- NAVY
- OLIVE
- PURPLE
- RED
- SILVER
- TEAL
- WHITE
- YELLOW

Remember that the syntax for specifying a characteristic has the form

```
{characteristic: value}
```

Multiple characteristic/value pairs should be separated by semicolons. For example:

```
P {font: 14 pt Times New Roman; line-height: 16 pt; color: black}
```

Part

II

Ch

9

> **CAUTION**
>
> When you first start to work with style sheets, you may be tempted to use the syntax "characteristic=value."
> Make sure you use the "{characteristic: value}" syntax previously noted.

The Cascading Style Sheet specification enables you to specify more than fonts, typefaces, and colors. Table 9.1 lists the different font and block level style attributes you can assign to a file containing style information.

Table 9.1 Font and Block Level Characteristics Permitted in Style Sheets

Characteristic	Possible Values
font-family	Any typeface available to the browser through Windows (the default font is used if one of the specified fonts is not available).
font-size	Any size in points (pt), inches (in), centimeters (cm), or pixels (px); larger or smaller (relative-size values); xx-small, x-small, small, medium, large, x-large, xx-large (absolute-size values); or a percentage relative to the parent font's size.
font-weight	Normal, bold; bolder, lighter (relative weights).
font-style	Normal, italic, oblique.
font-variant	Normal, small caps.
color	Any RGB hexadecimal triplet or HTML 4.0 English-language color name.
background-attachment	(Whether the background image stays fixed or scrolls with the content) scroll, fixed.
background-color	Transparent; any RGB hexadecimal triplet or HTML 4.0 English-language color name.
background-image	None; URL of image file.
background-repeat	Repeat-x (tile background image only in the horizontal direction), repeat-y (tile only in the vertical direction), repeat (tile in both directions), no-repeat (no tiling).
border-color	Any RGB hexadecimal triplet or HTML 4.0 English-language color name.

continues

Table 9.1 Continued

Characteristic	Possible Values
border-style	None, dashed, dotted, solid, double, groove, ridge, inset, outset.
border-bottom-width	Thin, medium, thick; any number of points (pt), inches (in), centimeters (cm), or pixels (px).
border-left-width	Thin, medium, thick; any number of points (pt), inches (in), centimeters (cm), or pixels (px).
border-right-width	Thin, medium, thick; any number of points (pt), inches (in), centimeters (cm), or pixels (px).
border-top-width	Thin, medium, thick; any number of points (pt), inches (in), centimeters (cm), or pixels (px).
float	Left, right, none; floats positioned content in left or right margin.
padding-bottom	Any number of points (pt), inches (in), centimeters (cm), or pixels (px); or a percentage of the parent element's width.
padding-left	Any number of points (pt), inches (in), centimeters (cm), or pixels (px); or a percentage of the parent element's width.
padding-right	Any number of points (pt), inches (in), centimeters (cm), or pixels (px); or a percentage of the parent element's width.
padding-top	Any number of points (pt), inches (in), centimeters (cm), or pixels (px); or a percentage of the parent element's width.
text-align	Left, center, right, justify.
text-decoration	None, underline, overline, line-through, blink.
text-indent	Any number of points (pt), inches (in), centimeters (cm), or pixels (px); or a percentage relative to the indentation of the parent element.
text-shadow	The shadow offset is required and can be set to any number of points (pt), inches (in), centimeters (cm), or pixels (px); specification of blur radius and shadow color is optional.
text-transform	Capitalize, uppercase, lowercase, none.
line-height	Normal; any number of points (pt), inches (in), centimeters (cm), or pixels (px); or a percentage of the font size.
letter-spacing	Normal; any number of points (pt), inches (in), centimeters (cm), or pixels (px).
word-spacing	Normal; any number of points (pt), inches (in), centimeters (cm), or pixels (px).
margin-left	Auto; any number of points (pt), inches (in), centimeters (cm), or pixels (px); or a percentage of the parent element's width.

Characteristic	Possible Values
margin-right	Auto; any number of points (pt), inches (in), centimeters (cm), or pixels (px); or a percentage of the parent element's width.
margin-top	Auto; any number of points (pt), inches (in), centimeters (cm), or pixels (px); or a percentage of the parent element's width.
margin-bottom	Auto; any number of points (pt), inches (in), centimeters (cm), or pixels (px); or a percentage of the parent element's width.
vertical-align	Baseline, sub, super, top, text-top, middle, bottom, text-bottom; or a percentage of the current line-height.

N O T E Line-height in Table 9.1 refers to the leading, or space between lines, that the browser uses. Padding refers to the amount of space left around an element. ▪

You can see from the table that you get control over a large number of presentation characteristics—certainly more than you get with HTML tags alone. In addition to the font and block level properties noted in Table 9.1, CSS2 includes characteristics that give you control over how your content is positioned on the browser screen. The content positioning characteristics, summarized in Table 9.2, enable you to precisely place any portion of your content, even overlapping other content in some cases.

Table 9.2   Content Positioning Characteristics Permitted in Style Sheets

Characteristic	Purpose and Possible Values
position	Specifies how content is to be positioned; possible values are static (content cannot be positioned or repositioned), absolute (content is positioned with respect to the upper-left corner of the browser window), and relative (content is positioned with respect to its natural position in the document).
top	Specifies the vertical displacement of the positioned content; values can be in points (pt), pixels (px), centimeters (cm), or inches (in) and can have negative values (negative value moves content above its reference point on the screen).
left	Specifies the horizontal displacement of positioned content; values can be in points (pt), pixels (px), centimeters (cm), or inches (in) and can have negative values (negative value moves content to the left of its reference point on the screen).
clip:rect(x1,y1,x2,y2)	Defines the size of the clipping region (rectangular area in which the positioned content appears); (x1,y1) are the coordinates of the upper-left corner of the rectangle and (x2,y2) are the coordinates of the lower-right corner.

continues

Part

II

Ch

9

Table 9.2 Continued

Characteristic	Purpose and Possible Values
overflow	Tells the browser how to handle positioned content that overflows the space allocated for it; possible values are visible, hidden, auto, and scroll.
visibility	Enables the document author to selectively display or conceal positioned content; possible values are show or hide.
z-index	Permits stacking of positioned content in the browser screen so that content overlaps; z-index is set to an integer value of 0 or higher (content with a smaller z-index will be positioned below content with higher z-index values).

Both Netscape and Microsoft have bundled their support for content positioning as part of the "Dynamic HTML" capabilities of the fourth release of each of their browsers. Although both browsers support content positioning by means of Cascading Style Sheets, Netscape initially tried to implement positioned content through the proprietary <LAYER> tag. Currently, Navigator 4.0 supports both the CSS and the <LAYER> tag approaches.

N O T E Content positioning is discussed in great detail in Chapter 24, "Introduction to Dynamic HTML," Chapter 25, "Advanced Netscape Dynamic HTML," and Chapter 26, "Advanced Microsoft Dynamic HTML." ▒

Using the *<LINK>* Tag

After you create your style sheet file, save it with a .css extension and place it on your server. Then you can reference it by using the <LINK> tag in the head of each of your HTML documents, as follows:

```
<HEAD>
<TITLE>A Document that Uses Style Sheets</TITLE>
<LINK REL=STYLESHEET HREF="styles/sitestyles.css">
</HEAD>
```

The REL attribute describes the relationship of the linked file to the current file, namely that the linked file is a style sheet. HREF specifies the URL of the style sheet file.

CAUTION

Style sheet files are of MIME type text/css, although not all servers and browsers register this automatically. If you set up a site that uses style sheets, be sure to configure your server to handle the MIME type text/css.

Embedded Style Information

Figure 9.2 shows Microsoft's Site Search page. The style information is stored in the document head, as shown in the excerpt of HTML source code in Listing 9.1. For the link styles defined near the bottom of the listing, the structure of the style information takes the same form that you saw for setting up style information in a separate file: an HTML tag name, followed by curly braces containing the style characteristics. The rest of the style information is devoted to setting up style classes. These classes can then be referenced by multiple tags by using the CLASS attribute.

Part
II
Ch
9

FIGURE 9.2

Microsoft defines several font classes for its search page. Each class is referenced by using the CLASS attribute in the tag where you want to apply the styles in that class.

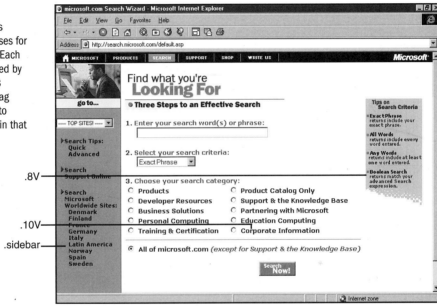

Listing 9.1 Embedded Style Information in Microsoft's Site Search Page

```
<STYLE TYPE="text/css">
<!--
.8V {font-size: 8pt; font-family: verdana, arial,
  helvetica, sans-serif;}
.10V {font-size: 10pt; font-family: verdana, arial,
  helvetica, sans-serif;}
.sidebar {font-size: 8pt; font-weight:bold; text-decoration: none;
  color:"#000000"; font-family: verdana, arial, helvetica, sans-serif;}
.COPY {font-size: 8pt; color:"#000000"; font-family: verdana,
  arial, helvetica, sans-serif;}
A:link {text-decoration:none;}
A:visited {text-decoration:none;}
-->
</STYLE>
```

Using the *<STYLE>* Tag

As you can see in Listing 9.1, embedded style information is placed between the <STYLE> and </STYLE> tags. When the W3C released HTML 3.2, it reserved the use of these tags specifically for the purpose of embedded style information. The HTML 4.0 recommendation now formalizes the use of the <STYLE> tag.

The TYPE attribute tells a browser what type of style information setup is used and is most often set equal to "text/css." Specifying other types allows for some flexibility in the implementation of other style information specification schemes in the future. This also makes it easier for browsers that do not support style sheets to ignore the style information between the two tags.

Style information of the MIME type text/css is set up the same way that style information is set up in a linked style sheet file. The first entry on each line is the keyword from an HTML tag, followed by a list of characteristic/value pairs enclosed in curly braces. You can use any of the characteristics shown in Tables 9.1 or 9.2 when specifying your embedded style information.

N O T E Note that the style information you see in Listing 9.1 is enclosed in comment tags (<!-- and -->) so that browsers that do not understand style sheets will ignore the style information rather than presenting it onscreen. ■

Style information that is specified in the head of a document by using the <STYLE> tag will only apply for that document. If you want to use the same styles in another document, you need to embed the style information in the head of that document as well.

Only use embedded style information for page-specific styles. If you have global style elements you want to implement, place them in a file and link the file as a style sheet in all your documents. Centralizing as much style information as possible is the best way to ensure a consistent implementation.

Inline Style Information

You can specify inline styles inside an HTML tag. The style information given applies to the document content up until the defining tag's companion closing tag is encountered. Consider the following <TABLE> tag used on the American Boxer Club's home page (see Figure 9.3):

```
<TABLE BORDER="5" WIDTH="600" STYLE="float: none; padding-left: 10px;
 padding-right: 10px; padding-top: 5px; padding-bottom: 5px"
BORDERCOLOR="#800080" CELLSPACING="0" CELLPADDING="10"
BORDERCOLORLIGHT="#800080" BORDERCOLORDARK="#800080" BGCOLOR="#EAEAEA">
```

The STYLE attribute in the tag suppresses floating and pads the table with 10 pixels on the left and right sides and 5 pixels on the top and bottom. This gives the table that contains the page's content a little bit of breathing room on all sides.

CAUTION

Don't forget the closing tag when embedding style information in an HTML tag. Otherwise, the effects of the style may extend beyond the point in the document where you wanted them to stop.

FIGURE 9.3

Many HTML tags now accept a STYLE attribute that specifies style information to apply along with the effect of the tag.

Padded table —

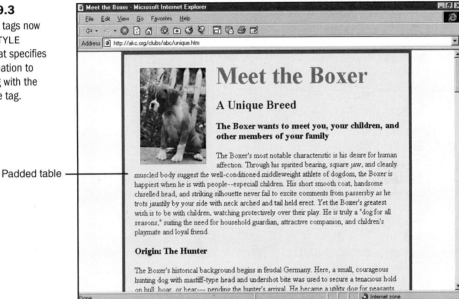

Other Tags That Take the *STYLE* Attribute

You saw in the preceding example that the <P> tag can take the STYLE attribute to define an inline style. Many other tags can take the style attribute as well, including the following:

- Physical style tags: <TT>, <I>, <B>, <U>, <S>, <STRIKE>, <BIG>, <SMALL>, <SUB>, <SUP>
- Logical style tags: <EM>, <STRONG>, <DFN>, <CODE>, <SAMP>, <KBD>, <VAR>, <CITE>, <ACRO-NYM>, <INS>, <DEL>, <Q>
- Block formatting tags: <BODY>, <BR>, <BLOCKQUOTE>, <ADDRESS>, <DIV>, <HR>, <CENTER>, <H1>, <H2>, <H3>, <H4>, <H5>, <H6>
- List tags: <UL>, <OL>, <LI>, <DL>, <DT>, <DD>, <DIR>, <MENU>
- Image and linking tags: <IMG>, <MAP>, <A>
- Form tags: <FORM>, <LABEL>, <INPUT>, <SELECT>, <TEXTAREA>, <FIELDSET>, <LEGEND>, <BUTTON>, <ISINDEX>
- Table tags: <TABLE>, <CAPTION>, <COLGROUP>, <COL>, <THEAD>, <TBODY>, <TFOOT>, <TR>, <TH>, <TD>

The *<SPAN>* Tag

For those times when you want to apply a style to part of a document that is not nicely contained between two tags, you can use the <SPAN> and </SPAN> tags to set up the part of the document that is to have the style applied. You assign style characteristics to the area set up by the <SPAN> tag by using the STYLE attribute, as in the previous example with the <P> tag.

As an example of how you might use the <SPAN> tag, consider the following HTML from the W3C's style sheets home page:

```
<P ID=p1><A HREF="#new"><SPAN ID=s1>What's new?</SPAN></A>
<P ID=p2><A HREF="#what"><SPAN ID=s2>What are style sheets?</SPAN></A>
<P ID=p3><A HREF="#press"><SPAN ID=s3>Press clippings</SPAN></A>
<P ID=p5><A HREF="./CSS"><SPAN ID=s5>CSS</SPAN></A>
<P ID=p6><A HREF="#dsssl"><SPAN ID=s6>DSSSL</SPAN></A>
<P ID=p7><A HREF="XSL"><SPAN ID=s7>XSL</SPAN></A>
```

The code in the example produces the stylized and overlapping set of links you see in Figure 9.4.

TIP Using inline styles is fine for changes to small sections of your document. However, you should consider using a linked style sheet or the <STYLE> tag if your styles are to be global.

FIGURE 9.4

The <SPAN> tags enable you to assign style characteristics to content that is not neatly contained between a set of tags.

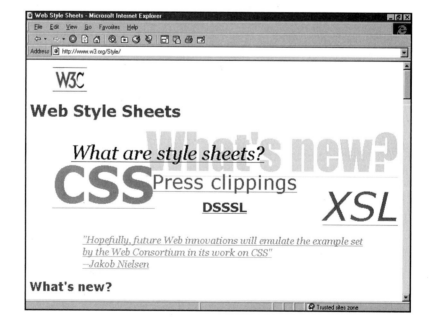

Tips for Style Sheet Users

Even though style sheets are relatively new, Web authors are already coming up with some good general rules for implementing them. The next few sections share some of these helpful hints.

Harnessing Inheritance

Inheritance refers to the fact that HTML documents are essentially set up as hierarchies, and styles applied at one level of the hierarchy necessarily apply to all subordinate levels as well. Therefore, if you assign style information inside of a <UL> tag, the information also applies to all the items in the unordered list because the <LI> tags are subordinate to the <UL> tag.

If you're not using embedded style information, you can make broader use of inheritance by setting up as much common style information in the <BODY> tag as you can. Because every tag between <BODY> and </BODY> is subordinate to the <BODY> tag, these tags will inherit the style information you specify in the <BODY> tag, and you should be spared from having to repeat it throughout the rest of the document.

Additionally, under CSS2, all presentation properties can take the keyword inherit, which forces an element to inherit the same value of the property as its parent element.

Grouping Style Information

If you want to assign the same style characteristics to a number of tags, you can do so in just one line rather than using a separate line for each tag. If you want all three kinds of links—unvisited, visited, and active—to be rendered in the same style, for example, you can list them all individually:

```
A:link {font-size: 10 pt; color: 00FF00; font-decoration: underline}
A:visited {font-size: 10 pt; color: 00FF00; font-decoration: underline}
A:active {font-size: 10 pt; color: 00FF00; font-decoration: underline}
```

or you can define them all at once:

```
A:link A:visited A:active {font-size: 10 pt; color: 00FF00;
font-decoration: underline}
```

Either set of code will make all hypertext links appear in 10-point type that is green and underlined.

N O T E   You may have noticed in CSS1 that the :link, :vlink, and :active link classes were all mutually exclusive. In CSS2, all three classes can be used together. ▪

You can also group style information applied to only one tag. For example, if you redefined your level 2 headings as

```
H2 {font-size: 16 pt; line-height: 18 pt; font-family: "Helvetica";
font-weight: bold}
```

you can express the same thing as

```
H2 {font: 16pt/18pt "Helvetica" bold}
```

and save yourself a bit of typing.

Part

II

Ch

9

Creating Tag Classes

The proposed style sheet specifications enable you to subdivide a tag into named classes and to specify different style information for each class. If you want three colors of unvisited links, for example, you can set them up as

```
A:link.red {color: red}
A:link.yellow {color: yellow}
A:link.fuschia {color: fuschia}
```

The period and color name that follow each A:link sets up a class of the A:link tag. The class name is whatever follows the period. You use the class names in the <A> tag to specify which type of unvisited link you want to create, as follows:

```
Here's a <A CLASS="red" HREF="red.html">red</A> link!
And a <A CLASS="yellow" HREF="yellow.html">yellow</A> one ...
And a <A CLASS="fuschia" HREF="fuschia.html">fuschia</A> one!
```

 TIP If you use multiple style sheet approaches, make sure you define the same set of classes in all of them so that the same set of class names is available to the browser in each case.

Using the *ID* Attribute

You can also set up your own style names if setting up a named class of an HTML tag doesn't suit your needs. For example, you can say:

```
<STYLE TYPE="text/css">
<!--
...
#style1 { font-size: 16 pt; text-decoration: underline }
#style2 { font-size: 20 pt; text-decoration: blink}
...
-->
</STYLE>
```

and then reference these styles using an ID attribute in a tag that can take the STYLE attribute; for example,

```
<BODY ID="style1" ...>
...
<P ID="style2">
Here is a paragraph done in style2 ...
</P>
...
</BODY>
```

In this code excerpt, all the body text will be rendered in underlined, 16-point type as defined by the style1 identifier, and text in the paragraph that starts "Here is a paragraph done in style2 ..." will be 20 points high and blinking, as specified by the style2 identifier.

NOTE Named identifiers have to start with the pound sign (#) when you define them in the style information section of your document. When you reference an identifier with the ID attribute, the pound sign isn't necessary. ▪

Style Sheet Software Tools

Even though Web style sheets are still fairly new, a number of document authoring software packages are rising to the occasion and providing support for including style information in your documents. Microsoft showed leadership in implementing the Cascading Style Sheet specification in Internet Explorer 3, so it should be no surprise that its Web development tool, FrontPage, is leading the way in providing style sheet support for document authors.

Microsoft FrontPage

To use FrontPage's style sheet functions, you need to work in the FrontPage Editor—the FrontPage component used to create Web documents.

In the FrontPage Editor, choosing Format, Stylesheet will reveal the Format Stylesheet dialog box you see in Figure 9.5. As you see in the figure, FrontPage assumes you're embedding your style information in the document head when you choose this option, as evidenced by the `<STYLE>` and `</STYLE>` tags you see in the dialog box.

FIGURE 9.5

The FrontPage Editor enables you to create embedded style specifications.

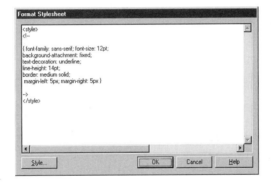

You can type the style information you want to apply directly into the dialog box, or you can click the Style button near the bottom left to open up the Style dialog box into which you can enter the information. Figure 9.6 shows you the Alignment tab of this dialog box, which enables you to specify values for margins, padding, and floating properties. Other tabs include

- Borders—For specifying type, color and width of borders.
- Font—For choosing a type family and size.
- Color—For choosing a background color, a foreground color, or a background image (including how to tile the image).
- Text—For choosing text style, weight, and decoration, line height, letter spacing, and alignment properties.

When you're done setting up the style information, click the OK button to apply the styles. Depending on what characteristics you've specified, you may not see any effect on the FrontPage Editor's Normal tab. To make sure that your style information was properly built into the source code of the document, click the HTML tab to look at the raw code. You should see your style information contained in the document head.

FIGURE 9.6

If you can't remember all those style characteristics, don't worry! FrontPage has them all stored in the Style dialog box.

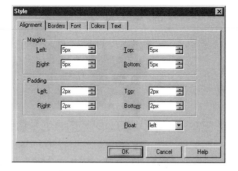

FrontPage can also help you if you want to place style information in a separate file, or if you want to use inline styles. If you need to create a separate style sheet file, you can still use the dialog boxes you see in Figures 9.5 and 9.6 to set up the style information. Then, after the style specifications are written into the document, you can copy and paste them to a blank document and then save the document as a text file with a .css extension.

If you plan to use inline styles, you'll find that many dialog boxes that insert tags have a Style button in them. Clicking the Style button will call up a dialog box much like the one you see in Figure 9.6, enabling you to specify the style information you want to associate with that instance of the tag.

N O T E The themes that come with FrontPage are *not* implemented by means of CSS style instructions. Rather, the server implements the theme (fonts, sizes, bullet graphics, and so on) according to instructions it gets in a <META> tag in the document head. ■

Allaire HomeSite

Another software package that can help you with the incorporation of style information is Allaire's HomeSite. HomeSite is not a WYSIWYG editor like the FrontPage Editor. Rather, it is focused on the composition of the raw HTML source code.

HomeSite has particularly good support for defining inline styles. When you have HomeSite's "What-You-See-Is-What-You-Need" (WYSIWYN) feature active and your cursor placed inside of a tag, the program will display a context-sensitive list of attributes that are appropriate to the tag (see Figure 9.7). HomeSite "knows" that the STYLE attribute is available for most HTML tags, and you'll typically find STYLE listed among the acceptable attributes in the context-sensitive list.

After you've placed the STYLE attribute, HomeSite can take you a step further by helping you to specify the style properties. When your cursor is between the quotation marks of the STYLE="" attribute, the WYSIWYN feature kicks in again and gives you the option to define an inline style (see Figure 9.8). Selecting this option launches HomeSite's Inline Style dialog box (see Figure 9.9). The dialog box has four tabs—Font, Text, Margins, and Position—where you can assign specific values to the properties grouped under the tab. You also get a small preview window in the dialog box and a button that will enable you to see the style sheet in an external browser.

FIGURE 9.7

HomeSite's WYSIWYN feature detects which tag you're inserting and provides a list of possible attributes to use inside the tag.

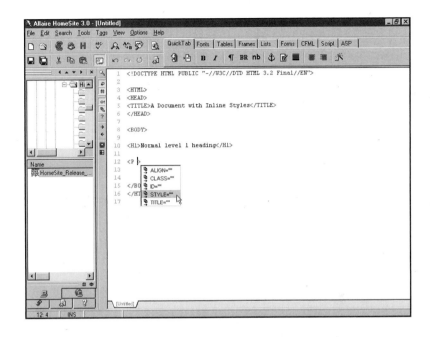

Part

II

Ch

9

FIGURE 9.8

HomeSite offers to help you define an inline style when it senses that you're placing a tag that has the STYLE attribute.

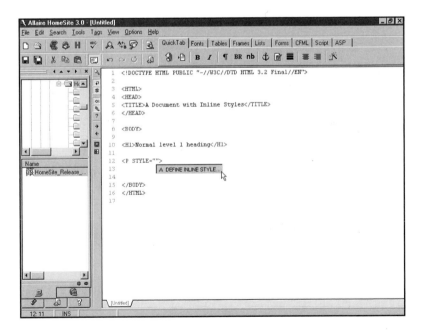

FIGURE 9.9

When you input the values you want for various font, text, margin, and positioning properties, HomeSite writes out the corresponding style sheet code.

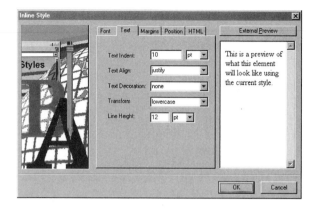

## CHAPTER 10

Microsoft FrontPage Components

by Eric Ladd

In this chapter

FrontPage Overview

Microsoft's FrontPage is probably one of the more misunderstood software tools available to Web content authors. Most people tend to think of it as being similar to Netscape's Composer or one of the other popular WYSIWYG Web page authoring programs. If you've only seen the FrontPage Editor, it's easy to understand why you might think this.

If you consider the entire FrontPage suite, however, you realize that FrontPage is actually an end-to-end Web site management tool. You can use FrontPage to get a Web site's basic structure in place, to prepare each of the individual documents in the site, to check for broken links, to assign and track Web site support tasks, and to set up site navigation resources. Additionally, you can integrate FrontPage with an image-editing tool, such as Microsoft's Image Composer, to support your graphics work or with your browser to make it easy to download pages from the Web and edit them. FrontPage makes page design a snap with seven site templates, more than fifty page templates (including many for framed documents), and dozens of ready-to-use graphic themes and clip art images. Tasks such as connecting to a back-end database or setting up an advanced page component, such as a Java applet, become simple, thanks to supporting wizards and dialog boxes. In short, FrontPage can help you with almost any Web site management task you can imagine from the initial creation of the site up through maintenance.

One feature that was introduced in earlier versions of FrontPage is the WebBot. WebBots are preprogrammed chunks of functionality that you can drop onto a page as easily as you would an HTML tag. When a server detects code in an HTML file that indicates the use of a WebBot, it takes the appropriate action to translate the code into something that a browser would understand—possibly an HTML tag or a call to a program residing on the server. The end result is that users see CGI-like functionality on their browser screen, and the page author didn't have to write a line of program code to accomplish it.

WebBots are still around in the current release of FrontPage, but they have been renamed *FrontPage Components*. This chapter introduces you to the various FrontPage Components, shows you how to place them on your pages, and shows how a FrontPage-compliant server interprets them to produce a result on a user's browser screen.

Before diving into a discussion about FrontPage Components, it's helpful to set the stage by taking a look at the entire FrontPage suite. In the broadest sense, FrontPage is a client-server application that supports a myriad of Web site management tasks. On the client side, you have two major program components:

- FrontPage Explorer—Helps you with duties such as setting up a site's structure, checking for broken links or missing image files, applying graphical themes to your site, and controlling editorial access to individual pages. The Explorer also enables you to view your site in several ways, including graphical depictions of navigation and hyperlinks (see Figure 10.1).

- FrontPage Editor —Meant for supporting you in page creation work. You can use one of the Editor's many templates to start a page, or you can begin with a blank page to create your own design. On the Editor's Normal tab (see Figure 10.2), you can compose a page as you would have it look in a Web browser by typing in your text, dropping in images, horizontal lines, and form fields, and using the extensive menu or toolbar options.

While you compose the page on the Normal tab, the code to produce the page is being generated on the HTML tab (see Figure 10.3). Authors who prefer to work with raw code can jump to this tab at any time to make quick edits as needed.

FIGURE 10.1

The FrontPage Explorer's Navigation view enables you to see your site's hierarchical structure.

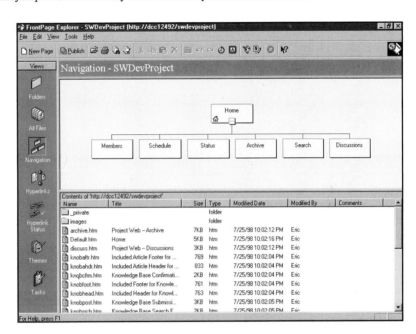

Part
II

Ch
10

FIGURE 10.2

The Normal tab is the WYSIWYG work area within the FrontPage Editor.

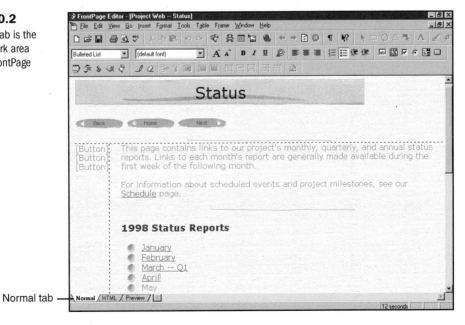

Normal tab

FIGURE 10.3

FrontPage also enables you to work with raw HTML code, although not much support is available for placing tags into the code other than by typing them in by hand.

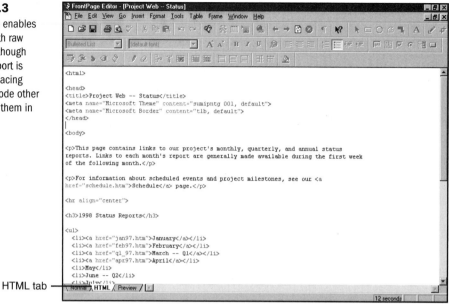

HTML tab

Because it's important to test your work by looking at it in a browser, the FrontPage Editor also comes with a Preview tab that gives you an idea of how a page will look to an end user. Figure 10.4 shows you a preview of the WYSIWYG page you saw in Figure 10.2.

FIGURE 10.4

The Preview tab gives you an idea of what a visitor to your site will see.

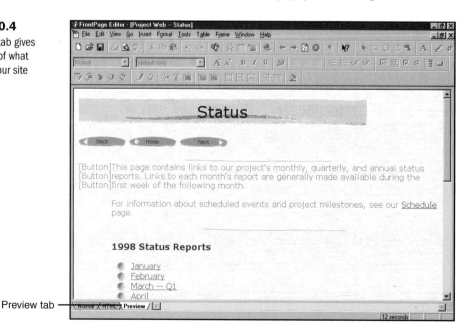

Preview tab

T I P Even if you look at your pages from the Preview tab, it's still a good idea to look at them in a full-fledged browser program, too. Additionally, some elements on a document you create with FrontPage may not be visible unless you're requesting the page from a FrontPage-compliant server.

On the server side of FrontPage, support needs to be in place for FrontPage's many interactions with the Web server. The FrontPage Explorer can read a Web site (or *Web*, in FrontPage lingo) right off a server and can publish a Web page you're working on back to a server. Additionally, automated functions such as FrontPage Components, page transitions, and hover buttons need to be processed by the server. It's easy to understand how you get the client-side components of FrontPage in place—you just install them on your hard drive—but it's probably less clear as to how you get FrontPage's server-side components installed.

N O T E If you outsource the hosting of your Web site, be sure to check with your provider to see if it supports FrontPage server extensions before you start developing in FrontPage. ■

If you use Microsoft's Internet Information Server (IIS) 3.0 or above, you're in luck because FrontPage's server-side components are already built in to IIS. When you direct your client-side components to work with an IIS server, the integration between the two is seamless.

If you use any other server software, you have to compensate by installing the FrontPage Server Extensions on your server. The Extensions enable a non-IIS server to

- Understand the code that the FrontPage Editor places into an HTML file when placing an automated function on a page.
- Act on that code by substituting an HTML tag, launching a program, downloading an applet, or performing whatever action is appropriate.

Microsoft has made FrontPage Server Extensions available for a wide variety of server platforms. Table 10.1 gives you the details on which servers have FrontPage Server Extensions available. After the extensions are installed, FrontPage's client-side components will work seamlessly with your server.

Part

II

Ch

10

Table 10.1 FrontPage Server Extensions

Operating System	Web Servers
Solaris 2.4, 2.5	NCSA 1.5.2; CERN 3.0; Apache 1.1.3, 1.2.4, and 1.2.5; Netscape Commerce Server 1.12; Netscape Communications Server 1.12; Netscape Enterprise Server 2.0 and 3.0; Netscape FastTrack 2.0
SunOS 4.1.3, 4.1.4	NCSA 1.5.2; CERN 3.0; Apache 1.1.3, 1.2.4, and 1.2.5; Netscape Commerce Server 1.12; Netscape Communications Server 1.12; Netscape Enterprise Server 2.0 and 3.0; Netscape FastTrack 2.0
IRIX 5.3, 6.2	NCSA 1.5.2; CERN 3.0; Apache 1.1.3, 1.2.4, and 1.2.5; Netscape Commerce Server 1.12; Netscape Communications Server 1.12; Netscape Enterprise Server 2.0 and 3.0; Netscape FastTrack 2.0

continues

Table 10.1   Continued

Operating System	Web Servers
HP/UX 9.03, 10.01	NCSA 1.5.2; CERN 3.0; Apache 1.1.3, 1.2.4, and 1.2.5; Netscape Commerce Server 1.12; Netscape Communications Server 1.12; Netscape Enterprise Server 2.0 and 3.0; Netscape FastTrack 2.0
BSD/OS 2.1, 3.0	NCSA 1.5.2; CERN 3.0; Apache 1.1.3, 1.2.4, and 1.2.5; Netscape Commerce Server 1.12; Netscape Communications Server 1.12; Netscape Enterprise Server 2.0 and 3.0; Netscape FastTrack 2.0
Digital UNIX 3.2c, 4.0	NCSA 1.5.2; CERN 3.0; Apache 1.1.3, 1.2.4, and 1.2.5; Netscape Commerce Server 1.12; Netscape Communications Server 1.12; Netscape Enterprise Server 2.0 and 3.0; Netscape FastTrack 2.0
Linux 3.0.3	NCSA 1.5.2; CERN 3.0; Apache 1.1.3, 1.2.4, and 1.2.5; Netscape Commerce Server 1.12; Netscape Communications Server 1.12; Netscape Enterprise Server 2.0 and 3.0; Netscape FastTrack 2.0
SCO OpenServer Release 5	NCSA 1.5.2; CERN 3.0; Apache 1.1.3, 1.2.4, and 1.2.5; Netscape Commerce Server 1.12; Netscape Communications Server 1.12; Netscape Enterprise Server 2.0 and 3.0; Netscape FastTrack 2.0
AIX 3.2.5, 4.x	NCSA 1.5.2; CERN 3.0; Apache 1.1.3, 1.2.4, and 1.2.5; Netscape Commerce Server 1.12; Netscape Communications Server 1.12; Netscape Enterprise Server 2.0 and 3.0; Netscape FastTrack 2.0
Windows 95/98, Windows NT, Intel x86	Internet Information Server 2.0 and later, Microsoft Peer Web Services (NT Workstation), Microsoft Personal Web Server, FrontPage 97 Personal Web Server, O'Reilly WebSite, Netscape FastTrack 2.0, Netscape Commerce Server 1.12, Netscape Enterprise Server 2.0 and 3.0
Alpha NT Server 4.0	Internet Information Server 2.0 and later; Microsoft Peer Web Services (NT Workstation)

When you install the FrontPage server extensions, you are placing several executable files on your server so that the FrontPage Editor can build calls to these executables into the HTML code it writes. This is the mechanism by which FrontPage supports the FrontPage Components you'll read about next.

CAUTION

Because the FrontPage server extension files are installed below the root directory of your HTTP server, you leave your server vulnerable to attack by hackers who can try to run one of the executables in an attempt to overwrite content on your server.

What Are FrontPage Components?

FrontPage Components are objects you place on a Web page that represent a piece of programming. You can drop a FrontPage Component anywhere you want on a page using the FrontPage Editor. It is up to the server to identify and interpret the component as it serves a page containing a component. How the server handles the component varies with what the component is supposed to do. A server may invoke the programming represented by the component when, for example,

- The file is published to the server.
- The file is served to a browser.
- The user performs a certain action.

The main thing is that the user never detects that you didn't have to do any programming to put program-like functionality on your Web pages. All you have to do is drop the component onto the page and let the server handle the rest.

FrontPage Components come in many flavors. Some are specific to certain types of HTML constructs, such as forms or imagemaps. Others handle routine tasks, such as counting how many visitors have accessed a page or maintaining a table of contents. The following list outlines the components discussed in this chapter. By reading subsequent sections of the chapter, you'll learn how to place each component on the page, what the component looks like in the raw HTML listing, and how a server processes the component.

- Comment Component
- Insert HTML Component
- Timestamp Component
- Include Page Component
- Scheduled Image Component
- Scheduled Include Page Component
- Table of Contents Component
- Hit Counter Component
- Substitution Component
- Confirmation Field Component
- Page Banner Component
- Navigation Bar Component

In addition to covering the preceding components, you'll also see how FrontPage uses a component to handle imagemap processing and how FrontPage supports many other compelling effects, such as banner ads, page transitions, and hover buttons.

Part
II

Ch
10

Using the Comment Component

The Comment Component enables you to add comments to your WYSIWYG page on the FrontPage Editor's Normal tab. The comment will appear in purple text and will be preceded by the word "Comment." Comments are remarks intended for authors and editors working on the document. They are not meant for consumption by the end user, so you'll never see a comment on the Preview tab.

To insert a Comment Component on a page, follow these instructions:

1. Choose Insert, FrontPage Component or click the Insert FrontPage Component button on the toolbar (the button has a picture of a robot on it). When you do, you'll see the Insert FrontPage Component dialog box shown in Figure 10.5. The box presents a listing of the FrontPage Components so that all you need to do to place one is to select it and click OK.

2. Select the Comment Component and click OK. The Comment dialog box shown in Figure 10.6 will appear.

3. Type the text of your comment into this dialog box and click OK when you finish.

FIGURE 10.5

The Insert FrontPage Component dialog box is your one stop for accessing most of FrontPage's Components.

Insert FrontPage Component button

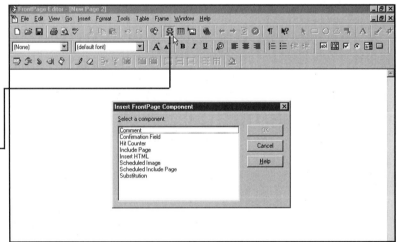

FIGURE 10.6

The Comment dialog box collects the comments you want to place in your documents.

After you click OK, you'll see your comment appear on the Normal tab of the FrontPage Editor. As previously noted, the comment should be painted purple and be preceded with the word "Comment." If you switch over to the HTML tab, you'll see something like the following:

```
<P><!--webbot bot="PurpleText"
preview=" This document created on 29 Sept 98 using Microsoft FrontPage." --></P>
```

When interpreted by the server, this code will invoke the PurpleText bot on the server and render the content stored under the preview parameter as a comment.

> **N O T E** A few things are worth noting about the preceding code. First, FrontPage still refers to components as WebBots in the code. This isn't a big deal because the FrontPage Server Extensions can handle the two names, and neither you nor a user should detect any difficulties.
>
> The second thing to note is that the component code is stored between HTML comment tags: <!-- and -->. This keeps the component code hidden in the event that the raw code is served to a browser. You'll find that most of the FrontPage Components show up in the HTML code this way.

Part
II
Ch
10

If you ever want to edit a comment, move your mouse pointer to it. When you do, you'll see the pointer cursor change to include a robot character, which means you're pointing at a FrontPage Component. Double-click the comment to open up the Comment dialog box you saw in Figure 10.6 and make the changes to your comment there.

Using the Insert HTML Component

HTML is changing all the time. New tags are proposed—and often implemented—at an alarming rate. No Web authoring program can keep releasing new versions to keep up with all the new tags, so most of them come with some means of inserting an unsupported HTML tag into a document's HTML code. In the case of the FrontPage Editor, this task is handled by the Insert HTML Component.

To insert an unsupported HTML tag, follow these steps:

1. Choose Insert, FrontPage Component, or click the Insert FrontPage Component toolbar button to call up a listing of available components.

2. Select the Insert HTML Component to reveal the HTML Markup dialog box (see Figure 10.7).

3. Type in the code you want to insert and then click OK. You won't see anything happen on the Normal tab, but you'll see something like the following on the HTML tab:

```
<P><!--webbot bot="HTMLMarkup" startspan -->
<OPTGROUP>
   <OPTION VALUE="1">Premium Plan
   <OPTION VALUE="2">Gold Plan
   <OPTION VALUE="3">Silver Plan
</OPTGROUP>
<!--webbot bot="HTMLMarkup" endspan --></P>
```

Again, the new code is not placed directly into the existing code. Rather it is passed as a parameter to the HTMLMarkup bot that will insert the tag into the file when the file is served.

FIGURE 10.7

You can enter new HTML tags using the Insert HTML Component.

CAUTION

FrontPage can't validate an HTML tag it doesn't know about. When you enter a new tag, you need to use the correct syntax.

Using the Timestamp Component

Marking your pages with the date and time of the last change or update shows visitors how "fresh" your content is. Unfortunately, it's easy to forget to adjust the date every time you make an edit to a page. The FrontPage Timestamp Component automates this process and places the date and time of the most current revision on the page whenever it is served.

To place a timestamp on your page

1. Move the cursor to the position on the page where you want the timestamp to appear.

2. Choose Insert, Timestamp to reveal the Timestamp Properties dialog box you see in Figure 10.8. Here you have the option of showing the date of the last edit or the last automatic update (other FrontPage Components enable you to automate content updates). You can choose from nearly 20 date formats and 8 time formats.

3. After you configure the timestamp to your liking, click OK to place it on your page.

You'll see the date and time appear on the FrontPage Editor's Normal tab. On the HTML tab, you'll see something like the following:

```
<!--webbot bot="Timestamp" s-type="EDITED"
s-format="%d %B %Y %I:%M %p" -->
```

This code prompts the server to activate the Timestamp bot and passes parameters to it corresponding to how you configured the timestamp.

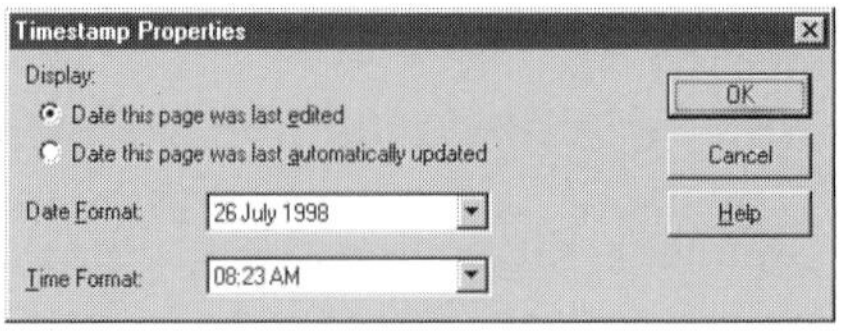

FIGURE 10.8

Automating the Last Updated date relieves you of an often-forgotten task.

N O T E The Timestamp Component is not available from the dialog box you saw in Figure 10.5. You can only select it from the Insert menu. ▨

Using the Include Page Component

The Include Page Component builds the HTML from another file into the HTML file being served. This is a convenient way to place standard, recurring page elements, such as copyright notices or disclaimer text. It also has the advantage of enabling you to store this content in one place. If you need to update the content, you only have to do so once in the master file rather than once for each HTML file on your site.

Using the Include Page Component is easy. Follow these steps:

1. Choose Insert, FrontPage Component, or click the Insert FrontPage Component toolbar button to call up the list of available components.
2. Choose the Include Page Component and click OK. This calls up the simple dialog box you see in Figure 10.9.
3. All you need to specify is the URL of the page you want to include. If the page is in the current Web, you can use the Browse button to find it. Otherwise, you have to type the URL into the Page URL field.

FIGURE 10.9

Includes are great for placing standard content on your pages.

N O T E Using the Include Page Component, you can include a file from a different server. All you need to do is specify the full URL of the file so that your server knows to look to another server for the file. ▨

When you click OK in the Include Page dialog box, you'll initially see the URL you entered displayed in italic on the Normal tab. FrontPage will try to access the file and build it in right then for you, but if it can't, you'll continue to see the italicized URL. On the HTML tab, you'll see a chunk of code such as the following:

```
<!--webbot bot="Include" u-include="copyright.htm" tag="BODY" -->
```

Using the Scheduled Image Component

Another Web site task that's often hard to keep track of is posting and removing time-sensitive content. You may remember to post the content at a certain time, but it is easy to forget about removing it after it has expired unless you marked it on your calendar. FrontPage can help you with these situations with its Scheduled Event Components. The first of these is the Scheduled Image Component that you can use to place an image on a page at a specific time and to remove or replace it at a later time.

To place a Scheduled Image Component, follow these instructions:

1. Choose Insert, FrontPage Components, or click the Insert FrontPage Component toolbar button to display the list of available components.

2. Highlight the Schedule Image option and then click OK. This calls up the Scheduled Image Properties dialog box you see in Figure 10.10. Here you can specify the image file to display, when to start displaying it, and when to stop displaying it. You also have the option of specifying an image to display before and after the scheduled times.

FIGURE 10.10

Scheduled Images are useful for placing a special image on a page for a limited period of time.

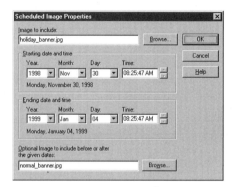

N O T E The image you choose to display doesn't have to be on your own server. You can specify an URL that points to an image file on another server as well. Keep in mind, though, that if the image file is removed from the remote server, your server won't be able to insert it when the page is served. Therefore, you may want to make a copy of the image on your server so that you'll always have access to it.

After you configure the Scheduled Image and click OK, the image or its alternate will show up on the Normal tab if FrontPage can access it. On the HTML tab, you'll see code similar to the following:

```
<P><!--webbot bot="ScheduledImage" U-Src="holiday_banner.jpg"
U-Else-Src="normal_banner.jpg" D-Start-Date="30 Nov 1998 08:25:47"
D-End-Date="04 Jan 1999 08:25:47" --></P>
```

Using the Scheduled Include Page Component

The Scheduled Include Page Component works in a way that is similar to the Schedule Image Component. The primary difference is that the Scheduled Include Page Component builds in the contents of an entire page for a specified period of time, rather than only an image.

When you choose Insert, FrontPage Component, or click the Insert FrontPage Component toolbar button and then select the Scheduled Include Page Component, you'll see a dialog box that's virtually identical to the one you saw in Figure 10.10. The only difference is that you are prompted to provide the URL of an HTML file and not the URL of an image. Note that you can display one file during the scheduled time and specify an alternate file to use before and after the scheduled display times.

Assuming FrontPage can access it, your Scheduled Include Page (or its alternate, depending on the timing) will appear on the Normal tab of the FrontPage Editor. The code for the Scheduled Include Page Component on the HTML tab will look something like the following:

```
<!--webbot bot="ScheduledInclude" u-include="pageone-halloween.htm"
u-else-include="pageone.htm" d-start-date="31 Oct 1998 00:01:00"
d-end-date="01 Nov 1998 00:01:00" -->
```

Using the Table of Contents Component

A table of contents can be another one of those site elements that is a "pain to maintain." Because tables of contents are also a valuable service to your visitors, it's important to make an effort to try to keep yours current. FrontPage can help you with this task by providing you with the Table of Contents Component.

To place a Table of Contents Component on your site, choose Insert, Table of Contents to reveal the Table of Contents Properties dialog box you see in Figure 10.11. Here you specify the file that is the starting point for your table of contents. FrontPage will follow all the links on the page and catalog the files it find along the way. Then FrontPage traverses the links it finds on these files, and so on, until it has generated a table of contents for the entire site.

Part

II

Ch

10

FIGURE 10.11

FrontPage will automatically generate and maintain a site table of contents, sparing you from having to track all the changes.

N O T E The Table of Contents Component is not available from the dialog box you saw in Figure 10.5. You can only select it from the Insert menu. ▪

Note also in the dialog box that you have control over the heading style used to render the table of contents. You can also specify that each file appear only once (a good idea if you have a lot of multiple linked files on your site) and that pages with no incoming hyperlinks appear (a good idea if you have many standalone pages). The Recompute feature is perhaps the nicest part of the Table of Contents Component because it will automatically redo the table if you make changes to any of the files.

 Recomputing your table of contents can place a temporary drain on server resources, so you should try to make changes that would trigger a recomputation at times when the load on the server is relatively low.

When the Tables of Contents Component is placed on your page, it will appear as a bulleted list of links on the Normal tab. You can follow the links by holding down the Control key while you click them. On the HTML tab, you'll see a call to the Outline bot as follows:

```
<!--webbot bot="Outline" U-URL="index.htm" B-Aggressive-Trimming="TRUE"
B-Show-Orphans="TRUE" B-Manual-Recalc="FALSE" I-Heading="1" TAG="BODY" -->
```

Using the Hit Counter Component

One popular element on the home page of many sites is a counter that indicates how many people have visited the page. When counters first started to appear on pages, they were simply text, but later Web content providers got fancy and sent images to the browser to represent the digits in the visitor count. This enabled counters to take on various looks—some looked like a car odometer and others looked like an LED readout. Either way, counters add a little pizzazz to a page and give the page's owner a sense of how popular the page is with Web surfers.

It used to be that you had to code a CGI script to retrieve the previous count, add one to it, and then display the result. Further coding was needed if you were going to parse the visitor count and send each digit as an image. But now, FrontPage relieves you of all that by providing a Hit Counter Component that you drop into place on a page.

To put a Hit Counter Component on one of your pages, follow these steps:

1. Choose Insert, FrontPage Component, or click the Insert FrontPage Component toolbar button to call up the list of available components.

2. Select Hit Counter and click OK to call up the Hit Counter Properties dialog box shown in Figure 10.12. FrontPage enables you to choose from five counter digit styles, or you can specify your own custom style. Additionally, you can reset the counter to a desired value, and you can restrict the counter to be a set number of digits.

FIGURE 10.12

Before FrontPage, hit counters required extensive server-side programming.

> **CAUTION**
>
> If you restrict the number of digits in your counter, make sure you leave enough digits to accommodate the traffic on your site.

When the Hit Counter appears on the Normal tab of the FrontPage Editor, you'll see the text "[Hit Counter]" rendered in boldface. If you switch to the HTML tab, you'll see code such as the following:

```
<!--webbot bot="HitCounter" i-image="1" i-digits="7"
b-reset="FALSE" PREVIEW="&lt;strong&gt;[Hit Counter]&lt;/strong&gt;"
u-custom i-resetvalue="0" -->
```

Using the Substitution Component

The Substitution Component inserts the value of a Web or page configuration variable into a document. The default configuration variables available to the Substitution Component are:

- Author
- Modified By
- Description
- Page URL

Any Web setting parameters you specify in the FrontPage Explorer will be available to the Substitution Component as well (choose Tools, Web Settings; see Figure 10.13).

FIGURE 10.13
You can establish global Web parameters that are available for placement on a page using the Substitution Component.

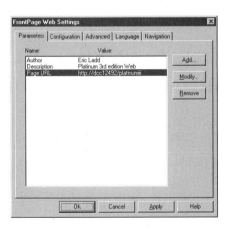

To use the Substitution Component, follow these steps:

1. Choose Insert, FrontPage Component, or click the Insert FrontPage Component toolbar button to reveal the dialog box that lists the components.

Part
II

Ch
10

2. Select the Substitution option and click OK to open the Substitution Component Properties dialog box you see in Figure 10.14.

3. Choose the configuration variable you want from the drop-down list and click OK to place the component.

FIGURE 10.14

The Modified By variable is a useful substitution for Webmasters who track changes to documents on their sites.

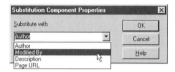

When the Substitution Component appears on the FrontPage Editor's Normal tab, you'll see the name of the variable you selected enclosed in square brackets. On the HTML tab, the Substitution Component is represented by code that resembles the following:

```
<!--webbot bot="Substitution" S-Variable="vti_modifiedby" -->
```

Using the Confirmation Field Component

Forms are a Web content provider's means of collecting information from end users. Data entered into a form is typically sent back to the server for some kind of processing, but before that happens, you can do a few things with the form data to ensure that it is as polished as it can be. One thing is to confirm the data in the form's key fields, and the FrontPage Confirmation Field Component can help you do it.

The first thing you need to make a form field confirmation is, not surprisingly, a form. Assuming you've already used the FrontPage Editor to compose a form, go back through the form and write down the names (as assigned in the NAME attributes) of the form fields you want to confirm. You'll need the field names when inserting the Field Confirmation Components.

Next, you need to create a confirmation page where the Field Confirmation Components will reside. To do this, follow these steps:

1. In the FrontPage Editor, choose File, New and then select the Normal Page option.

2. Put whatever banner, background, and text you want on the page, leaving spaces for where you want the form field confirmations to go.

3. Place your cursor at a position where you want a confirmation, and then choose Insert, FrontPage Component, or click the Insert FrontPage Component toolbar button. From the Components list, select the Confirmation Field option.

4. Enter the name of the form field you want confirmed in the Confirmation Field Properties dialog box (see Figure 10.15) and click OK.

5. Repeat steps 3 and 4 for each field you want to confirm.

6. Save the confirmation page to your open Web.

FIGURE 10.15

Confirming the data submitted in a form field is as simple as typing the field's name into a dialog box.

With the confirmation page created, the last thing you need to do is to link the form with the confirmation page. You can accomplish this by performing these steps:

1. Open the form page in the FrontPage Editor, right-click the form, and select the Form Properties option.

2. Click the Options button in the Form Properties dialog box.

3. In the Options for Saving Results of Form dialog box, click the Confirmation Page tab. You should see the dialog box shown in Figure 10.16.

FIGURE 10.16

You need to tell FrontPage if a form has an associated confirmation page.

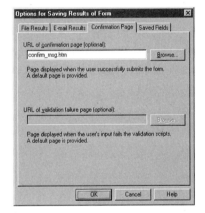

4. Enter the URL of the confirmation page or browse to the page itself if it's in your open Web.

5. Click OK in the Options for Saving Results of Form and Form Properties dialog boxes.

Now the chosen fields in the form will be confirmed before the data is sent along for processing. If you look at the Confirmation Field Components on the confirmation page, they will appear as the field name enclosed in square brackets. If you look at the HTML source code for the Confirmation Field Components, you'll see something such as the following:

```
<!--webbot bot="ConfirmationField" s-field="phone_number" -->
```

When users submit a form with fields set up for confirmation, they will be presented with your confirmation page that will repeat back to them what they entered. If the data entered is incorrect, users can make changes to it from the confirmation page.

Part

II

Ch

10

N O T E   Form field confirmation is different from form field validation. When you validate a field, you check to see if the input in the field conforms to a particular format. You might validate a phone number, for example, to see if it is in the form xxx-xxx-xxxx.

Form field validation is frequently done with client-side scripting. You can read about how to do form field validation with JavaScript in Chapter 21, "Using JavaScript to Create Smart Forms."

Using the Page Banner Component

The Page Banner Component places a banner across the top of the page in either an image-based or a text-based format. If you choose an image and one of the FrontPage graphic themes has been applied, the banner graphic will have the same look and feel as the theme (see Figure 10.17). A text-based banner will also have the same look and feel as the text within the theme. By default, the banner will display the page's title, regardless of whether you use the image or the text format.

T I P   You can change what is displayed on the banner from the Navigation view in the FrontPage Explorer.

FIGURE 10.17

Banners display a page's title in either image- or text-based form.

Text-based banner

Image-based banner

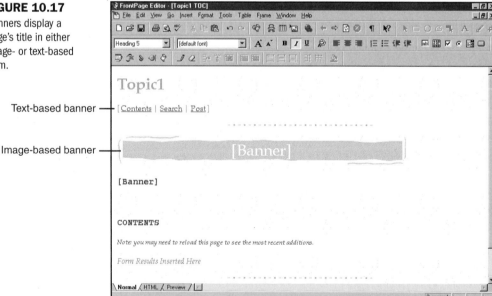

To place a banner on a page, place your cursor where you want the banner to appear and choose Insert, FrontPage Component, or click the Insert FrontPage Component toolbar button. In the dialog box that appears, select the Page Banner option and click OK. You'll then see the Page Banner Properties dialog box shown in Figure 10.18. All you need to do is to tell FrontPage whether you want the banner to be an image or text, and it will do the rest.

FIGURE 10.18

After FrontPage knows whether you want an image or text in your banner, it can proceed with the banner creation.

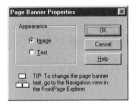

As you saw in Figure 10.17, a banner shows up on the Normal tab the same as it will look on a browser screen. When you look at the code for the banner, you'll see something resembling the following:

```
<!--webbot bot="Navigation" s-type="banner" s-rendering="graphics"
s-orientation b-include-home b-include-up -->
```

Part

II

Ch

10

Using the Navigation Bar Component

One final FrontPage Component enables you to automatically place Navigation Bars on your pages. You'll recall from the site and page design chapters that giving users consistent navigation to all parts of your site is an important measure of a usable site. By using FrontPage's Navigation Bar Component, you can implement site navigation across all your pages with ease.

To use the Navigation Bar Component, perform these steps:

1. From the Insert menu, choose the Navigation Bar option. This opens the Navigation Bar Properties dialog box you see in Figure 10.19.

2. First you need to specify what pages should be included in the navigation links. FrontPage enables you to choose from pages at the parent level (one level above the current level), pages at the same level of the current page, back and next pages, pages at the child level (one level below the current level), and pages at the top level. In addition to your level choice, you can also include links to a page's parent page and the site's home page.

 If you aren't clear as to the meaning of parent level, child level, and top level, look at the hierarchical diagram in the dialog box as you choose different levels. The diagram will change to match the selected level, and you'll have a visual representation of what pages will be linked in your navigation bar.

3. Next you need to choose how you want the navigation bar to appear on the page. You can choose either a horizontal or vertical orientation and either a button-based or text-based set of links.

4. When you're done configuring your navigation bar, click the OK button to place it on the page.

When the component appears on the Normal tab, you'll see some text that reads "[Button][Button][Button]." Over on the HTML tab, you'll see corresponding code that looks something like the following:

```
<P><!--webbot bot="Navigation" S-Type="arrows" S-Orientation="vertical"
S-Rendering="graphics" B-Include-Home="TRUE" B-Include-Up="true" --></P>
```

FIGURE 10.19

FrontPage can construct a set of navigation links based on its knowledge of your site's hierarchical structure.

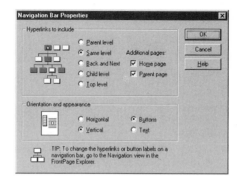

N O T E The Navigation Bar Component is not available from the dialog box you saw in Figure 10.5. You can only select it from the Insert menu. ■

How FrontPage Handles Imagemaps

The FrontPage Editor has toolbar buttons you can use to trace out hot regions on an image when you're creating an imagemap. After you've completed a trace, FrontPage prompts you for the URL to associate with the hot region. But what FrontPage does with the imagemap information after this may surprise you. This section looks at FrontPage's default approach to handling imagemaps, and how you can adjust it to your needs.

After you complete the definition of your hot regions, you should most likely switch to the HTML tab to examine the code FrontPage placed there to represent your imagemap. You probably expect to see the <MAP> tag and some <AREA> tags forming the imagemap code, but what you see instead is something like the following:

```
<!--webbot bot="ImageMap"
polygon=" (201,163) (237,139) (303,148) (329,180) (310,208) (259,204)
(213,202) (202,169) feedback.htm" rectangle=" (228,309) (278, 397)
services.htm" circle=" (281,83) 60  techsupport.htm" src="main.gif"
alt="main.gif (9219 bytes)" align="right" width="532" height="400" -->
```

As this code shows, FrontPage's default approach to processing imagemaps is to use a bot on the server, not to embed a client-side imagemap code into the HTML file.

Although the Imagemap bot works fine, you may prefer to have FrontPage write out <MAP> and <AREA> tags so that you can have a truly client-side imagemap (using a bot means that the server is still involved). To set up FrontPage to use client-side imagemaps, go to the FrontPage Explorer, choose Tools, Web Settings, and then click the Advanced tab. This opens the dialog FrontPage Web Settings box you see in Figure 10.20. Near the top of the dialog box, you will see options for creating imagemaps. Make sure the Generate Client-Side Imagemaps box is checked, select the Netscape option from the Style drop-down list, and then click OK. You should then find that additional imagemaps you create don't make use of the Imagemap bot.

FIGURE 10.20

You can alter FrontPage's approach to imagemap processing from the Advanced Web Settings dialog box.

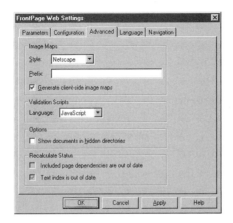

Other Automated FrontPage Features

FrontPage comes with a number of other automated features and functions beyond the FrontPage Components. To close the chapter, this last section takes you on a brief tour of some of FrontPage's other high-end features. In each case, FrontPage is taking a task that was previously labor intensive and reducing its setup to a few simple actions.

■ Search, Discussion, Save Results, and Registration Bots—If you've used previous versions of FrontPage, you might be wondering where some of the old FrontPage bots are among the FrontPage Components. Among the more popular of these are the Search, Discussion, Save Results, and Registration bots.

The answer is that they are available in the current release of FrontPage, but they are not listed with the FrontPage Components. Rather, you have to look elsewhere to create instructions that use these bots. To use the Search bot, which sets up a mini search engine in your FrontPage Web, choose Insert, Active Elements, Search Form to launch the dialog box that will enable you to configure your search.

You can use the Discussion bot to create a fully searchable threaded discussion group by choosing File, New FrontPage Web in the FrontPage Explorer. When you see the list of possible Webs, choose the Discussion Web Wizard to walk through the steps of creating the threaded discussion.

The Save Results bot is called the Save Results form handler in current release of FrontPage. To use the form handler, right-click your form and select Form Properties from the pop-up menu you see. Then click the Options button to configure the saving location and format.

Finally, the Registration bot is now tucked away in a User Registration page template in the FrontPage Editor. To load the template, in the Editor choose File, New and choose the User Registration document from the list you see. A registration page enables Web users to self-register, rather than burdening you with all the data entry.

■ Hover Buttons—Buttons that change their properties when a user's mouse pointer is over the button or when the user clicks the button. You can set up the button to be text- or image-based, and FrontPage can even bevel the image for you so that it looks more like a button.

To create a hover button, choose Insert, Active Elements, Hover Button to reveal the Hover Button dialog box. If you want a text-based button, you can set it up here, including how the button should be colored and what onscreen effect it should possess (glow, beveling, and so on). If you want to use an image, click the Custom button to open the Custom dialog box. In the lower half of the dialog box, you'll find fields for specifying the default button image and the image to display when a user's mouse is hovering over the image.

After your button is configured, click OK to place it on your page. If you peek at the HTML tag, you'll see that FrontPage renders the button by using a Java applet.

■ Page Transitions—One of the neat features found in Microsoft's PowerPoint presentation creation software is a set of transitions you can use between slides in the presentation. Now Microsoft brings those transitions to the Web through the FrontPage Editor. To add a transition to a page, choose Format, Page Transition to open the Page Transitions dialog box. Here you can choose from more than twenty transition effects. You can also set the duration of the transition and specify the event that triggers the transition (entering the page, leaving the site, and so on).

After the transition is in place, you can look at the HTML code to see that FrontPage accomplished the transition by using a <META> tag in the document head. The tag contains an HTTP-EQUIV value that corresponds to the triggering event that you selected. When the server detects the event, it uses Dynamic HTML to produce the transition effect.

N O T E   Because they use Microsoft's notion of Dynamic HTML, FrontPage page transitions are best viewed with Internet Explorer 4.0. ■

■ Text Animations—Text doesn't have to sit still with FrontPage. It can come flying onto the page from anywhere off the screen, or it can spiral into place gracefully. To animate text, highlight it with your mouse, choose Format, Animation, and then select one of the 14 animations available. When you preview the page in a Microsoft Dynamic HTML-capable browser, you'll see the text move onto the screen according to the animation technique you chose.

■ Banner Ad Manager—Sites that sell advertising can make use of the FrontPage Banner Ad Manager, which takes a list of ad graphics files and displays them in sequence. You can control how long each graphic appears, what the graphics link to, and the transition effect between graphics. To activate the Banner Ad Manager, choose Insert, Active Elements, Banner Ad Manager. The Banner Ad Manager enables you to specify the size of the banner, which images to display in the banner space, how banner transitions should occur, and how long each image should appear.

PART III

XML

Introduction to XML

by Eric Ladd

Why XML?

HTML is a fairly simple language—simple enough to have made Web publishing accessible to many people. Its rules are also straightforward enough that scores of programmers have written HTML editing tools that enable content publishers to prepare a document without knowing *any* HTML. This has opened up the Web to even more people. Indeed, HTML's ease of use is probably one of the biggest reasons for the explosive growth of the Web.

HTML, however, is not without its problems. For one thing, it is too restrictive. You probably know that HTML is an application of the Standard Generalized Markup Language (SGML), restricted to a certain set of rules. After you start using SGML in a specific way, you sacrifice much of the flexibility you get by using "less constrained" SGML. This means that you are less likely to be able to describe more complex documents with HTML or with any restricted form of SGML.

Yet another issue with HTML is that, as it evolved, its tags became more focused on describing how content should be presented rather than on what the content was. You read in Chapter 9, "Style Sheets," how the idea of a style sheet helps to separate the nature of content from its presentation. Style sheets are a step in the right direction, but they have only recently been adopted, and it will take some time before HTML becomes completely free of tags that describe presentation.

What's the solution to the problem with HTML then? The answer is the *eXtensible Markup Language* (XML). Because XML stays focused on content description, you don't run the risk of having any XML markup specifying how to present the content. Additionally, XML is highly extensible, meaning that it is flexible enough to handle a simple document, such as a home page, or a huge document, such as *War and Peace*. This chapter introduces you to XML, shows you how to use it, and explains why it is so important to the future of Web publishing.

To better understand why XML is the next wave in Web content markup, it is helpful to consider the alternatives and to see how they fall short of meeting the anticipated needs of both content providers and consumers. Discounting XML for the moment, only two options exist for marking up Web content: HTML and SGML.

Problems with HTML

The remarks in the previous paragraphs hint at some of the weaknesses inherent in HTML. The first of these is that many HTML tags are geared toward describing how content should look on a browser screen instead of saying what the content is (as a document description language should). Consider the many text formatting tags in HTML:

- `<B>` for boldface
- `<I>` for italic
- `<TT>` for fixed-width characters
- `<FONT>` for changing typeface, type size, and color
- `<CENTER>` for centering text, images, and other page elements

Each of these tags modifies a presentation-related property of an object on the page, but they give absolutely no indication of the meaning of the object. An indexing program, for example, would have no sense of the significance of the following markup:

```
<B>Warning! Pressing Ctrl+Alt+Del will restart your machine!</B>
```

A situation such as the one above is why someone tried to introduce a <NOTE> tag into HTML to handle admonishments. An indexer would have a much easier time understanding something like this:

```
<NOTE CLASS="WARNING">Warning! Pressing Ctrl+Alt+Del will restart
your machine!</NOTE>
```

In this case, it is clear from the markup that the text between <NOTE> and </NOTE> is a message encouraging caution.

To HTML's credit, it does have some tags that indicate the meaning of the text they mark up. The following tags, for example, all convey some sense of meaning:

- <ADDRESS> for email and postal addresses
- <BLOCKQUOTE> for indented, quoted text
- <CITE> for citations
- <DFN> for the defining instance of a term
- <EM> for text to be emphasized
- <KBD> for keyboard input
- <Q> for quoted text
- <STRONG> for strong emphasis

Part

III

Ch

11

You could easily generate a glossary of key terms from a document marked up with the <DFN> tag, for example. All the program would have to do is strip out all the words found between <DFN> and </DFN> tags and form a list from them. This simple example demonstrates what kind of automation is possible when you have marked text with tags that signify meaning.

N O T E A number of proposed tags indicate meaning, although many did not find their way into the HTML 4.0 recommendation. These include

- <AU> for an author's name
- <PERSON> for a person's name

With XML's star on the rise, it is unclear whether these tags will ever become part of the HTML standard.

HTML is not the best at describing what content means, but the problems don't stop there. Another issue is that HTML is not flexible enough to properly mark up the wide variety of documents that people want to publish electronically. The only pieces of a document that HTML can describe are a <HEAD> and a <BODY>. But what about document constructs, such as abstracts, chapters, and bibliographies? Currently, no HTML tags can accommodate these kinds of document divisions.

In response to the idea that HTML is not flexible enough, you may be thinking, "Hey, if HTML doesn't do what someone wants it to do, another tag will be introduced soon enough." That is actually another problem with HTML. Browser software companies have introduced scores of new, proprietary tags in an effort to lure users to their products. The World Wide Web Consortium (W3C) has, over time, incorporated many of these tags into the HTML standard, but many tags are still used in some HTML documents that won't be rendered properly on all browsers.

If the issues raised so far are not enough, here is one more browser-related problem: Browsers are too forgiving of bad HTML code. Consider the following HTML:

```
<HEAD>
<META KEYWORD="bad HTML document>
<BODY BGCOLOR="005MFF">
<H1>An Imperfect HTML Document</H2>
<UL>
<LI>Most browsers will render this document in a readable way.
<LI>An HTML validator would be required to catch the syntax errors.
</UL>
```

Syntactically speaking, this code contains several errors:

- <TITLE> is a required element, and the document has no title.

- The KEYWORD attribute in the <META> tag has a mismatched quotation mark (").

- The value of the BGCOLOR attribute is invalid because hexadecimal values can be made up only with the digits 0–9 and A–F. Also, the hexadecimal value should be offset by a pound sign (#).

- The heading style tags are mismatched.

- No closing </BODY> and </HTML> tags are present.

Despite these errors, look at Figure 11.1; this figure shows the document through Netscape Navigator. It looks pretty good, doesn't it? Why should authors adhere to proper HTML syntax when most popular browsers, in the absence of good syntax, can usually figure out what the user wants? The fact that browsers are so forgiving has led to very sloppy HTML authoring habits. This is a problem because, if the trend toward automated processing of Web documents continues, it will be imperative for all documents to adhere to proper syntax. Otherwise, it will be impossible for programs to correctly parse them.

By now you are probably losing confidence in HTML's capability to meet the electronic publishing needs of the future. Rest assured, you would not be alone in feeling that way. Many content providers also raised these concerns and escalated the situation to the point that the W3C began to consider alternatives. One of the easiest alternatives to consider was that of going back to HTML's parent language—SGML. As the next section illustrates, however, for a set of different reasons, SGML is not the markup language of the future.

FIGURE 11.1

Despite several syntax errors, Netscape Navigator still rendered this HTML document.

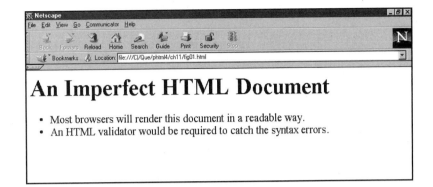

Problems with SGML

If you were to use SGML to mark up Web documents, you would certainly have no trouble with flexibility. After all, SGML is really a meta-language, or a language for defining other languages. It provides a vast set of features for devising description languages for documents as short as a single page or as long as several printed volumes.

But therein lies the problem. SGML is so vast that it is overkill for most kinds of Web publications. The SGML standard stretches on for pages and pages, making it more difficult for

- Content providers to mark up content
- Programmers to write parsers, browsers, and other processing programs

SGML has so many optional features that it is just too cumbersome for the needs of Web publishers. Yet it is much more extensible and structured—both very desirable features—than HTML. How then can the Web publishing world harness the best qualities of SGML without all its high maintenance features?

XML: The Best of Both Worlds

The answer is XML. XML is a simplified version of SGML that throws out many of the features of SGML that just don't apply to Web publishing activities. The result is a meta-language that provides SGML's structure and flexibility without all the complexities. Specifically, XML is

- Extensible. XML's flexibility comes from its capability to enable you to make up your own XML elements. This means that you can introduce tags into XML as appropriate to your publishing needs.
- Portable. The catch to being able to introduce your own tags is that you need to be able to communicate the syntax of those tags to others. Fortunately, it is fairly simple to produce files that capture the rules of your markup and enable others to properly read or process your XML documents.
- Structured. One feature that XML takes from SGML is a rigid adherence to a specific structure. If a document is not structured properly, it is not considered to be XML.

■ Descriptive. XML elements are necessarily divorced from specifying how content is to be presented. Thus, the elements are free to describe the meaning of what they contain. This permits more "intelligent" handling by parsers and other processing programs.

XML retains the best features of SGML without the intricacies of SGML, making it a much more accessible language. XML also retains some of the good things about HTML: It is easy for Web document authors to use and easy for programmers to write software to render XML code. The balance of this chapter is dedicated to introducing you to the work that has been done so far in developing an XML standard. After an overview of some basic concepts, you will read about elements and entities, the two major components of XML. You will then learn how to set up different kinds of links in XML documents. Finally, you will read about how style sheets can be used with XML files to specify presentation and how XML is already slated for use in a number of specialty publishing areas.

NOTE XML is a very young language. The XML 1.0 recommendation was published in early 1998, and only now are software developers moving toward producing XML parsers and browsers. Content developers have begun to devise different applications of XML—for example, the Mathematical Markup Language (MathML) is a specialized markup language derived from XML. Many other disciplines have their own XML-based markup languages in the works.

XML is eventually expected to supplant HTML as the "mother tongue" for Web publishing, but this will not happen overnight. When the World Wide Web Consortium (W3C) finalized the HTML 4.0 recommendation earlier this year, it announced that the next version of HTML would be the first important step toward migrating to XML. It also said that it would take approximately 18 months to develop this transitional language, so you have plenty of time to learn the basics of XML and develop markup languages appropriate to your Web publishing activities. ■

XML Overview

Before you dive into the specifics of XML, it is helpful to be grounded in some of the basic ideas. From what you have read so far, you understand the motivation for creating XML. (HTML is too limited; SGML is too broad.) In addition, some fundamental concepts—if mastered now—will make it easier to read the remaining sections of this chapter. These concepts include

■ The different types of XML markup
■ Document Type Definitions (DTDs)
■ Valid XML documents
■ Well-formed XML documents

The next three sections examine these ideas.

Types of XML Markup

Five types of markup exist in XML. Some of these might be familiar from your knowledge of HTML. If you know some SGML, all of them should ring a bell. The great thing is that no single one of them is much harder to learn than HTML; therefore, XML should be much more accessible than SGML.

The five classes of markup in XML are as follows:

- Elements. XML elements describe the meaning of the text they contain. Elements typically occur in pairs with a start tag and an end tag that enclose the text they mark up. Inside the start tag, a keyword indicates the meaning of the markup. The end tag contains the same keyword with a forward slash (/) in front of it. Both kinds of tag start with the less than sign (<) and end with the greater than sign (>).

N O T E Although subtle differences exist between what constitutes an element and what constitutes a tag, the words "element" and "tag" are sometimes used interchangeably. Specifically, <ADDRESS> is a tag, but the notion of an <ADDRESS>...</ADDRESS> container captures the idea of an element.

Some elements do not occur in pairs. These elements are said to be *empty*. Because it is important for parsers to know whether an element is empty, the tag for the element ends with /> rather than >. A line break element, for example, might look like

```
<BR/>
```

rather than the <BR> tag you are used to in HTML. The additional forward slash makes it clear to parsers that they should not look for a corresponding end tag.

N O T E The XML 1.0 recommendation makes allowances for empty tags to have an end tag, provided it immediately follows the start tag. Under this provision, you could use

```
<BR></BR>
```

rather than

```
<BR/>
```

This addition makes XML a bit more like HTML and will help ease the transition from authoring HTML documents to authoring XML documents.

Some elements take *attributes* that modify or expand on the meaning they impart to the content they contain. Attributes are set equal to values that must be offset by quotation marks. You could add an attribute to the previously mentioned <BR/> tag, for example, to make it read

```
<BR CLEAR="LEFT"/>
```

This makes it break to the first clear left margin.

- Entities. Entities in XML are very similar to entities in HTML. Recall that in HTML you need entities to represent reserved characters such as < or >. The same idea applies in XML, and you would use the same entities—< and >—to render these characters. XML also enables you to use any Unicode character you want; thus, producing documents in languages other than English is less of a chore. Finally, you can define your own entities right inside your XML code and reference them later on.

Part
III

Ch
11

XML entities can also reside externally to the document. You can incorporate a separate XML file by mapping it to an entity name and then referencing the entity in your main file.

- Comments. Commenting your code is always prudent, and XML supports you in commenting with the <!-- and --> tags for enclosing comments. These are the same tags you use for comments in both HTML and SGML.

  You can place any text you like between the <!-- and --> tags, except for the double hyphen construct --. This character sequence is reserved, so it can help to denote the comment.

- Processing instructions. Processing instructions (PIs) enable you to embed information to be passed to an application right in your XML document. All PIs have the following syntax:

  ```
  <?name data?>
  ```

  The name, or *PI target,* should be one that an application will recognize. You can give the target any name you like, but targets beginning with "XML" are reserved for standardization purposes.

  The data component of the PI can be anything that the processing application understands. Therefore, it is important for processing applications to act only on PIs whose targets they recognize.

- Ignored sections. Sometimes it is necessary to pass characters that are XML reserved characters. In these cases, you can define a section that will be ignored by the XML parser and be passed to a processing application. A good example of this is mathematical code, which is likely to contain greater than (>) or less than (<) signs. A parser would normally treat these characters as parts of a start or end tag, but if you put them into an ignored section, like this:

  ```
  <![CDATA[
  4 < 3 is FALSE.
  ]]>
  ```

  the expression with the less than sign passes to the application. All ignored sections start with <![CDATA[and end with]]>. You can put any text you want between these containers except for the]]> combination.

N O T E Comments found in an ignored section get passed to the processing application as well.

With a sense of what the major types of markup are, you could probably get started with some XML yourself. You could mark up a letter, for example, as follows:

```
<LETTER>
<DATE ALIGN="RIGHT">
September 29, 1998
</DATE>
<INSIDEADDRESS>
```

```
Trans Union Corporation<BR/>
Consumer Disclosure Center<BR/>
P.O. Box 390<BR/>
Springfield, PA  19064-0390<BR/>
</INSIDEADDRESS>
<SALUTATION>
Dear Customer Relations Representative:
</SALUTATION>
<BODY>
<P ALIGN="JUSTIFY">
Please send me a copy of my credit file.  Enclosed please find a page of
 personal data and a check for $8.00 for your services.
</P>
<P ALIGN="JUSTIFY">
You may send the report to the address indicated on the personal
data page.
</P>
<P>
Thank you for your assistance.
</P>
</BODY>
<CLOSING>
Very truly yours,
</CLOSING>
<SIGNATURE>
Mary Consumer
</SIGNATURE>
</LETTER>
```

Because you are probably familiar with the structure of a business letter, the preceding markup makes sense. Note how the elements describe the nature of the text they contain, rather than how it should be presented. In fact, the only reference to presentation you see is the ALIGN attribute in the <DATE> and <P> tags.

Note also that the elements used are not part of any specification—they were made up to describe each part of the letter. The freedom to make up your own elements is one of XML's chief strengths. What happens, however, when you try to share one of your XML documents with someone else? You understand what all the markup means, of course, but if you share with others who do not understand it, their XML parsers may not be able to handle your document correctly. Fortunately, you can share the XML structures you devise with others. By writing a Document Type Definition (DTD), you specify your XML elements, their attributes, and their syntax. Then you can reference your DTD at the top of your XML document so that any parser knows where to find the DTD file. After the parser has the DTD, it "understands" your document as well as you do. Composing a DTD is the subject of the next section.

Document Type Definitions (DTDs)

A *DTD* is a set of rules that specifies how to use XML markup. It contains specs for each element, including what the element's attributes are, what values the attributes can take on, and what elements can be contained in others. Additionally, you can define entities in the DTD. You can define entities right in the DTD or in reference code in an external file.

For the business letter example in the preceding section, you might compose a DTD that looks like this:

```
<!ELEMENT letter (date, insideaddress, salutation, body, closing,
signature?)>
<!ELEMENT date (#PCDATA)>
<!ATTLIST date align (left¦right) "left">
<!ELEMENT insideaddress (#PCDATA ¦ br*)>
<!ELEMENT br EMPTY>
<!ELEMENT salutation (#PCDATA)>
<!ELEMENT body (p+)>
<!ELEMENT p (#PCDATA)>
<!ATTLIST p align (left¦justify¦right) "left">
<!ELEMENT closing (#PCDATA)>
<!ELEMENT signature (#PCDATA)>
```

This code may not be as clear as the markup it specifies, so here is a line-by-line description of what the DTD says:

- A LETTER has exactly one DATE, one INSIDEADDRESS, one SALUTATION, one BODY, one CLOSING, and an optional SIGNATURE.
- A DATE contains only text.
- The DATE element has an attribute called ALIGN that can take on values of LEFT and RIGHT. In the absence of a specification for ALIGN, its value should be taken to be equal to LEFT.
- An <INSIDEADDRESS> contains text and zero or more <BR/> elements.
- The <BR/> element is empty (that is, it has no end tag).
- A <SALUTATION> contains only text.
- The <BODY> comprises one or more <P> elements.
- The <P> element contains only text.
- The <P> element also has an ALIGN attribute that can equal LEFT, JUSTIFY, or RIGHT. Its default value is taken to be LEFT.
- The <CLOSING> element contains only text.
- The <SIGNATURE> element contains only text.

Just by knowing these rules, any XML parser could properly process your document. In addition to being useful for XML parsers and browsers, a DTD is useful in a few other situations:

- XML authoring tools use DTDs to validate the code you write. If the syntax in your XML document is incorrect, the program can detect and flag it for you. As the next section explains, the program should not even enable you to save the document unless it conforms to a DTD.
- An XML browser can't know the default values of any attributes without a DTD.
- Just as with HTML, XML ignores extra whitespace characters (spaces, carriage returns, tabs) beyond a single space. Specifically, if an element's content model is *mixed* (meaning it can be both text and other elements), whitespace within the element is taken to be significant. Elements that contain only other elements are said to have *element content*; whitespace in these elements is ignored.

Most importantly, DTDs enable you to publish your documents for consumption by others. To accomplish this, however, you must include instructions in your documents that tell an XML processing program how to find your DTD. Adding a simple `<!DOCTYPE>` element at the start of your XML file takes care of this. For the letter example, you might reference its DTD as follows:

```
<!DOCTYPE LETTER SYSTEM "http:/www.server.com/DTDs/letter.dtd">
<LETTER>
<DATE ALIGN="RIGHT">
September 29, 1998
</DATE>
<INSIDEADDRESS>
...
</LETTER>
```

The first line in the code directs the XML processor to the DTD at `http://www.server.com/DTDs/letter.dtd`. The processor can then download the DTD and use it to check the document for appropriate syntax and to determine default attribute values.

Valid and Well-Formed XML Documents

For all the value a DTD provides, you may be surprised to learn that DTDs are not absolutely necessary. If an XML document conforms to a few key rules, a parser should still be capable of handling it. Specifically, a document is said to be *well-formed* if

Part

III

Ch

11

- It contains one or more elements.

- The document conforms to the grammar put forward in the XML specification.

- One element called the *root or document element* is present whose start and end tags are not contained by any other element. The `<LETTER>` element would be the root element for the letter example.

- All other non-empty elements are properly nested.

- All attribute values are contained by quotation marks.

- All entities have either been declared in the DTD or, if no DTD is specified, are one of the following reserved entities: `&amp;`, `&lt;`, `&gt;`, `&apos;`, and `&quot;`.

Even in the absence of a DTD, an XML parser should correctly parse a well-formed document. This means that the parser can build the document tree (the logical structure that the parser creates as it processes the document), but it cannot assess the proper use of the elements.

The key thing to remember about well-formed documents is this: If it is not well formed, it is not XML. A document that is not well formed will be summarily rejected by any XML parser. This seemingly rigid approach has two important advantages:

- It ensures that XML never "breaks" a browser the way extended HTML tags can. If a document is well formed, an XML browser is guaranteed to be capable of rendering it. If a document isn't well formed, the browser just ignores it.

- It forces XML authors to get into good coding habits, as opposed to the sloppy habits that have come to plague HTML documents. Because the rules of being well-formed are well established, any XML editing program should be capable of checking an author's work to determine whether it is well formed before saving.

If a DTD is specified for a well-formed document and the document conforms to the DTD, the document is said to be *valid*. Validity is a stronger requirement than being well-formed. However, because validity implies the presence of a DTD, it is certainly the preferred state of the two. The primary benefit of having a valid document is that it is widely publishable. A valid document has to have a DTD, and if you make that DTD available with the document, any XML processing program can use the DTD to facilitate the parsing and rendering of the document. Because the DTD formally defines the document, it also becomes easier to bring other functionality to bear on the document, such as search engines, style sheets, nonvisual browsers, and printing applications.

Linking with XML

The first phase of the W3C's rollout of XML was issuing the recommendation for basic XML grammar. That recommendation is really just a set of rules for how elements, entities, processing instructions, and so on must be structured for a document to be considered an XML document. The draft does not specify any particular elements because XML authors are free to create their own. The same is true for entities, except for the five reserved entity characters (<, >, &, ", '). Although the draft may seem vague, remember that, in a sense, it is supposed to be. The "extensibility" part of XML comes from the capability to form your own sets of elements and entities according to your needs.

One important idea that the recommendation does not address is that of linking documents. If you are familiar with HTML, you know that you use an <A> element with the HREF attribute to link text or graphics to another document. But because no specific elements exist in XML, you may be wondering how XML documents get linked together. The answer lies in the second phase of the XML rollout—the draft proposal for XML linking using the XML Linking Language (XLink) and the XML Pointer Language (XPointer). In keeping with the "extensible and flexible" philosophy inherent in XML, XLink and XPointer call for more than the traditional, unidirectional linking you get with HTML. Instead, you can do extended linking that allows for multidirectional links or links to special kinds of information. The next few sections look at what is possible in linking XML documents.

N O T E The XLink proposal is constantly evolving, so be sure to check the W3C site at `http://www.w3.org/TR/WD-xlink` for the most recent changes to the proposal. ▓

XLink

The W3C published a proposed XLink 1.0 standard in March 1998. That proposal put forth the notion of two classes of links:

- ▓ Simple links—Simple links are one-directional links from one resource to another, similar to how you use the <A> element in HTML. Simple links are usually *inline*, which means that the content of the element describing the link serves as a resource of the link. The <A> element, for example, produces inline links because its contents (the HREF attribute) specify the link's resource (the document the link points to).

■ Extended links—Extended links are links that can be multidirectional. Additionally, you can use the notion of extended links to define what is known as an extended link group (described later in the chapter).

You are free to make up whatever element you like to specify an XML link, but that link must contain the XML:LINK attribute, which is reserved so that parsers and browsers have some way of knowing that the element is defining a link. To create links, you usually set XML:LINK to one of two values: SIMPLE or EXTENDED. You can also use other values of XML:LINK when defining extended links. The next two sections review the specifics of each type of link.

Simple Links   The simple XML link is very much like the link you get with the <A> element in HTML. Because it is up to the XML author as to what to name an element, no specific element name is reserved for use when linking. For the purposes of this section, the simple linking element is <SIMPLINK>. You are welcome to call the simple link element whatever you would like in your own documents.

What sets simple linking apart from basic linking in HTML is the much greater number of attributes that a simple link element can take. Table 11.1 summarizes these attributes.

Table 11.1   Attributes for a Simple Link Element

Attribute	Purpose
ACTUATE="AUTO¦USER"	Specifies what event should trigger the traversal of the link
BEHAVIOR	Provides more detail about how the traversal should occur
CONTENT-ROLE	Describes the meaning of the content in the document you're linking to
CONTENT-TITLE	Provides a title for the linked content that can be displayed to the user
HREF	Specifies the URL of the document you're linking to
INLINE="TRUE¦FALSE"	Says whether the link is inline
ROLE	Describes the meaning of the link
SHOW="EMBED¦REPLACE¦NEW"	Tells the processing application how to display the information in the linked document
TITLE	Provides a title for the link that can be displayed to the user
XML:LINK	Specifies what kind of XML link the element supports

Part
III

Ch
11

Many of these attributes would strike even a veteran HTML author as strange; thus, a few additional words of explanation are probably in order. The ACTUATE attribute tells the processing application when the link should be traversed. If it is set to AUTO, the link is traversed when it is encountered. ACTUATE="USER" means that the link should not be traversed until the user explicitly requests it. After the link traversal begins, the processing application can get more details about how to carry out the traversal from the BEHAVIOR attribute.

The SHOW attribute tells the processing application how to display the linked content with respect to the content it is currently displaying. Setting SHOW to REPLACE tells the application to overwrite the current content with the linked content. A SHOW value of EMBED means to embed the linked content inside the current content. Finally, setting SHOW to NEW directs the application to display the linked content in a new context that does not change the nature of the display of the current content (much like a Web browser launching a new instance to display a page instead of replacing the loaded page).

If a link is an inline link (as most simple links are), it is appropriate to use the CONTENT-ROLE and CONTENT-TITLE attributes to provide meaning and title information for the content. If the link is out-of-line, you can still specify CONTENT-ROLE and CONTENT-TITLE attributes, but they have no meaning in that context. Recall that out-of-line links are useful for creating multidirectional links, but they have meaning only in the context of a link group, which tells a processing application where to look for linking information.

N O T E Attribute names that start with XML are reserved for the further standardization of the linking specification. Therefore, you should not introduce an attribute name that starts with the string "XML" in any of your XML markup. ▪

When setting up your link element, you can specify some default attribute values in your DTD that eliminate the need for a lot of extra typing. You know that <SIMPLINK> is intended to be a SIMPLE link, for example, and that it will most likely be inline, that users will probably want control over traversal of the link, and that the linked content should replace existing content. You can express all this in a DTD as follows:

```
<!ELEMENT simplink ANY>
<!ATTLIST simplink
       ACTUATE          (AUTO|USER)            "USER"
       BEHAVIOR         CDATA                  #IMPLIED
       CONTENT-ROLE     CDATA                  #IMPLIED
       CONTENT-TITLE    CDATA                  #IMPLIED
       HREF             CDATA                  #REQUIRED
       INLINE           (TRUE|FALSE)           "TRUE"
       ROLE             CDATA                  #IMPLIED
       SHOW             (REPLACE|EMBED|NEW)    "REPLACE"
       TITLE            CDATA                  #IMPLIED
       XML:LINK         CDATA                  #FIXED "SIMPLE"
>
```

With this DTD, you could specify a link as simple as

```
<SIMPLINK HREF="linked_doc.xml">element_content</SIMPLINK>
```

Values of XML:LINK="SIMPLE", ACTUATE="USER", INLINE="TRUE", and SHOW="REPLACE" are understood from the DTD.

Extended Links   Extended links differ from simple links in that they can point to any number of resources that may or may not be co-located with the document in which the link is found. The result is a "multilinked" link that can take a user to one of many places.

Two types of elements are needed to specify an extended link. The first is one to contain link text for each individual linked resource, and the second is one to contain the elements that define the linked resources. As stated earlier, you can name XML elements in whatever way you choose. For this discussion, however, <EXTLINK> is the container element for the elements that specify individual resources, and <LOCATOR> is the element that contains link text for each resource. What that yields for a general extended link syntax is

```
<EXTLINK ...>
    <LOCATOR ...>Link text</LOCATOR>
    <LOCATOR ...>Link text</LOCATOR>
    ...
    <LOCATOR ...>Link text</LOCATOR>
</EXTLINK>
```

Each of these elements has a number of attributes, but they are the same as those used with the <SIMPLINK> element to define simple links. <EXTLINK> takes the following attributes:

- ACTUATE
- BEHAVIOR
- CONTENT-ROLE
- CONTENT-TITLE
- INLINE
- ROLE
- SHOW
- TITLE
- XML:LINK

For the <EXTLINK> element, you should set the XML:LINK attribute equal to EXTENDED or assign a default value of EXTENDED in the DTD. Otherwise, values and functions of the attributes are the same as specified in Table 11.1. Note that <EXTLINK> does not take the HREF attribute. This is because it contains the pointers to individual resources instead of pointing to something itself.

The <LOCATOR> element takes these attributes:

- ACTUATE
- BEHAVIOR
- HREF
- ROLE
- SHOW
- TITLE
- XML:LINK

<LOCATOR> elements do not point to linked resources. Because of this, the HREF attribute is necessary. You should set the XML:LINK attribute in a <LOCATOR> element to LOCATOR. Beyond that, the attributes are the same as in Table 11.1.

Part
III

Ch
11

By putting it all together and including a DTD that specifies default attribute values, you might see a sample extended link that looks like this:

```
You can find a lot of good online references about
<EXTLINK>
<LOCATOR XML:LINK="LOCATOR" HREF="http://www.w3.org/XML/">W3C XML Page</LOCATOR>
<LOCATOR XML:LINK="LOCATOR" HREF="http://www.ucc.ie/xml/">XML FAQ</LOCATOR>
<LOCATOR XML:LINK="LOCATOR" HREF="http://developer.netscape.com/news/viewsource/
bray_xml.html">Beyond HTML: XML and Automated Web Processing
by Tim Bray</LOCATOR>
XML
</EXTLINK>
```

In a browser, the text "XML" would be hyperlinked. However, when a user clicks the text, the browser needs to do something to present the multiple linking options. This might take the form of a pop-up menu that lists W3C XML Page, XML FAQ, and "Beyond HTML: XML and Automated Web Processing" by Tim Bray. Users could then choose from among these three options.

N O T E   XLink does not say how an XML browser has to render an extended link. The method of rendering is up to whoever is programming the browser. ▪

Extended Link Groups   With the possibility of extended, out-of-line links, a processing application may find it necessary to process a number of separate files to determine all the links and their resources. To facilitate this processing, XML supports the notion of an *extended link group*—a logical grouping of linked documents. The group is defined by and contained in a grouping element, and each document in the group is specified by an empty document element. Calling the grouping and document elements <XLINKGROUP> and <DOCUMENT>, respectively, you could set up the following extended link group:

```
<XLINKGROUP XML:LINK="GROUP" STEPS=3>
    <DOCUMENT XML:LINK="DOCUMENT" HREF="doc1.xml"/>
    <DOCUMENT XML:LINK="DOCUMENT" HREF="doc2.xml"/>
    <DOCUMENT XML:LINK="DOCUMENT" HREF="doc3.xml"/>
    ...
    <DOCUMENT XML:LINK="DOCUMENT" HREF="docn.xml"/>
</XLINKGROUP>
```

The STEPS attribute of the <XLINKGROUP> elements recognizes that the linked documents may include extended link groups themselves and places a limit on how many document levels deep the processing application should go when processing the extended group. The HREF attribute of the <DOCUMENT/> element gives the URL of each linked document.

N O T E   Values of the XML:LINK attribute for the <XLINKGROUP> element and the <DOCUMENT/> element are GROUP and DOCUMENT, respectively. Note that these values could have been set up as defaults in the DTD. ▪

XPoint

Borrowing from the Text Encoding Initiative (TEI)—a project whose objective is to identify standards and guidelines for the electronic publication of scholarly work—XML also includes the notion of *extended pointers,* or *XPointers.* The W3C document that puts forward the notion of XPointers is called the XML Pointer Language or XPoint.

XPointers basically enable you to link to a position in a document's parsing tree (the logical structure the parser uses to represent the document). This saves you from having to set up named anchors the same as you do in an HTML document. In the business letter example, you could link to

```
child(1,body) (3)
```

This would refer to the third child of the first (and only) BODY element in the letter.

Links can also point to a span of the document tree. For example, the code

```
child(3,p)..child(5,p)
```

selects the third, fourth, and fifth <P> elements of the letter. A pointer that spans multiple element in the document tree is called *spanning XPointer.*

XPointers will be most useful to programmers writing applications that parse or display XML documents because they provide a convenient way to reference the document's internal structure. For more information about using XPointers, consult the W3C site at http://www.w3.org/TR/WD-xptr.

Part III

Ch 11

Using Style Sheets with XML

One of the important points made at the start of this chapter was that XML elements do not specify how content is presented. Instead, an XML browser should use a *style sheet* to determine how content in each element should be displayed. The delivery of a second draft specification for XML style sheet language (XSL) 1.0 is expected shortly after this book is published; thus, at the time of this writing, the exact details of how to implement XML style sheets are not known. However, some documents are available through the W3C that give a flavor for what XSL might ultimately be like: the draft XSL specification and the XSL Requirements Summary.

The Draft XSL Specification

The first is the draft XSL specification submitted to the W3C in August 1997. Authors of the draft expect that XML document authors will be able to use the Cascading Style Sheet (CSS) standard for specifying presentation attributes for simple XML documents. Documents requiring more complex formatting would use XSL.

▶ See "Style Sheets," **p. 261**.

The XSL draft spec is based largely on the Document Style Semantics and Specification Language (DSSSL), an ISO standard for specifying how a document is to be formatted. It consists of two parts: a transformation language, which is used to apply structural transformations to

SGML files; and a style language, which is used to provide formatting instructions. Together, these languages take raw SGML code and prepare it for display through a browser. The XSL Working Group is adapting DSSSL to work with XML. After their work is complete, XML authors will have a way to specify presentation for their documents the same as they use a DTD to specify syntax.

The XSL Requirements Summary

The W3C's XSL Working Group has put forward a number of requirements that the XSL standard should address. This requirements summary is something like a "wish list" given to the designers of XSL to guide their work. It is not expected that the first draft of XSL will address all the requirements, but by having all the requirements out on the table from the start, designers can create XSL in such a way that it is easier to implement the full set of requirements in future revisions.

The Summary places the requirements into several logical groupings, including:

- General formatting issues
- Columns, floats, keeps, and so on
- Fonts
- Colors
- Math
- Internationalization
- Scripting
- Interactivity
- Accessibility
- Extensibility
- Packaging
- Meta-information

The General formatting issues section, for example, contains specific requirements for content positioning, alignment, animation, cross-references, drop caps, headers, hyphenation, indenting, justification, kerning, leading, margins, run-arounds (whitespace around an object), tables, and tiling—all basic attributes of most Web documents.

NOTE You can look up specific requirements under each of the groupings listed previously by directing your browser to http://www.w3.org/TR/WD-XSLReq. ▉

Applications

At this point, you may be wondering how you might be able to use XML in your work as a Web content developer. XML's best and highest use is for the creation of specialized markup languages. Therefore, if you want to determine how you can use XML, think about the content you are publishing and what special needs you have based on the nature of the content. Perhaps your content is related to a specific scientific discipline, or your documents may have an unusual structure to them. You can capture these characteristics by using XML to define a customized markup language that supports them. If you take it a step further and develop a DTD for your XML application, you open the possibilities of making your documents more easily formatted and searched. This is because the applications that perform these tasks can use the DTD to teach themselves the rules you create for marking up the content.

Despite XML's newness, it is already being used by some companies as the foundation for specialized markup languages. Some of these applications include

- Synchronized Multimedia Integration Language (SMIL)—SMIL is intended for authoring presentations of multimedia content. The premise behind SMIL is to provide a simple, text-based language for creating multimedia presentations and to allow for controlling the order of presentation and any special effects within the presentation (control panels, slow motion, hyperlinks, and so on).

- Channel Definition Format (CDF)—Microsoft's vision for push technology on the Web is supported by CDF. Web site administrators can turn all or part of their sites into "Webcasting channels" by building a CDF file that drives the channel. XML is useful in creating CDF because it was necessary to create elements to define the channel and the schedule for updating the channel content.

▶ **See** "CDF and Active Desktop Components," **p. 415**.

- Mathematical Markup Language (MML)—Mathematics is a discipline with many unique publishing requirements, especially when it comes to special characters such as operator symbols or Greek letters. MML enables documents with heavy mathematical content to be rendered on the Web.

- Chemical Markup Language (CML)—Publications in chemistry need to be capable of expressing descriptions of chemical formulas, equations, and molecule structures. CML supports chemists who want to publish their research to the Internet.

The preceding list of applications covers a diverse range of content. No one of these areas could have been handled by HTML, yet XML has the flexibility to define a electronic publication markup language for each one.

XML Software

Now that XML is moving toward having a relatively stable standard to grow from, more and more XML-related software is becoming available. These programs tend to fall into one of three classes:

- XML browsers
- XML parsers/validators
- XML editors

Part
III

Ch
11

Because the XML style sheet specification has yet to come into sharp focus, few XML browsers exist at the moment; those that do exist are fairly primitive in their presentation capabilities. After XSL is on a firmer foundation, you can expect XML browsers to be more adept at presenting information marked up with XML.

It's a fairly easy matter to produce an XML parser/validator because the rules for what composes a valid XML document are rigidly defined. Such a program would first need to check whether the document is well formed. If it is, the next step is to scan the document's DTD and check to see whether the document conforms to the rules in the DTD. If it does, then it is a valid document.

Finally, more and more XML editors are emerging. These are also fairly straightforward to program because all an editor has to do is give users an environment in which they can create their own tags. One editor that has received favorable press is XML <PRO> from Vervet Logic (http://www.vervet.com/). After you create a root element for your XML document, XML <PRO> enables you to define other elements and associate attributes with those elements. Any element you define is listed in the floating Elements box (see Figure 11.2).

FIGURE 11.2

XML <PRO> gives you an environment for defining your own XML elements and their attributes.

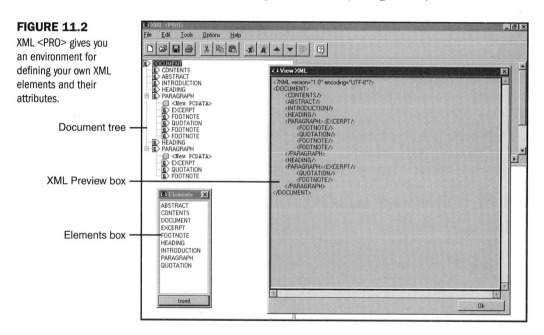

Document tree

XML Preview box

Elements box

After you have some elements defined, you can begin to build your document tree in the left side of the XML <PRO> window. You insert an element from the Elements box into the tree by clicking the element to select it and then clicking the Insert button at the bottom of the box. The tree is shown in a hierarchical structure—much the same way folders and files are displayed in the Windows Explorer (refer to Figure 11.2).

After you've built up a document tree, you can ask XML <PRO> to generate the corresponding XML code. By choosing the View XML option from the Tools menu, you'll get a pop-up box containing the XML that would be parsed to produce the document tree you've built (refer to Figure 11.2). When you save the document, XML <PRO> will save the code you see displayed in the pop-up box.

Other useful features of XML <PRO> include

- DTD Association—XML <PRO> won't help you to write a DTD for your document, but after you've written one, you can associate it with your document. XML <PRO> will insert the appropriate tag into your document, linking it to the DTD you specify.

- Document validation—If you've associated a DTD with a document, you can use the XML <PRO> validator to test the document for validity.

- Entity palette—A floating palette is available for inserting any entities you define. Choose Options, Show Entity Palette to activate the palette.

XML <PRO> retails for $149.95. You can download a demo version of XML <PRO> from the Vervet Logic Web site at `http://www.vervet.com/`.

N O T E As more public XML-related software becomes available, you can find it posted on Robin Cover's Public SGML/XML Software page at `http://www.sil.org/sgml/publicSW.html`. ▨

References

XML is in the early stages of development and is sure to evolve beyond the draft specifications that have already been put forward. What's more, these changes will probably occur rapidly because there is such a push to stop extending HTML and to start using a more flexible alternative.

The following list identifies some online resources that you can use to keep apprised of all the developments surrounding XML. Be sure to check them frequently so that you know the status of the "next wave" for Web document markup.

- The World Wide Web Consortium is the arbiter of the XML specification. You can find the W3C XML page at `http://www.w3.org/XML/`. Here you will find links to the most recent XML, XLink, XPoint, and XSL drafts, and listings of XML-related software, such as parsers and browsers.

- The XML Frequently Asked Questions (FAQ) list at `http://www.ucc.ie/xml/` is an excellent reference, with separate sections for general, user-, author-, and developer-related questions.

- Norman Walsh maintains a good set of XML-related bookmarks at `http://nwalsh.com/sgml/index.html`.

■ Jon Bosak of Sun Microsystems authored the highly regarded article "XML, Java, and the Future of the Web," which looks into the type of automated processing that will be possible with XML-based documents. You can find the article online at `http://sunsite.unc.edu/pub/sun-info/standards/xml/why/xmlapps.htm`.

■ You can learn all about DSSSL, the basis for the XML style specification, at `http://www.jclark.com/dsssl/`.

Anatomy of an XML Document

by Simon North and Jim O'Donnell

Just as student doctors begin their medical training by dissecting a human body and learning the nature and relation of the parts before they learn how to treat them, so this exploration of XML can begin with an examination of a small XML document with all its parts identified. In this chapter, we will look more closely at a sample XML document and break it down into its component parts. We will cover the following topics:

- The components of an XML document
- Logical and physical structures used in XML

XML Markup

XML has very simple rules for distinguishing between the content of a document and the XML markup elements used to describe it. Most of these rules are described in the following list:

- The start of XML markup elements is identified by either the less than symbol (<) or the ampersand (&) character.
- Three other characters, the greater than symbol (>), the apostrophe or single quote ('), and the double quotation mark ("), are used by XML for markup.
- To use these special characters as content within your document, you must use the corresponding general XML entity (shown in Table 12.1). XML entities are discussed in greater detail in Chapter 15, "XML Characters, Notations, and Entities."
- Everything else not used to denote XML markup represents the content of the document.

▶ **See** "Entities," **p. 391**.

Table 12.1 Predefined XML Entities

Character	Replacement
&	&amp;
'	&apos;
>	&gt;
<	&lt;
"	&quot;

A Sample XML Document

Listing 12.1 shows the XML code for a simple home page. This is a simple example, but it does contain all the important parts that you will find in nearly all XML documents.

Listing 12.1 *Home.xml*—A Simple XML Home Page

```xml
<?xml version="1.0"?>
<home.page>
   <head>
      <title>
         My Home Page
      </title>
      <banner source="topbanner.gif"/>
   </head>
   <body>
      <main.title>
         Welcome to My Home Page
      </main.title>
      <rule/>
      <text>
         <para>
            Sorry, this home page is still under construction.
            Please come back soon!
         </para>
      </text>
   </body>
   <footer source="foot.gif"/>
</home.page>
```

In the following sections, we will break apart the above XML home page and describe what each part of it achieves and how it is set up.

The XML Declaration

```xml
<?xml version="1.0"?>
```

The XML declaration identifies what follows as being XML code, states what version of the XML standard the code complies with, and specifies whether the document can be treated as a standalone document (yes) or whether a DTD must also be retrieved to be able to make full sense of the contents. Creating XML DTDs will be discussed in Chapter 14, "Creating XML Document Type Definitions."

▶ **See** "Getting Sophisticated with External DTDs," **p. 364**.

The XML declaration is, in fact, a "processing instruction" (identified by the ? at its start and end), but for now it's enough to treat it as a standard declaration. This declaration is not strictly compulsory (the fact that the document is XML code can also be announced by the Web server in the same way that is often done for HTML documents), but it is a good idea to get into the habit of always including such a declaration because it will increase the portability of your code.

The Root Element

```
<home.page>
  ...
</home.page>
```

Each XML document must have only one root element, and all the other elements must be completely enclosed in that element. In this document, the root element is defined by the start tag of the `<home.page>` element and the end tag of the `</home.page>` element.

In XML, a non-empty element must consist of three things: a start tag, content (either text or other elements), and an end tag. The name that you use in the element start tag must exactly match the name you use in the end tag. If you want to use an odd combination of cases to increase the legibility of long names (for example, `ThisIsAnIntelligibleName`), you must be careful to exactly match the case usage in both the opening and the closing tags.

Empty XML Elements

```
<banner source="topbanner.gif"/>

<rule/>

<footer source="foot.gif"/>
```

Empty elements are a special case in XML. In SGML and HTML, it is obvious from the definition of an element (in the DTD) that it is empty and has no comment. XML, in keeping with its developers' design goals, requires you to be much more explicit. Indeed, you may well not be using a DTD at all, and so it could be quite hard to decide whether an element is—or should be—empty. Empty elements, therefore, have to be clearly identified as such, and to do so, a special empty tag close delimiter is used, `/>` as in

```
<empty_element/>
```

To maintain a certain degree of backward compatibility with SGML and HTML, instead of using the special empty tag close delimiter, you can simply use a closing tag. The equivalent to the preceding code is

```
<empty_element/></empty_element>
```

In our sample document, the three empty elements are used to denote a graphic image to be used as the banner and footer of the XML home page, as well as to indicate a rule, representing a division between the title and the main body of the home page.

Attributes to XML Element Tags

Element start tags can include one or more optional or mandatory attributes that give further information about the elements they delimit. The syntax for specifying an attribute is

```
<element_type_name attribute_name="attribute.value">
```

If elements were nouns, then attributes would be adjectives. We could, therefore, say

```
<fruit taste="sharp">
```

or even:

```
<problem size="huge" cause="unknown" solution="run.away">
```

In direct contrast to SGML and HTML, where multiple declarations are considered to be fatal errors, XML deals with multiple declarations of attributes in a unique manner. If an element appears once with one set of attributes and then appears again with a different set of attributes, the two sets of attributes are simply merged. The first time you use the `fruit` element, for instance, you might include the `taste` attribute, as shown above. In a subsequent use of `fruit`, you can introduce a different attribute, such as `color`. Each time you do this, the complete set of attributes is merged to form the set of all possible attributes for that element.

N O T E   An XML processor is a software package, library, or module that is used to read XML documents. The XML processor makes it possible for an XML application, such as a formatting engine or a viewer, to access the structure and content of an XML document. ▪

Logical Structure

Conceptually, a big difference usually exists between XML and HTML markup. With a few exceptions, most HTML tags perform functions related to how the content is displayed. XML markup, on the other hand, is meant to convey what the content means.

XML uses its start tags and end tags as containers; the start tag, the content, and the end tag form a single element. Therefore, elements can be considered to be the objects out of which an XML document is assembled. Each XML document must have only one root element, and all the other elements must be perfectly nested inside that element. *Perfectly nested* means that if an element contains other elements, those elements must be completely enclosed within that element.

Now look at what that means for our simple example of Listing 12.1. If we sketch out the structure of the elements in this XML document, we obtain the kind of tree structure of elements shown in Figure 12.1.

As you can see from Figure 12.1, the document has a tree-like structure with the root element (`<home.page>`) at the top of the tree (or base, depending on how you look at it). All the elements that are inside this element are neatly contained within each other. An XML document must contain one—and only one—root element, and no elements can be either partially or completely outside, after or before that element.

To make it easier to refer to the relationships between elements and to elements with respect to other elements, we say that an element is the *parent* of the elements that it contains. The elements that are inside an element are called its *children*. Elements that share the same parent element are called *siblings*.

In our simple example of Listing 12.1, `<home.page>` is the parent of all the other elements, `<text>` is the parent of `<para>`, `<title>` is a child of `<head>`, and `<title>` and `<banner>` are siblings. Going down the element tree, each child element must be fully contained within its parent element. Sibling elements may not overlap.

Part

III

Ch

12

FIGURE 12.1

The logical structure of elements.

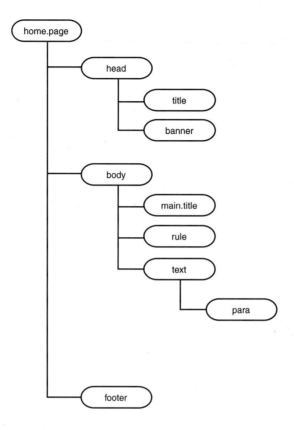

The arrangement of the elements in an XML document is called the logical structure. As you will see next, an XML document also has a physical structure, and to be usable (technically, in order to be "well formed"), the logical and the physical structure of an XML document must be consistent.

Physical Structure

One of the key concepts in XML is that of the entity. If you are to really understand XML, it is essential that you fully understand what entities are. Various types of entities exist, and it is the entities—far more than the elements—that determine how the XML processor deals with XML code. You will learn about entities in some detail in a later chapter, but for now it is enough to think of an entity as being a physical storage unit—an object; although in fact, most entities will usually be separate computer files.

The main entity that you work with all the time, although you will hardly ever notice it is there, is the document entity. This document (or *root*) entity, as we have seen, is logically divided into elements (other logical components exist that we will discuss later, but for now it is enough to concentrate on the elements).

Entities can reference other entities and cause them to be included in the XML document. You've already met some entities; the entities listed in Table 12.1 that we use to include markup characters in normal text are in fact internal entities. For now, we'll examine the basic reference to a graphics file that is so common in HTML Web pages, and it is our derivative example in Listing 12.1:

```
<banner source="topbanner.gif"/>
```

The banner element's source attribute refers to an external entity (it isn't contained in the current document), which is an external graphics file. If this were HTML code, the graphic would appear in your Web browser at this point in the document. In XML terms, this graphics file is called an *unparsed entity*; the XML processor ignores the content of the entity and simply passes it on to the application.

XML is a little stricter than HTML about the inclusion of external graphics files. (As you will learn later, XML requires you to specify the notation or format that the graphic is in.) XML is also able to include far more than a simple graphic—it is possible to include an external XML source as an entity within another XML document. However, that is where potential problems can be started.

XML is able to include entities that contain XML code, text, HTML code—almost anything. Depending on how the referenced entity is identified, it could be processed (parsed) by the XML processor as if the XML code had been in the original document (root entity) and not in an external file. To further complicate matters, that entity could reference another entity, and so on to infinity. Apart from the practical problems that this might cause (you can imagine trying to open a small document and getting several thousand linked pages!), this creates special problems when the included entities also contain markup.

Just as the arrangement of the elements gives a logical structure, so the arrangement of the entities gives a physical structure. Now, suppose that an included entity also contains elements. On the face of it, this might not pose such a problem. It certainly does become a problem, however, if the included entity contains elements with the same element type name as elements already present in the document. This problem will be addressed by a mechanism called namespaces, which will be available in a future release of the XML specification.

Element conflicts are one problem; there is another. Suppose that you had opened an element in the root entity (your XML document) and referenced an external entity. Again, it's not a problem; rather, it's a normal thing to do. Suppose, however, that the external entity contains an end tag for the element you just opened. Suddenly, your whole logical structure is ruined.

To try and limit the occurrence of these problems, the logical and physical structures of XML entities must be synchronous; logical entities cannot span physical entity boundaries. When this isn't the case, it can cause a lot of problems.

Markup Delimiters

Table 12.2 identifies the parts of XML's element tags. It is worth remembering that where HTML relies on recognizing pre-programmed tags, XML is *triggered* by these specific parts of the element tags and the XML processor's behavior, and what it expects to see next is directly controlled by the named symbols.

Table 12.2   The Parts of an XML Element Tag

Symbol	Description
<	start tag open delimiter
</	end tag open delimiter
foo	example of an XML element name
>	tag close delimiter
/>	empty tag close delimiter

Element Markup

XML is concerned with element markup. This might sound like an obvious point to make, but it is worth repeating because it indicates a deeply rooted conceptual difference between XML as a markup language and as an arbitrary tag language. As you have already seen, HTML often tends toward being a tag language rather than a markup language, which is a direct consequence of Web browsers being so intentionally lenient in accepting bad markup.

Instead of XML's tags being markers that indicate where a style should change or where a new line should begin, most of XML's element markup should be considered as objects composed of three parts: a start tag, the contents, and the end tag, as shown in Table 12.3. The start tag and end tags should be treated like wrappers, and when you think of an element, you should have a mental picture of a piece of text with both tags in place.

Table 12.3   The Parts of an XML Element

Symbol	Name	Description
<foo>	start tag	at the start of an element, the opening tag
text	content	in the middle of an element, its content
</foo>	end tag	at the end of an element, the closing tag

Note that the element name that appears in the start tag must be the same as the name that appears in the end tag; the following would be wrong because XML is case sensitive:

```
<simple.element>This element won't close!</simple.Element>
```

Attribute Markup

As you learned in the previous chapter, attributes are used to attach additional information to XML elements. The general form for using an attribute is

```
<element_name property="value">
```

or

```
<element_name property='value'>
```

The technical description of the markup of this attribute specification is given in Table 12.4.

Table 12.4 Specifying an Attribute

Symbol	Description
<	start tag open delimiter
element_name	element name
property	attribute name
=	value indicator
"	literal string delimiter
'	alternative literal string delimiter
value	value of the attribute
"	literal string delimiter
'	alternative literal string delimiter
>	start tag close delimiter

Note that an attribute value must be enclosed in quotation marks. You can use either single quotes (`<lie size='big'>`) or double quotes (`<lie size="massive">`), but you cannot mix the two in the same specification.

When you are working without a DTD (all the XML code shown in this chapter does not require you to associate a DTD with the XML document—we'll discuss creating DTDs in Chapter 14), you can specify the attribute and its value when you use the element for the first time, as shown below. When you specify attributes for the same element more than once, the specifications are simply merged. For instance, in the following code, the second use of the para element adds the color attribute to the number attribute that is used in the first use:

```
<?xml version="1.0"?>
<home.page>
    <para number="first">This is the first paragraph.</para>
    <para number="second" color="red">This is the second paragraph.</para>
</home.page>
```

Part

III

Ch

12

One attribute—the `xml:lang` attribute—is reserved for XML's own use. This attribute is reserved to identify the human language in which the element is written. The value of the attribute is one of the ISO 639 country codes; some of the most common language codes are shown in Table 12.5.

Table 12.5 Common ISO 639 Language Codes

Code	Language
ar	Arabic
ch	Chinese
de	German
en	English
es	Spanish
fr	French
gr	Greek
it	Italian
ja	Japanese
nl	Dutch
pt	Portugese
ru	Russian

Optionally (where several versions of the language exist, such as British and American English), the language code can be followed by a hyphen (-) and one of the ISO 3166 country codes. Some of the most common country codes are shown in Table 12.6; if you have spent much time on the Internet, you may recognize these as the same codes that are used in email addresses and URLs. An element written in American English could then be identified like this (note the cases; the language code is in lowercase and the country code is in uppercase):

```
<para xml:lang="en-US">My country 'tis of thee.</para>
```

Table 12.6 Common ISO 3166 Country Codes

Code	Country
AT	Austria
BE	Belgium
CA	Canada
CN	China

Code	Country
DE	Germany
DK	Denmark
EN	England
ES	Spain
FR	France
GR	Greece
IT	Italy
JA	Japan
NL	The Netherlands
PT	Portugal
RU	Russia
US	United States

On the CD

The codes given in Tables 12.5 and 12.6 are not complete. Another coding scheme registered by the Internet Assigned Numbers Authority (IANA) is defined in RFC 1766, and if you really need to, you can devise your own language code. User-defined codes must be prefixed with the string 'x-', in which case you could declare an element as being in computer geek, like this:

```
<para xml:lang="x-cg">Do you grok this code?</para>
```

Naming Rules

So far you have seen examples of the markup used for elements and attributes, and in each a name has been given to the XML markup element. XML has certain specific rules governing what names you can use for all its markup objects. XML's naming rules are as follows:

- A name consists of at least one letter: a to z, or A to Z.
- If the name consists of more than one character, it may then start with an underscore (_) or a colon (:).
- The initial letter (or underscore) can be followed by one or more letters, digits, hyphens, underscores, full stops, and so-called *combining characters*, *extender characters* and *ignorable characters*. (These last three classes of character are taken from the Unicode character set and include some of the special Unicode character symbols and accents. For more information about Unicode, you can look up http://www.unicode.org/.)

Note that spaces and tabs are not allowed in element names (`<one two>` would be interpreted as two separate names), and the only two punctuation signs allowed are the hyphen (-) and the period or full stop (.).

Part
III

Ch
12

No rule requires that your choice of a name should make sense. As long as you obey the naming rules, you can call XML objects whatever you like, and the names can be as long and as meaningless as you like. However, it is worth remembering that one of the major benefits of using XML in the first place is that it is self describing. If you are using elements such as `<thingamajig>`, `<whatsit>`, and `<doohickey>`, you will be defeating one of the major purposes of XML. Try to choose names that are suggestive of the nature or purpose of the object.

Comments

No self-respecting language, whether it's a programming language or a markup language, could hold its head up without enabling comments to be added to the code. From a maintenance point of view, it is also pretty important that you should have some lasting record of why you did particular things. The best way to document your code is to include the explanation with the code by means of comments.

In keeping with the design constraint of keeping XML simple, its comment facilities are also simple.

Comments have the form

```
<!-- this is comment text -->
```

> **CAUTION**
>
> The comment start tag (`<!--`) and end tag (`-->`) must be used exactly as they are shown here; inserting spaces or any other characters into these strings can lead to the tags—or anything inside the comment—being mistakenly interpreted by the XML processor as markup.

Provided that you use the comment start tag and end tag correctly, everything in the comment text will be completely ignored by the XML processor. The following comment, therefore, is quite valid:

```
<!-- These are the declarations for the <title> and <body> -->
```

Only one restriction exists on what you can place in your comment text: The string `--` is not allowed (this keeps XML backward compatible with SGML). (The string `-->` will end the comment.)

Comments can be placed anywhere in an XML document—outside other markup. Therefore, the following is allowed:

```
<para>This is simple <!-- So everyone tells me --> to do.</para>
```

But this is not allowed:

```
<para <!-- blatant lie --> >This is simple to do.</para>
```

Character References

Unlike SGML (and as a result, HTML too), which is very much ASCII based, XML was developed right from the start with a view to supporting languages other than English. In HTML, you can enter the code for certain non-English characters. For example, è would be è, í would be í and û would be û. As you will see at the beginning of the next chapter, these codes are, in fact, entity references. The abbreviations egrave, iacute, and ucirc are taken from the ISO 8859/1 character set (SGML's character set), which is derived from the ISO/IEC 646 version of the ASCII alphabet (the first 128 characters). ISO 8859/1 is also the basis for the Microsoft Windows fonts. Although these character entity references will enable you to deal with most European and Scandinavian languages, they are completely insufficient for displaying many Asian or Middle Eastern languages, such as Japanese, Hindi, or Arabic.

XML solves this problem by being based on Unicode and on the even more extensive ISO/IEC 10646 standards (the latter even allows the use of Chinese characters). If you need them, XML enables you to use these exotic characters—even if your keyboard doesn't support them. You do this by entering a *character reference*.

A character reference consists of the string &#, followed by the number of the character in the ISO/IEC 10646 alphabet and terminated by a semicolon (;). The character number may be either a decimal number, in which case you enter the number as is, or in hexadecimal form, in which case you must precede the number with the letter x, such as x12ABC. The character reference for the copyright symbol (©), for example (written in HTML as ©), is © (in decimal) or © (in hexadecimal). You can get more information on these character references at http://wwwold.dkuug.dk/jtc1/sc2/wg2/. ●

Part
III

Ch
12

## CHAPTER 13

Creating XML Documents

by Simon North and Jim O'Donnell

In this chapter

Entity References

As you learned in Chapter 12, "Anatomy of an XML Document," entities are normally external objects, such as graphics files that are meant to be included in the document. To be able to reference these external entities, you must have a DTD for your XML document. You will learn about these entities when you learn about DTDs, but one other type of entity, called an internal entity, you can use already, and it can save you a lot of unnecessary typing.

Internal entities look very much like character references but have one important difference—you must declare an internal entity before you can use it.

Entity Declarations

The declaration of an internal entity has the following form:

```
<!ENTITY name "replacement text">
```

Having declared this entity, every time that the string &name; now appears in your XML code, it will be automatically replaced with the replacement text (which can be as long as you like) by the XML processor. Judiciously used, entity references can save you a lot of typing.

Predefined Entities

Character references enable you to enter characters that you might not be able to enter normally from your keyboard. A variation on this theme is the set of so-called predefined entities. These are characters that you can enter quite normally, but you shouldn't because they can all too easily be mistaken for markup characters. To refresh your memory, the set of predefined entities is shown in Table 13.1.

Table 13.1 The Predefined Entities

Character	Replacement	
&	&	or &#38;
'	'	or '
>	>	or >
<	<	or &#60;
"	"	or "

You will see that the table now gives you two options: You can enter a named entity, for example ', or you can enter character reference ' to represent the character. The character references for the ampersand (&) and the less than (<) character are, however, special cases, and so the character references are "double escaped"; the reasons for this will be explained next when you learn about entity references.

The Benefits of Entities

You can think of entity references as being almost a kind of macro. They can be real time savers when you want to use sections of text several times. Consider the example shown below, where the person's name is an entity reference:

```xml
<?xml version="1.0"?>
<!DOCTYPE home.page [
    <!ENTITY club "Antidisestablishmentarianism Club of America">
]>
<home.page>
    <head>
        <title>The &club; Home Page</title>
    </head>
    <body>
        <h1>Welcome to the &club; Home Page!</h1>
        <para>Hello, I am the chairman of the &club; and this is our
              club's Home Page...</para>
    </body>
</home.page>
```

By using an entity reference in this way, you would only have to enter the name once, in the entity declaration, instead of having to search for and change every occurrence of the string in the text. Used in this way, entity references can make the task of creating and maintaining XML documents quite a bit easier.

Some of the Dangers of Using Entities

You've seen how handy internal entity references can be as a kind of shorthand for entering pieces of text and as a means of dealing with variable content. Obviously, with a little thought and advance preparation, entity references can save you a lot of time and effort later on.

A feature this handy naturally raises a simple question: Could this be used to insert markup, too? It's an attractive idea and a natural thing to want to do. You can put markup into replacement text, subject to a few restrictions. You need to think it out quite carefully beforehand to avoid some unpleasant surprises.

The first thing you must remember is that the XML will process the contents of the entity replacement text when it expands the entity reference. Therefore, you must not *escape* any markup characters in the replacement text, you must *double escape* the characters. Consider this simple example:

```xml
<!ENTITY dangerous "Black &#38; White">
```

When the XML processor sees the entity reference &dangerous; in the XML document, it will immediately expand (de-reference) the predefined entity before it inserts the replacement text. The following XML code seems harmless enough, but we'll look at what happens, step by step:

```xml
<text>This is not a &dangerous; choice.</text>
```

1. The XML processor sees the entity reference `&dangerous;` and looks for the replacement text.

2. Finding `Black &#38; White`, the XML processor de-references this to `Black & White`.

3. The XML processor inserts the replacement text and the resulting XML code is

   ```
   <text>This is not a Black & White choice.</text>
   ```

4. The XML processor then tries to parse the ampersand and will report an error because `&` has not been declared as an entity.

Avoiding the Pitfalls

You've seen some of the problems that entity references can create when their contents are de-referenced. At worst, they can make a complete mess of your XML code. Of course, these problems can be avoided. One of the best ways to avoid the de-referencing problems is to *double escape* any markup contained in the replacement text, like this:

```
<!ENTITY safe "Harry &#38;#38; Fred &amp;amp; Joe">
```

Now when the XML processor sees the entity reference `&safe;` in the XML document

```
<text>The job was left to &safe; to fix.</text>
```

the expansion will still leave you with valid code. We'll look at what happens, step by step, as the XML processor de-references the entity reference:

1. The XML processor sees the entity reference `&safe;` and looks for the replacement text.

2. Finding `"Harry &#38;#38; Fred &amp;amp; Joe">`, the XML processor de-references this to `Harry &#38; Fred &amp; Joe`.

3. The XML processor inserts the replacement text and the resulting XML code is

   ```
   <text>The job was left to Harry &#38; Fred &amp; Joe to finish.</text>
   ```

4. The XML processor then parses the resulting code, sees the entity reference `&#38;`, and de-references that to give

   ```
   <text>The job was left to Harry & Fred & Joe to finish.</text>
   ```

As you can see from the examples, you can escape the markup by using either the entity reference form (in the example, `&#38;`) or the character reference form (`&amp;`) of the predefined entity.

Synchronous Structures

Other than the problems that I have described, one very important restriction exists on using markup in entities. In the last chapter, you learned that the logical and physical structures in the XML document must be synchronous. At the time, the restriction might not have made too much sense because it can be difficult to imagine an example of when the two structures are not synchronous. However, this is an example of when the two structures can become asynchronous. The logical structure is composed of the elements in the XML document and in the replacement text. The physical structure is composed of the document entity (the root entity of the XML document containing the entity reference) and the internal entity (which is the replacement text). The two objects are discrete physical entities as far as XML is concerned, even though in this case they are actually in the same file.

For the two structures to be synchronous, any element that is inside the replacement text must start and finish inside the replacement text (in other words, inside the entity).

The following would be allowed:

```
<!ENTITY safe "&#38#60;emph&#62;Harry&#38#60;/emph&#62; and Joe">
<text>The job was left to &safe; to finish.</text>
```

because the de-referenced entity reference would yield this:

```
<text>The job was left to <emph>Harry</emph> and Joe to finish.</text>
```

The following, however, could create a lot of problems:

```
<!ENTITY unsafe ""&#38#60;emph&#62;Harry and Joe">
<text>The job was left to &safe;</emph> to finish.</text>
```

even though, when the entity reference has been de-referenced, the resulting markup would actually be legal:

```
<text>The job was left to <emph>Harry and Joe</emph> to finish.</text>
```

Although we are still talking about *internal* entities, which are completely within our control, the restriction is really pretty logical. The same de-referencing mechanism applies for external entities as well as internal entities, and bearing in mind that the intention is that XML can be used easily on the Web (one of the design goals), we have absolutely no control over what is contained in external entities. XML's developers could have made a distinction between internal and external entities, but that would go against two more of XML's basic design goals—simplicity and clarity.

Where to Declare Entities

You have learned what an internal entity reference looks like, and you've seen some of the benefits and drawbacks of using entity references. Before we move on to something else, you still need to learn where to put the entity declarations.

Entity references are normally allowed only in the DTD that accompanies the XML document. The declarations of element structures and entities are in fact the only reason for having a DTD at all. You will learn all about DTDs in detail in the next chapter; for now, all you need to know is illustrated by the following:

```
<?xml version="1.0"?>
<!DOCTYPE home.page [
   <!ENTITY shortcut "This is the replacement text.">
]>
<home.page>
   ...
</home.page>
```

Part
III

Ch
13

The second line in this listing is a document type declaration. This is the line that will later be used to make the association between the XML document and the DTD that describes its structure. The declaration takes the form:

```
<!DOCTYPE name external.pointer [ internal.subset ]>
```

where the `external.pointer` points to a separate file that contains the so-called external subset of the DTD. Don't worry too much about this for now; the trick is that you can leave this out and concentrate on the so-called internal subset of the DTD. The declaration you will need then looks like this:

```
<!DOCTYPE name [ internal.subset ]>
```

In this internal subset you can declare as many elements, attributes, and entities as you like, without having an external DTD at all.

As you will discover later, you can perform all sorts of other tricks with the internal DTD subset. Anything you put in the internal subset takes precedence over anything in an external subset. This means, for example, that you can declare a default set of global values for a whole suite of XML documents and then override the global values in an individual XML document whenever you want.

Before we leave the subject of DTDs altogether, there is one last thing about the document type declaration that you should get into the habit of doing now, even if it doesn't make much sense at this point. Although you aren't using an external DTD yet, if and when you do, the name that you give to the document type must be the same as the name of the root element in the XML document. This is shown in the preceding listing, where the document type name (`home.page`) is the same as the root element name. This isn't a requirement when an external DTD isn't present, but it is still a good practice.

CDATA Sections

You have learned how to escape markup characters by using the predefined entities and character references. It doesn't take much imagination to realize that replacing every markup character in a piece of text could be a long and tedious process. In addition, cases may occur (such as when you are sending the XML code on for further processing by a different application) when you really want to keep all those characters exactly as they are.

The way to do this is to use a CDATA (character data) section, like this:

```
<![CDATA[This is the text < 5 lines > that I want
        the &!%# XML processor to leave alone!]]>
```

Anything—absolutely anything—that appears between the opening tag (`<![CDATA[`) and the closing tag (`]]>`) will not be recognized as markup. You do not need to "escape" any markup characters in a CDATA section (in fact, you can't because the escape itself won't be recognized). The only thing that will be recognized is the end of section tag (`]]>`), so this string cannot be included in a CDATA section, and as a logical consequence, you cannot put one CDATA section inside another.

CAUTION

Using markup characters in a CDATA section like this in an XML document, whose existence is built around markup, goes against the grain. An XML processor is therefore intended to be very strict with this feature. The opening string and closing string for a CDATA section must be used exactly as shown here. The slightest deviation—a tab or a space character somewhere inside one of the strings—will be punished immediately. Should you do this, the content of the CDATA section will either be treated as markup, or the rest of your document (as far as the next CDATA section that is closed properly) will be treated as part of the CDATA section and all the markup will be ignored.

CDATA sections are one of the recommended ways to embed application code (JavaScript or Perl code, for instance) in your XML code. You could place the embedded code in comments (as is often done in HTML documents), but the XML processor is not required to pass the comment text to an application. Therefore, a risk exists that the contents of comments will be stripped out before the application sees them.

You could declare your own type of element to contain the embedded code (like the <SCRIPT> element in HTML 4), but by doing so, you are implicitly breaking the spirit of generic markup even though it is permitted to do so. This would not, however, prove to be much help if your embedded code contained characters that could be interpreted as markup because the contents of these elements would be parsed in the normal way by the XML processor.

The other way to embed code, and probably the best way, is by using processing instructions, which will be discussed in the next section.

Processing Instructions

The XML declaration that is (or at least should be) at the start of every XML document is a processing instruction:

```
<?xml version="1.0"?>
```

XML markup is meant to be generic, and in a perfect world, it would be. However, times will occur when you really do need to enter instructions for specific applications. One of these applications could be a script interpreter, and so, like CDATA sections, processing instructions are good places to put embedded code. Better still, although CDATA sections are purely a way of avoiding having characters interpreted as markup, processing instructions can be targeted to your application. This would enable you, for example, to have two or more sets of embedded script code intended for different processors or interpreters and enable you to identify them separately, as shown in this listing of a partial XML document:

```
<para>
    This is text containing two processing instructions,
        <?javascript I can put whatever I like here?>
        <?perl And I can put whatever I like here too?>
    one for each interpreter.
</para>
```

Part
III

Ch
13

No restrictions exist at all on the content of the processing instructions (the content is not even considered by the XML processor to be part of the document's character data), but the name that you choose must comply with XML's naming rules.

Markup Declarations

Before we get into the details of declaring elements and attributes, we'll quickly review where in the XML document these are made, as shown in the following:

```
<?xml version="1.0"?>
<!DOCTYPE page [
   <!-- this is where the internal DTD subset is located. -->
]>
<page>
   <!-- this is where the content of the root element is located. -->
</page>
```

As shown, the XML document begins with the XML declaration. At this stage, the document still does not have an external DTD, so the declaration as shown is sufficient. The DOCTYPE declaration follows, in which the internal DTD subset information can be entered. Finally, between the root element, <page>, is the content of the document.

Although the full syntax can be somewhat more complex than that which is shown here (the full syntax for DTDs will be shown in the next chapter), for use with an internal DTD subset only, the syntax takes the form

```
<!DOCTYPE document.type.name [ internal.subset ]>
```

where the document type name should be the same as the name of the XML document's root element (<page> above).

Element Declarations

The first kind of declaration is the element declaration. This takes the form

```
<!ELEMENT name content>
```

The name is a standard XML name constructed in accordance with the naming rules discussed in Chapter 12. The content part of the element declaration describes either a specific content in the form of the keyword EMPTY or the keyword ANY, or it consists of a so-called content model that describes the sequence and repetition of elements that are contained inside (are children of) this element.

Empty Elements

Empty elements have no content (they are forbidden to have any content) and they are marked up as either

```
<empty.element/>
```

or

```
<empty.element></empty.element>
```

An empty element is declared like this:

```
<!ELEMENT empty.element EMPTY>
```

Unrestricted Elements

The opposite pole to an empty element is an unrestricted element. An unrestricted element can contain any element that is declared elsewhere in the XML document's DTD (in either the internal or the external DTD subset). Because we aren't using an external DTD subset at this point, the XML processor cannot know about any elements declared in an external DTD subset.

An unrestricted element's content is declared like this:

```
<!ELEMENT any.element ANY>
```

and you cannot declare that the content should be in any order.

Element Content Models

An element content model consists of a description, using a very simple grammar, of the elements that may appear in the content of the current element, in what order they may or must appear, and how often they may or must appear. They are used to describe the structure of your XML documents, for instance, declaring that chapter elements must appear within section elements. Other examples of situations these models describe will be given in the following sections.

Element Sequences

The simplest form of element content model is a sequence consisting of a list of the possible elements, enclosed in parentheses and separated by commas:

```
<!ELEMENT counting (first,second,third,fourth)>
```

This example means that a counting element must consist of a first element, followed by a second element, followed by a third element, and ending with a fourth element.

In this example, all four elements must be present in a counting element, and each may be present only once (you can specify how often an element may appear by using an occurrence indicator, which you will learn about later in this chapter).

An element model with a sequence such as this would be used whenever you have an element that must be made up of a specific number of parts, which must occur in a specific order, and all of which must be present. For instance, you could create a business.letter element defined as follows:

```
<!ELEMENT business.letter (date,address,greeting,body,salutation)>
```

Part

III

Ch

13

A sequence such as this could also be used to count up the chapters in a book; however, remember that all the elements in the sequence must appear. Therefore, this will only work if you know precisely how many chapters you wish to use.

Choices

A choice of elements in an element content model is indicated by a ¦ between the alternatives:

```
<!ELEMENT choose (this.one ¦ that.one)>
```

so that a `choose` element consists of either a `this.one` element or a `that.one` element.

Notice once again that without an occurrence indicator, the chosen element can appear only once. Note also that only one element can be selected, no matter how long the list of alternatives is:

```
<!ELEMENT choose (this.one ¦ that.one ¦ the.other.one ¦ another.one ¦
no.that.one.silly)>
```

The choice element content model works best when a number of choices are available, one and only one of which must be selected. A `correspondence` element, for example, might include a number of choices to describe the type of correspondence:

```
<!ELEMENT correspondence (business.letter ¦ personal.letter ¦ quick.note)>
```

Combined Sequences and Choices

You can combine content sequence and choices by grouping the element content into model groups. For example:

```
<!ELEMENT lots.of.choice (maybe ¦ could.be), (this.one, that.one)>
```

Here, a `lots.of.choice` element can consist of either a `maybe` element or a `could.be` element, followed by one `this.one` element and then one `that.one` element. This type of combination model could be used for address data, for instance:

```
<!ELEMENT return.address (business.name ¦
personal.name),(street.address,city,state,zip)>
```

In this example, the address can belong to either a business or a person, and then must include a street address, city, state, and zip code.

Ambiguous Content Models

Although you can combine sequences and choices like this, you need to be very careful. You can create compatibility problems if your content model can be interpreted in more than one way. Consider this possibility:

```
<!ELEMENT confused ((this.one, that.one) ¦ (this.one, the.other.one))>
```

When the XML processor checks the content of the XML document to see whether the elements are in an allowed order (when it "validates" the document), it is going to be able to decide what is allowed and what isn't. In this case, once it sees the `this.one` element, it's impossible for it to work out which element is supposed to come next.

The XML processor could, of course, read further and then check to see if what occurs next is allowed, but XML processors are not meant to be able to look ahead. Remember, XML processors are meant to be simple and fast; if the processor has to look ahead, it is going to have to save what it has seen in memory, then look ahead, read in the next part, save that in memory, compare the two memory contents and then decide. All this takes extra processing and time.

By careful consideration, you can avoid ambiguous content models with a little rewriting:

```
<!ELEMENT unconfused (this.one, (that.one ¦ the.other.one))>
```

Generally, any time that you start combining these two operators, you should be on the lookout for ambiguities. Consider another example:

```
<!ELEMENT confused.again (this.one, that.one, the.other.one) ¦
no.that.one)>
```

This could easily lead you (and the XML processor) to believe that the no.that.one element is an alternative for all the other elements, or is it an alternative for a the.other.one element? Again, some rewriting can resolve the ambiguity and make your intention clearer:

```
<!ELEMENT explained (this.one, that.one, (the.other.one ¦ no.that.one))>
```

Occurrence Indicators

Using an occurrence indicator, you can specify how often (or not) an element or group of elements may appear in an element. Three occurrence indicators exist (without an occurrence indicator, the element or group of elements must appear only once):

- The ? character indicates that the element or group of elements may be omitted or may occur only once (zero or one time). The following content model:
  ```
  <!ELEMENT testing (one, two?, three)>
  ```
  would allow you to have
  ```
  <testing><one>tock</one><two>tock</two><three>tock</three></testing>
  ```
  or
  ```
  <testing><one>tock</one><three>tock</three></testing>
  ```
  in your XML document.
- The * character indicates that an element or group of elements may be omitted or may appear any number of times (zero or more times).
  ```
  <!ELEMENT nice (mmm, mmmm*)>
  ```
  would allow you to have
  ```
  <nice><mmm>I can't complain.</mmm></nice>
  ```
  or
  ```
  <nice><mmm>I like this one.</mmm><mmmm>More, </mmmm><mmmm>more, </mmmm>
  <mmmm>more, </mmmm><mmmm>more, <mmmm>more.</mmmm></testing>
  ```
- The + character indicates that an element or group of elements must appear at least once and may appear any number of times (one or more times).

```
<!ELEMENT funny (ha, haha+)>
```

would allow you to have

```
<funny><ha>Who?</ha><haha>is he?</haha></funny>
```

or

```
<funny><ha>I laughed </ha><haha>until </haha><haha>I </haha>
<haha>thought </haha><haha>I'd <haha>die!</haha></funny>
```

Using occurrence indicators, we could generalize our `return.address` element as follows:

```
<!ELEMENT return.address ((business.name,attn?) ¦
personal.name*),(street.address+,city,state,zip)>
```

This element breaks down as follows:

■ First, a choice exists between either `business.name` and `attn` or `personal.name`. The `?` after `attn` indicates that it can occur either zero or one time. The `*` after `personal.name` indicates it can occur any number of times, including zero. This leads to the following possibilities for this part of the content model:

   • Business name by itself

   • Business name with one `attn` name

   • One or more personal names

   • Nothing (the zero option of the `*` on `personal.name`)

■ Then, one or more `street.address` elements can be included.

■ Finally, one each of `city`, `state`, and `zip` must be used.

N O T E   As you can see, occurrence indicators give you a little control over the frequency of occurrence of an element or group of elements (not at all, once, or an unlimited number of times). This all-or-nothing approach is a little too loose for a lot of possible XML applications. Therefore, initiatives such as Microsoft's proposed XML-Data standard are very important. This standard, described at `http://www.microsoft.com/standards/xml/default.asp`, would give XML content authors more control over the data in their documents. ■

Character Content

One more type of element content is a little bit different from what we have discussed so far. Where text—and only text—is allowed inside an element, this is identified by the keyword PCDATA in the content model (parsable character data). To prevent you from confusing this keyword with a normal element name (and to make it impossible for you to use it as a name), the keyword is prefixed by a hash character (#), which is called the *reserved name character* (RNI).

The following element declarations:

```
<!ELEMENT para (title, text)>
<!ELEMENT title (#PCDATA)>
<!ELEMENT text (#PCDATA)>
```

would enable you to write this in your XML document:

```
<para>
   <title>My Life</title>
   <text>
      My life has been very quiet of late.
   </text>
</para>
```

A parsable character data element that cannot contain any further markup is therefore where the markup stops and normal text takes over.

Character Data Models

Don't lose sight of the fact that XML's content models are only concerned with the structure of an XML document; they make no attempt to control its content. An element that is totally devoid of data content will still match a #PCDATA content model.

Mixed Content

Elements that can contain either text (parsable character data), elements, or both are a real problem sometimes. They are given the name *mixed content* models, and they require extra care. The important point is that it is difficult for an XML processor to distinguish between unintentional PCDATA (spaces, tabs, line endings, and so on) and element content. An accidental space between an end tag and the next start tag could lead to some confusion on the part of the XML processor.

To declare mixed content, you use the content model grammar you have learned so far, but you must use it in a particular way. The content model has to take the form of a single set of alternatives, starting with #PCDATA and followed by the element types that can occur in the mixed content, each declared only once. Except when #PCDATA is the only option (as you saw earlier), the * qualifier must follow the closing parenthesis:

```
<!ELEMENT pick (#PCDATA ¦ eeney ¦ meeney ¦ miney ¦ mo)*>
```

Attribute Declarations

Although you can declare only one element at a time, elements can have lots of attributes, and so the attributes are all declared at once in an attribute specification list. An attribute declaration has the form

```
<!ATTLIST element.name attribute.definitions>
```

It is normal practice to keep the attribute declaration for an element close to the declaration of the element itself, but there is absolutely no requirement to do so; it just makes maintenance easier.

Attribute Specification Lists

An attribute specification list consists of one or more attribute specifications (for readability they are often put on separate lines, but this is not required). An attribute specification list does the following for an element:

- It declares the names of allowed attributes.
- It states the type of each attribute.
- It may provide a default value for each attribute.

Each attribute specification consists of a simple attribute name and attribute type pair statement of the form

```
attribute.name attribute.type
```

Attribute Types

Three types of attributes exist:

- A string attribute is one whose value consists of any amount of character data.
- A tokenized attribute is an attribute whose value consists of one or more *tokens* that are significant to XML.
- An enumerated attribute type is an attribute whose value is taken from a list of declared possible values.

String Types   The values of string types are simple strings of characters. Any attributes used in an XML document that does not have a DTD (either an internal DTD subset or an external DTD subset) is automatically treated as a string type attribute. An example of a string type declaration is

```
<!ATTLIST owner CDATA>
```

and you would then use it like this:

```
<book owner="Hammersmith Public Library">
```

You can also use an internal entity (in this case it's given the more generic name *general entity*) in the value of a string type attribute:

```
<book owner="&my.local; Public Library">
```

Tokenized Types   Tokenized attributes are classified according to what their value or values can be:

- ID—This type of attribute serves as an identifier for the element. No two elements can have the same ID value in the same document. An ID value must comply with the standard XML naming rules. An ID attribute type can be applied to any attribute, but it is standard practice to restrict its use to an attribute that is also called ID because this makes it easier to find.

  An example of an ID type declaration is

```
<!ATTLIST book
    id ID>
```

and you would then use it like this:

```
<book id="A51">
```

■ IDREF—This type of attribute is a pointer to an ID (an ID reference). The value must match the value of an ID type attribute that is declared somewhere in the same document.

■ IDREFS—The value of this type of attribute consists of one or more IDREF type values, separated by spaces.

An example of an IDREFS type declaration is

```
<!ATTLIST book
        authors IDREFS>
```

and you would then use it like this:

```
<book authors="A51 A62 B87">
```

■ ENTITY—This type of attribute is a pointer to an external entity that has been declared (in the DTD, in either the external or internal DTD subset). The value of the attribute is the name of the entity, which can consist of name characters only. The XML document can no longer be a standalone document if you use external entities. It is a little early to learn about external entities, but we will return to them in Chapter 15, "XML Characters, Notations, and Entities."

▶ **See** "Entities," **p. 391**.

■ ENTITIES—The value of this type of attribute consists of one or more ENTITY type values, separated by spaces.

ENTITY and ENTITIES type attributes are normally used to refer to things such as graphics files and other unparsed data:

```
<!ELEMENT graphic EMPTY>
<!ATTLIST graphic boardno ENTITY>
```

■ NMTOKEN—The value of this type of attribute is a "name token" string consisting of any mixture of name characters.

■ NMTOKENS—The value of this type of attribute consists of one or more NMTOKEN type values, separated by spaces.

Enumerated Types   Enumerated attributes have values that are simply a list of possible values. Each value has to be a valid name token (NMTOKEN). The following is an example:

```
<!ATTLIST paint
        COLOR (RED ¦ YELLOW ¦ GREEN) "RED">
```

When the list of possible values is prefixed by the keyword NOTATION, the notations listed as possible values must have been declared already:

```
<!ATTLIST image
        type NOTATION (GIF ¦ JPEG ¦ PNG) "GIF">
```

▶ **See** "Notations," **p. 389**.

Part
III

Ch
13

When matching an attribute value against the allowed values specified in the attribute defini-tion, the XML processor carries out a match (not case sensitive) for all attributes except those that are of the CDATA, IDREF, or IDREFS type.

Attribute Defaults   You can add a keyword to the end of an attribute specification to specify what action the XML processor should take when you leave out (or forget) the attribute in a particular start tag.

Three keywords are possible:

- #REQUIRED means that the attribute is required and should have been there. If it's missing, it makes the document invalid. An example of a required declaration is

```
<!ATTLIST book
          author ID #REQUIRED>
```

Normally, ID type attribute values are specified as being required (and you will learn later that they must be specified as required if the document is to be validated).

- #IMPLIED means that the XML processor must tell the application that no value was specified (it is then up to the application to decide what it is going to do). An example of an implied declaration is

```
<!ATTLIST section
          number #IMPLIED>
```

Implied attribute values are often used for things such as section and list item number-ing, where the application can calculate the value itself simply by counting.

- If the default value is preceded by the keyword #FIXED, any value that is specified must match the default value, or the document will be invalid.

The following are examples of attribute declarations with default values:

```
<!ATTLIST termdef
          id ID #REQUIRED
          name CDATA #IMPLIED>
<!ATTLIST list
          type (roman ¦ arabic ¦ Roman ¦ Arabic) "roman">
<!ATTLIST form
          method CDATA #FIXED "POST">
```

Well-Formed XML Documents

Elements, attributes, and entities are the three primary building blocks for XML documents. Using only elements, you can create true XML documents. Using all three objects, you can create quite complex XML documents; you could fulfill the needs of about 90% of the applica-tions for which you would want to use XML.

For such documents to be properly usable—for an XML processor to parse these documents successfully—they must be *well formed*. According to the XML standard, a data object is not officially an XML document until it is well formed. You have already encountered most of the rules that an XML document must obey in order to be well formed, but to round out this dis-cussion of XML documents, we'll review them all:

A document that you are able to create now using only elements, attributes, and entities is well formed if

- It contains one or more elements.
- It has only one element (the document, or root element) that contains all the other elements.
- Its elements (if it contains more than one element) are properly nested inside each other (no element starts in one element and ends in another).
- The names used in its element start tags and end tags match exactly.
- The names of attributes do not appear more than once in the same element start tag.
- The values of its attributes are enclosed in either single or double quotes.
- The values of its attributes do not reference external entities, either directly or indirectly.
- The replacement text for any entity referenced in an attribute value does not contain a < character (it can contain the string <).
- Its entities are declared before they are used.
- None of its entity references contains the name of an unparsed entity.
- Its logical and physical structures are properly nested.

Sample XML Applications

To get a better idea of what kinds of real-world applications can be created using XML, you can check out the following:

- Synchronized Multimedia Integration Language (SMIL)—Enables integrating a set of independent multimedia objects into a synchronized multimedia presentation (`http://www.w3.org/TR/REC-smil/`).
- Mathematical Markup Language (MathML)—Can be used to allow the description of mathematical notation, capturing both its structure and content (`http://www.w3.org/TR/REC-MathML/`).
- Chemical Markup Language (CML)—Enables the markup of information from the fields of molecular and biological chemistry (`http://www.venus.co.uk/omf/`).

Part
III

Ch
13

Creating XML Document Type Definitions

Why Have a DTD at All?

Recall from Chapter 11, "Introduction to XML," that an XML Document Type Definition (DTD) is simply a set of rules that explains how to use XML markup. As long as an XML document is well formed, no need exists to have a DTD at all. In fact, as will be shown later in this chapter, it is possible to derive a DTD just by looking at the XML document. However, some important restrictions apply to an XML document that does not have a DTD.

If you want to be able to validate an XML document without a DTD:

- All the attribute values in the XML document must be specified; you cannot have default values for them.
- No references to entities can be in the XML document (except of course `amp`, `lt`, `gt`, `apos`, and `quot`).
- No attributes can be present whose values are subject to normalization.
- In elements whose content consists of only elements, there can be no whitespace (space, tab, or other whitespace characters) between the starting tag of the container element and the start tag of the first element contained in it. The following, for example, would be illegal:

`<CHAPTER>   <SECTION>................. </SECTION></CHAPTER>`

This is a complicated point, but without the help of a DTD to tell the XML processor whether this whitespace is to be treated as meaningful (as PCDATA or a preserved whitespace), it has no way of knowing whether to delete it.

DTDs and Validation

The DTD describes a model of the structure of the content of an XML document. This model says what elements must be present, which are optional, what their attributes are, and how they can be structured in relation to each other. Although HTML has only one DTD, XML enables you to create your own DTDs for your applications, which gives you complete control over the process of checking the content and structure of the XML documents created for that application. This checking process is called *validation*. Depending on what you, as the DTD developer, want to achieve, you can exercise almost complete control over the structure and create a *strict* DTD. When you validate XML documents that were created using this strict DTD, you can insist that certain elements be present, and you can enforce the set order you require. You can check that certain attribute values have been set and, to a limited degree, you can even check that these attribute values are of the right general type.

On the other hand, you can also make almost everything optional and create a *loose* DTD. You could even have parallel versions of the same DTD, one that enables you to create *draft* versions of the XML that aren't complete and another that rigidly checks that everything is present. It is even possible to insert switches into a DTD that can be used to turn the degree of strictness on and off.

Based on what you have declared in the DTD, when the completed XML document is then validated, what is allowed, and what is not will be completely determined by the choices you made in designing the DTD. The author of the document can then be warned, for example, if elements are not in the right place, as shown in Figure 14.1, or if required elements are missing, as shown in Figure 14.2. (You'll learn more about the application that generated these messages in Chapter 16, "XML DTD and Document Validation.")

FIGURE 14.1

Faulty structure warning.

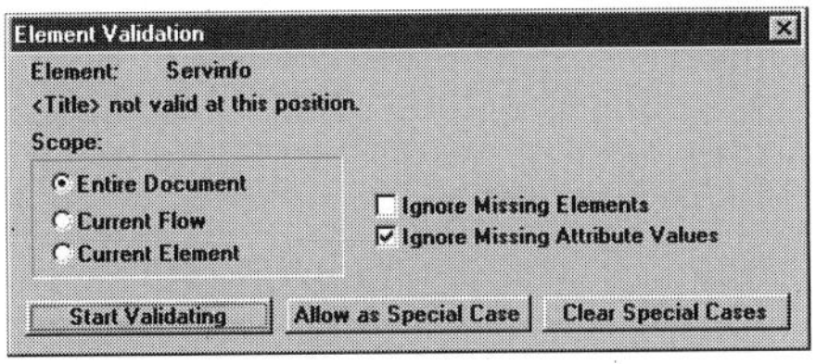

FIGURE 14.2

Missing XML element warning.

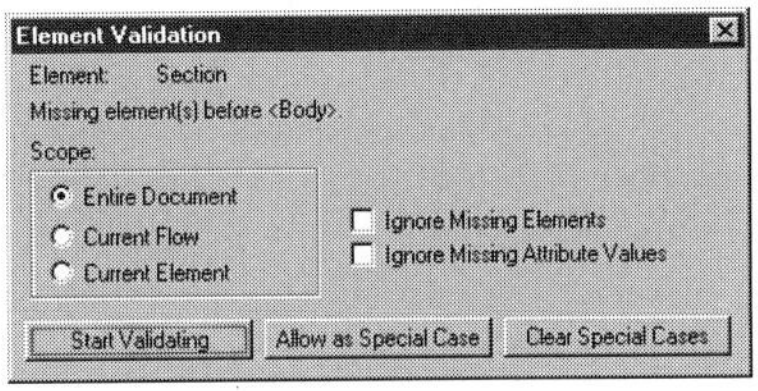

Document Type Declarations

After you have decided to use a DTD, the first step is to associate it with an XML document with a document type declaration. The document type definition (DTD) is an XML description of the content model of a type (or class) of documents. The document type declaration is a statement in an XML file that identifies the DTD that belongs to the document, and if an external DTD file is used, it identifies where the DTD entity (the file) can be found.

At its very simplest, a document type declaration looks like the following:

```
<!DOCTYPE DTD.name [ internal.subset ]>
```

`DTD.name` is the name of the DTD. When we come to the topic of validity later on, you will discover that the DTD name should be the same as the root element of the document. So, a DTD designed for a document would be called book, or something similar, and the root element in the document would also be book. Don't forget that XML is case sensitive; if you call the DTD Book, then you should have a root element Book.

`internal.subset` is the contents of the internal DTD subset, the part of the DTD that stays in the XML document itself. We will investigate the internal DTD subset shortly; it contains local element, attribute, and entity declarations. Without the internal DTD subset, there wouldn't really be much point in including a document type declaration.

Part

III

Ch

14

Internal DTD Subset

For an XML document to be well formed, all the external entities must be declared in the DTD. If you design your application carefully, it may be possible for you to put all the declarations in the internal DTD subset. With all the declarations in the internal DTD subset, the XML processor would not need to read and process external documents.

Note that having an internal subset does not affect the XML document's status as a standalone document. This can be a little confusing at first. When you start off the XML document, the first line is the XML declaration, which can include a standalone document declaration:

```
<?xml version="1.0" standalone="yes"?>
```

The statement standalone="yes" means that no markup declarations are external to the document entity. In the XML document, it is still perfectly acceptable to reference external entities (graphics files, included text, and so on), provided that the declarations of the external entities are contained inside the document entity (in other words, inside the internal DTD subset).

Standalone XML Documents

A document type declaration and the contents of an internal DTD subset are all you need to be able to define the structure of an XML document. Without any external support, without referring to any other files, an XML document containing an internal DTD subset contains enough information for it to be used for quite complex applications.

Listing 14.1 shows an XML document describing a basic catalog that uses the internal DTD subset.

Listing 14.1 *Catalog.xml*—Standalone XML Document with Internal DTD Subset

```
<?xml version="1.0" standalone="yes"?>
<!DOCTYPE CATALOG [
    <!ELEMENT CATALOG (PRODUCT+)>
    <!ELEMENT PRODUCT (SPECIFICATIONS+, PRICE+, NOTES?)>
    <!ATTLIST PRODUCT NAME CDATA #REQUIRED>
    <!ELEMENT SPECIFICATIONS (#PCDATA)>
    <!ATTLIST SPECIFICATIONS SIZE CDATA #REQUIRED
                             COLOR CDATA #REQUIRED>
    <!ELEMENT PRICE (#PCDATA)>
    <!ATTLIST PRICE WHOLESALE NMTOKEN #REQUIRED
              RETAIL NMTOKEN #REQUIRED
              SALES.TAX NMTOKEN #IMPLIED>
    <!ELEMENT NOTES (#PCDATA)>
]>
<CATALOG>
    <PRODUCT NAME="T-shirt">
        <SPECIFICATION SIZE="XL" COLOR="WHITE"/>
        <PRICE WHOLESALE="9.95" RETAIL="19.95" SALES.TAX="2.56" SHIPPING="5.00"/>
        <NOTES>Dilbert</NOTES>
```

```
   </PRODUCT>
   <PRODUCT NAME="Shirt">
      <SPECIFICATION SIZE="38" COLOR="BLACK" />
      <PRICE WHOLESALE="69.95" RETAIL="79.95" SALES.TAX="4.54" SHIPPING="10.00">
         Euro
      </PRICE>
   </PRODUCT>
</CATALOG>
```

Listing 14.1 starts with the now familiar XML prolog that identifies what follows as being a standalone XML version 1.0 document—one that doesn't use an external DTD. The second line declares the document type as being a CATALOG and opens the internal DTD subset. The internal DTD subset itself follows; it describes a CATALOG element that contains one or more PRODUCT elements, a PRODUCT element containing one or more SPECIFICATION elements, followed by one or more PRICE elements, and then optional NOTES elements.

The SPECIFICATION and PRICE elements, as shown in the markup, are actually empty, and their information is included in the form of attributes. These elements could have been declared as being empty, but in this case they were not. Just because an element isn't declared as being empty, this doesn't stop someone from leaving the element empty. Validation can check the markup, but it actually does little or nothing to check what's between the markup (the content), other than looking for more markup. You can have perfectly structured garbage if you wish, or even perfectly structured space and tab characters.

In this case, no currency attribute is attached to the PRICE element, so all the prices are assumed to be in the local currency. This might not always be true, so the document author has the option to add this information as text inside the PRICE element.

Note that the internal DTD subset uses elements to identify the main objects and properties of those objects; a PRODUCT has SPECIFICATION elements inside it. Most of the real property data, however, is declared as the attribute values of the SIZE, COLOR, and PRICE elements. The decision of when to use elements and when to use attributes is a difficult one to make. We will explore this problem later in this chapter. Most of the attribute values are being declared as #REQUIRED, which means that they must be given. One exception exists, though—the SALES.TAX attribute, which is #IMPLIED. This means that if the value isn't given, the XML application running on the computer system will be able to calculate the value.

The XML document described can be validated. It contains enough of a DTD, the internal DTD subset, to enable the content and structure of the XML document to be checked. In this form, the XML document is pretty portable and good arguments exist for leaving it at that. By adding a few additional lines to the XML markup, we've succeeded in making the document reasonably self describing. The recipient can even perform a rough check that parts of it are complete. The fact that a complete product is missing could only be detected by the lack of a closing CATALOG tag (assuming the file was clipped in transit). You wouldn't be able to tell through validation how many products were missing (although you could easily modify the DTD—even on-the-fly—to enable this to be checked).

Part

III

Ch

14

Getting Sophisticated with External DTDs

So far you have already learned that you can achieve quite a lot with a standalone XML document. Although you have all the benefits of portability by keeping the DTD inside the XML document itself, you are only just touching the surface of what can be achieved when you take the next logical step and use an external DTD subset.

The fact that it's called a document type definition already gives a clue that a DTD is intended for use with more than one XML document. Indeed, by not using an external DTD subset, you miss out on a lot of features of XML as well as the capability to use the DTD as a kind of template for a limitless set of XML documents. In XML contexts, the external DTD subset is often called an external DTD. XML has one DTD, but it's a composite of both the internal DTD subset and the external DTD subset.

In XML, the internal DTD subset is read before the external DTD subset, and so it takes precedence. This enables you to use an external DTD subset to make global declarations and then override them on an individual basis by putting different declarations in the internal DTD subset. You've already learned how to associate an internal DTD subset with an XML document. The association of an external DTD subset with an XML document is rather more complicated and uses either a system identifier (`system` keyword) or a public identifier (`public` keyword) and a system identifier:

```
<!DOCTYPE name public.identifier system.identifier [ internal.subset ]>
```

Both the system identifier and the public identifier are entity identifiers.

System Identifier

A system identifier is a URI (uniform resource identifier), which may be used to retrieve the DTD. If you've ever opened a Web page in a browser or downloaded a file from an FTP site, you have already seen one form of a URI called a URL (uniform resource locator). URLs are special forms of URIs intended for network (Internet) use. You will see the more technically precise name of URI used more often than URL, but for the majority of uses, the two terms are virtually interchangeable.

A system identifier can reference an absolute location, as in

```
<!DOCTYPE book SYSTEM "/mount/usr/home/dtds/book.dtd">
<!DOCTYPE book SYSTEM "http://wwwin.synopsys.com/~north/dtds/book.dtd">
```

or it can be a reference to a relative location:

```
<!DOCTYPE book SYSTEM "dtds/book.dtd">
<!DOCTYPE book SYSTEM "../../dtds/book.dtd">
```

Public Identifier

A public identifier is the officially recorded identifier for a DTD. Obviously, it would be impossible to register every DTD. Instead, the person or company who creates DTD registers itself. The International Standards Organization (ISO) is responsible under the provisions of ISO

9070 for the registrations, but authority to issue identifiers and the associated recordkeeping are delegated to the American Graphic Communication Association (AGCA). A public identifier has the following form:

```
reg.type // owner //DTD description // language
```

These parts have the following meanings:

- `reg.type` is a plus (+) if the owner is registered according to the ISO 9070 standard. Normally, this will not be the case and so `reg.type` is a minus (-) sign.
- `owner` is the name of the owner—your name or your company's name.
- `description` is a simple text description. You can make this description as long as you like, but it is a good idea to keep it as short and informative as possible. Spaces are allowed in the description, so you could make it something really meaningful such as `Simple Email Message`.
- `language` is the two-character language code taken from the ISO 639 standard.

An example of the public identifier for a DTD developed by me could then be

```
-//Jim O'Donnell//DTD Simple Web Page//EN
```

An XML processor attempting to retrieve the DTD's content may use the public identifier to try to generate a location. This is not always possible, so the public identifier must be followed by a so-called *system literal*, which is simply a URI. Using the public identifier and the system literal, the documentation type declaration would then look like this:

```
<!DOCTYPE home.page PUBLIC "-//Jim O'Donnell//DTD Simple Web Page//EN"
"home.dtd">
```

Note that before a match is attempted, all strings of whitespace in the public identifier are normalized to single space characters, and leading and trailing whitespace is removed.

Developing the DTD from XML

Many ways exist to describe information models, technically known as *schemas*. Indeed, several XML development activities are devoted to defining schemas for describing XML data. One such schema is the XML DTD.

The task of developing a DTD can be as simple or as difficult as you make it. It all depends on what you want to do with the information you intend to model with the DTD and what you intend to do with the information after it has been marked up. The easiest, quickest, and simplest method of creating an XML DTD is to start by creating an XML document and working backward.

Identifying Elements

For relatively simple Web pages—and some of the simple applications that we have discussed so far— typing out the intended XML document and then marking it up will most likely give you a flying start on developing your DTD. Before you do, though, make sure that you have a clear idea of what you want to achieve with the DTD. You will learn about this in more detail later in this chapter, but you need to be aware of what kind of markup you want to support. It can be

- Content—Here you are trying to describe what the information means or represents. You would then be looking for abstractions that represent real-world objects, such as part numbers and house addresses.

- Structure—Here you are more concerned with grouping elements such as lists, paragraphs, and tables. These are elements that break the information into units but do not add anything informational.

- Presentation—Here you are concerned only with the way things look and how they are presented when the XML document is displayed.

Avoiding Presentation Markup

As far as generic markup is concerned (and the portability of your XML documents), presentation elements are the worst kind of element and should be avoided as much as possible. Where you feel you need some kind of typographic embellishment, such as boldface, in an XML document, try and relate it to a function by asking yourself why you want it bold in the first place. Is it a keyword? Well, then, call it a KEYWORD element.

Although you should be able to get rid of all the purely presentation elements, inevitably, some will be left. A line break element might be useful, but some of the more familiar candidates that you might think you'd need aren't worth it. An example of this kind of presentation element is the horizontal line element, HR, in HTML. Yes, you can do some neat things with horizontal lines, but you should be asking yourself where you actually use them. If you can couple a presentation feature to an element, such as putting a horizontal line before the start of a section, or if you can link it to a context, such as indenting paragraphs inside lists, you should think carefully about whether you could achieve the required effect by using a style sheet of some kind.

ON THE WEB

`http://www.w3.org/Style/XSL/`   This Web site is the home of the work that the World Wide Web Consortium is doing on Extensible Style Sheets (XSL), the companion language to XML meant for describing the presentation format to be used with an XML document.

Structure the Elements

Having identified and named the elements in your XML document, the next step is to arrange the elements into some kind of hierarchical (tree) arrangement. The complexity of the tree that you make will largely depend on your application. If you are modeling a database, then you might want to keep the hierarchy fairly flat, but at the very least you must obey the rules of being well formed and having only one root element that contains all the other elements. You will probably find that a pencil-and-paper sketch of the structure will be a great help.

While structuring, look for group and container elements. Group elements are things such as lists, definition lists, and glossaries that arrange sets of elements as units. Sometimes you will need to consciously create extra elements to collect other elements to make processing easier. A container list for a set of numbered paragraphs, for instance, makes it easier to number the paragraphs and reset the number each time you start a new set. A useful clue to the need for a container element is that if you find yourself thinking of a set, a list, or a group of elements, you should automatically start thinking container.

Examples of container elements are the HEAD and BODY elements in HTML, or perhaps separate MESSAGE.HEADER and MESSAGE.TEXT elements for an email message DTD. A rough, general rule for containers is to look at the content model for the element. If you cannot easily understand what it means without having to stop and think, it is too complex, and you should consider breaking it up with a container element.

Enforce the Rules

So far, you should have been concentrating on getting everything identified and organized. Only when these stages have been completed should you start to think about enforcing your model, making elements optional and required. Think carefully about how strict you want to be and how much validation you need. If your XML code is to be computer generated, perhaps from a database, there probably isn't much point in wasting time and energy in tightening up the DTD. After all, you then have complete control over the generation of the XML markup. On the other hand, if the XML markup is to be created by humans, you will probably want to make sure that certain elements are not forgotten.

When you make elements optional, be careful that you don't make the content model ambiguous. Remember that XML parsers are not very complex and are unable to look ahead at what comes next in the XML document. At each point in the content model, it must be absolutely clear what element is allowed next. Sometimes you will have to use some clever tricks to get around these ambiguities.

Assigning Attributes

Only after you have arranged your elements into a hierarchical structure and grouped them as necessary should you assign attributes to them (size, color, ID and so on). At this point, you may find that you will want to move some of the information into attributes, which is why it helps to keep the two tasks separate.

No real rules exist about when to use attributes and when to use elements, although there is still a lot of discussion about it. This issue will be discussed in greater depth later in this chapter, but you can usually use common sense as a guide. One good way to divide them up is that things that are nouns should be elements, and things that are adjectives or adverbs should be attributes. So, in our Catalog example from Listing 14.1, the products themselves are elements, but the characteristics of those products, such as price and color, are attributes.

Tool Assistance

A number of quite good XML editors are already available. Although some of them are still in early stages of development and it is still unclear what features are actually required by users, a trend is apparent. In less than a year, along a path that very roughly parallels that followed by

Part

III

Ch

14

HTML tools, we have moved from markup-aware text editors to a kind of word processor package attuned to editing XML code. The XML editors that are now appearing on the market are beginning to add dedicated XML capabilities such as validation.

A Home Page DTD

Listing 14.2 shows an example of a simple XML document used to show a sample home page. In this section, I will build on this example to demonstrate how to put together a simple DTD.

> **Listing 14.2** *Home.xml*—**Home Page XML Document**

```
<?xml version="1.0"?>
<home.page>
   <head>
      <title>
         My Home Page
      </title>
      <banner source="topbanner.gif"/>
   </head>
   <body>
      <main.title>
         Welcome to My Home Page
      </main.title>
      <rule/>
      <text>
         <para>
            Sorry, this home page is still under construction.
            Please come back soon!
         </para>
      </text>
   </body>
   <footer source="foot.gif"/>
</home.page>
```

By pulling this document into an XML tool such as the XMLPro Editor, which can be found on the Web at http://www.vervet.com/, without a DTD (see Figure 14.3), you can then add elements, delete them, and move them around. After you've finished and are satisfied with the results, you can use the tree structure shown in the left window to see the way you have structured things. You can easily explore your tree, expanding and collapsing branches. The tree structure you will see gives you a good head start on describing the structure you want in your DTD.

If you pull the same XML markup into a different application, STILO WebWriter, it isn't quite as easy to navigate the structure as in XMLPro, but WebWriter compensates by enabling you to actually generate the DTD (see Figure 14.4).

Listing 14.3 shows the extracted DTD (slightly edited to enhance readability) derived from the sample XML document home page.

FIGURE 14.3

Exploring the structure in XMLPro Editor.

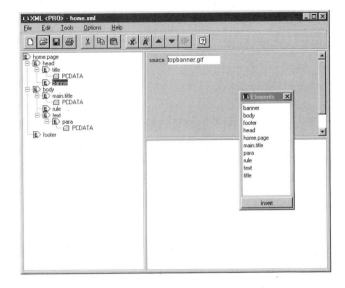

FIGURE 14.4

Creating the DTD in STILO WebWriter.

Listing 14.3 *Home_WW.dtd*—DTD Generated from *Home.xml*

```
<?xml version = "1.0"?>
<!ELEMENT home.page (#PCDATA | head | body | footer)*>
<!ELEMENT head (#PCDATA | title | banner)*>
<!ELEMENT title (#PCDATA)>
<!ELEMENT banner EMPTY>
<!ATTLIST banner source CDATA "">
<!ELEMENT body (#PCDATA | main.title | rule | text)*>
<!ELEMENT main.title (#PCDATA)>
<!ELEMENT rule EMPTY>
<!ELEMENT text (#PCDATA | para)*>
<!ELEMENT para (#PCDATA)>
<!ELEMENT footer EMPTY>
<!ATTLIST footer source CDATA "">
<!ENTITY lt "<">
<!ENTITY gt ">">
<!ENTITY apos "'">
<!ENTITY quot """>
<!ENTITY amp "&">
```

Part

III

Ch

14

WebWriter has played it safe in allowing every element to have mixed content (#PCDATA is allowed in all the content models), and it was wise not to guess about the nature of the element attributes. This gives you a good framework for your DTD. To complete it, you can tighten up the content models and fill in the attribute declarations. One possible end result is shown in Listing 14.4.

Listing 14.4 *Home.dtd*—Final *Home.dtd* DTD

```
<?xml version = "1.0"?>
<!ELEMENT home.page (head ¦ body ¦ footer)>
<!ELEMENT head (title ¦ banner?)>
<!ELEMENT title (#PCDATA)>
<!ELEMENT banner EMPTY>
<!ATTLIST banner
          src CDATA #REQUIRED
          alt CDATA #IMPLIED
          align (top ¦ middle ¦ bottom) #IMPLIED>
<!ELEMENT body (main.title ¦rule ¦ text)>
<!ELEMENT main.title (#PCDATA)>
<!ELEMENT rule EMPTY>
<!ATTLIST rule
          align (left¦right¦center) #IMPLIED
          size NMTOKEN #IMPLIED
          width CDATA #IMPLIED >
<!ELEMENT text (#PCDATA ¦ para)*>
<!ELEMENT para (#PCDATA)>
<!ELEMENT footer EMPTY>
<!ATTLIST footer
          src CDATA #REQUIRED
          alt CDATA #IMPLIED
          align (top¦middle¦bottom) #IMPLIED>
<!ENTITY lt "<">
<!ENTITY gt ">">
<!ENTITY apos "'">
<!ENTITY quot """>
<!ENTITY amp "&">
```

N O T E In accordance with the XML specification, now that we are using a DTD, we have included the declarations of the default character entities (lt, gt, apos, quot, and amp). ▇

Richness and Entropy

If you want to do something with a piece of information in an XML document, you must identify it. It doesn't matter whether you mark it up using elements or attributes, but if you haven't marked it up, you either won't be able to find it at all, and even if you can find it, you won't be able to do anything with it.

A DTD that contains a lot of (informative) markup is called a *rich* DTD. As the DTD designer, you will always face a difficult compromise between the complexity of the DTD and the information richness of XML documents that conform to that DTD. Where humans are the authors of those documents, the complexity of the DTD can become a major obstacle.

When you have the room to make choices, always choose the richest information model you can:

- It is far easier to throw away information than it is to add it afterward.

  Consider what happens when you go from XML, or even HTML, to plain text with no markup at all. It's a simple conversion to make because you are moving from a higher information richness to a lower one. Going the other way is not easy at all. The same applies for moving from SGML to XML, and from XML to HTML. At each conversion you throw information away, moving from an information-rich level (SGML) to a relatively poor level (HTML).

- You cannot always account for all media and all intended uses. No matter how carefully you research your application in advance, something you haven't thought of will occur.

  With SGML, it is often the case that it's only after you've got all your data marked up that you really start to appreciate what you can do with it. If you limit yourself to the minimum necessary for the current application, you may design yourself into a corner where there is no room left for expansion.

Visual Modeling

Earlier in this chapter, you learned that one of the basic DTD design process steps is to construct the hierarchy, to use the content models in the DTD to arrange the elements in an XML document that uses the DTD in a hierarchical, tree-like structure. Many information modeling techniques are available, but detailed discussion of them falls outside the scope of this book. What is of interest to us here is that all recommend some kind of visual aid to help you. The same applies for DTD development, but each expert has his or her own set of symbols. Some prefer to model using the blocks familiar from flow diagrams, as shown in Figure 14.5.

FIGURE 14.5
Block diagram DTD modeling.

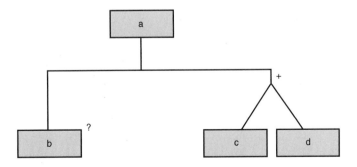

<!ELEMENT a (b?, (c|d)+>

An alternative is the somewhat sparser representation form shown in Figure 14.6.

FIGURE 14.6

Simplified diagram DTD modeling.

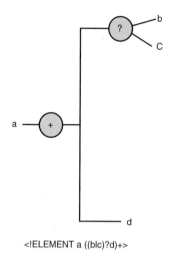

<!ELEMENT a ((b|c)?d)+>

Note that both types of modeling graphics try to represent the sequence and *OR* models by using different kinds of connecting lines between the objects (diagonal for an *OR* choice, straight lines for a simple relationship, and rectangular connections for sequences). This type of modeling graphics is also incorporated in the top-of-the-line SGML DTD modeling package, Microstar's NEAR & FAR, an example of which is shown in Figure 14.7.

FIGURE 14.7

Visual modeling in NEAR & FAR.

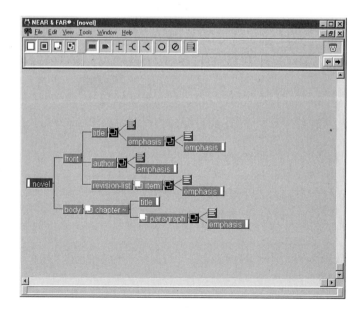

It is difficult to think of a better way of modeling DTDs visually than these kinds of models (different is easy; better is hard), especially in a software package where you can expand and collapse branches of the DTD tree as you work on them. However, as the DTD gets larger and larger, it becomes harder and harder to maintain a sensible overview. You shouldn't forget that these are primarily SGML tools where people are mostly working on a different scale than is probably useful in XML. Where an XML application might need a few tens of elements and a couple hundred lines in a DTD, SGML applications routinely think in terms of several hundred elements and several thousand lines of declarations in a DTD. It isn't only the number of elements that makes the DTD bulky, though. Often, elements that have a presentational function (such as emphasized text) will be reused in almost every element. When you expand these models, as you can see from Figure 14.8, unless you start finding other ways to manage DTDs of this scale or complexity, even a well-designed visual presentation can become too cluttered for it to be of much use.

FIGURE 14.8

Reaching the limits of useful visual modeling.

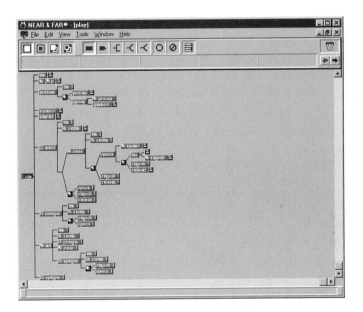

Of course, techniques exist for mastering DTDs of this scale. You can do this by breaking the DTD into modules of a more manageable size (you will learn about this technique later in the chapter), but a point also comes where you must ask yourself whether it is really worth continuing in this way. Figure 14.9 shows a public domain software package called ez DTD that gives a kind of tabular display of the elements in the DTD.

Here all you have is a list of elements, and you can display the content model for one model at a time. For simple XML applications and smaller DTDs, this kind of tool could quite possibly be as much as you will ever need, especially as you become more proficient in creating DTDs. Unfortunately, no way exists of displaying any kind of tree to show the relations between elements. Again, after the scale of the DTD increases beyond a certain point, the usefulness starts to tail off, as you can see from Figure 14.10.

FIGURE 14.9

Tabular modeling in ez DTD.

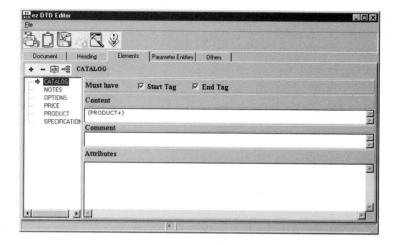

FIGURE 14.10

Reaching the limits of usefulness of a simplified form of visual modeling.

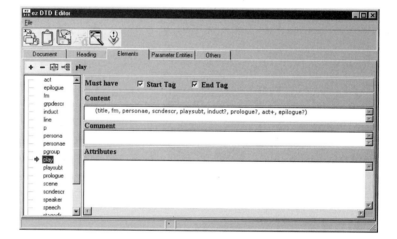

It may make more sense to give up on trying to visualize the DTD altogether, although a recommended tool is Earl Hood's public domain Perl script, DTD2HTML. This package converts a DTD into a set of interlinked HTML pages. The output isn't a great deal of help while you're actually developing the DTD, but it is extremely useful for checking the results of your work and is excellent as a means of documenting the completed DTD. Instead of visually modeling the DTD, you may ultimately find it easier to learn to use a more conservative package, such as Innovation Partners' DTD Generator package, shown in Figure 14.11.

In this no-frills package, you have a halfway point between the two camps. In this package, you have all the ease of dedicated buttons that enable you to add the parts of content models quickly, but there is no attempt to give any kind of visual display. Instead, you can very quickly flip backward between the ease-of-use interface and the raw DTD code.

FIGURE 14.11

DTD creating in the XML DTD Generator package from Innovation Partners.

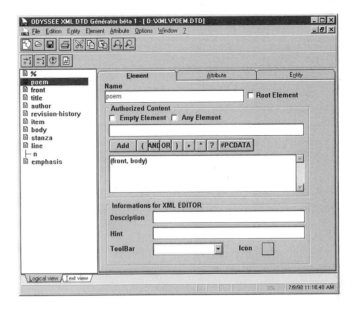

XML DTDs from Other Sources

One alternative to getting involved in the complexities of DTD design and development is to leave the DTD design to one side and work on a representative XML document. You must, of course, ensure that you consider all the likely variations of the document, and you will probably need several documents as your XML application becomes larger. However, after you have explored all the possibilities in the XML document, you can then use tools to create at least the core of the DTD for you. Although this would be almost impossible for an SGML application, this approach will often be a realistic choice for XML applications. As you can see from the real-life document loaded in XMLPro in Figure 14.12, a good XML editor will enable you to browse through the structure of the document, adding elements and attributes wherever you need them. Although you may find yourself repeating some steps unnecessarily, it is easy enough to consolidate the multiple declarations afterward. One significant benefit is gained from this approach that no specialized DTD tool can give you. By exposing you to what amounts to being a completed XML document using your (proposed) DTD, you get a first-hand taste of what it would be like for a human author to work with your DTD.

Many of the mainstream software packages, such as Adobe's FrameMaker and even Microsoft's Office suite, will be supporting XML as an output format in the near future. This opens up all sorts of possibilities for getting the structure of an intended XML correct in one of those software packages and then either creating the DTD from that document, or even skipping the DTD altogether.

An interesting development in this direction is the Majix software package from Tetrasix. This software package, shown in Figure 14.13, enables you to create an XML document from a Microsoft RTF format document. If you use Microsoft Word, for example, and you use Word styles properly, you can use these styles to drive the conversion into XML elements.

Part
III

Ch

14

FIGURE 14.12

Modeling the document before creating a DTD.

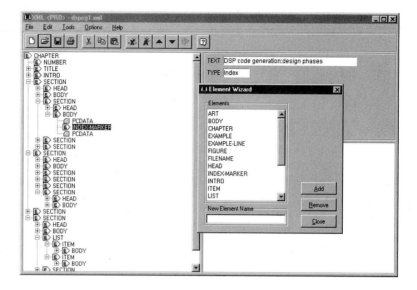

FIGURE 14.13

Converting RTF into XML with Majix from Tetrasix.

Modeling Relational Databases

In this discussion of developing DTDs, the elements have consistently been structured hierarchically. Generally, this really is what you need to do, but instances might occur where you might want to—or even need to—avoid having too much of a hierarchy, and you want to keep the model flat. Such an application would be when you are using XML to model a relational database, an application that XML is ideally suited for (subject to the planned XML data typing initiatives bearing fruit).

Consider the simple relational database description shown in Listing 14.5. Although the topic of database modeling in XML deserves more extensive treatment than can be given here, even a quick appraisal shows that you don't really need that much depth. The simple database shown here, in fact, only needs four levels:

- The database (the root element, `music`)
- The database tables (the `artists` and `discs` elements)
- The database records (the `artist` and `disc` elements)
- The database fields (the `name`, `label`, `title`, `date`, and `number` elements)

After you have this structure, it's a simple matter to add table and record keys by assigning attributes. In this way, you could create a forced division between using the elements to describe the content and structure of the database itself and reserve the use of attributes for the (internal) data that describes the relations between the data.

Listing 14.5 *Music.xml*—XML Description of a Music Database

```
<?xml version="1.0"?>
<!DOCTYPE music SYSTEM "mymusic.dtd">
<music>
    <artists>
        <artist>
            <name>Cyndi Lauper</name>
            <label>Sony</label>
            <title>Twelve Deadly Guns</title>
        </artist>
        <artist>
            <name>Kate Bush</name>
            <label>EMI</label>
            <title>Hounds of Love</title>
        </artist>
    </artists>
    <discs>
        <disc>
            <title>Twelve Deadly Guns</title>
            <date>1994</date>
            <number>EPC 477363 2</number>
        </disc>
        <disc>
            <title>Hounds Of Love</title>
            <date>1985</date>
            <number>CDP 7 46164 2</number>
        </disc>
    </discs>
</music>
```

Elements or Attributes?

The idea of separating elements and attributes in an XML database description is one of the many ways that a distinction can be made between the use of elements and attributes. This question surfaces regularly in SGML circles, and even now it has never really been answered with any degree of conviction. The database example shows one possible answer, but it is only one of many. The following are some things to keep in mind:

Part
III

Ch

14

▩ Elements can be remapped using architectural forms, and attributes can be remapped using XLink; this is, therefore, not a decisive reason for selecting either an element or an attribute.

▩ Historically, attributes have been reserved for intangible, abstract properties, such as color and size, and elements are reserved for physical components. To deviate from this usage, especially in an SGML context, may confuse people.

▩ It may be easier to edit elements in XML editing tools than attributes, and attribute values may not be so readily displayed as element content. This would favor elements when dealing with human authors.

▩ An XML processor is able to check the content of an attribute value more easily than it can check the content of an element. It can't check an attribute value for much, but it can barely check the content of an element at all.

▩ The attributes of elements from separate XML documents can be merged quite easily. It can be extremely hard to merge elements, and so, in a distributed environment, attributes may have the edge over elements.

▩ In collaborative (multiple) author environments, it is reasonably easy to split XML documents into fragments based on the element structure rather than the attribute values.

▩ Sensibly named elements can make (human) authoring easier and less confusing. When selecting an element to contain a list, for example, it's pretty obvious to the human writer that she should choose a list element. However, the selection of the correct attribute (and you will quite often see such cryptic attribute values as ordered and unordered, which come from HTM) can be less than obvious and not very visible. The choice of container elements instead, such as list.numbered and list.bulleted, may make the author's life much simpler.

From these concepts, you may notice a general trend. Generally speaking, when human beings are expected to create or work with the XML documents, it can be better to use elements rather than attributes.

Saving Yourself Typing with Parameter Entities

You will learn a lot more about entities in the next chapter. For the moment, we are concerned with one particular type of entity called the parameter entity, which can be extremely useful in XML DTDs. Parameter entities are basically like the character entities you learned about earlier. They, too, behave like macros and can be used as abbreviations for strings. However, where character entities serve as abbreviations for character strings, parameter entities serve as shortcuts for markup declarations and parts of declarations. Obviously, because they are concerned with markup declarations, they can be used only in DTDs. In fact, their use is a little more restrictive than this:

▩ In the internal DTD subset, parameter entities can be used only between other markup declarations.

■ In the external DTD subset, parameter entities can be used both between and inside other markup declarations.

To make sure no confusion occurs between parameter entities and character entities, the syntax for declaring and referring to parameter entities is quite different from the syntax for a character entity; a parameter entity uses a percent sign, as in the following example:

```
<!ENTITY % heading "H1 ¦ H2 ¦ H3 ¦ H4 ¦ H5 ¦ H6">
<!ENTITY % body.content "(%heading ¦ %text ¦ %block ¦ ADDRESS)*">
<!ELEMENT BODY %body.content>
```

The heading parameter entity saves a lot of typing (note that you could use this particular trick only in the external DTD subset). Parameter entities can also be used to make DTD declarations a little more comprehensible, as in the following example:

```
<!ENTITY % color "CDATA">
<!ENTITY % body-color-attrs "
        bgcolor %color #IMPLIED
        text    %color #IMPLIED
        link    %color #IMPLIED
        vlink   %color #IMPLIED
        alink   %color #IMPLIED
">
<!ELEMENT BODY  %body.content>
<!ATTLIST BODY
          background %URL #IMPLIED
          %body-color-attrs;>
```

Both examples shown here use internal parameter entities; no external file is required for the XML processor to be able to determine the contents of the entities. It is also possible to have external parameters, as you will learn next, and these are used for quite different purposes.

Modular DTDs

Earlier, you learned that techniques can be used to split up particularly complex DTDs. This is another use for external parameter entities. For example, the following DTD fragment declares and then immediately references a set of character entity declarations contained in an external file (this is such a common use for parameter entities that an extensive set of public identifiers exists that covers most of the less commonly used characters):

```
<!ENTITY % ISOnum PUBLIC "ISO 8879:1986//ENTITIES Numeric and Special Graphic//
EN">
%ISOnum;
```

External parameter entities really come in handy when you decide to reuse the results of work that you have invested in the development of other DTDs. Over the years, the declarations of the elements in a table, for example, have gradually become standardized around a model called the *cals table* model (named after the American Department of Defense Computer Assisted Logistic Support initiative, under which a lot of early SGML developments were funded). It is quite hard to improve on this model (tables are pretty standard), and so it is often provided as a common DTD fragment that all other DTDs can reference when they need it:

```
<?xml version="1.0" standalone="no"?>
<!DOCTYPE book SYSTEM "book.dtd" [
    <!ENTITY % calstable SYSTEM "cals.dtd">
    %calstable;
]>
```

Note that this external parameter entity declaration and the reference to it are located in the internal DTD subset. Note, too, that I have explicitly stated that the XML document is not a standalone document.

If you are not going to validate an XML document, you must always be wary of what can go wrong with external parameter entities that contain markup declarations. The following shows an external parameter entity being used in an internal DTD subset to include some declarations from an external file:

```
<?xml version="1.0" standalone="yes"?>
<!DOCTYPE menu [
    <!ELEMENT menu (#PCDATA, front, meals+, back)*>
    <!ATTLIST menu title CDATA "Carte Blanche">
    <!ENTITY % entrees SYSTEM "entrees.xml">
    %entrees;
    <!ATTLIST menu desserts CDATA "Sweet Temptations">
]>
<menu>
    <front>Sunday, July 11, 1998</front>
    …
</menu>
```

When this XML document is parsed but not validated, the value of the menu element's `title` attribute will be `"Carte Blanche"`. The XML processor sees the declaration of the `title` attribute, even though it is inside the internal DTD subset. Because it isn't validating (the document claims that it is a standalone document), the XML processor is not allowed to process any external entity references. The value of the `desserts` attribute has to remain unknown.

The default value (`"Sweet Temptations"`) has been declared, but the XML processor isn't allowed to use it. Maybe it does seem odd, but what is contained in the `entrees.xml` file that is referenced by the `entrees` external parameter entity? It doesn't really matter because the XML processor is not allowed to know, either. Suppose, though, that the `entrees.xml` file contained element declarations; the entity reference is inside the internal DTD subset, so it would be quite legal to do so. Suppose, too, that the file contained the following attribute declaration:

```
<!ATTLIST menu desserts CDATA "Bitter Experiences">.
```

This would mean that the `desserts` attribute could not have the value `"Sweet Temptations"`. So, be careful with external parameter entities in the internal DTD subset, and consider the possible confusion they could cause when the recipient is not validating (something you have little or no control over). The only way you can protect yourself from this is to always use a standalone document declaration.

The purpose of this declaration is really to indicate to the recipient that the DTD could change the document and that the DTD should be retrieved if the recipient wants to be certain that what it sees is the same as what the application that created the document sees. Parsing the

DTD would mean that external entity references would be dereferenced, and so the external declaration would then be found. Although the declaration has no effect on the XML processor, by changing the value of the standalone document declaration to "no," you can simply inform the recipient that validation is needed if the document is to be seen as intended.

Conditional Markup

When you learned about the DTD design step of constraining the model, one recommendation was that you could consider making two versions of the same DTD. You could use a loose DTD during authoring when, for example, not all the content may have been filled in, but you still want to validate the document, and you could use another, tighter DTD for the finished XML document. A way to do this uses conditional sections of the DTD and parameter entities.

This involves blocking the two variant declarations of the DTD inside blocks and starting the block with a reference to a parameter entity:

```
<![%AuthoringSwitch;[
   <!ENTITY % body "chapter, intro?, section*">
]]>
<![%FinalSwitch;[
   <!ENTITY % body "chapter, intro, section+">
]]>
```

The parameter entities `AuthoringSwitch` and `FinalSwitch` can then be declared as the keyword `INCLUDE` or `IGNORE`, according to which version of this entity you want to use. For the first, loose, version you would insert these declarations before these conditional sections:

```
<!ENTITY % AuthoringSwitch "INCLUDE">
<!ENTITY % FinalSwitch     "IGNORE">
<![%AuthoringSwitch; [
   <!ENTITY % body "chapter, intro?, section*">
]]>
<![%FinalSwitch; [
   <!ENTITY % body "chapter, intro, section+">
]]>
```

And for the second, tighter, version you would insert these declarations before these conditional sections:

```
<!ENTITY % AuthoringSwitch "IGNORE">
<!ENTITY % FinalSwitch     "INCLUDE">
<![%AuthoringSwitch; [
   <!ENTITY % body "chapter, intro?, section*">
]]>
<![%FinalSwitch; [
   <!ENTITY % body "chapter, intro, section+">
]]>
```

Part
III

Ch
14

This might seem to be a trivial feature because only a small section is affected like in the examples, but you can use pairs of parameter entities like this to control many separate sections of a DTD. By changing the values of these two parameter entities, you could radically change the whole DTD.

Optional Content Models and Ambiguities

When you review a DTD you are working on, take a close look at the occurrence indicators. If a lot of optional elements exist in a content model, this will often be an indication that something is wrong with the model.

An example of this comes from the SGML world of books. Consider the back part of a book. You might create an XML DTD for a book, for instance, and create a container element BACK to make it easier to process the parts together. The BACK element consists, as books often do, of any number (including zero) of appendixes, followed by an optional glossary and then an optional index. When you can describe a content model in plain English such as the following, it is quite easy to model:

```
<!ELEMENT BACK (appendix*, glossary?, index?)
```

The content model might look good, but a problem exists. Everything is now optional, making it possible for a document to have an empty BACK element, which certainly wasn't the idea. Well, one way to get around this is to break the content model into inner groups, where each group explicitly describes one of the possibilities:

```
<!ELEMENT BACK ( (appendix+, glossary?, index?) ¦
                 (appendix*, glossary, index?) ¦
                 (appendix*, glossary?, index) )>
```

That seems to cover it. Now we'll check:

- Group 1—You can have one or more appendixes, followed by an optional glossary and then an optional index.
- Group 2—You can have zero or more appendixes, which must be followed by a glossary and then an optional index.
- Group 3—You can have zero or more appendixes, followed by an optional glossary and an index, which is required.

It seems pretty complete—and no empty BACK elements are allowed. But now an even bigger problem exists. This markup won't work!

Parsers aren't intelligent. They are not able to remember what they've seen; they can't look ahead at what comes next and then backtrack to confirm that your markup agrees with content model. When the parser sees an appendix element, it really cannot tell what's supposed to happen next. Should a glossary element be next? This content model is ambiguous.

One way to get around this problem is to adopt what is called the waterfall approach, where you take each element in turn and work out only the new cases you need to cover. For the first element, you'd have to consider a lot of possibilities; then you'd consider fewer for the second and even fewer for the third, until, with the last element, hardly any possibilities are left. We'll adopt this approach here and follow the process step by step, re-examining the three groups defined earlier as we go:

- Group 1—You can have one or more appendixes, followed by an optional glossary and then an optional index. The first group seems OK.

- Group 2—You can have zero appendixes (we've already covered the one or more possibility), which must be followed by a glossary and then an optional index.

- Group 3—You can have zero appendixes and no glossary, but then an index must be present.

This is much better, and after we write it out in the DTD, it turns out to be the answer:

```
<!ELEMENT BACK ( (appendix+, glossary?, index?) ¦
                 (glossary, index?) ¦
                 (index) )>
```

XML Characters, Notations, and Entities

by Simon North and Jim O'Donnell

Character Data and Character Sets

At its most basic level, an XML document consists of a sequence of *characters*. Internally, computers generally always used 7 bits to store letters and characters in digital form. This representation was standardized (as ISO/IEC 646) as the now familiar ASCII scheme. XML allows you to use more than the standard ASCII set of characters. The range of *legal characters*, the characters that can appear in an XML document, are those with the following hexadecimal values:

- `09` (the tab character)
- `0D` (the carriage return character)
- `0A` (the line feed character)
- `20` to `D7FF`, `E000` to `FFFD`, and `10000` to `10FFFF` (the legal text and graphics characters of Unicode and ISO 10646)

Unicode and ISO 10646 are standardized character sets, which will be discussed in the next section.

Character Sets

In the ASCII alphabet, only 128 different 7-bit patterns are possible, so 7-bit ASCII is able to represent only 128 characters. These 128 characters are known as the standard ASCII character set and have been the basis of computing for many years. As computers became more advanced, and as they become more of an international phenomenon, extra characters were needed to cover things such as the accented characters used so much in European countries. The eighth bit was therefore repurposed to give 8-bit character sets, thereby doubling the number of possible characters to 256, and is standardized as the ISO 8859 character set. In fact, many ISO 8859 variants exist, each tailored for a specific language; the version we probably meet most often is 8859/1, which is the character set used for HTML and understood by Web browsers. This character set includes accented characters, drawing shapes, a selection of the most common Greek letters used in science and technology, and various other symbols. The first 128 characters of ISO 8859/1 are the same as ISO 646; therefore, it is backward compatible.

Eight bits are fine for most Western languages but are nearly useless for Asian and Oriental languages. To allow for languages such as Arabic, Chinese, Urdu, and so on, first Unicode (with 16-bit encoding) and then ISO 10646 took the next logical steps to support the use of up to 32-bit patterns to represent characters. These allow more than 2 billion characters to be represented. ISO 10646 provides a standard definition for all the characters found in many European and Asian languages. Unicode is used in Microsoft Windows NT.

Unicode actually includes a number of encoding schemes, named according to the number of bits they need. UCS-2 uses 16 bits (2 bytes), which is identical to Unicode, and UCS-4 uses a full 32 bits (4 bytes). ISO 10646 is even more sophisticated than this. Using mapping schemes (called a UTF for UCS Transformation Format), ISO 10646 allows a variable number of bits to be used. There's little point in using so many bits if you're only sending the basic 128 ASCII characters, so ISO 10646 allows you to claim extra bits as you need them.

XML supports two UTF formats, UTF-8 (8-bit to 48-bit encoding) and UTF-16 (up to 32-bit but using a mapping that gives more than a million characters).

Entity Encoding

Every text entity in XML may use a different encoding for its characters. Therefore, you can declare separate text entities or elements to hold sections of an XML document that contain, for example, Chinese or Arabic characters, and assign the 16-bit UCS-2 encoding to these sections. The rest of the document can then use more efficient 8-bit encoding.

By default, the ISO 10646 UTF-8 encoding is assumed. If the text entity uses some other encoding, you must declare what that encoding is at the beginning of the entity:

```
<?xml encoding="Encoding.Name"?>
```

Where Encoding.Name is a character set name consisting of only the Latin alphabetic characters (A to Z and a to z), digits, full stops, hyphens, and underscores. The XML processor has to recognize a number of character sets, most commonly UTF-8 and UTF-16. A more complete list can be found with the XML specification at http://www.w3.org/XML/.

Examples of encoding declarations are

```
<?xml version="1.0" encoding='UTF-16'?>
<?xml version="1.0" standalone="yes" encoding="EUC-JP"?>
```

The default (UTF-8) encoding is detected by the first four bytes of an XML text entity having the hexadecimal values 3C, 3F, 58, and 4D, which are the first characters of the encoding declaration. If no declaration exists, or if none of the other encoding schemes can be made to fit, the entity is assumed to be in UTF-8.

Entities and Entity Sets

Switching to a different encoding isn't the only way to represent characters that are not included in the UTF-8 character set. Don't forget that you can always reference any character by quoting its ISO 10646 character number in a character reference (such as &).

You can also declare an entity that represents the character you need, such as this declaration of the degree sign (?) taken from the ISO 8859-1 character set:

```
<!ENTITY deg "&#176;">
```

You can then reference this entity in an XML document wherever you need it:

```
<para>The temperature today in the south will be 82 &deg;C.</para>
```

Not all computer systems and transfer media can handle the advanced character sets that you have learned about. The 7-bit ASCII character set is still the lowest common denominator. Therefore, these kinds of character entity declarations have been around since the early days of SGML and have been collected into so-called entity sets.

These entity sets are included as part of the SGML standard (ISO 8879) and go under the somewhat cryptic names of ISOlat1 (Latin alphabet, accented characters), ISOnum (numeric and special characters), ISOcyr1 (Cyrillic characters used in Russian), and so on. They are really an SGML facility and cannot be used as they are in XML (XML does not allow the use of an SDATA *system data* notation). However, XML versions of the most important of these entity sets are being made publicly available, as you can see from the XML version of the ISOdia (diacritical marks) entity set shown in the following:

```
<!-- (C) International Organization for Standardization 1986
     Permission to copy in any form is granted for use with
     conforming SGML systems and applications as defined in
     ISO 8879, provided this notice is included in all copies.
-->
<!-- Character entity set. Typical invocation:
     <!ENTITY % ISOdia PUBLIC
          "ISO 8879:1986//ENTITIES Diacritical Marks//EN//XML">
     %ISOdia;
-->
<!-- This version of the entity set can be used with any SGML document
     which uses ISO 10646 as its document character set.
     This includes XML documents and ISO HTML documents.
     This entity set uses hexadecimal numeric character references.

     Creator: Rick Jelliffe, Allette Systems

     Version: 1997-07-07              -->

<!ENTITY acute   "&#180;" ><!--=acute accent-->
<!ENTITY breve   "&#x2D8;" ><!--=breve-->
<!ENTITY caron   "&#x2C7;" ><!--=caron-->
<!ENTITY cedil   "&#184;" ><!--=cedilla-->
<!ENTITY circ    "^" ><!--=circumflex accent-->
<!ENTITY dblac   "&#x2DD;" ><!--=double acute accent-->
<!ENTITY die     "&#168;" ><!--=dieresis-->
<!ENTITY dot     "&#x2D9;" ><!--=dot above-->
<!ENTITY grave   "`" ><!--=grave accent-->
<!ENTITY macr    "&#175;" ><!--=macron-->
<!ENTITY ogon    "&#x2DB;" ><!--=ogonek-->
<!ENTITY ring    "&#x2DA;" ><!--=ring-->
<!ENTITY tilde   "&#x2DC;" ><!--=tilde-->
<!ENTITY uml     "&#168;" ><!--=umlaut mark-->
```

The entity sets are provided as separate files, one for each set. If you know that you are going to need a particular set of characters for an XML document, you can include the necessary declaration in your XML DTD:

```
<?xml version="1.0" standalone="no"?>
<!DOCTYPE chapter SYSTEM "chapter.dtd" [

<!ENTITY % ISOlat1 PUBLIC "ISO 8879-1986//ENTITIES
                   Added Latin 1//EN//XML" "isolat1.xml">
%ISOlat1;
```

```
<!ENTITY % ISOnum PUBLIC "ISO 8879:1986//ENTITIES
                  Numeric and Special Graphic//EN//XML" "isonum.xml">
%ISOnum;

<!ENTITY % ISOpub PUBLIC "ISO 8879:1986//ENTITIES
                  Publishing//EN//XML" "isopub.xml">
%ISOpub;
]>
<chapter><number/> … </chapter>
```

Note that the declaration differs slightly from that shown in the entity file itself; a system identifier has to be used as well as the public identifier.

Notations

Notations identify by name the format of unparsed entities (binary files such as external graphics files), the format of elements that bear a notation attribute, or the helper application (capable of processing the data) to which a processing instruction is addressed.

A notation must be declared in the DTD before it is used. The absolute minimum acceptable form of a notation declaration is

```
<!NOTATION Name SYSTEM "">
```

where *Name* is something meaningful to you or the registered public identifier for a particular format.

If your system supports it (as most Microsoft Windows will, provided that the extension is associated with an application), you may be able to use a notation declaration such as this:

```
<!NOTATION GIF  SYSTEM "GIF">
```

This declaration takes advantage of the fact that as far as the XML processor is concerned, it is quite acceptable if nothing is on the system that can interpret data in this notation. As far as the XML processor is concerned, interpreting the data, or handling the error when it can't handle the data, is entirely the application's problem.

If you know that an application is on the system that can handle data in a certain notation, you can help the application out by pointing to the application:

```
<!NOTATION TIFF SYSTEM "C:\Program Files\Paint Shop Pro\psp.exe">
```

Obviously, this will work only if you know the name of the application that can handle a particular notation, if you know exactly where the application is, and if no one moves it. As you can imagine, this isn't very useful on the Internet.

It is also possible to use an existing SGML facility and use a public identifier. Many registered public identifiers are available, covering everything from the C programming language (ISO/IEC 9899:1990//NOTATION Programming languages - C) to time itself (ISO 8601:1988//NOTATION Representation of dates and times). Some of the most well-known notations and their SGML public identifiers, as they would be used in an SGML notation declaration, are shown in the following:

```
<!NOTATION JPEG PUBLIC "ISO/IEC 10918:1993//NOTATION
                Digital Compression and Coding of Continuous-tone Still Images
                (JPEG)//EN">

<!NOTATION JPEG PUBLIC "ISO/IEC 10918:1993//NOTATION
                Digital Compression and Coding of Continuous-tone Still Images
                (JPEG)//EN">

<!NOTATION BMP  PUBLIC "+//ISBN 0-7923-9432-1::Graphic Notation//NOTATION
                Microsoft Windows bitmap//EN">

<!NOTATION CGM-CHAR PUBLIC "ISO 8632/2//NOTATION Character encoding//EN">

<!NOTATION CGM-BINARY PUBLIC "ISO 8632/3//NOTATION Binary encoding//EN">

<!NOTATION CGM-CLEAR PUBLIC "ISO 8632/4//NOTATION Clear text encoding//EN">

<!NOTATION FAX PUBLIC "-//USA-DOD//NOTATION
                CCITT Group 4 Facsimile Type 1 Untiled Raster//EN">

<!NOTATION GIF87a PUBLIC "-//CompuServe//NOTATION
                Graphics Interchange Format 87a//EN">

<!NOTATION GIF89a PUBLIC "-//CompuServe//NOTATION
                Graphics Interchange Format 89a//EN">

<!NOTATION PCX  PUBLIC "+//ISBN 0-7923-9432-1::Graphic Notation//NOTATION
                ZSoft PCX bitmap//EN">

<!NOTATION WMF PUBLIC "+//ISBN 0-7923-9432-1::Graphic Notation//NOTATION
                Microsoft Windows Metafile//EN">
```

Nothing prevents you from using these SGML declarations in XML documents, and there are some very good reasons why you should, but the SGML public identifiers have to be combined with system identifiers to enable you to do so, like this:

```
<!NOTATION GIF89a PUBLIC "-//CompuServe//NOTATION
                Graphics Interchange Format 89a//EN" 'C:\Program
                Files\lviewpro.exe'>
```

Note that you use a system identifier, but you do not need the SYSTEM keyword.

After (and only after) you have declared the notation, you can use that notation by name in an entity declaration with the NDATA (notation data) keyword:

```
<!ENTITY figure1 SYSTEM 'figure1.gif' NDATA BMP>
```

You can also use the notation in one of the attribute declarations for an element using the NOTATION keyword:

```
<!ELEMENT IMG  EMPTY >
<!ATTLIST IMG
        src     %URL    #REQUIRED
        alt     CDATA   #IMPLIED
        type    NOTATION (GIF ¦ JPEG ¦ BMP) "GIF" >
```

When you use enumerated notations in an attribute declaration such as this, every notation you name must have been declared in the DTD before the XML processor reaches this part of the DTD. This means, for example, that if you use notations in the internal DTD subset, you must declare the notation in the internal DTD subset, too, and not in the external DTD subset (as you may remember, the internal DTD subset is read before the external DTD subset).

As you will have noticed, no doubt, typing in the public identifiers for notations can quickly become a very tedious and error-prone business. It is a good idea to collect all your notation declarations into one file. It will also help you to remember what the file is if you give it an obvious name, such as "graphics.ent"—and then reference that file in all the DTDs you create by using an external entity declaration that points to this file:

```
<?xml version="1.0" standalone="no"?>
<!DOCTYPE chapter SYSTEM "chapter.dtd" [
    <!ENTITY % myentities SYSTEM "mysymbols.ent">
    %myentities;
]>
<chapter>
    <number/>
    …
</chapter>
```

If for no other reason, keeping all your notation declarations in a separate file will mean that you will have to edit the file only once if something changes, instead of having to edit every separate DTD, and you are less likely to forget a declaration you need.

Entities

Without getting too involved in the precise technicalities of the terminology, XML brings markup a step closer to the world of object orientation, as in object-oriented programming. The basic *object* in XML's world is the entity, be it the XML document entity itself, the elements it contains, or the internal and external entities that it references.

The DTD itself is, of course, also an external entity (a special type of parameter entity, in fact) that the document references, but the relationship is a little more complex than this. The DTD describes a class of XML document entities, of which the actual XML document is an instantiation.

The entities (excluding the XML document entity because it really isn't of any further interest in this context) are divided into three types: character entities, general entities, and parameter entities. General entities can then be further subdivided into two other types: internal entities and external entities. To confuse things a little more, external entities are subdivided into parsed entities (these contain character data) and unparsed entities (these usually contain binary data). This hierarchy is shown in Figure 15.1. Finally, common usage plays with the terms so that parsed general entities are usually referred to as internal and external text entities, and unparsed external general entities are often just called binary entities.

You might find it easier, however, to just think of text entities, which can be either internal or external, and binary entities, which have to be external. This classification is actually helped by the way that you declare the entities. An internal text entity declaration looks like this:

```
<!ENTITY name "replacement text">
```

and an external text entity declaration looks like this:

```
<!ENTITY name SYSTEM "system.identifier">
<!ENTITY name PUBLIC public.identifier "system.identifier">
```

But character entity declarations (they are a special case of an internal text entity) look like this:

```
<!ENTITY name "&#code;">
```

and text and character entity references (they are identical) look like this:

```
&name;
```

Note that an entity reference must not contain the name of an unparsed entity. Unparsed entities may be referred to only in attribute values declared to be of the type ENTITY or ENTITIES.

FIGURE 15.1

XML entity types follow a specific hierarchy.

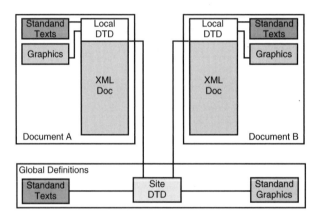

Internal Entities

Internal entities are entities whose definitions contain their values. No separate physical storage object (file) exists, and the content of the entity is given in the declaration, although it may be necessary for the XML processor to resolve any entity and character references in the entity value to produce the correct replacement text. Internal entities are parsed and must not contain references to themselves, either directly or indirectly.

Binary Entities

Binary entities contain unparsed data (graphics data, sound data, and so on). When they are declared, they must be identified as a notation. The notation must also have been declared in the DTD:

```
<!NOTATION notation.name "public.identifier" "helper.application">
<!ENTITY entity.name NDATA notation.name>
```

Binary entities can only be referenced in the value of an attribute that has been declared to be of type ENTITY or ENTITIES in the DTD.

```
<!ELEMENT element.name EMPTY>
<!ATTLIST element.name
          attribute.name NDATA notation.name>
```

And this binary would then be referred to in the XML document like this:

```
<element.name attribute.name="entity.name"/>
```

System Identifiers

A system identifier can be either a relative path to a filename (for example, `..\..\graphics\home.gif`) or an absolute path to a filename (for example, `C:\Program Files\LView\lview.exe`).

A system can also be a universal resource name (URN). The URN is an enhancement of the URL (universal resource locator) system; you are probably used to seeing URLs in the form of World Wide Web addresses:

`http://www.rpi.edu/~odonnj/index.html`

In this case, `www.rpi.edu` is my service provider's Web server, and `~odonnj` is a pointer that the UNIX system translates into my login (home) directory. The Web server then directs the Web browser to the designated Web page directory coupled to my login name, and `index.html` is the name of the file. URIs are a type of URN, and URNs are a kind of superset. As far as we are concerned, the two are more or less synonymous, so I will simply call it a URL and be done with it. The syntax for a full URL looks like the following:

`scheme://login-name:password@host:port//path`

`scheme` is a "protocol" and most of host information (`login-name`, `password`, and `port`) is only entered when it is really needed. The scheme could be `http` (Hypertext Transfer Protocol), `ftp` (File Transfer Protocol), `gopher` (the Gopher protocol), `news` (Usenet news; this one breaks the rule because protocol is actually `nntp`, which stands for Net News Transfer Protocol), `wais` (for Wide Area Information Servers), or `file` (for local file access). Several more exist, but many of them, such as `mailto`, wouldn't make much sense for retrieving information.

Public Identifier Resolution

The system identifier is reasonably straightforward. The public identifier is far more complicated, but in practice it is a lot simpler.

> **CAUTION**
>
> No *official* method exists yet for resolving public identifiers in XML. An SGML method has been used for years, however, and because most of the major XML tools come from SGML developers, the same method has quietly been implemented in their XML tools without any real discussion about whether it was needed.

SGML uses a public identifier resolution commonly known as the SGML Open Catalog (SOC), which uses a catalog file located in the same directory as the document (the application is free to change this location, of course). This file is usually called `catalog.soc` or, more frequently, just `catalog`.

There is little point in going into all the technical details because the `catalog` file is really an SGML facility. As far as we are concerned, the `catalog` file is basically an ASCII file consisting of lines that couple a public identifier (officially a "Formal System Identifier" (FSI)) with a *system object identifier*. A system object identifier is basically a file, but it could also be some other kind of identifier that the system is able to convert into something meaningful. A typical `catalog` file looks like the following:

```
-- catalog: SGML Open style entity catalog for HTML --
-- $Id: catalog,v 1.3 1995/09/21 23:30:23 connolly Exp $ --
-- Hacked by jjc --
-- Ways to refer to Level 2: most general to most specific --
PUBLIC   "-//IETF//DTD HTML//EN"                    "html.dtd"
PUBLIC   "-//IETF//DTD HTML 2.0//EN"                "html.dtd"
PUBLIC   "-//IETF//DTD HTML Level 2//EN"            "html.dtd"
PUBLIC   "-//IETF//DTD HTML 2.0 Level 2//EN"        "html.dtd"

-- Ways to refer to Level 1: most general to most specific --
PUBLIC   "-//IETF//DTD HTML Level 1//EN"            "html-1.dtd"
PUBLIC   "-//IETF//DTD HTML 2.0 Level 1//EN"        "html-1.dtd"

-- Ways to refer to Strict Level 2: most general to most specific --
PUBLIC   "-//IETF//DTD HTML Strict//EN"             "html-s.dtd"
PUBLIC   "-//IETF//DTD HTML 2.0 Strict//EN"         "html-s.dtd"
PUBLIC   "-//IETF//DTD HTML Strict Level 2//EN"     "html-s.dtd"
PUBLIC   "-//IETF//DTD HTML 2.0 Strict Level 2//EN" "html-s.dtd"

-- Ways to refer to Strict Level 1: most general to most specific --
PUBLIC   "-//IETF//DTD HTML Strict Level 1//EN"     "html-1s.dtd"
PUBLIC   "-//IETF//DTD HTML 2.0 Strict Level 1//EN" "html-1s.dtd"

-- ISO latin 1 entity set for HTML --
PUBLIC   "ISO 8879-1986//ENTITIES Added Latin 1//EN//HTML"  ISOlat1.sgm
```

Note that this example is a modified XML version of an SGML entities file; in XML the filename has to be enclosed in quotes, but in SGML it does not.

Nothing prevents you from creating this file by hand using a text editor, but a few free catalog management packages (also called entity management packages) are available on the Internet. Some software packages have their own built-in facility, often called an *entity manager*, for resolving entities.

Parameter Entities

Parameter entity references may only appear in a DTD. To keep them distinct from general entities (and to prevent them from being used in a document), parameter entities are declared and referenced with a percent sign (%):

```
<!ENTITY % "front ¦ body ¦ back" >
```

Parameter entities are extremely useful as shortcuts for parts of declarations that occur often in DTD. They are not, however, allowed to contain markup (complete declarations); they can only contain parts of declarations:

```
<!ENTITY often-used "(para ¦ body ¦ text)">
<!ELEMENT chapter ((%common;)*, section+)>
<!ELEMENT section (%common;)>
```

When a parameter entity reference is resolved, one leading and one trailing space character is added to the replacement text to make sure that it contains an integral number of grammatical tokens.

Entity Resolution

The rules governing entity resolution (when they are interpreted and when they are ignored) can be quite complicated.

Table 15.1 shows what happens to entity references and character references. The leftmost column describes where the entity reference appears:

Table 15.1 Entity Resolution

Where Referenced	Entity Type			Character Reference
	Parameter	**Internal General**	**External Parsed General**	
Inside an element	ignored	replaced	replaced if validating	replaced
In an attribute value	ignored	replaced	not allowed	replaced
Name in attribute value	ignored	not allowed	tell application	ignored
In an entity value	replaced*	ignored	not allowed	replaced
In the DTD	replaced if validating	not allowed	not allowed	not allowed

When the entity reference appears in an attribute value or a parameter reference appears in an entity value, single and double quotes are ignored so that the value isn't prematurely terminated.

The following list describes the different places in which an entity reference can occur and how it is treated there.

- Inside an element—The reference appears anywhere after the start tag and before the end tag of an element.
- In an attribute value—The entity reference occurs within either the value of an attribute in a start tag, or a default value in an attribute declaration.

- Name in attribute value—The entity reference appears as a name, not as an entity reference, but as the value of an attribute that has been declared as type ENTITY or ENTITIES:

```
<?xml version="1.0" standalone="yes"?>
<!DOCTYPE graphic SYSTEM "graphic.dtd" [
  <!ELEMENT graphic (icon)+>
  <!ELEMENT icon EMPTY>
  <!ATTLIST icon
            height   NMTOKEN #IMPLIED
            nsoffset NMTOKEN #REQUIRED
            width    NMTOKEN #IMPLIED >
  <!ENTITY icon8 SYSTEM "icon813.gif" NDATA gif>
]>
<graphic>
  <icon source="icon8"
        height="0.391in" nsoffset="0.000in"
        width="0.429in"/>
</graphic>
```

- In an entity value—The reference appears in a parameter or entity's value in the entity's declaration.

- In the DTD—The reference appears within either the internal or external subset of the DTD, but outside of an entity or attribute value.

An entity's replacement text may contain character entity, parameter entity, and general entity references. Character references and parameter entity references in the value of an entity are resolved when the entity is resolved. General entity references are ignored.

When an entity reference is replaced, the entity's replacement text is retrieved and processed in place of the reference itself, as though it were part of the document at the location the reference was recognized. The replacement text may contain both character data and (except for parameter entities) markup, which is recognized in the usual way, except that the replacement text of the entities amp, lt, gt, apos, and quot is always treated as data.

To validate a document, the replacement text for parsed entities also has to be parsed. If the entity is external and the document is not being validated, the replacement text doesn't have to be parsed. If the replacement text isn't parsed, the application is told of this, and it is up to the application to handle it.

When the name of an unparsed entity appears, as in the value of an attribute whose declared type is ENTITY or ENTITIES, the system and public (if any) identifiers for both the entity and its associated notation are simply passed to the application. The application is then responsible for any further processing (such as displaying the graphic file in a window).

Getting the Most Out of Entities

As you may remember, a fixed order exists in which the external and internal DTD subsets are read and interpreted. First the internal DTD subset is read and then the external DTD subset. If something is declared in the internal DTD subset, its declaration cannot be changed in the external DTD subset, although some things (such as additional attributes) can be added to declarations.

Used with a little careful planning, this hierarchical arrangement can enable you to construct your information collection (such as a Web site) to make the maximum use of shared data (see Figure 15.2):

Part III
Ch
15

- Global declarations can be placed in a central DTD that governs all the documents. As far as each document is concerned, this central DTD is the (common) external DTD subset.

  The central DTD references entities that contain common graphics (company logo graphics and letterhead material, special characters, and so on).

- Local declarations can be placed in the internal DTD subset of each document. This enables each document to override the global declarations and tailor them for its own purposes.

  The internal DTD subset in each document references any graphics and text that the particular document needs.

FIGURE 15.2

Using local and global entities.

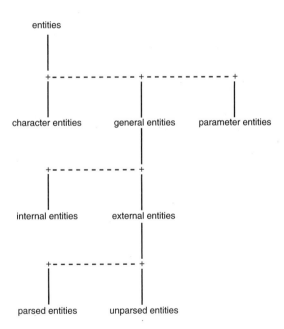

Breaking the documents into modules and exploiting the order in which the internal and external DTD subsets occur allow you to modularize a lot of documents, but you can go even further than this when you need to. You can even modularize the DTD itself and collect the parts you need for a particular document type (although in this context you could almost call it a subtype).

Many (large) industrial implementations of SGML use this scheme. Some people call this a "pizza model" because you build your DTD out of a base (core) of essential elements and then add the toppings that you need for the particular document. Examples of major DTDs that use this are the Text Encoding Initiative DTD and the American Department of Defense DTDs used for Interactive Electronic Technical Manuals (IETM).

This same approach could just as easily be used in XML. In fact, it could probably be used more easily because XML's capability to include Internet URLs as the locators for fragments makes it far easier to physically distribute data while still being able to bring it all together as a coherent set of information.

Although you have to use external entities to include binaries, such as graphics files, in your formatted XML output, entities can be a wonderful tool for breaking up the task of managing a complex collection of many documents into manageable chunks. By the considered use of internal and external text entities combined with the hierarchical ordering applied to interpreting the two DTD subsets, you can implement a staged hierarchy of template content. At the global level, you can safely set up default settings and then let individual XML documents implement local overriding changes as you need them. ●

## CHAPTER 16

XML DTD and Document Validation

In this chapter

By now, you're aware that an XML document must adhere to the very specific syntax put forward in its Document Type Definition (DTD). As you design an XML document, you are essentially designing its DTD, which resides in a separate file that you must also write. Given an XML document and its DTD, you will find yourself asking two important questions:

- How can I check that my DTD is correct?
- How can I check that my documents comply with the rules defined in the DTD?

The answer to both questions is to use a program called a validating parser. In this chapter you will learn how to check your DTD using programs called DXF and XML for Java. Additionally, you'll also see how to verify that your XML files comply with the rules of your DTD using these programs.

Checking Your DTD Using DXP

DXP stands for Datachannel XML Parser and is based on NXP (Norbert Mikula's XML Parser), one of the first XML parsers. DXP is written in Java, which is the most popular language for the development of XML parsers. You can use this parser to make sure your XML documents are both well formed and valid.

How to Install DXP

You can download DXP from `http://www.datachannel.com/`. You need to click through several pages to get to the actual download page. Once there, you should look for the file `DXP.zip` (about 535KB in size). In addition to the necessary Java class files, you'll find a fair amount of documentation and examples.

To install DXP, follow these steps:

1. Unzip the `DXP.zip` file.
2. Make sure you have a Java Virtual Machine version 1.x running. You can use Sun's JDK (Java Development Kit) (`http://www.javasoft.com/products/jdk/`), Sun's JRE (Java Runtime Environment) (`http://www.javasoft.com/products/`), or Microsoft's SDK for Java (`http://www.microsoft.com/java/`).
3. Make sure that your Java Virtual Machine can find the DXP classes by adding the packages directory of the DXP parser to your classpath environment variable, such as `c:\datachannel\dxp\classes` or, in the case of JRE, setting the `-cp` parameter to the path on the command line, such as `jre -cp c:\datachannel\dxp\classes`.

Running DXP

Once you've completed the steps above, you're ready to run DXP. To do this, type the following from a DOS command prompt:

```
jre -cp .;c:\datachannel\dxp\classes dxpcl -s -v c:\xmlex\file.xml
```

Here's a breakdown of what you just typed:

- jre invokes the Java Runtime Engine.
- -cp sets the classpath (where to find the classes used). In this case we specified two paths, separated by ;—the first (.) refers to the current working directory, and the second is c:\datachannel\dxp\classes.
- dxpcl is the name of the Java program (class).
- -s stands for "silent mode."
- -v stands for "validation on."
- c:\xmlex\file.xml is the file to be checked.

Because you've asked for silent mode, the program will only output the error messages.

Here the markup declarations exist in an external file (a special kind of external entity). The document type declaration in the XML file needs to point to this external file. For example:

```
<!DOCTYPE helptopic SYSTEM http://www.server.com/help.dtd []>
```

Use the DTD (external subset) shown in Listing 16.1. When invoking the parser, assume that this DTD is in the file dtdv.dtd.

Listing 16.1   DTD for Sample Document to Parse with DXP

```
<!ENTITY % admonitions "(tip ¦ warning ¦ note)" >
<!ENTITY % paracontent "(#PCDATA ¦ icon ¦ menu ¦ xref ¦ iconbmp)*" >

<!ELEMENT helptopic (title, rule, procedure, rule?, %admonitions;) >
<!ATTLIST helptopic id ID #IMPLIED>

<!ELEMENT title (#PCDATA) >
<!ATTLIST title keyword CDATA>

<!ELEMENT procedure (step+)>
<!ELEMENT step (action, (%admonitions;)*) >

<!ELEMENT action %paracontent; >
<!ELEMENT tip %paracontent; >
<!ATTLIST tip targetgroup (beginners ¦ specialists) "beginners" >

<!ELEMENT warning %paracontent; >
<!ELEMENT note %paracontent; >

<!ELEMENT icon (#PCDATA) >
<!ELEMENT menu (#PCDATA¦shortcut)+>

<!ELEMENT xref (#PCDATA) >
<!ATTLIST xref linkend idref #REQUIRED>

<!ELEMENT shortcut (#PCDATA)>
<!ELEMENT tip (#PCDATA) >
```

continues

Part

III

Ch

16

Listing 16.1   Continued

```
<!ELEMENT iconbmp EMPTY>
<!ATTLIST iconbmp src ENTITY #REQUIRED
                  type NOTATION (bmp | gif) "gif">
```

To check the preceding declarations, you need an XML file referring to this file as its DTD:

```
<?xml version="1.0" ?>
<!DOCTYPE helptopic SYSTEM "dtdv.dtd" [
]>
```

The preceding code starts the XML file with a document type declaration that refers to the external subset in the file dtdv.dtd.

> **N O T E**   For the purposes of this example, assume that the XML document and the DTD file are in the same directory. If they are not, you need to account for directory paths in your declaration. ■

When you run DXP with these files, you'll see several errors. The first is as follows:

```
FATAL ERROR: encountered ">". Was expecting one of: <EOF> , <S>
Location: file:///c:/xmlex/dtdv.dtd:8:30
```

```
Found errors/warnings: 1 fatal error(s), 0 error(s) and 0 warning(s)
```

The problem has to do with this line:

```
<!ATTLIST title keyword CDATA>
```

This declares the attributes for the title element—in this case, title just has the attribute keyword.

Recall that when you specify an attribute, you need to provide the following information:

- The name of the attribute
- The type of the attribute
- A default

These are all separated by a space. In this case, you have defined:

- The name (keyword)
- The type (CDATA)
- No default

This default needs to be one of the following:

- #REQUIRED
- #IMPLIED
- An attribute value, optionally preceded by #FIXED

This needs to be preceded by a space.

If you choose `#IMPLIED`, for example, the line becomes

```
<!ATTLIST title keyword CDATA #IMPLIED>
```

Parsing the document again, you get the following:

```
FATAL ERROR: encountered "+". Was expecting: "*"
Location: file:///c:/xmlex/dtdv.dtd:21:34

Found errors/warnings: 1 fatal error(s), 0 error(s) and 0 warning(s)
```

Now the problem lies with the following line:

```
<!ELEMENT menu (#PCDATA¦shortcut)+>
```

When you have mixed content—character data interspersed with child elements—the content model needs to have the * occurrence indicator. Thus, the line needs to become

```
<!ELEMENT menu (#PCDATA¦shortcut)*>
```

Reparsing the document, you now get

```
FATAL ERROR: encountered "idref". Was expecting one of: "ID" , "IDREF" , "IDREFS
" , "ENTITY" , "ENTITIES" , "NMTOKEN" , "NMTOKENS" , "NOTATION" , "CDATA" , "%"
, "("
Location: file:///c:/xmlex/dtdv.dtd:24:24

Found errors/warnings: 1 fatal error(s), 0 error(s) and 0 warning(s)
```

All keywords (including `IDREF`) need to be in uppercase in XML. Making the necessary correction and running the parser again produces

```
ERROR: element declared twice "tip"
Location: file:///c:/xmlex/dtdv.dtd:27:11

ERROR: notation not declared "bmp"
Location: file:///c:/xmlex/dtdv.dtd:31:41

ERROR: notation not declared "gif"
Location: file:///c:/xmlex/dtdv.dtd:31:44

FATAL ERROR: encountered end of file
Location: :3:4

Found errors/warnings: 1 fatal error(s), 3 error(s) and 0 warning(s)
```

Before encountering the fatal error, the parser found three errors that were not fatal. Note that non-fatal errors do not stop the parser from continuing its work.

The first non-fatal error occurs because the element `tip` is declared twice. The XML specification states that no element type may be declared more than once. This is a validity constraint, and violations against validity constraints are considered non-fatal errors. Fortunately, this error is simple to correct—you just need to delete the second declaration of the `tip` element.

The next two non-fatal errors have to do with the bmp and gif notations. This is understandable because, according to the specification, all notation names in the declaration must be explicitly declared. You can compensate for this by adding the following code:

```
<!NOTATION bmp SYSTEM "paint.exe">
<!NOTATION gif SYSTEM "">
```

After this, there is just one error left:

```
FATAL ERROR: encountered end of file
Location: :3:4

Found errors/warnings: 1 fatal error(s), 0 error(s) and 0 warning(s)
```

This is actually a little tricky to diagnose. The problem is no longer with the DTD, but with the XML file itself. The XML file passed to the parser has a prologue with an xml declaration and a doctype declaration, but nothing more—not even a root element! Every XML document must have a root element, and this is what led to the fatal error.

The good news is that there are no longer any errors in your DTD. The final corrected DTD is shown in Listing 16.2.

Listing 16.2   Corrected DTD for DXP Example

```
<!NOTATION bmp SYSTEM "paint.exe">
<!NOTATION gif SYSTEM "">

<!ENTITY % admonitions "(tip | warning | note)" >
<!ENTITY % paracontent "(#PCDATA | icon | menu | xref | iconbmp)*" >

<!ELEMENT helptopic (title, rule, procedure, rule?, %admonitions;) >
<!ATTLIST helptopic id ID #IMPLIED>

<!ELEMENT title (#PCDATA) >
<!ATTLIST title keyword CDATA #IMPLIED>

<!ELEMENT procedure (step+)>
<!ELEMENT step (action, (%admonitions;)*) >

<!ELEMENT action %paracontent; >
<!ELEMENT tip %paracontent; >
<!ATTLIST tip targetgroup (beginners | specialists) "beginners" >

<!ELEMENT warning %paracontent; >
<!ELEMENT note %paracontent; >

<!ELEMENT icon (#PCDATA) >
<!ELEMENT menu (#PCDATA|shortcut)*>

<!ELEMENT xref (#PCDATA) >
<!ATTLIST xref linkend IDREF #REQUIRED>

<!ELEMENT shortcut (#PCDATA)>
```

```
<!ELEMENT iconbmp EMPTY>
<!ATTLIST iconbmp src ENTITY #REQUIRED
                type NOTATION (bmp | gif) "gif">
```

Parser Warnings

One thing you'll note in the corrected DTD is that there are some elements for which there is no declaration. You may be wondering why the parser did not flag these instances.

If you read the XML specification, you'll find the following: "At user option, an XML processor may issue a warning when a declaration mentions an element type for which no declaration is provided, but this is no error."

Does DXP give you this user option? The answer is yes—you can add the parameter -w to receive warnings.

```
jre -cp .;c:\datachannel\dxp\classes dxpcl -s -v -w c:\xmlex\dtdv.xml
```

But DXP doesn't seem to catch this one, which technically isn't a problem because the standard says that an XML processor "*may* issue a warning," not that it always *will*.

Declarations in the Internal Subset

The declarations in the internal subset are those you find between [and] in the document type declaration:

```
<!DOCTYPE helptopic [
<!ELEMENT helptopic (title, procedure)>
<!ATTLIST helptopic id ID #REQUIRED>
…
]
<helptopic>….
```

N O T E Remember that the DTD of a document consists of both internal and external subsets taken together.

Suppose for the moment that all your declarations are in the external subset of your document type declaration. What will happen if you copy the content of your file inside your internal subset and don't refer to the external file with the declarations (as in Listing 16.3)?

Listing 16.3   DTD Declarations in the Internal Subset

```
<?xml version="1.0" ?>
<!DOCTYPE helptopic [
<!NOTATION bmp SYSTEM "paint.exe">
<!NOTATION gif SYSTEM "">

<!ENTITY % admonitions "(tip | warning | note)" >
<!ENTITY % paracontent "(#PCDATA | icon | menu | xref | iconbmp)*" >
```

continues

Listing 16.3   Continued

```
<!ELEMENT helptopic (title, rule, procedure, rule?, %admonitions;) >
<!ATTLIST helptopic id ID #IMPLIED>

<!ELEMENT title (#PCDATA) >
<!ATTLIST title keyword CDATA #IMPLIED>

<!ELEMENT procedure (step+)>
<!ELEMENT step (action, (%admonitions;)*) >

<!ELEMENT action %paracontent; >
<!ELEMENT tip %paracontent; >
<!ATTLIST tip targetgroup (beginners ¦ specialists) "beginners" >

<!ELEMENT warning %paracontent; >
<!ELEMENT note %paracontent; >

<!ELEMENT icon (#PCDATA) >
<!ELEMENT menu (#PCDATA¦shortcut)*>

<!ELEMENT xref (#PCDATA) >
<!ATTLIST xref linkend IDREF #REQUIRED>

<!ELEMENT shortcut (#PCDATA)>

<!ELEMENT iconbmp EMPTY>
<!ATTLIST iconbmp src ENTITY #REQUIRED
                  type NOTATION (bmp ¦ gif) "gif">

]>
```

Parsing this file with DXP produces the following:

```
FATAL ERROR: parameter entity reference in entity value in internal subset
for "admonitions"

Location: file:/c:/xmlex/dtdv.xml:9:65
```

In the internal DTD subset, parameter-entity references (`%admonitions;` and `%paracontent;`) can occur only where markup declarations can occur, and not within markup declarations such as the declaration of the element `tip`.

What does this mean? It means that code like the following is allowed:

```
<!DOCTYPE helptopic [
<!ATTLIST helptopic a CDATA "A11">
<!ENTITY % buttons SYSTEM "button.ent">
%buttons;
]>
```

You can include the parameter entity reference `%buttons;` at that place because markup declarations could be entered also.

Conversely, it means that code like the following is *not* allowed:

```
<!DOCTYPE helptopic [
<!ENTITY % paracontent "(#PCDATA | emphasis)*">
<!ELEMENT tip %paracontent; >
]>
```

This is because the parameter entity reference appears in a markup declaration.

The best way to resolve this situation is not to get into it in the first place. You can accomplish this in one of two ways:

Part

III

Ch

16

- Bring everything back to the external subset.
- Replace the parameter references with their declared content.

Listing 16.4 shows what the internal subset looks like with parameter references replaced by declared content.

Listing 16.4 Replacing Parameter References with Declared Content

```
<?xml version="1.0" ?>
<!DOCTYPE helptopic [
<!NOTATION bmp SYSTEM "paint.exe">
<!NOTATION gif SYSTEM "">
<!ELEMENT helptopic (title, rule, procedure, rule?, (tip | warning | note)) >
<!ATTLIST helptopic id ID #IMPLIED>

<!ELEMENT title (#PCDATA) >
<!ATTLIST title keyword CDATA #IMPLIED>

<!ELEMENT procedure (step+)>
<!ELEMENT step (action, ((tip | warning | note))*) >

<!ELEMENT action (#PCDATA | icon | menu | xref | iconbmp)* >
<!ELEMENT tip (#PCDATA | icon | menu | xref | iconbmp)* >
<!ATTLIST tip targetgroup (beginners | specialists) "beginners" >

<!ELEMENT warning (#PCDATA | icon | menu | xref | iconbmp)* >
<!ELEMENT note (#PCDATA | icon | menu | xref | iconbmp)* >

<!ELEMENT icon (#PCDATA) >
<!ELEMENT menu (#PCDATA|shortcut)*>

<!ELEMENT xref (#PCDATA) >
<!ATTLIST xref linkend IDREF #REQUIRED>

<!ELEMENT shortcut (#PCDATA)>

<!ELEMENT iconbmp EMPTY>
<!ATTLIST iconbmp src ENTITY #REQUIRED
                  type NOTATION (bmp | gif) "gif">

]>
```

Checking Your DTD Using XML for Java

XML for Java is a validating XML parser written in Java. The package (`com.ibm.xml.parser`) contains Java classes and methods for parsing, generating, manipulating, and validating XML documents. XML for Java is a robust XML processor and is very complete.

To download and install XML for Java, follow these steps:

1. Download XML for Java from `http://www.alphaworks.ibm.com/formula/xml/`. The file `xml4j.1.0.0.zip` is 1.039KB in size.

2. Unzip `xml4j.1.0.0.zip` into a new directory on your system's hard drive.

N O T E This is another Java implementation, so make sure you have a Java Virtual Machine version 1.x running. ▉

With the class and method files unzipped, you are ready to run XML for Java. Type the following from a DOS prompt:

```
jre -cp c:\xml4j\xml4j.jar trlx c:\xmlex\dtdv.xml
```

Here's a breakdown of what you just typed:

- `jre` invokes the Java Runtime Engine.
- `-cp` sets the classpath. In this case, you refer to the jar (Java archive file) as `xml4j.jar`.
- `trlx` is the Java class that does the parsing.
- `c:\xmlex\dtdv.xml` is the file to be checked.

Note that the preceding command is telling XML for Java to parse and validate the file `dtdv.xml`, which is the same file used in the discussion of DXP. When you hand this file to XML for Java, you get the following set of error messages:

```
dtdv.dtd: 8, 30: Spaces are expected.
dtdv.dtd: 8, 30: '#REQUIRED' or '#IMPLIED' or '#FIXED' or attribute value
is expected.
dtdv.dtd: 21, 35: This content model is not matched with the mixed model
'(#PCDATA|FOO|BAR|...|BAZ)*': '(#PCDATA|shortcut)+'
dtdv.dtd: 24, 29: 'CDATA' or 'ID' or 'IDREF' or 'IDREFS'or 'ENTITY' or
'ENTITIES' or 'NMTOKEN' or 'NMTOKENS' or 'NOTATION' or '(' is expected.
dtdv.dtd: 27, 24: Element 'tip' is already declared.
dtdv.dtd: 31, 27: NOTATION 'bmp' is not declared.
dtdv.dtd: 31, 33: NOTATION 'gif' is not declared.
c:\xmlex\dtdv.xml: 3, 3: The document has no element.
```

Every error message consists of the following:

- The file in which the error appears
- The line number
- The character position where the problem was detected
- A description of the error

Note that XML for Java gives you all of the errors at once. This is very different from DXP, which presents errors up until a fatal error is encountered.

With XML for Java, it is possible to check the DTD directly by adding the parameter -dtd to the command line, and to read the file with the external subset directly:

```
jre -cp c:\xml4j\xml4j.jar trlx -dtd c:\xmlex\dtdv.dtd
```

This is a much cleaner approach that will generate the same set of error messages (except for the last error, which points out that "the document has no element").

N O T E   XML for Java handles declarations in the internal subset in much the same way DXP does.

Checking the Validity of XML Files with DXP

You have seen how to use two different tools to parse and validate your XML DTDs. As noted earlier in the chapter, you can use both tools to validate an XML file as well. This section examines how to validate an XML document using DXP.

To use DXP as a document validator, enter a command like the following at the DOS prompt:

```
jre -cp .;c:\datachannel\dxp\classes dxpcl -s -v c:\xmlex\wfq.xml
```

Here's a breakdown of what you just typed:

- jre invokes the Java Runtime Engine.
- -cp sets the classpath (where to find the classes used). In this case you specified two paths: the first (.) refers to the current working directory, and the second is c:\datachannel\dxp\classes). They're separated by ;.
- dxpcl is the name of the Java program (class).
- -s stands for "silent mode."
- -v stands for "validation on."
- c:\xmlex\wfq.xml is the file to be checked.

The file wfq.xml that is being submitted to DXP is shown in Listing 16.5.

Listing 16.5   XML Document to Check for Validity

```
<?xml version="1.0" ?>
<?protext objid="I5678" ?>
<!DOCTYPE helptopic [
<!ENTITY doubleclick "Double-click">
]>
<helptopic>
<title keyword="printing,network;printing,shared printer">How to use a
shared network printer?</title>
<procedure>
```

continues

Listing 16.5   Continued

```
<step><action>In <icon>Network Neighborhood</icon>, locate and
double-click the computer where the printer you want to use is located.
</action>
<tip targetgroup="beginners">To see which computers have shared printers
attached, click the <menu>View</menu> menu,
click <menu>Details</menu>, &amp; look for printer names or descriptions
in the Comment column of the Network Neighborhood window.</tip>
</step>
<step>
<action>&doubleclick; the printer icon in the window that appears.
</action>
</step>
<step>
<action>
To set up the printer, <xref linkend="id45">follow the instructions</xref>
 on the screen.
</action></step>
</procedure>
<rule form="double"/>
<tip>
<p>After you have set up a network printer, you can use it as if it were
attached to your computer. For related topics, look up
&quot;printing&quot; in the Help Index.
</p>
</tip>
</helptopic>
```

Earlier in the chapter, you validated the DTD shown in Listing 16.6 for `helptopic` documents.

Listing 16.6   Validated DTD for *helptopic* Documents

```
<!NOTATION bmp SYSTEM "paint.exe">
<!NOTATION gif SYSTEM "">

<!ENTITY % admonitions "(tip | warning | note)" >
<!ENTITY % paracontent "(#PCDATA | icon | menu | xref | iconbmp)*" >

<!ELEMENT helptopic (title, rule, procedure, rule?, %admonitions;) >
<!ATTLIST helptopic id ID #IMPLIED>

<!ELEMENT title (#PCDATA) >
<!ATTLIST title keyword CDATA #IMPLIED>

<!ELEMENT procedure (step+)>
<!ELEMENT step (action, (%admonitions;)*) >

<!ELEMENT action %paracontent; >
<!ELEMENT tip %paracontent; >
<!ATTLIST tip targetgroup (beginners | specialists) "beginners" >

<!ELEMENT warning %paracontent; >
<!ELEMENT note %paracontent; >
```

```
<!ELEMENT icon (#PCDATA) >
<!ELEMENT menu (#PCDATA¦shortcut)*>

<!ELEMENT xref (#PCDATA) >
<!ATTLIST xref linkend IDREF #REQUIRED>

<!ELEMENT shortcut (#PCDATA)>

<!ELEMENT iconbmp EMPTY>
<!ATTLIST iconbmp src ENTITY #REQUIRED
                  type NOTATION (bmp ¦ gif) "gif">
```

DXP will use this DTD to check `wfq.xml` for validity. DXP will know to use this DTD once the filename `dtdv.dtd` is included in the `doctype` declaration of `wfq.xml`:

```
<!DOCTYPE helptopic SYSTEM "dtdv.dtd" []>
```

Thus, the file becomes the following:

```
<?xml version="1.0" ?>
<?protext objid="I5678" ?>
<!DOCTYPE helptopic SYSTEM "dtdv.dtd" [
<!ENTITY doubleclick "Double-click" >
]>
<helptopic>
...
<tip>
<p>After you have set up a network printer, you can use it as if it were
attached to your computer. For related topics, look up &quot;printing&quot;
in the Help Index.
</p>
</tip>
</helptopic>
```

When you submit `wfq.xml` to DXP, you get the following response:

```
ERROR: Invalid content : procedure
Possible: rule
Location: file:/c:/xmlex/wfq.xml:8:2

ERROR: element not declared in DTD "rule"
Location: file:/c:/xmlex/wfq.xml:21:2

ERROR: attribute hasn't been declared in the DTD "form"
Location: file:/c:/xmlex/wfq.xml:21:7

FATAL ERROR: java.lang.NullPointerException:
Location: :0:0
```

According to the DTD, a `helptopic` needs to start with a title, followed by a rule, and then the procedure. That is not the case in the file `wfq.xml`.

Suppose that you add a rule to `wfq.xml` and run the parser again. This time you get the following:

```
ERROR: element not declared in DTD "rule"
Location: file:/c:/xmlex/wfq.xml:8:2

ERROR: element not declared in DTD "rule"
Location: file:/c:/xmlex/wfq.xml:21:2

ERROR: attribute hasn't been declared in the DTD "form"
Location: file:/c:/xmlex/wfq.xml:21:7

FATAL ERROR: java.lang.NullPointerException:
Location: :0:0
```

The XML specification puts forward the following validity constraints:

- An element is valid if there is a declaration for the element.
- All attributes must be declared.

If one of these constraints doesn't hold, the document cannot be valid. This means you need to add declarations for the missing elements and attributes. The following code will do the trick:

```
<!ELEMENT rule EMPTY>
<!ATTLIST rule form (single | double | dotted) "single">
```

Once this is done and DXP is rerun, you get the following output:

```
ERROR: Invalid content : p
Possible: iconbmp, icon, menu, #PCDATA, , xref
Location: file:/c:/xmlex/wfq.xml:23:2

ERROR: element not declared in DTD "p"
Location: file:/c:/xmlex/wfq.xml:23:2

ERROR: unknown ID referred "id45"
Location: file:/c:/xmlex/wfq.xml:26:14

Found errors/warnings: 0 fatal error(s), 3 error(s) and 0 warning(s)
```

The tip after the second rule contains a p element, which isn't allowed by the DTD. Removing this element and running DXP one more time produces the following:

```
ERROR: unknown ID referred "id45"
Location: file:/c:/xmlex/wfq.xml:25:14

Found errors/warnings: 0 fatal error(s), 1 error(s) and 0 warning(s)
```

IDREF values must match the value of some ID attribute in the XML document, which isn't the case in the sample document. There is no element in wfq.xml with an attribute of type ID and a value of id45. Once the xref element is removed, the document will finally be valid.

Checking the Validity of XML Files with XML for Java

This section investigates how to use XML for Java to check the validity of an XML document. Assuming you have the class files downloaded and unzipped, you can type the following commands at a DOS prompt:

```
jre -cp c:\xml4j\xml4j.jar trlx c:\xmlex\wfq.xml
```

Here's a breakdown of what you just typed:

- jre is used to invoke the Java Runtime Engine.
- -cp is used to set the classpath. In this case you refer to the jar (Java archive file) as xml4j.jar.
- trlx is the Java class that does the parsing.
- c:\xmlex\wfq.xml is the file to be checked.

If you submit the original version of wfq.xml to XML for Java, you get the following set of error messages:

```
c:\xmlex\wfq.xml: 21, 22: Attribute 'form' of element 'rule' is not declared.
c:\xmlex\wfq.xml: 21, 22: Can't find content model of '<rule>'.
c:\xmlex\wfq.xml: 24, 5: Can't find content model of '<p>'.
c:\xmlex\wfq.xml: 25, 7: Content mismatch in '<tip>'.  Content model is
"(#PCDATA¦icon¦menu¦xref¦iconbmp)*'.
c:\xmlex\wfq.xml: 26, 13: Content mismatch in '<helptopic>'.  Content model is '
'(title,rule,procedure,rule?,(tip¦warning¦note))'.
c:\xmlex\wfq.xml: 18, 45: ID 'id45' is not defined in the document.
```

Note that all of these errors correspond exactly to the errors you saw using DXP. The one advantage to using XML for Java is that the error messages tell you where the error occurs in the file. Also, XML for Java's error messages tend to be more explicit than those generated by DXP.

Other XML Parsers

The two Java-based XML parsers you've read about in this chapter are by no means the only two available. Indeed, more and more XML-related software is becoming available every day. Here are two more parsers that are worth checking into:

- MSXML—This is a Java-based validating XML parser written by Microsoft. You can visit http://www.microsoft.com/workshop/xml/parser/xmldl.asp to learn how to download and install MSXML.
- Larval—Written by Tim Bray of Textuality, Larval is a validating XML parser based on the non-validating parser Lark. You can find out more about both of these programs at http://www.textuality.com/Lark/.

ON THE WEB

http://www.sil.org/sgml/publicSW.html   Because new XML software is always being written, you should consult Robin Cover's list of SGML and XML software to stay current with the most recent releases.

CDF and Active Desktop Components

by Eric Ladd

Microsoft's Approach to Webcasting

When Microsoft released Internet Explorer 4.0, it put out an integrated suite of Internet-related software tools that enables you to create and browse Web pages, read electronic mail and UseNet newsgroups, participate in virtual meetings with colleagues at a distance, and collaboratively work on Microsoft Office documents. The browser component of the Internet Explorer suite also included support for *Webcasting channels*—a medium by which content providers could "broadcast" their work right to a user's desktop.

The word "desktop" in the last sentence isn't used metaphorically, either. Another facet of Internet Explorer 4 is the Active Desktop, a Windows configuration that blurs the boundaries between the traditional desktop and the Internet. Under the Active Desktop, you have a single "Explorer" that enables you to examine files on your system as well as view documents on the Web. Users with the Active Desktop turned on are also able to view Active Desktop Components that content providers build into their Webcast channels.

▶ **See** Chapter 11, "Introduction to XML," **p. 305.**

This chapter introduces the ideas of Webcasting, channels, and Active Desktop Components. After gaining an understanding of Microsoft's Webcasting philosophy, you'll explore the Channel Definition Format (CDF)—a channel description language derived from the eXtensible Markup Language (XML)—and learn how to use it to convert your Web site into a Webcast channel. Finally, you'll see how to build Active Desktop Components into your channel so that users can have dynamic content sitting right on their desktop (no browser required!).

At some point during your experience with the Web, you've probably heard about the concept of "push technology," in which content is selectively pushed down to a user's computer at that user's request. Push technology has also found a role in corporate intranets because it gives system administrators an easy way to distribute software updates to all users.

But what exactly is push technology? In many cases, what some people call "push" is actually a misnomer. That's why Microsoft has proposed a three-tiered model of what it calls Webcasting. Push technology is part of this model, as are some simpler, less "intelligent" ways of managing content delivery.

The three components of the Microsoft Webcasting model are

- Subscriptions—The most basic form of Webcasting, in which a user subscribes to a specific Web page and is notified by Internet Explorer whenever the page changes.
- Channels—An intermediate form of Webcasting, in which content providers can create a "channel" from their existing content, enabling them to manage what users see and how frequently updates are made.
- Push technology—True push technology, content delivery that's handled completely on the server side, is the highest form of Webcasting.

According to Microsoft, the first two tiers of the model do not represent true push technology. Rather, they are more accurately described as an "intelligent pull" of content. "Pull" suggests that the movement of content is initiated by the browser rather than by a server, and the intelligence comes in through regularly scheduled site crawls, also initiated by your browser, which looks for information that has changed.

N O T E For a full treatment of Microsoft's take on Webcasting, consult its Webcasting white paper at `http://www.microsoft.com/ie/press/techinfo-f.htm?/ie/press/whitepaper/pushwp.htm`.

The next few sections take a closer look at each of these tiers.

Subscriptions

When visitors use Internet Explorer to subscribe to a page, they're really giving the browser instructions to look for changes to the page on a regular basis. If any changes are found, Internet Explorer can notify the users in the following ways:

Part
III

Ch
17

- By placing a "gleam" (red asterisk) on an updated Favorite
- By sending an email message

N O T E Internet Explorer assumes that if you like a page enough to subscribe to it, it should also have a place in your Favorites folder. That's why a change in a page you've subscribed to shows up as a gleam in the Favorites listing.

Either way, users find out about the changed content and make a decision about whether to go to the page and check out what's been updated. And if they don't want to look at the page right then, Internet Explorer can download it and store a copy locally for later offline browsing. This can save you big bucks in connect time charges if your Internet service provider charges you based on how long you've been connected.

Subscriptions, although considered to be the most basic form of Webcasting, have several inherent advantages:

- They're free and easy to use.
- Users have complete control over how often Internet Explorer checks a page for changes.
- Downloading of updated pages enables portability of content to a laptop, which means you can take the pages with you.
- Site administrators don't have to make any changes to their sites so that users can subscribe to them.
- Subscriptions are maintained by Internet Explorer rather than by a separate add-on program.

One major drawback to subscriptions is that Internet Explorer has to do a site crawl to determine whether a page has changed. A site crawl might end up generating too much information, leaving users to sift through everything it found to figure out what's relevant. Additionally, some sites do not permit site-crawling programs (frequently called *spiders*) to access them at all, so even if you do subscribe to a page, Internet Explorer might not be able to check whether any updates were made.

Channels

To overcome some of the limitations associated with subscriptions, Microsoft has developed the notion of a Webcast channel that starts with the content provider rather than with the user. Channels enable content providers to better manage what they put out on the Web, as well as when they put it out, just as a television station needs to manage its programming and schedule. Users tune in to Webcast channels using Internet Explorer the same as they would use their television sets to tune into a TV broadcast channel. Figure 17.1 shows the Warner Brothers Studio Store Webcast channel.

FIGURE 17.1

Webcast channels can be used for information, entertainment, and even electronic commerce sites.

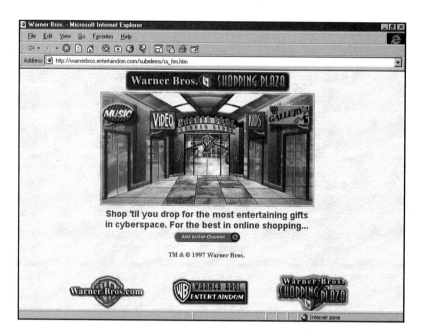

Channel authoring begins with Microsoft's Channel Definition Format (CDF), a markup language based on the eXtensible Markup Language (XML) standard. A CDF file defines a channel by specifying the following:

- Basic channel information, such as its title, a descriptive statement of the channel's content, and what iconography and graphics to use to represent the channel
- What Web pages on a site should be part of the channel
- How frequently the channel should be updated

This information is stored in a file ending with the `.cdf` extension. When a user tunes in to a channel and subscribes to it, Internet Explorer accesses the CDF file and notes the pages and update schedule specified there. Users don't need to know exactly which pages they're subscribing to and don't have to guess at what an appropriate update schedule is because all that is now supplied by the content provider (who would know best about what pages are essential to a channel and when those pages might change).

Channels allow for another important benefit, as well. Because CDF files can be generated on-the-fly, it's possible for channels to be customized to a user's preferences. A user can specify these preferences when subscribing to the channel, and the Web server stores the preferences in a cookie file on the user's machine. Later, when the channel is accessed again, the cookie file is retrieved and the information is used to display channel content according to the user's interests.

Television Channels and Webcasting Channels

The word "channels" in this chapter may lead you to think about how Webcasting channels are like those found on your television set. The concepts are similar in that the content on each is managed by the content provider—a television station determines what content it will broadcast the same as you determine what content will appear on your Webcasting channel. The nature of the content, however, may not be the same. Television stations broadcast audio and video-based content, but Webcasting channels can feature any type of Web content, such as text, graphics, audio and video files, application files, and binary executables.

With the W3C's release of the Synchronized Multimedia Integration Language (SMIL), it is now possible to more closely replicate television-like content (synchronized audio and video files) on the Web. In this case, you could essentially embed a television-like channel into your Webcasting channel to more truly simulate the way a television station manages its broadcasts. To learn more about SMIL, point your browser to `http://www.w3.org/AudioVideo/`.

Push Technology

Although channels represent a more advanced form of Webcasting than subscriptions, they are also examples of "intelligent pull" rather than "push" technology because the browser is still initiating the update step (with channels, however, the intelligence is based on information from the content provider rather than the user). True push technology in the Microsoft Webcasting scheme involves the use of *multicast* protocols, which is one server broadcasting to many clients. These special protocols make efficient use of available bandwidth to distribute content across a network. Note that this is different from subscriptions or channels because they only involve an interaction between one server and one browser.

Internet Explorer provides an open architecture for implementation of push technology client software. Although many such client programs are provided by third-party vendors, you can also use Microsoft's Windows Media Player to tune into a true push broadcast.

On the server side, push delivery cannot be provided by your common, everyday HTTP server alone. Rather, you have to use some kind of streaming media server that knows the Multicast File Transfer Protocol (MFTP), and Microsoft's NetShow Server is one such server product.

N O T E For more information about the NetShow server or client, visit the NetShow Web site at `http://www.microsoft.com/netshow/`.

Microsoft's Channel Definition Format (CDF)

If you've subscribed to some of Microsoft's premium channels, you may have seen some filenames that ended with the extension `.cdf`. These files are Channel Definition Format (CDF) files and are at the heart of Internet Explorer Webcasting. Microsoft developed the CDF standard so that content providers can quickly and easily author Webcast channels. This section introduces you to CDF and shows you how you can use it to create a channel of your own.

> **N O T E**   Microsoft has submitted its CDF specification to the World Wide Web Consortium (W3C) for
> consideration as a standard. You can view the CDF spec online at `http://www.w3.org/`
> `TR/NOTE-CDFsubmit.html`. Additionally, Microsoft maintains an updated list of CDF elements at
> `http://www.microsoft.com/standards/cdf/default.asp`. ■

Recall from the last section that three levels exist in Internet Explorer Webcasting. These are

- Subscriptions
- Channels
- Push technology

CDF comes in at the channel Webcasting level. By enabling the content developer to decide which content to deliver and when, the situation becomes more akin to a television station making decisions about a broadcast schedule. Accordingly, sites whose content is managed in this way are referred to as *channels*. Site administrators create channels out of their sites by authoring a CDF file to support the channel. No change is necessary to the HTML files that compose the site.

CDF is a markup language based on the XML and is intended to be an open, scalable solution for creating managed content channels. A CDF file provides a map of the information on a site, grouped into logical categories. Along with the information map, the CDF file also specifies which information should be Webcast and when, giving a site administrator complete control over what content becomes part of the channel. The basic elements of CDF are discussed over the next several sections.

To use a CDF file you've created, place it in the root directory of your Web server and set up hyperlinks on your Web page that point to it. CDF-compliant browsers such as Internet Explorer 4 will then parse the file and set up the channel.

The `<CHANNEL>` Element

The `<CHANNEL>` element or tag is used to define a channel in a CDF file. `<CHANNEL>` is a container tag, meaning that it has a companion `</CHANNEL>`. All content between these two tags defines the properties of the channel. The `<CHANNEL>` tag can take several attributes, as shown in Table 17.1.

Table 17.1   Attributes of the *<CHANNEL>* Element

Attribute	Purpose
BASE="url"	specifies the base URL of the channel (for use in resolving relative references later in the CDF file)
HREF="url"	denotes the channel's cover page, a document that prompts the user to subscribe to the channel
LASTMOD="date"	date the channel was last modified
LEVEL="n"	specifies how many levels below the cover page the browser should look when seeking content
PRECACHE="YES¦NO"	tells the browser whether to precache the channel content

Of the five attributes in Table 17.1, only HREF is really required. The LEVEL attribute, which controls how many levels deep the channel content goes, is useful for a couple of reasons. For the content provider, it is a means of controlling how much content goes into the channel. For end users, it helps to reduce the amount of time their browsers spend crawling a site looking for updated content. The default value of LEVEL is 0. You can set PRECACHE to YES so that your channel's content is preloaded in the user's cache, but keep in mind that this will add significantly to initial download time, and that may frustrate your users.

N O T E   If you set PRECACHE to NO, Internet Explorer ignores the LEVEL attribute.

N O T E   If you specify a time in your LASTMOD attribute, it should reflect Universal Coordinated Time (UCT) and not the local time. The offset between the two is handled by the TIMEZONE attribute of the <SCHEDULE> element discussed later in the chapter.

One important thing to note is that <CHANNEL> tags can be nested, which means you can have one <CHANNEL> ... </CHANNEL> pair inside of another. Nesting channels enables you to set up subchannels to your main channel and better organize your content.

CAUTION

A nested <CHANNEL> tag should not have an HREF attribute. If you specify a BASE attribute in a nested <CHANNEL> tag, it will override a BASE specified in the parent <CHANNEL> tag.

So far, then, if you are setting up a channel, your CDF file might look as follows:

```
<CHANNEL HREF="http://www.server.com/channelz/subscribe.html" LEVEL=4>
...
</CHANNEL>
```

Part
III

Ch

17

As you might guess, some work still needs to be done. Specifically, you need to specify the channel's content and how frequently it gets updated. Before getting into the CDF elements that handle those duties, however, a few other channel housekeeping chores should be tended to—such as giving the channel a title, an abstract, and a logo.

The *<TITLE>* Element

The CDF <TITLE> tag is much like the corresponding tag in HTML. It is a container tag used to specify the title of the channel. The same as in HTML documents, the title should be sufficiently descriptive without exceeding 40 characters or so. Longer titles are cut off when displayed on the Internet Explorer title bar.

After you give your developing channel a title, the corresponding CDF code will look as follows:

```
<CHANNEL HREF="http://www.server.com/channelz/subscribe.html" LEVEL=4>
  <TITLE>Channel Z</TITLE>
...
</CHANNEL>
```

<TITLE> takes the XML-SPACE attribute, which controls how whitespace is handled and can be set to "DEFAULT" or "PRESERVE." The DEFAULT value tells the browser to ignore any extra whitespace, and PRESERVE means that all whitespace characters should be retained.

Next, you'll see how to give your channel an abstract—a more detailed statement of what's available to users when they subscribe to your channel.

The *<ABSTRACT>* Element

The abstract of a paper gives a brief overview of the entire paper's content, and a channel abstract does the same thing for a Webcasting channel. The <ABSTRACT> tag is a container tag that contains a statement describing the nature of your channel's content. You can be a little more descriptive here than you were in the title, but you should still keep your abstract brief because this is the text that appears in the pop-up box when users hold their mouse pointers over the icon for your channel. These pop-up boxes can accommodate only around 100 characters before cutting off the message or becoming too cumbersome to read.

When updating your CDF code to include a title, you might have something like the following:

```
<CHANNEL HREF="http://www.server.com/channelz/subscribe.html" LEVEL=4>
  <TITLE>Channel Z</TITLE>
  <ABSTRACT>Welcome to Channel Z, your Internet movie site.</ABSTRACT>
...
</CHANNEL>
```

<ABSTRACT> can also take the XML-SPACE attribute. The values and meanings of XML-SPACE are the same for the <ABSTRACT> element as they are for the <TITLE> element.

The last housekeeping item to deal with before giving the channel some content and an update schedule is to provide a logo that Internet Explorer can use when displaying the channel on the Channel Bar.

The *<LOGO/>* Element

The `<LOGO/>` tag is a standalone tag that tells Internet Explorer where it can find an image file containing the logo for your site. The `<LOGO/>` tag's syntax is

```
<LOGO HREF="url_of_image " STYLE="ICON¦IMAGE¦IMAGE-WIDE"/>
```

N O T E The additional slash (/) you see in the `<LOGO/>` tag above is not a typo. It is part of the XML syntax for empty elements. ▪

The `HREF` attribute is set to the logo image's URL, enabling Internet Explorer to download it. The `STYLE` attribute denotes the context in which the image is used. If you choose the `ICON` style, your image must be 16 pixels wide by 16 pixels high (see Figure 17.2). It is used together with the channel title to identify the channel in places such as the Internet Explorer title bar. If you go with the `IMAGE` style, the image must be 80 pixels wide by 32 pixels high. This type of image is what users see in the Channels Bar. Finally, the `IMAGE-WIDE` image, which is used to provide a link to the channel main page, has to be 194 pixels wide by 32 pixels high.

Part

III

Ch

17

FIGURE 17.2

The Channels Bar is a framelike window for choosing which channels you want to view.

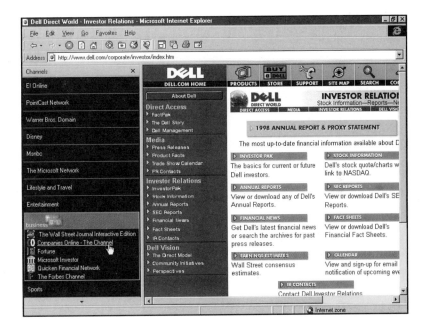

With a logo added in, your CDF code now changes to

```
<CHANNEL HREF="http://www.server.com/channezl/subscribe.html" LEVEL=4>
    <TITLE>Channel Z</TITLE>
    <ABSTRACT>Welcome to Channel Z, your Internet movie site.</ABSTRACT>
    <LOGO HREF="http://www.server.com/channelz/images/zlogo.gif"
    STYLE="ICON"/>
...
</CHANNEL>
```

With the channel structure and supporting items in place, you're now ready to put some content in the channel. For our sample channel, we will create three major content areas: new releases, reviews, and show times. You'll see how to add each of these in the next section.

The <*ITEM*> Element

<ITEM> is a container tag that you use to place content in your channel. Each <ITEM> ...
</ITEM> tag pair corresponds to one page of your site, so each page you want as part of the channel needs its own <ITEM> tag.

The <ITEM> tag takes the mandatory HREF attribute, which is set equal to the URL of the document you want to include in the channel. You can modify the <ITEM> tag further by using one of the attributes shown in Table 17.2.

Table 17.2   Attributes of the <*ITEM*> Element

Attribute	Purpose
HREF="url"	specifies the URL of the document to add to the channel
LASTMOD="date"	denotes when the document was last modified
LEVEL="n"	tells the browser how many levels below the document it should look and precache content
PRECACHE="YES"¦"NO"	indicates whether the browser should precache content

N O T E If you set PRECACHE to NO, Internet Explorer ignores the LEVEL attribute. ▨

You read above that <ITEM> is a container tag, so you may be wondering what you can put between <ITEM> and </ITEM>. The answer is that you can give the item its own title, abstract, and logo using the tags discussed in the previous few sections. Thus, a full-blown <ITEM> specification might look like

```
<ITEM HREF="http://www.server.com/new/index.html">
   <TITLE>New Movie Releases</TITLE>
   <ABSTRACT>New releases from the major studios this weekend</ABSTRACT>
   <LOGO HREF="http://www.server.com/channelz/images/new.gif"
    STYLE="ICON">
</ITEM>
```

If you build an <ITEM> such as the one above for the other two areas of your site, your CDF code now looks like the following:

```
<CHANNEL HREF="http://www.server.com/channelz/subscribe.html" LEVEL=4>
   <TITLE>Channel Z</TITLE>
   <ABSTRACT>Welcome to Channel Z, your Internet movie site.</ABSTRACT>
   <LOGO HREF="http://www.server.com/channelz/images/zlogo.gif"
   STYLE="ICON" />
...
   <ITEM HREF="http://www.server.com/new/index.html">
      <TITLE>New Movie Releases</TITLE>
      <ABSTRACT>New releases from the major studios this
      weekend</ABSTRACT>
      <LOGO HREF="http://www.server.com/channelz/images/new.gif"
      STYLE="ICON">
   </ITEM>

   <ITEM HREF="http://www.server.com/reviews/index.html">
      <TITLE>From the Critics</TITLE>
      <ABSTRACT>Find out what the critics said before you buy
      your ticket.</ABSTRACT>
      <LOGO HREF="http://www.server.com/channelz/images/reviews.gif"
      STYLE="ICON">
   </ITEM>

   <ITEM HREF="http://www.server.com/showtimes/index.html">
      <TITLE>When and Where?</TITLE>
      <ABSTRACT>Find out what films are playing near you.
      </ABSTRACT>
      <LOGO HREF="http://www.myserver.com/channelz/images/times.gif"
      STYLE="ICON">
   </ITEM>
...
</CHANNEL>
```

Now that you have content in your channel, one issue is left: setting up the update schedule.

The <SCHEDULE> Element

The <SCHEDULE> tag is a container tag that specifies the update schedule for the content you place in your channels. You can specify a <SCHEDULE> for the entire channel by placing it after the topmost <CHANNEL> tag and before the first nested <CHANNEL> tag. You can also assign a <SCHEDULE> to each <ITEM> by placing the <SCHEDULE> ... </SCHEDULE> tag pair inside the <ITEM> ... </ITEM> tag pair.

<SCHEDULE> takes three attributes: STARTDATE indicates the date that the update schedule should take effect, STOPDATE says when its schedule should terminate, and TIMEZONE tells the offset between local time and Universal Coordinated Time (UCT). Both STARTDATE and STOPDATE are set equal to dates in the ISO 8601:1988 format (YYYY-MM-DD).

NOTE STOPDATE replaces the ENDDATE attribute, which is now obsolete. ■

Between the <SCHEDULE> and </SCHEDULE> tags, you can have one of three standalone tags:

- ■ `<INTERVALTIME ... />`—Specifies the time interval between updates
- ■ `<EARLIESTTIME ... />`—Indicates the earliest time during an interval that an update can occur
- ■ `<LATESTTIME ... />`—Indicates the latest time during an interval that an update can occur

Each of the above standalone tags can take one of the following attributes: DAY, HOUR, or MIN. These attributes are set to the number of days (values of 1 through 7), hours (values of 1 through 23), or minutes (values of 1 through 59) that are appropriate to your scheduling needs. To do an update every half hour, for example, you would use

```
<INTERVALTIME MIN=30/>
```

To ensure that an update happens sometime in the 10 minutes before each hour, you would use

```
<INTERVALTIME HOUR=1/>
<EARLIESTTIME MIN=50/>
<LATESTTIME HOUR=1/>
```

Inserting a schedule that calls for a weekly update every Wednesday morning at exactly 8 a.m. into the channel you're building, you'd have the following:

```
<CHANNEL HREF="http://www.server.com/channelz/subscribe.html" LEVEL=4>
    <TITLE>Channel Z</TITLE>
    <ABSTRACT>Welcome to Channel Z, your Internet movie site.</ABSTRACT>
    <LOGO HREF="http://www.server.com/channelz/images/zlogo.gif"
    STYLE="ICON"/>
...
    <SCHEDULE STARTDATE="1998-08-19"> <!-- 8/19 is a Wednesday -->
        <INTERVALTIME DAY=7/>  <!- Weekly update -->
        <EARLIESTTIME DAY=7 HOUR=8/> <!-- Not earlier than 8 on Wed -->
        <LATESTTIME DAY=7 HOUR=8/>  <!-- Not later than 8 on Wed -->
    </SCHEDULE>
...
    <ITEM HREF="http://www.server.com/new/index.html">
        <TITLE>New Movie Releases</TITLE>
        <ABSTRACT>New releases from the major studios this
         weekend</ABSTRACT>
        <LOGO HREF="http://www.server.com/channelz/images/new.gif"
         STYLE="ICON">
    </ITEM>

    <ITEM HREF="http://www.server.com/reviews/index.html">
        <TITLE>From the Critics</TITLE>
        <ABSTRACT>Find out what the critics said before you buy
         your ticket.</ABSTRACT>
        <LOGO HREF="http://www.server.com/channelz/images/reviews.gif"
         STYLE="ICON">
    </ITEM>

    <ITEM HREF="http://www.server.com/showtimes/index.html">
        <TITLE>When and Where?</TITLE>
        <ABSTRACT>Find out what films are playing near you.
        </ABSTRACT>
        <LOGO HREF="http://www.myserver.com/channelz/images/times.gif"
```

```
        STYLE="ICON">
    </ITEM>
...
</CHANNEL>
```

The code above completes your channel setup. Note that you do not have to recode your content in any way. This is a key feature of CDF—it is content-independent, so no need exists to overhaul your content as you need to do with channel authoring for other software.

With your CDF file complete, you simply place it in the root directory of your Web server and set up hyperlinks that point to it. CDF-compliant browsers, such as Internet Explorer 4, will parse the file and set up the channel.

Setting Up a Software Distribution Channel

The elements discussed in the previous sections are enough to get you going with your own Webcast channel, but CDF is able to support much more than assigning content to a channel and saying when the channel should be updated. Corporations, for example, are looking to do more and more of their software distribution over their intranets. True push technology is one way to support this objective, but not every company has the financial means to set up the necessary servers or bandwidth. A less costly solution would be to use CDF to create a software update channel by which intranet users can stay current with the most recent software releases. This section shows you how to create a CDF file specifically for software distribution.

N O T E Since the initial release of the CDF standard, Microsoft has split off the CDF elements that support a software distribution channel into the Open Software Description (OSD) standard. These elements are maintained separately on Microsoft's site at `http://www.microsoft.com/standards/osd/default.asp.`

The primary element involved in creating a software distribution is <SOFTPKG>. The attributes of the <SOFTPKG> tag appear in Table 17.3.

Table 17.3 Attributes of the *<SOFTPKG>* Element

Attribute	Purpose
AUTOINSTALL="YES¦NO"	determines whether the browser is to download and install the software automatically
HREF	specifies the launch URL for the distribution
NAME	gives the distribution a unique name
PRECACHE="YES¦NO"	determines whether the browser downloads the software and holds it in its cache
STYLE	specifies the download and install procedure to use
VERSION="a,b,c,d"	provides a list of major, minor, custom, and build version numbers

N O T E Typically, you wouldn't have PRECACHE set to YES when you also have AUTOINSTALL set to
YES because no reason exists to hold the software in a cache when it is automatically installed. ▪

The STYLE attribute can be set to one of two established values: "ActiveSetup," which tells the browser to use the ActiveSetup ActiveX engine, or "MSICD" (Microsoft Internet Component Download), which instructs the browser to look in the Open Software Distribution (.osd) file for how to do the install. Additionally, developers are free to create their own download STYLEs.

A <SOFTPKG> element resides inside a <CHANNEL> element. Inside the <SOFTPKG> element, you can have many other elements, including some you've already seen, such as <TITLE>, <ABSTRACT>, and <LOGO/>. Beyond those elements, a few others are useful. The <LANGUAGE/> element can be used to specify which languages the software's user interface can support. <LANGUAGE/> takes the VALUE attribute, which is set equal to a semicolon-delimited list of ISO 639 language codes.

Another important element inside the <SOFTPKG> element is the <IMPLEMENTATION> element. <IMPLEMENTATION> provides information on the configuration necessary to install and run the software. Inside the <IMPLEMENTATION> element, you can specify various system configurations using these standalone elements:

- ▪ <LANGUAGE VALUE="list_of_languages"/> for which languages the software supports
- ▪ <OS VALUE="MAC¦WIN32¦WIN95¦WINNT"/> for the operating system
- ▪ <PROCESSOR VALUE="ALPHA¦MIPS¦PPC¦x86"/> for the type of processor

In addition to these, you can also use the <CODEBASE/> element inside the <IMPLEMENTATION> element. <CODEBASE/> takes the required attribute VALUE, which is set equal to the URL of the downloadable file. You can also have a SIZE attribute, set equal to the maximum number of kilobytes to allow in the download, and a STYLE attribute, which can be set equal to ActiveSetup, MSICD, or a style created by the developer.

Putting it all together, a sample software distribution channel might be coded like the following:

```
<CHANNEL HREF="http://www.server.com/channelz/download.html">
   <TITLE>Software Channel</TITLE>
   <ABSTRACT>Upgrades of the latest movie screensaver software that are
   available on this channel.</ABSTRACT>
   <LOGO HREF="http://www.server.com/channelz/images/download.gif"
   STYLE="ICON"/>
...
<SOFTPKG HREF="http://www.server.com/channelz/download-launch.html"
   NAME="download" PRECACHE="YES" VERSION="4,2,0,0" STYLE="MSICD">
   <TITLE>Upgrade Screen Saver</TITLE>
   <LOGO HREF="http://www.server.com/channelz/images/scrsaver.gif"
    STYLE="ICON"/>
   <LANGUAGES VALUE="en;es"/>
...
   <IMPLEMENTATION>
       <CODEBASE VALUE="http://www.server.com/channelz/scrsaver.exe"/>
   </IMPLEMENTATION>
...
</SOFTPKG>
```

```
...
</CHANNEL>
```

The preceding channel enables users to download version 4.2 of the screensaver program, which is stored at `http://www.myserver.com/channelz/scrsaver.exe`.

If you have multiple platforms to which you need to distribute software, you don't need to set up separate channels for each. A given <SOFTPKG> element can contain many <IMPLEMENTA-TION> elements, so you need to specify an <IMPLEMENTATION> element only for each platform. If you are distributing to Macintosh, Windows 95, and Windows NT platforms, you might alter the preceding code to read

```
<CHANNEL HREF="http://www.server.com/channelz/download.html">
    <TITLE>Software Channel</TITLE>
    <ABSTRACT>Upgrades of the latest movie screensaver software that are
    available on this channel.</ABSTRACT>
    <LOGO HREF="http://www.server.com/channelz/images/download.gif"
    STYLE="ICON"/>
...
<SOFTPKG HREF="http://www.server.com/channelz/download-launch.html"
    NAME="download" PRECACHE="YES" VERSION="4,2,0,0" STYLE="MSICD">
    <TITLE>Upgrade Screen Saver</TITLE>
    <LOGO HREF="http://www.server.com/channelz/images/scrsaver.gif"
     STYLE="ICON"/>
    <LANGUAGES VALUE="en;es"/>
...
    <IMPLEMENTATION>
        <OS VALUE="MAC"/>
        <CODEBASE VALUE="http://www.server.com/channelz/scrsaver.hqx"/>
    </IMPLEMENTATION>
...
    <IMPLEMENTATION>
        <OS VALUE="WIN95"/>
        <CODEBASE VALUE="http://www.myserver.com/channel/email95.exe"/>
    </IMPLEMENTATION>
...
    <IMPLEMENTATION>
        <OS VALUE="WINNT"/>
        <OSVERSION VALUE="4,0,0,0"/>
        <CODEBASE VALUE="http://www.myserver.com/channel/emailnt.exe"/>
    </IMPLEMENTATION>
...
</SOFTPKG>
...
</CHANNEL>
```

Part

III

Ch

17

Setting Up an Active Desktop Component

Active Desktop Components are really HTML files that sit on your Windows desktop. Because you aren't viewing them through a browser, they don't seem like HTML files, but that's all they really are (see Figure 17.3).

You can specify a channel <ITEM> to be an Active Desktop Component by using the <USAGE> element. <USAGE> takes the single attribute VALUE, which can be set to one of the following:

FIGURE 17.3

The Active Desktop Component from the *National Geographic* channel launches its GeoBee game.

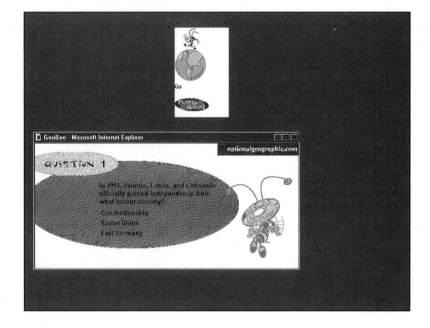

- ▨ Channel—Specifies the <ITEM> to be a component of the channel. This is the default behavior in the absence of any <USAGE> elements.
- ▨ DesktopComponent—Designates the <ITEM> to appear in a frame on the Active Desktop.
- ▨ Email—Specifies that the <ITEM> is to be emailed whenever the channel is updated.
- ▨ None—Specifies that the <ITEM> should be left out of the channel.
- ▨ ScreenSaver—Designates the <ITEM> for use as an Internet Explorer screensaver.
- ▨ SoftwareUpdate—Specifies that the component's purpose is to deliver a software update.

If you had an HTML file that contains your Active Desktop Component setup on a server, you could place the component into the channel with CDF code such as the following:

```
<ITEM HREF="http://www.server.com/channelz/desktop-comp.html">
  <USAGE VALUE="DesktopComponent"></USAGE>
</ITEM>
```

If you set the VALUE attribute of the <USAGE> element to DesktopComponent, then you can use several other elements between the <USAGE> and </USAGE> elements. These include

- ▨ <CANRESIZE VALUE="YES¦NO"/>—Enables the user to resize the desktop component. The default value is YES. This element has precedence over the <CANRESIZEX/> and <CANRESIZEY/> elements.
- ▨ <CANRESIZEX VALUE="YES¦NO"/>—Enables the user to resize the desktop component in the horizontal direction. The default value is YES.
- ▨ <CANRESIZEY VALUE="YES¦NO"/>—Enables the user to resize the desktop component in the vertical direction. The default value is YES.

- <HEIGHT VALUE="pixels"/>—Sets the initial height of the desktop component.
- <OPENAS VALUE="HTML¦Image"/>—Specifies how to open the component. An HTML document is opened using the HTML <IFRAME> element. Images are opened using the <IMG> element. The default value is HTML.
- <WIDTH VALUE="pixels"/>—Sets the initial width of the desktop component.

Controlling Log Recording

If you want to make sure that an entry appears in the page hit logs every time a certain <ITEM> is served, you can use the <LOG/> element to accomplish that. <LOG/> takes the VALUE attribute, which, for now, can take on only the value "document:view". By placing the <LOG/> element between the <ITEM> and </ITEM> tags, you instruct Internet Explorer to make a log entry whenever a document specified in the <ITEM> is accessed.

You can also specify where the log files should be sent by using the <LOGTARGET> element. <LOGTARGET> takes the attributes shown in Table 17.4.

Part

III

Ch

17

Table 17.4   Attributes of the *<LOGTARGET>* Element

Attribute	Purpose
HREF	specifies the URL of the directory to where the log file should be sent
METHOD="POST"	specifies the HTTP method to use when sending the log file
SCOPE="OFFLINE¦ONLINE¦ALL"	indicates which type of page hit to include in the log file transfer

The SCOPE attribute splits page hits into two categories: OFFLINE for browsing that has occurred from a local disk cache, and ONLINE for browsing over a connection to the Internet. The default value of SCOPE is ALL, so that all page hits are sent during the log file transfer.

The <LOGTARGET> element may only occur once in a channel, and it can contain the following two standalone elements:

- <HTTP-EQUIV NAME="header_name" VALUE="header_value"/>—<HTTP-EQUIV/> specifies what kind of HTTP header should be put in front of the log file as it is sent. The most common value for NAME is "Encoding-Type." An <HTTP-EQUIV/> element that handles a compressed zip file, for example, might look like

  <HTTP-EQUIV NAME="Encoding-Type" VALUE="zip"/>

- <PURGETIME HOUR="hours"/>—Suppose you want log entries only from the past 12 hours and nothing prior to that. You could use the <PURGETIME/> element as follows:

  <PURGETIME HOUR="12"/>

  to ensure that the entries in the transferred log file are not more than 12 hours old.

Making a Channel Password-Protected

Security is uppermost in people's minds when they're on the Internet, so any precautions you can take to ensure the security of channels—particularly channels with sensitive information—will be appreciated by end users. The CDF specification includes a <LOGIN/> element that you can use to require authentication before a user enters a channel. When initially subscribing to a CDF-based channel, a user would be prompted for a username and password to use with the channel.

CDF-Compliant Software

For users to fully appreciate the work you put into creating your channel, they have to have a client program that is CDF compliant. Internet Explorer is an obvious choice for this, but other push technology vendors have embraced CDF as the way to go for authoring managed content channels. Some of these companies include

- AirMedia
- BackWeb
- DataChannel
- FirstFloor
- Torso
- Wayfarer

Additionally, PointCast has thrown its support behind the CDF specification. Netscape's Netcaster can support CDF in a limited way because of a less powerful site-crawling scheme.

Creating Channels with Microsoft FrontPage

CDF is a markup language the same as HTML is, and creating a CDF file can be as easy as creating an HTML file. You can open up a simple text editor such as Notepad and type out your CDF file, or if you prefer a more automated approach, you can use the Channel Definition Wizard that comes with Microsoft FrontPage. The wizard walks you through several steps during which you'll build the channel by adding items, setting up update schedules, and configuring log files. This last section of the chapter takes a look at the Channel Definition Wizard and shows you how simple it is to make a channel out of an existing Web page.

To start the Channel Definition Wizard, go to the FrontPage Explorer and open up your Web page, if you don't have it open already. Then choose Tools, Define Channel to launch the wizard. The first option is the choice between creating a new channel or editing an existing CDF file (see Figure 17.4). Because this is probably your first stab at making your own channel, choose the option for creating a new channel and then click the Next button.

FIGURE 17.4

The FrontPage Channel
Definition Wizard can
build a CDF file from
scratch or help you edit
an existing one.

The first step in creating a new channel is to set up the basic channel parameters, including its
<TITLE>, <ABSTRACT>, and <LOGO/> information, as well as its Introduction Page (corresponding
to the HREF attribute in the <CHANNEL> element). Figure 17.5 shows the Channel Definition
Wizard dialog box that collects this information from you. Note that you can specify both a logo
and an icon image for the channel. When you have all your channel parameters set up, click the
Next button to continue.

FIGURE 17.5

The Channel Definition
Wizard first collects
basic channel
information.

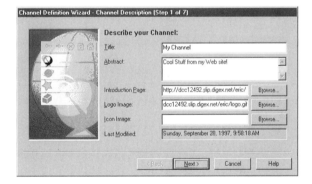

With the channel created, you now need to place items into it. The first step for this is to tell
the wizard which folder it should look in to find the items. The dialog box in Figure 17.6 enables you to browse to whichever folder you want to use for the source of your content. Be sure
to check the Include Subfolders box if you want to use content in subfolders for the channel.

Now that FrontPage knows where your channel content is, it prepares a list of all the files in
that folder and presents them to you as items to appear in the channel (see Figure 17.7). You
aren't obliged to place all the contents of a folder into a channel—only the pages you want. The
Channel Definition Wizard enables you to remove any of the displayed files from the list by
highlighting the file and clicking the Exclude button. If you accidentally remove a file that you
want on the channel, you can click the Restore button to put things back the way they were
when the dialog box first popped up. After you're happy with your list of channel items, you can
click the Next button to begin setting up parameters for each item.

Part
III

Ch
17

FIGURE 17.6

After FrontPage knows where you want to draw content from, it can create a list of potential channel items.

FIGURE 17.7

You can pick and choose which files should become items in your channel.

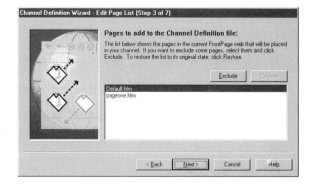

Each item in your channel has its own set of properties that you can configure in the next Channel Definition Wizard dialog box (see Figure 17.8). You can give each item an <AB-STRACT>, specify its <USAGE>, and say whether to use page caching. If for some reason you want to remove a file from the list of channel items, you can do that by clicking the Delete button. After you have properties set up for each item you're placing in the channel, click the Next button.

FIGURE 17.8

You can assign properties for each channel item, including whether it should be a regular channel component, an Active Desktop Component, or a screen saver.

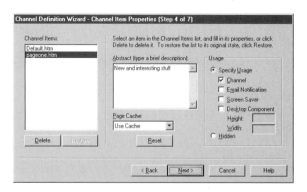

The next task in creating your channel is to set up the update schedule. Figure 17.9 shows you the Channel Definition Wizard's interface for specifying your schedule. You can choose the range of dates over which updates should occur and how frequently updates should be done during that time period. You can also specify that update checks be delayed during peak server usage times so that your server isn't overwhelmed with requests. With an update schedule configured to your satisfaction, you can click the Next button to continue.

 TIP It's best to specify that updates occur when the load on your server is typically the lowest.

FIGURE 17.9

Channel update schedule information tells a browser when it should come back and check for new content.

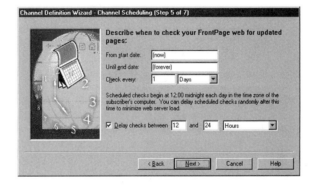

Log files help you examine how channel subscribers are using the content on your channel. You can specify a URL that the channel log file is sent to by using the dialog box shown in Figure 17.10. When using a FrontPage Web, you'll want to direct the log file to a URL that has a form handler behind it so it can store the log information in your Web for analysis at a later time. The dialog box in Figure 17.10 enables you to browse right to the URL to which log files should be sent. After you have the URL specified, click the Next button to move on to the last step.

FIGURE 17.10

CDF-compliant browsers send channel log information back to your server, enabling you to document subscriber behavior.

Part
III

Ch
17

At this point, the Channel Definition Wizard is all set to write your CDF file for you. All you need to do is tell the wizard where to put the file and what to name it (see Figure 17.11). Additionally, you can instruct the wizard to place a button that links to the channel on your Web's main page. If you're publishing the channel to a remote server, you can give the server's URL, and the wizard modifies the CDF code to reflect the new publishing target. With your last few parameters in place, click the Save button to save the CDF file.

FIGURE 17.11

The last step in creating a channel is to tell the wizard where to save the CDF file.

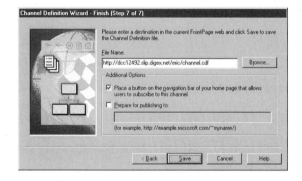

Because Microsoft created CDF, it's not a big shock that it was the first company to produce an automated tool for authoring a CDF file. As CDF moves toward becoming a standard, you should look for other Web authoring tools to include support for CDF files, as well. ●

JavaScript

Introduction to JavaScripting

by Jim O'Donnell

Introduction to JavaScript

JavaScript enables you to embed commands in an HTML page. When a compatible Web browser, such as Netscape Navigator 2 or higher or Internet Explorer 3 or higher, downloads the page, your JavaScript commands are loaded by the Web browser as a part of the HTML document. These commands can be triggered when the user clicks page items, manipulates gadgets and fields in an HTML form, or moves through the page history list.

N O T E   Microsoft's Internet Explorer Web browser supports JScript, Microsoft's own implementation of Netscape's JavaScript language. JScript is compatible with JavaScript, but some differences exist. When programming in JavaScript, it is always a good idea to test your scripts by using both browsers. ▧

Some computer languages are *compiled*—you run your program through a compiler, which performs a one-time translation of the human-readable program into a binary that the computer can execute. JavaScript is an *interpreted* language—the computer must evaluate the program every time it is run. You embed your JavaScript commands within an HTML page, and any browser that supports JavaScript can interpret the commands and act on them.

JavaScript is powerful and simple. If you've ever programmed in C++ or Java, you will find JavaScript easy to pick up. If not, don't worry. This chapter will have you working with JavaScript in no time. This chapter examines the basic syntax of the language, and the other chapters in this section show you how to apply it. In Chapter 19, "The Web Browser Object Model," you will find out how to use JavaScript to interact with your Web pages and how to build it in to your HTML. Chapters 20 through 23 then show you in greater detail how to use JavaScript with windows and frames, HTML forms, and Web browser cookies, and how to control other Web browser objects—such as Java applets and ActiveX Controls—with JavaScript.

Why Use a Scripting Language?

HTML provides a good deal of flexibility to page authors, but HTML by itself is static; after being written, HTML documents can't interact with the user other than by presenting hyperlinks. Creative use of CGI scripts (which run on Web servers) and the newer Web technologies, such as Java, ActiveX Controls, and Dynamic HTML, have made it possible to create more interesting and effective interactive sites. Even so, a scripting language is very often what ties all the elements of a Web page together.

JavaScript enables Web authors to write small scripts that execute on the users' browsers rather than on the server. An application that collects data from a form and then posts it to the server can validate the data for completeness and correctness, for example, before sending it to the server. This can greatly improve the performance of the browsing session because users don't have to send data to the server until it has been verified as correct.

Another important use of Web browser scripting languages such as JavaScript comes as a result of the increased functionality being introduced for Web browsers in the form of Java applets, plug-ins, Dynamic HTML elements, ActiveX Controls, and VRML objects and worlds. Web authors can use each of these things to add extra functions and interactivity to a Web page. Scripting languages act as the glue that binds everything together. A Web page might use an HTML form to get some user input and then set a parameter for a Java applet based on that input. It is usually a script that carries this out.

What Can JavaScript Do?

JavaScript provides a fairly complete set of built-in functions and commands, enabling you to perform math calculations, manipulate strings, play sounds, open new windows and new URLs, and access and verify user input to your Web forms.

Code to perform these actions can be embedded in a page and executed when the page is loaded. You can also write functions containing code that is triggered by events you specify. You can write a JavaScript method that is called when the user clicks the Submit button of a form, for example, or one that is activated when the user clicks a hyperlink on the active page.

JavaScript can also set the attributes, or *properties*, of Web page elements, ActiveX Controls, Java applets, and other objects present in the browser. This way, you can change the behavior of plug-ins or other objects without having to rewrite them. Your JavaScript code could automatically set the text of an ActiveX Label Control, for example, based on what time the page is viewed.

What Does JavaScript Look Like?

JavaScript commands are embedded in your HTML documents. Embedding JavaScript in your pages requires only one new HTML element: `<SCRIPT>` and `</SCRIPT>`. The `<SCRIPT>` element takes the attributes LANGUAGE, which specifies the scripting language to use when evaluating the script, and SRC, which can be used to load a script from an external source.

JavaScript itself resembles many other computer languages. If you are familiar with C, C++, Pascal, HyperTalk, Visual Basic, or dBASE, you will recognize the similarities. If not, don't worry—the following are some simple rules to help you understand how the language is structured:

- JavaScript is case sensitive.
- JavaScript is flexible about statements. A single statement can cover multiple lines, and you can put multiple short statements on a single line—just make sure to add a semicolon (;) at the end of each statement.
- Braces (the { and } characters) group statements into blocks; a *block* may be the body of a function or a section of code that gets executed in a loop or as part of a conditional test.

N O T E   If you program in Java, C, or C++, you might be puzzled when looking at JavaScript programs—sometimes each line ends with a semicolon, sometimes not. In JavaScript, unlike those other languages, the semicolon is not required at the end of each line. ■

JavaScript Programming Conventions

Even though JavaScript is a simple language, it is quite expressive. This section reviews a small number of simple rules and conventions that will ease your learning process and speed your use of JavaScript.

Hiding Your Scripts   You will probably be designing pages that may be seen by browsers that don't support JavaScript. To keep those browsers from interpreting your JavaScript commands as HTML—and displaying them—wrap your scripts as follows:

```
<SCRIPT LANGUAGE="JavaScript">
<!-- This line opens an HTML comment
document.write("You can see this script's output, but not its source.")
//   This is a JavaScript comment that also closes the comment -->
</SCRIPT>
```

The opening `<!--` comment causes Web browsers that do not support JavaScript to disregard all text they encounter until they find a matching `-->`; therefore, they don't display your script. You do have to be careful with the `<SCRIPT>` tag, however; if you put your `<SCRIPT>` and `</SCRIPT>` block inside the comments, the Web browser ignores them also.

Comments   Including comments in your programs to explain what they do is usually good practice—JavaScript is no exception. The JavaScript interpreter ignores any text marked as comments; therefore, don't be shy about including them. You can use two types of comments: single-line and multiple-line.

Single-line comments start with two slashes (`//`) and are limited to one line. Multiple-line comments must start with `/*` on the first line and end with `*/` on the last line. A few examples are

```
    // this is a legal comment
/ illegal -- comments start with two slashes
/* Multiple-line comments can
   be spread across more than one line, as long as they end. */
/* careful -- this comment doesn't have an end!
/// this comment's OK because extra slashes are ignored //
```

CAUTION

Be careful when using multiple-line comments—remember that these comments don't nest. If you commented out a section of code in the following way, for example, you would get an error message:

```
/* Comment out the following code
 * document.writeln(DumpURL()) /* write out URL list */
 * document.writeln("End of list.")
 */
```

To avoid error messages, the preferred way to create single-line comments is as follows:

```
/* Comment out the following code
 * document.writeln(DumpURL()) // write out URL list
 * document.writeln("End of list.")
 */
```

Using <*NOSCRIPT*> You can improve the compatibility of your JavaScript Web pages through the use of the <NOSCRIPT>...</NOSCRIPT> HTML tags. Any HTML code placed between these container tags will not display on a JavaScript-compatible Web browser but will display on one that cannot understand JavaScript. This enables you to include alternative content for your users who are using Web browsers that don't understand JavaScript. At the very least, you can let them know that they are missing something, as in this example:

```
<NOSCRIPT>
<HR>If you are seeing this text, then your web browser
   doesn't speak JavaScript!<HR>
</NOSCRIPT>
```

The JavaScript Language

JavaScript was designed to resemble Java, which, in turn, looks a lot like C and C++. The difference is that Java was built as a general-purpose object language; JavaScript, on the other hand, is intended to provide a quicker and simpler language for enhancing Web pages and servers. This section describes the building blocks of JavaScript and teaches you how to combine them into legal JavaScript programs.

On the CD

N O T E You can find a complete language reference for JavaScript in Appendix A, "JavaScript 1.2 Language Reference," and on the CD-ROM that accompanies this book. You can also find this information and more at Netscape's DevEdge Online Web site at http://developer. netscape.com.

Part

IV

Ch

18

Using Identifiers

An *identifier* is a unique name that JavaScript uses to identify a variable, method, or object in your program. As with other programming languages, JavaScript imposes some rules on what names you can use. All JavaScript names must start with a letter or the underscore character; they can contain both upper and lowercase letters and the digits 0 through 9. JavaScript supports two ways for you to represent values in your scripts: literals and variables. As their names imply, *literals* are fixed values that don't change while the script is executing, and *variables* hold data that can change at any time.

Literals and variables have several types; the type is determined by the kind of data that the literal or variable contains. The following are some of the types supported in JavaScript:

- Integers—Integer literals are made up of a sequence of digits only; integer variables can contain any whole-number value. You can specify octal (base-8) and hexadecimal (base-16) integers by prefixing them with a leading 0 or 0x, respectively.

- Floating-point numbers—The number 10 is an integer, but 10.5 is a floating-point number. Floating-point literals can be positive or negative and can contain either positive or negative exponents (which are indicated by an "e" in the number). For example, 3.14159265 is a floating-point literal, as is 6.023e23 (6.023×10^{23}, or Avogadro's number).

- Strings—Strings can represent words, phrases, or data and are set off by either double (") or single (') quotation marks. If you start a string with one type of quotation mark,

> you must close it with the same type. Special characters, such as \n for newline and \t, can also be utilized in strings.

■ Booleans—Boolean literals can have values of either TRUE or FALSE; other statements in the JavaScript language can return Boolean values.

Using Functions, Objects, and Properties

JavaScript is modeled after Java, an object-oriented language. An *object* is a collection of data and functions that have been grouped together. A *function* is a piece of code that plays a sound, calculates an equation, sends a piece of email, and so on. The object's functions are called *methods* and its data are called its *properties*. The JavaScript programs you write will have properties and methods and will interact with objects provided by the Web browser, its plug-ins, Java applets, ActiveX Controls, and other things.

N O T E Although the words "function" and "method" are often used interchangeably, they are not the same. A method is a function that is part of an object. For instance, writeln is one of the methods of the object document. ■

T I P Here's a simple guideline: An object's properties are the information it knows; its methods are how it can act on that information.

Using Built-In Objects and Functions   Individual JavaScript elements are *objects*. String literals are string objects, for example, and they have methods that you can use to change their case, and so on. JavaScript can also use the objects that represent the Web browser in which it is executing, the currently displayed page, and other elements of the browsing session.

To access an object, you specify its name. Consider, for example, an active document object named document. To use document's properties or methods, you add a period (.) and the name of the method or property you want. For example, document.title is the title property of the document object, and explorer.length calls the length member of the string object named explorer. Remember, literals are objects too.

You can find out more about the objects built in to JavaScript and the Web browser in the next chapter.

Using Properties   Every object has properties, even literals. To access a property, use the object name followed by a period and the property name. To get the length of a string object named address, you can write the following:

```
address.length
```

You get back an integer that equals the number of characters in the string. If the object you use has properties that can be modified, you can change them in the same way. To set the color property of a house object, for example, use the following line:

```
house.color = "blue"
```

You can also create new properties for an object simply by naming them. If you define a class called `customer` for one of your pages, for example, you can add new properties to the `customer` object as follows:

```
customer.name = "Joe Smith"
customer.address = "123 Elm Street"
customer.zip = "90210"
```

Finally, knowing that an object's methods are properties is important. You can easily add new methods to an object by writing your own function and creating a new object property using your own function name. If you want to add a `Bill` method to your `customer` object, you can do so by writing a function named `BillCustomer` and setting the object's property as follows:

```
customer.Bill = BillCustomer;
```

To call the new method, you use the following:

```
customer.Bill()
```

Array and Object Properties   JavaScript objects store their properties in an internal table that you can access in two ways. You have already seen the first way—just use the properties' names. The second way, *arrays*, enables you to access all an object's properties in sequence. The following function prints out all the properties of the specified object:

```
function DumpProperties(obj, obj_name) {
    result = ""     // set the result string to blank
    for (i in obj)
        result += obj_name + "." + i + " = " + obj[i] + "\n"
    return result
}
```

Part
IV
Ch
18

You can access all the properties of the `document` object, for instance, both by property name—using the dot operator (for example, `document.href`)—and by the object's property array (`document[1]`, although this may not be the same property as `document.href`). JavaScript provides another method of array access that combines the two: associative arrays. An *associative array* associates a left- and a right-side element; the value of the right side can be used by specifying the value of the left side as the index. JavaScript sets up objects as associative arrays with the property names as the left side and their values as the right. You can, therefore, access the `href` property of the `document` object by using `document["href"]`.

Programming with JavaScript

JavaScript has a lot to offer page authors. It is not as flexible as C or C++, but it is quick and simple. Most importantly, it's easily embedded in your Web pages; thus, you can maximize their impact with a little JavaScript seasoning. This section covers the gritty details of JavaScript programming and includes a detailed explanation of the language's features.

Expressions

An *expression* is anything that can be evaluated to get a single value. Expressions can contain string or numeric literals, variables, operators, and other expressions, and they can range from simple to quite complex. The following are examples of expressions that use the assignment operator (more on operators in the next section) to assign numeric or string values to variables:

```
x = 7;
str = "Hello, World!";
```

In contrast, the following is a more complex expression whose final value depends on the values of the `quitFlag` and `formComplete` variables:

```
(quitFlag == TRUE) & (formComplete == FALSE)
```

Operators

Operators do just what their name suggests: They operate on variables or literals. The items that an operator acts on are called its *operands*. Operators come in the following two types:

- Unary operators—These operators require only one operand, and the operator can come before or after the operand. The `--` operator, which subtracts one from the operand, is a good example. Both `--count` and `count--` subtract one from the variable count.

- Binary operators—These operators need two operands. The four math operators (+ for addition, - for subtraction, * for multiplication, and / for division) are all binary operators, as is the = assignment operator.

Assignment Operators   *Assignment operators* take the result of an expression and assign it to a variable. JavaScript doesn't enable you to assign the result of an expression to a literal. One feature of JavaScript not found in most other programming languages is that you can change a variable's type on-the-fly. Consider the HTML document shown in Listing 18.1.

Listing 18.1   *VarType.htm*—JavaScript Enables You to Change the Data Type of Variables

```
<HTML>
<HEAD>
<SCRIPT LANGUAGE="JavaScript">
<!-- Hide this script from incompatible Web browsers!
function typedemo() {
    var x;
    document.writeln("<DL>");
    document.writeln("<DT>Undefined...</DT>");
    document.writeln("<DD>x = " + x + "</DD>");
    document.writeln("<DT> </DT>");
    x = 17;
    document.writeln("<DT>Integer...</DT>");
    document.writeln("<DD>x = " + x + "</DD>");
    document.writeln("<DT> </DT>");
    x = Math.PI;
    document.writeln("<DT>Floating-Point...</DT>");
    document.writeln("<DD>x = " + x + "</DD>");
    document.writeln("<DT> </DT>");
    x = 'Hi, Mom!';
    document.writeln("<DT>String...</DT>");
    document.writeln("<DD>x = " + x + "</DD>");
    document.writeln("<DT> </DT>");
```

```
    x = false;
    document.writeln("<DT>Boolean...</DT>");
    document.writeln("<DD>x = " + x + "</DD>");
    document.writeln("</DL>");
}
//   Hide this script from incompatible Web browsers! -->
</SCRIPT>
<TITLE>Changing Data Types On-The-Fly...</TITLE>
</HEAD>
<BODY BGCOLOR=#FFFFFF>
<H1>Changing Data Types On-The-Fly...</H1>
<HR>
<SCRIPT LANGUAGE="JavaScript">
<!-- Hide this script from incompatible Web browsers!
typedemo();
//   Hide this script from incompatible Web browsers! -->
</SCRIPT>
<HR>
<A HREF="mailto:odonnj@rpi.edu"><EM>Jim O'Donnell</EM></A>
</BODY>
</HTML>
```

N O T E Math is a JavaScript object used to access many of its math functions. The next chapter introduces you to more of the Math object's properties. ▤

▶ **See** "JavaScript Objects," **p. 479**.

This short program shows that you can use the same variable in JavaScript to represent any or all of the different data types. If you tried to do something like this in most other languages, you would either generate a compiler error or a runtime error. JavaScript happily accepts the change and prints x's new value at each step (see Figure 18.1).

The most common assignment operator, =, assigns the value of an expression's right side to its left side. In the preceding example, the variable x got the floating-point value of 3.141592653589793 or the Boolean value of FALSE after the expression was evaluated. For convenience, JavaScript also defines some other operators that combine common math operations with assignment. Table 18.1 shows these.

Table 18.1 Assignment Operators that Provide Shortcuts to Doing Assignments and Math Operations at the Same Time

Operator	What It Does	Two Equivalent Expressions
+=	adds two values	x+=y and x=x+y
	adds two strings	string += "HTML" and string = string + "HTML"
-=	subtracts two values	x-=y and x=x-y
*=	multiplies two values	a*=b and a=a*b
/=	divides two values	e/=b and e=e/b

FIGURE 18.1

Because JavaScript variables are loosely typed, not only their value can be changed, but also their data type.

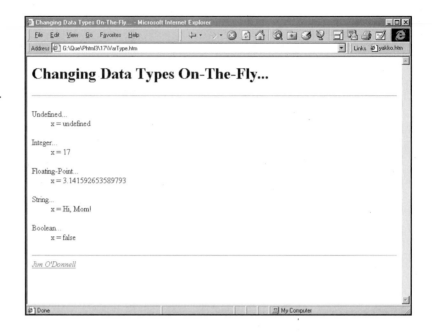

Math Operators The previous sections gave you a sneak preview of the math operators that JavaScript furnishes. You can either combine math operations with assignments, as shown in Table 18.1, or use them individually. As you would expect, the standard four math functions (addition, subtraction, multiplication, and division) work the same as they do on an ordinary calculator. The negation operator, -, is a unary operator that negates the sign of its operand. Another useful binary math operator is the modulus operator, %. This operator returns the remainder after the integer division of two integer numbers. For instance, in the expression

```
x = 13%5;
```

the variable x would be given the value of 3.

JavaScript also adds two useful unary operators, -- and ++, called, respectively, the *decrement* and *increment* operators. These two operators modify the value of their operand, and they return the new value. They also share a unique property: You can use them either before or after their operand. If you put the operator after the operand, JavaScript returns the operand's value and then modifies it. If you take the opposite route and put the operator before the operand, JavaScript modifies it and returns the modified value. The following short example might help to clarify this seemingly odd behavior:

```
x = 7;   // set x to 7
a = --x; // set x to x-1, and return the new x; a = 6
b = a++; // set b to a, so b = 6, then add 1 to a; a = 7
x++;     // add one to x; ignore the returned value
```

Comparison Operators Comparing the value of two expressions to see whether one is larger, smaller, or equal to another is often necessary. JavaScript supplies several comparison operators that take two operands and return TRUE if the comparison is true and FALSE if it is not. (Remember, you can use literals, variables, or expressions with operators that require expressions.) Table 18.2 shows the JavaScript comparison operators.

Table 18.2 Comparison Operators that Allow Two JavaScript Operands to Be Compared in a Variety of Ways

Operator	Read It As	Returns TRUE When
==	equals	The two operands are equal.
!=	does not equal	The two operands are unequal.
<	less than	The left operand is less than the right operand.
<=	less than or equal to	The left operand is less than or equal to the right operand.
>	greater than	The left operand is greater than the right operand.
>=	greater than or equal to	The left operand is greater than or equal to the right operand.

You might find it helpful to think of the comparison operators as questions. When you write the following:

```
(x >= 10)
```

you're really saying, "Is the value of variable x greater than or equal to 10?" The return value answers the question, TRUE or FALSE.

TROUBLESHOOTING

You may be asking yourself, "Why do my tests for equality always succeed, even when I know that the two quantities are sometimes different?"

A common mistake in JavaScript, as in C, C++, or Java, is mixing up the = operator—used to set one quantity equal to another—and the == operator—used to test two quantities for equality. The following code tests to see whether the variable a is equal to 10. If it is, this code writes out the following line:

```
if (a == 10)
document.writeln("a is equal to 10!")
```

On the other hand, the following code sets a equal to 10 and returns TRUE, and thus always writes out the following line:

```
if (a = 10)
document.writeln("a is equal to 10!")
```

Logical Operators   Comparison operators compare quantity or content for numeric and string expressions. Sometimes, however, you need to test a logical value such as whether a comparison operator returns TRUE or FALSE. JavaScript's logical operators enable you to compare expressions that return logical values. The following are JavaScript's logical operators:

- &&, read as "and." The && operator returns TRUE if both its input expressions are true. If the first operand evaluates to false, && returns FALSE immediately, without evaluating the second operand. Here's an example:

```
x = TRUE && TRUE;        // x is TRUE
x = FALSE && FALSE;      // x is FALSE
x = FALSE && TRUE;       // x is FALSE
```

- ¦¦, read as "or." This operator returns TRUE if either of its operands is true. If the first operand is true, ¦¦ returns TRUE without evaluating the second operand. Here's an example:

```
x = TRUE ¦¦ TRUE;        // x is TRUE
x = FALSE ¦¦ TRUE;       // x is TRUE
x = FALSE ¦¦ FALSE;      // x is FALSE
```

- !, read as "not." This operator takes only one expression and returns the opposite of that expression; !TRUE returns FALSE, for example, and !FALSE returns TRUE.

Note that the "and" and "or" operators don't evaluate the second operand if the first operand provides enough information for the operator to return a value. This process, called *short-circuit evaluation*, can be significant when the second operand is a function call. For example:

```
keepGoing = (userCancelled == FALSE) && (theForm.Submit())
```

If userCancelled is TRUE, the second operand, which submits the active form, is not called.

String Operators   You can use a few of the operators previously listed for string manipulation as well. All the comparison operators can be used on strings, too; the results depend on standard lexicographic ordering (ordering by the ASCII values of the string characters), but comparisons aren't case sensitive. Additionally, you can use the + operator to concatenate strings, returning a string made up of the original strings joined together. The expression

```
str = "Hello, " + "World!";
```

would assign the resulting string "Hello, World!" to the variable str.

Controlling Your JavaScripts

Some scripts you write will be simple. They will execute the same way every time, one time per page. If you add a JavaScript to play a sound when users visit your home page, for example, it doesn't need to evaluate any conditions or do anything more than one time. More sophisticated scripts might require that you take different actions under different circumstances. You might also want to repeat the execution of a block of code—perhaps by a set number of times or as long as some condition is TRUE. JavaScript provides constructs for controlling the execution flow of your script based on conditions, as well as for repeating a sequence of operations.

Testing Conditions   JavaScript provides a single type of control statement for making decisions: the `if...else` statement. To make a decision, you supply an expression that evaluates to
TRUE or FALSE; which code is executed depends on what your expression evaluates to.

The simplest form of `if...else` uses only the `if` part. If the specified condition is TRUE, the code
following the condition is executed; if not, it's skipped. In the following code fragment, for
example, the message appears only if the condition (that the `lastModified.year` property of
the `document` object says it was modified before 1995) is TRUE:

```
if (document.lastModified.year < 1995)
    document.write("Danger! This is a mighty old document.")
```

You can use any expression as the condition. Because you can nest expressions and combine
them with the logical operators, your tests can be pretty sophisticated. For example:

```
if ((document.lastModified.year >= 1995) && (document.lastModified.month >= 10))
    document.write("This document is reasonably current.")
```

The `else` clause enables you to specify a set of statements to execute when the condition is
FALSE. For instance,

```
if ((document.lastModified.year >= 1995) && (document.lastModified.month >= 10))
    document.write("This document is reasonably current.")
else
    document.write("This document is quite old.")
```

Repeating Actions   JavaScript provides two loop constructs that you can use to repeat a set
of operations. The first, called a `for` loop, executes a set of statements some number of times.
You specify three expressions: an *initial* expression that sets the values of any variables you
need to use, a *condition* that tells the loop how to see when it is done, and an *increment* expression that modifies any variables that need it. Here's a simple example:

```
for (count=0; count < 100; count++)
    document.write("Count is ", count);
```

This loop executes 100 times and prints out a number each time. The initial expression sets the
counter, `count`, to zero. The condition tests to see whether `count` is less than 100 and the increment expression increments `count`.

You can use several statements for any of these expressions, as follows:

```
for (count=0, numFound = 0; (count < 100) && (numFound < 3); count++)
    if (someObject.found()) numFound++;
```

This loop either loops 100 times or as many times as it takes to "find" three items—the loop
condition terminates when `count >= 100` or when `numFound >= 3`.

The second form of loop is the `while` loop. It executes statements as long as its condition is
TRUE. You can rewrite the first `for` loop in the preceding example, for instance, as follows:

```
count = 0
while (count < 100) {
    count++;
    if (someObject.found()) numFound++;
    document.write("Count is ", count)
}
```

Which form you use depends on what you are doing; for loops are useful when you want to perform an action a set number of times, and while loops are best when you want to keep doing something as long as a particular condition remains TRUE. Notice that by using braces, you can include more than one command to be executed by the while loop. (This is also true of for loops and if...else constructs.)

JavaScript Reserved Words

JavaScript reserves some keywords for its own use. You cannot define your own methods or properties with the same name as any of these keywords; if you do, the JavaScript interpreter complains.

 TIP Some of these keywords are reserved for future use. JavaScript might enable you to use them, but your scripts may break in the future if you do.

Table 18.3 shows some of JavaScript's reserved keywords.

Table 18.3   JavaScript Reserved Keywords Should Not Be Used in Your JavaScripts

abstract	double	instanceof	super
boolean	else	int	switch
break	extends	interface	synchronized
byte	FALSE	long	this
case	final	native	throw
catch	finally	new	throws
char	float	null	transient
class	for	package	TRUE
const	function	private	try
continue	goto	protected	var
default	if	public	void
do	implements	return	while
import	short	with	in
static			

CAUTION

Because JavaScript is still being developed and refined, the list of reserved keywords might change or grow over time. Whenever a new version of JavaScript is released, it might be a good idea to look over its new capabilities with an eye toward conflicts with your JavaScript programs.

Using JavaScript Statements

This section provides a quick reference to some of the more important JavaScript statements. Those listed here are in alphabetical order—many have examples. The formatting of these entries means the following:

- All JavaScript keywords are in monospaced font.
- Words in *monospace italic* represent user-defined names or statements.
- Any portions enclosed in square brackets ([and]) are optional.
- {*statements*} indicates a block of statements, which can consist of a single statement or multiple statements enclosed by braces.

The *break* Statement   The break statement terminates the current while or for loop and transfers program control to the statement that follows the terminated loop.

Syntax

```
break
```

Example

The following function scans the list of URLs in the current document and stops when it has seen all URLs or when it finds a URL that matches the input parameter searchName:

```
function findURL(searchName) {
   var i = 0;
   for (i=0; i < document.links.length; i++) {
      if (document.links[i] == searchName) {
         document.writeln(document.links[i] + "<BR>")
         break;
      }
   }
}
```

Part
IV
Ch
18

The *continue* Statement   The continue statement stops executing the statements in a while or for loop and skips to the next iteration of the loop. It doesn't stop the loop altogether like the break statement; instead, in a while loop, it jumps back to the condition. In a for loop, it jumps to the update expression.

Syntax

```
continue
```

Example

The following function prints the odd numbers between 1 and x; it has a continue statement that goes to the next iteration when i is even:

```
function printOddNumbers(x) {
   var i = 0
   while (i < x) {
      i++;
```

```
        if ((i % 2) == 0) // the % operator divides & returns the remainder
            continue
        else
            document.write(i, "\n")
    }
}
```

The *for* Loop   A for loop consists of three optional expressions, enclosed in parentheses and separated by semicolons, followed by a block of statements executed in the loop. These parts do the following:

- The starting expression, initial_expr, is evaluated before the loop starts. It is most often used to initialize loop counter variables. You are free to use the var keyword here to declare new variables.

- A *condition* is evaluated on each pass through the loop. If the condition evaluates to TRUE, the statements in the loop body are executed. You can leave the condition out. If you do, it always evaluates to TRUE. If you leave the condition out, make sure to use break in your loop when it is time to exit.

- An update expression, update_expr, is usually used to update or increment the counter variable or other variables used in the condition. This expression is optional; you can update variables as needed within the body of the loop if you prefer.

- A block of statements is executed as long as the condition is TRUE. This block can have one or multiple statements in it.

Syntax

```
for ([initial_expr;] [condition;] [update_expr]) {
    statements
}
```

Example

This simple for statement prints out the numerals from 0 to 9. It starts by declaring a loop counter variable, i, and initializing it to 0. As long as i is less than 9, the update expression increments i, and the statements in the loop body are executed.

```
for (var i = 0; i <= 9; i++) {
    document.write(i);
}
```

The *for...in* Loop   The for...in loop is a special form of the for loop that iterates the variable variable-name over all the properties of the object named object-name. For each distinct property, it executes the statements in the loop body.

Syntax

```
for (var in obj) {
    statements
}
```

Example

The following function takes as its arguments an object and the object's name. It then uses the `for...in` loop to iterate through all the object's properties and writes them into the current Web page.

```
function dump_props(obj,obj_name) {
    for (i in obj)
        document.writeln(obj_name + "." + i + " = " + obj[i] + "<br>");
}
```

The *function* Statement   The `function` statement declares a JavaScript function; the function may optionally accept one or more parameters. To return a value, the function must have a return statement that specifies the value to return. All parameters are passed to functions *by value*—the function gets the value of the parameter but cannot change the original value in the caller.

Syntax

```
function name([param] [, param] [..., param]) {
    statements
}
```

Example

This example defines a function called `PageNameMatches`, which returns `TRUE` if the string argument passed to the function is the title of the current document.

```
function PageNameMatches(theString) {
    return (document.title == theString)
}
```

The *if...else* Statement   The `if...else` statement is a conditional statement that executes the statements in `block1` if `condition` is `TRUE`. In the optional `else` clause, it executes the statements in `block2` if `condition` is `FALSE`. The blocks of statements can contain any JavaScript statements, including further nested `if` statements.

Syntax

```
if (condition) {
        statements
}
[else {
        statements
}]
```

Example

This `if...else` statement calls the `Message.Decrypt()` method if the `Message.IsEncrypted()` method returns `TRUE` and calls the `Message.Display()` method otherwise.

```
if (Message.IsEncrypted()) {
    Message.Decrypt(SecretKey);
}
else {
    Message.Display();
}
```

Part
IV

Ch

18

The *new* Statement   The new statement is the way that new objects are created in JavaScript. If, for example, you defined the following function to create a house object:

```
function house (rms,stl,yr,garp) { // define a house object
   this.room = rms;        // number of rooms (integer)
   this.style = stl;       // style (string)
   this.yearBuilt = yr;    // year built (integer)
   this.hasGarage = garp;  // has garage? (boolean)
}
```

Example

You could then create an instance of a house object by using the new statement, as in the following:

```
var myhouse = new house(3,"Tenement",1962,false);
```

A few notes about this example. First, note that the function used to create the object doesn't actually return a value. The reason that this method can work is that the function makes use of the this object, which always refers to the current object. Second, although the function defines how to create the house object, none is actually created until the function is called using the new statement.

The *return* Statement   The return statement specifies the value to be returned by a function.

Syntax

```
return expression;
```

Example

The following simple function returns the square of its argument, x, where x is any number.

```
function square( x ) {
   return x * x;
}
```

The *this* Statement   You use this to access methods or properties of an object within the object's methods. The this statement always refers to the current object.

Syntax

```
this.property
```

Example

If setSize is a method of the document object, this refers to the specific object whose setSize method is called:

```
function setSize(x,y) {
   this.horizSize = x;
   this.vertSize = y;
}
```

This method sets the size for an object when called as follows:

```
document.setSize(640,480);
```

The *var* Statement   The var statement declares a variable *varname*, optionally initializing it to have *value*. The variable name *varname* can be any JavaScript identifier, and *value* can be any legal expression (including literals).

Syntax

```
var varname [= value] [, var varname [= value] ] [..., var varname [= value] ]
```

Example

This statement declares the variables num_hits and cust_no, and initializes their values to zero.

```
var num_hits = 0, var cust_no = 0;
```

The *while* Statement   The while statement contains a condition and a block of statements. The while statement evaluates the condition; if *condition* is TRUE, it executes the statements in the loop body. It then re-evaluates *condition* and continues to execute the statement block as long as *condition* is TRUE. When *condition* evaluates to FALSE, execution continues with the next statement following the block.

Syntax

```
while (condition) {
    statements
}
```

Example

The following simple while loop iterates until it finds a form in the current document object whose name is "OrderForm" or until it runs out of forms in the document:

```
x = 0;
while ((x < document.forms[].length) && (document.forms[x].name != "OrderForm"))
{
    x++
}
```

The *with* Statement   The with statement establishes *object* as the default object for the statements in block. Any property references without an object are then assumed to be for *object*.

Syntax

```
with object {
    statements
}
```

Example

This statement uses with to apply the write() method and set the value of the bgColor property of the document object.

```
with document {
    write "Inside a with block, you don't need to specify the object.";
    bgColor = gray;
}
```

JavaScript and Web Browsers

The most important thing you will be doing with your JavaScripts is interacting with the content and information on your Web pages, and through it, with your user. JavaScript interacts with your Web browser through the browser's object model. Different aspects of the Web browser exist as different objects, with properties and methods that can be accessed by JavaScript. For instance, `document.write()` uses the `write` method of the `document` object. Understanding this Web Browser Object Model is crucial to using JavaScript effectively. Also, understanding how the Web browser processes and executes your scripts is also necessary.

When Scripts Execute

When you put JavaScript code in a page, the Web browser evaluates the code as soon as it is encountered. Functions, however, don't get executed when they're evaluated; they get stored for later use. You still have to call functions explicitly to make them work. Some functions are attached to objects—buttons or text fields on forms, for example, which are called when some event happens on the button or field. You might also have functions that you want to execute during page evaluation. You can do so by putting a call to the function at the appropriate place in the page.

Where to Put Your Scripts

You can put scripts anywhere within your HTML page, as long as they are surrounded with the `<SCRIPT>...</SCRIPT>` tags. One good system is to put functions that will be executed more than one time into the `<HEAD>` element of their pages; this element provides a convenient storage place. Because the `<HEAD>` element is at the beginning of the file, functions and VBScript code that you put there are evaluated before the rest of the document is loaded. Then you can execute the function at the appropriate point in your Web page by calling it, as in the following:

```
<SCRIPT language="JavaScript">
<!-- Hide this script from incompatible web browsers!
myFunction();
//   Hide this script from incompatible web browsers! -->
</SCRIPT>
```

Another way to execute scripts is to attach them to HTML elements that support scripts. When scripts are matched with events attached to these elements, the script is executed when the event occurs. This can be done with HTML elements, such as forms, buttons, or links. Consider Listing 18.2, which shows a simple example of two ways of attaching a JavaScript function to the `onClick` attribute of an HTML forms button (see Figure 18.2); it also shows how a JavaScript call can be executed in response to clicking a hypertext link.

Listing 18.2 *CallJS.htm*—**Calling a JavaScript Function with the Click of a Button or Hypertext Link**

```
<HTML>
<HEAD>
<SCRIPT LANGUAGE="JavaScript">
```

```
<!-- Hide this script from incompatible Web browsers! -->
function pressed() {
    alert("I said Don't Press Me!");
}
//   Hide this script from incompatible Web browsers! -->
</SCRIPT>
<TITLE>JavaScripts Attached to HTML Elements...</TITLE>
</HEAD>
<BODY BGCOLOR=#FFFFFF>
<FORM NAME="Form1">
<H1>JavaScripts Attached to HTML Elements...</H1>
<HR>
<DL>
<DT>Attach Javascript user function to button with onClick event...</DT>
<DD><INPUT TYPE="button" NAME="Button1" VALUE="Don't Press Me!"
        onClick="pressed()"></DD>
<DT> </DT>
<DT>Attach Javascript system function to button with onClick event...</DT>
<DD><INPUT TYPE="button" NAME="Button2" VALUE="Don't Press Me!"
        onClick="alert('I said Don\'t Press Me!')"></DD>
</FORM>
<DT>Attach Javascript user function to hypertext link with
➥"javascript:" url...</DT>
<DD><A HREF="javascript:pressed()">Don't Press Me!</A></DD>
</DL>
<HR>
<A HREF="mailto:odonnj@rpi.edu"><EM>Jim O'Donnell</EM></A>
</BODY>
</HTML>
```

Part
IV

Ch
18

FIGURE 18.2
JavaScript functions can be attached to form fields through several methods.

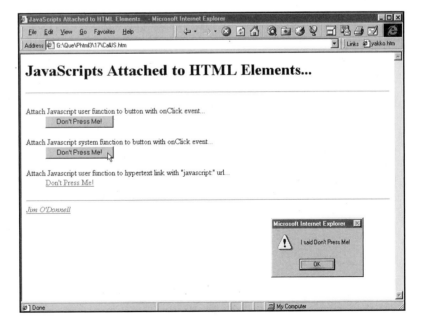

Three ways to call a JavaScript function from an HTML element are shown in Listing 18.2. The first attaches a user function call to the onClick event of an HTML forms element. The second way shows that you can directly call built-in JavaScript functions using the onClick event. This works particularly well when you are trying to do something simple. Finally, you can use the "javascript:" URL protocol to attach a JavaScript function call to a hypertext link. In the example shown in Listing 18.2, clicking either button or the hypertext link pops up the alert box shown in Figure 18.2.

JavaScript also provides you with an alternative way to attach functions to objects and their events. For simple actions, you can attach the JavaScript directly to the attribute of the HTML form element. This listing produces the output shown in Figure 18.2.

Sometimes you have code that should not be evaluated or executed until after all the page's HTML has been parsed and displayed. An example would be a function to print out all the URLs referenced in the page. If this function is evaluated before all the HTML on the page has been loaded, it misses some URLs. Therefore, the call to the function should come at the page's end. You can define the function itself anywhere in the HTML document; it is the function call that you should put at the end of the page.

N O T E   JavaScript code to modify the actual HTML contents of a document (as opposed to merely changing the text in a form text input field, for instance) must be executed during page evaluation. The only exception to this is when using Dynamic HTML, which, in some cases and on some browsers, enables you to change page content after initial evaluation. ▨

The Web Browser Object Model

by Jim O'Donnell

In this chapter

In Chapter 18, "Introduction to JavaScripting," you learned the basics of JavaScript—its syntax, control structures, and how to use it to access and manipulate objects. To be useful, however, something to manipulate is needed. How does JavaScript (or any other scripting language, for that matter) interact with your Web browser?

The answer is the Web Browser Object Model. Each script-compatible Web browser, mainly Netscape Navigator and Microsoft Internet Explorer, exposes a number of objects that can be used to control and interact with the browser. The sum total of these objects is the browser's object model.

As you would expect, the object models that Netscape and Microsoft have developed for their Web browsers are not completely compatible. Not only do differences exist between the models from the two vendors, but each revision of their Web browsers also differs from the last— they are largely backward compatible but include a number of new capabilities. This chapter examines those elements of the Web Browser Object Model that are (for the most part) common to all Netscape and Microsoft Web browsers, version 3 and higher. (Differences are noted in the discussion.) Later chapters discuss some of the major changes that have occurred with the advent of support for Cascading Style Sheets and Dynamic HTML.

▶ **See** "Web Browser Object Model," **p. 596**.

▶ **See** "Internet Explorer Document Object Model," **p. 638**.

Web Browser Object Hierarchy and Scoping

Figure 19.1 shows the hierarchy of objects that the Web browser provides and that are accessible to JavaScript. As shown, window is the topmost object in the hierarchy, and the other objects are organized underneath it. Using this hierarchy, the full reference for the value of a text field named text1 in an HTML form named form1 would be

`window.document.form1.text1.value.`

FIGURE 19.1
Objects defined by the Web browser are organized in a hierarchy and can be accessed and manipulated by JavaScript.

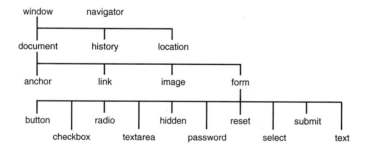

Because of the object-scoping rules in JavaScript, however, it is not necessary to specify this full reference. *Scoping* refers to the range over which a variable, function, or object is defined. A variable defined within a JavaScript function, for instance, is only scoped within that function— it cannot be referenced outside the function. JavaScripts are scoped to the current window, but not to the objects below the window in the hierarchy. Thus, for the preceding example, the text field value could also be referenced as `document.form1.text1.value`.

As in Figure 19.1, all Web pages will have the `window`, `navigator`, `document`, `history`, and `location` objects. Depending on the contents of the Web page, other objects may also be defined. The remainder of this chapter reviews the objects shown in Figure 19.1—what information is defined for them (properties), what functions they can perform (methods), and the actions to which they can respond (events).

The *window* Object

The Web browser creates at least one `window` object for every document. Think of the `window` object as an actual window and the `document` object as the content that appears in the window. As briefly discussed in this chapter and then in more detail in Chapter 20, "Manipulating Windows and Frames with JavaScript," one document can create more than one window, using the `window` object's `open()` method.

window Object Properties

Your HTML documents can access and manipulate a number of attributes of the current Web browser window through the `window` object. Some of the more useful `window` object properties are the following:

- `closed`—Specifies whether a window has been closed (Boolean).
- `defaultStatus`—The default message that appears in the status line of the Web browser window (string).
- `length`—The number of frames in the current window (integer).
- `name`—The name of a window (string).
- `opener`—When a window is opened using the `open()` method, the name of the window from which it was created is in this property (string).
- `parent`—Refers to a window that contains a frameset (object).
- `self` or `top`—Refers to the current window (object).
- `status`—Can be used to read or set the contents of the Web browser's status line (string).

In addition to the properties in the preceding list, remember that the `document`, `history`, and `location` objects are also properties of the `window` object.

window Object Methods

You can use JavaScript to create or operate on existing windows by using the methods associated with the `window` object. The following are some of these methods:

Part

IV

Ch

19

- alert(*string*)—Puts up an alert dialog box and displays the message specified in *string*. Users must dismiss the dialog box by clicking the OK button before the Web browser will enable them to continue.

- blur()—Removes the focus from the specified window.

- clearTimeOut(*timerID*)—Clears the timer function with ID *timerID* (see the setTimeOut() method in this list).

- close()—Closes the specified window.

- confirm(*string*)—Puts up a confirmation dialog box with two buttons (OK and Cancel) and displays the message specified in *string*. Users can dismiss the dialog box by clicking Cancel or OK; the confirm function returns true if users click OK and false if they click Cancel.

- eval(*string*)—Evaluates *string* as JavaScript code and returns the result.

- focus()—Puts the focus on the specified window.

- open(*arguments*)—Opens a new window.

- prompt(*string*,[*inputDefault*])—Opens a prompt box, which displays *string* as a prompt and asks the user for input. If *inputDefault* is specified, it is shown as the default value of the prompt box.

- scroll(*x*,*y*)—Scrolls the window to the given *x* and *y* coordinates.

- setTimeOut(*expression*,*msec*)—Evaluates *expression* after the specified number of milliseconds have passed. This method returns a timer ID that can be used by clearTimeOut.

N O T E   Each of these methods—as well as the events in the following section—are applied to the window object to which they belong. For instance, blur() or self.blur() would remove the focus from the window in which the document was located. MyWindow.blur() would remove it from the window called MyWindow. ▨

window Object Events

Finally, the window object can respond to the following events:

- onBlur—Triggered when the focus is removed from the window.

- onError—Triggered when an error occurs in the window.

- onFocus—Triggered when the focus is applied to the window.

- onLoad—Triggered when the Web browser finishes loading a document into the window.

- onUnload—Triggered when the user exits from the document within the window.

Window methods can be placed in either the <BODY> or <FRAMESET> tag of the document. To attach a JavaScript function to the onLoad event, for example, you could use this <BODY> tag:

```
<BODY onLoad="alert('Document download complete!')">
```

Chapter 20 includes an extensive example of how to use JavaScript to create and manipulate windows.

▶ **See** "JavaScript Windows Example," **p. 498**.

The *location* Object

As mentioned earlier, one of the properties of every window is the `location` object. This object holds the current URL, including the hostname, path, CGI script arguments, and even the protocol. Table 19.1 shows the properties and methods of the `location` object.

Table 19.1   The *location* Object Contains Information on the Currently Displayed URL

Properties

Name	What It Does
`href`	contains the entire URL, including all the subparts; for example, `http://www.rpi.edu:80/~odonnj/index.html`
`protocol`	contains the protocol field of the URL, including the first colon; for example, `http:`
`host`	contains the hostname and port number; for example, `www.rpi.edu:80`
`hostname`	contains only the hostname; for example, `www.rpi.edu`
`port`	contains the port number; for example, `80`
`path`	contains the path to the actual document; for example, `~odonnj/index.html`
`hash`	contains any CGI arguments after the first # in the URL
`search`	contains any CGI arguments after the first ? in the URL

Method

`assign(string)`	sets `location.href` to the value you specify

Part
IV

Ch
19

Listing 19.1 shows an example of how you access and use the `location` object. First, the current values of the `location` properties are displayed on the Web page (see Figure 19.2). As you can see, not all of them are defined. Additionally, when the button is clicked, the `location.href` property is set to the URL of my home page. This causes the Web browser to load that page (see Figure 19.3).

Listing 19.1 *location.htm*—The *location* Object Enables You to Access and Set Information About the Current URL

```
<HTML>
<HEAD>
<SCRIPT LANGUAGE="JavaScript">
<!-- Hide this script from incompatible Web browsers! -->
function gohome() {
    location.href = "http://www.rpi.edu/~odonnj/";
}
//  Hide this script from incompatible Web browsers! -->
</SCRIPT>
<TITLE>The Location Object</TITLE>
</HEAD>
<BODY BGCOLOR=#FFFFFF>
<H1>The Location Object</H1>
<HR>
<SCRIPT LANGUAGE="Javascript">
<!-- Hide this script from incompatible Web browsers! -->
document.writeln("Current location information:");
document.writeln("<UL>");
document.writeln("<LI>location.href = " + location.href);
document.writeln("<LI>location.protocol = " + location.protocol);
document.writeln("<LI>location.host = " + location.host);
document.writeln("<LI>location.hostname = " + location.hostname);
document.writeln("<LI>location.port = " + location.port);
document.writeln("<LI>location.pathname = " + location.pathname);
document.writeln("<LI>location.hash = " + location.hash);
document.writeln("<LI>location.search = " + location.search);
document.writeln("</UL>");
//  Hide this script from incompatible Web browsers! -->
</SCRIPT>
<FORM NAME="Form1">
    <INPUT TYPE="button" NAME="Button1" VALUE="Goto JOD's Home Page!"
        onClick="gohome()">
</FORM>
<HR>
<A HREF="mailto:odonnj@rpi.edu"><EM>Jim O'Donnell</EM></A>
</BODY>
  </HTML>
```

N O T E The document.write() method is discussed later in this chapter, in the "The document Object" section. ▨

The *history* Object

The Web browser also maintains a list of pages that you have visited since running the program; this list is called the *history list*, and it can be accessed through the history object. Your JavaScript programs can move through pages in the list by using the properties and functions shown in Table 19.2.

FIGURE 19.2

Manipulating the `location` object gives you another means of moving from one Web page to another.

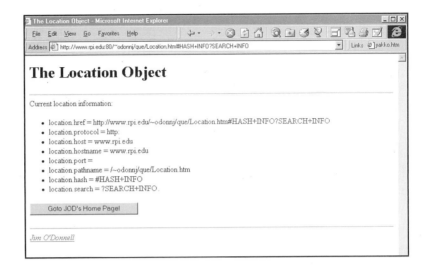

FIGURE 19.3

By setting its `href` property, you can use the `location` object to change the URL your Web browser is looking at.

The `history.length`, therefore, would return the number of entries in the history list. The methods `history.back()` and `history.forward()` would cause the Web browser to load the previous and next entry in the history list, if any.

Table 19.2   The *history* Object Contains Information on the Browser's History List

Property	Type	What It Does
current	property	contains the URL of the current history entry
length	property	contains the number of entries in the history list
previous	property	contains the URL of the previous history stack entry
next	property	contains the URL of the next history stack entry
back()	method	goes back one entry in the history list
forward()	method	goes forward one entry in the history list
go(*num*)	method	goes forward *num* entries in the history stack if *num* > 0, otherwise it goes backward *-num* entries
go(*string*)	method	goes to the newest history entry whose title or URL contains *string* as a substring; the string case doesn't matter

The *document* Object

Web browsers also expose an object called document. As you might expect, this object exposes useful properties and methods of the active document. The location object refers only to the URL of the active document, but document refers to the document itself. Chapter 20 discusses the document object in more detail, but its basic properties and methods are shown here.

▶ **See** "Filling Your Windows II: The document Object," **p. 496**.

document Object Properties

You can access and manipulate a number of attributes of the current Web browser document through the document object. Some of the more useful document object properties are the following:

- alinkColor—The color of the document's active link
- bgColor—The background color of the document
- cookie—The document's cookie
- domain—Domain name of the server that served the document
- fgColor—The foreground color of the document
- lastModified—The date the document was last modified
- linkColor—The color of the document's links
- referrer—The URL of the document from which this document was called

- title—The contents of the <TITLE> tag
- URL—The complete URL of the document
- vlinkColor—The color of the document's visited links

In addition to the properties in the preceding list, remember that the anchor, link, form, and image objects are also properties of the document object.

document Object Methods

You can use JavaScript to operate on documents by using the methods associated with the document object. The following are some of these methods:

- close()—Closes the specified document.
- eval(*string*)—Evaluates *string* as JavaScript code and returns the result.
- open()—Opens a stream for a new document. This document is meant to be filled with the output of calls to the document.write() and/or document.writeln() methods.
- write(*expression*, [*expression...*])—Writes one or more HTML expressions.
- writeln(*expression*, [*expression...*])—Identical to write(), except this method appends a newline.

Listing 19.2 shows a JavaScript that accesses and displays some of the properties of the document object. Notice that the link object is accessed through the links array, one for each URL link on the current Web page (see the "JavaScript Object Arrays" section later in this chapter). Figure 19.4 shows the results of loading this Web page.

Listing 19.2 *Document.htm*—The *document* Object Enables You to Access and Set Information About the Current Document

Part **IV** Ch **19**

```
<HTML>
<HEAD>
<TITLE>The Document Object</TITLE>
</HEAD>
<BODY BGCOLOR=#FFFFFF>
<A HREF="http://www.rpi.edu/~odonnj/">JOD's Home Page</A>
<A HREF="http://www.rpi.edu/~odonnj/que/Window.htm">The Window Object</A>
<A HREF="http://www.rpi.edu/~odonnj/que/Location.htm">The Location Object</A>
<A HREF="http://www.rpi.edu/~odonnj/que/Document.htm">The Document Object</A>
<HR>
<A HREF="mailto:odonnj@rpi.edu">Jim O'Donnell</A>
<HR>
<SCRIPT LANGUAGE="JavaScript">
<!-- Hide this script from incompatible Web browsers! -->
var n
document.writeln("Current document information:<PRE>")
document.writeln("<UL>");
document.writeln("<LI>document.title      = ",document.title)
document.writeln("<LI>document.location   = ",document.location)
document.writeln("<LI>document.lastModified = ",document.lastModified)
```

continues

Listing 19.2   Continued

```
for (n = 0;n < document.links.length;n++)
    document.writeln("<LI>document.links[",n,"].href = ",
        document.links[n].href)
document.writeln("<LI>document.linkColor    = ",document.linkColor)
document.writeln("<LI>document.alinkColor   = ",document.alinkColor)
document.writeln("<LI>document.vlinkColor   = ",document.vlinkColor)
document.writeln("<LI>document.bgColor      = ",document.bgColor)
document.writeln("<LI>document.fgColor      = ",document.fgColor,"<PRE><BR>")
document.writeln("</UL>");
//  Hide this script from incompatible Web browsers! -->
</SCRIPT>
</BODY>
</HTML>
```

FIGURE 19.4

document object properties contain information about the current document displayed in the Web browser.

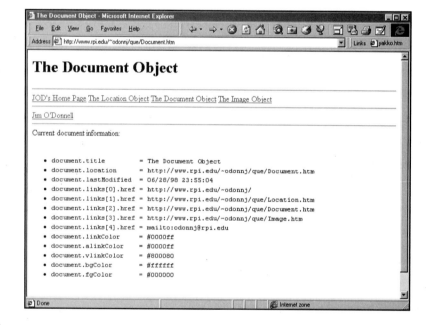

Some of the real power of the document object, however, is realized by making use of the objects underneath it in the hierarchy—particularly the different HTML forms elements available. This is because HTML forms can be one of the primary ways of interacting with the user of a Web page. The next few sections of this chapter discuss the objects used to interact with HTML forms.

JavaScript Object Arrays

Before you read about the other objects in the Web browser object hierarchy, now is a good time to learn about JavaScript's object array. An *object array* is what JavaScript uses to reference objects when more than one of the objects is in the current window or document (known as multiple instances of the object). An HTML document is likely to contain more than one hypertext link, for example, so more than one `link` and `anchor` object will be present. Each form requires a separate `form` object, each image an `image` object, and so on.

JavaScript gives you multiple ways of referencing and accessing these objects. Consider the following excerpt of HTML code, for example:

```
<FORM NAME=MyForm1 ACTION=… METHOD=…>
    HTML Form elements…
</FORM>
<FORM NAME=MyForm2 ACTION=… METHOD=…>
    HTML Form elements…
</FORM>
```

The first way to use JavaScript to reference these forms is to use the conventional object hierarchy that you have seen thus far. To set the value of a text field named `MyText1` in the first form, for example, you would use something like this:

```
document.MyForm1.MyText1.value = "Some Value"
```

JavaScript, on the other hand, gives you several other ways to reference these objects using JavaScript's object arrays. Objects are contained in an object array in the order in which they are defined in the document. Assuming that the two previously mentioned forms are the only two forms in the document, the first can be referenced using

```
document.forms[0]
```

and the second with

```
document.forms[1]
```

Thus, the same text field could be set using

```
document.forms[0].MyText1.value = "Some Value"
```

The third way to reference objects in an object array is to use JavaScript's associative arrays. With associative arrays, the array element is referenced by including its name as the argument of the array. Using this method, the two forms would be referenced as

```
document.forms["MyForm1"]
```

and

```
document.forms["MyForm2"]
```

and the text field set using

```
document.forms["MyForm1"].MyText1.value = "Some Value"
```

These examples show the three ways to reference JavaScript objects when multiple instances of them exist. Which should you use? That depends on the application:

- Object Hierarchy Referencing. For example,

  ```
  document.MyForm1.MyText1.value
  ```

Part

IV

Ch

19

Use this method when you are dealing with one or two objects, each with a predefined name and separate actions associated with each.

- Object Array with Numerical Index. For example,

```
document.forms[0].MyText1.value
```

Use this method when you want to repeat an action over multiple objects using a JavaScript `for` or `while` loop.

- Object Associative Array. For example,

```
document.forms["MyForm1"].MyText1.value
```

Use this method when you want to operate on one or two objects only, but the specific object may vary.

> **CAUTION**
>
> If you are designing HTML documents and wish to remain compatible with Netscape Navigator 2.0 (if you are programming for a corporate intranet that hasn't upgraded in a long while, for instance), you can use only the numerical index method of referencing object arrays.

For a given HTML document, some of the predefined object arrays that JavaScript can access (depending on what is defined in the document) are the following:

- `anchors`—One for each of the `<A>` tags containing a `NAME` attribute
- `applets`—One for each `<APPLET>` tag
- `arguments`—One for each argument of a JavaScript function
- `elements`—One for each element in an HTML form
- `embeds`—One for each `<EMBED>` tag
- `forms`—One for each HTML form
- `frames`—One for each `<FRAME>` tag in a window containing a `<FRAMESET>`
- `history`—One for each entry in the history list for a window
- `images`—One for each `<IMG>` tag
- `links`—One for each `<AREA>` and/or `<A>` tag containing an `HREF` attribute
- `mimeTypes`—One for each MIME type supported by the client Web browser, its helper applications, plug-ins, and (primarily for Internet Explorer) ActiveX Controls
- `options`—One for each `<OPTION>` tag
- `plugins`—One for each plug-in installed on the client Web browser

The *link*, *area*, and *anchor* Objects

These objects are created within a document when hypertext links or targets are created using the `<A>` or `<AREA>` tag. A `link` object is created when the `<A>` tag uses the `HREF` attribute, and the anchor object is created when it uses the NAME attribute. area objects are created for each <AREA> tag used for creating client-side imagemaps.

▶ **See** "Client-Side Imagemaps," **p. xxx**. (Ch. 4, "Imagemaps")

link and area objects are referenced through the link's object array. Each object in this array has the same properties as a location object (see Table 19.1 earlier in the chapter). In addition, these objects have the events listed in Table 19.3.

Table 19.3   Events of the HTML *form* Object

Event	When It Occurs
onClick	triggered when a link object is clicked
onMouseOver	triggered when the mouse passes over a link or area object
onMouseOut	triggered when the mouse passes out of a link or area object

anchor objects are also referenced using an object array—the anchors array. The only property of this object array, however, is the length property, which returns the number of elements in the array.

The *form* Object

The HTML form object is the primary way for Web pages to solicit different types of input from the user. JavaScript will often work along with HTML forms to perform its functions. The object model for HTML forms includes a wide variety of properties, methods, and events. If you use these with each form, JavaScript can manipulate and access those forms.

form Object Properties

Tables 19.4, 19.5, and 19.6 show some of the properties, methods, and events attached to HTML form objects. These can be used in JavaScripts—the properties and methods can be used to access or manipulate information and to perform certain functions, and the events can be used to trigger JavaScript functions related to the form itself. If a form is named Form1, for instance, the method document.Form1.submit() can be called in JavaScript to submit the form. On the other hand, if the Submit button calls a function in response to an onSubmit event, the submission of the form can be disabled if the function returns a false value. This is a good way to perform form validation within the Web browser and to allow submission of the form only if all fields are validated.

Note that the HTML form elements that can be included within the form, <INPUT>, <RADIO>, <CHECKBOX>, and other form tags, are also represented as objects and can be referenced by JavaScript. These form element objects are also properties of their parent form—they are discussed in the next section.

Table 19.4   Properties of the HTML *form* Object

Property	What It Contains
name	the value of the form's NAME attribute
method	the value of the form's METHOD attribute
action	the value of the form's ACTION attribute
elements	the elements array of the form
length	the number of elements in the form
encoding	the value of the form's ENCODING attribute
target	window targeted after submit for form response

Table 19.5   Methods of the HTML *form* Object

Method	What It Does
reset()	resets the form to its initial values
submit()	submits the form

Table 19.6   Events of the HTML *form* Object

Event	When It Occurs
onReset	triggered when the <RESET> button is clicked or the reset() method is called
onSubmit	triggered when the <SUBMIT> button is clicked or the submit() method is called

Using Objects to Manipulate *Form* Elements

A good place to use JavaScript is in forms; this is so because you can write scripts that process, check, and perform calculations with the data the user enters. JavaScript provides a useful set of properties and methods for text <INPUT> elements and buttons and the other form elements.

You use <INPUT> elements in a form to enable the user to enter text data; JavaScript provides properties to get the objects that hold the element's contents as well as methods for doing something when the user moves into or out of a field. Table 19.7 shows some of the properties, methods, and events defined for <INPUT> form element objects.

Table 19.7 HTML Form *input* Object Properties, Methods, and Events

Property	What It Contains
name	the value of the element's NAME attribute
value	the field's contents
defaultValue	the initial contents of the field

Method	What It Does
focus()	moves the input focus to the specified object
blur()	moves the input focus away from the specified object
select()	selects the specified object
submit()	submits the form according to its ACTION and METHOD attributes

Event	When It Occurs
onFocus	triggered when the user moves the input focus to the field, either via the Tab key or a mouse click
onBlur	triggered when the user moves the input focus out of this field
onSelect	triggered when the user selects text in the field
onSubmit	triggered when the form is submitted
onChange	triggered only when the field loses focus and the user has modified its text; use this action to validate data in a field

Individual buttons and check boxes have properties, too; JavaScript provides properties to get objects containing a button's data, as well as methods for doing something when the user selects or deselects a particular button. Table 19.8 shows some of the properties, methods, and events defined for button elements.

Table 19.8 HTML Form *radio* and *checkbox* Object Properties, Methods, and Events

Property	What It Contains
name	the value of the button's NAME attribute
value	the VALUE attribute
checked	the state of a check box
defaultChecked	the initial state of a check box

continues

Part
IV

Ch
19

Table 19.8 Continued

Method	What It Does
focus()	moves the input focus to the specified object
blur()	moves the input focus away from the specified object
click()	clicks a button and triggers whatever actions are attached to it
submit()	submits the form according to its ACTION and METHOD attributes

Event	When It Occurs
onClick	triggered when the button is pressed
onFocus	triggered when the user moves the input focus to the field, either via the Tab key or a mouse click
onBlur	triggered when the user moves the input focus out of this field
onSubmit	triggered when the form is submitted
onChange	triggered only when the field loses focus and the user has modified its text; use this action to validate data in a field

For more details and examples of what you can do with JavaScript and the objects, properties, and methods associated with HTML forms, see Chapter 21, "Using JavaScript to Create Smart Forms."

▶ **See** "Client-Side Form Validation," **p. 514**.

The *image* Object

The last Web browser object to be discussed in this chapter is the image object. One image object is created in a document by each <IMG> tag on the page. These objects are referenced through an image's object array; the object's array has a length property that you can use to find out how many images are present. Table 19.9 shows some of the other properties and events associated with the image object.

Table 19.9 HTML *image* Object Properties and Events

Property	What It Contains
border	the value of the BORDER attribute
complete	indicates whether the image has been completely loaded
height	the value of the HEIGHT attribute
hspace	the value of the HSPACE attribute
lowsrc	the value of the LOWSRC attribute

Property	What It Contains
name	the value of the NAME attribute
src	the value of the SRC attribute
vspace	the value of the VSPACE attribute
width	the value of the WIDTH attribute

Event	When It Occurs
onAbort	triggered when the user aborts the loading of an image, such as by clicking the Stop button
onError	triggered when an error occurs when an image is being loaded
onLoad	triggered when an image is completely loaded

image Object Example

Listing 19.3 shows an example that uses the onMouseOver and onMouseOut events of the link object, along with the properties of the image object, to create a hypertext link whose anchor changes whenever the mouse is passed over it. This is often done to highlight hypertext link anchors to make them stand out more as the mouse passes over them—for instance, the changed image can be a glowing version of the original image. Figure 19.5 demonstrates how this will appear in the Web page.

Listing 19.3 *image.htm*—Use JavaScript to Create Changing Hypertext Link Anchors

```
<HTML>
<HEAD>
<SCRIPT LANGUAGE="JavaScript">
<!-- Hide this script from incompatible Web browsers! -->
function changeImage(i,j) {
   document.images[i].src = "clickme" + j + ".gif"
}
//  Hide this script from incompatible Web browsers! -->
</SCRIPT>
<TITLE>The Image Object</TITLE>
</HEAD>
<BODY BGCOLOR=#FFFFFF>
<H1>The Image Object</H1>
<HR>
<A HREF="Document.htm" onMouseOver="changeImage(0,2)"
                       onMouseOut="changeImage(0,1)">
   <IMG SRC="clickme1.gif" WIDTH=200 HEIGHT=50>
</A>
<A HREF="Location.htm" onMouseOver="changeImage(1,2)"
                       onMouseOut="changeImage(1,1)">
```

Part
IV

Ch
19

continues

Listing 19.3 Continued

```
    <IMG SRC="clickme1.gif" WIDTH=200 HEIGHT=50>
</A>
<HR>
<A HREF="mailto:odonnj@rpi.edu">Jim O'Donnell</A>
</BODY>
</HTML>
```

FIGURE 19.5

The properties, events, and methods of different objects can be combined, using JavaScript, to produce cool effects.

Using the Image Constructor

You might have noticed in the example shown in Listing 19.3 that the first time you passed your mouse over the image, a slight pause occurred before the new image displayed. This is because the image needed to be downloaded into your cache the first time. (If you viewed this example right from the accompanying CD-ROM, you might not have noticed this delay.)

Along with the image object, an Image constructor can be used to preload your cache with images that will subsequently be shown on your page. This is done by creating a new image object with the JavaScript new statement and then setting the src property of this object to the URL of your image. This creates what is, in essence, an undisplayed image that is part of the current Web page. Although the image is not displayed, it is loaded into your cache so that if it is displayed later it will load much more quickly.

With Listing 19.3, if the following code was included in the <SCRIPT> tag that is in the <HEAD> section, it would preload the two images used in the example.

```
function loadImages() {
    this[1] = new Image();
    this[1].src = "clickme1.gif";
    this[2] = new Image();
    this[2].src = "clickme2.gif";
}
if (document.images) {
    loadImages();
}
```

JavaScript Objects

This chapter concludes by discussing a few of JavaScript's built-in objects. Strictly speaking, these objects are not part of the Web Browser Object Model; instead, they are part of JavaScript itself. However, their properties and methods are used in the same manner. JavaScript includes a number of its own objects—two of the most useful are the Date object and the Math object.

JavaScript objects, because they are outside the Web Browser Object Model hierarchy, are not the properties of any other object. In other words, to reference a JavaScript object, you need to use the object name itself instead of prefacing it with window or document, as shown in the next two sections below.

Using the *Date* Object

The JavaScript Date object is the easiest way to use dates and times within your scripts. JavaScript's new statement is used to create an instance of the Date object. The following list shows some of the ways you can create the Date object:

- today = new Date()—Gives the current date
- birthday = new Date("October 17, 1963 13:45:00")
- birthday = new Date(1963,9,17)
- birthday = new Date(1963,9,17,13,45,0)

In the previous two examples, the general syntax is as follows:

newdate = new Date(year, month, day, hour, minute, second)

Note that the month is specified as an integer from 0 to 11, where 0 represents January and 11 represents December, and that the hour is in 24-hour format.

Table 19.10 shows some of the methods of the Date object.

Table 19.10 HTML *Date* Object Methods

Property	What It Does
getYear()	returns the year
getMonth()	returns the month
getDate()	returns the day of the month
getDay()	returns the day of the week
getHours()	returns the hours
getMinutes()	returns the minutes
getSeconds()	returns the seconds

continues

Part

IV

Ch

19

Table 19.10 Continued

Property	What It Does
getTime()	returns the number of milliseconds since January 1970 00:00:00
getTimezoneOffset()	returns the number of hours of time zone offset from GMT in the current location
setYear(*arg*)	sets the year to *arg*
setMonth(*arg*)	sets the month to *arg*
setDate(*arg*)	sets the day of the month to *arg*
setHours(*arg*)	sets the hours to *arg*
setMinutes(*arg*)	sets the minutes to *arg*
setSeconds(*arg*)	sets the seconds to *arg*
setTime(*arg*)	sets the number of milliseconds since January 1970 00:00:00 to *arg*
toGMTString()	returns a string representation of the date in GMT
toLocalString()	returns a string representation of the date in the local time zone

Using the *Math* Object

JavaScript's Math object gives you access to various mathematical constants and functions. These are represented as properties and methods of the Math object. Table 19.11 shows the properties.

Table 19.11 HTML *Math* Object Properties

Property	What It Does
E	returns the constant e
LN2	returns the natural logarithm of 2
LN10	returns the natural logarithm of 10
LOG2E	returns the base-10 logarithm of e
LOG10E	returns the base-2 logarithm of e
PI	returns the constant pi
SQRT1_2	returns the square root of 1/2
SQRT2	returns the square root of 2

Table 19.12 shows the Math object methods, which are the different functions that you can use.

Table 19.12 HTML *Math* Object Methods

Method	What It Does
abs(x)	absolute value of x
acos(x)	arc cosine of x
asin(x)	arc sine of x
atan(x)	arc tangent of x
atan2(x,y)	arc tangent of x,y
ceil(x)	x rounded up to the nearest integer
cos(x)	cosine of x
exp(x)	e raised to the x power
floor(x)	x rounded down to the nearest integer
log(x)	logarithm of x
max(x,y)	maximum of x and y
min(x,y)	minimum of x and y
pow(x,y)	x raised to the y power
random()	returns a random number
round(x)	x rounded to the nearest integer
sin(x)	sine of x
sqrt(x)	square root of x
tan(x)	tangent of x

Part
IV

Ch
19

Manipulating Windows and Frames with JavaScript

As discussed in Chapter 19, "The Web Browser Object Model," you can create, manipulate, and access the properties of Web browser windows by using the window object. Chapter 18 showed the properties, methods, and events associated with the window object. This chapter shows some practical examples of this; it is meant to show you how to create and then use multiple windows.

Listing 20.1 shows the HTML document Window1.htm. This document uses a single JavaScript statement to create a window and load that window with another document (Form1.htm, shown in Listing 20.2). The new window is created using the window object's open() method. Figure 20.1 shows the result of loading Window1.htm into Internet Explorer. (In many of the examples shown in this chapter, the created windows may be rearranged for improved visibility—all appear in their original size, however).

Listing 20.1   *Window1.htm*—Create New Web Browser Windows with *window.open()*

```
<HTML>
<HEAD>
<TITLE>Window1.htm</TITLE>
</HEAD>
<BODY BGCOLOR=#FFFFFF>
<CENTER>
<H1>Window Example #1</H1>
<HR>
</CENTER>
<ADDRESS>
Jim O'Donnell, <A HREF="mailto:odonnj@rpi.edu">odonnj@rpi.edu</A>
</ADDRESS>
<SCRIPT LANGUAGE="JAVASCRIPT">
<!-- Hide script from incompatible browsers! -->
MyWindow = window.open("Form1.htm","MyWindow",
    "toolbar=no,location=no,directories=no,status=no," +
    "menubar=no,scrollbars=no,resizable=no," +
    "width=475,height=155")
//    Hide script from incompatible browsers! -->
</SCRIPT>
</BODY>
</HTML>
```

When loaded into a Web browser, the HTML document in Listing 20.1 creates a new window and displays the HTML form given in Listing 20.2.

Listing 20.2   *Form1.htm*—HTML Documents for Created Windows Should Be Sized Carefully

```
<HTML>
<HEAD>
<TITLE>Form1.htm</TITLE>
```

```
</HEAD>
<BODY BGCOLOR=#FFFFFF>
<CENTER>
<TABLE WIDTH=95% BORDER>
<FORM NAME="MyForm">
<TR><TD><B>Form Element Type</B></TD>
    <TD><B>Name</B></TD>
    <TD> </TD></TR>
<TR><TD><B>TEXT</B> Element</TD>
    <TD><I>MyText</I></TD>
    <TD><INPUT TYPE="TEXT" NAME="MyText"></TD></TR>
<TR><TD><B>CHECKBOX</B> Element</TD>
    <TD><I>MyCheckBox1</I></TD>
    <TD><INPUT TYPE="CHECKBOX" NAME="MyCheckBox1"></TD></TR>
<TR><TD><B>CHECKBOX</B> Element</TD>
    <TD><I>MyCheckBox2</I></TD>
    <TD><INPUT TYPE="CHECKBOX" NAME="MyCheckBox2"></TD></TR>
<TR><TD><B>CHECKBOX</B> Element</TD>
    <TD><I>MyCheckBox3</I></TD>
    <TD><INPUT TYPE="CHECKBOX" NAME="MyCheckBox3"></TD></TR>
</FORM>
</TABLE>
</BODY>
</HTML>
```

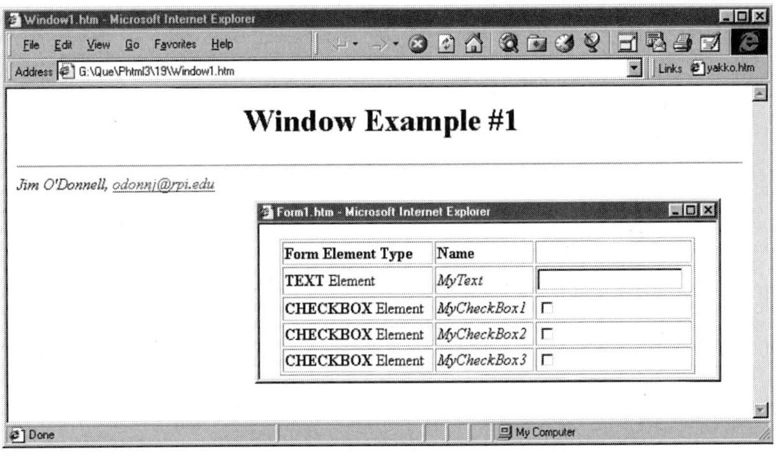

FIGURE 20.1
JavaScript can create new Web browser windows and configure them to look the way you would like for your applications.

Three arguments apply to the window.open() method, with the following meanings:

- The first argument is the URL of the HTML document to be loaded into the new window.

- The second argument is the name of the window that can be used as the TARGET attribute of the <A> tag.

- The third argument is optional and contains a comma-separated list of configuration options for the created window. The configuration options are the following:

Part
IV

Ch
20

- `toolbar = [yes¦no]`—Controls the display of the Web browser window toolbar
- `location = [yes¦no]`—Controls the display of the Web browser window location bar
- `directories = [yes¦no]`—Controls the display of the Web browser window directory bar
- `status = [yes¦no]`—Controls the display of the Web browser window status line
- `menubar = [yes¦no]`—Controls the display of the Web browser window menu bar
- `scrollbars = [yes¦no]`—Controls the display of the Web browser window scrollbars
- `resizable = [yes¦no]`—Controls whether the created window can be resized
- `width = # pixels`—Sets the width of the new window, in pixels
- `height = # pixels`—Sets the height of the new window, in pixels

T I P If you want to set one of the options for a new window, set them all; otherwise, your results may not be what you expect because each Web browser (and even the same browser on different platforms) handles the default options differently. It is better to play it safe and completely specify exactly how you want your windows to look.

In addition to the arguments for the `window.open()` method, it also has a return value. The method returns a handle that gives you the name of the newly created window. This enables you to access and manipulate the objects in the new window from the original.

Referencing Multiple Windows with JavaScript

Just creating a new window with the `window.open()` method does not accomplish that much. Your users can create new windows on their own—for instance, from Netscape Navigator's File, New menu selection. The window shown in Figure 20.1 was created without any of the controls, such as the menu bar. To enable it to be used as a full-fledged Web browser window, it could just as easily have been created with a menu bar, as well as with any of the other window user-interface elements.

To be able to create *and use* new windows, you need to be able to reference them. After you know where a new window fits into the Web browser object hierarchy detailed in Chapter 19, you can use the elements of that hierarchy to manipulate what appears in the new window. The next two sections of this chapter show you how to do just that.

▶ **See** "Web Browser Object Hierarchy and Scoping," **p. 462**.

Referencing Child Windows

Listing 20.3 shows `Window2.htm`—this HTML document is similar to `Window1.htm` shown in Listing 20.1. It loads the same document, `Form1.htm`, into the new window. It also includes a JavaScript, which shows you how you can access and manipulate the objects in a child window from the parent window. The parent window is the window in which the original document—`Window2.htm`, in this case—is loaded. The window it creates is the child window.

In this case, the JavaScript function updateWindow() is attached to the onChange event of the HTML form text field and the onBlur events of the check boxes. In this way, whenever the text field is changed or a check box is checked or unchecked (and the focus moved elsewhere), updateWindow() is called. This function then copies all the values of the HTML form in the parent window into the corresponding fields of the child window.

Listing 20.3 *Window2.htm*—JavaScripts Enable You to Manipulate Multiple Windows from a Single Document

```
<HTML>
<HEAD>
<TITLE>Window2.htm</TITLE>
<SCRIPT LANGUAGE="JAVASCRIPT">
<!-- Hide script from incompatible browsers! -->
function updateWindow() {
    self.MyWindow.document.MyForm.MyText.value = document.MyForm.MyText.value
    self.MyWindow.document.MyForm.MyCheckBox1.checked =
document.MyForm.MyCheckBox1.checked
    self.MyWindow.document.MyForm.MyCheckBox2.checked =
document.MyForm.MyCheckBox2.checked
    self.MyWindow.document.MyForm.MyCheckBox3.checked =
document.MyForm.MyCheckBox3.checked
}
//   Hide script from incompatible browsers! -->
</SCRIPT>
</HEAD>
<BODY BGCOLOR=#FFFFFF>
<CENTER>
<H1>Window Example #2</H1>
<HR>
<TABLE WIDTH=95% BORDER>
<FORM NAME="MyForm">
<TR><TD><B>Form Element Type</B></TD>
    <TD><B>Name</B></TD>
    <TD> </TD></TR>
<TR><TD><B>TEXT</B> Element</TD>
    <TD><I>MyText</I></TD>
    <TD><INPUT TYPE="TEXT" NAME="MyText" onChange="updateWindow()"></TD></TR>
<TR><TD><B>CHECKBOX</B> Element</TD>
    <TD><I>MyCheckBox1</I></TD>
    <TD><INPUT TYPE="CHECKBOX" NAME="MyCheckBox1" onBlur="updateWindow()">
</TD></TR>
<TR><TD><B>CHECKBOX</B> Element</TD>
    <TD><I>MyCheckBox2</I></TD>
    <TD><INPUT TYPE="CHECKBOX" NAME="MyCheckBox2" onBlur="updateWindow()">
</TD></TR>
<TR><TD><B>CHECKBOX</B> Element</TD>
    <TD><I>MyCheckBox3</I></TD>
    <TD><INPUT TYPE="CHECKBOX" NAME="MyCheckBox3" onBlur="updateWindow()">
</TD></TR>
</FORM>
</TABLE>
```

Part

IV

Ch

20

continues

Listing 20.3 Continued

```
<HR>
</CENTER>
<ADDRESS>
Jim O'Donnell, <A HREF="mailto:odonnj@rpi.edu">odonnj@rpi.edu</A>
</ADDRESS>
<SCRIPT LANGUAGE="JAVASCRIPT">
<!-- Hide script from incompatible browsers! -->
MyWindow = window.open("Form1.htm","MyWindow",
    "toolbar=no,location=no,directories=no,status=no," +
    "menubar=no,scrollbars=no,resizable=no," +
    "width=475,height=155")
//   Hide script from incompatible browsers! -->
</SCRIPT>
</BODY>
</HTML>
```

The `document` object of the child window is accessed by this JavaScript, running in the parent window, through the `self.MyWindow` object. The `self` object indicates the current window; the `MyWindow` is the return value of the `window.open()` method, indicating that you want to access the objects of the child object. Therefore, `self.MyWindow.document` gets to the `document` object of the child window, and from there you can access the child window's objects.

FIGURE 20.2

New windows fit into the object model, enabling you to create scripts to access their objects and properties.

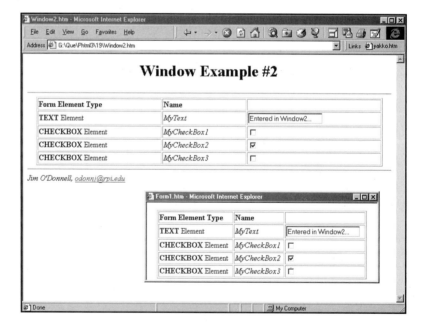

Referencing Parent Windows

Is it possible to go the other way? Can scripts running in the child window access and manipulate objects in the parent window? Yes, they can. The next example uses the HTML documents `Window3.htm` (which is the same as `Window2.htm` from Listing 20.3, except for a new title and heading) and `Form3.htm` (shown in Listing 20.4). `Form3.htm` uses a similar JavaScript, also called `updateWindow()`, to automatically update the fields of the parent window with information entered into the child window form fields. To reference the parent window from a child, the `opener` object is used. Thus `opener.document` gets the JavaScript in the child window to the `document` object of the parent, from which the other objects can be referenced. Figure 20.3 shows the values entered into the child window forms automatically reflected into the parent.

Listing 20.4 *Form3.htm*—Child-to-Parent as Well as Parent-to-Child Communication Is Possible

```
<HTML>
<HEAD>
<TITLE>Form3.htm</TITLE>
<SCRIPT LANGUAGE="JAVASCRIPT">
<!-- Hide script from incompatible browsers! -->
function updateWindow() {
    opener.document.MyForm.MyText.value = document.MyForm.MyText.value
    opener.document.MyForm.MyCheckBox1.checked =
document.MyForm.MyCheckBox1.checked
    opener.document.MyForm.MyCheckBox2.checked =
document.MyForm.MyCheckBox2.checked
    opener.document.MyForm.MyCheckBox3.checked =
document.MyForm.MyCheckBox3.checked
}
//   Hide script from incompatible browsers! -->
</SCRIPT>
</HEAD>
<BODY BGCOLOR=#FFFFFF>
<CENTER>
<TABLE WIDTH=95% BORDER>
<FORM NAME="MyForm">
<TR><TD><B>Form Element Type</B></TD>
    <TD><B>Name</B></TD>
    <TD> </TD></TR>
<TR><TD><B>TEXT</B> Element</TD>
    <TD><I>MyText</I></TD>
    <TD><INPUT TYPE="TEXT" NAME="MyText" onChange="updateWindow()"></TD></TR>
<TR><TD><B>CHECKBOX</B> Element</TD>
    <TD><I>MyCheckBox1</I></TD>
    <TD><INPUT TYPE="CHECKBOX" NAME="MyCheckBox1" onBlur="updateWindow()">
</TD></TR>
<TR><TD><B>CHECKBOX</B> Element</TD>
    <TD><I>MyCheckBox2</I></TD>
    <TD><INPUT TYPE="CHECKBOX" NAME="MyCheckBox2" onBlur="updateWindow()">
</TD></TR>
<TR><TD><B>CHECKBOX</B> Element</TD>
```

Part
IV

Ch
20

continues

Listing 20.4   Continued

```
      <TD><I>MyCheckBox3</I></TD>
      <TD><INPUT TYPE="CHECKBOX" NAME="MyCheckBox3" onBlur="updateWindow()">
</TD></TR>
</FORM>
</TABLE>
</BODY>
</HTML>
```

FIGURE 20.3

You can use JavaScript to coordinate the contents of multiple Web browser windows.

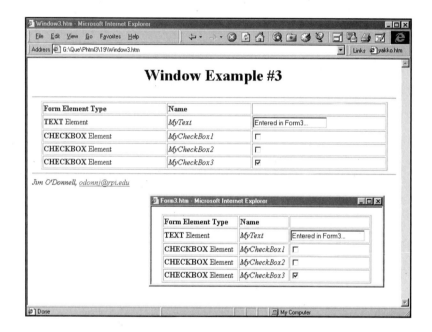

Making Use of Window Events

You can use a number of events associated with the window object in your scripts to control what they do and when they do it. The events are listed in Chapter 19. This section gives you an example of how you might use a few of them. Listing 20.5 shows Window4.htm. This HTML document creates another Web browser window, loads another document (Text.htm, which is not listed here but is included on the CD-ROM) into it, and automatically scrolls through the document. Figure 20.4 shows these two windows after they are first created.

▶ **See** "window Object Events," page **464**.

FIGURE 20.4
Small child windows are a good way to show additional information related to your Web site.

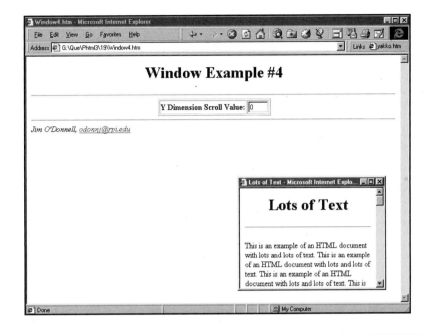

Listing 20.5 *Window4.htm*—**HTML Documents Can Be Automatically Scrolled**

```
<HTML>
<HEAD>
<TITLE>Window4.htm</TITLE>
<SCRIPT LANGUAGE="JAVASCRIPT">
<!-- Hide script from incompatible browsers! -->
var scrollVal = 0
function scrollWindow() {
   scrollVal += 10
   if (scrollVal <= 1500) {
      self.MyWindow.scroll(0,scrollVal)
      document.MyForm.ScrollY.value = scrollVal
         setTimeout("scrollWindow()",100)
   }
}
//   Hide script from incompatible browsers! -->
</SCRIPT>
</HEAD>
<BODY BGCOLOR=#FFFFFF onLoad="setTimeout('scrollWindow()',5000)">
<CENTER>
<H1>Window Example #4</H1>
<HR>
<TABLE BORDER>
<FORM NAME="MyForm">
<TR><TD><B>Y Dimension Scroll Value:</B></TD>
    <TD><INPUT TYPE="TEXT" NAME="ScrollY" SIZE=4></TD></TR>
</FORM>
</TABLE>
<HR>
```

continues

Listing 20.5 Continued

```
</CENTER>
<ADDRESS>
Jim O'Donnell, <A HREF="mailto:odonnj@rpi.edu">odonnj@rpi.edu</A>
</ADDRESS>
<SCRIPT LANGUAGE="JAVASCRIPT">
<!-- Hide script from incompatible browsers! -->
MyWindow = window.open("Text.htm","MyWindow",
    "toolbar=no,location=no,directories=no,status=no," +
    "menubar=no,scrollbars=yes,resizable=no," +
    "width=300,height=200")
document.MyForm.ScrollY.value = scrollVal
//    Hide script from incompatible browsers! -->
</SCRIPT>
</BODY>
</HTML>
```

This example uses one window event and three methods to accomplish its purpose. First, the
window.open() method is used to create the new window and to load the second HTML document into it. When the window is fully loaded, as indicated by the window object's onLoad
event—included as an attribute in its <BODY> tag—the setTimeout() method is used to set up a
call to the scrollWindow() JavaScript after five seconds (5,000 milliseconds) have passed. At
the end of this time, scrollWindow() is called, which, in turn, uses the window.scroll()
method to automatically scroll the second window. The JavaScript also uses setTimeout() to
set up another call to itself. This repeats until the document in the second window is scrolled all
the way through. Additionally, the HTML form text field in the main document is used to display the current scroll value (see Figure 20.5).

FIGURE 20.5
Use the
setTimeout()
method to create timed
effects in your HTML
documents.

Current scroll value —

Automatic scrolling
begins after 5 seconds

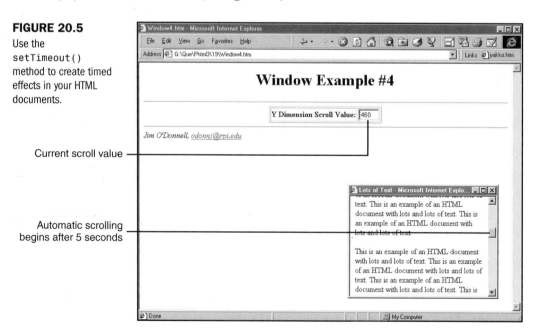

CAUTION

The x- and y-dimension scroll value passed to the `window.scroll()` method is in pixels, so it is very difficult to know how many pixels are needed to scroll through a given document. This is particularly true when the scrolled document is primarily text, which can be sized differently in different Web browsers. It is best to use this method when the document being viewed is primarily graphics, making it easier to scroll accurately.

Window Methods for Getting User Input

You can use three window object methods to solicit input from your users. You can use JavaScript to create windows and display custom-made forms to get any kind of input from your user that you would like. The three built-in methods, on the other hand, give you quick, easy ways to get input. These methods are

- `alert()`
- `confirm()`
- `prompt()`

Notification Using the *Alert* Method

Listing 20.6 shows an example of using the `window.alert()` method. This method is used to notify your user of something, and can only be responded to by clicking OK. Figure 20.6 shows an example of the alert using this method.

Listing 20.6   *Alert.htm*—Use This Method to Inform Your User of Important Information

```
<HTML>
<HEAD>
<TITLE>Alert.htm</TITLE>
</HEAD>
<BODY BGCOLOR=#FFFFFF>
<CENTER>
<H1>Alert Method Example</H1>
<HR>
</CENTER>
<ADDRESS>
Jim O'Donnell, <A HREF="mailto:odonnj@rpi.edu">odonnj@rpi.edu</A>
</ADDRESS>
<SCRIPT LANGUAGE="JAVASCRIPT">
<!-- Hide script from incompatible browsers! -->
window.alert("The alert method of the window object is used to " +
    "notify you of some condition; it does not present you with " +
    "any choice other than to click OK.")
//   Hide script from incompatible browsers! -->
</SCRIPT>
</BODY>
</HTML>
```

Part
IV

Ch
20

Using the *confirm* Method to Get a Yes or No

Listing 20.7 shows an example of using the `window.confirm()` method. This method is used to
solicit a yes or no from your user. It returns a Boolean `true` or `false` to indicate what the user
selected. This value can then be used by a JavaScript to decide what to display or what to do
based on the user input (see Figure 20.7).

**Listing 20.7 *Confirm.htm*—A Confirmation Box Gives the User a Yes or
No Decision**

```
<HTML>
<HEAD>
<TITLE>Confirm.htm</TITLE>
</HEAD>
<BODY BGCOLOR=#FFFFFF>
<CENTER>
<H1>Confirm Method Example</H1>
<HR>
<FORM NAME="MyForm">
Result of <U>confirm</U> method: <INPUT TYPE=TEXT NAME="MyText">
</FORM>
<HR>
</CENTER>
<ADDRESS>
Jim O'Donnell, <A HREF="mailto:odonnj@rpi.edu">odonnj@rpi.edu</A>
</ADDRESS>
<SCRIPT LANGUAGE="JAVASCRIPT">
<!-- Hide script from incompatible browsers! -->
res = window.confirm("The confirm method of the window " +
    "object is similar to the alert method in that it is " +
    "used to notify you of some condition; unlike the alert " +
    "method it presents you with a choice to either click " +
    "OK or Cancel, and returns true or false, respectively.")
document.MyForm.MyText.value = res
//   Hide script from incompatible browsers! -->
```

```
</SCRIPT>
</BODY>
</HTML>
```

FIGURE 20.7
You can use the
window.confirm()
method to create a
"gateway" condition to
your site. Users must
agree to this condition
before they can access
your site.

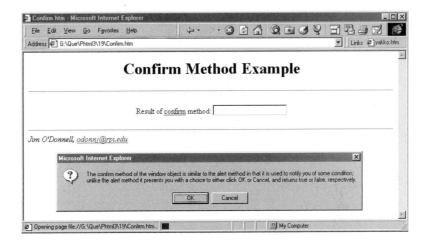

Asking the User for Input with the *prompt* Method

Listing 20.8 shows the window.prompt() method, which enables you to get a single line of input from your user. You can use this to ask users for their names, email addresses, URLs, or anything else that can be entered in a single line. It is also possible with this method, as shown in Figure 20.8, to include a default answer with the prompt() method.

Listing 20.8   *Prompt.htm*—The User Can Enter any Single Line of Input in the Prompt

```
<HTML>
<HEAD>
<TITLE>Prompt.htm</TITLE>
</HEAD>
<BODY BGCOLOR=#FFFFFF>
<CENTER>
<H1>Prompt Method Example</H1>
<HR>
<FORM NAME="MyForm">
Result of <U>prompt</U> method: <INPUT TYPE=TEXT NAME="MyText" SIZE=30>
</FORM>
<HR>
</CENTER>
<ADDRESS>
Jim O'Donnell, <A HREF="mailto:odonnj@rpi.edu">odonnj@rpi.edu</A>
</ADDRESS>
<SCRIPT LANGUAGE="JAVASCRIPT">
<!-- Hide script from incompatible browsers! -->
```

Part
IV

Ch
20

continues

Listing 20.8 Continued

```
res = window.prompt("The prompt method of the window " +
    "object enables you to ask the user for input; you can " +
    "also specify a default input, such as URL of my home " +
    "shown below.","http://www.rpi.edu/~odonnj")
document.MyForm.MyText.value = res
//   Hide script from incompatible browsers! -->
</SCRIPT>
</BODY>
</HTML>
```

FIGURE 20.8

Using the `window.prompt()` method's simple dialog box makes it easy to get simple input from your user.

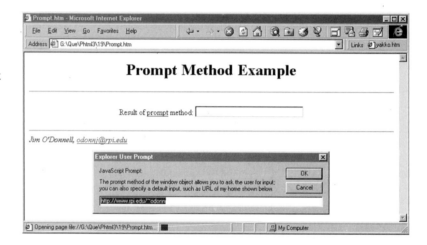

Filling Your Windows I: The *location* Object

Instead of specifying a URL in the `window.open()` method, you have several other ways to specify the contents of a new `window` object. The first of these ways is the simplest of the two: by using the new window's `location` object. Referring to the first example in this chapter, for instance, instead of specifying `Form1.htm` as the first argument of the `window.open()` method, you could do the same thing by using the following after the new window is created:

```
self.MyWindow.location.href = "Form1.htm"
```

Filling Your Windows II: The *document* Object

A second way of specifying content for new windows—or for your original Web browser window, for that matter—is by using methods of the `document` object. The following document object methods are used to create content within an HTML document:

- `document.open()`— The `open()` method is used to open the document for writing. If the method is used within an existing Web page, the content created will replace the current contents.

- `document.write()` or `document.writeln()`—Each of these methods is used to write HTML code into the currently opened document. If these statements are encountered while the current document is being loaded—in the following example, the document is already open—the content they generate will be included along with the other contents of the page.

  If these methods are used after the current document has been opened, but without a preceding `document.open()` method, they will generate an error. If the `document.open()` method is used, all the content generated will replace the current contents.

  The only difference between the `write()` and `writeln()` method is that the `writeln()` method includes a new line after the content. This does not affect the HTML generated, but makes it easier to view.

- `document.close()`— This method closes and causes to be displayed a document opened using the `document.open()` method.

Listing 20.9 shows `WindowJS.htm`. This HTML document reproduces the first example shown in this chapter (shown in Listings 20.1 and 20.2) with only one file. Instead of loading a second HTML document into the new window, the `document.write()` method is used to dynamically generate the HTML to be displayed. The results of this file are identical to that shown in Figure 20.1, except that the title and heading are changed.

Listing 20.9 *WindowJS.htm*—HTML Documents Can Be Generated On-the-Fly

```
<HTML>
<HEAD>
<TITLE>WindowJS.htm</TITLE>
</HEAD>
<BODY BGCOLOR=#FFFFFF>
<CENTER>
<H1>Window Example #5</H1>
<HR>
</CENTER>
<ADDRESS>
Jim O'Donnell, <A HREF="mailto:odonnj@rpi.edu">odonnj@rpi.edu</A>
</ADDRESS>
<SCRIPT LANGUAGE="JAVASCRIPT">
<!-- Hide script from incompatible browsers! -->
MyWindow = window.open("","MyWindow",
    "toolbar=no,location=no,directories=no,status=no," +
    "menubar=no,scrollbars=no,resizable=no," +
    "width=475,height=155")
str = "<HTML>" +
    "<HEAD>" +
    "<TITLE>Form1.htm</TITLE>" +
    "</HEAD>" +
    "<BODY BGCOLOR=#FFFFFF>" +
    "<CENTER>" +
    "<TABLE WIDTH=95% BORDER>" +
    "<FORM NAME='MyForm'>" +
    "<TR><TD><B>Form Element Type</B></TD>" +
```

Part

IV

Ch

20

continues

Listing 20.9 Continued

```
"      <TD><B>Name</B></TD>" +
"      <TD> </TD></TR>" +
"<TR><TD><B>TEXT</B> Element</TD>" +
"      <TD><I>MyText</I></TD>" +
"      <TD><INPUT TYPE='TEXT' NAME='MyText'></TD></TR>" +
"<TR><TD><B>CHECKBOX</B> Element</TD>" +
"      <TD><I>MyCheckBox1</I></TD>" +
"      <TD><INPUT TYPE='CHECKBOX' NAME='MyCheckBox1'></TD></TR>" +
"<TR><TD><B>CHECKBOX</B> Element</TD>" +
"      <TD><I>MyCheckBox2</I></TD>" +
"      <TD><INPUT TYPE='CHECKBOX' NAME='MyCheckBox2'></TD></TR>" +
"<TR><TD><B>CHECKBOX</B> Element</TD>" +
"      <TD><I>MyCheckBox3</I></TD>" +
"      <TD><INPUT TYPE='CHECKBOX' NAME='MyCheckBox3'></TD></TR>" +
"</FORM>" +
"</TABLE>" +
"</BODY>" +
"</HTML>"
self.MyWindow.document.open()
self.MyWindow.document.write(str)
self.MyWindow.document.close()
//   Hide script from incompatible browsers! -->
</SCRIPT>
</BODY>
</HTML>
```

JavaScript Windows Example

This example shows one application of how to create and use other Web browser windows. In this example, JavaScripts are attached to the onClick events of HTML forms buttons and are used to open and/or fill two other windows. The object of the windows, in this application, is to display pictures and accompanying biographical information.

This example shows how it is possible to create HTML forms-based buttons that call JavaScripts and use them to create, to assign content to, and to destroy other windows. In addition, this example shows you how a script in a created window can manipulate the content back in the window that created it.

Listing 20.10 shows WindEx.htm, the top-level HTML document for this example. The four buttons shown by this document each have JavaScripts attached to their onClick attributes. Clicking each button executes the appropriate JavaScript.

Listing 20.10 WindEx.htm—Create and Manipulate Browser Windows with JavaScript

```
<HTML>
<HEAD>
<TITLE>JavaScript Window Example</TITLE>
```

```
<SCRIPT LANGUAGE="JavaScript">
<!-- Hide this script from incompatible Web browsers!
var picwin = null;
var biowin = null;
var n = 0;
function openpic() {
    if (!picwin)
        picwin =
open("","PicWindow","width=200,height=250,screenX=70,screenY=270");
}
function openbio() {
    if (!biowin)
        biowin =
open("","BioWindow","width=400,height=250,screenX=320,screenY=270");
}
function closeboth() {
    if (picwin) {
        picwin.close();
        picwin = null;
    }
    if (biowin) {
        biowin.close();
        biowin = null;
    }
}
function loadnex() {
    if (!picwin) openpic();
    if (!biowin) openbio();
//
    n++;
    if (n > 5) n = 5;
    picname = "Pic" + n + ".htm";
    bioname = "Bio" + n + ".htm";
//
    self.picwin.location.href = picname;
    self.biowin.location.href = bioname;
    self.picwin.focus();
    self.biowin.focus();
}
function loadpre() {
    if (!picwin) openpic();
    if (!biowin) openbio();
//
    n--;
    if (n < 1) n = 1;
    picname = "Pic" + n + ".htm";
    bioname = "Bio" + n + ".htm";
//
    self.picwin.location.href = picname;
    self.biowin.location.href = bioname;
    self.picwin.focus();
    self.biowin.focus();
}
//   Hide script from incompatible browsers! -->
</SCRIPT>
```

Part

IV

Ch

20

continues

Listing 20.10 Continued

```
</HEAD>
<BODY BGCOLOR=#FFFFFF onUnload="closeboth()">
<FORM NAME="MyForm">
<CENTER>
<TABLE>
<TR><TD><INPUT TYPE="button" NAME="OpenWin"  VALUE="Open Windows"
        onClick="openpic();openbio()"></TD>
    <TD><INPUT TYPE="button" NAME="PreBut"    VALUE="Load Previous"
        onClick="loadpre()"></TD>
    <TD><INPUT TYPE="button" NAME="NexBut"    VALUE="Load Next"
        onClick="loadnex()"></TD>
    <TD><INPUT TYPE="button" NAME="CloseWin" VALUE="Close Windows"
        onClick="closeboth()"></TD>
</TR>
</TABLE>
</CENTER>
</FORM>
<HR>
<ADDRESS>
Jim O'Donnell, <A HREF="mailto:odonnj@rpi.edu">odonnj@rpi.edu</A>
</ADDRESS>
</BODY>
</HTML>
```

The four buttons created by this HTML document (see Figure 20.9)—through the attached JavaScript functions—perform the following functions:

- Open Windows—Clicking this button calls the openpic() and openbio() JavaScript functions, which will each open up a new window (one for pictures, one for biographical information), as shown in Figure 20.10. If the windows have already been opened, then clicking this button does nothing.

- Load Previous—Clicking this button calls the loadpre() function, which will first call openpic() and/or openbio() to create those windows, if necessary. Then, it will decrement the current number, display the appropriate picture and bio, and bring those windows focus (which will usually bring them to the top).

- Load Next—Clicking this button calls the loadnex() function, which works the same as the loadpre() function, except that it increments the current number.

- Close Windows—Clicking this button calls the closeboth() function to close the picture and bio window and also sets the picwin and biowin variables back to null.

N O T E The screenX and screenY window attributes used to provide the initial placement of the created windows are recent additions to JavaScript and will not work in all browsers. ▪

The last thing we want to do is to enable the user, from the last picture/bio combination, to link back to another Web site for additional information. But, we want that Web site to appear in the main window (the one where the control buttons are) and we want the two created windows to be closed. These two tasks are accomplished as follows. Listing 20.11 shows the HTML loaded with the last bio information. When the button created there is pressed, a JavaScript is called, which changes where the main window is looking by referring to the `location.href` property of the `self.opener` object. The `self.opener` object refers to the window that opened the current window—the main window, in this case.

FIGURE 20.9

HTML forms buttons provide a great way for your users to trigger JavaScripts.

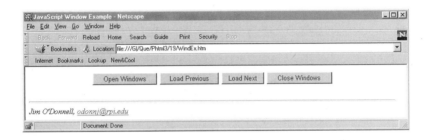

FIGURE 20.10

JavaScripts can easily manipulate information and content in multiple windows simultaneously.

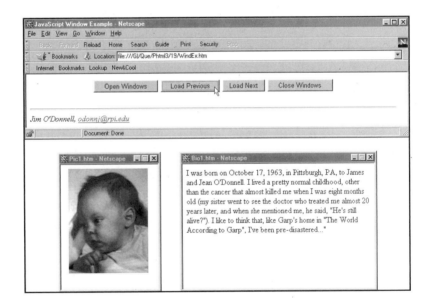

How do we get the two created windows to be closed when the main window moves to another location? This is done with the `onUnload` window event, placed into the `<BODY>` tag of the main window and used to call the `closeboth()` JavaScript function.

Listing 20.11 *Bio5.htm*—**Created Windows Can Access and Manipulate the Contents of Their Creators**

```
<HTML>
<HEAD>
<TITLE>Bio5.htm</TITLE>
<SCRIPT LANGUAGE="JavaScript">
```

continues

Part

IV

Ch

20

Listing 20.11   Continued

```
<!-- Hide this script from incompatible Web browsers!
function loadmain() {
    self.opener.location.href="http://www.rpi.edu/~odonnj"
}
//    Hide script from incompatible browsers! -->
</SCRIPT>
</HEAD>
<BODY BGCOLOR=#FFFFFF>
For more exciting (?) and (hopefully) current information about me, my life, my
interests, and whatever else catches my fancy, be sure to check out my Web
site...
<FORM NAME="MyForm">
<CENTER>
<TABLE>
<TR><TD><INPUT TYPE="button" VALUE="The House of JOD"
          onClick="loadmain()"></TD>
</TR>
</TABLE>
</CENTER>
</FORM>
</BODY>
</HTML>
```

Creating and Using Frames

Chapter 7, "Frames," showed you how to create and use frames in your Web site. You can access and manipulate the contents of these frames by using the `frame` object. Each of the frames created in a document can be accessed through the `frames` object array, which is attached to the `document` object. The most important thing to remember about a `frame` object is that *it is a* `window` *object.* This means that each frame created is a separate `window` object, and all the properties, methods, and events associated with `window` objects can be applied.

▶ **See** "Frames," page **211**.

Communicating Between Frames

After you have created a series of frames by using the `<FRAMESET>` and `<FRAME>` tags, how do you use JavaScript to access and manipulate each frame? As mentioned in the preceding section, each frame is a separate `window` object. Therefore, if you can reference each frame, you can use the same techniques that were used with windows for each frame.

The Web Browser Object Model includes several properties that apply to frame and window objects that make referencing different frames much easier. These properties are the `self`, `window`, `parent`, and `top` properties. Their meanings are as follows:

- `self` or `window`— These properties are used to refer to the current window or frame.
- `parent`— This property is used to refer to the `window` or `frame` object that contains the current frame.
- `top`— This property is used to refer to the topmost `window` or `frame` object that contains the current frame.

Understanding the Frames Object Hierarchy

Consider a simple frameset created using the following HTML code:

```
<FRAMESET ROWS="50%,50%">
    <FRAMESET COLS="50%,50%">
        <FRAME SRC="Form.htm" NAME="MyFrame1">
        <FRAME SRC="Form.htm" NAME="MyFrame2">
    </FRAMESET>
    <FRAME SRC="Frameset2.htm" NAME="MyFrame3">
</FRAMESET>
```

This divides the window into three frames: two side-by-side on the top half of the window, and a third occupying the entire bottom half. The object model for this document will appear as shown in Figure 20.11.

FIGURE 20.11

Each frame is associated with a window object, and each can access and manipulate the others.

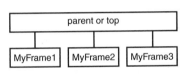

Given the object hierarchy shown in Figure 20.11, you would reference the `frame` objects as follows:

- To reference any of the child frames from the parent document, you could use `self.frame_name`. You could access the `document` object of the first frame, for example, through `self.MyFrame1.document`.
- To reference the parent document from any of the child frames, you could use `parent` or `top`. Any of the child frames could access the `document` object of the parent document, for example, through `parent.document`.

> **CAUTION**
> Whenever possible, you should use `parent` rather than `top` because `parent` always refers to the immediate parent of the frame in question. You can use `top` to refer to the topmost parent containing your frame. If your document is included as a frame in someone else's HTML document, however, it is likely that your reference to `top` will result in an error.

- To reference a child frame from another child frame, you would just combine the two already discussed in this list. The `document` object of the second frame, for instance, could be accessed by either of the other child frames through `parent.MyFrame2.document`.

Now, what if you introduce another generation to your framed document? The third frame might load an HTML document that itself contains a `<FRAMESET>` tag to further divide the window into more frames, as in the following:

```
<FRAMESET COLS="33%,33%,*">
    <FRAME SRC="Form.htm" NAME="MyFrame1">
    <FRAME SRC="Form.htm" NAME="MyFrame2">
    <FRAME SRC="Form.htm" NAME="MyFrame3">
</FRAMESET>
```

This would result in the object hierarchy shown in Figure 20.12.

FIGURE 20.12

Through multiple framesets, it is possible to produce an intricate hierarchy of `frame` objects.

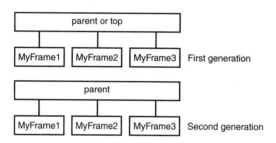

This would result in a window showing a total of five frames. The top half of the window would show two frames, part of the first generation of `frame` objects. The bottom half of the window would show three frames, part of the second generation of `frame` objects. The following examples show you ways to reference the `document` object of the different generations of frames and parent framesets:

- Reference first-generation `MyFrame1` document object from topmost parent:

  `self.MyFrame1.document`

- Reference second-generation `MyFrame1` document object from topmost parent:

  `self.MyFrame3.MyFrame1.document`

- Reference first-generation `MyFrame1` document object from the first-generation frame (`MyFrame2`) or the second-level parent (`MyFrame3`):

  `parent.MyFrame1.document`

- Reference first-generation `MyFrame1` document object from any of the second-generation frames:

  `parent.parent.MyFrame1.document`, or

  `top.MyFrame1.document`

■ Reference second-generation MyFrame1 document object from any of the other second-generation frames:

```
parent.MyFrame1.document
```

Multiple Frame Access Example

Listings 20.12 through 20.14 show an example of the kind of multiple frame, multiple generation frame setup discussed in the preceding section. Notice that a few things from this example demonstrate the object-oriented nature of JavaScript, which gives you the flexibility to accomplish multiple things.

■ The same HTML document is loaded into each of the five frames that results from this example. Thus, each form element has the same name. Because of the object hierarchy that results from the multiple frames, however, it is possible to uniquely specify each element.

■ Likewise, both the first and second-generation frames are given the same names. Again, the object hierarchy enables the frames to be uniquely addressed, accessed, and manipulated.

Listing 20.12   Frameset1.htm—Top-level Frameset

```
<HTML>
<HEAD>
<TITLE>Frameset1.htm</TITLE>
</HEAD>
<FRAMESET ROWS="50%,50%">
   <FRAMESET COLS="50%,50%">
      <FRAME SRC="Form.htm" NAME="MyFrame1">
      <FRAME SRC="Form.htm" NAME="MyFrame2">
   </FRAMESET>
   <FRAME SRC="Frameset2.htm" NAME="MyFrame3">
</FRAMESET>
</HTML>
```

Listing 20.13   Frameset2.htm—Second Generation Frameset

```
<HTML>
<HEAD>
<TITLE>Frameset2.htm</TITLE>
</HEAD>
<FRAMESET COLS="33%,33%,*">
   <FRAME SRC="Form.htm" NAME="MyFrame1">
   <FRAME SRC="Form.htm" NAME="MyFrame2">
   <FRAME SRC="Form.htm" NAME="MyFrame3">
</FRAMESET>
</HTML>
```

Part

IV

Ch

20

Listing 20.14 *Form.htm*—HTML Document to Be Included in Each Frame

```
<HTML>
<HEAD>
<TITLE>Form.htm</TITLE>
</HEAD>
<BODY BGCOLOR=#FFFFFF>
<CENTER>
<TABLE>
<FORM NAME="MyForm">
<TR><TD>
    <INPUT TYPE=TEXT NAME="MyText1"
       onChange="self.document.MyForm.MyText4.value =
          document.MyForm.MyText1.value">
    </TD></TR>
<TR><TD>
    <INPUT TYPE=TEXT NAME="MyText2"
       onChange="parent.MyFrame2.document.MyForm.MyText4.value =
          document.MyForm.MyText2.value">
    </TD></TR>
<TR><TD>
    <INPUT TYPE=TEXT NAME="MyText3"
       onChange="top.MyFrame2.document.MyForm.MyText4.value =
          document.MyForm.MyText3.value">
    </TD></TR>
<TR><TD>
<INPUT TYPE=TEXT NAME="MyText4">
    </TD></TR>
</FORM>
</TABLE>
<HR>
<CENTER>
<ADDRESS>
Jim O'Donnell, <A HREF="mailto:odonnj@rpi.edu">odonnj@rpi.edu</A>
</ADDRESS>
</BODY>
</HTML>
```

The HTML form specified in the document shown in Listing 20.14 has small JavaScript functions attached to the onChange events of each of the first three text elements. The first copies any entered text into the fourth text element of the current frame. The second copies entered text into the fourth text element of the parent's MyFrame2 frame. The third copies entered text into the fourth text element of the grandparent's MyFrame2 frame.

Figure 20.13 shows how this works when text is entered into the first of the second-generation frames. Line 1 is copied into line 4 in the same frame. Line 2 is copied into line 4 of the second of the second-generation frames. Line 3 is copied into line 4 of the second of the first-generation frames.

Figures 20.14 and 20.15 show the effects of typing the same lines into the first three lines in one of the first-generation frames. Note that when line 3 is entered, it overwrites line 4 of the second of the first-generation frames. This is because parent refers to itself when you are already at the top level. Therefore, for first-generation frames, parent.parent and parent are equivalent.

FIGURE 20.13
Any frame can be accessed by scripts in any other frame in a multiple-frame document.

Text typed by the user in these fields

Appears here, here, and here

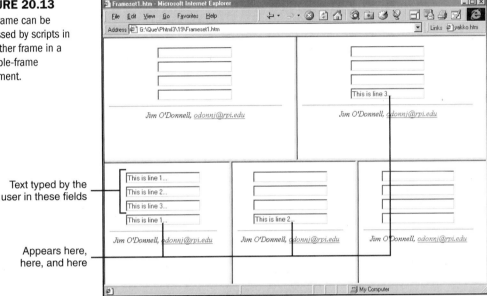

FIGURE 20.14
You can use HTML frames to solicit input from the user and then use that input in other frames and windows.

Text typed by the user in these fields

Appears here and here

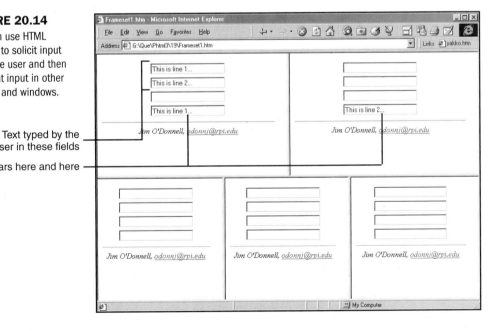

FIGURE 20.15

The parent and top properties of the frame or window object refer to themselves when you are already at the top level.

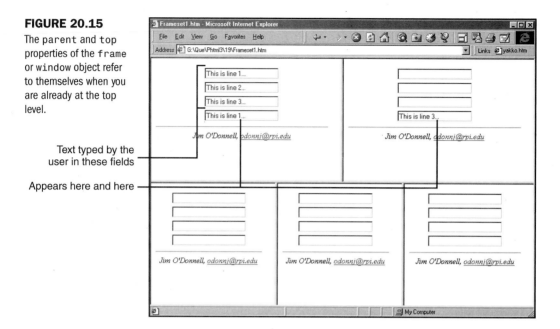

Text typed by the user in these fields

Appears here and here

Using Hidden Frames

You can build frame-based pages another way, too—by placing all the HTML and JavaScript code that you don't want changed into a hidden frame. Depending on the Web browser your users are using to look at your site and how you specify the borders of your frames, this frame may not actually be completely invisible. It might appear as a tiny space with one or two borders shown on it. To specify a hidden frame, add another frame to your frameset, but make sure the other frames take up all the available space. If you are using two frames, for example, as in the following:

```
<FRAMESET ROWS="50%,50%">
   <FRAME NAME="MyFrame1" SRC="Frame1.htm">
   <FRAME NAME="MyFrame2" SRC="Frame2.htm">
</FRAMESET>
```

you could add a hidden frame this way:

```
<FRAMESET ROWS="50%,50%,*">
   <FRAME NAME="MyFrame1" SRC="Frame1.htm">
   <FRAME NAME="MyFrame2" SRC="Frame2.htm">
   <FRAME NAME="MyHidden" SRC="Hidden.htm">
</FRAMESET>
```

With this, the first two frames take up 100% of the page, which means that the last frame will be made as small as the browser can make it. You can then place the JavaScript code that you wish to persist in the hidden HTML document and use the techniques shown in this chapter to manipulate the contents of the other frames in the document.

JavaScript Frames Example

In this frames example, you will see how to set up a Web page that is roughly equivalent to the windows example shown earlier in this chapter. A Web page will be created with three frames; the top one will have buttons that use attached JavaScripts to change the contents of the other two. Listing 20.15 shows the main document, which simply defines the frameset to be used.

Listing 20.15 *FramEx.htm*—The Main Document of a Framed Web Page Will Usually Be Pretty Simple, Just Setting Up the Frameset

```
<HTML>
<HEAD>
<TITLE>JavaScript Frames Example</TITLE>
</HEAD>
<FRAMESET ROWS="25%,*">
   <FRAME SRC="Buttons.htm" NAME="MyFrameBut">
   <FRAMESET COLS="200,*">
      <FRAME SRC="" NAME="MyFramePic">
      <FRAME SRC="" NAME="MyFrameBio">
   </FRAMESET>
</FRAMESET>
</HTML>
```

As shown in Listing 20.15, the only HTML document loaded initially is Buttons.htm, which loads the buttons into the top frame used to manipulate the other two (see Figure 20.16). This file is listed in Listing 20.16; it is similar to the buttons used in the window example. No buttons are needed to open and close the windows (or frames, in this case) because the frames already exist. Also, the contents of the frames are manipulated using the location.href property of the parent.MyFramePic and parent.MyFrameBio objects, respectively, as shown in Figure 20.17.

Listing 20.16 *Buttons.htm*—Frames and Windows Can Both Be Easily Controlled Using JavaScript

```
<HTML>
<HEAD>
<TITLE>Buttons.htm</TITLE>
<SCRIPT LANGUAGE="JavaScript">
<!-- Hide this script from incompatible Web browsers!
var n = 0;
function loadnex() {
   n++;
   if (n > 5) n = 5;
   picname = "Pic" + n + ".htm";
   bioname = "Bio" + n + ".htm";
   if (n == 5) bioname = "Bio5f.htm";
//
   parent.MyFramePic.location.href = picname;
```

continues

Part
IV

Ch
20

FIGURE 20.16

Frames can be created with nothing in them initially, then subsequently filled using targeted links or JavaScript.

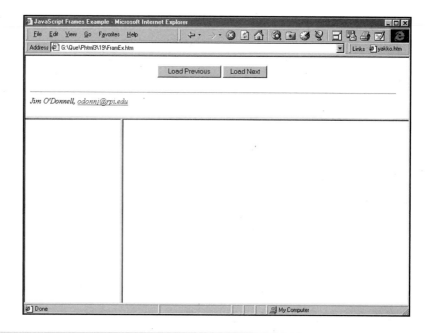

Listing 20.16   Continued

```
    parent.MyFrameBio.location.href = bioname;
}
function loadpre() {
    n--;
    if (n < 1) n = 1;
    picname = "Pic" + n + ".htm";
    bioname = "Bio" + n + ".htm";
//
    parent.MyFramePic.location.href = picname;
    parent.MyFrameBio.location.href = bioname;
}
//   Hide script from incompatible browsers! -->
</SCRIPT>
</HEAD>
<BODY BGCOLOR=#FFFFFF>
<FORM NAME="MyForm">
<CENTER>
<TABLE>
<TR><TD><INPUT TYPE="button" NAME="PreBut" VALUE="Load Previous"
        onClick="loadpre()"></TD>
    <TD><INPUT TYPE="button" NAME="NexBut" VALUE="Load Next"
        onClick="loadnex()"></TD>
</TR>
</TABLE>
</CENTER>
</FORM>
<HR>
<ADDRESS>
```

```
Jim O'Donnell, <A HREF="mailto:odonnj@rpi.edu">odonnj@rpi.edu</A>
</ADDRESS>
</BODY>
</HTML>
```

FIGURE 20.17

The use of frames and JavaScript enables multiple views to be used to present coordinated information.

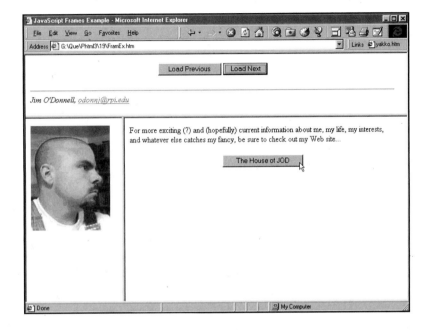

It is interesting to note that the same HTML documents for the pictures and biographies can be used in this example as in the preceding window example. The only exception to this is the final biography entry, which provides a link to an outside document that will replace the entire frameset. This document is shown in Listing 20.17 and uses the `location.href` property of the parent object to do this (see Figure 20.18).

Part

IV

Ch

20

Listing 20.17 *Bio5f.htm*—**Each of the Frames Can Manipulate the Others or Load a Completely New Document**

```
<HTML>
<HEAD>
<TITLE>Bio5.htm</TITLE>
<SCRIPT LANGUAGE="JavaScript">
<!-- Hide this script from incompatible Web browsers!
function loadmain() {
    parent.location.href="http://www.rpi.edu/~odonnj"
}
//  Hide script from incompatible browsers! -->
</SCRIPT>
</HEAD>
<BODY BGCOLOR=#FFFFFF>
```

continues

Listing 20.17 Continued

```
For more exciting (?) and (hopefully) current information about me, my life, my
interests, and whatever else catches my fancy, be sure to check out my Web
site...
<FORM NAME="MyForm">
<CENTER>
<TABLE>
<TR><TD><INPUT TYPE="button" VALUE="The House of JOD"
        onClick="loadmain()"></TD>
</TR>
</TABLE>
</CENTER>
</FORM>
</BODY>
</HTML>
```

FIGURE 20.18

Make sure your documents that use frames close down cleanly when they are done.

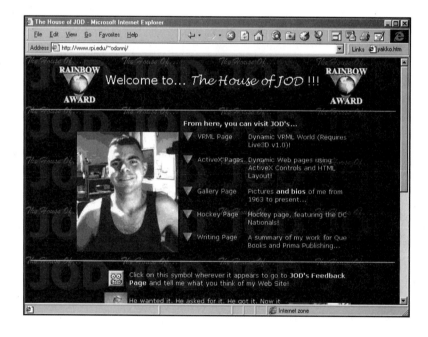

## CHAPTER 21

Using JavaScript to Create Smart Forms

by Jim O'Donnell

In this chapter

Client-Side Form Validation

One of the most common tasks for JavaScripting is to do form validation. Many Web applications need to gather input from users. Traditionally, this data is entered in the browser and then transmitted to the server. The server checks the validity of the data and either stores the data on the server or sends back a message requesting additional information or asking the user to enter valid data. Not only does this slow down your Web server, but it creates unnecessary Web traffic as well. With just a few lines of code, you can validate much of this data on the client's machine and send it to the server only after it is complete. Of course, you still need to completely validate data on the server as well, because people still use browsers that either don't support JavaScript or they have it turned off.

This chapter discusses ways of using JavaScript to make your HTML forms smarter. First, a few examples give you some ideas on how to use JavaScript to prefill, validate, and format HTML form elements. After that, the discussion focuses on how you can make sure a credit card number is well formed—obviously, it is not possible to truly validate a credit card number at the client, but it is possible to determine whether the number is a valid format. Finally, this chapter reviews a couple of collections of JavaScript form validation scripts that are freely available on the Web. These should get you well on your way to adding form validation to your Web pages.

HTML Form Text Field Validation and Formatting with JavaScript

Listing 21.1 is an example of a traditional HTML page used to gather input from a user. Take a closer look at a few of the elements of this page.

Listing 21.1   *Form.htm*—An HTML Document Using a Standard HTML Form

```
<HTML>
<HEAD>
<TITLE>Forms Verification</TITLE>
</HEAD>
<BODY BGCOLOR="#FFFFFF">
<H1>Credit Card Payment Information</H1>
<HR>
<B>All information must be entered before the form can be submitted...</B>
<HR>
<FORM NAME="MyForm">
<TABLE>
<TR><TD>First Name:</TD>
    <TD> </TD>
    <TD><INPUT TYPE=TEXT NAME="FirstName" SIZE=21 VALUE=""></TD></TR>
<TR><TD>Last Name:</TD>
    <TD> </TD>
    <TD><INPUT TYPE=TEXT NAME="LastName"  SIZE=21 VALUE=""></TD></TR>
<TR><TD COLSPAN=4><HR></TD></TR>
```

```
<TR><TD>Payment Date:</TD>
    <TD> </TD>
    <TD><INPUT TYPE=TEXT NAME="PayDate"    SIZE=10 VALUE=""></TD>
    <TD>(enter as mm/dd/yy)</TD></TR>
<TR><TD>Payment Amount:</TD>
    <TD><B>$</B></TD>
    <TD><INPUT TYPE=TEXT NAME="Amount"     SIZE=10 VALUE=""></TD></TR>
<TR><TD>Credit Card Number:</TD>
    <TD> </TD>
    <TD><INPUT TYPE=TEXT NAME="CCNumber"   SIZE=20 VALUE=""></TD>
    <TD>(must be 13 or 16 digits long)</TD></TR>
<TR><TD>Expiration Date:</TD>
    <TD> </TD>
    <TD><INPUT TYPE=TEXT NAME="ExpDate"    SIZE=10 VALUE=""></TD>
    <TD>(enter as mm/dd/yy)</TD></TR>
</TABLE>
<HR>
<INPUT TYPE=SUBMIT NAME="MySubmit" SIZE=20 VALUE="SUBMIT INFORMATION">
</FORM>
<HR>
<ADDRESS>
Jim O'Donnell, <A HREF="mailto:odonnj@rpi.edu">odonnj@rpi.edu</A>
</ADDRESS>
</BODY>
</HTML>
```

This HTML document, when viewed in Netscape Navigator, appears as shown in Figure 21.1.

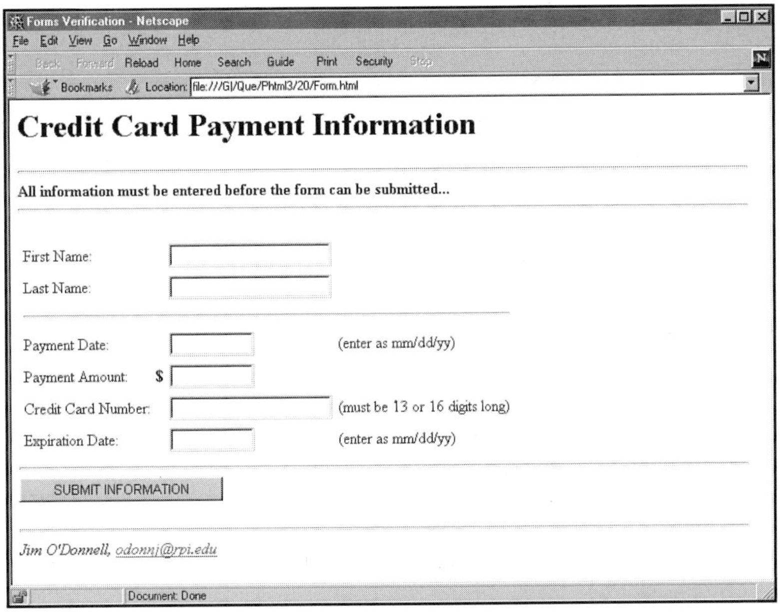

FIGURE 21.1
You can use standard
HTML Forms elements
to set up a document
for receiving user input.

Part
IV

Ch

21

The different elements of the HTML document, as shown in Listing 21.1, are as follows:

- ▮ `<FORM>...</FORM>` tags—These are the container tags that must surround the HTML Forms input elements. The `NAME="MyForm"` attribute is used to help identify the form from which that data came when the form is being processed. You might notice that neither the `METHOD` nor the `ACTION` attribute for the `<FORM>` tag has been sent. This is because this form is being used as an example. Normally you would set `METHOD=POST`, and set the `ACTION` to the appropriate URL of where on your Web server you want the data to be sent.

- ▮ `<INPUT TYPE=TEXT>` tags—Each of these tags is used to receive one piece of information from the user. Each is named, using the `NAME` attribute, to enable the resulting data to be identified.

- ▮ `<INPUT TYPE=SUBMIT>` tag—This tag puts the button on the form used to submit it. Like the other elements, it is named using the `NAME` attribute, and the `VALUE` attribute is used to customize the text appearing on the button.

▶ **See** "Creating Forms," page **234**.

Scripting HTML Form Text Fields

HTML documents can include JavaScripts to perform a variety of client-side scripting functions to validate elements of the form before it is submitted to the Web server. Note that not all the form validation can be done at the client—for instance, for this example you would definitely need to validate the payment information at the server—but some of the simpler things definitely can be done.

> **CAUTION**
>
> This is meant to be an illustrative example designed to show some of the types of user input that can be validated using JavaScript at the client. It is not meant to be a realistic example of how to implement a Web-based payment system. If you want to do that, a lot of concerns exist with security and validation of payment information that are not addressed here. However, you can find some of this information elsewhere in this book.

A couple of ways enable you to validate the information entered into a form. For text fields, the best way to do it is as you go. By calling a JavaScript from the `onChange` method of the HTML Form text field, you can validate the data entered into a field any time it has changed. An example of the syntax used to do this follows:

```
<INPUT TYPE=TEXT NAME="PayDate" SIZE=10 VALUE=""
     onChange="checkDate(document.MyForm.PayDate)">
```

In this example, whenever the information in the text field named `PayDate` is changed, the JavaScript `checkDate()` function is called. The argument of the `checkDate()` function, in this case, is the text field object (assuming that the name of the form is `MyForm`).

Prefilling Entries

The only apparent change from the unscripted to scripted version of this example in Figure 21.2 is that the payment date has been prefilled. Because an obvious default entry exists for this field—the current date—it makes sense to enable JavaScript to do this and save the user a little bit of effort. This is done by executing the JavaScript statements shown in Listing 21.2 when the document is loaded:

Listing 21.2   *FormScr.htm* (excerpt)—Prefilling Entries Makes Your Pages Easier to Use and Less Error Prone

```
//
////////////////////////////////////////////////////////////////////////////
//
// This function formats a date as mm/dd/yy.
//
function formatDate(dateVar) {
   newDate = dateVar.toLocaleString()
   newDate = newDate.substring(0,newDate.indexOf(" "))
   return newDate
}
//
// Prefill payment date with current date
//
today = new Date()
document.MyForm.PayDate.value = formatDate(today)
```

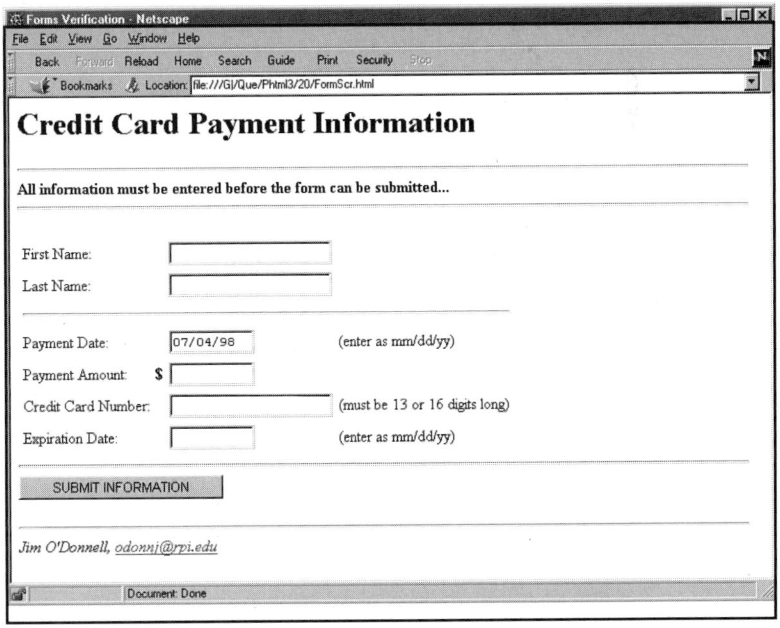

FIGURE 21.2

Other than having the payment date entry prefilled, this JavaScripted form doesn't look very different from the unscripted version.

```
Forms Verification - Netscape                                          _ □ ×
File  Edit  View  Go  Window  Help
  Back   Forward  Reload   Home   Search   Guide   Print   Security   Stop        N
    Bookmarks    Location: file:///G|/Que/Phtml3/20/FormScr.html                   ▼
```

Credit Card Payment Information

All information must be entered before the form can be submitted...

First Name: [   ]

Last Name: [   ]

Payment Date: [07/04/98]   (enter as mm/dd/yy)

Payment Amount: $ [   ]

Credit Card Number: [   ] (must be 13 or 16 digits long)

Expiration Date: [   ] (enter as mm/dd/yy)

[SUBMIT INFORMATION]

Jim O'Donnell, odonnj@rpi.edu

```
            Document: Done
```

> **N O T E** The complete listings of this HTML document and all the other documents used in this chapter are on the accompanying CD-ROM in the file named `FormScr.htm`. ■

The `today` variable is set equal to a JavaScript `Date` object containing the current date. The `formatDate()` function takes a `Date` object as an argument and returns a string with the date in the format "mm/dd/yy".

Note that the user can change this entry, picking a payment date that is after the current date. You might not want to allow the user to select a payment date prior to the current date, however—if his payment is late, for instance, you don't want him to be able to "predate his check." You can easily prevent this with JavaScript, as will be shown later in this chapter.

Formatting Proper Name Entries

Listing 21.3 shows the JavaScript function `capitalizeName()`. This function formats a proper name entry by capitalizing the first letter. This is not terribly important to do as forms validation topics go, but it is a nicety. Another feature of this function (included here because of personal bias), is that it also capitalizes the letter immediately following an apostrophe.

Listing 21.3 *FormScr.htm* (excerpt)—JavaScript Subroutine to Format Proper Name Entries

```
//
// This function capitalizes proper names; it also capitalizes the
// letter after the apostrophe, if one is present
//
function capitalizeName(Obj) {
//
// Set temp equal to form element string
//
    temp  = new String(Obj.value)
    first = temp.substring(0,1)
    temp  = first.toUpperCase() + temp.substring(1,temp.length)
    apnum = temp.indexOf("'")
    if (apnum > -1) {
       aplet = temp.substring(apnum+1,apnum+2)
       temp  = temp.substring(0,apnum) + "'" +
               aplet.toUpperCase() +
               temp.substring(apnum+2,temp.length)
    }
    Obj.value = temp
}
```

Validating and Formatting Currency Entries

Listing 21.4 shows the JavaScript function `checkAmount()`. This function validates and formats an entry meant to be an amount of money. Primarily, this entry needs to be a numeric value, but it is a little more forgiving than that; it will remove a leading dollar sign if the user has put one in. Then, after making sure that the value is numeric, the subroutine formats it as dollars and cents and writes it back out to the form field from which it came.

Listing 21.4 *FormScr.htm* (excerpt)—JavaScript Subroutine to Validate and Format Currency

```
//
/////////////////////////////////////////////////////////////////////////
//
// This function checks to see if the value of the object that is
// passed to it is a valid currency, and then formats it.
//
function checkAmount(Obj) {
//
// Set temp equal to form element string
//
   temp = new String(Obj.value)
//
// Remove leading $, if present
//
   temp = temp.substring(temp.indexOf("$")+1,temp.length)
//
// Convert into a floating point number and format as dollars
// and cents
//
   temp = parseFloat(temp)
   temp = Math.floor(100*temp)/100
   temp = String(temp)
   if (temp.indexOf(".") == -1) {
      temp = temp + ".00"
   }
   if (temp.indexOf(".") == temp.length -2) {
      temp = temp + "0"
   }
//
// If zero value, make blank
//
   if (temp == "0.00") {
      temp = ""
   }
//
// Write back out to the form element
//
   Obj.value = temp
}
```

If you are not familiar with JavaScript, you might be confused a little by the checkAmount() function because it seems to treat the same variable alternatively as a number or as a string. Because JavaScript enables its variables to have their types changed dynamically, you can use the same variable to store any kind of data that JavaScript recognizes. JavaScript generally treats data as the subtype—such as integer, floating point, or string—appropriate to the operation.

As a final note, you see that for an entry incorrectly formatted, `checkAmount()` will blank the entry. How your JavaScripts respond to incorrect entries is up to you. You can remove the incorrect entry—as is done in this example—leave it but set an error flag that prevents the form from being submitted until it is corrected, bring up an Alert box, or anything else you would like to do.

Validating and Formatting Date Entries

The `checkDate()`, shown in Listing 21.5, is similar to `checkAmount()`, except that it validates a correct date entry rather than amount. If the user inputs the date as requested, in the form `mm/dd/yy`, this value can be passed to the JavaScript `Date` object, which will return a valid `Date` object with that date; then the `formatDate()` function can be called to format the date as desired.

Listing 21.5   *FormScr.htm* **(excerpt)—JavaScript Subroutine to Validate and Format Date**

```
//
////////////////////////////////////////////////////////////////////
//
// This function checks to see if the value of the object that is
// passed to it is a valid date, and then formats it.
//
function checkDate(Obj) {
//
// Grab the form element value and, if it's a valid date, format
// it as mm/dd/yy
//
    temp = new Date(Obj.value)
    temp = formatDate(temp)
//
// If it's not a valid date, assume that it's mm/dd and create a
// valid date by appending the current year to it
//
    if (temp == "Invalid") {
//
//    Parse out the month, subtracting one because JavaScript months
//    are numbered from 0 to 11
//
        temp  = Obj.value
        month = temp.substring(0,temp.indexOf("/")) - 1
//
//    Parse out the day of the month
//
        day = temp.substring(temp.indexOf("/")+1,temp.length)
//
//    Find the current year from today's date
//
        today = new Date()
        today = formatDate(today)
        year  = today.substring(6,8)
```

```
//
//    Create a date object from the year, month, and day, and
//    format it as mm/dd/yy; if this date is still invalid,
//    then the string "Invalid" will be displayed in the form
//    element
//
      temp = new Date(year,month,day)
      temp = formatDate(temp)
   }
//
// Write back out to the form element
//
   Obj.value = temp
}
```

Unfortunately, JavaScript's Date object is not smart enough to correctly interpret a date argument entered as mm/dd; you would like it to append the current year. The checkDate() function looks for dates entered as mm/dd and appends the current year to them.

If the information entered into a date field cannot be interpreted as a valid date, this function places the string Invalid in the field.

Validating Numeric Entries

Even if it would be possible to do so, you would probably not want to verify a credit card number on the client, for reasons of account security. You can perform a little bit of validation on the numeric credit card number entry, however, before the form data is sent along for final validation at the Web server. checkCCNumber(), shown in Listing 21.6, makes sure that this entry is numeric and is a proper length for a credit card number (defined here as either 13 or 16 digits, although this can be adjusted if necessary). It also formats a valid number and redisplays it; for example, a 16-digit number displays formatted as in 1234 5678 1234 5678. Like the checkDate() function, this function also puts the string Invalid in the field if the number entered is not valid.

Listing 21.6 *FormScr.htm* **(excerpt)—JavaScript Subroutine to Validate Numerical Entry**

```
//
///////////////////////////////////////////////////////////////////////
//
// This subroutine checks to see if the value of the object that is
// passed to it is a valid credit card number.
//
// Specify minimum and maximum length of valid credit card numbers
//
minLength = 13
maxLength = 16
//
function checkCCNumber(Obj) {
```

Part
IV

Ch
21

continues

Listing 21.6 Continued

```
//
// Get object value
//
   temp = Obj.value
//
// Remove all embedded spaces to make sure the credit card
// number is the right length (either minLength of maxLength
// digits long)
//
   while (temp.indexOf(" ") > -1) {
      temp = temp.substring(0,temp.indexOf(" ")) +
             temp.substring(temp.indexOf(" ")+1,temp.length)
   }
//
// Add back embedded spaces in the appropriate spots for
// valid length numbers, else return "Invalid"
//
   if (temp.length == minLength)
      temp = temp.substring( 0, 4) + " " +
             temp.substring( 4, 7) + " " +
             temp.substring( 7,10) + " " +
             temp.substring(10,13)
   else if (temp.length == maxLength)
      temp = temp.substring( 0, 4) + " " +
             temp.substring( 4, 8) + " " +
             temp.substring( 8,12) + " " +
             temp.substring(12,16)
   else
      temp = "Invalid"
//
// Write back out to the form element
//
   Obj.value = temp
}
```

You will notice that the minLength and maxLength variables are defined in the preceding listing outside of the JavaScript checkCCNumber() function. This enables these variables to have a global scope, making them accessible outside of that function. In the HTML document, these variables are used to correctly print in the Web page itself the number of digits expected in the credit card number:

```
document.write("<TD>(must be " + minLength + " or " + maxLength +
               " digits long)</TD>")
```

N O T E Credit card numbers are not "random." Mathematical tests can be applied at the client-side to verify that a given number is "well formed"—in other words, that a given number can or cannot be a valid credit card number for a given type of card. The checkCCNumber() function checks only the length of the number. You can read about a function for verifying that a credit card number is well formed later in this chapter in the section, "Verifying Well-Formed Credit Card Numbers."

Validating Forms Before Submission

After all the information has been entered into the form and each individual entry has been validated, you might still want to perform some form-level checks before the form is submitted. You can do this in several ways. The most common way is to attach a JavaScript function to the onSubmit event of the Submit button (for example, with onSubmit="checkForm(document. MyForm)". If the function returns true, the form is submitted; if it returns false, it is not.

Another way to do the same thing is to attach a JavaScript function to a regular forms button—for example, onClick="checkForm(document.MyForm)". Then, if all the validation checks are passed, the submit() method of the HTML Form can be called to submit the form. This is how the checkForm() function, shown in Listing 21.7, is attached to the HTML Form in this example.

> **Listing 21.7** *FormScr.htm* **(excerpt)—JavaScript Function to Validate Form Prior to Submission**

```
//
///////////////////////////////////////////////////////////////////////////
//
// This function will verify that the current form is ready to
// be submitted before allowing it to be submitted
//
function checkForm(formObj) {
//
// Verify that all fields have valid information in them
//
   for (i = 0;i < formObj.length;i++)
      if (formObj.elements[i].value == "" |
          formObj.elements[i].value == "Invalid") {
         alert("All fields must be completed with valid "
               "information for submission!")
         formObj.elements[i].focus()
         return
      }
//
// Verify that the payment date is on or after the current date, and
// on or before the expiration date
//
   today   = new Date()
   today   = formatDate(today)
   today   = new Date(today)
   paydate = new Date(formObj.PayDate.value)
   expdate = new Date(formObj.ExpDate.value)
//
   if (paydate.getTime() < today.getTime()) {
      alert("Payment date must be on or after current date!")
      formObj.PayDate.focus()
      return
   }
```

Part

IV

Ch

21

continues

Listing 21.7 Continued

```
    if (paydate.getTime() > expdate.getTime()) {
        alert("Payment date must be on or before expiration date!")
        formObj.PayDate.focus()
        return
    }
//
// Submit form
//
    formObj.submit()
    alert("Form successfully submitted!")
}
```

The checkForm() function does three things. First, it verifies that valid information has been entered into each field on the form. Rather than referring to each form field by name, it does this by using the elements object array of the form object, with the following for loop:

```
for (i = 0;i < formObj.length;i++)
    if (formObj.elements[i].value == "" ¦
        formObj.elements[i].value == "Invalid") {
        alert("All fields must be completed " +
            "for submission!")
        formObj.elements[i].focus()
        return
    }
```

If all the fields are not completed, an Alert box appears (see Figure 21.3), the form is not submitted, and the focus is moved to the first empty field.

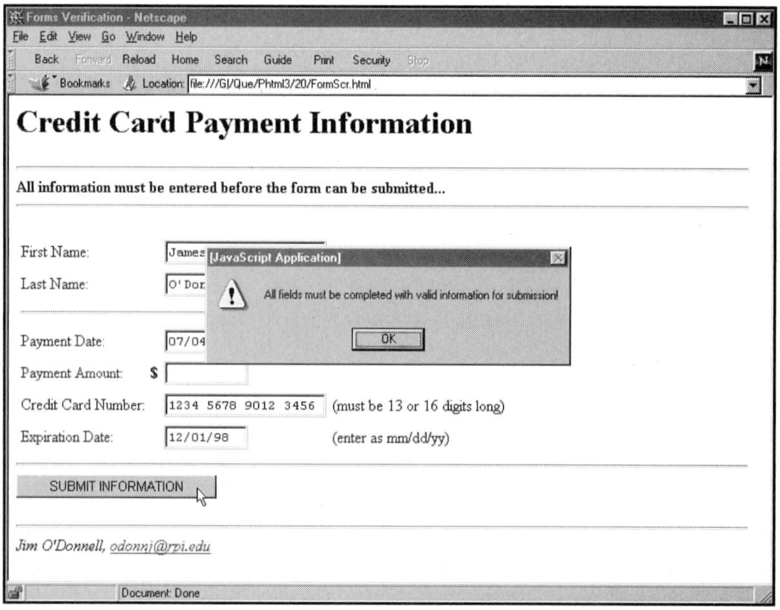

FIGURE 21.3
Client-side processing is ideal for catching situations, such as this incomplete form, prior to submission.

Even if the form is completely filled out and each of the entries has the correct type of data in it, problems still might exist that you can catch at the client with JavaScript. checkForm() also checks for two types of invalid entries that can occur with either the payment or credit card expiration date. It is incorrect if either the payment date is after the expiration date of the card or the payment date is before the current date. In either of these cases, an appropriate Alert box appears, as shown in Figure 21.4, and the form is not submitted.

FIGURE 21.4
You can save effort on your Web server by using scripting to catch simple errors, such as an expired credit card, at the client.

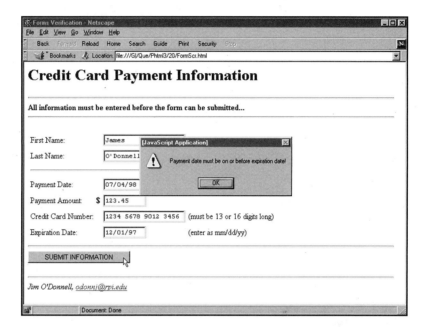

After all the entries in the form have been verified, it is then ready to be submitted to the Web server for further verification of the payment information. You can also use JavaScript to put up an Alert box that tells you that your information is on its way (see Figure 21.5).

Verifying Well-Formed Credit Card Numbers

The only way to completely verify the validity of a credit card number is through a Web server specifically set up to handle credit card transactions. However, you can apply some checks at the client-side, using JavaScript, that enable you to determine whether the number is well formed. A well-formed number is one that *could* be a valid number for that type of credit card. Passing the test for being well formed does not mean that the number is from a good credit card; failing the test, however, does mean that the number can't be from a good card.

You can apply two easy tests using JavaScript at the client-side. These tests enable you to determine whether a credit card number for a given card type is well formed. The first is to check the prefix (the first one to four numbers) and the length—each major credit card type has a given prefix and length. Second, most algorithms are encoded with a "check digit." This digit is added to the number and can also be determined from the rest of the digits in the card by using a simple algorithm. Therefore at the client-side, you can apply the algorithm to generate the check digit and compare it to the digit actually present. If they do not match, the number is not well formed.

FIGURE 21.5

After all the entries are validated at the client as much as possible, they can be submitted to processing at the server.

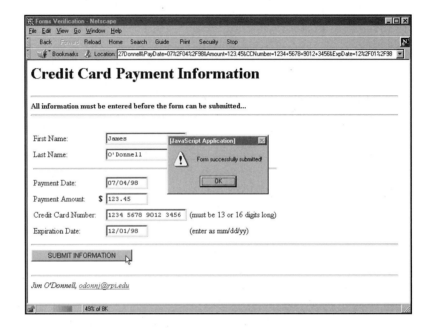

Checking Card Prefix and Length

Table 21.1 outlines the major credit cards you might want to validate, along with their allowed prefixes and lengths. (Note that the JCB card type has two entries because it is *either* 16 digits beginning with a 3 *or* 15 digits beginning with 2131 or 1800.)

Table 21.1   Major Credit Cards, Their Prefixes, and Lengths

Card Type	Prefixes	Length
MasterCard	51–55	16
VISA	4	13,16
American Express	34,37	15
Diner's Club, Carte Blanche	300–305,36,38	14
Discover	6011	16
enRoute	2114,2149	15
JCB	3	16
JCB	2131,1800	15

Validation Using the Luhn Algorithm

The algorithm used to validate the credit card number is known as the Luhn Algorithm, and it employs the following steps:

1. Double the value of alternating digits of the credit card number, beginning with the second digit from the right.

   Example: For the number 1234 5678 1234 5678

1	2	3	4	5	6	7	8	1	2	3	4	5	6	7	8
×2		×2		×2		×2		×2		×2		×2		×2	
2		6		10		14		2		6		10		14	

2. Add the separate digits of the products found in step 1 (10 yields the separate digits 1 and 0) along with all the credit card digits not used in step 1.

   Example: Products = 2+6+(1+0)+(1+4)+2+6+(1+0)+(1+4) = 28

   Unaffected Digits = 2+4+6+8+2+4+6+8 = 40

   Total = 28 + 40 = 68

The total found by following the preceding steps must be divisible by 10 (must end in 0) for it to be a well-formed credit card number.

Example: Total = 68. This number is *not* well formed.

If the original number in the preceding example had been

   1234 5678 1234 5670

the total would have worked out to be 60, and it would be well formed. This number would not have passed the complete well-formed test, however, because its prefix and length do not match any of the major credit cards shown in Table 21.1.

If you are planning on using JavaScript functions to verify that credit card numbers are well formed, you should have a set of sample numbers to use to verify that the functions are working correctly. (It is not a good idea to test these functions by using your own credit card numbers unless you are sure their information won't be accessible over the Web.) Table 21.2 shows a set of sample well-formed credit card numbers, available from the Netscape Web site. (The next section of this chapter discusses this Netscape site in more detail.)

Table 21.2—Sample Well-Formed Credit Card Numbers

Card Type	Sample Number
MasterCard	5500 0000 0000 0004
VISA	4111 1111 1111 1111
American Express	3400 0000 0000 009
Diner's Club or Carte Blanche	3000 0000 0000 04

continues

Table 21.2—Continued

Card Type	Sample Number
Discover	6011 0000 0000 0004
enRoute	2014 0000 0000 009
JCB	3088 0000 0000 0009

A number of freely available JavaScripts implement the test for a well-formed credit card number. You can find one of them, developed by Simon Tneoh, at the following URL:

http://www.tneoh.zoneit.com/javascript/cardobject.html

On the CD

A slightly altered version (to fix some minor typographical mistakes) of the CardType.js JavaScript source file available from this Web site is included with the accompanying CD-ROM. You can find it in the file named ChkCard.js. Listing 21.8 shows ChkCard.htm, an HTML document that makes use of this JavaScript source file to implement its credit card number tests.

Listing 21.8   *ChkCard.htm*—Checking for Well-Formed Credit Card Numbers Can Be the First Step in Validating Them; You Still Need to Verify Them on the Server

```
<HTML>
<HEAD>
<TITLE>Check for Well-Formed Credit Card Number</TITLE>
<SCRIPT LANGUAGE="JAVASCRIPT" src="ChkCard.js"></SCRIPT>
</HEAD>
<BODY BGCOLOR=#FFFFFF>
<CENTER>
<H1>Check for Well-Formed Credit Card Number</H1>
<HR>
</CENTER>
<FONT COLOR=#FF0000>Alert!
Please do not use a real card number and valid expiration date
to test. If you really want to do it, please check the source
first, make sure it will not submit the card number.
</FONT>
<CENTER>
<TABLE>
<FORM NAME="MyForm">
<TR><TD>Card Number:</TD>
    <TD><INPUT TYPE=TEXT NAME="CardNumber" SIZE=16 MAXLENGTH=19></TD></TR>
<TR><TD>Card Type:</TD>
    <TD><SELECT NAME="CardType">
            <OPTION VALUE="MasterCard">MasterCard
            <OPTION VALUE="VisaCard">Visa
            <OPTION VALUE="AmExCard">American Express
            <OPTION VALUE="DinersClubCard">Diners Club
            <OPTION VALUE="DiscoverCard">Discover
            <OPTION VALUE="enRouteCard">enRoute
```

```
                <OPTION VALUE="JCBCard">JCB
                <OPTION VALUE="LuhnCheckSum">Luhn Check Only
        </SELECT></TD></TR>
<TR><TD>Expiration Month:</TD>
    <TD><SELECT NAME="ExpMon">
                <OPTION VALUE=01>January
                <OPTION VALUE=02>February
                <OPTION VALUE=03>March
                <OPTION VALUE=04>April
                <OPTION VALUE=05>May
                <OPTION VALUE=06>June
                <OPTION VALUE=07>July
                <OPTION VALUE=08>August
                <OPTION VALUE=09>Septembet
                <OPTION VALUE=10>October
                <OPTION VALUE=11>November
                <OPTION VALUE=12 SELECTED>December
        </SELECT></TD></TR>
<TR><TD>Expiration Year:</TD>
    <TD><SELECT NAME="ExpYear">
                <OPTION VALUE=97 selected>1997
                <OPTION VALUE=98>1998
                <OPTION VALUE=99>1999
                <OPTION VALUE=00>2000
                <OPTION VALUE=01>2001
                <OPTION VALUE=02>2002
        </SELECT></TD></TR>
<TR><TD> </TD>
    <TD><INPUT TYPE=BUTTON VALUE="Check"
                OnClick="CheckCardNumber(document.MyForm)"></TD></TR>
</FORM>
</TABLE>
<HR>
</CENTER>
<ADDRESS>
Jim O'Donnell, <A HREF="mailto:odonnj@rpi.edu">odonnj@rpi.edu</A>
</ADDRESS>
</BODY>
</HTML>
```

The JavaScripts implement a number of tests. In addition to making sure that the expiration date entered has not passed, the credit card number entered is checked to see whether it is well formed. The JavaScript checks employ both the prefix and length text, as well as the Luhn Algorithm check digit test. Figure 21.6 shows the results of a well-formed credit card number of the card type selected.

As shown in Figure 21.7, the JavaScript tests are even smart enough to determine when a well-formed card number of a type other than the one selected has been entered. If the number is not a well-formed card number for any known type of card, an Alert box with that information appears (see Figure 21.8).

Part
IV

Ch
21

FIGURE 21.6

Both the check digit and prefix and length test need to pass to correctly identify the card number as well formed for the given type.

FIGURE 21.7

Using the prefix and length information, it is possible to automatically determine the type of a misidentified card.

FIGURE 21.8

If the check digit test is failed, the number cannot be a valid credit card number of any known type.

Netscape's Sample Form Validation Scripts

A veritable treasure trove of freely available JavaScripts for form validation is available from the Netscape Web site, available on the accompanying CD-ROM and also at the following URL:

```
http://developer.netscape.com/library/examples/javascript/formval/
overview.html
```

The JavaScript source file that you can download from that site is called FormChek.js. In addition, a number of sample HTML files show the functions in operation. The JavaScript functions defined there come under a number of general categories, as described in the header information in the FormChek.js file (summarized in the following sections).

Data Validation Functions

The purpose of these JavaScripts is to check strings and characters, normally those entered into HTML Form text fields. The functions can also be more generally applied to determine whether the strings are a given type of data. The basic functions are the following:

- isWhitespace(s)—Check whether string s is empty or whitespace.
- isLetter(c)—Check whether character c is an English letter.
- isDigit(c)—Check whether character c is a digit.
- isLetterOrDigit(c)—Check whether character c is a letter or digit.
- isInteger(s,ok_if_empty?)—True if all characters in string s are numbers.

Part
IV

Ch
21

- `isSignedInteger(s,ok_if_empty?)`—True if all characters in string s are numbers; leading + or - allowed.

- `isPositiveInteger(s,ok_if_empty?)`—True if string s is an integer > 0.

- `isNonnegativeInteger(s,ok_if_empty?)`—True if string s is an integer >= 0.

- `isNegativeInteger(s,ok_if_empty?)`—True if s is an integer < 0.

- `isNonpositiveInteger(s,ok_if_empty?)`—True if s is an integer <= 0.

- `isFloat(s,ok_if_empty?)`—True if string s is an unsigned floating point (real) number. (Integers also okay.)

- `isSignedFloat(s,ok_if_empty?)`—True if string s is a floating point or integer number; leading + or - allowed.

- `isAlphabetic(s,ok_if_empty?)`—True if string s is English letters.

- `isAlphanumeric(s,ok_if_empty?)`—True if string s is English letters and numbers only.

The preceding functions are used to build up more specialized data validation functions, as shown in the list below:

- `isSSN(s,ok_if_empty?)`—True if string s is a valid U.S. Social Security number.

- `isUSPhoneNumber(s,ok_if_empty?)`—True if string s is a valid U.S. phone number.

- `isInternationalPhoneNumber(s,ok_if_empty?)`—True if string s is a valid international phone number.

- `isZIPCode(s,ok_if_empty?)`—True if string s is a valid U.S. zip code.

- `isStateCode(s,ok_if_empty?)`—True if string s is a valid U.S. postal code.

- `isEmail(s,ok_if_empty?)`—True if string s is a valid email address.

- `isYear(s,ok_if_empty?)`—True if string s is a valid year number.

- `isIntegerInRange(s,a,b,ok_if_empty?)`—True if string s is an integer between a and b, inclusive.

- `isMonth(s,ok_if_empty?)`—True if string s is a valid month between 1 and 12.

- `isDay(s,ok_if_empty?)`—True if string s is a valid day between 1 and 31.

- `daysInFebruary(year)`—Returns number of days in February of that year.

- `isDate(year,month,day)`—True if string arguments form a valid date.

Data Formatting Functions

As you saw with the JavaScript example presented in the beginning of this chapter, it is often necessary or desirable to reformat information entered into the HTML Form text fields, either before processing it or afterward for redisplay. By doing this, it is possible to strip dollar signs or commas from entered currency amounts, format phone number or credit card numbers to display in a uniform way, or to perform any other function meant to manipulate data for processing or display. The following list identifies the JavaScripts available from the Netscape Web site for doing these functions:

- `stripCharsInBag(s,bag)`—Removes all characters in string `bag` from string `s`.
- `stripCharsNotInBag(s,bag)`—Removes all characters *not* in string `bag` from string `s`.
- `stripWhitespace(s)`—Removes all whitespace characters from `s`.
- `stripInitialWhitespace(s)`—Removes leading whitespace characters from `s`.
- `reformat(target,[string,integer,...])`—Function for inserting formatting characters or delimiters into target string.
- `reformatZIPCode(ZIPString)`—If 9 digits, inserts separator hyphen.
- `reformatSSN(SSN)`—Reformats as 123-45-6789.
- `reformatUSPhone(USPhone)`—Reformats as (123) 456-789.

User Prompting Functions

Other than soliciting the user for input in the HTML Form, it is possible to use the other methods and properties available to help the user correctly fill out the form. You can use Alert, Confirm, or Prompt boxes, for example, to inform the user of something or to solicit simple input. You can also make use of the status line at the bottom of the Web browser window. The following list identifies the JavaScript functions included in `FormChek.js` for doing this:

- `prompt(s)`—Display prompt string `s` in status bar.
- `promptEntry(s)`—Display data entry prompt string `s` in status bar.
- `warnEmpty(theField,s)`—Notify user that required field `theField` is empty.
- `warnInvalid(theField,s)`—Notify user that contents of field `theField` are invalid.

HTML Form Field Checking Functions

The following functions call some of the more basic functions previously described to directly check whether the contents of a given HTML form field contain valid data of the appropriate type:

- `checkString(theField,s,ok_if_empty?)`—Check that `theField.value` is not empty or all whitespace.
- `checkStateCode(theField)`—Check that `theField.value` is a valid U.S. state code.
- `checkZIPCode(theField,ok_if_empty?)`—Check that `theField.value` is a valid zip code.
- `checkUSPhone(theField,ok_if_empty?)`—Check that `theField.value` is a valid U.S. phone number.
- `checkInternationalPhone(theField,ok_if_empty?)`—Check that `theField.value` is a valid international phone number.
- `checkEmail(theField,ok_if_empty?)`—Check that `theField.value` is a valid email address.
- `checkSSN(theField,ok_if_empty?)`—Check that `theField.value` is a valid Social Security number.

- checkYear(theField,ok_if_empty?)—Check that theField.value is a valid year.
- checkMonth(theField,ok_if_empty?)—Check that theField.value is a valid month.
- checkDay(theField,ok_if_empty?)—Check that theField.value is a valid day.
- checkDate(yearField,monthField,dayField,labelString, OKtoOmitDay)—Check that field values form a valid date.
- getRadioButtonValue(radio)—Get checked value from radio button.
- checkCreditCard(radio,theField)—Validate credit card information.

Credit Card Validation Functions

Finally, Netscape's FormChek.js form validation script collection contains a full set of JavaScripts to check that credit card numbers are well formed for a given credit card. The following list identifies and describes these functions:

- isCreditCard(st)—True if credit card number passes the Luhn Algorithm test.
- isVisa(cc)—True if string cc is a valid VISA number.
- isMasterCard(cc)—True if string cc is a valid MasterCard number.
- isAmericanExpress(cc)—True if string cc is a valid American Express number.
- isDinersClub(cc)—True if string cc is a valid Diner's Club number.
- isCarteBlanche(cc)—True if string cc is a valid Carte Blanche number.
- isDiscover(cc)—True if string cc is a valid Discover card number.
- isEnRoute(cc)—True if string cc is a valid enRoute card number.
- isJCB(cc)—True if string cc is a valid JCB card number.
- isAnyCard(cc)—True if string cc is a valid card number for any of the accepted types.
- isCardMatch(Type,Number)—True if number is valid for credit card of type.

FormChek JavaScript Collection Example

Along with the FormChek.js JavaScript source file for forms validation, Netscape has a number of sample HTML documents that exercise the JavaScript functions. These functions, and the way they are implemented, provide a good example of ways to create smart HTML forms with JavaScript.

Figure 21.9 shows one of the sample HTML documents, which shows a partially filled-out form. Notice that the zip code and phone number have been formatted using a standard format. The data was not entered into those fields in that format—JavaScript functions were called to reformat and redisplay those fields in that standard format.

You should notice one other thing about Figure 21.9. Notice that the cursor is located in the Email field and that the status line of the Web browser window contains the text, "Please enter a valid email address (like foo@bar.com)." This is a way of providing context-sensitive help to your user with a JavaScript that sets the window.status property—and thus the contents of the current status line—to an informative string for the current field being entered. This is done using the onFocus event of each <INPUT> tag, as shown here:

```
<INPUT TYPE="text" NAME="Email" onFocus="promptEntry(pEmail)"
                    onChange="checkEmail(this,true)">
```

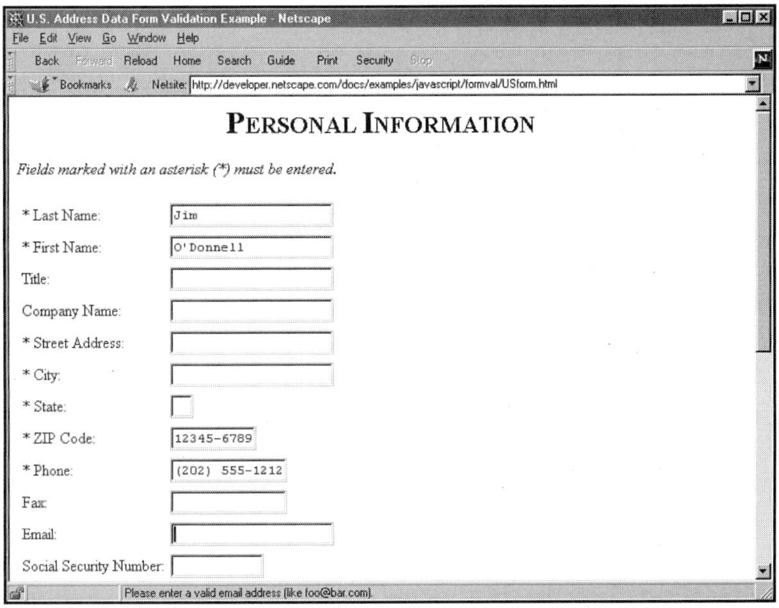

FIGURE 21.9
JavaScript can reformat your data to standardize the appearance of the information entered.

The onFocus event is triggered when the cursor enters the form field in question. When this happens, the preceding code calls the promptEntry() function, which is as follows:

```
function promptEntry(s) {
   window.status = pEntryPrompt + s
}
```

This function sets the status line to the passed string. (pEntryPrompt and pEmail are predefined global strings that, in this case, result in the status line shown in Figure 21.9.)

What about the other side of the equation? How does the entered information get validated? The onChange event triggers a call to the checkEmail() function, which is as follows:

```
function checkEmail(theField,emptyOK) {
   if (checkEmail.arguments.length == 1) emptyOK = defaultEmptyOK;
   if ((emptyOK == true) && (isEmpty(theField.value))) return true;
   else if (!isEmail(theField.value,false))
      return warnInvalid(theField,iEmail);
   else return true;
}
```

The checkEmail() function calls the isEmail() function with the contents of the Email field, which returns true or false, depending on whether it was found to be valid. If it was not valid, the warnInvalid() function is called, as shown in the following code, which displays the Alert box shown in Figure 21.10.

Part
IV

Ch

21

```
function warnInvalid(theField,s) {
    theField.focus()
    theField.select()
    alert(s)
    return false
}
```

FIGURE 21.10

The FormChek
JavaScript routines
display an Alert
immediately when an
invalid form field is
found.

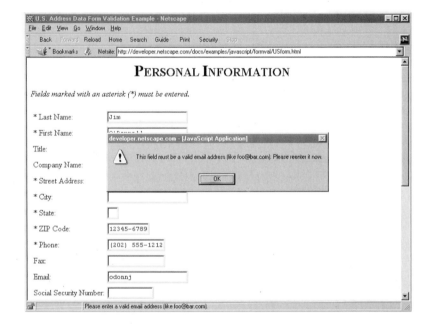

In addition to displaying the Alert box, `warnInvalid()` also does two other things: It moves the cursor to the field in question, using the `theField.focus()` method, and then selects the current contents of the field with `theField.select()`. This makes it easy for you to edit the contents of the field (see Figure 21.11).

The `FormChek` routines also include credit card validation functions that perform the same prefix, length, and check digit tests as those discussed earlier in this chapter. As shown in Figure 21.12, these routines are not quite as forgiving if you enter a valid number with the wrong card type.

When you attempt to submit the form, it calls a routine that checks to make sure that you have input valid data in all the required fields. If you have not, you get an alert box that tells you about the first such field, and the cursor is moved to that field (see Figure 21.13). When you have finally completed all required elements of the form correctly, you can successfully submit the form; in this sample program, the dynamically generated HTML document shown in Figure 21.14 results.

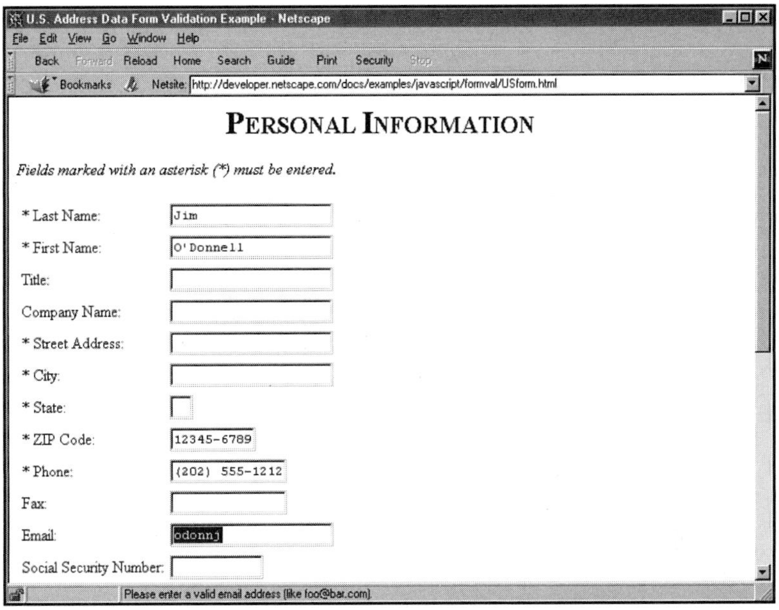

FIGURE 21.11

You can make it easy for your users to correct invalid fields by selecting the current contents.

FIGURE 21.12

If the credit card number you enter is not a valid number for the selected card type, you will receive this Alert box and be given the opportunity to re-enter the number.

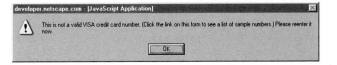

FIGURE 21.13

You can easily make any field in your form a required field and require your users to enter valid data there.

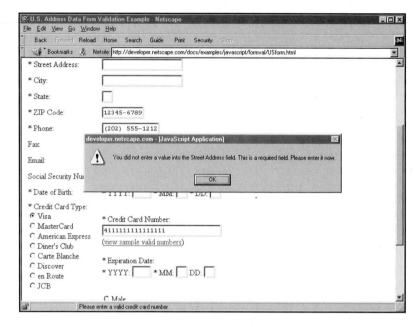

FIGURE 21.14

Upon successful completion of the form, its data can be submitted for processing.

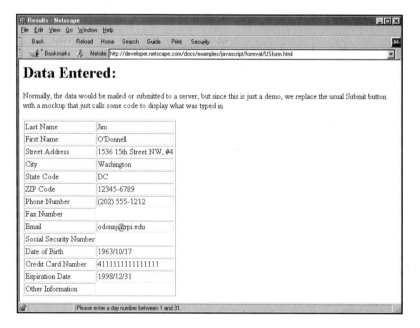

## CHAPTER 22

Cookies and State Maintenance

by Bill Chosiad and Jim O'Donnell

The Trouble with Stateless HTTP

Most Web servers have very short memories. When you request a page, the server usually doesn't really know who you are, what you entered on a form three pages ago, or whether this is your first visit to the site or your 75th. One of the challenges of using the Hypertext Transfer Protocol (HTTP) is that it doesn't track the state of your interactions with the server. State refers to any information about you or your visit to a Web site. It is maintained as you move from page to page within the site, and it may be used by the Web server or a JavaScript program (or both) to customize your experience at the site. But if HTTP doesn't maintain the state, what does?

This chapter shows you how to get around HTTP's limitations by using cookies, URL query string parameters, and hidden form variables. Although the bulk of this chapter deals with cookies, time is spent investigating other techniques, as well as where and how they may best be used.

Maintaining State

Maintaining state means remembering information while the user moves from page to page within a Web site. With this information in hand, you can set user preferences, fill in default form values, track visit counts, and do many other things that make browsing easier for users and that give you more information about how your pages are used.

You can maintain state information in a number of ways:

- Store it in cookies
- Encode it in URL links
- Send it in hidden form variables
- Store it in variables in other frames
- Store it on the Web server

Be aware, however, that some technical challenges regarding state maintenance can occur. While browsing a site, a user might suddenly zoom off to another Web site and return minutes, hours, or days later, only to find that any saved state information is out of date or has been erased. He or she might return by clicking the browser's Back button, by using a bookmark, or by typing in the URL directly, causing state information encoded in the URL to be overwritten or lost.

The Web developer must maintain state information regardless of whether the user navigates through the site using buttons on a form or a URL link on a page. This could mean adding information to both hidden form variables and every URL <A HREF...> tag that appears on the page.

With all these difficulties to overcome, these state maintenance mechanisms had better be useful. Luckily, they are. Many advantages exist to maintaining state, both within a single site visit and from one visit to the next. Consider the following scenarios:

- A shopping cart application. Users could browse through the site while selecting items and adding them to a virtual shopping cart. At any time, they can view the items in the cart, change the contents of their cart, or take the cart to the checkout counter for purchase. Keeping track of which user owns which shopping cart is essential.

- Custom home pages. Many Web sites have now set up home pages where users can customize what they see when they arrive. After giving the user a choice of layouts, color schemes, and favorite destinations, it stores the preferences on the user's own computer through the use of cookies. The user can return to the site any time and get the previously configured page.

- Frequent visitor bonuses. By storing information on the client computer, this application keeps track of how many times a browser has hit a particular page. When the user reaches a certain level of hits, he or she gets access to more or better services.

- Change banners. You can make graphic banners and text changes each time the user hits a page. This technique is often used to cycle through a list of advertisements.

- Bookmarks. Remember where a user was when he last visited the site. Was he reading a story, filling out a questionnaire, or playing a game? Let him pick up where he left off.

- Games. Remember current or high scores. Present new challenges based on past answers and performance.

Cookies: An Introduction

Cookies—sometimes called magic cookies, but more formally known as persistent client state HTTP cookies—enable you to store information on the client browser's computer for later retrieval. Although they have their drawbacks, cookies are the most powerful technique available for maintaining state within a Web site.

Netscape came up with the original cookie specification. There doesn't seem to be any good reason why Netscape chose that particular name. In fact, on their cookie specification page, they even admit that "the state object is called a cookie for no compelling reason."

In their simplest form, cookies store data in the form of name=value pairs. You, the developer, can pick any name and value combination you want. More advanced cookie features include the capability to set an expiration date and to specify what Web pages may see the cookie information.

Advantages of Cookies

One of the most powerful aspects of cookies is their persistence. When a cookie is set on the user's browser, it may persist for days, months, or even years. This makes it easy to save user preferences and visit information and keep this information available every time the user returns to your site.

Cookies prove especially helpful when used in conjunction with JavaScript. Because JavaScript has functions for reading, adding, and editing cookies, your JavaScript programs can use them to store global information about a user as she surfs through your Web site.

Limitations of Cookies

Some limitations of cookies could prove problematic. Cookies are stored on the user's computer, usually in a special cookie file. As with all files, this cookie file might be accidentally (or purposefully) deleted, taking all the browser's cookie information with it. The cookie file could be write protected, thus preventing any cookies from being stored there. Browser software may impose limitations on the size and number of cookies that may be stored, and newer cookies may overwrite older ones.

Because cookies are associated with a particular browser, problems come up if users switch from one browser to another. If you usually use Netscape Navigator and have a collection of cookies, they will no longer be available for you to use if you decide to switch to Microsoft Internet Explorer.

Finally, if several people use the same computer and browser, they might find themselves using cookies that belong to someone else. The reason for this is that cookie information is stored in a file on the computer, and the browser has no way to distinguish between multiple users.

Disadvantages of Cookies

Some problems, both real and imagined, also occur with the use of cookies. Because many browsers store their cookie information in an unencrypted text file, you should never store sensitive information, such as a password, in a cookie. Anyone with access to the user's computer could read it.

Newer Web browsers, such as the latest versions of Netscape Navigator and Microsoft Internet Explorer, have a feature that alerts the user every time an attempt is made to set a cookie. These browsers can even be configured to prevent cookies from being set at all. This sometimes results in confusion on the user's part when a dialog box informs her that something strange involving a cookie is happening to her computer. If cookies are disabled, your carefully designed Web application might not run at all.

Cookie Myths

The biggest problem facing cookies could be a psychological one. Some savvy Web users believe that all cookies are a tool used by "Big Brother" to violate their privacy. Considering that cookies are capable of storing information about where users have visited on a Web site, how many times they have been there, what advertising banners they have viewed, and what they have selected and placed on forms, some people think that their privacy is being invaded whenever a cookie gets set on their computer.

In reality, cookies are seldom used for these purposes. Although technically these things are possible, better and easier ways of getting the same type of information now exist without using cookies.

Other users complain about Web sites being able to write information to their computers and taking up space on their hard drives. This is somewhat true. Web browser software limits the total size of the cookies stored, as well as the amount of space that can go to the cookies of a particular Web site. Consider, however, that this number probably is small when compared to the size of the pages and graphic images that Web browsers routinely store in their page caches.

Other users are concerned that cookies set by one Web site might be read by other sites. This is completely untrue. Your Web browser software prevents this from happening by making cookies available only to the sites that created them.

If your users understand the usefulness of cookies, this "cookie backlash" shouldn't be a problem.

ON THE WEB

Netscape came up with the original cookie specification. You can find more information on the Netscape Web site at http://www.netscape.com/newsref/std/cookie_spec.html.

Using Cookies

By now you have considered the pros and cons of cookies and have decided that they are just what you need to make your JavaScript application a success.

This section discusses a number of handy functions for reading and setting cookies, which will help you make your Web sites smarter and more user friendly. Also included in this section are Internet references for finding additional information concerning cookies.

Retrieving Cookie Values

Cookie names and values are stored and set using the cookie property of the document object. To store the raw cookie string in a variable, you would use a JavaScript command such as the following:

```
var myCookie = document.cookie;
```

To display it on a Web page, use the following command:

```
document.write ("Raw Cookies: " + document.cookie + "<BR>");
```

JavaScript stores cookies in the following format:

```
name1=value1; name2=value2; name3=value3
```

Individual name=value pairs are separated by a semicolon and a blank space. No semicolon is used after the final value. To retrieve a particular cookie, you can use a JavaScript routine such as the one shown in Listing 22.1.

Listing 22.1 *FavList.htm* (excerpt)—JavaScript Function for Retrieving a Specific Cookie

```
// GetCookie - Returns the value of the specified cookie or null
//             if the cookie doesn't exist
//
function GetCookie(name) {
   var result = null;
   var myCookie = " " + document.cookie + ";";
   var searchName = " " + name + "=";
   var startOfCookie = myCookie.indexOf(searchName)
   var endOfCookie;
   if (startOfCookie != -1) {
      startOfCookie += searchName.length; // skip past cookie name
      endOfCookie = myCookie.indexOf(";",startOfCookie);
      result =
         unescape(myCookie.substring(startOfCookie,endOfCookie));
   }
   return result;
}
```

N O T E Most of the listings that will appear in this chapter are excerpts from the FavList.htm document that is discussed in the "A Cookie Example" section, later in this chapter. ■

In Listing 22.1, the myCookie string helps avoid annoying boundary conditions by making sure all cookie string names start with a space and end with a semicolon. From there, it is easy to find the start of the name= portion of the string, skip it, and retrieve everything from that point until the next semicolon.

Setting Cookie Values

The name=value combination is the minimum amount of information you need to set up a cookie. However, there may be more to cookies than just this. The complete list of parameters, which should be separated by a space and semicolon, that can be used to specify a cookie is as follows:

- name=value
- expires=date
- path=path
- domain=domainname
- secure

Cookie Names and Values The name and value can be anything you choose. In some cases, you might want it to be very explanatory, such as FavoriteColor=Blue. In other cases, it could just be code that the JavaScript program interprets, such as CurStat=1:2:1:0:0:1:0:3:1:1. In any case, the name and value are completely up to you.

In its simplest form, a routine to add a single name=value pair to a cookie looks like that shown in Listing 22.2.

Listing 22.2 *FavList.htm* (excerpt)—Adding Cookies Is Easy with JavaScript

```
// SetCookieEZ - Quickly sets a cookie which will last until the
//               user shuts down his browser
//
function SetCookieEZ(name,value) {
    document.cookie = name + "=" + escape(value);
}
```

Notice that the value is encoded using the JavaScript escape function. If there were a semicolon in the value string itself, it might prevent you from achieving the expected results. Using the escape function eliminates this problem.

Also notice that the document.cookie property works rather differently from most other properties. In most other cases, using the assignment operator (=) causes the existing property value to be completely overwritten with the new value. This is not the case with the cookie property. With cookies, each new name you assign is added to the active list of cookies. If you assign the same name twice, the second assignment replaces the first.

Some exceptions exist to this last statement, but these are explained in the section "Path" later in this chapter.

Expiration Date   The expires=date tells the browser how long the cookie will last. The cookie specification page at Netscape states that dates are in the form of

```
Wdy, DD-Mon-YY HH:MM:SS GMT
```

Here's an example:

```
Mon, 08-Jul-96 03:18:20 GMT
```

This format is based on Internet RFC 822, which you can find at http://www.w3.org/hypertext/WWW/Protocols/rfc822/#z28.

The only difference between RFC 822 and the Netscape implementation is that in Netscape Navigator, the expiration date must end with GMT (Greenwich Mean Time). Happily, the JavaScript language provides a function to do just that. By using the toGMTString() function, you can set cookies to expire in the near or distant future.

 TIP

Even though the date produced by the toGMTString() function doesn't match the Netscape specification, it still works under JavaScript.

If the expiration date isn't specified, the cookie remains in effect until the browser is shut down.

The following is a code segment that sets a cookie to expire in one week (where one week equals 7 days/week times 24 hours/day times 60 minutes/hour times 60 seconds/minute times 1000 milliseconds/second):

```
var name="foo";
var value="bar";
var oneWeek = 7 * 24 * 60 * 60 * 1000;
var expDate = new Date();
expDate.setTime(expDate.getTime() + oneWeek);
document.cookie = name + "=" + escape(value) + "; expires=" +
                  expDate.toGMTString();
```

Deleting a Cookie   To delete a cookie, set the expiration date to some time in the past—how far in the past doesn't generally matter. To be on the safe side, a few days ago should work fine. The following is a routine to delete a cookie, shown in Listing 22.3.

Listing 22.3   *FavList.htm* (excerpt)—Use the Cookie Expiration Date to Delete an Unwanted Cookie

```
// ClearCookie   - Removes a cookie by setting an expiration date
//                 three days in the past
//
function ClearCookie(name) {
   var ThreeDays = 3 * 24 * 60 * 60 * 1000;
   var expDate = new Date();
   expDate.setTime(expDate.getTime() - ThreeDays);
   document.cookie = name + "=ImOutOfHere; expires=" +
                     expDate.toGMTString();
}
```

When deleting cookies, it doesn't matter what you use for the cookie value—any value will do.

CAUTION

Some versions of Netscape do a poor job of converting times to GMT. Some common JavaScript functions for deleting a cookie consider the past to be one millisecond behind the current time. Although this is usually true, it doesn't work on all platforms. To be on the safe side, use a few days in the past to expire cookies.

Path   By default, cookies are available to other Web pages within the same directory as the page on which they were created. The Path parameter enables a cookie to be made available to pages in other directories. If the value of the Path parameter is a substring of a page's URL, cookies created with that path are available to that page. You could create a cookie, for example, with the following command:

```
document.cookie = "foo=bar1; path=/javascript";
```

This would make the cookie foo available to every page in the javascript directory and all those directories beneath it. If, instead, the command looked like this:

```
document.cookie = "foo=bar2; path=/javascript/sam";
```

the cookie would be available to sample1.html, sample2.html, sammy.exe, and so on.

Finally, to make the cookie available to everyone on your server, use the following command:

```
document.cookie = "foo=bar3; path=/";
```

What happens when a browser has multiple cookies on different paths but with the same name? Which one wins?

Actually, they all do. When this situation arises, it is possible to have two or more cookies with the same name but with different values. If a page issued all the commands listed previously, for example, its cookie string would look like the following:

```
foo=bar3; foo=bar2; foo=bar1
```

To help be aware of this situation, you might want to write a routine to count the number of cookie values associated with a cookie name. It might look like this:

```javascript
function GetCookieCount(name) {
   var result = 0;
   var myCookie = " " + document.cookie + ";";
   var searchName = " " + name + "=";
   var nameLength = searchName.length;
   var startOfCookie = myCookie.indexOf(searchName)
   while (startOfCookie != -1) {
      result += 1;
      startOfCookie = myCookie.indexOf(searchName,startOfCookie + nameLength);
   }
   return result;
}
```

Of course, if a GetCookieCount function exists, a GetCookieNum function should be available to retrieve a particular instance of a cookie. That function would look like this:

```javascript
function GetCookieNum(name,cookieNum) {
   var result = null;
   if (cookieNum >= 1) {
      var myCookie = " " + document.cookie + ";";
      var searchName = " " + name + "=";
      var nameLength = searchName.length;
      var startOfCookie = myCookie.indexOf(searchName);
      var cntr = 0;
      for (cntr = 1; cntr < cookieNum; cntr++)
         startOfCookie = myCookie.indexOf(searchName,startOfCookie + nameLength);
      if (startOfCookie != -1) {
         startOfCookie += nameLength; // skip past cookie name
         var endOfCookie = myCookie.indexOf(";",startOfCookie);
         result = unescape(myCookie.substring(startOfCookie,endOfCookie));
      }
   }
   return result;
}
```

CAUTION

A bug is present in Netscape Navigator version 1.1 and earlier. Only cookies whose Path attribute is set explicitly to / are properly saved between sessions if they have an Expires attribute.

To delete a cookie, the Name and the Path must match the original Name and Path used when the cookie was set.

Domain   Usually, after a page on a particular server creates a cookie, that cookie is accessible only to other pages on that server. Just as the Path parameter makes a cookie available outside its home path, the Domain parameter makes it available to other Web servers at the same site.

You can't create a cookie that anyone on the Internet can see. You may only set a Path that falls inside your own Domain. This is because the use of the Domain parameter dictates that you must use at least two periods (for example, .mydomain.com) if your domain ends in .com, .edu, .net, .org, .gov, .mil, or .int. Otherwise, it must have at least three periods (.mydomain.ma.us). Your Domain parameter string must match the tail of your server's domain name.

Secure   The final cookie parameter tells your browser that this cookie should be sent only under a Secure connection with the Web server. This means that the server and the browser must support HTTPS security. (HTTPS is Netscape's Secure Socket Layer Web page encryption protocol.)

If the Secure parameter is not present, it means that cookies are sent unencrypted over the network.

N O T E   You can't set an infinite number of cookies on every Web browser that visits your site. The following list shows the number of cookies you can set and how large they can be:

- Cookies per each server or domain: 20
- Total cookies per browser: 300
- Largest cookie: 4KB (including both the Name and Value parameters)

If these limits are exceeded, the browser might attempt to discard older cookies by tossing out the least recently used cookies first.

Now that you have seen all the cookie parameters, it would be helpful to have a JavaScript routine set cookies with all the parameters. Such a routine might look like that shown in Listing 22.4.

Listing 22.4   *FavList.htm* (excerpt)—JavaScript Routine to Add a Cookie, Including Any Optional Parameters

```
// SetCookie - Adds or replaces a cookie. Use null for parameters
//             that you don't care about
//
function SetCookie(name,value,expires,path,domain,secure) {
```

```
    var expString =
        ((expires == null) ? "" : ("; expires=" + expires.toGMTString()))
    var pathString = ((path == null) ? "" : ("; path=" + path))
    var domainString =
        ((domain == null) ? "" : ("; domain=" + domain))
    var secureString = ((secure == true) ? "; secure" : "")
    document.cookie = name + "=" + escape(value) +
                        expString + pathString + domainString +
                        secureString;
}
```

To use this routine, you call it with whatever parameters you care about and use null in place of parameters that don't matter.

A Cookie Example

On the CD

The JavaScript program in this example is in the HTML document FavList.htm, which is included on the CD-ROM that comes with this book. Excerpts of the program were shown in Listings 22.1 through 22.4; these showed the JavaScript functions used to create and manipulate the document cookies used in this example. Listing 22.5 shows the actual <BODY> section of the FavList.htm example, which enables the user to create a personalized "News-of-the-Day" page containing links to sites of general interest in a number of categories. The user's favorite links are stored in cookies.

Listing 22.5 *FavList.htm* **(excerpt)—The** *<BODY>* **Section of the Cookie Example**

```
<BODY BGCOLOR=#FFFFFF>
<SCRIPT LANGUAGE="JavaScript">
<!-- Hide script from incompatible browsers!
//
// Here's where we select the page to send. Normally we send the
// personalized favorites page (by calling SendPersonalPage). However,
// If the cookie ShowOptions is set, we'll send the options selection
// page instead (by calling SendOptionsPage).
//
if (GetCookie("ShowOptions") == "T") {
    ClearCookie("ShowOptions");
    SendOptionsPage();
} else
    SendPersonalPage();
//  Hide script from incompatible browsers! -->
</SCRIPT>
<HR>
<H2>Current Document Cookie Contents...</H2>
<CENTER>
<FORM NAME="MyForm">
<TEXTAREA NAME="MyTextArea" ROWS=1 COLS=60>
</TEXTAREA>
</FORM>
```

continues

Listing 22.5 Continued

```
</CENTER>
<SCRIPT LANGUAGE="JavaScript">
<!-- Hide script from incompatible browsers!
document.MyForm.MyTextArea.value = document.cookie;
//   Hide script from incompatible browsers! -->
</SCRIPT>
<HR>
<ADDRESS>
Jim O'Donnell, <A HREF="mailto:odonnj@rpi.edu">odonnj@rpi.edu</A>
</ADDRESS>
</BODY>
</HTML>
```

As shown in Listing 22.5, when this page is loaded, one of two JavaScripts will be called to actually "fill" the page: either SendOptionsPage() or SendPersonalPage(). The former enables the user to select from a list of sites to be included as favorites; the latter is used to display those sites (or to display all the possible sites). Figure 22.1 shows this page when it is first loaded, before the user has selected a list of favorites (so all possible sites are shown).

FIGURE 22.1

The Favorites page displays all possible sites when first loaded.

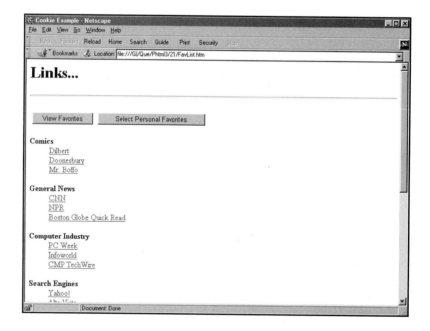

Before JavaScript, a task such as this would have been handled at the server. Each hit would have involved having the server run some type of script or program to read the user's cookies and generate his page on-the-fly. With JavaScript, all this processing takes place on the client's browser. The server just downloads the static page—and it might not even do that because the page might come from the client's local cache. When the page is loaded, all the links, selected or not, are sent. The client, with the help of cookies and JavaScript, decides which ones to show the user.

This program makes use of three cookies. The Favorites cookie contains a unique code for each favored link. The ViewAll cookie toggles between showing the user's favorites and all possible links. The program may also display either of two pages: one for displaying the selected links, and the other for changing the configuration and options. When the ShowOptions cookie is set, the Options selection page is displayed. Otherwise, the regular page is shown.

When the screen shown in Figure 22.1 is displayed after the page is first loaded, the value of the document cookie is

```
Favorites=null; ViewAll=T
```

This indicates that no favorites have been selected, but that all the options should be displayed. If View Favorites is clicked at this point, then the Document cookie will be

```
Favorites=null ,
```

and the screen shown in Figure 22.2 will be displayed—empty, because no favorites have been selected yet. Clicking the Select Personal Favorites button gets the screen shown in Figure 22.3, where favorites can be selected from the list of choices. One such selection might result in the Favorites list shown in Figure 22.4, which has the document cookie value of

```
Favorites=null%3Ccdilb%3E%3Cmjod%3E%3Cmgunther%3E%3Csyah%3E%3Csav%3E
```

N O T E   You may notice in Figures 22.2 and 22.4 that the current contents of the document cookie are displayed in a text area box at the bottom of the page. This is done in this example for educational purposes—to enable you to see the changes to the cookie as they occur; in an actual "production" page, you probably wouldn't include it. ◾

FIGURE 22.2

An empty Favorites list doesn't yield a very exciting Web page.

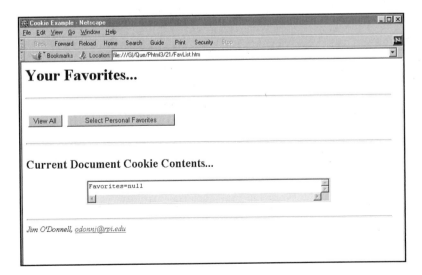

FIGURE 22.3

The Select Favorites page displays all the possible sites as check boxes and enables the user to select and deselect which to use as favorites.

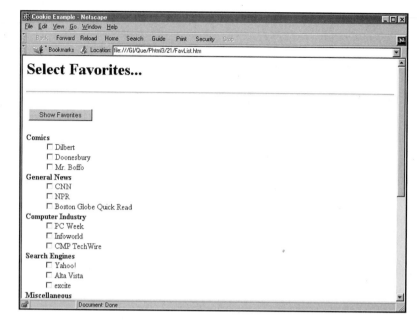

FIGURE 22.4

By enabling users to personalize their copy of your Web page, you allow a more personal experience without a greater burden on your server.

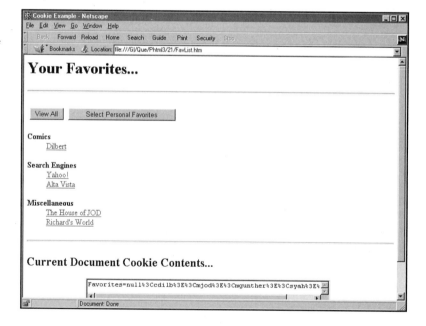

The program creates objects called "favorites." Each favorite is, in essence, a Web link to another page. The favorite contains information on the link's URL, a user-friendly page description, and the code that identifies it in the Favorites cookie string. The favorite also knows how to print itself on a Web page as a regular link for the Favorites page or in a check box format for the Options page. The functions used to manipulate the cookies in the FavList.htm example were shown in Listings 22.1 through 22.5. The other functions used in this example are summarized in the following list (the full HTML source code for this example is available on the CD-ROM).

- SendOptionsPage—Loads the Web browser with a page that enables the user to select which sites to be included as favorites.
- SendPersonalPage—Loads the Web browser with a page that shows either the user's favorites or all the sites as hypertext links.
- WriteAsCheckBox—Used by SendOptionsPage to display each potential favorite site as a check box, to enable the user to select or deselect it.
- WriteAsWebLink—Used by SendPersonalPage to display each site as a hypertext link.
- LoadOptions—This function is called to initiate the display of the options page.
- ToggleView—This function is called to toggle the personal page between displaying favorites and all sites.
- favorite—This function is used to create a JavaScript object that is used to store the information used to define a favorite site.
- Enabled—This JavaScript function is used as a method by the favorite object; it returns true if the link corresponding to this object is enabled.
- Checked— This JavaScript function is used as a method by the favorite object; it returns the string CHECKED if the link corresponding to this object is enabled.
- isEnabled—Returns true if the favorite identified by the Name parameter passed to the function is enabled.
- AddFavorite—Enables the favorite identified by the Name parameter passed to the function.
- ClearFavorite—Disables the favorite identified by the Name parameter passed to the function.
- SetFavoriteEnabled—Enables or disables the favorite identified by the Name parameter passed to the function by calling AddFavorite or ClearFavorite.
- ReloadPage—Reloads the Web browser with the current page; what is displayed, however, will change according to the current state of the Document cookie.

Where Are Cookies Going?

As mentioned earlier, cookies were designed and first implemented by Netscape. However, the Internet Engineering Task Force (IETF) has a committee—the Hypertext Transfer Protocol (HTTP) Working Group—whose charter is to examine, document, and suggest ways to improve HTTP.

ON THE WEB

You can find a link to the HTTP Working Group's latest Internet Draft, called "Proposed HTTP State Management Mechanism," at `http://www.ietf.cnri.reston.va.us/html.charters/http-charter.html`.

Although the draft specification resembles Netscape cookies in theory, if not in syntax, it does have a few notable differences. It doesn't encourage having cookies around much longer than the browser session. If the new specification is accepted, cookies are given a Max-Age lifetime rather than an expires date. All cookies expire when their time comes; but in all cases, they go away when the browser shuts down.

Reading the specification provides insight into the complexities that surround the inner workings of cookies; it is well worth the read, regardless of whether the specification is approved.

Which Servers and Browsers Support Cookies?

Although other ways of Web programming, such as CGI and special server interfaces, require that the server as well as the browser understand cookies, only the browser matters to JavaScript. This means, in general, that you can use JavaScript with impunity as long as you know your clients are JavaScript-capable.

Many JavaScript Web applications probably mix the language with other development tools, however, which would require the server to understand cookies. Because new servers and browsers are coming to the net so quickly, it is impossible for a printed book to keep up with the latest software.

ON THE WEB

You can find cookie information at the following locations on the Web:

Netscape cookie spec page (referenced previously in this chapter): `http://www.netscape.com/newsref/std/cookie_spec.html`

Browsers supporting cookies: `http://www.research.digital.com/nsl/formtest/stats-by-test/NetscapeCookie.html`

Cookie Central: `http://www.cookiecentral.com/`

Robert Brooks's Cookie Taste Test: `http://www.geocities.com/SoHo/4535/cookie.html`

Article about tracking cookies at the HotWired Web site: `http://www.arctic.org/~dgaudet/cookies`

Netscape World cookie article: `http://www.netscapeworld.com/netscapeworld/nw-07-1996/nw-07-cookies.html`

Other State Maintenance Options

As mentioned earlier in this chapter, a few drawbacks exist to using cookies. Perhaps you would rather just avoid the controversy and find some other way to maintain state from one page to the next. Two ways of doing this are available. Which one you use depends on how you, the developer, will have the users get from one page to the next.

The main limitation of these methods is that they work only from one page to the page immediately following. If state information is to be maintained throughout a series of pages, these mechanisms must be used on every single page.

Query String

If most of your navigation is done through hypertext links embedded in your pages, you can add extra information to the end of the URL. This is usually done by adding a question mark (?) to the end of your Web page URL, followed by information in an encoded form, such as that returned by the escape method. To separate one piece of information from another, place an ampersand (&) between them.

If you want to send the parameters color=blue and size=extra large along with your link, for example, you use a link such as this:

```
<A HREF="MyPage.htm?color=blue&size=extra+large">XL Blue</A>
```

This format is the same as the format used when submitting forms using the get method. A succeeding page can read this information by using the search property of the location object. This property is called search because many Internet search engines use this part of the URL to store their search criteria.

The following is an example of how to use the location.search property. In this example, the name of the current page is sent as a parameter in a link to another page. The other page reads this property through the search property and states where the browser came from. Listing 22.6 shows the first page that contains the link.

Listing 22.6 *Where1.htm*—You Can Include Extra Parameters in the HREF to Pass State Information

```
<HTML>
<HEAD>
<TITLE>Where Was I? (Page 1)</TITLE>
</HEAD>
<BODY>
<H1>Where Was I? (Page 1)</H1>
<HR>
This page sets information which will allow the page it is linked
to figure out where it came from. It uses values embedded in the link
URL in order to do this
<P>
We'll assume that any URL parameters are separated by an ampersand.
<P>
Notice that there doesn't need to be any JavaScript code in this page.
<P>
And now...
<A HREF="Where2.htm?camefrom=Where1.htm&more=needless+stuff">
```

continues

Listing 22.6   Continued

```
    ON TO PAGE 2!!!
</A>
<HR>
<ADDRESS>
Jim O'Donnell, <A HREF="mailto:odonnj@rpi.edu">odonnj@rpi.edu</A>
</ADDRESS>
</BODY>
</HTML>
```

Listing 22.7 shows the second page, which demonstrates how to use location.search to find where the browser came from.

Listing 22.7   *Where2.htm*—Access HREF Information Using the *window.location.search* Property

```
<HTML>
<HEAD>
<TITLE>Where Was I? (Page 2)</TITLE>
</HEAD>
<BODY>
<H1>Where Was I? (Page 2)</H1>
<HR>
This page reads information which allows it to figure out where it
came from.
<P>
<SCRIPT LANGUAGE="JavaScript">
<!-- Hide script from incompatible browsers!
//
// WhereWasI - Reads the search string to figure out what link
//             brought it here.
//
function WhereWasI() {
//
// start by storing our search string in a handy place (so we don't
// need to type as much)
//
    var handyString = window.location.search;
//
// find the beginning of our special URL variable
//
    var startOfSource = handyString.indexOf("camefrom=");
//
// if it's there, find the end of it
//
    if (startOfSource != -1) {
        var endOfSource = handyString.indexOf("&",startOfSource + 9);
        var result = handyString.substring(startOfSource + 9,
                                           endOfSource);
    }
```

```
        else
            var result = "Source Unknown";
        return result;
    }
    if (WhereWasI() != "Source Unknown")
        document.write("You just came from <B>" + WhereWasI() + "</B>...")
    else
        document.write("Unfortunately, we don't know where you came from...");
    //  Hide script from incompatible browsers! -->
</SCRIPT>
<HR>
<ADDRESS>
Jim O'Donnell, <A HREF="mailto:odonnj@rpi.edu">odonnj@rpi.edu</A>
</ADDRESS>
</BODY>
</HTML>
```

Figures 22.5 and 22.6 show the two Web pages, demonstrating that the first was able to pass information to the second.

FIGURE 22.5

Extra information can be included in a hypertext link using the ? and # characters.

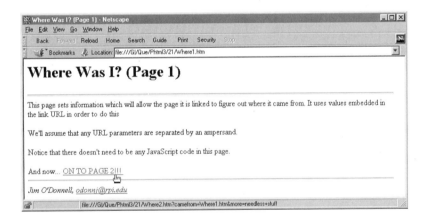

FIGURE 22.6

By including extra information in your hypertext links, you can enable some state information to be passed among pages in your Web site.

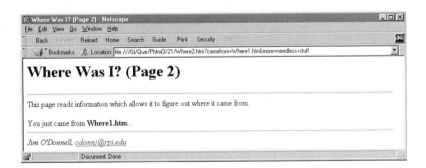

Hidden Form Variables

The method used in the preceding section works fine as long as the user navigates from one page to another using links. To do the same thing with forms, you can use hidden form variables rather than the `location.search` parameter.

Hidden form variables have the following format:

```
<INPUT TYPE=HIDDEN NAME="HiddenFieldName" VALUE="HiddenFieldValue">
```

You can specify whatever you like for `HiddenFieldName` and `HiddenFieldValue`.

Using hidden fields does not necessarily require the use of JavaScript code. They are defined, instead, in the `INPUT` tag of normal HTML documents. You do, however, need to have some sort of server-based script, such as a CGI program or a server API program, to read the values of these hidden fields. The form containing the hidden variables is submitted to a server script, which spills out everything it knows about your browser on to a single Web page, including the form's field information. You find your hidden field information listed at the bottom of the page. ●

## CHAPTER 23

Finding Records Is Sometimes Difficult

by Jim O'Donnell

What Are Web Browser Objects?

In Chapter 19, "The Web Browser Object Model," you learned about the Web Browser Object Model, which dictates how your JavaScripts can access and manipulate aspects of the Web browser and the HTML document that it is viewing. The Web browser, whether Netscape Navigator or Microsoft Internet Explorer, exposes a collection of objects—these objects control just how much you can do with your scripts. (As you will see in a few chapters, both Microsoft and Netscape extend their respective object models with their varieties of Dynamic HTML, which greatly extends the number of aspects of an HTML document that can be accessed and changed using JavaScript.)

▶ **See** "Putting the "Dynamic" in Dynamic HTML with JavaScript," **p. 621**.

▶ **See** "Internet Explorer Document Object Model," **p. 638**.

In addition to the objects exposed that are part of the Web browser (such as the window object) or part of the current HTML document itself (such as the document or image object), a number of other Web browser objects can occur within a Web page. These are objects included in the HTML document via the <APPLET>, <EMBED>, or <OBJECT> tags.

In general, the following types of content can be included in your Web pages by using one of these three tags. In many cases, although not all, the addition of this content provides additional objects that you can access and change with JavaScript.

■ Java applets. Java applets are normally included in a Web page using the <APPLET> tag, although Internet Explorer 4 also supports the use of the <OBJECT> tag to include them. Both Netscape and Microsoft have provided ways to access Java objects, properties, and methods through JavaScript, and vice versa, as long as the Java applet is set up to do so. Netscape does this by using their LiveConnect technology, discussed later in the "Netscape's LiveConnect" section. Microsoft provides the same functionality through its own ActiveX technology and Java Virtual Machine.

■ Plug-in content. Normally, content that is in a form that is not natively supported by the Web browser is included in an HTML document by using the <EMBED> tag. At the client browser, when this tag is encountered, the appropriate plug-in and/or ActiveX Control is loaded. As with Java applets, if the plug-in is set up to do so, it can expose its properties and methods that can be accessed through JavaScript. Later in this chapter, you will see examples of how this is done with the Envoy Viewer from Tumbleweed Software and with Macromedia's Shockwave Flash Viewer.

Again, both Netscape and Microsoft provide this same functionality but use different methods. Netscape's LiveConnect technology enables JavaScript to access plug-in properties and methods through Java; Microsoft, which supports many of Netscape Navigator's plug-ins, enables scripts to interface with the plug-ins directly.

■ ActiveX Controls. ActiveX controls are a technology developed by Microsoft; Microsoft's Internet Explorer is the only Web browser that fully supports them, although Netscape

Navigator also supports them through Ncompass Labs ScriptActive plug-in (`http://www.ncompasslabs.com`). As you will see in the "Interfacing with ActiveX Controls with JavaScript" section later in this chapter, it is very easy to use scripts to control ActiveX controls.

■ VRML. The VRML 2.0 standard also supports scripting in general—and JavaScript in particular—through the use of its `Script` node. The way you include JavaScripts with a VRML source file is a lot different than in HTML and is beyond the scope of this chapter. To find more information, see the VRML Repository Web site at `http://www.sdsc.edu/vrml/`.

Part

IV

Ch

23

Referencing Web Browser Objects

After the objects have been included in your HTML documents, you need only to know how to reference them to access them from your JavaScripts. Objects supplied by Java applets, plug-in content, and ActiveX controls fit into the same Web browser object hierarchy discussed in Chapter 19. To use them, you must know where they fit.

▶ **See** "Web Browser Object Hierarchy and Scoping," **p. 462**.

You can access these Web browser objects in many ways, depending on how they are included in your HTML documents. Objects exposed through the `<APPLET>` tag can be accessed through the `applet` object. Plug-ins called by the `<EMBED>` tag can be accessed through either the `embed` or the `plugin` object. Both these types of objects are included in the Web Browser Object Model hierarchy under the `document` object. Objects that are included through the use of the `<OBJECT>` tag are directly accessible by name through the `window` object, and because of the scoping rules of JavaScript, if you are controlling an object in the current window, the opening `window.` can be omitted.

▶ **See** "The `window` Object", **p. 463**.

Java Applets Using the *<APPLET>* Tag

As mentioned earlier, Java applets placed in your HTML documents via the `<APPLET>` tag can be referenced by using the `applet` object. Depending on how you include the `<APPLET>`, however, the object can be referenced a number of ways. Consider Listing 23.1, which shows a simple Web page with a controllable Java applet.

Listing 23.1   *Applet1.htm*—Controlling an Applet Using Its Name

```
<HTML>
<HEAD>
<TITLE>JavaScript Control of a Java Applet I</TITLE>
</HEAD>
<BODY BGCOLOR=#FFFFFF>
<H1>JavaScript Control of a Java Applet I</H1>
<HR>
```

continues

Listing 23.1   Continued

```
<APPLET NAME="Counter" CODE="Counter.class" WIDTH=200 HEIGHT=100></APPLET>
<FORM>
<INPUT TYPE=BUTTON VALUE="Add 1" NAME="AddButton"
       onClick="document.Counter.increment()">
<INPUT TYPE=BUTTON VALUE="Subtract 1" NAME="SubtractButton"
       onClick="document.Counter.decrement()">
</FORM>
</BODY>
</HTML>
```

As shown in Listing 23.1, the Java applet's `increment()` and `decrement()` methods are called through the JavaScript attached to the `onClick` event of the two HTML forms buttons. The applet's methods are accessed by referring to the Java `applet` object, which is included in the object hierarchy under the `document` object.

What if the applet isn't named? You can still access Java applets in your HTML documents, even if you don't specify a NAME attribute in the `<APPLET>` tag. This is done using JavaScript's object arrays, in this case the `applets` array associated with the `applet` object. Listing 23.2 shows the same example as Listing 23.1, demonstrating how to reference the Java applet without using a name.

▶ **See** "JavaScript Object Arrays," **p. 470**.

Listing 23.2   *Applet2.htm*—Controlling an Applet Without Using Its Name

```
<HTML>
<HEAD>
<TITLE>JavaScript Control of a Java Applet I</TITLE>
</HEAD>
<BODY BGCOLOR=#FFFFFF>
<H1>JavaScript Control of a Java Applet I</H1>
<HR>
<APPLET CODE="Counter.class" WIDTH=200 HEIGHT=100></APPLET>
<FORM>
<INPUT TYPE=BUTTON VALUE="Add 1" NAME="AddButton"
       onClick="document.applets[0].increment()">
<INPUT TYPE=BUTTON VALUE="Subtract 1" NAME="SubtractButton"
       onClick="document.applets[0].decrement()">
</FORM>
</BODY>
</HTML>
```

Because the Java applet is the only one in the HTML document, it is referenced through the first position in the `applet` object array, as `applets[0]`.

Plug-in Content from the *<EMBED>* Tag

Accessing plug-in objects, properties, and methods included in an HTML document through the `<EMBED>` tag is done in the same manner as with Java applets, which was discussed in the preceding section. Consider, for example, the following tag included as the first embed in your HTML document:

```
<EMBED NAME="MyPlug" SRC="MyMovie.dcr" WIDTH=300 HEIGHT=200></EMBED>
```

If the plug-in that was called to support this content type exposed object and methods to the Web browser and to JavaScript, you could access them in any of three ways. If the plug-in had an `initialize()` method you wanted to call, for example, you could do so by using one of the following:

- `document.MyPlug.initialize()`
- `document.embeds[0].initialize()`
- `document.embeds["MyPlug"].initialize()`

The last syntax shown is known as an associative array and was discussed in Chapter 19. That chapter also discussed when each of the syntaxes in this list is most appropriate.

Accessing *<OBJECT>* Tag Included Objects

By comparison with the `<APPLET>` and `<EMBED>` tags, objects included with the `<OBJECT>` tag are a bit easier to reference with JavaScript. That is because these objects are attached to the window object, and so can be referenced directly. If, for example, an object were included in your HTML document using the following:

```
<OBJECT NAME="MyControl"...></OBJECT>
```

And if it had an `initialize()` method, for example, it could be called from JavaScript by using just `MyControl.initialize()`.

Netscape's LiveConnect

Since its introduction, Netscape has introduced many new technologies into its Navigator Web browser. In addition to HTML extensions and multimedia capabilities such as LiveAudio, LiveVideo, and Live3D, three technologies in particular were introduced, or first became widely used, with Netscape Navigator. These are Web browser scripting with JavaScript, Java applet support, and Web browser plug-ins.

Until the release of Netscape Navigator 3, these technologies suffered from the handicap of being completely separate applications within a Web browser. JavaScripts, Java applets, and Navigator plug-ins ran within Navigator on their own, without the capability to interact. However, with Navigator 3 and now 4, Netscape has introduced its LiveConnect technology, enabling its three systems to interact.

Figure 23.1 shows how LiveConnect works within the Netscape Navigator runtime environment. JavaScripts can call Java methods and plug-in functions. Java applets can call both JavaScript and plug-in functions. Plug-ins can call Java methods and, through Java, call JavaScript functions. The objects and properties of each LiveConnect-compatible Java applet and plug-in are available to be manipulated through JavaScripts, applets, and other plug-ins.

FIGURE 23.1

Netscape's LiveConnect technology enables JavaScript, Java, and plug-ins to work together within Netscape Navigator.

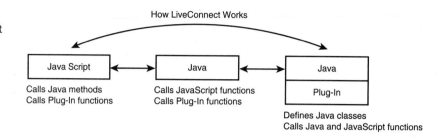

More extensive information on Netscape's LiveConnect technology is available on its Web site at `http://developer.netscape.com/docs/technote/javascript/liveconnect/liveconnect_rh.html`.

Enabling LiveConnect

By default in Netscape Navigator, Java and JavaScript are enabled—whenever these languages are enabled, LiveConnect is enabled as well. To confirm that they are enabled in your copy of Navigator, choose Edit, Preferences. Then, in the Categories list, select Advanced, make sure that the Enable Java and Enable JavaScript boxes are checked, and then click OK.

What About Internet Explorer?

As you might expect, Microsoft Internet Explorer does not explicitly support the LiveConnect technology. However, this doesn't mean that Internet Explorer authors and users are left out in the cold. Far from it.

The foundation of Microsoft's Web offerings is its ActiveX technology. These are a series of Web capabilities that enable authors to make use of scripting, ActiveX Controls, and Navigator plug-ins, and view and edit legacy documents (such as Microsoft Word documents) right in their Internet Explorer window. The ActiveX technologies were designed to enable the different components running within Internet Explorer to communicate with one another.

Although Internet Explorer does not support LiveConnect *per se*, its ActiveX technology achieves the same thing. Later in this chapter, you will find out how to control ActiveX Controls within Microsoft Internet Explorer using JavaScript.

The Java Console

Netscape Navigator has a Java Console that can be displayed by choosing Window, Java Console. Messages sent using `java.lang.System.out` or `java.lang.System.err` appear in this console.

Now, because of the communication possible between JavaScript and Java using LiveConnect, messages can be sent to the Java Console from JavaScript as well. To write a message to the Java Console from JavaScript, use the `println` method of `java.lang.System.out` or `java.lang.System.err`, as in the following:

```
java.lang.System.err.println("JavaScript checkpoint #1")
```

> **TIP** You can use the Java Console to help debug JavaScript applications. Output messages and intermediate values to the Java Console and watch it while browsing your pages. If you create JavaScripts to validate HTML forms, for instance, while you are debugging the scripts, you can print out intermediate form data to the console.

The Netscape Packages

Netscape Navigator includes several Java packages used to enable LiveConnect communication. The first, `netscape`, is used to enable communication back and forth between JavaScript and Java applets. Additionally, replacement `java` and `sun` packages are provided. These feature security improvements for LiveConnect. The following `netscape` packages are included:

- `netscape.javascript`—This package implements the `JSObject` and `JSException` classes, which enable Java applets to access JavaScript properties and throw exceptions when JavaScript returns an error.

- `netscape.plug-in`—This package implements the `Plugin` class, which enables cross communication between JavaScript and plug-ins. Plug-ins must be compiled with this class to make them LiveConnect compatible.

- `netscape.applet` and `netscape.net`—These are direct replacements for the `sun.applet` and `sun.net` classes provided in Sun's Java Development Kit.

▶ **See** "Leveraging Java Classes and Packages," **p. 984**.

JavaScript to Java Communication

With LiveConnect, JavaScript can make calls directly to Java methods. As already shown in the "Java Console" section, this is how JavaScript can output messages to the Java Console. To JavaScript, all Java packages and classes are properties of the `packages` object. Therefore, the full name of a Java object in JavaScript would be something like
`Packages.packageName.className.methodName`.

> **TIP** The packages name is optional for the `java`, `sun`, and `netscape` packages.

Java applets can be controlled through JavaScript without knowing too much about the internal construction of the applet, as long as a few conditions are true. The first step is to attach a `NAME` attribute to the `<APPLET>` tag when including the Java applet in your HTML document. Then all public variables, methods, and properties of the applet are available for access to JavaScript.

Any time you want to pass information into a Java applet, you might want to consider using JavaScript to do this. If you have a Java applet that implements a calendar, for example, you could create an HTML form with attached JavaScripts to enable the user to select what month should be displayed. By using JavaScript in this way, you avoid the need to give the applet itself the capability to interact with the user. Netscape shows a simple demo of controlling a Java applet by using JavaScript at `http://developer.netscape.com/docs/technote/javascript/liveconnect/Fade.html`.

The Java applet is included in the HTML document by using the following:

```
<APPLET CODE="Fade.class" NAME="Fader" WIDTH=400 HEIGHT=100>
<PARAM NAME="text1" VALUE="Look at this text carefully!">
<PARAM NAME="url1"  VALUE="http://www.netscape.com">
<PARAM NAME="font1" VALUE="Helvetica,PLAIN,36">
</APPLET>
```

The name Fader attached to the applet is how the Java applet is controlled. When any of the parameters entered in the form elements are changed, one of the public Java methods of this applet (setFont, setText, setUrl, setAnimateSpeed, or setBackgroundColor) is called through its onChange event.

For this to work, therefore, the Java methods need to be defined as public methods. When called, each method takes the parameter supplied and changes the characteristics of the applet (see Figure 23.2). As an example, the setText method is defined as a public method, as shown here:

```
public void setText(int which,String text) {
    bgChange = true;
    thoughts.theThoughts[which] = text;
    thoughts.Reset();
}
```

FIGURE 23.2

JavaScript is LiveConnect's link between the HTML form user input and Java applets.

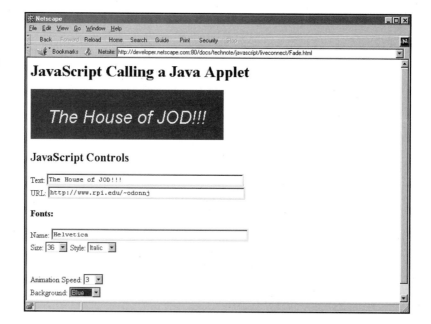

N O T E As mentioned a little earlier in this chapter, Internet Explorer achieves the same JavaScript to Java communication by using Microsoft's own ActiveX technology rather than Netscape's LiveConnect. Figure 23.3 demonstrates this, showing the same Netscape demo page shown in Figure 23.2 displayed instead in Internet Explorer.

However, this example also shows that Microsoft and Netscape don't quite have compatible versions of JavaScript. Although Internet Explorer enables you to change most of the parameters of the Fader applet, it does not support the JavaScript 1.2 font object used to change the display font. (If you look at this Web page with Internet Explorer, you'll get a few error dialogs, such as that shown in Figure 23.4; as long as you choose to keep running scripts, you'll be able to change everything but the display font for the applet.) ■

Part
IV

Ch
23

FIGURE 23.3

Microsoft accomplishes the same goal of JavaScript to Java communication with different means—but the same HTML and JavaScript will work with both browsers.

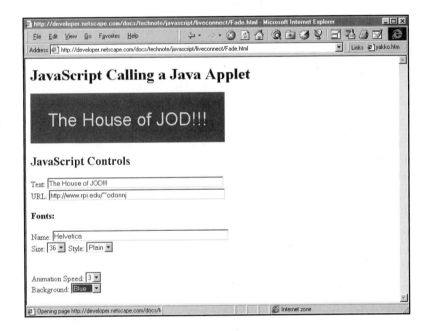

FIGURE 23.4

Internet Explorer and Navigator do not yet support completely compatible versions of JavaScript.

Java to JavaScript Communication

The first step in enabling your Java applets to access JavaScript properties is to import the `javascript` package into your Java applet, as shown here:

```
import netscape.javascript.*
```

This enables the Java applet to access JavaScript properties through the JSObject class. However, the author of the HTML document must still enable access to his JavaScript by including the MAYSCRIPT attribute in the <APPLET> tag used to include the Java applet. If the Fader used in the last example needed to access JavaScript, for example, the <APPLET> tag would look like the following:

```
<APPLET CODE="Fade.class" NAME="Fader" MAYSCRIPT WIDTH=400 HEIGHT=100>
<PARAM NAME="text1" VALUE="Look at this text carefully!">
<PARAM NAME="url1"  VALUE="http://www.netscape.com">
<PARAM NAME="font1" VALUE="Helvetica,PLAIN,36">
</APPLET>
```

If these two conditions have been satisfied, accessing JavaScript objects or methods is a two-step process, as follows:

1. Get a handle for the Navigator window containing the JavaScript objects or methods you want to access. This can be done using the getWindow() method of the netscape.javascript.JSObject package:

```
// winhan is a variable of type JSObject
public void initialize() {
    winhan = JSObject.getWindow(this);
}
```

2. To access JavaScript objects and properties, do the following:

Use the getMember() method in the netscape.javascript.JSObject package to access each JavaScript object in turn. To access the JavaScript object document.testForm using the window handle found in step 1, you could do the following:

```
public void accessForm(JSObject winhan) {
    JSObject myDoc = (JSObject) winhan.getMember("document");
    JSObject myForm = (JSObject) myDoc.getmember("testForm");
}
```

3. To call a JavaScript method:

Use either the call() or eval() method of the netscape.javascript.JSObject class. The syntax for the two commands (using the window handle found in step 1) is as follows:

```
winhan.call("methodName",arguments)
winhan.eval("expression")
```

In the former, *methodName* is the name of the JavaScript method, and *arguments* is an array of arguments to be passed on to the JavaScript method. In the latter, *expression* is a JavaScript expression that, when evaluated, has a value that is the name of a JavaScript method.

Similar to JavaScript to Java communication, Java to JavaScript communication can be useful when you don't want to re-create an input or output interface within your Java applet. You might create a Java applet that makes use of Java's network and Internet capabilities to access data from a database server on some other machine. Rather than using Java to display this data, you can access JavaScript objects to display it within a conventional HTML form.

JavaScript and Plug-Ins

JavaScript can be used with the client to determine what plug-ins the client has installed and what MIME types are supported. This is done through the `navigator` object, through two of its properties: `plugins` and `mimeTypes`. JavaScripts can also be used to call plug-in functions.

N O T E Internet Explorer also supports the `navigator` object, so the techniques in this section should work for both Netscape Navigator and Microsoft Internet Explorer. Be aware, however, that Internet Explorer does not support all Navigator plug-ins. ▨

By determining at the client whether a particular plug-in is installed or MIME-type supported, you can write scripts that generate content dynamically. If a particular plug-in is installed, the appropriate plug-in data can be displayed; otherwise, some alternative image or text can be shown.

If you have developed an inline VRML scene to embed in a Web page, for instance, you might want to know whether the user has a plug-in installed that supports VRML. Then, a VRML world or a representative GIF image could be displayed, as appropriate, such as the following:

```
<SCRIPT LANGUAGE="JavaScript">
<!-- Hide script from incompatible browsers -->
var isVrmlSupported,VrmlPlugin
isVrmlSupported = navigator.mimeTypes["x-world/x-vrml"]
if (isVrmlSupported)
    document.writeln("<EMBED SRC='world.wrl' HEIGHT=200 WIDTH=400>")
else
    document.writeln("<IMG SRC='world.gif' HEIGHT=200 WIDTH=400>")
//   Hide script from incompatible browsers -->
</SCRIPT>
```

N O T E As the next section shows, the `<OBJECT>` tag is the preferred method of including plug-in content for Internet Explorer; Navigator uses `<EMBED>`. Internet Explorer does, however, support the `<EMBED>` tag. ▨

Including and Referencing Plug-in Objects

The first step in using plug-ins within a Web page is to include them in the first place. The recommended way to do this is to use the `<OBJECT>` tag; however, both Internet Explorer and Navigator support the `<EMBED>` tag as well. If you want to include plug-in content in a Web page that will work with browsers that support both tags, use something like the following, which shows an example using the Flash Player by Macromedia:

```
<OBJECT CLASSID="clsid:D27CDB6E-AE6D-11cf-96B8-444553540000"
   ID="objID" WIDTH=100 HEIGHT=100
   CODEBASE="http://active.macromedia.com/flash2/cabs/
➥swflash.cab#version=2,0,0,11">
<PARAM NAME="Movie" VALUE="controls.swf">
<EMBED NAME="objID" MAYSCRIPT SRC="controls.swf"
   WIDTH=100 HEIGHT=100
   PLUGINSPAGE="http://www.macromedia.com/shockwave/download/
➥index.cgi?P1_Prod_Version=ShockwaveFlash">
</OBJECT>
```

N O T E Note that the preceding example actually is used to either call the Macromedia Flash
ActiveX control or plug-in, depending on whether Internet Explorer or Navigator is used. You
can use the same technique, however, to include plug-in content for each browser. You can read more
about accessing and manipulating ActiveX controls later in this chapter. ▪

This HTML code segment consists of the following tags:

- ▪ The <OBJECT> tag is used to include the plug-in content meant for Internet Explorer; its
  ID attribute gives it the name that will be used to script it.

- ▪ The <PARAM> tag (there can be as many of them as necessary) includes a NAME and a
  VALUE attribute used to configure the plug-in.

- ▪ The <EMBED> tag is included within the <OBJECT> container tag; this provides alternate
  content for browsers that do not understand the <OBJECT> tag. In this case, the plug-in
  content would be included either via the <OBJECT> or <EMBED> tag, but not both. The NAME
  attribute performs the same function as the ID attribute of the <OBJECT> tag—in this
  case, the SRC attribute.

Plug-ins included with the <OBJECT> and <EMBED> commands are also referenced differently.
When included with the <OBJECT> tag, plug-in objects are members of the window object; those
with <EMBED> are members of window.document.

Determining Which Plug-ins Are Installed

The navigator.plugins object has the following properties:

- ▪ description—A description of the plug-in, supplied by the plug-in itself
- ▪ filename—The filename on the disk in which the plug-in resides
- ▪ length—The number of elements in the navigator.plugins array
- ▪ name—The plug-in's name

Listing 23.3 shows an example of a JavaScript that uses the navigator.plugins object to display the names of the installed plug-ins right on the Web page. You can place this JavaScript at
the bottom of any Web page to display this information (see Figure 23.5).

Listing 23.3 *PlugIn.htm*—JavaScript to Detect Locally Installed Plug-ins

```
<HTML>
<HEAD>
<TITLE>JavaScript Plug-Ins Check</TITLE>
</HEAD>
<BODY BGCOLOR="#FFFFFF">
<H1>JavaScript Plug-Ins Check</H1>
<HR>
<SCRIPT LANGUAGE="JavaScript">
<!-- Hide script from incompatible browsers -->
var i,n
n = navigator.plugins.length
document.writeln("This Web browser has " + n + " plug-ins installed:<P>")
for (i=0;i<n;i++)
   document.writeln(navigator.plugins[i].name + "<BR>")
//   Hide script from incompatible browsers -->
</SCRIPT>
<HR>
<ADDRESS>
Jim O'Donnell, <A HREF="mailto:odonnj@rpi.edu">odonnj@rpi.edu</A>
</ADDRESS>
</BODY>
</HTML>
```

Part
IV

Ch
23

FIGURE 23.5

The navigator.plugins object enables you to use JavaScript to determine whether a plug-in is installed.

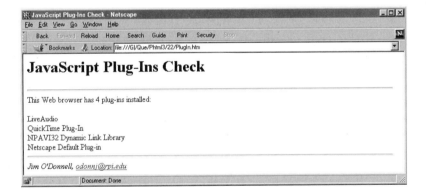

Client-Supported MIME Types

The navigator.mimeTypes object is similar to the navigator.plugins object and can be used to determine supported MIME types at the client. It has the following properties:

- description—A description of the MIME type
- enabledPlugin—A reference to the particular navigator.plugins object that handles this MIME type
- length—The number of elements in the navigator.mimeTypes array

- `suffixes`—A string listing the filename extensions, separated by commas, for this MIME type

- `type`—The MIME type name (for example, `x-world/x-vrml`)

Listing 23.4 shows an HTML document that contains a JavaScript that displays all the client-supported MIME types in an HTML table. Along with the MIME type, the supported file extensions are shown, as well as the name of the associated plug-in, if any (see Figure 23.6).

Listing 23.4 *MimeType.htm*—JavaScript to Detect Locally Supported MIME types

```
<HTML>
<HEAD>
<TITLE>JavaScript MIME Types Check</TITLE>
</HEAD>
<BODY BGCOLOR="#FFFFFF">
<H1>JavaScript MIME Types Check</H1>
<HR>
<SCRIPT LANGUAGE="JavaScript">
<!-- Hide script from incompatible browsers -->
var i,n
n = navigator.mimeTypes.length
document.writeln("The following MIME types are recognized:<P>")
document.writeln("<TABLE BORDER WIDTH=100%>")
document.writeln("<TR><TH COLSPAN=2>MIME Type</TH></TR>")
document.writeln("<TR><TH>Extensions</TH><TH>" +
   "Associated Plug-In (if any)</TH></TR>")
for (i=0;i<n;i++)
   if (navigator.mimeTypes[i].enabledPlugin)
      document.writeln("<TR><TD COLSPAN = 2><B>" +
         navigator.mimeTypes[i].type + "</B></TD></TR><TR><TD>" +
         navigator.mimeTypes[i].suffixes + "</TD><TD>" +
         navigator.mimeTypes[i].enabledPlugin.name + "</TD></TR>" )
   else
      document.writeln("<TR><TD COLSPAN = 2><B>" +
         navigator.mimeTypes[i].type + "</B></TD></TR><TR><TD>" +
         navigator.mimeTypes[i].suffixes + "</TD><TD></TD></TR>" )
document.writeln("</TABLE>")
//   Hide script from incompatible browsers -->
</SCRIPT>
<HR>
<ADDRESS>
Jim O'Donnell, <A HREF="mailto:odonnj@rpi.edu">odonnj@rpi.edu</A>
</ADDRESS>
</BODY>
</HTML>
```

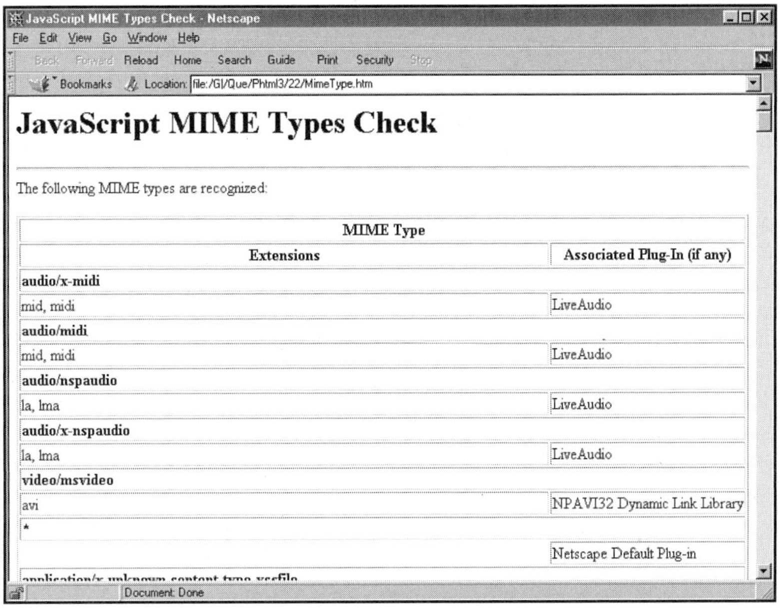

FIGURE 23.6

JavaScript can use the `navigator.mimeTypes` to determine the built-in MIME type support in the client Web browser.

Calling Plug-in Functions from JavaScript

For plug-in variables and methods to be accessible from JavaScript and Java applets, the plug-in must be LiveConnect compatible and associated with the `netscape.plugin.Plugin` Java class. If that is true, the plug-in variables and methods are available to JavaScript—in much the same way as the public variables and methods of Java applets are available.

JavaScript gives you two ways to access and control compatible plug-ins active in the Web environment. Similar to Java applets, the first is to use the `NAME` attribute of the `<EMBED>` tag to give a name to the embedded document. This enables the plug-ins' functions to be accessed through the document object. If `NAME=myenvoydoc` is used with the `<EMBED>` tag to embed an Envoy document using the Envoy Plug-In Viewer, for example, you can access the viewer functions by using the `document.myenvoydoc` object.

It is possible to access plug-ins even if they are not named by using the `embeds` array of the `document` object. If an Envoy document is the first embedded document in the Web page, it can be accessed with `document.embeds[0]`.

Figure 23.7 shows a simple example from the Netscape site of an HTML forms button that calls a JavaScript used to start the LiveAudio plug-in. The plug-in content is included in the Web page with the following HTML code:

```
<EMBED SRC="suspens1.wav"
       HIDDEN=TRUE
       NAME="Mysound"
       MASTERSOUND
```

```
AUTOSTART=yes
LOOP=NO
>
```

The JavaScript used to interface with the plug-in is

```
<input type="button" value="Play Sound" onClick="document.Mysound.play(false)">
<input type="button" value="Stop Sound" onClick="document.Mysound.stop()">
```

This example can be found at the following location on the Netscape site: http://
developer.netscape.com:80/docs/technote/javascript/liveconnect/js_plugin.html.

FIGURE 23.7
HTML forms and
JavaScripts are the
perfect combination for
creating user interfaces
to Java applets and
plug-ins.

Using JavaScript to Control the Shockwave Flash Player

One of the more popular types of multimedia content to include in a Web page is content created for Shockwave using one of Macromedia's applications, such as Macromedia Director,
Authorware, or FreeHand. Typically, Shockwave content is displayed using the Macromedia
Shockwave Flash Player. This free player gives the user a number of options for viewing the
content.

You can also make use of the methods of the Shockwave Flash Player to control precisely how
your Shockwave for Director movie, for example, appears to your users. This is done by including JavaScripts that respond to timers or user input to control the display of your movie
through the Flash Player. Following is a list of some of the more useful methods available from
the Shockwave Flash Player:

- GotoFrame(*frame_number*)—Moves the player to the specified frame number.
- IsPlaying()—Returns TRUE or FALSE, depending on whether the movie is currently
  playing.
- Pan(*x*,*y*,*mode*)—If the movie has been zoomed in, this method enables you to pan right
  or left, up or down.
- PercentLoaded()—This method returns the percentage of the movie that has been
  downloaded so far.

- `Play()`—Starts playing the movie through the player.
- `Rewind()`—Rewinds the movie.
- `SetZoomRect(left,top,right,bottom)`—Zooms in on a rectangular area of the movie.
- `StopPlay()`—Stops the movie.
- `Zoom(percent)`—Zooms the movie by the specified percentage.

For more information on Macromedia Shockwave, you can visit their Web site at `http://www.macromedia.com`. You can find more specific information on controlling the Flash Player in your Web pages at `http://www.macromedia.com/support/flash/`.

Part
IV
Ch
23

Interfacing with ActiveX Controls with JavaScript

This is an example of using JScript, Microsoft's implementation of the JavaScript language, to manipulate another Web browser object, ActiveX Controls—in this case the ActiveX Label Control. ActiveX Controls are a Microsoft technology, similar to plug-ins, that enables developers to dynamically increase the capabilities of the Web browser. Many major software developers that produce plug-ins for Netscape Navigator produce ActiveX Control versions as well. Therefore, controlling ActiveX Controls would be done for many of the same reasons as for plug-ins.

The Label Control enables the Web author to place text on the Web page, select the text, font, size, and an arbitrary angle of rotation. One of the exciting things about the Label Control is that it can be manipulated in real-time, producing a variety of automated or user-controlled effects.

In the following example, the Label Control is used to place text on the Web page, and form input is used to enable the user to change the text used and the angle at which it is displayed. Figure 23.8 shows the default configuration of the label and Figure 23.9 shows it after the text and the rotation angle have been changed.

FIGURE 23.8

The ActiveX Label Control enables arbitrary text to be displayed by the Web author in the size, font, position, and orientation desired.

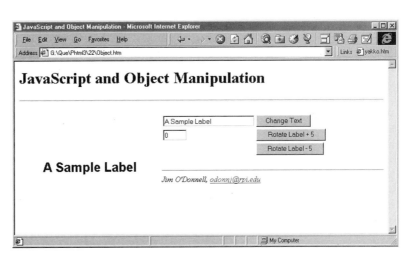

FIGURE 23.9

JavaScript's capability to manipulate Web browser objects enables label parameters to be changed dynamically.

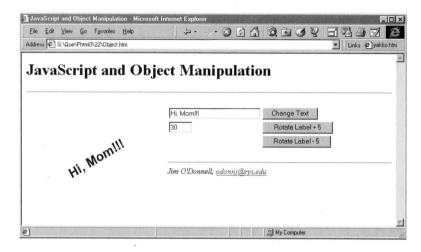

Listing 23.5 shows the code used to produce this example. The following are some things to note about the example:

- The `<OBJECT>...</OBJECT>` container tag is where the ActiveX Label Control is included and its default parameters assigned. The `classid` attribute must be included exactly as shown. The `id` attribute is the object name used by JavaScript to reference the `Label Control` object. The other attributes define the size and placement of the control.

- The `<PARAM>` tags within the `<OBJECT>...</OBJECT>` container enable the Web author to define attributes of the ActiveX Label Control. The `NAME`, `VALUE` pairs are unique to each ActiveX Control and should be documented by the ActiveX Control author. For the Label Control, they define various aspects of the appearance of the label. The `NAME` is also used to manipulate the value with JavaScript.

- An HTML form is used to accept input and print output for information about the Label Control. The first text area is used to set the label text, and the second text area is used to output the current label text angle. The buttons call the appropriate JavaScript routine to change the label text or angle.

- One final note about the placement of the JavaScripts in this HTML document: The functions are defined in the `<HEAD>` section—although not necessary, this is common practice so that they will be defined before use. Note that the last `<SCRIPT>...</SCRIPT>` section, which initializes the value of the form text area showing the current angle, is placed at the end of the HTML document to ensure that the object is defined and value set before it is called.

Listing 23.5   *Object.htm*—JavaScript Can Interact with Objects

```
<HTML>
<HEAD>
<SCRIPT LANGUAGE="JAVASCRIPT">
<!-- Hide this script from incompatible Web browsers -->
```

```
function ChangeIt() {
   lblActiveLbl.caption = document.LabelControls.txtNewText.value
}
function RotateP() {
   lblActiveLbl.angle = lblActiveLbl.angle + 5
   document.LabelControls.sngAngle.value = lblActiveLbl.angle
}
function RotateM(){
   lblActiveLbl.Angle = lblActiveLbl.Angle - 5
   document.LabelControls.sngAngle.value = lblActiveLbl.angle
}
//   Hide this script from incompatible Web browsers -->
</SCRIPT>
<TITLE>JavaScript and Object Manipulation</TITLE>
</HEAD>
<BODY BGCOLOR=#FFFFFF>
<H1>JavaScript and Object Manipulation</H1>
<HR>
<OBJECT classid="clsid:99B42120-6EC7-11CF-A6C7-00AA00A47DD2"
        id=lblActiveLbl
        width=250
        height=250
        align=left
        hspace=20
        vspace=0
>
<PARAM NAME="Angle" VALUE="0">
<PARAM NAME="Alignment" VALUE="4">
<PARAM NAME="BackStyle" VALUE="0">
<PARAM NAME="Caption" VALUE="A Sample Label">
<PARAM NAME="FontName" VALUE="Arial">
<PARAM NAME="FontSize" VALUE="20">
<PARAM NAME="FontBold" VALUE="1">
<PARAM NAME="ForeColor" VALUE="0">
</OBJECT>
<FORM NAME="LabelControls">
<TABLE>
<TR><TD><INPUT TYPE="TEXT" NAME="txtNewText" SIZE=25></TD>
    <TD><INPUT TYPE="BUTTON" NAME="cmdChangeIt" VALUE="Change Text"
              onClick="ChangeIt()">
    </TD></TR>
<TR><TD><INPUT TYPE="TEXT" NAME="sngAngle" SIZE=5></TD>
    <TD><INPUT TYPE="BUTTON" NAME="cmdRotateP" VALUE="Rotate Label + 5"
              onClick="RotateP()">
    </TD></TR>
<TR><TD></TD>
    <TD><INPUT TYPE="BUTTON" NAME="cmdRotateM" VALUE="Rotate Label - 5"
              onClick="RotateM()">
    </TD></TR>
</TABLE>
</FORM>
<SCRIPT LANGUAGE="JAVASCRIPT">
<!-- Hide this script from incompatible Web browsers -->
document.LabelControls.sngAngle.value = lblActiveLbl.angle
```

Part

IV

Ch

23

continues

Listing 23.5   Continued

```
document.LabelControls.txtNewText.value = lblActiveLbl.caption
//   Hide this script from incompatible Web browsers -->
</SCRIPT>
<HR>
<ADDRESS>
Jim O'Donnell, <A HREF="mailto:odonnj@rpi.edu">odonnj@rpi.edu</A>
</ADDRESS>
</BODY>
</HTML>
```

JavaScript

## CHAPTER 24

Introduction to Dynamic HTML

by Jim O'Donnell

In this chapter

What Is Dynamic HTML?

When HTML was first developed, its mixing of text and graphics, as well as the inclusion of the hypertext link for linking information, revolutionized the way information was presented and distributed across the Internet. Since the inception of HTML, Web developers and vendors have been looking for ways to present information more dynamically and to create more ways to interact with the user. Animated GIFs, Web browser plug-ins and ActiveX Controls, Java applets, and scripting languages are all examples of ways to make Web pages more exciting.

HTML itself is basically a static language, however; information is sent to a client Web browser, which renders it for the viewer. To add movement or animation to an HTML document, it was necessary to embed some other element, such as the Java applets or ActiveX Controls mentioned in the preceding paragraph. Macromedia's Shockwave, for example, has long been used to add increased animation and interactivity to many Web pages.

With version 4 of their latest Web browser applications, however, both Netscape and Microsoft have introduced a new technology, dubbed "Dynamic HTML," which seeks to make HTML more interactive in its own right. Through each company's version of Dynamic HTML, Web developers have increased control over the appearance of an HTML document as rendered on a compatible Web browser and have more ways to make the document dynamic and interactive, capable of better detection and response to user actions.

What exactly is Dynamic HTML? Unlike the current state of such languages and technologies as HTML, Java, and VRML, Dynamic HTML is not a standard; it is not enacted, proposed, or even being developed by any Internet standards organization. Rather, Dynamic HTML is a term applied by both Netscape and Microsoft to a collection of technologies that they are developing for making HTML documents more dynamic and interactive. Although a few common elements exist, the question "What is Dynamic HTML?" has a different answer, depending on whom you ask.

The remainder of this chapter will give you an introduction to the different capabilities in Netscape Navigator and Microsoft Internet Explorer under the guise of "Dynamic HTML." The next two chapters will take a more in-depth look, first at Netscape and then at Microsoft Dynamic HTML. Finally, you will finish this section by learning how to use Dynamic HTML to develop your Web pages in such a way that they are compatible with both browsers.

Netscape's Answer

Netscape's documentation for its version of Dynamic HTML, along with a lot of other documentation, demos, and other good information about Netscape software and technologies, is located on its DevEdge Online Web site, which can be found at

```
http://developer.netscape.com/
```

The specific URL for its Dynamic HTML documentation can be found at

```
http://developer.netscape.com/tech/dynhtml/index.html
```

According to this information, Netscape's answer to the question "What is Dynamic HTML?" would consist of the following elements, which were first introduced into Netscape Navigator version 4:

- Style sheets— Microsoft first implemented support for Cascading Style Sheets (CSS), MicrosoftCSS, in its Internet Explorer version 3.0, and Netscape added it to its Web browser with version 4 and above. Both Netscape and Microsoft support the Cascading Style Sheets standard adopted by the World Wide Web Consortium (W3C). You can find these standards on W3C's CSS Web site.

▶ **See** "What Are Style Sheets?," **p. 262**.

Netscape considers style sheets a part of its implementation of Dynamic HTML because it has extended its Web Browser Object Model to include style sheets and styles attached to tags within an HTML document. This enables the formatting information for the content within the HTML document to be changed dynamically using JavaScript.

ON THE WEB

`http://www.w3.org/Style/`   This Web site houses the W3C's complete Cascading Style Sheet definition, as well as a number of links you can follow to find out more.

- Content positioning—With the early beta releases of Netscape Navigator version 4, Netscape introduced the `<LAYER>` and `<ILAYER>` tags, which were their proposed HTML tags to allow for precise 2D and 3D positioning of elements within an HTML document. These tags were rejected by the W3C, although Netscape still supports them in the release version of its Web browser.

  With the rejection of the `<LAYER>` and `<ILAYER>` tags, Netscape added support for what is known as CSS positioning. In addition to the formatting options that can be specified using style sheets, Netscape also includes support for positioning the elements to which they are attached. Whether you create your HTML elements to be positioned using the `<LAYER>` or `<ILAYER>` tags, or whether you use CSS positioning, Netscape enables you to use JavaScript to reference those elements the same way, enabling you to dynamically change their positions.

- Downloadable fonts—One problem with using style sheets to achieve your desired formatting effects is that they work only if your users have the same fonts installed on their local systems. If they do not, your carefully constructed Web page will be rendered using a font different from the one you intended, potentially destroying the desired effect.

  Netscape has developed a solution to this problem, which it groups as a part of its Dynamic HTML. It has added a way for you to set up and embed fonts in your HTML documents, which are then downloaded over the Web along with the document so that you can be sure it will be correctly rendered.

Other than the specific elements mentioned in the preceding list—which are also contained in the introductory section of Netscape's own Dynamic HTML documentation—Netscape has added other new features related to Dynamic HTML to version 4 of its Web browser. These include the changes to its JavaScript scripting language and to the Navigator Web Browser Object Model that supports these new capabilities.

Microsoft's Answer

Microsoft's answer to the "What is Dynamic HTML?" question is a bit longer than Netscape's and reveals a greater number of new possibilities and capabilities of its Internet Explorer Web browser. Microsoft has very good documentation for its technologies at its SiteBuilder Network, located at

```
http://www.microsoft.com/sitebuilder/
```

The documentation for Dynamic HTML is located at the following location on Microsoft's Web site:

```
http://www.microsoft.com/workshop/author/default.asp
```

The elements listed there as being a part of Microsoft's version of Dynamic HTML are the following:

- Dynamic HTML object model—The heart of Microsoft's Dynamic HTML is its extensions to the Web Browser Object Model. As shown in Chapter 19, "The Web Browser Object Model," previous object models for Netscape Navigator and Microsoft Internet Explorer enabled you to create scripts to interact with a small portion of HTML elements—images could be swapped, forms could be processed, hypertext links could be manipulated, and so on.

  With Microsoft's version of Dynamic HTML, it has extended the Web Browser Object Model to include every HTML tag. Therefore, events such as responding to mouse movements or keypresses can be attached to any element in an HTML document. The format and style of any element on a page can be dynamically changed, either separately or as a group. Not only can the format be changed, but the actual contents of an HTML tag can be changed—the text within a <P> paragraph container tag can be changed on-the-fly, without going back to the Web server, in response to a user action or some other event.

- Dynamic content—Microsoft achieves *dynamic content*—the capability to change the displayed content of an HTML document without getting more information from a Web server—through its enhanced object model. Unlike Netscape Navigator, Internet Explorer also supports the dynamic redisplay of the content of a Web page when something on it has changed. Therefore, when something on a Web page is added, removed, or replaced, the other contents on the page automatically adjust themselves to display correctly.

- Dynamic styles—As with Netscape, Microsoft's Dynamic HTML achieves the capability to dynamically change the style of the contents of an HTML document through style sheets and its object model. In Microsoft's Dynamic HTML, as implemented in its Internet Explorer Web browser, whenever the contents (as described in the preceding item in this list) or format of a Web page are dynamically changed, the rest of the document automatically reformats itself to display properly.

- Positioning—Microsoft uses CSS positioning and its object model to implement the precise positioning and repositioning of HTML elements. CSS formatting and positioning are the only aspects of Dynamic HTML that Netscape and Microsoft really share.

- Data binding—Data binding is a way of attaching data from an external source to an HTML element. In addition to using special new attributes to certain HTML tags, data binding makes use of Microsoft's ActiveX Control Data Source Object. In this way, for instance, an HTML table can be filled with data from an external file, such as a flat ASCII file or database, through the Data Source Object. Methods of that object can then be called to sort the data using any of the columns of data.

- Multimedia effects—Microsoft also uses its ActiveX Control technology to add multimedia effects to its Dynamic HTML. You can add filters to your document to create visual effects or use Microsoft's DirectAnimation system to easily add animations. The effects possible with Microsoft's filters and other technologies are similar to those offered by animated GIFs or Shockwave; because they are built into the Web browser, however, you can often achieve these possibilities much more simply.

In addition to the topics covered in the preceding list—the only technologies listed by Microsoft as part of its implementation of Dynamic HTML—Microsoft has other technologies that add related capabilities. For instance, Microsoft has its own system for embedding and downloading fonts into an HTML document. Although this technique is not technically considered part of Microsoft's Dynamic HTML, it is discussed in the "Dynamic Fonts" section later in this chapter and compared with Netscape's system.

The World Wide Web Consortium's Answer

For the most part, the W3C considers the bulk of the Dynamic HTML implementations introduced by Netscape and Microsoft to be extensions to the Web Browser Object Model (also known as the Document Object Model, or DOM). The W3C has undertaken the task of developing a DOM standard, but its work on that topic is not as far along as its work on other standards. You can find out where it stands on a Document Object Model standard by looking at

```
http://www.w3.org/DOM/
```

As of August 18, 1998, the W3C has released a Document Object Model Level 1 Proposed Recommendation. Until the W3C's specification is officially released, the efforts and advances of Netscape and Microsoft with Dynamic HTML will likely continue to diverge. Only the market and the efforts of the community of Web developers will determine which technologies survive and thrive.

Web Page Layout and Content Positioning

Because of their support for the W3C's CSS standard, most similarities between Netscape's and Microsoft's Dynamic HTML technologies occur with the elements that make use of style and style sheets. The main use of style sheets, discussed extensively in Chapter 9, "Style Sheets," is in the specification of formatting information for HTML elements. The benefit of

Part
V

Ch
24

using style sheets for this purpose is the capability of the Web page designer to separate the content of the document from its formatting information. (This makes it much easier to change the format while keeping the information the same.)

A newer use of style sheet attributes is to perform positioning of HTML elements through the CSS positioning attributes. Both Microsoft and Netscape support these attributes in their Web browsers—although, as a new standard, neither Web browser offers perfect support for them. This section focuses on how you can use style sheet attributes to specify positioning of HTML elements within a Web page. You will also see how to do this for Netscape Navigator by using Netscape's <LAYER> and <ILAYER> tags. Finally, you can learn how to create scripts that can dynamically change the positioning information and how to achieve a measure of cross-plat-form compatibility between the two flavors of Dynamic HTML.

CSS Positioning

The following list shows the most important style sheet attributes concerning positioning and manipulation of elements within an HTML document. Through the use and manipulation of these attributes, it is possible to precisely determine the two-dimensional positioning of every-thing within the Web browser window. In situations where HTML elements overlap, it is also possible to specify the relative three-dimensional placement.

The list shows the name of the attribute, followed by its possible values, and a description of what it is used for. The default value for each attribute is shown in **bold** type.

■ position

Possible values: absolute | relative | **static**

This determines whether the element will accept further positioning attributes and whether they will be referenced absolutely to the Web browser window or relative to the location of the element on the page. If an element is static, it cannot be positioned further and will behave like a conventional, static HTML element.

■ left

Possible values: absolute length | percentage | **auto**

Defines the left edge of the element, either with an absolute length or as a percentage.

■ top

Possible values: absolute length | percentage | **auto**

Defines the top edge of the element, either with an absolute length or as a percentage.

■ width

Possible values: absolute length | percentage | **auto**

Defines the width of the element, either with an absolute length or as a percentage.

■ height

Possible values: absolute length | percentage | **auto**

Defines the height of the element, either with an absolute length or as a percentage.

- `clip`

  Possible values: bounding box | **auto**

  If specified, the bounding box gives the four numbers that define a rectangle that is the visible portion of the element.

- `overflow`

  Possible values: scroll | visible | hidden | **auto**

  Specifies how parts of the HTML element outside the visible area defined by the bounding box are displayed, if at all.

- `z-index`

  Possible values: stacking order | **auto**

  Determines the three-dimensional stacking order of HTML elements. The higher the `z-index` value, the farther to the front it is displayed.

- `visibility`

  Possible values: visible | hidden | **auto**

  You can use this attribute to make an HTML element visible or not visible.

Part

V

Ch

24

N O T E By default, location and lengths in CSS attributes are given in units of pixels. You can specify other units by giving the unit abbreviation (for example, "1in"). ■

Listing 24.1 shows an example in Internet Explorer of how to position HTML elements—in this case, three copies of an image and a block of text—using CSS positioning attributes. Styles are defined for two of the images using an embedded style sheet, defined by the <STYLE> tag, and attached to the HTML tags using the CLASS attribute (the third copy of the image uses the default style). The block of text is assigned style parameters using the STYLE attribute of the <DIV> container tag.

Listing 24.1 *CssPos.htm*—**Using CSS Attributes to Position HTML Elements**

```
<HTML>
<HEAD>
<TITLE>CSS Positioning</TITLE>
<STYLE TYPE="text/css"> <!--
.sample1 {
   position: absolute;
   left: 100px;
   top: 100px;
   width: 150px;
   height: 150px;
}
.sample2 {
   position: relative;
```

continues

Listing 24.1   Continued

```
    left: 275px;
    top: -300px;
    width: 200px;
    z-index: -1;
} -->
</STYLE>
</HEAD>
<BODY BGCOLOR=#FFFFFF>
<H1>CSS Positioning</H1>
<HR>
<CENTER>
<IMG SRC="Tux.jpg" WIDTH=450 HEIGHT=335 BORDER=0>
<BR>
<IMG CLASS="sample1" SRC="Tux.jpg" WIDTH=450 HEIGHT=335 BORDER=0>
<BR>
<IMG CLASS="sample2" SRC="Tux.jpg" WIDTH=450 HEIGHT=335 BORDER=0>
</CENTER>
<BR>
<DIV STYLE="position: absolute; top: 1.75in; left: 1.5in;
            z-index: 4;color: yellow; font: 36pt Verdana">
   Works With Text, Too!
</DIV>
<HR>
<ADDRESS>
Jim O'Donnell, <A HREF="mailto:odonnj@rpi.edu">odonnj@rpi.edu</A>
</ADDRESS>
</BODY>
</HTML>
```

This HTML document produces a Web page with three renderings of the same image and a block of text (along with the header and footer information identifying the example and author). As shown in Figure 24.1, one of these images is placed inline, the way images are conventionally placed within a Web page. The second image uses as its class name "sample1," which attaches the corresponding style to it. As a result, this image is absolutely positioned 100 pixels down and to the left of the upper-left corner of the Web browser window. Also, because the width and height defined in the style are smaller than the actual width and height of the image, it is scaled to fit. Because no value for the z-index attribute is specified, this image appears above the first image defined.

The third image uses the style class "sample2." This style defines a relative position for the image—defined relative to where the image would have appeared. This image would have appeared directly under the first inline image, so the left and top attributes are relative to that position. As a result, the image appears 50 pixels farther to the left and 200 pixels above this position. In addition, the height of the style is less than the height of the image, so it is scaled in this axis. This image is made to appear below the other two by specifying a z-index attribute value of −1.

Finally, the block of text is positioned absolutely, to overlay all three images.

FIGURE 24.1

HTML element positioning enables you to place objects within a Web page exactly where you want them instead of letting the client Web browser decide how to render them.

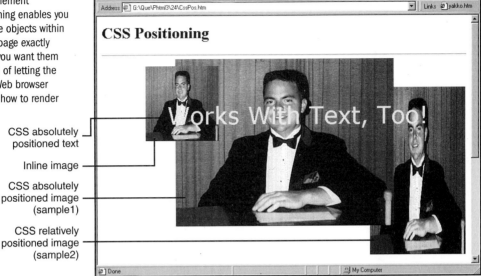

CSS absolutely positioned text

Inline image

CSS absolutely positioned image (sample1)

CSS relatively positioned image (sample2)

CAUTION

Netscape Navigator supports only values of z-index that are positive integers. If you try to design Web pages that will appear correctly in both Navigator and Internet Explorer, keep this in mind.

Netscape's *<LAYER>* Tag

Although the <LAYER> and <ILAYER> tags will not become standard HTML, they are supported in Netscape Navigator; therefore, you might want to learn how to position HTML elements by using them. Sometimes these tags work better in Navigator than the CSS positioning attributes. If you are designing documents for an audience predominantly using Netscape's Web browser, you might want to use the <LAYER> tag.

Listing 24.2 shows an HTML document designed to achieve roughly the same HTML element layout as achieved by that shown in Listing 24.1 using the <LAYER> and <ILAYER> tags. Figure 24.2 demonstrates that the result is, in fact, very similar.

Listing 24.2   *LayerPos.htm*—Using Netscape's *<LAYER>* Tag to Position HTML Elements

```
<HTML>
<HEAD>
<TITLE>LAYER Positioning</TITLE>
</HEAD>
```

continues

Listing 24.2 Continued

```
<BODY BGCOLOR=#FFFFFF>
<CENTER>
<H1>LAYER Positioning</H1>
<HR>
<ILAYER Z-INDEX=2>
   <IMG SRC="Tux.jpg" WIDTH=450 HEIGHT=335 BORDER=0>
</ILAYER>
<LAYER PAGEX=100 PAGEY=100 Z-INDEX=3>
   <IMG SRC="Tux.jpg" WIDTH=150 HEIGHT=150 BORDER=0>
</LAYER>
<ILAYER LEFT=275 TOP=-300 Z-INDEX=1>
   <IMG SRC="Tux.jpg" WIDTH=200 HEIGHT=335 BORDER=0>
</ILAYER>
<DIV STYLE="position: absolute; top: 1.75in; left: 1.5in;
            z-index: 4;color: yellow; font: 36pt Verdana">
   Works With Text, Too!
</DIV>
<HR>
</CENTER>
<ADDRESS>
Jim O'Donnell, <A HREF="mailto:odonnj@rpi.edu">odonnj@rpi.edu</A>
</ADDRESS>
</BODY>
</HTML>
```

FIGURE 24.2

Netscape's nonstandard <LAYER> and <ILAYER> tags give you another way to position HTML elements in documents meant for Navigator version 4 and higher.

CSS absolutely positioned text

Inline <ILAYER> image

<LAYER> image

Repositioned <ILAYER> image

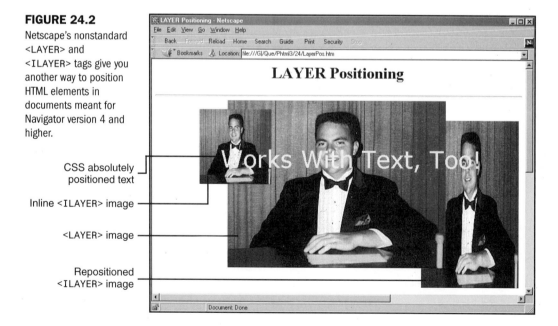

Some important differences between these two examples are noted, along with other points of interest, as follows:

- <LAYER> tags define layers that are absolutely positioned; <ILAYER> tags define layers that are positioned relative to where they would otherwise have appeared in the HTML document.

- As mentioned in the preceding section, Netscape Navigator supports only positive integer values of the z-index attribute—images with the highest z-index value appear on top. To achieve the desired three-dimensional layout, therefore, it was necessary to place each copy of the image in a layer of its own and assign appropriate z-index attributes to each.

  Note that if the first image's <ILAYER> tag had been named with an ID attribute, the desired layering of images could have been achieved by using the BELOW and ABOVE attributes in the other two images' <LAYER> and <ILAYER> tags.

- The WIDTH and HEIGHT attributes of the <LAYER> and <ILAYER> tags do not perform the same scaling function that the corresponding style sheet attributes perform. Therefore, to achieve the same scaling in this example as in the last, it was necessary to alter the WIDTH and/or HEIGHT attributes of the <IMG> tag.

- Did you notice that the positioning and other styles applied to the text block were done with the exact same code as in the previous example? They could have been done with a <LAYER> tag, but they were done this way to emphasize that Navigator also supports style sheets and CSS positioning.

The <LAYER>/<ILAYER> tags are currently the centerpiece of Netscape's Dynamic HTML implementation, although that is changing as Netscape moves to a more CSS-oriented approach. Chapter 25, "Advanced Netscape Dynamic HTML," discusses the use of these tags in much greater depth.

▶ **See** "Content Positioning," **p. 618**.

Scripting Positioning Elements

Both Microsoft and Netscape enable you to access the positioning information of individual HTML elements via a scripting language and their object model. Microsoft's Dynamic HTML object model automatically enables you to set and access the attributes of every tag within an HTML document. This is done with the all object, which is underneath the document object in the Web browser object hierarchy. You can write out the names of all the HTML tags on a page, for instance, with the following:

```
for (i=0;i < document.all.length;i++) {
    document.write(document.all[i].tagName + "<BR>")
}
```

To access a tag's positioning elements, you simply need a reference to that tag. If the tag has a NAME or ID attribute set for it, this is pretty straightforward. If an <IMG> tag is given the ID="MyImage" attribute, for instance, you could check the value of its z-index style attribute with

```
document.write("MyImage z-index is: " +
   document.all.MyImage.style.zIndex)
```

Or, using associative arrays:

```
document.write("MyImage z-index is: " +
   document.all['MyImage'].style.zIndex)
```

N O T E   Notice that the z-index style attribute is scripted using the zIndex property. Dashes
cannot be used in an object property name and are replaced by intercaps (the letter
immediately after where the dash would have been is capitalized). ▪

Netscape Navigator, on the other hand, enables you to access only the attributes of a subset of
the HTML tags within a document—for instance, those tags that either have a style attached to
them or that are within a <LAYER> or <ILAYER> container tag. In either case, the syntax for
writing scripts to access or change any of the positioning attributes is the same and is referenced through the layers object array of the document object. To look at a similar example as
that given above for Internet Explorer, for a layer that has been given the ID="MyLayer" attribute, you could check its visibility style attribute value with either

```
document.write("MyLayer z-index is: " +
   document.layers.MyLayer.zIndex)
```

or

```
document.write("MyLayer z-index is: " +
   document.layers['MyLayer'].zIndex)
```

▶ **See** "Referencing Web Browser Objects," **p. 561**.

Dynamic Styles with Cascading Style Sheets

Similar to CSS positioning, discussed in the preceding section, both Internet Explorer and
Navigator have the capability to specify and/or dynamically change the format and style of
HTML elements through style sheets and the object model that each browser uses. Navigator
can use JavaScript only to specify formatting styles at load time, whereas Internet Explorer can
establish them at load time and also dynamically change them.

Table 9.1 in Chapter 9 gives a very good listing of the formatting attributes of style sheets.
These attributes can be manipulated by scripts running in either Netscape Navigator or
Microsoft Internet Explorer, although, like CSS positioning, the object reference in each
browser differs slightly.

Chapter 25, "Advanced Netscape Dynamic HTML," and Chapter 26, "Advanced Microsoft
Dynamic HTML," discuss this topic in greater detail. These chapters show you how to use
Dynamic HTML in either browser to change the format of your documents on-the-fly.

▶ **See** "JavaScript Accessible Style Sheets," **p. 610**.

▶ **See** "Using Dynamic HTML with Styles," **p. 650**.

Listing 24.3 shows an example of an HTML document that uses JavaScript to change the format of its content. This example also demonstrates some of the differences between what can be achieved with Netscape versus Microsoft Dynamic HTML.

Listing 24.3 *DynStyle.htm*—JavaScript for Specifying and (in Internet Explorer) Changing Formats

```
<HTML>
<HEAD>
<TITLE>Dynamic HTML Example</TITLE>
<STYLE>
    .clicked {font-size:36pt;color:red}
</STYLE>
<STYLE TYPE="text/javascript">
    classes.myClass.P.fontSize = "12pt"
    classes.myClass.P.fontFamily = "Verdana"
</STYLE>
<SCRIPT LANGUAGE="JavaScript">
if (navigator.appName == "Netscape")
    ieflag = false
else
    ieflag = true
function changeStyle() {
    if (ieflag) {
        document.all.tags("H1").item(0).className = "clicked"
        document.all.tags("P").item(1).style.fontSize = "18pt"
    }
}
</SCRIPT>
</HEAD>
<BODY BGCOLOR=#FFFFFF>
<CENTER>
<H1>Dynamic HTML and Styles</H1>
<HR>
<P CLASS="myClass">
    In this example, JavaScript (or JavaScript Accessible
    Style Sheets, for Navigator) is used to change the
    style of this paragraph when the document is loaded.
    This will work in version 4.0 or higher of either
    Netscape Navigator or Microsoft Internet Explorer.</P>
<P>When you click the button below, the style of the
    heading and this paragraph is changed; however, this
    only works in Internet Explorer.</P>
<HR>
<FORM>
<INPUT TYPE=BUTTON onClick="changeStyle()" VALUE="Click Me!">
</FORM>
<HR>
</CENTER>
```

Part
V

Ch
24

continues

Listing 24.3   Continued

```
<ADDRESS>
Jim O'Donnell, <A HREF="mailto:odonnj@rpi.edu">odonnj@rpi.edu</A>
</ADDRESS>
</BODY>
<SCRIPT LANGUAGE="JavaScript">
if (ieflag) {
    document.all.tags("P").item(0).style.fontSize = "12pt"
    document.all.tags("P").item(0).style.fontFamily = "Verdana"
}
</SCRIPT>
</HTML>
```

This example works as follows. First, a flag is set establishing whether the browser is Netscape Navigator or Microsoft Internet Explorer:

```
if (navigator.appName == "Netscape")
    ieflag = false
else
    ieflag = true
```

This flag is used throughout the rest of the document to determine which actions to perform.

N O T E   If you are trying to design pages that work on more than one browser, you need to be a little more thorough than performing only the check shown. Not only do you need to check for the browser type, you also need to check for version number and platform. If you are designing a personal Web site, it is usually enough to display a "Works best with..." message to indicate your preferred browser. Corporate sites, however, need to be designed for use with different browsers. ■

▶ **See** "Browser Detection Scripts," **p. 672**.

If this page is loaded into Netscape Navigator (see Figure 24.3), the second `<STYLE>` tag contains the information that is used to change the formatting information of the first paragraph of text.

```
<STYLE TYPE="text/javascript">
    classes.myClass.P.fontSize = "12pt"
    classes.myClass.P.fontFamily = "Verdana"
</STYLE>
```

This is what Netscape refers to as a "JavaScript Accessible Style Sheet." It specifies the format of the paragraph class known as `myClass`. This style is applied to the first paragraph through its `<P CLASS="myClass">` tag. After the document is loaded and displayed into Netscape Navigator, however, the format cannot be changed.

If this page is loaded into Internet Explorer, the following JavaScript lines change the format of the first paragraph of text after it is loaded and displayed:

```
if (ieflag) {
    document.all.tags("P").item(0).style.fontSize = "12pt"
    document.all.tags("P").item(0).style.fontFamily = "Verdana"
}
```

FIGURE 24.3

Netscape Navigator can use JavaScript to set formats as the document is being loaded, but it cannot change them after that.

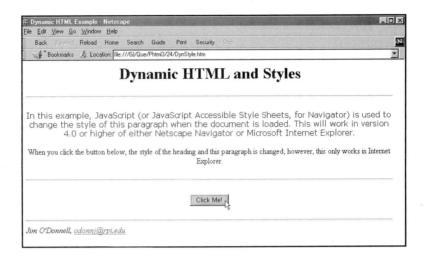

Unlike Navigator, Internet Explorer can also change the format of text dynamically. This is done in this document by attaching the `changeStyle()` function to the `onClick` event of the button.

```
function changeStyle() {
    if (ieflag) {
        document.all.tags("H1").item(0).className = "clicked"
        document.all.tags("P").item(1).style.fontSize = "18pt"
    }
}
```

The `changeStyle()` function changes the format of the second paragraph by directly manipulating its style properties, and it changes the format of the heading by attaching a different style sheet class to it (see Figure 24.4).

FIGURE 24.4

Microsoft Dynamic HTML surpasses that of Netscape in at least one area: enabling document formats to be changed and redisplayed on-the-fly.

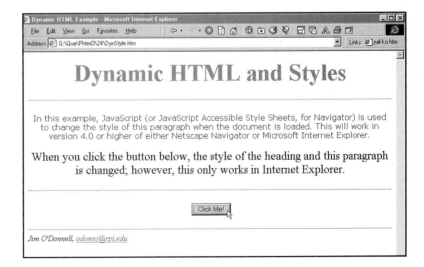

Web Browser Object Model

The Document Object Model used by Netscape Navigator and Microsoft Internet Explorer lies at the heart of their implementations of Dynamic HTML. Netscape's implementation, and its extensions to the object model, are not as extensive as Microsoft's. Still, a number of important extensions enable you to increase capability in your HTML documents.

Microsoft's new object model, on the other hand, is a much more significant extension of the object models of the past for either browser. In the past, you were limited mainly to accessing and manipulating the Web browser windows and only a few aspects of the current document, such as the hypertext links, HTML Forms, and images. Now, Microsoft's Dynamic HTML has extended the object model to every HTML tag. It is now possible to examine or set properties for any tag within an HTML document or to set up events that are attached anywhere. Microsoft's Dynamic HTML documentation Web site includes some good examples of this, enabling you to dynamically change the content included in an outline, expanding or compressing it in response to user input.

The differences and additions to the Web Browser Object Models introduced by Netscape and Microsoft are discussed in greater depth and detail in the following two chapters. The next two sections highlight some of the more important additions—in this case, changes to the Web browser event model and how you use it.

▶ **See** "Internet Explorer Document Object Model," **p. 638**.

The traditional event model enabled you to respond to a limited number of events that could be triggered by the actions of your users. Table 24.1 summarizes the most important of these events, along with their description and the HTML elements to which they applied.

Table 24.1   Traditional Web Browser Event Model

Event	Triggered When...	Where It Applies
onChange	object contents change	HTML form text fields
onClick	object is clicked	links and HTML form elements
onLoad	object loading is completed	document and images
onMouseOut	mouse is no longer over object	links and imagemaps
onMouseOver	mouse is over object	links and imagemaps
onReset	object contents are reset	HTML forms
onSubmit	object contents are submitted	HTML forms

The Netscape Navigator Event Model

Netscape Navigator version 4 and higher adds support for several new classes of events, enabling you to create scripts that respond to a greater variety of user input. The new categories and events are as follows:

■ Mouse events—Added events for `onMouseDown`, `onMouseUp`, and `onMouseMove`

■ Keystroke events—Added events for `onKeyDown`, `onKeyUp`, and `onKeyPress`

■ Window events—Added events for `onMove` and `onResize`

In addition to the new events, Netscape has added a new `event` object that you can use to access information about the triggered events. This object is created whenever an event is being processed, and it has the following properties:

■ `target`—The name of the object to which the event belongs

■ `type`—The event type (for example, `onMouseDown`, `onMouseUp`, and so forth)

■ `pageX`—The mouse's horizontal position relative to the HTML page

■ `pageY`—The mouse's vertical position relative to the HTML page

■ `screenX`—The mouse's horizontal position relative to the screen

■ `screenY`—The mouse's vertical position relative to the screen

■ `which`—A number specifying the mouse button or ASCII value of the key that was pressed

The `event` object is used a little differently than other objects. It comes into being in response to an event and can then be passed to an event handler for that event, as in

```
<FORM NAME="MyForm">
<INPUT TYPE="BUTTON" VALUE="Hi!" NAME="MyButton" onClick="hello(event)">
</FORM>
```

The event handler then takes the `event` object as a parameter and can access its properties to process the event, such as this:

```
<SCRIPT LANGUAGE="JAVASCRIPT">
function hello(MyEvent) {
    alert("Hello " + MyEvent.target.name);
}
</SCRIPT>
```

The Microsoft Internet Explorer Event Model

Microsoft's new event model is similar to Netscape's model in many respects and different in a few others. It includes most of the new events that Netscape has included, with the exception of the `onMove` and `onResize` events. It also creates an `event` object in response to events within the HTML document. Unfortunately, the `event` object itself and how it is used within a script are quite different from Netscape's system.

Microsoft's event model has a large number of properties for identifying the nature of the event and the state of the mouse and/or keyboard when the event was triggered. The properties that correspond to the properties of the Netscape event model shown previously are as follows:

■ `srcElement`—The name of the object to which the event belongs

■ `reason`—The event type (for example, `onMouseDown`, `onMouseUp`, and so forth

■ `x`—The mouse's horizontal position relative to the HTML page

■ `y`—The mouse's vertical position relative to the HTML page

Part
V

Ch
24

- `screenX`—The mouse's horizontal position relative to the screen
- `screenY`—The mouse's vertical position relative to the screen
- `button`—A number specifying the mouse button that was pressed
- `keyCode` A number specifying the UNICODE value of the key that was pressed

The syntax used for the Microsoft event object differs from that used with Netscape. It also comes into being in response to an event, but you do not need to pass it to the event handler:

```
<FORM NAME="MyForm">
<INPUT TYPE="BUTTON" VALUE="Hi!" NAME="MyButton" onClick="hello()">
</FORM>
```

The event handler can automatically access the properties of the event object, as in the following:

```
<SCRIPT LANGUAGE="JAVASCRIPT">
function hello() {
    alert("Hello " + event.srcElement.name);}
}
</SCRIPT>
```

Dynamic Fonts

The introduction of the FACE attribute of the <FONT> tag gave Web developers the capability to choose the font in which their content should be rendered, giving them much greater control over the final appearance of their documents. The advent of style sheets and the CSS standard—now supported by the two most popular Web browsers—add an even greater capability for you to specify the precise font, format, and position of everything on your Web page. Increasingly, the visual effects that you develop through HTML, without having to rely on large graphics or other types of plug-in content, are limited only by your imagination.

Unfortunately, one implicit assumption is made that might get you into trouble when using <FONT FACE> or style sheets: These techniques work only if your user has the desired font installed on his or her local system. Although this should not be a problem for the "standard" fonts installed with Windows 95, you may run into problems if you want to use less popular fonts, or when your documents are viewed on other computer platforms. Many of your carefully constructed documents and effects can be ruined if your page is rendered in fonts other than the desired ones.

Both Netscape and Microsoft have introduced solutions to this problem. It will come as no surprise to you that the two solutions are not compatible, but they each achieve the same effect—they enable fonts to be embedded and used within an HTML document in such a way that, when the document is served to a Web browser, the fonts can also be downloaded and used for that document. Of course, it takes time to download fonts, the same as with graphics and other hypertext media; font files tend to be not very large, and Web fonts can be designed to have only the characters you need. Both these technologies are new, but they offer you the capability to truly design Web pages that will appear to your user exactly as designed.

Netscape's Downloadable Fonts

Netscape Dynamic HTML's downloadable fonts capability enables you to use any font in your HTML documents. You do this by creating a font definition file that would be placed on your Web server along with your other documents and content. When a user accesses a page that uses one of these fonts, the font definition file downloads with the HTML document the same as images, sounds, and other content displayed on the page. These downloaded fonts remain on the user's system only while the page is in their cache. Thus, users cannot make use of the fonts for their own purposes.

To make use of Netscape's downloadable fonts, you need to follow these steps:

1. Identify the font(s) that you want to use and make sure they are installed on your local system.

> **CAUTION**
>
> Remember that fonts, like all information on the Internet and the Web, are subject to copyright laws. Make sure you have a right to use any font that you plan to use as a downloadable font in any of your documents.

2. Create a font definition file. The easiest way to do this is with an authoring tool for font definition files, such as Typograph from HexMac Web sites (`http://www.hexmac.com`) or Netscape's Font Composer Plug-in for Communicator.

   The specific steps necessary to produce the file will depend on the tool used, but the output of the operation will be the font definition.

N O T E Netscape's font definition files enable you to specify the domain from which they may be served. This enables you to make sure that other people don't "hijack" fonts from your server to be used in their documents. ■

3. You must link the font definition file to your HTML document. You can do this either by using style sheets or with the `<LINK>` tag. Using style sheets, for example, to refer to a font definition file named `myfont.pfr` looks like this:

```
<STYLE TYPE="text/css">
<!-- Hide from incompatible browsers! -->
@fontdef url(http://www.rpi.edu/fonts/myfont.pfr);
<!-- Hide from incompatible browsers! -->
</STYLE>
```

   Linking the same font definition file by using the `<LINK>` tag looks like this:

```
<LINK REL=FONTDEF SRC="http://www.rpi.edu/fonts/myfont.pfr">
```

4. Add a new MIME type to your Web server for the font definition file. The MIME type is application/font-tdpfr, with file type `.pfr`.

5. Specify the font in your HTML documents. The name of the font will be specified within the font definition file, so you can use the font with `<FONT FACE>` or style sheets the same as you would use any other font.

Figure 24.5 shows an example of Netscape's downloadable fonts at work—a sample file located on the DevEdge Online Web site at

```
http://developer.netscape.com/library/documentation/communicator/dynhtml/
fontdef1.htm
```

If you watch this file load into your Web browser, you will notice that the text first renders in the default font. Then, as the desired fonts download, the text re-renders.

FIGURE 24.5

Netscape's downloadable fonts enable you to specify any font face, size, and weight that you have access to.

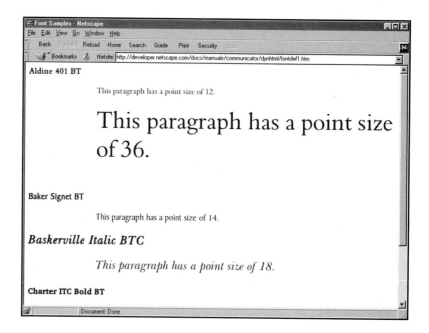

Microsoft Web Embedding Fonts

If you look through Microsoft's Dynamic HTML documentation, you won't find any mention of a capability to download fonts to be used with your HTML documents. Microsoft has, in fact, developed technology to perform this function—they just don't call it part of Dynamic HTML. You can find this technology, dubbed the Web Embedding Fonts Tool (WEFT), on Microsoft's Typography Web site at

```
http://www.microsoft.com/typography/
```

In practice, using the WEFT is similar to using Netscape's downloadable fonts technology. As with Netscape, you can use a special tool to produce what Microsoft calls the font object to be linked to and downloaded with an HTML document. These font object files differ from regular fonts files in that they are prepared especially to be downloaded over the Web—they are compressed and made up of the subset of font characters actually used. These techniques can result in a savings of at least half the time otherwise required—far more if only a small number of characters is used.

After the WEFT is used to create the font object file, it is linked into the HTML document. The syntax Microsoft uses to define an embedded font, included within a style sheet, is the following:

```
@font-face {
    font-family: MyFont;
    font-style:  normal;
    font-weight: normal;
    src: url(MYFONT0.eot);
}
```

In this case, the `src` attribute defines the actual location of the font object file.

Although the tools used to define the font file and the format of the file itself differ between Microsoft's and Netscape's systems—as well as the way that the fonts are linked into an HTML document—the other features of the two systems are very similar. Both systems enable you to determine the domain from which the fonts can be served, and both allow the font to remain on the user's system only as long as the user is viewing your pages.

Figures 24.6 and 24.7 show an example of pages created using Microsoft's font-embedding technology. The second figure shows what can happen to your carefully constructed Web page if, for some reason, the fonts it uses cannot be downloaded (or are otherwise unavailable).

FIGURE 24.6

Downloading small subsets of fonts makes it easy to create neat effects and special displays without having to create large graphics.

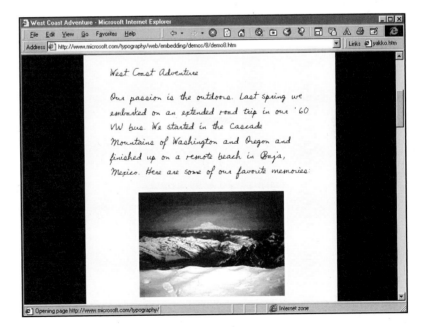

FIGURE 24.7

If the font to be downloaded can't be found, or some other problem occurs, your Web page won't have the desired effect.

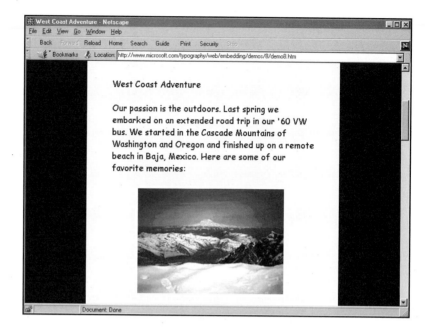

Advanced Netscape Dynamic HTML

by Eric Ladd and Jim O'Donnell

Different Approaches to Dynamic HTML

In Chapter 24, "Introduction to Dynamic HTML," you learned about the different claims as to what constitutes Dynamic HTML as put forward by Netscape and Microsoft. The two claims have a number of similarities—the differences lie in the implementation. Both takes on Dynamic HTML involve the following ideas:

■ Positioning content on a page, either absolutely or relative to where the content would otherwise go

■ Use of a Web Browser Object Model to make all or part of a document accessible to a scripting language

■ The capability to download fonts to a user's machine so that your pages are displayed with the typefaces you designate

Again, the differences are in how you implement each of the preceding ideas on Navigator or Internet Explorer. Both browsers more or less conform to the Cascading Style Sheets 1 (CSS1) recommended standard for content positioning, for example, but Netscape also has a proprietary HTML tag that can do many of the same things. Another difference is in the scripting language. Navigator uses JavaScript, whereas Internet Explorer uses its own JScript, which is largely compatible with Netscape's JavaScript, but not completely. Internet Explorer's object model is much more extensive than Navigator's. The mechanism that each program uses to download fonts to a user's hard drive is different. The list could go on and on, but the point is that if you develop a Dynamic HTML document for one browser, it is likely that it will not work in the other. This might hinder your development efforts if your audience is using a mix of browsers. If you are developing for a consistent desktop platform (a corporate intranet, for example, where everyone is using the same browser), however, you can make use of one definition of Dynamic HTML or the other and not have to worry about your content being lost on some users.

> **N O T E**   Microsoft's version of Dynamic HTML also calls for dynamic redisplay and reformatting of dynamic content, attaching data from an external source to an HTML element, and multimedia capabilities using ActiveX Controls. Netscape Navigator does not support these additional Dynamic HTML components. ■

This chapter digs deeper into Netscape's implementation of Dynamic HTML on the Netscape Navigator 4.0 browser. By more closely examining Netscape's approach to Dynamic HTML and considering some examples, you will be better prepared to develop pages for a user base that has Navigator as its "standard-issue" browser.

A Standard Deployment of Dynamic HTML?

Even if your entire audience is using one browser or another, you should also keep in mind that people are working on a standard deployment of some of the common Dynamic HTML elements listed at the start of the chapter. This means that you could develop Dynamic HTML content for one browser or another, and it may never be considered "standard."

Content positioning by Cascading Style Sheets is covered in the CSS specification found at `http://www.w3.org/Style/`. The good news here is that both major browsers more or less conform to the standard.

Additionally, the World Wide Web Consortium (W3C) is working on a Document Object Model (DOM), the details of which are covered at `http://www.w3.org/DOM/`. Both Netscape's and Microsoft's Web Browser Object Models are extensions of the W3C DOM.

Chapter 27, "Cross-Browser Dynamic HTML," contains more tips on how to create Web pages that use Dynamic HTML and that can be successfully viewed with both Netscape Navigator and Microsoft Internet Explorer.

▶ **See** "What Is Cross-Browser Dynamic HTML?," **p. 670**.

The Three Main Elements of Netscape's Dynamic HTML

Netscape considers something to be Dynamic HTML if it includes the following three major elements:

- Styles sheets accessible through the browser object model
- Content positioning in two and three dimensions
- Downloadable fonts

Netscape Navigator supports the Cascading Style Sheet specification just like other browsers do, but what makes its support dynamic is that style sheet elements are part of the Navigator browser object model. This means that you can specify style information through JavaScript in addition to the CSS way of doing it. Figure 25.1 shows a Web page that formats content style through both JavaScript and CSS (see Listing 25.1). As you can see, it is possible to manipulate the same style parameters with either method.

Part
V

Ch
25

Listing 25.1 *StyleApp.htm*—**JavaScript and CSS Styles**

```
<HTML>
<HEAD>
<STYLE TYPE="text/css">
.css {color: red;
      font-family: Comic Sans MS;
      font-size: 18pt;
      line-height: 18pt;
      margin-left: 40px}
</STYLE>
<STYLE TYPE="text/javascript">
document.tags.P.color = "blue";
document.tags.P.fontFamily = "Verdana";
document.tags.P.fontSize = "12pt";
```

continues

Listing 25.1 Continued

```
document.tags.P.fontWeight = "bold";
document.tags.P.lineHeight = "20pt";
document.tags.P.marginLeft = "80px";
</STYLE>
<TITLE>Applying Styles: CSS vs JavaScript</TITLE>
</HEAD>
<BODY>
<H1>Applying Styles: CSS vs JavaScript</H1>
<HR>
<P><EM>[JavaScript Syntax]</EM><BR>
   In this example, we show that styles can be changed in
   Netscape Navigator using either CSS or JavaScript syntax.
   This paragraph gets its style with &lt;STYLE&gt; information
   assigned to the &lt;P&gt; tag via JavaScript.</P>
<HR>
<P CLASS="css"><EM>[CSS Syntax]</EM><BR>
   In this example, we show that styles can be changed in
   Netscape Navigator using either CSS or JavaScript syntax.
   This paragraph gets its style via a style sheet class
   defined using CSS syntax.</P>
<HR>
<ADDRESS>
Jim O'Donnell, <A HREF="mailto:odonnj@rpi.edu">odonnj@rpi.edu</A>
</ADDRESS>
</BODY>
</HTML>
```

FIGURE 25.1

Navigator enables you to specify style parameters using a couple of syntaxes.

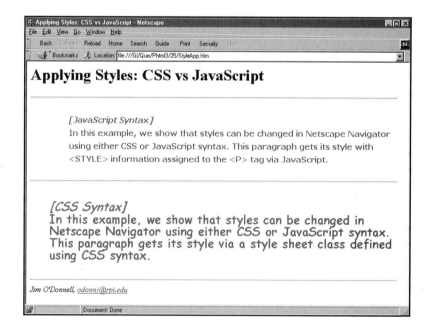

Note the object orientation of the JavaScript code in Listing 25.1. The first style assignment says "set the `color` property of the `P` property of the `tags` property of the `document` property to blue." The Navigator browser object model makes many tags available to you in this way.

 The `document` object reference is understood whenever you reference the `tags` object. Thus, instead of saying

```
document.tags.P.color = "blue";
```

you can equivalently say

```
tags.P.color = "blue";
```

 When assigning multiple style characteristics to the same tag, you can use the JavaScript `with` instruction to reference the tag and then all styles inside the `with` instruction will be assigned to the tag. For the `P` tag assignments in Listing 25.1, you could have used the following abbreviated code:

```
with (tags.P) {
    color = "blue";
    fontFamily = "Verdana";
    fontSize = "12pt";
    fontWeight = "bold";
    lineHeight = "20pt";
    marginLeft = "80px";
}
```

Content positioning was introduced in Navigator 4.0 through use of the `<LAYER>` and `<ILAYER>` tags for absolute and relative positioning, respectively. Unfortunately for Netscape, using HTML tags to specify content presentation information flies in the face of the direction that the W3C wants to move—namely, to reserve HTML for describing the meaning of the content and to specify presentation through style sheets. The W3C rejected the Netscape proposal for the `<LAYER>` tag, and Netscape was forced to scramble to make Navigator compliant with the CSS approach to content positioning. Currently, Navigator supports both positioning techniques, although you should always consider developing according to the CSS specification because this will make your content more portable.

Figures 25.2 and 25.3 show a page done with Netscape layers. Each figure has two layers nested within an outer layer. The two layers, Layer A and Layer B in the example, are each made up of text with some style information attached. The containing layer has functions attached to its `onMouseOver` and `onMouseOut` events that toggle which layer is shown by manipulating their visibility properties. Figure 25.2 shows the `onMouseOut` condition, with Layer A visible. Figure 25.3 shows the `onMouseOver` condition, with Layer B visible. Note that the `onMouseOver` event is triggered even though it appears the mouse cursor is not over the layer. Because the `onMouseOver` event of the outer layer is used, more of the screen area of the browser window is included in it than just the visible inner layers. The HTML code for this example is shown in Listing 25.2.

Part
V

Ch

25

FIGURE 25.2

When you open this page, it displays only one of two nested layers.

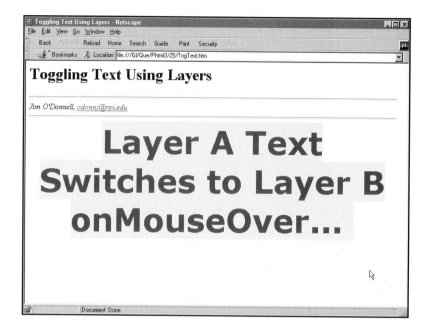

FIGURE 25.3

By clicking the layer, you instruct the browser to swap the hidden and displayed nested layers.

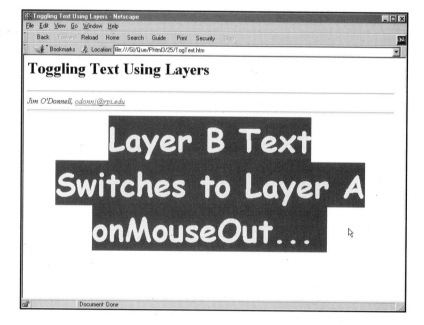

Listing 25.2 *TogText.htm*—**Dynamic Content in Netscape Navigator Using Layers**

```html
<HTML>
<HEAD>
<TITLE>Toggling Text Using Layers</TITLE>
<SCRIPT LANGUAGE="JavaScript">
function layerUp(show,hide) {
   show.visibility = "SHOW";
   hide.visibility = "HIDE";
}
</SCRIPT>
</HEAD>
<BODY BGCOLOR=#FFFFFF>
<H1>Toggling Text Using Layers</H1>
<HR>
<ADDRESS>
Jim O'Donnell, <A HREF="mailto:odonnj@rpi.edu">odonnj@rpi.edu</A>
</ADDRESS>
<HR>
<CENTER>
<LAYER NAME=togLayer
       onMouseOver="layerUp(layerb,layera)"
       onMouseOut="layerUp(layera,layerb)"
       VISIBILITY=INHERIT>
   <LAYER NAME=togLayerA
       STYLE="font-family: Verdana; font-size: 48pt;
              font-weight: bold; text-align: center;
              color: blue; background-color: yellow"
       VISIBILITY=INHERIT>
   Layer A Text<BR>Switches to Layer B onMouseOver...
   </LAYER>
   <LAYER NAME=togLayerB
       STYLE="font-family: Comic Sans MS; font-size: 48pt;
              font-weight: bold; text-align: center;
              color: yellow; background-color: blue"
       VISIBILITY=HIDE>
   Layer B Text<BR>Switches to Layer A onMouseOut...
   </LAYER>
</LAYER>
</CENTER>
</BODY>
<SCRIPT LANGUAGE="JavaScript">
var layera = document.layers['togLayer'].document.togLayerA;
var layerb = document.layers['togLayer'].document.togLayerB;
</SCRIPT>
</HTML>
```

Part

V

Ch

25

TIP Netscape has many useful Dynamic HTML JavaScript routines available through its DevEdge site at
http://developer.netscape.com/tech/dynhtml/index.html.

For all your hard work in coming up with attractive style information, you may end up having your effect lost on users who don't have the font you specified in your style sheet. Rather than take chances on fonts a user may or may not have, you can bundle the font you want to use with a Web page and have it download along with the page. This assures both you and the reader that the page will display the way you wanted it to.

Figure 25.4 shows an example of a page that uses a downloaded font. The type face you see is used for Japanese language pages, one not commonly found on most users' systems.

FIGURE 25.4

By downloading fonts along with a page, you ensure that readers see content the way you intended.

Now that you have the major ideas behind Netscape's Dynamic HTML fresh in your mind, it is time to take a closer look at each one. The remaining sections of this chapter examine each idea in turn and provide you with more details about how to implement Dynamic HTML on your pages.

JavaScript Accessible Style Sheets

Netscape Navigator does support the CSS specification, and using the CSS approach is a perfectly good way to build style information into your documents. But, as you saw earlier in the chapter, Navigator also includes style properties in the browser object model, which means you can use JavaScript to access and set style characteristics. Netscape call this approach JavaScript Accessible Style Sheets; it is the first major feature of Netscape's version of Dynamic HTML.

The advantage of JavaScript Accessible Style Sheets is that by using the browser object model, you can dynamically change style information by using scripts triggered by certain events that come about from user actions. This section focuses solely on the JavaScript implementation of styles so that you can be prepared to use them by themselves and also as part of content positioning.

To get started, it is helpful to recall some of the style-related code—both CSS and JavaScript—that you saw earlier in the chapter. Go back a few pages and look at Listing 25.1. Both techniques apply the same style information, yet one is an implementation of CSS style sheets and the other is an implementation of JavaScript Accessible Style Sheets. If you are familiar with one approach, you can see that it would be pretty easy to learn the other. Most of the style characteristics you can set have the same name (although the names differ in the use of hyphens, capitalization, and so on). The chief difference between the two approaches is how the style characteristics are assigned. The CSS approach uses name/value pairs separated by a colon. The JavaScript approach is more object based in that you reference an object's (a tag's) style property and set it to the value you want. Beyond the syntactical difference in assigning values, the two approaches are—in most respects—equivalent.

Table 25.1 summarizes the style characteristics you can assign by either approach and includes the keyword for the characteristic that you would use in either the CSS or JavaScript approach. The table should make a handy reference for all style sheet authors, regardless of how they are assigning style information.

Table 25.1   Style Characteristics in CSS and JavaScript Accessible Style Sheets

Style Characteristic	CSS Keyword	JavaScript Property
font family	font-family	`fontFamily`
font size	font-size	`fontSize`
font style	font-style	`fontStyle`
font weight	font-weight	`fontWeight`
text alignment	text-align	`textAlign`
text decoration	text-decoration	`textDecoration`
text indent	text-indent	`textIndent`
text transform	text-transform	`textTransform`
line height	line-height	`lineHeight`
alignment	float	`align`
border color	border-color	`borderColor`
border style	border-style	`borderStyle`
border widths (all)	border-width	`borderWidths()`
border width (bottom)	border-bottom-width	`borderBottomWidth`
border width (left)	border-left-width	`borderLeftWidth`

continues

Table 25.1 Continued

Style Characteristic	CSS Keyword	JavaScript Property
border width (right)	border-right-width	`borderRightWidth`
border width (top)	border-top-width	`borderTopWidth`
margins (all)	margin	`margins()`
margin (bottom)	margin-bottom	`marginBottom`
margin (left)	margin-left	`marginLeft`
margin (right)	margin-right	`marginRight`
margin (top)	margin-top	`marginTop`
padding (all)	paddings	`paddings()`
padding (bottom)	padding-bottom	`paddingBottom`
padding (left)	padding-left	`paddingLeft`
padding (right)	padding-right	`paddingRight`
padding (top)	padding-top	`paddingTop`
width	width	`width`
background color	background-color	`backgroundColor`
background image	background-image	`backgroundImage`
color	color	`color`
display	display	`display`
list style type	list-style-type	`listStyleType`
whitespace	white-space	`whiteSpace`

You are probably familiar with most of the characteristics in Table 25.1, except possibly for the last three. Display controls how an element is displayed and can take values of `block` (display as a block-level element), `inline`, `list-item`, or `none`. List style type refers to the different styles of ordered and unordered lists HTML supports. You may set the `list-style-type` keyword or the `listStyleType` property to values of `disc`, `circle`, `square`, `decimal`, `lower-alpha`, `upper-alpha`, `lower-roman`, `upper-roman`, or `none`. Finally, the whitespace characteristic specifies how extra whitespace should be treated. A whitespace value of `normal` means that extra whitespace characters will be ignored, and a value of `pre` means that all whitespace characters will be rendered.

With what you have learned so far, you can probably handle most of the style sheet challenges that come your way. Be aware, however, that both the CSS and JavaScript approaches support some more advanced techniques. These include the following:

- Setting up different classes of the same element
- Creating a named style that you can apply to any element
- Selecting an element based on context
- Making use of block-level styles

Each of these points is covered in the sections that follow, with emphasis on the JavaScript implementation of each.

TROUBLESHOOTING

My JavaScript code is not working in Netscape Navigator and I can't tell what the error is!

Make sure that JavaScript is enabled in your Netscape Navigator. You can do this by choosing Edit, Preferences, and then clicking the Advanced item in the category listing in the Preferences dialog box. After you do this, you will see a list of check box options. Make sure that the check box labeled Enable JavaScript is checked. Then click OK.

Because Netscape is capable of processing JavaScript, you should find that the next time you load your JavaScript document, Netscape will interpret the script code and note in a pop-up dialog box any syntax errors it finds. The error messages are usually very specific and should help you clean up your code.

Setting Up Style Classes

Suppose you assign the following style characteristics to the `<H1>` element:

```
<STYLE TYPE="text/javascript">
with (tags.H1) {
   backgroundColor = "black";
   color = "white";
   fontSize = "36pt";
   lineHeight = "40pt";
   align = "center";
   width = "100%";
}
</STYLE>
```

Using the preceding code, each level 1 heading would appear centered in a black box that is 40 points high and spans the width of the browser screen. The text of the headline would be 36 points high and rendered in white. But what if you don't want every level 1 heading to look like this? Suppose you want some of them to be in yellow on a red background so that they are more prominent. In that case, you can define two classes of the H1 element style—one for the white on black heading and one for the yellow on red.

Classes are set up using the JavaScript `classes` object. To set up the two types of level 1 headings just discussed, for example, you could use this code:

```
<STYLE TYPE="text/javascript">
with (tags.H1) {
```

```
        fontSize = "36pt";
        lineHeight = "40pt";
        align = "center";
        width = "100%";
}
classes.whiteOnBlack.H1.backgroundColor = "black";
classes.whiteOnBlack.H1.color = "white";
classes.yellowOnRed.H1.backgroundColor = "red";
classes.yellowOnRed.H1.color = "yellow";
</STYLE>
```

The `with` operator makes all level 1 headings 36 point on 40 point, centered, and the full width of the browser screen. The last four lines of code define the two classes: `whiteOnBlack`, which produces white text on a black background; and `yellowOnRed`, which produces yellow text on a red background. With the two classes defined, you can invoke one class or another by using the `CLASS` attribute in the `<H1>` tag as follows:

```
<H1 CLASS="yellowOnRed">Yellow headline on red background</H1>
<H1 CLASS="whiteOnBlack">White headline on black background</H1>
```

The one limitation in the way the classes are set up is that they can be used only with the `H1` element. If you want your classes applicable to more than just the `H1` element, you could duplicate the code for the other elements you want to use the classes with, or you could make the classes available to every element by using the `all` object as follows:

```
classes.whiteOnBlack.all.backgroundColor = "black";
classes.whiteOnBlack.all.color = "white";
classes.yellowOnRed.all.backgroundColor = "red";
classes.yellowOnRed.all.color = "yellow";
```

The preceding code makes the `whiteOnBlack` and `yellowOnRed` classes available to all HTML elements, not just `H1`. If you don't want to apply either class to an element, don't use a `CLASS` attribute with that element.

N O T E The properties assigned in these classes are only applicable to block-level formats such as headings, paragraphs, blockquotes, and lists. Trying to apply the classes to text-level formatting tags would have no effect.

CAUTION

You can only specify one CLASS per HTML tag. If you put multiple CLASS attributes in a tag, Netscape Navigator uses the first one it encounters and ignores the rest.

Setting Up Named Styles

Besides creating classes of the same tag, you can also create a specific named style that you can build into any tag. The JavaScript `ids` object enables you to set up the named style, and then the style can be referenced by any tag using the `ID` attribute.

As an example of a named style, consider the following code:

```
<STYLE TYPE="text/javascript">
ids.allCaps.textTransform = "uppercase";
ids.bigText.fontSize = "125%";
</STYLE>
```

After executing the script code, Navigator recognizes two named styles: `allCaps`, which transforms all text to uppercase; and `bigText`, which magnifies text to 125% of its default size. If you had a paragraph you wanted to appear in all uppercase letters, you could set it up with this:

```
<P ID="allCaps">This paragraph is all uppercase letters...</P>
```

Suppose you still had the `whiteOnBlack` and `yellowOnRed` classes available to you from the preceding section. You could then use a class and a named style together as follows:

```
<H1 CLASS="yellowOnRed" ID="allCaps">
   Yellow Uppercase Heading on Red Background
</H1>
```

One popular effect on Web pages is *small caps* —text that is all in uppercase and the first letter of each word is larger than the rest of the letters in the word. You can accomplish this with the two named styles already defined, but you have to use the `<SPAN>` tag to apply the `bigText` style. For example:

```
<H1 CLASS="whiteOnBlack" ID="allCaps">
<SPAN ID="bigText">V</SPAN>ery
<SPAN ID="bigText">I</SPAN>mportant
<SPAN ID="bigText">S</SPAN>tory!
</H1>
```

Listing 25.3 shows an example that combines these methods of applying style information and shows that their effects are cumulative on subject text. In this example, the text within the `<H1>` container tag is given the `Impact` style through the `CLASS` attribute, and the named `allCaps` through the `ID` attribute. Further, the small caps font style is achieved by applying the named `bigText` style to the first letter of each word. The effects accumulate; the text is first given the font characteristics of 48pt Impact through the `Impact` class, then it is made all capital letters with the `allCaps` style, and finally, its initial letters are enlarged using the `bigText` style (see Figure 25.5).

Listing 25.3 *StyleApp2.htm*—Applied Style Effects Are Cumulative

```
<HTML>
<HEAD>
<STYLE TYPE="text/javascript">
classes.Impact.all.fontFamily = "Impact";
classes.Impact.all.fontSize = "48pt";
ids.allCaps.textTransform = "uppercase";
ids.bigText.fontSize = "125%";
</STYLE>
<TITLE>Applying Styles: Classes and Named Styles</TITLE>
</HEAD>
<BODY>
<H1 CLASS="Impact" ID="allCaps">
```

continues

Part

V

Ch

25

Listing 25.3 Continued

```
    <SPAN ID="bigText">A</SPAN>pplying
    <SPAN ID="bigText">S</SPAN>tyles:
    <SPAN ID="bigText">C</SPAN>lasses
    and
    <SPAN ID="bigText">N</SPAN>amed
    <SPAN ID="bigText">S</SPAN>tyles</H1>
<HR>
<ADDRESS>
Jim O'Donnell, <A HREF="mailto:odonnj@rpi.edu">odonnj@rpi.edu</A>
</ADDRESS>
</BODY>
</HTML>
```

FIGURE 25.5

You can use style classes and named styles together to produce complex typographic effects.

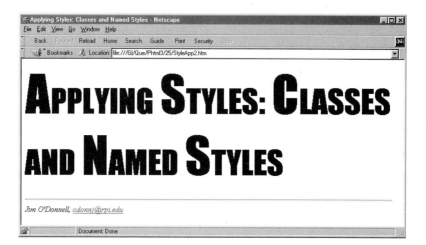

Doing Contextual Selection

Sometimes it is necessary to apply style information to an element only when it appears in the context of another. With CSS, doing this is fairly straightforward. As an example, the following code:

```
<STYLE TYPE="text/css">
H1 STRONG {color:red};
</STYLE>
```

says that any level 1 heading text marked up with the <STRONG> element should be rendered in red. This makes some sense because headings are already in boldface. Adding the <STRONG> element, which usually produces boldface rendering, would not change the appearance of the text. By making <STRONG> text red within a level 1 heading, you make it stand out even more and thereby convey your strong emphasis.

To accomplish the same effect with JavaScript, you need to use the contextual() method. contextual() takes a list of element objects that represent the usage context to which you want to apply style information. The following replicates the effect of the CSS code just discussed:

```
<STYLE TYPE="javascript"
contextual(tags.H1,tags.STRONG).color = "red";
</STYLE>
```

After you have the context set up, you don't need to do anything special in the HTML code to invoke it. You just nest the tags and the browser detects the context.

Applying Styles to Block-Level Elements

Block-level formatting tags require some extra attention because of how the browser treats them. Block-level formatting in HTML 4.0 includes <P>, <DIV>, <H1>–<H6>, and <BLOCKQUOTE>.

You can think of each block-level element on a page as having an invisible box that contains it. The boundaries of that box define the extent of the block-formatted text, and the browser treats that box as an object that has many properties, such as borders, indentation, and background colors. Figure 25.6 shows the extent of a box around an <H1> heading by turning on the box's border and making the background color yellow. This example was made using virtually the same code as shown in Listing 25.3, with the addition of the <STYLE> information shown in Listing 25.4, which is used to add the background color and borders.

Listing 25.4   *StyleApp3.htm* (excerpt)—HTML Block-Level Elements

```
<STYLE TYPE="text/javascript">
with (tags.H1) {
   backgroundColor = "yellow";
   borderWidths("10pt");
   borderStyle = "solid";
}
</STYLE>
```

Part
V

Ch
25

FIGURE 25.6

Block-level formats are contained in an invisible box, but you can modify the box's properties to make it visible.

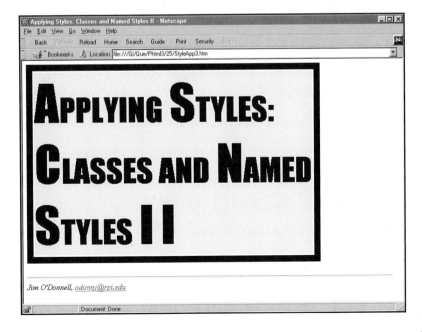

Because of the boxes that surround them, block-level elements have style characteristics that other elements do not. These characteristics include the following:

- Alignment with respect to the rest of the document
- Background colors or images
- Borders of varying width, style, and color
- Margins from the left, right, top, and bottom boundaries of the box
- Padding (the distance from the elements' content to the edges of the box) along the left, right, top, and bottom of the content within the box
- Width of the box with respect to the rest of the document

Refer back to Table 25.1 for the JavaScript property names for each of these; each is fairly intuitive. As you specify values for these properties, keep the image of the invisible box in mind, and it will help you visualize what your results will look like.

One important thing to note is the relationship between the width and margin characteristics. Mathematically, you could describe the relationship between the width of the block element, the margins, and the width of the content of the block element as this:

```
block element width = left margin + content width + right margin
```

After the content is specified, its width is determined and becomes a fixed value. This means you can set either of the following:

- The margins, and let the margin sizes and the content width determine the total width
- The total width, and let the margins split the balance of the remaining space

The point is that it does not make sense to specify *both* the margins and the total width. After you choose values for one, the value of the other is determined by the preceding equation.

Content Positioning

In the previous section, you saw how you could use JavaScript to assign values to style characteristics and dynamically format your document. One class of style characteristics was deliberately left out of the section, however: those for specifying content position. Content positioning is a much different activity than assigning styles, and you can bring many more JavaScript commands to bear on a content-positioning challenge. This section looks at how you can do content positioning with Netscape Navigator. Again, the focus is on Netscape's implementation of content positioning. This means that it will be "legal" to make use of the nonstandard <LAYER> element as well as CSS techniques to do positioning.

The *<LAYER>* and *<ILAYER>* Elements

Chapter 24 showed you some examples of content positioning. Specifically, you saw how you could position an element with respect to the upper-left corner of the browser window (*absolute positioning*) or with respect to the location where the element would ordinarily be placed (*relative positioning*). In addition to being able to specify the x and y coordinates of where the element should appear, you were also able to control a z coordinate, which determined how the elements overlap. You could think of each element as sitting on a transparent sheet that you could move around the browser screen and stack one on top of the other to create different effects. Netscape's term for these transparent sheets is *layers*. You can implement layers in Navigator by using the CSS specification for content positioning or by using the proprietary <LAYER> and <ILAYER> elements to do absolute and relative positioning, respectively. This section introduces you to the <LAYER> and <ILAYER> tags and their many attributes.

N O T E   <LAYER> and <ILAYER> take the same set of attributes, so this section focuses only on using the <LAYER> tag. The <ILAYER> (inline layer) tag behaves the same as the <LAYER> tag. Although the <ILAYER> allows for positioning of content relative to where the content would appear in the flow of the document, the <LAYER> tag is used for absolute positioning of content with respect to the upper-left corner of the browser window. ▪

The <LAYER> tag is a container tag that can take the following attributes:

- BACKGROUND—The BACKGROUND attribute is set equal to the URL of an image to tile in the background of the layer. In the absence of a background image or background color (see BGCOLOR next in this list), the layer background is transparent and enables any layers stacked beneath it to show through.

- BGCOLOR—You can set BGCOLOR equal to a reserved English-language color name, an RGB triplet, or a hexadecimal triplet that specifies a background color for the layer. Otherwise, the layer background is transparent.

- SRC—You have two ways to place content in layers. You can place the content between the <LAYER> and </LAYER> tags or you can import the content from another file by using the SRC attribute. SRC is set equal to the URL of the document you want to import.

- ID—The ID attribute is used to assign a unique name to a layer so that it can be referenced in other <LAYER> tags or in JavaScript code.

- LEFT and TOP—LEFT and TOP are set equal to the number of pixels from the upper-left corner of the browser screen where the layer should begin. These two attributes permit exact positioning of the layer on the screen. Note that if you're using <ILAYER>, LEFT and TOP specify displacement from the left of and below the point where the layer would ordinarily start, rather than from the upper-left of the browser screen. Also, when using relative positioning, you can set LEFT and TOP equal to negative values.

- Z-INDEX, ABOVE, and BELOW—These three attributes help to specify how the layers stack up along the z-axis (the axis coming out of the browser screen toward the user). Z-INDEX is set equal to a positive integer, and a layer with a larger Z-INDEX value will appear stacked on top of layers that have lower Z-INDEX values. You can place a new layer above or below an existing named layer by setting ABOVE or BELOW equal to the named layer's name. In the absence of Z-INDEX, ABOVE, or BELOW attributes, new layers are stacked on top of old layers.

- VISIBILITY—VISIBILITY can take on one of the following three values: SHOW, HIDE, or INHERIT. If a layer's VISIBILITY is set to SHOW, the content of the layer will be displayed.

Setting VISIBILITY to HIDE conceals the layer content. A VISIBILITY value of INHERIT means that the layer will have the same VISIBILITY behavior as its parent layer.

- CLIP—The *clipping region* of a layer is a rectangular area that defines how much of the layer content is visible. You can control the size of the clipping region by using the CLIP attribute. CLIP is set equal to a comma-delimited list of four numbers that represent the coordinates of the upper-left and lower-right corners of the clipping region. Measurements for clipping region coordinates are taken with respect to the upper-left corner of the layer. By default, the clipping region is large enough to display all the contents of the layer.

- HEIGHT—In the absence of a CLIP attribute, HEIGHT controls the height of the clipping region. HEIGHT may be set equal to a number of pixels or to a percentage of the layer's height.

- WIDTH—The WIDTH attribute specifies the width at which layer contents begin to wrap to new lines. Like HEIGHT, you can set WIDTH equal to a number of pixels or to a percentage of the layer width.

- PAGEX and PAGEY—Because it is possible to nest layers inside of layers, you may end up in a situation where you want to position a layer with respect to the entire browser screen and not its parent element (the layer that contains it). In such a case, you can use the PAGEX and PAGEY attributes to specify where the layer should begin with respect to the upper-left corner of the browser screen.

The <LAYER> tag's extensive set of attributes makes many interesting effects possible. By changing the size of the clipping region, for example, you can show or hide different parts of the layer's content. You can change the Z-INDEX of a layer to make it rise above or drop below other layers. You could even adjust the TOP and LEFT values to make a layer move to a new position. All these changes are possible thanks to the capability to use JavaScript to modify layer properties. The following section provides some examples of that. To complete the discussion of the <LAYER> tag's syntax, however, the following is a list of JavaScript event handlers you can use with the <LAYER> tag:

- OnMouseOver—The OnMouseOver event is invoked when a user's mouse pointer enters the layer.

- OnMouseOut—When the mouse pointer leaves a layer, the OnMouseOut event is fired.

- OnFocus—If the layer acquires keyboard focus (for example, a user clicks a form field in a layer so as to be able to type in it), an OnFocus event is triggered.

- OnBlur—Blurring refers to the loss of focus. When a layer blurs, Navigator invokes an OnBlur event.

- OnLoad—The OnLoad event is triggered when the layer is initially loaded.

Using these event handlers is the first step in making your positioned content dynamic. Depending on what JavaScript code you execute upon an event firing, you can change a layer's content or move it to a new position to create an animation effect. You will read about some of the possibilities in subsequent sections of this chapter. However, you should first know about one other layer-related tag.

The *<NOLAYER>* Tag

Netscape knew it was creating proprietary tags when it introduced <LAYER> and <ILAYER>, so it also included a <NOLAYER> element for specifying nonlayered versions of layered content. You might use <NOLAYER>, for example, as shown in Listing 25.5.

Listing 25.5 *NoLayer.htm* **Providing Alternate Content for Other Browsers**

```
<HTML>
<HEAD>
<TITLE>Welcome to Our Site!</TITLE>
</HEAD>
<LAYER LEFT=50 TOP=35 ID="layer1" SRC="toplayer.html"></LAYER>
<LAYER LEFT=100 TOP=152 ID="layer2" SRC="bottomlayer.html"></LAYER>
<NOLAYER>
<BODY BGCOLOR="white">
<H1>Whoops!</H1>
You must not be using Netscape Navigator, so you'd probably be interested
in a <A HREF="nolayers/index.html">non-layered version</A> of our site.
</BODY>
</NOLAYER>
</HTML>
```

Netscape Navigator ignores anything between <NOLAYER> and </NOLAYER>, so it will render the preceding example just fine. A browser that does not understand the layer-related tags ignores the two <LAYER> elements and the <NOLAYER> element and displays the HTML between the <NOLAYER> and </NOLAYER> tags.

N O T E When using layers, you don't use the <BODY> tag in the document except between
<NOLAYER> and </NOLAYER> tags. ■

Putting the "Dynamic" in Dynamic HTML with JavaScript

Everything you have read about so far in this chapter has largely been about how to create static content, so you might be wondering whether the term "Dynamic HTML" really applies. Now that you understand how to access style characteristics with JavaScript and how to use the <LAYER> tag to position content, however, you are ready to see how you can use JavaScript to make your pages come alive. This section gives an overview of some of the many things possible with JavaScript, layers, and style information.

▶ **See** "The Netscape Navigator Event Model," page **xxx.** (chapter 24, "Introduction to Dynamic HTML").

The capability to use JavaScript to create dynamic pages hinges on the Netscape browser object model, which provides for many different events and responses to those events. You read in Chapter 24 about the traditional events that Navigator supports and some extras added by Netscape to handle `mouse`, `keystroke`, and `window` events. Any of these can be used to trigger the execution of some JavaScript code in response to some kind of user action.

Two other aspects of the Netscape browser object model make Dynamic HTML possible. The first is the new `event` object that is created whenever an event occurs. As noted in Chapter 24, you can access properties of the `event` object to determine which kind of event was triggered, what mouse button or keystroke initiated the event, and to which object the event belongs.

The other helpful feature of the Netscape browser object model is that every layer—regardless of whether it was created using CSS properties or the `<LAYER>` tag—is accessible through the `layers` object. The `layers` object is actually an arrayed property of the `document` object, which means that you can reference a particular layer in the following manner:

```
document.layers["layer1"]
```

This code says to select the layer named "layer1" from the `layers` array of the `document` object. You can also reference the array by a number if you know the layer's position in the stacking order. If you want to make a direct reference to layer1, you could also say this:

```
document.layer1
```

N O T E　Only top-level layers in a document are listed in the layers array.

The properties of a layer selected from the `layers` object map very closely to the attributes of the `<LAYER>` tag discussed in the preceding section. Beyond those properties, one other thing could cause some confusion: Each layer has its own `document` property! A layer's `document` property refers to the content inside the layer and not the main document. Other than that, you can use the `document` property just as you always have. Thus, to reference a `<BLOCKQUOTE>` tag inside a layer named "imagelayer," you would use the following:

```
document.layers["imagelayer"].document.tags.BLOCKQUOTE
```

This may not seem too bad, but your references can get fairly complicated if you have layers nested inside a layer. Suppose "layer2" and "layer3" are top-level layers nested inside "layer1." Then, to reference the H5 tag in "layer3," you would have to say:

```
document.layers["layer1"].document.layers["layer3"].document.tags.H5
```

Table 25.2 provides a full listing of the properties of a selected layer. Note that you can't modify all the properties by using JavaScript commands. The layer's `parentLayer`, for example, is a fixed property that cannot be changed.

In addition to the many layer properties you can reference, JavaScript also supports several methods that you can apply to a layer. Table 25.3 summarizes these methods.

Now that you know about the `layer` object, its properties, its methods, and the event handlers available in the Netscape browser object model, you are finally ready to take a look at some examples of truly Dynamic HTML—pages that change right in the browser window without going back to the server to get more content.

Table 25.2   Properties of a Selected Layer

Property	Description
above	the layer above the selected layer or the browser window if you have selected the topmost layer
background.src	the URL of the image file to use as the background
below	the layer below the selected layer or null if the selected layer is at the lowest level
bgColor	color specification for the background
clip.bottom	controls the position of the bottom edge of the clipping region
clip.left	controls the position of the left edge of the clipping region
clip.right	controls the position of the right edge of the clipping region
clip.top	controls the position of the top edge of the clipping region
clip.height	controls the distance between the top and bottom edges of the clipping region
clip.width	controls the distance between the left and right edges of the clipping region
document	object that enables you to reference the contents of a layer
left	controls the horizontal position of where the layer begins
name	the unique name of the layer as assigned by the ID attribute of the <LAYER> tag
pageX	the horizontal position of the layer with respect to the browser screen
pageY	the vertical position of the layer with respect to the browser screen
parentLayer	the layer that contains the object layer or the browser window if the object layer is a top-level layer
siblingAbove	the sibling layer (same parent layer) that is above the object layer in the stacking order, or null if there is no layer above it
siblingBelow	the sibling later (same parent layer) that is below the object layer in the stacking order, or null if there is no layer above it
src	the URL of the document to be loaded into the layer
top	controls the vertical position of where the layer begins
visibility	determines whether the content of the layer is shown or hidden
zIndex	determines the layer's position in the stacking order

Part
V

Ch
25

Table 25.3 JavaScript Methods for the *layer* Object

Method Name	Function
load(URL,$width$)	loads the document at the URL specified into the layer (replacing existing content in the layer) and changes the width of the layer to the value in the second argument
moveAbove($layer$)	moves a layer to a position in the stacking order above the layer in the argument
moveBelow($layer$)	moves a layer to a position in the stacking order below the layer in the argument
moveBy(dx,dy)	moves a layer dx pixels to the left and dy pixels down
moveTo(x,y)	moves an absolutely positioned layer to the specified coordinates with the containing document or layer; moves a relatively positioned layer to the specified coordinates, taken with respect to the layer's natural position
moveToAbsolute(x,y)	moves a layer to the specified coordinates, taken with respect to the browser screen
resizeBy(dw,dh)	adds dw to the layer width and dh to the layer height
resizeTo($width$,$height$)	resets the layer's width and height to the specified values

Animated Buttons Using Layers

When you push a button on an appliance or dashboard, you get visual and tactile feedback from the button that tells you something about its status. If the button is depressed, you know that what it controls is on. Conversely, you know that the function the button controls is off if the button is raised. When you press the button to toggle its state, you feel a click as it moves to its new position. This tells you that you have changed states successfully. Unfortunately, this kind of feedback has been tough to provide for buttons on Web pages. Although you will probably never be able to provide tactile feedback to a user pressing a button, Dynamic HTML enables you to give visual feedback about whether the button is depressed or raised, whether the user's mouse is over it, and whether the button is being pressed.

Suppose you are designing an interface where you want your buttons to have the following three states:

- Raised
- Selected (meaning the user's mouse is over it)
- Depressed

One way to accomplish this task that has worked in Navigator since version 3 and in Internet Explorer since version 4 is to come up with GIF or JPG images of the three button "states" and to use the image object to switch them in and out in response to the appropriate mouse events.

However, using Netscape Dynamic HTML, it is possible to create an animated, state-dependent button without requiring any images to be created or downloaded.

Listing 25.6 shows the Dynamic HTML and JavaScript code used to implement the animated button. Two style classes are used to create the buttons; three layers nested within an outer layer hold each button; and a series of JavaScripts selects the displayed button depending on the state of various mouse events.

Listing 25.6 *Button.htm*—Layers Enable You to Create Dynamic Content

```
<HTML>
<HEAD>
<SCRIPT LANGUAGE="JavaScript">
active = 0;
function layerSet(show,hide1,hide2) {
    if (active < 1) {
        show.visibility = "SHOW";
        hide1.visibility = "HIDE";
        hide2.visibility = "HIDE";
    }
}
</SCRIPT>
<STYLE TYPE="text/javascript">
with (classes.Button.P) {
    fontFamily = "Verdana";
    fontSize = "24pt";
    fontWeight = "bold";
    textAlign = "center";
}
with (classes.Out.all) {
    backgroundColor = "white";
    borderWidths("10pt");
    borderStyle = "outset";
    color = "black";
    width = "275pt";
}
with (classes.Over.all) {
    backgroundColor = "yellow";
    borderWidths("10pt");
    borderStyle = "outset";
    color = "black";
    width = "275pt";
}
with (classes.Down.all) {
    backgroundColor = "black";
    borderWidths("10pt");
    borderStyle = "inset";
    color = "yellow";
    width = "275pt";
}
</STYLE>
<TITLE>Animated Buttons without GIFs</TITLE>
</HEAD>
```

continues

Part
V

Ch
25

Listing 25.6 Continued

```
<BODY>
<H1>Animated Buttons without GIFs</H1>
<HR>
<ADDRESS>
Jim O'Donnell, <A HREF="mailto:odonnj@rpi.edu">odonnj@rpi.edu</A>
</ADDRESS>
<HR>
<LAYER NAME=buttons
        onMouseOut="layerSet(layera,layerb,layerc)"
        onMouseOver="layerSet(layerb,layera,layerc)"
        VISIBILITY=INHERIT>
    <LAYER NAME=buttonOut  CLASS="Out"  VISIBILITY=INHERIT>
      <P CLASS="Button">SUBMIT</P>
    </LAYER>
    <LAYER NAME=buttonOver CLASS="Over" VISIBILITY=HIDE>
        <P CLASS="Button">ARE YOU SURE?</P>
    </LAYER>
    <LAYER NAME=buttonDown CLASS="Down" VISIBILITY=HIDE>
        <P CLASS="Button">SENT!!!</P>
    </LAYER>
</LAYER>
</BODY>
<SCRIPT LANGUAGE="JavaScript">
var layera = document.layers['buttons'].document.buttonOut;
var layerb = document.layers['buttons'].document.buttonOver;
var layerc = document.layers['buttons'].document.buttonDown;
//
var buttons = document.layers['buttons'];
//
buttons.document.captureEvents(Event.MOUSEDOWN);
buttons.document.onmousedown = buttonDown;
function buttonDown() {
   layerSet(layerc,layera,layerb);
   active++;
}
</SCRIPT>
</HTML>
```

The first step in animating the button is to set each button up in a layer. The main button layer will contain three child layers—one for each state of the button. By changing the VISIBILITY properties of the layers as different mouse events occur, you can show the graphic appropriate to the button's state. Figure 25.7 shows the initial state of these layers in which the button is in the raised state.

The elements of the button appearance are as follows:

- Style Sheet Button Class—The Button class is defined and attached, via the CLASS attribute of the <P> tag, to the text used to make up the button in each layer.

- Style Sheet Out Class—Attached via the CLASS attribute to the layer containing the button representing the up state (when the mouse is completely "out" of the button). This class defines the color scheme and border of the layer—using the outset border style to generate a raised, three-dimensional appearance, and also defines a layer width the same as that used in each of the other two button styles, Over and Down, so that they will all be sized equivalently.

■ Style Sheet Over Class—Attached via the CLASS attribute to the layer containing the button representing the selected state (when the mouse is "over" the button, but no button has been pressed). This class is identical to the Out class, except that it changes the background color to highlight the button (see Figure 25.8).

■ Style Sheet Down Class—Attached via the CLASS attribute to the layer containing the button representing the down or clicked state (when the mouse is over the button, and a button has been clicked "down"). This class uses an "inverse video" color scheme to denote the clicked button, and changes the border style to inset, for a lowered three-dimensional appearance.

FIGURE 25.7
The outset border style can give the contents of a layer a three-dimensional appearance.

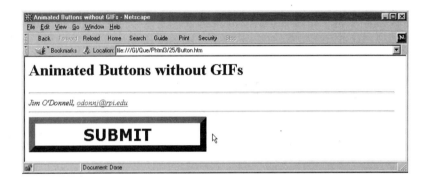

FIGURE 25.8
Prudent use of background colors can highlight important information.

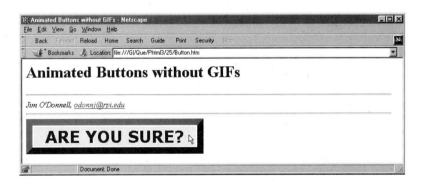

What you need to do next is put in the JavaScript code to handle the changes to the state of the button. The first two states, Out and Over, are easy because the <LAYER> tag supports the onMouseOut and onMouseOver events. In this example, onMouseOut and onMouseOver event handlers in the initial <LAYER> tag call the layerSet() function, which uses the layers' VISIBILITY property to make the desired button visible and hide the other two.

The last mouse event that we want to catch, the button click when the mouse is over the button layers, is a little trickier. That's because the `<LAYER>` tag doesn't support `onClick` or `onMouseDown` events. In order to detect a pressed mouse button when the mouse cursor is over the button layers, we need to catch the event at the `document` level. The JavaScript code located at the bottom of Listing 25.6 shows how this is done:

```
var buttons = document.layers['buttons'];
//
buttons.document.captureEvents(Event.MOUSEDOWN);
buttons.document.onmousedown = buttonDown;
function buttonDown() {
    layerSet(layerc,layera,layerb);
    active++;
}
```

First, the variable `button` is created and defined to be the outermost layer containing the three layers representing the three button states. Then, its `captureEvents` method is used to instruct JavaScript to capture `onMouseDown` events that occur within the layer and assigns the JavaScript `buttonDown` function to be called in that case. The `buttonDown` function simply displays the "down" button (see Figure 25.9) and sets the active variable so that no further changes in button appearance are possible (in this example, after the button is pressed, it can't be unpressed).

FIGURE 25.9

You can define as many layers as you want to manipulate their visibility to dynamically change your pages in response to events.

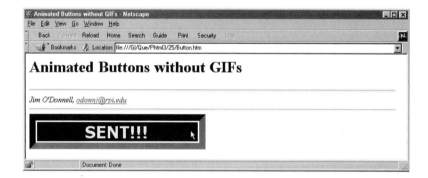

Dynamic HTML Pop-Up Menus

Pop-up menus are used in many applications to give users a context-sensitive listing of program options. These menus are usually accessed by right-clicking the mouse or by some special keystroke. By using Dynamic HTML techniques, you can make a pop-up menu appear on a Web page as well. This can prove helpful in a situation where you need to conserve space on a page. Instead of having all the options presented all the time, you can have a menu with the options pop up when the user requests it.

Look at the example shown in Figure 25.10. The "menu bar" shown in the Web page is set up for this example to look like a typical menu bar (this one looks a lot like the one you will find in Notepad, actually). You could use a menu like this, for instance, to contain your site's navigation options. A listing of this example is shown in Listing 25.7.

FIGURE 25.10
Netscape Dynamic HTML layers can be used to show context-sensitive information on your Web pages.

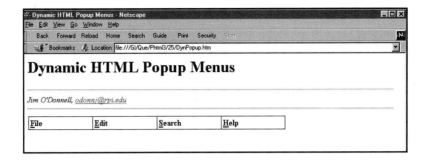

Listing 25.7 DynPopup.htm

```
<HTML>
<HEAD>
<TITLE>Dynamic HTML Pop-up Menus</TITLE>
<STYLE TYPE="text/javascript">
with (classes.Border.all) {
    borderStyle = "SOLID";
    borderWidths("1pt");
    width = "100pt";
}
</STYLE>
</HEAD>
<H1>Dynamic HTML Pop-up Menus</H1>
<HR>
<ADDRESS>
Jim O'Donnell, <A HREF="mailto:odonnj@rpi.edu">odonnj@rpi.edu</A>
</ADDRESS>
<HR>
<LAYER TOP=125 LEFT=10 NAME=fileT CLASS=Border VISIBILITY=SHOW
        onMouseOver="swapLayers(fileMLayer,fileTLayer)">
    <B><U>F</U>ile</B>
</LAYER>
<LAYER TOP=125 LEFT=10 NAME=fileM CLASS=Border VISIBILITY=HIDE
        onMouseOut="swapLayers(fileTLayer,fileMLayer)">
    <B><U>F</U>ile</B><BR>
    <HR>
    <U>N</U>ew<BR>
    <U>O</U>pen<BR>
    <U>S</U>ave<BR>
    S<U>a</U>ve as...<BR>
    <HR>
    Page Se<U>t</U>up...<BR>
    <U>P</U>rint<BR>
    <HR>
    E<U>x</U>it
</LAYER>
<LAYER TOP=125 LEFT=142 NAME=editT CLASS=Border VISIBILITY=SHOW
        onMouseOver="swapLayers(editMLayer,editTLayer)">
    <B><U>E</U>dit</B>
</LAYER>
<LAYER TOP=125 LEFT=142 NAME=editM CLASS=Border VISIBILITY=HIDE
```

continues

Listing 25.7   Continued

```
        onMouseOut="swapLayers(editTLayer,editMLayer)">
    <B><U>E</U>dit</B><BR>
    <HR>
    <U>U</U>ndo<BR>
    <HR>
    Cu<U>t</U><BR>
    <U>C</U>opy<BR>
    <U>P</U>aste<BR>
    De<U>l</U>ete<BR>
    <HR>
    Select <U>A</U>ll<BR>
    Time/<U>D</U>ate<BR>
    <HR>
    <U>W</U>ord Wrap<BR>
</LAYER>
<LAYER TOP=125 LEFT=274 NAME=findT CLASS=Border VISIBILITY=SHOW
        onMouseOver="swapLayers(findMLayer,findTLayer)">
    <B><U>S</U>earch</B>
</LAYER>
<LAYER TOP=125 LEFT=274 NAME=findM CLASS=Border VISIBILITY=HIDE
        onMouseOut="swapLayers(findTLayer,findMLayer)">
    <B><U>S</U>earch</B><BR>
    <HR>
    <U>F</U>ind<BR>
    Find <U>N</U>ext<BR>
</LAYER>
<LAYER TOP=125 LEFT=406 NAME=helpT CLASS=Border VISIBILITY=SHOW
        onMouseOver="swapLayers(helpMLayer,helpTLayer)">
    <B><U>H</U>elp</B>
</LAYER>
<LAYER TOP=125 LEFT=406 NAME=helpM CLASS=Border VISIBILITY=HIDE
        onMouseOut="swapLayers(helpTLayer,helpMLayer)">
    <B><U>H</U>elp</B><BR>
    <HR>
    <U>H</U>elp Topics<BR>
    <HR>
    <A HREF="http://www.rpi.edu/~odonnj">The House of JOD</A>
</LAYER>
</BODY>
<SCRIPT LANGUAGE="JavaScript">
var fileTLayer = window.document.fileT;
var fileMLayer = window.document.fileM;
var editTLayer = window.document.editT;
var editMLayer = window.document.editM;
var findTLayer = window.document.findT;
var findMLayer = window.document.findM;
var helpTLayer = window.document.helpT;
var helpMLayer = window.document.helpM;

function swapLayers(showLayer,hideLayer) {
    showLayer.visibility = "SHOW";
    hideLayer.visibility = "HIDE";
}
</SCRIPT>
</HTML>
```

This example has four main features that it uses to display and hide the context-sensitive menus that go with each of the menu options shown in Figure 25.9.

- Style Sheet `Border` Class—This class is attached to each layer in order for them to have a fixed width and a visible border.

- Title and Menu Option Layers—Each of the four menus shown is implemented using two layers. The first is the layer that just shows the title of that menu option—for example, `File`. The second layer has both the title of the menu and its contents.

- Layer-Based Mouse Events   The `onMouseOver` event of each "title" layer and the `onMouseOut` event of each "menu" layer are used to trigger a JavaScript function to show and hide the appropriate layer in each case.

- JavaScript `swapLayers` Function   The `swapLayers` function is called by the layer mouse events to display the appropriate menu, depending on the location of the mouse. It uses the `VISIBILITY` properties of the title and menu layers to hide one and show the other (see Figure 25.11).

FIGURE 25.11

Pop-up menus enable you to greatly increase the amount of information on your page without making it cluttered.

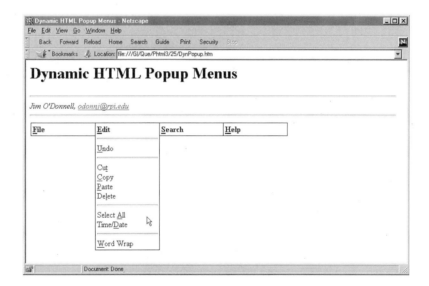

You can use these context-sensitive pop-up menus for any number of purposes. They can be used to display useful information that you don't want cluttering up your Web pages all the time. Or, as shown in Figure 25.12, you can include hypertext links in these menus to enable your users to navigate to another Web page.

Downloadable Fonts

Setting up a document with downloadable fonts is a multistep process that begins with your securing copies of the fonts you want to use in your design. If you are a skilled digital typographer, you may be able to create your own. Most, however, will have to be content to purchase them or to download a publicly available font from somewhere on the Internet.

FIGURE 25.12

Any HTML elements can be included within pop-up layers.

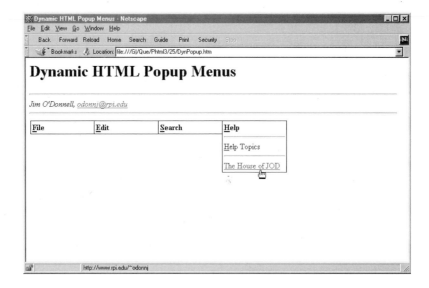

After you have the fonts you want in hand, you need to apply them to text on your page. Ultimately, what you want to produce is what is called a *font definition file*—a file downloaded with the page to provide font information to Navigator. To accomplish this, you need a software tool of some kind. A good bet for this is to use Typograph, a font definition generation tool from HexMac.

Figure 25.13 shows the Typograph screen with an HTML document loaded. By using Typograph's simple menus, you select text and apply a font to it, the same as you would if you were using a word processing program. When the document looks the way you want it, you use the Typograph Burn option to save the file, to set up the link in the document to the font definition file, and to create the font definition file itself.

N O T E HexMac has standalone versions of Typograph for Macintosh and Windows 95/NT platforms, as well as plug-in versions for BBEdit (Macintosh) and FrontPage (Windows 95/NT). For more information on Typograph, visit http://www.hexmac.com/. ■

CAUTION

As part of the burning process, you need to tell Typograph from which Internet domain the font information will be served. After the domain is stored in the font definition file, the font information in the definition file can be served *only* from that domain. If you are serving the same documents on multiple domains, you must burn a new definition file for the other domains.

If you use a different font definition file generation program, you may need to place the link to the definition file into your document manually. Two ways exist to link a definition file to a document. The first is to use the <LINK> tag in the document head. When linking to a font definition file with the <LINK> tag, you need to use the following attributes:

■ REL—REL is set equal to FONTDEF, signifying that the linked file is a font definition file.

■ SRC—SRC points to the URL where the font definition file can be found.

Thus a <LINK> tag that links to a font definition file might look like this:

```
<LINK REL="FONTDEF" SRC="http://www.myserver.com/fonts/mydoc.pfr">
```

FIGURE 25.13

HexMac's Typograph simplifies the application of fonts to text and creates a font definition file for you.

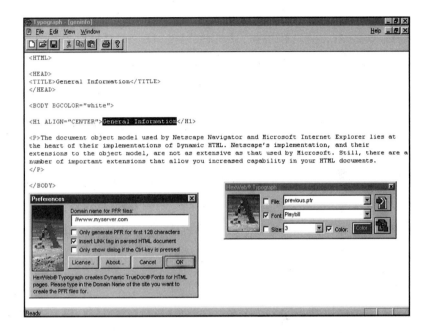

The other approach is to link the font definition file inside the HTML <STYLE> element. The CSS specification supports a link such as the following:

```
<STYLE TYPE="text/css">
<!--
  @fontdef url(http://www.myserver.com/fonts/mydoc.pfr)
-->
</STYLE>
```

The <STYLE> implementation here is equivalent to the <LINK> implementation shown previously.

N O T E Font definition files end with the .pfr extension. ■

With the font definition file linked to your HTML document, you are free to use the fonts contained in the file anywhere in your document. Two approaches to this exist as well. One is to use the FACE attribute of the <FONT> tag just as you always would. FACE is set equal to a comma-delimited list of fonts to use in the order that the browser should try to apply them. For example, the HTML

```
<FONT FACE="Palatino, Garamond, Clarendon, serif">
This will be in Palatino, if possible.
</FONT>
```

will render the sentence "This will be in Palatino, if possible." in Palatino. If Palatino is not available, the browser looks for Garamond, and then Clarendon, and finally, if none of the named fonts are available, it uses a serif font.

The other way to go is to use the font-family characteristic available through the Cascading Style Sheet specification. Using CSS, you could express the same font choices in the preceding <FONT> tag as follows:

```
<STYLE TYPE="text/css">
<!--
  P {font-family: "Palatino", "Garamond", "Clarendon", serif}
-->
</STYLE>
...
<P>This will be in Palatino, if possible.</P>
```

 T I P   Try to use the CSS approach to choosing a typeface wherever possible. When style sheets are more common on the Web, it is likely that the <FONT> tag will be deprecated and your document will not conform to standards.

You get some additional flexibility if you opt to use the <FONT> tag because Netscape has extended the tag with a few more attributes. These are as follows:

- POINT_SIZE—You can control the point size of the font by setting POINT_SIZE to the number of points high you want the text to be.

- WEIGHT—WEIGHT controls the boldness of the font and can be set to a value between 100 and 900 in increments of 100. A value of 100 is the least bold and a value of 900 is the most bold. Using WEIGHT gives you finer control over boldness than the <B> tag, which always uses the highest level of boldness.

With the downloaded typefaces specified in your HTML document, you are almost done. As a final step, you need to put the HTML file and the font definition file out on your server. Remember that the server must be in the domain you specified when creating the font definition file. You should publish both files to a location from which the server can serve them.

Additionally, you need to add a MIME type to your server for the font definition file. MIME information is sent in front of a file to give Navigator a heads up as to what kind of file is coming down the pipe. For font definition files, you should add the MIME type application/font-tdpfr, paired with the file extension .pfr, to your server. After you or your server administrator make this addition to the MIME types file, you probably need to restart the server to get it to recognize the new MIME type. Netscape Navigator is already configured to handle the application/font-tdpfr MIME type and uses the information in the font definition file to render the typefaces in the file.

ON THE WEB

http://developer.netscape.com/dynhtml/   Netscape's own take on Dynamic HTML, how its functionality is integrated into the Navigator browser, and how to develop Dynamic HTML content.

http://www.all-links.com/dynamic/   The Dynamic HTML Index contains frequently asked questions about Dynamic HTML and provides links to sites that answer the questions.

http://www.dhtmlzone.com/   Hosted by Macromedia, this site looks at developing Dynamic HTML for both Netscape and Microsoft browsers.

Part
V

Ch
25

## CHAPTER 26

Advanced Microsoft Dynamic HTML

by Jim O'Donnell

In this chapter

Microsoft's Implementation of Dynamic HTML

Dynamic HTML is Microsoft's term for the new technology it has embedded in its Internet Explorer Web browser, versions 4 and higher. Through Dynamic HTML, you can create Web pages that can change dynamically and have a much higher degree of interaction than in the past. The heart of Dynamic HTML is Microsoft's new Document Object Model. This model is what provides you, and scripts that you write, with the capability to interact with and change any element in an HTML document.

This chapter shows some examples of the kinds of things you can do with Dynamic HTML (and related technologies, such as *Scriptlets*). None of the examples shown represents anything you could not have done in the past—now, however, it is possible to do them using HTML alone. Dynamic HTML is a new technology still under development. People are just scratching the surface of what is possible with it. This chapter identifies some of the best places to look for examples and more information.

Internet Explorer Document Object Model

The heart of Dynamic HTML is the new Document Object Model that Internet Explorer supports. You can think of every element in an HTML document as an object—including the HTML tags and information that they contain—as well as aspects of the Web browser itself and any included Java applets, ActiveX Controls, or other elements. The Document Object Model is what *exposes* these objects, making them accessible to you through scripts that you can write and include with the document.

Before Internet Explorer 4 and Dynamic HTML, the Document Object Model was very limited. It could expose Java applets, ActiveX Controls, and the Web browser window properties, such as window size and location. The model exposed a very limited number of HTML elements, however. The HTML tags that were supported by past object models were primarily limited to HTML Forms elements.

Microsoft's Dynamic HTML changes all that. With Dynamic HTML, every HTML tag is exposed through the Document Object Model. Not only that, but the contents of all HTML container tags are also exposed. Therefore, not only can you change the styles or formats associated with a <P> tag, for instance, but you can also change its text contents. And, this is all done on the client side, without any need to interact with the Web server.

The remainder of this section discusses aspects of the Document Object Model for Internet Explorer 4. It is important to at least understand the different terms used with the object model—object, property, method, collection, and event— and what they mean. This section gives you a good basis for understanding the Dynamic HTML samples later in the chapter.

N O T E   For the remainder of this chapter, references to Internet Explorer should be interpreted to mean Internet Explorer version 4 and higher (unless otherwise noted). Although Internet Explorer version 5 may support the W3C Document Object Model standard if the standard is available before version 5 is finalized, the browser will probably be backward compatible with the version 4 object model.

Understanding Objects and the Object Hierarchy

Figure 26.1 shows the hierarchy of objects that is part of the Internet Explorer Document Object Model. In the simplest terms, an *object* in this model is a recognizable element of the whole. Objects can contain other objects, however; thus, all the objects are organized into an object hierarchy.

FIGURE 26.1

The preceding boxed elements of the Document Object Model represent the additions that Dynamic HTML uses.

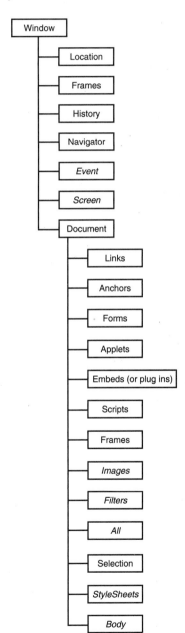

As you look at Figure 26.1, the `window` object, at the top of the hierarchy, includes everything you see within a given Web browser window. That object can and will, in turn, contain other objects. This object hierarchy is used when referencing these objects, with the following sample notation:

```
window.document.links[0]
```

This line of code refers to the first `link` object contained in the current `document` of a given Web browser `window`. (Normally, unless you are authoring Web pages that use multiple windows, you can omit `window`.)

A description of each type of object in the Internet Explorer Document Object Model follows:

- `window`—Represents an open Web browser window.
- `location`—Information for the current URL.
- `frames`—A collection of `window` objects, one for each separate frame in the current window.
- `history`—Information for the recently visited URLs.
- `navigator`—Information about the browser itself.
- `event`—Maintains the state of events occurring within the browser.
- `screen`—Statistics on the physical screen and the rendering capabilities of the client.
- `document`—Contains all the information attached to the current HTML document.
- `links`—A collection of links referenced in the current document.
- `anchors`—A collection of anchors present within the current document.
- `forms`—Can contain a number of other objects corresponding to the forms elements within it; there is one `forms` object for each HTML form in the document.
- `applets`—Contains information about the Java applets present.
- `embeds`—Has information about all objects included using the `<EMBED>` tag; this object can also be referenced using the synonym `plugins`.
- `scripts`—A collection of all the script elements within the document.
- `images`—A collection that contains one element for each image in the document.
- `filters`—Contains a collection of the `filter` objects associated with the document.
- `all`—Allows access to all the HTML tags that are a part of the document.
- `selection`—Represents the current active selection, a user-selected block of text within the document.
- `styleSheets`—A collection of the style sheets attached to the current document.
- `body`—Accesses the `<BODY>` section of the document.

Note that many of these objects are collections of other objects. The `images` object, for instance, is a collection of objects associated with all the images in the current document. You can access elements in these collections either by name or by number. If the first image in an HTML document, for example, is defined by the following tag:

```
<IMG SRC="ryan.jpg" ID=Ryan>
```

you can use the `images` object to access that image in one of three ways:

```
document.images[0]
```

```
document.images("Ryan")
```

```
document.images.Ryan
```

Note that arrays in the object model are zero based, so the first element in an array is referenced using zero.

Using Properties

Every object has properties. To access a property, use the object name followed by a period and the property name. To get the length of the `images` object, which would tell you how many images are in the current document, you can write the following:

```
document.images.length
```

If the object you are using has properties that can be modified, you can change them in the same way. You can change the URL of the current window, for example, by setting the `href` property of the `location` object, as in the following line:

```
Location.href = "http://www.rpi.edu/~odonnj/"
```

If this line is executed within a script, the HTML document referenced by it (my home page) will be loaded into your Web browser window.

Listing 26.1 shows an example of a program that uses Dynamic HTML's `all` object to access all the HTML tags included within the document. In this case, when the document is loaded, a script writes out on the bottom of the document a list of all the HTML tags included in the document (with the exception of the ones written out by the script itself). The script does this by using the `length` property of the `all` object to see how many tags there are and then stepping through them using the `tagName` property to display what the tags are (see Figure 26.2).

Part
V

Ch
26

Listing 26.1 *DispTags.htm*—The *all* Object Enables You to Access Every HTML Tag

```
<HTML>
<HEAD>
<TITLE>Document Object Model: all Object</TITLE>
</HEAD>
<BODY>
<CENTER>
<H1>Document Object Model: <EM>all</EM> Object</H1>
<HR>
<P>
The script in this example will put up a series of alert boxes
showing all the HTML tags used in this document. The script
uses the <EM>length</EM> and <EM>tagName</EM> properties of
```

continues

Listing 26.1 Continued

```
the <EM>all</EM> object.
</P>
<HR>
</CENTER>
<ADDRESS>
Jim O'Donnell, <A HREF="mailto:odonnj@rpi.edu">odonnj@rpi.edu</A>
</ADDRESS>
</BODY>
<SCRIPT LANGUAGE="JavaScript">
imax = document.all.length
document.write("<PRE>")
for(i = 0;i < imax;i++)
    if (i < 9)
        document.write("Tag 0" + (i+1) + " of " + imax + ": " +
            "document.all[0" + i + "].tagName = " +
            document.all[i].tagName + "<BR>")
    else if (i == 9)
        document.write("Tag " + (i+1) + " of " + imax + ": " +
            "document.all[0" + i + "].tagName = " +
            document.all[i].tagName + "<BR>")
        else
        document.write("Tag " + (i+1) + " of " + imax + ": " +
            "document.all[" + i + "].tagName = " +
            document.all[i].tagName + "<BR>")
document.write("</PRE>")
</SCRIPT>
</HTML>
```

FIGURE 26.2

Dynamic HTML enables you to access all the information in the current HTML document.

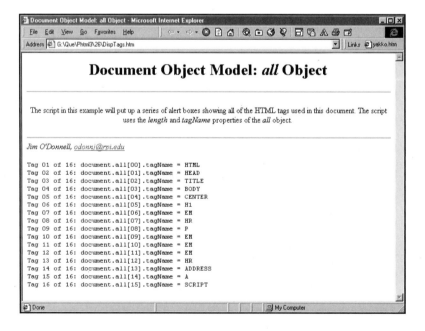

Many properties are associated with HTML element objects in Microsoft's new object model—too many to go over in any detail here. However, you should be aware of two properties in particular; they are one of the ways that Microsoft's Dynamic HTML enables you to easily change the content of HTML documents on-the-fly, without going back to the Web server:

- innerHTML—This is a property of an HTML tag object, and its value is whatever text, information, and HTML code are included within the HTML container tags corresponding to that object.

- outerHTML—This is a property of an HTML tag object, and its value is whatever text, information, and HTML code are included within the HTML container tags corresponding to that object, *including* the container tags themselves.

Listing 26.2 shows a sample HTML document that demonstrates these two properties and the difference between them. In this case, the tag objects being referenced are attached to the <H1> tag by using the attribute ID="MyHeading" and to the <P> tag by using the attribute ID="MyParagraph". At the end of the document, the JavaScript shown displays the value of the innerHTML and outerHTML properties of the objects corresponding to each of these tags. Notice that the outerHTML value for the <H1> tag is in the H1 heading format and that of the <P> tag has an extra space in it. This occurs, in each case, because outerHTML includes the effects of the container tag as well as its contents (see Figure 26.3).

Listing 26.2 *ContentP.htm*—HTML Document Contents Can Be Accessed Using the *innerHTML* and *outerHTML* Properties

```
<HTML>
<HEAD>
<TITLE>Document Object Model: innerHTML and outerHTML Properties</TITLE>
</HEAD>
<BODY>
<CENTER>
<H1 ID="MyHeading">Document Object Model:<BR>
                   <EM>innerHTML</EM> and
                   <EM>outerHTML</EM> Properties</H1>
<HR>
<P ID="MyParagraph">
The <EM>contents</EM> of the &lt;P&gt; tag "MyParagraph"...
</P>
<HR>
</CENTER>
<ADDRESS>
Jim O'Donnell, <A HREF="mailto:odonnj@rpi.edu">odonnj@rpi.edu</A>
</ADDRESS>
<SCRIPT LANGUAGE="JavaScript">
document.write("<PRE>")
document.write("document.all['MyHeading'].innerHTML = " +
    document.all['MyHeading'].innerHTML + "<BR>")
document.write("document.all['MyHeading'].outerHTML = " +
    document.all['MyHeading'].outerHTML + "<BR>")
document.write("<HR>")
```

Part
V

Ch
26

continues

Listing 26.2 Continued

```
document.write("document.all['MyParagraph'].innerHTML = " +
    document.all['MyParagraph'].innerHTML + "<BR>")
document.write("document.all['MyParagraph'].outerHTML = " +
    document.all['MyParagraph'].outerHTML + "<BR>")
document.write("</PRE>")
</SCRIPT>
</BODY>
</HTML>
```

Listing 26.3 shows another example, this one using the `innerHTML` property to dynamically *change* the contents of a Web page.

FIGURE 26.3

Not only the format, but the actual contents of your HTML documents can be accessed and changed with Microsoft Dynamic HTML.

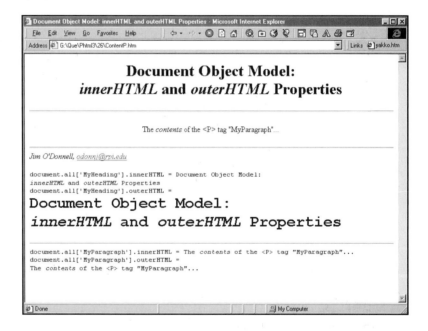

Listing 26.3 *DynCon.htm*—Real-time Changing of HTML Document Contents Using the *innerHTML* Property

```
<HTML>
<HEAD>
<STYLE>
SPAN,P {font-family: Verdana;
        font-size: 18pt;
        font-weight: bold}
</STYLE>
<SCRIPT>
function errortrap(msg,url,line){
   return true
}
```

```
onerror = errortrap;
</SCRIPT>
<TITLE>Dynamic Content Using innerHTML</TITLE>
</HEAD>
<BODY onload="stuff()" onmouseover="update()">
<CENTER>
<H1>Dynamic Content Using <EM>innerHTML</EM></H1>
<HR>
<P>
<SPAN>This</SPAN>
<SPAN>paragraph</SPAN>
<SPAN>contains</SPAN>
<SPAN ID=wordCount>???</SPAN>
<SPAN>words</SPAN>.
<SPAN>The</SPAN>
<SPAN>mouse</SPAN>
<SPAN>is</SPAN>
<SPAN>currently</SPAN>
<SPAN>over</SPAN>
<SPAN>the</SPAN>
<SPAN>word</SPAN>
<BR><SPAN ID=currentWord STYLE="color:#0000FF;font-size:36pt">n/a</SPAN><BR>
<SPAN>In</SPAN>
<SPAN>this</SPAN>
<SPAN>paragraph</SPAN>,
<SPAN>this</SPAN>
<SPAN>is</SPAN>
<SPAN>word</SPAN>
<SPAN>number</SPAN>
<BR><SPAN ID=currentWordNum STYLE="color:#0000FF;font-size:36pt">n/a</SPAN>
</P>
<HR>
</CENTER>
<ADDRESS>
Jim O'Donnell, <A HREF="mailto:odonnj@rpi.edu">odonnj@rpi.edu</A>
</ADDRESS>
</BODY>
<SCRIPT LANGUAGE="JScript">
var oldObject
function stuff() {
    oldObject = null
    wordCount.innerHTML = document.all.tags("SPAN").length
}
function update() {
    if (window.event.srcElement.tagName == "SPAN") {
        if (oldObject)
            oldObject.style.fontFamily = "Verdana"
        oldObject = window.event.srcElement
        oldObject.style.fontFamily = "Lucida Handwriting"
        for (i = 0;i < document.all.tags("SPAN").length;i++)
            if (oldObject == document.all.tags("SPAN").item(i))
                currentWordNum.innerHTML = i + 1
        currentWord.innerHTML = oldObject.innerHTML
    } else {
        if (oldObject) {
```

continues

Part

V

Ch

26

Listing 26.3 Continued

```
        oldObject.style.fontFamily = "Verdana"
        oldObject = null
        currentWordNum.innerHTML = "n/a"
        currentWord.innerHTML = "n/a"
      }
    }
  }
  function errortrap(msg,url,line){
  //   alert(msg);
      return true;
  }
  onerror = errortrap;
  </SCRIPT>
  </HTML>
```

The three main sections of interest in this example are the main document text (contained within the <P> container tag) and the two JavaScript functions, stuff() and update(). This application determines which word in the paragraph (if any) the mouse is over and changes the text to display this word as well as its position within the paragraph. To help accomplish this, each of these sections does the following:

■ Body text within the <P> container tag—Each separate word in this paragraph is set off by a <SPAN> container tag to enable you to access and manipulate it separately from the rest. In addition, three of the words are also given an ID because the JavaScripts will be using their innerHTML properties to dynamically change their contents.

■ JavaScript stuff() function—This function is called when the page has completely loaded by the onload event of the <BODY> tag. It is used to fill in the total number of words in the paragraph. This is done by counting the number of <SPAN> tags, then inserting this number into the paragraph using the appropriate innerHTML property.

■ JavaScript update() function—This function is called whenever an onmouseover event is triggered. Because the onmouseover event is given in the <BODY> tag, such an event is generated whenever the mouse passes over *any* element in the page!

The update() function first determines whether the element that triggered the event is one of the <SPAN> elements in the paragraph. If it is, it changes the font of the corresponding word and places the word and word number in the appropriate spaces in the paragraph (see Figure 26.4). If the triggering element was not one of the <SPAN> tags, the function changes the text to read "n/a."

Dynamic HTML Events and the *event* Object

In addition to making HTML documents more responsive by enabling you to attach events and manipulate the properties of virtually any HTML tag, Microsoft's Dynamic HTML also has increased the number of HTML events that the Web browser can sense and respond to. This section identifies what most of these events are and shows what triggers them.

FIGURE 26.4
Internet Explorer automatically adjusts the other contents of the page to correctly display dynamically altered information.

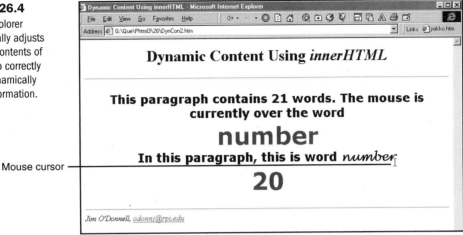

Mouse cursor

Mouse Events

These events are the events triggered in response to mouse movements or mouse button presses. A few of these are familiar events, having been part of the Document Object Model before; some are new as a result of Dynamic HTML.

- onclick—This event is normally triggered when the user presses and releases the left mouse button. It can also occur when the user presses certain keys, such as Enter and Esc, in an HTML form.

  A JavaScript onclick event handler is shown later. This event handler is triggered when a mouse click is recorded anywhere in the current document, and it uses the event object to pop up an Alert box to give the name of the HTML tag in which the click occurred.

  ```
  <SCRIPT FOR=document EVENT=onclick LANGUAGE="JAVASCRIPT">
      alert("Clicked in " + window.event.srcElement.tagName);
  </SCRIPT>
  ```

- ondblclick—This event is triggered when the user clicks twice over an object. If an event handler assigned to this event returns a false value, it cancels the default action.

- ondragstart—This event is triggered when the user begins a drag selection.

- onmousedown—This event is triggered when the user presses the mouse button.

- onmousemove—This event is triggered when the mouse is moved.

- onmouseover—This event is triggered when the mouse is moved into an object. It occurs when the mouse first enters the object and does not repeat unless the user moves the mouse out and then back in.

- onmouseout—This event is triggered when the user moves the mouse out of a given element. When the user moves the mouse pointer into an element, one onmouseover event occurs, followed by one or more onmousemove events as the user moves the pointer

Part

V

Ch

26

within the element; and finally, one `onmouseout` event occurs when the user moves the pointer out of the element.

■ `onmouseup`—This event is triggered when the mouse button is released.

Note that some of the events described in the preceding list actually trigger multiple events. The events leading to a valid `ondblclick` event, for example, occur in the following steps:

1. `onmousedown`
2. `onmouseup`
3. `onclick`
4. `onmousedown`
5. `onmouseup`
6. `ondblclick`

Keystroke Events

New to Microsoft Internet Explorer with its support for Dynamic HTML are events triggered by user keypresses. Three general purpose events and one special purpose event respond to keys:

■ `onkeydown`—This event is triggered when the user presses a key and returns the number of the keycode for the key pressed. An event handler assigned to service this event can return a different value and override the original key.

■ `onkeyup`—Triggered when the user releases a key.

■ `onkeypress`—The last event triggered for a valid key press: First the `onkeydown` event is triggered, and then `onkeyup`, and then `onkeypress`. Event handlers assigned to any of these three events can be used to intercept, override, and/or nullify the actual key pressed.

■ `onhelp`—This event is triggered when the user presses the F1 key or clicks the Help key on the Web browser.

Focus Events

These events are used to follow the focus of the cursor around the HTML document. They can be used to good effect when performing HTML form validation but can also be used with non-form elements.

■ `onfocus`—This event is triggered when the element in question receives the input focus.

■ `onblur`—This event is triggered when an object loses the input focus.

■ `onchange`—This event is triggered when the contents of the object, normally a text or text area HTML form field, are changed.

Note that this event is triggered only after the object has lost focus and if its contents have changed. If an event handler exists for the `onblur` event for the same object, the `onchange` event is triggered and executed first.

<MARQUEE> Events

Although Microsoft's <MARQUEE> tag is a nonstandard HTML element, it has come into increasing use. Microsoft's Dynamic HTML implementation includes three events specifically tied to that tag:

- onbounce—This event can only be triggered when the contents of the <MARQUEE> tag are set to alternately scroll one way and then the other. It is actually triggered when the scrolling content changes direction.

- onstart—This event is triggered when a scrolling loop begins or, for alternate behavior, when a bounce cycle begins.

- onfinish—This event is triggered when a scrolling loop ends.

Page Events

In addition to the onload event, which has existed in the past and is triggered when a Web page is completely loaded, Dynamic HTML adds a couple of other events associated with loading and unloading documents into your Web browser. This enables you to set the entrance and exit behaviors of the Web browser for a given document.

- onload—This event is triggered after the Web browser loads the given object. It is normally used with the HTML document itself, but can also be applied to images, applets, and any other Web browser object loaded along with the HTML document itself.

- onbeforeunload—This event is triggered prior to an HTML document being unloaded. By attaching an event handler to this event, you can give the user a chance to change his or her mind and remain on the current page.

- onunload—This event is triggered immediately before the current page is unloaded. Unlike the onbeforeunload event, after this event is triggered it is too late to prevent the user from leaving the page.

HTML Form Events

As you would expect, Microsoft's Dynamic HTML supports the traditional onreset and onsubmit events associated with an HTML form's Reset and Submit buttons. Each of these events is triggered when the corresponding button is clicked. If an event handler for the onsubmit event returns a value of false, the form is not submitted.

Other Events

The following list describes the other events supported by Microsoft's implementation of Dynamic HTML. Note also that a collection of events is associated with the data binding capabilities of Dynamic HTML—these events are discussed later in this chapter.

- onabort—This event is triggered when the user aborts the download of an image, normally by pressing the Stop button.

Part

V

Ch

26

- onerror—This event is triggered when an error occurs when loading an image or other Web browser object. You can suppress error messages that occur when an image fails to load by setting the onerror attribute in the element to "null."

- onfilterchange—This event fires when a filter changes state or completes a transition from one state to another. Filter effects of Microsoft Dynamic HTML are discussed in the "Dynamic HTML Filters" section later in this chapter.

- onresize—This event is triggered when the object to which it is attached is resized.

- onscroll—This event is triggered when the user scrolls the window, either by using the scrollbar, arrow keys, or some other means.

- onselect—This event is triggered when the current selection changes. The event continues to fire as the mouse moves from character to character during a drag selection.

- onselectstart—This event is triggered at the beginning of a user-initiated select.

Using Dynamic HTML with Styles

Dynamic HTML works very well with another aspect of Internet Explorer for dynamically changing the formatting of elements in an HTML document: styles and style sheets. One property associated with all HTML tags—which, as you will recall, you can access through the all object—is that tag's style. The style property, in turn, has properties of its own that you can access and change to immediately change the appearance of the Web page.

Listing 26.4 shows an example of dynamically changing the style of elements of an HTML document. In this example, the format is applied to two elements in different ways—either through an embedded style sheet created with the <STYLE> tag or through the STYLE attribute. No matter which way you do it, the script changes the format in response to the onMouseDown and onMouseUp events. Figures 26.5 and 26.6 show the before and after screen shots of this HTML document.

FIGURE 26.5

You can attach formatting styles to HTML elements in a variety of ways.

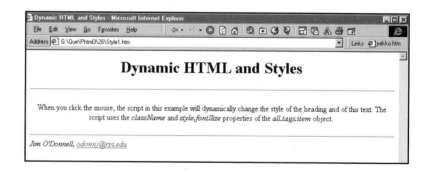

Dynamic HTML and Styles - Microsoft Internet Explorer

File   Edit   View   Go   Favorites   Help

Address G:\Que\Phtml3\26\Style1.htm

Dynamic HTML and Styles

When you click the mouse, the script in this example will dynamically change the style of the heading and of this text. The script uses the *className* and *style.fontSize* properties of the *all.tags.item* object.

Jim O'Donnell, odonnj@rpi.edu

FIGURE 26.6

You can change formats and immediately update the Web browser window in response to any event.

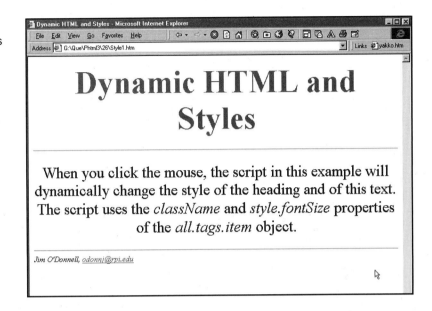

Listing 26.4   *Style1.htm*—Dynamic HTML Can Change Document Styles

```
<HTML>
<HEAD>
<TITLE>Dynamic HTML and Styles</TITLE>
<STYLE>
    .mousedown {font-size:48pt;color:red}
    .mouseup {font-size:24pt;color:black}
</STYLE>
<SCRIPT LANGUAGE="JScript">
function changeStyles(mousedown) {
    if (mousedown) {
        document.all.tags("H1").item(0).className = "mousedown";
        document.all.tags("P").item(0).style.fontSize = "24pt";
    } else {
        document.all.tags("H1").item(0).className = "mouseup";
        document.all.tags("P").item(0).style.fontSize = "12pt";
    }
}
</SCRIPT>
</HEAD>
<BODY onMouseDown="changeStyles(1)" onMouseUp="changeStyles(0)">
<CENTER>
<H1 CLASS="mouseup">Dynamic HTML and Styles</H1>
<HR>
<P STYLE="font-size: 12pt">
When you click the mouse, the script in this example will
dynamically change the style of the heading and of this
text. The script uses the <EM>className</EM> and
<EM>style.fontSize</EM> properties of the
<EM>all.tags.item</EM> object.
```

Part

V

Ch

26

continues

Listing 26.4   Continued

```
</P>
<HR>
</CENTER>
<ADDRESS>
Jim O'Donnell, <A HREF="mailto:odonnj@rpi.edu">odonnj@rpi.edu</A>
</ADDRESS>
</BODY>
</HTML>
```

Dynamic HTML and the Data Source Object

Another Dynamic HTML capability works hand in hand with Microsoft's Data Source Object to enable what is called *data binding*. The Data Source Object is an ActiveX Control that references an external file to provide data for the HTML document. Dynamic HTML enables you to use the DATASRC and DATAFLD attributes to bind this data to HTML elements. This way, the data displayed within a document can be kept separate from the formatting. Also, after the data is transmitted to the client Web browser, the Data Source Object can perform operations on it locally.

Data Binding Events

A collection of events is associated with HTML elements that are data bound using the DATASRC and DATAFLD attributes. The following list describes these events:

- ondataavailable—This event is triggered as data arrives from an asynchronous data source object; how often it fires depends on the data source object.

- ondatasetchanged—This event is triggered when the data set used by a data source object changes.

- ondatasetcomplete—This event is triggered when all the data available to a data source object has been loaded.

- onrowenter—This event is triggered when the current row of data has changed, and new data values are available.

- onrowexit—This event is triggered just prior to a data source object changing the current row in response to new data.

- onbeforeupdate—This event is triggered before the transfer of data from an element to a data provider.

- onafterupdate—This event is triggered after the transfer of data from an element to a data provider.

- onerrorupdate—This event is triggered when the handler for the onbeforeupdate event cancels the data transfer and fires instead the onafterupdate event.

Data Binding Example

Listing 26.5 shows an example of data binding using the Data Source Object and Dynamic HTML. In this example, a data file of chapter, page count, and author information is bound to the columns of an HTML table. The Data Source Object's `SortColumn()` method is attached to the table headings, using the `onClick` event. When a column heading is clicked, the table is sorted by the contents of that column and immediately redisplayed. Figures 26.7 and 26.8 show examples of this, with the table sorted either by chapter number or chapter title.

Listing 26.5 *DataBind.htm*—**Dynamic HTML and Data Binding Enable Easy Client-Side Data Manipulation**

```
<HTML>
<HEAD>
<TITLE>Data Binding with Dynamic HTML</TITLE>
</HEAD>
<BODY>
<OBJECT ID="inputdata"
        CLASSID="clsid:333C7BC4-460F-11D0-BC04-0080C7055A83"
        align="baseline" border="0" width="0" height="0">
<PARAM NAME="DataURL"   VALUE="authors.txt">
<PARAM NAME="UseHeader" VALUE=TRUE>
</OBJECT>
<CENTER>
<H1>Data Binding with Dynamic HTML</H1>
<HR>
<P>
   This example shows an example of how you can use
   Dynamic HTML to bind an HTML element, in this case
   the columns of a table, to a Data Source Object.
   This enables the data to be kept separately from the
   formatting information in the HTML document. It
   also enables the data to be operated on at the client.
   In this example, if you click the table headers
   of the table below, it will be sorted by the
   elements in that column.
</P>
<HR>
<TABLE DATASRC="#inputdata" BORDER>
<THEAD>
<TR><TH><U><DIV ID=ChapNum onclick="sort1()">
        Chapter<BR>Number</DIV></U></TH>
    <TH><U><DIV ID=ChapTitle onclick="sort2()">
       Chapter<BR>Title</DIV></U></TH>
    <TH><U><DIV ID=PageCount onclick="sort3()">
       Estimate<BR>Page Count</DIV></U></TH>
    <TH><U><DIV ID=Author onclick="sort4()">
       Author</DIV></U></TH></TR>
</THEAD>
<TBODY>
<TR><TD ALIGN=RIGHT><DIV DATAFLD="ChapNum"></DIV></TD>
    <TD>            <DIV DATAFLD="ChapTitle"></DIV></TD>
    <TD ALIGN=RIGHT><DIV DATAFLD="PageCount"></DIV></TD>
```

continues

Listing 26.5 Continued

```
    <TD>                   <DIV DATAFLD="Author"></DIV></TD></TR>
</TBODY>
</TABLE>

<SCRIPT LANGUAGE="JavaScript">
function sort1() {
  inputdata.SortColumn = "ChapNum";
  inputdata.Reset();
}
function sort2() {
  inputdata.SortColumn = "ChapTitle";
  inputdata.Reset();
}
function sort3() {
  inputdata.SortColumn = "PageCount";
  inputdata.Reset();
}
function sort4() {
  inputdata.SortColumn = "Author";
  inputdata.Reset();
}
</SCRIPT>
<HR>
</CENTER>
<ADDRESS>
Jim O'Donnell, <A HREF="mailto:odonnj@rpi.edu">odonnj@rpi.edu</A>
</ADDRESS>
</BODY>
</HTML>
```

FIGURE 26.7

The Data Source Object enables you to include external data within an HTML document by Dynamic HTML.

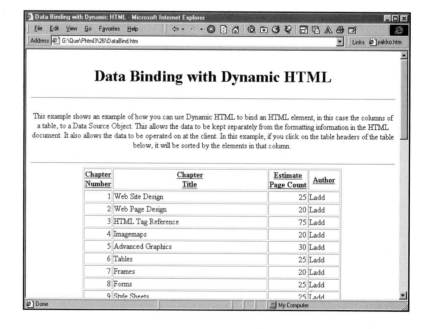

FIGURE 26.8

Using Dynamic HTML, you can automatically sort—or otherwise operate on—and immediately redisplay data.

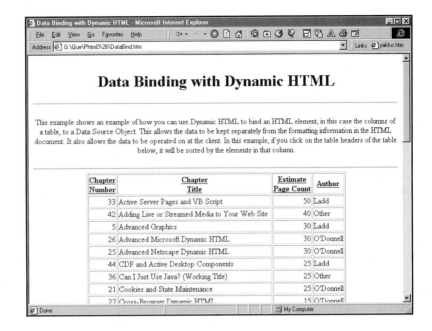

Position HTML Elements with Dynamic HTML

One exciting thing possible with Dynamic HTML is the capability to reposition HTML elements on the Web page. To do this, change the `left` and `top` properties of the element's `style` object (which, in turn, is a property of the element). This change can be done either automatically or in response to user interaction.

Listing 26.6 shows an example of a Dynamic HTML document that enables the user to position an HTML element—in this case a group of pictures—on the Web page. In this example, a table containing three images is contained within a `<SPAN>` tag. An `onClick` event is attached to the `<SPAN>`, which is used to toggle whether it can be moved and to initialize the coordinates for the move. An `onMouseMove` event is attached to the document itself; when the `<SPAN>` region has moving enabled, the position of the mouse determines where the region is moved. Figure 26.9 shows the Web page immediately after it is loaded, and Figure 26.10 shows it while it is being moved. Note that the movement status and the current x,y coordinate are shown in the text boxes near the bottom of the page.

N O T E The "x-ray" effect shown in Figure 26.10 is applied using the Internet Explorer "xray" filter. Dynamic HTML filters will be discussed in the "Dynamic HTML Filters" section later in this chapter. ■

Part
V

Ch
26

FIGURE 26.9

You can use the HTML <SPAN> container tag to group other HTML elements into one region.

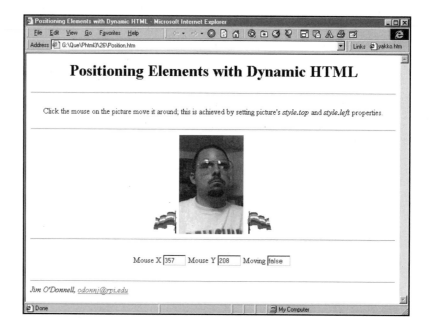

FIGURE 26.10

The `top` and `left` style properties make it easy to move HTML elements around the page.

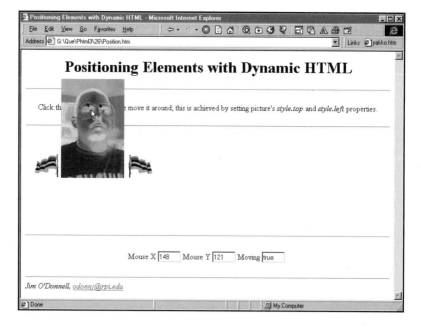

Listing 26.6 *Position.htm*—**With Dynamic HTML, You Can Change the Position of any HTML Element**

```html
<HTML>
<HEAD>
<SCRIPT LANGUAGE="JavaScript">
basex  = 0;
basey  = 0;
deltax = 0;
deltay = 0;
moving = false;
function toggleMove() {
   moving = !moving;
   document.MyForm.Moving.value = moving;
   if (moving) {
      Author.style.filter = "xray(enabled=1)"
      deltax += window.event.x - basex;
      deltay += window.event.y - basey;
   } else
      Author.style.filter = "xray(enabled=0)"
}
function moveAuthor() {
   if (moving) {
      basex = window.event.x;
      basey = window.event.y;
      Author.style.left = basex - deltax;
      Author.style.top  = basey - deltay;
      document.MyForm.PicX.value = basex;
      document.MyForm.PicY.value = basey;
   }
}
</SCRIPT>
<TITLE>Positioning Elements with Dynamic HTML</TITLE>
</HEAD>
<BODY onMouseMove="moveAuthor()">
<CENTER>
<H1>Positioning Elements with Dynamic HTML</H1>
<HR>
<P>
Click the mouse on the picture to move it around; this is achieved by
setting picture's <EM>style.top</EM> and <EM>style.left</EM>
properties.
</P>
<HR>
<CENTER>
<SPAN ID=Author STYLE="position:relative;width:132" onClick="toggleMove()">
   <TABLE>
   <TR VALIGN="BOTTOM">
      <TD><IMG SRC="rbflag_ls.gif" WIDTH=50  HEIGHT=47  BORDER=0></TD>
      <TD><IMG SRC="Author.jpg"    WIDTH=132 HEIGHT=198 BORDER=0><TD>
      <TD><IMG SRC="rbflag_rs.gif" WIDTH=50  HEIGHT=47  BORDER=0></TD></TR>
   </TABLE>
</SPAN>
</CENTER>
```

continues

Listing 26.6 Continued

```
<HR>
<FORM NAME="MyForm">
<TABLE>
<TR><TD>Mouse X</TD><TD><INPUT TYPE="TEXT" SIZE=5 NAME="PicX">  </TD>
    <TD>Mouse Y</TD><TD><INPUT TYPE="TEXT" SIZE=5 NAME="PicY">  </TD>
    <TD>Moving </TD><TD><INPUT TYPE="TEXT" SIZE=5 NAME="Moving"></TD></TR>
</TABLE>
</FORM>
<HR>
</CENTER>
<ADDRESS>
Jim O'Donnell, <A HREF="mailto:odonnj@rpi.edu">odonnj@rpi.edu</A>
</ADDRESS>
</BODY>
</HTML>
```

Changing HTML Documents On-the-Fly

The last example shows the use of Dynamic HTML to create dynamic content—HTML elements that are changed within the Web browser on-the-fly. Listing 26.7 is an example of two ways HTML elements can be changed on-the-fly. The digital clock (see Figure 26.11) is an HTML element, but it changes automatically each second to reflect the local time. The paragraph following it, on the other hand, is changed in response to user input—when the user clicks the Change HTML button, the contents of the text box above the button are substituted for the paragraph. As you can see in Figure 26.12, this substitution can also include any HTML elements, as shown with the <MARQUEE> and hypertext link in this example.

Listing 26.7 *DynCon2.htm*—Dynamic HTML Can Change HTML Documents Without Going Back to the Web Server

```
<HTML>
<HEAD>
<TITLE>Dynamic Content</TITLE>
</HEAD>
<BODY>
<CENTER>
<H1>Dynamic Content</H1>
<HR>
<DIV ID=digitalClock STYLE="font-size: 60">
    
</DIV>
<HR>
<DIV ID=dynContent>
   <P>
   This example shows how HTML content can be dynamically
   changed. The clock shown above is updated with the local
   time on your system once a second. This text will be
```

```
          replaced by any HTML elements that are entered in the
          text box below when the <EM>Change HTML</EM> button is
          clicked.
          </P>
     </DIV>
     <HR>
     <INPUT ID=newContent TYPE=TEXT STYLE="width: 100%"><BR>
     <INPUT TYPE=BUTTON VALUE="Change HTML"
          onclick="dynContent.innerHTML = newContent.value">
     <HR>
     </CENTER>
     <ADDRESS>
     Jim O'Donnell, <A HREF="mailto:odonnj@rpi.edu">odonnj@rpi.edu</A>
     </ADDRESS>
     </BODY>
     <SCRIPT LANGUAGE="JScript">
     function runClock() {
          var d,h,m,s;
     //
          d = new Date();
          h = d.getHours();
          m = d.getMinutes();
          s = d.getSeconds();
     //
          if (h < 10) h = "0" + h;
          if (m < 10) m = "0" + m;
          if (s < 10) s = "0" + s;
     //
          digitalClock.innerHTML = h + ":" + m + ":" + s;
          window.setTimeout("runClock();",100);
     }
     window.onload = runClock;
     </SCRIPT>
     </HTML>
```

Part
V

Ch
26

FIGURE 26.11

Real-time clocks appearing in Web pages are common; with Dynamic HTML, however, you can make them appear using only HTML elements.

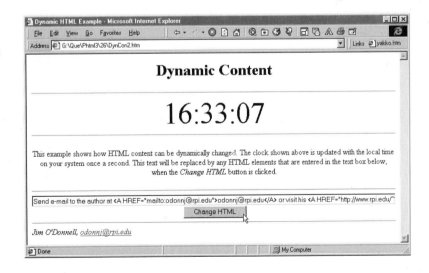

FIGURE 26.12

Dynamic HTML can dynamically change the contents of a displayed HTML document, which is automatically redisplayed by Internet Explorer.

Dynamically changed HTML content

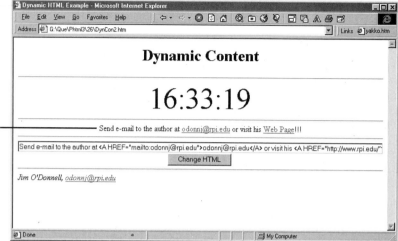

Dynamic HTML Filters

Microsoft has included some new capabilities in its newer Internet Explorer Web browsers through a series of ActiveX Controls and Web browser objects as part of its implementation of Dynamic HTML. You have already seen one of them in action: the Data Source Object that works along with Dynamic HTML data binding to enable HTML elements to import data from external sources. In addition to this component, Microsoft has included a series of controls used to create and manipulate graphic objects and the appearance of an HTML document as a whole.

Microsoft has included a series of filters you can add to Web pages to achieve a number of interesting visual effects that were previously possible only by creating large graphic images in a program such as Adobe Photoshop. These filters are accessed through style sheet attributes and can be applied to text, images, and graphic objects—in short, anything that can appear in an HTML document.

Microsoft has an excellent example of the possible effects users can achieve with the Dynamic HTML filters, along with the other Dynamic HTML demos. The demo Web site is at

```
http://www.microsoft.com/ie/ie40/demos/
```

The filter example is at

```
http://www.microsoft.com/ie/ie40/demos/filters.htm
```

Figure 26.13 shows the default, unfiltered state of this demo page, and it has the following elements:

- HTML text
- GIF image

- Graphic object
- Buttons attached to Dynamic HTML filters

FIGURE 26.13
Dynamic HTML filters
can apply visual effects
to any HTML element—
text, images, even other
objects.

HTML text
GIF image
Graphic object

Buttons attached to
Dynamic HTML filters

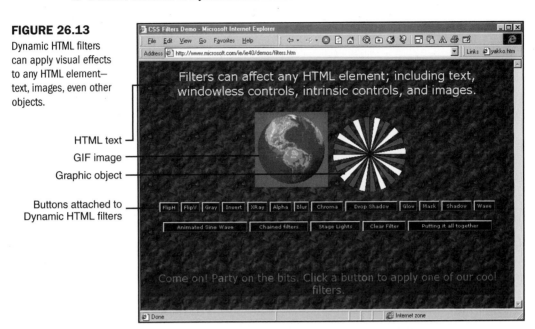

Table 26.1 shows a listing of the different filters included with Dynamic HTML and supported by Internet Explorer 4, along with a description of their effects.

Table 26.1 Dynamic HTML Filters in Internet Explorer 4

Filter	Description
Alpha	Used to make an object more or less opaque.
Blur	Used to blur an object in a specified direction; this can be used to make it appear as if the object is moving very quickly in that direction.
Chroma	Used to make a specific color in an object transparent.
Drop Shadow	Used to give an object a solid silhouette in a specified direction.
Flip Horizontal	Used to flip an object horizontally.
Flip Vertical	Used to flip an object vertically.
Glow	Used to add a radiance effect to an object.
Grayscale	Used to display an object in shades of gray.
Invert	Used to invert the colors of an object.
Light	Used to add simulated light sources to an object.

continues

Table 26.1 Continued

Filter	Description
Mask	Used to take a visual object, make the transparent pixels a specific color, and make a transparent mask from the nontransparent pixels.
Shadow	Used to give an object a solid silhouette in a specific direction. This filter is similar to the Drop Shadow filter, but is more configurable.
Wave	Used to give a sine wave distortion to an object along its vertical axis.
XRay	Used to change an object's color depth and display it in black and white, making it look somewhat like a black-and-white x-ray.

Placing *graphic* Objects

Before you see how the filters are applied, it is first helpful to see how the `graphic` object is created. Listing 26.8 shows an excerpt from the example shown, showing how the `graphic` object is included and configured in the HTML document.

Listing 26.8 Embedding *graphic* Objects

```
<OBJECT ID=SG1>
        STYLE="HEIGHT:150; WIDTH:150"
        CLASSID="CLSID:369303C2-D7AC-11D0-89D5-00A0C90833E6">
    <PARAM NAME="Line0001" VALUE="SetFillStyle(1)">
    <PARAM NAME="Line0002" VALUE="SetFillColor(255,255,255)">
    <PARAM NAME="Line0003" VALUE="Pie(-75,-75,150,150,0,10,0)">
    <PARAM NAME="Line0004" VALUE="SetFillColor(0,90,200)">
    <PARAM NAME="Line0005" VALUE="Pie(-75,-75,150,150,0,10,18)">
    ...
    <PARAM NAME="Line0042" VALUE="SetFillColor(255,255,255)">
    <PARAM NAME="Line0043" VALUE="Pie(-75,-75,150,150,0,10,360)">
</OBJECT>
```

This HTML `<OBJECT>` tag and parameters use the following information:

- The `ID` attribute of the `<OBJECT>` tag defines the name of the object that will be used by scripts and other objects.

- The `STYLE` attribute of the `<OBJECT>` tag defines, in this case, the desired height and width of the object.

- The `CLASSID` attribute of the `<OBJECT>` tag is its most important attribute because it is what uniquely identifies this ActiveX Control that the `<OBJECT>` tag is attempting to include in the HTML document.

- The `<PARAM>` tags given inside the `<OBJECT>` container are used to configure the object. The `NAME`, `VALUE` attribute pairs used are unique to any given object and are used to configure it appropriately. In this case, they define a series of pie wedges used to make up the `graphic` object.

Applying Dynamic HTML Filters

Dynamic HTML filters are implemented by Microsoft as style sheet attributes. To apply them to all or part of an HTML document, therefore, a region needs to be defined and (optionally) named. You can then write scripts that reference the `style` property of the region to apply different filters.

Listing 26.9 shows the outline of the region defined in the example shown in Figure 26.13. Notice that HTML text, an image, and a graphic object are all included within the bounds of a `<DIV>` container tag. The `NAME` attribute of the `<DIV>` tag enables the entire region to be treated as one and to be referred to by name within the object hierarchy.

Listing 26.9 Use the *<DIV>* Tag to Group HTML Elements

```
<DIV ID=theImg style parameters…>
   HTML text…
   <IMG image parameters…>
   <OBJECT graphic object parameters…>
      <PARAM graphic object parameters…>
      …
</DIV>
```

Figure 26.14 shows what the document looks like when the Blur filter effect is selected. This is implemented by using the `onClick` method of one of the buttons, as shown here:

```
<INPUT CLASS=clsbtn VALUE="Blur" TYPE=BUTTON NAME=BLUR
   onClick="theImg.style.filter =
'blur(direction=45,strength=15,add=0,enabled=1)';
           progress.innerText = 'explanatory text…';">
```

The different attributes of this `<INPUT>` tag do the following:

- The `CLASS` attribute attaches a style to the label of the button, enabling you to change its appearance. (This was not possible in earlier versions of Internet Explorer.)

- The `TYPE`, `VALUE`, and `NAME` attributes are the familiar attributes used for HTML form elements, defining the type of element, label, and object name, respectively.

- The `onClick` attribute attaches the inline JavaScript shown so that it gets executed whenever the button is clicked. The inline JavaScript does two things. First, it attaches the Blur filter to the style sheet `filter` property for the region named `theImg` (as defined in Listing 26.9). Second, it sets the `innerText` property of the region named `progress`, which displays explanatory text in that region for the filter selected.

A number of filter effects are possible. It is even possible to combine the effects of more than one filter within a given region, or to apply a filter and animate it through JavaScript. Figure 26.15 shows a snapshot of an animated sine wave filter. This is achieved by applying the Wave filter, and then dynamically changing its parameters with a JavaScript, as shown in this code excerpt:

Part
V

Ch
26

FIGURE 26.14

Filter effects are quickly applied by the client browser and save the need for creating graphic images to achieve the same look.

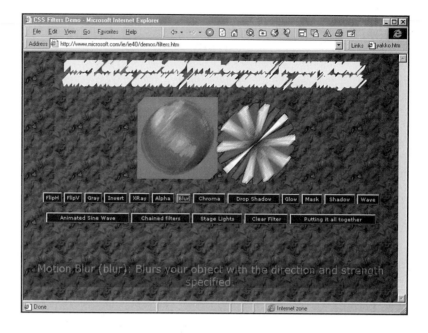

FIGURE 26.15

Because you can dynamically change the filter applied to a given region, it is very easy to quickly achieve an assortment of effects.

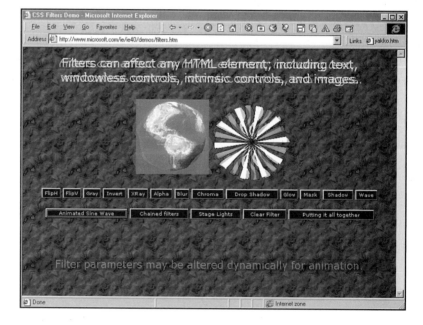

```
function animatwav() {
   if (wavable) {
      wavphase = (wavphase + 10) % 100;
      if (theImg.style.filter == "wave(freq=4,strength=8,phase=0,
➡lightstrength=25,add=1,enabled=1)") {
         theImg.filters[0].phase = wavphase;
      }
      window.setTimeout("animatwav()", 0400, "JavaScript");
   }
}
```

Microsoft's Scriptlets

With version 4 of Internet Explorer, Microsoft also introduced another new technology known as *Scriptlets*. Microsoft calls Scriptlets "components for the Web." Although not technically a part of Dynamic HTML, Scriptlets enable you to create small, reusable Web applications that can be used in any Web page. Scriptlets are created using HTML, scripting, and Dynamic HTML. To include them in an HTML document, use the <OBJECT> tag.

What is meant by "Web component?" A software component is a self-contained piece of software designed to be used within a container application through a clearly defined interface. ActiveX Controls and Java applets represent two examples of Web objects that act as components within a browser. Until now, it has been possible to obtain some component functionality with HTML scripting by using the SRC attribute of the HTML <SCRIPT> tag. You could also achieve some measure of reuse either by making use of server-side includes or by simply cutting and pasting from one document to another.

Microsoft's Scriptlets add more complete component architecture for reusing scripted HTML documents and applications within other documents. Using Scriptlets as components in your HTML documents offers the following benefits:

- Scriptlets are isolated from the surrounding HTML document, except through a predefined interface. This way, errors that occur elsewhere in the document do not affect the Scriptlet, and vice versa. This simplifies the development process of both the Scriptlet and the containing document.

- A second benefit of Scriptlet Web components is that they can be easily reused within other HTML documents. A component can be designed, developed, and debugged one time, and then can be easily reused without further investment of time.

- The final benefit of Scriptlet Web components is that you can use Scriptlets to interact with any other Web component developed using any other compatible language or technology. In this way, Scriptlets (components developed using HTML and scripts), Java applets, and ActiveX Controls can work together without the need to recode them into a common language.

Part

V

Ch

26

 ON THE WEB

`http://www.microsoft.com/scripting/`   This Web site contains the latest information about all of Microsoft's scripting languages, including Scriptlets.

Creating Scriptlets

Scriptlets are created like any other HTML document, with HTML and scripts. Scriptlet properties and methods are made accessible to containing HTML documents by prefacing them with `public`. For instance, if the following appears in the Scriptlet:

```
<SCRIPT LANGUAGE="JAVASCRIPT">
public_Value = "Hello";
function public_myFunction(par1,par2,…) {

    …

}
</SCRIPT>
```

and if the Scriptlet is included in an HTML document with `<OBJECT ID="MyScriptlet">`, the property and method shown in the preceding code can be accessed using this:

```
MyScriptlet.Value = "Goodbye";
x = MyScriptlet.myFunction();
```

Scriptlets can initiate two kinds of events that can be received and acted on by the containing HTML document. These are `onscriptletevent` events and standard `window` events such as mouse clicks and keypresses. The `onscriptletevent` event includes a string and an object parameter; the external HTML document can base its action on the contents of the string and interpret the object parameters appropriately.

Using Scriptlets in HTML Documents

After a Scriptlet is created, including it and using it within an HTML document is a simple procedure. A Scriptlet is included in an HTML document by using the `<OBJECT>` tag with the following syntax:

```
<OBJECT ID="Calendar" WIDTH=400 HEIGHT=270 TYPE="text/x-scriptlet">
    <PARAM NAME="URL" VALUE="Calendar.htm">
</OBJECT>
```

Like other Web browser objects, the `ID` attribute is used to name the object so that it can be accessed by scripts within the page. The `WIDTH` and `HEIGHT` attributes define the size of the object within the page. The Scriptlet `<OBJECT>` tag's `TYPE` attribute uses the MIME type `text/x-scriptlet` to tell Internet Explorer that this object is a Scriptlet. Finally, the `<PARAM>` tag is used to give the URL of the Scriptlet itself.

Scriptlet Example

Microsoft maintains a collection of samples of many of its technologies, including Dynamic HTML and Scriptlets, at `http://www.microsoft.com/workshop/c-frame.htm#/gallery/samples/default.asp`. Figure 26.16 shows one of the demos from this site, the Calculator Scriptlet Demo, in action. Notice the following features of this demonstration:

- The HTML needed to implement the table containing the calculator, as well as the supporting scripts, is all contained within the Calculator Scriptlet.

- Scriptlet methods are attached to each of the buttons shown in the page below the calculator; these buttons are part of the external document, not the Scriptlet itself.

Clicking any of them calls a Scriptlet method with the contents of the adjacent text field to set the corresponding property of the Scriptlet.

■ Dynamic HTML is used to dynamically change the contents of the calculator display when any of its buttons are pressed.

■ Figure 26.16 shows how the document can respond to two kinds of Scriptlet events. The number of the day that the mouse is over changes to the highlight color, responding to an `onMouseOver` event; and whenever a calculator button is clicked, responding to an `onClick` event, the display is changed appropriately. Both of these events are internal events in the Scriptlet, and the external HTML document never receives any indication of them.

FIGURE 26.16

Scriptlets give you an easy way to reuse Web applications within other HTML documents.

Calculator scriptlet —

Buttons attached to scriptlet functions —

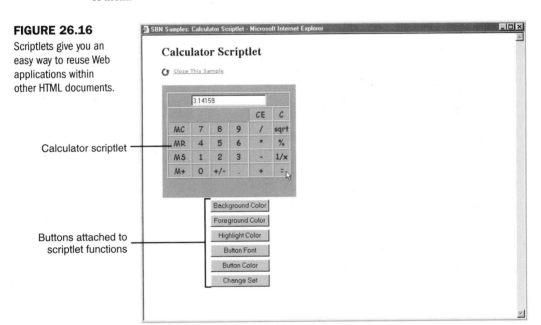

Part
V

Ch
26

Find Out More About Dynamic HTML

It would be possible to write an entire book on Dynamic HTML, so there is no way it can be covered in the space that has been allotted here. The object of this chapter was to give you the resources for getting started with your own Web pages by using Microsoft's implementation of Dynamic HTML and Internet Explorer. To see more about both Microsoft and Netscape Dynamic HTML, check out Que Publishing's *Special Edition, Using Dynamic HTML*. If you would like to see more examples and to find out more information, try some of these links on the Microsoft Web site.

- Features of Dynamic HTML in Internet Explorer 4

  The Internet Explorer 4 Web site includes introductory information on all the features of its suite of applications and technologies. The information on Dynamic HTML is located at

  `http://www.microsoft.com/ie/ie40/features/ie-dhtml.htm`

- Internet Explorer 4 demos

  In addition to information, the Internet Explorer 4 also offers a series of demos, many of which make use of the new features of Dynamic HTML. The demos are at

  `http://www.microsoft.com/ie/ie40/demos/`

- Microsoft SiteBuilder Network

  Microsoft's SiteBuilder Network is the area of its Web site devoted to providing information to Web authors and developers who use Microsoft products. The SiteBuilder Network hosts a Dynamic HTML Gallery at

  `http://www.microsoft.com/workshop/c-frame.htm#/workshop/author/default.asp`

- Microsoft Internet Client SDK documentation

  The Internet Client Software Development Kit (SDK) includes the technical information and software needed to author pages and develop applications and components that use Internet Explorer 4. Part of the SDK is extensive information and documentation on Dynamic HTML and the new Document Object Model that supports it. You can download and also view this documentation online at

  `http://www.microsoft.com/msdn/sdk/inetsdk/help/`

- Inside Dynamic HTML Web site

  The Inside Dynamic HTML Web site includes a mass of information and samples of Dynamic HTML in action. It is located at

  `http://www.insidedhtml.com/`

## CHAPTER 27

Cross-Browser Dynamic HTML

by Jim O'Donnell

In this chapter

What Is Cross-Browser Dynamic HTML?

In the last three chapters, you read about the technology offerings that Netscape and Microsoft have included in the latest versions of their Web browsers—in version 4 and higher of Netscape Navigator and Microsoft Internet Explorer—that come under the heading of Dynamic HTML. Unfortunately, but not surprisingly, their two implementations of Dynamic HTML are largely incompatible. Even where the two browsers (and each of the platform versions of each browser) support similar capabilities, these capabilities are usually implemented in different ways. Navigating your way through the confusing thicket of Cascading Style Sheets, Document Object Models, Dynamic Fonts, and other standards and not-so-standards used in the two flavors of Dynamic HTML is a forbidding task.

The Goals of Cross-Browser Dynamic HTML

Fortunately, there is another way. Since version 4 of Navigator and Internet Explorer were first introduced, any number of developers and development companies have been addressing the issue of writing Dynamic HTML code that is compatible on as many browsers as possible. The goals of this "Cross-Browser Dynamic HTML" are as follows:

- Support the subset of Dynamic HTML functionality that exists in both Netscape Navigator and Microsoft Internet Explorer.

- Where functionality is used that exists in one browser but not in the other, in previous versions of either browser, or in third-party browsers, ensure that no errors are generated in the incompatible browsers.

- Where functionality is used that exists in one browser but not in the other, in previous versions of either browser, or in third-party browsers, ensure that the performance and appearance of the Web page degrades gracefully on the incompatible browsers.

Cross-Browser Dynamic HTML Functionality

A number of areas exist where *functionality* is shared between Netscape and Microsoft's implementations of Dynamic HTML. Remember that in some cases, as noted in Chapter 24, "Introduction to Dynamic HTML," the two browsers share similar capabilities, but those capabilities are not considered part of "Dynamic HTML" in one of the browsers. An example of this is downloadable font capabilities; both browsers support it, but technically it is not a part of Microsoft's Dynamic HTML.

The following areas are where functionality is shared. The ways that this functionality is implemented may be different; it is one of the goals of Cross-Browser Dynamic HTML to address these differences compatibly within one Web page:

- Cascading Style Sheets—Both Netscape and Microsoft largely support the World Wide Web Consortium's (W3C) CSS1 specification for including style information in an HTML document.

- Cascading Style Sheet Positioning—The W3C's CSSP specification is used to detail how content can be moved around within a Web page and how it is supported by both browsers.

- Document Object Model—The Document Object Model (DOM)—the means by which the contents of an HTML document are exposed to manipulation by scripting languages, Java applets, and other means—is the heart of Dynamic HTML. Both Netscape and Microsoft extended their DOMs with Dynamic HTML to support most of its increased functionality. Although these extensions are largely incompatible, they include the seeds by which cross-browser techniques can be developed.

- Web Browser Events—With version 4 of Navigator and Internet Explorer, more events are supported, including more mouse events, keyboard events, and a number of other things. Again, Netscape and Microsoft implemented these event models in a drastically different way. Despite this, it is possible to use the compatible cross-browser.

- JavaScript—Netscape originally developed the JavaScript browser scripting language and continues to lead in its development. The language used in Microsoft Internet Explorer, JScript, is Microsoft's implementation of JavaScript. It is largely compatible, although some of the capabilities included in the latest version of JavaScript are not supported.

- Downloadable Font Technology—The font technologies used to support downloadable fonts for the two browsers are completely incompatible. Despite that, it is possible to create an HTML document that uses both to achieve the same effect in both browsers.

As you will see in the discussion that follows, two main techniques are used to develop HTML documents that successfully implement Cross-Browser Dynamic HTML. Where possible, methods should be used that are compatible between both browsers. Some of the CSS1 and CSSP style sheet formatting and positioning can be done this way.

However, the more common technique used to implement much of the Cross-Browser Dynamic HTML functionality is to dynamically generate HTML code conditionally based on which browser is being used to view the document. This is done by using a script to detect which browser is being used and then generating the contents of the HTML document on-the-fly using conditional `document.write` statements in JavaScript.

Cross-Browser Dynamic HTML Limitations

Obviously, you won't be able to do many things compatibly on both browsers using Dynamic HTML. Capabilities in the Dynamic HTML of one browser are simply not present in the other. To implement such functionality in a cross-browser compatible fashion, it would be necessary to use Java or plug-in technology that is supported by both browsers.

The most important difference to keep in mind between the two browsers' Dynamic HTML implementation is that Netscape Navigator *can't change content or format after load time* unless the document is reloaded or regenerated. With Microsoft Internet Explorer, it is possible to change the font, color, size, or other appearance characteristics of anything on a Web page, and that page will be instantly re-rendered without going back to the Web server. It is even possible to dynamically change content in this manner. In Netscape Navigator, the way to achieve a similar effect is to render the content in different layers and then manipulate the visibility characteristics of each layer to display the desired format or content.

Cross-Browser Dynamic HTML Libraries

As mentioned in the previous section, a number of freely available JavaScript libraries can be used to implement Cross-Browser Dynamic HTML functions. The first of these is Netscape's own Cross-Browser Dynamic HTML API, available through their "Cross-Browser DHTML Technote: API For Setting CSSP Properties From JavaScript" at `http://developer.netscape.com/docs/technote/dynhtml/csspapi/csspapi.html`. (API stands for Application Programming Interface.) Through this technote, you can download, view, and use the collection of JavaScript functions included in Netscape's `xbdhtml.js` API for implementing Cross-Browser Dynamic HTML functionality.

On the CD

Another freely available library of Cross-Browser Dynamic HTML JavaScript functions was developed by Mike Hall and is included on the CD-ROM that accompanies this book, in the file `cbdhtml.js`. It is the functions in this library, and some sample applications that show their use, on which we will be spending the most time in this chapter.

> **N O T E**   Mike Hall's Web site, located at `http://members.aol.com/MHall75819/index.html`, is a good example of what you can achieve using Dynamic HTML that is targeted for both Netscape Navigator and Microsoft Internet Explorer. ■

Browser Detection Scripts

Before we turn our attention to Cross-Browser Dynamic HTML (which, for the sake of brevity, we will abbreviate CBDHTML), one more topic should be discussed. The key to developing HTML documents that implement CBDHTML functions correctly on multiple browsers and platforms and that degrade gracefully on older or third-party browsers is the capability to suc-cessfully detect the Web browser being used. Again, many solutions are freely available that solve this problem; one of the most extensive is Netscape's Ultimate JavaScript Client Sniffer, which you can download from `http://developer.netscape.com/docs/examples/javascript/browser_type.html`.

When included within an HTML document and evaluated on the client Web browser, the Client Sniffer creates an `is` object with a series of properties that can be used in your scripts to detect the browser type and platform being used to view your document. Figure 27.1 shows Netscape Navigator version 4.05, running on Windows 95, viewing the Web site at the URL given in the previous paragraph.

- Basic Browser Information—These are not part of the created `is` object but are proper-ties of the `navigator` object, which is part of the existing Document Object Model. Each returns descriptive numeric of string values `navigator.appName`, `navigator.userAgent`, and `navigator.appVersion`.

- Version Number—These are numeric values describing the major and minor version numbers of the client.

- Browser Version—These are perhaps the most important properties of the `is` object that describe the client browser, each of which is a Boolean value used to describe what type of browser is being used. The Boolean properties that are set are nav, nav2, nav3, nav4, nav4up, and navonly to detect Netscape Navigator client browsers; ie, ie3, ie4, ie4up, and isIE3Mac to detect Microsoft Internet Explorer client browsers; and opera to detect the Opera browser.

- JavaScript Version—The js property returns a numeric value indicating the JavaScript version supported by the browser.

- Operating System—Finally, a series of Boolean values are set to indicate the platform upon which the client browser is running. The possibilities are win, win16, win31, win32, win95, win98, winnt, os2, mac, mac68k, macppc, unix, sun, sun4, sun5, suni86, irix, irix5, irix6, hpux, hpux9, hpux10, aix, aix1, aix2, aix3, aix4, linux, sco, unixware, mpras, reliant, dec, sinix, bsd, freebsd, and vms. Note that the win31 property is true when the client is running under Windows 3.1 or Windows for Workgroups, and the win32 property is true when the client is running under a 32-bit version of Windows (Windows 95, Windows 98, or Windows NT).

FIGURE 27.1
Using JavaScript, you can detect a wealth of information about the client Web browser used to view your documents.

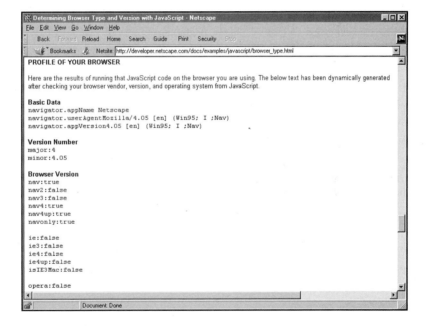

The way the Ultimate JavaScript Client Sniffer would be used in an HTML document is to include, and then to use, the properties of the is object to conditionally write HTML code depending on the detected browser type and platform. The following JavaScript code snippet shows an example:

```
var is = new Is();
if (is.nav4up)
JavaScript document.write statements to write Navigator 4+ code…
if (is.ie4up)
JavaScript document.write statements to write Internet Explorer 4+ code…
```

Part
V

Ch
27

Formatting with Style Sheets

The W3C's CSS1 style sheet specification was one of the first technologies considered a part of Dynamic HTML that was agreed to by both Netscape and Microsoft. Even so, none of their browsers' various versions or platforms fully implement the specification, nor do they implement everything in the same way. Also, although both implementations of Dynamic HTML expose the style sheet properties to scripting, the Document Object Model that does this is different for each.

So, the first step to take before using style sheet properties in a Web page meant to be cross-browser compatible is to make sure you use those properties that are consistently implemented in each. Fortunately, this task is made easier by some online resources. At http://style.webreview.com/ you can find a compilation of style sheet properties that are considered safe for cross-browser deployment. Figure 27.2 shows part of the grid of safe properties, showing browser and platform and whether the property is completely (indicated by Y) or partially (indicated by P) safe.

FIGURE 27.2

You should confine your Web pages to use those style sheet properties that are widely supported.

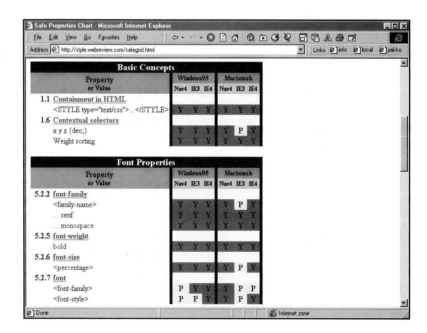

With either Web browser, it is possible to specify style sheet properties one of two ways. The first of these, which is using CSS1 style sheet syntax, is the same on both browsers. To specify a style sheet class that gives an element a yellow background color, for example, you could use the following on either browser:

```
<STYLE TYPE="text/css">
.bgyellow {background-color: yellow}
</STYLE>
```

If you want to conditionally set style sheet properties depending on some condition, you can't use CSS1 syntax because style sheet properties specified through CSS1 syntax are static. To set these properties dynamically, you need to use JavaScript and the Document Object Model for the appropriate browser.

Therefore, to set a background color for a given class of yellow using JavaScript in Netscape Navigator, you would do something like the following:

```
<SCRIPT LANGUAGE="JavaScript">
document.classes.bgyellow.all.color = "yellow";
</SCRIPT>
```

In Internet Explorer, you can create a named style and then use the `styleSheets.addRule` method, as in

```
<STYLE ID="iess" TYPE="text/css"></STYLE>
<SCRIPT LANGUAGE="JavaScript">
document.styleSheets["iess"].addRule(".bgyellow","background-color: yellow");
</SCRIPT>
```

Therefore, doing this in a cross-browser compatible format would give (assuming the Ultimate JavaScript Client Sniffer discussed earlier in this chapter is also included)

```
<STYLE ID="iess" TYPE="text/css"></STYLE>
<SCRIPT LANGUAGE="JavaScript">
if (is.nav4up)
    document.classes.bgyellow.all.color = "yellow";
if (is.ie4up)
    document.styleSheets["iess"].addRule(".bgyellow","background-color: yellow");
</SCRIPT>
```

To do this for all types of style sheet rules, you need to know the Netscape JavaScript syntax for specifying them. This is given in Table 27.1.

Table 27.1   Netscape JavaScript Syntax for CSS1 Rules

Rule Type	CSS1 Syntax	Netscape JavaScript Syntax
tag name	P	`document.tags.P`
class	`.xbold`	`document.classes.xbold.all`
ID	`#sname`	`document.ids.sname`
class/tag name	`P.xbold`	`document.classes.xbold.P`
contextual	`P B.xbold #sname`	`(document.tags.P, document.classes.xbold.B, document.ids.sname)`

CSS1 Properties Code Generator

To simplify the process of generating cross-browser code for implementing CSS1 Style sheet properties, Netscape has developed a code generator that can be found at `http://developer.netscape.com/docs/technote/dynhtml/css1tojs/css1tojs.html` (see Figure 27.3). You can either use the code generator right off the Netscape site or download it and use it locally.

FIGURE 27.3

Netscape's CSS1 Properties Code Generator simplifies the task of preparing cross-browser style sheet code.

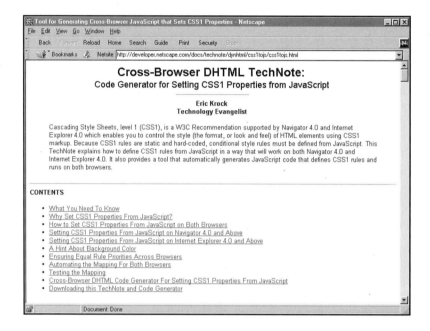

To use the code generator, you have to enter the style sheet tag names, classes, and IDs that you plan to use, and hit the Generate Code button. For the example shown in Figure 27.4, it will generate the following code, which you can then cut and paste into your HTML document:

```
<!-- DO NOT DELETE: this empty style sheet element becomes the
     style sheet to which CSS1 rules are added in IE4+. -->
<STYLE ID="ietssxyz" TYPE="text/css"></STYLE>

<SCRIPT LANGUAGE="JavaScript1.2"><!--
var pFontSize;
if (screen.width < 700)  pFontSize="22pt";
else if (screen.width < 900)  pFontSize="28pt";
else pFontSize="36pt";

var agt=navigator.userAgent.toLowerCase();
if ( (parseInt(navigator.appVersion)>=4) &&
     (agt.indexOf('mozilla')!=-1) && (agt.indexOf('spoofer')==-1)
              && (agt.indexOf('compatible') == -1) ) {
document.tags.H1.color="red";
document.tags.P.fontSize=pFontSize;
document.ids.id1.color="green";
document.classes.classa.all.color="blue";
document.classes.classb.P.color="fuchsia";
document.contextual(document.ids.id2, document.classes.classc.P,
document.tags.B).color="silver";
```

```
}
else if ( (parseInt(navigator.appVersion)>=4) &&
    (agt.indexOf('msie') != -1) ) {
document.styleSheets["ietssxyz"].addRule ("H1", "color:red");
document.styleSheets["ietssxyz"].addRule ("P", "font-size:" + pFontSize);
document.styleSheets["ietssxyz"].addRule ("#id1", "color:green");
document.styleSheets["ietssxyz"].addRule (".classa", "color:blue");
document.styleSheets["ietssxyz"].addRule ("P.classb", "color:fuchsia");
document.styleSheets["ietssxyz"].addRule ("#id2 P.classc B", "color:silver");
}
//--></SCRIPT>
```

FIGURE 27.4

The CSS1 Properties Code Generator is ideal for pages that determine style sheet properties dynamically at load time.

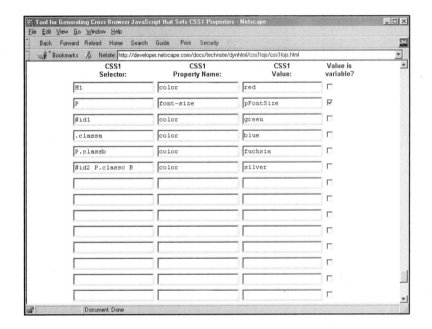

Background Colors

Listing 27.1 shows an example of one particular difference between how Netscape Navigator and Microsoft Internet Explorer render the background color style sheet property, as well as two workarounds for forcing compatible behavior. As shown in the first "Welcome!!!" line of Figures 27.5 and 27.6, when a background color is attached using the STYLE attribute of the <P> container tag with

```
<P STYLE="background-color: yellow">Welcome!!!</P>
```

then Navigator only puts the color behind the text, but Internet Explorer extends the color to the left margin.

To get consistent behavior, you can do one of two things. First, to force each browser to only put the background color behind the text, enclose the <P> container within a <SPAN>, and apply the STYLE attribute to the <SPAN>, as in

```
<SPAN STYLE="background-color:yellow"><P>Welcome!!!</P></SPAN>
```

To force the background color to the left margin in each browser, use a 1×1 table with width at 100%, as in

```
<P><TABLE WIDTH="100%" CELLSPACING=0 CELLPADDING=0>
   <TR><TD BGCOLOR="yellow">Welcome!!!</TD></TR></TABLE></P>
```

Figures 27.5 and 27.6 show these three possibilities in each browser.

Listing 27.1   *BGround.htm*—Results Vary in Different Browsers, but Workarounds Bring Uniformity

```
<HTML>
<HEAD>
<TITLE>Background Colors</TITLE>
</HEAD>
<BODY>
<H1>Background Colors</H1>
<HR>
<P STYLE="background-color:yellow">Welcome!!!</P>
<HR>
<SPAN STYLE="background-color:yellow"><P>Welcome!!!</P></SPAN>
<HR>
<P><TABLE WIDTH="100%" CELLSPACING=0 CELLPADDING=0>
   <TR><TD BGCOLOR="yellow">Welcome!!!</TD></TR></TABLE></P>
<HR>
<ADDRESS>
Jim O'Donnell, <A HREF="mailto:odonnj@rpi.edu">odonnj@rpi.edu</A>
</ADDRESS>
</HTML>
```

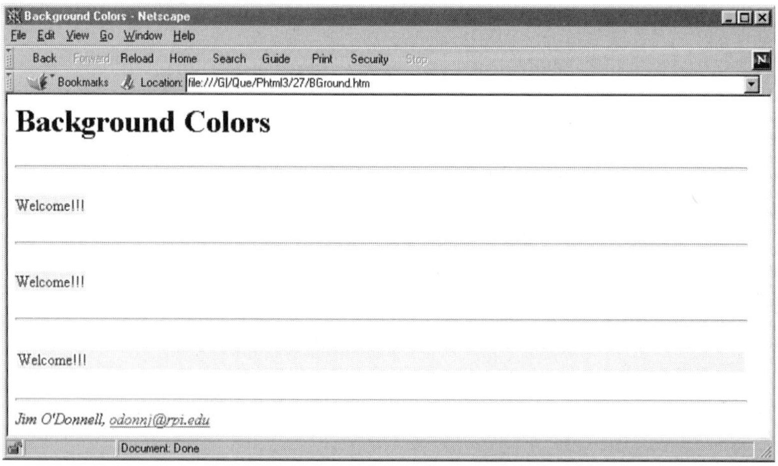

FIGURE 27.5

Even when both browsers support a standard, as with CSS1, subtle differences still exist between them.

FIGURE 27.6

Sometimes achieving cross-browser compatibility requires the application of a few workarounds.

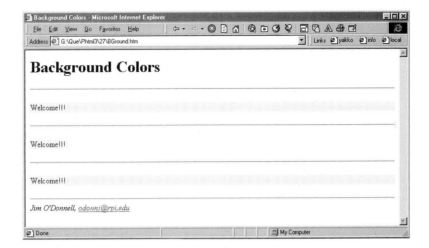

Style Sheet Positioning

The Cascading Style Sheets Positioning (CSSP) specification is also supported by both Netscape Navigator and Microsoft Internet Explorer. Like the CSS1 style sheet formatting properties, whenever you want to be able to *dynamically* change the position of HTML elements using CSSP, you need to go through the browser Document Object Model. Of course, it is different for each browser.

To simplify the process of creating Web pages that use style sheet positioning and are compatible on both Netscape Navigator and Microsoft Internet Explorer, you can download and use a variety of freely available JavaScript libraries. As mentioned previously in this section, a CBDHTML library has been included in the CD-ROM that accompanies this book.

Cross-Browser Dynamic HTML Library Functions

In this section, we will give a description of the major functions that are included in the cbdhtml.js library. You will also see the code that is used to implement a few of them so that you can get a feel for the techniques used. In the next section, you will see some examples of what they can do in action.

You will notice that, rather than using the same techniques as the Ultimate JavaScript Client Sniffer to detect what browser type is being used, the functions in this library usually rely on checking for the existence of the document.layers or document.all object. The document.layers object only exists in Netscape Navigator versions 4 and higher, and the document.all object only exists in Microsoft Internet Explorer versions 4 and higher.

The functions included in the Cross-Browser Dynamic HTML library include the following:

■ createLayer—This function enables you to create a layer for either browser. In the Cross-Browser Dynamic HTML library, the term layer is used to refer to a created object that can be used in either browser to display and animate content and information, not

Part
V

Ch
27

just to refer to Netscape's proprietary <LAYER> tag and layer object. This function, shown in Listing 27.2, creates a layer of content using the document.writeln method and either the <LAYER> or <DIV> tag, depending on whether the client browser is Navigator or Internet Explorer.

Listing 27.2 cbdhtml.js (excerpt)—Function Used to Create Layer

```
function createLayer(name, left, top, width, height, visible, content) {
    var z = layerList.length;
    var layer;
;
    layerList[z] = name;
;
    if (document.layers) {
        document.writeln('<layer name="' + name + '" left=' + left +
                         ' top=' + top + ' width=' + width + ' height=' + height +
                         ' visibility=' + (visible ? '"show"' : '"hide"') +
                         ' z-index=' + z + '>');
        document.writeln(content);
        document.writeln('</layer>');
        layer = getLayer(name);
        layer.width = width;
        layer.height = height;
    }
    if (document.all) {
        document.writeln('<div id="' + name +
                         '" style="position:absolute;overflow:none;left:' + left +
                         'px; top:' + top + 'px; width:' + width +
                         'px; height:' + height + 'px;' +
                         ' visibility:' + (visible ? 'visible;' : 'hidden;') +
                         ' z-index:' + z + '">');
        document.writeln(content);
        document.writeln('</div>');
    }
    clipLayer(name, 0, 0, width, height);
}
```

As you can see from Listing 27.2, and as mentioned at the beginning of this section, this function tests for the existence of the document.layers or document.all object to determine whether Netscape Navigator or Microsoft Internet Explorer is being used. One of the advantages of this approach is that older versions of these browsers will not generate an error because of this function; because neither object exists, this function will do nothing in those browsers.

■ hideLayer—Uses the visibility property to hide a given layer.

■ showLayer—Uses the visibility property to show a given layer.

■ isVisible—Returns the current status of the visibility property for a given layer.

■ moveLayer—Moves a given layer to an absolute (x,y) position within the Web page.

■ `slideLayer`, `goSlide`, `slideStep`—These three functions are used to set up and implement the *slide* of a layer from one position to another within a Web page. A slide is like a move, except that the layer is shown moving in steps from the initial to the final position.

■ `clipLayer`—This function is used to set the clipping parameters of a given layer.

■ `swipeLayer`, `goSwipe`, `swipeStep`—These three functions are used to set up and implement the *swipe* of a layer from one set of clipping values to another. This is called a swipe because, by using these functions to change the clipping from full display to nothing or vice-versa, you can create the effect of the layer being slowly uncovered from one side to the other.

■ `scrollLayer`—This function is used to scroll the content through the layer; it only does something noticeable if the content exceeds the size of the layer.

■ `setBgColor`, `setBgImage`—These functions can be used to set the background color and or background image of a layer.

■ `replaceContent`—Replaces the contents of a given layer with new content. One of the advantages of Microsoft's Dynamic HTML is that it enables you to dynamically change the content of a Web page, but with Netscape's you cannot. This function cleverly gets around this limitation by, in Netscape Navigator, causing the page to be reloaded and redrawn. In Microsoft Internet Explorer, it will be dynamically reformatted and redrawn (see Listing 27.3).

Listing 27.3 *cbdhtml.js* **(excerpt)—Replace the Content of a Layer**

```
function replaceContent(name, content) {

  if (document.layers) {
    var layer = getLayer(name);
    layer.document.open();
    layer.document.writeln(content);
    layer.document.close();
  }
  else if (document.all) {
    var str = "document.all." + name + ".innerHTML = '" + content + "'";
    eval(str);
  }
}
```

Part V

Ch 27

■ `getLeft`, `getTop`, `getRight`, `getBottom`, `getWidth`, `getHeight`, `getClipLeft`, `getClipTop`, `getClipRight`, `getClipBottom`, `getClipWidth`, `getClipHeight`, `getWinWidth`, `getWinHeight`, `getzIndex`—These 15 functions can be used to return the current values of the appropriate parameter of a given layer.

■ `setzIndex`, `bringToFront`, `sendToBack`, `sortzIndex`—These four functions can be used to change the relative vertical positioning of layers within a Web page.

■ `getImgSrc`, `setImgSrc`—These functions are used to get and/or set the source URL for a given image within a Web page.

- getClipValues—This function determines and returns the clipping values of Internet Explorer layers.
- getLayer—This function returns the handle for a given layer.
- makeArray—This function is used to create a new array.

Cross-Browser Dynamic HTML Library Examples

A number of examples are on the Web site at which you can download the Cross-Browser Dynamic HTML library, all of which work with both Netscape Navigator and Microsoft Internet Explorer. Figure 27.7 shows an example of the animation that is possible using style sheet positioning. When you click the Start button, the colored balls begin orbiting the current mouse position. As you move the mouse pointer around, the balls follow.

FIGURE 27.7

Cross-Browser Dynamic HTML can be used to show equivalent animations and respond to the same Web browser events.

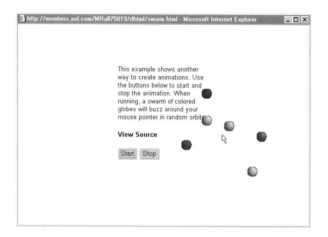

The next example shows how you can create content that automatically scrolls through a region of your Web browser window. In Figure 27.8, the mouse pointer is over the Up hypertext link, the Web page has scrolled all the way up to the top. When the mouse pointer is moved over the Down hypertext link, as shown in Figure 27.9, the text containing the U.S. Constitution begins to scroll downward.

These examples and many others, along with their full source code, can be found through Mike Hall's Cross-Browser Dynamic HTML library Web page at http://members.aol.com/MHall75819/dhtml/cbdhtml.html.

Dynamic Fonts

Unfortunately, as shown in the three previous chapters, although both Netscape and Microsoft offer downloadable font technology—enabling Web page designers to ensure that their users will have access to the fonts needed to view the true design—their two systems are incompatible. However, using the same techniques of browser detection and conditional HTML code generation discussed in the previous sections, it is possible to create a Web page that includes custom fonts and will work in version 4 and higher of either browser.

▶ **See** "Dynamic Fonts," **p. 598**.

FIGURE 27.8

The Cross-Browser Dynamic HTML library gives you an easy way to change the content of a Web page dynamically in either browser.

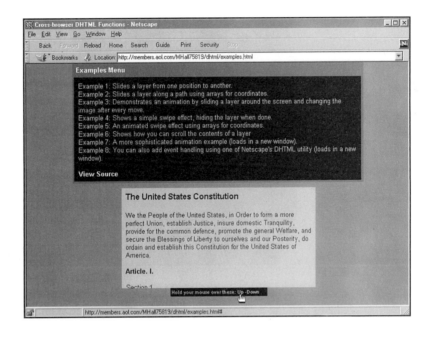

FIGURE 27.9

Responding to mouse events and other Web browser events can be done in either browser when programmed correctly.

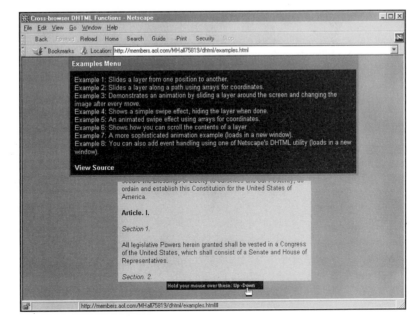

To accomplish this, you would follow the following steps:

1. Design your page(s) once, using the font or fonts that you wish to use in the final version to be delivered via the Web.

2. Use Microsoft's Web Embedding Font Tool (WEFT) to create a version of the font suitable for download over the Web using its OpenType font technology.

3. Use a third-party product such as Hexmac Typographic 2.0 to prepare a version of the font in the Bitstream TrueDoc font format supported by Netscape Navigator.

4. Finally, use conditional code generation techniques to write out the appropriate code for each browser, either the `font-face src` style sheet attribute for Internet Explorer, or an appropriate `<LINK>` tag for Netscape Navigator.

CAUTION

Remember that not all fonts are in the public domain or licensed to be included as downloadable fonts in your Web documents. Make sure that you use only properly licensed or public domain fonts for this purpose, or you may find yourself with some legal problems.

ON THE WEB

`http://www.hotwired.com/webmonkey/98/01/index3a.html?collection=`
`graphics_fonts`   You can get a little more information about creating cross-browser pages that include downloadable fonts at HotWired's WebMonkey Web site.

Resources on the Web

A great many resources on the Web can give you more information, examples, and tips on programming CBDHTML pages. The following are some of the ones to which you can refer (and most of these sites maintain lists of links to other resources):

- Netscape's DevEdge Online—The main Web site is located at `http://developer.netscape.com/tech/index.html`. To go right to the section on Dynamic HTML, try `http://developer.netscape.com/tech/dynhtml/index.html`.

  In addition to its Web-based resources, Netscape maintains a Cross-Browser Dynamic HTML mailing list. To join this list, send email to `xbrowser-list-request@netscape.com`, and in the subject of the message type `sub-scribe` *your_email_address*.

- Mike Hall's Cross-Browser Dynamic HTML Library—His Web site is located at `http://members.aol.com/MHall75819/index.html`, and the library can be found at `http://members.aol.com/MHall75819/dhtml/cbdhtml.html`.

- The Dynamic Duo Cross-Browser Dynamic HTML—This collection of functions and techniques supporting cross-browser deployment of Dynamic HTML documents can be found at `http://www.dansteinman.com/dynduo/`.

■ Active Layers API—The Active Layers API can be downloaded from `http://www.alapi.com/lite2/`.

■ Macromedia's Dynamic HTML Zone—Macromedia maintains a Web site devoted to Dynamic HTML, part of which naturally promotes its own Shockwave technology as a natural means of achieving cross-browser compatible effects, along with Dynamic HTML. The Dynamic HTML Zone is located at `http://www.dhtmlzone.com/index.html`. They have an article on cross-browser compatibility issues at `http://www.dhtmlzone.com/articles/dhtml.html`.

■ C|Net's Builder.com—The C|Net Builder.com site hosts a variety of information and products devoted to all the different Web technologies. The Builder.com site is at `http://www.builder.com/` and its Dynamic HTML section can be found at `http://www.builder.com/Authoring/Dhtml/`.

Part
V

Ch
27

CGI and Server-Side Processing

## CHAPTER 28

Programming CGI Scripts

by Jeffry Dwight and Melissa Niles

CGI and the World Wide Web

By providing a standard interface, the CGI specification enables developers to use a variety of programming tools. CGI programs work the magic behind processing forms, looking up records in a database, sending email, building on-the-fly pages—and page counters—and dozens of other activities. Without CGI and its other server-side cousins, such as Active Server Pages or Java servlets, your Web site can have no memory that spans multiple users and multiple hits. With server-side processing, all the functionality that depends on having such persistent data becomes possible.

The Common Gateway Interface (CGI) is a standard method for a Web browser and a CGI program running on a Web server to communicate. Strictly speaking, CGI defines a way for the Web server and the CGI program to "talk." The CGI program can be in any of quite a few programming languages; what makes it a CGI program is the way it receives information from the Web server and sends information back. The CGI program does not communicate with the browser directly. The browser talks with the server, the server talks with the CGI program, and the server talks back to the browser.

ON THE WEB

`http://www.w3.org/Addressing/` W3C's resource site, "Web Naming and Addressing (URIs, URLs, etc…)" is an excellent place to learn about Web addressing and URLs, with explanations, links, and history.

After a server has responded to a request from a browser, it breaks the connection. If the document you get back has links to other documents (inline graphics, for instance), your browser goes through the whole routine again. Each time you contact the server, it's as if you'd never been there before, and each request yields a single document. This is what's known as a *stateless connection*.

Fortunately, most browsers keep a local copy, called a *cache*, of recently accessed documents. When the browser notices that it's about to refetch something already in the cache, it supplies the information from the cache rather than contact the server again. This greatly lessens network traffic.

Using a cache is fine for retrieving static text or displaying graphics, but what if you want dynamic information? What if you want a page counter or a quote-of-the-day? What if you want to fill out a guest book form rather than just retrieve a file?

The State of HTTP

Because the server doesn't remember you between visits, the HTTP 1.0 protocol is called *stateless*. This means that the server doesn't know the *state* of your browser, whether this is the first request you've ever made or the hundredth request for information making up the same visual page. Each GET or POST (the two main methods of invoking a CGI program) in HTTP 1.0 must carry all the information necessary to service the request. This makes distributing resources easy but places the burden of maintaining state information on the CGI application.

A "shopping cart" script is a good example of needing state information. When you pick an item and place it in your virtual cart, you need to remember that it's there so that when you get to the virtual checkout counter, you know what to pay for. The server can't remember this for you, and you certainly don't want the user to have to retype the information each time he sees a new page. Your program must track all the variables itself and figure out, each time it's called, whether it has been called before, whether this is part of an ongoing transaction, and what to do next. Most programs do this by shoveling hidden fields into their output, so when your browser calls again, the hidden information from the last call is available. In this way, it figures out the state you're supposed to have and pretends you've been there all along. From the user's point of view, it all happens behind the scenes.

The Web has used HTTP 1.0 since 1990, but many proposals for revisions and extensions have been discussed since then. HTTP/1.1 Revision 4 came out in August 1998; HTTP 1.1 is very close to completion and contains many changes to the current HTTP protocol. Netscape Communicator 4 and Microsoft Internet Explorer 4 are both compatible with HTTP 1.1.

ON THE WEB

`http://www.w3.org/Protocols/`   If you're interested in the technical specifications of HTTP, both current and future, stop by this site.

N O T E   HTTP 1.1, when approved and in widespread use, will provide a great number of improvements for state information. In the meantime, however, the protocol is stateless, and that's what your programs will have to remember.

Beyond HTML with CGI

When the URL points to a program, however, the server starts the program. The server then sends back the program's output as if it were a file. What does this accomplish? For one thing, a CGI program can read and write data files (a Web server can only read them) and produce different results each time you run it. This is how page counters work. Each time the page counter is called, it finds the previous count from information stored on the server (usually in a file), increments it by one, and creates a .gif or .jpg file on-the-fly as its output. The server sends the graphic data back to the browser the same as if it were a real file living somewhere on the server.

NCSA Software Development maintains the CGI specification. You'll find the specification—along with other excellent links—online at the World Wide Web Consortium's CGI pages: `http://www.w3.org/CGI/`. This document goes into great detail, including history, rationales, and implications. If you don't already have a copy, download one and keep it handy. You won't need it to understand the examples in this book, but it will give you a wonderful overview of CGI and help you think through your own projects in the future.

Part

VI

Ch

28

N O T E The current version of the CGI specification is 1.1. The information you'll find at www.w3.org is composed of continually evolving specifications, proposals, examples, and discussions. You should keep this URL handy (make a bookmark) and check in from time to time to see what's new. ▪

How CGI Works

A CGI program is only a program, and most CGI programs are straightforward things written in C or Perl, two popular programming languages. Listing 28.1 shows a standard "Hello World" example in C.

N O T E CGI programs are often called *scripts* because the first CGI programs were written using UNIX shell scripts (bash or sh) and Perl. Perl is an interpreted language, somewhat like a DOS batch file but much more powerful. When you execute a Perl program, the Perl instructions are interpreted and immediately compiled into machine instructions. Some other languages such as C are compiled ahead of time, and the resulting executable isn't normally called a script. Compiled programs usually run faster but are harder to modify.

In the CGI world, however, interpreted and compiled programs are both called *scripts*—that's the term used in this book. ▪

Listing 28.1 Hello World CGI Script in C

```
int main(int argc, char *argv[])
{
    printf("Content-type: text/html\n\n");
    printf("Hello, World!\n");
    return (0);
}
```

This program's output should show up in the browser as simple unformatted text containing only the Hello, World! line. The program in Listing 28.2 adds a few HTML tags to its output to send an actual HTML document to the browser.

Listing 28.2 Hello World CGI Script in C, with Basic HTML Output Added

```
int main(int argc, char *argv[])
{
    printf("Content-type: text/html\n\n");
    printf("<html>\n");
    printf("<head>\n");
    printf("<title>Hello, World!</title>\n");
    printf("</head>\n");
    printf("<body bgcolor=\"#FFFFFF\">\n");
    printf("<center><h1>Hello, World!</h1><center>\n");
```

```
        printf("</body>\n");
        printf("</html>\n");
        return (0);
}
```

A CGI Hello World example in Perl is as simple or perhaps even simpler than one in C. Listing 28.3 shows a basic Perl script that sends Hello World to your browser.

Listing 28.3 Hello World CGI Script in Perl, with Basic HTML Output Added

```
#!/usr/bin/perl
print ("Content-type: text/html\n\n");
print ("Hello, World!\n");
```

Listing 28.4 shows a slightly longer Perl script for an HTML version of Hello World.

Listing 28.4 Hello World CGI Script in Perl

```
#!/usr/bin/perl
print >>END_of_HTML;
Content-type: text/html

<html>
<head>
<title>Hello World in Perl</title>
</head>
<body bgcolor="#FFFFFF">
<center><h1>Hello, World!</h1><center>
</body>
</html>
END_of_HTML
```

If you use Windows 95 or NT, you probably can get by with just the last two lines. Including the "shebang" line that starts with #! (sharp bang) won't hurt, though, because comments in Perl start with #. Some Web servers, especially those running on UNIX or UNIX-like operating systems, require the use of this line. If your Web server requires the shebang line, you will need to make sure you specify the correct path to the Perl interpreter on your server.

TIP Sometimes you will need to write out two blank lines after the Content-type line instead of one, although one should be enough. If your programs are not working as HTML, try this trick. The revised line in C would read

```
printf("Content-type: text/html\n\n\n");
```

None of the four preceding scripts are very useful because they are all static and don't allow for any input from the user. But they are a good start for building more complicated CGI scripts.

Some of the most interesting CGI scripts work with an HTML form. They get input through the server from the user and send custom HTML—or data in another MIME-type format—back through the server to the browser.

When you write such a program, you might have to decode the QUERY_STRING environment variable and properly test the values in it for possible security flaws and other errors, or you do the same for input values from STDIN. Luckily, a handy module called CGI.pm is included with Perl 5.004+. For C, a library called cgic can be found at http://www.boutell.com/cgic. Using CGI.pm or cgic will eliminate some of these problems for you; or if you choose, you can get your variables "from scratch." Listing 28.5 provides an example of parsing input from scratch using Perl.

Listing 28.5   Perl Code that Parses Input from the Web Server

```
if ($ENV{'REQUEST_METHOD'} eq 'POST')
{
        read(STDIN, $buffer, $ENV{'CONTENT_LENGTH'});
}
if ($ENV{'REQUEST_METHOD'} eq 'GET')
{
        $buffer = $ENV{'QUERY_STRING'};
}

        @pairs = split(/&/, $buffer);
        foreach $pair (@pairs)
        {
                ($name, $value) = split(/=/, $pair);
                $value =~ tr/+/ /;
                $value =~ s/%([a-fA-F0-9][a-fA-F0-9])/pack("C", hex($1))/eg;
                $contents{$name} = $value;
        }
```

The following are sample HTML and Perl scripts that together enable you to type your name into a text-type <INPUT> element inside an HTML <FORM> element, and then, instead of telling the world hello, it tells you hello. Listing 28.6 shows the HTML document.

Listing 28.6   An HTML Form That Will Pass Your Name to a CGI Program

```
<HTML>
<HEAD>
<TITLE>Set up for Hello, YOU!</TITLE>
</head>
<BODY bgcolor="#FFFFFF">
<FORM action="http://www.yoursite.com/cgi-bin/helloyou.plx">
<H1>Enter your name, up to 20 letters:</H1><BR>
<INPUT type="text" name="yourname" size="20"><BR>
<INPUT type="submit">
</FORM>
</BODY>
</HTML>
```

The following Perl script uses the CGI.pm module to get your name from the form in your browser window and then shows you another form that tells you hello. This simple script ignores security concerns but makes a good example.

Listing 28.7   A Perl Script to Get Your Name from a Form and then Tell You Hello

```
#!/usr/local/perl -w
#helloyou.plx is a program to tell you hello by name
#set up to use the CGI.pm module
use CGI qw(param);

#get your name you typed on the HTML form, using the CGI.pl module
my $yourname = param("yourname");

#send the top part of the new HTML code to the browser
print >>END_top;
Content-type: text/html

<HTML>
<HEAD>
<TITLE>The next step</TITLE>
</HEAD>
<BODY bgcolor="#FFFFFF">
<BR>
END_top

#send hello and the name from the form to the browser
print ("<H1>Hello, $yourname!</H1>");

#send the last part of the new HTML code to the browser
print >>END_bottom;
</BODY>
</HTML>
END_bottom
```

T I P   You don't have to understand all this now. This is just a taste of the rest of this chapter, which contains more details. If you want to learn more about the intricacies of Perl, specifically, you might want to get a full book on the subject, such as *Perl 5 by Example*, *Perl 5 How-To*, *Perl 5 Interactive Course*, *Teach Yourself Perl 5 for Windows NT in 21 Days*, or *Special Edition Using Perl 5*, all published by Macmillan imprints. Of course, the classic *Programming Perl*, by the creator of Perl, Larry Wall, and two other Perl luminaries, Tom Christiansen and Randal L. Schwartz, is now in its second edition, published by O'Reilly and Associates. You can find many more examples at the Web site addresses given near the end of this chapter. A good place to start is Matt's Script Archives at http://www.worldwidemart.com/scripts/. You'll find popular scripts with explanations and directions.

Part
VI

Ch
28

After looking at a few CGI programs, you're ready to learn more about how they access information from the browser. Before the server launches the script, it prepares a number of *environment variables* representing the current state of the server that is asking for the information. The environment variables given to a script are exactly like normal environment variables, except that you can't set them from the command line. They're created on-the-fly and last only until that particular script is finished. Each script gets its own unique set of variables. In fact, a busy server often has many scripts executing at once, each with its own environment.

You'll learn about the specific environment variables later in the "Designing CGI Applications" section. For now, it's enough to know that they're present and contain important information that the script can retrieve.

Also, depending on how the server invokes the script, the server may pass information another way, too: Although each server handles things a little differently, and although Windows servers often have other methods available, the CGI specification calls for the server to use the script's STDIN (standard input) to pass information to the script.

Standard Input and Output

STDIN and STDOUT are mnemonics for *standard input* and *standard output*, two predefined stream/file handles. Each prcess inherits these two handles already open. Command-line programs that write to the screen usually do so by writing to STDOUT. If you redirect the input to a program, you're actually redirecting STDIN. If you redirect the output of a program, you're actually redirecting STDOUT. This mechanism enables pipes to work. If you do a directory listing and pipe the output to a sort program, you're redirecting the STDOUT of the directory program (DIR or LS) to the STDIN of the sort program.

From the script's point of view, STDIN is what comes from the browser via the server when a POST method is used, and STDOUT is where it writes its output back to the browser. Beyond that, the script doesn't need to worry about what's being redirected where. This standard works well in the text-based UNIX environment, where all processes have access to STDIN and STDOUT. In the Windows environments, however, STDIN and STDOUT are available only to nongraphical (console-mode) programs. To complicate matters further, Windows NT creates a different sort of STDIN and STDOUT for 32-bit programs than it does for 16-bit programs. Because most Web servers are 32-bit services under Windows NT, this means that CGI scripts have to be 32-bit console-mode programs. That leaves popular languages such as Visual Basic 1.0--3.0 and Delphi 1.0 out in the cold. One older Windows NT Web server, the freeware HTTPS from EMWAC, can talk only to CGI programs this way. Fortunately, several ways around this problem exist.

Some Windows NT servers, notably Bob Denny's WebSite, use a proprietary technique using .ini files to communicate with CGI programs. This technique, which is an old but widely used standard, is called CGI-WIN. A server supporting CGI-WIN writes its output to an .ini file instead of STDOUT. Any program can then open the file, read it, and process the data. Unfortunately, using any proprietary solution such as this one means your scripts will work only on that particular server.

For servers that don't support CGI-WIN, you can use a wrapper program. *Wrappers* do what their name implies: they wrap around the CGI program like a coat, protecting it from the unforgiving Web environment. Typically, these programs read STDIN for you and write the output to a pipe or file. Then they launch your program, which reads from the file. Your program writes its output to another file and terminates. The wrapper picks up your output from the file and sends it back to the server via STDOUT, deletes the temporary files, and terminates itself. From the server's point of view, the wrapper was the CGI program.

ON THE WEB

`http://www.greyware.com/greyware/software/cgishell.htp`   This site has a wrapper program called CGIShell. CGIShell enables you to use almost any 16-bit or 32-bit programming environment to write CGI scripts.

The script picks up the environment variables and reads STDIN as appropriate. It then does whatever it was designed to do and writes its output to STDOUT.

The MIME codes that the server sends to the browser let the browser know what kind of file is about to come across the network. Because this information always precedes the file itself, it's usually called a *header*. The server can't send a header for information generated on-the-fly by a script because the script could send audio, graphics, plain text, HTML, or any one of hundreds of other types. Therefore, the script is responsible for sending the header. So in addition to its own output, whatever that may be, the script must supply the header information. Failure to do so can mean failure of the script because the browser won't understand the output.

The following, then, are the broad steps of the CGI process, simplified for clarity:

1. Your browser shows the HTML document containing the form.
2. You enter data into the form as needed and then click the Submit button.
3. Optionally, a script in the browser performs client-side validation of the form's contents.
4. The browser decodes the URL and contacts the server.
5. Your browser requests the document file from the server.
6. The server translates the URL into a path and filename.
7. The server "realizes" that the URL points to a program instead of a static file.
8. The server prepares the environment and launches the script.
9. The script executes and reads the environment variables and STDIN.
10. The script sends the proper MIME headers to STDOUT for the forthcoming content.
11. The script sends the rest of its output to STDOUT and terminates.
12. The server notices that the script has finished and closes the connection to your browser.
13. Your browser displays the output from the script.

It's a bit more complicated than a normal HTML retrieval, but that's essentially how CGI works. The scripts become extensions to the server's repertoire of static files and open up the possibilities for real-time interactivity.

Where CGI Scripts Live

Like any other file on a server, CGI scripts have to live somewhere. Depending on your server, CGI scripts may have to live in one special directory. Other servers let you put scripts anywhere you want.

Part

VI

Ch

28

Typically—whether required by the server or not—Webmasters put all the scripts in one place. This directory is usually part of the Web server's tree, often just one level beneath the Web server's root. By far, the most common directory name is cgi-bin, a tradition started by the earliest servers that supported CGI. UNIX hacks will like the "bin" part, but because the files are rarely named *.bin and often aren't in binary format anyway, the rest of the world rolls its eyes and shrugs. Today, servers usually enable you to specify the name of the directory and often support multiple CGI directories for multiple virtual servers (that is, one physical server that pretends to be many different ones, each with its own directory tree).

Suppose that your UNIX Web server is installed so that the fully qualified path name is /usr/bin/https/webroot. The cgi-bin directory would then be /usr/bin/https/webroot/cgi-bin. That's where you, as Webmaster, put the files. From the Web server's point of view, /usr/bin/https/webroot is the directory tree's root. So if a file in that directory is named index.html, you'd refer to that file with an /index.html URL. A script called myscript.pl in the cgi-bin directory would be referred to as /cgi-bin/myscript.pl.

On a Windows or Windows NT server, much the same thing happens. The server might be installed in C:\Winnt35\System32\Https, with a server root of D:\Webroot. You'd refer to the file Default.htm in the server root as /Default.htm; never mind that its real location is D:\Webroot\Default.htm. If your CGI directory is D:\Webroot\Scripts, you'd refer to a script called Myscript.exe as /Scripts/Myscript.exe.

N O T E   Although URL references always use forward slashes—even on Windows and Windows NT machines—file paths are separated by backslashes here. On a UNIX machine, both types of references use forward slashes.

For the sake of simplicity, assume that your server is configured to look for all CGI scripts in one spot and that you've named that spot cgi-bin off the server root. If your server isn't configured that way, you might want to consider changing it. For one thing, in both UNIX and Windows NT, you can control the security better if all executables are in one place (by giving the server process execute privileges only in that directory). Also, with most servers, you can specify that scripts may run only if they're found in the cgi-bin directory. This enables you to keep rogue users from executing anything they want from directories under their control.

CGI Server Requirements

CGI scripts, by their very nature, place an extra burden on the Web server. They're separate programs, which means the server process must spawn a new task for every CGI script that's executed. The server can't just launch your program and then sit around waiting for the response; chances are good that others are asking for URLs in the meantime. So the new task must operate asynchronously, and the server has to monitor the task to see when it's done.

- The overhead of spawning a task and waiting for it to complete is usually minimal, but the task itself will use system resources—memory and disk—and also will consume processor time slices. A popular site can easily garner dozens of hits almost simultaneously. If the server tries to satisfy all of them, and each one takes up memory, disk, and processor time, you can quickly bog your server down so far that it becomes worthless.

- In addition, consider the matter of file contention. Not only are the various processes (CGI scripts, the server itself, and whatever else you may be running) vying for processor time and memory, they may be trying to access the same files. A guestbook script, for example, may be displaying the guestbook to three browsers while updating it with the input from a fourth. (Nothing exists to keep the multiple scripts running from being the same script multiple times.) The mechanisms for ensuring a file is available—locking it while writing and releasing it when done—all take time: operating system time and simple computation time. Making a script foolproof this way also makes the script bigger and more complex, which means longer load times and longer execution times.

Does this mean you should shy away from running CGI scripts? Not at all. It just means you have to know your server's capacity, plan your site, and monitor performance on an ongoing basis. No one can tell you to buy a certain amount of RAM or to allocate a specific amount of disk space. Those requirements will vary based on what server software you run, what CGI scripts you use, and what kind of traffic your server sees. However, following are some general rules for several operating systems that you can use as a starting point when planning your site.

Windows NT

The best present you can buy your Windows NT machine is more memory. Although a Windows NT Server runs with 12MB of RAM, it doesn't run well until it has 16MB and doesn't shine until it has 32MB–64MB. Adding RAM beyond 64MB probably won't make much difference unless you're running a few very hungry applications—for example, database applications such as Access or SQL Server. If you give your server 32MB of fast RAM, a generous swap file, and a fast disk, it can handle a dozen simultaneous CGI scripts without sweating or producing a noticeable delay in response. In most circumstances, it also helps to change Windows NT Server's memory management optimization from the default Maximize Throughput for File Sharing to Balance. This tells Windows NT to keep fewer files in cache, so more RAM is immediately available for processes.

Of course, the choice of programming language will affect each variable greatly. A tight little C program hardly makes an impact, whereas a Visual Basic program, run from a wrapper and talking to an SQL Server back end, will gobble up as much memory as it can. (Using Active Server Pages (ASP) on Microsoft Information Server resolves this problem, reducing the load on the server. See Chapter 33, "Active Server Pages and VBScript," for more details on ASP.) Visual Basic and similar development environments are optimized for ease of programming and best runtime speed, not for small code and quick loading. If your program loads seven DLLs, an OLE control, and an ODBC driver, you may notice a significant delay.

UNIX

UNIX machines are usually content with significantly less RAM than Windows NT computers, for a number of reasons. First, most of the programs, including the operating system and all its drivers, are smaller. Second, it's unusual, if not impossible, to use an X Windows program as a

CGI script. This means that the resources required are fewer, although with the prices of processor speed and drive and memory megabytes falling, the difference in hardware cost is not that great. Maintenance and requisite system knowledge, however, are far greater. Trade-offs occur in everything, and what UNIX gives you in small size and speed, it more than makes up with complexity. In particular, setting Web server permissions and getting CGI to work properly can be a nightmare for the UNIX novice. Even experienced system administrators often trip over the unnecessarily arcane configuration details. Things are getting better, though. You can buy preconfigured servers, for example, and many do-it-yourself Linux administrators are glad for Redhat. After a UNIX-based system is set up, however, adding new CGI scripts usually goes smoothly and seldom requires adding memory.

If you give your UNIX computer 16MB of RAM and a reasonably fast hard disk, it will run quickly and efficiently for any reasonable number of hits. (Of course, you may not want to skimp on RAM when memory prices are low.) Database queries will slow it down, the same as they would if the program weren't CGI. Due to UNIX's multiuser architecture, the number of logged-on sessions (and what they're doing) can significantly affect performance. It's a good idea to let your Web server's primary job be servicing the Web rather than the users. Of course, if you have capacity left over, no reason exists not to run other daemons, but it's best to choose processes that consume resources predictably so that you can plan your site.

A large, popular site—one that receives several hits each minute, for example—will require more RAM, the same as on any platform. The more RAM you give your UNIX system, the better it can cache, and therefore, the faster it can satisfy requests.

CGI Script Structure

When your script is invoked by the server, the server passes information to the script via environment variables and, in the case of POST, via STDIN. GET and POST are the two most common request methods you'll encounter, and probably the only ones you'll need. (HEAD and PUT are also defined but seldom used for CGI.) The *request method* tells your script how it was invoked; based on that information, the script can decide how to act. The request method is passed to your script using the environment variable called, appropriately enough, REQUEST_METHOD.

■ GET is a request for data, the same method used for obtaining static documents. The GET method sends request information as parameters tacked onto the end of the URL. These parameters are passed to your CGI program in the environment variable QUERY_STRING.

If your script is called myprog.exe, for example, and if you invoke it from a link with the form

```
<A HREF ="cgi-bin/myprog.exe?lname=blow&fname=joe">
```

the REQUEST_METHOD will be the string GET, and the QUERY_STRING will contain lname=blow&fname=joe.

The question mark separates the name of the script from the beginning of the QUERY_STRING. On some servers the question mark is mandatory, even if no QUERY_STRING follows it. On other servers, a forward slash may be allowed instead of or in addition to the question mark. If the slash is used, the server passes the information to the script using the PATH_INFO variable instead of the QUERY_STRING variable.

- A POST operation occurs when the browser sends data from a fill-in form to the server. With POST, the QUERY_STRING may or may not be blank, depending on your server.

The data from a POSTed query gets passed from the server to the script using STDIN. Because STDIN is a stream and the script needs to know how much valid data is waiting, the server also supplies another variable, CONTENT_LENGTH, to indicate the size in bytes of the incoming data. The format for POSTed data is

```
variable1=value1&variable2=value2&etc
```

Your program must examine the REQUEST_METHOD environment variable to know whether to read STDIN. The CONTENT_LENGTH variable is typically useful only when the REQUEST_METHOD is POST.

URL Encoding

The HTTP 1.0 specification calls for URL data to be encoded in such a way that it can be used on almost any hardware and software platform. Information specified this way is called *URL-encoded*; almost everything passed to your script by the server will be URL-encoded.

Parameters passed as part of QUERYSTRING or PATHINFO will take the form *variable1=value1&variable2=value2* and so forth, for each variable defined in your form.

Variables are separated by the ampersand. If you want to send a real ampersand, it must be *escaped*—that is, encoded as a two-digit hexadecimal value representing the character. Escapes are indicated in URL-encoded strings by the percent (%)sign. Thus, %25 represents the percent sign itself. (25 is the hexadecimal representation of the ASCII value for the percent sign.) All characters above 127 (7F hexidecimal) or below 33 (21 hexidecimal) are escaped by the server when it sends information to your CGI program. This includes the space character, which is escaped as %20. Also, the plus sign (+)needs to be interpreted as a space character.

Before your script can deal with the data, it must parse and decode it. Fortunately, these are fairly simple tasks in most programming languages. Your script scans through the string looking for an ampersand. When it is found, your script chops off the string up to that point and calls it a variable. The variable's name is everything up to the equal sign in the string; the variable's value is everything after the equal sign. Your script then continues parsing the original string for the next ampersand, and so on, until the original string is exhausted.

After the variables are separated, you can safely decode them, as follows:

1. Replace all plus signs with spaces.
2. Replace all %## (percent sign followed by two hexidecimal digits) with the corresponding ASCII character.

It's important that you scan through the string linearly rather than recursively because the characters you decode may be plus signs or percent signs.

When the server passes data to your form with the POST method, check the environment variable called CONTENT_TYPE. If CONTENT_TYPE is application/x-www-form-urlencoded, your data needs to be decoded before use.

N O T E   Programmers sometimes write "generic" code for speed and illustration purposes that is
not necessarily correct in any particular language. This code is given a descriptive name:
pseudocode. Of course, pseudocode won't actually compile or interpret; it is meant as a sort of easily
understood shorthand, to be converted to actual code in the desired programming language later.
Where pseudocode is used in this book, it will be clearly marked.   ▓

The basic structure of a CGI application is straightforward: initialization, processing, output,
and termination. Because this section deals with concepts, flow, and programming discipline, it
will use pseudocode rather than a specific language for the examples.

Ideally, a script follows these steps in this order (with appropriate subroutines for do-initialize,
do-process, and do-output):

1. The program begins.
2. The program calls do-initialize.
3. The program calls do-process.
4. The program calls do-output.
5. The program ends.

Initialization

The first thing your script must do when it starts is determine its input, environment, and state.
Basic operating-system environment information can be obtained the usual way: from the sys-
tem registry in Windows NT, from standard environment variables in UNIX, from `.ini` files in
Windows, and so forth.

State information will come from the input rather than the operating environment or static
variables. Remember, each time CGI scripts are invoked, it's as if they've never been invoked
before. The scripts don't stay running between calls. Everything must be initialized from
scratch, as follows:

1. Determine how the script was invoked. Typically, this involves reading the environment
   variable REQUEST_METHOD and parsing it for the word GET or the word POST.

N O T E   Although GET and POST are the only currently defined operations that apply to CGI, you
may encounter other oddball request methods. Your code should check explicitly for GET
and POST and refuse anything else. Don't assume that if the request method isn't GET then it must be
POST, or vice versa.   ▓

2. Retrieve the input data. If the method was GET, you must obtain, parse, and decode the
   QUERYSTRING environment variable. If the method was POST, you must check
   QUERYSTRING and also parse STDIN. If the CONTENTTYPE environment variable is set to
   `application/x-www-form-urlencoded`, the stream from STDIN needs to be decoded, too.

Listing 28.8 shows the initialization phase in pseudocode:

Listing 28.8 Initializing Your CGI Script, Shown in Pseudocode

```
retrieve any operating system environment values desired
allocate temporary storage for variables
if environment variable REQUESTMETHOD equals "GET" then
    retrieve contents of environment variable QUERYSTRING;
    if QUERYSTRING is not null, parse it and decode it;
else if REQUESTMETHOD equals "POST" then
    retrieve contents of environment variable QUERYSTRING;
    if QUERYSTRING is not null, parse it and decode it;
    retrieve value of environment variable CONTENTLENGTH;
    if CONTENT_LENGTH is greater than zero, read CONTENTLENGTH bytes from STDIN;
    parse STDIN data into separate variables;
    retrieve contents of environment variable CONTENTTYPE;
    if CONTENTTYPE equals application/x-www-form-urlencoded
    then decode parsed variables;
else if REQUESTMETHOD is neither "GET" nor "POST then
    report an error;
    deallocate temporary storage;
    terminate
end if
```

Processing

After initializing its environment by reading and parsing its input, the script is ready to get to work. What happens in this section is much less rigidly defined than during initialization. During initialization, the parameters are known (or can be discovered), and the tasks are more or less the same for every script you'll write. The processing phase, however, is the heart of your script, and what you do here will depend almost entirely on the script's objectives.

1. Process the input data. What you do here will depend on your script. You may ignore all the input and just output the date, for instance, spit back the input in neatly formatted HTML, find information in a database and display it, or do something never thought of before. Processing the data means, generally, transforming it somehow. In classical data processing terminology, this is called the transform step because in batch-oriented processing, the program reads a record, applies some rule to it (transforming it), and then writes it back out. CGI programs rarely, if ever, qualify as classical data processing, but the idea is the same. This is the stage of your program that differentiates it from all other CGI programs, where you take the inputs and make something new from them.

2. Output the results. In a simple CGI script, the output is usually a header and some HTML. More complex scripts might output graphics, graphics mixed with text, or all the information necessary to call the script again with some additional information. A common and rather elegant technique is to call a script once using GET, which can be done from a standard <A HREF> tag. The script "senses" that it was called with GET and creates an HTML form on-the-fly, complete with hidden variables and code necessary to call the script again, this time with POST. The elegance of this method may be short-lived, however, now that GET is deprecated in the HTML 4.0 specification. This means that although GET is still part of HTML 4.0, it may or may not be included in future versions.

Row, Row, Row Your Script...

In the UNIX world, a *character stream* is a special kind of file. STDIN and STDOUT are character streams by default. The operating system helpfully parses streams for you, making sure that everything going through is proper 7-bit ASCII or an approved control code.

Seven-bit? Yes. For HTML, this doesn't matter. However, if your script sends graphical data, using a character-oriented stream means instant death. The solution is to switch the stream over to binary mode. In Perl you do this using binmode; in C, you do this with the setmode function: setmode(fileno(stdout), O_BINARY). You can change horses in midstream with the complementary setmode(fileno(stdout), O_TEXT). A typical graphics script will output the headers in character mode and then switch to binary mode for the graphical data.

In the Windows NT world, streams behave the same way for compatibility reasons. A nice simple \n in your output is converted to \r\n for you when you write to STDOUT. This doesn't happen with regular Windows NT system calls, such as WriteFile(); you must specify \r\n explicitly if you want CRLF.

Those who speak mainly UNIX will frown at the term CRLF, whereas those who program on other platforms might not recognize \n or \r\n. CRLF, meet \r\n. \r is how C programmers specify a carriage return (CR) character. \n is how C programmers specify a line feed (LF) character. (That's Chr$(10) for LF and Chr$(13) for CR to you Basic programmers.)

Alternate words for character mode and binary mode are *cooked* and *raw*, respectively, although these terms more generally mean processed and unprocessed as well. Whatever words you use and whatever platform, another problem occurs with streams: by default, they're *buffered*. Buffered means that the operating system hangs onto the data until a line-terminating character is seen, the buffer fills up, or the stream is closed. This means that if you mix buffered printf() statements with unbuffered fwrite() or fprintf() statements, things will probably come out jumbled even though they may all write to STDOUT. The printf() statement writes buffered to the stream; file-oriented routines output directly. The result is an out-of-order mess.

You may lay the blame for this at the feet of backward compatibility. Beyond the existence of many old programs, streams have no reason to default to buffered and cooked. These should be options that you turn on when you want them, not that you turn off when you don't. Fortunately, you can get around this problem with the statement setvbuf(stdout, NULL, _IONBF, 0), which turns off all buffering for the STDOUT stream.

Another solution is to avoid mixing types of output statements; even so, that won't make your cooked output raw, so it's a good idea to turn off buffering anyway. Many servers and browsers are cranky and dislike receiving input in drabs and twaddles.

Listing 28.9 shows a pseudocode representation of a simple processing phase whose objective is to have the browser display all the environment variables gathered in the initialization phase.

This has the effect of creating a simple HTML document containing a bulleted list. Each item in the list is a variable, expressed as name=value.

Listing 28.9   A Pseudocode Script to Show Variables Gathered During Initialization

```
output header "content-type: text/html\n"
output required blank line to terminate header "\n"
output "<HTML>"
output "<HEAD><TITLE>Variable Report</TITLE></HEAD>"
output "<BODY bgcolor=\"#FFFFFF\">"
output "<H1>Variable Report</H1>"
output "<UL>"
for each variable known
    output "<LI>"
    output variable-name
    output "="
    output variable-value
loop until all variables printed
output "</UL>"
output "</BODY>"
output "</HTML>"
```

TROUBLESHOOTING TIP

If your document displays without explicit error but is empty, make sure that you included a blank line following the header line(s) at the beginning of the `.cgi` script, before the output for the body of your document. Sometimes you may even need to use two blank lines to get your document content to show.

TROUBLESHOOTING TIP

If your script shows in the browser, instead of its output, your script is not being executed. Three usual causes exist for your script being treated as data instead of running as a program. One is that your server may not be properly configured for CGI. Another is that your script may be in the incorrect directory. Your scripts may need to be in a designated CGI script directory, often called `cgi-bin`. Lastly, your script's filename may not have the proper filename extension for your server's configuration. This extension is usually `.cgi`, `.plx`, or `.pl`. In short, check your filename and location, and your server's CGI-related configuration values.

Termination

Termination is nothing more than cleaning up after yourself and quitting. If you've locked any files, you must release them before letting the program end. If you've allocated memory, semaphores, or other objects, you must free them. Failure to do so may result in a "one-shot wonder" of a script: one that works only the first time. Worse yet, your script may hinder—or even break—the server itself or other scripts by failing to free up resources and release locks.

On some platforms, most noticeably Windows NT, and to a lesser extent, UNIX, your file handles and memory objects are closed and reclaimed when your process terminates. Even so, it's unwise to rely on the operating system to clean up your mess. For instance, under Windows NT, the behavior of the file system is undefined when a program locks all or part of a file and then terminates without releasing the locks.

Make sure that your error-exit routine, if you have one (and you should), knows about your script's resources and cleans up just as thoroughly as the main exit routine does.

Planning Your Script

Now that you've seen a script's basic structure, you're ready to learn how to plan a script from the ground up:

1. Take your time defining the program's task. Think it through thoroughly. Write it down and trace the program logic. When you're satisfied that you understand the input, output and the transform process you'll have to do, proceed.

2. Order a pizza and a good supply of your favorite beverage, lock yourself in for the night, and come out the next day with a finished program. This sounds cute, but it is oddly good advice. Sometimes, it seems as if more bugs stem from interruptions while programming—which cause loss of concentration—than from any other source. And while you're sequestered, don't forget to document your code as you write it.

3. Test, test, test. Use every browser known to mankind and every sort of input you can think of. Especially test for the situations in which users enter 32KB of data in a 10-byte field (using MAXSIZE within your input tag does not protect you from receiving more input than expected), or they enter control codes where you're expecting plain text.

4. Document the program as a whole, too—not just the individual steps within it—so that others who have to maintain or adapt your code will understand what you were trying to do.

Step 1, of course, is this section's topic, so we'll look at that process in more depth:

- If your script will handle form variables, plan out each one: its name, expected length, and data type.

- As you copy variables from QUERY_STRING or STDIN, check for proper type and length. A favorite trick of UNIX hackers is to overflow the input buffer purposely. Because of the way some scripting languages (notably sh and bash) allocate memory for variables, this sometimes gives the hacker access to areas of memory that should be protected, enabling them to place executable instructions in your script's heap or stack space.

- Use sensible variable names. A pointer to the QUERY_STRING environment variable should be called something such as pQueryString, not p2. This not only helps debugging at the beginning but makes maintenance and modification much easier. No matter how brilliant a coder you are, chances are good that a year from now you won't remember that p1 points to CONTENT_TYPE and p2 points to QUERY_STRING.

- Distinguish between *system-level parameters* that affect how your program operates and *user-level parameters* that provide instance-specific information. In a script to send email, for example, don't let the user specify the IP number of the SMTP host. This information shouldn't even appear on the form in a hidden variable. It's instance independent and should therefore be a system-level parameter. In Windows NT, store this information in the Registry or an `.ini` file. In UNIX, store it in a configuration file or system environment variable.

- If your script will *shell out* to the system to launch another program or script, don't pass user-supplied variables unchecked. Especially in UNIX systems, where the `system()` call can contain pipe or redirection characters, leaving variables unchecked can spell disaster. Clever users and malicious hackers can copy sensitive information or destroy data this way. If you can't avoid `system()` calls altogether, plan for them carefully. Define exactly what can get passed as a parameter and know which bits will come from the user. Include an algorithm to parse for suspect character strings and exclude them.

- If your script will access external files, plan how you'll handle concurrency. You may lock part or all of a data file, you may establish a semaphore, or you may use a file as a semaphore. If you take chances, you'll be sorry. Never assume that because your script is the only program to access a given file that you don't need to worry about concurrency. Five copies of your script might be running at the same time, satisfying requests from five users.

- If you lock files, use the least-restrictive lock required. If you're only reading a data file, lock out writes while you're reading and release the file immediately afterward. If you're updating a record, lock just that one record (or byte range). Ideally, your locking logic should immediately surround the actual I/O calls. Don't open a file at the beginning of your program and lock it until you terminate. If you must do this, open the file but leave it unlocked until you're actually about to use it. This will enable other applications or other instances of your script to work smoothly and quickly.

- Prepare graceful exits for unexpected events. If, for instance, your program requires exclusive access to a particular resource, be prepared to wait a reasonable amount of time and then die gracefully. Never code a *wait-forever* call. When your program dies from a fatal error, make sure that it reports the error first. Error reports should use plain, sensible language. When possible, also write the error to a log file so the system administrator knows of it.

- If you're using a GUI language (for example, Visual Basic) for your CGI script, don't let untrapped errors result in a message box onscreen. This is a server application; chances are excellent that no one will be around to notice and clear the error, and your application will hang until the next time an administrator chances by. Trap all errors! Work around those you can live with and treat all others as fatal.

- Write pseudocode for your routines at least to the point of general logical structure before firing up the editor. It often helps to build stub routines so that you can use the actual calls in your program while you're still developing. A *stub routine* is a quick and dirty routine that doesn't actually process anything; it just accepts the inputs the final routine will be expecting and outputs a return code consistent with what the final routine would produce.

Part

VI

Ch

28

- For complex projects, a data flow chart can be invaluable. Data flow should remain distinct from logic flow; your data travels in a path through the program and is "owned" by various pieces along the way, no matter how it's transformed by the subroutines.

- Try to encapsulate private data and processing. Your routines should have a defined input and output: one door in, one door out, and you know who's going through the door. How your routines accomplish their tasks isn't any of the calling routine's business. This is called the *black box* approach. What happens inside the box can't be seen from the outside and has no effect on it. A properly encapsulated lookup routine that uses flat file tables, for example, can be swapped for one that talks to a relational back end database without changing any of the rest of your program.

- Document your program as you go along. Self-documenting code is the best approach, with generous use of comments and extra blank lines to break up the code. If you use sensible, descriptive names for your variables and functions, half your work is already done. But good documentation doesn't just tell *what* a piece of code does; it tells *why*. "Assign value of REQUESTMETHOD to pRequestMethod," for example, tells what your code does. "Determine if you were invoked by GET or POST" tells why you wrote that bit of code and, ideally, leads directly to the next bit of code and documentation: "If invoked via GET, do this," or "If invoked via POST, do this."

- Define your output beforehand as carefully as you plan the input. Your messages to the user should be standardized. For instance, don't report a file-locking problem as Couldn't obtain lock. Please try again later, and report a stack overflow error as ERR4332. Your success messages should be consistent as well. Don't return You are the first visitor to this site since 1/1/96 one time and You are visitor number 2 since 01-01-96 the next.

  If you chart your data flow and group your functions logically, each type of message will be produced by the appropriate routine for that type. If you hack the code with error messages and early-out success messages sandwiched into your program's logic flow, you'll end up with something that looks inconsistent to the end user and looks like a mess to anyone who has to maintain your code.

Standard CGI Environment Variables

The following is a brief overview of the standard environment variables you're likely to encounter. Each server implements the majority of them consistently, but variations, exceptions, and additions exist. In general, you're more likely to find a new, otherwise undocumented variable omitted rather than a documented variable. The only way to be sure, though, is to check your server's documentation.

This section is taken from the NCSA specifications and is the closest thing to "standard" as you'll find. The following environment variables are set each time the server launches an instance of your script and are private and specific to that instance:

- AUTH_TYPE—If the server supports basic authentication and if the script is protected, this variable will provide the authentication type. The information is protocol and server-specific. An example of AUTH_TYPE is BASIC.

- CONTENT_LENGTH—If the request includes data using the POST method, this variable will be set to the length of valid data supplied in bytes through STDIN; for example, 72.

- CONTENT_TYPE—If the request includes data, this variable will specify the type of data as a MIME header; for example, application/x-www-form-urlencoded.

- GATEWAY_INTERFACE—Provides the version number of the CGI interface supported by the server in the format CGI/version-number; for example, CGI/1.1.

- HTTP_ACCEPT—Provides a comma-delimited list of MIME types that are acceptable to the client browser; for example, image/gif, image/x-xbitmap, image/jpeg, image/pjpeg, and */*. This list actually comes from the browser itself; the server just passes it on to the CGI script.

- HTTP_USER_AGENT—Supplies the name, possibly including a version number or other proprietary data, of the client's browser, such as Mozilla/2.0b3 (WinNT; I).

- PATH_INFO—Shows any extra path information supplied by the client, tacked onto the end of the virtual path. This is often used as a parameter to the script. For example, with the URL http://www.yourcompany.com/cgi-bin/myscript.pl/dir1/dir2, the script is myscript.pl and the PATH_INFO is /dir1/dir2.

- PATH_TRANSLATED—Supported by only some servers, this variable contains the translation of the virtual path to the script being executed (that is, the virtual path mapped to a physical path). If, for example, the absolute path to your Web server root is /usr/local/etc/httpd/htdocs and your cgi-bin folder is in the root level of your Web server (that is, http://www.mycorp.com/cgi-bin), a script with the URL http://www.mycorp.com/cgi-bin/search.cgi would have the PATH_TRANSLATED variable set to /usr/local/etc/httpd/htdocs/cgi-bin/search.cgi.

- QUERY_STRING—Shows any extra information supplied by the client, tacked onto the end of a URL and separated from the script name with a question mark; for example, http://www.yourcompany.com/hello.html?name=joe&id=45 yields a QUERY_STRING of name=joe&id=45.

- REMOTE_ADDR—Provides the IP address of the client making the request. This information is always available; for example, 199.1.166.171.

- REMOTE_HOST—Furnishes the resolved host name of the client making the request; for example, dial-up102.abc.def.com. Often, this information is unavailable for one of two reasons: Either the caller's IP is not properly mapped to a host name via DNS, or the Webmaster at your site has disabled IP lookups. Webmasters often turn off lookups because they mean an extra step for the server to perform after each connect, and this slows down the server.

- REMOTE_IDENT—If the server and client support RFC 931, this variable will contain the identification information supplied by the remote user's computer. Very few servers and clients still support this protocol, and the information is almost worthless because the user can set the information to be anything he wants. Don't use this variable even if it's supported by your server.

- REMOTE_USER—If AUTH_TYPE is set, this variable will contain the user name provided by the user and validated by the server. Note that AUTH_TYPE and REMOTE_USER are only set after a user has successfully authenticated (usually via a username and password) his identity to the server. Hence, these variables are useful only when restricted areas have been established and then only in those areas.

- ▪ REQUEST_METHOD—Supplies the method by which the script was invoked. Only GET and POST are meaningful for scripts using the HTTP/1.0 protocol.

- ▪ SCRIPT_NAME—This is the name of the script file being invoked. It's useful for self-referencing scripts. For example, scripts use this information to generate the proper URL for a script that gets invoked using GET, only to turn around and output a form that, when submitted, will reinvoke the same script using POST. By using this variable instead of hard-coding your script's name or location, you make maintenance much easier; for example, /cgi-bin/myscript.exe.

- ▪ SERVER_NAME—Your Web server's host name, alias, or IP address. It's reliable for use in generating URLs that refer to your server at runtime; for example, www.yourcompany.com.

- ▪ SERVER_PORT—The port number for this connection; for example, 80.

- ▪ SERVER_PROTOCOL—The name/version of the protocol used by this request; for example, HTTP/1.0.

- ▪ SERVER_SOFTWARE—The name/version of the HTTP server that launched your script, for example, HTTPS/1.1.

CGI Script Portability

CGI programmers face two portability issues: platform independence and server independence. *Platform independence* is the capability of the code to run without modification on a hardware platform or operating system different from the one for which it was written. *Server independence* is the capability of the code to run without modification on another server using the same operating system.

Platform Independence

The best way to keep your CGI script portable is to use a commonly available language and avoid platform-specific code. It sounds simple, right? In practice, this means using either C or Perl and not doing anything much beyond formatting text and outputting graphics.

Does this leave Visual Basic, AppleScript, and UNIX shell scripts out in the cold? Yes, I'm afraid so, for now. However, platform independence isn't the only criterion to consider when selecting a CGI platform. The speed of coding, the ease of maintenance, and the capability to perform the chosen task should also be considered.

Certain types of operations simply aren't portable. If you develop for 16-bit Windows, for instance, you'll have great difficulty finding equivalents on other platforms for the VBX and DLL functions you use. If you develop for 32-bit Windows NT, you'll find that all your asynchronous Winsock calls are meaningless in a UNIX environment. If your shell script does a system() call to launch grep and pipe the output back to your program, you'll find nothing remotely similar in the Windows NT environment, unless you add an NT version of grep to the system. And AppleScript is good only on Macintoshes.

If one of your mandates is the capability to move code among platforms with a minimum of modification, you'll probably have the best success with C. Write your code using the standard functions from the ANSI C libraries and avoid making other operating system calls. Unfortunately, following this rule will limit your scripts to very basic functionality. If you wrap your platform-dependent code in self-contained routines, however, you minimize the work needed to port from one platform to the next. As you saw in the section "Planning Your Script," when talking about encapsulation, a properly designed program can have any module replaced in its entirety without affecting the rest of the program. Using these guidelines, you may have to replace a subroutine or two, and you'll certainly have to recompile; however, your program will be portable.

Perl scripts are easier to maintain than C programs, mainly because no compile step is used. You can change the program quickly when you figure out what needs to be changed. And there's the rub: Although learning to write simple Perl is easier than learning C for many people, Perl has many obscure subtleties, and the libraries tend to be much less uniform—even between versions on the same platform—than do C libraries. You pay for all that wonderful string-processing and pattern-handling power. Also, Perl for Windows NT is fairly new and still quirky, although the most recent versions are much more stable. And in fairness to Perl, Win32 is not the only compiler or interpreter to be quirky on a relatively new operating system such as NT 4.0 and now 5.0.

Server Independence

Far more important than platform independence is server independence. Server independence is fairly easy to achieve, but for some reason, it seems to be a stumbling block to beginning script writers. To be server independent, your script must run without modification on any server using the same operating system. Only server-independent programs can be useful as shareware or freeware, and without a doubt, server independence is a requirement for commercial software.

Most programmers think of obvious issues, such as not assuming that the server has a static IP address. The following are some other rules of server independence that, although obvious once stated, nevertheless get overlooked time and time again:

- Don't assume your environment—For example, just because the temp directory was C:\Temp on your development system, don't assume that it will be the same wherever your script runs. Never hard code directories or filenames. This goes double for Perl scripts, where this travesty of proper programming happens most often. If your Perl script to tally hits needs to exclude a range of IP addresses from the total, don't hard code the addresses into the program and say, "Change this line" in the comments. Use a configuration file.

- Don't assume privileges—On a UNIX machine, the server (and therefore your script) may run as the user nobody, as root, or as any privilege level in between. On a Windows NT machine, too, CGI programs usually inherit the server's security attributes. Check for access rights and examine return codes carefully so you can present intelligible error information to the user in case your script fails because it can't access a resource. Some NT servers enable you to specify a user account for CGI programs that's separate from the user account for the Web server. Microsoft's IIS does this and goes one step beyond: For CGI programs with authentication, the CGI runs in the security context of the authenticated user.

- Don't assume consistency of CGI variables—Some servers pass regular environment variables (for instance, PATH and LIB variables) along with CGI environment variables; however, the ones they pass depend on the runtime environment. Server configuration can also affect the number and the format of CGI variables. Be prepared for environment-dependent input and have your program act accordingly.

- Don't assume version-specific information—Test for it and include workarounds or sensible error messages telling the user what to upgrade and why. Both server version and operating system version can affect your script's environment.

- Don't assume LAN or WAN configurations—In the Windows NT world, the server can be Windows NT Workstation or Windows NT Server; it may be standalone, part of a workgroup, or part of a domain. DNS (Domain Name Services) may or may not be available; lookups may be limited to a static hosts file. In the UNIX world, don't assume anything about the configurations of daemons, such as inetd, sendmail, or the system environment, and don't assume directory names. Use a configuration file for the items that you can't discover with system calls, and give the script maintainer instructions for editing it.

- Don't assume the availability of system objects—As with privilege level, check for the existence of such objects as databases, messaging queues, and hardware drivers, and output explicit messages when something can't be found or is misconfigured. Nothing is more irritating than downloading a new script, installing it, and getting only Runtime error #203 for the output.

CGI Libraries

When you talk about CGI libraries, two possibilities exist: libraries of code you develop and want to reuse in other projects and publicly available libraries of programs, routines, and information.

Personal Libraries

If you follow the advice given earlier in this chapter in the "Planning Your Script" section about writing your code in a black box fashion, you'll soon discover that you're building a library of routines that you'll use over and over. After you puzzle out how to parse out URL-encoded data, for instance, you don't need to do it again. And when you have a basic main() function written, it will probably serve for every CGI program you ever write. This is also true for generic routines, such as querying a database, parsing input, and reporting runtime errors.

How you manage your personal library depends on the programming language you use. With C and assembler, you can precompile code into actual .Lib files, with which you can then link your programs. Although possible, this likely is overkill for CGI, and it doesn't work for interpreted languages, such as Perl and Visual Basic. (Although Perl and VB can call compiled libraries, you can't link with them in a static fashion the way you can with C.) The advantage of using compiled libraries is that you don't have to recompile all your programs when you make a change to code in the library. If the library is loaded at runtime (a DLL), you don't need to change anything. If the library is linked statically, all you need do is relink.

Another solution is to maintain separate source files and include them with each project. You might have a single, fairly large file that contains the most common routines, but put seldom used routines in files of their own. Keeping the files in source format adds a little overhead at compile time but not enough to worry about, especially when compared to the time savings you gain by writing the code only once. The disadvantage of this approach is that when you change your library code, you must recompile all your programs to take advantage of the change.

Nothing can keep you from incorporating public-domain routines into your personal library, either. As long as you make sure that the copyright and license allow you to use and modify the source code without royalties or other stipulations, then you should strip out the interesting bits and toss them into your library.

Well-designed and well-documented programs provide the basis for new programs. If you're careful to isolate the program-specific parts into subroutines, you can cannibalize an entire program's structure for your next project.

You can also develop platform-specific versions of certain subroutines and, if your compiler will allow it, automatically include the correct ones for each type of build. At the worst, you'll have to manually specify which subroutines you want.

N O T E The key to making your code reusable is to make it as generic as possible. Don't make it so generic that, for instance, a currency printing routine needs to handle both yen and dollars, but make it generic enough that any program that needs to print out dollar amounts can call that subroutine. As you upgrade, swat bugs, and add capabilities, keep each function's inputs and outputs the same, even when you change what happens inside the subroutine. This is the black box approach in action. By keeping the calling convention and the parameters the same, you're free to upgrade any piece of code without fear of breaking older programs that call your function.

Another technique to consider is using function stubs. Suppose you decide that a single routine to print both yen and dollars is actually the most efficient way to go. But you already have separate subroutines, and your old programs wouldn't know to pass the additional parameter to the new routine. Rather than going back and modifying each program that calls the old routines, just "stub out" the routines in your library so that the only thing they do is call the new, combined routine with the correct parameters. In some languages you can do this by redefining the routine declarations; in others, you actually need to code a call and pay the price of some additional overhead. But even so, the price is far less than that of breaking all your old programs.

Public Libraries

The Internet is rich with public-domain sample code, libraries, and precompiled programs. Although most of what you'll find is UNIX-oriented (because it has been around longer), no shortage exists of routines for Windows NT.

The following is a list of some of the best sites on the Internet with a brief description of what you'll find at each site. This list is far from exhaustive. Hundreds of sites are dedicated to or contain information about CGI programming. Hop onto your Web browser and visit your favorite search engine. Tell it to search for "CGI" or "CGI libraries," and you'll see what I mean. To save you the tedium of wading through all the hits, I've explored many of them for you. The following are the ones that struck me as most useful:

- `http://www.worldwidemart.com/scripts/`—The justifiably famous Matt's Script Archive. Look here first for tested, practical scripts in Perl and C for many common business uses.

- `http://www.ics.uci.edu/pub/websoft/libwww-perl/`—This is the University of California's public offering, libwww-perl. Based on Perl version 5.003, this library contains many useful routines. If you plan to program in Perl, this library is worth the download just for ideas and techniques.

- `http://www.w3.org/CGI/`— The W3C standards organization CGI site. W3C is always worth a periodic visit.

- `http://www.itm.com/cgicollection/`—A vast collection of CGI script that you can use and learn from. It covers CGI security and contains tutorials and other examples.

- `http://www-genome.wi.mit.edu/WWW/tools/scripting/cgi-utils.html`—cgi-utils.pl is an extension to cgi-lib.pl from Lincoln D. Stein at the Whitehead Institute, MIT Center for Genome Research.

- `http://www-genome.wi.mit.edu/ftp/pub/software/WWW/cgi_docs.html`—cgi.pm is a Perl 5 library for creating forms and parsing CGI input.

- `http://www-genome.wi.mit.edu/WWW/tools/scripting/CGIperl/`—This is a useful list of Perl links and utilities.

- `http://www.boutell.com/gd/`—A C library for producing GIF images on-the-fly, gd enables your program to create images complete with lines, arcs, text, multiple colors, and to cut and paste from other images and flood fills, which get written out to a file. Your program can then suck this image data in and include it in your program's output. Although these libraries are difficult to master, the rewards are well worth it. Many map-related Web sites use these routines to generate map location points on-the-fly.

- `http://www.boutell.com/cgic/`—A CGI library providing an easier method to parse CGI input using C.

- `http://stein.cshl.org/WWW/software/GD/GD.html`—GD.pm, a Perl wrapper and extender for gd, is written by Thomas Boutell of Cold Spring Harbor Labs.

- `http://www.iserver.com/cgi/library.html`—This is Internet Servers Inc.'s wonderful CGI library. Among the treasures here, you'll find samples of image maps, building a Web index, server-push animation, and a guest book.

- `http://www.charm.net/~web/Vlib/Providers/CGI.html`—This collection of links and utilities will help you build an editor, use C++ with predefined classes, join a CGI programmer's mailing list, and best of all, browse a selection of Clickables, Plug and Play CGI Scripts.

- `http://www.greyware.com/greyware/software/`—Greyware Automation Products provides a rich list of shareware and freeware programs for Windows NT. Of special interest are the free SSI utilities and the CGI-wrapper program, CGIShell, which enables you to use Visual Basic, Delphi, or other GUI programming environments with the freeware EMWAC HTTP server.

- `http://www.greyware.com/greyware/bulletins/iis-cgi-faq.html`—FAQ on enabling CGI on Microsoft's Internet Information Server (IIS) Web server.

- `http://www.bhs.com/`—Although not specifically geared to CGI, the Windows NT Resource Center, sponsored by Beverly Hills Software, provides some wonderful applications, some of which are CGI-related. In particular, you'll find EMWAC's software, Perl for Windows NT and Perl libraries, and SMTP mailers.

- `http://mfginfo.com/htm/website.htm`—Manufacturer's Information Net provides a rich set of links to Windows NT utilities, many of which are CGI-related. Of special interest are links to back end database interfaces and many Internet server components.

- `http://website.oreilly.com/`—Bob Denny, author of WebSite, has probably done more than any other individual to popularize HTTP servers on the Windows NT platform. At this site, you'll find a collection of tools, including Perl for Windows NT, VB routines for use with the WebSite server, and other interesting items.

- `ftp://ftp.ncsa.uiuc.edu/Web/httpd/Unix/ncsa_httpd/cgi`—NSCA's CGI Archive. Don't miss this one!

- `http://www.cgi-resources.com/`—The CGI Resource Index, another good CGI site.

- `http://www.perl.com/perl/faq/`—The Perl Language Home Page's list of Perl FAQs. Check out the rest of the site while you're there.

- `http://www.w3.org/Security/Faq/www-security-faq.html`—Frequently asked questions about CGI security issues.

These sites should be enough to get you started. For a fresh list of sites, start looking on `http://www.yahoo.com/` or use your favorite search engine.

The Future of CGI Scripting

The tips, techniques, examples, and advice in this book will enable you to create your own scripts immediately. You should be aware, however, that the CGI world is in a constant state of change, more so perhaps, than most of the computer world. Fortunately, most servers will stay compatible with existing standards, so you won't have to worry about your scripts not working. Here's a peek at other *CGI-like* options available for programming interactive sites.

Part
VI

Ch
28

FastCGI

FastCGI, created by Open Market Inc., extends the capabilities of CGI while removing the overhead associated with executing CGI scripts. Much like CGI, FastCGI is a non-proprietary system in which script run continuously in the background, handling requests as needed.

Like CGI, FastCGI is language independent. You can create scripts in the language that you are most comfortable with. Like CGI, scripts created with FastCGI run separately from the Web server maintaining the security associated with CGI.

N O T E The Apache Web server is one of the most used Web servers that supports the FastCGI specification. If you're interested in FastCGI and Apache, you should also check out mod_perl, which will greatly increase the speed of CGI scripts.

FastCGI also makes use of distributed computing. Instead of serving documents and executing CGI scripts on one machine, you can use multiple machines sharing the load.

ON THE WEB

`http://www.fastcgi.com/` Contains additional information on the FastCGI specification, along with examples on how to convert your current CGI applications to take advantage of the FastCGI specification.

Java Servlets

Java Servlets were created to eliminate the problems that currently exist when using Java as CGI applications. Normally server-side Java applications require the use and overhead of the Java Virtual Machine. Each time a server-side Java application runs, the virtual machine needs to be loaded as well. Also, server-side Java applications have difficulty accessing environmental variables, which are commonly used in CGI scripting. Java servlets reduce these problems. Sun Microsystems has started development that includes an API that enables Java applications to act as CGI applications. Of course, your applications are not limited to serving requests from the Web, they can access existing sockets, protocols created by the developer, or both.

▶ **See** Chapter 36, "Introduction to Java," **p. 963**, to find out more information on Java and building Java applications.

Applications created that use the Java Server API are commonly known as servlets. *Servlets* are simply server-side applets. The difference between server-side applets and client-side applets, however, is that servlets do not utilize a user interface like that associated with client-side Java applets.

Servlets are Java applications that extend the traditional functionality of Web servers. Even so, servlets are not confined to the world of the Web. When a connection is made to the servlet, the servlet can create a connection between a client-side applet and a servlet, which communicate using a custom protocol with a new connection.

N O T E Java servlets work with many Web servers, including Sun's Java Web server, the Apache Web server using the mod_jserv module, and with Microsoft's Web server (MIIS) using LiveSoftware's JRun. ▓

You can run servlets continuously in the background or dynamically load them in a running server (if the server allows this function). You can also execute them either from a local disk or from the network. As such, a new servlet does not have to be executed for every request, thus greatly reducing the load of the server. The Web server calls the servlet, which in turn, responds to the request. Lastly, servlets don't need to be running in a Web server environment. The servlet API was designed so that servlets can run in conjunction with other types of servers as long as those servers can be accessed via the net.

ON THE WEB

`http://jserv.java.sun.com/products/java-server/servlets/`
`environments.html`   Lists various Web servers that allow the use of Java servlets.

`http://www.javasoft.com/products/java-server/servlets/index.html`   The Java servlet white paper and the Servlet Development Kit can be found at this site.

`http://www.javasoft.com/products/java-server/alpha2/doc/servlet_tutorial/`
`examples.html`   Provides an example of a counter servlet and contains additional examples on how to use Java servlets.

Server-Side JavaScript

Just as Java has been used to run on the server side, Netscape, using LiveWire, has created an environment to do the same thing with JavaScript (Microsoft provides some reference to using server-side JavaScript as a batch file with ScriptEase 4.0). JavaScript as a server-side application can be used to extend the capabilities of the server. By using JavaScript, the Web server can do more without calling external programs. This makes it easier for Web developers to add features to their pages where the browser is used in conjunction with the application running on the server while reducing the load on the Web server.

▶ **See** Chapter 18, "Introduction to JavaScripting," **p. 439**, for more information on JavaScript.

Visual Basic, Scripting Edition and Active Server Pages

Following the incredible popularity of the Internet and the unprecedented success of companies such as Netscape, Microsoft entered the arena and declared war. With its own Web server, its own browsers, and a plethora of back end services—and don't forget unparalleled marketing muscle and name recognition—Microsoft has already made an impact on the way people look at and use the Internet.

Along with some spectacular blunders, Microsoft has had its share of spectacular successes. One such success is Visual Basic, the all-purpose, almost-anyone-can-learn-it Windows programming language. VB was so successful that Microsoft made it the backbone of their office application suite. Visual Basic for Applications (VBA) has become the *de facto* standard

Part
VI

Ch
28

scripting language for Windows. Although not as lean as some other options (Borland's Delphi in some regards, or C programs in general), VB nevertheless has two golden advantages: it's easy to learn, and it has widespread support from third-party vendors and users.

When Microsoft announced it was getting into the Web server business, no one was terribly surprised to learn that they intended to incorporate a variant of VB or that they wanted everyone else to incorporate VB, too. VBScript, similar to a subset of VBA, has been useful on the client side, especially with ActiveX controls, and it should become even more useful with the Document Object Model's expansion of HTML's programmability. Server-side, VBScript has shone in Microsoft's Active Server Page (ASP) technology built in to Internet Information Server. Fans of ASP, which is a powerful alternative to Perl and C CGI programs, are glad that third-party ASP capability is now available for other Web servers through Chili!soft. So far, Chili!ASP versions of ASP are available for Netscape's FastTrack and Enterprise Servers on Windows 95, NT 3.51 and NT 4.0, the Lotus Go Web Server on Windows 95, NT 3.51 and NT 4.0, IBM's ICS for Windows NT, and O'Reilly's WebSite for Windows 95 and NT. Versions for Netscape Enterprise for Solaris 2.5 and Apache for Solaris 2.5 are in alpha and coming soon, and more are planned. For more information on Chili!ASP and some excellent ASP links and content in general, see `http://www.chilisoft.net/`. You can read more about Active Server Pages in Chapter 33, "Active Server Pages and VBScript."

You can get the latest technical specifications and other VBScript information from `http://www.microsoft.com/vbscript/`. VBScript, when Active Server Pages are available on even more servers and when server-side VBScript gets implemented more widely, should remove many of the arcane aspects from CGI programming. No more fussing with Perl arcana, C++ constructors, or worrying about stray pointers. Distribution should be a snap; Microsoft even currently provides code on its Web site for developers to include with their HTML, which will take the (willing) user straight to the scripting engine download area should an update be needed. Debugging can be done on-the-fly, with plain-English messages and help as far away as the F1 key. Code runs both server side and client side, whichever makes the most sense for your application. Versions of the runtimes may soon be available for Sun, HP, Digital, and IBM flavors of UNIX and are already available to developers for Windows 95, Windows 3.1, Windows NT for Intel-based computers, Windows NT for DEC Alpha-based computers, and the Macintosh. Also, Microsoft is licensing VBScript for free to browser developers and application developers. They want VBScript to become a standard. It may well do so, when combined with ASP and other powerful tools from third-party vendors and Microsoft.

VBScript

On the CD-ROM accompanying this book, you'll find `Aclist.exe` and `Vbsdoc.exe`. `Aclist.exe` is a self-extracting archive file containing all the runtime DLLs, source code examples, and ActiveX controls currently available for VBScript. `Vbsdoc.exe` is a self-extracting archive containing all the documentation for VBScript.

So where's the rub? All that, if true, sounds pretty good—even wonderful. Well, yes; it is, but VB applications of whatever flavor have a two-fold hidden cost: RAM and disk space. With each release, GUI-based products tend to become more powerful and more friendly but also take up more disk space and more runtime memory. And don't forget that managing those resources in a GUI environment also racks up computing cycles, mandating a fast processor. Linux users with a 286 clone and 640KB of RAM won't see the benefits of VBScript for a long, long time.

Although text-only UNIX machines don't comprise a large share of the paying market, they do nevertheless make up a large percentage of Internet servers. Historically, the Internet community has favored large, powerful servers rather than large, powerful desktops. In part, this is due to the prevalence of UNIX on those desktops. In a text-based environment where the most demanding thing you do all day is the occasional grep, processing power and RAM aren't constant worries. Although early DOS machines were considered "loaded" if they had 640KB RAM, UNIX machines in use today often use that amount—or even less—for most applications. Usually, only high-end workstations for CAD-CAM or large LAN servers come equipped with substantial RAM and fast processors.

In the long run, of course, such an objection is moot. Already, except in third-world areas, worries about those with 286s are becoming only memories. But in the meantime, developers need to keep current users in mind and try to keep from disenfranchising them. The Internet thrives on its egalitarianism. Just as a considerate Webmaster produces pages that can be read by Lynx or Netscape Navigator, developers using Microsoft's fancy—and fascinating—new tools must keep in mind that many visitors won't see their work…for now. ●

## CHAPTER 29

Custom Database Query Scripts

by Melissa Niles

In this chapter

Understanding Database Design

In this chapter, you'll take a look at three kinds of databases: flat file, DBM, and SQL. You'll build a different database using each of these databases so that you can see the differences among the three methods of storing information. The three methods used here require little or no money to use and build. Nearly everyone will be able to work with databases, and most database applications—free or commercial—work with the same basic principles.

The most difficult and daunting task is how to go about designing your database to store and retrieve information. What would happen if you wanted to upgrade your database or if you needed to insert additional information (fields or tables, for example) to your database?

When requesting information that derives from a database, you set into motion quite a few steps to complete that request:

1. Your Web server receives the request from the visitor to your site, then sends that information on to your CGI script.

2. The CGI script acts as the main gateway tying two very different systems together. The CGI script performs the actual query, receives the results from the database, formulates a proper reply, and sends it off to the Web server.

3. The Web server, in turn, sends it to the person visiting your site.

Why Access a Database?

Most likely, your organization already has an existing database in which it has stored information about its products, its customers, and other aspects of business life. Some of this information you might want to allow your customers to see, or you might even want to make the information in the database available to your workers stationed away from the office. If so, you would have to create HTML documents that contain all this information several times, which, if you're part of a large organization, can be a tedious task. Integrating the Web with your databases can save you tremendous amounts of time in the long run, especially when it comes to maintaining that information. As the database changes, your Web pages change.

Another good reason to use the World Wide Web to access your database is that any Web browser that supports forms can access information from the database—no matter which platform is being used.

Database Access Limitations

Consider the following events:

1. Person one accesses the database for editing.

2. Next, person two comes along and does the same thing.

3. Person one makes changes and saves that information to the database.

4. Person two saves information as well, possibly writing over what person one just saved.

5. A short time later, person one is wondering what happened to his or her data.

The browser and the server are stateless in relation to each other. Except in certain instances with certain products, the browser makes a request, the server processes the query and sends the result back to the browser, and the connection is closed. This creates a problem with databases because a connection to a database is usually constant. Normally, someone accesses the database, which keeps a connection open, locking a record if any editing is performed, and closes the connection only when the person is finished. Accessing a database doesn't work the same way when you're using a CGI script.

N O T E Application Programming Interfaces (APIs) have been created to alleviate the problem with stateless connections. You have to use proprietary software to utilize these APIs, but they are well worth it. Active Server Pages using ODBC and NSAPI are two examples.

Accessing a database using a Java client/server application can also eliminate the problems associated with stateless connections.

Two ways exist to handle the problem described previously. The first method involves keeping track of all entries with a time stamp. This will enable both entries to be maintained by the database, without the possibility of either person's entry being overwritten.

Another solution is to only provide information from the database and not allow someone on the Web to edit, remove, or insert information to the database. Although this limits some of the possibilities for having the database on the Web, it also alleviates some of the security problems.

N O T E With the exception of ODBC for NT and a few other proprietary methods, no official standard exists that you can use to connect to a database. If you create a script to access one type of database, that same script won't necessarily work on a different database—even if the query used was the same. Because of this, you may be required to learn a lot about each database application that you come across.

Security Issues

The major problem with having those on the Web accessing your database is that your CGI script is trusted by your database program. That is, your database has to accept commands from your CGI script, and your CGI script needs to perform queries based upon what you want to provide to those on the Web. This can lead to problems if someone with ill intentions gains access to a script and is able to edit your database.

In addition, most databases require the use of a password. Because your CGI script stores user information in the database as well as retrieves information from the database, your script needs to have the password to access your database. You need to ensure that your script cannot be read by others within your organization and outside your organization.

Creating and Using Flat File Databases

Flat file databases are about the easiest databases you can create. To create a small ASCII text database, you need nothing more than a language with which to program and a text editor.

A flat file database consists mainly of lines of text, where each line is its own entry. If you have more than one field for each record, the records are usually separated by a *delimiter*. No special technique is used to index the database. Therefore, flat file databases usually are relatively small (about 1,000–2,000 records). The larger the database, the longer it takes to perform queries to it.

In a flat file database, each record is contained on its own line. How many fields are in each record is completely up to you, but they are usually separated by some sort of delimiter. Often commas or tabs are used to delimit a record. A record containing, for example, a name, email address, home phone, work phone, and country may look like this:

```
Melissa Niles,mniles@itm.com,555-5555,555-5566,USA
```

It doesn't matter which delimiter you use, but you want to ensure that the delimiter (in this case, a comma) isn't going to be used anywhere in each field. An address may contain commas and can present problems when retrieving information; for example:

```
Melissa Niles,555 E. Lane, Suite 600,Anywhere, WA.,99999
```

In the example, the street address would become two separate fields when it was meant to be one. You would either have to use a different delimiter, or you would have to have your script catch any use of the delimiter when receiving information to add to the database. The latter can be easily accomplished using Perl, with something like

```
$incoming{'address'} =~ s/,/ /g;    #Replace any commas with a space
```

No matter what delimiter you use, it is always good practice to check the information coming in to ensure that it will comply with how you have your database structured.

You can build your database using any text editor or spreadsheet that will export a delimited text file (such as Microsoft Excel). After the database has been created, you will need to add, remove, and browse information within the database.

Adding Information

In a flat file database, nothing exists to check and ensure that the data you are receiving is the data that you are expecting. We already talked about checking to ensure that the new information doesn't contain the delimiter you are using. When writing your script, you will also have to ensure that you are getting what you need. If you are expecting a name, then you might want to ensure that you are not receiving an email address. A database is only as good as the information contained in it. Incorrect information can create problems.

Adding information to a flat file database is quite easy, no matter which programming language you use. The basic idea is that you want to append a new record to the end of the database. Rarely do you find that you have to place a new record somewhere in the middle of the database. If you would like to display your listing in a numerical or alphabetical order, then you can easily sort the contents of the database any time you read from the database.

Using Perl, only a few lines of code are needed to add a new entry to a flat file database. If you need to store a name, address, city, and state, this could be easily accomplished with the following:

```
open(FILE, ">>database.txt");
print FILE "$name¦$address¦$city¦$state\n";
close(FILE);
```

With Perl, you open the file using ">>", which appends the information to whatever already exists. Next, using the FILE filehandle, you add information using a pipe (¦) for the delimiter, and then you finish your entry by printing a newline.

> **N O T E**   Although Perl was used in the example, you can easily perform the same operation using any other programming language. The functions may work differently, but the programming concept is the same. Perl is used here because it is easy to read and to follow and because Perl is widely available for various platforms. ■

Of course, you will want to ensure that you were able to successfully open the database and that the program produced an error if you could not.

Removing Information

Although adding information is crucial to any database application, so is the capability to remove any old information from the database. No matter which programming language is used, removing information is relatively easy. The basic idea is to read the database into an array and then print the database back out to the file, excluding the records that you do not wish to keep.

Again, using Perl, it takes only a few lines of code to accomplish this task. If $remove_key contained the string "smith," then Listing 29.1 would remove any instance of "smith."

Listing 29.1   Search Through a Database and Remove a Record

```
open(FILE, "database.txt"); @lines = <FILE>; close(FILE);
open(FILE, ">database.txt");
foreach $line (@lines) {
  print FILE "$line" unless $line =~ /$remove_key/i; }
close(FILE);
```

If you had a database containing information about people and needed to remove an entry with the name "John Smith," then you will have to ensure that your script will only remove the "John Smith" that you no longer want. Often, you would find in this instance that more than one person has the same name. The following code stores the text "smith" in the variable $remove_key. Next, we write everything back into the database unless any record matches "smith":

```
$remove_key = "smith";
print FILE "$line" unless $name =~ /$remove_key/i;
```

This could remove any entry such as "John Smith," "Jill Smithy," and "Jennifer Wilsmithmire." When deleting information from a database, you need to be as specific as possible so that you don't remove any records that you want to keep.

Browsing the Database

Now that you have the capability to add and remove entries to the database, you need to create a script that will enable you to display the contents of your database.

If the database is expected to be small in size, the easiest thing to do is to simply display all entries, formatting each record as you deem fit. With Perl, you read the database into an array and then print each line, as shown in Listing 29.2. Each field is provided within the record by using a comma as the delimiter.

Listing 29.2 Here You Open the Database and then Print Out Each Line as You Would Like to Display the Contents

```
open(FILE, "database.txt");
@lines = <FILE>;
close(FILE);
foreach $line (@lines) {
$line =~ s/\n//g;
($name, $address, $city, $state) = split(/,/, $line);
print "$name - $address - $city - $state<br>\n";
}
undef $lines;
```

It is quite possible that displaying the database in its entirety would not be visually appealing. Looking for one specific entry in a list of 200 records, for instance, would be daunting. The best solution would be to allow the visitor to enter a keyword and list only those entries that match the keyword. You can allow queries against specific fields or against the entire record.

As shown, flat file databases are handy and simple to use. Of course, using flat file databases is economical, as well, because they do not cost a penny. If your database is going to be relatively small, using flat file databases can provide a professional look and provide dynamic content without any expenses.

DBM Databases

Most UNIX systems have some kind of DBM database; in fact, I have yet to find a system that runs without one. DBM is a set of library routines that manages data files consisting of key and value pairs. The DBM routines control how users enter and retrieve information from the database. Although it is not the most powerful mechanism for storing information, using DBM is a faster method of retrieving information than using a flat file. Because most UNIX sites use one of the DBM libraries, the tools you need to store your information to a DBM database are readily available.

Almost as many flavors of the DBM libraries exist as those of UNIX systems. Although most of these libraries are not compatible with each other, all work basically the same way. This section explores each of the DBM flavors to give you a good understanding of their differences. Afterward, you'll create an address book script, which should give you an idea of how DBM databases work.

A list follows of some of the most popular DBM libraries available:

- DBM—DBM stores the database in two files. The first has the extension .Pag and contains the bitmap. The second, which has the extension .Dir, contains the data.

- NDBM—NDBM is much like DBM with a few additional features; it was written to provide better storage and retrieval methods. Also, NDBM enables you to open many databases, unlike DBM, in which you are allowed to have only one database open within your script. Like DBM, NDBM stores its information in two files using the extensions .Pag and .Dir.

- SDBM—SDBM comes with the Perl archive, which has been ported to many platforms. Therefore, you can use DBM databases as long as a version of Perl exists for your computer. SDBM was written to match the functions provided with NDBM, so portability of code shouldn't be a problem. Perl is available for most of the popular platforms, including Amiga, Macintosh, MS-DOS, and UNIX.

ON THE WEB

http://www.perl.com/perl/   For more information on SDBM and Perl, visit the Perl home page.

- GDBM Version 1.7.1—GDBM is the GNU version of the DBM family of database routines.

  GDBM also enables you to cache data, reducing the time that it takes to write to the database. The database has no size limit; its size depends completely on your system's resources. GDBM database files have the extension .Db. Unlike DBM and NDBM, both of which use two files, GDBM uses only one file.

- Berkeley db Version 1.85—The Berkeley db expands on the original DBM routines significantly. The Berkeley db uses hashed tables the same as the other DBM databases, but the library also can create databases based on a sorted balanced binary tree (BTREE) and store information with a record line number (RECNO). The method that you use depends completely on how you want to store and retrieve the information from a database. Berkeley's db creates only one file, which has no extension.

If you can't find a particular DBM database on your system, search the Web for DBM databases.

Writing to a DBM Database

Perl provides the capability to work with a DBM database as if it were an associative array. This enables you to manipulate a DBM database using Perl with very little difficulty. Include files for C exist for using DBM databases as well, making a DBM database with C simplistic (see the

UNIX db main page). Unfortunately, the "how-to" of using DBM databases isn't well documented, and trying to figure out how to use DBM databases can be a daunting task.

In actuality, using DBM databases is quite simple and much easier than using flat file databases. Adding an entry, for example, only requires a couple of lines in Perl. Perl provides various modules, depending on which DBM database you are using, and also supplies a module called `AnyDBM_File.pm`, which covers all the common DBM databases. The full documentation on `AnyDBM` can be found at

```
http://www.perl.com/CPAN-local/doc/manual/html/lib/AnyDBM_File.html
```

DBM databases store information using a key and a value. The contents of each key cannot be repeated, although the value can. Therefore, you want to treat the contents of each key the same as if the key were a primary key in an SQL database. Because the key cannot be duplicated, you want to figure out what information you want to store would be unique. For a simple phone book, the email address would make a good unique identifier because some names are common (look in your phone book and see how many occurrences of "James Smith" you find).

For the value, you can store either one field or multiple fields using a delimiter, such as those used when accessing a flat file database. Using the email address as the key, you could store the name, work phone, and home phone in the value. The following is an example:

```
use AnyDBM_File;
$database=tie(%db, 'NDBM_File', "database", O_RDWR¦O_CREAT, 0666);
$db{'mniles@itm.com'} = "Melissa Niles,555-5555,555-6666";
untie %db;
undef $database;
```

As you can see, the key contains an email address, and the value contains the name and phone numbers—using a comma to delimit the record. With these few lines, the DBM database now contains a new entry.

Reading from a DBM Database

To retrieve information from a database, all you have to do is create a loop that reads the contents of the database and separates the value of each key at the colon. In your script, the following

```
while (($key,$value)= each(%db)) {
```

starts the loop that accomplishes this. Within the loop, the value of each key is split and assigned to the array `part`. When that is done, you can format the result in any manner you choose. In Listing 29.3, I have placed the name to be printed as part of a `mailto:` anchor, using each entry's email address if it was entered.

Listing 29.3   We Read Each Record and Display the Contents

```
use AnyDBM_File;
$database=tie(%db, 'NDBM_File', "database", O_RDWR¦O_CREAT, 0666);
while (($key,$value)= each(%db)) {
  ($name, $work_phone, $home_phone) = split(/,/, $value);
  print "Name: $name\n";
```

```
    print "Email: $key\n";
    print "Work Phone: $work_phone\n";
    print "Home Phone: $home_phone\n";
}
untie %db;
undef $database;
```

If desired, we could print out only those entries matching a query by matching a query against the value of each record. Also, if you know the email address you are looking for, you can retrieve the associated information by reading only that record (see Listing 29.4).

Listing 29.4   Using a DBM Database, You Can Access a Specific Record Without Reading the Whole Database

```
use AnyDBM_File;
$database=tie(%db, 'NDBM_File', "database", O_RDWR¦O_CREAT, 0666);
if ($db{'mniles@itm.com'}) {
    $value = $db{'mniles@itm.com'};
    ($name, $work_phone, $home_phone) = split(/,/, $value);
    print "Name: $name\n";
    print "Email: mniles@itm.com\n";
    print "Work Phone: $work_phone\n";
    print "Home Phone: $home_phone\n";
}
untie %db;
undef $database;
```

Searching a DBM Database

If your database starts to get large, it's convenient to provide a means by which visitors to your site can search for a specific keyword. Performing a search works much the same as displaying the whole database, except that rather than immediately displaying each entry, you check it first to see whether it matches the keyword entered by the visitor. If the keyword matches the key, you print the line; otherwise, you simply skip ahead and check the next entry (see Listing 29.5).

Listing 29.5   By Matching Each Field Against a Query, You Can Limit What Information Is Returned to the Visitor

```
$database=tie(%db, 'NDBM_File', "database", O_READ, 0660);
while (($key,$value)= each(%db)) {
    if ($key =~ /$query/i) {
        ($name, $work_phone, $home_phone) = split(/,/, $value);
        print "Name: $name\n";
        print "Email: mniles@itm.com\n";
        print "Work Phone: $work_phone\n";
        print "Home Phone: $home_phone\n";
    }
}
```

Now that you have seen how DBM databases work, you can take the same concepts from these scripts and apply them to something different. You could use them in a hotlinks script for example, in which you can store information for all your favorite Web sites or in a proper address book that stores the names, addresses, and phone numbers of all your customers. You can also create a database that stores names and email addresses and use it as a mailing list, providing friends and customers news about you or your organization—or your products. Three files, called dbbookadd.pl, dbbook.pl, and dbbooksearch.pl, are provided on the CD that accompanies this book. These files work together as a phone book application using DBM databases.

Relational Databases

Most relational database servers consist of a set of programs that manage large amounts of data, offering a rich set of query commands that help manage the power behind the database server. These programs control the storage, retrieval, and organization of the information within the database. This information can be changed, updated, or removed after the support programs or scripts are in place.

Unlike DBM databases, relational databases don't link records together physically like the DBM database does by using a key/value pair. Instead, they provide a field in which information can be matched, and the results can be sent back to the person performing the query, as if the database were organized that way.

Relational databases store information in tables. A table is similar to a smaller database that sits inside the main database. Each table can usually be linked with the information in other tables to provide a result to a query. Take a look at Figure 29.1, which shows how this information could be tied together.

FIGURE 29.1

A relational database stores certain information in various parts of the database; this information can later be called with one query.

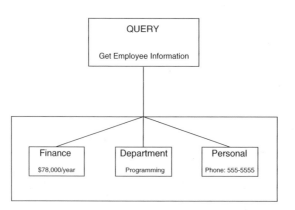

Figure 29.1 depicts a query in which it requests employee information from a database. To get a complete response, information is retrieved from three tables, each of which stores only parts of the information requested. In the figure, information about the person's pay rate is retrieved, and departmental information and personal information are retrieved from other

tables. This can produce a complete query response with an abundant amount of information on an individual.

Introduction to Database Design

SQL databases consist largely of tables, records, and fields. The table(s) hold all information that is stored in the database, and each table contains one or more records. A record contains one or more fields grouping the fields for a specific entry. A field is given a specific data type, which specifies what kind of information is to be stored in that field. For instance, a field may contain a date, a number, a set of characters, and so on.

N O T E Tables are formally called *relations*, records are called *tuples*, and fields are called *attributes*. More often, you will hear a record being called a column and a field being called a row. The rows and columns seem to be the most used when talking among database developers.

As stated, each table consists of columns and rows. The columns identify the data by a name, and the rows store information relevant to that name. Take a look at the following example:

Name	Number	Email
Fred Flintstone	01–43	ff@bedrock.com
Barney Rubble	01–44	br@bedrock.com

The column heads give a name to each item below it. Information within a table is stored in much the same way.

If you add more tables to the database, you could have something that looks like the following:

Name	PayRate
Fred Flintstone	$34/month
Barney Rubble	$29/month

You could have department information as well:

Name	Department	Tardy Record
Fred Flintstone	Dino-Digger	17
Barney Rubble	Pebble Pusher	3

With this information, you can perform a query to get a complete look at an individual.

When designing a database, you need to decide what tables you require and what data each table will contain. You will also need to decide how each table will work with other tables.

You need to decide what bits (*entities*) of information you want to store and how this information is related to other entities. The usual technique, when designing a database, is to draw a graphical display of the database. This drawing is called an Entity-Relationship (E-R) diagram. If you take a look at Figure 29.2, you can see that each box corresponds to a table. Each line in the box represents a specific field. When required, each box is connected to another where an entity is related to an entity in another table.

FIGURE 29.2

An E-R diagram shows how the information in various tables is to be related.

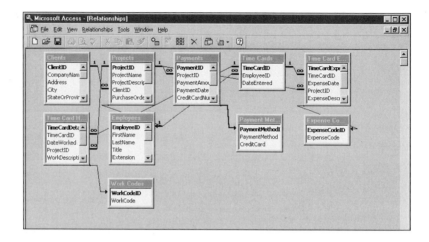

The purpose of having relational databases is to limit the amount of repetitive information contained in the database. After someone's address is entered in one table, for example, you should never have to provide an address in any other table.

Making SQL Queries

Structured Query Language (*SQL*) is a language that provides a user interface to relational database management systems (RDBMS). Originally developed by IBM in the 1970s, SQL is the de facto standard for storing and retrieving information for relational databases, as well as being an ISO and ANSI standard. The current standard is SQL2, with SQL3, which was released in 1998. The purpose of SQL is to provide a language, easily understandable by humans, that interfaces with relational databases.

When adding, removing, and retrieving information from SQL databases, you perform what is called a *query*. A query is a command that is sent to the database, telling the database engine what to do to manipulate the contents of a database.

One example of a query is provided below using the `select` command. The select command enables you to specifically define what information you want retrieved from the database. You can be as broad or as specific as you want when retrieving information from the database.

```
select * from personal,department,finance where Name='Fred Flintstone'
```

This would pull up all information on Fred Flintstone—from all the tables. You could even be more specific, pulling only certain parts from each table:

```
select Name.finance,Name.department,Tardy.department
     from department,finance
     where Tardy > 5 AND Name.finance = Name.department
```

Many commands are used to query a database, providing you with quite a bit of power when working with a relational database. Most SQL servers use basic commands such as `select`, but minor differences can be noticed. It is best to check the documentation provided with your SQL server for a complete list of commands and the proper syntax for each command.

Debugging Database Applications

One of the biggest problems when dealing with databases on the Web is trying to fix any problems that may occur when you are writing your script. First, you can have problems because of a bug in your script. Second, you can have problems because of an improper query.

The best way to see whether the problem lies within your script is to create a copy of the script that includes dummy variables—variables that contain information as if a visitor actually entered something into a form. Using the previous scripts, for example, you can create a set of variables that mimics information that a visitor might have entered:

```
$contents{'fname'} = "John";
$contents{'lname'} = "Doe";
```

After you have the dummy variables set, you can execute your script using the command line

```
% /usr/bin/perl phone.pl
```

Perl will report any problems with your script if you have programmed any code improperly.

To figure out what may be wrong with your SQL query, you can usually use the console interface provided with your SQL server. If you construct the query with the console interface and everything works fine, then look at your script and see if an error can be produced there.

 TIP Last, try to keep things simple and build up from what you know works. At first, create a script that contains the query you need to perform, making sure that you use the `Content-type text/plain`. This will enable you to make sure that your script is providing a proper query. If all goes well, access your database using the same query from the command line. If the query produces the proper results, you can move on and try to access your script through the Web server. If you are having problems here, make sure that you have specified the `Content-type` *before* anything is sent out to the server. This is probably one of the biggest problems with any script. An error occurs and your script sends information back to the Web server without specifying the `Content-type`.

## CHAPTER 30

Web Database Tools

by Melissa Niles

In this chapter

Database Considerations

It is an appealing idea to take information that is stored in your database and allow its access to those visiting your site (for either Internet or intranet purposes). Not only can it save you the time of reentering all that data to create an HTML document, but it also can enable you to use your database to create Web pages that change the moment the information in your database changes.

Integrating your existing databases with the Web enables you to create Internet and intranet applications that can be beneficial to the customers visiting your site and to those within your organization who need up-to-date information.

For customers, a database enables them to place orders and purchase goods that you have for sale. Most businesses take customer information and store that information in a database whenever an order is placed. This enables you to keep track of who ordered what, when items were shipped, how much and by what method they paid, as well as the personal information used to ship each item.

The old method of purchasing goods on the Web was to take an order through a form and then email the order to the appropriate person. This person would enter the customer and order information into the database, and at that point any online order would be processed as expected.

Integrating your database with the Web removes the "middle person." Each order can be placed in the database and processed from that point, lessening the chances of lost paperwork or misdirected email.

You can use the information that already exists in your databases to create up-to-date Web documents. These documents can be used to provide a product listing in which visitors can select the items that they would like to purchase. The information in your databases can also be used to provide support.

For intranet purposes, you can provide your employees with information no matter where they are or what platform they are using. Many businesses have employees working in the field who need to quickly access company information. Direct access to a database of information enables your employees to be more efficient. Providing information via the Web even enables access to a database that wouldn't normally be accessible over a network. Accessing a database also eliminates the need for specific (oftentimes custom) client software that must be installed and maintained on the PC of everyone who's going to access the database.

All the databases and database tools described in this chapter can be used for these purposes, although some are better suited for a particular task than others.

Which database is best suited for your needs depends on how much you are willing to pay for a database and the tools needed to create dynamic Web pages. How much horsepower you are going to need to serve your customers will also have to be considered:

- The smaller databases available, such as Access and mSQL, work well and are within the budget of most small businesses. Even so, they wouldn't be able to handle a hundred thousand or more queries a day.

■ Database engines such as Oracle and Sybase are better suited for larger companies and those companies that receive a large number of queries each day. At the same time, Oracle or Sybase would be overkill for a business that sells only a handful of goods and that receives a few hundred queries a day.

You often have to consider what database a company is already using. Many companies have spent a lot of time training their employees to use a particular database, or they have spent a lot of money on a database that has worked well for them for years. At times, you will have to convince a company to change its database to something more Web worthy. First, you need to find out whether tools exist that can help a company use its existing database and whether the database it currently has is well within the bounds of the company's particular needs.

Not too long ago, it was quite difficult to create Web pages based on information from a database. Now, so much support is available that trying to figure out which way to go can be an intimidating task. This chapter briefly covers the favorite databases available and the gateways used to access and place that information on the Web.

Databases Available

In this section, you take a quick look at the most commonly used databases on the Web and where you can look for further information and support.

Oracle

Oracle is the largest database developer in the World. Oracle provides databases for Windows NT and various UNIX flavors and has created its own set of tools called the Oracle Web Developer Suite. This suite integrates the Oracle8 Server, Oracle WebServer, Designer/2000, and the Developer/2000 kit, along with additional kits. With the Web Developer Suite, you can get your database information on the Web in minutes using a graphical point-and-click environment. With some additional time, you can make your Web site more interactive, storing and retrieving information with the Oracle database. A storefront, where you can sell goods or provide up-to-date product support, makes good use of the Oracle Web Developer suite.

ON THE WEB

`http://www.oracle.com/products/tools/WDS/`   For more information on Oracle and how you can use Oracle with the World Wide Web, visit its Web page.

Sybase

Sybase's Adaptive Server is the most powerful of Sybase's database servers. Provided with the Adaptive Server are tools that can be used to produce dynamic Web pages from the information data in your database. Sybase's newest product to help build Web applications is called Power Studio.

Power Studio is a suite of programs that enables you to access your Sybase database and create interactive Web applications through a beautifully designed graphical interface. The heart of

Sybase's Power Studio is PowerBuilder. With PowerBuilder, you can create applications that easily integrate with the database, enabling those new to the environment to perform advanced queries. PowerSite, another kit that is provided with the Studio, is the key element to tying the information in the database to the Web.

ON THE WEB

`http://www.sybase.com/`   For more information on Sybase, Power Studio, web.sql, and other Sybase-related APIs, visit the Sybase home page.

mSQL

On the CD

As introduced in Chapter 29, "Custom Database Query Scripts," mSQL is a mid-sized SQL database server for UNIX; it is much more affordable than te commercial SQL servers available on the market. Written by David Hughes, it was created to enable users to experiment with SQL and SQL databases. It is free for noncommercial use (nonprofit, schools, and research organizations)—for individual and commercial use, the price is quite fair, at about $250 per server.

ON THE WEB

`http://www.Hughes.com.au/`   This site provides additional information on mSQL, along with documentation and a vast array of user-contributed software.

Informix

Informix has grown up quite a bit. Originally called Illustra, Informix has been completely revamped and now has quite a few complementary tools to help with the design and integration of database information with the Web environment. The main component for creating Web applications lies with a suite of tools called Universal Web Architecture (UWA).

UWA comprises the Informix Universal Web Connect, the Web Datablade, and the Data Director for Java. These tools enable you to easily create Web applications in a minimal amount of time.

ON THE WEB

`http://www.informix.com/`   Visit this site for detailed information on Informix, along with additional information on how you can use Informix with your Web-based applications.

Microsoft SQL

Microsoft released its own SQL database server as a part of its BackOffice suite. Microsoft is trying to compete heavily with Oracle and Sybase by providing its own set of development tools and products to get database-driven information on the Web.

Microsoft SQL works well with any Web development tool that complies with Microsoft's ODBC. Even so, Microsoft has been working hard to tie the SQL server, Microsoft Internet

Information Server, and Microsoft Web browser together to provide one environment for those providing Web content and those who come to your site.

ON THE WEB

`http://www.microsoft.com/sql/`   For additional information about Microsoft's SQL server and how you can use Microsoft's SQL server in conjunction with the World Wide Web, visit Microsoft's Web site.

PostgreSQL

PostgreSQL (formerly Postgres95) is a SQL database server developed by the University of California at Berkeley. Older versions of Postgres are still available but no longer supported.

ON THE WEB

`http://s2k-ftp.CS.Berkeley.EDU:8000/postgres/`   For additional information on PostgreSQL, along with the source code that is available for downloading, see this site.

Ingres

Ingres (Interactive Graphics Retrieval System) comes in both a commercial and a public domain version. The University of California at Berkeley originally developed this retrieval system, but Berkeley no longer supports the public domain version. You can still find it on the university's Web site.

Ingres uses the QUEL query language as well as SQL. QUEL is a superset of the original SQL language, making Ingres more powerful. Ingres was developed to work with graphics in a database environment. The public domain version is available for UNIX systems.

ON THE WEB

`ftp://s2k-ftp.cs.berkeley.edu/pub/ingres/`   Visit this site to download the public domain version of Ingres.

`http://www.cai.com/products/ingr.htm`   Computer Associates owns the commercial version of Ingres. This version is quite robust and capable of managing virtually any database application. The commercial version is available for UNIX, VMS, and Windows NT. To find out more about the commercial version of Ingres (called Ingress II), visit them at this site.

`http://www.naiua.org/`   For information about both the commercial and public domain versions of Ingres, visit the North American Ingres Users Association.

FoxPro

Microsoft's Visual FoxPro has been a favorite for Web programmers, mostly because of its long time in the database community and its third-party support. FoxPro, available for MS-DOS, Macintosh, and some flavors of UNIX, is an Xbase database system that is widely used for smaller business and personal database applications.

ON THE WEB

`http://www.microsoft.com/products/prodref/269_ov.htm`   Visit the FoxPro home page
on Microsoft's Web site for more information on FoxPro.

Microsoft Access

Microsoft Access is a relational database management system that is part of the Microsoft
Office suite. Microsoft Access can be used to create HTML documents based on the information stored in the Access database with the help of Microsoft's Internet Assistant. Microsoft's
Internet Assistant is an add-on that is available free of charge for Access users. Microsoft Access can also support ActiveX controls, which makes Access even more powerful when used
with the Microsoft Internet Explorer.

You can also query an Access database without having Access on the Web server. If you have
the Access ODBC driver installed, you can access any `.mdb` file with your Web server to retrieve or update database information.

A Job forum page was created to enable you to see how Access can be used in conjunction with
the World Wide Web.

ON THE WEB

`http://www.microsoft.com/accessdev/`   Details on Microsoft Access and how you can use
Access with your Web-based applications can be found at this URL. Additionally, you can test the Job
forum and look at the code used to create this application.

MySQL

Developed by T.c.X, MySQL (pronounced My Ess Que Ell) was created to handle large
amounts of data. According to one of the benchmark tests, MySQL provides a robust SQL
engine comparable to the major commercial database servers. MySQL can be accessed using
Perl, ODBC, C, and Tcl; it provides you with the means to provide database-generated Web
content. For more information, visit `http://www.mysql.com/`.

Solid

Solid Information Technology, Ltd., provides a low-cost commercial Web database solution for
providing dynamic database-driven content. One product, the Solid Web Engine, was created
and optimized specifically for Web/database use. Various programming languages can be used
to interface with the Solid Web Engine, including C/C++, Perl, Tcl, and Python. With the capability to handle large amounts of data, the Solid Web Engine is definitely a viable option for use
in providing Web/database content. For more information see `http://www.solidtech.com/`.

Database Tools

Now that you have taken a look at the various databases available, it's time to take a look at the third-party tools that help you create applications to tie your databases to the Web.

Some of the tools work with only one specific database; other tools work with a couple of different databases; and some tools work with most databases available.

Which tool you use depends on several factors:

Which database are you using? I know that this sounds like a simple thing to consider, but I've repeatedly seen companies that have purchased a Web/database tool that doesn't work with their existing database. Most of the time, they purchased a particular tool because they liked that tool's features or ease of use. They didn't realize that some of the tools work with specific databases. You will want to know which tools work with each particular database. MsqlPerl doesn't work at all with Microsoft Access, for example, and Oracle can't be used with web.sql.

Which platform are your database and Web servers running on? On NT you have the capability to use the ODBC driver to access a database, making programming Web/database applications easier. This doesn't help much, though, if your company's SQL server is on a UNIX machine. If you are programming the database application on a UNIX machine, it doesn't help if the SQL server is on an NT. How you go about programming your database application will depend on what platform your Web server is running on, what platform your database is on, and what tools you have at your disposal.

How do you want to access a database (using CGI or a proprietary API)? Portability used to be the biggest concern when constructing a database application for the Web. Now it is not. Because of the ease of use with most proprietary APIs, they have become quite commonplace but may create problems if the technology changes drastically in the future. Web/database tools such as Visual Interdev and DBI enable a bit more flexibility when porting scripts or applications to be used with different databases. Other tools are quite limited and restrictive (MORE, for example, which is discussed later in this chapter).

How much money is your company willing to spend? This may not be a major consideration for most larger companies, but smaller businesses have to watch every nickel and dime. If you weigh the tools available with how much money a company is willing to spend, you will most likely be able to create a rock-solid application for even the most frugal company.

With these ideas in mind, take a look at the tools available, as described in the next sections, and see which Web/database tool will suit your needs.

PHP

On the CD

PHP (originally called PHP/FI) was developed by Rasmus Lerdorf, who needed to create a script that enabled him to log visitors to his page. The script replaced a few other smaller ones that were creating a load on Lerdorf's system. This script became PHP, which is an acronym for Lerdorf's Personal Home Page tools. Lerdorf later wrote a script that enabled him to embed commands within an HTML document to access a SQL database. PHP grew into a small language that enables developers to add commands within their HTML pages instead of running multiple smaller scripts to do the same thing. PHP is actually a CGI program written in C that can be compiled to work on any UNIX or NT system. The embedded commands are parsed by the PHP script, which then prints the results through another HTML document. PHP is browser independent because the script is processed through the PHP executable that is on the server. For those using Apache, a module is provided that enables you to parse PHP embedded HTML files without having to directly call the PHP parser.

PHP can be used to integrate MySQL along with Oracle, Sybase, mSQL, Postgres95, and on any database using ODBC on NT to create dynamic HTML documents. It's fairly easy to use and quite versatile.

ON THE WEB

`http://www.php.net/`   Visit this site for more information on PHP, which includes examples of how PHP can be used.

ColdFusion

Allaire created ColdFusion as a system that enables you to write scripts within an HTML document. ColdFusion, a database interface, processes the scripts and then returns the information within the HTML written in the script. Allaire wrote ColdFusion to work with just about every Web server available for Windows NT and to integrate with just about every SQL engine using ODBC.

ColdFusion works by processing a form, created by you, that sends a request to the Web server. The server starts ColdFusion and sends the information to ColdFusion that is used to call a template file. After reading the information that the visitor entered, ColdFusion processes that information according to the template's instructions. It returns an automatically generated HTML document to the server and then returns the document to the visitor.

▶ **See** "Using ColdFusion" for more information on using ColdFusion, **p. 879**.

ON THE WEB

`http://www.allaire.com/`   Visit Allaire's site for the complete details on ColdFusion.

W3-mSQL

W3-mSQL was created by David Hughes, the creator of mSQL, to simplify accessing an mSQL database from within your Web pages. It works as a CGI script that your Web pages go through to be parsed. The script reads your HTML document, performs any queries required, and sends the result back out to the server to the visitor. W3-mSQL is much like PHP/FI, but on a smaller scale. W3-mSQL makes it easy for you to create Web documents that contain information based on what is in your database.

A sample bookmarks script and database dump is included within the W3-mSQL archive.

ON THE WEB

`http://www.hughes.com.au/software/w3-msql.htm`   For additional information W3-mSQL,
visit this site.

MsqlPerl

MsqlPerl is a Perl interface to the mSQL database server. Written by Andreas Koenig, it utilizes the mSQL API and enables you to create CGI scripts in Perl, complete with all the SQL
commands available to mSQL.

ON THE WEB

`ftp://Bond.edu.au/pub/Minerva/msql/Contrib/`   Visit this site for additional information
on MsqlPerl.

MsqlJava

MsqlJava is an API that enables you to create applets that can access an mSQL database server.
The package has been compiled with the Java Development Kit version 1 and tested using
Netscape 3.

ON THE WEB

`http://mama.minmet.uq.oz.au/msqljava/`   For additional information on MsqlJava and to
download the latest version and view the online documentation, visit this site.

Microsoft's Active Server Pages

Active Server Pages (ASP) enables you to produce dynamic content with the use of ActiveX on
the server (MS Internet Information Server). Commonly, VBScript is used to write ASP applications, but JScript and PerlScript are also used. Using VBScript, you can easily write applications that access a database, enabling you to provide dynamic content based on the information
in the database.

▶ For more information, **see** "Active Server Pages and VBScript," **p. 835**.

ON THE WEB

`http://www.microsoft.com/vinterdev/`   For more information, visit Microsoft.

WDB

WDB is a suite of Perl scripts that helps you create applications enabling you to integrate SQL
databases with the World Wide Web. WDB provides support for Sybase, Informix, and mSQL
databases, but it has been used with other database products as well.

WDB uses what its author, Bo Frese Rasmussen, calls "form definition files," which describe how the information retrieved from the database should display to the visitor. WDL automatically creates forms on-the-fly that enable the visitor to query the database. This saves you a lot of work when you prepare a script to query a database. The user submits the query and WDB then performs a set of conversions, or links, so the visitor can perform additional queries by clicking one of the links.

ON THE WEB

`http://arch-http.hq.eso.org/wdb/html/wdb.html`   Visit the WDB home page for further information on WDB.

Web/Genera

Web/Genera is a software toolset that is used to integrate Sybase databases with HTML documents. Web/Genera can be used to retrofit a Web front end to an existing Sybase database, or it can be used to create a new one. When using Web/Genera, you are required to write a schema for the Sybase database indicating what fields are to be displayed, what type of data they contain, what columns they are stored in, and how you want the output of a query formatted. Next, Web/Genera processes the specification, queries the database, and formats an HTML document. Web/Genera also supports form-based queries and whole-database formatting, which turns into text and HTML.

The main component of Web/Genera is a program called symfmt, which extracts objects from Sybase databases based on your schema. After the schema is written, compile it using a program called sch2sql, which creates the SQL procedures that extract the objects from the database.

When you have compiled the schema, you can retrieve information from the database using URLs. When you click a link, the object requested is dynamically loaded from the Sybase database, formatted as HTML, and displayed to the visitor.

Web/Genera was written by Stanley Letovsky and others for UNIX.

ON THE WEB

`http://gdbdoc.gdb.org/letovsky/genera/`   For additional information on Web/Genera, along with downloading the latest version, visit its page.

MORE

MORE is an acronym for Multimedia Oriented Repository Environment, which was developed by the Repository Based Software Engineering (RBSE) Program. MORE is a set of application programs that operates in conjunction with a Web server to provide access to a relational (or Oracle) database. It was designed to enable a visitor to access the database using a set of CGI scripts written in C. It was also designed so that a consistent user interface can be used to work with a large number of servers, enabling a query to check information on multiple machines.

This expands the query and gathers a large amount of information.

ON THE WEB

`http://rbse.jsc.nasa.gov:81/DEMO/`   Visit the MORE Web site for additional information on MORE and RBSE.

DBI

On the CD

DBI's founder, Tim Bunce, wanted to provide a consistent programming interface to a variety of databases using Perl. Since the beginning, others have joined to help build DBI so that DBI can support a wide variety of databases through the use of a database driver, or DBD. The DBD is simply the driver that works as a translator between the database server and DBI. A programmer has to deal with only one specification, and the drivers handle the rest transparently.

So far, the following databases have database drivers. Most are still in testing phases, although they are stable enough to use.

Oracle	mSQL
Ingres	Informix
Sybase	Empress
Fulcrum	C-ISAM
DB2	Quickbase
Interbase	

ON THE WEB

`http://www.hermetica.com/technologia/DBI/`   Visit this site for the latest developments on DBI and on various database drivers; authors continue to develop this interface where DBDs are being built for additional databases.

DBGateway

On the CD

DBGateway is a 32-bit Visual Basic WinCGI application that runs on a Windows NT machine as a service to provide World Wide Web access to Microsoft Access and FoxPro databases. It is being developed as part of the Flexible Computer Integrated Manufacturing (FCIM) project. DBGateway is a gateway between your CGI applications and the database servers. Because your CGI scripts only "talk" with the database gateway, you need to be concerned only with programming for the gateway instead of each individual database server. This performs two functions—programming a query is much easier because the gateway handles the communication with the database, and scripts can be easily ported to different database systems.

The gateway enables a visitor to your site to submit a form that is sent to the server. The server hands the request to the gateway, which decodes the information and builds a query forming the result based on a template; or, it can send the result of the query raw.

ON THE WEB

`http://fcim1.csdc.com/` Visit this site to view DBGateway's user manual, view the online FAQ, and see how DBGateway has been used.

Additional Resources on the Web

Additional information on Web database gateways is found at the Web-Database Gateways page at

`http://gdbdoc.gdb.org/letovsky/genera/dbgw.html`

and also on Yahoo! at

`http://www.yahoo.com/Computers_and_Internet/World_Wide_Web/Databases_and_Searching`

## CHAPTER 31

Indexing and Adding an Online Search Engine

by Mike Ellsworth and Melissa Niles

In this chapter

Understanding Searching

How can you find what you're looking for? If you are looking for something on the Web, chances are you will use a search engine instead of plodding through dozens or hundreds of pages in hopes of uncovering items of interest. These search services are made possible by programs known as robots, spiders, Web crawlers, or worms; they are on the job 24 hours a day, 365 days a year. They do nothing but wander around from site to site, reading and cataloging whatever they find. They store the results of their searches in huge databases, which anyone can access.

That's the easy part: assembling the haystack. But how to find that needle? This section examines search techniques used by search engines to sift through masses of information to bring back results that satisfy your request.

Understanding Literal Searching

Many search engines use a technique called full-text indexing and retrieving. *Full-text* refers to the fact that each word in each document scanned becomes part of the index. Listings 31.1, 31.2, and 31.3 show three files that might be included in an index.

Listing 31.1 *Holidays.txt*—Sample Text File #1

```
Holiday Schedule
New Year's Day, Monday, January 2.
Memorial Day, Monday 29 May
July 4th, Independence Day, Thursday
```

Listing 31.2 *Birthdays.txt*—Sample Text File #2

```
John, Jan 17 (Thursday this year)
Mary, May 29
```

Listing 31.3 *Taxes.txt*—Sample Text File #3

```
Fiscal year ends 31 December
Expect big write-off in May or June
Estimates due July 1
```

Suppose you search for any file containing the word "Jan." The search engine would return Holidays.txt (which has "January") and Birthdays.txt (which has "Jan"). You would not see Taxes.txt because "Jan" doesn't appear anywhere in it. If you ask for "May," you will get back all three files because all three contain the word "May."

Commonly Used Search Qualifiers

"" (quotation marks)—Specify that documents must contain the exact phrase within the quotation marks: "history of computing"

AND—Indicates a search for documents containing all the terms joined by the operator: UNIX AND Solaris

OR—Indicates a search for documents containing any of the terms joined by the operator: SCO OR HP/UX

NOT—Excludes documents containing the term that follows the operator: UNIX NOT Solaris

NEAR—Finds documents in which two words appear within a certain number of words of each other: Linux NEAR UNIX

+ (plus sign)—Placed at the beginning of a word to indicate that the word is required: UNIX +NetBSD

- (minus sign)—Placed at the beginning of a word to indicate that the word must be excluded: UNIX -SCO

Part

VI

Ch

31

If you ask for anything containing either "February" or "tax," the search engine will return Taxes.txt. Although none of the files contains the word "February," the Taxes.txt file contains the word "tax" as part of the title. This satisfies the request for either the first word *or* the second word. This kind of search is called a Boolean OR.

If you search for both "May" and "29," you will see Birthdays.txt and Holidays.txt. At this point, you will find out that Mary's birthday is on Memorial Day this year. Taxes.txt contains the word "May," but not the number "29," so the file fails the "find files with the first term *and* the second term" test. This kind of search is called a Boolean AND.

You can stretch a bit by asking for only files that have both "May" and "29," but not "Mary." A Boolean expression might state this search as follows:

```
((May AND 29) AND (NOT Mary))
```

This search first finds files matching the first term (it must have both "May" and "29"), and then excludes files having "Mary," leaving only Holidays.txt as the result. Suppose the search expression had been:

```
((May AND 29) OR (NOT Mary))
```

The search engine would have found all three files under this search expression. The Holidays.txt file is included because it has both "May" and "29"; the Birthdays.txt file is included for the same reason; and the Taxes.txt file shows up because it *doesn't* have the word "Mary."

A full-text index is obviously very powerful. Even in this limited example, you can clearly see the usefulness and flexibility of this kind of tool. Yet in a large database of files, thousands might include the word "May." If the database includes source code files, hundreds of thousands of references to "29" might be found. Wouldn't it be nice to find only dates that look like birthdays, or the word "May," but only if it is near the word "29," and not in any source code files?

Advanced search engines go one step beyond literal Boolean searches and give you the means to do more.

Advanced Searches

Advanced searching techniques go beyond literal matching. A search that doesn't rely on exact matches is often called a *fuzzy* search. It is not based on Boolean algebra, with its mixture of AND, OR, and NOT operators, although these might come into play if appropriate. Instead, it tries to identify concepts and patterns and deal with *information* rather than *data*.

Feel the Heat

Information is data that has been assigned meaning by a human. In a simple example, "It's 98 degrees" is data, whereas "It's hot" is information. As the amount of data on the Internet grows, the importance of distinguishing information from data skyrockets.

The ultimate artificial-intelligence search engine would have a DWIM, or "Do What I Mean" command. Putting data in context with other data is one way to derive information. Human language abounds with contextual references and implied scopes.

When you say "It's hot," for example, you probably don't mean "Somewhere in the world the temperature is such that someone might refer to it as hot."

You mean that you're feeling hot right now, regardless of the actual temperature.

The context and scope of your original statement is implied; the concomitant associations derive from the context, your knowledge of human behavior in general, and your behavior in particular.

If you searched the Internet for "Hot Babes" (not that you would ever do so), you would be disappointed if you got back pointers to the National Weather Service's reports mingled with articles about infant care. How can search engines figure out what kind of "hot" you mean? Can DWIM ever be achieved?

This question is a hot topic—the basis for an ongoing and bitter debate among philologists, linguists, artificial-intelligence theorists, and natural-language programmers. Almost as many sides exist as participants in the debate, and no one view clearly outstrips the rest. If you are interested in this sort of debate, check out the `comp.ai.fuzzy` newsgroup on Usenet, or stop by your local library or favorite online search engine and find references to *AI* and *natural language*.

Evaluating Search Results

When you perform a search, not only do you want information, you want information relevant to the question at hand. In a perfect world, every search returns only information that completely satisfies your request—no more, no less. But this is not a perfect world, so how can do you compare the effectiveness of various searches? Two major parameters are commonly used to judge the results of a search:

- *Recall* indicates what fraction of the relevant documents are retrieved by the query.
- *Precision* measures the degree to which the returned documents satisfy the request.

Each query can be graded as a fraction, with a perfect score being 1.00. In that mythical perfect world, every search would score a 1.00 on both measures because only relevant documents would be retrieved, and those documents would be exactly what you are looking for. Assume that you have a site containing 100 documents, for example, and of these 100, 10 are about search engines. If a query is made for "Perl-based search engines," the query might retrieve four documents about search engines and two others about Perl. In this case, the search would have a precision of 0.66 (four of the six documents returned were relevant) and a recall of 0.40 (4 of a possible 10 relevant documents were returned).

Search engines use a variety of search strategies to increase recall and precision, and some of them are quite complex. The following sections examine various search techniques used to find potential matches, as well as weighting methods used to rank these results in an attempt to present the most likely matches first.

Some of the following material is adapted from Rod Clark's excellent discussion in *Special Edition Using CGI* (Que Publishing, 1996).

Understanding Search Techniques

People think and remember in imprecise terms. You might ask a friend, "Tell me everything about piranha mating," or "Who were the six actors who portrayed James Bond?" Depending on the company you keep, you might get accurate answers. You are likely to get unsatisfactory answers, however, from today's search engines. Unfortunately, conventional query syntax follows very precise rules, even for simple queries. Search engines are evolving toward being capable of handling natural language queries, but there is a long way to go. Toward that end, search engines commonly use the following search techniques to enhance recall and precision.

Substringing   Suppose a friend mentions a reference to "dogs romping in a field." It could be that what he actually saw, months ago, was the phrase "while three collies merrily romped in an open field." In a very literal search system, searching for "dogs romping" would turn up nothing at all. "Dogs" are not "collies," and "romping" is not "romped."

If you entered the query "romp field," however, you might get the exact reference if the search tool understands *substrings*. A substring is part of the a string—but figuring out which part is meaningful isn't easy. The search engine takes the word "romp" and searches for it, as well as its variants: romps, romped, and romping and even brompton. Obviously, language-specific rules are required to generate the variants from the root word.

Stemming   Some search engines, but by no means all, offer *stemming*. Stemming is related to substringing, but involves an even greater understanding of the language. Rather than requiring the user to enter root terms in a query, stemming involves trimming a query word to its root and then looking for other words that match the same root. The word "wallpaper," for example, has "wall" as its root word; so does "wallboard," which the user might never have entered as a separate query. When a user enters "wallpaper," a stemmed search might serve up unwanted additional references to "wallflower," "wallbanger," "Wally," and "walled city," but it would also catch "wall" and "wallboard" and probably provide useful information that way.

Stemming has at least the following two advantages over plain substring searching:

- It doesn't require the user to mentally determine and then manually enter the root words.

- It allows assigning higher relevance scores to results that exactly match the entered query and lower relevance scores to the other stemmed variants.

But stemming is also language specific: The rules of stemming in English, for example, are quite different from those for German or Finnish. Human languages are complex, and a search program can't just trim English suffixes from words in another language.

Thesauri   One way to broaden the reach of a search is to use a *thesaurus,* a separate file that links words with lists of their common equivalents. Most thesauri enable you to add special words and terms, either linked to a dictionary or directly to synonyms. A thesaurus-based search engine automatically looks up words related to the terms in your submitted query and then searches for those related words. If you publish several technical briefs on the cellular mitosis, for example, a thesaurus-based search engine would show your articles under biology and physiology as well as cytology.

Pattern Matching   Building specific language rules into a search engine is difficult. What happens when the program encounters documents in a language that it hasn't seen before?

Several newer search engines concentrate on some more general techniques that are not language based. Some of these tools can analyze a file, even if it is in an unknown language or file format, and then search for similar files. The key to this kind of search is matching *patterns* within the files rather than matching the contents of the files.

Even if you don't know or can't explain the rules for constructing the patterns that you see— whether those patterns are in human language, graphics, or binary code—you can still rank them for similarity. "Yes, this one matches." Or "No, that one doesn't. This one is very similar, but not exact. This one matches a little. This one is more exact than that one." To analyze files for content similarity, keyword nearness, and other such qualities, some of the newer search engines look for patterns. Such engines use fuzzy logic and a variety of weighting schemes.

The theory behind sophisticated pattern analysis is far beyond the scope of this book. A good explanation of just the algorithms, *sans* theory, would cover several chapters. You should be aware that these techniques exist, however, and that some of the indexing engines you will encounter use variants of these techniques to enhance their searching power.

Understanding Weighting Methods

The search engine has done its job, but it has brought back dozens, hundreds, or thousands of items that might be what you're looking for. Scrolling through all this material looking for something truly relevant is probably not what you would like to spend your time doing. It is common, therefore, for indexing search engines to assign confidence factors or weights to the documents returned from a search and to use these measures to rank the list of documents. That way, if you're lucky, what you're looking for is close at hand, and not at the end of a long list.

Common methods for establishing weights include evaluating adjacency, frequency, and relevance.

Adjacency   *Adjacency* is a type of phrase searching method that examines the relationship between words in the search phrase. The search engine increases the relevance score based on how closely the words in the search term occur in the target document. If you search for the phrase "hearing aids," the search engine can use adjacency to determine that you aren't interested in documents containing the phrase "Senate hearing on medical research on AIDS."

Obviously, adjacency only comes into play when more than one search term is used. Yet, findings by Webcrawler (see `http://info.webcrawler.com/bp/WWW94.html`) indicate that the average search comprises only 1.5 words. If you can encourage your users to specify search phrases, however, a good indexing engine can employ adjacency to increase the effectiveness of the search.

Frequency   Indexing search engines can use the *frequency* of hits on search terms within a page to increase the page's relevancy score. If you're like most fans of the Blue Devils, it is far more likely that you are interested in a page that lists "Duke Blue Devils" seven times than in a page that only contains one mention of the phrase. The former page is much more likely to be an article about the subject; the other could just be a listing of teams or a passing mention.

Relevance Feedback   *Relevance feedback* is a form of query by example. With this method, a user first performs a search using normal search terms. The user samples one or more of the found documents and determines whether a particular document is close to what he or she wants. The user can inform the search engine to "find more documents like this one." The search engine then parses the relevant document and uses its profile to perform another search.

Relevance feedback can be an especially powerful means of searching. Instead of using the one or two search terms the user originally provides, the search is done using *all* the keywords from the found document.

Indexing Your Own Site

So far in this chapter, you have learned the theory behind site searching and have seen the techniques used by search engines to improve search effectiveness. In this section, you learn how to improve the accuracy of site indexing. This enables you to maximize the effectiveness of the search engine, whether you use an external, commercial engine, or implement your own.

Using Keywords

Before you start studying indexing programs and individual search engines, you need to examine the kinds of information that you can provide for the indexers to index. Some of the code examples and supporting text in this section are adapted from Rod Clark's excellent discussion in *Special Edition Using CGI*.

Adding keywords to files is particularly important when using simple search tools, many of which are very literal. These tools need all the help they can get.

Manually adding keywords to existing files is a slow and tedious process. Doing so isn't particularly practical when you are faced with a mountain of seldom-read archival documents. When you first create new documents that you know people will search online, however, you can stamp them with an appropriate set of keywords. This stamping (or *keying*) provides a consistent set of words that people can use to search for the material in related texts, in case the exact wording in each text doesn't happen to include some of the relevant general keywords. Using equivalent nontechnical terminology that users are likely to understand also helps.

Sophisticated search engines can yield good results when searching documents with little or no intentional keying, but well-keyed files produce better and more-focused results with these search tools. Even the best search engines, when they set out to catch all the random, scattered, unkeyed documents that you want to find, return information that is liberally diluted with *noise*—irrelevant data. Keying your files helps keep them from being missed in relevant lists for closely related topics.

Using Keywords in Plain Text   To help find HTML pages, you can add an inconspicuous line at the bottom of each page that lists the keywords you want, like this:

```
Poland Czechoslovakia Czech Republic Slovakia Romania Rumania
```

This line is useful, but ugly and distracting. Also, many search engines assign a higher relevance to words in titles, headings, emphasized text, `<A NAME=...>` tags and other areas that stand out from a document's body. The next few sections consider how to key your files in more sophisticated and effective ways.

Using Keywords and Descriptions in HTML *META* Tags   You can put more information than simply the page title in an HTML page's `<HEAD>...</HEAD>` section. Specifically, you can include a description of your page, or a standard `Keywords` list in a `META` tag. Some confusion seems to exist about how to implement these tags. `META` tags that include `HTTP-EQUIV` as part of the statement in the tag are considered to be part of the HTTP header. You can insert these tags in your `HEAD` section, and the browser is supposed to interpret them as if they were a true HTTP header. To change the date a page expires, for example, add a `META` tag similar to the following:

```
<META HTTP-EQUIV="Expires" CONTENT="Thu, 01 Jan 1998 12:00:00 GMT">
```

N O T E   HTTP 1.0 header content is defined in RFC 1945, included on the CD-ROM that accompanies this book. Also included on the CD-ROM is draft 8 of the HTTP 1.1 specification. ■

`keywords` and `description`, however, are not officially defined components of HTTP headers, although they can be implemented as part of the `META NAME` tag, such as the following:

```
<META NAME="keywords" CONTENT="keyword1 keyword2 keyword3">
<META NAME="description" CONTENT="This site contains...">
```

Despite this, you will see many pages that utilize the improper `<META HTTP-EQUIV="Keywords" NAME="Keywords" CONTENT="blah, blah">` construction. This may seem to be a quibble, yet what's important is getting search engines to recognize your keywords and descriptions. Some search engines, including AltaVista, InfoSeek, and HotBot, pay particular attention to META description and META keywords entries. These services index terms in both the Description and keywords tags and use the META description rather than the first few lines of the page to identify the URL in returned searches. All three of these engines look for the proper syntax, and it is not known what they will do with META HTTP-EQUIV tags.

Other search engines, such as Excite, may explicitly ignore these fields due to the potential for abuse. See http://www.clackamas.cc.or.us/instruct/cs/classes/178/search/s-meta.htm for more information. In fact, at least one lawsuit has been filed regarding keyword abuse.

Use of these META tags is becoming more popular. According to an analysis by Dave Beckett of the University of Kent at Canterbury (http://www.hensa.ac.uk/uksites/survey/1996-12-01/META-HTTP-Equiv-Field-Names.html), 11.44% of HTTP headers from sites in the .uk domain contain META Keywords. An earlier study of the various metadata attributes found in 17,000 documents in the Nordic Web Index during early summer of 1996 found that 48.7% contained META keywords and 48.9% contained META descriptions.

The following is an example of using the META keywords tag within an HTML header:

```
<HEAD>
      <META name="description" content="ACNielsen Consumer Information">

      <META name="keywords" content="consumer panel,
                              consumption,
                              marketing research">
<TITLE>Buying Habits of Internet Users</TITLE>
</HEAD>
```

After the search engine indexes this page, if a user searches for "marketing research," the engine will find this page even if the words "marketing research" do not appear anywhere in the text of the page.

Using Keywords in HTML Comments

This section presents some lines from an HTML file that lists links to English language newspapers. The lines aren't keyed; to find a match, therefore, you must enter a query that exactly matches something in either a particular line's URL or its visible text. Such matches are not too likely with some of these example lines. Only one of them comes up in a search for "Sri Lanka." None of them comes up in a search for "South Asia."

```
<B><A HREF="http://www.lanka.net/lakehouse/anclweb/dailynew
➡ /select.html">Sri Lanka Daily News</A></B><BR>

<B><A HREF="http://www.is.lk/is/times/index.html">Sunday Times
➡ </A></B><BR>

<B><A HREF="http://www.is.lk/is/island/index.html">Sunday Island<
➡ /a></B><BR>
```

To improve the search results, you can key each line with one or more likely keywords. The keywords can be contained within <!--comments -->, in <A NAME=...> statements or in ordinary visible text. Some of these approaches are more successful than others. The following are examples of each.

First, add some keywords as HTML comments on each line. The following example already looks better:

```
<!--South Asia Sri Lanka -->
<B><A HREF="http://www.lanka.net/lakehouse/anclweb/dailynews
➥ /select.html">Sri Lanka Daily News</A></B><BR>

<!--South Asia Sri Lanka -->
<B><A HREF="http://www.is.lk/is/times/index.html">Sunday Times
➥ </A></B><BR>

<!--South Asia Sri Lanka -->
<B><A HREF="http://www.is.lk/is/island/index.html">Sunday Island<
➥ /a></B><BR>
```

You could put the keywords in `<A NAME=...>` statements also, but HTML prohibits spaces in `<A NAME=...>` statements. Therefore, keys in an `<A NAME=...>` statement are limited to single keywords rather than phrases. This *might* suffice if you can always be sure of using an AND or OR search instead of searching for exact phrases. But many scripts don't support Boolean operators, and even when Booleans are allowed, most users don't use them. So, overall, using `<A NAME=...>` statements for keying isn't the best choice. Nevertheless, the following is an example of using an `<A NAME=...>` statement to provide a keyword:

```
<A NAME="Tamil">
```

Leveraging Commercial Indexes

Fortunately, you don't have to be a natural language or artificial-intelligence expert to incorporate indexing into your home page or Web site. If you want to offer your users the capability to search the Web for items of interest, you can include links on your site to the commercial search engines. You may also want to help your users define their searches by topic by passing parameters to these commercial search engines. Many fine public search engines are available. This section examines some of the more common commercial indexes and how you can use them to provide services for your site.

Public indexes are available for free through sponsoring corporations, groups, or individuals and are usually accessed through an HTML form and a CGI program.

You don't have to rely on a list of bookmarks or your browser's setting to use a search page. You can put a page on your site that links directly to your favorite search engines. You can even tailor the form so that it comes preloaded with specific search terms, or, with a little more effort, make a massive commercial index return only pages from your own site when queried.

Using AltaVista to Search Your Site

AltaVista provides a helpful index of Web sites and newsgroups (see Figure 31.1). You can find AltaVista at the following address:

```
http://www.altavista.digital.com/
```

FIGURE 31.1

The AltaVista Web page offers a wide range of searching options.

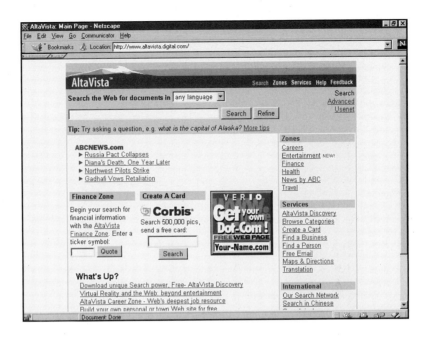

Listing 31.4 shows a generic form for invoking AltaVista's gigantic search engine. Listing 31.5 shows a modification to restrict the search to one of several predefined terms. Notice how Listing 31.5 takes the same form fields defined in Listing 31.4 and hard-codes some of them. The result is that Listing 31.5 always searches the newsgroups, and only for CGI by Example, Using CGI, or Que Corporation.

N O T E HTML examples are not provided for the other sites. The concept is the same for each site: You take the HTML used by the site itself to invoke its CGI script, and then modify the HTML to suit your needs. ▨

Listing 31.4 A Generic AltaVista Search Form

```
<H1>Search AltaVista</H1>
<FORM METHOD=get
        ACTION="http://www.altavista.digital.com/cgi-bin/query">
<INPUT TYPE=hidden name=pg value=q>
<B>Search
<SELECT name=what>
<OPTION value=web  SELECTED>the Web
<OPTION value=news >Usenet
</SELECT>
and Display the Results
<SELECT name=fmt>
<OPTION value="." SELECTED>in Standard Form
<OPTION value=c >in Compact Form
```

continues

Listing 31.4   Continued

```
<OPTION value=d >in Detailed Form
</SELECT></B>
<INPUT TYPE=text name=q size=55 maxlength=200 value="">
<INPUT TYPE=submit value=Submit>
<BR>
</FORM>
```

Listing 31.5   A Customized AltaVista Search Form

```
<H1>Search AltaVista</H1>
<FORM METHOD=get
      ACTION="http://www.altavista.digital.com/cgi-bin/query">
<INPUT TYPE=hidden name=pg value=q>
<INPUT TYPE=hidden name=what value=news>
<INPUT TYPE=hidden name=fmt value=d>
<B>Search Newsgroups for</B>
<SELECT name=q>
<OPTION>CGI by Example
<OPTION>Using CGI
<OPTION>Que Corporation
</SELECT><BR>
<INPUT TYPE=submit value=Submit>
<BR>
</FORM>
```

Because of a particular feature available on AltaVista and few other indexes, you can effectively use it as a local search engine to search out information on your own site.

One of the advanced keywords available on AltaVista is the `host:` keyword. You use this keyword to limit AltaVista's search to only those hosts you specify. Assume, for example, that you want to limit the search to your site and that your site has been visited and fully indexed by the AltaVista robot. To narrow a search, first specify `host:www.yoursite.com` and then follow it with the search terms you desire. AltaVista produces a list of files on your site that contains the search terms. To find pages on the following site that concern merchandising, use this query:

```
host:acnielsen.com merchandising
```

Thus, you could modify Listing 31.5 to look like Listing 31.6.

Listing 31.6   A Customized Form to Use AltaVista to Search Your Site

```
<FORM METHOD=get
      ACTION="http://www.altavista.digital.com/cgi-bin/query">
<INPUT TYPE=hidden name=pg value=q>
<INPUT TYPE=hidden name=what value=web>
<INPUT TYPE=hidden name=fmt value=d>

<B>Search Our Site for</B>
```

```
<SELECT name=q>
<OPTION VALUE="host:www.mcp.com 'CGI by Example'">CGI by Example
<OPTION VALUE="host:www.mcp.com 'Using CGI'">Using CGI
<OPTION VALUE="host:www.mcp.com 'Que Corporation'">Que Corporation
</SELECT><BR>
<INPUT TYPE=submit value=Submit>
<BR>
</FORM>
```

Note the use in this example of the VALUE keyword of the OPTION tag to specify the host and the search terms. If you want to enable freeform searching, you must write a CGI program that adds the host keyword before submitting the query to the search engine.

The HotBot (www.hotbot.com) and InfoSeek search engines also enable you to specify a particular site to search.

Using Lycos Search Resources

You can get HTML that links to Lycos by email. Lycos will even provide a link back to your site on the resulting search page.

Stop by http://www.lycos.com/lycosinc/backlink.html and fill out the online form. Within a day or so, you will get back some sample HTML. Lycos provides you with an identifying number so that when users search with Lycos from your site, the resulting search page contains an image you provide and a link back to your site.

Lycos is available at the following site:

http://www.lycos.com/

Linking to Starting Point

For many users, Starting Point is *the* starting point when they conduct Web searches.

When you visit Starting Point, you can add a link for your site at the following address:

http://www.stpt.com/general/setup.html#WEBPAGE

You can find the Starting Point main page at the following site:

http://www.stpt.com/

Linking to Infoseek

Infoseek makes it easy to add a link to its service to your site. Just go to the following site and follow the instructions:

http://www.infoseek.com/webkit?pg=webkit.html&sv=A2

You can find the main Infoseek page at the following site:

http://www.infoseek.com/

Using Excite on Your Site

Excite is more than a public index. Excite makes search engines that you can install on your own system, and it is working closely with Web server companies to provide integrated solutions. See the section "Implementing an Indexing Search Engine with Excite for Web Servers" later in this chapter for more information.

You can find the Excite Web site at the following address:

```
http://www.excite.com/
```

Using Other Search Engines

You can find dozens of other search engines on the Web—too many to hope to list them all. Each has its own advantages and disadvantages. "Meta" search engines, such as MetaCrawler, All4one, MetaFind, and 1Blink will even submit your query to several other search engines and collate the results.

The following listing identifies other important search engines. You can find a comprehensive list at `http://www.albany.net/allinone/all1www.html#WWW`.

Yahoo!	Lycos' A2Z	Go2.com
HotBot	Open Text	WebCrawler
WWW Yellow Pages	Thunderstone What U Seek	
PlanetSearch	Magellan All4one	

Using Web Servers' Built-In Search Tools

Another alternative to implementing your own search engine is to use search services already built in to your Web server. Several Web servers for UNIX and Windows NT include built-in utilities to index and search the files at a site. Some of these tools have fewer capabilities than the search engines previously mentioned.

Searching with OraCom WebSite Server

O'Reilly's WebSite server for Windows NT includes the company's WebIndex indexing and WebFind searching tools. WebIndex can index the full text of every page in the server's directory structure or only selected parts of the directories. WebFind runs as a CGI program and is a conventional search tool. It does keyword searches and supports AND and OR operators.

O'Reilly publishes a book (or manual), *Building Your Own WebSite,* that goes into considerable detail about setting up and using its WebSite server. Before you install the company's software, you can read all about it at

```
http://www.ora.com/
```

The following site is running WebSite and has set up several search databases:

```
http://www.videoflicks.com/
```

Searching with Netscape SuiteSpot Servers

Netscape SuiteSpot Standard and Professional Editions run on Windows NT and UNIX. They include a built-in indexing and searching system, although Netscape's lower-priced FastTrack Server does not. You can find out more about Netscape's servers at

> http://home.netscape.com/servers/index.html

Searching with Microsoft Index Server

Designed for zero maintenance and complete Web-site indexing, Microsoft's Index Server search engine supports multiple languages (Dutch, U.S. and International English, French, German, Italian, Spanish, and Swedish) and attempts to index by content type as well as contents. It can index documents in several formats: text in a Microsoft Word document, statistics on a Microsoft Excel spreadsheet, or the content of an HTML page. Index Server enables the user to search using both keywords and content types. You may read about Index Server and download a free copy at

> http://www.microsoft.com/ntserver/info/indexserver.htm

Index Server requires NT 4.0 and is designed to work with Microsoft's Internet Information Server (IIS).

Considerations when Adding a Search Engine to Your Site

For purposes of this discussion, you have evaluated the alternatives and decided that you need to implement a site-resident search engine. Perhaps you don't like the idea of sending your users off to a commercial index, and your Web server doesn't have a built-in search capability, or maybe you just want more control. Before you get started, however, you should consider the type of search engine you want to use.

Indexing Versus Grepping Search Engines

Two main types of approaches can be used for creating an online search facility for your Web site:

- Indexing—Using this method, you periodically run a process that examines and pulls out keywords from every document on the entire Web site. The main advantage of this method is speed. When a user does a search, the search engine needs to look only at the index instead of searching every file on the site. A disadvantage of this approach is timeliness because a user's search can be only as current as your last index.

- Grepping—Using this method, you provide a search engine that searches all files on your site each time the user performs a search. The term *grepping* is taken from the UNIX grep facility that enables users to search for keywords within files. Timeliness is a major advantage of this approach because the user is searching the actual files on your site and any changes are automatically reflected. The major disadvantages of this method are

Part
VI

Ch
31

performance and high resource utilization. Because each search touches every file on your site, searches can run for a long time and consume significant server resources.

Indexing search engines predigest your Web site and create indexes containing all its words. The major commercial Web search engines, such as AltaVista, Lycos, Excite, and Web Crawler, are all indexing engines. In fact, it is not practical to have a search engine that searches the whole Web with the grepping method. To accomplish this, the search engine would have to either add the full text of every site to a database or search every site in real-time.

With an indexing search engine, when a user requests a search, the search engine needs to refer only to the index to find relevant pages. Because indexes are often a small fraction of the size of the documents indexed, this takes much less time. More important, such an approach makes the major commercial search engines practical by enabling them to store only the indexes of sites rather than site images.

Indexing search engines generally employ more sophisticated searching algorithms to improve their chances of returning relevant documents.

Although easy to implement, most grepping search engines are somewhat limited in the types of search queries they support. Grepping, after all, is a rather brute-force method of searching. Each file is opened and then scanned for the search terms. The amount of system resources consumed by these activities can limit the sophistication of the search strategies. Most grepping engines use only simple keyword searches, although some offer searching via regular expressions.

To determine which searching method to employ, you must first decide what kinds of search services you want to offer and how many resources—both disk space and processor time—to dedicate to those services.

Evaluating Performance and Processor Efficiency   As you might imagine, a big difference exists between the performance and efficiency of grepping and indexing search engines.

N O T E   Performing a grepping search on one section of my site, which contains about 600 average-size files, takes 8 CPU seconds and 40 elapsed seconds on a Sun Sparcstation 20. Because our user load is not very high, this is an acceptable amount of overhead for a search. If your site is very busy, however, with a hundred simultaneous users, for example, it is probably not feasible to dedicate this amount of resources to user searching.

In contrast, performing an index-based search on the same site takes about one CPU second and five or six elapsed seconds. Because the size of the site is not large, about 90MB, and indexes average between 10% and 20% of the total size of the site, the amount of disk overhead is acceptable. Because the information on our site doesn't change much from day to day, I can run the indexing software overnight and provide a day-old index for our users to search. ▪

One approach that adds no disk overhead and a small amount of processor overhead is to have someone else maintain your index and run the search process. An example of this approach is Pinpoint, from Netcreations (http://www.netcreations.com/pinpoint/). This commercial service sends its robot to your site about once a month. The site index is maintained on the

Netcreations site, and it also maintains and runs the search engine. You maintain a query form on your site that points to the Pinpoint URL. Some trade-offs, of course, exist for this type of solution. You give up a lot of control over what is indexed, how it is indexed, and how often the index is updated. In addition, performance of search queries is likely to be slower when conducted over the Internet.

You may also worry about the security aspects of turning over so much information about your site to a third party. In reality, however, many other third parties already index your site (AltaVista, Lycos, Excite, and all the rest). If you are going to worry, you might as well worry about them. When a third party provides an important service such as this for your site, you are giving up a lot of control. You are trusting the third party to maintain the search engine, as well as to only index those sections of the site that you want your users to see. You are also trusting them to maintain a timely index of your site and to be available to your users constantly. If these compromises work for you, this approach is quick and easy. If, on the other hand, you don't want to give up control of such an important function of your site, you should consider implementing your own search engine.

Evaluating Complexity of Searching   Your choice of a search engine depends, in part, on how complex the searches on your site are likely to be. If relevant documents can be found with the use of a simple keyword, not much difference exists between the grepping and the indexing approaches. If, on the other hand, the average user wants to implement multiple-word searches or searches involving concepts other than keywords, an indexing search engine is the better choice.

In general, indexing search engines can accomplish more complex searches than grepping engines. A grepping engine basically does string compares. It may support regular expressions, wildcards, fuzzy and normal Boolean matching, but it is difficult to implement more sophisticated context matching or concept searching in this type of engine. The sheer overhead of a grepping engine makes it difficult to do multipass searching of any kind.

Using an indexing approach, a search engine can spend more time examining the relationships between search terms and found pages. Because the engine doesn't need to burn processor time churning through all the pages in a site, it can offer nice features such as relevancy ranking and concept searching.

Understanding Indexing Issues

Issues to consider when evaluating an indexing search engine include the following:

- Resource usage—The size of the index, the speed of search, and the impact on the CPU
- Handling of "stop" words—How the engine deals with commonly occurring words such as "the," "a," and "an"
- Control over indexed material—How files to index are included or excluded from the process

Comparing Index Size and Speed   Typically, the larger the index, the longer it takes to search. Most indexing search engines create indexes that are a small fraction of the size of the material to be searched (usually between 10% and 20%). If your site is massive, however, you need to consider whether the index can fit in memory all at once or whether your server needs to swap it in and out as the engine does its searching. Excessive disk thrashing dramatically slows the search process and may even affect overall server performance.

If yours is a high-volume site and your users do a lot of searches, you may need to consider holding the index in memory or even limiting the number of simultaneous searches.

One way to reduce the size of the index on your site is to exclude certain common words from the index. By default, most indexing engines exclude words known as *stop* words—commonly occurring articles and pronouns, for example. But additional *noise* words may be on your site that you may not want to include in your index (the name of your organization, for example). Excluding words such as these reduces the size of the index and improves searching efficiency.

Understanding Stop Words   Most indexing search engines have some capability to ignore *stop* words, also known as garbage or noise words. These are commonly occurring words such as articles, pronouns, and many adjectives. The indexing engine should ignore such words when indexing, and the query engine should discard them from the search terms when performing a search. Table 31.1 lists commonly used stop words.

Table 31.1   Some Common Stop Words

after	by	he	many	old	their	was
all	can	her	may	on	them	way
also	come	hers	me	only	then	we
am	did	hid	more	onto	there	were
an	do	him	most	or	these	what
and	does	his	much	other	they	when
any	each	how	must	out	this	where
are	etc	however	my	over	those	whether
aren	far	ie	near	per	til	which
as	few	if	new	put	to	who
at	fix	in	next	same	too	why
be	for	into	no	say	try	will
because	from	is	none	since	under	with
been	get	it	nor	so	unto	within
before	go	its	not	some	up	without
between	got	just	now	such	upon	yet
big	had	led	of	than	us	
both	has	less	off	that	very	
but	have	let	oh	the	vs	

One feature to look for in an indexing search engine is the capability to add words to the stop words list. On my site, for example, I would like to add the name of our company, ACNielsen, to the list. Because this word is mentioned in almost every file on the site, it doesn't make sense to waste indexing space, nor do we need to enable users to search for this term.

Controlling Items to Index An important feature of any search engine is the capability to determine which files on your site to include in a search. If your site is like many, various directories are either password-protected or developmental in nature and not linked to the main pages. Certainly you don't want files from these directories to turn up when users search your site.

Two approaches generally are used to control what material is indexed by the search engine. Either you specify all the directories you want to search, or you specify only those directories you want to exclude from searches. This latter approach usually results in less maintenance for the Webmaster. An even easier method is for the indexing engine to automatically skip directories protected with an access control file, such as the .htaccess file used by the NCSA Web server. This way you don't have to remember to include or exclude new directories as they are added to your site.

As mentioned in the section "Using Keywords and Descriptions in HTML META Tags" earlier in this chapter, some indexing search engines enable you to use the <META> tag to control how a page is indexed. Using this tag, you place a page description and keywords in the heading of your documents. The search engine then gives this information special treatment when it performs its index.

Evaluating Search Engine Security Concerns

You must think about two main security concerns when implementing a search facility on your site:

- Does the search engine itself represent a threat to site security?
- Does the search engine allow users access to information that ordinarily they are prevented from seeing?

Any time you add a piece of software to your site, you need to be concerned with its impact on site security. Can the software be overwhelmed by an attack and provide direct access to the site? Does it offer a way for users to execute programs on your server? Before releasing a search engine for production use, you may want to experiment with it, to try to overwhelm it or get it to produce unpredictable results.

> **CAUTION**
>
> Be aware of security concerns regarding implementations of Perl on Windows NT. See
> `http://www.perl.com/perl/news/latro-announce.html` for more information.

Part
VI

Ch
31

The potential for users to use your search engine to execute arbitrary code on your Web server is obviously a serious security concern. If the search engine uses the Perl `eval` command to perform the search, you need to be sure to screen search terms to remove potentially harmful characters and code before passing them to the search engine. On UNIX systems, this means preventing the user from entering a search term containing the escape symbol (!) or any commands that could be used to invoke a command interpreter (`!sh`, for example).

Even if your search engine doesn't offer a security hole, you still need to be sure that users can't see information on your site that they usually are prevented from seeing. It is common on sites using the NCSA Web server, for example, to use access control files (typically `.htaccess`) to control access to sensitive directories. If the search engine ignores these access control files, it can return links to or summaries of the files contained in protected directories. At best, your users will be frustrated at seeing links that they are prevented from following. At worst, file summaries can compromise the confidentiality of protected information.

And finally, a security concern that is really a resource concern: You may want to limit the amount of resources any one user of your search engine can consume, or the number of simultaneous searches that occur. A malicious user can bring your server to its knees by launching a large number of time-consuming searches. Most search engines do provide a method of controlling access in this way. You may need to use other system-management tools to regulate search engine use.

Making the Decision

Which search engine you select depends in part on whether you prefer the timely, but resource-hungry, grepping approach or the faster, CPU-friendly, indexing approach. Regardless of the approach you pick, you should evaluate several requirements before selecting your engine:

- How easy is it to maintain?

  Indexing engines take more maintenance by their very nature. But if maintaining your search engine means remembering to update variables or rerun indexes when new information is added, you need to decide if you're willing to spend the time. By the same token, if your grepping engine looks at all directories on your site, you need to keep that in mind when creating new directories. The best search engine is probably one that you can set and forget.

- Does it automatically recurse directories?

  This is a security question closely related to maintenance concerns. If the engine needs to be told explicitly what to search for, you will spend more time maintaining it. If it automatically searches new directories, you need to be aware of sensitive or password-protected information when creating new ones.

- Does it honor access control files?

  These files are a simple way to control access to information on your site, but if your search tool gives users access to these files or their summaries, security is breached. At best, users are frustrated if they cannot access the files that turn up in an index.

- Does it reject searches for garbage, noise, or stop words?

  No matter which type of engine you select, you don't want to waste resources running down all instances of the word "the" on your site.

- Does it allow for complex searches?

  A good search engine will at least allow for Boolean searches and searches that are not case-sensitive. The capability to search for regular expressions is also desirable. More sophisticated engines evaluate word proximity or enable users to search on concepts.

- Does it index offsite links?

  You have to make up your own mind as to whether you want your engine to index such links.

- Does it provide a context so that the user can evaluate the suitability of the found file?

  At a minimum, the search engine needs to offer a hyperlink to the relevant file. It is more helpful, however, if a summary of the file is available, especially if the files are large.

- Does it present search results in small groups or in one big list?

  To avoid overwhelming your users with a huge results page that takes forever to download, some control is needed. The engine can either present the results in small groups, offering a link to the next set, or enable the user or Webmaster to control the number of files returned by any one search.

- Does it enable you to capture information about what users are searching for?

  You can better design your site to serve your users if you know just what they are looking for. Data on user searches can be a very important tool in determining the organization of your site.

These are just some of the questions you should ask yourself as you plan to add a search capability to your site. The discussion that follows examines how well various approaches satisfy these requirements.

Implementing a Grepping Search Engine

Grepping search engines share a common methodology: Start at an arbitrary point in the directory tree, open each HTML file in the tree, and search the file for the search term. Optionally, the engine might recursively follow each subsequent directory branch encountered and repeat the search process.

This allows for unsophisticated searches, although it is possible to enable support for searches using regular expressions.

Building Your Own Grepping Search Engine

To help you better understand how grepping search engines work, this section shows how you can use the Perl language to build your own. In building your own grepping search engine, you will need to tackle two problems: finding files to search, and searching those files for search terms.

First, it is important to examine the problem of finding files to search. Using a couple of key Perl capabilities, it is easy to build a recursive routine that will identify the types of files contained within a directory tree, perform an operation on them, and continue the process with underlying directories. The Perl script in Listing 31.7 demonstrates this approach.

Listing 31.7   *Tfind.pl*—Perl Script to Recursively Find Files in Subdirectories

```perl
#!/usr/local/bin/perl
# define the directory to start at
# you could prompt user for this
$BASEDIR = "/web/home/acn";

# print page preamble to STDOUT
print "Content-type: text/html\n\n";
print "<HEAD><TITLE>Test Find Capability</TITLE>\n";
print "<BODY bgcolor=#FFFFFF>\n";

# call subroutine to find files
&finddir($BASEDIR);
# close the page
print "<\/BODY><\/HTML>\n";

sub finddir
{
    local ($$BASEDIR) = @_;

# open directory and load file names into array
    opendir(BASE, $BASEDIR) || die("Can't open directory $BASEDIR");
    @files = grep(!/^\.\.?$/, readdir(BASE));
    closedir(BASE);

    ITEM:
# for every file in the array
    foreach $file (@files)
    {
# check to see if it's a directory
        if (-d "$BASEDIR/$file")
        {
# if it is, recursively call the subroutine
            $next = "$BASEDIR/$file";
            &finddir($next);
# if not a directory, you've got a hit
        }
        else
        {
            print "<P>Found a file called $BASEDIR/$file\n";
            next ITEM ;
        }
    }
}
```

When you run this Perl program, you see a display similar to that shown in Figure 31.2.

FIGURE 31.2

The basic file recursion script produces a listing line for each file found.

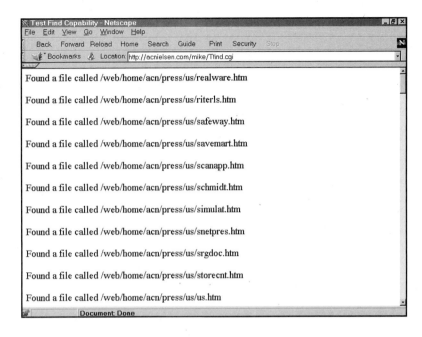

Note that all HTML files are found in both the base directory (/web/home/acn) as well as in all subdirectories (/web/home/acn/press).

You can create your own directory walking code, as in this example, or you can use Find.pl, part of the Perl distribution library (available at http://www.perl.com/). This Perl script steps through all files recursively and executes a subroutine that you define for each file found. Find returns the name of a file in the variable $name and executes a subroutine in your wrapper script called wanted. You can refer to the $name variable in the wanted subroutine to display the name of the file or grep for a search string. It is easy use Find.pl to develop a slightly more sophisticated find routine (see Listing 31.8).

Listing 31.8 *Tsfind.pl—Using Find.pl to Recursively Search Directories*

```perl
#!/usr/local/bin/perl

# requires find.pl
require("/public/local/lib/perl5/find.pl");
$BASEDIR = "/web/home/acn";

print "Content-type: text/html\n\n";
print "<HEAD><TITLE>Test Find Capability Using Find.pl</TITLE>\n";
print "<BODY bgcolor=#FFFFFF>\n";

&find("$BASEDIR");

# close the page
print "<\/BODY><\/HTML>\n";
```

continues

Listing 31.8 Continued

```perl
sub wanted
{
# if it's an HTML file
    if (($name =~ /.htm/) && !($name =~ /.html/))
    {
# print its name
                print "<P>Found a file called $BASEDIR/$name\n";


    }
}
```

Like the previous script, this script merely prints the name of each file in which the search string is found. You can easily insert a call to a grepping routine in place of the code that prints out the name of the file.

The grepping routine needs to open the file and read through it to search for instances of the search string. The normal Perl searching function works nicely. This approach is demonstrated in Listing 31.9.

Listing 31.9 *Tsrch.pl*—A Basic Search Script

```perl
#!/usr/local/bin/perl
# define the directory, file name, and search string
# you could prompt user for these, or find files
# using find.pl

$BASEDIR = "/web/home/acn";
$file = "acn.htm";
$term = "ACNielsen";

# print page preamble to STDOUT
print "Content-type: text/html\n\n";
print "<HEAD><TITLE>Test Find Search Engine</TITLE>\n";
print "<BODY bgcolor=#FFFFFF>\n";

# call subroutine to search the file
&findstr($BASEDIR);
print "<\/BODY><\/HTML>\n";

sub findstr
{
# open the file
    open(FILE,"$file");
# read all lines into an array
    @LINES = <FILE>;
    close(FILE);

# create one huge string to search
    $string = join(' ',@LINES);
    $string =~ s/\n/ /g;
```

```
                    if (!($string =~ /$term/i))
{
# don't include this file name
                last;
                }
# if string is found
                else
{
# include the file name
        print "<P>Found string in $BASEDIR/$file\n";
                }

}
```

Now if you combine these two scripts, as in Listing 31.10, you will have a rudimentary search engine that still produces output similar to Figure 31.2.

Listing 31.10   *Tstfind.pl*—A Basic Recursive Search Engine

```perl
#!/usr/local/bin/perl

# requires find.pl
require("/public/local/lib/perl5/find.pl");
$BASEDIR = "/web/home/acn";
# hardcode the search term - you could prompt user
$term = "ACNielsen";

print "Content-type: text/html\n\n";
print "<HEAD><TITLE>A Basic Recursive Search Engine</TITLE>\n";
print "<BODY bgcolor=#FFFFFF>\n";

&find("$BASEDIR");

# close the page
print "<\/BODY><\/HTML>\n";

sub wanted
{
# if it's an HTML file
    if (($name =~ /.htm/) && !($name =~ /.html/))
        {
# search for string
                $findstr($BASEDIR/$name, $term);

        }
} # sub wanted
sub findstr
{
# get the name of the file and search term as a parameter
my ($file,$term) = @_;
# open the file
        open(FILE,"$file");
# read all lines into an array
```

continues

Listing 31.10 Continued

```
        @LINES = <FILE>;
        close(FILE);

# create one huge string to search
        $string = join(' ',@LINES);
        $string =~ s/\n//g;
                if (!($string =~ /$term/i))
    {
# don't include this file name
                last;
                }
# if string is found
                else
    {
# include the file name
            print "<P>Found string $term in $BASEDIR/$file\n";
                }

} # sub findstr
```

This script works; it finds instances of a search string in all files in a directory tree. But it ignores some problems and is definitely lacking in features. It would be nice, for example, to be
able to specify the search to be case sensitive and whether multiple words should be treated as
Boolean AND or OR. The display does not provide a link to the found files. Another missing feature is the context of the search hit. You know that the search terms are found in these files,
but you have no idea if the use of them is trivial or important. You don't know how many times
the search string was found, and you have no way to evaluate the relevance of a file.

N O T E   Rarely on a site is there a directory tree in which every HTML file and directory is available
to the public. On my own site, many protected directories require a user ID and password
to access. In addition, a number of experimental files, backup files, or other files are not linked to the
main site and are not for public consumption. This rudimentary script searches all files on the site
regardless of whether they are protected.

Implementing a Third-Party Grepping Search Engine

Several very popular grepping search engines are available on the Web. The following sections
examine three of them:

- Matt's Simple Search Engine by Matthew M. Wright, author of the famous Matt's Perl
  Script Archive
- Htgrep by Oscar Nierstrasz
- Hukilau 2 from Adams Communications

All are written in Perl, and each has a little something to recommend it. All solve many of the
problems mentioned in the last section and provide added functionality.

Implementing Matt's Simple Search Engine You can find Matt's Simple Search Engine in Matt's Script Archive at `http://www.worldwidemart.com/scripts/`, one of the most popular Perl script archives on the Web.

Implementing Matt's search engine is fairly simple: get the distribution archive, install it on your site, configure it, and create a search form. To configure the script, you need to edit several lines at the top to point to the base directory. The base directory is the base URL for the site and is used to create links to the found pages. You also need to insert a title to put on the resulting page and furnish links for the home page and search page.

Because Matt's script does not do recursion, you also need to specify all the subdirectories you want searched. This can be tedious to maintain as your site changes, so you may want to modify the file finding script from the previous example and combine it with calls to Matt's engine to perform the search.

After you finish configuring, you need to create a page that incorporates something similar to Listing 31.11.

Part
VI

Ch

31

Listing 31.11 *mattform.txt*—A Simple Form Allowing the Selection of Search Parameters

```
<FORM method=POST
     action="http://worldwidemart.com/scripts/cgi-bin/demos/search.cgi">
<CENTER><TABLE border>
<TR>
<TH>Text to Search For: </TH>
<TH><INPUT type=text name="terms" size=40><BR></TH>
</TR><TR>
<TH>Boolean: <SELECT name="boolean">
<OPTION>AND
<OPTION>OR
</SELECT> </TH><TH>Case <SELECT name="case">
<OPTION>Insensitive
<OPTION>Sensitive
</SELECT><BR></TH>
</TR><TR>
<TH colspan=2><INPUT type=submit value="Search!">
<INPUT type=reset><BR></TH>
</TR></TABLE></FORM></CENTER>
<HR size=7 width=75%><P>
```

This form produces a Web page similar to that shown in Figure 31.3.

You may wish to design your own search interface. If so, your form needs to present the following three parameters to the search script:

■ Terms—A text string containing one or more words

■ Boolean—The Boolean AND or OR

■ Case—Whether the search should be case sensitive or not case insensitive

FIGURE 31.3

You can use the generic form provided with Matt's Search Engine to allow user input.

 TIP   Make sure you use the POST method to call Matt's Simple Search Engine. If you use GET, the script won't work because Matt's script reads form input from <STDIN>.

The result of a search using Matt's Simple Search Engine interface will look similar to that shown in Figure 31.4.

FIGURE 31.4

The results page from Matt's Search Engine provides links to the found pages.

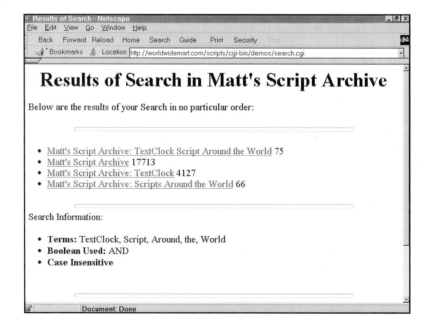

Notice that each found page is represented by a link to that page. The search terms are also provided, along with the Boolean and case sensitivity settings.

Matt's script works fine and is fairly fast. It took 3 CPU seconds and about 10 elapsed seconds to search about 250 files on my site.

Some desirable features are lacking, however—for example, only the titles of found files are displayed. No context indicates whether the search term is merely mentioned in the file or whether significant information about the term is contained in it. When presented with a list of dozens of files as the result of a search, with no way to distinguish between them, users may become weary of trying to find the information and visit a different site.

File titles are presented in no particular order, which is not very helpful in determining their relevance.

The results also do not indicate how many times a search term was found in a particular file or, in the case of multiple-word search terms, whether the words were found in close proximity. The user has no control over partial matches such as finding "state" within "estate" and "intestate." Whatever the user types becomes the search string.

In addition, various implementation problems exist with this simple search engine. Because it does not support recursion, control over which directories are searched rests entirely in the hands of the Webmaster, who must remember to add new directories to the variable in the script file. Files or directories also are not easily excluded from a search. In addition, no limit is placed on the number of files that can be returned, nor are stop words ignored. Given the way that directories must be explicitly specified, this may not seem to be a big drawback, but what if you have painstakingly added all directories on your site to the script and someone searches for the word "the"? A better way is definitely needed to control the directories that are searched.

Fortunately, Htgrep satisfies many of these objections.

Implementing the Htgrep Search Engine

Htgrep, written by Oscar Nierstrasz, can be obtained at `http://iamwww.unibe.ch/~scg/Src/Doc/htgrep.html` or in the Software Composition Group Software Archives at `http://iamwww.unibe.ch/~scg/Src/`.

The major differences between Htgrep and Matt's script is that Htgrep automatically recurses subdirectories, and it supports Boolean AND searches as well as case-sensitive searches.

After you have installed the Perl script `htgrep.pl` and the associated scripts `find.pl`, `html.pl`, and `bib.pl`, you configure the base directory by changing a variable at the beginning of `htgrep.pl`. Other variables you configure include the path to users' public HTML directories and any pseudo URLs (URLs that have been aliased) that you want included in the search.

On the CD

Included in the package is a basic search form and a basic CGI wrapper script that you can use to control the behavior of `htgrep.pl`. The CGI wrapper appears on the accompanying CD-ROM as `htgrep.cgi`.

You will need to modify the wrapper to configure the location of your Perl library files. The CGI wrapper assumes that `find.pl`, which was used in an earlier example, is located in the library. You can find the `find.pl` program in the Htgrep distribution, if you don't already have it.

The Htgrep wrapper script enables you to use either the POST method or the GET method to process the form. It first looks for information from a POST, using $ENV{'PATH_INFO'}, and then from a GET, using $ENV{'QUERY_STRING'}.

After you have configured the CGI wrapper, you need to build a form for your users to specify parameters. The form provided with the distribution appears in Listing 31.12.

Listing 31.12 *Htform.txt*—Sample Form for Use with HTGREP

```
<H2>Generic Form</H2>

<FORM ACTION="/~scg/cgi-bin/htgrep.cgi">
<P>
<INPUT
     NAME="file"
     SIZE=30
     VALUE="/~scg/Src/Doc/htgrep.html"
>
<!
     VALUE="/~scg/Src/Doc/htgrep.html"
!>
<B>File to search</B> (relative to WWW home)
<BR>
<INPUT NAME="isindex" SIZE=30>
<B>Query</B>
<INPUT TYPE="submit" VALUE="Submit">
<INPUT TYPE="reset" VALUE="Reset">

<DL>

<DT><B>Query style:</B>
<DD>
<INPUT type="checkbox" name="case" value="yes">
Case Sensitive
<DD>
<INPUT type="radio" name="boolean" value="auto" checked="yes">
Automatic Keyword/Regex
<INPUT type="radio" name="boolean" value="yes">
Multiple Keywords
<INPUT type="radio" name="boolean" value="no">
Regular Expression

<DT><B>HTML Files:</B>
<DD>
<INPUT type="radio" name="style" value="none" checked="yes">
Ordinary Paragraphs
<INPUT type="radio" name="style" value="ol">
Numbered list
<INPUT type="radio" name="style" value="ul">
Bullet list
<INPUT type="radio" name="style" value="dl">
Description list

<DT><B>Plain Text:</B>
```

```
<INPUT type="radio" name="style" value="pre">
(preformatted)
<DD>
<INPUT type="checkbox" name="grab" value="yes">
Make URLs live (works with plain text only)

<DT><B>Refer Bibliography files:</B>
<INPUT type="checkbox" name="refer" value="yes">
<DD>
<INPUT type="checkbox" name="abstract" value="yes">
Show Abstract
<INPUT type="checkbox" name="ftpstyle" value="dir">
Link to directories, not files (for refer files)
<DD>
<INPUT type="radio" name="style" value="ul">
Bullet list (instead of numbered)

<DT><B>Max records to return:</B>
<INPUT NAME="max" VALUE="250" SIZE=10>
</DL>

</FORM>
```

Part
VI

Ch
31

This code produces a form similar to the one shown in Figure 31.5.

FIGURE 31.5

You can use the generic form provided with Htgrep to allow user input.

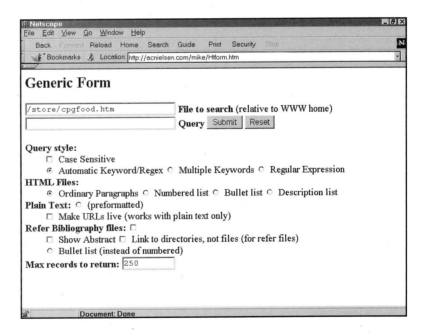

A welcome feature of Htgrep is its support for regular expressions. Although most users are probably not well-versed in the use of regular expressions, most at least can understand using the asterisk to fill out portions of words. Additionally, unless you use regular expressions, Htgrep searches on whole words, which is a nice feature.

Using the default search form, you can also determine the format of the resulting hits page—either full paragraphs or various types of listings.

N O T E The capability to return full paragraphs was the key in my decision to use Htgrep on my site. Because a high proportion of the words that users are likely to search for occur in many documents on the site, I felt it was important to provide this context to help guide users to relevant pages quickly and easily.

To enable the return of entire paragraphs from a search, Htgrep takes a different approach to finding text in files. Rather than assembling one huge string from all the lines in the files, Htgrep enables you to specify a record delimiter and then searches each record in a file. You may decide, for example, that you want HTML paragraph tags (<P>) to be your record delimiter. It is the record orientation of the search that allows Htgrep to return the context for a search hit. Htgrep returns the entire record in which it found the search term. The user thus sees the entire paragraph and can better determine whether the page meets his or her needs. Htgrep does this by using Perl's capability to define a record delimiter. This is demonstrated in the following code fragment:

```
# the default record separator is a blank line
#$separator = "";
$separator = "<P>";
[. . .]
    # normally records are separated by blank lines
    # if linemode is set, there is one record per line
    if ($tags{'linemode'} =~ /yes/i) { $/ = "\n"; }
    else { $/ = "$separator"; }
```

Unfortunately, a side effect of this context approach is that multiple paragraphs from each found page can be returned. Although this may help further guide the user, many may find it an annoyance. You may want to modify the Htgrep code to cause it to proceed to the next file upon finding a search hit. Doing this, however, might cause the search to skip particularly relevant material. What is really needed is a more sophisticated approach that evaluates the fitness of a document based on other rules, such as the number of hits per document and the proximity of words found as a result of multiple-word searches. It is difficult to add this level of sophistication to a grepping search engine. As discussed later in this chapter, you can find such features in some indexing search engines.

TROUBLESHOOTING

If you make any changes in these scripts, you can test them for syntax errors before installing the script in your CGI-bin directory. Give the script execute permission for your account, and then type its filename at the command line. The output will be either the default form (if the syntax is correct) or a syntax error message (if it's not).

Htgrep also enables you to set the maximum number of records to return. This is an important feature because no provision exists in Htgrep to ignore stop words. Unfortunately, there is also no way to prevent Htgrep from returning really long records. Assume, for example, that you define <P> as your record delimiter. If you add a new document that uses <p> for paragraphs, or if you have long material contained within <PRE> tags, the result can be huge amounts of text returned on the results page. To solve this problem, you can modify the code to include a line counter that aborts the paragraph retrieval if it is longer than 200 words. The following code fragment contains this modification:

```
# this is where Htgrep actually searches the file
        while (<FILE>) {
# call the subroutine that evaluates the search terms
            $queryCommand
# optional filter definition
            $filter
# remove all the nasty tags that can disturb paragraph display
        s/\<table/\<p/g ;
        s/\<hr/\<p/g ;
        s/\<HR/\<p/g ;
        s/\<IMG/\<p/g ;
        s/\<img/\<p/g ;
# transform relative URLs in found pages to full URLs
        if ((/\<A HREF/) && !(/http/) && !(/home/)) {
            s/\<A HREF \= \"/\<A HREF \= \"\$dirname/g ;}
        print \$url;
# count the number of words
        \@words = split(' ', \$_);
        \$wordcount = 0;
        foreach \$word (\@words)
        {
            \$wordcount++;
        }
# if it's too large, don't print the record
        if (\$wordcount >= 200)
        {
            print "\<H4\>Excerpt would be greater than 200 \n";
            print "words. Select link above to see entire \n";
            print "page.\<\/H4\>\\n";
# skip to next record
            next;
        }
# otherwise print out the record
        print;
# if you've printed up to the limit, stop
        last if (++\$count == $maxcount);
    }
```

Another side effect of returning the whole paragraph concerns what else besides text is returned. Because Htgrep grabs the whole paragraph, it also grabs links to images, bits of Java, JavaScript, or ActiveX code, and anything else contained in the paragraphs. This is probably not what the user wants when using a search engine. The resulting hits page can contain dozens of large GIFs and take a long time to download.

TIP

If your search engine returns blocks of text from the found files, be sure your script processes the text before displaying it to remove image references or program code. Failure to do so can result in pages containing many large images that are time-consuming to download.

Because of this limitation, I modified the Htgrep script to remove all <IMG> tags. I must confess, I did this in a decidedly low-tech way by replacing all instances of <IMG with <P in all found paragraphs (see the previous example). It is crude, but effective. The resulting hits page is devoid of image tags (see Figure 31.6).

FIGURE 31.6

All image references are removed from the search results page produced by a modified Htgrep.

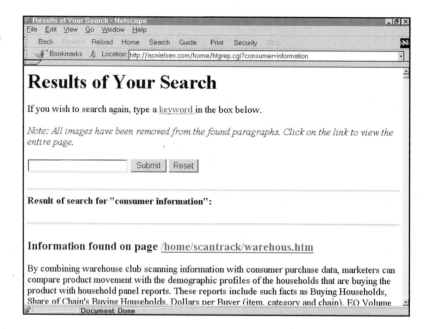

You will notice that another script modification produces a hyperlink to the found page, something that the base Htgrep script only provides if you elect plain-text formatting.

A security problem occurs with using Htgrep that you must take care of in the wrapper script. Because the search string can be a Perl regular expression, it executes using Perl's eval function. This can allow your users to execute arbitrary commands on your Web server. To prevent this from happening, be sure to prescreen search terms for dangerous characters or expressions, especially !sh, in the CGI wrapper that you use to call Htgrep.

> **CAUTION**
>
> If your Perl script uses the eval command to execute the search, you need to preprocess the search terms to prevent users from executing processes on your Web server.

Another nice feature of Htgrep is that, on NCSA servers, it ignores any directories that contain an access control file (.Htaccess). Chances are, you don't want users searching these directories anyway. If you want finer control over what directories are searched, you can put a .Htaccess file in your backup, administration, or internal directories. Other search engines require you to explicitly exclude such directories from the search and that leads to administrative overhead for the poor Webmaster.

Implementing the Hukilau 2 Search Engine Hukilau is a search script that searches through all the files in a directory. It can be very slow, so it is not practical for every site.

You may use this script for noncommercial purposes free of charge. A single-site commercial license is available for $250.

Hukilau searches one directory, which you specify in the script. (The registered version enables you to choose other directories from the search form.) Its search results page includes filenames, relevance scores, and context samples. The files on a search results page are in directory order, not sorted by relevance.

An option is available to show text excerpts from all the files in a directory, listed alphabetically by filename. This is useful when you are looking for something ill-defined, or when you need a broad overview of what is in the directory.

A quick file list feature reads only the directory file itself, not the individual files in the directory. It is fast, but it includes only filenames, not page titles or context samples.

The defaults are to apply an AND operator to all the words, to search for substrings rather than whole words, and to conduct a search that is not case sensitive. If you would like to change these defaults, you can edit the search form that the script generates. Listing 31.13 shows the part of the form that applies to the radio button and check box settings, edited a bit here for clarity.

Part VI Ch 31

Listing 31.13 Excerpt from a Hukilau Search Form

```
sub PrintBlankSearchForm
{
...
<INPUT TYPE="RADIO" NAME="SearchMethod" value="or"><B>Or</B>
<INPUT TYPE="RADIO" NAME="SearchMethod"
value="and" CHECKED><B>And</B>
<INPUT TYPE="RADIO" NAME="SearchMethod"
value="exact phrase"><B>Exact phrase</B> /

<INPUT TYPE="RADIO" NAME="WholeWords" value="no" CHECKED><B>Sub</B>strings
<INPUT TYPE="RADIO" NAME="WholeWords" value="yes"><B>Whole</B> Words<BR>

<INPUT TYPE="CHECKBOX" NAME="CaseSensitive" value="yes">Case sensitive<BR>

<INPUT TYPE="RADIO" NAME="ListAllFiles" value="no" CHECKED><B>Search</B> (enter
terms in search box above) <BR>
<INPUT TYPE="RADIO" NAME="ListAllFiles" value="yes">
List all files in directory (search box has no effect)<BR>
<INPUT TYPE="RADIO" NAME="ListAllFiles" value="quick">
Quick file list<BR>

<INPUT TYPE="RADIO" NAME="Compact" value="yes">
Compact display<BR>
<INPUT TYPE="RADIO" NAME="Compact" value="no" CHECKED>
Detailed display<BR>
```

continues

Listing 31.13   Continued

```
<INPUT TYPE="CHECKBOX" NAME="ShowURL" value="yes">URLs<BR>
<INPUT TYPE="CHECKBOX" NAME="ShowScore" value="yes" CHECKED>Scores<BR>
<INPUT TYPE="CHECKBOX" NAME="ShowSampleText" value="yes"
CHECKED>Sample text<BR>
...
```

To change the default from AND to OR in Listing 31.13, for example, move the word CHECKED from one line to the other on these two lines:

```
<INPUT TYPE="RADIO" NAME="SearchMethod" value="or"><B>Or</B>
<INPUT TYPE="RADIO" NAME="SearchMethod" value="and" CHECKED><B>And</B>
```

The result should look like the following:

```
<INPUT TYPE="RADIO" NAME="SearchMethod" value="or" CHECKED><B>Or</B>
<INPUT TYPE="RADIO" NAME="SearchMethod" value="and"><B>And</B>
```

Changing the value of a check box is a little different. To make searching case sensitive by default, for example, add the word CHECKED to the statement that creates the unchecked box. Here's the original line:

```
<INPUT TYPE="CHECKBOX" NAME="CaseSensitive"
value="yes">Case sensitive<BR>
```

Here is the same line, but set to display a checked box. It now looks like this:

```
<INPUT TYPE="CHECKBOX" NAME="CaseSensitive"
value="yes" CHECKED>Case sensitive<BR>
```

An unchecked box sends no value to the CGI program. It would not matter if you changed "yes" to "no" (or even "blue elephants"), as long as the box remains unchecked. The quoted value never gets passed to the program unless the box is checked.

This is the importance behind choosing values for the defaults. If you remove all the radio and check box fields from the form, leaving only the SearchText text entry field, the hidden Command field, and the Submit button, the program sets a range of reasonable, often used defaults.

This makes it practical to use relatively simple hidden Hukilau forms as drop-in search forms on your pages. To change the defaults and still use a hidden form, you can include the appropriate extra fields, but hide them, as shown in Listing 31.14.

Listing 31.14   Hiding All Form Variables

```
<FORM METHOD="POST"
➥ACTION="http://www.substitute_your.com/cgi-bin/hukilau.cgi">
<INPUT TYPE="HIDDEN" NAME="Command" VALUE="search">
<INPUT TYPE="TEXT" NAME="SearchText" SIZE="48">
<INPUT TYPE="SUBMIT" VALUE=" Search "><BR>
<INPUT TYPE="HIDDEN" NAME="SearchMethod" value="and">
<INPUT TYPE="HIDDEN" NAME="WholeWords" value="yes">
<INPUT TYPE="HIDDEN" NAME="ShowURL" value="yes">
</FORM>
```

The current version of the Hukilau Search Engine is available from Adams Communications at

    http://www.adams1.com/

Updates regarding new features being added or tested may be found on the Small Hours site at

    http://www.aa.net/~rclark/scripts/

The complete source code for the original Hukilau Search Engine is on the accompanying CD-ROM, as well as a modified version called Hukilau 2 that includes some added routines that Rod Clark wrote for this chapter.

Implementing an Indexing Search Engine

As you have learned from the previous discussion, implementing a grepping search engine can be quite easy. The discussion focused on only three popular Perl-based grepping engines, but many more are available with various features. Using the grepping approach represents a trade off between minimal disk usage and up-to-the-minute timeliness with high CPU usage and long elapsed times. You certainly can't beat the price (usually free) or the ease of setup and maintenance.

More sophisticated searching, however, is hard to implement using the grepping approach. For larger, more complex sites, an indexing search engine can be the best choice.

Several indexing search engines are available for use on your Web site. In addition to an array of shareware or free engines, several of the large commercial search sites make their technology available for use on a local site. Commercial indexing search engines include those listed in Table 31.2.

Part

VI

Ch

31

Table 31.2 Some Available Commercial Indexing Search Engines

Company	Tool Name	URL	Free?
Verity	Search 97	http://www.verity.com/ products/datasheets/ dk.html	No
Thunderstone	The Webinator Web Index & Retrieval System	http://www. thunderstone.com/ webinator/	Yes (shareware)
AltaVista	AltaVista Search eXtensions	http://altavista. software.digital.com/ search/index.htm	No
Inmagic/Lycos	DB/SearchWorks	http://www.inmagic.com/ textprod.htm#sm	No
Excite	Excite for Web Servers	http://www.excite.com /navigate/home.html	Yes

continues

Table 31.2   Continued

Company	Tool Name	URL	Free?
Netcreations	Pinpoint	`http://www.netcreations.com/pinpoint/`	No (free trial)
SDSU	ht://dig	`http://htdig.sdsu.edu`	Yes

The sections that follow focus on implementing the following five indexing search engines:

- WebGlimpse, developed by the University of Arizona
- ICE by Christian Neuss
- Simple Web Indexing System for Humans - Enhanced (SWISH-E) by Kevin Hughes
- freeWAIS from the University of Dortmund, Germany
- Excite for Web Servers

Implementing WebGlimpse

GLIMPSE (which stands for GLobal IMPlicit SEarch) and its Web companion, WebGlimpse, are projects of the University of Arizona's Computer Science Department. WebGlimpse is available for free for nonprofit use. A small licensing fee is charged for commercial users. The University has recently developed a new program called the Search Broker. The Search Broker forwards your query to a search engine dealing specifically with the subject of your question, which you specify as the first word of your query.

A recent search of the Web turned up hundreds of sites that are using this popular tool or its precursor, GlimpseHTTP. A partial list of sites is available at `http://glimpse.cs.arizona.edu/ghttp/sites.html`. GLIMPSE is also used as a basis for Harvest Information Discovery and Access System (`http://harvest.cs.colorado.edu/`).

As the name implies, the program displays glimpses of context samples from the files. This makes it a particularly useful tool, even though it doesn't offer relevance ranking.

GLIMPSE is available at

```
ftp://ftp.cs.arizona.edu/glimpse/
```

You can obtain WebGlimpse at

```
http://glimpse.cs.arizona.edu/webglimpse/
```

CAUTION

Be sure to get the most recent version of WebGlimpse. In July 1997, a security hole was discovered in the program and fixed.

The distribution comprises GLIMPSE, written in C, glimpseindex, another C program that creates the index, the webglimpse script itself, written in Perl, and an assortment of Perl utilities that you use to create and manage your indexes.

Installation is mostly automated but definitely not foolproof. Sometimes several attempts are needed to get it installed smoothly. After it is installed, you need to run a Perl script that creates the WebGlimpse index using glimpseindex. GLIMPSE can build indexes of several sizes, from tiny (about 1% of the size of the source files) to large (up to 30% of the size of the source files). Even small indexes are practical and offer good performance.

Other welcome features include the capability to index pages that have been added only since the last index, a facility to index offsite links, the capability to set a tolerance for spelling errors, and the capability to establish neighborhoods. *Neighborhoods* are defined as all links within an arbitrary number of hops from a page or all pages within a directory.

N O T E Running the index can consume quite a lot of time. Using WebGlimpse's option that enables indexing of external links as well as local pages, indexing took 45 minutes to index almost 600 files on my site. After that index was done, however, a re-index without the external option took only a few minutes. ■

After the index has been established, you can use a `cron` job (a program which executes applications for you at defined times) to run it periodically to maintain it. The installation routine even creates the job for you.

Using the WebGlimpse Perl script (created by the install) to perform searches is easy. After aliasing to the proper directory, you call the script with a parameter that indicates where the index resides. The user sees a basic search form if the script is called directly.

Alternatively, you can include either of two code fragments in your Web pages to provide a nicer looking interface. The two interface styles are created using the HTML code fragments in Listing 31.15.

Part
VI

Ch
31

Listing 31.15   *Glimform.txt*—Two Forms for Calling WebGlimpse

```
<H2>Basic WebGlimpse Interface</H2>

<CENTER>
<TABLE border=5><TR border=0>
<TD align=center valign=middle>
<A HREF=http://glimpse.cs.arizona.edu/webglimpse>
<IMG src=/images/glimpse-eye.jpg alt="WG" align=middle width=50><BR>
<FONT size=-3>WebGlimpse</FONT></A></TD>
<TD> <FORM method=get ACTION=/$CGIBIN/webglimpse$ARCHIVEPWD>
<INPUT NAME=query size=20>
<INPUT TYPE=submit VALUE="Search">
<INPUT name=file type=hidden value="$FILE">
<A HREF=/$CGIBIN/webglimpse-fullsearch$ARCHIVEPWD?file=$FILE>
Search Options</A></TD></TR>
<TR><TD colspan=2>
```

continues

Listing 31.15 Continued

```
Search:
<INPUT TYPE=radio NAME=scope VALUE=neighbor CHECKED>
The neighborhood of this page
<INPUT TYPE=radio NAME=scope VALUE=full>The full archive
</TD></TR></FORM></TABLE></CENTER><HR>


<H2>Full-Featured WebGlimpse Interface</H2>
<TABLE border=5>
<TR><TD align=center valign=middle>
<A HREF=http://glimpse.cs.arizona.edu/webglimpse>
<IMG src="/images/glimpse-eye.jpg"
align=middle></TD>
<TD align=center valign=middle>
<A HREF=http://glimpse.cs.arizona.edu/webglimpse>
<FONT size=+3>WebGlimpse </A> Search<BR></FONT></TD>
</TR>


<TR><TD colspan=2>
<FORM method=get ACTION=>
<INPUT name=file type=hidden value=/home/msmith/public_html/big/index.html>
Search:
<INPUT TYPE=radio NAME=scope VALUE=neighbor>
The neighborhood of <Ahref="">the ACNielsen Web Site
</A>
<INPUT TYPE=radio NAME=scope VALUE=full CHECKED>The full archive:
<AHREF="">the ACNielsen Site including links offsite</A>
</TD></TR>


<TR><TD colspan=2>
String to search for: <INPUT NAME=query size=30>
<INPUT TYPE=submit VALUE=Submit>
<BR>
<CENTER>
<INPUT NAME=case TYPE=checkbox>Case sensitive
<!SPACES>   
<INPUT NAME=whole TYPE=checkbox>Partial match
<!SPACES>   
<INPUT NAME=lines TYPE=checkbox>Jump to line
<!SPACES>   
<SELECT NAME=errors align=right>
<OPTION>0
<OPTION>1
<OPTION>2
</SELECT>
misspellings allowed
<BR>
</CENTER>
Return only files modified within the last <INPUT NAME=age size=5>
days.
<BR>
Maximum number of files returned:
```

```
<SELECT NAME=maxfiles>
<OPTION>10
<OPTION selected>50
<OPTION>100
<OPTION>1000
</SELECT>
<BR>Maximum number of matches per file returned:
<SELECT NAME=maxlines>
<OPTION>10
<OPTION selected>30
<OPTION>50
<OPTION>500
</SELECT>
<BR>
</FORM>
</TD></TR>
<TR><TD colspan=2>
<CENTER>
<FONT size=-2><A HREF=http://glimpse.cs.arizona.edu>
Glimpse</A> and <A HREF=http://glimpse.cs.arizona.edu/webglimpse>
WebGlimpse</A>, Copyright &copy; 1996,
Arizona Board of Regents.
</CENTER>
</FONT></TD></TR>
</TABLE></CENTER>
</CENTER>
```

The sample page in Figure 31.7 demonstrates the two available user interfaces for WebGlimpse.

FIGURE 31.7

The default search forms provided with WebGlimpse enable you to choose the level of search complexity.

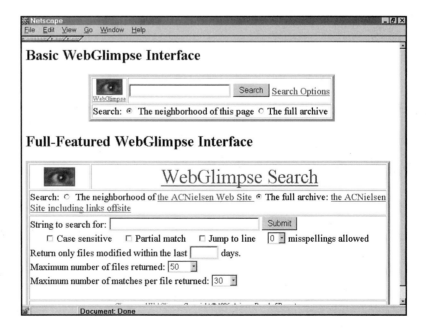

The first interface is short, sweet, and perfect for an unobtrusive search facility. The second interface enables the user to select a neighborhood search or a full archive search; choose case sensitivity, partial match, and spelling-error settings; to optionally jump to the line in a found document; and to control the date and number of documents returned.

> **CAUTION**
>
> One annoying aspect of the WebGlimpse indexing routine is that it automatically appends the user interface code at the bottom of each page it indexes unless you comment out the appropriate line. Although this feature is a nice service for those who want it, being able to turn it off is a must. My personal preference is to add a link to the search facility rather than the entire user interface. Due to WebGlimpse's concept of page neighborhood, however, putting this code on every page can make sense.

A page neighborhood is obviously context sensitive. You can define a page's neighborhood, for example, as every other page that is within two jumps (a link to a page that links to one other page). If page A has a link to page B and page C, and each of those pages links to one other page, pages BA and CA, page A's neighborhood is pages B, C, BA, and CA. However, if you follow the links to page BA, for example, you may find it links to pages D and E, making its neighborhood much different. Because the context determines the neighborhood, you need a unique call to WebGlimpse on each page rather than a generic (search the whole site) search page.

By the same token, if you define a neighborhood as all files in the same directory, the context of the WebGlimpse search changes depending on the starting page.

If your site is massive, or if you want to allow for more context-sensitive searching, you may prefer to have unique calls to WebGlimpse embedded on each page of your site. You might, for example, have a site that offers a number of Web utilities. Each utility is available in a variety of languages and for a variety of operating systems. If a user is reading about one of the programs and wants to know more about its implementation in Perl, he or she doesn't want to search the entire site and then have to wade through scads of listings for irrelevant utilities. In this instance, a neighborhood search is appropriate. If the site is organized properly, the information should be available either within a few hops or within the same directory.

The output of WebGlimpse looks similar to that shown in Figure 31.8.

This output from WebGlimpse shows that a link is provided to the found document. In addition, context is provided by including all lines in which the search terms are found. WebGlimpse automatically limits the number of found files as well.

An interesting feature of WebGlimpse is its setting for spelling errors. The example given in the documentation is a search for the name "Schwarzkopf." Many people do not know how to spell this name. Therefore, spelling errors may occur both in the user's search terms or in the documents on the site. Because WebGlimpse uses GLIMPSE, which in turn builds on the powerful agrep, it supports approximate matching that allows for spelling errors. Thus, if the material on your site comes from a variety of sources, varies in grammatical quality, or if your users can't spell, the capability to be forgiving of spelling errors is a definite plus.

FIG. 31.8

The search result page from WebGlimpse contains a link to the found page as well as a listing of all found lines.

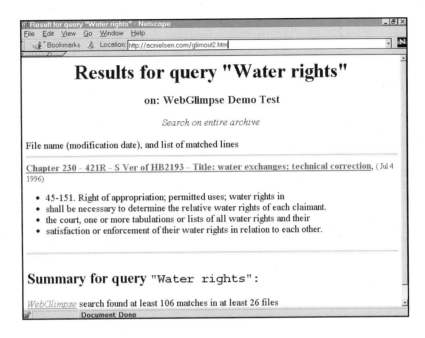

WebGlimpse basically uses a modified grepping approach, but applies the grepping to an index. Although some flexibility is offered in the spelling–error tolerance feature, complex searches are not offered and no ranking of results by confidence level occurs.

WebGlimpse takes the grepping approach just about as far as it can go. To achieve better results, a more complicated search methodology is needed.

Implementing ICE

Christian Neuss's ICE search engine produces relevance-ranked results and lists the search words that it finds in each file. It is written in Perl.

There are two scripts. The indexing script, `ice-idx.pl`, creates an index file that ICE can later search. The indexer runs from the UNIX command line as a standard non-CGI program. The search script, `ice-idx.pl`, is a CGI script. It searches the index and displays the results on a Web page.

ICE can use an optional external thesaurus in Thesaurus Interchange Format. Christian Neuss notes that ICE has worked well with small thesauri of a few hundred technical terms, but that anyone who wants to use a large thesaurus should contact him for more information.

You can find the current version of ICE on the Net at these two distribution sites, although the German site generally has a much later version:

```
http://www.informatik.th-darmstadt.de/~neuss/ice/ice.html

http://ice.cornell-iowa.edu/
```

Part
VI

Ch
31

Indexing Your Files with ICE   ICE searches the directories that you specify in the script's configuration section. When ICE indexes a given directory, it also indexes all its subdirectories.

Five configuration items are at the top of the indexer script. You will need to edit three of them:

```
@SEARCHDIRS=(
   "/home/user/somedir/subdir/",
   "/home/user/thisis/another/",
   "/home/user/andyet/more_stuff/"
);

$INDEXFILE="/user/home/somedir/index.idx"

# Minimum length of word to be indexed
$MINLEN=3;
```

The first directory path in @SEARCHDIRS is the default that will appear on the search form. You can add more directory lines in the style of the existing ones, or you can include only one directory if you want to limit what people can see of your files.

TIP Remember that ICE automatically indexes and searches all the subdirectories of the directories you specify.

ICE's index is a plain ASCII text file. The following is a sample from the beginning of an ICE index file:

```
@f /./bookmark.htm
@t Rod Clark s Bookmarks
@m 823231844
1 ABC
1 AFGHANISTAN
1 AGREP
1 AIP
1 ALTNEWS
1 AND
1 ANIMAL
1 ANU
1 ATM
1 AUSTRALIA
1 AsiaLink
```

After you have set the configuration variables, run the script from the command line to create the index. Whenever you want to update the index, run the ice-idx.pl script again. It overwrites the existing index with the new one.

TIP You can use the UNIX cron utility to schedule your index updates.

Searching from a Web Browser with ICE   The search form presents a choice of directories in a drop-down selection box. You can specify these directories in the script. Listing 31.16 shows how to accomplish this task.

Listing 31.16 A Sample ICE Search Script

```
# Title or name of your server:
local($title)="ICE Indexing Gateway";

# search directories to present in the search dialogue
local(@directories)=(
    "Public HTML Directory",
    "Another HTML Directory"
);
```

Now you can install the script in your CGI directory and call it from your Web browser.

Implementing SWISH-E (Simple Web Indexing System for Humans-Enhanced)

SWISH-E is easy to set up and offers fast, reliable searching for Web sites. In indexing HTML files, SWISH-E can ignore data in most tags while giving higher relevance to information in header and title tags. You can also limit your search to words in HTML titles, comments, emphasized tags, and META tags. SWISH-E creates a small and portable index consisting of a single file averaging around 1% to 5% of the size of the original source files.

Kevin Hughes wrote the original SWISH program in C for UNIX Web servers. In autumn 1996, The Library of UC Berkeley received permission from Kevin Hughes to implement bug fixes and enhancements to the original binary. SWISH-E is freeware, available from the Berkeley Digital Library Sunsite at

> http://sunsite.berkeley.edu/SWISH-E/

Installing SWISH-E is straightforward. After uncompressing and untarring the source files, you edit the SRC/CONFIG.H file and compile SWISH-E for your system.

Configuring SWISH-E isn't very hard either. You set up a configuration file, Swish.CONF, which the indexer uses. Listing 31.17 shows a sample SWISH-E configuration file.

Listing 31.17 *Swish.conf*—A Sample SWISH-E Configuration File

```
# SWISH-E configuration file

IndexDir /home/rclark/public_html/
# This is a space-separated list of files and directories you
# want indexed. You can specify more than one of these directives.

IndexFile index.swish
# This is what the generated index file will be.

IndexName "Index of Small Hours files"
IndexDescription "General index of the Small Hours Web site"
IndexPointer "http://www.aa.net/~rclark/"
IndexAdmin "Rod Clark (rclark@aa.net)"
```

continues

Listing 31.17 Continued

```
# Extra information you can include in the index file.

IndexOnly .html .txt .gif .xbm .jpg
# Only files with these suffixes will be indexed.

IndexReport 3
# This is how detailed you want reporting. You can specify numbers
# 0 to 3 - 0 is totally silent, 3 is the most verbose.

FollowSymLinks yes
# Put "yes" to follow symbolic links in indexing, else "no".

NoContents .gif .xbm .jpg
# Files with these suffixes will not have their contents indexed -
# only their file names will be indexed.

ReplaceRules replace "/home/rclark/public_html/"
➡  "http://www.aa.net/~rclark/"
# ReplaceRules allows you to make changes to file path names
# before they're indexed.

FileRules pathname contains test newsmap
FileRules filename is index.html rename chk 1st bit
FileRules filename contains ~ .bak .orig .000 .001 .old old. .map
➡ .cgi .bit .test test log- .log
FileRules title contains test Test
FileRules directory contains .htaccess
# Files matching the above criteria will *not* be indexed.

IgnoreLimit 80 50
# This automatically omits words that appear too often in the files
# (these words are called stopwords). Specify a whole percentage
# and a number, such as "80 256". This omits words that occur in
# over 80% of the files and appear in over 256 files. Comment out
# to turn of autostopwording.

IgnoreWords SwishDefault

# The IgnoreWords option allows you to specify words to ignore.
# Comment out for no stopwords; the word "SwishDefault" will
# include a list of default stopwords. Words should be separated
# by spaces and may span multiple directives.
```

After you set up SWISH-E for your site, create the indexes by running SWISH-E from the command line:

```
swish -c swish.conf
```

You can use cron to update the indexes regularly or run the job manually when needed. Alternatively, you can use the AutoSWISH script that is part of the distribution, and which automates the indexing process from an HTML form.

Now that you have your indexes, you need some CGI to access them. The distribution includes a sample script, which is also available on the accompanying CD-ROM as `swish.cgi`.

Using Swish-Web, a SWISH-E Gateway   Swish-Web is in the public domain. If you would like to practice a little programming on it, here are a few ideas for additions to the script.

N O T E   The complete Perl source code for the Swish-Web gateway is on the accompanying CD-ROM as `swishweb.cgi`. It is an example of a Web gateway for a UNIX command-line program. ▓

SWISH-E provides relevance scores, but the scoring algorithm seems to favor small files with little text, among which keywords loom large. Because SWISH-E reports file sizes, it is possible to add a routine to Swish-Web to sort SWISH-E's output by file size. Another useful addition would be a second relevance ranking option that weights file size more heavily.

A selection box on the form to limit the results to the first 10, 25, 50, 100, or 250 (or all) results might be another useful addition.

Implementing freeWAIS

In October 1989, a group of companies composed of Dow Jones, Thinking Machines Corporation, Apple Computer, and KPMG Peat Marwick saw the need for an easy way to provide text-based information systems on the corporate level and decided to do something about it. Their goal was to create a system for searching that was easy to use, flexible, built on an established standard, and which could search large amounts of distributed information in various formats. In April 1991, the group released the first Internet version of Wide Area Information Systems (abbreviated WAIS and pronounced "ways").

The benefits of WAIS are ease of use (for clients and developers), full-text search capability, and support for a variety of document types. It also has a far-reaching knowledge base; it can draw on remote databases to continue the query by example. Using results from one search can lead to a more appropriate server, and so on until the desired result is found.

Almost any time you encounter a discussion of WAIS on the Internet, freeWAIS will also be mentioned. The term freeWAIS is fairly self explanatory—it is a freeware version of WAIS. Much of the material in this section is adapted directly from Bill Schongar's comprehensive discussion of WAIS in Chapter 12 of *Special Edition Using CGI.*

Implementing freeWAIS on UNIX   Most WAIS tools are still primarily designed for use on UNIX servers. These tools include the servers themselves as well as the client scripts. It only makes sense, therefore, that one of the most significant public extensions to original WAIS functions first appeared on UNIX servers. *freeWAIS-SF,* designed by the University of Dortmund, Germany, takes advantage of built-in document structures to make more sense out of queries. It even enables you to specify your own document types for its use.

In addition, freeWAIS-SF gives you more power to search the way you want to search. Wild cards, "sounds-like" searches, and more conditions for what does and doesn't match are all components that make finding what you're looking for much easier. You no longer have to worry about whether the author wrote "Color" or "Colour," "Center" or "Centre."

Part
VI

Ch
31

Unlike many things that you use with your server, especially in the UNIX world, the freeWAIS-SF package is easy to install. A shell script leads you through the basic configuration by asking questions; when you finish answering the questions, you're finished installing freeWAIS-SF.

At the time of this writing, the current version of freeWAIS was 2.2.10. You can obtain the freeWAIS-SF package at the following site:

```
ftp://ftp.germany.eu.net/pub/infosystems/wais/Unido-LS6/
```

If you want the original freeWAIS instead (which you can certainly use, although it was last updated in 1996), you can get it from the Center for Networked Information Discovery and Retrieval. To get the main distribution directory so that you can choose the appropriate build, visit the following site:

```
ftp://cnidr.org/pub/NIDR.tools/freewais/
```

Whichever freeWAIS build you use will be a tarred and GNUZIPped file. To unpack the build, therefore, you must enter a command such as the following:

```
gunzip -c freeWAIS-0.X-whatever.tar.gz ¦ tar xvf -
```

freeWAIS comes with its own longer set of installation instructions within the distribution, so double-check the latest information for the build that you obtain to make sure that you don't skip any steps.

Implementing freeWAIS on Windows NT   A port of freeWAIS 0.3 is available for Windows NT from EMWAC (the European Microsoft Windows Academic Center) in its WAIS Toolkit. EMWAC's current version of the toolkit is 0.7. You should, however, check with EMWAC before obtaining the toolkit to find out what is the latest version. Versions are available for all types of Windows NT: 386-based, Alpha, and PowerPC. You can obtain the toolkit from the following site:

```
ftp://emwac.ed.ac.uk/pub/waistool/
```

After you obtain the ZIP file, decompress it to retrieve the files that compose the distribution. Move them to an NTFS drive partition, and then rename the file Waisindx.exe to Waisindex.exe.

If you plan to use the entire WAIS Toolkit with your server, put all three .exe programs into the %SYSTEMROOT%\SYSTEM32 directory (usually C:\WINNT\SYSTEM32).

TIP   If you are using UNIX, the WAIS program to query the WAIS indexes is called WAISQ. The query tool provided for Windows NT is called WAISLOOK. Keep this in mind when you see references to WAISQ, and just substitute WAISLOOK if you are using Windows NT.

Building a WAIS Database   Now that you have the software installed and running, you are ready to make a database (a set of index files).

The WAISINDEX program looks through your files and creates an index that the WAIS query tool can use later. This index consists of seven distinct files that are either binary or plain text, as shown in Table 31.3.

Table 31.3 WAIS Index Database Files

File Extension	Purpose	File Type
.Cat	A catalog of indexed files with a few lines of information about each one.	text
.Dct	A dictionary of indexed words.	binary
.Doc	A document table.	binary
.Fn	A filename table.	binary
.Hl	A headline table, featuring the descriptive text used to identify documents that the search returns.	binary
.Inv	An inverted file index.	binary
.Src	A structure for describing the source. The structure includes the creation date and other similar information.	text

The files with the extensions listed in Table 31.3 all share the same first name, as in Index.cat, Index.dct, Index.doc, and so on. You can name the first file anything you want, but if the file containing the HTML for the search form is called Index.html, INDEX is what you should use for the database. If your HTML file is called Default.htm (as it would be using EMWAC's HTTP server), DEFAULT is the correct first name for your database.

TIP Many Web servers have built-in support for WAIS databases and determine which files to look at by matching the first name of the HTML file with the first name of the database files. Therefore, naming your database files correctly is important if you expect the built-in support to function.

The command line options that you use when executing WAISINDEX determine these database files' contents. You might want to use a variety of options, depending on your objective and the nature of the files that you want to index. The following is a simple command line to create an index:

```
waisindex -d Data\database1 Data\*.html
```

This command line uses only one option, the -d switch, which specifies that the next argument is the name that you want to give the index. The command specifies that the name is DATA-BASE1 and that the database is to reside in the DATA directory. Arguments following the switches are the file names to index. In this example, the command indexes all the HTML files (those with an .html extension) in the DATA directory.

One of the more powerful features of WAISINDEX is that it enables you to index a variety of file types. To find out exactly which file types your version supports, check your version's documentation. The versions of WAISINDEX vary in the file-type support that they offer. In particular, freeWAIS-SF enables you to specify your own document types, and the EMWAC Toolkit supports such formats as Microsoft's Knowledge Base.

Part
VI

Ch
31

Accessing the WAIS Database   If your Web server has built-in support for WAIS (as many Web servers do), accessing the WAIS database is quite simple. You just create an HTML file to make the query and put the file in the same directory as the WAIS database files. (Remember that the first names of the HTML file and the database files must match.)

The HTML itself could not be simpler. Listing 31.18 shows a sample. All you have to do is include an <ISINDEX> tag somewhere on the form, and the Web server does the rest.

Listing 31.18   A Sample WAIS Search HTML

```
<HEAD>
<TITLE>Sample WAIS Search</TITLE>
</HEAD>
<BODY>
<H1>Sample WAIS Search</H1>
This page has a built-in index.  Give it a whirl!
<P>
<ISINDEX>
</BODY>
</HTML>
```

If your Web server doesn't support WAIS directly, you must use a CGI script to access the data. You might also want to use a script when you need to format the output or filter the input.

Your script must gather data from a fill-in form and run a query against the WAIS index, and then format the data appropriately for the visitor.

You can have your script perform the same function Web servers directly supporting WAIS perform: Call the WAISQ (or WAISLOOK) program. You can test this call from the following command line:

```
waisq -d -http Data\database1 stuff
```

In this simple example, you run a query against the DATA\DATABASE1 index files, using stuff as the query term. The result returns STDOUT as properly formatted HTML code, which makes the result perfect for use in a CGI script.

WAIS is so popular that dozens of scripts are available in the public domain for managing your queries. The following are the three most generic and useful scripts:

- WAIS.PL `ftp://ftp.ncsa.uiuc.edu/Web/httpd/Unix/ncsa_httpd/cgi/wais.tar.Z`
- Son-of-WAIS.PL `http://dewey.lib.ncsu.edu/staff/morgan/son-of-wais.html`
- Kid-of-WAIS.PL `http://www.cso.uiuc.edu/grady.htmlhttp://jordal.cso.uiuc.edu/kidofwais.pl`

Implementing Excite for Web Servers

Architext's popular search engine, Excite for Web Servers (EWS), is available for SunOS, Solaris, HP-UX, SGI Irix, AIX, BSDI UNIX, and Windows NT. EWS is a full-featured, fast indexing search tool based on the same technology as the Excite search service. Despite being a commercial search engine, it is available for use on your Web site for free. The only restriction in the user license is that you cannot use it to provide services for a third party (by establishing a service to compete with Excite, for example).

Excite enables people to enter queries in ordinary language, without using specialized query syntax. Excite claims that EWS understands plain English queries such as, "How to stay healthy by eating well" or "Learn to speak Tagalog." Queries using concepts are more likely to produce effective results than simple keyword searches, according to the company.

The user can choose either a concept-based search or a conventional keyword AND search. When you run a search, EWS lists search results in decreasing order of confidence. Each result consists of a title, an URL, a confidence rating, and an automatically generated summary of what the page is about. Relevance ranking is the default, but a click of the mouse enables the user to see the same results grouped by subject or topic.

Excite also supports relevance feedback, or query-by-example, searching. Using this technique, if you visit a found page and find it is pretty much what you're looking for, you can return to the search results and click the icon next to the listing to initiate another search. The subsequent search uses the found page as a parameter and returns similar pages.

Excite doesn't require a thesaurus to do concept-based searching, but the company indicates that an external thesaurus can improve results. Because a thesaurus is not necessary, adding support for new languages supposedly is not as difficult as with some other software. Architext claims that independent software developers can also write modules to support additional data file formats without facing too many obstacles.

Architext currently offers the software at no charge and sells annual support contracts. Further information about Excite for Web Servers can be found at

```
http://www.excite.com/navigate/
```

Quite a few sites are running the Excite search engine. One good example is the *Houston Chronicle* search page at

```
http://www.chron.com/content/search/
```

Installing Excite is described as Plug and Play, and it couldn't be easier. Download the distribution archive (along with the C++ libraries if you need them), run a shell script that asks a few questions, and you're just about ready to go. You need to run an administrative script that creates the index and another script that creates the search page. Both scripts are run from Web forms.

N O T E   EWS took 16 minutes, 40 seconds of CPU time to index my UNIX site; elapsed time was
23 minutes. It thoughtfully provided status pages that enabled me to keep tabs on the
progress of the indexing. EWS created an index that was around 7MB in size on a collection 4,490
files consisting of slightly more than 90MB. It even emailed me when it was done. ▪

After generating the index, you then generate the search page by using an HTML form. EWS
creates a page that includes a search form and a link to the custom-generated search script for
this collection. The resulting search page looks similar to that shown in Figure 31.9.

FIGURE 31.9

The Excite for Web
Servers search form
enables users to search
for keywords or
concepts.

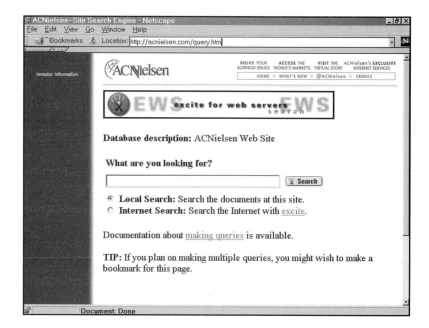

Notice that the form does not provide options for case sensitivity or Boolean searches. This is
because Excite employs concept matching to do its searching. The company suggests creating
queries that are descriptions of information rather than lists of keywords.

Excite for Web Servers will search for documents that are a best match for the words in your
query. Excite for Web Servers will also search for documents that are about the same concepts
that your query describes, so sometimes Excite for Web Servers will bring back articles that
don't mention any of the words in your original query.

The more search words, the better the query. Unfortunately, because the search algorithm is
proprietary, you have to trust that EWS will perform.

Excite for Web Servers uses Excite's proprietary Intelligent Concept Extraction (ICE) search
method (which is apparently not related to Christian Neuss' ICE engine). An excellent discussion of search strategies can be found on Excite's site at `http://www.excite.com/ice/`
`tech.html`. Although Excite does not provide a lot of detail about its patent-pending proprietary

search techniques, ICE is described as a means to find and score documents based on a correlation of their concepts as well as actual keywords. Excite states that this capability to go beyond simple Boolean searches of keywords is the key to its technology.

Using techniques similar to Latent Semantic Indexing (for more information on LSI, visit `http://n106.is.tokushima-u.ac.jp/member/kita/EPrint/index-LSI.html`), Excite claims that it can perform rapid searches without significant resources as well as maintain performance when the size of the index is scaled up. According to Excite, "Unlike other systems which need more time to perform a query as the size of the database increases, the Excite search engine can perform most queries in a constant amount of time."

A typical results page resembles that shown in Figure 31.10.

FIGURE 31.10

The results page from Excite for Web Servers includes links to the found file, a summary, and the confidence rating. The icon on each line enables you to submit a new query to find similar pages.

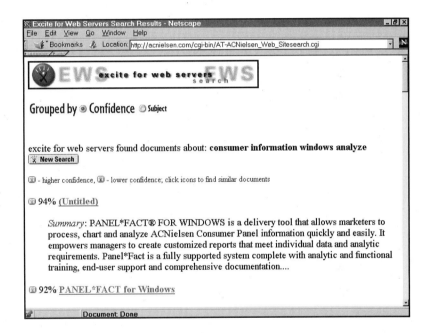

Part VI

Ch 31

Producing this search page took a little more than a second of CPU time and five or six seconds of elapsed time.

If you click the icon beside a page listing, Excite performs a query by example search using that document as the criteria.

A nice touch to the search display is the inclusion of confidence scores. Just the fact that the search hits are ranked conveys information. If you receive 20 responses with the highest confidence of only 50%, you might want to reformulate your search terms and try again rather than examining pages with low probability of satisfying your request.

EWS ignores stop words. These words are maintained in a table, but no way seems to be available to edit or add to them.

Excite for Web Servers is quite an impressive search tool that is easy to install and easy to implement. It creates a small index file and searches consume little system resources and are quite rapid. The inability to maintain the stop words tables and the lack of significant documentation on the operation of the system are its only drawbacks. Given its ease of use and strong features, however, such complaints are minor. ●

Server-Side Includes

by Jeffry Dwight and Melissa Niles

A Web server normally doesn't look at the files it passes along to browsers. It checks security—that is, it makes sure the caller has the right to read the file—but otherwise it just hands the file over.

A Web page is often more than one document. The most common addition is an inline graphic or two, plus a background graphic. As you learned in Chapters 28, "Programming CGI Scripts," and 29, "Custom Database Query Scripts," a page can contain information about other resources to display at the same time. When the browser gets back to the first page, it scans the page, determines whether more parts exist, and sends out requests for the remaining parts. This scanning and interpretation process is called *parsing*, and it normally happens on the client's side of the connection.

Under certain circumstances, though, you can talk the server into parsing the document before it ever gets to the client. Instead of blindly handing over the document, ignorant of the contents, the server can interpret the documents first. When this parsing occurs on the server's side of the connection, the process is called a *server-side include (SSI)*.

Why *include*? Because the first use of server-side parsing was to allow files to be included along with the one being referenced. Programmers love abbreviations, and SSI was established quickly. Changing the term later on, when other capabilities became popular too, seemed pointless.

If you are the Webmaster for a site, you might be responsible for 50, 100, or 250 pages. Because you're a conscientious Webmaster, you include your email address at the bottom of each page so that people can tell you about any problems. But what happens when your email address changes? Without SSI, you need to edit 50, 100, or 250 pages individually. Hope you're a good typist!

With SSI, however, you can include your email address on each page. Your email address actually resides in one spot—say, a file called webmaster.email.txt somewhere on your server—and each page uses SSI to include the contents of this file. Then, when your email address changes, all you have to do is update webmaster.email.txt with the new information. All 250 pages referencing it will have the new information automatically and instantly.

SSI can do more than include files. You can use special commands to include the current date and time. Other commands let you report the date that a file was last modified, or its size. Yet another command lets you execute a subprogram in the manner of CGI and incorporate its output right into the flow of the text.

N O T E The hallmark of SSI, generally, is that the end result is text. If you implement an SSI page hit counter, for instance, it would report the hits using text, not inline graphical images. From your browser's point of view, the document is all text, with nothing odd about it. SSI works without the browser's consent, participation, or knowledge. The magic is that the text is generated on-the-fly by SSI, not hard-coded when you created the HTML file. ▪

SSI Specification

Unfortunately, there is no formal set of specifications for SSI that applies to the servers of all manufacturers. There is NCSA SSI documentation available at `http://hoohoo.ncsa.uiuc.edu/docs/tutorials/includes.html`, but the syntax and usage given applies only to NCSA-style Web servers, like the Apache Web server. Even so, most Web servers follow the basic rules outlined by NCSA, and usually there are only minor variances from the basic rules. We'll cover the rules that apply to the NCSA's documentation because they'll probably be compatible with the Web server you are using.

- Unlike many protocols, options, and interfaces, SSI isn't governed by an Internet RFC (Request For Comment) or other standard. Each server manufacturer is free to implement SSI on an ad hoc basis, including whichever commands suit the development team's fancy and using whatever syntax strikes it as reasonable. Some servers, such as the freeware EMWAC server for Windows NT, don't support SSI at all.

- No one can give you a list of commands and syntax rules that apply in all situations. Most servers follow NCSA's specification up to a point. Although you may not find the exact commands, you can probably find functions similar to those in NCSA's arsenal.

- Because SSI isn't defined by a standard, server developers tend to modify their implementations of SSI more frequently than they modify other things. Even if I listed all the known servers and how they implement SSI today, the list would be out of date by the time you read this book.

- The only way to determine which SSI functions your server supports and which syntax your server uses for each command is to find and study your server's documentation. This chapter shows you the most common functions on the most common servers, and you'll probably find that the syntax is valid. However, the only authority is your particular server's documentation, so get a copy and keep it handy as you work through this chapter.

Part
VI

Ch
32

Configuring SSI

Although plenty of SSI FAQ (Frequently Asked Questions) sheets are available on the Internet, most of them are not that detailed. Configuring SSI to work on NCSA or Apache remains a common stumbling block. The other servers are a little easier to use. In addition to the NCSA site previously given, the following is one of the better sites for configuration information, and relates to the popular Apache server:

`http://www.apache.org/docs/mod/mod_include.html`

On most servers, SSI must be "turned on" before it will work. By default, SSI is not enabled. This is for your protection, because mismanaged SSI can be a huge security risk. For instance, what if you give any caller user on the system privileges to run any program or read any file anywhere on the server? Maybe nothing bad would happen, but that's not the safe way to bet.

In an NCSA or Apache (UNIX) environment, you enable SSI by editing the configuration files. You must have administrative privileges on the server to edit these files, although you can probably look at them with ordinary user privileges.

You need to change the following directives to enable SSI on NCSA or Apache servers:

- The `Options` directive—Used to enable SSI for particular directories. Edit `access.conf` and add `Includes` to the `Options` lines for the directories in which you want SSI to work. If a line reads `Options All`, SSI is already enabled for that directory. If it reads anything else, you must add `Includes` to the list of privileges on that line. Note that adding this line enables SSI in whatever directory you select and all subdirectories under it. So if you add this line to the server root section, you effectively enable SSI in every directory on the server.

- The `AddType` directive—Used to designate the MIME type for SSI files. For example, use

  `AddType text/x-server-parsed-html .shtml`

  to enable SSI parsing for all files ending with `.shtml`. This information is normally stored in `srm.conf`. Also use

  `AddType application/x-httpd-cgi .cgi`

  if you want to allow the `exec` command to work. Specifying `.cgi` here means that all your SSI scripts must have that extension. Most `srm.conf` files already have these two lines, but they are commented out. Just skip down to the bottom of the file and either uncomment the existing lines or add them manually.

Learning to find the configuration files for your server, and to use the `Options` and `AddType` directives, is all you need to do to edit the configuration files.

Enabling SSI on Windows NT machines is usually a matter of naming your HTML files correctly and clicking a check box somewhere in the Configuration dialog box. Process Software's Purveyor server uses `.htp` as the default filename extension for parsed files. Most other servers emulate NCSA and use `.shtml` instead. However, changing the extension is usually simple. Hunt up the MIME Types dialog box and add a MIME type of `text/x-server-parsed` for whichever filename extension you want. (As always, check your particular server's documentation to find out whether this technique works.)

One last note on configuration: most servers allow you either to require that all SSI executables be located in your `cgi-bin` or `Scripts` directory, or require this by default. If your server doesn't require this behavior by default, find the documentation to learn how to enable it. If the only programs that can be run are located in a known, controlled directory, the chances for errors (and hacking) are greatly reduced.

Using SSI in HTML

Now that you've enabled SSI on your server (or talked your system administrator into doing it for you), you're ready to learn how to use SSI. Sit back and relax a bit. What you've done already is by far the hardest part. From here on, you simply need to find the syntax in your particular server's documentation and try things out.

TIP Of special interest at this point is the one thing all SSI implementations have in common: all SSI commands are embedded within regular HTML comments.

Having embedded commands makes it easy to implement SSI while still making the HTML portable. A server that doesn't understand SSI passes the commands to the browser, and the browser ignores them because they're formatted as comments. A server that does understand SSI, however, does not pass the commands to the browser. Instead, the server parses the HTML from the top down, executing each comment-embedded command and replacing the comment with the output of the command.

This process is not as complicated as it sounds. You will go through some step-by-step examples later in this chapter, but first you'll examine HTML comments.

HTML Comment Syntax

Because anything not tagged in HTML is considered displayable text, comments must be tagged like any other directive. Tags are always marked with angle brackets—the less-than sign (<) and greater-than sign (>)—and a keyword, which may be as short as a single letter. For example, the familiar paragraph tag, <p>, is *empty*, so no closing tag is necessary. *Nonempty* tags, such as <A href...>...</a>, enclose displayable information, or "content," between the opening and closing tags.

The comment tag is empty and is of the form:

```
<!--comment text here-->
```

NOTE Although many servers and browsers can understand the nonstandard <!--comment text here> syntax, the remaining ones want the comment to end with -->, as required by the HTML specifications. Why? Because this lets you comment out sections of HTML code, including lines containing < and > symbols. Although not all servers and browsers require comments to end with -->, all of them will understand the syntax. Therefore, you're better off following the standard and surrounding your comments with <!-- at the front and --> at the end.

In summary, an HTML comment is anything with the format <!--commenttexthere-->. Browsers know to ignore this information, and servers don't even see it unless SSI is enabled.

Turning Comments into Commands

What happens to comments when SSI is enabled? The server looks for comments and examines the text inside them for commands. The server distinguishes comments that are really SSI commands from comments that are just comments by following a simple convention: inside the comment, all SSI commands start with a pound sign (#).

All SSI commands therefore begin with <!--#, followed by information meaningful to your server. Typically, each server supports a list of keywords, and it expects to find one of these keywords immediately following the pound sign. After the keyword are any parameters for the command—with syntax that varies both by command and by server—and then the standard comment closing (-->).

Syntax of SSI Commands

Most SSI commands have the form

```
<!--#command tagname="parameter" -->
```

where command is a keyword indicating what the server is supposed to do, tagname is a keyword indicating the type of parameter, and parameter is the user-defined value for that command.

Note that the first space character is after the command keyword. Most servers refuse to perform SSI if you don't follow this syntax exactly. SSI syntax is among the fussiest you'll encounter. For example, Microsoft's Internet Information Server (IIS) recognizes the following command:

```
<!--#include file=fname.inc-->
```

But only in lowercase. Different versions of IIS also gave new users problems with syntax peculiarities and restrictions. For example, some versions of IIS reportedly required an extra bang at the end of the comment tag:

```
<!--#include file=fname.inc--!>
```

And for some versions, files containing SSI had to end in the .stm extension—except for IIS 3.0 Active Server Page (.asp) files. The ASP DLLs introduced with IIS 3.0 and higher offer better SSI support, but only for ASP files.

The important thing to remember is that SSI syntax is highly idiosyncratic. Each server is different, and each server is fussy. Read the documentation!

Another implementation variation to watch for is that various servers have rules about which kinds of files can be included and what the default file extension is. O'Reilly's current WebSite Pro, for instance, assumes an extension of .html-ssi unless you configure it otherwise. Some others can only include files with a .txt extension, and yet others only allow an .stm extension.

Common SSI Commands

You can use SSI commands for a variety of tasks, including inserting (echoing) a value into the document, running a program, inserting the contents of a file into the document, setting the way file sizes appear, inserting the hit count or a file size into the document, and more. The following sections provide step-by-step examples of SSI commands in action.

N O T E Microsoft's IIS has some important peculiarities. IIS 2.0, and Microsoft's Personal Web Server, only support one SSI command—#include—and only in lowercase. IIS 3.0 supports the #include, #flastmod, #fsize, #echo, #config, and #exec directives. However, ASP versions 1.0 and 1.0b only support the #include directive. You can obtain more information on SSI in IIS in the installed documentation at http://yourserver/iasdocs/aspdocs/ssi/isiall.htm.

There are some security concerns with IIS and SSI. If you use the FrontPage Server Extensions with SSI, you should install the updated FrontPage Server Extensions, which do not allow the user to enter HTML into FrontPage feedback forms. If you allow the user to enter HTML, and you enable SSI, you are risking a serious security problem.

Apache has expanded its Web server to use Extended Server Side Includes (XSSI). XSSI provides additional functionality to SSI, including the use of condition statements. For more information, see `http://www.apache.org/docs/mod/mod_include.html`.

Most other servers support all of the commands listed here or a variant command to accomplish the same task. ▉

echo

The following is the syntax for `echo`:

```
The current date is <!--#echo var="DATE_LOCAL" -->
```

This syntax expands to something like the following when executed by an NCSA or Apache server:

```
The current date is 28 Feb 1999 12:00:13 GMT-6
```

The command is `echo`, the tagname is `var` (short for *variable*), and the parameter is `DATE_LOCAL`, which is a variable defined by the NCSA server that represents the local time on the server. When the server processes this line, it sees that the command requires it to echo (print) something. The `echo` command takes only one parameter, the keyword `var`, which is followed by a value specifying which variable you want to be echoed.

Most servers let you echo at least a subset of the standard CGI variables, if not all of them. You can usually find some special variables that are available only to SSI. `DATE_LOCAL` is one of them.

Again on the NCSA or Apache server, you can change the time format using the SSI `config` command, as follows:

```
<!--#config timefmt="format string" -->
```

Substitute a valid time format string for `"format string"` in the preceding example. The syntax of the format string is compatible with the string you pass to the UNIX `strftime()` system call. For example, `%a %d %b %y` gives you `Sun 28 Feb 99`.

Here are some other useful variables you can echo:

```
You are calling from <!--#echo var="REMOTE_ADDR" -->
```

This outputs a line like

```
You are calling from 38.247.88.150
```

Here's another example:

```
This page is <!--#echo var="DOCUMENT_NAME" -->
```

This yields a line resembling

```
This page is /home/joeblow/ssitest.shtml
```

Spend some time learning which variables your server lets you echo and the syntax for each. Related commands, such as the `config timefmt` command, often affect the way a variable is printed.

Part
VI

Ch
32

include

The include command typically takes one of two attributes, file or virtual, with a single parameter specifying which file to include. Using the file attribute, the included file must be something relative to, but not above, the current directory. Thus, ../ is disallowed, as is any absolute path, even if the httpd server process would normally have access there. The virtual attribute allows you to include any file relative to the document root. For example, /otherdir/file.html can be included as long as the Web server can access the file.

Other servers let you specify any path at all, or work with the operating system to limit access in a more flexible way than hard-coding forbidden paths. Purveyor, for instance, lets you use UNC file specifications, thus allowing your include to pull its data from anywhere reachable on the network. Regular Windows NT file permission requirements must be met, of course. Don't give the user ID under which Purveyor runs access to areas you don't want to include.

A typical use for the include command is a closing tag line at the bottom of a page. Let's say you're working in the directory /home/susan, and you create a simple text file called email.htm:

```
Click <A HREF="mailto:susan@nowhere.com">here</A> to send me email.
```

Next, you create index.shtml, which is the default page for /home/susan, as follows:

```
<HTML>
<HEAD><TITLE>Susan's Home Page</TITLE></HEAD>
<BODY>
<H1>Susan's Home Page</H1>
Hi, I'm Susan.  <!--#include file="email.htm"-->
See you later!
</BODY>
</HTML>
```

When index.shtml appears, the contents of email.htm are inserted, resulting in the following being sent to the browser:

```
<HTML>
<HEAD><TITLE>Susan's Home Page</TITLE></HEAD>
<BODY>
<H1>Susan's Home Page</H1>
Hi, I'm Susan.  Click <A HREF="mailto:susan@nowhere.com">here</A>
to send me email.  See you later!
</BODY>
</HTML>
```

You can use the email.htm file in as many other files as you want, limiting the places where you need to change Susan's email address to exactly one.

exec

You can turn off the exec command on some servers while leaving other SSI functions enabled. If you are the system administrator of your server, study your setup and security arrangements carefully before enabling exec.

exec is a very powerful and almost infinitely flexible command. An SSI exec is very much like regular CGI in that it spawns a subprocess and lets it open files, provide output, and do just about anything else an executable can do.

> **N O T E**   On Netscape and NCSA servers, your SSI executable must be named *.cgi and probably will have to live in a centrally managed cgi-bin directory. (The Apache server gives you a bit more flexibility, allowing you to control the extensions of programs used for SSI.) Check your particular server's documentation and your system setup to find out. Again, keep the documentation handy—you'll need it again in just a moment. ■

The exec command typically takes one attribute, most frequently called cgi but also exe, script, and cmd on various servers. Some servers let you specify two different ways to execute programs. For example, <!--#exec cgi or <!--#exec exe usually means to launch a program and treat it just like a CGI program. <!--#exec cmd usually means to launch a shell script (called a *batch file* in the PC world). Shell scripts are often, but not always, treated specially by the server. In addition to launching the shell, or command processor, and passing the script name as the parameter, the server often forges the standard MIME headers, relieving the script of that duty. You have only one way of knowing how your server handles this process: If you haven't found your server's documentation yet, stop right now and get it. There are no rules of thumb, no standards, and no rational ways to figure out the syntax and behavior.

Here's a trivial example of using a shell script on a UNIX platform to add a line of text. Start with a file called myfile.shtml, which contains the following somewhere in the body:

```
Now is the time
<!--#exec cgi="/cgi-bin/foo.cgi" -->
to come to the aid of their country.
```

Then create the shell script foo.cgi and place it in the /cgi-bin directory:

```
#!/bin/sh
echo "for all good persons"
```

When you then access myfile.shtml, you see the following:

Now is the time for all good persons to come to the aid of their country.

Note that this example assumes you have configured your server to require that SSI scripts live in the /cgi-bin subdirectory, and that you have designated .cgi as the correct extension for scripts.

> **N O T E**   Some implementations of SSI allow you to include command-line arguments. Sadly, NCSA isn't one of them (although Apache is). Each server has its own way of handling command-line arguments, of course. Consult your trusty documentation yet again to find out if, and how, your server allows this feature.

The SPRY Mosaic server from Compuserve actually uses an args key for arguments. A typical SPRY Mosaic script might be invoked the following way:

```
<!--#exec script="scriptname.exe" args="arg1 arg2 arg3" -->
```

Process Software's Purveyor allows arguments, even though no documentation is available to support the mechanism. With Purveyor, you supply the arguments exactly as you would on a real command line:

```
<!--#exec exe="\serverroot\cgi-bin\scriptname arg1 arg2 arg3" -->
```

Other Commands

Your server probably supports as many as a dozen commands in addition to the three covered in the preceding sections. Following are some of the most common, with a brief explanation of each:

- `config errmsg="message text"`   Controls which message is sent back to the client if the server encounters an error while trying to parse the document.
- `config timefmt="format string"`   Sets the format for displaying time and date information from that point in the document on.
- `sizefmt`   Format varies widely among servers. This command controls how file sizes appear—as bytes, formatted bytes (1,234,567), kilobytes (1234K), or megabytes (1M).
- `fsize file="filespec"`   Reports the size of the specified file.
- `flastmod file="filespec"`   Reports the last modification date of the specified file.
- `counter type="type"`   Displays the count of hits to the server as of that moment.

Sample SSI Programs

This section presents the complete C code for several useful SSI programs. Some of them are platform-independent; others make use of some special features in the Windows NT operating system. You can find the source code, plus compiled executables for the 32-bit Windows NT/ Windows 95 environment, on the CD-ROM accompanying this book.

SSIDump

The SSIDump program is a handy debugging utility that dumps the SSI environment variables and command-line arguments back to the browser (see Listing 32.1).

Listing 32.1   *ssidump.c*—SSI Program for Dumping SSI Environment Variables

```
// SSIDUMP.C
// This program dumps the SSI environment variables
// to the screen.  The code is platform-independent.
// Compile it for your system and place it in your
// CGI-BIN directory.

#include <windows.h>  // only required for Windows machines
#include <stdio.h>

void main(int argc, char * argv[]) {
```

```
        // First declare our variables.  This program
        // only uses one, i, a generic integer counter.

        int i;

        // Print some nice-looking header
        // information.  Note that unlike a CGI
        // program, there is no need to include the
        // standard HTTP headers.

        printf("<H1>SSI Environment Dump</H1>\n");
        printf("<B>Command-Line Arguments:</B>\n");

        // Now print the command-line arguments.
        // By convention, arg[0] is the path to this
        // program at run-time.  args[1] through
        // arg[argc-1] are passed to the program as
        // parameters.  Only some servers will allow
        // command-line arguments.  We'll use a nice
        // bulleted list format to make it readable:

printf("<ul>\n");
        for (i = 0; i < argc; i++) {
            printf("<li>argv[%i]=%s\n",i,argv[i]);
        }
        printf("</ul>\n");

        // Now print out whatever environment variables
        // are visible to us.  We'll use the bulleted
        // list format again:

        printf("<b>Environment Variables:</b>\n<ul>\n");
        i = 0;
        while (_environ[i])
    {
            printf("<li>%s\n",_environ[i]);
            i++;
    }
        printf("</ul>\n");

        // Flush the output and we're done

        fflush(stdout);
        return;
    }
```

RQ

The RQ program hunts up a random quotation or other bit of text from a file and outputs it. The quotation file uses a simple format: Each entry must be contiguous, but can span any number of lines. Entries are separated by a single blank line. Listing 32.2 is a sample quotation file. The entries were chosen randomly by RQ itself. Make of that what you will.

Listing 32.2 *Rq.txt*—Sample Text File for Use with the *RQ* Program

```
KEEPING THIS A HAPPY FILE:
o All entries should start flush-left.
o Entries may be up to 8K in length.
o Entries must be at least one line.
o Entries may contain 1-9999 lines (8K max).
o Line length is irrelevant; CRs are ignored.
o Entries are separated by ONE blank line.
o The last entry must be followed by a blank line, too.
o The first entry (these lines here) will never get picked,
o so we use it to document the file.
o Length of the file doesn't change retrieval time.
o Any line beginning with "--" it is treated as a byline.
o It must be the last line in the block, otherwise the
o quotation might get cut off.
o You can use HTML formatting tags.

Drunk is feeling sophisticated when you can't say it.
--Anon

What really flatters a man is that you think him worth
flattery.
--George Bernard Shaw

True patriotism hates injustice in its own land more
than anywhere else.
--Clarence Darrow

If by "fundies" we mean "fanatics," that's okay with
me, but in that case shouldn't we call them fannies?
--Damon Knight

My <I>other</I> car is <I>also</I> a Porsche.
--Bumper Sticker

The death sentence is a necessary and efficacious means for
the Church to attain its ends when rebels against it disturb
the ecclesiastical unity, especially obstinate heretics who
cannot be restrained by any other penalty from continuing to
disturb ecclesiastical order.
--Pope Leo XIII
```

Note that although the preceding sample file has text quotations in it, you can just as easily use RQ for random links or graphics. For random links or graphics, leave off the bylines and use standard <A HREF> format. You can even use RQ for single words or phrases used to complete a sentence in real-time. For example, the phrases in parentheses can come from an RQ file to complete this sentence: "If you don't like this page, you're (a pusillanimous slug) (a cultured person) (pond scum) (probably dead) (quite perceptive) (drunk) (an editor)." I'll leave it to you to figure out which are compliments and which are insults.

NOTE RQ has security precautions built in. It does not read from a file that's located anywhere other than the same directory as RQ itself or a subdirectory under it. This precaution prevents malicious users from misusing RQ to read files elsewhere on the server. It looks for two periods in case the user tries to evade the path requirement by ascending the directory tree. It checks for a double-backslash in case it finds itself on an NT server and the user tries to slip in a UNC file specification. Finally, it checks for a colon in case the user tries to specify a drive letter. If RQ finds any of these situations, it writes out an error message and dies. ▪

RQ can accept the name of a quotation file from a command-line argument. If you're unlucky enough to run RQ on a server that doesn't support command-line arguments, or if you leave the command-line arguments off, RQ tries to open Rq.txt in the same directory it's in. You can have multiple executables, each reading a different file, simply by having copies of RQ with different names. RQ looks for its executable name at runtime, strips the extension, and adds .txt. So if you have a copy of RQ named RQ2, it opens Rq2.txt.

Listing 32.3 shows the code for the rq.c program.

Listing 32.3   *rq.c*—A Simple Random Quotation Script Used as an SSI

```
// RQ.C
// This program reads a text file and extracts a random
// quotation from it.  If a citation line is found, it
// treats it as a citation; otherwise, all text is treated
// the same.  HTML tags may be embedded in the text.

// RQ is mostly platform-independent.  You'll have to change
// path element separators to the correct slash if you
// compile for UNIX.  There are no platform-specific system
// calls, though, so a little bit of customization should
// enable the code to run on any platform.

#include <windows.h>  // only required for Windows
#include <stdio.h>
#include <stdlib.h>
#include <io.h>

char      buffer[16000];      // temp holding buffer

void main(int argc, char * argv[]) {
      FILE          *f;          // file-info structure
      fpos_t        fpos;        // file-pos structure
      long          flen;        // length of the file
      char          fname[80];   // the file name
      long          lrand;       // a long random number
      BOOL          goodpos;     // switch
      char          *p;          // generic pointer
      char          *soq;        // start-of-quote pointer
      char          *eoq;        // end-of-quote pointer

      // Seed the random number generator
```

Part

VI

Ch

32

continues

Listing 32.3   Continued

```
srand(GetTickCount());

// Set all I/O streams to unbuffered

setvbuf(stdin,NULL,_IONBF,0);
setvbuf(stdout,NULL,_IONBF,0);

// Open the quote file

// If a command-line argument is present, treat it as
// the file name.  But first check it for validity!

if (argc > 1) {
    p = strstr(argv[1],"..");
    if (p==NULL) p = strstr(argv[1],"\\\\");
    if (p==NULL) p = strchr(argv[1],':');

    // If .., \\, or : found, reject the filename
    if (p) {
        printf("Invalid relative path "
                "specified: %s",argv[1]);
        return;
    }

    // Otherwise append it to our own path
    strcpy(fname,argv[0]);
    p = strrchr(fname,'\\');
    if (p) *p = '\0';
    strcat(fname,"\\");
    strcat(fname,argv[1]);

} else {

    // No command-line parm found, so use our
    // executable name, minus our extension, plus
    // .txt as the filename

    strcpy(fname,_pgmptr);
    p = strrchr(fname,'.');
    if (p) strcpy(p,".txt");
}

// We have a filename, so try to open the file

f = fopen(fname,"r");

// If open failed, die right here

if (f==NULL) {
    printf("Could not open '%s' for read.",fname);
    return;
}
```

```
// Get total length of file in bytes.
// We do this by seeking to the end and then
// reading the offset of our current position.
// There are other ways of getting this
// information, but this way works almost
// everywhere, whereas the other ways are
// platform-dependent.

fseek(f,0,SEEK_END);
fgetpos(f,&fpos);
flen = (long) fpos;

// Seek to a random point in the file.  Loop through
// the following section until we find a block of text
// we can use.

goodpos = FALSE;            // goes TRUE when we're done

while (!goodpos) {

    // Make a random offset into the file.  Generate
    // the number based on the file's length.

    if (flen > 65535) {
        lrand = MAKELONG(rand(),rand());
    } else {
        lrand = MAKELONG(rand(),0);
    }

    // If our random number is less than the length
    // of the file, use it as an offset.  Seek there
    // and read whatever we find.

    if (lrand < flen) {
        fpos = lrand;
        fsetpos(f,&fpos);
        if (fread(buffer, sizeof(char),
            sizeof(buffer),f) !=0 ) {
            soq=NULL;
            eoq=NULL;
            soq = strstr(buffer,"\n\n");
            if (soq) eoq = strstr(soq+2,"\n\n");
            if (eoq) {
                // skip the first CR
                soq++;
                // and the one for the blank line
                soq++;
                // mark end of string
                *eoq='\0';
                // look for citation marker
                p = strstr(soq,"\n--");
                // if found, exempt it & remember
                if (p) {
                    *p='\0';
                    p++;
```

continues

Part

VI

Ch

32

Listing 32.3   Continued

```
                                    }
                                    // print the quotation
                                    printf(soq);
                                    if (p)
                                    // and citation if any
                                    printf("<br><cite>%s</cite>",p);
                                    // exit the loop
                                    goodpos=TRUE;
                                }
                            }
                        }
                    }

            fclose(f);
            fflush(stdout);
                return;
        }
```

XMAS

The XMAS program prints out the number of days remaining until Christmas. It recognizes Christmas Day and Christmas Eve as special cases, and solves the general case problem through brute force. You can certainly find more elegant and efficient ways to calculate elapsed time, but this method doesn't rely on any platform-specific date/time routines.

The code in Listing 32.4 is short enough and uncomplicated enough that it needs no further explanation.

Listing 32.4   *xmas.c*—A Simple SSI Script that Counts Down the Days Until Christmas

```
// CHRISTMAS.C
// This program calculates the number of days between
// the time of invocation and the nearest upcoming 25
// December.  It reports the result as a complete sentence.
// The code is platform-independent.


#include <windows.h>      // only required for Windows
#include <stdio.h>
#include <time.h>

void main() {

        // Some variables, all self-explanatory

        struct tm       today;
        time_t          now;
        int             days;
```

```
// Get the current date, first retrieving the
// Universal Coordinated Time, then converting it
// to local time, stored in the today tm structure.

time(&now);
today = *localtime(&now);
mktime(&today);

// month is zero-based (0=jan, 1=feb, etc);
// day is one-based
// year is one-based
// so Christmas Eve is 11/24

// Is it Christmas Eve?

if ((today.tm_mon == 11) && (today.tm_mday==24)) {
    printf("Today is Christmas Eve!");

} else {

    // Is it Christmas Day?

    if ((today.tm_mon == 11) && (today.tm_mday==25)) {
        printf("Today is Christmas Day!");

    } else {

        // Calculate days by adding one and comparing
        // for 11/25 repeatedly

        days =0;
        while ( (today.tm_mon  != 11) |
                (today.tm_mday != 25) )
        {
            days++;
            today.tm_mday = today.tm_mday + 1;
            mktime(&today);
        }

        // Print the result using the customary
        // static verb formation

        printf("There are %i days until Christmas."
                ,days);
    }
}

// Flush the output and we're done

fflush(stdout);
return;
}
```

Part
VI

Ch
32

HitCount

The HitCount program creates that all-time favorite, a page's hit count. The output is a cardinal number (1, 2, 3, and so on) and nothing else. HitCount works only on Windows NT. See Listing 32.5 for the C source code.

Listing 32.5   *hitcount.c*—A Counter Script Used as an SSI

```
// HITCOUNT.C
// This SSI program produces a cardinal number page hit
// count based on the environment variable SCRIPT_NAME.

#include <windows.h>
#include <stdio.h>
#define     ERROR_CANT_CREATE "HitCount:  Cannot open/create
➥registry key."
#define  ERROR_CANT_UPDATE "HitCount:  Cannot update registry key."
#define  HITCOUNT "Software\\Greyware\\HitCount\\Pages"

void main(int argc, char * argv[]) {
     char     szHits[33];      // number of hits for this page
     char     szDefPage[80];   // system default pagename
     char     *p;              // generic pointer
     char     *PageName;       // pointer to this page's name
     long     dwLength=33;     // length of temporary buffer
     long     dwType;          // registry value type code
     long     dwRetCode;       // generic return code from API
     HKEY     hKey;            // registry key handle

     // Determine where to get the page name.  A command-
     // line argument overrides the SCRIPT_NAME variable.

     if ((argc==2) && ((*argv[1]=='/') ¦ (*argv[1]=='\\')))
          PageName = argv[1];
     else
          PageName = getenv("SCRIPT_NAME");

     // If invoked from without SCRIPT_NAME or args, die

     if (PageName==NULL)
     {
          printf("HitCount 1.0.b.960121\n"
                  "Copyright (c) 1995,96 Greyware "
                  "Automation Products\n\n"
                  "Documentation available online from "
                  "Greyware's Web server:\n"
                  "http://www.greyware.com/"
                  "greyware/software/freeware.htp\n\n");
     }
     else
     {

          // Open the registry key
```

```
dwRetCode = RegOpenKeyEx (
    HKEY_LOCAL_MACHINE,
    HITCOUNT,
    0,
    KEY_EXECUTE,
    &hKey);

// If open failed because key doesn't exist,
// create it

if ((dwRetCode==ERROR_BADDB)
    || (dwRetCode==ERROR_BADKEY)
    || (dwRetCode==ERROR_FILE_NOT_FOUND))
    dwRetCode = RegCreateKey(
        HKEY_LOCAL_MACHINE,
        HITCOUNT,
        &hKey);

// If couldn't open or create, die

if (dwRetCode != ERROR_SUCCESS) {
    printf (ERROR_CANT_CREATE);

} else {

    // Get the default page name

    dwLength = sizeof(szDefPage);
    dwRetCode = RegQueryValueEx (
        hKey,
        "(default)",
        0,
        &dwType,
        szDefPage,
        &dwLength);

    if ((dwRetCode == ERROR_SUCCESS)
        && (dwType == REG_SZ)
        && (dwLength > 0)) {
        szDefPage[dwLength] = '\0';
    } else {
        strcpy(szDefPage,"default.htm");
    }

    // If current page uses default page name,
    // strip the page name

    _strlwr(PageName);
    p = strrchr(PageName,'/');
    if (p==NULL) p = strrchr(PageName,'\\');
    if (p) {
        p++;
        if (stricmp(p,szDefPage)==0) *p = '\0';
    }
```

continues

Listing 32.5 Continued

```c
// Get this page's information

dwLength = sizeof(szHits);
dwRetCode = RegQueryValueEx (
    hKey,
    PageName,
    0,
    &dwType,
    szHits,
    &dwLength);

if ((dwRetCode == ERROR_SUCCESS)
    && (dwType == REG_SZ)
    && (dwLength >0)) {
    szHits[dwLength] = '\0';
} else {
    strcpy (szHits, "1");
}

// Close the registry key

dwRetCode = RegCloseKey(hKey);

// Print this page's count

printf("%s",szHits);

// Bump the count by one for next call

_ltoa ((atol(szHits)+1), szHits, 10);

// Write the new value back to the registry

dwRetCode = RegOpenKeyEx (
    HKEY_LOCAL_MACHINE,
    HITCOUNT,
    0,
    KEY_SET_VALUE,
    &hKey);

if (dwRetCode==ERROR_SUCCESS) {
    dwRetCode = RegSetValueEx(
        hKey,
        PageName,
        0,
        REG_SZ,
        szHits,
        strlen(szHits));
    dwRetCode = RegCloseKey(hKey);
} else {
    printf(ERROR_CANT_UPDATE);
}
```

```
                }
            }
            fflush(stdout);
            return;
        }
```

HitCount takes advantage of one of NT's unsung glories, the system Registry. Counters for other platforms need to worry about creating and updating a database file, file locking, concurrency, and a number of other messy issues. HitCount uses the hierarchical Registry as a database, letting the operating system take care of concurrent access.

HitCount is actually remarkably simple compared to other counters. It uses the SCRIPT_NAME environment variable to determine the name of the current page. Therefore, you have no worries about passing unique strings as parameters. HitCount takes the page name and either creates or updates a Registry entry for it. The information is always available and can be rapidly accessed.

HitCount works on most NT servers. One notable exception is WebSite. WebSite supplies the SCRIPT_NAME variable, but also supplies spurious arguments in the argv[] array. To make HitCount work with WebSite, delete the section of code that checks for command-line arguments.

HitCount, like the other samples in this chapter, is freeware from Greyware Automation Products (http://www.greyware.com/). You can find more extensive documentation online at its site. The code is unmodified from the code distributed by Greyware for a good reason: Registry keys are named, so having multiple versions of the software running around loose with different key names just wouldn't do. Therefore, the code retains the key names for compatibility.

The only bit of configuration you might need to do is if your server's default page name isn't default.htm. In that case, add this key to the Registry before using HitCount for the first time:

```
HKEY_LOCAL_MACHINE
    \Software
        \Greyware
            \HitCount
                \Pages
```

After you create the key, add a value under Pages. The name of the value is (default) and its type is REG_SZ. Fill in the name of your system's default page. Case doesn't matter.

HitCount uses this information to keep from falsely distinguishing between a hit to http://www.yourserver.com/ and one to http://www.yourserver.com/default.name. Some Web servers would report these two as different URLs in the SCRIPT_NAME environment variable, even though they refer to the same physical page. By setting the default in the registry, you tell HitCount to strip the page name off, if found, thus reconciling any potential problems before they arise. The default is default.htm, so you need to set this value only if your SSI pages use a different name.

HitCntth

HitCntth is a variation of HitCount. Its output is an ordinal number (1st, 2nd, 3rd, and so on). You probably understand the name by now. HitCntth provides the HitCount-th number. Get it?

HitCntth is designed to work alongside HitCount. It uses the same Registry keys, so you can switch from one format to the other without having to reset the counter or worry about duplicate counts. See the HitCount documentation for configuration details.

Creating an ordinal takes a bit more work than printing a cardinal number because the English method of counting is somewhat arbitrary. HitCntth looks for exceptions and handles them separately, and then throws a *th* on the end of anything left over. Otherwise, the function is identical to HitCount. Listing 32.6 shows the source code for HitCntth.

Listing 32.6 *hitcntth.c*—A Counter Script that Provides the Count Using Ordinal Numbers

```
// HITCNTTH.C
// This SSI program produces an ordinal number page hit
// count based on the environment variable SCRIPT_NAME.

#include <windows.h>
#include <stdio.h>
#define     ERROR_CANT_CREATE "HitCntth:  Cannot open/create
➥registry key."
#define  ERROR_CANT_UPDATE "HitCntth:  Cannot update registry key."
#define  HITCOUNT "Software\\Greyware\\HitCount\\Pages"

void main(int argc, char * argv[]) {
    char     szHits[36];      // number of hits for this page
    char     szDefPage[80];   // system default pagename
    char     *p;              // generic pointer
    char     *PageName;       // pointer to this page's name
    long     dwLength=36;     // length of temporary buffer
    long     dwType;          // registry value type code
    long     dwRetCode;       // generic return code from API
    HKEY     hKey;            // registry key handle


    // Determine where to get the page name.  A command-
    // line argument overrides the SCRIPT_NAME variable.

    if ((argc==2) && ((*argv[1]=='/') | (*argv[1]=='\\')))
        PageName = argv[1];
    else
        PageName = getenv("SCRIPT_NAME");

    // If invoked from without SCRIPT_NAME or args, die
    if (PageName==NULL)
    {
        printf("HitCntth 1.0.b.960121\n"
               "Copyright (c) 1995,96 Greyware "
               "Automation Products\n\n"
```

```
                        "Documentation available online from "
                        "Greyware's Web server:\n"
                        "http://www.greyware.com/"
                        "greyware/software/freeware.htp\n\n");
}
else
{

    // Open the registry key

    dwRetCode = RegOpenKeyEx (
        HKEY_LOCAL_MACHINE,
        HITCOUNT,
        0,
        KEY_EXECUTE,
        &hKey);

    // If open failed because key doesn't exist,
    // create it

    if ((dwRetCode==ERROR_BADDB)
        || (dwRetCode==ERROR_BADKEY)
        || (dwRetCode==ERROR_FILE_NOT_FOUND))
        dwRetCode = RegCreateKey(
            HKEY_LOCAL_MACHINE,
            HITCOUNT,
            &hKey);

    // If couldn't open or create, die

    if (dwRetCode != ERROR_SUCCESS) {
        printf (ERROR_CANT_CREATE);
    } else {    // Get the default page name
        dwLength = sizeof(szDefPage);
        dwRetCode = RegQueryValueEx (
            hKey,
            "(default)",
            0,
            &dwType,
            szDefPage,
            &dwLength);
        if ((dwRetCode == ERROR_SUCCESS)
            && (dwType == REG_SZ)
            && (dwLength > 0)) {
            szDefPage[dwLength] = '\0';
        } else {
            strcpy(szDefPage,"default.htm");
        }

        // If current page uses default page name,
        // strip the page name

        _strlwr(PageName);
        p = strrchr(PageName,'/');
```

continues

Listing 32.6 Continued

```c
        if (p==NULL) p = strrchr(PageName,'\\');
        if (p) {
            p++;
            if (stricmp(p,szDefPage)==0) *p = '\0';
        }

        // Get this page's information

        dwLength = sizeof(szHits);
        dwRetCode = RegQueryValueEx (
            hKey,
            PageName,
            0,
            &dwType,
            szHits,
            &dwLength);
        if ((dwRetCode == ERROR_SUCCESS)
            && (dwType == REG_SZ)
            && (dwLength >0)) {
            szHits[dwLength] = '\0';
        } else {
            strcpy (szHits, "1\0");
        }

        // Close the registry key

        dwRetCode = RegCloseKey(hKey);

        // Check for special cases:
        // look at count mod 100 first

        switch ((atol(szHits)) % 100) {
            case 11:    // 11th, 111th, 211th, etc.
                printf("%sth",szHits);
                break;
            case 12:    // 12th, 112th, 212th, etc.
                printf("%sth",szHits);
                break;
            case 13:    // 13th, 113th, 213th, etc.
                printf("%sth",szHits);
                break;
            default:
                // no choice but to look at last
                // digit
                switch (szHits[strlen(szHits)-1]) {
                    case '1':    // 1st, 21st, 31st
                        printf("%sst",szHits);
                        break;
                    case '2':    // 2nd, 22nd, 32nd
                        printf("%snd",szHits);
                        break;
                    case '3':    // 3rd, 23rd, 36rd
                        printf("%srd",szHits);
                        break;
```

```
                        default:
                                printf("%sth",szHits);
                                break;
                        }
                }
                // Bump the count by one for next call
                _ltoa ((atol(szHits)+1), szHits, 10);

                // Write the new value back to the registry
                dwRetCode = RegOpenKeyEx (
                    HKEY_LOCAL_MACHINE,
                    HITCOUNT,
                    0,
                    KEY_SET_VALUE,
                    &hKey);
                if (dwRetCode==ERROR_SUCCESS) {
                    dwRetCode = RegSetValueEx(
                        hKey,
                        PageName,
                        0,
                        REG_SZ,
                        szHits,
                        strlen(szHits));
                    dwRetCode = RegCloseKey(hKey);
                } else {
                    printf(ERROR_CANT_UPDATE);
                }
            }
        }
        fflush(stdout);
        return;
}
```

FirstHit

FirstHit is a companion program for HitCount or HitCntth. It tracks the date and time of the first hit to any page. FirstHit uses the same registry scheme as HitCount or HitCntth, but it stores its information in a different key. You have to set the (default) page name here, too, if it's something other than Default.htm. The proper key is

```
HKEY_LOCAL_MACHINE
    \Software
        \Greyware
            \FirstHit
                \Pages
```

You may notice a pattern in a number of areas. First, all these programs use the registry to store information. Second, they use a similar naming scheme—a hierarchical one. Third, they share great quantities of code. Some of these functions can be moved into a library, and probably should be.

You use FirstHit, typically, right after using HitCount. To produce the line You are visitor 123 since Fri 19 Sep 1997 at 01:13 on the Purveyor server, your source would look like this:

```
You are visitor <!--#exec exe="cgi-bin\hitcount" --> since
<!--#exec exe="cgi-bin\firsthit" -->.
```

Listing 32.7 shows the source code. It's no more complicated than HitCount or HitCntth, and writes to the Registry only the first time any page is hit. Thereafter, it just retrieves the information it wrote before.

Listing 32.7 *firsthit.c*—Provides Information on when the File Was First Hit

```
// FIRSTHIT.C
// This SSI program keeps track of the date and time
// a page was first hit.  Useful in conjunction with
// HitCount or HitCntth.

#include <windows.h>
#include <stdio.h>
#define     ERROR_CANT_CREATE "FirstHit:  Cannot open/create
➥registry key."
#define  ERROR_CANT_UPDATE "FirstHit:  Cannot update registry key."
#define  FIRSTHIT "Software\\Greyware\\FirstHit\\Pages"
#define     sdatefmt "ddd dd MMM yyyy"

void main(int argc, char * argv[]) {
    char      szDate[128];      // number of hits for this page
    char      szDefPage[80];    // system default pagename
    char      *p;               // generic pointer
    char      *PageName;        // pointer to this page's name
    long      dwLength=127;     // length of temporary buffer
    long      dwType;           // registry value type code
    long      dwRetCode;        // generic return code from API
    HKEY      hKey;             // registry key handle
    SYSTEMTIME st;              // system time
    char      szTmp[128];       // temporary string storage

    // Determine where to get the page name.  A command-
    // line argument overrides the SCRIPT_NAME variable.

    if ((argc==2) && ((*argv[1]=='/') | (*argv[1]=='\\')))
        PageName = argv[1];
    else
        PageName = getenv("SCRIPT_NAME");

    // If invoked from without SCRIPT_NAME or args, die
    if (PageName==NULL)
    {
        printf("FirstHit 1.0.b.960121\n"
                "Copyright (c) 1995,96 Greyware "
                "Automation Products\n\n"
                "Documentation available online from "
                "Greyware's Web server:\n"
                "http://www.greyware.com/"
                "greyware/software/freeware.htp\n\n");
    }
    else
```

```
{
    // Open the registry key
    dwRetCode = RegOpenKeyEx (
        HKEY_LOCAL_MACHINE,
        FIRSTHIT,
        0,
        KEY_EXECUTE,
        &hKey);

        // If open failed because key doesn't exist,
    // create it
    if ((dwRetCode==ERROR_BADDB)
        || (dwRetCode==ERROR_BADKEY)
        || (dwRetCode==ERROR_FILE_NOT_FOUND))
            dwRetCode = RegCreateKey(
                HKEY_LOCAL_MACHINE,
                FIRSTHIT,
                &hKey);

    // If couldn't open or create, die
    if (dwRetCode != ERROR_SUCCESS)
    {
        strcpy(szDate,ERROR_CANT_CREATE);
    }
    else
    {
        // Get the default page name
        dwLength = sizeof(szDefPage);
        dwRetCode = RegQueryValueEx (
            hKey,
            "(default)",
            0,
            &dwType,
            szDefPage,
            &dwLength);
        if ((dwRetCode == ERROR_SUCCESS)
            && (dwType == REG_SZ)
            && (dwLength > 0)) {
            szDefPage[dwLength] = '\0';
        } else {
            strcpy(szDefPage,"default.htm");
        }

        // If current page uses default page name,
        // strip the page name
        _strlwr(PageName);
        p = strrchr(PageName,'/');
        if (p==NULL) p = strrchr(PageName,'\\');
        if (p) {
            p++;
            if (stricmp(p,szDefPage)==0) *p = '\0';
        }

        // Get this page's information
        dwLength = sizeof(szDate);
```

continues

Part

VI

Ch

32

Listing 32.7 Continued

```
dwRetCode = RegQueryValueEx (
    hKey,
    PageName,
    0,
    &dwType,
    szDate,
    &dwLength);
if ((dwRetCode == ERROR_SUCCESS)
    && (dwType == REG_SZ)
    && (dwLength >0)) {
    szDate[dwLength] = '\0';
} else {
    GetLocalTime(&st);
    GetDateFormat(
        0,
        0,
        &st,
        sdatefmt,
        szTmp,
        sizeof(szTmp));
    sprintf(
        szDate,
        "%s at %02d:%02d",
        szTmp,
        st.wHour,
        st.wMinute);
     // Write the new value back to the
    // registry
    dwRetCode = RegOpenKeyEx (
        HKEY_LOCAL_MACHINE,
        FIRSTHIT,
        0,
        KEY_SET_VALUE,
        &hKey);
    if (dwRetCode==ERROR_SUCCESS)
    {
        dwRetCode = RegSetValueEx(
            hKey,
            PageName,
            0,
            REG_SZ,
            szDate,
            strlen(szDate));
        dwRetCode = RegCloseKey(hKey);
    }
    else
    {
        strcpy(szDate,ERROR_CANT_UPDATE);
    }
}

// Close the registry key
dwRetCode = RegCloseKey(hKey);
}
```

```
        printf("%s",szDate);
    }

    fflush(stdout);
    return;
}
```

LastHit

LastHit is yet another Windows NT SSI program. It tracks visitor information (date, time, IP number, and browser type). Like FirstHit, LastHit uses the same Registry scheme as HitCount or HitCntth, but it stores its information in its own key. You have to set the (default) page name here, too, if it's something other than Default.htm. The proper key is

```
HKEY_LOCAL_MACHINE
    \Software
        \Greyware
            \LastHit
                \Pages
```

LastHit isn't actually related to HitCount or FirstHit, other than by its common code and its nature as an SSI program. LastHit tracks and displays information about the last visitor to a page. Each time the page is hit, LastHit displays the information from the previous hit and then writes down information about the current caller for display next time.

The source code for LastHit is a little more complicated than FirstHit's, as Listing 32.8 shows. It uses a subroutine. If nothing else, these programs should demonstrate how easily SSI lets you create dynamic documents. There's no rocket science here.

Part VI

Ch 32

Listing 32.8 *lasthit.c*—Provides Information on the Last Person Who Accessed the Page

```
// LASTHIT.C
// This SSI program tracks visitors to a page, remembering
// the most recent for display.

#include <windows.h>
#include <stdio.h>
#define    ERROR_CANT_CREATE "LastHit:  Cannot open/create
➥registry key."
#define  ERROR_CANT_UPDATE "LastHit:  Cannot update registry key."
#define  LASTHIT "Software\\Greyware\\LastHit\\Pages"

// This subroutine builds the info string about the
// current caller.  Hence the name.  It uses a pointer
// to a buffer owned by the calling routine for output,
// and gets its information from the standard SSI
// environment variables.  Since "standard" is almost
// meaningless when it comes to SSI, the program
// gracefully skips anything it can't find.
```

continues

Listing 32.8 Continued

```c
void BuildInfo(char * szOut) {
    SYSTEMTIME    st;
    char          szTmp[512];
    char          *p;

    szOut[0]='\0';

    GetLocalTime(&st);
    GetDateFormat(0, DATE_LONGDATE, &st, NULL, szTmp, 511);
    sprintf(szOut,
        "Last access on %s at %02d:%02d:%02d",
        szTmp,
        st.wHour,
        st.wMinute,
        st.wSecond);

    p = getenv("REMOTE_ADDR");
    if (p!=NULL) {
        szTmp[0] = '\0';
        sprintf(szTmp,"<br>Caller from %s",p);
        if (szTmp[0] != '\0') strcat(szOut,szTmp);
    }
    p = getenv("REMOTE_HOST");
    if (p!=NULL) {
        szTmp[0] = '\0';
        sprintf(szTmp," (%s)",p);
        if (szTmp[0] != '\0') strcat(szOut,szTmp);
    }
    p = getenv("HTTP_USER_AGENT");
    if (p!=NULL) {
        szTmp[0] = '\0';
        sprintf(szTmp,"<br>Using %s",p);
        if (szTmp[0] != '\0') strcat(szOut,szTmp);
    }
}

void main(int argc, char * argv[]) {
    char    szOldInfo[512];
    char    szNewInfo[512];
    char    szDefPage[80];
    char    *p;
    char    *PageName;      // pointer to this page's name
    long    dwLength=511;   // length of temporary buffer
    long    dwType;         // registry value type code
    long    dwRetCode;      // generic return code from API
    HKEY    hKey;           // registry key handle

    // Determine where to get the page name.  A command-
    // line argument overrides the SCRIPT_NAME variable.

    if ((argc==2) && ((*argv[1]=='/') | (*argv[1]=='\\')))
        PageName = argv[1];
    else
        PageName = getenv("SCRIPT_NAME");
```

```
// If invoked from without SCRIPT_NAME or args, die
if (PageName==NULL)
{
    printf("LastHit 1.0.b.960121\n"
            "Copyright (c) 1995,96 Greyware "
            "Automation Products\n\n"
            "Documentation available online from "
            "Greyware's Web server:\n"
            "http://www.greyware.com/"
            "greyware/software/freeware.htp\n\n");
}
else
{

    // Build info for next call

    BuildInfo(szNewInfo);

    // Open the registry key

    dwRetCode = RegOpenKeyEx (
        HKEY_LOCAL_MACHINE,
        LASTHIT,
        0,
        KEY_EXECUTE,
        &hKey);

    // If open failed because key doesn't exist,
    //create it

    if ((dwRetCode==ERROR_BADDB)
        || (dwRetCode==ERROR_BADKEY)
        || (dwRetCode==ERROR_FILE_NOT_FOUND))
        dwRetCode = RegCreateKey(
            HKEY_LOCAL_MACHINE,
            LASTHIT,
            &hKey);

    // If couldn't open or create, die

    if (dwRetCode != ERROR_SUCCESS) {
        printf (ERROR_CANT_CREATE);
    } else {

        // Get the default page name
        dwLength = sizeof(szDefPage);
        dwRetCode = RegQueryValueEx (
            hKey,
            "(default)",
            0,
            &dwType,
            szDefPage,
            &dwLength);
        if ((dwRetCode == ERROR_SUCCESS)
            && (dwType == REG_SZ)
            && (dwLength > 0)) {
```

Part

VI

Ch

32

continues

Listing 32.8   Continued

```
            szDefPage[dwLength] = '\0';
    } else {
            strcpy(szDefPage,"default.htm");
    }

    // If current page uses default page name,
    // strip the page name
    _strlwr(PageName);
    p = strrchr(PageName,'/');
    if (p==NULL) p = strrchr(PageName,'\\');
    if (p) {
        p++;
        if (stricmp(p,szDefPage)==0) *p = '\0';
    }

    // Get this page's information
    dwLength = sizeof(szOldInfo);
    dwRetCode = RegQueryValueEx (
        hKey,
        PageName,
        0,
        &dwType,
        szOldInfo,
        &dwLength);
    if ((dwRetCode == ERROR_SUCCESS)
        && (dwType == REG_SZ)
        && (dwLength >0)) {
        szOldInfo[dwLength] = '\0';
    } else {
        strcpy (szOldInfo, szNewInfo);
    }

    // Close the registry key
    dwRetCode = RegCloseKey(hKey);

    // Print this page's info
    printf("%s",szOldInfo);


    // Write the new value back to the registry
    dwRetCode = RegOpenKeyEx (
        HKEY_LOCAL_MACHINE,
        LASTHIT,
        0,
        KEY_SET_VALUE,
        &hKey);
    if (dwRetCode==ERROR_SUCCESS) {
        dwRetCode = RegSetValueEx(
            hKey,
            PageName,
            0,
            REG_SZ,
            szNewInfo,
            strlen(szNewInfo));
        dwRetCode = RegCloseKey(hKey);
```

```
            } else {
                printf(ERROR_CANT_UPDATE);
            }
        }
    }
    fflush(stdout);
    return;
}
```

Server Performance Considerations

Real-time programs can affect server performance. SSI doesn't bring anything new to the table in that regard.

In general, SSI programs tend to be less of a drain on the server than full-fledged CGI. SSI programs are usually small—they only have to produce text, after all—and seldom do much of any significance with files. Page hit counters that rely on generating inline graphics put far more stress on a server than an SSI counter does.

Still, a dozen—or a hundred—instances of your SSI program running at once can steal memory and processor slices needed by the server to satisfy client requests. Imagine that you are Webmaster of a large site. On each of the 250 pages for which you're responsible, you include not one, but all the SSI examples in this chapter. Each page hit would produce seven separate processes, each of which has to jostle with the others in resource contention. In a worst-case scenario, with 100 pages being hit per minute, you would have 700 scripts running each minute, 10 or more simultaneously, at all times. This kind of load would seriously affect your server's capability to do anything else—such as serve up pages to users who stop by to see your wonderful SSI handiwork.

You won't find much difference among platforms either. Some SSI utilities run more efficiently in UNIX, others work better under Windows NT, and in the end, everything balances out. Programs that use the NT Registry have a distinct advantage over programs that hit the file system to save data. The Registry functions as a back-end database—always open, always ready for queries and updates. The code for handling concurrency is already loaded and running as part of the operating system, so your program can be smaller and tighter. However, pipes and forks tend to run more efficiently under some flavors of UNIX, so if your program does that sort of thing, you are better off in that environment.

Don't pick your server operating system based on which SSI programs you plan to run. If you run into performance problems, adding RAM usually gives your server the extra headroom it needs to handle the load imposed by SSI.

ON THE WEB

For additional sites containing examples on using SSI, see:

`http://www.cgi-resources.com/Programs_and_Scripts/Perl/`

`http://www.itm.com/cgicollection/index.cgi?page=1`

Part
VI

Ch
32

Active Server Pages and VBScript

by Ramesh Chandak, Eric Ladd, and Jim O'Donnell

In this chapter

Introduction to VBScript

Like JavaScript, Microsoft's Visual Basic Scripting Edition (VBScript) enables you to embed commands into an HTML document. When a user of a compatible Web browser (for example, Internet Explorer or Netscape Navigator with the ScriptActive plug-in from Ncompass Labs) downloads your page, your VBScript commands are loaded by the Web browser along with the rest of the document and are run in response to any of a series of events. Again, like JavaScript, VBScript is an *interpreted* language; Internet Explorer interprets the VBScript commands when they are loaded and run. They do not first need to be *compiled* into executable form by the Web author who uses them.

VBScript is a fast and flexible subset of Microsoft's Visual Basic and Visual Basic for Applications languages and is designed to be easy to program in and quick in adding active content to HTML documents. The language elements are mainly ones that should be familiar to anyone who has programmed in just about any language: If…Then…Else blocks and Do, While, and For…Next loops, and a typical assortment of operators and built-in functions. The first half of this chapter takes you to the heart of the VBScript language and shows you examples of how to use it to add interaction and increased functionality to your Web pages. Then, in the second part of the chapter, you'll learn how to use VBScript on the server side to create applications using Active Server Pages.

VBScript Identifiers

An *identifier* is a unique name that VBScript uses to identify a variable, method, or object in your program. As with other programming languages, VBScript imposes some rules on what names you can use. All VBScript names must start with an alphabetic character and can contain both uppercase and lowercase letters and the digits 0 through 9. They can be as long as 255 characters, although you probably don't want to go much more than 32 or so for readability's sake.

Unlike JavaScript, which supports two ways for you to represent values in your scripts, literals and variables, VBScript has only variables. The difference in VBScript, therefore, is one of usage. If you wish to use a constant value in your VBScript programs, set a variable equal to a value and don't change it. This discussion will continue to refer to literals and variables as distinct entities, although they are interchangeable.

Literals and variables in VBScript are all of type *variant*, which means that they can contain any type of data that VBScript supports. It is usually a good idea to use a given variable for one type and explicitly convert its value to another type as necessary. The following are some of the types of data that VBScript supports:

- Integers—These types can be 1, 2, or 4 bytes in length, depending on how big they are.
- Floating point—VBScript supports single- and double-precision floating point numbers.
- Strings—Strings can represent words, phrases, or data, and they are set off by double quotation marks.

■ Booleans—Booleans have a value of either `true` or `false`.

■ Objects—A VBScript variable can refer to any object within its environment.

Objects, Properties, Methods, and Events in VBScript

Before you proceed further, you should take some time to review some terminology that may or may not be familiar to you. VBScript follows much the same object model followed by JavaScript and uses many of the same terms. In VBScript, as in JavaScript—and in any object-oriented language for that matter—an *object* is a collection of data and functions that have been grouped together. An object's data is known as its *properties*, and its functions are known as its *methods*. An *event* is a condition to which an object can respond, such as a mouse click or other user input. The VBScript programs that you write make use of properties and methods of objects, both those that you create and those objects provided by the Web browser, its plug-ins, ActiveX Controls, Java applets, and so on.

TIP The following is a simple guideline: An object's *properties* are the information it knows; its *methods* are how it can act on that information; and *events* are what it responds to.

N O T E A very important, and a little confusing, thing to remember is that an object's methods are *also* properties of that object. An object's properties are the information it knows. The object certainly knows about its own methods, so those methods are properties of the object right along with its other data. ■

Using Built-In Objects and Functions

Individual VBScript elements are objects. Literals and variables are objects of type *variant*, which can be used to hold data of many types. These objects also have associated methods—ways of acting on the different data types. VBScript also enables you to access a set of useful objects that represent the Web browser, the currently displayed page, and other elements of the browsing session.

You access objects by specifying their names. The active document object, for example, is named `document`. To use `document`'s properties or methods, you add a period (.) and the name of the method or property you want. For example, `document.title` is the `title` property of the `document` object.

Using Properties

Every object has properties, even literals. To access a property, use the object name followed by a period and the property name. To get the length of a string object named `address`, you can write the following:

```
address.length
```

You get back an integer that equals the number of characters in the string. If the object you are using has properties that can be modified, you can change them in the same way. To set the `color` property of a house object, just write the following:

```
house.color = "blue"
```

You can also create new properties for an object by naming them. Assume, for example, that you define a class called `customer` for one of your pages. You can add new properties to the `customer` object as follows:

```
customer.name = "Jim O'Donnell"
customer.address = "1757 P Street NW"
customer.zip = "20036-1303"
```

Because an object's methods are properties, you can easily add new properties to an object by writing your own function and creating a new object property using your own function name. If you want to add a `Bill` method to your `customer` object, you can write a function named `BillCustomer` and set the object's property as follows:

```
customer.Bill = BillCustomer;
```

To call the new method, you write the following:

```
customer.Bill()
```

VBScript Language Elements

Although VBScript is not as flexible as C++ or Visual Basic, it is quick and simple. Because it is easily embedded in your Web pages, adding interactivity or increased functionality with a VBScript is easy—a lot easier than writing a Java applet to do the same thing. (Although, to be fair, you *can* do a lot more with Java applets.) This section covers some of the nuts and bolts of VBScript programming.

A full language reference for VBScript, as well as Microsoft's tutorial for VBScript programming, is included on the accompanying CD-ROM. Because VBScript is a new and evolving language, you can get up-to-the-minute information on it at the Microsoft VBScript Web site at `http://www.microsoft.com/vbscript/`.

VBScript Variables

All VBScript variables are of the type *variant*, which means that they can be used for any of the supported data types. Table 22.1 summarizes the types of data that VBScript variables can hold:

Table 33.1   Data Types that VBScript Variables Can Contain

Type	Description
empty	Uninitialized and is treated as 0 or the empty string, depending on the context
null	Intentionally contains no valid data

Type	Description
Boolean	`true` or `false`
byte	Integer in the range –128 to 127
integer	Integer in the range –32,768 to 32,767
long	Integer in the range –2,147,483,648 to 2,147,483,647
single	Single-precision floating point number in the range –3.402823E38 to –1.401298E-45 for negative values and 1.401298E-45 to 3.402823E38 for positive values
double	Double-precision floating point number in the range –1.79769313486232E308 to –4.94065645841247E-324 for negative values; 4.94065645841247E-324 to 1.79769313486232E308 for positive values
date	Number that represents a date between January 1, 100 to December 31, 9999
string	Variable-length string up to approximately 2 billion characters in length
object	Any object
error	Error number

Forming Expressions in VBScript

An *expression* is anything that can be evaluated to get a single value. Expressions can contain string or numeric variables, operators, and other expressions, and they can range from simple to quite complex. The following expression uses the assignment operator (more on operators in the next section), for example, to assign the result 3.14159 to the variable pi:

```
pi = 3.14159
```

By contrast, the following is a more complex expression whose final value depends on the values of the two Boolean variables Quit and Complete:

```
(Quit = TRUE) And (Complete = FALSE)
```

Using VBScript Operators

Operators do just what their name suggests: They operate on variables or literals. The items that an operator acts on are called its *operands*. Operators come in the following two types:

- Unary—These operators require only one operand and the operator can come before or after the operand. The Not operator, which performs the logical negation of an expression, is a good example.

- Binary—These operators need two operands. The four math operators (+ for addition, – for subtraction, × for multiplication, and / for division) are all binary operators, as is the = assignment operator you saw earlier.

Assignment Operators   *Assignment operators* take the result of an expression and assign it to a variable. One feature that VBScript has that most other programming languages do not is the capability to change a variable's type on-the-fly. Consider the example shown in Listing 33.1.

Listing 33.1   *Pi-fly.htm*—VBScript Variables Can Change Type On-the-Fly

```
<HTML>
<HEAD>
<SCRIPT LANGUAGE="VBS">
<!-- Hide this script from incompatible Web browsers!
Sub TypeDemo
    Dim pi
    document.write("<HR>")
    pi = 3.14159
    document.write("pi is " & CStr(pi) & "<BR>")
    pi = FALSE
    document.write("pi is " & CStr(pi) & "<BR>")
    document.write("<HR>")
End Sub
<!-- -->
</SCRIPT>
<TITLE>Changing Pi on-the-Fly!</TITLE>
</HEAD>
<BODY BGCOLOR=#FFFFFF>
If your Web browser doesn't support VBScript, this is all you will see!
<SCRIPT LANGUAGE="VBS">
<!-- Hide this script from incompatible Web browsers!
TypeDemo
<!-- -->
</SCRIPT>
</BODY>
</HTML>
```

N O T E   The Cstr function converts a numerical value into a string. ■

This short function first prints the (correct) value of pi. In most other languages, however, trying to set a floating point variable to a Boolean value either generates a compiler error or a runtime error. Because VBScript variables can be any type, it happily accepts the change and prints pi's new value: false (see Figure 33.1).

The assignment operator, =, assigns the value of an expression's right side to its left side. In the preceding example, the variable pi gets the floating point value 3.14159 or the Boolean value false after the expression is evaluated.

Math Operators   The previous sections gave you a sneak preview of the math operators that VBScript furnishes. As you might expect, the standard four math functions (addition, subtraction, multiplication, and division) work the same as they do on an ordinary calculator and use the symbols +, -, ×, and /.

FIGURE 33.1

Because all VBScript variables are of type `variant`, not only can their values be changed, but also their data types.

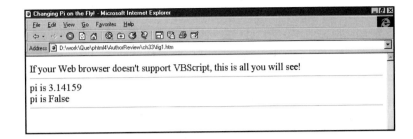

VBScript supplies three other math operators:

- ▨ \—The backslash operator divides its first operand by its second, after first rounding floating point operands to the nearest integer, and returns the integer part of the result. For example, `19 \ 6.7` returns 2 (6.7 rounds to 7, 19 divided by 7 is a little over 2.71, the integer part of which is 2).

- ▨ `Mod`—This operator is similar to \ in that it divides the first operand by its second, again after rounding floating point operands to the nearest integer, and returns the integer remainder. Therefore, `19 Mod 6.7` returns 5.

- ▨ `^`—This exponent operator returns the first operand raised to the power of the second. The first operand can be negative only if the second, the exponent, is an integer.

Comparison Operators Comparing the value of two expressions to see whether one is larger, smaller, or equal to another is often necessary. VBScript supplies several comparison operators that take two operands and return `true` if the comparison is true and `false` if it is not. Table 33.2 shows the VBScript comparison operators:

Part VI

Ch 33

Table 33.2   VBScript Comparison Operators

Operator	Read It As	Returns true When:
=	equals	The two operands are equal.
<>	does not equal	The two operands are unequal.
<	less than	The left operand is less than the right operand.
<=	less than or equal to	The left operand is less than or equal to the right operand.
>	greater than	The left operand is greater than the right operand.
>=	greater than or equal to	The left operand is greater than or equal to the right operand.

Thinking of the comparison operators as questions may be helpful. When you write

```
(x >= 10)
```

you are really saying, "Is the value of variable x greater than or equal to 10?" The return value answers the question true or false.

Logical Operators   Comparison operators compare quantity or content for numeric and string expressions, but sometimes you need to test a logical value—whether a comparison operator returns true or false, for example. VBScript's logical operators enable you to compare expressions that return logical values. The following are VBScript's logical operators:

- And—The And operator returns true if both its input expressions are true. If the first operand evaluates to false, And returns false immediately, without evaluating the second operand. The following is an example:

```
x = TRUE And TRUE      ' x is TRUE
x = TRUE And FALSE     ' x is FALSE
x = FALSE And TRUE     ' x is FALSE
x = FALSE And FALSE    ' x is FALSE
```

- Or—This operator returns true if either of its operands is true. If the first operand is true, ¦¦ returns true without evaluating the second operand. The following is an example:

```
x = TRUE Or TRUE       ' x is TRUE
x = TRUE Or FALSE      ' x is TRUE
x = FALSE Or TRUE      ' x is TRUE
x = FALSE Or FALSE     ' x is FALSE
```

- Not—This operator takes only one expression and it returns the opposite of that expression. Thus Not true returns false, and Not false returns true.

- Xor—This operator, which stands for "exclusive or," returns true if either, but not both, of its input expressions is true, as in the following:

```
x = TRUE Xor TRUE      ' x is FALSE
x = TRUE Xor FALSE     ' x is TRUE
x = FALSE Xor TRUE     ' x is TRUE
x = FALSE Xor FALSE    ' x is FALSE
```

- Eqv—This operator, which stands for "equivalent," returns true if its two input expressions are the same—either both true or both false. The statement x Eqv y is equivalent to Not (x Xor y).

- Imp—This operator, which stands for "implication," returns true according to the following:

```
x = TRUE Imp TRUE      ' x is TRUE
x = FALSE Imp TRUE     ' x is TRUE
x = TRUE Imp FALSE     ' x is FALSE
x = FALSE Imp FALSE    ' x is TRUE
```

N O T E Note that the logical implication operator `Imp` is the only logical operator for which the order of the operands is important. ▪

Note that the `And` and `Or` operators don't evaluate the second operand if the first operand provides enough information for the operator to return a value. This process, called *short-circuit evaluation*, can be significant when the second operand is a function call.

N O T E Note that all six of the logical operators can also operate on non-Boolean expressions. In this case, the logical operations described previously are performed bitwise, on each bit of the two operands. For the two integers 19 (00010011 in binary) and 6 (00000110), for example:

```
19 And 6 =    2 (00000010 in binary)
19 Or 6  =   23 (00010111 in binary)
Not 19   =  -20 (11101100 in binary) ▪
```

String Concatenation   The final VBScript operator is the string concatenation operator &. Although you can also use the addition operator + to concatenate strings (returning a string made up of the original strings joined together), using & proves better because it is less ambiguous.

Testing Conditions in VBScript

VBScript provides one control structure for making decisions—the `If…Then…Else` structure. To make a decision, you supply one or more expressions that evaluate to `true` or `false`; which code is executed depends on what your expressions evaluate to.

The simplest form of `If…Then…Else` uses only the `If…Then` part. If the specified condition is `true`, the code following the condition is executed; if not, that code is skipped. In the following code fragment, for example, the message appears only if the variable x is less than `pi`:

```
if (x < pi) then document.write("x is less than pi")
```

You can use any expression as the condition. Because you can nest and combine expressions with the logical operators, your tests can be pretty sophisticated. Also, using the multiple statement character, you can execute multiple commands, as in the following:

```
if ((test = TRUE) And (x > max)) then max = x : test = FALSE
```

The `else` clause enables you to specify a set of statements to execute when the condition is `false`. In the same single line form shown in the preceding line, your new line appears as follows:

```
if (x > pi) then test = TRUE else test = FALSE
```

A more versatile use of the If…Then…Else allows multiple lines and multiple actions for each case. It looks something like the following:

```
if (x > pi) then
    test = TRUE
    count = count + 1
else
    test = FALSE
    count = 0
end if
```

Note that with this syntax, additional test clauses using the elseif statement are permitted. You could, for example, add one more clause to the preceding example:

```
if (x > pi) then
    test = TRUE
    count = count + 1
elseif (x < -pi) then
    test = TRUE
    count = count - 1
else
    test = FALSE
    count = 0
end if
```

Executing VBScript Loops

If you want to repeat an action more than one time, VBScript provides a variety of constructs for doing so. The first, called a For…Next loop, executes a set of statements some number of times. You specify three expressions: an *initial* expression, which sets the values of any variables you need to use; a *final value*, which tells the loop how to see when it is done; and an *increment* expression, which modifies any variables that need it. The following is a simple example:

```
for count = 0 to 100 step 2
    document.write("Count is " & CStr(count) & "<BR>")
next
```

In this example, the expressions are all simple numeric values—the initial value is 0, the final value is 100, and the increment is 2. This loop executes 51 times and prints out a number each time.

The third form of loop is the While…Wend loop. It executes statements as long as its condition is true. You can rewrite the first For…Next loop, for example, as follows:

```
count = 0
while (count <= 100)
    document.write("Count is " & CStr(count) & "<BR>")
    count = count + 2
wend
```

The last type of loop is the Do…Loop, which has several forms, and which either test the condition at the beginning or the end. The test can either be a Do While or Do Until, and can occur at the beginning or end of the loop. If a `Do While` test is done at the beginning, the loop executes as long as the test condition is true, similar to the `While...Wend` loop. The following is an example:

```
count = 0
do while (count <= 100)
    document.write("Count is " & CStr(count) & "<BR>")
    count = count + 2
loop
```

An example of having the test at the end, as a `Do...Until`, can also yield equivalent results. In that case, the loop looks like the following:

```
count = 0
do
    document.write("Count is " & CStr(count) & "<BR>")
    count = count + 2
loop until (count > 100)
```

One other difference between these two forms is that when the test is at the end of the loop, as in the second case, the commands in the loop are executed at least one time. If the test is at the beginning, that is not the case.

Which form you prefer depends on what you are doing. `For...Next` loops prove useful when you want to perform an action a set number of times. `While...Wend` and `Do...Loop` loops, although they can be used for the same purpose, are best when you want to keep doing something as long as a particular condition remains true.

N O T E The For...Next and Do...Loop loops also have a way to exit the loop from inside—the End For and End Do statements, respectively. Normally, these tests would be used as part of a conditional statement, such as the following:

```
for i = 0 to 100
    x = UserFunc()
    document.write("x[" & CStr(i) & "] = " & CStr(x) & "<BR>")
    if (x > max) end for
next
```

Using Other VBScript Statements

This section provides a quick reference to some of the other VBScript statements. The following formatting is used:

- All VBScript keywords are in a `monospace` font.
- Words in *`monospace italic`* represent user-defined names or statements.
- Any portions enclosed in square brackets ([and]) are optional.
- Portions enclosed in braces ({ and }) and separated by a vertical bar (¦) represent an option, of which one must be selected.
- The word *`statements...`* indicates a block of one or more statements.

The *Call* Statement

The Call statement calls a VBScript Sub or Function procedure as follows:

Syntax:

```
Call MyProc([arglist])
```

or

```
MyProc [arglist]
```

Note that *arglist* is a comma-delimited list of zero or more arguments to be passed to the procedure. When the second form is used, omitting the Call statement, the parentheses around the argument list, if any, must also be omitted.

The *Dim* Statement

The Dim statement is used to declare variables and also to allocate the storage necessary for them. If you specify subscripts, you can also create arrays.

Syntax:

```
Dim varname[([subscripts])][,varname[([subscripts])],...]
```

The *Function* and *Sub* Statements

The Function and Sub statements declare VBScript procedures. The difference is that a Function procedure returns a value, and a Sub procedure does not. All parameters are passed to functions *by value*—the function gets the value of the parameter but cannot change the original value in the caller.

Syntax:

```
[Static] Function funcname([arglist])
    statements...
    funcname = returnvalue
End
```

and

```
[Static] Sub subname([arglist])
    statements...
End
```

Variables can be declared with the Dim statement within a Function or Sub procedure. In this case, those variables are local to that procedure and can only be referenced within it. If the Static keyword is used when the procedure is declared, all local variables retain their value from one procedure call to the next.

The *On_Error* Statement

The On Error statement is used to enable error handling.

Syntax:

```
On Error Resume Next
```

`On Error Resume Next` enables execution to continue immediately after the statement that provokes the runtime error. Alternatively, if the error occurs in a procedure call after the last executed `On Error` statement, execution commences immediately after that procedure call. This way, execution can continue despite a runtime error, enabling you to build an error-handling routine inline within the procedure. The most recent `On Error Resume Next` statement is the one that is active, so you should execute one in each procedure in which you want to have inline error handling.

VBScript Functions

VBScript has an assortment of intrinsic functions that you can use in your scripts. The VBScript documentation on the accompanying CD contains a full reference for these functions. Table 33.3 shows the functions that exist for performing different types of operations. (Because you can use some functions for several types of operations, they appear multiple times in the table.)

Table 33.3   VBScript Functions

Type of Operation	Function Names
array operations	IsArray, LBound, UBound
conversions	Abs, Asc, AscB, AscW, Chr, ChrB, ChrW, Cbool, CByte, CDate, CDbl, CInt, CLng, CSng, Cstr, DateSerial, DateValue, Hex, Oct, Fix, Int, Sgn, TimeSerial, TimeValue
dates and times	Date, Time, DateSerial, DateValue, Day, Month, Weekday, Year, Hour, Minute, Second, Now, TimeSerial, TimeValue
input/output	InputBox, MsgBox
math	Atn, Cos, Sin, Tan, Exp, Log, Sqr, Randomize, Rnd
objects	IsObject
strings	Asc, AscB, AscW, Chr, ChrB, ChrW, Instr, InStrB, Len, LenB, LCase, UCase, Left, LeftB, Mid, MidB, Right, RightB, Space, StrComp, String, LTrim, RTrim, Trim
variants	IsArray, IsDate, IsEmpty, IsNull, IsNumeric, IsObject, VarType

Part

VI

Ch

33

Active Server Pages and the Active Server Platform

The Active Server Platform refers to Microsoft's take on server-side application development. As with the Active Desktop, you can author on the server side with three standard components: HTML, scripting, and software components, such as Java applets and ActiveX server components. This enables you to leverage your client-side development skills to start building dynamic applications on your server.

In addition, you can take advantage of a number of Microsoft server technologies and services, such as Transaction Server, Merchant Server, Proxy Server, and so on, to implement specialized business solutions. Microsoft's server technology is tightly integrated with Windows NT operating system and Internet Information Server (IIS). As a result, your Active Platform solution will benefit from the operating system's services and features. Your Web application, for example, can inherit Windows NT's built-in security mechanism.

N O T E As you probably guessed from the preceding paragraph, the Active Server development environment is only available on servers running the Windows NT operating system. If you have a UNIX-based server, you will not be able to develop server-side applications with Active Server Pages.

Advantages of the Active Server Platform

If yours is a Microsoft shop, then you can harness the many advantages of developing on the Active Server Platform. These include:

- Active Server components offer a different dimension to Web programming. Active Server components are, in fact, ActiveX controls implemented on the server. By using Active Server components on the server, your application will need a very thin client because the components will reside on the server. This means the application will benefit from the server's processing power. In addition, the server can generate the HTML dynamically. And because the components will reside on the server, multiple applications can share them.

- As with ActiveX controls, you can use (and reuse) Active Server components across applications and with a variety of development tools. You can also use any standard Windows development tool, such as Visual C++ and Visual Basic, to create the Active Server components for your application.

- The Active Server is fully scalable. You can start development, for example, with the Personal Web Server running on Windows 98 and, after testing the Web site, port the site to your IIS server without changing or rewriting any component. Thus, you can use the Personal Web Server as your development server and the IIS as your production server.

■ By using the Active Server, you can implement multi-tier architecture for your application. Your application's business rules and application logic will reside on the server. The server, in turn, will connect and communicate with a database server or any other server that supports back-end processes. The database server may reside on a platform different from the Web server's platform.

Active Server Pages

You can create Active Server Pages (ASP) by using the same set of components you use to implement client-side scripting. That is, you can integrate Active Server components and Java applets within your ASP code by using scripting languages such as VBScript, JavaScript, and JScript.

The Active Server includes a number of prebuilt, pretested Active Server components, such as the Browser Capabilities Component and Active Data Object (ADO) Component. By using the Browser Capabilities Component, you can detect the type of client browser. In response, you can create the HTML that the browser will be capable of handling. For instance, if the browser does not support frames and tables, you can create and send a simple HTML page that will not use the <FRAME> and <TABLE> tags.

In addition, you can use the ADO with your server-side scripts to query back-end databases and integrate the query results into a dynamically generated page. A server-side script, for example, can communicate a SQL query to the ADO. The ADO, in turn, will pass the query to a database server. The database server processes the query and sends the results back to the ADO. The ADO then returns the results to the Active Server Page script. Finally, the script uses the query data to generate and send an HTML page to the browser. As you can see, each component within the architecture performs a specific role, and each component communicates with its immediate neighbor to get the job done.

 TIP ASP is a good alternative to Common Gateway Interface (CGI) programming. Traditionally, CGI has been the primary protocol to build dynamic, data-driven Web pages. With server-side scripting, you can use an Active Server component that will keep the connection alive with the database server. As a result, you will reduce the traffic to the database server and improve the response time of the requests because your application will make the connection to the database only once.

N O T E If the prepackaged components do not meet your application's requirements, you can write your own components. Alternatively, you can use a third-party component that will meet your application's criteria.

In addition, like Active Desktop, Active Server also supports Java. This means you can integrate Java applets with your server-side scripts. ■

Part
VI

Ch
33

Building Active Server Page Applications

You can use the same technologies and languages you use to implement client-side scripting. You can use Visual Basic 5, for example, to create ActiveX controls and Active Server components. You can use VBScript to bring together Java applets, ActiveX controls (or Active Server components), and HTML to create ASP.

The chief ingredients in any ASP application are scripted instructions embedded in an HTML document. When a browser requests a file containing an Active Server Page document, the server parses out and executes the scripted instructions. Any HTML output from the script is inserted back into the document in place of the original script code. The result is a pure HTML page that is sent back to the browser.

N O T E   ASPs are not precompiled. Rather, they are interpreted when they are requested by a browser. IIS does cache interpreted ASPs so that later requests can occur more quickly. ▓

To execute a script on the server, you must include the RUNAT="SERVER" option in your <SCRIPT> tags. The code is as follows:

```
<SCRIPT LANGUAGE="VBScript" RUNAT="SERVER">
```

<SCRIPT> tags without this attribute define scripts that are to run on the client side. Listing 33.2 shows some script code that will execute on the client. Notice the line of code that displays a message box. Because the script will execute on the client, displaying a message box is meaningful.

Listing 33.2   A Client-Side Script

```
<SCRIPT LANGUAGE=VBScript>
<!--
Option Explicit

Dim validCreditCardNumber

Sub Submit_OnClick
validCreditCardNumber = True
Call CheckCreditCardNumber(CreditCardNumberField.Value,
"Please enter your credit card number.")
If validCreditCardNumber then
Msgbox "Thank you for your order"
End if
End Sub
</SCRIPT>
```

If you tried to execute the same script on the server, displaying a message box would be meaningless because no user interface exists on the server. As a result, the server will bypass the line of code that displays the message box.

The server-side scripts you embed inside of HTML code should reside in a text file with the extension .asp. An HTML file is a text file the browser can render on the client machine. The HTML file has the extension `.htm` or `.html`. Similarly, an ASP file is a text file the IIS will process on the server. Within an ASP file, you integrate server components through your scripted instructions. Microsoft recommends using VBScript or JScript as your default ASP scripting language.

 TIP If you are an experienced C++ or Java programmer, you will find JavaScript or JScript easy to learn. If you are an experienced Visual Basic programmer, you will probably find VBScript easier to use.

Listing 33.3 shows an example of an ASP file done with VBScript, the scripting language discussed in the first portion of this chapter.

Listing 33.3 A Sample ASP File

```
<HTML>
<HEAD>
<TITLE>Hello World in ASP</TITLE>
</HEAD>
<BODY BGCOLOR="WHITE">
<% '=== Active Server Scripting begins
sub HelloWorld()
        dim Greeting
        Greeting = "Hello World!"
        Response.write Greeting
End sub
%>
<% Call HelloWorld %>   '=== Calling the Active Server subroutine
</BODY>
</HTML>
```

As you can see, this ASP file includes both traditional HTML and scripted instructions. Note that all script code is enclosed within the <% %> tags.

Listing 33.4 shows a more complex ASP example that uses three of the five ASP component objects (Session, Response, and Request) to process information. First, you will retrieve information from the form using the Request object and store the information within the Session object's variables. Within this example, you will use the Session variables User_ID, nba_Online, and nfl_Online to store information from the form fields User_Id, nba_online, and nfl_online.

Next, you will check whether the User_Id variable is empty. If the variable is empty, you will use the Response object's Redirect method to redirect the browser to the "invalid.htm" file. If the variable is not empty, you will use the Request object to retrieve the report_type variable's value. If the value is "nba" and the value of the Session variable "nba_Online" = "Y", you will use the Response object's Redirect method to redirect the browser to the "latest_nba.htm" file. The "latest_nba.htm" file, in turn, will display the latest NBA scores.

On the other hand, if the value of the Session variable "nba_Online" = "N", you will redirect the browser to the "invalid.htm" file. You will process similarly for the "nfl_Online" option. In the next section, you will learn more about these ASP objects and their variables, properties, methods, and events.

Listing 33.4   Using the ASP Objects

```
<%@ LANGUAGE="VBSCRIPT" %>
<% Session("User_ID")    = Request.Form("User_Id") %>
<% Session("nba_Online") = Request.Form("nba_online") %>
<% Session("nfl_Online") = Request.Form("nfl_online") %>
<%
If IsEmpty(Session("User_Id")) Then
        Response.Redirect "invalid.htm"
Else
        If Request.Form("report_type") = "nba" Then
                If Session("nba_Online") = "Y" Then
                        Response.Redirect "latest_nba.htm"
                Else
                        Response.Redirect "invalid.htm"
                End If
        Else
                If Session("nfl_Online") = "Y" Then
                        Response.Redirect "latest_nfl.htm"
                Else
                        Response.Redirect "invalid.htm"
                End If
        End If
End If
%>
```

Note that no HTML is in this file. That's because all output sent to the browser is handled through the redirects, not by dynamically writing out any HTML.

Active Server Page Objects

Five fundamental server objects typically form the core of ASP applications:

- Application—The Application object manages your Web application's information.
- Session—The Session object manages and tracks individual user sessions within your Web application.
- Server—The Server object controls behavior of your Web server.
- Response—The Response object transmits information from the Web server to the browser.
- Request—The Request object retrieves information from the browser for processing at the server.

Like any other object within an object-oriented programming world, the five ASP objects have specific events, methods, and properties. You can use an ASP object's events, methods, and properties to configure the object per your application and business requirements. You will learn more about the methods and properties of ASP objects in the following sections. These five ASP objects are extremely critical for developing an ASP application.

The *Application* Object

By using the Application object, you can manage your Web application's information. You can pass application-level information between different users of the application. In addition, you can lock and unlock an application-level variable. When you lock an application-level variable, users of the application cannot modify the variable's value. After you release the lock, users can modify the variable's value.

Events The Application object supports the following two events:

- Application_OnStart—Triggered when the application starts
- Application_OnEnd—Triggered when the application terminates

You will find the Application object's two events within your application's global.asa file.

> **N O T E** The global.asa file is an Active Server application file you can use to track and manage the application and session events, variables, and objects. When you start the application, the server will load the global.asa file into memory.

Variables You declare application-level variables within your application's global.asa file. The following line of code, for example, declares an application-level variable myAppTitle. After you declare the variable, all users of the application will have access to the variable

```
Application("myAppTitle") = "My First ASP application"
```

In the next section, you will learn how you can use the Application object's Lock and UnLock methods with your application-level variables.

Methods Two primary types of methods are used in the Application object:

- Lock—By using the Lock method, you can prevent another user from updating or changing the application-level variable's value.
- UnLock—By using the UnLock method, you can release the control on the application-level variable. The following code demonstrates the use of Lock and UnLock methods:

```
<%
Application.Lock
Application(""errMsg"") = ""Please contact the Plan Administrator""
Application.UnLock
%>
```

The *Session* Object

By using the Session object, you can manage information about a specific user of your Web application. The user information is specific only to the user, and one user cannot access or modify another user's information. The Session object includes the events, properties, and methods described in the following sections.

N O T E The Session object is extremely useful because HTTP does not allow for tracking of state information. ▨

Events

Like the Application object, the Session object also supports the following two events:

- ▇ Session_OnStart—Triggered when the server starts a new user session
- ▇ Session_OnEnd—Triggered when the server terminates the user session

You will find the Session object's two events within your application's global.asa file.

N O T E By using the Abandon method that falls under the Session object, you can explicitly close a user's session rather than waiting for the user to close it. As a result, the server will automatically release all resources consumed by the user session and destroy the user Session object. The syntax for the Abandon method is

Session.Abandon

where Session is the current Session object. ▨

Properties

The Session object has four properties:

- ▇ CodePage—By using the CodePage property, you can set your Web pages' attributes. The syntax for the CodePage property is

  Session.CodePage = CodePage

  where CodePage is a valid code page for the scripting engine.

- ▇ LCID—You use the LCID property to set the local date, time, and currency formats. As a result, you can control the display formatting of your ASP pages based on a particular locale or region. The syntax for using the LCID property is

  Session.LCID(=LCID)

  where LCID is a valid local identifier.

- ▇ SessionID—The SessionID property represents a unique user session. When a user initiates a session with your Web application, the Web server will automatically generate a SessionID for the user's session. The syntax for using the SessionID property is

  Session.SessionID

■ TimeOut—The TimeOut property represents the amount of time the user session will remain active before the Web server will close the Session object. The syntax for using the TimeOut property is

```
Session.Timeout [ = nMinutes]
```

where Session is the Session object and you specify the TimeOut in number of minutes. The default is 20 minutes. The server will store the TimeOut within your system's Registry. The following line of code, for example, will override the default value:

```
<%Session.Timeout = 1%>
```

The *Server* Object

By using the Server object, you can manage and administer your Web server. The Server object includes the methods and properties described in the following sections.

Methods   The following methods are supported by the Serverobject:

■ CreateObject—By using the CreateObject method, you can create a Server object's instance. The CreateObject method's syntax is

```
Server.CreateObject( progID )
```

where progID is the class ID of the object's instance you want to create. The following line of code, for example, will create the Browser Detection Active Server object's instance:

```
Set BrowserType = Server.CreateObject("MSWC.BrowserType")
```

After you create a Server object's instance, you can access the object's methods and properties within your ASP file. An object whose instance you create within an ASP file will have page-level scope. An object whose instance you create within the global.asa file will have application or session-level scope, depending on whether you use the application or session object.

■ MapPath—By using the MapPath method, you can map a physical or virtual path to a directory on the server. The MapPath method's syntax is

```
Server.MapPath( path )
```

where Server is the Active Server and path is the virtual or physical directory.

■ HTMLEncode—By using the HTMLEncode method, you can encode a string using the HTML encoding methods. Typically, you will use the HTMLEncode method to pass encoded information from the server to the client. The HTMLEncode method's syntax is

```
Server.HTMLEncode( string )
```

where Server is the Active Server and string is the string to be HTML-encoded.

■ ULREncode—By using the URLEncode method, you can encode a string using the URL encoding methods. Typically, you will use the URLEncode method to pass encoded information from the client to the server. The URLEncode method's syntax is

```
Server.URLEncode( string )
```

where Server is the Active Server and string is the string to be encoded.

Properties   The following property is supported under the `Server` object:

■ `ScriptTimeOut`—The `ScriptTimeOut` property indicates the amount of time the server will wait to process a script before the server will terminate the script processing. The `ScriptTimeOut` property's syntax is

```
Server.ScriptTimeout = Seconds
```

where `Server` is the Active Server and you specify the script timeout in seconds. The default timeout value is 90 seconds. The value is stored within your system's Registry. To change the default value to 30 seconds, for example, you can use the following line of code within your ASP file:

```
Server.TimeOut = 30
```

The *Response* Object

By using the `Response` object, you can send information from the server to the client. The `Response` object includes the methods and properties described in the following sections.

Properties   The `Response` object has the following properties:

■ `Buffer`—You can use the `Buffer` property to turn the server's buffering on or off. The syntax for using the `Buffer` property is

```
Response.Buffer = [flag]
```

where `flag` equals `True` if you want to turn the buffering on or `False` if you want to turn the buffering off. The following line of code, for example, will turn the server's buffering on:

```
<%Response.Buffer = True%>
```

■ `Expires`—By using the `Expires` property, you can control the amount of time before the browser will remove the page from its cache. The syntax for using the `Expires` property is

```
Response.Expires = [number]
```

where `number` equals the number of minutes you want the browser to keep the page active within its cache.

■ `ExpiresAbsolute`—By using the `ExpiresAbsolute` property, you can specify the exact date and time when the browser should remove the page from its cache. The syntax for using the `ExpiresAbsolute` property is

```
Response.ExpiresAbsolute = [[date][time]]
```

■ `IsClientConnected`—By using the `IsClientConnected` property, you can determine whether the client was disconnected since the last time the Web server sent data to the browser. The syntax for using the `IsClientConnected` property is

```
Response.IsClientConnected()
```

- Status—The Status property controls the status line the Web server will return. The syntax for using the Status property is

```
Response.Status = StatusCodeAndDescription
```

where StatusCodeAndDescription includes the status code and description.

- PICS—By using the PICS property, you can control the rating values of the PICS-label field. The syntax for using the PICS property is

```
Response.PICS(PicsLabel)
```

where PicsLabel is the formatted PICS label.

- ContentType—By using the ContentType property, you can specify the MIME content type the Web server will send to the browser. The syntax for using the ContentType property is

```
Response.ContentType = [ContentType]
```

where ContentType is a valid content type. Examples of valid content types are image/ GIF, image/JPEG, text/HTML, and so on.

- CharSet—The CharSet property controls the character set of the content type the browser will display. The syntax is

```
Response.CharSet(CharSetName)
```

where CharSetName is a valid character set name.

Methods   The following methods are supported by the Response object:

- Write—By using the Write method, you can send output to the client. The Write method's syntax is

```
Response.Write variant
```

where variant is a VBScript data type. You can use the following line of code, for example, to send the current date and time to the client's browser:

```
<%Response.Write now%>
```

- BinaryWrite—By using the BinaryWrite method, you can send binary information, such as an image, to the client. The BinaryWrite method's syntax is

```
Response.BinaryWrite binarydata
```

- Redirect—Redirect is used to direct the client to a different URL. You will find the Redirect method useful if your site's URL has changed, but a visitor to your site has not updated its link to your site. This way, when the visitor connects to your site at the old URL, the Redirect method will automatically redirect the visitor's browser to the new URL. The Redirect method's syntax is

```
Response.Redirect URL
```

You can use the following line of code, for example, to redirect the client browser to the default.asp Active Server Page on your server:

```
<%Response.Redirect ""default.asp""%>
```

Part

VI

Ch

33

▨ AppendToLog—By using the AppendToLog method, you can record information within the Web server's log file. As a result, you can use the AppendToLog method and the log file for debugging and tracking purposes. The AppendToLog method's syntax is

```
Response.AppendToLog string
```

where string is the string you will record to the log file.

▨ AddHeader—AddHeader adds information to the existing HTTP header. The AddHeader method's syntax is

```
Response.AddHeader header_name, header_value
```

where header_name is the name of the header, and header_value is the header's value.

▨ Clear—By using the Clear method, you can direct the Web server to clear its buffer. The Clear method's syntax is

```
Response.Clear
```

▨ Flush—The Flush method directs the Web server to send the buffered output to the client browser. The Flush method's syntax is

```
Response.Flush
```

N O T E You can use the Clear and Flush methods only if the buffering is on. If buffering is turned off, no data will be within the server's buffer. Using either method in such a case will result in an error. ▨

▨ End—By using the End method, you can control the amount of data within the Web server's buffer. The End method's syntax is

```
Response.End
```

When the server that processes the script comes across the End command, the server, in turn, will stop the data buffering.

The *Request* Object

The Request object enables you to retrieve information from the client. The Request object includes five collections:

▨ ClientCertificate—By referencing the ClientCertificate collection within the Request object, the Web server can collect information about certification fields from the browser. The certification fields include the following:

- Certificate—The Certificate field contains the entire certificate content in ASN.1 format.
- SerialNumber—The SerialNumber field contains the certification serial number.
- ValidFrom—The ValidFrom field specifies when the certificate will come into effect.

- ValidUntil—The ValidUntil field specifies when the certificate will expire.
- Issuer—The Issuer field contains information about the issuer of the certificate.
- Subject—The Subject field contains information about the subject of the certificate.

■ Cookies—By using the Cookies collection within the Request object, the Web server can collect information from the cookies on the client machine. The syntax for using the Cookies collection is

```
Request.Cookies(cookie)[(key)¦.attribute]
```

where cookie is the cookie's name, key is the index of subkey values, and attribute is the specified cookie's property.

■ Form—The Form collection is extremely useful because it enables you to retrieve information the user enters on a form within the browser. The syntax for using the Form collection is

```
Request.Form(parameter)[(index)¦.Count]
```

where parameter is the form collection's name, index is the specific form element, and count is the number of elements on the form.

■ QueryString—Sometimes data is passed to the server on a URL. By using the QueryString collection, the Web server can parse the information contained with the URL string. The syntax for using the QueryString collection is

```
Request.QueryString(variable)[(index)¦.Count]
```

where variable is the variable's name within the query string, index is the element index, and count represents the total number of elements within the query string.

■ ServerVariables—The ServerVariables collection enables you to access values of server environment variables. The syntax for using the ServerVariables collection is

```
Request.ServerVariables (ServerVariable)
```

where ServerVariable is the server variable's name. Table 33.4 lists the server variables.

Part VI

Ch 33

Table 33.4 The Server Variables

Variable Name	Description
AUTH_TYPE	specifies the server's authentication method
AUTH_PASSWORD	specifies the password the user entered within the client browser
CONTENT_LENGTH	returns the content's length
CONTENT_TYPE	returns the content's data type
GATEWAY_INTERFACE	returns the version of the server's CGI specification
HTTP_<HeaderName>	returns information contained within <HeaderName>

continues

Table 33.4   Continued

Variable Name	Description
LOGON_USER	specifies the NT login account that made the request
PATH_INFO	specifies the server's path information
PATH_TRANSLATED	returns a translated version of PATH_INFO
QUERY_STRING	returns the query string contained within the URL
REMOTE_ADDR	specifies the client machine's IP address
REMOTE_HOST	specifies the requesting host's name
REQUEST_METHOD	returns the method initiating the request
SCRIPT_NAME	specifies the executing script's virtual path
SERVER_NAME	returns the server's host name, DNS alias, or IP address
SERVER_PORT	returns the server's port number on which the request is made
SERVER_PORT_SECURE	returns a 1 if the request is made on the server's secure port, 0 if unsecured
SERVER_PROTOCOL	returns the requesting protocol's name and version
SERVER_SOFTWARE	returns the HTTP server's name and version
URL	returns the URL's base portion

N O T E   If you've done any CGI programming, you'll recognize the variables in Table 33.4 as the CGI environment variables. ▓

In addition, the Request object includes the following property and method:

▓   TotalBytes—The TotalBytes property tells you the total number of bytes the client sends. The syntax for using the TotalBytes property is

Request.TotalBytes

where Request is the Active Server Request object and TotalBytes represents the total number of bytes the client sends.

▓   BinaryRead—By using the BinaryRead method, the Web server can read binary information the client sends through the POST request. The BinaryRead method's syntax is

aBinaryArray = Request.BinaryRead(count)

where Request is the Active Server Request object, aBinaryArray is the binary array the BinaryRead method will create, and count is the total number of bytes for aBinaryArray.

Using Existing ASP Components

In addition to the `Application`, `Session`, `Server`, `Response`, and `Request` objects, IIS comes with a number of predefined, pretested Active Server components you can readily use within your ASP application. You will find these existing server-side components extremely useful in building your ASP application:

- Active Data Object (ADO)—The ADO is probably one of the most important ASP components. By using the ADO, you can communicate with back-end databases and create dynamic, data-driven Web sites.

- Browser Capabilities—By using the Browser Capabilities component, you can detect the type of client browser, determine the browser's capabilities through an INI file, and display appropriate HTML.

- Advertisement Rotator—The Advertisement Rotator component displays ad banners within your Web site. In addition, you can change the ad banners dynamically.

- Permission Checker Component—By using the Permission Checker component, you can determine whether a user has access permission to a given file.

- Content Linking Component—The Content Linking component helps you to design and develop a navigation scheme for your Web site.

- Page Counter Component—The Page Counter component tracks the number of times a page from your Web site has been requested. As a result, you can determine the amount of interest your Web site generates.

This chapter discusses the first two components: the Active Data Object and Browser Capabilities.

Active Data Object (ADO)

ADO is based on OLE DB, a C++ based applications programming interface (API). OLE DB is Microsoft's new database technology based on object linking and embedding. Because the technology is based on C++, its API is object oriented. ADO includes *data providers* and *data consumers*. The data providers access the OLE DB interface, and the data consumers take data from the interface. ADO is similar to Microsoft's Data Access Object (DAO) and Remote Data Object (RDO). However, Microsoft designed ADO specifically with Internet-based applications in mind.

ADO enables you to add database connectivity to your ASP application. To create an instance of the ADO component, you use the `Server` object's `CreateObject` method. The following line of code shows an example of creating a database connection:

```
Set myDBConnection = Server.CreateObject(""ADODB.Recordset"")
```

Next, you can use the ADO object's `Open` method to store the results of executing a given SQL statement. The following line of code shows an example of executing the given SQL statement and storing the results within the result set:

```
myDBConnection.Open "SELECT * FROM Transactions"
```

Part
VI

Ch
33

Next, you use the data connection's BOF (beginning-of-file) and EOF (end-of-file) methods to determine whether the current record within the recordset is the first or last record, respectively. If you are not at the beginning or end of the recordset, you can display the fields, for example. The following code uses a Do...While loop to print the transaction IDs in the recordset:

```
<%
If myDBConnection.EOF
    '=== you are at the end of the record set
Else If myDBConnection.BOF
    '=== you are at the beginning of the record set
Else
    Do While Not myDBConnection.EOF    '=== loop through the result set
        Response.Write (myDBConnection("Transaction_ID") & <BR>)
    Loop
End if
%>
```

The ADO object model includes the following objects, each of which is covered in detail in subsequent sections:

- Connection—By using the Connection object, you establish a connection with your application's data source. In addition, you can use the Connection object to send SQL commands for a database server to process.

- Command—The Command object executes parameterized queries and stored procedures.

- Parameter—You pass parameters to a stored procedure by using the Parameter object.

- Recordset—The Recordset object holds the data the server returns as a result of processing a SQL command.

- Field—The Recordset object uses the Field object because each record returned will contain one or more fields.

- Error—The Error object logs any errors from the data source.

The *Connection* Object   The Connection object establishes a connection with a system data source. In addition, you can use the Connection object to pass SQL instructions for the database server to process. Like most objects, Connection has a set of useful properties that you can reference. These include

- Attribute—The Attribute property specifies whether the database server will start a new transaction after the previous transaction's commit or rollback.

- CommandTimeOut—The CommandTimeOut property specifies the amount of time the server will wait to process the command. The default is 30 seconds.

- ConnectionString—ConnectionString specifies the connection string used to connect to the database.

- ConnectionTimeOut—The ConnectionTimeOut property specifies the amount of time to wait for a connection to the data source.

- DefaultDatabase—DefaultDatabase is set equal to the default database to use if your application's data source supports connecting to multiple databases.

- ▓ Isolation—The Isolation property specifies the isolation level of your application's connection to the data source.

- ▓ Mode—You use the Mode property to specify the connection type: either read-only or read/write.

- ▓ Provider—The Provider property is used to determine the provider of the connection to the data source.

- ▓ Version—You use the Version property to determine the ADO's version.

You can also perform operations on the Connection object by employing one of the following methods:

- ▓ BeginTrans—By using the Connection object's BeginTrans method, you can initiate a new transaction. Transactions are useful for maintaining data integrity within the database.

- ▓ CommitTrans—The CommitTrans method commits the current transaction to the database. If the commit is successful, your application will write all changes to the database since the previous CommitTrans or RollBackTrans.

- ▓ RollBackTrans—The RollBackTrans method cancels the current transaction. As a result, all changes to the database will revert since the previous CommitTrans or RollBackTrans.

- ▓ Close—To close your application's connection to the database, use the Close method.

- ▓ Execute—The Execute method is used to instruct the database server to execute a SQL command. If the Execute is successful, the database server will return a result set. You can then use the Recordset object to process the result set.

- ▓ Open—To open a connection to your application's data source, use the Open method.

The *Recordset* Object   In the ADO model, the Recordset object holds the results of a database query. You can create a Recordset object in a number of ways. You can create the object by using the Connection or Command objects, or by using the Recordset object itself. If you use the ADO Recordset object, you get to set the resulting recordset's properties. If you establish a Recordset using the Connection or Command object, you cannot set the resulting recordset's properties. Listing 33.5 shows an example of using the ADO Recordset to create a new Recordset object.

Listing 33.5   Creating a New *Recordset* Object with *ADO.Recordset*

```
Set myRecordset = Server.CreateObject("ADO.Recordset")
myRecordset.Source = ''
myRecordset.RecordCount = 20
myRecordset.Open
```

Table 33.6 lists the Recordset object's many properties.

Table 33.6   The *Recordset* Object Properties

Property	Description
AbsolutePage	indicates the current record's page
AbsolutePosition	indicates the current record's position within the recordset
ActiveConnection	indicates the active connection the recordset is using
BOF	indicates the beginning of file within the recordset
Bookmark	indicates a bookmark reference for the recordset
CacheSize	indicates the cache size for the recordset
CursorType	indicates the cursor type for the recordset
EditMode	indicates whether the current record is being edited or added
EOF	indicates the end of file within the recordset
Filter	indicates the filter applied to the recordset
LockType	indicates the type of lock applied to the recordset
MaxRecords	indicates the maximum number of records the recordset will return
PageCount	indicates the number of pages within the recordset
PageSize	indicates the number of records within a page
RecordCount	indicates the recordset's total number of records
Source	indicates the recordset's source (table or query)
Status	indicates the given record's status

The Recordset object also has several methods that you can use to manipulate it. These methods are outlined in Table 33.7.

Table 33.7   *The Recordset* Object Methods

Method	Description
AddNew	creates a new record
CancelBatch	cancels the pending batch update
CancelUpdate	cancels changes made to the current recordset
Clone	creates a new recordset by copying the records from the current recordset
Close	closes the current recordset

Method	Description
Delete	deletes the current record
GetRows	copies the given records into an array
Move	moves to the given record within the recordset
MoveFirst	moves to the recordset's first record
MoveLast	moves to the recordset's last record
MoveNext	moves to the next record within the recordset
MovePrevious	moves to the previous record within the recordset
NextRecordset	closes the current recordset and then opens the next recordset
Open	opens a recordset
Requery	refreshes the recordset by re-executing the query
Resync	syncs the current recordset with the database
Supports	verifies whether the database supports the given function
Update	saves the current record to the database
UpdateBatch	saves changes from the batch update to the database

The *Field* Object

Recall that the Recordset object also has a Field object associated with it because each record returned will contain one or more fields. Table 33.8 lists the Field object's properties.

Table 33.8 The *Field* Object Properties

Property	Description
ActualSize	the data's actual length
Attribute	the field's data
DefinedSize	the field's maximum size
Name	the field's name
NumericScale	scale for numeric field values
OriginalValue	the field's value before it was changed
Precision	precision scale for numeric field values
Type	the field's data type
UnderlyingValue	the field's value as stored within the database
Value	the field's actual value

Part
VI

Ch
33

You can use the two methods shown in Table 33.9 to modify the `Field` object.

Table 33.9 The *Field* Object Methods

Method	Description
AppendChunk	appends data to the field
GetChunk	gets data from the field

The Command Object   You can use the `Command` object to execute parameterized queries and stored procedures. To execute the query, you must specify the `ActiveConnection` and query. Listing 33.6 shows an example of creating a new `Recordset` object by using the `Command` object.

Listing 33.6 Creating a New *Recordset* Object by Using the *Command* Object

```
Set myRecordset = Server.CreateObject(ADODB.Command)
myRecordset.ActiveConnection = "myCompany"
myRecordset.CommandText = "qryGetActiveEmployees"
myRecordset.Execute
```

Table 33.10 details the properties associated with the `Command` object.

Table 33.10 The *Command* Object Properties

Property	Description
ActiveConnection	Indicates the `Connection` object for the `Command` object.
CommandText	Indicates the command the data source will execute.
CommandTimeout	Specifies the amount of time (in seconds) the data source will wait for the command to execute. The default is 30 seconds.
CommandType	Indicates the type of command the data source will execute.
Prepared	Used to tell the data provider to compile the command before execution.

Table 33.11 lists the `Command` object methods.

Table 33.11 The *Command* Object Methods

Method	Description
CreateObject	creates a new `Command` object
Execute	executes the command contained within the `Command` object's `CommandText` property

***Error* Object Methods**   The Error object logs any error messages returned from a database query. The entire group of error messages is known as the Error collection. Tables 33.12 and 33.13 list the Error collection properties and methods, respectively.

Table 33.12   The *Error* Collection Properties

Property	Description
Count	Indicates the total number of Error objects within the Error collection.
Item	Indicates the specific Error object within the Error collection. The object is identified by number or name.

Table 33.13   The *Error* Collection Methods

Method	Description
Clear	removes all Error objects from the Error collection

The Error object itself has the properties described in Table 33.14.

Table 33.14   The *Error* Object Properties

Property	Description
Description	description of the error
HelpContext	help topic within the help file to provide context-sensitive information about the error
HelpFile	help file's name
NativeError	error code specific to the data provider
Number	ID uniquely identifying the error
Source	name of the application returning the error
SQLState	five-digit SQL error code

The *Parameter* Object   The Parameter object is used to pass names of values of parameters to a stored procedure. It has the properties and methods detailed in Tables 33.15 and 33.16, respectively.

Table 33.15   The *Parameter* Object Properties

Property	Description
Attributes	indicates the type of data the Parameter object will accept
Direction	indicates whether the parameter is an input, output, or both
Name	parameter's name
NumericScale	scale for numeric parameter values
Precision	precision for numeric parameter values
Size	Parameter object's maximum size
Type	parameter's data type
Value	parameter's value

Table 33.16   The *Parameter* Object Methods

Method	Description
AppendChunk	appends a large amount of data to the parameter object

Browser Capabilities Component

The Browser Capabilities Component enables you to detect the type of client browser accessing your Web site. To create an instance of the Browser Capabilities Component, you use the Server object's CreateObject method. The following code shows an example of creating an instance of the Browser Capabilities Component:

```
Set bc = Server.CreateObject(""MSWC.BrowserType"")
```

You can use the Browser Capabilities Component along with the Browscap.ini file to determine the type of browser and its capabilities. The Browscap.ini file will contain information about the different industry-standard browsers. If the client browser does not support ActiveX controls, for example, you can decide to send alternate content to that browser instead of an ActiveX control. By using the Browser Capabilities Component, you can design your Web site irrespective of the browser the visitors to your site will use. This way, your target audience will not be limited by the type of browser.

Once instantiated, a Browser Capabilities object has properties whose values tell you what the target browser is able to process. The key properties of a Browser Capabilities object are outlined in Table 33.17.

Table 33.17   Properties of a Browser Capabilities Object

Property	Description
BackgroundSounds	whether the browser supports background sounds
Browser	the name of the browser ("Mozilla" for Netscape Navigator, "Explorer" for Microsoft Internet Explorer, and so on)
Cookies	whether the browser supports cookies
Frames	whether the browser supports frames
JavaScript	whether the browser supports JavaScript
Majorver	browser's major version number
Minorver	browser's minor version number
Tables	whether the browser supports tables
VBScript	whether the browser supports VBScript
Version	browser's complete version number

Developing ASP Applications with Visual InterDev

Visual InterDev is a Web programming tool for the advanced Web programmer and developer. Visual InterDev provides an integrated, visual development environment that includes all the tools you need to design and develop dynamic, data-driven Web applications. By using Visual InterDev, you can build Active Server Pages applications that incorporate server-side scripts, and access via ODBC to database formats such as Microsoft SQL Server, Oracle, and Informix, site management, and reusable server components.

Visual InterDev also enables you to integrate components such as Java applets, ActiveX controls, Active Server components, COM objects, and so on within your HTML and ASP pages. Furthermore, you can integrate third-party components.

You have access to a powerful set of tools within Visual InterDev that you can use to make your Web application data-aware and data-driven. Visual InterDev's main database components include the following:

- Database Designer—You use the Database Designer to design and manage Microsoft SQL Server 7.0 databases. By using the Database Designer, you can create, set up, and manage SQL Server databases.

- Query Designer—The integrated Query Designer constructs your queries visually. The Query Designer, in turn, will automatically translate the queries into Data Manipulation Language (DML) statements. In addition, you can use the Query Designer to test the SQL queries you build and to construct stored procedures for your application.

■ Database Wizards—The Database Wizard builds data-aware ASP pages. The Wizard will step you through the process of creating such pages, saving you from having to write much code on your own.

Visual InterDev supports both standard and design-time ActiveX controls. The design-time ActiveX controls will automatically generate the client-side or server-side scripts for your application. In addition, they can also generate the HTML content you can view by using any browser on any platform.

Just as you can integrate Visual SourceSafe with your Visual C++ and Visual Basic development environment, you can also integrate Visual SourceSafe with your Visual InterDev development environment to enable team development and version control.

Besides the tightly integrated database component, Visual InterDev also includes a version of FrontPage WYSIWYG HTML Editor, Microsoft Image Composer, which you can use to create, edit, and manipulate all kinds of images, and Microsoft Music Producer to integrate sounds into your Web pages. Visual InterDev also includes a Media Manager you can use to track your multimedia resources, such as sound clips, video clips, and images.

Putting It All Together: A Simple ASP Application

In the first part of this chapter, you read about VBScript In the first and how you could use it to create client-side scripts. Then, you learned quite a bit about Active Server Page applications and some of the built-in objects and components that support ASP development. Now it is time to join these two bodies of knowledge by looking at a short ASP application developed in VBScript. Suppose your company is running a Web-based marketing campaign. You have sent mailers to your clients assigning a unique promotional identifier to each one and inviting them to check out the promotion on your site. At your site, you will verify their contact information, ask them a few marketing questions, and then thank them for their participation. A back-end data source named "promotion" holds the current contact information and promotion IDs for each of your clients.

To begin the application, you need prompt your client for his or her promotion ID. A simple HTML form will suffice for this. What's unique in this case is that the ACTION attribute of the <FORM> tag will point to the ASP file promo1.asp and not at a CGI program. Listing 33.7 shows one possible way to code the form.

Listing 33.7   Form to Prompt User for Promotion ID

```
<HTML>
<HEAD>
<TITLE>Your Company: Marketing Promotion</TITLE>
</HEAD>
<BODY BGCOLOR="WHITE">
<BLOCKQUOTE>
Please enter your ID number below and click the "Enter Promotion" button.<P>
<FORM ACTION="promo1.asp" METHOD="POST">
```

```
<INPUT TYPE="TEXT" NAME="ID" SIZE=10><P>
<INPUT TYPE="SUBMIT" VALUE="Enter Promotion">
</FORM>
</BODY>
</HTML>
```

Next you need to create the file promo1.asp that will use the ID number entered by the user to query your "promotion" data source and present the information found in a second HTML form where the user can confirm his or her information and then answer your marketing question. You also need to be prepared to handle the cases where the ID entered is not a valid one and where the database query returns no results. In Listing 33.8, both the confirmation form and the error messages are handled by VBScript subroutines called by the main VBScript code block. Figure 33.2 shows the response to a valid ID number.

Listing 33.8   Code Listing for *promo1.asp*

```
<%
dim error
dim ID
error=""

if Not(IsNumeric(request.form("ID"))) then    'ID Not Numeric - stop
    call sub_error                 ' call error and don't come back
else
    ID = request.form("ID")        ' ID Fine, continue

' Create Connection
set dConn = Server.CreateObject("ADODB.Connection")
dConn.Open "promotion"

' Build SQL statement
SQL =       "Select * "
SQL = SQL + "FROM Clients "
SQL = SQL + "WHERE ClientID = " & request.form("ID")

' Execute Query
Set dRS = dConn.Execute(SQL)

if (dRS.EOF) AND (dRS.BOF) then    ' No record exists, print error
    call sub_empty
else
    call sub_Confirm
end if

' Clean Up RecordSets for Better
 ' memory management
dRS.Close
Set dRS=Nothing

end if   ' Else from Login Error
```

continues

Part

VI

Ch

33

Listing 33.8 Continued

```
' BEGIN SUBPROCEDURES

' Sub ERROR:  Provide user with message stating that entered ID is
' invalid, provide link to return to main page and start again

Sub sub_error
%>
<HTML><HEAD><TITLE>Invalid ID Number</TITLE></HEAD>
<BODY BGCOLOR="WHITE">
<H1>Invalid ID Number</H1>
The ID number you entered is not valid.  Please click the Continue
button below and re-enter the number from the letter you received in the
 mail.<P>
<FORM ACTION="index.html" MEHOD="POST">
<INPUT TYPE="SUBMIT" VALUE="Continue">
</FORM>
</BODY></HTML>
<%
end sub

' Sub empty:  Tells user no matching records were found and reprompts for
 promotion ID number.
Sub sub_empty
%>
<HTML><HEAD><TITLE>No Matches Found</TITLE></HEAD>
<BODY BGCOLOR="WHITE">
<H1>No Matches Found</H1>
No records in our database matched the ID number you entered.  Please
click the Continue button below and re-enter the number from the letter
you received in the mail.<P>
<FORM ACTION="index.html" MEHOD="POST">
<INPUT TYPE="SUBMIT" VALUE="Continue">
</FORM>
</BODY></HTML>
<%
end sub

' Sub Confirm:  Provide user with current data from database and
' allow user to update/modify information.

sub sub_confirm
%>
<HTML><HEAD><TITLE>Contact Information</TITLE></HEAD>
<BODY BGCOLOR="WHITE">
Please review the information below, making corrections where necessary.
 Click the "Continue" button when you're finished.

<FORM ACTION="promo2.asp" METHOD="POST">
<TABLE>
  <TR>
   <TD><B>First Name</B></TD>
   <TD><INPUT TYPE="TEXT" NAME="FirstName" VALUE="<%=dRS("FirstName")%>"
        SIZE=35></TD>
  </TR>
```

```
<TR>
 <TD><B>Last Name</B></TD>
 <TD><INPUT TYPE="TEXT" NAME="LastName" VALUE="<%=dRS("LastName")%>"
      SIZE=35></TD>
</TR>
<TR>
 <TD><B>Title</B></TD>
 <TD><INPUT TYPE="TEXT" NAME="Title" VALUE="<%=dRS("Title")%>" SIZE=35></TD>
</TR>
<TR>
 <TD><B>Company</B></TD>
 <TD><INPUT TYPE="TEXT" NAME="Company" VALUE="<%=dRS("Company")%>"
      SIZE=35></TD>
</TR>

    <%if (NOT IsEmpty(Address2)) then%>
<TR>
 <TD ROWSPAN=2 VALIGN="TOP"><B>Address</B></TD>
 <TD><INPUT TYPE="TEXT" NAME="Address1" VALUE="<%=dRS("Address1")%>"
      SIZE=35></TD>
</TR>
<TR>
 <TD><INPUT TYPE="TEXT" NAME="Address2" VALUE="<%=dRS("Address2")%>"
      SIZE=35></TD>
</TR>
    <%else%>
<TR>
 <TD ROWSPAN=2 VALIGN="TOP"><B>Address</B></TD>
 <TD><INPUT TYPE="TEXT" NAME="Address1" VALUE="<%=dRS("Address1")%>"
      SIZE=35></TD>
</TR>
<TR>
 <TD><INPUT TYPE="TEXT" NAME="Address2" VALUE="<%=dRS("Address2")%>"
      SIZE=35></TD>
</TR>
    <%end if%>
        <TR>
 <TD><B>City</B></TD>
 <TD><INPUT TYPE="TEXT" NAME="City" VALUE="<%=dRS("City")%>" SIZE=35>
 </TD>
</TR>
<TR>
 <TD><B>State</B></TD>
 <TD><INPUT TYPE="TEXT" NAME="State" VALUE="<%=dRS("State")%>" SIZE=35>
 </TD>
</TR>
<TR>
 <TD><B>Zip Code</B></TD>
 <TD><INPUT TYPE="TEXT" NAME="Zip" VALUE="<%=dRS("Zip")%>" SIZE=35>
 </TD>
</TR>
<TR>
 <TD><B>Phone</B></TD>
 <TD><INPUT TYPE="TEXT" NAME="Phone" VALUE="<%=dRS("Phone")%>"
```

continues

Listing 33.8 Continued

```
   SIZE=35></TD>
</TR>
<TR>
 <TD><B>Fax</B></TD>
 <TD><INPUT TYPE="TEXT" NAME="Fax" VALUE="<%=dRS("Fax")%>" SIZE=35>
 </TD>
</TR>
<TR>
<TD><B>Email</B></TD>
 <TD><INPUT TYPE="TEXT" NAME="Email" VALUE="<%=dRS("Email")%>" SIZE=35>
 </TD>
</TR>
<TR>
 <TD COLSPAN="2"><HR NOSHADE WIDTH="100%"></TD>
</TR>
<TR>
 <TD COLSPAN="2"><B>Are you a decision maker for
  technology purchases?</B></TD>
</TR>
<TR>
   <TD><INPUT TYPE="RADIO" NAME="Decide" VALUE="1">
       Yes</TD>
   <TD><INPUT TYPE="RADIO" NAME="Decide" VALUE="0">
       No</TD>
</TR>
<TR>
   <TD COLSPAN="2"><B>How much will you spend on new
    equipment this year?</B><BR>
    </TD>
</TR>
<TR>
   <TD COLSPAN="2"><INPUT TYPE="TEXT" NAME="Amount"></TD>
</TR>
<TR>
   <TD COLSPAN="2"><INPUT TYPE="Submit" NAME="Continue"></TD>
</TR>
</TABLE>
<INPUT TYPE="HIDDEN" NAME="ID" VALUE="<%=ID%>">
</FORM>
</BODY>

</HTML>
<%
end sub
%>
```

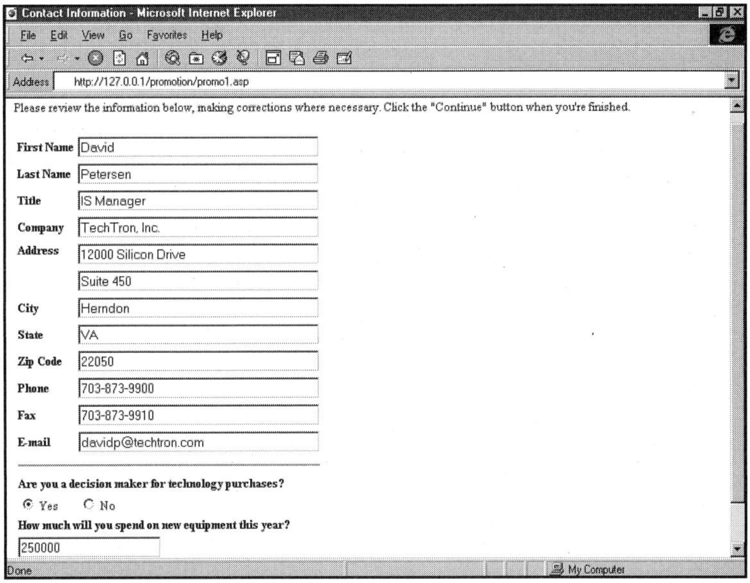

FIGURE 33.2

If a user's ID number is found in the database, you present him with his information as it currently exists and invite him to update it.

Note the use of many of the things you've seen so far in this chapter:

- VBScript for validation of the form input and general control of the processing through if-then-else type statements
- Use of the Request object to get the form data submitted by the user
- Use of the ADO component to initiate a query against the database
- Referencing the ADO object to get the values of the fields returned in the query

Part

VI

Ch

33

Users entering a valid ID into the initial form will now see their current contact information displayed in a HTML form that they can update if required. Then, after they click the Continue button, the ASP promo2.asp is launched to process the submitted form data. promo2.asp, shown in Listing 33.9 builds the SQL statement to update the database with the submitted information and then presents a thank-you message to the user (see Figure 33.3).

Listing 33.9 Code Listing for *promo2.asp*

```
<%
dim ID
dim FirstName
dim LastName
dim Title
dim Company
```

continues

Listing 33.9   Continued

```
dim Address1
dim Address2
dim City
dim State
dim Zip
dim Phone
dim Fax
dim Email
dim Decide
dim Amount

FirstName = request.form("FirstName")
LastName  = request.form("LastName")
Title     = request.form("Title")
Company   = request.form("Company")
Address1  = request.form("Address1")
Address2  = request.form("Address2")
City      = request.form("City")
State     = request.form("State")
Zip       = request.form("Zip")
Phone     = request.form("Phone")
Fax       = request.form("Fax")
Email     = request.form("Email")
Decide    = request.form("Decide")
Amount    = request.form("Amount")
ID        = request.form("ID")

' Build SQL statement

SQL = "UPDATE  Clients "
SQL = SQL + "SET FirstName='" & FirstName  & "',LastName='" & LastName
SQL = SQL + ",Title= '" & Title & "',Company='" & Company & "',"
SQL = SQL + "Address1='" & Address1 & "',Address2='" & Address2 &"',"
SQL = SQL + "City='" & City & "',State='" & State & "',"
SQL = SQL + "Zip='" & Zip & "',Phone='" & Phone & "',"
SQL = SQL + "Fax='" & Fax & "',Email='" & Email & "',"
SQL = SQL + "Decide='" & Decide & "',"
SQL = SQL + "Amount='" & Amount
SQL = SQL + "WHERE ClientID = " & ID

' Execute Query - execute the update

Set dRS = dConn.Execute(SQL)

' Clean Up RecordSets for Better
 ' memory management
dRS.Close
Set dRS=Nothing

%>

<HTML>
<HEAD>
```

```
<TITLE>Information Updated!</TITLE>
</HEAD>
<BODY BGCOLOR="WHITE">
<H2>Thank you, <%=FirstName%></H2>
Thanks for participating in our survey.  We look forward to
supporting you in the future.
</BODY>
</HTML>
```

FIGURE 33.3

A second ASP takes care of updating the database and presenting a closure message to the user.

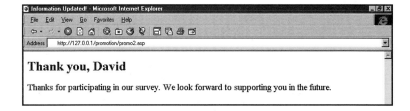

Again, the ASP file uses the `Request` object and the ADO Component to take the user's input, compose a SQL statement that will update the user's record, and then perform the update.

Now that you have seen some of the basics of VBScript and ASP development, it would not be hard to extend this sample application to include greater functionality, such as assigning a client ID number to someone who does not have one or doing some basic error-checking. Additionally, you should be able to easily adapt the approaches used in this example to build other ASP applications for your Web site. For more information on ASP development, consult the ASP developer resource site found at `http://www.activeserverpages.com/`.

Part
VI

Ch
33

Using ColdFusion

by Eric Ladd

What Is ColdFusion?

With the soaring popularity of dynamically generated pages created from server-side databases, it should come as no surprise that many software tools have emerged to assist Web developers with the programming required to produce such pages. Software of this kind is often called *middleware* because it acts as an intermediary between the Web server software and the target database.

One middleware product that has proved to be immensely popular with developers is Allaire's ColdFusion. References to chemistry aside, ColdFusion is an application that runs on the same machine as your Web server. Figure 34.1 shows an overview of how ColdFusion works with your Web server. The major steps in the delivery of a ColdFusion based page are

1. A user requests a file containing ColdFusion code (called a ColdFusion *template*) or submits a form that has a ColdFusion template as its ACTION attribute.

2. The Web server hands the template over to the ColdFusion Application Server for processing.

3. The ColdFusion Application Server parses out the programmatic instructions, makes all necessary calls to server-side databases via Open Database Connectivity (ODBC) drivers, performs any required data manipulation, and then prepares an HTML document as its response to the server.

4. The HTML document is returned to the Web server which, in turn, sends it to the user's browser.

FIGURE 34.1

This diagram illustrates how ColdFusion works with a Web server and other services on your server.

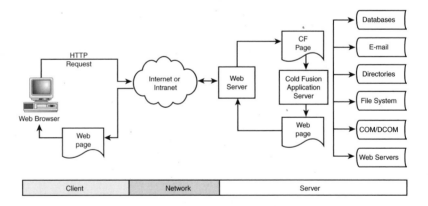

You give instructions to the ColdFusion Application Server through the ColdFusion Markup Language (CFML), a tag-based language that you embed inside HTML code to produce a ColdFusion template. In addition to the tags, CFML features scores of useful built-in functions that make it easy to handle data structures such as queries, arrays, strings, lists, dates, and variables.

In addition to its capability to interact with ODBC-compliant databases, ColdFusion extends its usefulness with the capability to interact with other services running on your server. These include

- Mail servers
- Lightweight Directory Access Protocol (LDAP) directory servers
- Verity search engine collections
- Java applets
- COM/DCOM objects

Thus, it becomes easy to perform basic tasks common to many Web-based applications. In an electronic commerce application, for example, you could gather a user's purchases as he or she shops, storing them in a backend database table. At checkout time, you query the database for the user's purchases and present them for confirmation. Then you collect the user's credit card information, stashing that in your database as well, and email a receipt confirming the purchase. All these steps are simple to implement using ColdFusion.

This chapter introduces you to the ColdFusion application development environment. The major components of this environment include

- The ColdFusion Application Server, which can be installed on either a Windows NT/98 or Solaris platform
- The ColdFusion Administrator, a browser-based interface that enables you to configure the ColdFusion Application Server
- ColdFusion Studio, a useful tool for authoring ColdFusion templates

Over the course of the chapter, you'll also learn about many of the useful CFML tags and functions that make Web-based application development with ColdFusion a straightforward and enjoyable task.

N O T E A single chapter cannot do justice to the power and utility of the ColdFusion development environment. For a fuller treatment, you should consult Ben Forta's popular book, *The ColdFusion Web Application Construction Kit, Second Edition*, published by Que.

Part VI Ch 34

What Else Do I Need to Know to Develop ColdFusion Applications?

Understanding the ColdFusion development environment and mastering CFML are two important steps in becoming proficient in developing ColdFusion applications. However, to do serious application development, you should also be versed in the following skills:

- HTML—CFML instructions are embedded inside HTML code, so to excel at ColdFusion development, you need to truly understand HTML and be able to work with raw HTML code.
- Relational database design—You should have a command of data modeling theory and how to express your model in terms of fields and tables in a relational database.

continues

continued

- Structured Query Language (SQL)—SQL (pronounced "sequel") is the language used to pose queries to, insert data into, update data in, or delete data from a backend database. You can find an excellent SQL tutorial on the Web at w3.one.net/~jhoffman/sqltut.htm.

- JavaScript—You can combine JavaScript and ColdFusion to produce applications more powerful and flexible than those you could create with ColdFusion alone.

You will most definitely need to have a basic understanding of HTML, SQL, and relational database design to become a competent ColdFusion developer. After you feel well grounded in these basics, you can then move on to building JavaScript-enabled ColdFusion applications. But knowing JavaScript is not an absolute prerequisite for being able to develop with ColdFusion.

Installing the ColdFusion Application Server

As noted earlier in the chapter, the Cold Fusion Application Server can run on both Windows NT/98 and Solaris platforms. On a Windows server, ColdFusion is compatible with the following kinds of HTTP servers:

- Netscape servers, such as FastTrack or Enterprise
- Microsoft servers, such as Internet Information Server (IIS) or Peer Web Services (PWS)
- O'Reilly WebSite Pro
- Apache for NT

If you're installing ColdFusion on a Solaris machine, it will need to be running with one of the following Web servers:

- Apache
- Netscape Enterprise or FastTrack servers

Installing ColdFusion on either platform is fairly straightforward. On a Windows machine, you'll be walked through the process over the course of several dialog boxes that prompt you for information such as the directory where you want to install ColdFusion, which Web server ColdFusion will be working with, and what password you want to use with the ColdFusion Administrator and ColdFusion Studio. If you're doing a Solaris installation, you'll find that all you need to do is launch the installation file and respond to the few questions you are asked during the install.

After you've installed the application server, you can immediately check to see if it is working properly by accessing the ColdFusion Getting Started page at http://127.0.0.1/CFDOCS/index.htm. There you will find links to an application where you can test your installation, as well as links to help and documentation in HTML format (see Figure 34.2).

FIGURE 34.2

The ColdFusion Getting Started page enables you to test your installation and serves as a reference while you're developing applications.

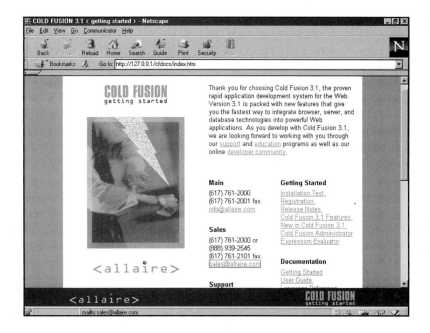

NOTE The IP address 127.0.0.1 is reserved for addressing the Web server running on the machine on which you did the ColdFusion installation. ▦

With the ColdFusion Application Server installed, you can then configure the server using the ColdFusion Administrator. The many functions of the Administrator are discussed in the next section.

Using the ColdFusion Administrator

A lot is going on behind the scenes within the ColdFusion development environment, and you can orchestrate all aspects of this activity through the ColdFusion Administrator. Specifically, you can do things such as

- Stop and start the ColdFusion Application Server.
- Create and configure ODBC data sources.
- Activate debugging messages that make it easier to troubleshoot your applications.
- Specify how and where the ColdFusion Application Server should log certain events.
- Configure the ColdFusion Application Server to work with an electronic mail server.
- Create searchable Verity collections.
- Install custom CFML tags.
- Register Java applets.

Part
VI

Ch
34

To access the ColdFusion Administrator, access the URL `http://127.0.0.1/CFIDE/adminis-trator/index.cfm` and enter the Administrator password you specified during the installation of the ColdFusion Application Server. After you're authenticated, you'll see a screen such as the one in Figure 34.3.

FIGURE 34.3

You can control the ColdFusion development environment through a browser-based interface.

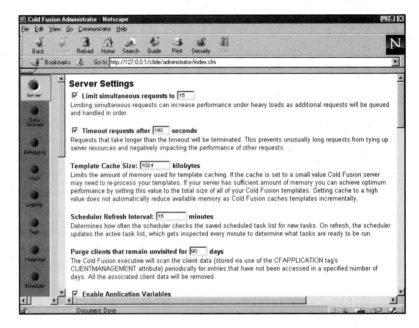

The main administrator page is split into two frames. The left frame contains buttons that enable you to quickly navigate to the major parts of the Administrator. The right frame displays the settings that you can change within a given part. The next several sections of this chapter walk you through the various parts of the Administrator and point out the ColdFusion environment parameters that you can control through the Administrator.

Configuring the ColdFusion Application Server

The right frame in Figure 34.3 shows the many server settings you can configure using the Administrator. These include

- Number of simultaneous requests—You can enhance the application server's performance by limiting the number of requests that it can simultaneously process. Any requests beyond this limiting number are queued in memory and processed in the order in which they are received.

T I P

A good rule of thumb is to make the maximum number of simultaneous requests equal to the number of processors on your server.

- Request timeout—You can specify a certain number of seconds after which the processing of a template will time out. This helps to avoid situations where infinite loops or especially large query result sets might bog down your server.

N O T E Even if you specify a timeout value, you should keep in mind that users can override this value by adding a `RequestTimeOut` parameter to the URL of the ColdFusion template that they are calling. If you have the timeout set to 30 seconds, for example, a user could circumvent this by entering a URL such as:

`http://www.cfserver.com/template.cfm?RequestTimeOut=300`

The `RequestTimeOut` parameter passed with the URL will increase the timeout value for that request to 300 seconds instead of the 30 seconds that you specified in the Administrator.

- Template caching—A cached template will be processed much more quickly than one that is not cached, so you should set this value as high as your server's memory will allow. In an ideal setting, you would set this value equal to the total size in kilobytes of all your ColdFusion templates. That way, all your templates could be cached after they are initially processed, and subsequent calls to those templates would run much more quickly.

- Schedule refresh interval—The ColdFusion Scheduler enables you to submit templates for processing at specified times. This setting in the Administrator tells the Scheduler how frequently it should check for new scheduled tasks.

- Client data retention—ColdFusion can store individual client data and retain it for a certain number of days. You can instruct ColdFusion to purge this data after a set number of days of inactivity using this Administrator setting.

- Application and session variables—ColdFusion also supports the storage of application-specific and user session-specific variables on the server. You can control the maximum and default timeout times for these variables with the ColdFusion Administrator.

N O T E If your server's memory resources are limited, you may want to think about turning off application and session variables because they increase the amount of memory that the ColdFusion Application Server uses.

- Passwords—You can enable password-protected access to the ColdFusion Application Server from both the Administrator and from ColdFusion Studio by putting a check in the appropriate box and specifying the password you want to use. You are strongly encouraged to do this so that users are not able to alter your ColdFusion environment's settings.

Setting Up Data Sources

Clicking the Data Sources button in the left frame yields a screen such as the one you see in Figure 34.4. This is where you create, modify, test, and delete ODBC data sources. These data sources are pointers to database files, together with specifications on how ColdFusion should interact with the database.

Part
VI

Ch
34

FIGURE 34.4

The Data Sources section of the ColdFusion Administrator is where you specify which databases ColdFusion is able to use and how it should connect to those databases.

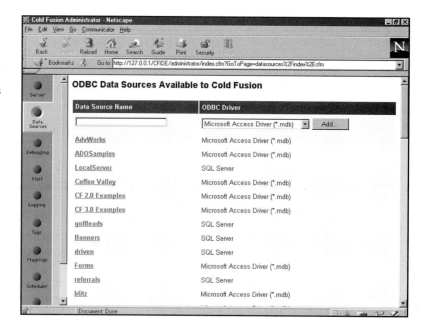

On the initial page of the Data Sources section, you'll see a list of all the available data sources and what kind of ODBC driver is being used to access the data source. Below this list, you'll see a drop-down list that contains the names of all the data sources. By selecting one of these and clicking the Verify button, ColdFusion will test its connection to that data source and let you know if the test succeeded or failed.

To create a new data source, follow these steps:

1. Type the name of the data source into the text field at the top of the Data Source Name column.

2. Select which kind of ODBC driver you want to use from the drop-down list at the top of the ODBC Driver column. The list of ODBC drivers available depends on your operating system. If you're using a Windows machine, you'll see drivers for all the Microsoft database formats (Access, SQL Server, FoxPro, Excel), as well as Oracle drivers and any other drivers you may have installed yourself. On a Solaris machine, you will not find drivers for the Microsoft database formats.

3. Click the button labeled Add to create the data source. The right frame will change to show you the Create ODBC Data Source page similar to the one you see in Figure 34.5.

N O T E   The Create ODBC Data Source page will look slightly different for each kind of ODBC driver because each driver has its own specific parameters that need to be set. ▪

4. Fill in the information requested on the Create ODBC Data Source page, making sure to specify the drive and directory path to the database file. ColdFusion comes with a Java applet that enables you to browse the drives and directories until you find the file you want.

FIGURE 34.5

When setting up a data source, you need to give it a name, specify the location of the database file, and set other driver-specific parameters.

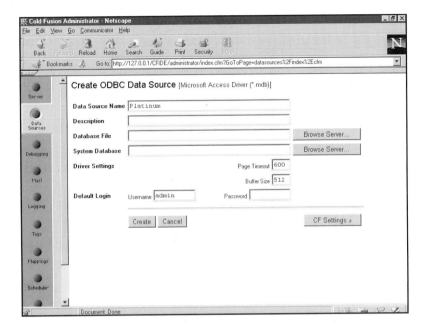

5. At this point, you have two options. You can click the Create button to create the data source and return to the initial data source page, or you can click the CF Settings button to reveal a more detailed version of the Create ODBC Data Source page (see Figure 34.6).

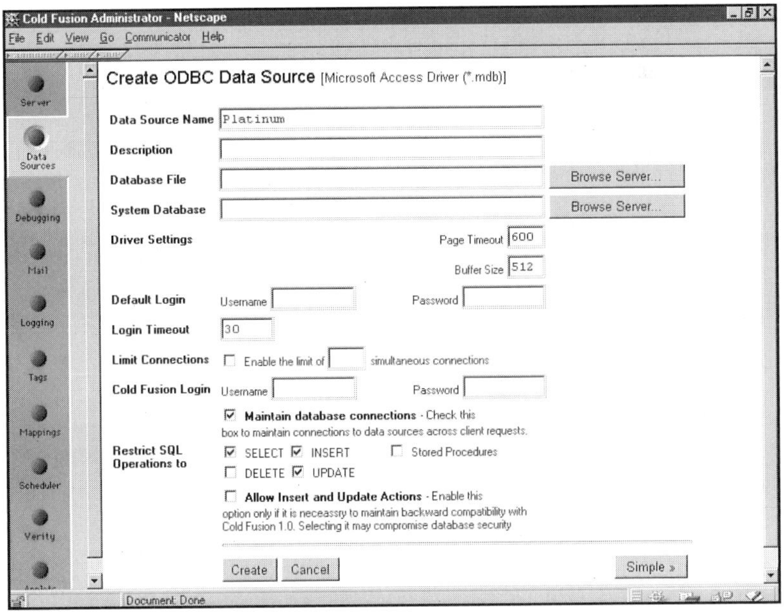

FIGURE 34.6

You can also configure how ColdFusion interacts with the data source when you create it.

Part

VI

Ch

34

6. Choose values for the ColdFusion settings to associate with the data source. This includes values for the login timeout (how long ColdFusion will try to connect to the data source), how many simultaneous connections to allow to the database, a special username and password for ColdFusion to use when logging into the database, whether or not to maintain a connection to the database between requests, and any restrictions on SQL operations done against the database.

TIP

Don't maintain connections to the database if you frequently have to upload updated copies of the database. If ColdFusion maintains the connection, then it keeps a lock on the database file and you can't overwrite it with the new file without stopping the ColdFusion service.

7. Click the Create button to create the data source and return to the main data source page.

To edit an existing data source, click its name from the main data source page. This will take you to a page that looks almost like the one you saw in Figure 34.5. From there, you can edit the data source's properties or click the CF Settings button to get an expanded edit page that is similar to what you saw in Figure 34.6. After you're done making your changes, click the Update button to save them.

If you need to delete a data source, click the data source's name to go to the edit page, and then click the Delete button.

CAUTION

After you delete a data source, it will no longer be available to any of your ColdFusion applications. Before deleting a data source, make sure that none of your applications contain references to it.

Also, keep in mind that deleting a data source is not the same as deleting a database file. If you want to delete the database file, you'll need do that through your operating system's interface.

Using Debugging

ColdFusion's debugging feature is invaluable when you're troubleshooting an application. Figure 34.7 shows you the Debug Settings section of the ColdFusion Administrator. The four check boxes at the top control what kinds of debugging messages you get from the server. You can choose any combination of

- Variables—If checked, you get a list of all form, URL, cookie, and CGI environment variables as well as the values of each variable.
- Processing time—Knowing the total processing time for a request can help you determine if changes to your code are making it more efficient or if they are impairing performance.
- SQL and data source name—In the event of a query error, ColdFusion will show you the SQL statement and the target data source that caused the error.
- Query information—ColdFusion can tell you the processing time, how many records were returned, and what SQL statement was used for each query in the request.

FIGURE 34.7

You can choose which kinds of debugging messages you want displayed during application development and testing.

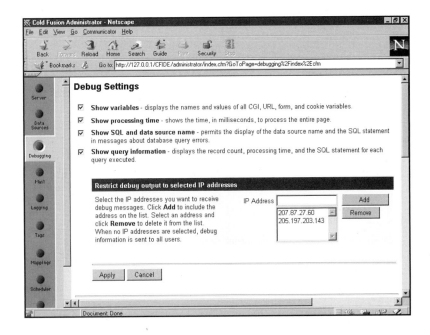

ColdFusion appends debugging information to the bottom of the HTML page it generates in response to a browser's request. As you can see in Figure 34.8, the debugging information is rendered in a typewriter font, so it is easy to pick out from the rest of the document.

FIGURE 34.8

Debugging information always appears at the end of the ColdFusion page.

Debugging information—

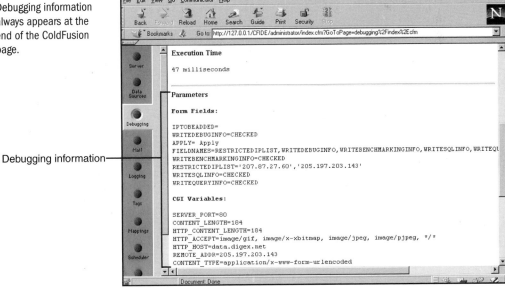

Part
VI

Ch
34

One nice feature about ColdFusion debugging information is that you can restrict the delivery of the information to a specific set of IP addresses but not to every user. Thus, if you and/or your development team all have fixed IP addresses, you can insert these addresses into the IP Address listing you see in Figure 34.7. That way, your developers will see debugging messages, but regular application users will not.

TIP If your IP addresses are dynamically assigned, you may want to do your ColdFusion development and testing on a separate server and then port the finished application to a production server when you are done. You can then turn on debugging for the development server without restricting the output to specific IP addresses, and your developers will still be able to get debugging feedback.

Using ColdFusion with a Mail Server

You can send electronic mail messages from your ColdFusion applications after you have ColdFusion configured to work with your mail server. Figure 34.9 shows the Mail portion of the ColdFusion Administrator. Here you can tell the ColdFusion Application Server the name or IP address of your mail server, which server port it should use (typically port 25), and a connect timeout value. You can also verify the connection to your mail server by clicking the Send button under the Verify Mail Server Settings heading on the page.

FIGURE 34.9

Telling ColdFusion some things about your mail server is an important prerequisite for sending electronic mail through ColdFusion applications.

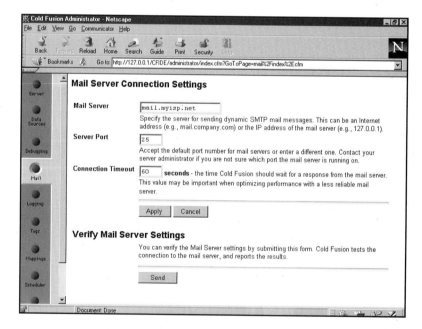

Setting Up Logging

Like many applications, ColdFusion will log any errors in encounters while processing your templates. Under the Logging section of the ColdFusion Administrator, you can tell ColdFusion the directory where you want the ColdFusion logs stored and provide an email address for the server administrator so that users can mail any error occurrences to the administrator (see Figure 34.10).

FIGURE 34.10

ColdFusion Application Server errors are logged in files stored in a directory of your choosing.

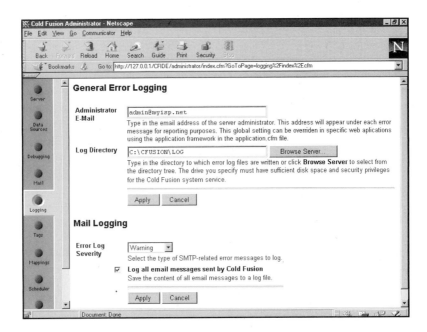

You can also log any mail-related errors ColdFusion encounters when composing and sending email messages. You can log mail server messages by their severity (Information, Warning, or Error) and you can choose to log the content of every email that ColdFusion sends.

 TIP If you opt to log all email messages, make sure you archive the contents of the file periodically so it does not become so large as to become unmanageable.

Restricting File-Related Tags and Using Custom Tags

Some CFML tags can manipulate files, and an ill-intentioned user could exploit these tags to upload content to, modify content on, or delete content from your server. To prevent this from happening, you can choose to enable or disable these tags from the Tags section of the ColdFusion Administrator. As you can see in Figure 34.11, you can activate the <CFDIRECTORY>, <CFFILE>, <CFCONTENT>, and <CFOBJECT> tags by checking the box next to each one.

FIGURE 34.11

If you're administering a ColdFusion server and are concerned about file security, you will probably want to disable the file-related CFML tags.

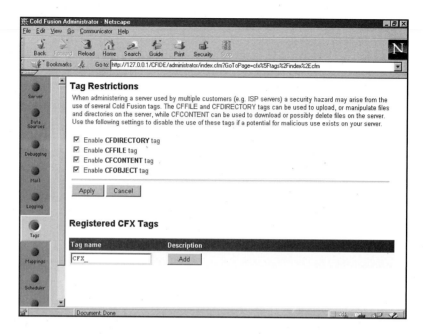

Another of ColdFusion's many great features is that you can develop your own tags when existing CFML tags won't do the job. Custom ColdFusion tags can be developed in CFML or in more complicated programming languages such as C++. After you have developed a custom tag, you need to register it with the ColdFusion Administrator. To do this, you enter the tag's name in the text field you see under the Registered CFX Tags heading in Figure 34.11 and then click the Add button. You then need to specify a few additional pieces of information, such as the supporting DLL file, procedure, whether to keep the DLL loaded in memory, and a description of the tag.

N O T E All custom tags that you write in C++ must begin with CFX_. Custom tags written in CFML begin with CF_ and can reside in the same directory as your other application templates.

Setting Up Mappings

Sometimes it's much easier to set up a logical path or *alias* to a long directory path than type out that path again and again. You can do this through the ColdFusion Administrator's Mappings page (see Figure 34.12). To set up a directory mapping, enter the logical path in the first text field, then enter the actual directory path into the second text field and click the Add Mapping button.

T I P It's easier to use the built-in Java applet to browse the server when specifying the directory path. It also reduces the chance of your making a mistake while typing in the path.

FIGURE 34.12

You can shorten long, tedious directory paths by setting up aliases in the ColdFusion Administrator.

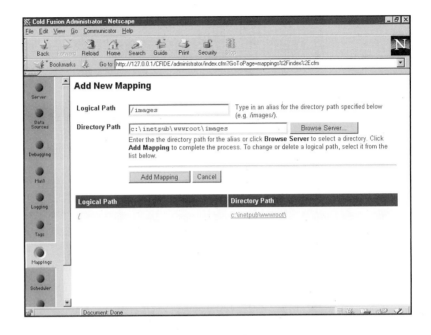

Scheduling ColdFusion Templates

The ColdFusion Scheduler will submit templates for processing at intervals you specify. This might be useful, for example, when developing a survey application. As part of the application, you could write a daily summary template that looks at the survey entries for a 24-hour period and emails a summary of the day's results to the survey administrator.

To schedule a template, you first need to go to the Scheduler page of the ColdFusion Administrator. There you type in the name of the task you want to schedule and click the Add New Task button. When you do, you'll see a screen similar to the one shown in Figure 34.13.

When scheduling the task, you will have to provide information such as

- Start and end dates for the task (ColdFusion will assume no end date if none is specified).
- The frequency of the task (once, daily, every 45 minutes, and so on).
- The URL of the template and any login and proxy information needed to invoke the template.
- Where to write the output from the template, should you choose to record it.

After you have all the scheduling parameters entered, click the Create button to schedule the task. If you need to modify the task later on, click the task name from the main Tasks page and make the edits on the Edit Scheduler Task page (which looks exactly like the page in Figure 34.13). When you're done making your changes, click the Update button to apply them.

Part

VI

Ch

34

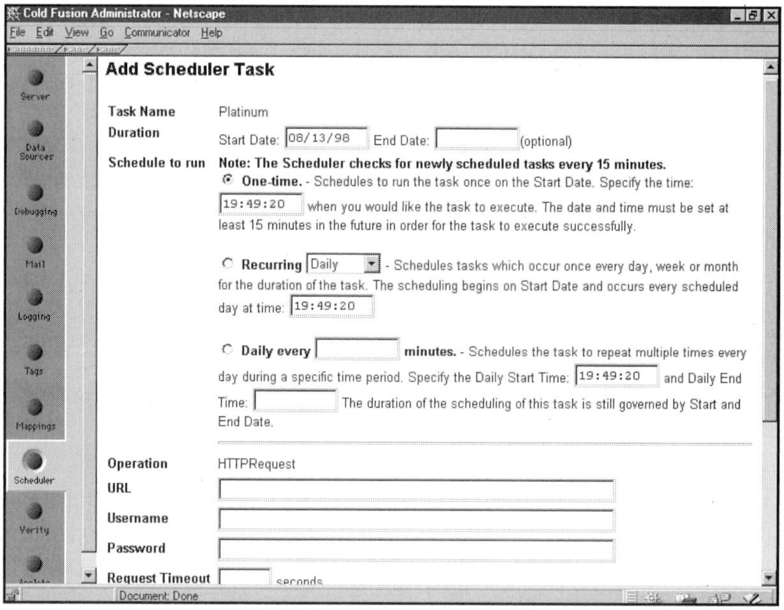

FIGURE 34.13

ColdFusion templates can be run automatically according to schedules that you create.

NOTE Tasks are automatically deleted after the end date specified in the task duration has passed. If you did not specify an end date, you can delete the task by going to the Edit Scheduler Task page and clicking the Delete button. ▇

Using the Verity Search Engine

ColdFusion comes bundled with a version of the popular Verity search engine, making it easy to set up searchable sets of documents. In Verity vernacular, these sets of documents are called *collections*, and you can create your own collections from the ColdFusion Administrator's Verity page (see Figure 34.14).

The Verity page is divided into two parts. The top part shows any existing Verity collections and enables you to perform different operations on those collections. The most common task is to index a collection. When you click the Index button, you get the option of specifying (by file extension) which type of files you want to index, the directory you want to index, and whether you want to recursively index subdirectories. When Verity indexes a collection, it examines the contents of each file and builds a database to support search engine queries against those files.

The lower part of the Verity page enables you to create a new Verity collection. To do this, you type in a name for the collection, specify the directory where ColdFusion should store the collection, and provide a language context for the collection.

FIGURE 34.14

Verity collections are groups of searchable documents that you can access through ColdFusion.

Registering Applets

ColdFusion works well with Java applets, but only after you have registered the applet with the ColdFusion Administrator. To do this, go to the Applet page in the Administrator, type in a name for the applet, and click the Register New Applet button. When you do, you'll see the page shown in Figure 34.15.

The information you have to provide on the Register New Applet page may look familiar to you if you use the <APPLET> tag a lot. The values for the CODE, CODEBASE, METHOD, HEIGHT, WIDTH, VSPACE, HSPACE, and ALIGN attributes are exactly what you would put in the corresponding fields on the registration page. ColdFusion will use this information to write out an <APPLET> tag for you. The text entered in the Java Not Supported Message is exactly what you might specify in an ALT attribute, except what you enter through the ColdFusion Administrator can be marked up with HTML code.

In the applet parameters section, you can specify the parameter/value pairs that get passed to the applet. This is analogous to using the <PARAM> tag to pass parameters to an applet placed with the <APPLET> tag.

Part
VI

Ch
34

Stopping and Starting ColdFusion

One other important piece of ColdFusion administration that does not appear as an option in the main Administrator interface is stopping and starting the ColdFusion Application Server. Occasionally, you'll need to stop the Application Server to update a database file or to refresh the service in the event of a crash. To do this, direct your browser to http://127.0.0.1/ CFIDE/administrator/startstop.html. This will load an HTML page with an embedded Java applet that will present you with buttons that stop and start the Application Server (see Figure 34.16).

FIGURE 34.15

You can embed Java applets in your ColdFusion templates after you register them.

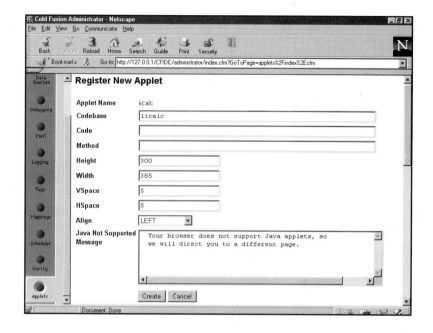

FIGURE 34.16

The ColdFusion Administrator also comes with a simple two-button control panel that you can use to stop and start the ColdFusion service.

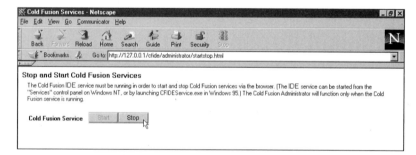

N O T E   You will need to enter the ColdFusion Administrator password before being able to stop and start the ColdFusion Application Server. ■

The ColdFusion Markup Language (CFML)

Now that you are familiar with the basics of ColdFusion administration, you can begin to learn CFML—the language used to develop ColdFusion applications. Two important things to remember about CFML are

- CFML code is located in the same file as HTML code.
- CFML is a tag-based language, so if you're comfortable with HTML, it will be easier to pick up CFML.

As you read earlier, CFML also comes with more than 175 functions for processing specific data structures. These functions are used within tags and make ColdFusion application development that much easier.

The next two major sections look at the most useful CFML tags and functions in the context of common tasks you would need to code when developing a ColdFusion application. Documentation covering every CFML tag and function can be found in ColdFusion's built-in help and reference material (`http://127.0.0.1/CFDOCS/index.html`) or in the Help section of the ColdFusion Studio Resource Tab.

▶ **See** "Using ColdFusion Studio," later in this chapter, **p. 928**.

CFML Tags

CFML tags are similar to HTML tags in that

■ They can occur as standalone tags or in an opening tag/closing tag pair.

■ They have attributes that modify the effect of the tag.

One thing common to all CFML tags is that the keyword for each tag always begins with the letters CF. This is especially important to remember because some CFML tags, such as `<CFFORM>` and `<CFTABLE>`, would be reduced to regular HTML tags if you left the CF off the keywords.

The next several sections examine many of the useful tags that make up CFML, including

■ Assigning values to ColdFusion variables with `<CFSET>` and printing their values with `<CFOUTPUT>`

■ Querying, inserting, updating, and deleting records in a database using `<CFQUERY>`

■ Implementing conditional logic with `<CFIF>`

■ Creating looping constructs with `<CFLOOP>`

■ Sending email using `<CFMAIL>`

■ Using several other useful tags such as `<CFINCLUDE>`, `<CFLOCATION>`, `<CFCOOKIE>`, `<CFTRANSACTION>`, and `<CFFORM>`

Setting Variables and Displaying Their Values

In any programming language, it is common to create named areas in memory called *variables* and store key values there for reference during the execution of the program. ColdFusion is no different in this regard and enables you to create variables of many types, including

■ Numeric

■ Strings

■ Boolean (TRUE or FALSE)

Part
VI

Ch
34

- Date/Time
- Lists (items delimited by commas or another character of your choosing)
- Arrays
- Queries

Each type of variable is instantiated by the `<CFSET>` tag. `<CFSET>` is a standalone tag with the following syntax:

```
<CFSET variable = value>
```

Some sample variable assignments might look like

```
<CFSET sorted = FALSE>
<CFSET total = 0>
<CFSET name = "Allaire">
<CFSET today = DateFormat(Now(),'mm/dd/yy')>
<CFSET flavors = "Vanilla,Chocolate,Strawberry">
```

N O T E The Now() function fetches the system date and time, and the DateFormat function applies the mm/dd/yy format to the date. ■

You also use `<CFSET>` to update the value of an existing variable. For example,

```
<CFSET total = total + item_cost>
```

takes the value currently stored in the variable `total`, adds `item_cost` to that amount, and then stores the result back in the variable `total`.

Creating arrays and queries requires a few other ColdFusion functions in addition to the `<CFSET>` tag because these data structures are more complex than the other variable types. To create an array, you first have to use the `ArrayNew()` function:

```
<CFSET planets = ArrayNew(1)>
```

N O T E The number you pass to the ArrayNew() function specifies how many indexes the array is to have. Arrays can have up to three indexes.

Also, ColdFusion array indexes start at the value 1. This is different from languages such as JavaScript, with array indexes beginning at 0. ■

With the array declared, you can then use `<CFSET>` to assign values to the array:

```
<CFSET planets[1] = "Mars">
<CFSET planets[2] = "Venus">
<CFSET planets[3] = "Earth">
...
<CFSET planets[9] = "Pluto">
```

Query variables are structured much like a query result set in memory. In fact, after you've defined a query variable, you can use it just as you would if it were generated by a call to a database, meaning you can loop over the query variable with `<CFLOOP>` or output the contents of the query variable using `<CFOUTPUT>`.

To instantiate the query variable, you use the ColdFusion `QueryNew()` function:

```
<CFSET contact_info = QueryNew("Name,Address,City,State,Zip")>
```

The quoted list of values you pass to the `QueryNew()` function is the column names you want to use in the query. With the query created, you can add empty rows to the query so that you can populate it with data. You do this with the `QueryAddRow` function. Because you have to call this function from within a tag, you most commonly see `QueryAddRow` used as follows:

```
<CFSET temp = QueryAddRow(contact_info,20)>
```

The number following the name of the query indicates how many blank rows to add to the query. If you don't specify a value, ColdFusion will assume you just want to insert one row. If successful, the `QueryAddRow` function returns a value of `TRUE`, and this is what is assigned to the variable `temp`. Otherwise, `temp` ends up being set to `FALSE`.

Finally, to place values into the individual cells of the query, you use the `QuerySetCell` function. `QuerySetCell` is used in a `<CFSET>` tag in much the same way as `QueryAddRow`. For example, the code

```
<CFSET temp = QuerySetCell(contact_info,"City","Alexandria",12)>
```

places the value `"Alexandria"` in the City column of the 12th row of the query variable `contact_info`. If no row number is specified, ColdFusion will insert the value into the last row. If the insert is successful, `temp` will take on a value of `TRUE`; otherwise, `temp` is set to `FALSE`.

When it comes time to print the value of a ColdFusion variable on an HTML page, you need to know two things:

- You have to use the `<CFOUTPUT>` tag.
- You have to enclose the name of the variable in pound signs (#) to indicate to ColdFusion that it should replace the variable name with its value.

To illustrate what can happen if you miss one or the other, consider the following code:

```
<CFSET holiday = "Christmas">
<CFOUTPUT>holiday</CFOUTPUT><P>
#holiday#<P>
<CFOUTPUT>#holiday#</CFOUTPUT>
```

When ColdFusion processes this code, it produces the HTML page you see in Figure 34.17. In the first line, you just see the word "holiday" because no pound signs tell ColdFusion to replace the variable with its value. You see `#holiday#` on the second line because ColdFusion will only do variable value substitution inside of `<CFOUTPUT>` and `</CFOUTPUT>` tags. The third line reads `Christmas` because both the `<CFOUTPUT>` tag and the pound signs are used.

FIGURE 34.17
Getting ColdFusion to output variable values can be tricky initially.

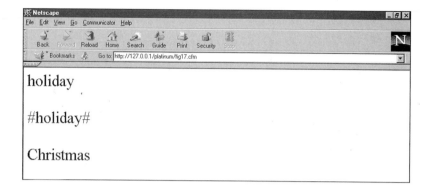

A useful variant of the `<CFOUTPUT>` tag is to use its QUERY attribute to make the output loop over an entire query result set. If you have done a query that retrieves students' names and exam scores, for example, you could print them all out in a table using the following code:

```
<TABLE BORDER=1>
<TR><TH>Name</TH><TH>Exam Score</TH></TR>
<CFOUTPUT QUERY="grades">
<TR><TD>#name#</TD><TD>#score#</TD></TR>
</CFOUTPUT>
</TABLE>
```

In this case, the variables name and score are column names from the database containing the names and exam scores. When flanked with pound signs and enclosed in `<CFOUTPUT>` and `</CFOUTPUT>` tags, the values of these variables are printed instead. And because you used the QUERY attribute of the `<CFOUTPUT>` tag, ColdFusion will automatically loop over the entire query set and produce a table row for each name and exam score. Imagine how long it would take you to code such a table for a class of 30 students! With ColdFusion, you can produce the output table with just a few lines of code.

Sometimes query result sets can be rather long, and it's helpful to limit the amount of output the user gets at one time. To assist with this, you can use the MAXROWS attribute of the `<CFOUTPUT>` tag to specify a maximum number of rows from the result set that the tags should loop over. You might set MAXROWS to 20, for example, so that a user only sees, at most, 20 records at a time.

You can also control the record where the output begins by using the `<CFOUTPUT>` tag's START attribute. This enables you to set up a link pretty easily to see the next 20 records. All you need to do is pass the value of the last record printed, add one to it, and set the START attribute equal to that value.

Performing Database Operations

ColdFusion's strength lies in its capability to communicate with any ODBC-compliant database and retrieve, store, update, or delete records in those databases. Regardless of the type of database operation you're doing, you use the `<CFQUERY>` and `</CFQUERY>` tags to enclose the SQL statement that does the operation. The next four sections look at how to use `<CFQUERY>` for the basic operations of retrieving, inserting, updating, and deleting.

Retrieving Database Records   Querying a database to find records that match specific search criteria is probably the most popular of the fundamental database operations. ColdFusion makes each part of this task easy—from incorporating search criteria entered on an HTML form into the SQL statement, to performing the actual query, to receiving and printing out the results of the query in HTML format.

Suppose you are assigned to create an intranet page for your company's sales force that prints a list of your clients in a state that the user can specify. To begin, you would set up a form that asks the user for which state they want a list. The HTML for that form might look like this:

```
<FORM ACTION="statelist.cfm" METHOD="POST">
<B>Show me clients in the following state:</B><P>
<SELECT NAME="state">
<OPTION VALUE="AL">Alabama
<OPTION VALUE="AK">Alaska
<OPTION VALUE="AR">Arkansas
...
<OPTION VALUE="WY">Wyoming
</SELECT>
<INPUT TYPE="SUBMIT" VALUE="Generate List">
</FORM>
```

This produces a drop-down list of all the states. The user chooses one of them and then clicks the Generate List button to submit the request to the server. Seeing an ACTION attribute that ends in .cfm (the file extension for ColdFusion templates), the server hands over the template and the form data to the ColdFusion Application Server for processing.

The challenge now is to write the template called statelist.cfm so that it

  1. Queries the database for clients located in the state the user selects.
  2. Produces an HTML page that will display the client listing.

Both of these are easy to accomplish with CFML. First, you need to write a query that pulls client information based on the selected state. You can do this with the following code:

```
<CFQUERY DATASOURCE="clients" NAME="ByState">
SELECT company, city
FROM Clients
WHERE state = '#Form.state#'
</CFQUERY>
```

Note first that <CFQUERY> takes a few attributes. The DATASOURCE attribute is mandatory and should be set equal to the name of a data source you set up in the ColdFusion Administrator. The NAME attribute is also required and enables you to assign a unique name to the query so you can reference the results set by that name.

Next, note the WHERE clause in the SQL statement. Instead of a specific state's name, you see #Form.state#. ColdFusion treats submitted form data as an object that you can reference by the name Form. To key in on a particular form field, you can say Form.field_name. That's why you see Form.state in the code above—it references the state field of the form that was submitted. By enclosing Form.state in pound signs, you instruct ColdFusion to substitute in the value it finds at `Form.state`. So in this case, if the user chose the state of California, the resulting SQL statement (after ColdFusion substitutes in the value) would be

```
SELECT company, city, state
FROM Clients
WHERE state = 'CA'
```

In response to this SQL statement, the database would return the company name and city of each client in the state of California and store the result set under the name `"ByState"`. You can then use the `<CFOUTPUT>` tag with the `QUERY` attribute to produce a table that prints out the entire list of clients. The complete listing for this template is shown in Listing 34.1.

Listing 34.1 *statelist.cfm* Code Listing

```
<CFQUERY DATASOURCE="clients" NAME="ByState">
SELECT company, city
FROM Clients
WHERE state = '#Form.state#'
</CFQUERY>

<HTML>

<HEAD>
<TITLE>Client Listing for <CFOUTPUT>#Form.state#</CFOUTPUT></TITLE>
</HEAD>

<BODY BGCOLOR="WHITE">

<H1>Client Listing for <CFOUTPUT>#Form.state#</CFOUTPUT></H1>

<CFOUTPUT>#ByState.RecordCount#</CFOUTPUT> records found
<P>
<TABLE>
<TR><TH>Company</TH><TH>Location</TH></TR>
<CFOUTPUT QUERY="ByState">
<TR><TD>#company#</TD><TD>#city#, #Form.state#</TD></TR>
</CFOUTPUT>
</TABLE>

</BODY>

</HTML>
```

N O T E   A query's `RecordCount` property contains the number of records found when performing the query. You can access the value by referencing `query_name.RecordCount`, but be sure to enclose it in pound signs and `<CFOUTPUT>` tags if you want to write its value into your resulting HTML document.

This short template file should begin to give you an inkling of ColdFusion's power. In just a few lines of code, you have taken the form input, used it to dynamically build a SQL statement, passed the SQL statement to a database engine, retrieved the query results, and generated an

HTML table that presents the results in a readable format. If you've ever coded any CGI programs in a language such as Perl, think about how much code you would need to replicate the same functionality and compare it to Listing 34.1. You'll very likely conclude that ColdFusion wins handily in terms of power and efficiency.

N O T E Always use METHOD="POST" with a form that uses a ColdFusion template as its ACTION attribute. Otherwise, the form data will be passed on the URL, in which case you would have to reference the URL object to get the submitted values. ■

Inserting Records into a Database   Another common database operation is to insert a new record into a database table. Suppose, for example, you were gathering subscription information for an email-based newsletter. You would need to collect the subscriber's name and email address so that you could send the newsletter whenever it is published. In support of this, you could write a form similar to the following:

```
<FORM ACTION="subscribe.cfm" METHOD="POST">
<B>Name: </B>
<INPUT TYPE="TEXT" NAME="subscriber_name" SIZE=20>
<P>
<B>E-mail: </B>
<INPUT TYPE="TEXT" NAME="subscriber_email" SIZE=20>
<P>
<INPUT TYPE="SUBMIT" VALUE="Sign me up!">
</FORM>
```

After you write the form, next you need to write the ColdFusion template named subscribe.cfm. The important thing for this template to do would be to insert the name and email address information into the database, but it would also be nice if the user received some kind of confirmation message to let them know that the subscription has been entered.

To handle the insertion of the new record, you can use the following code:

```
<CFQUERY DATASOURCE="newsletter" NAME="NewSubscriber">
INSERT
INTO Subscribers (name,email)
VALUES ('#Form.subscriber_name#','#Form.subscriber_email#')
</CFQUERY>
```

Note in the VALUES specification that you reference the subscriber_name and subscriber_email fields of the submitted form, and that by enclosing them in pound signs, you instruct ColdFusion to substitute the values passed in those fields. Thus, the resulting SQL statement for a user named Mabel Anderson with email address manderson@isp.net would look like

```
INSERT
INTO Subscribers (name,email)
VALUES ('Mabel Anderson','manderson@isp.net')
```

You can round out the template with some kind of message back to the user that repeats her information and confirms the insertion of her record into the database. Listing 34.2 shows one possible way of accomplishing this.

Listing 34.2   *subscribe.cfm* Code Listing

```
<CFQUERY DATASOURCE="newsletter" NAME="NewSubscriber">
INSERT
INTO Subscribers (name,email)
VALUES ('#Form.subscriber_name#','#Form.subscriber_email#')
</CFQUERY>

<HTML>

<HEAD>
<TITLE>Subscription Confirmation</TITLE>
</HEAD>

<BODY BGCOLOR="WHITE">

<H1>Thank you, <CFOUTPUT>#Form.subscriber_name#</CFOUTPUT></H1>

Your subscription has been entered and will be sent to you each
month at <CFOUTPUT>#Form.subscriber_email#</CFOUTPUT>.

</BODY>

</HTML>
```

If you're not that comfortable with SQL INSERT statements, ColdFusion can relieve you of some of the burden with the <CFINSERT> tag. <CFINSERT> will automatically generate the SQL call to insert submitted form data into a database—all you need to provide is the data source name and the name of the table where the data should be inserted. The one catch, however, is that the names of the form fields and the names of the corresponding columns in the database have to be an *exact match*. Looking back at the form that collects subscriber information, you can see that the form field names are subscriber_name and subscriber_email. However, the SQL in Listing 34.2 above tells you that the column names you're inserting into are name and email. The names of the form fields and columns are different in this case, so you are not set up properly to use <CFINSERT>. If you abbreviated the form field names to name and email, then you would be able to successfully use <CFINSERT>. In that case, you could replace the <CFQUERY> code with

```
<CFINSERT DATASOURCE="newsletter" TABLENAME="Subscribers">
```

and achieve the same result.

N O T E   <CFINSERT> also takes the FORMFIELDS attribute, which is set equal to the names of the fields you want to insert. If FORMFIELDS is not specified, ColdFusion tries to insert every form field that was submitted. ▪

Updating an Existing Database Record   A third common database operation is to make a change to an existing record or records. Again, the <CFQUERY> tag plays a pivotal role in doing the update.

For this example, suppose that you are a developer for a credit card company that wants to Web-enable many of its customer service functions. The function you are tasked with coding is the change of address. As part of this function, you have to code the following form to collect the new address information:

```
<FORM ACTION="updateaddr.cfm" METHOD="POST">
Please enter your credit card number:
<INPUT TYPE="TEXT" NAME="card_number">
<P>
Please enter your new address below:
<P>
Street:
<INPUT TYPE="TEXT" NAME="new_street" SIZE=20>
<P>
City:
<INPUT TYPE="TEXT" NAME="new_city" SIZE=20>
<P>
State:
<INPUT TYPE="TEXT" NAME="new_state" SIZE=20>
<P>
Zip:
<INPUT TYPE="TEXT" NAME="new_zip" SIZE=20>
<P>
<INPUT TYPE="SUBMIT" VALUE="Update my Address">
</FORM>
```

In addition to the new address information, you also have to ask for something to uniquely identify the customer. In this case, you can use the credit card number itself because you know that each customer has a unique number.

Now you need to write the template updateaddr.cfm to do the update operation and display a confirmation message so that customers know that their information was changed. To do the update, you would again use the <CFQUERY> tag:

```
<CFQUERY DATASOURCE="customers" NAME="UpdateAddr">
UPDATE Contact_Info
SET street='#Form.new_street#',city='#Form.new_city#',
   state='#Form.new_state#',zip='#Form.new_zip#'
WHERE customer_ID = '#Form.card_number#'
</CFQUERY>
```

The SQL UPDATE command is used to do the update, and you can see how each field is being set equal to the new values submitted on the form. What's very important in the SQL statement is the WHERE clause, which restricts the update to the record belonging to the user with the credit card number entered on the form. Without the WHERE clause, the street, city, state, and zip columns of *every record in the database* would have been updated to reflect the new address information! The moral of the story is this: When doing updates, make sure that you are keying in on the record or records that require the updates by using the WHERE clause in your SQL statement. Otherwise, your updates will be made globally—usually with disastrous results.

Part

VI

Ch

34

Unique Record Identifiers

In relational database theory, the column that uniquely identifies a record in a table is called the table's *primary key*. The table is indexed by the primary key values, so searching by the primary key value is typically rapid and efficient. In the credit card example above, you could conceivably use the customer's credit card number as a primary key, but primary keys are usually shorter than a 16-digit credit card number. In fact, primary keys are usually numeric fields that are automatically incremented each time a new record is inserted into the database. This ensures that each primary key is unique.

Tables in a well-designed relational database usually contain pointers to records in other tables. You might have a table, for example, where you store all transactions posted for an electronic commerce site. You know that a customer is associated with that transaction, but rather than put the customer's name and address into the transaction table, you can include the primary key of the customer's entry in your contact information table. That way, if you need that customer's contact information, you can use the primary key for the contact information table to do a quick query into that table and retrieve the information. When you use a primary key from one table as a pointer in a second table, you are said to be putting a *foreign key* into the second table.

Listing 34.3 shows a complete listing of one possible way to code the template `updateaddr.cfm` so that it does the update and notifies the user about the change.

Listing 34.3 *updateaddr.cfm* **Code Listing**

```
<CFQUERY DATASOURCE="customers" NAME="UpdateAddr">
UPDATE Contact_Info
SET street='#Form.new_street#',city='#Form.new_city#',
    state='#Form.new_state#',zip='#Form.new_zip#'
WHERE customer_ID = '#Form.card_number#'
</CFQUERY>

<HTML>

<HEAD>
<TITLE>Address Updated</TITLE>
</HEAD>

<BODY BGCOLOR="WHITE">

<H1>Address Updated</H1>

We have updated your address information as you requested.
<P>
Your monthly bill will now be sent to:
<BLOCKQUOTE>
<CFOUTPUT>
#Form.new_street#<BR>
#Form.new_city#, #Form.new_state# #Form.new_zip#
```

```
</CFOUTPUT>
</BLOCKQUOTE>

</BODY>

</HTML>
```

Just as you could use <CFINSERT> instead of <CFQUERY> to do a database insert, you can use the <CFUPDATE> tag to do an update. <CFUPDATE> works much the same way as <CFINSERT> —you specify the data source and table names and ColdFusion writes the SQL code to do the update. Again, you have to make sure that the form field names and the database column names are the same, or the tag won't work.

Deleting Database Records   The fourth common database operation you can do with the <CFQUERY> tag is to delete records from a database. Like updating, deleting is something that you have to do selectively because after a record is gone, there's no getting it back. This means you will almost always want to use a WHERE clause in your SQL DELETE statements so that you do not do a wholesale deletion of all the records in a table.

N O T E   One way to delete records without really losing any information is to do what's called a *logical* or *soft delete*. This involves adding a Boolean field to your database table so that if the field is set to TRUE, the record is considered to be deleted and not included in any query results. With such a field in place, all you have to do to "delete" a record is to update it so that the field has a value of TRUE. Similarly, you can "undelete" the record by setting the Boolean field to FALSE. Regardless of the value of the Boolean field, the record information is still in the database and could be retrieved by the database administrator if it became necessary.

Another technique to preserve deleted records is to write a copy of the record into an archival database before deleting it. This is fairly easy to do, but it does mean you have to manage the archival database pretty closely so that it does not become too large. ▪

Suppose that you maintain a comments page on your personal Web site and that you want to remove any comments that are more than 30 days old. You can accomplish this by setting up a template with the following <CFQUERY> tag:

```
<CFQUERY DATASOURCE="feedback" NAME="PurgeOldComments">
DELETE
FROM Comments
WHERE entry_date < #CreateODBCDate(Now() - CreateTimeSpan(30,0,0,0))#
</CFQUERY>
```

The SQL statement is fairly straightforward except for what you see in the WHERE clause. Recall that the Now() function grabs the current system date and time. The CreateTimeSpan function creates a date differential that you can add or subtract from a valid date. In this example, we use this function to create a differential of 30 days, 0 hours, 0 minutes, and 0 seconds and then subtract that differential from the current date. The result is the date from 30 days ago.

We then apply the CreateODBCDate function so that date is in the appropriate format for doing a comparison. This sets us up to check the entry_date value of the comment to see if it is "less than" (occurred before) the current date minus 30 days. If it is, then the comment is deleted by the DELETE statement.

This is a good example of a maintenance query that you can automate to keep your site fresh. You could set up a task in the Scheduler that will submit the template once a day, and ColdFusion will then automatically remove any old comments for you. If you wanted to know which comments were deleted, you could retrieve the delete candidates first with a SELECT statement, output them with a <CFOUTPUT> tag, and then do the delete query. The Scheduler will enable you to capture the template's output in an HTML file that you can review each morning to see which comments have been deleted. Listing 34.4 shows the ColdFusion code that accomplishes this.

Listing 34.4   Automatic Deletion of Old Comments

```
<CFQUERY DATASOURCE="feedback" NAME="GetDeleteCandidates">
SELECT visitor,comment
FROM Comments
WHERE entry_date < #CreateODBCDate(Now() - CreateTimeSpan(30,0,0,0))#
</CFQUERY>

<HTML>

<HEAD>
<TITLE>Deleted Comments</TITLE>
</HEAD>

<BODY BGCOLOR="WHITE">

<B>The following comments have been deleted:</B>
<P>

<TABLE>
<TR><TH>Visitor Name</TH><TH>Comment</TH></TR>
<CFOUTPUT QUERY="GetDeleteCandidates">
<TR><TD>#visitor#</TD><TD>#comment#</TD></TR>
</CFOUTPUT>
</TABLE>

</BODY>

</HTML>
```

```
<CFQUERY DATASOURCE="feedback" NAME="PurgeOldComments">
DELETE
FROM Comments
WHERE entry_date < #CreateODBCDate(Now() - CreateTimeSpan(30,0,0,0))#
</CFQUERY>
```

N O T E The delete query in Listing 34.4 could have occurred before the HTML output section. After you have the delete candidate information stored in the query named `GetDeleteCandidates`, it doesn't matter where in the template you do the deletion.

Using Decision Statements

Conditional logic is another basic component of any programming language, and ColdFusion enables you to build conditional processing into your applications with the <CFIF> tag. Instead of taking a particular attribute, the <CFIF> tag has to contain one of ColdFusion's eight decision operators:

- IS
- IS NOT
- GREATER THAN
- LESS THAN
- GREATER THAN OR EQUAL TO
- LESS THAN OR EQUAL TO
- CONTAINS
- DOES NOT CONTAIN

Each of these operators is evaluated to a Boolean TRUE or FALSE value. If the operator evaluates to TRUE, the code between the <CFIF> and </CFIF> tags is executed. Otherwise, the code is ignored.

 T I P Many of the decision operators can be abbreviated to a more compact form. For example, you can abbreviate LESS THAN to LT and GREATER THAN OR EQUAL TO to GE.

You can expand your programming logic by using the <CFELSE> and <CFELSEIF> tags inside a <CFIF> and </CFIF> tag pair. <CFELSE> enables you to define a block of code to execute if the condition in the <CFIF> tag evaluates to FALSE. For example:

```
<CFQUERY DATASOURCE="customers" NAME="GetCustomers">
SELECT name, phone
FROM Customers
WHERE city = 'Springfield'
</CFQUERY>
```

```
<CFIF GetCustomers.RecordCount IS NOT 0>
   <H1>Customers Living in Springfield</H1>
   <TABLE BORDER=1>
   <TR><TH>Name</TH><TH>Phone Number</TH></TR>
   <CFOUTPUT QUERY="GetCustomers">
   <TR><TD>#name#</TD><TD>#phone#</TD></TR>
   </CFOUTPUT>
   </TABLE>
<CFELSE>
   <H1>No customers in Springfield</H1>
</CFIF>
```

After doing the query named GetCustomers, ColdFusion will check to see how many records were returned. If the number of records is not zero, ColdFusion prints out a table of the names and phone numbers of the records selected in the query. Otherwise, the number of query results was zero, so ColdFusion outputs a message saying that no customers were found.

 TIP   It's helpful to indent code inside of <CFIF>, <CFELSE>, <CFELSEIF>, and </CFIF> tags because it makes troubleshooting the code much easier.

In addition to the <CFELSE> tag, you can also place as many <CFELSEIF> tags as you'd like between the <CFIF> and </CFIF> tags. Suppose, for example, you had a string variable named residence that could take on one of four values. You could the use the following code to do conditional processing based on the four values:

```
<CFIF residence IS "apartment">
   <B>Please enter your monthly rent: </B>
<CFELSEIF residence IS "condo">
   <B>Please enter your total monthly mortgage payment + condo fee: </B>
<CFELSEIF residence IS "home">
   <B>Please enter your total monthly mortgage payment: </B>
<CFELSEIF residence IS "other">
   <B>Please enter your monthly housing expense: </B>
</CFIF>
<INPUT TYPE="TEXT" NAME="housing_expense">
```

Technically, if you were absolutely sure that residence could only take on values of "apartment", "condo", "home", or "other", you could change the <CFELSEIF residence IS "other"> tag to a <CFELSE> tag because that would be the only possibility left at that point in the processing.

The <CFIF> tag is also flexible enough to work with other constructs that evaluate to either TRUE or FALSE. These include

■ Compound decision operators—You can join decision operators with logical ANDs and ORs to produce more complex decision criteria. For example:

```
<CFIF (Sex IS "Male") AND (Age GE 16)>
   <B>You must register with the Selective Service.</B>
</CFIF>
```

It's a good idea to group each individual decision operator in parentheses so that it's easier to troubleshoot the expression later.

■ Negation operator—You can also use the NOT operator to logically negate one of the decision operators:

```
<CFIF NOT(Age GE 21)>
    <B>You are not old enough to drink.</B>
</CFIF>
```

■ Boolean variables—You can also use Boolean variables in place of a decision operator in a <CFIF> tag. This is useful when the variable is a flag in the program. In the following example, a set of names taken from a query is printed out in a comma-delimited list. Each name from the query needs a comma and a space in front of it, except for the first name printed. You can control for this by introducing the printed_one flag, which has a value of TRUE if the first item in the list has been printed.

```
<CFSET printed_one = FALSE>
<CFOUTPUT QUERY="names">
<CFIF printed_one>
    , #name#
<CFELSE>
    #name#
    <CFSET printed_one = TRUE>
</CFIF>
</CFOUTPUT>
```

■ CFML functions—Many of the ColdFusion functions evaluate to values of TRUE or FALSE. Any of these functions is valid to use inside the <CFIF> tag. The IsNumeric function, for example, checks a variable to see whether it is a number. You can use IsNumeric together with a <CFIF> tag to do some basic data checking as follows:

```
<CFIF NOT(IsNumeric('Form.price'))>
    The price you entered is not valid.
</CFIF>
```

Using Looping Constructs

Looping enables you to execute a set of instructions again and again until a certain condition is met. ColdFusion loops are implemented with the <CFLOOP> tag and can be one of four types:

■ Looping over an index

■ Looping while a specified condition is TRUE

■ Looping over a query result set

■ Looping over the items in a list

Each type of loop is considered in the following five sections.

Part

VI

Ch

34

N O T E You can also loop over a COM/DCOM collection object, but this type of object is a bit too advanced for an introductory discussion on ColdFusion looping. For more details, consult Chapter 34, "Interfacing with COM and DCOM Objects," in Ben Forta's *The ColdFusion Web Application Construction Kit, Third Edition*. ■

CAUTION

Whenever you're doing any kind of looping, make sure that you have a reasonable `Request Timeout` value set in the ColdFusion Administrator. This prevents an infinite loop from consuming all your server's resources and crashing it.

Looping Over an Index   When looping over an index variable, you need to specify the name of the variable, the initial value of the variable, and the terminating value of the variable. This is done in the `<CFLOOP>` tag with the INDEX, FROM, and TO attributes, respectively. Each of these attributes is required when looping over an index. `<CFLOOP>` can also take the optional STEP attribute, which you can use to specify the value by which the index variable should change after each pass through the loop. The default value of STEP is 1, which means that the loop index is increased by 1 after each iteration.

As a simple example of index-based looping, consider the following code:

```
<CFIF (#Form.value# GE 1) AND (#Form.value# LE 9)>
   <CFLOOP INDEX="count" FROM="1" TO="#Form.value#">
      <CFOUTPUT>#count#. #planets[count]#<BR></CFOUTPUT>
   <CFLOOP>
</CFIF>
```

This code takes a value specified by the user through an HTML form and checks to make sure that the value is between 1 and 9. If it is, then a loop is used to print out the elements of the array called `planets`, beginning with the first element and ending with the element the user specified through the form. If a user entered the value 6 on the form, ColdFusion would generate the output you see in Figure 34.18.

FIGURE 34.18

Index-based loops are useful for referencing arrays.

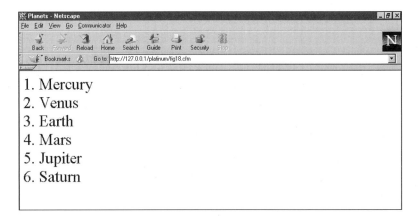

Looping While a Condition is *TRUE*   You can also loop based on the value of one of the ColdFusion decision operators by using the CONDITION attribute of the `<CFLOOP>` tag. As long as the condition is TRUE, the loop will continue to iterate. When the condition becomes FALSE, the loop will terminate.

The following code illustrates a conditional loop:

```
<CFIF (IsNumeric('Form.value')) AND (#Form.value# GE 1)>
    <CFSET count = 1>
    <CFLOOP CONDITION="count LE Form.value">
        <CFOUTPUT>#count#<BR></CFOUTPUT>
        <CFSET count = count + 1>
    </CFLOOP>
</CFIF>
```

This code produces the output you see in Figure 34.19. After checking to make sure that a user's form input is a numeric value that is greater than 1, ColdFusion enters a loop and prints out the values between 1 and the value entered by the user.

FIGURE 34.19

Conditional looping enables you to repeat a set of CFML or HTML instructs as long as the looping condition is TRUE.

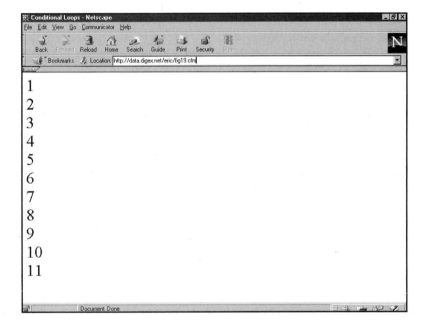

N O T E Remember that when you use conditional looping, it's up to you to manage the variables in the condition so that it eventually evaluates to FALSE and exits the loop.

Looping Over Query Results   Looping over a query result set is a useful capability in many settings. You've already seen how you can use <CFOUTPUT> with the QUERY attribute to loop over and print out a query result set. The example shown here will also use a set of query results, but in a different way.

Suppose your company assigns sales leads to representatives on your sales force through a ColdFusion-based lead management system. If you were coding a page for the lead administrator to make the assignment, you would most likely include a drop-down list of the representatives' names so that the administrator could select one from the list and then click a submit button to make the assignment. Although you could hard-code all the representatives' names into the drop-down list, a far more elegant way to do this is with a query to pull all the representatives' names out of a database table and then loop over that result set to create the HTML code that produces the drop-down list.

In addition to being programmatically more efficient, this approach also has a maintenance advantage: If an existing representative leaves or a new representative joins the company, all that has to be done is to enter him into the database table that contains the representative information. Because ColdFusion is dynamically generating the drop-down list based on the query results, you are assured that any departed representatives will no longer show up and that any new representatives will appear as options in the list. Best of all, you will be spared from having to go through your forms to manually edit HTML code.

To see how you accomplish this, you first need to do a query that pulls the representative information:

```
<CFQUERY DATASOURCE="employees" NAME="GetReps">
SELECT Rep_ID, Rep_Last, Rep_First
FROM Reps
ORDER BY Rep_Last, Rep_First
</CFQUERY>
```

The ORDER BY clause orders the query results according to the database column or columns you specify. In this case, the results are sorted alphabetically by the representative's last name and, in the event of the same last name, the representative's first name.

With the query results in hand, you can now dynamically generate the drop-down list as follows:

```
<FORM ACTION="assignrep.cfm" METHOD="POST">
Please select a rep to be responsible for this lead:<P>
<SELECT NAME="rep">
<CFLOOP QUERY="GetReps">
   <CFOUTPUT><OPTION VALUE=#Rep_ID#>#Rep_Last#, #Rep_First#</CFOUTPUT>
</CFLOOP>
</SELECT>
<INPUT TYPE="SUBMIT" VALUE="Assign a Rep">
</FORM>
```

The <CFLOOP> used here loops over each result in the query, plucking off the values of Rep_ID, Rep_First, and Rep_Last as it goes. During each pass through the loop, ColdFusion uses these values to construct an <OPTION> tag for the representative. The result is an alphabetized drop-down list with one entry for each sales representative—all generated by just a few lines of code.

N O T E   When looping over a query result set, you don't necessarily have to loop over the entire set. You can use the STARTROW and ENDROW attributes of the <CFLOOP> tag to specify starting and ending rows for the looping.

Looping Over a List ColdFusion lists are simply a collection of items separated by some kind of delimiter character. The default delimiter is a comma, but you can choose other delimiters as well. ColdFusion enables you to loop over the items in a list by using the <CFLOOP> tag with the LIST and INDEX attributes. LIST is set equal to the list you want to loop over. INDEX specifies the name of the "holding variable" that takes on the values of the individual list items as the loop progresses.

As a simple example of looping over a list, consider the following example:

```
<CFSET xfiles = "Mulder,Scully,Cigarette Smoking Man,Black Oil Aliens">
Who is your favorite X-Files character?
<FORM ACTION="favchar.cfm" METHOD="POST">
<CFLOOP LIST="#xfiles#" INDEX="character">
   <CFOUTPUT>
   <INPUT TYPE="RADIO" NAME="favorite" VALUE="#character#"> #character#
   </CFOUTPUT>
</CFLOOP>
<INPUT TYPE="SUBMIT" VALUE="Register my Favorite">
</FORM>
```

This code produces a set of four radio buttons—one for each *XFiles* character in the list. Note how the INDEX variable character is used to populate the VALUE attribute of the <INPUT> tag as well as to produce the text that appears next to the radio button.

N O T E To change the list delimiter from a comma to another character, you use the ListChangeDelims function. The syntax of this function is explained in the "CFML Functions" section later in this chapter. ■

If you want to loop over a one-dimensional array, you can use the ArrayToList function to convert the array into a list and then loop over the list.

Breaking Out of a Loop You can break out of a loop before it would ordinarily terminate by using the <CFBREAK> tag. Suppose, for example, you were using a loop to look for the first non-zero element of a list:

```
<CFLOOP LIST="0,0,4,7,0,9,0" INDEX="value">
   <CFIF value IS NOT 0>
      <CFSET magic = value>
      <CFBREAK>
   </CFIF>
</CFLOOP>
```

The first non-zero value is <CFOUTPUT>#magic#</CFOUTPUT>.

On each pass through the loop, the variable value takes on the next value of the next list item. The <CFIF> tag checks to see if the current value is non-zero. If it is, it sets magic equal to that value and then breaks out of the loop because there is no point in continuing the search. Thus, the loop will stop after its third iteration (when it encounters the value of 4) rather than looping through all seven values.

Part
VI

Ch
34

TIP Try to use <CFBREAK> whenever you can. <CFLOOP> is somewhat notorious for being the most resource-intensive of the CFML tags, so if you can break out of the loop early, you increase the efficiency of your application.

Sending an Email Message

When you read about the ColdFusion Administrator, you learned that ColdFusion can interface with an electronic mail server to send email messages. But all you could do through the Administrator was to tell ColdFusion which mail server to use. When it comes time to actually compose and send a message, you need to use the <CFMAIL> tag. <CFMAIL> is a container tag, which means that there is a companion </CFMAIL> closing tag. You place the contents of the message you want to send between these two tags, as follows:

```
<CFMAIL>
... message to send ...
</CFMAIL>
```

The message doesn't have to be plain text. In fact, it often includes ColdFusion variables. As long as the variable names are enclosed in pound signs, ColdFusion will replace the variable name with its value as it composes the message.

Certainly more components are part of an email than the body of the message, and ColdFusion enables you to handle these other message components through attributes of the <CFMAIL> tag. Following is a complete list of the <CFMAIL> tag's attributes:

- TO—Set equal to the email address of the recipient of the message.
- FROM—Set equal to the name or the email address of the sender.
- SUBJECT—Specifies the subject of the message.
- CC—Set equal to a list of email addresses that should receive a copy of the message.
- QUERY—Denotes a query to use to generate the message. The query information can be used in one of two ways. You can loop over the query set and generate a separate email for each record in the set, or you can send the results of the entire query in a single message.
- STARTROW—If a QUERY attribute is given, you can start processing it in a row other than the first row by setting STARTROW equal to the row where the processing should commence.
- MAXROWS—If you're looping over a query and want to limit the number of messages you're sending, you can set MAXROWS equal to the maximum number of messages to send.
- GROUP—Specifies the query column by which to group records together. This is only applicable when sending an entire set of query results in a single message.

- MIMEATTACH—Set equal to the path and filename of a file to attach to the message.

- TYPE—If you know your recipients are using mail readers that are capable of parsing HTML-based email, you can set TYPE="HTML" so that the message is sent in HTML format.

- SERVER—By default, ColdFusion uses the server specified in the Mail section of the ColdFusion Administrator. You can override this choice of server by specifying a different mail server with the SERVER attribute.

- PORT—ColdFusion will automatically use the port set up in the ColdFusion Administrator (which is almost always port 25). Should you need to direct a mail message to a different port, you can specify the port number with the PORT attribute of the <CFMAIL> tag.

- TIMEOUT—If specified, the TIMEOUT attribute will override the timeout set up in the ColdFusion Administrator.

The capability to dynamically generate and send email messages enables you to add many useful features to your ColdFusion applications. You could do the following, for example, on an electronic commerce site:

- Send email to customers who make purchases from your site, confirming their order and thanking them for shopping with you. This can be sent right away so that customers feel that they are getting an immediate response from you.

- Send status messages to customers as their orders are filled. This enables you to inform them when their orders are shipped, if an item has to be back-ordered, and when they can expect to receive their orders.

- Send follow-up messages to assess satisfaction and to notify customers about upcoming specials.

Indeed, you could create and maintain an entire mailing list using ColdFusion. Subscribers could add themselves to the database and post messages to the list through HTML forms. Then, when it's time to send a message to the list, you would query the list of recipients to get everyone's email address:

```
<CFQUERY DATASOURCE="mailinglist" NAME="GetAddresses">
SELECT name, emailaddress
FROM Subscribers
</CFQUERY>
```

Then you can use <CFMAIL> with the QUERY attribute to send a submitted message to each member of the list:

```
<CFMAIL QUERY="GetAddresses" TO="#name#" FROM="Mailing List Admin"
  SUBJECT="#Form.subject#">
#Form.message#
</CFMAIL>
```

Part
VI

Ch
34

How ColdFusion Handles the Message Text

The content you place between the <CFMAIL> and </CFMAIL> tags is what ColdFusion uses to generate the body of the email message. An important thing to keep in mind is that ColdFusion may insert blank lines into the message where it has parsed out any CFML tags it encounters. Consider the following code, for example:

```
<CFMAIL TO="#email# FROM="confirm@yourserver.com"
  SUBJECT="Address Confirmation" QUERY="GetAddressInfo">
Your name and address are shown below.  If any of this information
is incorrect, please reply to this message with the correct information.

#GetAddressInfo.name#
#GetAddressInfo.address1#
<CFIF #GetAddressInfo.address2# IS NOT "">#GetAddressInfo.address2#</CFIF>
#GetAddressInfo.city#, #GetAddressInfo.state# #GetAddressInfo.zip#
</CFMAIL>
```

Notice in the body of the message that a <CFIF> tag checks the value of #GetAddressInfo.address2# to see if it is not blank. If it isn't, then ColdFusion will output its value. If it is, then ColdFusion will parse out the entire line and keep going. Unfortunately, this produces a blank line in the resulting email and the recipient sees something like

```
Your name and address are shown below. If any of this information
is incorrect, please reply to this message with the correct information.

John Doe
123 Main Street

New York, NY 10033
```

To avoid this problem, what you can do is to compose a string that contains the contents of the message, and then place the variable containing the string between the <CFMAIL> and </CFMAIL> tags. The trick to doing this is to account for breaks to a new line, but ColdFusion makes this fairly easy with the Chr function. In the following code, the concatenation of Chr(13) and Chr(10) produces the carriage returns in the message. The ampersand (&) operator concatenates the strings.

```
<CFSET message = #GetAddressInfo.name# & Chr(13) & Chr(10)>
<CFSET message = message & #GetAddressInfo.address1# & Chr(13) & Chr(10)>
<CFIF #GetAddressInfo.address1# IS NOT "">
 <CFSET message = message & #GetAddressInfo.address2# & Chr(13) & Chr(10)>
</CFIF>
<CFSET message = message & #GetAddressInfo.city# & ", " &
 #GetAddressInfo.state# & " " & #GetAddressInfo.zip#>

<CFMAIL TO="#email# FROM="confirm@yourserver.com"
  SUBJECT="Address Confirmation" QUERY="GetAddressInfo">
Your name and address are shown below.  If any of this information
is incorrect, please reply to this message with the correct information.

#message#
</CFMAIL>
```

Other Useful CFML Tags

Fifty-one CFML tags are available, and to fully describe them all would require several chapters instead of just this one. The tags you have read about so far are the ones that form the core of most ColdFusion applications, but many others are deserving of mention. This section briefly surveys some of the other CFML tags that are popular with developers.

These tags include:

- <CFABORT>—If ColdFusion encounters the <CFABORT> tag, it stops processing the template at that point and sends whatever HTML it has generated to the server. <CFABORT> is useful when you're doing error checking on form data:

```
<CFIF NOT(IsNumeric('Form.age'))>
   <H1>Invalid age</H1>
   Please use your browser's Back button and enter a valid age on the form.
   <CFABORT>
</CFIF>
...
```

- <CFLOCATION>—<CFLOCATION> enables you to put redirects into your applications. It takes the URL attribute, which is set equal to the URL of the page where you want to redirect your users. You might do some queries to insert some information into one of your data sources, for example, and redirect the user back to the main page of your site with the following code:

```
<CFQUERY DATASOURCE="info" NAME="add".
INSERT
INTO Transactions (Item_number,quantity)
VALUES ('#Form.item_number#', #Form.quantity#)
</CFQUERY>
...
<CFLOCATION URL="index.cfm">
```

- <CFCOOKIE>—If you need to write a cookie to a user's browser, you can do so easily with the <CFCOOKIE> tag. <CFCOOKIE> has two required attributes: NAME, which is set equal to the name of the cookie, and VALUE, which is set equal to the cookie's value. Additionally, you can use the EXPIRES attribute to specify the cookie's expiration date and the SECURE attribute to require secure transmission of the cookie. For example:

```
<CFCOOKIE NAME="ID" VALUE="#User_ID#" EXPIRES="01/01/99" SECURE="YES">
```

You can also specify the domain for which the cookie is valid with the DOMAIN attribute and the paths on the server to which the cookie applies with the PATH attribute.

- <CFTRANSACTION>—Data integrity is important on transaction-oriented databases where several users might be accessing the database at any given time. Suppose you have the following three queries that insert a new record in the Contact_Info table, query the Contact_Info table for the primary key of the record that was just inserted, and then insert that primary key value into the Orders table, respectively:

```
<CFQUERY DATASOURCE="store" NAME="InsertInfo">
INSERT
INTO Contact_Info (name,address,city,state,zip,phone)
VALUES ('#Form.name#','#Form.address#','#Form.city#','#Form.state#',
'#Form.zip#', '#Form.phone#')
</CFQUERY>

<CFQUERY DATASOURCE="store" NAME="GetPrimaryKey">
SELECT MAX(Customer_ID) as pk
FROM Contact_Info
</CFQUERY>

<CFQUERY DATASOURCE="store" NAME="InsertPrimaryKey">
INSERT
INTO Orders (Customer)
VALUE (#GetPrimaryKey.pk#)
</CFQUERY>
```

These queries will work just fine, so long as no other queries are processed between them. Suppose, for example, that immediately after the contact information for customer A is inserted, contact information for customer B is also inserted. Then, when ColdFusion goes to query the database for customer A's primary key, it will really get customer B's primary key and customer B will then be associated with customer A's order in the Orders table. This creates the potential for erroneous orders throughout your entire electronic commerce application and sows the seeds for some pretty unhappy customers.

Fortunately, you can eliminate the potential by wrapping queries that should occur together in <CFTRANSACTION> and </CFTRANSACTION> tags. Queries grouped this way are treated as a single entity, and ColdFusion will not attempt any other queries until those in the <CFTRANSACTION> have finished.

■ <CFFORM>—CFML has some souped-up versions of the HTML form tags that enable you to automatically build JavaScript into your pages that will enable you to check for required fields and for appropriate formatting of input items such as phone numbers and zip codes. To use these tags, you have to use <CFFORM> and </CFFORM> tags where you would normally use <FORM> and </FORM> tags. After you've declared your intention to build a ColdFusion form, you can use tags such as <CFINPUT> for text fields, <CFSELECT> for drop-down lists, <CFSLIDER> for a Java-based slider control, <CFTREE> for a Java-based tree control, and <CFGRID> for a Java-based spreadsheet-like control.

The automated JavaScript comes into play when you use attributes such as REQUIRED or VALIDATE in the CFML form tags. For example, the tag

```
<CFINPUT TYPE="TEXT" NAME="fax" REQUIRED="YES" VALIDATE="telephone">
```

sets up a text input field rigged with JavaScript that checks to make sure the user entered a value into the field (REQUIRED="YES") and that what was entered is in a telephone number format (VALIDATE="telephone").

Of all the available CFML tags, you have read about slightly more than one-third of them here. But these should be enough to get you started with ColdFusion application development.

Remember that the online documentation that comes with ColdFusion and ColdFusion Studio contains full documentation on all the CFML tags in the event that you need to look up one of them.

CFML Functions

If you thought 51 was a lot of CFML tags, you'll be overwhelmed by the number of CFML functions—178 of them! Although that may seem like a huge number of new things to learn, you should make your best effort to get as familiar with as many of the CFML functions as you can. By using the built-in functions, you can accomplish critical tasks quickly and efficiently instead of trying to write your own tags to do the same work (which is almost always less efficient).

In reading about CFML tags, you were introduced to a few of the CFML functions as well. This section reviews several more of the key CFML functions. To help you understand them a little better, they are grouped as follows:

- String functions
- Formatting functions
- Array functions
- List functions
- Date and time functions
- Math functions
- Query functions
- Two other useful functions: IsDefined and URLEncodedFormat

As you read about these functions, try to focus on developing an awareness of the functions and what they do. You can always look up the details of the syntax later.

String Functions

CFML comes with a wealth of functions that make string manipulation a breeze. In fact, nearly one quarter of all CFML functions operate on strings. The following list summarizes some of the more commonly used string functions:

- Asc(*str*)—Returns the ASCII numeric value of the first character of *str*.
- Chr(*val*)—Returns the character with the ASCII value equal to *val*.
- CJustify(*str,len*)—Centers *str* in a field of length *len*.
- Compare(*str1,str2*)—Does a case-sensitive comparison of *str1* and *str2*, returning -1 if *str1* is less than *str2*, 0 if the strings are equal, and 1 if *str1* is greater than *str2*.
- CompareNoCase(*str1,str2*)—Does a case-sensitive comparison of *str1* and *str2*, returning -1 if *str1* is less than *str2*, 0 if the strings are equal, and 1 if *str1* is greater than *str2*.

Part

VI

Ch

34

- Find(*str1*,*str2*,*start*)—Returns the position in *str2* where there is an occurrence of *str1*. The case-sensitive search begins at the first character unless you specify a different value with the *start* parameter. The function returns 0 if no occurrence of *str1* is found.

- FindNoCase(*str1*,*str2*,*start*)—Returns the position in *str2* where there is an occurrence of *str1*. The not case-sensitive search begins at the first character unless you specify a different value with the *start* parameter. The function returns 0 if no occurrence of *str1* is found.

- Insert(*str1*,*str2*,*pos*)—Inserts *str1* into *str2* at position *pos*. If *pos* is 0, the function concatenates *str1* and *str2*.

- LCase(*str*)—Converts *str* to lowercase.

- Left(*str*,*pos*)—Returns the leftmost *pos* characters from *str*.

- Len(*str*)—Returns the number of characters in *str*.

- LTrim(*str*)—Removes any leading spaces from *str*.

- Mid(*str*,*start*,*num*)—Extracts *num* characters from *str*, starting at position *start*.

- REFind(*rexpr*,*str*,*start*)—Returns the position of an occurrence of the regular expression *rexpr* in *str*, beginning its search at position *start*.

- Replace(*str1*,*str2*,*str3*,*scope*)—Replaces occurrences of *str2* in *str1* with *str3*. *scope* controls how many replacements should be made (one or all).

- RERplace(*str1*,*rexpr*,*str2*,*scope*)—Replaces occurrences of the regular expression *rexpr* in *str1* with *str2*. *scope* controls how many replacements should be made (one or all).

- Reverse(*str*)—Reverses the order of the characters in *str*.

- Right(str,pos)—Returns the rightmost *pos* characters from *str*.

- RJustify(*str*,*len*)—Right-justifies *str* in a field of length *len*.

- RTrim(*str*)—Removes trailing spaces from *str*.

- UCase(*str*)—Converts str to uppercase.

Formatting Functions

ColdFusion can do some of the preparatory work that needs to be done before displaying a value. The following are some of the more popular CFML formatting functions:

- DateFormat(*date*,*mask*)—Formats *date* according to the specified mask. A *mask* of mm/dd/yy, for example, would yield a date in the form 12/31/98.

- DollarFormat(*number*)—Returns *number* formatted as a dollar amount with a dollar sign, decimal point, and commas where necessary.

- HTMLEditFormat(*HTMLcode*)—Removes reserved characters within the string *HTMLcode* and replaces them with their escaped values. The less than sign (<), for example, would be replaced with <.

- `NumberFormat(`*`number,mask`*`)`—Returns *number* formatted according to the specified *mask*. For example, a mask of '_,___.__' would produce a number in the form 1,000.00.

- `ParagraphFormat(`*`str`*`)`—Removes consecutive carriage return and line feed characters from *str* and replaces them with <P> tags.

- `TimeFormat(`*`time,mask`*`)`—Formats *time* according to the specified *mask*. A mask of hh:mm:ssTT, for example, produces a time in the form 07:25:00AM.

Array Functions

Arrays are a convenient way to store related information for quick reference throughout your template. You create an array with the `ArrayNew` function. For example:

```
stats = ArrayNew(2)
```

creates a new, two-dimensional array. This means the array will have two subscripts: stats[*subs1*][*subs2*]. ColdFusion supports one-, two-, and three-dimensional arrays.

N O T E   One-dimensional arrays are essentially the same as a ColdFusion list.

CFML comes with a large number of functions to handle array manipulation. These include

- `ArrayAppend(`*`arr,element`*`)`—Adds *element* to the end of the array *arr*. Returns a value of TRUE if successful.

- `ArrayAvg(`*`arr`*`)`—Returns the average value of the elements in the array *arr*.

- `ArrayClear(`*`arr`*`)`—Clears all elements from the array *arr*. Returns a value of TRUE if successful.

- `ArrayDeleteAt(`*`arr,index`*`)`—Removes the element at position *index* from the array *arr*. Returns a value of TRUE if successful.

- `ArrayInsertAt(`*`arr,index,element`*`)`—Inserts *element* into the array *arr* at position *index*. Returns a value of TRUE if successful.

- `ArrayIsEmpty(`*`arr`*`)`—Returns TRUE if *arr* has no elements or FALSE if *arr* has at least one element.

- `ArrayLen(`*`arr`*`)`—Returns the length of the array *arr*.

- `ArrayMax(`*`arr`*`)`—Returns the maximum value in the array *arr*.

- `ArrayMin(`*`arr`*`)`—Returns the maximum value in the array *arr*.

- `ArrayPrepend(`*`arr,element`*`)`—Adds *element* at the front of the array *arr*. Returns a value of TRUE if successful.

- `ArrayResize(`*`arr,min_size`*`)`—Resizes the array *arr* to have at least *min_size* elements.

- `ArraySort(`*`arr,type,order`*`)`—Sorts the array *arr* according to the *type* of sort specified (*numeric*, *text*, or *textnocase*). The sort *order* can be ascending (*asc*) or descending (*desc*).

- `ArraySum(`*`arr`*`)`—Returns the sum of the elements in the array *arr*.

Part
VI

Ch

34

■ `ArrayToList(arr,del)`—Converts the array *arr* to a list with the delimiter character *del*.

■ `IsArray('variable')`—Returns TRUE if *variable* is an array.

List Functions

ColdFusion lists are delimited sets of items. The default delimiter is a comma (,), but you can use any other character you would like to delimit your lists. You can even choose to have more than one delimiter character.

The same as with arrays, CFML comes with many functions that support rapid processing of lists. Some of the key CFML list functions follow. In each case, *del* is a string of list delimiters.

■ `ListAppend(lst,item,del)`—Adds *item* to the end of the list *lst*.

■ `ListChangeDelims(lst,new_del,del)`—Replaces all delimiters in the list *lst* with *new_del*.

■ `ListContains(lst,str,del)`—Returns the position of the first item in the list *lst* that contains *str* as a substring. The substring search is case sensitive.

■ `ListContainsNoCase(lst,str,del)`—Returns the item number of the first item in the list *lst* that contains *str* as a substring. The substring search is not case sensitive.

■ `ListDeleteAt(lst,pos,del)`—Deletes the item at position *pos* from the list *lst*.

■ `ListFind(lst,item,del)`—Returns the position of the first instance of *item* in the list *lst*. Search is case sensitive.

■ `ListFindNoCase(lst,item,del)`—Returns the position of the first instance of *item* in the list *lst*. Search is not case sensitive.

■ `ListFirst(lst,del)`—Returns the first item from the list *lst*.

■ `ListGetAt(lst,pos,del)`—Returns the item at position *pos* from the list *lst*.

■ `ListInsertAt(lst,pos,item,del)`—Inserts *item* at position *pos* of the list *lst*.

■ `ListLast(lst,del)`—Returns the last item from the list *lst*.

■ `ListLen(lst,del)`—Returns the number of items in the list *lst*.

■ `ListPrepend(lst,item,del)`—Adds *item* to the front of the list *lst*.

■ `ListRest(lst,del)`—Returns all items in the list *lst* except for the first one.

■ `ListSetAt(lst,pos,item,del)`—Sets the value of the item at position *pos* in the list *lst* to *item*.

■ `ListToArray(lst,del)`—Converts the list *lst* to a one-dimensional array.

Date and Time Functions

Handling date and time variables can be somewhat tricky, especially when you're using the SQL calls, in which case they have to be in a format that ODBC can interpret correctly. CFML supports 31 functions that operate on date and time variables. The following list provides a sampling of these functions. If you specify a year quantity less than 100, it is interpreted as a twentieth century value.

- CreateDateTime(*year*,*month*,*day*,*hour*,*minute*,*second*)—Creates a date/time variable with the value corresponding to the year, month, day, hour, minute, and second information provided.

- CreateODBCDateTime(*year*,*month*,*day*,*hour*,*minute*,*second*)—Creates a date/time variable in ODBC format with the value corresponding to the year, month, day, hour, minute, and second information provided.

- DateCompare(*datetime1*,*datetime2*)—Compares *datetime1* and *datetime2* and returns -1 if *datetime1* is less than *datetime2*, 0 if *datetime1* equals *datetime2*, and 1 if *datetime1* is greater than *datetime2*.

- Day(*date*)—Returns the day of the month (1–31) on which that *date* falls.

- Hour(*date*)—Returns the hour (0–23) specified by *date*.

- IsDate('*variable*')—Returns TRUE if *variable* is a valid date/time variable or FALSE if *variable* is not.

- IsLeapYear(*year*)—Returns TRUE if *year* is a leap year or FALSE if *year* is not.

- Minute(*date*)—Returns the value of the minutes (0–59) specification in the variable *date*.

- Month(*date*)—Returns the numeric value of the month (1–12) in the variable *date*.

- Now()—Returns the current system date and time.

T I P The Now() function makes it easy to timestamp database transactions.

- ParseDateTime(*str*)—Converts the string *str* to a valid date/time variable.

- Second(*date*)—Returns the value of the seconds (0–59) specification in the variable *date*.

- Week(*date*)—Returns the numerical week of the year (1–53) during which *date* occurs.

- Year(*date*)—Returns the value of the year specification in the variable *date*.

Math Functions

You may not need to do much mathematical computation as part of your ColdFusion applications, but CFML includes a large library of math functions for you to use when the need arises. Some of these include:

- Abs(*num*)—Returns the absolute value of *num*.

- Ceiling(*num*)—Returns the closest integer bigger than *num*.

- DecrementValue(*num*)—Subtracts one from the value of *num*.

- IncrementValue(*num*)—Adds one to the value of *num*.

- Int(*num*)—Returns the closest integer smaller than *num*.

- Log(*num*)—Returns the natural logarithm of *num*.

Part
VI

Ch

34

- Log10(*num*)—Returns the base-10 logarithm of *num*.
- Max(*num1,num2*)—Returns the larger of *num1* and *num2*.
- Min(*num1,num2*)—Returns the smaller of ***num1*** and *num2*.
- pi()—Returns the value of the constant pi, 3.14159265358979. pi represents the ratio of the circumference of a circle to its diameter.
- Rand()—Returns a random number between 0 and 1.
- RandRange(*num1,num2*)—Returns a random number between *num1* and *num2*.
- Round(*num*)—Rounds *num* to the closest integer.
- Sgn(*num*)—Returns -1 if *num* is negative, 0 if *num* is zero, and 1 if *num* is positive.
- Sqr(*num*)—Returns the positive square root of *num*.

Two Other Useful Functions

Two other valuable functions should be part of your basic ColdFusion awareness:

- IsDefined('*variable*')—Returns TRUE if *variable* is defined and FALSE if it is not defined.
- URLEncodedFormat(*str*)—Converts *str* so that it can be passed to the next template as a URL variable.

IsDefined is ideal for handling radio button and check box form controls. The problem with both of these controls is that no name/value pairs are passed for them if nothing is selected. In the following set of check boxes, for example:

```
<B>Additional Pizza Toppings</B>
<INPUT TYPE="TEXT" NAME="TOPPING" VALUE="Pepperoni"> Pepperoni
<INPUT TYPE="TEXT" NAME="TOPPING" VALUE="Mushrooms"> Mushrooms
<INPUT TYPE="TEXT" NAME="TOPPING" VALUE="Pineapple"> Pineapple
<INPUT TYPE="TEXT" NAME="TOPPING" VALUE="Onions"> Onions
<INPUT TYPE="TEXT" NAME="TOPPING" VALUE="Anchovies"> Anchovies
```

a user may not select any of them. You could check for this in the template that processes the pizza order form as follows:

```
<CFIF IsDefined('Form.Topping')>
        ... extra topping processing code ...
<CFELSE>
        You did not select any extra toppings.
</CFIF>
```

If the user did select extra toppings, Form.Topping will be defined and ColdFusion will execute the block of code that processes the user's selections.

TIP By naming all the check boxes with the same NAME attribute, any selected check box values will be passed to ColdFusion as a list. If a user selects pepperoni, onions, and anchovies, for example, the value of Form.Topping would be Pepperoni,Onions,Anchovies, and you could process the toppings like so:

```
<CFIF IsDefined('Form.Topping')>
   <CFSET ToppingList = #Form.Topping#>
   You requested the following additional toppings:
   <UL>
   <CFLOOP LIST="ToppingList" INDEX="top">
      <CFOUTPUT><LI>#top#</CFOUTPUT>
   </CFLOOP>
   </UL>
<CFELSE>
   You did not select any extra toppings.
</CFIF>
```

The URLEncodedFormat function is essential if you plan to pass strings of data on a URL. Recall that the browser encodes form data before sending it, doing things such as replacing spaces with plus signs (+) and replacing special characters with hexadecimal escape codes. To have to do this conversion yourself would be nightmarish, but thankfully the URLEncodedFormat function spares you the agony.

URLEncodedFormat is especially useful when you are setting up links that users can click to invoke other templates. For example:

```
<CFQUERY DATASOURCE="sales" NAME="GetAll">
SELECT ID, region
FROM Territories
</CFQUERY>

<B>Please click a region's ID number for more information.</B>
<P>
<TABLE>
<TR><TH>ID</TH><TH>Region</TH></TR>
<CFOUTPUT QUERY="GetAll">
<TR>
<TD>
<A HREF="regiondetail.cfm?region=#URLEncodedFormat(region)#>#ID#</A>
</TD>
<TD>#region#</TD>
</TR>
</CFOUPTUT>
</TABLE>
```

If region had the value Central Region, for example, it would need to be converted to Central+Region before passing it on the URL for the regiondetail.cfm template. In the code above, the URLEncodedFormat function takes care of this conversion for you.

Part
VI

Ch
34

N O T E   If you're familiar with JavaScript, the URLEncodedFormat function does the same thing as the JavaScript escape function. ▨

Using ColdFusion Studio

As you've seen throughout the chapter, CFML code coexists in the same file as HTML code. Therefore, ColdFusion templates have to be plain text files, just as HTML documents are. So technically, all you need to write ColdFusion templates is an editor that can write out plain text files. This means that you could compose your templates using Notepad, Microsoft Word, or any HTML authoring tool that enables you to edit the raw code.

Although any text editor is fine, you should seriously consider using Allaire's ColdFusion Studio as your development tool of choice for ColdFusion templates. Based on the popular HTML authoring program HomeSite, ColdFusion Studio comes with many helpful features that directly support you as you write CFML code. This final section of the chapter introduces you to ColdFusion Studio and how to use Studio to make your development work much less tedious.

The ColdFusion Studio Interface

Figure 34.20 shows the ColdFusion Studio user interface. The interface is toolbar oriented, and you have the option of displaying any or none of the toolbars. Additionally, you can customize many of the toolbars to include only the buttons you use frequently or buttons that you create.

FIGURE 34.20

The ColdFusion Studio user interface strongly resembles that of HomeSite.

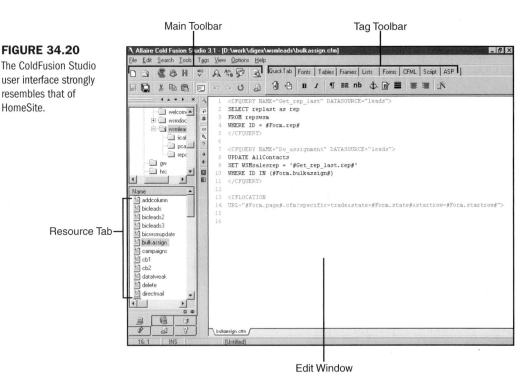

The major components of the interface include:

- Main Toolbar—The Main Toolbar contains buttons that do common file related tasks such as opening, saving, and printing and editing tasks such as cut, copy, and paste. Buttons also launch Studio's verification tools: a link checker, a document weight computation tool (how long it will take to download the document and its dependent files), and an HTML validator.

- Tag Toolbar—The Tag Toolbar plays host to several tabs (all of which you can display or hide easily), including QuickTab, Fonts, Tables, Frames, Lists, Forms, CFML, Script, and Active Server Pages (ASP). Each tab, in turn, contains buttons that place HTML and CFML tags into your documents. By putting the tags into logical grouping on the tabs, it becomes easy to switch back and forth between sets of buttons as you need them.

 TIP

If you're writing JavaScript and you've forgotten some part of the browser object model, the Script tab contains a drop-down box with a collapsible tree that outlines the entire model for you (see Figure 34.21).

FIGURE 34.21

A reference for the browser object model is built right in to the Script tab of the Tags Toolbar.

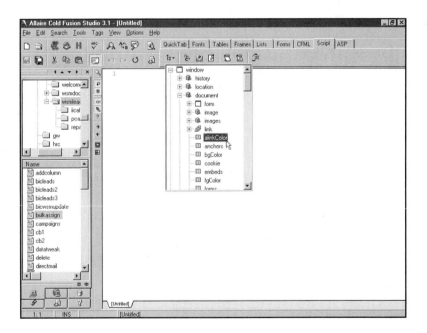

- Editor Toolbar—The behavior of the editing window is controlled by the Editor Toolbar (located along the left side of the editing window). Buttons on this toolbar control properties such as word wrapping, block indenting, and numbering of the lines of code. In addition, you can toggle the window between browser preview mode and edit mode and between full-screen and partial-screen modes.

The remaining buttons on the Editor Toolbar support what Allaire calls Studio's What-You-See-Is-What-You-Need (WYSIWYN) feature. This includes Tag Completion (a container tag's closing tag will automatically appear when you finish typing in the opening tag), Tag Tips (pop-up messages that show all the possible attributes permitted by the tag's syntax), and Tag Insight (which provides a drop-down list of attributes the tag can take, enabling you to easily choose the ones you want). Figure 34.22 shows the Tag Insight in action.

FIGURE 34.22

With Tag Insight activated, you can select which attributes you want to place inside a tag from a context-sensitive list.

Tag Insight drop-down list

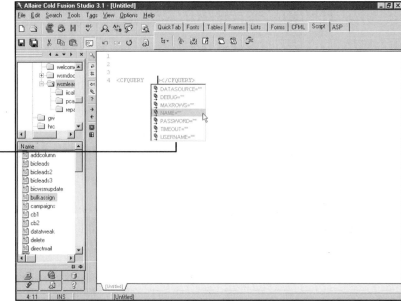

NOTE With some practice, most users acclimate themselves to the WYSIWYN features and are able to develop more rapidly. If you find them more of a hindrance, you can suppress them by deselecting their buttons on the Edit Toolbar.

- Resource Tab—The Resource Tab typically appears to the left of the edit window, although you can change its position easily enough. The Resource Tab is itself tabbed to give you access to local and remote disk drives, ColdFusion data sources on remote servers, groups of related templates called *projects*, tag *snippets* (chunks of reusable code), and the full set of ColdFusion and ColdFusion Studio documentation in HTML format.

- Palette—The bar running along the bottom of the Resource Tab and the edit window is called the Palette. From here, you can select colors for backgrounds, text, links, and any other situation where you might need a hexadecimal color triplet. The default color palette is the "browser safe" color palette advanced by Lynda Weinman (http://www.lynda.com/).

> **CAUTION**
>
> Be careful when using hexadecimal color triplets because the pound sign (#) that precedes them can confuse the ColdFusion Application Server when it parses the file. As long as you keep the color triplets outside of any CFML container tags, your code should be parsed without any problems.

Using the Resource Tab

The Resource Tab is an incredibly useful window to many of the resources developers need while creating a ColdFusion application. This section takes a closer look at the tabs on the Resource Tab and what they let you access.

The tab you see open in Figure 34.20 is the Local Tab. When this tab is selected, the Resource Tab is divided into two windows. In the upper window, you can navigate drives and folders on your machine. As you change from one folder to another, the files in that folder appear in the lower window. Having the list of files at your disposal is very valuable. You can double-click a file to open it, drag and drop an HTML file or a ColdFusion template into the edit window to set up a link to it, or drag and drop an image file into the edit window to place the image in your document.

The Remote Tab is shown open in Figure 34.23. Again, the Resource Tab is split into two windows and both windows perform similar functions. But in this case, you are working with files on a remote server via FTP. When you double-click a file, the file is downloaded to your machine and presented in the edit window so you can work on it. When you save your changes, Studio uploads the modified file to the remote machine.

FIGURE 34.23

No need to use a separate FTP client because ColdFusion Studio has one built right in.

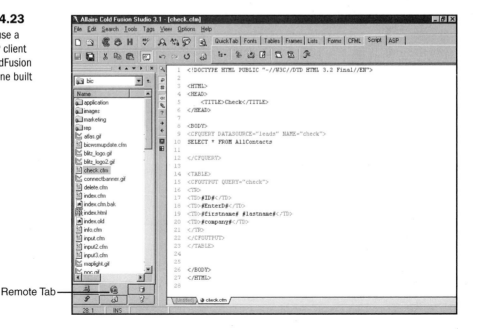

Remote Tab

N O T E When you first open the Remote Tab, you see a list of the FTP server profiles you have set up. If you haven't set up any yet, right-click the Resource Tab and select the Add FTP Server option.

CAUTION

If you don't save frequently, your FTP connection may time out, and you'll have to reconnect to the remote server.

The Database Tab enables you to access the system data sources on a remote server that's running ColdFusion. This can be incredibly valuable during development, especially when writing queries. Each data source on the server is presented in a tree that you can expand to display the tables, views, and queries stored in the corresponding database file. You can also expand a given table to display the database columns that compose the table. Studio will show you not only the name of the column, but its type and length as well (see Figure 34.24).

FIGURE 34.24

By connecting to a remote ColdFusion server through the Database Tab, you can view the tables, fields, and queries available under each data source on the server.

Database Tab

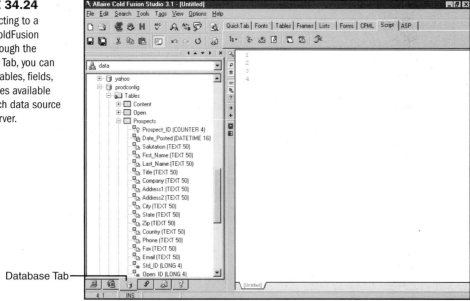

Projects are groups of related files stored together. For example, you can group all the templates that support a single application into a project. Once grouped, you can open, close, and save all the files simultaneously. Furthermore, you can do search and replace operations across all the files, making it simple to deploy global changes in your applications. You can access the projects you've created through the Projects Tab on the Resources Tab.

The Tag Snippets Tab enables you to set up folders to hold frequently used blocks of code (see Figure 34.25). This is an excellent place to store code for things such as standard headers and footers, common form controls (for example, a drop-down list of all 50 states—something that is painful to have to type out each time you need it!), and client-side imagemaps.

FIGURE 34.25

The Tag Snippets Tab is like a big Clipboard where you can store chunks of code that you use frequently.

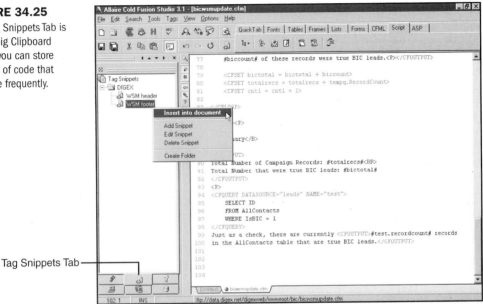

Tag Snippets Tab

Finally, the Help Tab gives you access to complete documentation on all CFML tags and functions, explanations of how to use and customize ColdFusion Studio, references for HTML and Cascading Style Sheets, and information on how to contact Allaire for technical support.

Using Special ColdFusion Studio Tools

In addition to the excellent tag support provided by the Tag Toolbar and the easy access to resources through the Resource Tab, ColdFusion Studio also comes with a few other useful tools. The chapter closes with a brief look at three of them: the Tag Chooser, the Expression Builder, and the Insert SQL Statement tool.

The Tag Chooser   Figure 34.26 shows the Tag Chooser, which you can activate by pressing Ctrl+E. Within the Chooser, all HTML and CFML tags are stored in an easy-to-navigate tree structure that enables you to zero in on the tags you want quickly. As you move through the tree structure, the various tags available are displayed in the right side of the Chooser. To insert one of the tags into your document, click it and then click the Select button in the lower right.

Part
VI

Ch
34

FIGURE 34.26

If you don't like using the toolbars, the Tag Chooser can put all the HTML and CFML tags at your fingertips.

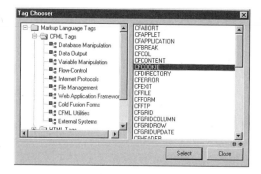

The Expression Builder   You launch the ColdFusion Studio Expression Builder by pressing Ctrl+Shift+E. The Expression Builder is useful in two ways. First, it is helpful when you're building complicated expressions that involve ColdFusion functions. You can see the expression in the window at the top of the Builder and make edits to it there as necessary (see Figure 34.27).

The other useful feature of the Expression Builder is that it catalogs all CFML functions, constants, operators, and variables in the tree you see on the left side of the builder. By navigating the tree, you can easily look up one of the CFML functions that are otherwise too numerous to commit to memory. As you move through the tree, the available functions, constants, operators, and variables are displayed in the right side of the Builder. After you're done composing your expression, clicking the Insert button places it into your template.

FIGURE 34.27

Can't remember one of the CFML list functions? Look it up through the Expression Builder.

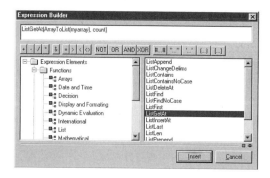

The Insert SQL Statement Tool   If you need to use a query stored in one of your data sources or if you need to construct a new query, you can choose the Insert SQL Statement option under the Tools menu to open the window you see in Figure 34.28. From this window, you can connect to one of the ColdFusion servers that Studio is configured to work with and navigate to the Queries subtree of the data source you're using. From there you can choose one of the queries and insert it directly into your template.

FIGURE 34.28
ColdFusion Studio can easily grab a pre-existing query from one of your data sources.

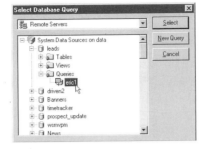

If you need to compose a brand new query, you can click the New Query button you see in Figure 34.28 to launch the Query Builder you see in Figure 34.29. The Query Builder gives you a visual environment in which to construct your query. You can open as many tables as you need in the Query Builder window and do joins on the tables by simply dragging the joining fields from one table to another. As you do, the corresponding SQL statement is constructed at the bottom of the Query Builder. When you're done building the query and click the close button, the Query Builder will give you the option to insert the SQL statement right into your template.

FIGURE 34.29
The ColdFusion Studio Query Builder is similar to the Microsoft Access Query Builder and can place the SQL statements you build directly into your template file.

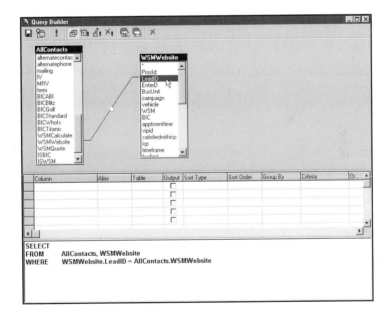

Server-Side Security Issues

by Greg Knauss and Melissa Niles

In this chapter

Scripts Versus Programs

Shell scripts, Perl programs, and C executables are the most common forms that a CGI script takes, and each has advantages and disadvantages when security is taken into account. No single language is the best; depending on other considerations such as speed and reuse, each has a place.

- Although shell CGI programs are often the easiest to write, it can be difficult to fully control them because they usually do most of their work by executing other, external programs. This can lead to several possible pitfalls because your CGI script instantly inherits any of the security problems that those called programs have. The common UNIX utility awk has some fairly restrictive limits on the amount of data it can handle, for instance, and your CGI program will be burdened with all those limits, as well.

- Perl is a step up from shell scripts. It has many advantages for CGI programming and is fairly secure, in itself. But Perl can offer CGI authors just enough flexibility and peace of mind that they might be lulled into a false peace of mind. Perl is interpreted, for example, and this makes it easier for bad user data to be included as part of the code.

- The third language option is C. Although C is popular for many uses, it is because of this popularity that many of its security problems are well known and can be exploited fairly easily. For instance, C is bad at string handling; it does no automatic allocation or clean up, leaving coders to handle everything on their own. Many C programmers, when dealing with strings, will set up a predefined space and hope that it will be big enough to handle whatever the user enters. Robert T. Morris, the author of the infamous Internet Worm, exploited such a weakness in attacking the C-based sendmail program, overflowing a buffer to alter the stack and gain unauthorized access. The same can happen to your CGI program.

CGI Security Issues: Recognizing Problems, Finding Solutions

Almost all CGI security holes come from interaction with the user. By accepting input from an outside source, a simple, predictable CGI program suddenly takes on any number of new dimensions, each of which might have the smallest crack through which a hacker can slip. It is interaction with the user—through forms or file paths—that gives CGI scripts their power but also make them the most potentially dangerous part of running a Web server.

> **CAUTION**
>
> Writing secure CGI scripts is largely an exercise in creativity and paranoia. You must be creative to think of all the ways that users, either innocently or otherwise, can send you data that has the potential to cause trouble. And you must be paranoid because, somehow, users will try every one of them.

Two Roads to Trouble

When users log on to your Web site and begin to interact with it, they can cause headaches in two ways. One is by not following the rules, by bending or breaking every limit or restriction you've tried to build into your pages; the other is by doing just what you've asked them to do.

- Most CGI scripts act as the back end to HTML forms, processing the information entered by users to provide some sort of customized output. Therefore, most CGI scripts are written to expect data in a very specific format. They rely on input from the user matching the information that the form was designed to collect. This, however, isn't always the case. A user can get around these predefined formats in many ways, sending your script seemingly random data. Your CGI programs must be prepared for it.

- Secondly, users can send a CGI script exactly the type of data it expects, with each field in the form filled in, in the format you expect. This type of submission can be from an innocent user interacting with your site as you intended, or it can be from a malevolent hacker using his knowledge of your operating system and Web server software to take advantage of common CGI programming errors. These attacks, in which everything seems fine, are the most dangerous and the hardest to detect. The security of your Web site depends on preventing them.

Form Data: The Most Common Security Hole

Users are an unruly lot, and they're likely to find the handful of ways to send data that you never expect—even ways that you think are impossible. All your scripts must take this into account. For instance, each of the following situations—and many more like them—are possible:

- The selection from a group of radio buttons or `<SELECT>` element may not be one of the choices offered in the form. The options in the `<SELECT NAME="opinion">` element may be `"yes"` and `"no"`, for example, but the URL returned to the server may be `http://www.yourdomain.com/cgi-bin/fileproc.cgi?option=maybe`. The user may have edited the URL to include nearly any string.

- The length of the data returned from a text field may be longer than what is allowed by the MAXLENGTH attribute. As in the previous example, the user may have edited the URL to include a string of nearly any length. If your form has a text field `<INPUT NAME="city" TYPE="text" MAXLENGTH="15">`, for example, the URL returned to the server may be `http://www.yourdomain.com/cgi-bin/yourprog.pl/city=El+Pueblo+de+Nuestra+Senora+la+Reina+de+los+Angeles+de+Porciuncula`.

- The names of the fields themselves may not match what you specified in the form. If your survey form has three named fields: q1, q2, and q3, for example, you may still get a URL returned to the server ending in `?you_are=hacked`.

- Using "hidden" fields in your form provides no assurances that someone cannot read that value within the input tag. Also, anyone viewing a form can view the source, and all form tags are displayed. They can simply edit the HTML and enter their own values.

Part
VI

Ch
35

Where Bad Data Comes From

These situations can arise in several ways—some innocent, some not. For instance, your script can receive data that it doesn't expect because somebody else wrote a form (that requests input completely different from yours) and accidentally pointed the form's ACTION attribute to your CGI script. Perhaps they used your form as a template and forgot to edit the ACTION attribute's URL before testing it. This would result in your script getting data that it has no idea what to do with, possibly causing unexpected—and dangerous—behavior.

Or the user might have accidentally (or intentionally) edited the URL to your CGI script. When a browser submits form data to a CGI program, it simply appends the data entered into the form onto the CGI's URL (for GET methods). The user can easily modify the data being sent to your script by typing in the browser's Address bar.

Finally, an ambitious hacker might write a program that connects to your server over the Web and pretends to be a Web browser. This program, though, can do things that no true Web browser would do, such as send a hundred megabytes of data to your CGI script. What would a CGI script do if it didn't limit the amount of data it read from a POST method because it assumed that the data came from a small form? It would probably crash and maybe crash in a way that would allow access to the person who crashed it.

Fighting Bad Form Data

You can fight the unexpected input that can be submitted to your CGI scripts in several ways. You should use any or all of them when writing CGI.

- First, your CGI script should set reasonable limits on how much data it will accept, both for the entire submission and for each name/value pair in the submission. If your CGI script reads the POST method, for instance, check the size of the CONTENT_LENGTH environment variable to make sure that it's something that you can reasonably expect. Although most Web servers set an arbitrary limit on the amount of data that will be passed to your script via POST, you may want to limit this size further. For instance, if the only input your CGI script is designed to accept is a person's first name, it might be a good idea to return an error if CONTENT_LENGTH is more than, say, 100 bytes. No reasonable first name will be that long, and by imposing the limit, you've protected your script from blindly reading anything that gets sent to it.

N O T E In most cases, you don't have to worry about limiting the data submitted through the GET method. GET is usually self-limiting and won't deliver more than approximately one kilobyte of data to your script. The server automatically limits the size of the data placed into the QUERY_STRING environment variable, which is how GET sends information to a CGI program.

Of course, hackers can easily circumvent this built-in limit by changing the METHOD attribute of your form from "GET" to "POST". At the very least, your program should check that data is submitted using the method you expect; at most, it should handle both methods correctly and safely. ■

▶ **See** "Standard CGI Environment Variables," **p. 708**.

■ Next, make sure that your script knows what to do if it receives data that it doesn't recognize. If, for example, a form asks that a user select one of two radio buttons, the script shouldn't assume that just because one isn't clicked, the other is. The following Perl code makes this mistake.

```
if ($form_Data{"radio_choice"} eq "button_one")
{
        # Button One has been clicked
}
else
{
        # Button Two has been clicked
}
```

■ Your CGI script should anticipate unexpected or "impossible" situations and handle them accordingly. The preceding example is pretty innocuous, but the same assumption elsewhere can easily be dangerous. An error should be printed instead, as follows:

```
if ($form_Data{"radio_choice"} eq "button_one")
{
        # Button One selected
}
elsif ($form_Data{"radio_choice"} eq "button_two")
{
        # Button Two selected
}
else
{
        # Error
}
```

Of course, an error may not be what you want your script to generate in these circumstances. Overly picky scripts that validate every field and produce error messages on even the slightest unexpected data can turn users off.

T I P   The balance between safety and convenience for the user is important. Don't be afraid to consult with your users to find out what works best for them.

■ To have your CGI script recognize unexpected data, throw it away, and automatically select a default is a possibility, too. The following is C code that checks text input against several possible choices, for instance, and sets a default if it doesn't find a match. You can use this to generate output that might better explain to the user what you expect.

```
/* Notes for non-C programmers:                                  */
/* Contrary to what its name implies,                            */
/*    the C string comparison function strcmp used below         */
/*    returns 0 (false) when its two arguments match and     */
/*    returns nonzero (true)_when its two arguments differ.   */
/*    A better name might be strDIFF.                            */
/* In C, "&&" is logical AND.                                    */
/*                                                               */
/* If the help_Topic is not any of the three choices given...  */
```

```
if ((strcmp(help_Topic,"how_to_order.txt")) &&
 (strcmp(help_Topic,"delivery_options.txt")) &&
 (strcmp(help_Topic,"complaints.txt")))
{
      /* then set help_Topic to the default value here       */
      strcpy(help_Topic,"help_on_help.txt");
}
```

■ However, your script might try to do users a favor and correct any mistakes rather than send an error or select a default. If a form asks users to enter the secret word, your script can automatically strip off any whitespace characters from the input before doing the comparison, such as the following Perl fragment:

```
# Remove whitespace by replacing it with an empty string
$user_Input =~ s/\s//g;
if ($user_Input eq $secret_Word)
{
      # Match!
}
```

TIP

Although it's nice to try to catch the users' mistakes, don't try to do too much. If your corrections aren't really what users wanted, they'll be annoyed.

CAUTION

You should also be aware that trying to catch every possible user-entry error will make your code huge and nearly impossible to maintain. Don't over-engineer.

■ Finally, you might choose to go the extra mile and have your CGI script handle as many different forms of input as it can. Although you can't possibly anticipate everything that can be sent to a CGI program, often several common ways exist to do a particular thing, and you can check for each.

Just because the form you wrote uses the POST method to submit data to your CGI script, for example, that doesn't mean that the data will come in that way. Rather than assuming that the data will be on standard in (stdin) where you're expecting it, you can check the REQUEST_METHOD environment variable to determine whether the GET or POST method was used and read the data accordingly. A truly well-written CGI script will accept data no matter what method was used to submit it and will be made more secure in the process. Listing 35.1 shows an example in Perl.

TROUBLESHOOTING

If your script returns an error, there are five usual causes. The first is that your script is not returning the proper Content-type. The second may be that your server is not properly set up to handle CGI scripts. The third is that the script named in the form's ACTION attribute is not in your CGI-enabled directory, usually called cgi-bin. The fourth is that the path given in the form's ACTION attribute is misspelled, or the filename is misspelled. Check the spelling of the filename and path. The fifth cause is that the filename and path are correct, but the filename does not end in the proper extension (such as `.cgi` or `.plx` or `.pl`) for your server configuration.

Although you will usually get this error when the form is METHOD=`"POST"`, a user can cause this error to occur in a form with METHOD=`"GET"` by editing your page in his browser and substituting `"POST"` for `"GET"`.

Listing 35.1 *Cgi_read.pl*—A Robust Reading Form Input

```
# Takes the maximum length allowed as a parameter
# Returns 1 and the raw form data, or "0" and the error text
sub cgi_Read
{
      local($input_Max) = 1024 unless $input_Max = $_[0];
      local($input_Method) = $ENV{'REQUEST_METHOD'};

      # Check for each possible REQUEST_METHODs
      if ($input_Method eq "GET")
      {
            # "GET"
            local($input_Size) = length($ENV{'QUERY_STRING'});

            # Check the size of the input
            return (0, "Input too big") if ($input_Size > $input_Max);

            # Read the input from QUERY_STRING
            return (1,$ENV{'QUERY_STRING'});
      }
      elsif ($input_Method eq "POST")
      {
            # "POST"
            local($input_Size) = $ENV{'CONTENT_LENGTH'};
            local($input_Data);

            # Check the size of the input
            return (0,"Input too big") if ($input_Size > $input_Max);

            # Read the input from stdin
            return (0,"Could not read STDIN") unless
 (read(STDIN,$input_Data,$input_Size));

            return (1,$input_Data);
      }

      # Unrecognized METHOD
      return (0,"METHOD not GET or POST");
}
```

> **TIP** Many existing CGI programming libraries already offer good built-in security features. Rather than write your own routines, you may want to rely on some of the well-known, publicly available functions.

Don't Trust Path Data

Another type of data the user can alter is the PATH_INFO server environment variable. This variable is filled with any path information that follows the script's filename in a CGI URL. For instance, if sample.sh is a CGI shell script, the URL http://www.yourserver.com/cgi-bin/ sample.sh/extra/path/info will cause /extra/path/info to be placed in the PATH_INFO environment variable when sample.sh is run.

If you use this PATH_INFO environment variable, you must be careful to completely validate its contents. Just as form data can be altered in any number of ways, so can PATH_INFO—accidentally or on purpose. A CGI script that blindly acts on the path file specified in PATH_INFO can enable malicious users to wreak havoc on the server.

If a CGI script is designed to print out the file that's referenced in PATH_INFO, for instance, a user who edits the CGI URL can read almost any file on your computer, as in the following script:

```
#!/bin/sh

# Send the header
echo "Content-type: text/html"
echo ""

# Wrap the file in some HTML
echo "<HTML><HEADER><TITLE>File</TITLE></HEADER><BODY>"
echo "Here is the file you requested:<pre>\n"
cat $PATH_INFO
echo "</PRE></BODY></HTML>"
```

Although this script works fine if the user is content to click only predefined links—for example, http://www.yourserver.com/cgi-bin/showfile.sh/public/faq.txt—a more creative (or spiteful) user could use it to receive *any* file on your server. If she were to jump to http:// www.yourserver.com/cgi-bin/showfile.sh/etc/passwd, the preceding script would happily return your machine's password file, something you do not want to happen.

A much safer course is to use the PATH_TRANSLATED environment variable. It automatically appends the contents of PATH_INFO to the root of your server's document tree, which means that any file specified by PATH_TRANSLATED is probably already accessible to browsers and, therefore, safe. If your document root is /usr/local/etc/htdocs, for example, and PATH_INFO is /etc/passwd, then PATH_TRANSLATED is /usr/local/etc/htdocs/etc/passwd.

N O T E   In one case, however, files that may not be accessible through a browser can be accessed if PATH_TRANSLATED is used within a CGI script. The .htaccess file, which can exist in each subdirectory of a document tree, controls who has access to the particular files in that directory. It can be used, for example, to limit the visibility of a group of Web pages to company employees. Whereas the server knows how to interpret .htaccess and thus knows how to limit who can and who can't see these pages, CGI scripts don't. A program that uses PATH_TRANSLATED to access arbitrary files in the document tree may accidentally override the protection provided by the server. ■

Handling Filenames

Filenames, for example, are simple pieces of data that may be submitted to your CGI script and cause endless amounts of trouble—if you're not careful (see Figure 35.1).

FIGURE 35.1

Depending on how well the CGI script is written, the Webmaster for this site can get into big trouble.

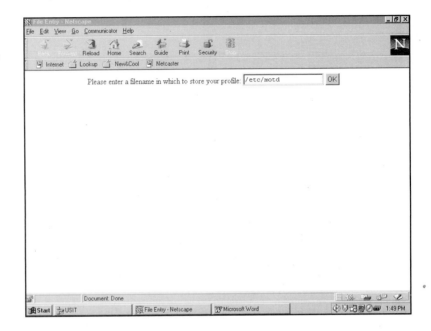

Any time you try to open a file based on a name supplied by the user, you must rigorously screen that name for any number of tricks that can be played. If you ask the user for a filename and then try to open whatever was entered, a problem may occur.

- For instance, what if the user enters a name that has path elements in it, such as directory slashes and double dots? Although you expect a simple filename—for example, `File.txt`—you can end up with `/file.txt` or `../../../file.txt`. Depending on how your Web server is installed and what you do with the submitted filename, you can be exposing any file on your system to a clever hacker.

- Furthermore, what if the user enters the name of an existing file or one that's important to the running of the system? What if the name entered is `/etc/passwd` or `C:\WINNT\SYSTEM32\KERNEL32.DLL`? Depending on what your CGI script does with these files, they may be sent out to the user or overwritten with garbage.

- Under Windows 95 and Windows NT, if you don't screen for the backslash character (\), you might enable Web browsers to gain access to files that aren't even on your Web server through Universal Naming Convention (UNC) filenames. If the script that's about to run in Figure 35.2 doesn't carefully screen the filename before opening it, it might give the Web browser access to any machine in the domain or workgroup.

Part

VI

Ch

35

FIGURE 35.2

Opening a UNC filename is one possible security hole that gives hackers access to your entire network.

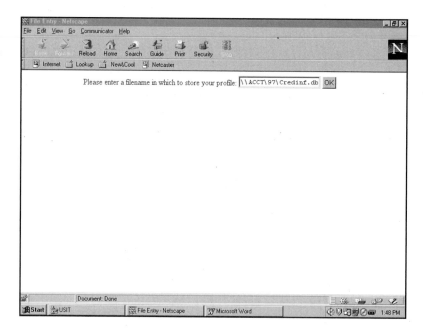

- What might happen if the user puts an illegal character in a filename? Under UNIX, any filename beginning with a period (.) will become invisible. Under Windows, both slashes (/ and \) are directory separators. It's possible, if the filename begins with the pipe (¦), to write a Perl program carelessly and allow external programs to be executed when you thought you were only opening a file. Even control characters (the Escape key or the Return key, for instance) can be sent to you as part of filenames if the user knows how. (See "Where Bad Data Comes From," earlier in this chapter.)

N O T E   Worse yet, in shell script, the semicolon ends one command and starts another. If your script is designed to `cat` the file the user enters, a user might enter `file.txt;rm -rf/` as a filename, causing `File.txt` to be returned and, consequently, the entire hard disk to be erased, without confirmation. ■

Verifying Input Is Legitimate

To avoid all the dangers associated with bad input and close all the potential security holes they open, you should screen every filename the user enters. You must make sure that the input is only what you expect.

The best way to do this is to compare each character of the entered filename against a list of acceptable characters and return an error if they don't match. This turns out to be much safer than trying to maintain a list of all the illegal characters and to compare against that—it's too easy to accidentally let something slip through.

The code snippet below is an example of how to do this comparison in Perl. It allows any letter of the alphabet (upper or lowercase), any number, the underscore, and the period. It also checks to make sure that the filename doesn't start with a period. Thus, this fragment doesn't allow slashes to change directories, semicolons to put multiple commands on one line, or pipes to play havoc with Perl's open() call.

```
if (($file_Name =~ /[^\w\.]/) ¦¦ ($file_Name =~ /^\./)){
    # File name contains an illegal character or starts with a period
}
```

T I P

When you have a commonly used test, such as the code above, it's a good idea to make it into a subroutine so you can call it repeatedly. This way, you can change it in only one place in your program if you think of an improvement.

Continuing that thought, if the subroutine is used commonly among several programs, it's a good idea to put it into a library so that any improvements can be instantly inherited by all your scripts.

CAUTION

Although the previous code snippet filters out most bad filenames, your operating system may have restrictions it doesn't cover. Can a filename start with a digit, for instance? With an underscore? What if the filename has more than one period, or if the period is followed by more than three characters? Is the entire filename short enough to fit within the restrictions of the file system?

You must constantly ask yourself these kinds of questions. The most dangerous thing you can do when writing CGI scripts is to rely on the users to follow instructions. They won't. It's your job to make sure they don't get away with it.

Handling HTML

Another type of seemingly innocuous input that can cause you endless trouble is receiving HTML when you request text from the user. The code snippet below is a Perl fragment that customizes a greeting to whomever has entered a name in the $user_Name variable; for example, John Smith (see Figure 35.3).

```
print("<HTML><TITLE>Greetings!</TITLE><BODY>\n");
print("Hello, $user_Name!  It's good to see you!\n");
print("</BODY></HTML>\n");
```

But imagine if, rather than entering only a name, the user types <HR><H1><P ALIGN="CENTER">Jane Smith</P></H1><HR>. The result would be Figure 35.4—probably not what you wanted.

Or imagine if a hacker entered

```
<IMG SRC="/secret/project/funnyface.jpg">
```

Part

VI

Ch

35

FIGURE 35.3

When the user enters what you requested, everything works well.

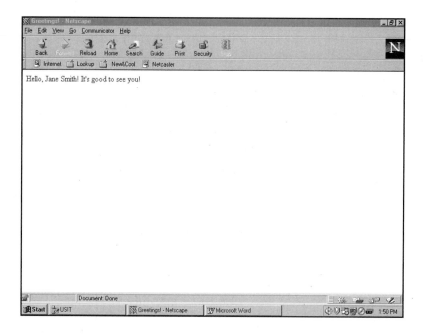

FIGURE 35.4

Entering HTML when a script expects plain text can change a page in unexpected ways.

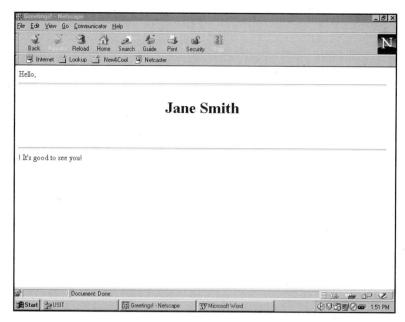

when you requested the user's name. Again, if the code from the preceding snippet were part of a CGI script with this HTML in the `$user_Name` variable, your Web server would happily show the hacker your secret adorable toddler picture! Figure 35.5 is an example.

FIGURE 35.5
Allowing HTML to be entered can be dangerous. Here a secret file is shown instead of the user's name.

Or what if `The last signee!<FORM><SELECT>` was entered as the user's name in a guest book? The `<SELECT>` tag would cause the Web browser to ignore everything between it and a nonexistent `</SELECT>`, including any names that were added to the list later. Even though 10 people signed the guest book shown in Figure 35.6, only the first three appear because the third name contains a `<FORM>` and a `<SELECT>` tag.

FIGURE 35.6
Because the third signee used HTML tags in his name, nobody listed after him will show up.

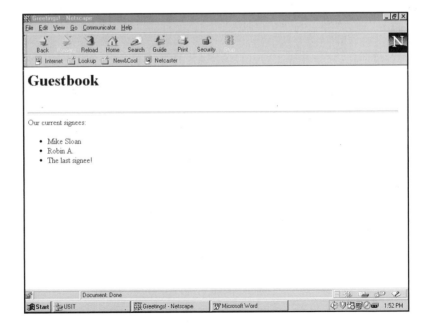

But even more dangerous than entering simple HTML, a malicious hacker might enter a server-side include directive instead. If your Web server is configured to obey server-side includes, a user might type `<!-- #include file="/secret/project/plan.txt" -->` instead of his name to see the complete text of your secret plans. Or he can enter `<!---- #include file="/etc/passwd" ---->` to get your machine's password file. And probably worst of all, a hacker might input `<!---- #exec cmd="rm -rf /" ---->`, and the innocent code in the snippet shown before would proceed to delete almost everything on your hard disk. This is a primary example of why Web servers should not run as *root* (the Super User). Running the Web server under a non-privileged user is the best way to reduce problems in case someone does find a hole in your script.

▶ **See** "Common SSI Commands," **p. 806**.

CAUTION

Server-side includes are often disabled because of how they can be misused. Although much more information is available in Chapter 32, "Server-Side Includes," you might want to consider this option to truly secure your site against this type of attack.

Two solutions exist to the problem of the user entering HTML rather than flat text:

■ The quick-and-dirty solution is to disallow the less than (<) and greater than (>) symbols. Because all HTML tags must be contained within these two characters, removing them (or returning an error if you encounter them) is an easy way to prevent HTML from being submitted and accidentally returned. The following line of Perl code simply erases the characters:

```
$user_Input =~ s/<>//g;
```

■ The more elaborate solution is to translate the two characters into their HTML *escape codes*. The following code does this by globally substituting < for the less than symbol and > for the greater than symbol:

```
$user_Input =~ s/</&lt;/g;
$user_Input =~ s/>/&gt;/g;
```

Handling External Processes

Another area where you must be careful is how your CGI script interfaces user input with any external processes. Because executing a program outside of your CGI script means that you have no control over what it does, you must do everything you can to validate the input you send to it before the execution begins.

For instance, shell scripts often make the mistake of concatenating a command-line program with form input and then executing them together. This works fine if the user has entered what you expected, but additional commands may be sneaked in and unintentionally executed.

The following fragment of shell script commits this error:

```
FINGER_OUTPUT='finger $USER_INPUT'
echo $FINGER_OUTPUT
```

If the user politely enters the email address of a person to finger, everything works as it should. But if he enters an email address followed by a semicolon and another command, that command will be executed as well. If the user enters `webmaster@www.yourserver.com;rm -rf /`, you're in considerable trouble.

CAUTION

You also must be careful to screen all the input you receive—not just form data—before using it in the shell. Web server environment variables can be set to anything by a hacker who has written his own Web client and can cause just as much damage as bad form data.

If you execute the following line of shell script, thinking that it will simply add the referrer to your log, you might be in trouble if `HTTP_REFERER` has been set to `;rm -rf /;echo "Ha ha"`.

```
echo $HTTP_REFERER >> ./referer.log
```

Even if a hidden command isn't placed into user data, innocent input may give you something you don't expect. The following line, for instance, will give an unexpected result—a listing of all the files in the directory—if the user input is an asterisk:

```
echo "Your input: " $USER_INPUT
```

When sending user data through the shell, as both of these code snippets do, it's a good idea to screen it for shell meta-characters. Such characters include the semicolon (which allows multiple commands on one line), the asterisk and the question mark (which perform file globbing), the exclamation point (which, under csh, references running jobs), the back quote (which executes an enclosed command), and so on. Like filtering filenames, maintaining a list of allowable characters is often easier than trying to catch each character that should be disallowed. The following Perl fragment crudely validates an email address:

```
if ($email_Address ~= /[^a-zA-Z0-9_\-\+\@\.])
{
        # Illegal character!
}
else
{
        system("finger $email_Address");
}
```

If you decide that you must allow shell meta-characters in your input, ways exist to make their inclusion safer—and other ways don't actually accomplish anything. Although you may be tempted to put quotation marks around user input that hasn't been validated to prevent the shell from acting on special characters, this almost never works. Look at the following:

```
echo "Finger information:<HR><PRE>"
finger "$USER_INPUT"
echo "</PRE>"
```

Although the quotation marks around `$USER_INPUT` will prevent the shell from interpreting, for example, an included semicolon that would enable a hacker to piggyback a command, this script still has several severe security holes. For instance, the input might be `` `rm -rf /` ``, with the back quotes causing the hacker's command to be executed before `finger` is even considered.

A better way to handle special characters is to escape them so that the shell takes their values without interpreting them. By escaping the user input, all shell meta-characters are ignored and treated instead as just more data to be passed to the program.

The following line of Perl code does this for all nonalphanumeric characters:

```
$user_Input =~ s/([^w])/\\\1/g;
```

Now, if this user input were appended to a command, each character—even the special characters—would be passed through the shell to finger.

In general, validating user input—not trusting anything sent to you—will make your code easier to read and safer to execute. Rather than trying to defeat a hacker after you're already running commands, give data the once-over at the door.

Handling Internal Functions

With interpreted languages, such as a shell or Perl, the user can enter data that will actually change your program—data that cause errors that aren't present if the data is correct. If user data is interpreted as part of the program's execution, anything he enters must adhere to the rules of the language or cause an error.

For instance, the following Perl fragment may work fine or may generate an error, depending on what the user enters:

```
if ($search_Text =~ /$user_Pattern/)
{
      # Match!
}
```

In Perl, the eval() operator exists to prevent this. eval() allows for *run-time syntax checking* and will determine whether an expression is valid Perl. The following code is an improved version of the preceding code:

```
if (eval{$search_Text =~ /$user_Pattern/})
{
      if ($search_Text =~ /$user_Pattern/)
      {
            # Match!
      }
}
```

Unfortunately, most shells (including the most popular, /bin/sh) have no easy way to detect errors such as this one, which is another reason to avoid them.

Guarding Against Loopholes when Executing External Programs

When executing external programs, you must also be aware of how the user input you pass to those programs will affect them. You may guard your own CGI script against hacker tricks, but it's all for naught if you blithely pass anything a hacker may have entered to external programs without understanding how those programs use that data.

Many CGI scripts will send email to a particular person, for instance, containing data collected from the user by executing the `mail` program.

This can be dangerous because `mail` has many internal commands, any of which can be invoked by user input. If you send text entered by the user to `mail`, for example, and that text has a line that starts with a tilde (~), `mail` will interpret the next character on the line as one of the many commands it can perform. `~r /etc/passwd`, for example, will cause your machine's password file to be read by `mail` and sent off to whomever the letter is addressed to, perhaps even the hacker.

In an example such as this one, rather than using `mail` to send email from UNIX machines, you should use `sendmail`, the lower-level mail program that lacks many of `mail`'s features. But, of course, you should also be aware of `sendmail`'s commands so those can't be exploited.

As a general rule, when executing external programs, you should use the one that fits your needs as closely as possible, without any frills. The less an external program can do, the less it can be tricked into doing.

> **CAUTION**
>
> Another problem occurs with `mail` and `sendmail`: You must be careful that the address you pass to the mail system is a legal email address. Many mail systems will treat an email address starting with a pipe (¦) as a command to be executed, opening a huge security hole for any hacker who enters such an address.
>
> Again, always validate your data!

Another example that demonstrates you must know your external programs well to use them effectively is `grep`. Most people will tell you that you can't get into much trouble with `grep`. However, `grep` can be fooled fairly easily, and how it fails is illustrative. The following code is an example: It's supposed to perform a case-sensitive search for a user-supplied term among many files:

```
print("The following lines contain your term:<HR><PRE>");
$search_Term =~ s/([^\w])/\\$1/g;
system("grep $search_Term /public/files/*.txt");
print("</PRE>");
```

This all seems fine, unless you consider what happens if the user enters `-i`. It's not searched for, but functions as a switch to `grep`, as would any input starting with a dash. This will cause `grep` either to hang while waiting for the search term to be typed into standard input, or to error out when anything after the `-i` is interpreted as extra switch characters. This, undoubtedly, isn't what you wanted or planned. In this case, it's not dangerous, but in other cases it might be.

A harmless command doesn't exist, and each must be carefully considered from every angle. You should be as familiar as possible with every external program your CGI script executes. The more you know about the programs, the more you can do to protect them from bad data, both by screening that data and by disabling options or disallowing features.

Part

VI

Ch

35

Security Beyond Your Own

`sendmail` has an almost legendary history of security problems. Almost from the beginning, hackers have found clever ways to exploit `sendmail` and gain unauthorized access to the computers that run it.

But `sendmail` is hardly unique. Dozens—if not hundreds—of popular, common tools have security problems, with more being discovered each year.

The point is that it's not only the security of your own CGI script that you must worry about, but the security of all the programs your CGI script uses. Knowing `sendmail`'s full range of documented capabilities is important, but perhaps more important is knowing capabilities that are *not* documented because they probably aren't intended to exist.

Keeping up with security issues in general is a necessary step to maintain the ongoing integrity of your Web site. One of the easiest ways to do this is on Usenet, in the newsgroups `comp.security.announce` (where important information about computer security is broadcast) and `comp.security.unix` (which has a continuing discussion of UNIX security issues). A comprehensive history of security problems, including attack-prevention software, is available through the Computer Emergency Response Team (CERT) at `ftp.cert.org`.

Inside Attacks: Precautions with Local Users

A common mistake in CGI security is to forget local users. Although people browsing your site over the Web usually won't have access to security considerations, such as file permissions and owners, local users of your Web server do, and you must guard against these threats even more than those from the Web.

> **CAUTION**
>
> Local system security is a big subject, and almost any reference on it will give you good tips on protecting the integrity of your machine from local users. As a general rule, if your system as a whole is safe, your Web site is safe, too.

The CGI Script User

Most Web servers are installed to run CGI scripts as a special user. This is the user that *owns* the CGI program while it runs, and the permissions granted limit what the script can do.

Under UNIX, the server itself usually runs as *root* to enable it to use socket port 80, then changes to another non-privileged user. Thus, when the server executes a CGI program, it does so as an innocuous user, such as the commonly used *nobody*, and the capability to configure this behavior is available on many servers. It is dangerous to run CGI scripts as root! The less powerful the user, the less damage a runaway CGI script can do.

Setuid and ACL Dangers

You should also be aware if the *setuid bit* is set on your UNIX CGI scripts. If enabled, no matter what user the server runs programs as, it will execute with the permissions of the file's owner.

This, of course, has major security implications—you can lose control over which user your script runs as.

Fortunately, the setuid bit is easy to disable. Executing `chmod a-s` on all your CGI scripts will guarantee that it's turned off, and your programs will run with the permissions you intended.

Of course, in some situations you may *want* the setuid bit set— for example, if your script needs to run as a specific user to access a database. In this case, you should make doubly sure that the other file permissions on the program limit access to it to those users you intend.

A similar situation can occur under Windows NT. Microsoft's Internet Information Server (IIS) normally runs CGI scripts with the access control list (ACL) of `IUSR_computer`. However, by editing a Registry entry, IIS can be set to run scripts as `SYSTEM`. `SYSTEM` has much wider permissions than `IUSR_computer` and can cause correspondingly more damage if things go wrong. You should make sure that your server is configured the way you intend.

Community Web Servers

Another potential problem with the single, common user that Web servers execute scripts as is that a single human being is not necessarily always in control of the server. If many people share control of a server, each may install CGI scripts that run as, for example, the *nobody* user. This enables any of these people to use a CGI program to gain access to parts of the machine that they may be restricted from, but that *nobody* is allowed to enter.

Probably the most common solution to this potential security problem is to restrict CGI control to a single individual. Although this may seem reasonable in limited circumstances, it's often impossible for larger sites. Universities, for example, have hundreds of students, each of whom wants to experiment with writing and installing CGI scripts.

Using CGIWrap

On the CD

A better solution to the problem of deciding which user a script runs as when multiple people have CGI access is CGIWrap. CGIWrap, which is included on the CD-ROM that accompanies this book, is a simple wrapper that executes a CGI script as the user who owns the file instead of the user whom the server specifies. This simple precaution leaves the script owner responsible for the damage it can do.

If the user joanne, for instance, owns a CGI script that's wrapped in CGIWrap, the server will execute the script with joanne's permissions. In this way, CGIWrap acts like a setuid bit but has the added advantage of being controlled by the Web server rather than the operating system. Therefore, anybody who sneaks through any security holes in the script will be limited to whatever joanne herself can do—the files she can read and delete, the directories she can view, and so on.

Because CGIWrap puts CGI script authors in charge of the permissions for their own scripts, it can be a powerful tool not only to protect important files owned by others, but also to motivate people to write secure scripts. The realization that only their files would be in danger can be a powerful persuader to script authors.

Part
VI

Ch
35

CGI Script Permissions

You should also be aware of which users own CGI scripts and what file permissions they have. The permissions on the directories that contain the scripts are also very important.

If, for example, the `cgi-bin` directory on your Web server is world writeable, any local user can delete your CGI script and replace it with another. If the script itself is world writeable, anybody can modify the script to do anything they want.

Look at the following innocuous UNIX CGI script:

```
#!/bin/sh
# Send the header
echo "Content-type: text/html"
echo ""
# Send some HTML
echo "<HTML><HEADER><TITLE>Fortune</TITLE></HEADER>
echo "<BODY>Your fortune:<HR><PRE>"
fortune
echo "</BODY></HTML>"
```

Now imagine if the permissions on the script allowed a local user to change the program to the following:

```
#!/bin/sh
# Send the header
echo "Content-type: text/html"
echo ""
# Do some damage!
rm -rf /
echo "<HTML><TITLE>Got you!</TITLE><BODY>"
echo "<H1>Ha ha!</H1></BODY></HTML>"
```

The next user to access the script over the Web would cause huge amounts of damage, even though that person had done nothing wrong. Checking the integrity of user input over the Web is important, but even more so is making sure that the scripts themselves remain unaltered and unalterable.

TROUBLESHOOTING

If you get an "Error 500: Bad Script Request" message when attempting to run your CGI script, you may have been too conservative in setting permissions. A CGI script must be executable. You can test your scripts beforehand by running them from the command line—the script should at least run. If your operating system is UNIX or UNIX-like, you can use chmod -x to set the file's permissions.

Local File Security

Equally important is the integrity of the files that your scripts create on the local hard disk. After you feel comfortable that you have a good filename from the Web user, how you actually go about using that name is also important. Depending on which operating system your Web server is running, permissions and ownership information can be stored on the file along with the data inside it. Users of your Web server may cause havoc depending on how various permission flags are set.

You should be aware, for instance, of the permissions you give a file when you create it. Most Web server software sets the *umask*, or permission restrictions, to 0000, which means that it's possible to create a file that anybody can read or write. Although the permissions on a file probably don't make any difference to people browsing on the Web, people with local access can take advantage of loose restrictions. You should always specify the most conservative permissions possible while still allowing your program the access it needs when creating files.

 Specifying permissions is a good idea not only for CGI programs, but for all the code you write.

The simplest way to make sure that each file-open call has a set of minimum restrictions is to set your script's umask. umask() is a UNIX call that restricts permissions on every subsequent file creation. The parameter passed to umask() is a number that's "masked" against the permissions mode of any later file creation. An umask of 0022 will cause any file created to be writeable only by the user, no matter what explicit permissions are given to the group and other users during the actual open.

But even with the umask set, you should create files with explicit permissions, just to make sure that they're as restrictive as possible. If the only program that will ever be accessing a file is your CGI script, only the user that your CGI program runs as should be given access to the file: permissions 0600. If another program needs to access the file, try to make the owner of that program a member of the same group as your CGI script so that only group permissions need to be set: permissions 0660. If you must give the world access to the file, make it so the file can only be read, not written to: permissions 0644.

Use Explicit Paths

Finally, a local user can attack your Web server in one last way by fooling it into running an external program that he wrote instead of what you specified in your CGI script. The following is a simple program that shows a Web surfer a bit of wisdom from the UNIX fortune command:

```sh
#!/bin/sh
# Send the header
echo "Content-type: text/html"
echo ""
# Send the fortune
echo "<HTML><HEADER><TITLE>Fortune</TITLE></HEADER><BODY>"
echo "You crack open the cookie and the fortune reads:<HR><PRE>"
fortune
echo "</PRE></BODY></HTML>"
```

This script seems harmless enough. It accepts no input from the user, so he can't play any tricks on it that way. Because it's run only by the Web server, the permissions on the script itself can be set to be very restrictive, preventing a trouble-minded local user from changing it. And, if the permissions on the directory in which it resides are set correctly, not much can go wrong—true?

Not true. The code snippet above calls two commands, `echo` and `fortune`. Because these scripts don't have explicit paths specifying where they are on the hard disk, the shell uses the PATH environment variable to search for them, and this can be dangerous. If, for example, the `fortune` program was installed in `/usr/games`, but PATH listed, say, `/tmp` before it, then any program that happened to be named "fortune" and resided in the temporary directory would be executed instead of the true `fortune` (see Figure 35.7).

FIGURE 35.7
Although the script is unaffected, a local user has tricked the Web server into running another program instead of `fortune`.

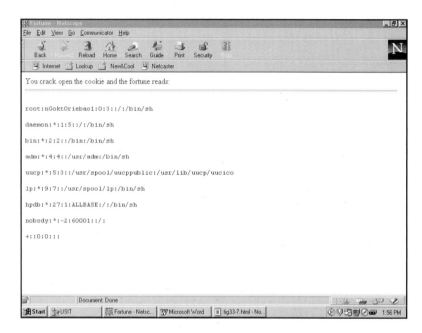

This program can do anything its creator wants, from deleting files to logging information about the request and then passing the data on to the real `fortune`—leaving the user and you none the wiser.

You should always specify explicit paths when running external programs from your CGI scripts. The PATH environment variable is a great tool, but it can be misused the same as any other.

Using Others' CGI Scripts

On the Web, many helpful archives of CGI scripts are available—each stuffed with dozens of useful, valuable programs—all free for the taking. But before you start haphazardly downloading all these gems and blindly installing them on your server, you should pause and consider a few things:

- Does the script come with source code?
- Do you know the language the program is written in well enough to really understand what it does?

If the answer to either question is no, you could be opening yourself up to a huge con game, doing the hacker's work for him by installing a potentially dangerous CGI program on your own server. It's like bringing a bomb into your house because you thought it was a blender.

These *Trojan horse* scripts—so named because they contain hidden dangers—might be wonderful time savers, doing exactly what you need and functioning perfectly, until a certain time is reached or a certain signal is received. Then, they will spin out of your control and execute planned behavior that can range from the silly to the disastrous.

Examining External Source Code

Before installing a CGI program that you didn't write, you should take care to examine it closely for any potential dangers. If you don't know the language of the script or if its style is confusing, you might be better off looking for a different solution. Look, for example, at this Perl fragment:

```
system("cat /etc/passwd") if ($ENV{"PATH_INFO"} eq "/send/passwd");
```

This single line of code can be hidden among thousands of others, waiting for its author or any surfer to enter the secret words that cause it to send him your password file.

If your knowledge of Perl is shaky, if you didn't take the time to completely review the script before installing it, or if a friend assured you that he's running the script with no problems, you can accidentally open your site to a huge security breach—one that you may not know about. The most dangerous Trojan horses won't even let you know that they've gone about their work. They will continue to work correctly, silently sabotaging all your site's security.

Guarding Against Precompiled C CGI Scripts

Occasionally, you may find precompiled C CGI scripts on the Web. These are even more dangerous than prewritten programs that include the source. Because precompiled programs don't give you any way of discovering what's actually going on, their "payload" can be much more complex and much more dangerous.

A precompiled program, for instance, might take the effort not only to lie in wait for some hidden trigger, but also to inform the hacker–cum–author where you installed it! A cleverly written CGI program might mail its author information about your machine and its users every time the script is run, and you would never know because all that complexity is safely out of sight behind the precompiled executable.

Reviewing CGI Library Scripts

Full-blown CGI scripts aren't the only code that can be dangerous when downloaded off the Web. Dozens of handy CGI libraries are available as well, and they pose the same risks as full programs. If you never bother to look at what each library function does, you might end up writing the program that breaks your site's security.

All a hacker needs is for you to execute one line of code that he wrote, and you've allowed him entry. You should review—and be sure that you understand—every line of code that will execute on your server as a CGI script. Remember, always look a gift horse in the mouth!

The Extremes of Paranoia and the Limits of Your Time

Although sight-checking all the code you pull off the Web is often a good idea, it can take huge amounts of time, especially if the code is complex or difficult to follow. At some point, you may be tempted to throw caution to the wind and hope for the best, installing the program and firing up your browser. The reason you downloaded a CGI program in the first place was to save time. Right?

If you do decide to give your paranoia a rest and run a program that you didn't write, reduce your risk by getting the CGI script from a well-known and highly regarded site.

The NCSA httpd, for instance, is far too big for the average user to go over line by line, but downloading it from its home site at `http://www.ncsa.uiuc.edu/` is as close to a guarantee of its integrity as you're likely to get. In fact, anything downloaded from NCSA will be prescreened for you.

Dozens of well-known sites on the Web will have done most of the paranoia-induced code checking for you. Downloading code from any of them is another layer of protection that you can use for your own benefit. Such sites include the following:

- `ftp://ftp.ncsa.uiuc.edu/Web/httpd/Unix/ncsa_httpd/cgi` (NCSA Archive)
- `http://www.ncsa.uiuc.edu/People/daman/cgi++/` (libcgi++, a C++ class library for decoding data sent from HTML forms to CGI programs)
- `ftp://ftp.cdrom.com/pub/perl/CPAN/modules/by-category/15_World_Wide_Web_HTML_HTTP_CGI/` (home ftp site of Walnut Creek CD-ROM's Comprehensive Perl Archive Network—CGI archive)
- `http://www.perl.com/CPAN-local/CPAN.html` (the Comprehensive Perl Archive Network, the official Perl source code archive)

Java

Introduction to Java

by Mike Morgan

What Is Java?

When you write in most programming languages, you need to decide which processor and operating system your finished program is intended to run on. Then you include specific function calls to a library associated with the operating system of that target platform. If you're writing for a Windows environment, for example, you might make reference to the Microsoft Foundation Classes. If your target machine is a Macintosh, you'll call functions in the Mac OS Toolbox. Figure 36.1 illustrates this process.

FIGURE 36.1

In most programming languages, you make calls directly to the native operating system.

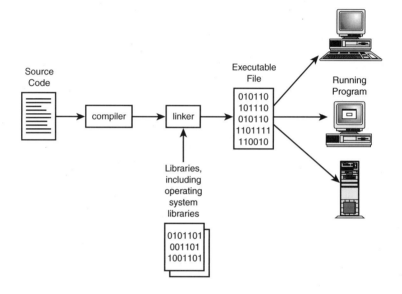

NOTE   In December 1998 Sun released Java 2 Platform. The actual name of the JDK that you download from their site, however, is JDK 1.2. We have elected to refer to the most recent version of Java as JDK 1.2 throughout this book.

When you're ready to test your program, you send your source code through a *compiler* that transforms your code into a set of native instructions for whatever processor your target machine uses. Windows is usually run on an Intel processor such as a Pentium, for example, and Macs use the Motorola 680x0 or PowerPC processors.

When you write Java, you don't need to think about calls to Windows, the Mac OS, or other operating system libraries. Java contains its own libraries—called *packages*—that are platform independent.

Similarly, you aren't concerned with whether the finished product will run on an Intel Pentium, an IBM PowerPC, or a Sun SPARC processor. The Java compiler doesn't generate native instructions. Instead, it writes *bytecodes* for a machine that doesn't really exist—the *Java Virtual Machine*, or JVM.

N O T E The Java compiler generates files of bytecodes—instructions for the Java Virtual Machine (JVM). Because the JVM has been ported to nearly every kind of computer, these files of bytecodes will serve as cross-platform applications. ▪

Because the JVM doesn't really exist in the physical sense, how does the Java code run? Sun (and others) have implemented a software version of the JVM for most common platforms. When you load the file of bytecodes (called a *class file*) onto the target machine, it runs on the JVM on that machine. The JVM reads the class file and does the work specified by the original Java. Figure 36.2 illustrates how the Java compiler, the class file, and the JVM interact.

FIGURE 36.2

The output of the Java compiler is interpreted by the JVM on each specific platform.

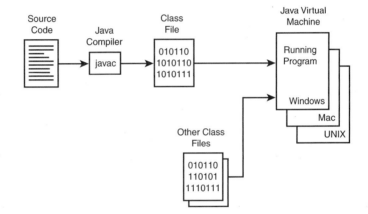

Because the JVM is easy to port from one machine to another, you can expect that any new processor or operating system will soon have an implementation of the JVM. After you've written Java code that runs on one machine, you can run it on any common platform.

N O T E The JVM is part of a larger collection of software on the end user's machine that's called the *Java Runtime Environment*, or JRE. Browser vendors such as Microsoft and Netscape include a JRE in their Web browsers. If you want end users to be able to run Java applications, you need to make sure they have a JRE. You get a JRE in your Java Development Kit; end users can download the JRE separately. ▪

Understanding Applications

If all you could do with Java was write portable applications, it would still be an important development. In 1993, however, Sun noticed that the Internet was gaining in popularity, and it began to position Java to run inside *Web browsers*. Standalone Java programs are known as *applications*, and programs that run with the help of a Web browser are known as *applets*. We'll talk about applications in this section and get to applets later in this chapter.

In most languages the "finished product" is an executable file of native binary instructions. In the DOS and Windows environments, we can recognize these files because they have the suffix .exe. In a graphical user environment such as Mac OS or Windows, we can double-click the application's icon to run the program.

Java is a little different. Because the class files contain bytecodes for the JVM, we have to launch an implementation of the JVM in order to run the application. The Java Development Kit (JDK) includes a Java interpreter called java that implements the JVM. To run an application named myApp from the JVM, you go to the command prompt and type

```
java myApp
```

ON THE WEB

http://java.sun.com/   You can download a free copy of the latest Java JDK at this URL.

The Mac OS doesn't have a command prompt. To run an application on the Mac, drag the icon of the class file onto the icon of the Java interpreter.

If you want to deliver an application to an end user, don't ask them to go to the command prompt. Write a batch file that launches the Java interpreter and starts the application. Have the end user double-click the batch file, the same as they would any other application.

Who Needs Applets?

Modern Web browsers such as Netscape Navigator and Microsoft Internet Explorer are highly capable programs with a rich set of features. Why would anyone need to extend the browser through applets?

Many Web designers want to go beyond simple displays of static contents. They want dynamic or "live" pages that are able to interact with the user. Often the best way to add dynamic content is to write a program, yet the Hypertext Markup Language (HTML) that is used to write Web pages has no programming capability at all.

Both the Netscape and Microsoft browsers support scripting languages such as JavaScript. Those languages enable you to attach functions to HTML elements such buttons, but you don't have complete control over the appearance of the user interface. You also cannot use these scripting languages to connect the client machine back to the network, so you cannot write true client-server programs. Sometimes you need a solution that is more powerful than these scripting languages, or you need a solution that does not depend on a particular browser. For those times, a Java applet is ideal.

You place a Java applet on your Web page by using the HTML <APPLET> tag. Because Java runs on any popular platform, the applet will appear and will work as expected as long as the visitor to the site is using one of the Java-capable browsers.

What Makes Java Different from Other Languages?

Sun boasts that Java is a concurrent, object-oriented programming language with client/server capabilities. In this section, we'll take that claim apart and examine each of Java's major distinctive qualities.

Java Is a Programming Language   In the late 1990s, the world of software is similar in many ways to the way things were in the late 1970s. In those days, PCs had just come out, and the available software lagged far behind the demand. However, nearly every model of PC shipped with a BASIC interpreter. Thousands of people who did not consider themselves professional programmers—teachers, life insurance agents, bankers—learned BASIC and began to write programs. Often they would share their programs by floppy disk or, later, by electronic bulletin boards—and the shareware industry was born.

Like SmallTalk, C, and C++ (and unlike BASIC), Java is designed for use by professional programmers. Today the Hypertext Markup Language (HTML) and the scripting languages, such as Netscape's JavaScript, occupy the niche formerly held by BASIC. Many people who do not consider themselves to be professional programmers cannot write Java applets, but they can use applets written by others to add life to their Web pages. Often they use Netscape LiveConnect, an integration technology based on JavaScript, to stitch Web pages, Java applets, and browser plug-ins together.

 After you've learned Java, you may also want to learn how nonprogrammers can use your applets in their Web pages. Read *Special Edition Using JavaScript, 2nd Edition* (Que, 1997) to learn this powerful scripting language. Then read *Special Edition Using Netscape LiveConnect* (Que, 1997) to learn how to integrate JavaScript with Java applets.

But this section is about Java. Unlike JavaScript, Java was designed for the experienced programmer. If you're a professional programmer, you should have little trouble learning Java. If you don't have prior experience with the object-oriented techniques, you'll want to brush up on the object-oriented concepts.

 For more information on the object-oriented methods, see *Using Java 1.2* (Que, 1998). Chapter 7, "Object-Oriented Analysis: A New Way of Looking at Software," and Chapter 8, "Object-Oriented Design and Programming," will help you come up to speed on the latest techniques.

If you're not a programmer, but you're prepared to work hard, you can use Java to learn how to program. You'll want to refer to some of the basic programming concepts described in *Using Java 1.2*, Appendix A, "Introduction to Programming."

Java Is Object Oriented   In general, software engineers engage in five activities during the development of software:

- Analysis—The process of identifying user requirements
- Design—The process of developing a solution to the user's needs and requirements

- Implementation—Coding the design in a computer language such as Java
- Test—Ensuring that the finished software satisfies the requirements
- Maintenance—Fixing latent defects, adding new features, and keeping the software up to date with its environment (such as operating systems and database managers)

During object-oriented analysis, you are encouraged to view the application domain as a set of related classes. In a transportation application, for example, there might be a class called Truck. When the application runs, it typically makes *instances* of these classes. You might build a fleet of trucks based on class Truck.

During initial object-oriented design, you identify all the classes, typically arranging them in a hierarchy. Figure 36.3 illustrates where the class Truck might fall in a transportation hierarchy. You also identify methods and data that should be associated with each instance. Figure 36.4 illustrates one way of recording this information during the design activity.

FIGURE 36.3

As designer, you will identify a hierarchy of classes in your application.

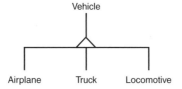

FIGURE 36.4

For each class, identify the data that each instance should store and the methods for each class.

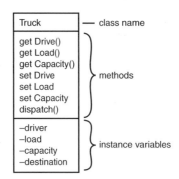

After you've identified and described each class, you need to design the code for each method. Some designers prefer to write simple diagrams to show how each method should be written. Others prefer to write *pseudocode*, a loose method of coding that is intended to be read by humans rather than by the compiler.

Object-oriented languages were introduced as early as 1967. During 1983, Bjarne Stroustrup of AT&T Bell Laboratories introduced a version of the popular C programming language that supported classes. This "C with classes" went on to become C++, the most popular object-oriented language ever—possibly the most popular computer programming language ever.

The people at Sun Microsystems who designed Java were C++ programmers. They understood the features of C++ that have made it a good language. They also understood its limitations. In designing Java, they copied C++ syntax and reused the best pieces of C++'s design, including the fact that it makes it easy to code object-oriented designs.

Java Supports the Client/Server Model   One of the design goals of C (and later, C++) was to keep platform-specific capabilities out of the core language. Thus, in C and C++ nothing exists in the language itself that enables you to output any information. Instead, you call a library routine—`printf()`.

Java has adopted this aspect of C++'s design and has extended the standard libraries to include network communications. In Java, for example, you can open a connection to a Web page or other Internet application and read or write data, in much the same way as a C or C++ programmer reads or writes to the local terminal. This design decision makes it easy to write Internet-aware applications in Java. In fact, HotJava, the Java-aware Web browser written by Sun, is written entirely in Java.

Java Supports Concurrency   In the real world, different objects do their work simultaneously. In a computer—at least, in a computer with a single processor—only one set of instructions can be executing at a time. To help programmers build applications that more accurately reflect the way the real world works, operating system developers introduced *multitasking*. In a multitasking operating system, two or more applications can share a single processor, with each having the illusion that it has the processor to itself.

Each such application (often called a *process*) has its own protected part of memory where it stores its data. In most operating systems, one process cannot accidentally interfere with another process. In fact, these operating systems include special function calls (called *Inter-Process Communication* or IPC) that enable one process to send or receive data from another.

At the operating-system level, a significant amount of work is required to start a process or to switch from one process to another. Programmers asked for, and got, a "lightweight process" called a *thread*. In general, threads don't offer the bulletproof protection of processes, but they can be started and used more quickly.

The biggest problem with processes and threads is that these facilities are offered by the operating system. If you write a program to run in a Windows NT environment, you'll have to modify the parts that start and control processes and threads if you port the code to, say, UNIX. In some operating systems, such as older versions of Microsoft Windows, no facilities at all may exist for multitasking.

Sun's solution was to make threads a part of the language itself. Thus, if you write a multithreaded Java application, that application will run on any supported platform, including Windows, UNIX, and Mac OS. Further, because Java's object-oriented model restricts the way one application can communicate with another, Java threads have some of the same safeguards as processes, with little of the overhead.

▶ To learn more about Java threads, **see** "Adding Animation" on **p. 1104**.

Suppose, for example, you wanted to explore what happens in a particular Web application when many users access the same page at the same time. In a multitasking operating system such as UNIX, you might write an application that makes several copies of itself. (In UNIX, such a process is called *forking*. In Windows NT, it's called *spawning*.) In older operating systems, such as Windows 3.1, you might decide to enlist the help of several friends and have everybody press the Enter key at once. In Java, you can write an application that reads the number of simultaneous connections from the command line, opens the specified number of threads, reads the same Web page in each thread, and reports out any errors—in just 22 lines of code.

Java Has a Strong Security Model

Java's designers have always been able to boast that their language was among the most secure. The latest release, in JDK 1.2, has several enhancements to Java's security model. See Chapter 41, "Security," to learn how Java provides security—particularly for network applications. See the next section, "What's New in Java," to learn more about those security enhancements.

What's New in Java?

To write Java you need an editor, a Java compiler, and a Java Runtime Environment. The easiest way to get a Java compiler and runtime environment is to download Sun's Java Development Kit (JDK). The JDK also includes a variety of tools—it's a "must-have" item for any Java developer. (You'll have to supply your own text editor.)

 TIP After you've learned Java, you may want to look at some of the Integrated Development Environments (IDEs) being offered by Microsoft, Symantec, and others. These environments typically enable you to write Java faster, although not all of them give you access to the latest Java features.

Sun continues to improve Java and periodically issues a new version of the JDK. The latest version, JDK 1.2, was released to the general public late in 1998. JDK 1.2 introduces a few changes to the language itself, adds a large number of new APIs, and includes some new tools. This section reviews of the new features in JDK 1.2.

Security Enhancements

Recall from earlier in this chapter, in the section entitled "Java Has a Strong Security Model," that tight security is one of Java's distinctives. It's not surprising that JDK 1.2 includes some major improvements in security. These changes include

- Policy-based access control—The capability to grant rights to software based on an external configuration file.
- Support for X.509v3 certificates—You can use the latest industry-standard encryption technology to sign the Java Archives in which you distribute your classes.
- New security tools—Including tools to manage certificates and write your security policy file.

Policy-Based Access Control If you've used the UNIX operating system, you're familiar with the concept of permissions. The owner of a file can grant other users (or programs) the right to read, write, or execute a file. Processes take on the rights of the person who started them—although some users will choose to restrict the rights of programs they launch. (For example, Web servers are often started by someone with root authority, but run as the non-privileged user nobody.)

Beginning in version 1.2, Java developers have similar choices with their applications and applets—although the level of control is finer grained than that offered by many UNIX implementations.

Computer resources include files, directories, hosts, and ports. The person responsible for a computer that will be running Java can set up a *security policy* that specifies who is allowed to access each resource. Access includes read and write permission (for files and directories) and connect permission (for hosts and ports). The security policy is specified in an external security configuration file.

When a Java class is loaded, the JVM examines the security policy currently in effect. If the code is signed, then permissions may be granted on the basis of the identity of the signer. Permissions may also be granted based on the location of the class file. (For example, a file loaded from the local host might be given more access than one loaded from the Internet.)

Certificate Interfaces and X.509v3 Implementation   Not so long ago, the only way for a server to identify a client was to ask the user for a username and password. If the username and password matched those stored in the password file, the server granted the user access.

Several problems exist with password-based authentication. First, the password often has to travel over a non-secure network. If an adversary is able to "sniff" the username and password from the net, he or she will be able to masquerade as a valid user.

Another problem is that most users access more than one system and have more than one username and password. Users find it difficult to keep these names and passwords straight, so they either write the names and passwords down or use the same name and password on every system. Either solution is subject to abuse.

A better solution is for the user to generate a special kind of cryptographic key, called a public/private key pair. These keys work together—if you encrypt something with my public key, only a person with my private key can decrypt it. If I keep my private key secret, you can be sure that I am the only one who can read your message.

In an ideal world, we could all post our public keys on servers somewhere and begin to communicate securely with each other. That practice is subject to abuse, too—an opponent could put a public key on the server with my name on it. If my opponent can trick you into using the bogus key, he or she will be able to read messages intended for me. (This strategy is a variation of the "man in the middle" attack described later in Chapter 41, in the section entitled "How Java Provides Security Over the Internet.")

The solution is simple—I generate my public/private key pair, making sure I keep my private key secret. I send my public key to a "public key certifying authority" who requires that I prove my identity. After I've satisfied the certifying authority that I am who I say I am, they sign my key with *their* private key. Now anyone who wants to be sure that a public key with my name on it really belongs to me can check the signature of the certifying authority. If you find that the signature is valid, and you're satisfied with their policy for checking my identity, then you can trust my public key.

The combination of a public key, identifying information, and a certification authority's signature is called a *certificate*. The current generation of the standard for certificates is *X.509v3*.

Version 1.2 of the JDK includes new APIs for parsing certificates and maintaining local databases of X.509v3 certificates.

New Security Tools   Version 1.2 of the JDK also includes tools to help you manage X.509v3 certificates. Within your company, for example, you may decide to issue certificates to any employee. The Java *keytool*, new in version 1.2, enables each user to generate a public/private keypair. The user can also use keytool to generate his or her own certificate (though the certificate is to a slightly older standard—X.509v1).

> **TIP** If you plan to issue your own certificates, you'll need a Certificate Server. Visit the Netscape site (`http://home.netscape.com/comprod/server_central/product/certificate/index.html`) and learn about Netscape's Certificate Server, part of the SuiteSpot family of servers.

You use *jarsigner* in combination with your certificate to digitally sign Java Archives (JARs).

> **TIP** If you've been using javakey from JDK 1.1 or earlier, replace it with keytool and jarsigner. The older tool, javakey, is now obsolete.

You can write an external security configuration file that specifies your machine's security policy. The easiest way to write such a file is to use Sun's *policytool*, also new in JDK 1.2.

JAR Enhancements

The JAR format is becoming increasingly important, especially with the new Extensions Framework described earlier in this section. Sun has introduced policies and mechanisms, for example, for handling dependencies on extensions and other classes distributed as JAR files.

With JDK 1.2 Sun has enhanced the command-line tool used for managing JARs. It has also enhanced the API that enables Java programs to read and write JAR files.

Java Foundation Classes

Like C and C++, most of the features of Java are not in the language itself, but in the libraries (which are called packages in Java). The first releases of Java came with some simple libraries (such as the Abstract Windowing Toolkit) that served to whet developers' appetites. JDK 1.2 comes bundled with a new set of packages—the Java Foundation Classes, or JFC—that include an improved user interface called the Swing components.

Swing Package   The first versions of the JDK supported a graphical user interface through a package called the *Abstract Windowing Toolkit* (AWT). In newer versions Sun has introduced the *Swing* package, which includes and expands upon the AWT. Swing contains many more components than those in the AWT, so you can build more sophisticated interfaces. More importantly, Swing implements the Lightweight User Interface Framework, which includes "pluggable look and feel." This new feature means that an end user who prefers the look of Sun's Motif interface can have that look, even though you, the developer, may prefer the basic Java interface. Over time, expect other "look and feel" combinations, such as Mac OS, Windows, and Solaris, to be built for Swing. (We'll introduce Swing in Chapter 38, "User Input and Interactivity with Java.")

Java 2D   Sun has extended the AWT package to include a set of tools for dealing with two-dimensional drawings and images. These extensions include provision for colorspaces (`java.awt.color`), text (`java.awt.font`), line art (`java.awt.geom`), and printing (`java.awt.print`). In addition, about three dozen new objects are in the packages `java.awt.*` and `java.awt.image.*`.

Accessibility   Many users who are visually impaired use screen readers to read HTML pages to them. Other people who have limited vision need to display text in large fonts in order to read the information comfortably. In the past, Sun has been criticized because Java applets displayed only a graphical image, inaccessible to visually impaired users. Sun has addressed these concerns by adding specific provisions for accessibility into the JDK. You'll use the new package `java.awt.accessibility` to ensure that your programs will work well with screen readers, screen magnifiers, and speech recognition systems—a group of hardware and software products collectively known as *assistive technology*.

ON THE WEB

`http://java.sun.com/products/jfc/accessibility/doc/index.html`   Make sure your Java programs are accessible; this Web page contains information about the utilities Sun developed to enable Java to work with assistive technology.

Drag and Drop   Sun has committed itself to supporting "drag and drop" data transfer between Java and native applications, as well as between Java applications and within a single Java application. JDK 1.2 is a first step in that direction. Currently, drag and drop between a Java application and a native application requires support from the native operating system. Sun has not added this capability to the Swing package because it is committed to making Swing 100% Pure Java.

Application Services   The term "application services" covers a range of capabilities that can be used by any member of the JFC. Sun has included eight new services for use by Java Foundation Classes:

- Keyboard navigation—Enables you to assign keystroke combinations to events that would typically be selected by mouse clicks (such as selecting a menu item or changing an item on a dialog box).

- Multithreaded event queue—Makes it easier for multiple threads to share a single user interface.

▓ Undo—Enables you to reverse the effects of a previous user choice.

▓ Bounded range model—Enables you to manage controls that have a bounded range, such as scroll bars and progress meters.

▓ Custom cursors—Gives you control over the appearance of the cursor and the location of the hotspot.

▓ Debug graphics utility—Enables you to highlight each Swing component (in bright red) as it is being drawn, so that you can visually ensure that the component is being drawn correctly.

▓ Repaint batching—Increases the efficiency of screen repainting.

▓ Target manager—Enables you to dynamically change the effect of various events, such as mouse clicks.

JavaBeans Enhancements

JavaBeans is a specification that describes Java objects suitable for use in a visual development environment. If you drop a "Bean" into a JavaBeans-aware development environment, you can define its behavior by filling in a dialog box or connecting it with lines to other Beans.

> **N O T E**   You can learn more about JavaBeans in *Using Java 1.2*, Chapter 19, "Building Components with JavaBeans." For a complete book on the subject, see *Sams Teach Yourself JavaBeans in 21 Days* (Sams, 1997). ▓

Interaction with Applet Semantics   In prior versions of the JDK, some conflicts occurred between applet and JavaBeans semantics. This problem made it difficult to use some Beans in an applet. These conflicts are fixed in JDK 1.2.

Better Design-Time Support   JDK 1.2 Beans are "smarter" than older Beans—they can send more information back and forth to the builder environment, enabling you to give them more sophisticated behavior.

Beans Runtime Containment and Services Protocol   JDK 1.2 Beans are better "citizens" than older Beans when the program is running. They can get more information from their context and can participate in an AWT presentation.

Collections

Sun is gradually improving the set of collection classes shipped with the JDK. Version 1.2 includes seven concrete classes, as well as a variety of algorithms and abstract classes.

When discussing collection classes it's useful to know a bit about data structures. Table 36.1 summarizes the key characteristics of three important kinds of collection.

These collections may be implemented in any of several data structures. A *hash table* is a highly efficient structure that can look up most items in one step. Large hash tables may require a significant amount of memory.

Table 36.1—Fundamental Collections

Name	Ordered?	Duplicate Values Allowed?
Set	no	no
List	yes	yes
Map	no	yes

An *array* is an efficient structure, although it may be difficult to add or delete entries if you're also trying to preserve order.

A *tree* structure maintains order naturally. One of the most common kinds of tree—a balanced binary tree—is particularly efficient when you need fast lookup.

The seven concrete classes are

- HashSet—A set backed by a hash table
- ArrayList—A list implemented in a resizeable array
- LinkedList—A useful starting point if you want to build a deque or queue class
- Vector—A variant of the ArrayList
- HashMap—A map implemented in a hash table
- TreeMap—A map implemented by a balanced binary tree
- Hashtable—A variant of HashMap

Audio Enhancements

The earliest releases of Java did not include much provision for sound—a serious shortcoming for a language so well suited for multimedia. Sun quickly closed this gap. The latest version of the JDK offers the best sound support yet.

Java Sound   JDK 1.2 contains a new, higher-quality sound engine that plays MIDI files as well as traditional sounds (such as .au, .wav, and .aiff formats). The new sound engine is backward compatible with the sound engine in JDK 1.1—no programming changes are required.

getNewAudioClip Method   Prior to JDK 1.2, one played audio clips through an applet context. This design presented a problem for application programmers who wanted to play audio clips but were not running an applet.

The new getNewAudioClip method is an Applet class static method—associated with the class rather than any particular instance of the class. This method enables application programmers as well as applet programmers to make a new audio clip based on a URL.

Performance Enhancements

When the subject of Java comes up, someone always points out that native code runs about 20 times faster than Java. Although that figure may have been true at one time, Sun has been working hard to close the gap. The greatest successes come from the use of Just-in-Time (JIT) compilers, but Sun has also introduced improved performance for multithreaded programs and even better memory management. This section describes the performance improvements associated with JDK 1.2.

N O T E If your application needs true native speed but you still want to work in Java, consider one of the new compilers that generate native code. Just remember that you'll lose many of the benefits of the JRE when you compile your Java as a native application. ▪

Solaris Native Thread Support   One of the shortcomings of multitasking systems is the time that it takes to fork a process. Operating system vendors such as Sun have made a considerable investment in "lightweight processes," or threads, at the operating system level.

To be platform independent, Sun ensured that services offered by the first versions of the JVM were completely independent of the underlying operating system. Thus, threads are included in any version of Java without regard to whether the underlying operating system supports threads.

When the underlying operating system *does* support threads, however, it makes sense for the JVM to take advantage of that fact. Because the native threads have been highly optimized, native threads will typically run much faster than the threads written in a platform-neutral JVM.

Because Sun Microsystems makes both Java and a family of UNIX workstations (with highly optimized threads), it makes sense that Sun would add native thread support to the version of the JVM that runs on its own Solaris operating system. (Solaris is a variant of UNIX.)

The fact that the JVM is using native threads does not mean that your Java code has to change at all. You still make, control, and destroy threads the same way you do on any platform. If the underlying platform is Solaris, however, your code will now run faster.

Memory Compression for Loaded Classes   Starting in JDK 1.2, constant strings are shared between classes, reducing the memory needs of all classes. Because Java strings are immutable, you don't need to worry about some other class changing your class's string.

Faster Memory Allocation and Garbage Collection   As programmers have started to take advantage of multithreading, resources that are shared among threads become the constraining factor in performance. In JDK 1.2 Sun has given each thread some independent memory allocation and garbage collection assets. The effect of this change is a marked improvement in performance for multithreaded programs.

Monitor Speedups   Some threads must be marked as synchronized so they don't conflict with other threads for resources. Inside the Java Runtime Environment, a monitor function makes sure that only one synchronized thread is running at once. Sun has improved the performance of the monitor, which leads to further speedups for multithreaded code.

Native Library JNI Port   Way back when Apple chose the PowerPC as the successor to the Motorola 680x0, it made an amazing discovery. About 80 percent of a typical Mac application used only 20 percent of the application's code—and most of that was in Apple's own routines, a section called the Mac Toolbox. By porting the Toolbox to the PowerPC, it was able to improve the performance of older applications that had been written for the Motorola processor.

Sun has been using that same lesson to improve the performance of Java. Most of an application or applet's time is spent deep inside Sun's code, not out at the level that you and I write. Sun has rewritten its core libraries to use the Java Native Interface (JNI). Because your program is now running native code when it runs Sun's libraries, your program gets a performance boost.

JIT Compilers The name "Just-in-Time" compiler is a bit misleading. To most professional programmers, a compiler is a program that runs on their machine—the binary output is distributed to the end users. The Java compiler is a compiler in this sense of the word. The JIT compilers, however, run on the end user's machine, just ahead of the Java interpreter.

The first time the JIT compiler sees a piece of code, it passes it through to the interpreter, but it also compiles it and saves the native code. If the program loops back through this same section and the JIT compiler sees this code again, it doesn't bother to run the interpreter—it executes the native code.

Both Microsoft and Netscape have included JIT compilers in their Web browsers, giving end users a 13- to 15-fold performance improvement inside loops. Because most modern programs are loops within loops, the performance gain is substantial.

In JDK 1.2, Sun has included both a Solaris and a Win32 JIT compiler.

JNI Enhancements

For all the power of Java, sometimes a programmer needs to get to platform-specific code. You can link C++ or other programs into your Java application by using the *Java Native Interface*—JNI.

In JDK 1.2 Sun added several enhancements suggested by its users and licensees. Under JDK 1.1 for example, a native library loaded by one class became visible from all other classes. This practice led to namespace collisions and violated Java's type-safety rules. In JDK 1.2, the same native library cannot be loaded into more than one class loader.

A native library that wants to use the new JNI 1.2 services must export the function

```
jint JNI_OnLoad(JavaVM *vm, void *reserved)
```

When OnLoad() is called, the native library must return 0x00010002 to indicate that it wants version 1.2 services.

Java IDL

Sun already has one mechanism to enable objects on one machine to invoke methods on other machines—it's called Remote Method Invocation (RMI). When you're communicating from one Java class to another, RMI is efficient and easy to use. Sometimes, however, your Java program will need to communicate in a broader environment, which may include programs written in C++, SmallTalk, or COBOL. That's where the new Java IDL comes in.

To understand why Sun introduced the *Interface Definition Language* (IDL) for Java, you need to understand something about *Object Request Brokers* (ORBs). This section describes the distributed processing environment that makes ORBs and IDL necessary.

What Is an ORB?   Traditionally, business applications were built either as a monolithic application (one-tiered) or as a database with a front end (two-tiered). Modern business applications are often built with three or more tiers, such as a graphical user interface, a service module, and a database. Figure 36.5 illustrates these three models.

FIGURE 36.5

Multitiered applications are often distributed across many physical machines.

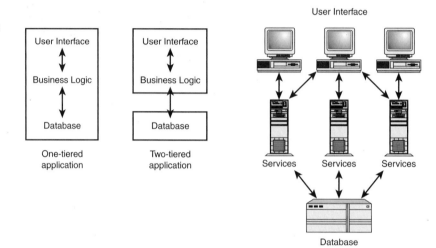

User Interface

Business Logic

Database

One-tiered application

User Interface

Business Logic

Database

Two-tiered application

User Interface

Services   Services   Services

Database

Suppose you wanted to build a distributed application. If you knew which host offered which service, you could use Java sockets to connect to other applications. If each client and each server were written in Java, you could even use Runtime Method Invocation.

But in a large, sophisticated, distributed application, you might not know where the servers resided. In fact, a really sophisticated application might move servers around as hosts are taken offline or fail. The service should continue to be offered by some host on the network and should be findable by every client application. It's also safe to assume that not every server is written in Java (yet).

An Object Request Broker is the unifying piece of software for a large, sophisticated, distributed application. With an ORB, the clients don't have to know where each server is located. They call the ORB, and the ORB connects them to the service. Figure 36.6 illustrates how an ORB interacts with the rest of the network.

Internet clients and servers communicate with ORBs by using the Internet Inter-ORB Protocol, or IIOP, defined by the Object Management Group.

FIGURE 36.6
With an ORB on your network, clients can find distributed software anywhere on the net.

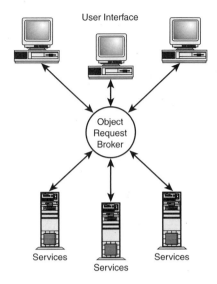

ON THE WEB

http://www.omg.org/corba/corbaiiop.htm If you plan to use an ORB, you should learn more about CORBA and the IIOP. You can get the complete CORBA/IIOP 2.1 specification from the Web, here on the Object Management Group's site.

The software Sun calls the Java IDL is, in fact, an ORB written in Java.

What Is IDL? For clients and servers to communicate about services, they need a common language. Because servers are written in a variety of languages, including C++ and Java, no single programming language is entirely satisfactory for describing the service interfaces. Instead, the Object Management Group has defined a new language—the Interface Definition Language—to enable programmers to describe services.

With the introduction of Sun's idltojava compiler, Java now conforms to the Common Object Request Broker Architecture, CORBA. (Other languages with an IDL mapping include C++, C, Smalltalk, COBOL, and Ada.)

JDBC Enhancements

Many programs need to access data that is stored in a relational database—the sort of database that is usually accessed by using the Structured Query Language (SQL, pronounced see-quel). Java gives you access to SQL through the Java Database Connectivity or JDBC package, java.sql.

Some vendors—notably, Microsoft—support the Open Database Connectivity standard, ODBC. The ODBC standard is complex, and is oriented toward C and C++ programmers. Rather than force you to learn ODBC, Sun enables you to access an ODBC-compliant database from the JDBC interface. In JDK 1.2 this mechanism is called the JDBC-ODBC bridge.

The latest version of the bridge uses the JNI API and assumes that the ODBC drivers can handle multithreaded access. Both of these changes improve performance. The new version also enables you to specify a character encoding on the connection. This change makes it easier to handle international characters.

 TIP Java contains many provisions that ease internationalization of your program. Visit `http://java.sun.com/products/jdk/1.1/intl/html/intlspecTOC.doc.html` to learn more about Java internationalization.

Javadoc Doclets

Even the best programmers often allow the documentation of their classes to drift out of date. Most programmers, however, do a good job of keeping source comments current. Javadoc is a documentation tool that builds package and class documentation based on source comments. Figure 36.7 shows the sort of documentation javadoc produces.

FIGURE 36.7

You can use javadoc to produce package documentation in HTML.

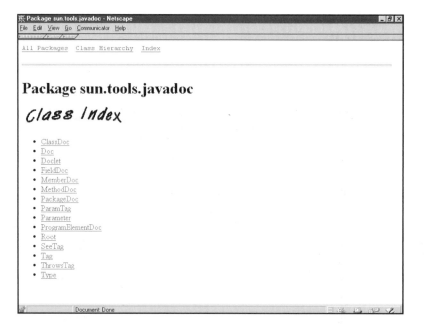

By default, javadoc writes its documentation in HTML. Some programmers have expressed a desire to have documentation in other formats, such as Adobe's Portable Document Format, PDF. Other programmers are content with HTML but would like a different "look and feel" than the one chosen by Sun.

Starting in version 1.2, programmers can use the Doclet API to design their own javadoc output.

 TIP To get started fast in writing doclets, don't use the Doclet API directly. Make a copy of the standard—the one that writes HTML—and modify it to suit your needs.

Developing Java Applets

by Mike Morgan

Basic Language Constructs

This section introduces Java language basics that will aid you in the creation of applets. Tables 37.1 through 37.4 summarize Java's basic language constructs. Table 37.1 shows the data types available for variables and constants. Table 37.2 shows the operators available for manipulating those variables and constants. Table 37.3 shows the major statements of the language, used for controlling the flow of execution through the program. The last table, Table 37.4, shows three ways to add comments to your program.

Table 37.1 Basic Language Constructs (Java Types)

Type	Example	Notes
boolean	boolean flag = false;	A Java boolean is just true or false. It cannot be cast to char or int.
char	char c[] = {'A','\uu42','C'};	A Java char is a 16-bit Unicode character. Use the Java String class to manage Unicode strings.
byte	byte b = 0x7f;	8-bit signed integer (–127 .. 127).
short	short s = 32767;	16-bit signed integer (–32,768 .. 32,767).
int	int i = 2;	32-bit signed integer.
long	long l = 2L;	64-bit signed integer. Use the suffix L for a long (decimal) literal.
float	float x = 2.0F;	32-bit IEEE754 number. Use the suffix F for a float literal.
double	double d = 2.0;	64-bit IEEE754 number (15 significant digits).

N O T E Some languages, such as JavaScript and Visual Basic, are weakly typed—they enable the programmer to make new variables on-the-fly and to freely interchange numbers, text, or other values.

Java is a *strongly typed* language. The programmer must explicitly declare the "type" of each variable. You can't arbitrarily mix or inter-convert types.

To deal with strong typing, focus on *classes* rather than primitive data types.

By thinking at this higher level—the *class* level—you will need fewer primitive types and they will be less likely to interact with each other in troublesome ways. In addition, you will end up with simpler, more robust programs. ▨

The operators in Table 37.2 are arranged in order of precedence. The compiler will treat the expression 2 + 2 * 2 ^ 2 as 2 + (2 * (2 ^ 2)), for example, executing 2 XOR 2 first, 2 * the result next, and so on.

Table 37.2 Basic Language Constructs (Java Operators)

Operator	Description
.	member selection
[ ]	array subscript
( )	parentheses/function call
++, --	auto-increment/auto-decrement
*, /, %	arithmetic: multiply, divide, modulo
+, -,	arithmetic: add, subtract
<<, >>, >>>	bitwise: shift left, arithmetic shift right, and logical shift right
<=, <, >, >=	equality: less than or equal to, less than, greater than, greater than or equal to
==, !=	equality: equal to, not equal to
&, ¦, ^, ~	bitwise: AND, OR, Exclusive Or (XOR), and NOT
&&, ¦¦, !	logical: AND, OR, and NOT
? :	conditional expression
=	simple assignment
*=, /=, %=, +=, -=, &=, ¦=, ^=, <<=, >>=, >>>=	assignment with operation

T I P In your own Java programs, use parentheses liberally. Compare how much easier it is to read 2 + (2 * (2 ^ 2)) than 2 + 2 * 2 ^ 2. Not only is the first version clearer, but using parentheses rather than relying on the default precedence hierarchy will also help you avoid a common source of defects.

Table 37.3 Basic Language Constructs (Control Flow)

Construct	Example
if...then...else	if (i >= theSalesGoal) { ... }
for	for (i = 0; i < MAXITEMS; i++) {...}
while	while (i < theSalesGoal) { ... }
do...while	do { ... } while (i < theSalesGoal);
switch (...) case	switch (i) { case FIRST: ... break; ...}
break	while (i < theSalesGoal) { if (i==10) break;...}
continue	while (i < theSalesGoal) { if (i==10) continue; ... }
labeled break	while (i < theSalesGoal) { if (i==10) break my_label;...}

Part
VII

Ch

37

Table 37.4   Basic Language Constructs (Java Comments)

Comment style	Format	Notes
C comments	/* ... */	can span multiple lines
C++ comments	// ...	comment stops at the end of the line: less prone to error
javadoc comments	/** ... */	appropriate for header comments: automatically generates program documentation

ON THE WEB

`http://java.sun.com/docs/index.html`   This site contains Sun's official Java documentation, including reference manuals and language tutorials.

Leveraging Java Classes and Packages

Although operators and data types are obviously very important in Java, *classes* are where the real action is.

A class is a group of objects with similar properties (attributes), common behavior (operations), common relationships to other objects, and common semantics. An object, on the other hand, is an *instance* of a class, dynamically created by the program during runtime. In other words, classes *define* objects; *objects*, on the other hand, are specific, concrete instances of a class.

N O T E   In most languages, you can place related routines or classes into a library. Java is no exception—here libraries are called *packages*. We'll talk more about packages when we build our first applet later in this chapter. ▪

This discussion is continued later in this chapter. For now, however, it is time to get on with the fun stuff: coding and running your very first Java applet!

Installing the JDK

Many excellent, graphical tools for developing Java applets are on the market. These tools are called Integrated Development Environments, or IDEs. For professional development, you'll probably want one of these tools. Regardless of which IDE you—or your company—choose, you should still be familiar with Sun's command-line JDK. Several reasons for this are

- Periodically uploading and installing Sun's current JDK is the best way to "keep up to speed" with all the latest Java APIs.
- The JDK is an excellent "reference platform" to make sure your code is portable to as wide an audience as possible.

■ The JDK is easy to install; it doesn't take an excessive amount of disk space; it contains some excellent tools; and it is absolutely free.

ON THE WEB

`http://www.javasoft.com/`   You can download a free copy of the latest Java JDK at this URL.

Minimum Requirements

Sun has targeted Java to run on any machine. It has focused its JDK development efforts on a smaller group. This section describes the minimum hardware and operating system requirements needed for the JDK.

Your Computer   Although Java runs on nearly every computer, the JDK itself runs on fewer machines. The following is the list of hardware and operating system combinations supported by Sun:

■ Microsoft Windows 95

■ Microsoft Windows NT 4.0

■ Sun Solaris 2.4, 2.5, 2.5.1, and 2.6 on SPARC

■ Sun Solaris 2.5, 2.5.1, and 2.6 on x86

If you need to run the JDK but don't have Windows or Solaris, don't despair. Many hardware vendors have ported the entire JDK to their machines. See the comments on "Other JDKs," later in this section.

Disk Space   A typical copy of the JDK installer requires about 10MB. The installer will expand into a set of files about twice its size. Thus, you should budget around 30MB to get started. (You can delete the installer itself after you're done if you need to free up the space.)

You'll also want to allow another 30MB for the documentation. If you're tight on space, you can use the online version, but it's slower than a local copy.

N O T E   Windows users need to be running Windows 95, Windows NT, or higher to develop Java applets because Java requires a 32-bit operating system and long, case-sensitive filenames. ■

Other JDKs

If you're not using a common operating system such as Sun's Solaris or Microsoft's Windows NT, don't worry. Even though a Sun JDK may not be available for your computer, you may still be able to develop Java programs. Check with your computer vendor to see if it has ported the JDK to your operating system.

IBM, for example, has released versions of the JDK for AIX (IBM's version of UNIX), OS/400 (which runs on the popular AS/400), and OS/390 (a mainframe operating system).

ON THE WEB

`http://java.sun.com/cgi-bin/java-ports.cgi`   Find out which operating systems support Java by running the Sun Web application at this address. Note that not all operating systems that support Java support a JDK.

Downloading to Windows NT, Step by Step

This section describes the process of downloading Sun's JDK to your desktop computer. In this example, we'll assume you use a Windows NT system—other operating systems work similarly.

Connecting to JavaSoft   The easiest way to find the current JDK is to start at `http://java.sun.com/`. Scroll down the page until you see the Spotlight section on the left margin. In that section you'll see a link for the Java Development Kit.

T I P   If you want to be sure to have access to the latest versions of the JDK, consider downloading public betas. Learn more about beta software at `http://developer.javasoft.com/` by becoming a member of the Java Developer Connection (JDC). Membership is free.

Downloading the JDK   After you're on the download page, read the information about the JDK, then scroll down until you see the "Java Development Kit Software" section. Note the version number; make sure you're getting the version you expect. Figure 37.1 shows the download section of a typical JDK release.

FIGURE 37.1
Start your download by selecting the version of the JDK.

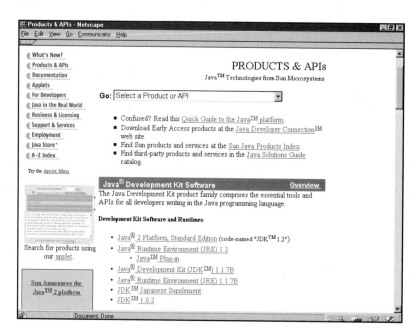

TIP From the download page, you'll find links to various text files, including a README file, a list of changes, and a list of features supported in this version of the JDK. Use the README file to get an overview of the download and installation process.

You might want to print out the README file because some of the recommendations about setting environment variables can get tricky. If you don't get them right, you'll get errors when you try to use the JDK tools.

Below the download section for the JDK, you'll see options for the documentation and other software. You can download either the documentation or the JDK first—in this example, we'll start with the JDK itself. When you're done, come back to this page and follow the same procedures to download the documentation.

Before leaving this page, scroll down to the end. Sun has put many useful links on this page, including links to Java documentation (beyond that supplied in the documentation kit). Consider bookmarking this page so you'll always have the latest information on Java.

Use the pull-down menu to select your operating system, and then click the Continue button. The license agreement for the JDK appears. Read the license agreement; if you want the JDK, you must accept the agreement.

N O T E Note that the license agreement prohibits you from distributing the JDK. If you develop a Java applet, you don't need to send the end user anything—most browsers contain a Java Runtime Environment (JRE), or the end user can install Sun's Java plug-in for Netscape Navigator or Microsoft Internet Explorer.

If you want to distribute a standalone application, you can download the Java Runtime Environment (JRE) from Sun and bundle it with your application, or you can instruct the user how to get the JRE directly.

After you navigate the license agreement, you finally arrive at the download page itself. Figure 37.2 shows this page. Note that you can download the JDK either from Sun's FTP server or via HTTP. If your network connection permits you to use FTP, do so; it's faster and more reliable. If you must, use HTTP.

 TIP If your network connection is slow or unreliable, consider getting the JDK via CD-ROM. Sun refers to this offer throughout the download process. If you take it up on the offer, it will include additional Java resources on the CD-ROM.

You can download the installation kit into any convenient directory; the installer will place the components into the proper directories.

Be sure to note the name of the file you're downloading—it's given at the top of the download page. Some network connections change the name of the downloaded file to match the name of the page from which it is downloaded. If your software makes this mistake, switch the name back to the one given by Sun before continuing the installation process.

FIGURE 37.2

This version of the download page enables you to get the Windows 95/NT version of the JDK.

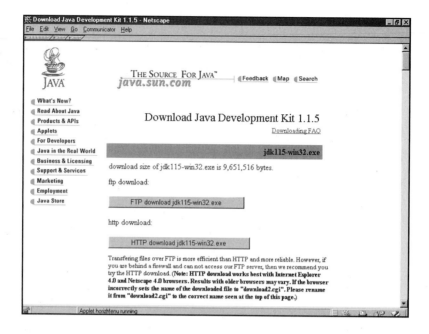

Installing the JDK   The JDK installer for Windows 95/NT is an executable archive. Double-click this file to start the installation process. Follow the instructions to make the JDK directory.

> **N O T E**   You should unpack both the documentation and the JDK into the same directory. The documentation installer will make a `docs` folder in the JDK directory. Sun's links are designed to look for the documentation in that folder. ∎

When you finish installation, feel free to delete the installer programs for both the JDK and the documentation. You won't need them again unless you need to reinstall the software.

> **N O T E**   As you explore your JDK and third-party products, you may run across zip files such as `lib/classes.zip`. Don't unzip these files—they are designed to be read directly by the Java runtime environment. In the newest JDK, these zip files are being replaced by Java Archives, or JAR files, which serve the same purpose but aren't likely to be confused with zip archives. ∎

Setting Environment Variables   Java uses the CLASSPATH environment variable to tell it where to look for Java classes. As a developer, you'll want to add new class libraries to the CLASSPATH variable.

If you've installed the JDK in the default location for your platform, the JDK tools will find the lib directory without searching CLASSPATH. You'll still need to set CLASSPATH if you install third-party programs.

To see if CLASSPATH is set on a Windows machine, type set at the command prompt. If you find that CLASSPATH is set, you can clear it by typing set CLASSPATH=. Of course, if you set

CLASSPATH in a startup file such as `Autoexec.bat`, you'll want to remove that entry in order to permanently unset CLASSPATH.

On a Windows 95 machine, you can edit the CLASSPATH entry in the `Autoexec.bat` file. On a Windows NT machine, use the System Control panel and this step-by-step procedure:

1. From the Start menu, choose Settings, Control Panel, as shown in Figure 37.3.

2. In the resulting folder, locate the System Control Panel and double-click it.

3. In the System Properties dialog box, choose the Environment tab, shown in Figure 37.4.

4. Select the CLASSPATH variable in the upper window (marked System Variables). When you click the variable name, the variable and its current value appear in the edit fields at the bottom of the dialog box.

5. Add the path of your library directories to the value of CLASSPATH.

FIGURE 37.3

On a Windows NT machine, set up your environment variables through the System control panel.

FIGURE 37.4

In the System Properties dialog box, select the Environment tab to change the CLASSPATH variable.

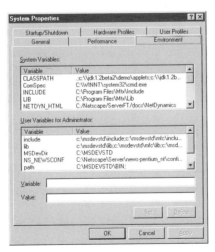

Part VII

Ch

37

When you're working in your development directory (described in the next section), you'll find it useful to be able to refer to the tools by name rather than having to specify the full path. Thus, you would prefer to type javac myClass.java rather than typing C:/jdk1.2/bin/javac myClass.java.

The solution is to set the PATH variable. Include the bin directory of your JDK in the PATH so that the operating system can find the JDK tools.

Setting Up a Development Directory   You can place a development directory anywhere you like on your hard drive. (Remember to set the PATH variable so you don't have to type the full path to every JDK tool.) You might store code for the Model 1000 project in C:\Projects\Model1000\ on a Windows machine, for example, or /home/myname/projects/model1000/ under UNIX. If you're using a development environment, such as Symantec Visual Cafè or Together/J, follow the instructions that came with your tools to set up a development directory.

As you gain experience in Java, you'll undoubtedly develop several libraries of classes (called packages). You can add these libraries to your CLASSPATH variable, or wrap your calls to Java tools in a batch file or shell script that sets its own version of CLASSPATH. To compile all the Java programs in the current directory on a Windows machine, for example, you could type

```
javac -classpath .;C:\usr\local\classes\;
ÂC:\projects\model1000\java\lib\classes.zip *.java
```

To avoid retyping this long line each time you need to compile, put this line into a batch file. If you name the file compile.bat, for instance, you now only need to type compile to invoke the javac compiler on all Java files. (If you're using UNIX, you can get the same effect by using a shell script.)

Testing Your Installation   To test your JDK installation, go to a command prompt. (On a UNIX system, go to a shell prompt.) Change to your development directory and type javac—the name of the Java compiler.

You should get a usage message back telling you about the dozen or so options available. If you get a message complaining that the command or program doesn't exist, check your PATH variable and make sure it includes the bin subdirectory of your JDK directory. Thus, if you placed the JDK in a directory called jdk1.2, make sure your PATH variable includes jdk1.2/bin (or jdk1.2\bin in Windows).

Building Your First Applet

To build an applet, you need to have the JDK installed. After that's done, you'll follow a four-step process.

Build a Java application:

1. Enter the code into a text file.
2. Compile all classes by using javac.

3. Write an HTML file that loads the applet.

4. Load the HTML file by using your Web browser.

This section walks you through the first two steps. The next section, "Running the Applet," describes the last two steps.

Writing the Code

Use any text editor to make a program source file, as shown in Listing 37.1.

> **N O T E** The listing shows line numbers for reference only. Don't enter the line numbers if you type in this program. ▪

On the CD

Complete source code for each of these programs is included on the accompanying CD-ROM.

Listing 37.1   *HelloApplet.java*—To Write an Applet, Start by Importing Sun's Classes

```
import java.applet.Applet;
import java.awt.Graphics;

public class HelloApplet extends Applet
{
  public void paint(Graphics theGraphics)
  {
    theGraphics.drawString("Hello, World!", 0, 50);
  }
}
```

Java is an object-oriented language, and the engineers at Sun have written a complete applet that you can use as a starting point. As you'll see in a moment, all you have to do is build a class that inherits from `java.applet.Applet`, then override any methods in `Applet` that don't meet your requirements. We'll walk through this code in detail later in this section—for now, just type in the code or copy it from the CD-ROM.

> **N O T E** You must use a text editor that supports long, case-sensitive filenames.
>
> The versions of Notepad, WordPad, and Edit that come with Windows 95 work fine. Microsoft Word 95 or higher also works. Older versions of Word for 16-bit Windows do not work.
>
> Be sure, too, to save your file as plain text. If you save the file as a word processing document, the compiler won't be able to process it. ▪

> **N O T E** Your Java source file must have the same name as the public class. That is, you must name this file `HelloApplet.java`, which corresponds to the public class `HelloApplet`.
>
> Furthermore, the capitalization must also match exactly. If your class is named `HelloApplet` (capital *H*, capital *A*) but your source file is named `helloapplet.java`, the program will not compile. ▪

Compiling the Applet

Open a command prompt window. Make sure you're in your development directory and then type `javac HelloApplet.java`. Remember that the filename must match the name of the class exactly—including capitalization. Even on a Windows system, which typically is case-insensitive, you must type the filename the way the compiler expects to see it. Four outcomes are possible whenever you run `javac`:

- The command interpreter cannot find `javac`—Check your PATH variable to make sure the `bin` subdirectory of your JDK folder is in the path.

- The compiler returns without comment—Your code has compiled successfully.

- Your compiler emits one or more warnings—You should examine the warning to see if you've made a coding error.

- Your compiler emits one or more errors—You have made a coding error.

You must eliminate the causes for all compiler errors before you can run the applet. You should strive to eliminate all warnings as well. Although your program may run, warnings are an indication that you may have made a mistake. You should almost always be able to rewrite the code in such a way as to eliminate the warnings.

Occasionally you may get a warning that tells you that you are using a deprecated method. Rerun the compiler with the `-deprecated` switch to find out the exact problem. *Deprecated methods* are those that are still supported but are no longer recommended—they may be removed completely in some future release. When writing new code, you should eliminate all deprecated calls.

After your code has compiled successfully, it's time to load your applet into a Web page.

▶ To learn more about the Graphics class, **see** "Displaying Graphics" on **p. 1078**.

Running the Applet

If we were writing an application, we could invoke the Java interpreter from the command line to run the class. An applet, however, requires a browser environment, so we'll have to write some HTML to display the applet.

Writing the HTML

Listing 37.2 shows a simple Web page that includes the `HelloApplet` applet. This Web page will work with the appletviewer—you'll want to improve the HTML by adding a head, title, background color, and perhaps some text before you use it on your Web site.

Listing 37.2   *helloApplet.html*—You Must Write an HTML File to Test an Applet

```
<HTML>
<BODY>
<APPLET CODE="HelloApplet.class" WIDTH="200" HEIGHT="200">
</APPLET>
```

```
</BODY>
</HTML>
```

TIP Your HTML source file is not subject to the same strict rules about long filenames and case sensitivity as your Java source files. The file here is called `helloApplet.html`. You can pretty much name yours anything you want, provided it has an `.htm` or `.html` suffix.

ON THE WEB

`http://java.sun.com/products/plugin/` You can ensure that the user is running your applet in the latest version of Java by configuring your HTML pages to use the Sun Java plug-in. See `http://java.sun.com/products/plugin/currentVersion/docs/tags.html#Any` to learn how to convert <APPLET> tags to JavaScript that will load the plug-in correctly on either a Microsoft or a Netscape browser. (In this URL, replace `currentVersion` with the current version number, such as 1.1.1 or 1.2.) You can convert your pages automatically by using Sun's Java Plug-In HTML Converter, described at `http://java.sun.com/products/plugin/features.html`.

Getting Started Quickly with a Simple <Applet> Tag   The <APPLET> tag shown in Listing 37.2 is about as simple as an <APPLET> tag can get. You must include the CODE attribute to tell the browser which class to load. You need to specify the height and width of the graphical space so the browser can allocate it. Other than that, everything in this tag is defaulted.

Note that you must close the applet tag with </APPLET>. Many new Java users forget the closing tag, leaving the appletviewer confused.

Using the Full <Applet> Tag   From time to time, you may need to add other elements to the <APPLET> tag. Listing 37.3 shows a more complete example.

Listing 37.3   *bigApplet.html*—You Can Use More Attributes, Parameters, and Even HTML in the *<APPLET>* Tag

```
<HTML>
<BODY>
<APPLET CODEBASE="http://myserver.mydomain.com/applets">
CODE="SomeApplet.class" WIDTH="200" HEIGHT="200"
ALT="A simple applet" NAME="hello"
ALIGN="Center" VSPACE="2" HSPACE="2">
<PARAM NAME="Auto" VALUE="True">
<PARAM NAME="Interface" VALUE="Full">
Your browser doesn't understand Java. If you had a Java-enabled
➥browser you'd see something like this:<BR>
<IMG SRC="applet.gif" ALT="Image of Applet" HEIGHT="200" WIDTH=
➥"200">
You can get a Java-aware browser from
<A HREF="http://home.netscape.com/">Netscape Communications</A>.
</APPLET>
</BODY>
</HTML>
```

In this version of the <APPLET> tag, we've specified a CODEBASE where the browser should look for the class file. (By default the browser asks for the applet from the same server and directory that provided the HTML page.) This version also includes some descriptive text about the applet (in ALT) and a NAME (for use by other applets or by JavaScript).

▶ For an example of JavaScript that communicates with an applet, **see** "JavaScript to Java Communication" on **p. 565**.

The final set of attributes, ALIGN, VSPACE, and HSPACE, provides alignment and vertical and horizontal spacing.

Following the opening <APPLET> tag, you may place parameters (in <PARAM> tags). Give each parameter a name and a value; the applet will be able to read the parameters.

It's a good idea to make your applets customizable with parameters. Parameterized applets are more useful as components.

TIP

Try to avoid having required parameters—if someone other than you uses your applet on their Web page, they may not know how to use all the parameters. Your applet should behave in a reasonable manner with no parameters at all.

You can make your applet more usable by implementing the getParameterInfo() method, which enables a tool such as AppletViewer to find out about the parameters you support.

Before you close the <APPLET> tag, you can include some HTML. This HTML will only be displayed if the browser did not understand the <APPLET> tag, so you should display a message telling the user what he or she is missing. The HTML in Listing 37.3 (lines 9 through 13) tells the user about the problem, puts up a graphic showing what the applet looks like, and then offers a link to the Netscape site so the end user can download Netscape Communicator.

Running Your Applet with *AppletViewer*

To start AppletViewer, type appletViewer HelloApplet.html at the command line. Figure 37.5 shows our applet in action. It doesn't do much, but it works!

FIGURE 37.5

The fastest and easiest way to test an applet is with the AppletViewer.

Seeing Your Applet in a Web Browser

Eventually you'll want your applet to appear on a Web page. Figure 37.6 shows `HelloApplet` viewed with Microsoft Internet Explorer. Figure 37.7 shows the same applet in Netscape Navigator.

FIGURE 37.6
Microsoft displays a gray rectangle to show the applet's reserved space.

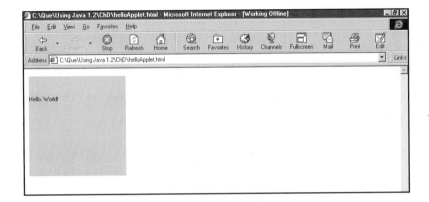

FIGURE 37.7
Netscape displays the applet against a transparent background.

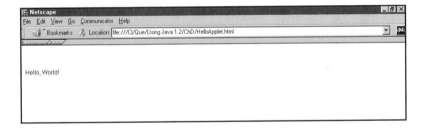

TIP

Even an applet as simple as this one can look different when run on different Web browsers.

Depending on how widely you expect your applets to be circulated, it is usually a good idea to have several browsers (on different machines with different resolutions and different operating systems) and several different versions handy for testing.

To ensure that users are using Sun's version of the Java Virtual Machine (rather than one written by the browser vendor), script your pages so that they load Sun's plug-in. That way you won't have as much variation from one machine to another.

Troubleshooting

If all doesn't go well when you compile and load your applet, double-check your CLASSPATH variable. The most common problem new Java programmers experience is an incorrect CLASSPATH variable. If either your compiler or interpreter complain about missing classes, make sure every class archive is listed in CLASSPATH. If your class files are "loose" files in a directory, list the directory. If they're archived into a `.zip` file or `.jar` file, you must name the archive in CLASSPATH. You shouldn't have much trouble with HelloApplet, but it does need to find Sun's `Applet` and `Graphics` classes.

> **N O T E**   If you'd like to know more about how the browser calls the various methods of your applet,
> look at "Life Cycle of an Applet," later in this chapter. ■

Step by Step Through the Code

This section walks through the code for the HelloApplet class so you can see why each line is written the way it is. Even though only one executable statement exists (in line 8), this tiny program illustrates many of the principles you'll use in writing any Java applet.

- ■ The class is declared to be public.
- ■ The class contains a member named paint().
- ■ paint() is declared to be public and to return void.

Importing Packages

The first two lines of HelloApplet.java tell the compiler to use class definitions from two specific packages: java.applet and java.awt. (AWT stands for the Abstract Windowing Toolkit.) Specifically, these directives tell the compiler to use the Applet object from java.applet and the Graphics object from java.awt.

The import statement is simply a shorthand notation. We could have written

```
public class HelloApplet extends java.applet.Applet
```

and

```
public void paint (java.awt.Graphics theGraphics)
```

but most programmers prefer the aesthetics of import. If we planned to use many classes from java.applet or java.awt, we could have written

```
import java.applet.*;
import java.awt.*;
```

to give the compiler permission to use any class from those packages. In practice, this asterisk notation is used frequently, although we lose the immediate capability to identify where a class is defined. If we didn't know Java well, we wouldn't know whether the Graphics class was part of java.applet or java.awt.

> **N O T E**   If two classes in different packages have the same name, you can run into problems if you
> use the asterisk (*) notation on both packages. To make sure you get the class you want,
> fully qualify it in your code or in the import statement. ■

Extending *Applet*

The most powerful statement in HelloApplet is in the class definition HelloApplet extends Applet. With that one statement, we've said that our little class, HelloApplet, inherits all the methods and variables of Sun's much larger class, `Applet`. `Applet` already knows how to communicate with the Web browser. It knows how to communicate with the graphical interface inside the browser window. It even knows how to redraw its content (although that content is empty). What it doesn't know is how to do any work. By extending `Applet`, we get a complete applet—ready to go. All we have to do is add content.

What's a *public* Class?

Java provides several levels of access—public, `protected`, `private`, and a default level. Anyone who wants can access classes and members that are public. When you write an applet, you need to declare the applet's class as public so that the Java environment can find it and run its methods.

Using *Applet's paint()* Method

An applet draws into a graphical space provided by the Web browser. Whenever that space is covered (by another window) or disappears (because the user has minimized the window) it becomes invalid. When it becomes visible again, the applet must repaint itself. In fact, internally, `Applet` calls a method called `repaint()`. That `repaint()` method, in turn, calls `paint()`. In order to draw something into the applet's graphical space, we need to do the work in `paint()`.

The `Graphics` space allocated for us by the browser is represented by a `Graphics` object, so we begin the `paint()` method by accepting that `Graphics` object (which we call `theGraphics`).

The `Graphics` class supports over three dozen public methods, including `drawLine()`, `draw3DRect()`, and `fillArc()`. Because we want to put a `String` into the graphic, the method we're interested in is `drawString()`. `drawString()` takes three parameters—the `String` we want to draw, and the x and y coordinates where we want to start drawing. We've chosen the coordinates 0 and 50 to start the `String` against the left margin, down a bit from the top.

> **N O T E** The paint() method is one of several methods that the browser calls. You can get
> sophisticated behavior from your applet by overriding other methods, such as start()
> and init(). See the comments on "Life Cycle of an Applet" in the next section. ■

Life Cycle of an Applet

We've seen `Applet`'s `paint()` method. As you might guess, repainting the screen is only one part of an applet's life cycle. This section shows the various stages of an applet's life and suggests various tasks you may want to undertake at each step. If you'd like to see these steps in action, compile `LifeCycle.java`, given in Listing 37.4. You can construct an HTML file based on the pattern given in `HelloApplet.html`—just change the name of the class file.

Listing 37.4 *LifeCycle.java*—This Applet Demonstrates the Stages in the Life of an Applet

```java
import java.applet.Applet;
import java.awt.Graphics;

public class LifeCycle extends Applet
{
  public LifeCycle()
  {
    System.out.println("Constructor running...");
  }
  public void init()
  {
    System.out.println("This is init.");
  }
  public void start()
  {
    System.out.println("Applet started.");
  }
  public void paint(Graphics theGraphics)
  {
    theGraphics.drawString("Hello, World!", 0, 50);
    System.out.println("Applet just painted.");
  }
  public void stop()
  {
    System.out.println("Applet stopped.");
  }
  public void destroy()
  {
    System.out.println("Applet destroyed.");
  }
}
```

If you run the LifeCycle applet from the appletviewer, you'll receive standard out messages in the command prompt window. If you're using a Web browser, you can open the Java console. To open the Java console in Netscape Communicator 4.0, for example, choose Communicator, Java Console. Figure 37.8 shows the console in action.

 T I P You can type commands into Navigator's Java console. Enter a question mark (?) to see a list of commands. If you enter nine (9) you'll put the console in maximum debugging mode—it will show you all kinds of information about your running applet.

Constructor

Every class has a constructor—you'll spot it because it has the same name as the class. You can put initialization code in the constructor. Restrict yourself to code that should be run only once during the life of the applet.

FIGURE 37.8

You can write to the Java console to help debug your applets.

> **CAUTION**
>
> Not all browsers load and unload applets in the same way. For best results, put once-only code into init() rather than the constructor.

init()

When the browser sees an `<APPLET>` tag, it instructs the Java class loader to load the specified class. The Java environment in the browser makes an instance of the class (by calling its constructor). It then calls the instance's init() method. The init() method is the best place to put code that should run only once during your applet's lifetime. Experiment with the LifeCycle applet in different browsers to see the circumstances under which the constructor and init() are called.

start() and stop()

After your applet is loaded and initialized, the Java environment calls start(). If the user leaves the page or minimizes it, the applet's stop() method is called. The start() method will be called again when the user returns to the page.

If your applet should take special action when the user enters or leaves the page, place the code for those actions in start() or stop().

paint()

The Java environment calls paint() whenever it suspects that the applet's graphic space may have been obscured. As a result, paint() gets called far more often than you might expect.

Experiment with the LifeCycle applet in various browsers to see when `paint()` gets called. Design your applets so that `paint()` is as efficient as possible—this method is where your program will spend much of its time.

destroy()

Put up Navigator's Java Console, open a page with the LifeCycle applet on it, and exit Navigator. If you watch the console closely, you'll see LiveCycle's "destroy" message just before the console itself disappears. In general, browsers will try to keep applets around (at least in their `stopped` state) as long as they can. When the browser's memory is full, or when the user exits the browser, the applet's resources are released. Just before the browser destroys the applet's memory, it calls `destroy()`. Use `destroy()` to release any resources your applet may have acquired.

Where's the Destructor?   If you're experienced in C++, you may be puzzled by Java's lack of a destructor. Java relies on garbage collection—you don't have to explicitly delete objects. Nevertheless, your C++ habits will stand you in good stead—most programmers prefer to release resources as soon as they know they're done with them. The code you put into `destroy()` should, therefore, resemble code you might write in a C++ destructor; look through your constructor and `init()` code, identify any resources (such as object references) you acquired, and release them. If your applet acquired other resources during its lifetime (such as nodes on a linked list), release them by setting the references to `null`.

You get a similar effect by writing a `finalize()` method. The garbage collector calls an object's `finalize()` method just before the object's memory is reclaimed. If you have a sophisticated applet with more than one class, you might want to write a `finalize()` method for each class that needs to dispose of resources. You can then use `finalize()` to dispose of system resources or perform other cleanup, and use `destroy()` to wrap up the applet itself.

Troubleshooting *HelloApplet*

Even with an applet as simple as this, a number of things could go wrong. Take a look at some common "gotchas":

- `javac: Bad command or filename` error—This message means that you didn't install the JDK correctly.

  If you are sure that you installed the JDK, all you need to do is set your DOS `PATH`. The easiest way to fix this problem is to make sure `PATH` and `CLASSPATH` are correctly defined in `AUTOEXEC.BAT` and then reboot your PC. Following is a sample `AUTOEXEC` entry:

  ```
  PATH=c:\windows;c:\windows\command;c:\java\bin
  CLASSPATH=c:\java\lib;.
  ```

  Remember to use the Control Panel if you're using Windows NT or a shell script if you're on a UNIX system. You may need to restart your shell or command prompt window for this change to take effect. If you've changed `AUTOEXEC.BAT`, you need to run that batch file or reboot the machine.

■ Extraneous `thread applet-HelloApplet.class find class HelloApplet` messages—This message means that `CLASSPATH` is not defined correctly. The solution is the same as for the preceding problem: double-check your definitions for `PATH` and `CLASSPATH` and reboot your PC.

`CLASSPATH` consists of a list of directory paths in which appletviewer looks for Java classes. Each different pathname is separated by a semicolon. Make sure that the current directory (represented by a dot) is in your `CLASSPATH` list.

■ `HelloApplet.java:26: Class gelloApplet not found in type declaration`—This message or any similar-sounding compiler error probably means you mis-typed something.

Carefully double-check every place in the program where you meant to type the name in question (here, `HelloApplet`). Be sure each occurrence matches exactly (including capitalization—Java is case sensitive).

In this case, you carefully double-check your program and discover that you typed `gelloApplet` rather than `HelloApplet`. It compiles correctly after you make this correction.

■ `HelloApplet.java:24: Warning: Public class HelloApplet must be defined in a file called HelloApplet.java`—The name of your Java source file must match the name of your public Java class exactly.

For the sample program, this requirement means the class needs to be called `HelloApplet`, the source file needs to be called `HelloApplet.java`, and the HTML `<APPLET>` tag needs to specify `HelloApplet.class`, or your program will neither compile cleanly nor execute.

To fix this problem, carefully double-check everything for exact spelling and capitalization, and then compile again.

■ Nothing happens—If you are running Internet Explorer and you see the HTML, but not your applet, your browser probably is not configured to run Java. Choose View, Options, Security, and look at your Active Content group to make sure Java is enabled.

You must check the following:

■ Allow downloading of active content.

■ Enable Java programs. You should also set your browser's Safety Level to Medium.

Sample Applets

Sometimes programming is better "caught than taught." This section shows three fairly advanced applets—each uses techniques that haven't been described in detail in this book. If you have a programming background, most of the logic of these applets should be clear; look in the Java documentation for details about the API. If you'd like a more detailed treatment of Java programming, read *Using Java 1.2* (Que, 1998).

SystemInfo

The applet in Listing 37.5 demonstrates how to build several "cards" of data into an applet. The file defines three classes:

■ LabelField—A derivative of Panel that knows how to lay out its data and a label.

■ SystemInfo—The applet class itself, which reads various system properties and displays them on the "cards" of a CardLayout.

■ ButtonAction—An "inner class" of SystemInfo that responds to clicks on the applet's two buttons.

Figure 37.9 shows the applet in action.

Listing 37.5   *SystemInfo.java*—This Applet Displays Several "Cards" of Information

```java
import java.applet.Applet;
import java.awt.Panel;
import java.awt.GridLayout;
import java.awt.BorderLayout;
import java.awt.CardLayout;
import java.awt.Label;
import java.awt.Button;
import java.awt.Font;
import java.awt.TextField;
import java.awt.Dimension;
import java.awt.event.ActionListener;
import java.awt.event.ActionEvent;

class LabelField extends Panel {
  int fLabelWidth;
  Label fLabel;
  TextField fField;

  public LabelField(int theLabelWidth, String theLabel, String theValue) {
    this.fLabelWidth = theLabelWidth;
    add(this.fLabel = new Label(theLabel));
    add(this.fField = new TextField(theValue));
    fField.setEditable(false);
  }
  public void doLayout() {
    Dimension theDimension = getSize();
    Dimension theLabelSize = fLabel.getPreferredSize();
    Dimension theFieldSize = fField.getPreferredSize();
    fLabel.setBounds(0, 0, fLabelWidth, theLabelSize.height);
    fField.setBounds(fLabelWidth + 5, 0, theDimension.width - (fLabelWidth + 5),
      theFieldSize.height);
  }
}

public class SystemInfo extends Applet {
  CardLayout fCardLayout;
  Panel fPanel;
```

```
Button fNextButton;
Button fPrevButton;

public void init() {
Font theFont = new Font("Helvetica", Font.BOLD, 14);
setLayout(new BorderLayout());
add("South", fPanel = new Panel());

fNextButton = new Button("Next");
fPrevButton = new Button("Previous");
ButtonAction aButtonAction = new ButtonAction();

fNextButton.addActionListener(aButtonAction);
fPrevButton.addActionListener(aButtonAction);

fPanel.add(fPrevButton);
fPanel.add(fNextButton);

add("Center", fPanel = new Panel());
fPanel.setLayout(fCardLayout = new CardLayout());

try {
  Panel aPanel = new Panel();
  aPanel.setLayout(new GridLayout(0, 1));
  aPanel.add(new Label("System Properties")).setFont(theFont);
  aPanel.add(new LabelField(100, "version:",
    System.getProperty("java.version")));
  aPanel.add(new LabelField(100, "vendor:",
System.getProperty("java.vendor")));
  aPanel.add(new LabelField(100, "vendor.url:",
➥System.getProperty("java.vendor.url")));
  fPanel.add("system", aPanel);

  aPanel = new Panel();
  aPanel.add(new Label("Java Properties")).setFont(theFont);
  aPanel.setLayout(new GridLayout(0, 1));
  aPanel.add(new LabelField(100, "class version:",
    System.getProperty("java.class.version")));
  fPanel.add("java", aPanel);

  aPanel = new Panel();
  aPanel.setLayout(new GridLayout(0, 1));
  aPanel.add(new Label("OS Properties")).setFont(theFont);
  aPanel.add(new LabelField(100, "OS:",
➥System.getProperty("os.name")));
  aPanel.add(new LabelField(100, "OS Arch:",
➥System.getProperty("os.arch")));
  aPanel.add(new LabelField(100, "OS Version:",
➥System.getProperty("os.version")));
  fPanel.add("os", aPanel);

  aPanel = new Panel();
  aPanel.setLayout(new GridLayout(0, 1));
  aPanel.add(new Label("Misc Properties")).setFont(theFont);
  aPanel.add(new LabelField(100, "File Separator:",
```

continues

Listing 37.5   Continued

```
      System.getProperty("file.separator")));
   aPanel.add(new LabelField(100, "Path Separator:",
      System.getProperty("path.separator")));
   aPanel.add(new LabelField(100, "Line Separator:",
      System.getProperty("line.separator")));
   fPanel.add("sep", aPanel);
} catch (SecurityException e) {
   System.out.println("Security Exception: " + e);
   }
}

class ButtonAction implements ActionListener {

   public void actionPerformed (ActionEvent theEvent) {
      Object anObject = theEvent.getSource();
      if (anObject == fNextButton)
        fCardLayout.next(fPanel);
      else if (anObject == fPrevButton)
        fCardLayout.previous(fPanel);
   }
 }
}
```

FIGURE 37.9
The first card of
`SystemInfo`.

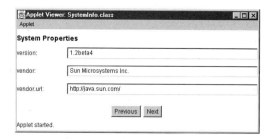

The Great Thread Race

Java enables your applet (or application) to have more than one thread of control. *TRaceApplet*,
shown in Listing 37.6, starts several "racing" threads and shows them moving across the
screen. You can use this applet to test your Web browser to see how well it shares time between threads of different priorities. (Most Web browsers do a poor job in this area—you
shouldn't rely upon relative priorities between threads for any critical feature.) Note, too, that
this program has a `main()` method and can be run as an application as well as an applet.

**Listing 37.6   *TRaceApplet.java*—This Program Sets Up the User Interface
and Starts the Race**

```
import java.applet.Applet;
import java.awt.Graphics;
```

```java
import java.awt.GridLayout;

public class TRaceApplet extends Applet implements Runnable,
➥TSuspendable
{
  private TRacer fRacers[];
  static private short fRacerCount = 0;
  private Thread fThreads[];
  static private Thread fMonitorThread;
  static private boolean fInApplet = true;
  private boolean fThreadSuspended = false;
  static private java.awt.Frame fFrame = null;
  private TWindowAdapter fWindowAdapter = null;

  public void init()
  {
    if (fInApplet)
    {
      String theParameter = getParameter("NUMBER");
      if (theParameter == null)
        fRacerCount = 0;
      else
        fRacerCount = Short.parseShort(theParameter);
    }
    if (fRacerCount <= 0)
      fRacerCount = 2;
    if (fRacerCount > Thread.MAX_PRIORITY -
➥Thread.MIN_PRIORITY + 1)
        fRacerCount = (short)(Thread.MAX_PRIORITY -
➥Thread.MIN_PRIORITY + 1);

    if (!fInApplet)
      fWindowAdapter = new TWindowAdapter();

    // have one column, with one row per Racer
    setLayout(new GridLayout(fRacerCount, 1));

    // initialize the fRacers and fThreads arrays
    fRacers = new TRacer[fRacerCount];
    fThreads = new Thread[fRacerCount];

    for (short i=0; i<fRacerCount; i++)
    {
      fRacers[i] = new TRacer("Racer# " + i, this);

      // scale the image so that all of the racers will fit
      fRacers[i].setSize(getSize().width,
➥getSize().height/fRacerCount);
      add(fRacers[i]);
    }
  }

  public void start()
  {
    // set up our own "monitor" thread
```

continues

Listing 37.6 Continued

```
      fMonitorThread = new Thread(null, this,
➥"Monitor Thread");
      fMonitorThread.start();
  }

  public void stop()
  {
      fMonitorThread = null;
  }

  public void run()
  {
    if (fMonitorThread == Thread.currentThread())
    {
      TMouseAdapter aMouseAdapter = new TMouseAdapter();
      for (short i=0; i<fRacerCount;i++)
      {
        // this version of the Thread constructor specifies a
➥Runnable target
        fThreads[i] = new Thread(fRacers[i]);

        // should guarantee that the high-number thread wins
        fThreads[i].setPriority(Thread.MIN_PRIORITY+i);
        fThreads[i].start();
        fRacers[i].addMouseListener(aMouseAdapter);
      }
      synchronized (fMonitorThread)
      {
        fMonitorThread.notify();
      }
    }

    // now the world knows that all the racers are running
    while (fMonitorThread == Thread.currentThread())
    try
    {
      fMonitorThread.sleep(100);
      synchronized(fMonitorThread)
      {
        while (fThreadSuspended)
        {
          fMonitorThread.wait();
        }
        synchronized(this)
        {
          notifyAll();
        }
      }
    } catch (InterruptedException e)
    {
      System.err.println("The monitor thread was interrupted
➥while sleeping.");
      System.exit(1);
```

```
    }
  }

  public String[][] getParameterInfo()
  {
   short theMaximumNumberOfThreads =
➡(short)(Thread.MAX_PRIORITY - Thread.MIN_PRIORITY + 1);
   String theParameterInfo[][] =
   {
     {"NUMBER",     "1-"+theMaximumNumberOfThreads,
➡"number of racers"},
   };
   return theParameterInfo;
  }

  public String getAppletInfo()
  {
    String theAppletInfo = "Author: Michael L. Morgan\nDate:
➡19 March 98\nInspired by the Great Thread Race
➡(Special Edition Using Java, Que, 1996, p. 551)";
    return theAppletInfo;
  }

  public boolean isSuspended()
  {
    return fThreadSuspended;
  }

  public static void main(String argv[])
  {
    fInApplet = false;

    //look for the number of racers on the command line
    if (argv.length>0)
    try {
      fRacerCount = Short.parseShort(argv[0]);
    } catch (NumberFormatException e)
    {
      fRacerCount = 5;
    }

    fFrame = new java.awt.Frame("Racing Threads");

    TRaceApplet theRace = new TRaceApplet();
    fFrame.setSize(400,200);
    fFrame.add(theRace, java.awt.BorderLayout.CENTER);
    fFrame.show();
    theRace.init();

    // be sure to wait until after init() to hook up listener
    fFrame.addWindowListener(theRace.fWindowAdapter);
    fFrame.pack();
    theRace.start();

    // don't pass here till all racers are started
```

continues

Listing 37.6 Continued

```
    synchronized (fMonitorThread)
    {
      try {
        fMonitorThread.wait();
      } catch (InterruptedException e)
      {
        System.err.println("Main thread interrupted while
➡waiting for racers to start.");
        System.exit(1);
      }
    }
    System.out.println("And they're off!");

    // wait till all the racers are finished
    for (short i=0; i<fRacerCount; i++)
    try
    {
      theRace.fThreads[i].join();
    } catch (InterruptedException e)
    {
      System.err.println("The monitor thread was interrupted
➡while waiting for the other threads to exit.");
    }
    System.exit(0);
  }

  class TWindowAdapter extends java.awt.event.WindowAdapter
  {
    public void windowClosing(java.awt.event.WindowEvent
➡anEvent)
    {
      fFrame.setVisible(false);
      fFrame.dispose();
      System.exit(0);
    }
  }
  class TMouseAdapter extends java.awt.event.MouseAdapter
  {
    public synchronized void mousePressed(
➡java.awt.event.MouseEvent anEvent)
    {
      anEvent.consume();
      fThreadSuspended = !fThreadSuspended;
      if (!fThreadSuspended)
        synchronized (fMonitorThread)
        {
          fMonitorThread.notifyAll();
        }
    }
  }
}
```

TIP Whenever possible, include code such as `main()` in your own `applets`. This is shown in `TraceApplet` beginning about 2/3 into the listing with

```
public static void main(String argv[])
```

and ending with

```
System.exit(0);
}
```

When you include code such as this, you can run your program as an applet or as an application. You'll want to run as an application when you regression test, or if you later reuse the code outside of a browser environment.

Note that TRaceApplet supports parameters from the HTML `<PARAM>` tag. Lines 21 through 28 (as follows) look for a parameter named NUMBER.

```
String theParameter = getParameter("NUMBER");
if (theParameter == null)
  fRacerCount = 0;
else
  fRacerCount = Short.parseShort(theParameter);
}
if (fRacerCount <= 0)
  fRacerCount = 2;
```

If the parameter is found, it is used as the number of racers (`fRacerCount`). If it can't be found, if it is unreadable, or if it is less than or equal to zero, the program defaults to two racers.

How is the HTML author to know that this applet supports this parameter? Many browsers can call the `getParameterInfo()` method. TRaceApplet implements this method in lines 114 through 124 (as follows).

```
public String[][] getParameterInfo()
{
  short theMaximumNumberOfThreads =
Â(short)(Thread.MAX_PRIORITY - Thread.MIN_PRIORITY + 1);
  String theParameterInfo[][] =
  {
    {"NUMBER",     "1-"+theMaximumNumberOfThreads,
Â"number of racers"},
  };
  return theParameterInfo;
}
```

If the user requests this information, the program returns the parameter name, type, and range. Figure 37.10 shows how `AppletViewer` handles this request.

Listing 37.7 shows an HTML file that takes advantage of this feature.

FIGURE 37.10

Choose Info from the Applet menu in `AppletViewer` to see the applet and parameter information.

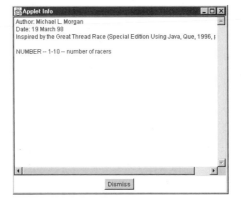

Listing 37.7   autogen_Race1.html—This HTML Was Originally Written by Visual Cafè, from Symantec

```html
<HTML>
<HEAD>
<TITLE>Autogenerated HTML</TITLE>
</HEAD>
<BODY>
<APPLET CODE="TRaceApplet.class" WIDTH=430 HEIGHT=270>
<PARAM NAME="NUMBER" VALUE="5">
</APPLET>
</BODY>
</HTML>
```

TRaceApplet requires two additional files: TRacer.java, which contains the class definition for the racer itself, and TSuspendable.java, an interface that supports pausing and unpausing the race with a mouse click. These files are shown in Listings 37.8 and 37.9, respectively.

Listing 37.8   TRacer.java—TRacer Is a Runnable Canvas and Is Responsible for Its Own User Interface

```java
import java.awt.Graphics;
import java.awt.Color;

public class TRacer extends java.awt.Canvas implements
➥Runnable
{
  private short fPosition = 0;
  private String fName;
  static private final short kNumberOfSteps = 1000;
  TSuspendable fAncestor;

  public TRacer(String theName, TSuspendable theAncestor)
  {
    fName = new String(theName);
    fAncestor = theAncestor;
  }
```

```java
public TRacer(String theName)
{
  fName = new String(theName);
  fAncestor = null;
}

public synchronized void paint(Graphics g)
{
  g.setColor(Color.black);
  g.drawLine(0,getSize().height/2, getSize().width,
getSize().height/2);
  g.setColor(Color.red);
  g.fillOval(fPosition*getSize().width/kNumberOfSteps, 0,
15, getSize().height);
}

public void run()
{
  while (fPosition < kNumberOfSteps)
  {
    fPosition++;
    repaint();
    try
    {
      Thread.currentThread().sleep(10);
      if (fAncestor != null)
      {
        synchronized (fAncestor)
        {
          if (fAncestor.isSuspended())
            fAncestor.wait();
        }
      }
    } catch (InterruptedException e)
    {
      System.err.println("Thread " + fName + " interrupted.");
      System.exit(1);
    }
  }
  System.out.println("Thread " + fName + " has finished
the race.");
}

public static void main(String argv[])
  {
    java.awt.Frame theFrame = new java.awt.Frame("One Racer");
    TRacer aRacer = new TRacer("Test");
    theFrame.setSize(400,200);
    theFrame.add(aRacer, java.awt.BorderLayout.CENTER);
    theFrame.show();
    aRacer.paint(theFrame.getGraphics());
    theFrame.pack();
    aRacer.run();
    System.exit(0);
  }
}
```

Listing 37.9 *TSuspendable.java*—Use This Interface to Ensure that the Ancestor Is Suspendable

```
public interface TSuspendable
{
  public boolean isSuspended();
}
```

Recall (lines 79 and 80 of TRaceApplet.java follow) that the highest-numbered thread should always win.

```
// should guarantee that the high-number thread wins
fThreads[i].setPriority(Thread.MIN_PRIORITY+i);
```

As Figures 37.11 and 37.12 show, you can't count on the priority mechanism to function as you'd expect. In AppletViewer, threads 2, 3, and 4 have a decided advantage over threads 0 and 1, but little difference exists within each group. Figure 37.12 shows that Netscape Navigator (a component of Netscape Communicator) ignores priority completely.

FIGURE 37.11

This version of the Great Thread Race is running on the JDK 1.2 AppletViewer.

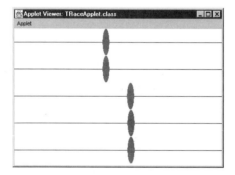

FIGURE 37.12

When run in Navigator 4.04, thread priority seems to have no effect.

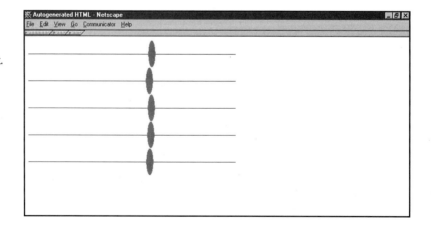

Working with an Object-Oriented Database

Sun supports an interface to relational databases called JDBC. For new applications, however, you may want to take advantage of the higher performance of an object-oriented database. Object Design, Inc. (http://www.odi.com/) offers a free version of its object-oriented database at http://www.odi.com/content/products/pse/PSEHome.html. It calls this version the Personal Storage Environment, or PSE.

After you've downloaded and installed the PSE, you can build and run applications such as DBDemo, shown in Listing 37.10. This program opens an existing database (demo.odb); if the database doesn't exist, the program makes a new one.

N O T E   After you've compiled this applet, you'll need to make class TNurse persistent. Follow the instructions that come with PSE and use its osjcfp utility to make TNurse persistent. ▨

Listing 37.10   *DBDemo.java*—**This Test Program Opens a Database and Reads and Writes Data Interactively**

```java
import java.awt.*;
import java.applet.*;
import java.util.Properties;
import java.util.Enumeration;
import COM.odi.*;
import COM.odi.util.*;

public class DBDemo extends Applet
{
    private Database fDb;
    private Transaction fTrans;

    // indicates that ObjectStore has been initialized
    private Thread fInitialized;
    private Session fSession;

        public void init()
        {
                // Take out this line if you don't use
➥symantec.itools.net.RelativeURL or
➥symantec.itools.awt.util.StatusScroller
                symantec.itools.lang.Context.setApplet(this);

                // This code is automatically generated by Visual Cafe
➥when you add
                // components to the visual environment.
➥It instantiates and initializes
                // the components. To modify the code,
➥only use code syntax that matches
                // what Visual Cafe can generate,
➥or Visual Cafe may be unable to back
                // parse your Java file into its visual environment.
                //{{INIT_CONTROLS
```

continues

Listing 37.10 Continued

```
                 setLayout(null);
                 setSize(426,400);
                 theAddNurseLabel = new java.awt.Label("Add Nurse to Database");
                 theAddNurseLabel.setBounds(48,192,360,32);
                 theAddNurseLabel.setFont(new Font("Dialog", Font.BOLD, 18));
                 add(theAddNurseLabel);
                 theNursesInDatabaseLabel = new java.awt.Label("Nurses in Data-
base");
                 theNursesInDatabaseLabel.setBounds(24,12,360,32);
                 theNursesInDatabaseLabel.setFont(new Font("Dialog", Font.BOLD,
18));
                 add(theNursesInDatabaseLabel);
                 theNurseIDLabel = new java.awt.Label("ID");
                 theNurseIDLabel.setBounds(48,240,40,36);
                 add(theNurseIDLabel);
                 theNurseNameLabel = new java.awt.Label("Last Name");
                 theNurseNameLabel.setBounds(48,276,72,54);
                 add(theNurseNameLabel);
                 theNurseIDField = new java.awt.TextField();
                 theNurseIDField.setText("the nurse ID");
                 theNurseIDField.setBounds(120,240,225,26);
                 add(theNurseIDField);
                 theNurseNameField = new java.awt.TextField();
                 theNurseNameField.setText("the nurse name");
                 theNurseNameField.setBounds(120,288,225,28);
                 add(theNurseNameField);
                 theAddButton = new java.awt.Button();
                 theAddButton.setLabel("Add");
                 theAddButton.setBounds(228,324,113,30);
                 theAddButton.setFont(new Font("Dialog", Font.BOLD, 12));
                 theAddButton.setBackground(java.awt.Color.lightGray);
                 add(theAddButton);
                 theNurseList = new java.awt.List(0,false);
                 add(theNurseList);
                 theNurseList.setBounds(36,60,329,103);
                 //}}

                 setupDatabase();

                 //{{REGISTER_LISTENERS
                 SymAction lSymAction = new SymAction();
                 theAddButton.addActionListener(lSymAction);
                 //}}
         }

     public void start()
     {
                 reload(theNurseList, TNurse.getAll());
     }


     public void destroy() {
         // save everything to the database
```

```
        if (fDb == null) {
            System.out.println("Database not open.");
            return;
        }
        fTrans.commit();

        // and close the database
        if (fDb == null) {
            System.out.println("No database to close.");
            return;
        }
        fDb.close();
        fDb = null;
    }

    private void maybeInitialize() {
        if (fInitialized != null) {
            return;
        }
        Properties properties = new Properties();
        String user = getParameter("user");
        if (user != null) {
            properties.put("COM.odi.user", user);
        }
        String password = getParameter("password");
        if (password != null) {
            properties.put("COM.odi.password", password);
        }
        ObjectStore.initialize(null, properties);
        fInitialized = Thread.currentThread();
    }

    public String[][] getParameterInfo() {
        String pinfo[][] = {
            {"user",     "String",    "username for database"},
            {"password", "String", "password for database"}
        };
    return pinfo;
}

public void setupDatabase()
{
vvvv// Here begins the ObjectStore connection
                fDb = null;
                fTrans = null;
                fInitialized = null;
                fSession = null;

                if (fDb != null) {
            System.out.println("Database already open.");
            return;
                }

                String theDbname = new String("demo.odb");

    // The following line starts a nonglobal session and joins this
```

continues

Listing 37.10 Continued

```
                // thread to the new session. This allows the thread to use
                // the ObjectStore API.
                        Session.create(null, null).join();
        fSession = Session.getCurrent();
                        try {
                    //db = Database.create(dbname, 0664);
                    System.out.println("Opening database");
                    fDb = Database.open(theDbname, ObjectStore.OPEN_UPDATE);
                    System.out.println("1a.Database open is " + fDb.isOpen());

                    // Enable this code if you want a new database each time
                    /* db.destroy();
                            System.out.println("Replacing database.");
                            db = Database.create(dbname, ObjectStore.ALL_READ |
➥ObjectStore.ALL_WRITE);
                    System.out.println("1b.Database open is " + db.isOpen());
                    */
                        } catch (AccessViolationException e) {
                    System.out.println("File system access violation.");
                    return;
                        } catch (DatabaseAlreadyExistsException e) {
                    System.out.println("Database already exists.");
                            } catch (DatabaseNotFoundException e) {
                                System.out.println("Making new database.");
                            fDb = Database.create(theDbname, ObjectStore.ALL_READ
➥ObjectStore.ALL_WRITE);
                            } catch (DatabaseException e) {
                    System.out.println("Invalid database: " + theDbname);
                    return;
                        }

                        if (fDb != null) {
                    fTrans = Transaction.begin(ObjectStore.UPDATE);
                    System.out.println("Made new transaction.");
                    System.out.println("2.Database open is " + fDb.isOpen());
                        }

                    System.out.println("About to initialize TNurse");
                    System.out.println("3.Database open is " + fDb.isOpen());
                    TNurse.initialize(fDb);
                }

                public void reload(java.awt.List theList, Enumeration e)
                {
                        // copy the elements of the enumeration into the list
                        for ( ; e.hasMoreElements();) {
                                theList.add((String) e.nextElement().toString());
                        }
                }

        public static void main(String args[])
        {
```

```
        System.out.println("Starting. . . ");
        DBDemo theApplet = new DBDemo();
        System.out.println("setting up database");
        theApplet.setupDatabase();

        System.out.println("populating database");
        try {
                    TNurse nurseSmith = TNurse.add("123S", "Smith");
                    TNurse nurseJones = TNurse.add("234J", "Jones");
                    TNurse nurseBrown = TNurse.add("345B", "Brown");
                } catch (Exception e) {
                        System.out.println("Exception: " + e);
                }

        System.out.println("destroying");
        theApplet.destroy();
        System.out.println("done");
        System.exit(0);
    }

    //{{DECLARE_CONTROLS
    java.awt.Label theAddNurseLabel;
    java.awt.Label theNursesInDatabaseLabel;
    java.awt.Label theNurseIDLabel;
    java.awt.Label theNurseNameLabel;
    java.awt.TextField theNurseIDField;
    java.awt.TextField theNurseNameField;
    java.awt.Button theAddButton;
    java.awt.List theNurseList;
    //}}

    class SymAction implements java.awt.event.ActionListener
    {
        public void actionPerformed(java.awt.event.ActionEvent event)
        {
            Object object = event.getSource();
            if (object == theAddButton)
                    theAddButton_Action(event);
        }
    }

    void theAddButton_Action(java.awt.event.ActionEvent event)
    {
        if (Session.getCurrent() == null)
    fSession.join();

TNurse.initialize(fDb);

        String theID = theNurseIDField.getText();
        String theName = theNurseNameField.getText();
        try {
          TNurse aNurse = TNurse.add(theID, theName);
        } catch (Exception e) {
                System.out.println("Exception: " + e);
        }
```

continues

Listing 37.10   Continued

```
            fTrans.commit();
        fTrans = Transaction.begin(ObjectStore.UPDATE);
        TNurse.initialize(fDb);

            //{{CONNECTION
            // Clear the text for TextField
            theNurseIDField.setText("");
            //}}

            //{{CONNECTION
            // Clear the text for TextField
            theNurseNameField.setText("");
            //}}

            //{{CONNECTION
            // Clear the List
            theNurseList.removeAll();
            reload(theNurseList, TNurse.getAll());
            //}}
        }
}
```

DBDemoApplet reads and writes a persistent object called TNurse to the database. TNurse is
defined in TNurse.java, given in Listing 37.11.

Listing 37.11   *TNurse.java*—Be Sure to Use ODI's osjcfp Utility to Make This Class Persistent

```
import java.util.*;
import COM.odi.*;
import COM.odi.util.*;

public class TNurse
{
  private String fID;
  private String fLastName;

  // Has table of all nurses
  private static OSHashtable all;

  private TNurse(String theID, String theLastName)
  {
    fID = theID;
    fLastName = theLastName;
    all.put(fID, this);
  }

  static public TNurse add(String theID, String theLastName)
➥throws Exception
  {
    if (all.containsKey(theID, true))
```

```
            throw new Exception("Nurse ID " + theID + " already exists.");
        else
            return (new TNurse(theID, theLastName));
    }

        static TNurse get(String theID) throws Exception
        {
                TNurse theResult = (TNurse)all.get(theID);
                if (theResult == null) {
                        throw new Exception("Nurse " + theID + " not found.");
                }
                return theResult;
        }

        public String toString()
        {
                return ("ID: " + fID + "; Name: "+ fLastName);
        }

        static void initialize(Database db)
        {
                try {
                System.out.println("Looking up nurses.");
                                System.out.println("N1.Database open is " +
db.isOpen());
                all = (OSHashtable)db.getRoot("Nurses");
                                System.out.println("N2.Database open is " +
db.isOpen());
                } catch (DatabaseRootNotFoundException e) {
                        System.out.println("Making new root.");
                        all = new OSHashtable();
                        db.createRoot("Nurses", all);
                }
        }

        public String getID()
        {
                return fID;
        }

        public String getLastName()
        {
                return fLastName;
        }

        static public Enumeration getAll()
        {
                return all.elements();
        }

        // This class is not to be used as a persistent hash key
        public int hashCode()
        {
                return super.hashCode();
        }
```

continues

Listing 37.11 Continued

```java
public static void main(String args[])
{
  System.out.println("TNurse class running.");
  String host = System.getProperty("COM.odi.host");
  String dbpath = System.getProperty("demo.dbpath");

  if (dbpath == null)
    dbpath = "demo.odb";

  ObjectStore.initialize(host, null);
  Database db = Database.open(dbpath, ObjectStore.UPDATE);

  Transaction t = Transaction.begin(ObjectStore.UPDATE);
  TNurse.initialize(db);

  System.out.println("Adding Nurse Jones");
  TNurse nurseJones = null;
  try {
    nurseJones = TNurse.add("12345A", "Jones");
    System.out.println("Nurse Jones is " + nurseJones.toString());
  } catch (Exception e) {
      System.out.println("Exception: " + e);
      return;
  }

  TNurse nurseJonesAgain = null;
  try {
      nurseJonesAgain = TNurse.add("12345A", "Jones");
  } catch (Exception e) {
      System.out.println("Exception: " + e); //expect duplicate
  }
  System.out.println("Nurse Jones is " + nurseJones.toString());
  System.out.println("Nurse Jones again is " +
➥nurseJonesAgain.toString());

  t.commit();
  db.close();
  ObjectStore.shutdown(true);
  System.out.println("TNurse class finished.");
  }
}
```

Figure 37.13 shows DBDemoApplet in action.

N O T E In order to read and write data on the local hard drive, an applet must be "trusted." Your browser will ask you if you want to trust this applet—you should answer "Yes." ▪

FIGURE 37.13

DBDemoApplet reads and writes data to an ObjectStore database.

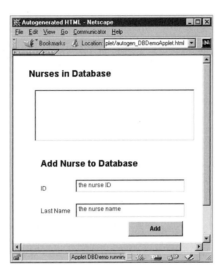

HelloApplet as a Standalone Application

Recall that our applet example (HelloApplet) ran in a Graphical User Interface (GUI) provided by the Web browser. You don't need to limit your Java GUI programming to writing applets that run only inside of Web pages—you can write a standalone application with its own graphical environment.

It is often more appropriate—or more convenient—to write a standalone Java application. A *Servlet*—a Java program that runs on your Web server—is one example of a Java application; it runs in the environment of a Web server such as Sun's Java Server. The HelloGUI program described here is another example.

Writing the Standalone Application

It is not much work at all to convert an applet into a standalone Java application. To do so, follow these steps:

1. A standalone application does not subclass Applet. Change this. Usually, your application's main class will be Frame instead:

   Applet version:

   ```
   public class HelloApplet extends Applet
   ```

   Standalone version:

   ```
   public class HelloGUI extends Frame
   ```

2. Delete the line import java.applet.Applet. Replace it with either import java.awt.Frame or import java.awt.*.

3. A Java applet overrides the init () method. A standalone application doesn't use init(). Instead, when the Java interpreter (java) runs an application, it looks for a public static void method named main().

Move all the code from the old init() into main() or into the Frame's constructor. Suppose, for example, you had written

```
public void init ()
{
  f = new Font ("Helvetica", Font.BOLD, 24);
}
```

In the standalone version, you'd write

```
// main: application initialization code goes here
public static void main (String[] args)
{
   Frame theFrame = new HelloGUI ();
   theFrame.setTitle ("Hello World!");
   theFrame.setSize (250, 100);
   f = new Font ("Helvetica", Font.BOLD, 24);
   theFrame.show ();
}
```

4. Delete your applet's init() method.

5. A standalone application typically needs to do a little more setup work: organize its frame layout, set the window title, and so on, as shown in step 3 of this list.

6. Finally, you need to run your standalone application by using the JDK java interpreter rather than the appletviewer or a Web browser.

Listing 37.12 shows a completed Java application.

Listing 37.12   *HelloGUI.java*—A Simple Standalone Java Application

```
/**
 * HelloGUI: Standalone Java application
 *
 * NOTES:
 * Compare this standalone Java application
 *    with "HelloApplet" applet.
 *
 * @version 1.0, DATE: 07.07.98
 * @author Mike Morgan
 */
import java.awt.*;                 // User Interface components

public class HelloGUI extends Frame
{
  private static Font f;

  private void drawCenteredString (Graphics g, String s)
  {
    Dimension d = getSize ();
    FontMetrics fm = getFontMetrics (f);
```

```
    int x =
      (d.width - fm.stringWidth (s)) / 2;
    int y =
      d.height -
        ( (d.height - fm.getHeight ()) / 2 );

    g.drawString (s, x, y);
}

// paint: window refresh code goes here
public void paint (Graphics g)
{
  g.setFont (f);
  g.setColor (Color.red);
  drawCenteredString (g, "Hello from Java!");
}

// main: application initialization code goes here
public static void main (String[] args)
{
  Frame theFrame = new HelloGUI ();
  theFrame.setTitle ("Hello World!");
  theFrame.setSize (250, 100);
  f = new Font ("Helvetica", Font.BOLD, 24);
  theFrame.show ();
}
}
```

Part

VII

Ch

37

The biggest practical difference between applets running on a Web page and standalone applications is that the application can generally be "trusted" and allowed to do more: open files, establish TCP/IP connections with arbitrary computers, and so on. Applets, on the other hand, are restricted from doing anything that might compromise the security of the host computer. The restricted environment that Java-enabled browsers set up for applets to run in is called a "sandbox."

▶ To learn more about the sandbox, **see** "Executable Content and Security" on **p. 1142**.

Compiling and Running the Standalone Application

You can compile and run the standalone application from the command line:

```
javac HelloGUI.java
java HelloGUI
```

If you were to run this application in AppletViewer, the output will look like what you saw earlier in this chapter as Figure 37.5.

N O T E If you look carefully at HelloGUI, you will see that a new method is there that was not in the applet version: drawCenteredString (). This code illustrates how you can use getSize() if you ever need to find out the height and width of your "Component" (here, a Frame).

drawCenteredString() also introduces FontMetrics objects and shows how you can use them. ▨

User Input and Interactivity with Java

by Mike Morgan

Interacting with People by Using Java

User interaction with your programs is by far the most important aspect of creating Java applets and applications. If your interface is bad, people will not want to use your program. Come up with an intuitive interface, however, and you could have the next "killer" app. But keep in mind that building those awesome interfaces requires you to start with some foundation.

It is that Java foundation that this chapter discusses. Learning about the different tools at your disposal enables you to build intuitive interfaces that empower your users.

The Abstract Windowing Toolkit

The Abstract Windowing Toolkit (AWT) was Java's primary user interface component package in JDK 1.0 and 1.1. You can still use the AWT, but now Sun has also introduced a new package code-named Swing. These packages contain all the programming tools you will need to interact with the user. This section describes the now-classic AWT tools; the next section describes Swing.

The AWT contains a number of familiar user interface elements. Figure 38.1 shows a Java applet with a sample of some of the components of the AWT.

FIGURE 38.1

The AWT features a number of familiar components.

Figure 38.2 shows a portion of the AWT's inheritance hierarchy.

The original AWT in version 1.0 of the JDK did its work by instantiating *peer objects* from the native operating system. Suppose you asked Java to put a button on the screen, for example, and then ran your application on a Windows machine. The Java runtime would handle your request by asking Windows to make a new button. After that, your Java object and the corresponding Windows object would communicate about mouse clicks and other events in order for the button to behave as you expected.

FIGURE 38.2
The AWT inherits all its user interface components from `Component`.

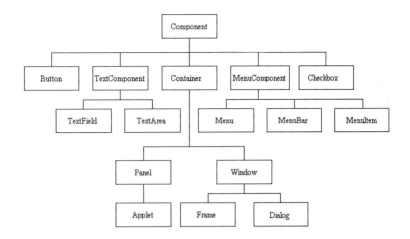

Java Foundation Classes and the Swing Components

Starting in JDK 1.1, Sun made substantial changes to the user interface components. Figure 38.3 illustrates the current state of affairs. The original AWT from JDK 1.0 is gone; in its place is the AWT that was introduced in JDK 1.1, as well as a new interface called Swing. (Swing, in turn, is part of the Java Foundation Classes, or JFC.) Java user interface classes that do their work through peer objects are still available; they're called *heavyweight components* now. As you might guess, there are also *lightweight components* that don't tie you to the peer objects of the native operating system. Instead, they support *pluggable look and feel*, enabling an end user to select from a Windows, Macintosh, or native Java appearance (among others).

N O T E In addition to pluggable look and feel, the JFC offers printing capability, clipboard data transfer, improved accessibility for people with disabilities, and much more. It's a major upgrade and well worth the time it takes to learn it. ▨

FIGURE 38.3
A revised version of the AWT is still available in the Java Foundation Classes.

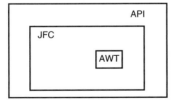

Using the Abstract Windowing Toolkit

As a platform-neutral language, Java makes many of the details of graphical user interface (GUI) programming invisible, but they don't go away. As we saw in Chapter 37, "Developing Java Applets," you can build a simple applet with a GUI interface in just 10 lines of code. (See

Listing 37.2, HelloApplet.java.) It takes just a few more lines to add a main() routine and a standalone Frame, enabling the applet to double as a GUI application. (Listing 38.1 shows such a program.)

Listing 38.1 *HelloApplication.java*—If You're Going to Write an Applet, Consider Adding the Code to Make It a Standalone GUI Application as Well

```java
import java.applet.*;
import java.awt.*;
import java.awt.event.*;

public class HelloApplication extends Applet {
  public static void main(String[] args) {
    HelloApplicationFrame theApplication =
      new HelloApplicationFrame("Hello Application");
    theApplication.setSize(200,200);
    theApplication.show();
  }

  public void paint(Graphics theGraphics) {
    theGraphics.drawString("Hello, World!", 0, 50);
  }
}

class HelloApplicationFrame extends Frame {
  private HelloApplication fApplet;

  public HelloApplicationFrame(String name) {
    super(name);
    addWindowListener(new HelloWindowAdapter());
    fApplet = new HelloApplication();
    fApplet.init();
    fApplet.start();
    add(fApplet);
  }
  class HelloWindowAdapter extends WindowAdapter {
    public void windowClosing(WindowEvent e) {
      fApplet.stop();
      fApplet.destroy();
      System.exit(0);
    }
  }
}
```

In this first section, we'll take some time to understand how this program works; then we'll use it as the foundation for building more sophisticated user interfaces with the AWT.

To learn more about programs that can run both as an application and as an applet, compile HelloApplication.java and experiment with it in both environments. (To use HelloApplication as an applet you'll need an HTML file. The one in Listing 38.2 works well.) Figure 38.4 shows this program in action.

Listing 38.2 *HelloApplication.html*—You'll Need an HTML File with an
<APPLET> Tag in Order to View *HelloApplication* as an Applet

```
<HTML>
<BODY>
<APPLET CODE="HelloApplication.class"
WIDTH="200" HEIGHT="200">
</APPLET>
</BODY>
</HTML>
```

FIGURE 38.4

HelloApplication
can be run as an applet
or as an application.

Understanding Components and Containers

You can write a one-line `main()` method and get a command-line application started. In order to
build a GUI program, however, someone needs to provide a place in which to draw. (In GUI
programs all elements of the interface are drawn—even text.) If you're writing an applet, the
browser is responsible for that detail. If you want your program to function as an application
you have to do that work yourself.

In AWT, the "place in which to draw" is called a *container*, and is derived from the Java
`java.awt.Container` class. The elements of the user interface itself are called *components*—
they all derive from `java.awt.Component`. Some of the components supplied with the AWT
include:

- `java.awt.Button`
- `java.awt.Canvas`
- `java.awt.Checkbox`
- `java.awt.Choice`
- `java.awt.Container`
- `java.awt.Label`
- `java.awt.List`
- `java.awt.Scrollbar`
- `java.awt.TextComponent`
- `java.awt.Composite`

Most of these components provide familiar functionality. A `Button`, for example, works the way you expect buttons to work in any GUI. The classes `Canvas` and `Composite` enable you to use drawing primitives to build a custom GUI component. What's most significant about this list is that it includes `java.awt.Container`, which means you can build a new drawable area and add it to an existing `Container`. The AWT supplies a variety of subclasses of `Container`, including `Panel`, `ScrollPane`, and `Window`.

`Window`, in turn, has two subclasses in the AWT: `Dialog` and `Frame`. (Each of those classes has further subclasses, but we're not concerned about those just now.) To add a GUI to an application, you must supply a top-level `Frame` into which the application can add `Components`. That's what we're doing in line 18 of Listing 38.1:

```
class HelloApplicationFrame extends Frame
```

N O T E   If you run `HelloApplication` as an application, you invoke `main()` which starts by
making a new `HelloApplicationFrame`, and then transfers control to it. If you load
`HelloApplication` as an applet, the browser and the Java runtime work together to make a new
frame inside the browser window. Then the Java runtime calls the applet's `init()`, `start()`, and
`paint()` methods. ■

Introducing the JDK 1.1 Delegation Event Model

Much of the work of writing a user interface has to do with communication. If the operating system detects a key being pressed or a mouse button coming up, it needs to notify the right application. The application, in turn, needs to find out which components are interested in that activity and send them a message. Starting with JDK 1.1, Sun introduced a new way of communicating information about events: the *delegation event model*. Prior to JDK 1.1 the model was, well, different. Don't worry about how the user interface worked in JDK 1.0—it's gone for good. Do be aware that the mechanism did change; if you have occasion to read old code or you have old books on Java, don't copy the way they do things. Its use is discouraged in JDK 1.1 or later because it doesn't support some of the newest features (such as Java's component model, JavaBeans).

N O T E   JavaBeans is an advanced topic not covered in this book. To learn more about Beans, see
Chapters 19 and 20 of *Using Java 1.2* (Que, 1998), or read *Sams Teach Yourself
JavaBeans in 21 Days* (Sams, 1997). ■

So how does the delegation event model work? Every element of communication between the GUI and the program is defined as an *event*. Application classes register their interest in particular events from particular components by asking the component to add their *listener* to a list. When the event occurs, the event source notifies all registered listeners.

Two kinds of events exist: low-level events and semantic events. All of them are derived from `java.awt.AWTEvent`. A low-level event is concerned with the physical aspects of the user interface—mouse clicks, key presses, and the like. Semantic events are based on low-level events. To choose a menu item, for example, a user may click the menu bar, then click a menu item. To "click" means to press the mouse button down and then up again. This series of low-level events (mouse-down on the menu bar, mouse-up on the menu bar, mouse-down on the menu item, and mouse-up on the menu item) is combined into one semantic event.

Class `ComponentEvent` includes a special type of event that is not used with the delegation event model: `PaintEvent`. A `PaintEvent` signals that the operating system wants to redraw a portion of the user interface. A component must override `paint()` or `update()` to make sure it handles the `PaintEvent` correctly.

Look at line 23 of Listing 38.1:

```
addWindowListener(new HelloWindowAdapter());
```

This line is part of `HelloApplicationFrame`'s constructor. As the new `Frame` is being built, this line tells the `Frame` that it is interested in certain events. Rather than notify it directly, however, the constructor tells it to send the notifications to an `adapter`—a convenience class that handles only one kind of event. Our adapter is called `HelloWindowAdapter`—it's an instance of `WindowAdapter`, which is interested in `WindowEvents`. When the frame sends a `WindowEvent`, `HelloWindowAdapter` looks to see if the message is `windowClosing`. If it isn't, `HelloWindowAdapter` ignores it, but if it is, the program starts the process of shutting down.

Because `HelloApplication` is written as both an applet and an application, it begins its shutdown by calling the methods a browser calls when it wants to shut down an applet—`stop()` and `destroy()`. Finally it calls `exit()`, ending the application and enabling the `Frame` to close.

Class `AWTEvent` also includes semantic events:

- `ActionEvent`—Notifies your program about component-specific actions such as button clicks
- `AdjustmentEvent`—Tells you that a scrollbar has been adjusted
- `ItemEvent`—Notifies your program when the user interacts with a choice, list, or check box
- `TextEvent`—Tells you when the user changes text in a `TextArea` or `TextField` component

> **N O T E** Many user actions, such as mouse clicks, send events at both the low level and the semantic level. If you move your mouse onto a button and click the mouse button, you'll get a series of `MouseEvents`: one for when the mouse enters the component, one for the button press, one for the button release, and one for the click itself. You'll also get a single `ActionEvent` from the button saying that it was clicked. Unless you need fine-grained control of the user interface, listen for semantic events.

Drawing and *add*ing—Constructing the User Interface

In Listing 38.1 we implemented the applet's `paint` method by calling `drawString()` on the `Graphics` object. The `drawString()` method is one of the drawing primitives that has been available in Java from its earliest days. `Graphics`' drawing methods also include

- draw3DRect()
- drawArc()
- drawBytes()
- drawChars()
- drawImage()
- drawLine()
- drawOval()
- drawPolygon()
- drawPolyline()
- drawRect()
- drawRoundRect()

Graphics also supports a whole range of fill..., get..., and set... methods. Much of the time, however, you're less interested in the image that appears on the screen than in the controls, such as Buttons and TextFields (which are implemented as Components). To add controls to your Container, you call the Container's add() method. See line 27 of Listing 38.1:

```
add(fApplet);
```

Listing 38.3 shows a more elaborate version of Listing 38.1. In this program, you see more AWT components at work: a Button, a TextField, a Checkbox, a Choice, and several Labels.

TIP You may have noticed that the AWT doesn't include *radio buttons*—a group of buttons designed so that, at most, one selection is active. To make radio buttons, just build a CheckboxGroup—it's documented in the JDK documentation.

Listing 38.3   *HelloPlus.java*—This Version of the Application/Applet Has Some Working AWT Components

```java
import java.applet.*;
import java.awt.*;
import java.awt.event.*;

public class HelloPlus extends Applet {
  private Button fButton;
  private TextField fTextField;
  private Label fLabelForTextField;
  private Checkbox fCheckbox;
  private OKDialog fDialog;
  private Label fLabelForChoice;

  public static void main(String[] args) {
    HelloApplicationFrame theApplication =
      new HelloApplicationFrame("Hello Application");
    theApplication.setSize(200,200);
    theApplication.show();
  }
```

```java
public void init() {
  add (new Label("Hello, World!"));

  fTextField = new TextField("TextField");
  add(fTextField);
  fLabelForTextField = new Label("Your text is TextField");
  add(fLabelForTextField);

  setBackground(java.awt.Color.red);
  fButton = new Button("White");
  fButton.setBackground(java.awt.Color.white);
  add(fButton);

  fCheckbox = new Checkbox("Checkbox");
  add(fCheckbox);
  fDialog = OKDialog.makeDialog("You clicked the checkbox!");
  Choice theChoice = new Choice();
  theChoice.addItem("Choice Item 1");
  theChoice.addItem("Choice Item 2");
  theChoice.addItem("Choice Item 3");
  add(theChoice);
  fLabelForChoice = new Label("You haven't chosen anything");
  add(fLabelForChoice);

  fButton.addActionListener(new ActionListener(){
    public void actionPerformed(ActionEvent e) {
      if (fButton.getLabel() == "White") {
        setBackground(java.awt.Color.white);
        fButton.setLabel("Red");
      }
      else {
        setBackground(java.awt.Color.red);
        fButton.setLabel("White");
      }
      Component theComponents[] = getComponents();
      try {
        if (theComponents.length == 0)
          throw (new AWTException("Cannot find the components"));
      } catch (AWTException theException) {
        System.err.println("Exception: " + theException.getMessage());
        theException.printStackTrace();
        System.exit(1);
      }
      for (short theIndex = 0;
           theIndex < theComponents.length; theIndex++)
            getComponent(theIndex).setBackground(getBackground());
      if (fButton.getLabel() == "White")
        fButton.setBackground(java.awt.Color.white);
      else
        fButton.setBackground(java.awt.Color.red);
    }
  });

  fTextField.addActionListener(new ActionListener() {
```

continues

Listing 38.3   Continued

```java
      public void actionPerformed(ActionEvent e) {
        fLabelForTextField.setText("Your text is " +
                                   fTextField.getText());
      }
    });

    fCheckbox.addItemListener(new ItemListener(){
      public void itemStateChanged(ItemEvent e) {
        if (fCheckbox.getState())  // the box is checked
          fDialog.show();
        else
          fDialog.setVisible(false);
      }
    });

    theChoice.addItemListener(new ItemListener() {
      public void itemStateChanged(ItemEvent e) {
        try {
          Object theSelectedItem[] =
            e.getItemSelectable().getSelectedObjects();
          if (theSelectedItem.length != 1)
            throw(
              new AWTException(
                "Number of selected items in choice is " +
                                theSelectedItem.length));
          fLabelForChoice.setText("Your choice is " +
            theSelectedItem[0]);
        } catch (AWTException theException) {
          System.err.println("Exception: " + theException.getMessage());
          theException.printStackTrace();
          System.exit(1);
        } // end catch
      } // end method
    }); // end addItemListener
  } // end init

} // end HelloPlus

class HelloApplicationFrame extends Frame {
  private HelloPlus fApplet;

  public HelloApplicationFrame(String name) {
    super(name);
    addWindowListener(new HelloWindowAdapter());
    fApplet = new HelloPlus();
    fApplet.init();
    fApplet.start();
    add(fApplet);
  }

  // We're still within HelloApplicationFrame;
  // these adapters are inner classes
  class HelloWindowAdapter extends WindowAdapter {
```

```
    public void windowClosing(WindowEvent e) {
      fApplet.stop();
      fApplet.destroy();
      System.exit(0);
    }
  } // end inner class HelloWindowAdapter
} // end HelloApplicationFrame

class OKDialog extends Dialog {
  private Button fOKButton;
  static private Frame fFrame;

  private OKDialog(Frame theParent, String theMessage) {
    super(theParent, true); // call Dialog's modal constructor
    fOKButton = new Button("OK");
    add(fOKButton, BorderLayout.CENTER );
    Label theMessageLabel = new Label(theMessage);
    add (theMessageLabel, BorderLayout.NORTH );
    pack();

    fOKButton.addActionListener(new ActionListener(){
      public void actionPerformed(ActionEvent e) {
        setVisible( false );
      }
    }
    );

  } // end constructor

  static public OKDialog makeDialog(String theMessage) {
    if (fFrame == null)
      fFrame = new Frame();
    OKDialog theResult = new OKDialog(fFrame, theMessage);
    fFrame.setSize(theResult.getSize().width,
                   theResult.getSize().height);
    return theResult;
  }
} // end OKDialog class
```

If you compile HelloPlus.java and run it as an application or as an applet, your screen will resemble Figure 38.5. This section describes how the code in HelloPlus.java works.

FIGURE 38.5

By default, HelloPlus fills a 200 × 200 pixel panel.

Part

VII

Ch

38

The first difference you'll notice between HelloPlus and HelloApplication is that we've added several data members to the class: fButton, fTextField, and so forth. Often you'll need to refer back to user-interface components during the life of the program—it's convenient to have all the components available as class members. (If you don't want to carry these references around in the class, you don't have to—theChoice is an example of a user interface component that is not referenced as an instance variable.)

The biggest area of change is in init(). We've used init() to build the user interface—that way, the components are added to the applet when we're running as an applet, and the application frame when we're running as an application.

Understanding *fTextField* and *fLabelForTextField*   We start init() by adding our ubiquitous Hello, World! label. Then we instantiate a new TextField and add it to the interface. We follow this with a new Label, likewise added to the interface. Now go down to lines 72 through 77:

```
fTextField.addActionListener(new ActionListener() {
    public void actionPerformed(ActionEvent e) {
        fLabelForTextField.setText("Your text is " +
                            fTextField.getText());
    }
});
```

Here's a construct we haven't seen before. Because we added a TextField, we're able to get a semantic event—the ActionEvent—which has only one method: actionPerformed(). Although the action differs from one component to the next, the method for listening to these events is the same. We don't need an adapter because only one method is in the event. Instead, we declare a new ActionListener and define it right here inside addActionListener(). In this case, the body of the method is quite simple:

```
fLabelForTextField.setText("Your text is " +
                    fTextField.getText());
```

When you change the text in the text field and press Enter, the Java runtime sends an ActionEvent to your listening program, which changes the text in fLabelForTextField.

 TIP   The components in HelloPlus.java don't need adapters because their events have only one method. If you want to receive events with more than one method, consider using adapters—abstract classes that implement an interface and "stub out" the methods.

Understanding *fButton*   This version of the program starts with a red background on the frame and a white button labeled "White." When you click the button, it sends an ActionEvent to the listening program. The definition of the listener starts at line 43 of Listing 38.3:

```
fButton.addActionListener(new ActionListener(){
    public void actionPerformed(ActionEvent e) {
        if (fButton.getLabel() == "White") {
            setBackground(java.awt.Color.white);
            fButton.setLabel("Red");
        }
        else {
            setBackground(java.awt.Color.red);
```

```
        fButton.setLabel("White");
      }
      Component theComponents[] = getComponents();
      try {
        if (theComponents.length == 0)
          throw (new AWTException("Cannot find the components"));
      } catch (AWTException theException) {
        System.err.println("Exception: " + theException.getMessage());
        theException.printStackTrace();
        System.exit(1);
      }
      for (short theIndex = 0;
           theIndex < theComponents.length; theIndex++)
          getComponent(theIndex).setBackground(getBackground());
      if (fButton.getLabel() == "White")
        fButton.setBackground(java.awt.Color.white);
      else
        fButton.setBackground(java.awt.Color.red);
    }
  });
```

We handle the button click in three steps:

1. Change the `Container`'s background and the label of the button to reflect the `Container`'s new state.

2. Step through each `Component` in the `Container`, setting its background to match the background of the `Container`.

3. Because step 2 changed the background of the button, change it back to match the button's label.

Understanding *fCheckbox* and *fDialog*   The `Checkbox`, named `fCheckbox`, is added in the same way as the other components we've seen, but then we do something different—we make a new `Dialog`. Our plan is to have a modal dialog box come up whenever the end user checks the `Checkbox`, and we have to go through a couple of extra steps to make this work.

> **N O T E**   Unlike `Button` and `TextField`, a `Checkbox` doesn't send an `ActionEvent`. Instead, it sends an `ItemEvent`. The principle is the same as the `ActionEvent`, however—we just instantiate a new `ItemListener`. ▪

If you examine the documentation for class `Dialog`, you'll see that all its constructors need an owner—a `Frame` or another `Dialog` that serves as the parent of the new `Dialog` in the `Window` hierarchy. If you're writing a pure application, you can use the application's `Frame` as the owner of the `Dialog`. In this case, we can be called as either an applet or an application. An `Applet` is a `Panel`, not a `Frame`, so we have to start up our own `Frame` to serve as the parent.

At the bottom of the `HelloPlus.java` listing you'll see a definition of class `OKDialog`. After the constructor (which is private) you'll see a factory method: `makeDialog()`:

```
static public OKDialog makeDialog(String theMessage) {
    if (fFrame == null)
      fFrame = new Frame();
```

```
        OKDialog theResult = new OKDialog(fFrame, theMessage);
        fFrame.setSize(theResult.getSize().width,
                       theResult.getSize().height);
        return theResult;
    }
} // end OKDialog class
```

> **N O T E**   A factory method returns a new object based on an existing object. For example,
> `java.awt.geom.Arc2D` supports `makeBounds()`, a factory method that returns a new
> `Rectangle2D` based on the bounding rectangle of the arc. ■

The class `OKDialog` has a static `Frame` member `fFrame`. When `makeDialog()` is first called, it instantiates a new `Frame` and assigns it to `fFrame`. Next, `makeDialog()` instantiates a new `OKDialog`, using `fFrame` as the parent. It scales the `Frame` to the same size as the `OKDialog` and returns a reference to the `OKDialog` for use by the calling class.

The `OKDialog` constructor instantiates a button and a label and adds them to the dialog, then calls `pack()` to shrink the dialog window down to a size that contains the components. The listener that is attached to the dialog's button makes the dialog window invisible.

> **N O T E**   You may have noticed that the calls to `add()` in `OKDialog()` include strings. For
> example, we add the message label by saying   ·
>
> `add(theMessageLabel, BorderLayout.NORTH);`
>
> These strings are part of the `BorderLayout`, which is described in the next section. ■

Understanding *theChoice*   In Java, a `Choice` is a pop-up list that displays one item at a time. We add a `Choice` (called `theChoice`—it's a local variable, not an instance variable) and a matching `Label`. Then we add an `ItemListener`. When we get an `itemStateChanged()` event, we use `getItemSelectable()` to get a reference back to `theChoice` and then call `getSelectedObjects()` to get an array of selected items. If `theChoice` is working correctly, we should be able to get back only a single item. (We throw an exception if that condition doesn't hold.) Finally, we modify `fLabelForChoice` to reflect the user's choice.

Working with Layouts

Recall that several of the sample applets shown in Chapter 37 use layout managers such as `CardLayout` or `GridLayout` to manage the placement of components on the screen. You can see the effect of a layout manager by resizing the HelloPlus window. Figure 38.6 shows a maximized window in which the components have room to spread out; in Figure 38.7, the window is tall and narrow—the components appear one above the other.

FIGURE 38.6

When the components have enough room, they're laid out one beside the other.

FIGURE 38.7

When the window is narrow, the components flow one above the next.

You don't have to worry about the precise location of every component or whether the user is working on a 640 × 480 screen or an older Macintosh with a 9-inch monitor. That's because every Java window has an associated LayoutManager. If you don't specify the manager, Java supplies one for you. This section walks you through the standard layouts:

- FlowLayout—The components are added left to right, top to bottom. This layout is the default layout for Panel and its derived classes, including Applet.
- GridLayout—Similar to FlowLayout, but each component gets an equal-sized cell.
- BorderLayout—Divides the container into five areas: North, South, East, West, and Center. This layout is the default layout for Windows (except special-purpose Windows such as FileDialog).
- CardLayout—Used to display one component at a time, like a stack of index cards.
- GridBagLayout—A flexible (and complicated) layout used when none of the other layout managers will do.

N O T E By default, Java supplies a layout manager for every new Container. It's possible to turn it off (by calling setLayout(null)) and then use absolute positioning to lay out your components. That's a poor idea, though—your application won't display correctly on different-sized monitors. ▪

 If you find that none of the standard layout managers meet your needs, you can make your own implementation of LayoutManager2. (LayoutManager, a simpler class, doesn't support a constraints object, so it's less useful.) You'll find details of this process in Chapter 11 of *Using Java 1.2* (Que, 1997).

Using *FlowLayout*

Figures 38.6 and 38.7 showed how HelloPlus.java looks when you use the default layout for Panel, FlowLayout. (Recall that an Applet is a kind of Panel.) If you're happy with this design— all the components laid out left to right, top to bottom, with each component taking up whatever amount of space it requires—you don't have to do anything. Just call `add()` to place each component into the `Container`.

If you're working in a `Window`, where the default layout is `BorderLayout`, you'll need to change the layout manager if you want a `FlowLayout`. Just write

```
setLayout(new FlowLayout());
```

before you `add()` any components.

Using *GridLayout*

Figure 38.8 shows how HelloPlus looks in a `GridLayout`. A `GridLayout` is similar to a `FlowLayout`, but each component gets the same size cell as all the others. The cell size is determined by the size of the largest component. To apply a `GridLayout` to `HelloPlus`, add this line to the top of `init()`:

```
setLayout(new GridLayout(rows, columns));
```

where *rows* gives the number of rows and *columns* gives the number of columns. If you set either value to zero, Java will use as many of that dimension as necessary to display all the components in the layout.

> **N O T E**   If you specify both the number of rows and the number of columns and then add more
> components than the product of those two numbers, the layout manager will behave as
> though you had specified a zero for the number of columns. I don't recommend that you rely upon this
> feature—it's not documented, so Sun could change the behavior in the future.

FIGURE 38.8

This grid was produced with `rows=0` and `columns=2`.

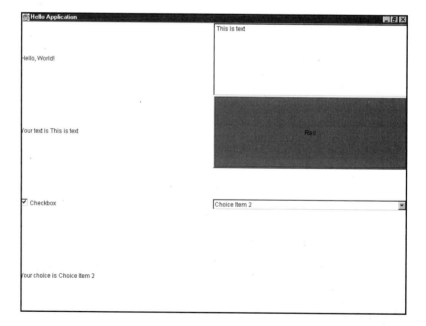

Using *BorderLayout*

`BorderLayout` is particularly appropriate when you have one large component and several smaller ones because you can place the large component in the center position. Figure 38.9 illustrates the general design of `BorderLayout`, and Figure 38.10 shows `HelloPlus.java` in this layout.

FIGURE 38.9

Think of BorderLayout as a compass, with the largest component in the center.

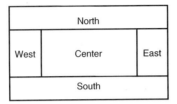

FIGURE 38.10

You need to put some components into panels to lay out more than five components in a BorderLayout.

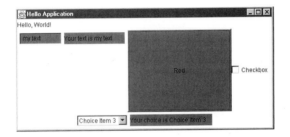

To modify `HelloPlus.java` to use a `BorderLayout`, you need to make three changes:

- Set the layout to `BorderLayout` in `init()`.
- Assemble some of the components into groups on `Panels`.
- Change `add()` so that it passes the location `String`.

Here's a code snippet that shows these changes in **bold**:

```
public void init() {
    setLayout(new BorderLayout());

    add (new Label("Hello, World!"), BorderLayout.NORTH);

    Panel theWestPanel = new Panel();
    fTextField = new TextField("TextField");
    theWestPanel.add(fTextField);
    fLabelForTextField = new Label("Your text is TextField");
    theWestPanel.add(fLabelForTextField);
    add(theWestPanel, BorderLayout.WEST);

    setBackground(java.awt.Color.red);
    fButton = new Button("White");
    fButton.setBackground(java.awt.Color.white);
    add(fButton, BorderLayout.CENTER);
```

```
fCheckbox = new Checkbox("Checkbox");
add(fCheckbox, BorderLayout.EAST);
fDialog = OKDialog.makeDialog("You clicked the checkbox!");

Panel theSouthPanel = new Panel();

Choice theChoice = new Choice();
theChoice.addItem("Choice Item 1");
theChoice.addItem("Choice Item 2");
theChoice.addItem("Choice Item 3");
theSouthPanel.add(theChoice);
fLabelForChoice = new Label("You haven't chosen anything");
theSouthPanel.add(fLabelForChoice);
add(theSouthPanel, BorderLayout.SOUTH);
```

TIP   At some point you'll change the layout and discover that your components are no longer visible. The reason is that you *must* use the two-parameter version of add() when you add components to a BorderLayout. Double-check the Constraint, too—the only valid Constraints are BorderLayout.NORTH, SOUTH, EAST, WEST, and CENTER. If you leave off the Constraint or mis-type it, you may not see your component.

Using *CardLayout*

Figure 38.11 shows how HelloPlus.java looks when you switch to CardLayout. Like BorderLayout, you need to do more than just call setLayout(). CardLayout shows one component at a time; you call next() and previous() to move from one card to another. In the design shown in Figure 38.11, there's a BorderLayout for the application, then a CardLayout in a Panel in the "South" position to hold the contents. Two buttons are in a Panel in the "North" position; by clicking those buttons you can issue calls to next() and previous(). The code changes from HelloPlus are

```
public void init() {

    setLayout(new BorderLayout());
    Panel theControls = new Panel();
    Button thePreviousButton = new Button("Previous");
    theControls.add(thePreviousButton);
    Button theNextButton = new Button("Next");
    theControls.add(theNextButton);

    add(theControls, BorderLayout.NORTH);

    fContents = new Panel();
    fContents.setLayout(new CardLayout());

    fContents.add (new Label("Hello, World!"), "Hello");

    Panel theTextPanel = new Panel();
    fTextField = new TextField("TextField");
    theTextPanel.add(fTextField);
    fLabelForTextField = new Label("Your text is TextField");
    theTextPanel.add(fLabelForTextField);
    fContents.add(theTextPanel, "Text");
```

```
        setBackground(java.awt.Color.red);
        fButton = new Button("White");
        fButton.setBackground(java.awt.Color.white);
        fContents.add(fButton, "Button");

        fCheckbox = new Checkbox("Checkbox");
        fContents.add(fCheckbox, "Checkbox");
        fDialog = OKDialog.makeDialog("You clicked the checkbox!");

        Panel theChoicePanel = new Panel();
        Choice theChoice = new Choice();
        theChoice.addItem("Choice Item 1");
        theChoice.addItem("Choice Item 2");
        theChoice.addItem("Choice Item 3");
        theChoicePanel.add(theChoice);
        fLabelForChoice = new Label("You haven't chosen anything");
        theChoicePanel.add(fLabelForChoice);
        fContents.add(theChoicePanel, "Choice");

        add(" fContents, BorderLayout.SOUTH);

        theNextButton.addActionListener(new ActionListener() {
          public void actionPerformed(ActionEvent e) {
            CardLayout theLayout = (CardLayout) fContents.getLayout();
            theLayout.next(fContents);
        }});

        thePreviousButton.addActionListener(new ActionListener() {
          public void actionPerformed(ActionEvent e) {
            CardLayout theLayout = (CardLayout) fContents.getLayout();
            theLayout.previous(fContents);
        }});
```

FIGURE 38.11

You can use CardLayout to simulate a deck of index cards, with one card showing at a time.

N O T E   In addition to next() and previous(), the CardLayout supports first(), last(), and show(). The latter enables you to display a card by name. ■

Using *GridBagLayout*

Although you can control such factors as alignment and horizontal and vertical gap in the other layout managers, the GridBagLayout gives you the ultimate in flexibility. At its simplest, GridBagLayout works much like a grid, except that it puts each component in a cell of its preferred size. The total area that a component occupies is called its "display area." You specify suggestions—called GridBagConstraints—that further control how the layout will appear.

The `GridBagConstraints` class has a number of variables to control the placement of a component:

- `gridx` and `gridy` are the coordinates of the cell where the next component should be placed. (If the component occupies more than one cell, these coordinates are for the upper-left cell of the component.) The upper-left corner of the `GridBagLayout` is at 0, 0. The default value for both `gridx` and `gridy` is `GridBagConstraints.RELATIVE`, which for `gridx` means the cell to the right of the last component that was added; for `gridy` it means the cell just below the last component added.

- `gridwidth` and `gridheight` tell how many cells wide and how many cells tall a component should be. The default for both `gridwidth` and `gridheight` is 1. If you want this component to be the last one on a row, use `GridBagConstraint.REMAINDER` for the `gridwidth`. (Use this same value for `gridheight` if this component should be the last one in a column.) Use `GridBagConstraint.RELATIVE` if the component should be the next-to-last component in a row or column.

- `fill` tells the `GridBagLayout` what to do when a component is smaller than its display area. The default value, `GridBagConstraint.NONE`, causes the component size to remain unchanged. `GridBagConstraint.HORIZONTAL` causes the component to be widened to take up its whole display area horizontally while leaving its height unchanged. `GridBagConstraint.VERTICAL` causes the component to be stretched vertically while leaving the width unchanged. `GridBagConstraint.BOTH` causes the component to be stretched in both directions to completely fill its display area.

- `ipadx` and `ipady` tell the `GridBagLayout` how many pixels to add to the size of the component in the x and y direction. The pixels are added on both sides of the component, so an `ipadx` of 4 causes the size of a component to be increased by 4 on the left and also 4 on the right. Remember that the component size grows by twice the amount of padding because the padding is added to both sides. The default for both `ipadx` and `ipady` is 0.

- `insets` is an instance of an `Insets` class and indicates how much blank space to leave between the borders of a component and edges of its display area. The `Insets` class has separate values for the top, bottom, left, and right insets.

- `anchor` is used when a component is smaller than its display area. It indicates where the component should be placed within the display area. The default value is `GridBagConstraint.CENTER`, which indicates that the component should be in the center of the display area. The other values are all compass points: `GridbagConstraints.NORTH`, `GridBagConstraints.NORTHEAST`, `GridBagConstraints.EAST`, `GridBagConstraints.SOUTHEAST`, `GridBagConstraints.SOUTH`, `GridBagConstraints.SOUTHWEST`, `GridBagConstraints.WEST`, and `GridBagConstraints.NORTHWEST`. As with the `BorderLayout` class, `NORTH` indicates the top of the screen; `EAST` is to the right.

- `weightx` and `weighty` are used to set relative sizes of components. A component with a `weightx` of 2.0, for instance, takes up twice the horizontal space of a component with a `weightx` of 1.0. Because these values are relative, no difference exists between all components in a row having a weight of 1.0 or a weight of 3.0. You should assign a weight to at least one component in each direction; otherwise, the GridBagLayout squeezes your components toward the center of the container.

Figure 38.12 shows HelloPlus.java laid out using a GridBagLayout. The code that produced this layout is as follows:

```
public void init() {
    GridBagLayout theGridBag = new GridBagLayout();
    setLayout(theGridBag);
    GridBagConstraints theConstraints =
      new GridBagConstraints();

    // have all components expand to their largest size
    theConstraints.fill = GridBagConstraints.BOTH;

    // set the first label to span a row
    theConstraints.gridwidth = GridBagConstraints.REMAINDER;
    theConstraints.weightx = 1.0;

    Label theHelloLabel = new Label("Hello, World!", java.awt.Label.CENTER);
    theGridBag.setConstraints(theHelloLabel, theConstraints);
    add(theHelloLabel);

    // the text field and its label are a row
    theConstraints.gridwidth = GridBagConstraints.RELATIVE;
    theConstraints.weightx = 1.0;
    fTextField = new TextField("TextField");
    theGridBag.setConstraints(fTextField, theConstraints);
    add(fTextField);
    fLabelForTextField = new Label("Your text is TextField");
    theConstraints.gridwidth = GridBagConstraints.REMAINDER;
    theConstraints.weightx = 0.0;
    theGridBag.setConstraints(fLabelForTextField, theConstraints);
    add(fLabelForTextField);

    // make the button double-height
    setBackground(java.awt.Color.red);
    theConstraints.gridwidth = 1;
    theConstraints.gridheight = 2;
    theConstraints.weightx = 0.0;
    theConstraints.weighty = 1.0;
    fButton = new Button("White");
    theGridBag.setConstraints(fButton, theConstraints);
    fButton.setBackground(java.awt.Color.white);
    add(fButton);

    // let the checkbox end its own row
    theConstraints.gridwidth = GridBagConstraints.REMAINDER;
    theConstraints.gridheight = 1;
    fCheckbox = new Checkbox("Checkbox");
    theConstraints.weightx = theConstraints.weighty = 0.0;
    theGridBag.setConstraints(fCheckbox, theConstraints);
    add(fCheckbox);
    fDialog = OKDialog.makeDialog("You clicked the checkbox!");

    // and the choice and corresponding label span another row
```

Part
VII

Ch
38

```
Choice theChoice = new Choice();
theChoice.addItem("Choice Item 1");
theChoice.addItem("Choice Item 2");
theChoice.addItem("Choice Item 3");
theConstraints.gridwidth = GridBagConstraints.RELATIVE;
theConstraints.weightx = 1.0;
theGridBag.setConstraints(theChoice, theConstraints);
add(theChoice);
fLabelForChoice = new Label("You haven't chosen anything");
theConstraints.gridwidth = GridBagConstraints.REMAINDER;
theConstraints.weightx = 0.0;
theGridBag.setConstraints(fLabelForChoice, theConstraints);
add(fLabelForChoice);
```

FIGURE 38.12

Use the data members of the GridBagConstraint to set up each row of a GridBagLayout.

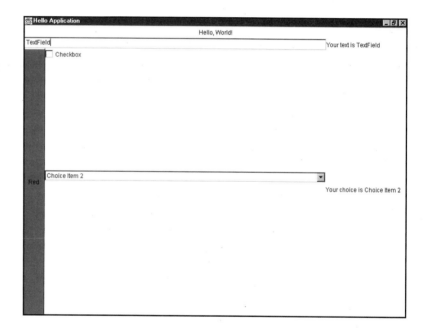

As you can see, most of the changes have to do with manipulating the data members of the GridBagConstraint as we move from row to row and cell to cell.

Adding Menus to Frames

We first saw a frame in Listing 38.1. You can attach a MenuBar class to a frame to provide drop-down menu capabilities. To make a menu bar and add it to a frame, write

```
MenuBar myMenuBar = new MenuBar();
myFrame.setMenuBar( myMenuBar );
```

After you have a menu bar, you can add menus to it. The following code fragment creates a menu called "File" and adds it to the menu bar:

```
Menu fileMenu = new Menu( "File" );
myMenuBar.add( fileMenu );
```

Some windowing systems enable you to create menus that stay up after you release the mouse button. These are referred to as "tear-off" menus. You can specify that a menu is a tear-off menu when you create it:

```
// true indicates it can be torn off
Menu tearOffMenu = new Menu( "Tear Me Off", true );
```

In addition to adding submenus, you will want to add menu items to your menus. Menu items are the parts of a menu the user actually selects. Menus are used to contain menu items as well as submenus. The File menu on many systems, for example, contains menu items such as New, Open, Save, and Save As. You can add menu items to a menu in two ways. You can add an item name by writing

```
// Add an "Open" option to the file menu
fileMenu.add( "Open" );
```

You can also add an instance of a MenuItem class to a menu:

```
// Make a "Save" menu item
MenuItem saveMenuItem = new MenuItem( "Save" );

// Add the "Save" option to the file menu
fileMenu.add( saveMenuItem );
```

Part
VII

Ch

38

You can enable and disable menu items by using setEnabled method. When you disable a menu item, it still appears on the menu, but it usually appears in gray (depending on the windowing system). You cannot select disabled menu items. The format for setEnabled is this:

```
// Disable the save option from the file menu
saveMenuItem.setEnabled( false );

// Enable the save option again
saveMenuItem.setEnabled( true );
```

In addition to menu items, you can add submenus and menu separators to a menu. A separator is a line that appears on the menu to separate sections of the menu. To add a separator, just call the addSeparator method:

```
fileMenu.addSeparator();
```

To add a submenu, make a new instance of a menu and add it to the current menu:

```
Menu printSubmenu = new Menu( "Print" );
fileMenu.add( printSubmenu );
printSubmenu.add( "Print Preview" );
        // Add print preview as option on Print menu
printSubmenu.add( "Print Document" );
        // Add print document as option on Print menu
```

You can also add special check box menu items. These items function like check box buttons. The first time you select one, it becomes checked or "on." The next time you select it, it becomes unchecked or "off." The code to add a check box menu item:

```
CheckboxMenuItem autoSaveOption = new CheckboxMenuItem( "Auto-save" );
fileMenu.add( autoSaveOption );
```

You can check to see whether a check box menu item is checked with getState:

```
if ( autoSaveOption.getState() )
{
    // autoSaveOption is checked, or "on"
}
else
{
    // autoSaveOption is off
}
```

You can set the current state of a check box menu item with `setState`:

```
autoSaveOption.setState( true );
```

Typically, menus are added to a menu bar in a left-to-right fashion. Some windowing systems, such as Microsoft Windows 95, have a special "Help" menu that is on the far right of a menu bar. You can add such a menu to your menu bar with the `setHelpMenu` method:

```
Menu helpMenu = new Menu();
myMenuBar.setHelpMenu( helpMenu );
```

Using AWT Menus   Whenever a menu item is selected, it generates an `ActionEvent`. Just add an `ActionListener` for each menu item to handle events.

Listing 38.4 shows an application that sets up a simple File menu with New, Open, and Save menu items, a check box called Auto-Save, and a Print submenu with two menu items on it:

Listing 38.4   *MenuApplication*—Add Menus and Menu Items to a Menu in a Frame

```
import java.awt.*;
import java.applet.*;

public class MenuApplication extends Frame {
  public static void main( String[] args ) {
    new MenuApplication();
  }

  public MenuApplication() {
    //  Construct the Frame
    super( "Menu Example" );

    // Add the menu bar
    MenuBar theMenuBar = new MenuBar();
    setMenuBar( theMenuBar );

    // Make the file menu and add it to the menubar...
    Menu aFileMenu = new Menu( "File" );
    theMenuBar.add( aFileMenu );

    // Add the New and Open menuitems
    aFileMenu.add( new MenuItem( "New" ) );
    aFileMenu.add( new MenuItem( "Open" ) );

    // Add a (disabled) Save menuitem
```

```
        MenuItem theSaveMenuItem = new MenuItem( "Save" );
        theSaveMenuItem.disable();
        aFileMenu.add( theSaveMenuItem );

        // Add an Auto-Save checkbox, followed by a separator
        aFileMenu.add( new CheckboxMenuItem( "Auto-Save" ) );
        aFileMenu.addSeparator();

        // Add the Print submenu
        Menu thePrintSubmenu = new Menu( "Print" );
        aFileMenu.add( thePrintSubmenu );
        thePrintSubmenu.add( "Print Preview" );
        thePrintSubmenu.add( "Print Document" );

        // Resize the frame before it can be shown
        setSize( 300, 200 );

        // Make the frame appear on the screen
        show();
    }
}
```

Part
VII

Ch
38

Figure 38.13 shows the output from the MenuApplication program, with the Print Document option in the process of being selected.

FIGURE 38.13

The AWT provides a number of popular menu features, including checked menu items, disabled menu items, and separators.

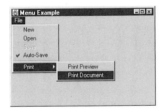

AWT Dialogs

Like Frames, Dialogs are windows. Unlike Frames, Dialogs are designed to be pop-up windows that are not quite as flexible as frames. Dialogs are used for things such as "Are you sure you want to quit?" pop-ups, better known as message boxes. You can set a dialog to be either "modal" or "non-modal." The term *modal* means the dialog box blocks input to other windows while it is being shown. This technique is useful for dialogs where you want to stop everything and get a crucial question answered, such as "Are you sure you want to quit?" An example of a non-modal dialog box is a control panel that changes settings in an application while the application continues to run.

Making Dialogs   To make a dialog, you must first have a frame. A dialog cannot belong directly to an applet. However, an applet may instantiate a frame to which the dialog can then belong. You must specify whether a dialog is modal or non-modal when you instantiate it; you cannot change its modality after it has been built. The following example makes a modal dialog whose parent is myFrame:

```
// true means model dialog
Dialog myDialog = new Dialog( myFrame, true );
```

You can also give a dialog a title:

```
Dialog myDialog = new Dialog( myFrame, "A Non-Modal Dialog", false );
```

N O T E Because a dialog cannot belong directly to an applet, your use of dialogs can be somewhat limited. One solution is to make a dummy frame as the dialog's parent. Unfortunately, you cannot make modal dialogs this way because only the frame and its children would have their input blocked—the applet would continue on its merry way. A better solution is to use the technique shown in `HelloPlus.java` (Listing 38.3) in which you make a standalone application using frames and then have a "bootstrap" applet make a frame and run the real applet in it. ■

After you have instantiated a dialog, you can make it visible using the show method:

```
myDialog.show();
```

Dialog Features The Dialog class has several methods in common with the Frame class:

```
void setResizable( boolean );
boolean isResizable();
void setTitle(String);
String getTitle();
```

In addition, the isModal method returns true if the dialog is modal.

A Reusable OK Dialog Box Listing 38.5 shows the OKDialog class that provides an OK dialog box that displays a message and waits for you to click OK.

Listing 38.5 *OKDialog*—Pop Up a Simple Dialog Box with an OK Button

```
import java.awt.*;

public class OKDialog extends Dialog {
  protected Button  fOKButton;
  protected static Frame  fFrame;

  public OKDialog( Frame theParent, String theMessage )
  {
    super( theParent, true );    // Call the parent's constructor

    // This Dialog box uses the GridBagLayout.
    GridBagLayout theGridBagLayout = new GridBagLayout();
    GridBagConstraints theConstraints = new GridBagConstraints();

    // Make the OK button and the message to display
    fOKButton = new Button( "OK" );
    Label aMessageLabel = new Label( theMessage );

    setLayout( theGridBagLayout );

    // The message should not fill, it should be centered within this area, with
    // some extra padding.  The gridwidth of REMAINDER means this is the only
```

```
    // thing on its row, and the gridheight of RELATIVE means there should only
    // be one thing below it.
    theConstraints.fill = GridBagConstraints.NONE;
    theConstraints.anchor = GridBagConstraints.CENTER;
    theConstraints.ipadx = 20;
    theConstraints.ipady = 20;
    theConstraints.weightx = 1.0;
    theConstraints.weighty = 1.0;
    theConstraints.gridwidth = GridBagConstraints.REMAINDER;
    theConstraints.gridheight = GridBagConstraints.RELATIVE;
    theGridBagLayout.setConstraints( aMessageLabel, theConstraints );
    add( aMessageLabel );

    // The button has no padding, no weight, takes up minimal width, and
    // is the last thing in its column.
    theConstraints.ipadx = 0;
    theConstraints.ipady = 0;
    theConstraints.weightx = 0.0;
    theConstraints.weighty = 0.0;
    theConstraints.gridwidth = 1;
    theConstraints.gridheight = GridBagConstraints.REMAINDER;
    theGridBagLayout.setConstraints( fOKButton, theConstraints );
    add( fOKButton );

    // Pack is a special window method that makes the window take up the minimum
    // space necessary to contain its components.
    pack();
  }

  // The action method just waits for the OK button to be clicked;
  // when it is it hides the dialog, causing the show() method to return
  // back to whoever activated this dialog.

  public boolean action( Event theEvent, Object whichAction ) {
    if ( theEvent.target == fOKButton ) {
      setVisible( false );
      if ( fFrame != null )
        fFrame.setVisible( false );
    }
    return( true );
  }

  // Shortcut to make a frame automatically
  public static void makeOKDialog( String theDialogString ) {
    if ( fFrame == null )
      fFrame = new Frame( "Dialog" );
    OKDialog theOKDialog = new OKDialog( fFrame, theDialogString );

    // Shrink the frame to just fit the dialog
    fFrame.setSize( theOKDialog.getSize().width, theOKDialog.getSize().height );

    theOKDialog.show();
  }
}
```

The `DialogApplet` in Listing 38.6 pops up an `OKDialog` whenever a button is pressed.

Listing 38.6   *DialogApplet.java*—Test Your New *OKDialog* with This Applet

```java
import java.awt.*;
import java.awt.event.*;
import java.applet.*;

public class DialogApplet extends Applet {
  protected Button fLaunchButton;

  public void init() {
    fLaunchButton = new Button( "Show OK Dialog" );
    add( fLaunchButton );
    fLaunchButton.addActionListener( new ActionListener() {
      public void actionPerformed( ActionEvent e ) {
        doLaunchClicked(); } } );
  }

  public void doLaunchClicked() {
    OKDialog.makeOKDialog( "Press OK to dismiss this dialog" );
  }
}
```

Figure 38.14 shows the `DialogApplet` with the OK dialog popped up.

FIGURE 38.14

The `OKDialog` class makes a pop-up dialog box with an OK button.

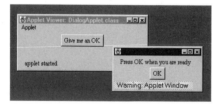

The Swing Architecture

When Java was first introduced, the only graphical user interface (GUI) available was the Abstract Windowing Toolkit (AWT). Recall from the first section of this chapter, "Interacting with People by Using Java," that AWT components are considered to be "heavyweight" in that each Java component has a peer object from the native GUI.

Sun also offers "lightweight" components that don't have a peer object. Instead, they offer "pluggable look and feel." If the end user is running on a Windows 95 machine but prefers the look and feel of Sun's Motif interface, for example, the user can select that interface in the running application. When Sun developed these lightweight components, it did so as part of a project called "Swing," so the lightweight user interface components are usually called Swing components.

Swing components are one part of the Java Foundation Classes (JFC). Figure 38.15 illustrates the relationship of the AWT and the Swing components to the JFC.

N O T E Many of the Swing components are derived from their AWT counterparts. Most developers, however, reserve the term "AWT component" for the heavyweight components, and refer to the components in `javax.swing` simply as "Swing components." ▓

FIGURE 38.15

The Swing components are the lightweight user-interface components of the JFC.

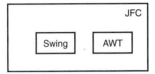

Understanding the JFC

Although the JFC was released well before JDK 1.2, Sun didn't make a big deal about it. Most of Sun's description of the new JFC has centered on Swing, so many people have the idea that Swing is all there is to the JFC and that the JFC came out as part of JDK 1.2. The link is so strong that Sun unofficially calls JFC 1.1 "Swing 1.0."

In fact, the JFC includes

- The lightweight user interface components (code named Swing)
- The delegation event model
- Printing capability
- Clipboard data transfer
- Better integration with system colors
- Mouseless operation
- Drag-and-drop operation
- Better support for assistive technology for people with disabilities
- Improved 2D graphics operations

N O T E Before JFC was developed, Netscape developed a set of classes called the Internet Foundation Classes, or IFC. Microsoft has also developed the Application Foundation Classes, or AFC. Netscape has announced that the JFC supersedes the IFC, leaving Microsoft and Sun to battle it out. ▓

A Short Tour of Swing

Sun supplies Swing in 14 packages:

- `javax.swing`—Components, adapters, default component models and interfaces
- `javax.swing.basic`—The user interface classes (known as delegates) for the Windows look and feel

- `javax.swing.beaninfo`—Support classes for use when Swing components are used as JavaBeans

- `javax.swing.border`—The Border interface and classes, which define specific border-rendering styles

- `javax.swing.event`—Swing-specific event types and listeners

- `javax.swing.jlf`—The user interface classes for the Java look and feel (sometimes known as "Metal")

- `com.sun.java.swing.plaf.motif`—The user interface classes for the Motif look and feel

- `javax.swing.multi`—The multiplexing user interface classes that enable you to make components from different factory classes

- `com.sun.java.swing.plaf`—Used by developers who want to write their own Pluggable Look and Feel (PLAF)

- `javax.swing.table`—The Swing `Table` class and its kin

- `javax.swing.target`—The support classes for `Action` target management

- `javax.swing.text`—Support for the Swing document framework

- `javax.swing.undo`—Support classes for implementing undo and redo

- `javax.accessibility`—Support for working with assistive technology to make Java programs accessible for people with disabilities

N O T E Swing is an emerging technology—not all Java-compatible browsers understand Swing, but most can be configured to run Swing applets. To test your browser (and to get instructions on reconfiguring your browser, if necessary) visit `http://java.sun.com/products/jfc/swingdoc-current/applets.html`.

Swing was first released as a separate set of classes that worked with JDK 1.1. Swing was not actually part of JDK 1.1, but had to be downloaded and installed separately. Swing remained a separate set of classes through much of the JDK 1.2 beta process. Now, however, Swing is fully integrated into JDK 1.2. Be sure to get the most up-to-date version of Swing by downloading the final version of Java 2/JDK 1.2 at `http://java.sun.com/products/jdk/1.2/`.

 T I P Before you begin to develop with Swing components, make sure you can run an existing Swing-based application. Sun includes SwingSet, an overview of the Swing components, in the JFC. You'll find it in `SWING_HOME/examples/SwingSet`. Follow the instructions in the `README.txt` file in that directory to run the application. Make sure it loads and runs without errors.

Swing Component APIs

With the AWT you can choose buttons, labels, lists, and a few other user interface components. With the Swing components, Sun provides a richer interface, more akin to the full range available in Microsoft Foundation Classes or the Macintosh Toolbox. More than twice as many Swing components are available as AWT components. The Swing components include

- Labels
- Bordered panes
- Progress bars
- Tool tips
- Buttons
- Radio buttons
- Check boxes
- Tool bars
- Sliders
- Combo boxes
- Menus
- Trees
- Scroll bars
- List boxes
- Tabbed panes
- Tables

All these components are lightweight—instead of building a peer component from the native operating system, they look for a library of pluggable look and feel classes. Three such libraries come with Swing 1.0:

- `SWING_HOME/windows.jar`—A look and feel strongly resembling Windows 95/ Windows NT 4.0.
- `SWING_HOME/motif.jar`—A look and feel based on Sun's own Motif interface.
- `SWING_HOME/metal.jar`—A platform-independent look and feel.

N O T E Sun has announced a Macintosh look and feel (`http://java.sun.com/products/jfc/tsc/swingdoc-current/mac_1-f.html`) that will be available in Swing 1.1. Swing 1.1 also includes a new version of the cross-platform Java look and feel, formerly known as Metal (`http://java.sun.com/products/jfc/tsc/swingdoc-current/plaf_report.html`). Use the Java look and feel if you want your application or applet to look the same on every platform. ▓

Part
VII

Ch
38

Most of Sun's demo applets enable you to change the look and feel from a control at runtime. Figure 38.16 shows Simple, one of the examples, in the default look and feel (called Metal).

FIGURE 38.16

Assume that some users will want to switch from one look and feel to another.

Compare Figure 38.16 with Figure 38.17. Figure 38.16 shows Simple with the Metal look and feel. By choosing the Windows radio button, you can switch Simple to the Windows look and feel, shown in Figure 38.17. Similarly, you can use the Motif look and feel, shown in Figure 38.18.

FIGURE 38.17

Compare the Windows look and feel to Metal (shown in Figure 38.16) and Motif (in Figure 38.18).

FIGURE 38.18

The Motif look and feel is based on an interface Sun designed to its UNIX operating system.

N O T E Pluggable Look and Feel (PLAF) is here to stay. Use SwingSet to explore all three PLAFs, as well as others that will become available in the future. Remember that the decision about which look and feel to use is left to the user. Strive to make sure your design looks good in all available PLAFs.

Using the *TPanelTester* Application

The examples in this section are based on subclasses of the Swing panel component, JPanel. To run the various panels, you need an application to display the panel. Listing 38.7 shows a generic panel tester.

Listing 38.7 *TPanelTester.java*—Change the Name in This Panel Tester to Match the Panel Under Test

```
import javax.swing.*;

public class TPanelTester extends JFrame {
  public TPanelTester() {
    super("Panel Tester");
```

```
    // change TLabelPanel to match the name of the panel under test
    JPanel thePanelUnderTest = new TLabelPanel();
    setContentPane(thePanelUnderTest);
  }

  public static void main(String[] args) {
    JFrame theFrame = new TPanelTester();
    theFrame.addWindowListener(new java.awt.event.WindowAdapter() {
      public void windowClosing(java.awt.event.WindowEvent e)
        {System.exit(0);}
      });
    theFrame.pack();
    theFrame.setVisible(true);
  }
}
```

Using *JPanel*

We first looked at panels earlier in this chapter in our discussion of the AWT. A JPanel is a lightweight version of panel; it is used in most of the examples in this section.

> **N O T E** In Chapter 39, "Graphics and Animation," we'll talk about how you can reduce flicker with double buffering. Double buffering is built into JComponent; check the documentation for the setDoubleBuffered() method. ▪

Working with Icons

In our discussion of the AWT, we noted that subclasses of java.awt.Container can contain java.awt.Components, and that Containers themselves are Components. It is this hierarchy that enables us to add Panels to Frames, for example. All the Swing components are derived from JComponent, which is a java.awt.Container. This design means that every JComponent can contain other components, either AWT or Swing. Therefore, you can add a graphical icon to a JButton, a JLabel, or other Swing component. Swing provides Icon as an interface; to implement it you must provide a paintIcon() method, a getIconWidth() method, and a getIconHeight() method. The paintIcon() method is

paintIcon(Component c, Graphics g, int x, int y);

where x and y specify the drawing origin; the drawing itself happens in Graphics g. You can use the Component to get properties such as the foreground or background color—in practice, it's usually ignored.

> **N O T E** In theory, any JComponent can contain either AWT or Swing components. Unfortunately, the words "in theory" often translate into "not really." Many programmers report that they have had difficulty mixing classic AWT components with Swing components. If you want to try, go ahead—you've been warned. ▪

Swing provides one Icon class for you—ImageIcon, used for displaying Images. Listing 38.8 is an example of an Icon.

Listing 38.8   *TBigBlackDot.java*—You Can Add This *Icon* to Swing Buttons and Labels

```java
public class TBigBlackDot implements javax.swing.Icon {
  public void paintIcon(java.awt.Component c,
                        java.awt.Graphics g, int x, int y) {
    g.setColor(java.awt.Color.black);
    g.fillOval(x, y, getIconWidth(), getIconHeight());
  }
  public int getIconWidth() {
    return 100;
  }
  public int getIconHeight() {
    return 100;
  }
}
```

Adding an Instance of *JLabel*

A label enables you to place static text onto the screen. We took our first look at Label when we discussed the AWT. The Swing JLabel improves upon java.awt.Label by enabling you to add an Icon and giving you better control over the position of the text. Listing 38.9 shows a JLabel in action on a JPanel.

Listing 38.9   *TLabelPanel.java*—This Panel Contains a Label with a *TBigBlackDot* Icon

```java
public class TLabelPanel extends javax.swing.JPanel {
  public TLabelPanel() {
    javax.swing.JLabel theLabel =
      new com.sun.java.swing.JLabel("Example of TBigBlackDot");

    // we don't have to settle for plain vanilla text
    java.awt.Font theBigBoldFont =
      new java.awt.Font("Serif",
                        java.awt.Font.BOLD,
                        32);
    theLabel.setFont(theBigBoldFont);

    // now add an icon
    javax.swing.Icon aDot = new TBigBlackDot();
    theLabel.setIcon(aDot);
    theLabel.setPreferredSize(new
      java.awt.Dimension(600, 150));

    // place the text to the right of the icon
    theLabel.setHorizontalAlignment(javax.swing.JLabel.RIGHT);

    // and add the whole thing to the panel
    add(theLabel);
  }
}
```

Figure 38.19 shows an instance of `TLabelPanel`.

FIGURE 38.19
You can add icons to a
JLabel and control
the text's position and
appearance.

Using *JButton*

`JButton` behaves much like `Button`; you add it to a `JPanel` and listen for its `Action` with an
`ActionListener`.

Part
VII
Ch
38

 By default, a new `JButton` has the same background color as the container. Some developers don't
like this design and prefer that it stand out more. Consider adding a line such as

`theButton.setBackground(SystemColor.control );`

to make the button highly visible.

As with `JLabel`, you can add an `Icon` to `JButton` by calling the `setIcon()` method.

 Several Swing components, including `JButton`, are derived from `AbstractButton`. Review the
documentation for `AbstractButton`—you'll find methods that enable you to enable and disable the
button, methods that enable you to control the internal alignment, and ways to associate an accelera-
tor key with the button.

Adding an Instance of *JCheckBox*

Recall from the earlier section of this chapter, "Using the Abstract Windowing Toolkit," that
you can implement check boxes with `java.awt.Checkbox`. You implemented radio buttons by
placing the `Checkbox` into a `CheckboxGroup`. In Swing, the concept of a radio button in handled
explicitly—Swing has its own `JRadioButton` class with an associated `ButtonGroup`. You use
`JCheckBox` just to implement check boxes.

N O T E JCheckBox has its own icons to signify the selected and unselected states. If you prefer,
you can make your own `Icons` and use them in `setIcon()` and
`setSelectedIcon()`.

Using *JRadioButton*

To make a group of radio buttons, make instances of `JRadioButton` and add them to a
`ButtonGroup`. Listing 38.10 shows an example of some radio buttons.

Listing 38.10   *TDoseNotGivenPanel.java*—This Panel Contains a Group of Radio Buttons

```java
public class TDoseNotGivenPanel extends javax.swing.JPanel {
  public TDoseNotGivenPanel() {

    // make room for a label and four buttons
    setLayout(new java.awt.GridLayout(5, 1));

    javax.swing.ButtonGroup aReason =
      new javax.swing.ButtonGroup();
    javax.swing.JLabel theLabel =
      new javax.swing.JLabel("Dose not given because");
    theLabel.setFont(new java.awt.Font("SansSrif",
                                       java.awt.Font.BOLD, 14));
    add(theLabel);

    javax.swing.JRadioButton thePatientNotAvailableButton =
      new javax.swing.JRadioButton("Patient not available");
    thePatientNotAvailableButton.setHorizontalAlignment(
      javax.swing.AbstractButton.LEFT);
    thePatientNotAvailableButton.setKeyAccelerator('A');
    thePatientNotAvailableButton.setSelected(true); //default
    add(thePatientNotAvailableButton);
    aReason.add(thePatientNotAvailableButton);

    javax.swing.JRadioButton thePatientOffWardButton =
      new javax.swing.JRadioButton("Patient off ward");
    thePatientOffWardButton.setHorizontalAlignment(
      javax.swing.AbstractButton.LEFT);
    thePatientNotAvailableButton.setKeyAccelerator('O');
    add (thePatientOffWardButton);
    aReason.add(thePatientOffWardButton);

    javax.swing.JRadioButton thePatientRefusedButton =
      new javax.swing.JRadioButton("Patient refused dose");
    thePatientRefusedButton.setHorizontalAlignment(
      javax.swing.AbstractButton.LEFT);
    thePatientNotAvailableButton.setKeyAccelerator('R');
    add (thePatientRefusedButton);
    aReason.add(thePatientRefusedButton);

    javax.swing.JRadioButton thePatientExpelledDoseButton =
      new javax.swing.JRadioButton("Patient expelled dose");
    thePatientExpelledDoseButton.setHorizontalAlignment(
      javax.swing.AbstractButton.LEFT);
    thePatientNotAvailableButton.setKeyAccelerator('X');
    add (thePatientExpelledDoseButton);
    aReason.add(thePatientExpelledDoseButton);
  }
}
```

Figure 38.20 shows the JPanel that results from the code in Listing 38.10.

FIGURE 38.20

Use a `ButtonGroup` to implement a set of radio buttons.

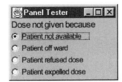

Remembering State with *JToggleButton*

`JToggleButton` is the parent class of both `JCheckBox` and `JRadioButton`, but it's a concrete class that you can use in your design. When unselected, a `JToggleButton` is indistinguishable from a `JButton`. When someone clicks it, it goes to its selected state and stays there. (By default, it looks like a push button that's locked in the "Down" state.)

Managing Text

Swing's `JTextComponent` gives you more than you'd expect from a simple field or text area. Its methods include

- `copy()`
- `cut()`
- `paste()`
- `getSelectedText()`
- `getSelectionStart()`
- `getSelectionEnd()`
- `getText()`
- `setText()`
- `setEditable()`
- `setCaretPosition()`

Figure 38.21 illustrates the inheritance hierarchy that derives from `JTextComponent`.

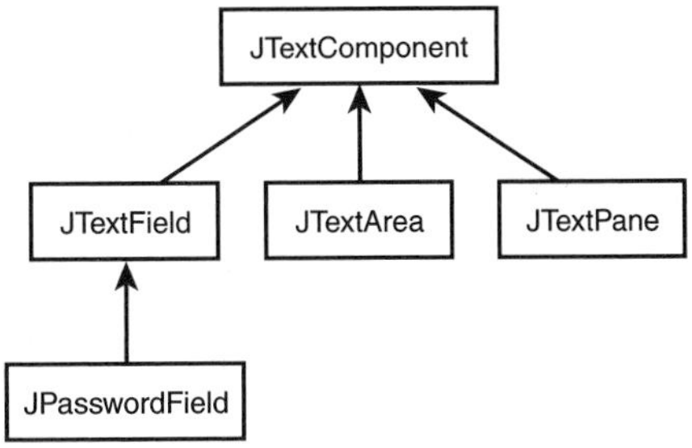

FIGURE 38.21

Each member of the `JTextComponent` family supports the methods of a simple text editor.

`JTextField` and `JTextArea` resemble their AWT counterparts, but `JTextPane` is something new. It implements a complete text editor; you can format text and embed images. Words will wrap where you expect them to, based on their current font, size, and style.

TProgressNotePanel, a class used in a pharmacy application, is shown in Listing 38.11. Figure 38.22 shows the TProgressNotePanel itself.

 TIP

When a user enters a password or other sensitive information, the information should not become visible on the screen. Use JPasswordField instead of JTextField to ensure privacy. Use setEchoChar() if you want to override the default echo character, asterisk (*).

Listing 38.11 *TProgressNotePanel.java*—Nurses Enter Progress Notes to Report Significant Events in the Care of Their Patients

```java
public class TProgressNotePanel extends javax.swing.JPanel
{
  public TProgressNotePanel() {
    setLayout(new java.awt.BorderLayout());
    setPreferredSize(new java.awt.Dimension(400,400));
    javax.swing.JTextPane theText = new javax.swing.JTextPane();

    javax.swing.text.MutableAttributeSet theAttributes =
      new javax.swing.text.SimpleAttributeSet();
    javax.swing.text.StyleConstants.setFontFamily(theAttributes,
                                                  "Serif");
    javax.swing.text.StyleConstants.setFontSize(theAttributes, 18);
    javax.swing.text.StyleConstants.setBold(theAttributes, true);
    theText.setCharacterAttributes(theAttributes, false);

    add(theText, java.awt.BorderLayout.CENTER);
  }
}
```

FIGURE 38.22

You can get a full text editor in only nine lines of code.

Giving Feedback with *JProgressBar*

In Chapter 39 we'll talk about starting up more than one independent thread of control. Sometimes you'll want a thread running in the background while the user goes on with other work. You can put up a progress bar to report on the progress in that thread and, if you like, enable the user to control that thread. Listing 38.12 and Figure 38.23 show one way to use a JProgressBar.

▶ To learn more about threads, **see** "Adding Animation" on **p. 1104**.

Listing 38.12 *TBackgroundPanel.java*—You Can Use a *JProgressBar* to Report the Progress of a Thread

```java
import javax.swing.*;
public class TBackgroundPanel extends JPanel {
  private Thread fThread;
  private Object fLock;
  private boolean fNeedsToStop = false;
  private JProgressBar fProgressBar;
  private JButton fStartButton;
  private JButton fStopButton;

  public TBackgroundPanel() {
    fLock = new Object();
    setLayout(new java.awt.BorderLayout());
    add(new JLabel("Status"), java.awt.BorderLayout.NORTH);
    fProgressBar = new JProgressBar();
    add(fProgressBar, java.awt.BorderLayout.CENTER);
    JPanel theButtons = new JPanel();

    fStartButton = new JButton("Start");
    fStartButton.setBackground(java.awt.SystemColor.control);
    theButtons.add(fStartButton);
    fStartButton.addActionListener(new java.awt.event.ActionListener() {
      public void actionPerformed(java.awt.event.ActionEvent e) {
        startTheThread();
      }
    });
    fStopButton = new JButton("Stop");
    fStopButton.setBackground(java.awt.SystemColor.control);
    theButtons.add(fStopButton);
    fStopButton.addActionListener(new java.awt.event.ActionListener() {
      public void actionPerformed(java.awt.event.ActionEvent e) {
        stopTheThread();
      }
    });
    add(theButtons, java.awt.BorderLayout.SOUTH);
  }

  public void startTheThread() {
    if (fThread == null)
      fThread = new TBackgroundThread();
```

continues

Listing 38.12 Continued

```
      if (!fThread.isAlive())
      {
        fNeedsToStop = false;
        fThread.start();
      }
    }

    public void stopTheThread() {
      synchronized(fLock) {
        fNeedsToStop = true;
        fLock.notify();
      }
    }

    // inner class, so it has access to private members of panel
    class TBackgroundThread extends Thread {
      public void run() {
        // run at a low priority; after all, we _
        // are_ a background thread
        Thread.currentThread().setPriority(Thread.MIN_PRIORITY);
        int theMinimum = 0;
        int theMaximum = 100;
        fProgressBar.setValue(theMinimum);
        fProgressBar.setMinimum(theMinimum);
        fProgressBar.setMaximum(theMaximum);
        for (int i=0; i<theMaximum; i++) {
          fProgressBar.setValue(i);

          // do the real work of the background thread
          // here

          synchronized(fLock) {
            if (fNeedsToStop)
              break;
            try {
              fLock.wait(100);
            } catch (InterruptedException e) {
              // ignore the exception
            }
          }
        }
        // clue the garbage collector that we're done with the thread
        fThread = null;
      }
    }
  }
}
```

FIGURE 38.23

For a nice touch, enable the user to start and stop the work of the background thread.

TBackgroundPanel is a generic JPanel that can be used to display and control a background thread. The class has six instance variables:

- Thread fThread—The background thread itself; see "Adding Animation" in Chapter 39 to learn more about threads.
- Object fLock—A simple object used to synchronize the foreground and background threads.
- boolean fNeedsToStop—A bit of shared data that tells the background thread that the foreground thread wants it to stop.
- JProgressBar fProgressBar—The Swing progress bar.
- JButton fStartButton and JButton fStopButton—The controls to start and stop the background thread.

The TBackgroundPanel constructor builds the user interface, including the pair of buttons that communicate with the background thread. The listeners are designed to start and stop the thread by calling TBackgroundPanel's methods startTheThread() and stopTheThread(). The class TBackgroundThread is an inner class, so it has access to all the instance variables of TBackgroundPanel. Like most threads, it has only one method: run().

When the user clicks fStartButton, startTheThread() instantiates a new TBackgroundThread and tells it to start(). When the thread starts, its run() method immediately sets the priority to the minimum value; the user interface has a higher priority, so the application feels responsive to the user. The TBackgroundThread sits in a tight loop doing whatever work it does—that work has been left as a comment in this version. You could download a file, query a database, or do anything else that takes so much time that you don't want the user to have to wait.

As it runs, TBackgroundThread continually reports its status to fProgressBar. Then it checks the state of fNeedsToStop. If the user has clicked fStopButton, then fNeedsToStop is true and run() breaks out of its loop.

 TIP The boolean variable fNeedsToStop is shared between the two threads. If you're not careful, it's possible that both threads could be using the variable at once. To prevent this, we use the Object fLock as a *semaphore* so that only one thread can work with fNeedsToStop at a time.

Adding Toolbars and ToolTips

It's easy to add toolbars and tooltips to your Swing components. If you have a JButton named fButton, just write

```
fButton.setToolTipText("This is the tooltip");
```

to add a ToolTip to the button. You can use this technique on any `JComponent`.

A `JToolBar` is simply another `JComponent`. You can write code such as

```
JToolBar theToolBar = new JToolBar();
JButton aButton = new JButton("One");
theToolBar.add(aButton);
JButton anotherButton = new JButton("Two");
theToolBar.add(anotherButton);
```

to build a toolbar.

 TIP   You can add `JButtons` and other components to your toolbar; use an `ActionListener` to handle mouse clicks, the same as you would with any other button. `ActionListeners` are part of the delegation event model described earlier in this chapter in the section, "Using the Abstract Windowing Toolkit."

The Long-Awaited Tabbed Pane

The Windows32 user interface (implemented in Windows95 and Windows NT 4.0) included a tabbed pane, which is commonly used throughout Windows applications. Unfortunately, the AWT interface did not include a tabbed pane—early Java programmers often cobbled one together by using the `CardLayout`.

Now, with Swing, we get our own `JTabbedPane`. You can add one to a `BorderLayout` with just a few lines of code, as shown in Listing 38.13.

Listing 38.13   *TTabbedPanel.java*—Add Tabs to a *JTabbedPanel*

```java
import javax.swing.*;
public class TTabbedPanel extends JPanel {
{
  private JTabbedPane fTabbedPane;
  public TTabbedPanel() {
    setLayout (new java.awt.BorderLayout());
    fTabbedPane = new JTabbedPane();
    fTabbedPane.addTab("One", null, makePane("One"));
    fTabbedPane.addTab("Two", null, makePane("Two"));
    fTabbedPane.addTab("Three", null, makePane("Three"));
    fTabbedPane.setSelectedIndex(0);
    add (fTabbedPane, java.awt.BorderLayout.CENTER);
  }
  protected void makePane(String theString) {
    // customize makePane to display the exact info you want
    // on each panel
    JPanel thePanel = new JPanel();
    thePanel.setBackground(SystemColor.control);
    thePanel.add(new JLabel(theString));
    return thePanel;
  }
}
```

Other Swing Components

Swing is a huge component library; in addition to the components described here, JSliders, JComboBoxes, JLists, and many other widgets are included. A JSlider resembles a JScrollBar, but you can add major and minor tick marks and display a Border around the slider. A JComboBox resembles the AWT's Choice component but has more capability. (You can use a JComboBox to supply a list of default choices, for example, and then enable the users to enter their own values if none of the defaults are appropriate.) Use JList the same as you would use List in the AWT. You can listen for ListSelectionEvents the same as you do other events—just add a ListSelectionListener.

 TIP Unlike its AWT counterpart, JList doesn't support scrolling directly. That's not a problem, though—just add it to a ScrollPane or JScrollPane to restore that capability.

Part
VII
Ch
38

Writing Swing Applets

Swing introduces a new class—JApplet—that is derived from Applet. Many of the new methods you'll find in JApplet have to do with accessibility for people with disabilities. The other new capability is called JRootPane.

JRootPane enables you to place contents into one of several layers. In order from front (closest to user) to back (farthest from user) the layers are

1. glassPane—A JComponent that fills the entire viewable area of the JRootPane. By default, the glassPane is not visible.

2. layeredPane—A subclass of JComponent designed to hold dialog boxes, menu pop-ups, and other components that should appear to be floating between the user and the content.

3. menubar—An optional component; if present, it appears anchored to the top of the JRootPane.

4. contentPane—The JComponent where most of the contents will be drawn.

Using the *contentPane* To add components to a JApplet, you should usually add them to the contentPane. Instead of writing

```
theApplet.add(theComponent);
```

as you would in AWT, write

```
theApplet.getContentPane().add(theComponent);
```

Working with the *JLayeredPane* By placing most of your components in the contentPane (which is farthest away from the user), you make it possible to add special components such as menu pop-ups or dialog boxes in a layer closer to the user (such as the layeredPane).

NOTE By default, the contentPane has a BorderLayout layout manager.

N O T E If you plan to use the layeredPane, be sure to read the JDK documentation on
javax.swing.JLayeredPane. This class—a layer in itself—supports six distinct layers
internally: from back to front, the FRAME_CONTENT_LAYER, the DEFAULT_LAYER, the
PALETTE_LAYER, the MODAL_LAYER, the POPUP_LAYER, and the DRAG_LAYER. In addition, you
can make up layers of your own.

Adding Menus to *JApplets*   If you've worked with the AWT, you know that you cannot easily
add menus to an applet. AWT menus need to be attached to a Frame, but an Applet is a Panel.
With JApplet, you can set a JMenuBar on the JRootPane. It will be positioned along the upper
edge of the JApplet's JRootPane.

Drawing on the *glassPane*   The glassPane is closest to the user. If you need to draw something that should appear in front of *all* components, including dialog boxes, menu pop-ups, and
other components on the layeredPane, add it to the glassPane.

T I P If you use the glassPane, remember to make it visible. It is not visible by default. In a JApplet, for
example, you might write

```
getGlassPane.setVisible(TRUE);
```

Using Swing-Specific Layouts

In addition to the AWT layouts that we've been using earlier in this chapter, Swing comes with
four layouts of its own:

- ScrollPaneLayout—Built into the ScrollPane component.
- ViewportLayout—Built into the Viewport component.
- BoxLayout—Built into the Box component, but also available as an option in other
  components.
- OverlayLayout—A layout manager in which every component is added on top of every
  previous component.

Taking Advantage of *ScrollPaneLayout* in *JScrollPanes*

You'll never need to instantiate a ScrollPaneLayout. Instead, just make a new JScrollPane.
You'll get the nine areas associated with the ScrollPaneLayout automatically:

- A JViewport, in the center—Use it for your contents.
- Two JScrollBars—One for horizontal scrolling, the other for vertical scrolling.
- Two JViewPorts—One for row headers, the other for column headers.
- Four Components—One for each corner.

N O T E ScrollPaneLayout includes named constants to make it easy for you to refer to the
parts of the layout. The corners, for example, are named LOWER_LEFT_CORNER,
LOWER_RIGHT_CORNER, UPPER_LEFT_CORNER, and UPPER_RIGHT_CORNER.

Each JViewport has its own layout manager, the ViewportLayout.

Working with *ViewportLayout* and *OverlayLayout*

Like the ScrollPaneLayout, you don't need to make your own ViewportLayout. You get it automatically with every Viewport. Just add a component to the Viewport—the ViewportLayout will position it based on the properties of your Viewport.

The OverlayLayout positions each component over the top of the others. The size of the complete layout is the size of the largest component.

Using *Box* and *BoxLayout*

The BoxLayout resembles the AWT FlowLayout, except that you can specify the axis—either x or y. Unlike GridLayout, each component can occupy a different size cell. To use the BoxLayout in the y axis, write

```
setLayout(new BoxLayout(this, BoxLayout.Y_AXIS));
```

Figure 38.24 illustrates a BoxLayout in the y axis.

FIGURE 38.24
This BoxLayout is set up for the y axis and has three components.

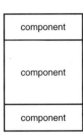

> **TIP** If you plan to use BoxLayout, just subclass Box rather than JPanel. BoxLayout is the default layout manager for Box and provides several methods that give you detailed control over the layout.

Swing Listeners and Events

Recall from the earlier sections of this chapter, "Using the Abstract Windowing Toolkit" and "The Swing Architecture," that one of the distinctives of the JFC is the delegation event model. Although the AWT components can still use the now-deprecated JDK-1.0 model for communicating about actions, Swing components use only the delegation event model. In fact, Swing takes the delegation event model to new heights, based on the *Model-View-Controller* (MVC) design pattern.

▶ To learn more about MVC, **see** Chapter 13 of *Using Java 1.2* (Que, 1998).

Understanding Swing Events

Earlier in this chapter, in "Using the Abstract Windowing Toolkit," we introduced the delegation event model and talked about low-level and semantic events. Swing has its own event package for Swing-specific events. Use the javax.swing.event package for the event listeners and the events themselves; the event sources are the Swing components. The following is a list of the Swing event classes—DocumentEvent is an interface—and their meanings:

N O T E   Many Swing events, such as those that refer to the "model," assume that you're using the MVC pattern. Read the Swing documentation on MVC or Chapter 13 of *Using Java 1.2* before attempting to use these Swing events. ▪

- AncestorEvent—Ancestor added, moved, or removed.
- ChangeEvent—A component has had a state change.
- DocumentEvent—A document has had a state change.
- ListDataEvent—Contents of a list have changed, or an interval has been added or removed.
- ListSelectionEvent—The selection on a list has changed.
- MenuEvent—A menu item has been selected or posted, deselected, or canceled.
- TableColumnModelEvent—The model for a table column has changed.
- TableModelEvent—The model for a table has changed.
- TreeExpansionEvent—A tree node has been expanded or collapsed.
- TreeModelEvent—A tree model has changed.
- TreeSelectionEvent—The selection in a tree has changed status.

N O T E   Sun divides events into two categories—semantic events and low-level events. Usually you'll get a better, more portable interface by listening for semantic events such as the ActionEvent. If you need special behavior, however, you can listen for low-level events such as mouse clicks and key presses. Refer back to Listing 37.6—TRaceApplet.java—to see how to use low-level events. Line 72 (copied below) constructs a new TMouseAdapter:

TMouseAdapter aMouseAdapter = new TMouseAdapter();

That adapter is defined in lines 202 to 215 (shown below). When the adapter "hears" a mouse press, it consumes the event (line 207—copied below)

anEvent.consume();

and toggles fThreadSuspended; if the thread was suspended, it is now unsuspended, and vice versa.

```
    class TMouseAdapter extends java.awt.event.MouseAdapter
    {
      public synchronized void mousePressed(
➥java.awt.event.MouseEvent anEvent)
      {
        anEvent.consume();
        fThreadSuspended = !fThreadSuspended;
        if (!fThreadSuspended)
```

```
       synchronized (fMonitorThread)
       {
         fMonitorThread.notifyAll();
       }
    }
  }
}
```

▶ To learn more about TRaceApplet.java, **see** "Sample Applets" on **p. 1001**.

Drag and Drop

In the latest version of the JDK, all drag-and-drop (DnD) operations (for both Swing and AWT components) are supported through the interface java.awt.dnd. Listing 38.14 shows a typical DnD program.

N O T E When a class implements an interface, the class must provide an implementation of every method in the interface. To implement a drag-and-drop target, a class must implement DropTargetListener. As shown in Listing 38.14, most of the work is done in dragEnter() and drop().

Listing 38.14 *DnDTest.java*—An Implementation of a *DropTargetListener*

```java
import java.awt.*;
import java.awt.dnd.*;
import java.awt.datatransfer.*;
import java.awt.event.*;
import java.io.*;

public class DnDTest extends Frame implements DropTargetListener {

  DropTarget fTarget;
  TextArea fTextArea;

  public DnDTest () {
    fTextArea = new TextArea("Grab some text and \npull it over here!");
    fTarget = new DropTarget(text, DnDConstants.ACTION_COPY, this);
    fTarget.setActive (true);
    add ("Center", fTextArea);
    enableEvents(AWTEvent.WINDOW_EVENT_MASK);
  }

  public static void main (String args[]) {
    DnDTest theFrame = new DnDTest();
    theFrame.setSize (400, 200);
    theFrame.setVisible (true);
  }

// required methods in DropTargetListener
```

continues

Listing 38.14 Continued

```java
public  void dragEnter (DropTargetDragEvent dtde) {
  System.out.println ("dragEnter");

  // use the DropTargetDragEvent to find out what flavors are offered
  DataFlavor df[] = dtde.getCurrentDataFlavors();
  for (int i = 0; i < df.length; i++)    {
    if (df[i].equals (DataFlavor.plainTextFlavor)) {

      // if the flavor is plain text, accept the drag
      dtde.acceptDrag (DnDConstants.ACTION_COPY);
      return;
    }
  }
  // otherwise reject this drag
  dtde.rejectDrag ();
}

public  void dragOver (DropTargetDragEvent dtde) {

  // dragOver is called repeatedly while the cursor is over
  // the target. Uncomment the println to see how often this
  // method is called.
  //System.out.println ("dragOver");
}

public void dropActionChanged(DropTargetDragEvent dtde) {
  System.out.println("dropActionChanged");
}

public  void dragScroll (DropTargetDragEvent dtde) {
  System.out.println ("dragScroll");
}

public  void dragExit (DropTargetEvent dte) {
  System.out.println ("dragExit");
}

public  void drop (DropTargetDropEvent dtde) {
  dtde.acceptDrop (DnDConstants.ACTION_COPY);
  System.out.println ("dropped");
  Transferable theTransferable = dtde.getTransferable();
  DataFlavor df[] = dtde.getCurrentDataFlavors();
  Object theObject = null;

  try {

    // search through the flavor looking for plain text
    // when you find it get the associated data and stuff
    // it into the Object.
    for (int i = 0; i < df.length; i++)    {
      if (df[i].equals (DataFlavor.plainTextFlavor)) {
        theObject = theTransferable.getTransferData(df[i]);
      }
    }
```

```
      // if the data comes from outside the JVM, it comes in
      // on an InputStream. Read in the stream.
      if (theObject != null && theObject instanceof InputStream) {
        InputStream theInputStream = (InputStream) theObject;
        StringBuffer theStringBuffer = new StringBuffer();
        byte[] aBuffer = new byte[64];
        int theCount = theInputStream.read(aBuffer);
        while (theCount != -1) {
          // keep stuffing data into the string buffer
          theStringBuffer.append (new String (aBuffer, 0, theCount));
          theCount = theInputStream.read(aBuffer);
        }
        // We've read in all the data. Now let's use it
        theInputStream.close();
        fTextArea.setText (theStringBuffer.toString());
      }
    } catch (Exception e) {
    e.printStackTrace();
    } finally {
      try {
        fTarget.getDropTargetContext().dropComplete(true);
      } catch (Exception ignore) {}
    }
  }
}

// let's handle a click on the window's close box
  protected void processWindowEvent (WindowEvent e) {
    if (e.getID() == WindowEvent.WINDOW_CLOSING)
      System.exit(0);
    super.processWindowEvent (e);
  }
}
```

Compile DnDTest and run it from the command line (by typing java DnDTest). Open a text editor or other native application that's DnD-capable and drag some text onto the Java application. Your Java program detects the drag event over the DropTarget (called a DropTargetDragEvent) and calls dragEnter(). Because the incoming data is plain text, dragEnter() accepts the drag—the user sees the default cursor showing a drag-copy in progress. If the user moves the cursor out of the target area, the program calls dragExit(). If the user drops the transferred object over the target, your program calls drop(). In this case, DnDTest extracts the plain text from the transferred flavor and places it in the TextArea.

Your Java program can be a source for a drag-and-drop operation as well as being a target. Your source should implement DragGestureListener so that Java recognizes a click-and-drag action as the start of a drag-and-drop. The source should also implement DragSourceListener, though you won't need its methods unless you want a special effect.

DragGestureListener requires that you implement only one method: dragGestureRecognized(). In this method, you should determine what data is to be transferred, then package that data into a flavor. If your interface stores data in a Vector called fModel, for example, and the user has selected theItem, you might write:

```
Transferable theTransferable = null;
theTransferable = (Transferable) fModel.elementAt(theItem);
DataFlavor theFlavors[] = theTransferable.getTransferDataFlavors();
try {
  theDragGestureEvent.startDrag(DragSource.DefaultCopyDrop,
                                theTransferable,
                                this);
  } catch (InvalidDnDOperationException e) {
    System.out.println("Invalid Drag and Drop operation: " + e);
  }
```

DragSourceListener requires that you implement five methods:

- dragDropEnd()
- dragEnter()
- dragExit()
- dragOver()
- dropActionChanged()

Unless you need a special effect, you can stub out all these methods. Now when you start a drag, dragGestureRecognized() runs, stuffs the data into one or more flavors, and attaches the array of flavors to the DragGestureEvent. When the cursor enters a drop target, your program examines the array of flavors; if it finds one that it can accept, it accepts the drag. Finally, when the user drops the transferred object, your program reads out the data from the flavor and puts it to work in the target.

Using Swing Event Listeners

Like their AWT counterparts, Swing event listeners are interfaces. Unlike AWT, Sun hasn't yet implemented adapter classes, so you'll need to override every listener method in order to implement a listener. To implement an AncestorListener (which has three methods), for example, you might write

```
public class myAncestorListener implements AncestorListener {
  public void ancestorAdded(AncestorEvent e) {
    // ignore this one
  }
  public void ancestorRemoved(AncestorEvent e) {
    // don't care about this one either
  }
  public void ancestorMoved(AncestorEvent e) {
    // do something in this case
    Here is code to handle the case of a moving ancestor
  }
}
```

N O T E In Windows jargon, an *ancestor* is a member of the path of containers that goes back to the root window. If you put a JPanel into a Frame, then put a JLabel on the JPanel, and finally put an Icon in the JLabel, then the JLabel, the JPanel, and the Frame are all ancestors of the Icon.

Understanding Swing Event Sources

Swing events originate in the Swing components. A list showing which events come from which sources follows. Remember the component hierarchy—an event sent by a JComponent is sent by every class that derives from JComponent.

- ActionEvent

    AbstractButton

    DefaultButtonModel

    JDirectoryPane

    JTextField

    Timer

- AdjustmentEvent

    JScrollBar

    Spinner

- AncestorEvent—JComponent
- CellEditorEvent—DefaultCellEditor
- ChangeEvent

    AbstractButton

    DefaultBoundedRangeModel

    DefaultButtonModel

    DefaultCaret

    DefaultSingleSelectionModel

    FontChooser.Patch

    JProgressBar

    JSlider

    JTabbedPane

    JViewport

    StandardDialog

    StyleContext

- DocumentEvent—AbstractDocument
- ItemEvent

    AbstractButton

    DefaultButtonModel

    JComboBox

- ListDataEvent—AbstractListModel
- ListSelectionEvent

    DefaultListSelectionModel

    JList

- MenuEvent—JMenu
- PropertyChangeEvent

    AbstractAction

    DefaultTreeSelectionModel

    DirectoryModel

    JComponent

    TableColumn

- TableColumnModelEvent—DefaultTableColumnModel
- TableModelEvent—AbstractTableModel
- TreeExpansionEvent—DefaultTreeModel
- TreeSelectionEvent

    DefaultTreeSelectionModel

    JTree

- VetoableChangeEvent—JComponent
- WindowEvent—JPopupMenu

Of course, you still have access to events sent by AWT components:

- ComponentEvent—From Component
- FocusEvent—From Component
- KeyEvent—From Component
- MouseEvent—From Component
- MouseMotionEvent—From Component
- ContainerEvent—From Container
- WindowEvent—From Window

Graphics and Animation

by Mike Morgan

Displaying Graphics

Colorful graphics and animation can change a dull, static, and gray Web page into an exciting and interesting place to visit. Java provides a wide range of tools for building and displaying graphics. These tools are found in Swing (package `javax.swing*`), the Abstract Windowing Toolkit (AWT) package (`java.awt`), and especially in the Graphics2D class (`java.awt.Graphics2D`). Most of what you need is part of the AWT. In fact, the majority of Java's graphics methods are contained in the `Graphics` class.

▶ For more information on the AWT, **see** "Using the Abstract Windowing Toolkit," **p. 1027**.

▶ For more information on Swing, **see** "The Swing Architecture," **p. 1052** and "Swing Component APIs," **p. 1055**.

Using Java's *Graphics* Class

Java's `Graphics` class provides methods for manipulating a number of graphics features, including the following:

- Drawing graphics primitives
- Displaying colors
- Displaying text
- Displaying images
- Creating flicker-free animation

The following sections discuss all these graphics features and show how to implement them in Java applets. Along the way, you will acquire a complete understanding of the `Graphics` class and its methods.

You can find Java's `Graphics` class in the `java.awt` (the Java Abstract Window Toolkit) package. Be sure to properly import the `Graphics` class when you use it in your code. Include the following line at the beginning of your file:

```
import java.awt.Graphics;
```

N O T E The Graphics class is a nice class with plenty of capabilities. To graphics professionals, however, Graphics seems a bit anemic. More mature GUI platforms, such as Windows 95 and the Macintosh, support features that are not present in Graphics.

If you need to go beyond Graphics, take a look at java.awt.Graphics2D, a richer, two-dimensional graphics class. It's described later in this chapter, in the section titled "Using the 2D API."

Using Java's Coordinate System

You display the various graphics you produce—lines, rectangles, images, and so on—at specific locations in an applet or application window. A simple Cartesian (x, y) coordinate system defines each location within a Java window, as shown in Figure 39.1. The upper-left corner of a window is its origin (0, 0). x increases by the number of screen pixels that you move to the right of the left edge of an applet's window. The number of pixels you move down from the top of a window is y.

FIGURE 39.1

Java's graphics coordinate system increases from left to right and from top to bottom.

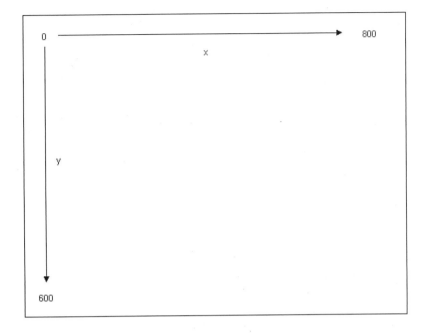

Part

VII

Ch

39

Displaying Graphics Primitives

The Java Graphics class provides you with methods that make it easy to draw two-dimensional graphics primitives. You can draw any two-dimensional graphics primitive, including

- Lines
- Rectangles
- Ovals
- Arcs
- Polygons

The following sections explain how to draw these graphics primitives.

Drawing Lines

Perhaps the simplest graphics primitive is a line. The Java Graphics class provides a single drawLine() method for drawing lines. The complete definition of the drawLine() method is:

```
public abstract void drawLine(int  x1, int  y1, int  x2,  int  y2)
```

The drawLine() method takes two pairs of coordinates—x1, y1 and x2, y2—and draws a line between them.

The applet in Listing 39.1 uses the drawLine() method to draw some lines. Figure 39.2 shows the output from this applet.

Listing 39.1   *DrawLines.java*—Use Graphics Primitives to Display Two Lines

```java
import java.awt.Graphics;

public class DrawLines extends java.applet.Applet
{
   public void paint(Graphics g)
   {
      g.drawLine(0, 0, 400, 200);
      g.drawLine(20, 170, 450, 270);
   }
}
```

FIGURE 39.2

This applet displays two lines drawn using the drawLine() method.

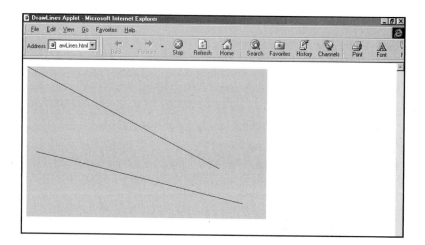

Drawing Rectangles

The Java Graphics class provides six methods for drawing rectangles: drawRect(), fillRect(), drawRoundRect(), fillRoundRect(), draw3DRect(), and fill3DRect(). You can use these methods to draw and fill three designs of rectangles.

To draw a simple rectangle using the drawRect() method, use this definition:

```java
public void drawRect(int  x, int  y, int  width, int  height)
```

Pass the x and y applet window coordinates of the rectangle's upper-left corner along with the rectangle's width and height to the drawRect() method. Assume, for example, that you want to draw a rectangle that is 300 pixels wide (width = 300) and 170 pixels high (height = 170). You also want to place the rectangle with its upper-left corner 150 pixels to the right of the left edge of the applet's window (x = 150) and 100 pixels down from the window's top edge (y = 100). You would write

```java
g.drawRect(150, 100, 300, 170);
```

N O T E   The preceding drawRect() call assumes that you already have a Graphics object g. See Listing 39.2 for an example of where such an object might come from. ▓

To build an applet named OneRectangle that uses the Graphics class drawRect() method, you might write code similar to that shown in Listing 39.2. Figure 39.3 shows the applet's output.

Listing 39.2   *OneRectangle.java*—Display a Simple Rectangle

```
import java.awt.Graphics;

public class OneRectangle extends java.applet.Applet
{
   public void paint(Graphics g)
   {
      g.drawRect(150, 100, 300, 170);
   }
}
```

FIGURE 39.3

The rectangle displayed by this applet was built with the drawRect() method.

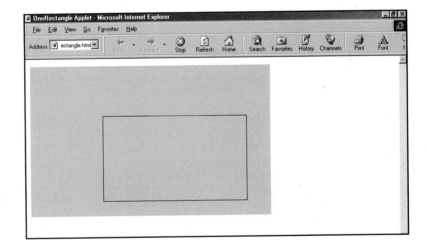

Use the fillRect() method if you want to draw a solid rectangle. The complete definition of the fillRect() method follows:

```
public abstract void fillRect(int  x, int  y, int  width,  int  height)
```

As you can see, the fillRect() method takes the same parameters as the drawRect() method. Figure 39.4 shows the result of using the drawRect() and fillRect() methods. The rectangle at the left of the figure is drawn with the drawRect() method, and the one at the right is drawn with the fillRect() method. The body of this applet contains the lines

```
g.drawRect(20, 20, 200, 100);
g.fillRect(240, 20, 200, 100);
```

The Java Graphics class also provides two methods for drawing rectangles with rounded corners. The drawRoundRect() and fillRoundRect() methods are similar to the drawRect() and fillRect() methods except that they take two extra parameters: the arcWidth and arcHeight parameters. Their complete definitions are

Part
VII

Ch
39

FIGURE 39.4

The left rectangle was drawn with `drawRect()`, and the one on the right was drawn with `fillRect()`.

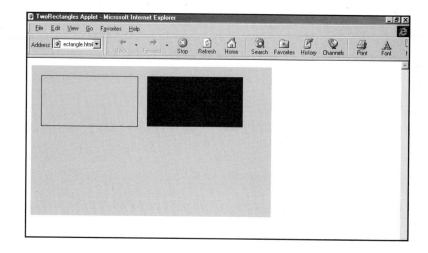

```
public abstract void drawRoundRect(int  x, int  y, int  width,
    ➥int  height, int  arcWidth, int  arcHeight)

public abstract void fillRoundRect(int  x, int  y, int  width,
    ➥int height, int  arcWidth,  int  arcHeight)
```

The `arcWidth` and `arcHeight` parameters determine how the corners will be rounded. Using an `arcWidth` of 10 results in including the leftmost 5 pixels and the rightmost 5 pixels of each horizontal side of a rectangle in the rectangle's rounded corners. Similarly, using an `arcHeight` of 8 includes the topmost 4 pixels and the bottommost 4 pixels of each vertical side of a rectangle in the rectangle's rounded corners. Figure 39.5 shows rectangles with rounded corners constructed using these parameter values. The body of this applet contains the lines

```
g.drawRoundRect(20, 20, 200, 100, 40, 20);
g.fillRoundRect(240, 20, 200, 100, 40, 20);
```

FIGURE 39.5

Rectangles with rounded corners were drawn using the `drawRoundRect()` and `fillRoundRect()` methods.

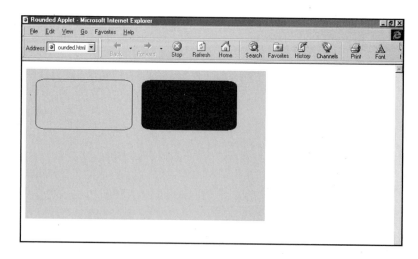

In addition to the regular rectangles and those with rounded corners, the Graphics class provides two methods for drawing three-dimensional rectangles: the draw3DRect() and fill3DRect() methods. The complete definitions of the three-dimensional rectangle methods are:

```
public void draw3DRect(int  x, int  y, int  width,
Âint  height, boolean  raised)

public void fill3DRect(int  x, int  y, int  width,
Âint  height, boolean  raised)
```

The syntax for the draw3DRect() and fill3DRect() methods is similar to the drawRect() and fillRect() methods except that they have an extra parameter added to the end of their parameter lists. It is a boolean parameter that results in a raised rectangle effect when set to true. If it is set to false, the face of the rectangle shows a sunken effect. The applet in Listing 39.3 draws raised and lowered, filled and unfilled rectangles.

N O T E The three-dimensional rectangles discussed here do not actually exist as three-dimensional objects. A shadow effect is used to give the illusion that they are three dimensional. This effect consists of a relatively dark color along two adjacent sides of a rectangle and a light color along the opposite two sides. Java assumes the light source to be from the upper-left corner of the screen. ▪

ON THE WEB

http://java.sun.com/products/java-media/3D/   Sun is developing a set of classes for writing true 3D objects. Learn more on this Web page.

Listing 39.3   *Rect3D.java*—3-D Rectangles Have a Shadow that Assumes Light Comes from the Upper-Left Corner

```java
import java.awt.Graphics;

// This applet draws four varieties of 3D rectangles.
// It sets the drawing color to the same color as the
// background.

public class Rect3D extends java.applet.Applet
{
   public void paint(Graphics g)
   {
     // Make the drawing color the same as the background
     g.setColor(getBackground());
     // Draw a raised 3D rectangle in the upper-left
     g.draw3DRect(20, 20, 200, 100, true);
     // Draw a lowered 3-D rectangle in the upper-right
     g.draw3DRect(240, 20, 200, 100, false);
     // Fill a raised 3D rectangle in the lower-left
     g.fill3DRect(20, 140, 200, 100, true);
     // Fill a lowered 3D rectangle in the lower-right
     g.fill3DRect(240, 140, 200, 100, false);
   }
}
```

Figure 39.6 shows the output from the Rect3D applet. The raised rectangles appear the same when filled or unfilled because the drawing color is the same color as the background. If a different drawing color were used, the filled rectangle would be filled with the drawing color, whereas the unfilled rectangle would still show the background color.

TIP Three-dimensional rectangles typically look best when their color matches the background color. Three-dimensional effects depend on several aspects of your system, including your computer graphics and color capabilities and the browser you use. If your three-dimensional effects are less than satisfactory, try using different colors. Color manipulation using Java is covered in detail later in this chapter in the section titled "Displaying Colors."

FIGURE 39.6

The draw3DRect() and fill3DRect() methods use shading to produce a three-dimensional effect.

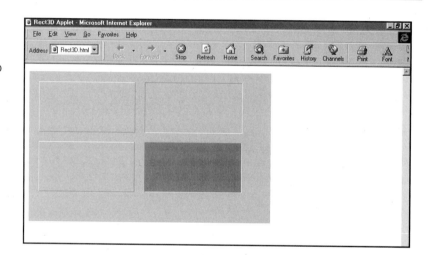

Drawing Ovals

The Java Graphics class provides two methods for drawing ovals or circles: the drawOval() and fillOval() methods. The full definitions of these methods are as follows:

```
public abstract void drawOval(int  x, int  y, int width, int  height)

public abstract void fillOval(int  x, int  y, int  width, int  height)
```

N O T E A circle is an oval with its width equal to its height.

To draw an oval, imagine surrounding the oval with a rectangle that just touches the oval at its widest and highest points as illustrated in Figure 39.7. Listing 39.4 shows the code.

FIGURE 39.7

The same oval is inside its bounding rectangle on the left and by itself on the right.

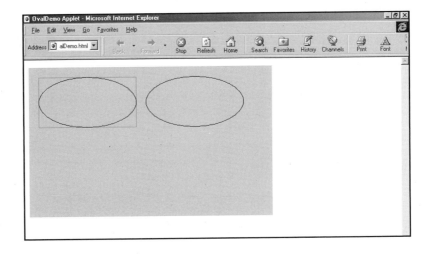

Listing 39.4   OvalDemo.java—Think of Ovals as Lying Inside a Bounding Rectangle

```java
import java.awt.Graphics;
import java.awt.Color;

public class OvalDemo extends java.applet.Applet
{
    public void paint(Graphics g)
    {
        // Draw a gray rectangle 200 pixels wide and 100 pixels
        //   high with its upper left corner at (20, 20).
        g.setColor(Color.gray);
        g.drawRect(20, 20, 200, 100);
        // Draw an oval inside the rectangle created above.
        g.setColor(Color.black);
        g.drawOval(20, 20, 200, 100);
        // Draw the oval again but to the right of the oval above.
        g.drawOval(240, 20, 200, 100);
    }
}
```

You pass the coordinates of the upper-left corner of the imaginary surrounding rectangle and the width and height of the oval to drawOval() or fillOval(). The width and height are equal to the width and height of the imaginary surrounding rectangle. The Ovals applet in Listing 39.5 draws a circle and a filled oval. Figure 39.8 shows the output from the Ovals applet.

Listing 39.5   Ovals.java—You Can Use the Oval Methods to Draw a Circle

```java
import java.awt.Graphics;

// This applet draws an unfilled circle and a filled oval
```

continues

Part
VII

Ch
39

Listing 39.5   Continued

```
public class Ovals extends java.applet.Applet
{
    public void paint(Graphics g)
    {
        // Draw a circle with a diameter of 150 (width=150, height=150)
        // With the enclosing rectangle's upper-left corner at (20, 20)
        g.drawOval(20, 20, 150, 150);
        // Fill an oval with a width of 150 and a height of 80
        // The upper-left corner of the enclosing rectangle is at (200, 20)
        g.fillOval(200, 20, 150, 80);
    }
}
```

FIGURE 39.8

Draw ovals and circles by using the Graphics class drawOval() and fillOval() methods.

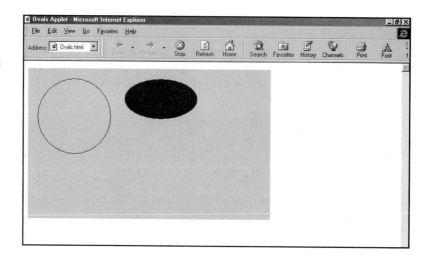

Drawing Arcs

An arc is a segment of the line that forms the perimeter of an oval, as demonstrated in Figure 39.9. This output is generated by the ArcDemo1 applet shown in Listing 39.6.

Listing 39.6   *ArcDemo1.java*—Think of an Arc as a Wedge of an Oval

```
import java.awt.Graphics;
import java.awt.Color;

public class ArcDemo1 extends java.applet.Applet
{
    public void paint(Graphics g)
    {
        // Draw a gray oval 200 pixels wide and 100 pixels
        //   high with the upper left corner of its
        //   enclosing rectangle at (20, 20).
```

```
    g.setColor(Color.gray);
    g.drawOval(20, 20, 200, 100);
    // Draw a black arc from 0 to 90 degrees inside
    //   the oval created above.
    g.setColor(Color.black);
    g.drawArc(20, 20, 200, 100, 0, 90);
    // Draw the same arc as above but to the right
    //   with the upper left corner of its enclosing
    //   rectangle at (240, 20).
    g.drawArc(240, 20, 200, 100, 0, 90);
  }
}
```

FIGURE 39.9

At the left are the arc and its associated oval, and at the right is the arc alone.

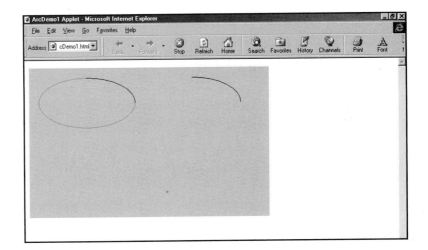

Two Graphics class methods are provided for drawing arcs: the drawArc() and fillArc() methods. Their complete definitions are as follows:

```
public abstract void drawArc(int  x,  int  y,  int  width,
  ➥int  height, int  startAngle, int  arcAngle)

public abstract void fillArc(int  x,  int  y,  int  width,
  ➥int  height, int  startAngle, int  arcAngle)
```

Use the first four parameters just as you did with the oval methods. In fact, you are drawing an invisible oval and the arc is a segment of the oval's perimeter defined by startAngle and arcAngle, the last two parameters.

The startAngle parameter defines where your arc starts along the invisible oval's perimeter. In Java, angles are set around a 360° circle as follows:

- 0° is at 3 o'clock.
- 90° is at 12 o'clock.
- 180° is at 9 o'clock.
- 270° is at 6 o'clock.

Part

VII

Ch

39

The arcAngle parameter defines the distance, in degrees, that your arc traverses along the invisible oval's perimeter. Angles are positive in the counterclockwise direction and negative in the clockwise direction.

The arc you saw in Figure 39.9 began at 0°, or at 3 o'clock, and traversed the invisible oval 90° in the positive, or counterclockwise, direction. The relevant line in Listing 39.6 is reproduced here:

```
g.drawArc(20, 20, 200, 100, 0, 90);
```

Notice that the last parameter is given in the angle traversed and not the angle at which the arc ends. Therefore, if you want an arc that starts at 45° and ends at 135°, you must provide a startAngle parameter value of 45° and an arcAngle parameter value of 90°.

N O T E   When you use a negative arcAngle parameter value, the arc sweeps clockwise along the invisible oval's perimeter. ▪

Using the fillArc() method results in a filled, pie-shaped wedge defined by the center of the invisible oval and the perimeter segment traversed by the arc.

Drawing Polygons

The Java Graphics class provides four methods for building polygons: two versions of the drawPolygon() method and two versions of the fillPolygon() method. Each has two methods so that you can either pass two arrays containing the x , y coordinate of the points in the polygon, or you can pass an instance of a Polygon class. The Polygon class is defined in the java.awt package.

Making a Polygon by Passing Coordinate Arrays   First look at how to make a polygon by using two arrays. The full definitions of the drawPolygon() and fillPolygon() methods for using arrays are

```
public abstract void drawPolygon(int  xPoints[], int yPoints[],
 Âint  nPoints)

public abstract void fillPolygon(int  xPoints[], int  yPoints[],
 Âint  nPoints)
```

The DrawPoly applet in Listing 39.7 draws a polygon using an array of x coordinates (xCoords) and an array of y coordinates (yCoords). Each x,y pair, the first x (50) and the first y (100) pair, for instance, defines a point on a plane (50, 100). Use the drawPolygon method to connect each point to the following point in the list. The first pair is (50, 100) and connects by a line to the second pair (200, 0), and so on. The drawPolygon method's third parameter, nPoints, is the number of points in the polygon and should equal the number of pairs in the x and y arrays. Figure 39.10 shows the DrawPoly applet's output.

Listing 39.7 *DrawPoly.java*—**This Applet Draws Polygons Based on Arrays of Coordinates**

```java
import java.awt.Graphics;

public class DrawPoly extends java.applet.Applet
{
    int xCoords[] = { 50, 200, 300, 150, 50 };
    int yCoords[] = { 100, 0, 50, 300, 200 };

    int xFillCoords[] = { 450, 600, 700, 550, 450 };

    public void paint(Graphics g)
    {
      // Draw the left polygon.
      g.drawPolygon(xCoords, yCoords, 5);
      // Draw the right filled polygon.
      g.fillPolygon(xFillCoords, yCoords, 5);
    }
}
```

 TIP The applets in this chapter assume that you have a graphics resolution of at least 800 pixels across by 600 pixels top to bottom (800×600). If your monitor displays a smaller number of pixels (640×480, for example), you can either use your browser's scroll bars to see the rest of the applet window, or you can change some of the coordinates in the example so that they are no larger than your largest screen coordinates.

Part
VII

Ch
39

FIGURE 39.10

Draw polygons using x and y arrays.

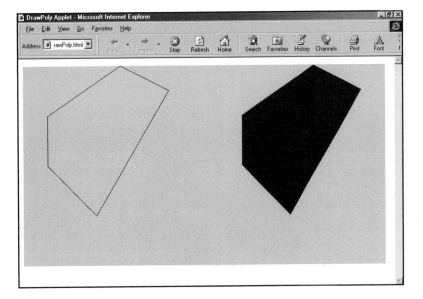

Using Java's *Polygon* Class   The Java `Polygon` class provides features that often make it the most convenient way to define polygons. The `Polygon` class provides the two constructors, defined as follows:

```
public Polygon()
public Polygon(int  xpoints[], int  ypoints[], int  npoints)
```

These constructors enable you to either instantiate an empty polygon or instantiate a polygon by initially passing an array of x and an array of y numbers and the number of points made up of the x and y pairs. If you do the latter, the parameters are saved in the following `Polygon` class fields:

```
public int xpoints[]
public int ypoints[]
public int npoints
```

Regardless of whether you started with an empty polygon, you can add points to it dynamically by using the `Polygon` class `addPoint()` method, defined as follows:

```
public void addPoint(int  x, int  y)
```

The `addPoint()` method automatically increments the `Polygon` class number of points field, named `npoints`.

The `Polygon` class includes two other methods: the `getBoundingBox()` and `inside()` methods, defined as follows:

```
public Rectangle getBoundingBox()
public boolean inside(int  x, int  y)
```

You can use the `getBoundingBox()` method to determine the minimum-sized box that can completely surround the polygon in screen coordinates. The `Rectangle` class returned by `getBoundingBox()` contains variables indicating the x , y coordinates of the rectangle along with the rectangle's width and height.

You determine whether a point is contained within the polygon or is outside it by calling the `inside` methods with the x,y coordinate of the point.

Use the `Polygon` class in place of the x and y arrays for either the `drawPolygon()` or `fillPolygon()` method as indicated in their definitions, shown here:

```
public void drawPolygon(Polygon  p)
public void fillPolygon(Polygon  p)
```

The `Polygon` class is used for both the `drawPolygon()` and the `fillPolygon()` methods in Listing 39.8. This applet's output is identical to Figure 39.10.

Listing 39.8   *Polygons.java*—This Applet Draws Polygons Based on a *Polygon* Object

```
import java.awt.Graphics;
import java.awt.Polygon;

public class Polygons extends java.applet.Applet
```

```
{
    int xCoords[] = { 50, 200, 300, 150, 50, 50 };
    int yCoords[] = { 100, 0, 50, 300, 200, 100 };

    int xFillCoords[] = { 450, 600, 700, 550, 450, 450 };

    public void paint(Graphics g)
    {
        Polygon myPolygon = new Polygon(xCoords, yCoords, 6);
        Polygon myFilledPolygon = new Polygon(xFillCoords, yCoords, 6);
        // Draw the left polygon.
        g.drawPolygon(myPolygon);
        // Draw the right filled polygon.
        g.fillPolygon(myFilledPolygon);
    }
}
```

Displaying Colors

Remember when you were in elementary school, and the teacher showed you how to make green by combining yellow and blue paint? Forget all that—those techniques applied to pigments on paper, in which colors are made by subtracting colors from the white light falling on the paper. Most of the graphics you make in Java need to look good on a computer screen—an additive process based on the primary colors red, green, and blue. Common combinations are

- Red and green, which results in yellow when the colors are bright and in brown when the colors are less intense
- Green and blue, resulting in cyan
- Red and blue, resulting in magenta

Black is formed by the absence of all light, and white is formed by the combination of all the additive primary colors. In other words, red, blue, and green, transmitted in equal amounts, result in white.

N O T E   The color effects of subtractive pigments and directly transmitted (additive) light are closely related. Each color pigment absorbs light, but not all of it. The color of a pigment is due to the wavelength of the light that the pigment does not absorb—and, therefore, the light that the pigment reflects. Because the absence of pigments results in all wavelengths of light being reflected, the result is white. This effect is the same as the transmission of all the additive primary colors of light. In contrast, all the colored pigments mixed together absorb all light. This effect is equivalent to the color black resulting from the absence of light. ■

Java uses the RGB (Red, Green, and Blue) color model. You define the colors you want by indicating the amount of red, green, and blue light that you want to transmit to the viewer. You can do this either by using integers between 0 and 255 or by using floating-point numbers between 0.0 and 1.0. Table 39.1 indicates the red, green, and blue amounts for some common colors. Note that you don't always have to specify the RGB values—the Color class includes some named colors, such as red, blue, and white, as shown in the first column of Table 39.1.

Part
VII

Ch
39

Table 39.1   Common Colors and Their RGB Values

Color Name	Red Value	Green Value	Blue Value
Color.black	0	0	0
Color.blue	0	0	255
Color.cyan	0	255	255
Color.darkGray	64	64	64
Color.gray	128	128	128
Color.green	0	255	0
Color.lightGray	192	192	192
Color.magenta	255	0	255
Color.orange	255	200	0
Color.pink	255	175	175
Color.red	255	0	0
Color.white	255	255	255
Color.yellow	255	255	0

You must import the Color class to use a Color class constant, but you don't need to make a new Color object. Just type the class name followed by the dot operator followed by the color name. For example, you can write

```
g.setColor(Color.yellow);
g.fillOval(50, 50, 200, 200);
```

to get a yellow oval.

N O T E   Although the Graphics class uses an informal version of the RGB model, the Graphics2D class is based on a proposed standard called *sRGB*. For more information, see "Using the 2D API" later in this chapter, or visit the standard's Web site, http://www.w3.org/pub/WWW/Graphics/Color/sRGB.html.

Java's Graphics class provides two methods for manipulating colors: the getColor() and setColor() methods. Their full definitions are:

```
public abstract Color getColor()
public abstract void setColor(Color c)
```

The getColor() method returns the Graphics object's current color encapsulated in a Color object, and the setColor() method sets the Graphics object's color by passing it a Color object.

Using Java's *Color* Class

The Color class is defined in the java.awt package and has three constructors. The first constructor enables you to instantiate a Color object using explicit red (r), green (g), and blue (b) integers between 0 and 255:

```
public Color(int  r, int  g, int  b)
```

The second constructor is similar to the first. Instead of integer values, it uses floating-point values between 0.0 and 1.0 for red (r), green (g), and blue (b):

```
public Color(float  r, float  g, float  b)
```

The third constructor enables you to make a Color using red, green, and blue integers between 0 and 255, but you combine the three numbers into a single, typically hexadecimal, value (rgb):

```
public Color(int  rgb)
```

In the 32-bit rgb integer, bits 16 through 23 (8 bits) hold the red value, bits 8 through 15 (8 bits) hold the green value, and bits 0 through 7 (8 bits) hold the blue value. The highest 8 bits, bits 24 through 32, are not manipulated. You usually write rgb values in hexadecimal notation so that it is easy to see the color values. A number prefaced with 0x is read as hexadecimal. For instance, 0xFFA978 would give a red value of 0xFF (255 decimal), a green value of 0xA9 (52 decimal), and a blue value of 0x78 (169 decimal).

After you make a Color object, set a Graphics object's drawing color by using its setColor method. The default drawing color for Graphics objects is black. The ColorPlay applet in Listing 39.9 gets the graphics context's default color and assigns it to the defaultColor variable by passing the color value encapsulated in a Color object. A new Color object is built by using a hexadecimal value and is assigned to the newColor variable. We draw a filled circle on the left using newColor and another on the right using the defaultColor variable. Figure 39.11 shows the resulting output.

TROUBLESHOOTING

How do you return to the original color assigned to your program's Graphics object?

It's a good policy to always save the color assigned to your program's Graphics object to a Color object variable before you assign it a new color. That way you can reassign the original color to the Graphics object after the program is finished using the new color.

Listing 39.9   *ColorPlay.java*—When You Set the Color You Affect All Subsequent Drawing

```
import java.awt.Graphics;
import java.awt.Color;

public class ColorPlay extends java.applet.Applet
```

continues

Listing 39.9   Continued

```
{
    public void paint(Graphics g)
    {
        // Assign the red Color object to newColor.
        Color newColor = new Color(0xFFA978);
        // Assign Graphic object's current color to default Color.
        Color defaultColor = g.getColor();
        // Draw a red oval 200 pixels wide and 200 pixels
        //  high with the upper left corner of its
        //  enclosing rectangle at (50, 50).
        g.setColor(newColor);
        g.fillOval(50, 50, 200, 200);
        // Draw an oval 200 pixels wide and 200 pixels
        //  high with the upper left corner of its
        //  enclosing rectangle at (300, 50) in the
        //  default color.
        g.setColor(defaultColor);
        g.fillOval(300, 50, 200, 200);
    }
}
```

FIGURE 39.11

Make color graphics by changing the graphics context's current color using the setColor method.

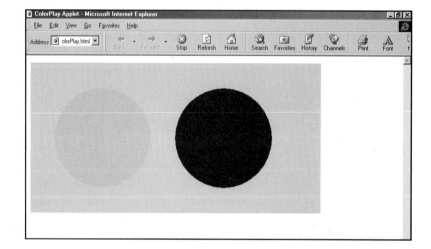

Displaying Text

Java's Graphics class provides seven methods related to displaying text. Before plunging into the various aspects of drawing text, however, you should be familiar with the following common terms for fonts and text:

- *Baseline* is the imaginary line that the text rests on.
- *Descent* is the distance below the baseline that a particular character extends. The letters *g* and *j,* for instance, extend below the baseline.

- *Ascent* is the distance above the baseline that a particular character extends. For instance, the letter *d* has a higher ascent than the letter *x*.

- *Leading* is the space between a line of text's lowest descent and the following line of text's highest ascent. Without leading, the letters *g* and *j* would touch the letters *M* and *h* on the next line.

Figure 39.12 illustrates the relationships among descent, ascent, baseline, and leading.

FIGURE 39.12

Java's font terminology originated in the publishing field.

CAUTION

The term "ascent," as used in Java, is slightly different from the way the term is used in the publishing world. The publishing term "ascent" refers to the distance from the top of a letter such as x to the top of a character such as d. In contrast, the Java term "ascent" refers to the distance from baseline to the top of a character.

N O T E You may hear the terms "*proportional*" and "*fixed*" associated with fonts. Characters in a proportional font take up only as much space as they need. In a fixed font, every character takes up the same amount of space.

Most of the text in this book is in a proportional font. Compare the width of the letters in a word with a proportional font with the letters of the same word in a fixed font:

```
FIXIM
FIXIM
```

One simple way to display text in Java is to draw from an array of bytes representing ASCII characters or from an array of 16-bit Unicode characters. You can use an array of ASCII codes when you use the drawBytes() method, or you can use an array of characters when you use the drawChars() method. Both of these methods are available in Java's Graphics class. They are defined as

```
public void drawBytes(byte  data[], int  offset, int  length,
⮑int  x, int  y)
public void drawChars(char  data[], int  offset, int  length,
⮑int  x, int  y)
```

The offset parameter refers to the position of the first character or byte in the array to draw. This is most often zero because you will usually want to draw from the beginning of the array.

The length parameter is the total number of bytes or characters in the array. The x coordinate is the integer value that represents the beginning position of the text, in number of pixels, from the left edge of the applet's window. The y coordinate is distance, in pixels, from the top of the applet's window to the text's baseline. The DrawChars applet in Listing 39.10 displays text from an array of ASCII codes in blue and text from an array of characters in red. Figure 39.13 shows the DrawChars applet's output.

Listing 39.10   *DrawChars.java*—This Applet Draws Text Based on Arrays of *bytes* and *chars*

```
import java.awt.Graphics;
import java.awt.Color;

public class DrawChars extends java.applet.Applet
{
   byte[] bytesToDraw = { 72, 101, 108, 108, 111, 32,
➥87, 111, 114, 108, 100, 33 };
   char[] charsToDraw = { 'H', 'e', 'l', 'l', 'o', ' ',
➥'W', 'o', 'r', 'l', 'd', '!' };

   public void paint(Graphics g)
   {
     // Draw Hello World! from bytes in blue.
     g.setColor(Color.blue);
     g.drawBytes(bytesToDraw, 0, bytesToDraw.length, 10, 20);
     // Draw Hello World! from characters in red.
     g.setColor(Color.red);
     g.drawChars(charsToDraw, 0, charsToDraw.length, 10, 50);
   }
}
```

N O T E   The numbers used in the byte array, bytesToDraw, are base-10 ASCII codes. They are the numbers that most computer systems use to represent letters. (Java uses the 16-bit Unicode, but for the common characters and punctuation marks of English the Unicode codes are identical to the ASCII codes.) You could use any base for these numbers, including the popular hexadecimal. ▪

Arrays are objects in Java. You made two array objects when you built the two arrays, bytesToDraw and charsToDraw, in Listing 39.10. That is why you could use the array property, length, to get the lengths of the arrays in number of bytes or characters.

Java provides another object type, the String object, which is similar to the array objects that you just built. It is, however, more convenient for manipulating text.

Using Java's *String* Class

The Java Graphics class provides a method for displaying text by drawing a string of characters. The method, the drawString() method shown here, takes a String object as a parameter:

```
public abstract void drawString(String  str, int  x, int  y)
```

FIGURE 39.13

The drawBytes method displays the first line of text in blue, and the drawChars method displays the second line of text in red.

If you put double quotation marks around a string, Java automatically makes a String object. You then pass an x coordinate—the integer value that represents the beginning position of the text in number of pixels from the left edge of the applet's window, and pass a y coordinate—the distance in pixels from the top of the applet's window to the text's baseline.

Making *Strings* Automatically   The StringObjects applet in Listing 39.11 demonstrates two ways of passing a String object to the drawString() method. A String object is automatically built in the argument list of line 12. The drawString method in line 15 is passed to a String object assigned to the myString variable, which was built in line 5. This call to the drawString method produces text displayed in red, because the color is changed in line 14. The StringObjects applet's output is identical to that shown in Figure 39.13.

Listing 39.11   *StringObjects.java*—You Can Make a *String* Automatically or Explicitly

```java
import java.awt.Graphics;
import java.awt.Color;

public class StringObjects extends java.applet.Applet
{
    String myString = new String("Hello World!");

    public void paint(Graphics g)
    {
      // Draw Hello World! in blue.
      g.setColor(Color.blue);
      g.drawString("Hello World!", 10, 20);
      // Draw Hello World! in red.
      g.setColor(Color.red);
      g.drawString(myString, 10, 50);
    }
}
```

Building One *String* from Another   The String object assigned to the myString variable was initiated with another String object through the following String class constructor:

```java
public String(String  value)
```

Building *Strings* from Byte Arrays   Java's String class provides nine constructors, including the preceding one, so you have several options for building a String object. In fact, you can build `String` objects from the byte arrays or character arrays you used for the `drawBytes` and `drawChars` methods previously discussed.

You can use one of the following two constructors when you create `String` objects from byte arrays:

```
public String(byte  bytes[])
public String(byte  bytes[], int  offset, int  length)
```

The first parameter in both constructors, `bytes[]`, is the byte array. In the second constructor, the `offset` parameter refers to the position of the first byte in the array to draw. The `length` parameter is the total number of bytes to include in the output. The StringsOne applet demonstrates these two `String` constructors in Listing 39.12.

The `String` object assigned to the `bytesString` variable is passed to an array of ASCII codes. The `String` object assigned to the `bytesAnotherString` variable is passed to the array of ASCII codes; in addition, a 6 is passed to the `offset` parameter and another 6 is passed to the `length` parameter.

TIP To count your offset, start with zero. An offset of six ends up on *W* in "Hello World!" Don't forget to count spaces as characters.

Listing 39.12   StringsOne.java—Build *Strings* from Byte Arrays

```
import java.awt.Graphics;
import java.awt.Color;

public class StringsOne extends java.applet.Applet
{
   byte[] bytesToDraw = { 72, 101, 108, 108, 111, 32,
 ➥87, 111, 114, 108, 100, 33 };

   String bytesString = new String( bytesToDraw );
   String bytesAnotherString = new String( bytesToDraw, 6, 6 );

   public void paint(Graphics g)
   {
     // Draw Hello World! in blue.
     g.setColor(Color.blue);
     g.drawString(bytesString, 10, 20);
     // Draw World! in red.
     g.setColor(Color.red);
     g.drawString(bytesAnotherString, 10, 50);
   }
}
```

The StringsOne applet output is identical to the output shown in Figure 39.13.

Building *Strings* From Character Arrays   You use one of the following two constructors when you make `String` objects from character arrays:

```
public String(char  value[])
public String(char  value[], int  offset, int  count)
```

These constructors behave analogously to the two constructors that use `byte` arrays.

Making an Empty *String*   If you pass nothing to a `String` object when you make it, you'll get an empty string:

```
public String()
```

You can then use the class's methods to dynamically change the content. Class `String` has more than 40 properties and methods—see your documentation to learn how to manipulate `Strings`.

> **CAUTION**
>
> For security reasons, Java's strings are *immutable*—after you make one, you cannot change it. When you manipulate it (for example, by extracting substrings) the Java runtime makes a new string. All this building and releasing of string storage can have an impact on performance.

 TIP
If your program manipulates passwords, store them as a `char` array rather than as a `String` object. After you've used the password, overwrite it, minimizing the time the password is in memory.

Using Java's *Font* Class

You may find that the default font you have been working with so far is not very interesting. Fortunately, you can select from a number of fonts. Java's `Graphics` class provides the `setFont()` method, defined here, so that you can change your text's font characteristics:

```
public abstract void setFont(Font  font)
```

The `setFont` method takes a `Font` object as its argument. Java provides a `Font` class that gives you a lot of text-formatting flexibility. The `Font` class provides a single constructor

```
public Font(String  name, int  style, int  size)
```

Pass the name of the font, surrounded by double quotation marks, to the name parameter. The availability of fonts varies from system to system, so it is a good idea to make sure that the user has the font you want. You can check the availability of a font by using the `Toolkit` class `getFontList` method defined here:

```
public abstract String[] getFontList()
```

 TROUBLESHOOTING

How do you avoid demanding the use of a font in your program that a user does not have?

Always query for the available fonts by using the `getFontList` method, and then use only those fonts in your program. This dynamic method of using fonts is the best policy for distributed computing software such as Java programs.

Typically, you don't import the `Toolkit` class. Instead, you use the `Applet` class `getToolkit()` method (which is inherited from the `Component` class), defined as follows:

```
public Toolkit getToolkit()
```

You use the `style` parameter to set the font style. Bold, italic, plain, as well as the combination (bold and italic) are available. The `Font` class provides three class constants: `Font.BOLD`, `Font.ITALIC`, and `Font.PLAIN`, which you can use in any combination to set the font style. To set a font to bold, for example, pass `Font.BOLD` to the `style` parameter. If you want to display a bold italic font, you pass `Font.BOLD + Font.ITALIC` to `Font` class's `style` parameter.

Finally, you set the point size of the font by passing an integer to `Font` class's `size` parameter. The point size is a printing term. When printing on a printer, an inch has 100 points, but this does not necessarily apply to screen fonts. Just as in your word processor, a typical point size value for printed text is 12 or 14. The point size does not indicate the number of pixels high or wide; it is a relative term. A point size of 24 is twice as big as a point size of 12.

All this information is pulled together in the ShowFonts applet, shown in Listing 39.13. Figure 39.14 shows the output from the ShowFonts applet.

Listing 39.13 *ShowFonts.java*—Use This Simple Applet to Display the Variety of Fonts Available

```java
import java.awt.Graphics;
import java.awt.Font;

public class ShowFonts extends java.applet.Applet
{
    public void paint(Graphics g)
    {
        String fontList[];
        int startY = 15;

        // Get the list of fonts installed on
        //   this computer.
        fontList = getToolkit().getFontList();

        // Go through the list of fonts and draw each
        //   to the applet window.
        for (int i=0; i < fontList.length; i++)
        {
            // Draw font name in plain type.
            g.setFont(new Font(fontList[i], Font.PLAIN, 12));
            g.drawString("This is the " + fontList[i] + " font.",
    ➥5, startY);
            startY += 15;

            // Draw font name in bold type.
            g.setFont(new Font(fontList[i], Font.BOLD, 12));
            g.drawString("This is the bold "+ fontList[i] + " font.",
    ➥5, startY);
            startY += 15;
```

```
        // Draw font name in italic type.
        g.setFont(new Font(fontList[i], Font.ITALIC, 12));
        g.drawString("This is the italic " + fontList[i] + " font.",
➡5, startY);
        startY += 20;
      }
    }
}
```

FIGURE 39.14

Java provides a number of fonts and font styles.

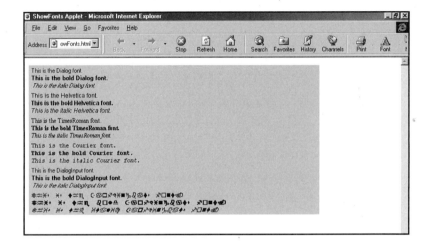

Displaying Images

To use Java to display images, you must first get the image, and then you must draw it. The Java `Applet` class provides methods for getting images, and the Java `Graphics` class provides methods for drawing them.

Java's `Applet` class provides two `getImage()` methods, listed here:

```
public Image getImage(URL  url)
public Image getImage(URL  url, String  name)
```

In the first method listed, you provide an URL class. You can just type the URL surrounded by double quotation marks, or you can create an URL object and then pass it to the `getImage()` method. If you do the latter, be sure to import the URL class. The URL class is part of the `java.net` package.

Whichever way you pass the URL, the first method takes the whole path, including the filename of the image itself. Because images are usually aggregated into a single directory or folder, it is usually handier to keep the path and filename separate.

The second method takes the URL path to the image as the `url` parameter, and it takes the filename—or even part of the path and the filename—as a string enclosed by double quotation marks and passed to the `name` parameter.

The `Applet` class provides two particularly useful methods, the `getDocumentBase()` and `getCodeBase()` methods, as follows:

```
public URL getDocumentBase()
public URL getCodeBase()
```

The `getDocumentBase()` method returns an `URL` object containing the path to where the HTML document resides that displays the Java applet. Similarly, the `getCodeBase()` method returns an `URL` object that contains the path to where the applet is running the code. Using these methods makes your applet flexible. You and others can use your applet on different servers, directories, or folders.

Java's `Graphics` class provides `drawImage()` methods to use for displaying images. The most basic method is listed here:

```
public abstract boolean drawImage(Image  img, int  x, int  y,
  ➡ImageObserver  observer)
```

The first parameter, `img`, takes an `Image` object. Often, you will get an `Image` object by using the `getImage()` method, as discussed previously. The second, `x`, and third, `y`, parameters set the position of the upper-left corner of the image in the applet's window. The last parameter, `observer`, takes an object that implements the `ImageObserver` interface. This design enables your code to make decisions based on an image's loading status. It is usually enough to know that the `Applet` class inherits the `ImageObserver` interface from the `Component` class. Just passing the applet itself (`this`) as the `observer` parameter is usually sufficient. You might use an alternative object with an `ImageObserver` interface if you are tracking the asynchronous loading of many images.

TROUBLESHOOTING

The image doesn't load into the applet. What do you do?

Make sure that the image is in the proper folder—either in the same folder as the Java code or in the same folder as the HTML document, depending on the method your program uses. See the section, "Loading Images over the Web," later in this chapter if the problem is due to slow or faulty network connections.

Basic image display is easier than it sounds. The DrawImageOne applet in Listing 39.14 displays an image residing in the same directory or folder as the applet itself. Figure 39.15 shows the output of the DrawImageOne applet.

N O T E   Place the `Earth1.gif` image file into the same folder as the `DrawImageOne.class` file before you try to run the DrawImageOne applet. ■

Listing 39.14 *DrawImageOne.java*—**Retrieve an Image from the Applet's Server and Display It**

```java
import java.awt.Graphics;

public class DrawImageOne extends java.applet.Applet
{
    public void paint(Graphics g)
    {
        // Load Earth image and draw it in the applet's window.
        g.drawImage(getImage(getCodeBase(), "Earth1.gif"), 0, 0, this);
    }
}
```

FIGURE 39.15

You can draw any JPG or GIF image in a Java applet window by using the `drawImage()` method.

The code in Listing 39.14 is simple—too simple. It is poor coding practice to put actions not directly related to putting something onscreen inside your applet's `paint()` method. Every time your applet's window needs updating, the `paint` method is called. In this case, the applet is forced to reload the image every time your applet's window is refreshed. You should override the `init()` method to take actions such as loading images that are only done one time, at the beginning of the applet's life. The `init()` method takes no arguments and returns void. Listing 39.15 shows a well-behaved applet that displays the same output as the applet in Listing 39.14.

N O T E Place the `Earth1.gif` image file into the same folder as the `DrawImageTwo.class` file before you try to run the DrawImageTwo applet.

Listing 39.15 *DrawImageTwo.java*—**Improve Performance by Loading Images Only Once, in *init()***

```java
import java.awt.Graphics;
import java.awt.Image;

public class DrawImageTwo extends java.applet.Applet
{
    private Image fImage;
```

continues

Listing 39.15   Continued

```
public void init()
{
  // Load image.
  fImage = getImage(getCodeBase(), "Earth1.gif");
}

public void paint(Graphics g)
{
  // Draw image in the applet's window.
  g.drawImage(fImage, 0, 0, this);
}
}
```

Notice that in Listing 39.15, the image from the Earth1.gif file loads only one time, in the init() method. When the applet window is refreshed, the Image object assigned to the fImage variable is passed to the drawImage() method without reloading the image from the Earth1.gif file.

Another version of the drawImage() method is similar to the one you have already seen and used, but it includes two additional parameters. These enable you to determine the size of the image displayed in an applet window. This version of the drawImage() method is as follows:

```
public abstract boolean drawImage(Image  img, int  x, int  y,
        int  width, int  height, ImageObserver  observer)
```

The width and height parameters take the width and height, in pixels, of the display area for the image regardless of the image's native size. You can stretch and shrink an image by using these parameters; the actual disk size of the image remains the same.

CAUTION

Changing the size of the image at runtime can degrade the quality of your image. For best results, use your graphics tools to scale the image to the desired size, and don't attempt to use Java for further scaling.

Adding Animation

As you develop your user interfaces—particularly user interfaces for applets—you may find a need for animation. The previous section explored drawImage(); it is the graphical analog of drawString() that we've been using for a while. It may occur to you to put up an animation using a technique similar to that shown in Listing 39.16.

Listing 39.16   *Animation1.java*—This Applet Loads and Displays a Series of Images in Rapid Succession

```
import java.awt.*;
import java.applet.Applet;
```

```
public class Animation1 extends Applet implements Runnable {
    int fFrame = -1;
    int fDelay;
    Thread fThread;
    Image[] fEarth;

    public void init() {
      fEarth = new Image[30];
      String theString;
      int theFramesPerSecond = 10;

      //load in the images
      for (int i=1; i<=30; i++)
      {
      System.err.println("Starting load from " +
         getCodeBase() +
         " of ./Earth" + i +".gif");
         fEarth[i-1] = getImage (getCodeBase(),
                                 "./Earth"+i+".gif");
      }

      //How many milliseconds between frames?
      theString = getParameter("fps");
      try {
        if (theString != null) {
            theFramesPerSecond = Integer.parseInt(theString );
        }
      } catch (NumberFormatException e) {}
      fDelay = (theFramesPerSecond > 0) ?
               (1000 / theFramesPerSecond) : 100;
    }

    public void start() {
      // start a new thread for the animation
      if (fThread == null) {
          fThread = new Thread(this);
      }
      fThread.start();
    }

    public void stop() {
      // stop the animation thread
      fThread = null;
    }

    public void run() {
      // run at a low priority; animation is second-place to content
      Thread.currentThread().setPriority(Thread.MIN_PRIORITY);
      long theStartTime = System.currentTimeMillis();

      //Here comes the show.
      while (Thread.currentThread() == fThread) {

        //Advance the frame.
        fFrame++;
```

continues

Listing 39.16   Continued

```
            //Display it.
            repaint();

            //Delay depending on how far we are behind.
            try {
                theStartTime += fDelay;
                Thread.sleep(Math.max(0,
                                  theStartTime-
                            System.currentTimeMillis()));
            } catch (InterruptedException e) {
                    break;
            }
        }
    }

    //Draw the current frame
    public void paint(Graphics g) {
      g.drawImage(fEarth[fFrame % 30], 0, 0, this);
    }
  }
```

This applet works, but it suffers from two problems. First, the animation is far from smooth. Even when the images are loading from the local hard drive, we notice a certain jerkiness as the frames change. Second, if we load this applet over the network, the animation may begin before all the image files have finished loading, resulting in an ugly half-drawn frame. In the next two sections we'll solve both of these problems.

We're going to use this applet as the basis for building a smooth, flicker-free animation applet. We'll examine Animation1.java in detail.

You'll notice that this applet implements an interface called Runnable. Runnable enables the applet to start a new *thread* of control so the animation can proceed independently of the user interface.

N O T E   Java interfaces are Sun's solution to multiple inheritance. A class can only subclass one base class, but it can implement as many interfaces as you like. When you subclass a class (such as Applet), you may override as many or as few of the class's methods as you like. When you implement an interface, you must provide an implementation for every method in the interface. ▨

Our list of instance variables includes a reference to the animation thread (fThread) and a reference to the array of images. We're using 30 frames of the revolving Earth, so we call this array fEarth.

In init() we loop from 1 to 30, loading the images of Earth. (They're stored in files named Earth1.gif through Earth30.gif.)

Next, we look for an applet <PARAM> called `fps` (frames per second). If we find it, we attempt to parse it into a number. If we don't find it or if we can't read it, we use 10 frames per second as the basis for calculating the delay between calls to `paint()`.

When the browser first shows the applet, it calls `init()` followed by `start()`. The browser will call `stop()` if the user iconifies the browser window or moves to a different page. We handle `start()` by checking to see whether the animation thread has already been set up. If it hasn't, we instantiate it. In either case, we `start()` the thread and destroy it in `stop()`.

The required method of `Runnable` is `run()`. The Java runtime environment calls this method whenever time is available to run our thread. Our version of `run()` starts by setting the animation thread's priority to a low value because any user interaction should take precedence over the animation. Then we simply step through the frames, `repaint` on each loop, and delay as necessary to match the desired frame rate.

Finally, the work is done in `paint()` itself (as it is in most graphics-intensive applets). We simply draw the current frame onto the screen.

Loading Images over the Web

As you experiment with this code you'll discover that it sometimes jerks a bit. This happens when the image doesn't load fast enough to support the animation, particularly when someone is loading this applet over the Internet.

A simple fix to this problem requires only six lines of code. You add an instance of the `MediaTracker` class to your applet. The `MediaTracker` knows which images are already loaded into memory and can prevent you from using an image that has not been fully loaded. A step-by-step procedure for adding a `MediaTracker` to any animation project follows:

1. Add a `MediaTracker` as an instance variable:

   ```
   MediaTracker fTracker;
   ```

2. In `init()`, instantiate a new `MediaTracker`:

   ```
   fTracker = new c1
   MediaTracker( this );
   ```

3. As each image is loaded, place it under the control of the `MediaTracker`:

   ```
   fTracker.addImage ( fEarth[i], 0 );
   ```

   The second parameter to this method, `0`, is an ID number that will be used to refer to this set of images.

4. Before the `while` loop in `run()`, call `waitForID()`:

   ```
   try {
     fTracker.waitForID( 0 );
   } catch (InterruptedException e) {
     return;
   }
   ```

5. Before using the images in `paint()`, double-check that they're loaded:

   ```
   if (fTracker.checkID( 0 ))
   ```

Fighting Flicker

You may have also noticed an annoying flicker in your animation program. This flicker occurs because a delay exists between the start of paint() and the time the image is actually loaded from the disk. You can eliminate the flicker by preloading the image into memory—a technique called *double-buffering*. Like the MediaTracker technique, double-buffering requires only a few lines of code. The following is a step-by-step procedure for adding double-buffering:

1. Add an offscreen buffer and its graphics context to the list of instance variables:

```
Image fOffScreenImage;
Graphics fOffScreenGraphics;
```

2. In init(), instantiate the offscreen buffer and paint it blue:

```
fOffScreenImage = createImage( getSize().width, getSize().height);
fOffScreenGraphics = fOffScreenImage.getGraphics();
fOffScreenGraphics.setColor(Color.blue);
fOffScreenGraphics.fillRect(0, 0, getSize().width, getSize().height);
```

3. Override update(), which is responsible for clearing the background and calling paint():

```
public void update( Graphics g ) {
  fOffScreenGraphics.setColor(Color.blue);
  fOffScreenGraphics.clearRect(0, 0, getSize().width, getSize().height);
  fOffScreenGraphics.fillRect(0, 0, getSize().width, getSize().height);
  paint(g);
}
```

4. Modify paint() so that it updates the offscreen image and draws the onscreen image from the offscreen image:

```
fOffScreenGraphics.drawImage(fEarth[i], 0, 0, this);
g.drawImage(fOffScreenImage, 0, 0, this);
```

Listing 39.17 shows the revised animation applet, with double-buffering and a MediaTracker. The new lines are shown in **boldface** font. You can use an HTML file to put the two applets up side-by-side, as a before-and-after demonstration. For smoothest performance, though, put Animation2 on a Web page without Animation1 so its thread doesn't compete with Animation1's thread.

Figure 39.16 shows a screen shot of an HTML page that shows all three versions of this applet—the original Animation1.java, a version with a MediaTracker, and a version that adds double-buffering.

 T I P AppletViewer's performance with animation is sometimes poor. Use a Web browser such as Netscape Navigator (part of Netscape Communicator) to view these applets.

FIGURE 39.16

The Earth spins in three versions of the animation applet.

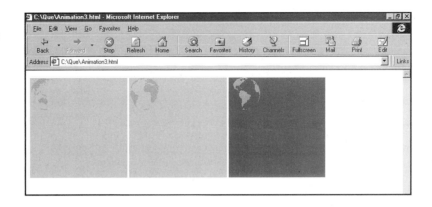

Listing 39.17 *Animation2.java*—This Version of the Animation Applet is Noticeably Smoother and Is Flicker Free

```java
import java.awt.*;
import java.applet.Applet;

public class Animation2 extends Applet implements Runnable {
    int fFrame = -1;
    int fDelay;
    Thread fThread;
    Image[] fEarth;
    MediaTracker fTracker;
    Image fOffScreenImage;
    Graphics fOffScreenGraphics;

    public void init() {
      fEarth = new Image[30];
      String theString;
      int theFramesPerSecond = 10;
      fTracker = new MediaTracker( this );
      fOffScreenImage = createImage(getSize().width,
                                    getSize().height);
      fOffScreenGraphics = fOffScreenImage.getGraphics();

      // fill the offsceen buffer with blue
      fOffScreenGraphics.setColor(Color.blue);
      fOffScreenGraphics.fillRect(0, 0,
                   getSize().width, getSize().height);

      //load in the images
      for (int i=1; i<=30; i++)
      {
         fEarth[i-1] = getImage (getCodeBase(),
                               "./Earth"+i+".gif");
         fTracker.addImage(fEarth[i-1], 0);
      }
```

continues

Part
VII

Ch

39

Listing 39.17 Continued

```
      //How many milliseconds between frames?
      theString = getParameter("fps");
      try {
        if (theString != null) {
            theFramesPerSecond = Integer.parseInt(theString );
        }
      } catch (NumberFormatException e) {}
      fDelay = (theFramesPerSecond > 0) ?
              (1000 / theFramesPerSecond) : 100;
  }

  public void start() {
    // start a new thread for the animation
    if (fThread == null) {
        fThread = new Thread(this);
    }
    fThread.start();
  }

  public void stop() {
    // stop the animation thread
    fThread = null;
  }

  public void run() {
    // run at a low priority; animation is second-place to content
    Thread.currentThread().setPriority(Thread.MIN_PRIORITY);
    long theStartTime = System.currentTimeMillis();

    //Here comes the show.
    try {
     fTracker.waitForID(0);
    } catch (InterruptedException e) {
      System.err.println("Interrupted Exception: " + e.getMessage());
      e.printStackTrace();
      return;
    }
    while (Thread.currentThread() == fThread) {

      //Advance the frame.
      fFrame++;

      //Display it.
      repaint();

      //Delay depending on how far we are behind.
      try {
          theStartTime += fDelay;
          Thread.sleep(Math.max(0,
                            theStartTime-
                      System.currentTimeMillis())));
      } catch (InterruptedException e) {
              break;
```

```
                }
            }
        }

    public void update( Graphics g) {

        // fill the offsceen buffer with blue
        fOffScreenGraphics.setColor(Color.blue);
        fOffScreenGraphics.clearRect(0, 0,
                      getSize().width, getSize().height);
        fOffScreenGraphics.fillRect(0, 0,
                      getSize().width, getSize().height);
        paint(g);
    }

    //Draw the current frame
    public void paint(Graphics g) {
      if (fTracker.checkID( 0 )) {
        fOffScreenGraphics.drawImage(fEarth[fFrame % 30], 0, 0, this);
        g.drawImage(fOffScreenImage, 0, 0, this);
      }
    }
  }
}
```

Using the 2D API

From its earliest days, Java has included a nice graphics class called `java.awt.Graphics`. To graphics professionals, however, `Graphics` left some features to be desired. More mature GUI platforms, such as Windows 95 and the Macintosh, support features that are not present in `Graphics`.

Now, in JDK 1.2, all that has changed. Sun has provided a much richer, two-dimensional graphics class called `java.awt.Graphics2D`. This section describes the major improvements available in `Graphics2D`. Listing 39.18 shows a demonstration program, `PathsFill.java`, that shows how to display shapes by using `Graphics2D`. The `PathsFill` class is a type of `Canvas`, so `Graphics2D` is able to draw on it by casting the `Graphics` parameter to `paint()` as a `Graphics2D`. The class also contains a `main()` method, enabling us to run it from the command line. Compile `PathsFill.java` by typing

`javac PathsFill.java`

and run it by typing

`java PathsFill`

at the command line. You should see a spiral of shapes in a variety of colors.

N O T E   Graphics2D is an abstract class—you must either subclass it yourself or rely on Sun's subclasses to actually draw anything. ■

ON THE WEB

`http://developer.java.sun.com/developer/technicalArticles/monicap/`
`2DGraphics/Intro/simple2D.html`   If you're a member of Sun's Java Developer Connection,
you can read this technical article, "New 2D Graphics Features," by Monica Pawlan. The extended
example in this section, Listing 39.18, is drawn from Pawlan's article.

Listing 39.18   *PathsFill.java*—**This Program, from Monica Pawlan's Article on the JDC Site, Demonstrates the Major Capabilities of 2D Graphics**

```java
import java.awt.*;
import java.awt.event.*;
import java.awt.geom.*;

public class PathsFill extends Canvas {

    public PathsFill() {
        setBackground(Color.cyan);
    }

    public void paint(Graphics g) {
        int n = 0;
        Dimension theSize = getSize();

        Graphics2D g2;
        g2 = (Graphics2D) g;
        g2.setRenderingHints(Graphics2D.ANTIALIASING,
➥Graphics2D.ANTIALIAS_ON);

        GeneralPath p = new GeneralPath(1);
        p.moveTo( theSize.width/6, theSize.height/6);
        p.lineTo(theSize.width*5/6, theSize.height/6);
        p.lineTo(theSize.width*5/6, theSize.height*5/6);
        p.lineTo( theSize.width/6, theSize.height*5/6);
        p.closePath();

        g2.setColor(Color.blue);
        g2.draw(p);

        AffineTransform at = new AffineTransform();
        at.scale(.5, .5);
        at.translate(theSize.width/2, theSize.height/2);
        g2.setTransform(at);
        g2.setColor(Color.red);
        g2.fill(p);

        Color colorArray[] = new Color[10];
        colorArray[0] = Color.blue;
        colorArray[1] = Color.green;
        colorArray[2] = Color.magenta;
        colorArray[3] = Color.lightGray;
        colorArray[4] = Color.pink;
```

```
        colorArray[5] = Color.white;
        colorArray[6] = Color.yellow;
        colorArray[7] = Color.black;
        colorArray[8] = Color.gray;
        colorArray[9] = Color.orange;

        for(n = 0;  n < 10; n++){
                at.scale(.9, .9);
                at.rotate(15, theSize.width/2, theSize.height/2);
                g2.setTransform(at);
                g2.setColor(colorArray[n]);
                g2.fill(p);
        }

    }

    public static void main(String s[]) {
       WindowListener l = new WindowAdapter() {
          public void windowClosing(WindowEvent e)
➥{System.exit(0);}
          public void windowClosed(WindowEvent e)
➥{System.exit(0);}
        };
        Frame f = new Frame("Simple 2D Demo ...");
        f.addWindowListener(l);
        f.add("Center", new PathsFill());
        f.pack();
        f.setSize(new Dimension(500,500));
        f.show();
    }
}
```

Understanding Coordinate Spaces

One reason that graphics display is an interesting problem is that not all graphics devices have the same coordinate system or resolution. This problem is compounded for Java, which has staked its reputation on being the "Write Once, Run Anywhere" language. In order to live up to this name, Sun needed a way for designers to produce graphics that look good regardless of the device's characteristics.

In some cases you may want to write a program that enables a user to draw—and then play back—that file of captured points. If the playback device has different characteristics than the one on which the original drawing was captured, a potential for error exists.

Sun solved this problem by introducing a *user coordinate space*, also known in some of Sun's documentation as *user space*.

Using Transforms   To actually display a Graphics2D object on a device, you must transform the object from user space to a specific *device space*. Although you may apply a transform at any time, you'll start with a default transform that is selected for you based on the target of your Graphics2D object.

All transforms from user space to device space share three characteristics:

- The origin is in the upper-left corner of the target space (such as a screen or printed page).
- Increasing numbers in the x dimension move to the right.
- Increasing numbers in the y dimension move down.

If you specify a screen or an image buffer as the target for your drawing, you'll get the identity transform. If your target is a printer or other high-resolution device, you'll get a default transform of 72 user-space coordinates per device inch.

Understanding Rendering

N O T E   You can use the Graphics2D class without understanding how the class places your shape, text, or image on the screen. If you're building sophisticated graphics that may be rendered on different devices (such as monitors and printers), you need to know the basics of both coordinate spaces and color spaces. If you like, skip this section while you're learning to use Graphics2D, then return here when you're ready to build a sophisticated graphic.

Rendering is the mechanism by which the graphics object is made to appear on the output device. With Graphics2D-based objects, rendering proceeds in four conceptual steps. (Because of optimization, Sun does not guarantee that each step will be performed each time an image is rendered—it guarantees only that the finished graphic will appear as though it has gone through all four rendering steps.)

The four steps are

1. Determine where to render.
2. Constrain the current rendering operation to the current Clip.
3. Determine what colors to render.
4. Apply the colors to the destination drawing space.

By understanding how the Graphics2D class processes each step, you'll be better able to produce high-quality graphics.

Determining Where to Render a Shape   The first step in rendering is to determine the area of the screen, printed page, or other output device that is affected by the rendering operation. Graphics2D objects may either be shapes, text, or images. If the object is a shape, the "where to render" question is answered by computing the outline of the shape. If the object is text, then Graphics2D computes the outline of the text by using information about the font. In the case of an image, the class computes a bounding box into which the image is rendered. This section provides details on how each of these three kinds of objects is rendered.

In Listing 39.18, for example, you see the lines:

```
Graphics2D g2;
g2 = (Graphics2D) g;
```

where g is the `Graphics` object passed in as the parameter of `paint()`. Next, the program constructs a new shape inside a `GeneralPath`:

```
GeneralPath p = new GeneralPath(1);
p.moveTo( theSize.width/6, theSize.height/6);
p.lineTo(theSize.width*5/6, theSize.height/6);
p.lineTo(theSize.width*5/6, theSize.height*5/6);
p.lineTo( theSize.width/6, theSize.height*5/6);
p.closePath();
```

Finally, the author uses the new shape:

```
g2.draw(p);
...
g2.fill(p);
...
for (n=0; n < 10; n++) {
  at.scale(.9, .9);
  at.rotate(15, theSize.width/2, theSize.height/2);
  g2.setTransform(at);
  ...
  g2.fill(p);
}
```

where at is an `AffineTransform`, described later.

When the object is a shape, as it is in this case, the `Graphics2D` class will determine where to render it by following a four-step procedure to compute the outline of the shape:

1. Compute a `Stroke` to fill based on the `Shape`.

2. Transform the `Shape` from user space into device space.

3. Call `Shape.getPathIterator()` to extract the outline of the `Shape`. (The outline is an instance of class `PathIterator`, which may contain curved segments.)

4. If the `Graphic2D` object cannot handle the curved segments in the `PathIterator`, it calls an alternative version of `Shape.getPathIterator()` that accepts a `flatness` parameter. This alternative version only returns straight line segments.

The `Shape`'s outline will be rendered by using an implementation of the `java.awt.Stroke` interface. To make an ellipse, you might write

```
draw(Ellipse2D.Float(10.0, 10.0, 150.0, 100.0));
```

but the `Graphics2D` class will implement that call as

```
BasicStroke theStroke = new BasicStroke();
theStroke.createStrokedShape(new Ellipse2D.Float(10.0, 10.0, 150.0, 100.0);
```

`BasicStroke` is a class that implements `Stroke`. Figure 39.17 illustrates the concept of a mitre limit, the part of `BasicStroke` that determines whether two lines are joined when they pass close to each other.

N O T E BasicStroke's default constructor specifies a line width of 1.0, a CAP_SQUARE style at the ends of lines, a JOIN_MITRE style where lines come together, a *mitre limit* of 10.0, and no dashing. (A mitre limit is the limit at which to trim the mitre join where two lines come together.)

Part
VII

Ch
39

FIGURE 39.17

Class `BasicStroke` supports three ways to join lines—`JOIN_MITRE` is the default.

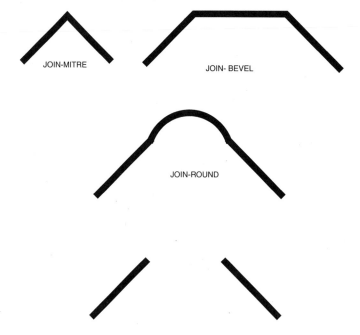

JOIN-MITRE

JOIN- BEVEL

JOIN-ROUND

`Ellipse2D` is an abstract `Shape`; `Ellipse2D.Float` is a concrete class that accepts floating point coordinates.

To transform the `Shape` into device space, `Graphics2D` calls the currently defined transform. Transforms are instances of class `AffineTransform`, which supports the following types of transform:

- `GENERAL_ROTATION`—Rotation through an arbitrary angle.
- `GENERAL_SCALE`—Scale by arbitrary factors in x and y.
- `GENERAL_TRANSFORM`—Arbitrary conversion of the input coordinates.
- `IDENTITY`—The output is identical to the input.
- `QUADRANT_ROTATION`—Rotation through a multiple of 90 degrees
- `TRANSLATION`—The graphic is moved in the x and y dimensions.
- `UNIFORM_SCALE`—The graphic is scaled uniformly in both dimensions.

In Listing 39.18 you see the lines that set up and use an `AffineTransform`:

```
AffineTransform at = new AffineTransform();
at.scale(.5, .5);
at.translate(theSize.width/2, theSize.height/2);
g2.setTransform(at);
```

and later

```
for(n = 0;  n < 10; n++){
  at.scale(.9, .9);
```

```
    at.rotate(15, theSize.width/2, theSize.height/2);
    g2.setTransform(at);
    . . .
}
```

Determining Where to Render Text   If the Graphics2D represents text rather than a shape, it is rendered by using *glyphs*—integer codes used by Fonts to represent text graphically. If the text is in a String, the String is sent to the current Font, which is asked to compute a java.awt.font.GlyphSet based on the Font's default layout.

If the text is in a StyledString, the StyledString itself computes the GlyphSet based on its own font attributes.

If the text is already a GlyphSet, then this step is skipped.

After Graphics2D has a GlyphSet, it asks the current Font to convert the glyphs to shapes. It then starts the process of rendering the shapes, as described earlier in this section.

Determining Where to Render an Image   If the Graphics2D is an image (as indicated by a call to the drawImage() method, the class computes a bounding rectangle for the image in a local coordinate system called *image space*. If the programmer has specified a transform, that transform is used to convert the bounding rectangle from image space coordinates to user space coordinates. If the programmer doesn't supply a transform, an identity transform is used.

The bounding rectangle—now in user coordinate space—is transformed again, into device space.

Constraining the Graphic with _Clip_   Graphics2D inherits getClip() and setClip() methods from its base class, Graphics. You can use setClip() to limit the rendering to a specified rectangle. You specify the clipRect in user space—Graphics2D transforms it into device space by using the current transform.

 TIP   Suppose you had a complex graphic, or an animation, in which performance was important. You could improve performance by limiting the rendering area by using setClip().

After Graphics2D has computed the rendering region (for either a graphic, text, or an image) it applies the clipRect to define the region that will actually be rendered.

Determining the Colors   If the Graphics2D object is an Image, the class samples the colors in the Image based on the current transform. (If you specify an Image transform, that transform is also applied during color sampling.)

For text and graphic instances of Graphics2D, the class looks at the current Paint implementation. You set the Paint instance by calling Graphics2D.setPaint(). Paint itself is an interface; Sun has provided GradientPaint and TexturePaint to enable you to implement special effects.

Instead of a Paint-based object, you can set a Color. PathsFill, in Listing 39.18, uses this approach. You'll notice lines such as

```
g2.setColor(Color.blue);
```

and

```
g2.setColor(Color.red);
```

Whether you've provided a `Paint` object or a `Color` object, `Graphics2D` uses it to obtain a `PaintContext`—a specific mapping of colors and textures into device space—and is now ready to apply the colors.

Applying the Colors `Graphics2D` objects are drawn on a `java.awt.Composite` object. The `Composite` interface contains predefined rules to combine the source with colors that have already been drawn.

N O T E Sun provides one example of a `Composite`-based class: `AlphaComposite`. This class implements a set of blending and transparency rules based on T. Porter and T. Duff's paper, "Compositing Digital Images," SIGGRAPH 84, 253-259. Read the API documentation on `AlphaComposite` to see the essence of these rules. ■

Dealing with Compatibility Issues

Not only does Sun have to deal with a range of device compatibility, it also has had to ensure that changes in JDK 1.2 don't break the `Graphics` API of JDK 1.1. To help your `Graphics2D` objects deal with the range of rendering environments they may encounter, use `Graphics2D.setRenderingHints()`. This method accepts hints that you may want to add to improve the performance and appearance of your graphics.

Suppose, for example, that you know that an image contains a number of diagonal lines that would benefit from antialiasing. You might specify `ANTIALIASING_ON`—at runtime, the environment and the device driver would negotiate whether to actually make the antialiasing pass. If you've specified `RENDER_SPEED`, the device driver may ignore the `ANTIALIASING_ON` directive entirely, but for `RENDER_QUALITY`, the driver may use the best antialiasing algorithm at its disposal, even though that algorithm may require extra time.

The hint list includes the following:

- `ANTIALIASING_ON` and `ANTIALIASING_OFF`—Controls whether an extra step is applied to smooth jagged edges.
- `RENDER_SPEED` and `RENDER_QUALITY`—Controls whether the rendering algorithm should optimize for performance or appearance.

Notice the line in Listing 39.18 that sets these hints:

```
g2.setRenderingHints(Graphics2D.ANTIALIASING,
ÂGraphics2D.ANTIALIAS_ON);
```

Java Resources on the Web

The Java language is continually being upgraded. New packages and versions are being released at a rapid pace. Many of these new features will increase the power and ease of Java graphics and animation programming. Continue to increase your Java graphics and animation knowledge and programming skills by keeping up with the latest developments over the Web.

The most important Web site is the Java home page provided by JavaSoft—the Java development branch of the Sun Corporation. The Java home page is at `http://java.sun.com/`.

Use the Search feature at the top of the page (or go to `http://java.sun.com/share/search.html`) and enter terms such as "graphics" or "animation" to see the latest information. You can also keep informed about the latest Java developments and software release dates at this Web site and download the latest production-quality Java development software. (For access to beta releases of the software, join the Java Developer Connection—it's free—at `http://developer.javasoft.com/`.)

While browsing the JavaSoft site, you'll want to visit `http://java.sun.com/products/java-media/2D/samples/README.html`—as the URL suggests, that page shows sample code using the features of the new JDK 1.2.

In addition to the JavaSoft site, you can find some excellent central Java news-gathering sources on the Web. These also include reviews, tutorials, and other useful information. The best of these includes JavaWorld at

`http://www.javaworld.com/`

For example, they have archives of articles on graphics at `http://www.javaworld.com/javaworld/topicalindex/jw-ti-graphics.html`. Go to `http://www.javaworld.com/javaworld/topicalindex/jw-ti-animation.html` for information on animation.

You can download sample programs and tutorials from the Java archive at Gamelan (`http://www.gamelan.com/`), the Java library of `http://www.developer.com/`. Their graphics information is at `http://www.developer.com/directories/pages/dir.java.programming.graphics.html`. ●

Part
VII

Ch
39

Network Programming

by Mike Morgan

In this chapter

Java Simplifies Network Programming

Not so long ago, programming network applications in any language was an ordeal. Sometimes it involved writing specialized system software that talked directly to network drivers—or even the network cards themselves. Programming IPX/SPX applications in DOS or Windows used to require the programmer to write software interrupt handlers. With Java, however, writing some kinds of network applications is as easy as using `println()`.

The thing that makes network programming in Java easier is encapsulation. Java hides the difficult, low-level network programming from you. This design enables you to concentrate on your application, not on the communications. In older systems, many steps were required to talk over a network. You had to

- Initialize the network card
- Set up buffers for inbound and outbound packets
- Create callback routines for the networking driver to notify you of data
- Write low-level (sometimes assembler!) code to talk with the network driver

If it sounds like a lot of work—it was! On the other hand, programming the network in Java is very slick. Just instantiate a `Socket` class and you are on your way. But more on that later.

This chapter discusses the network classes in Java (in the `java.net` package). These classes make writing programs for communication over the Internet, intranets, or even local area networks easier than in any other language you're likely to use.

How Do Java Programs Communicate with the Outside World?

Java's network classes use streams for their underlying communications. A *stream* is a path of communication between a source of information and a destination. For our purposes, our Java program is at one end of the stream. If we're the source, the stream is an output stream. If we're the destination, we call the stream an input stream.

Readers and *writers* are analogous to streams, except that streams are based on bytes, and readers and writers are based on chars. In older languages, such as C and C++, this distinction is not important. In Java, however, a char is a 16-bit entity designed to hold Unicode characters.

You've already used an output stream without realizing it, when you wrote `System.out.println("Hello, world!")`. Streams enable you to communicate with files, printers, the screen, and the network. Streams, readers, and writers are all part of the `java.io` package. You can find complete documentation on each class, interface, and method in `/docs/api/Package-java-io.html` in your JDK directory. You'll also need to import `java.io.*` or specify `java.io` as part of the class name in your code.

Connecting to the Internet: The *URL* Class

Back in Chapter 37, "Developing Java Applets," you learned how to write a tiny Java program—`HelloWorld.java`—with only one executable statement. The fact is, people have been writing tiny programs that write information to the screen ever since there were computer screens. One of the features that makes Java exciting is that you can connect to the Internet with a program that's not much more complex than `HelloWorld.java`.

N O T E   For years Sun has been telling us that "the network is the computer," and its design of Java reflects that philosophy. Java is the only major language that enables you to connect your program to the Internet in just one line of code, as shown in line 39 of Listing 40.1:

```
URL theURL = new URL(theURLString);
```

▶ **See** `HelloWorld.java` in Listing 37.1, **p. 990**.

Using *showDocument()* to Change Web Pages

Listing 40.1 shows `HelloNet.java`, a simple applet that connects you to a new Web page.

Listing 40.1   *HelloNet.java*—This Simple Applet Connects to Three URLs

```java
import java.awt.*;
import java.net.*;
import java.applet.Applet;
import java.awt.event.*;
  public class HelloNet extends Applet
{
  public void init()
  {
    setLayout(new GridLayout(3,1));
    Button theBookSiteButton = new Button("Platinum Edition");
   theBookSiteButton.addActionListener(new ActionListener(){
      public void actionPerformed(ActionEvent e) {
        linkTo("http://www.mcp.com/ info/0-7897/0-7897-1759-X");
      }
    });
    add(theBookSiteButton);

    Button theMCPButton = new Button("Macmillan Computer Publishing");
    theMCPButton.addActionListener(new ActionListener(){
      public void actionPerformed(ActionEvent e) {
        linkTo("http://www.mcp.com/");
      }
    });
    add(theMCPButton);

    Button theJavaSoftButton = new Button("JavaSoft");
    theJavaSoftButton.addActionListener(new ActionListener(){
      public void actionPerformed(ActionEvent e) {
        linkTo("http://java.sun.com/");
      }
    });
    add(theJavaSoftButton);
  }
```

continues

Part
VII

Ch
40

Listing 40.1 Continued

```
public void linkTo(String theURLString)
{
  try {
    URL theURL = new URL(theURLString);
    getAppletContext().showDocument(theURL, "_top");
  } catch (MalformedURLException e) {
    System.err.println("Bad URL: " + theURLString);
  }
}
}
```

Most of this applet is familiar to you by now. (If you're new to the Abstract Windowing Toolkit, take a look at Chapter 38, "User Input and Interactivity with Java.") This applet has three buttons, each with a Web destination name. When you click a button, it fires the `linkTo()` method. This code is where the new Web-specific information appears.

First, we make a new URL object from the `String`. If the URL constructor cannot make sense out of `theURLString`, it throws `MalformedURLException`. Given a valid URL, `linkTo()` now transfers control to the browser's `AppletContext` and asks it to show the specified URL in the browser's topmost window.

 TIP If your applet is buried down inside an HTML frame, the `showDocument(String)` page will also appear inside that frame. In this case, all three URLs should appear on a page by themselves, not in their own frames. You can get that behavior by adding "`_top`", as shown in line 40.

This code has only three executable lines per button and three executable lines in `linkTo()`. Of course, it takes advantage of the fact that it's running inside a Web browser. The browser supplies the `AppletContext`, and it's the browser that actually fetches the document specified by the URL.

Calling Back the Server with *openStream()*

From within either an applet or an application, you can open a connection to a URL and read back the contents. The basic mechanism is a URL method called `openStream()`:

```
try {
  DataInputStream theData =
    new BufferedReader(new
      InputStreamReader(theURL.openStream()));
  String aLine;
  while ((aLine = theData.readLine()) != null) {
    System.out.println(aLine);
  }
} catch (IOException e) {
  System.err.println("IOException: " + e.getMessage());
} finally {
  theData.close();
}
```

Line 4 uses openStream() to retrieve the InputStream. URL.openStream() is really shorthand for

theURL.openConnection().getInputStream();

but most programmers will appreciate the shorter version.

Also on the first line, we wrap the InputStream first in an InputStreamReader (in order to bridge between the byte-oriented world of streams and the char-oriented world of readers). Then we wrap the InputStreamReader in a BufferedReader for efficiency—we'd prefer to read the stream a buffer at a time, rather than a byte at a time!

Finally, we call theData.readLine() successively, bringing in lines of data from the server. For this simple code snippet, we just send the data back out to standard out.

If anything goes wrong, we'll throw an IOException somewhere in there and catch it on the way out. Whether we throw an exception or not, we'll always execute the finally clause, closing the stream.

> **CAUTION**
>
> If you compile the URL.openStream() code into an applet and attempt to fetch data from some Web server, it probably won't work. Most browsers include a SecurityManager that reports a SecurityException as soon as you attempt to contact a host other than the one you were downloaded from. To make this code work in an applet, either restrict yourself to connecting only to the applet's home server or negotiate higher rights with the browser's SecurityManager.

▶ To learn more about applet security, **see** "Executable Content and Security," **p. 1142**.

How the *URL* Class Works

The URL class contains constructors and methods for managing a URL—an object or service on the Internet. The TCP protocol requires two pieces of information: the IP address and the port number. So how is it possible that when you type

http://www.yahoo.com/

you get Yahoo!'s home page?

First, Yahoo! has registered its name, enabling yahoo.com to be assigned an IP address (say 205.216.146.71). This address is resolved by using your system's domain name resolution service.

Now what about the port number? If not specified, the server's default port is used—for the Web, that's port 80.

The URL class supports four constructor variations:

```
public URL(String spec) throws MalformedURLException;
public URL(String protocol, String host, int port, String file) throws
```

```
➥MalformedURLException;
public URL(String protocol, String host, String file) throws
➥MalformedURLException;
public URL(URL context, String spec) throws MalformedURLException;
```

You can thus specify each piece of the URL, as in

`URL("http","www.yahoo.com",80,"index.html")`, or enable the defaults to take over, as in
`URL("http://www.yahoo.com/")`, letting Java figure out all the pieces.

The Java Socket Classes

Java, of course, was developed by Sun. Sun earned its reputation as a leading developer of UNIX workstations—much of the Internet runs on Sun servers. It's not surprising, therefore, that Java is designed from the ground up as a networking language. This overview shows how Java makes network programming easier by encapsulating connection functionality in *socket classes*:

- ▦ `Socket` is the basic object in Internet communication, which supports the TCP/IP protocol. The Transmission Control Protocol/Internet Protocol (TCP/IP) is a reliable stream network connection. The `Socket` class provides methods for stream I/O, which make reading from and writing to `Socket` easy.

- ▦ `ServerSocket` is an object used for Internet server programs for listening to client requests. `ServerSocket` does not actually perform the service; instead, it creates a `Socket` object on behalf of the client. The communication is performed through that object.

- ▦ `DatagramSocket` is an object that uses the *User Datagram Protocol* (UDP). Datagram sockets are technically unreliable because no connection is involved. You send them out hoping they reach their destination, but you have no guarantee that a server is even listening. In addition, the networking software will not guarantee the delivery of UDP packages. However, communication using datagram sockets is faster because no connection is made between the sender and receiver. Think of UDP like a telegram, sent out in the hope that it will be delivered. TCP, in contrast, is more like a telephone call—you know the message is delivered because you delivered it yourself, through a connection. Streaming audio and video often use UDP.

- ▦ `SocketImpl` is an abstract class that enables you to implement your own flavor of data communication. As with all abstract classes, you subclass `SocketImpl` and implement its methods, as opposed to instantiating `SocketImpl` itself.

How the Internet Uses Sockets

You can think of an Internet server as a set of sockets, each of which provides additional capabilities called *services*. Examples of services are electronic mail, *Telnet* for remote login, and the

File Transfer Protocol (FTP) for transferring files around the network. If the server to which you are attached is a Web server, then you can retrieve Web pages as well.

Ports and Services

Each service is associated with a *port*. A port is a numeric address through which service requests (such as asking for a Web page) are processed. On a UNIX system, the particular services provided are in the /etc/services file. Here are a few lines from a typical /etc/services file:

daytime	13/udp	
ftp	21/tcp	
telnet	23/tcp	telnet
smtp	25/tcp	mail
www	80/tcp	

The first column displays the system name of the service (such as "daytime"). The second column displays the port number and the protocol, separated by a slash (as in "13/udp"). The third column displays an alias to the service, if any. For example, SMTP (the Simple Mail Transfer Protocol), also known as *mail*, provides the email service.

Mapping Java Sockets to Internet Sockets

Sockets are based on a client/server model. One program (the server) provides the service at a particular IP address and port. The server listens for service requests, such as requests for Web pages, and fills the order. Any program that wants to be serviced (a client, such as a Web browser) needs to know the IP address and port to communicate with the server.

An advantage of the socket model over other forms of data communication is that the server doesn't care where the client requests come from. As long as the client is sending requests according to the TCP/IP protocol, the requests will reach the server—provided the server is up and the Internet isn't too busy. What the particular server program does with the request is another matter.

This design also means that the client can be any type of computer. No longer are you restricted to UNIX, Macintosh, DOS, or Windows platforms. Any computer that supports TCP/IP can talk to any other computer that supports it through this socket model. This design is a potentially revolutionary development in computing. Instead of maintaining armies of programmers to *port* a system from one platform to another, you write it one time—in Java. Any computer with a Java Virtual Machine can run it.

Java socket classes fit nicely into this picture. You implement a server by creating subclasses of Thread and overriding the run() method. The Java Virtual Machine can then perform the thread management without the program having to worry. Thus, with a few lines of code, you can write a server that can handle as many data communication sessions as you want. And data transmission is just a matter of calling the Socket methods.

Part
VII

Ch
40

Writing Your Own Client and Server

Applets are restricted from connecting to just any Web server. They can only connect back to the server from which they were downloaded. If you want to give an applet access to the rest of the Internet, you'll need to place a server on the same machine that hosts the applet. You can use a commercial server such as a File Transfer Protocol (FTP) server, or you can write your own special-purpose server.

When you write a server, you write a program that opens a socket (typically on a *well-known port number*) and wait for some client to connect. The client calls in from some unused port number (called an *ephemeral port*). As soon as the client and the server connect, it's common for the server to propose that the conversation continue on a different port. This design frees up the well-known port number to handle a new connection. Table 40.1 shows some common, well-known port numbers. These services are offered both on TCP ports and on UDP ports. The RFC column refers to the Internet Request for Comments document, where you'll find the specification for the service.

ON THE WEB

`ftp://ds.internic.net/rfc/` You can download any RFCs that you'd like to read from this FTP server. Check the login message you get when you connect—FTP sites are on each continent. If you're not on the East Coast of North America, one may be closer to you than `ds.internic.net`.

Table 40.1 Common Internet Services and Their Port Numbers

Service Name	TCP Port	UDP Port	RFC	Description
echo	7	7	862	Server returns whatever the client sends.
discard	9	9	863	Server discards whatever the client sends.
daytime	13	13	867	Server returns the time and date in a human-readable format.
chargen	19		864	TCP server sends a continual stream of characters until the client terminates the connection.
chargen		19	864	UDP server sends a datagram containing a random number of characters each time the client sends a datagram.
time	37	37	868	Server returns the time as a 32-bit binary number—the number of seconds since midnight on January 1, 1900, UTC.

N O T E TCP/IP port numbers are managed by the Internet Assigned Numbers Authority (IANA). IANA has specified that well-known port numbers are always between 1 and 1023. A Telnet server listens on TCP port 23, for example, and the Trivial File Transfer Protocol (TFTP) server listens on UDP port 69. Most TCP/IP implementations allocate ephemeral port numbers between 1024 and 5000, but that design isn't specified by IANA. ▪

Java provides two kinds of sockets: client sockets, implemented in the Socket class, and server sockets, implemented in the ServerSocket class.

Understanding the Client *Socket* Class

To connect to a host, your client program should include a line such as

```
Socket theConnection = new Socket(hostname, portNumber);
```

(Remember the security restrictions that apply to applets.)

▶ To learn more about the restrictions browsers place on applets, **see** "Executable Content and Security," **p. 1142**.

The Socket constructor throws an IOException if it has a problem. Otherwise, you can presume that the Socket is open and ready for communication:

```
BufferedReader theReader = new BufferedReader(
  new InputStreamReader(theConnection.getInputStream()));
BufferedWriter theWriter = new BufferedWriter(
  new OutputStreamWriter(theConnection.getOutputStream()));
```

Now you can read and write theReader and theWriter in the usual fashion. When you're done with theConnection, call

```
theConnection.close();
```

This step will also close all the streams, readers, and writers you have associated with this Socket.

Understanding *ServerSockets*

If you choose to write a server, you'll need to write a ServerSocket. Such a socket binds a specified port. To bind port 8000, for example, you write

```
ServerSocket theServerConnection = new ServerSocket(8000);
```

 T I P When you install a server, it's a good idea to check /etc/services to make sure the port number is free. Likewise, after you choose a port number, add a corresponding entry in /etc/services to notify other programmers who might want to add a server to this machine.

This code tells the underlying operating system that you intend to offer a service on port 8000. (You aren't listening to that port quite yet.) If the runtime environment is able to bind to the specified port, it does so and sets the allowable backlog to a default of 50. (This means that once you have 50 pending requests to connect, all subsequent requests are refused. You can

Part

VII

Ch

40

specify a different backlog value in the `ServerSocket` constructor.) If the runtime environment cannot bind to the port (which happens if the port is already allocated to another service), you'll get an `IOException`.

After you've bound the port, you can attach the port and start listening for connections by calling `accept()`:

```
Socket aSocket = theServerConnection.accept();
```

When the connection is made, `accept()` unblocks and returns a `Socket`. You can open streams, readers, and writers on the `Socket` the same as you did from the client program.

Using Client and Server Sockets

Listing 40.2 shows a server framework. Our simple server sets up the `ServerSocket`, then implements four steps:

1. Waits for a client to connect

2. Accepts the client connection

3. Sends a message to the client

4. Tears down the connection

Listing 40.2   *TServer.java*—Use This Framework as the Basis for Your Own Server

```java
import java.net.*;
import java.io.*;

public class TServer extends Thread {
  private static final int PORTNUMBER = 8013;
  private ServerSocket fServerSocket;

  public TServer() {
    super("TServer");
    try {
      fServerSocket = new ServerSocket(PORTNUMBER);
      System.out.println("TServer up and running...");
    } catch (IOException e) {
      System.err.println("Exception: couldn't make server socket.");
      System.exit(1);
    }
  }

  public void run() {
    Socket theClientSocket;

    while (true) {

      // wait for a client to connect
      if (fServerSocket == null)
        return;
      try {
        theClientSocket = fServerSocket.accept();
```

```
        // accept the client connection

        // send a message to the client
        PrintWriter theWriter = new PrintWriter(new
          OutputStreamWriter(theClientSocket.getOutputStream()));
        theWriter.println(new java.util.Date().toString());
        theWriter.flush();

        // tear down the connection
        theWriter.close();
        theClientSocket.close();
      } catch (IOException e) {
        System.err.println("Exception: " + e.getMessage());
        System.exit(1);
      }
    }
  }

  public static void main(String[] args) {
    TServer theServer = new TServer();
    theServer.start();
  }
}
```

Listing 40.3 shows a client designed to work with the server in Listing 40.2. This client has four steps:

1. Connect to the server.
2. Wait for a message.
3. Display the message to the user.
4. Tear down the connection.

Listing 40.3 *TClient.java*—This Class Will Help You Design Your Client Program

```
import java.net.*;
import java.io.*;

public class TClient {
  private static final int PORTNUMBER = 8013;
  public static void main(String args[]) {
    Socket theSocket;
    BufferedReader theReader;
    String theAddress = "";

    // check the command line for a host address
    if (args.length != 1) {
     System.out.println("Usage: java TClient <address>");
     System.exit(1);
    }
    else
      theAddress = args[0];
```

continues

Listing 40.3 Continued

```
// connect to the server
try {
  theSocket = new Socket(theAddress, PORTNUMBER);
  theReader =
    new BufferedReader(new
      InputStreamReader(theSocket.getInputStream()));

  // wait for a message
  StringBuffer theStringBuffer = new StringBuffer(128);
  String theLine;
  int c;
  while ((theLine = theReader.readLine()) != null) {

    // show the message to the user
    System.out.println("Server: " + theLine);
    break;
  }

  // Tear down the connection
  theReader.close();
  theSocket.close();
} catch (IOException e) {
  System.err.println("Exception: " + e.getMessage());
}
}
}
```

N O T E As long as you keep the server on the machine that hosts your applet, you can put the code from Listing 40.3 into an applet. Just move the code in `main()` into `init()`. You don't have to look for the server's address in a parameter. Just use the `Applet` method `getCodeBase()`; it returns the complete URL of the applet itself. ■

To test this code, first start the server:

```
java TServer
```

Now run the client. Note that `"localhost"` is a common name for a TCP/IP machine to use for itself—this invocation specifies that the server is running on the same machine as the client. We could also have used `127.0.0.1`, the local loopback address.

```
java TClient "localhost"
Server: someDateandTime
```

To fault-isolate between the client and the server, use your computer's Telnet client to access the server by port number. Figure 40.1 shows this step. If you're able to connect and the server works as you expect, you have a problem with your client. Otherwise, you have a problem with the server.

FIGURE 40.1

Use your platform's Telnet client to attempt to connect to your new server's well-known port.

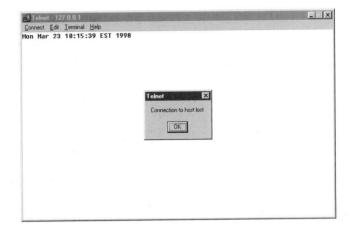

Communicating with Datagram Sockets

Communicating using datagram sockets is simpler than using the TCP-based sockets (`Socket` and `ServerSocket`) that you used for the `TServer`. Communication is also faster because no connection overhead exists. There is also no attempt to send packets again if an error occurs or sequencing of multiple packets, as occurs in TCP/IP transmissions.

A datagram packet is sent as an array of bytes to a receiving program, presumably listening at a particular IP address and port. If the receiving program gets the datagram and wants to send a reply, it becomes the sender, addressing a datagram back to a known IP address and port. The conversation style is a bit like those two-way radios in airplanes in which the pilot sends a message, says "Over," and waits for the controller to respond.

You might use datagram socket communication if you are writing an interactive game—returning a small piece of information such as the time. You don't want the overhead of establishing a connection, or perhaps the communication takes place locally.

Part
VII

Ch

40

Sending a Datagram Packet

Listing 40.4 shows a prototype program for sending a datagram packet. It sends a 27-byte message ("I'm a datagram and I'm O.K.") to the IP address mapped to `"localhost"` at port number 6969. When you try this, use an IP address and port that you know is available. These values should work on most machines.

Listing 40.4 *DatagramSend.java*—A Prototype Program to Transmit a Datagram Packet

```
import java.net.*;
import java.net.*;
import java.io.IOException;
```

continues

Listing 40.4 Continued

```java
public class TDatagramSend {
  static final int PORT = 6969;
  public static void main( String args[] ) throws Exception {
    String theStringToSend = "I'm a datagram and I'm O.K.";
    byte[] theByteArray = new byte[ theStringToSend.length() ];
    theByteArray = theStringToSend.getBytes();

    // Get the IP address of our destination...
    InetAddress theIPAddress = null;
    try {
      theIPAddress = InetAddress.getByName( "localhost" );
    } catch (UnknownHostException e) {
      System.out.println("Host not found: " + e);
      System.exit(1);
    }

    // Build the packet...
    DatagramPacket thePacket = new DatagramPacket( theByteArray,
      theStringToSend.length(),
      theIPAddress,
      PORT );

    // Now send the packet
    DatagramSocket theSocket = null;
    try {
      theSocket = new DatagramSocket();
    } catch (SocketException e) {
      System.out.println("Underlying network software has failed: " + e);
      System.exit(1);
    }
    try {
      theSocket.send( thePacket );
    } catch (IOException e) {
      System.out.println("IO Exception: " + e);
    }
    theSocket.close();
  }
}
```

You need to use only one socket: the DatagramSocket. There is no concept of the server listening for client requests. The idea is to establish a DatagramSocket object and then send and receive messages. The messages are sent in a DatagramPacket object. An additional object—InetAddress—is needed to construct the IP address to send the packet.

The DatagramSend class has only one method—main()—so it is a standalone Java program. This demonstration program sends only one message. You can, of course, modify main() to pass any message to any IP address and port.

The DatagramPacket constructor used here has the following four arguments:

- theByteArray—An array of bytes containing the message to send
- theStringToSend.length()—The length of the string you are going to send

- theIPAddress—the InetAddress object containing the resolved IP address of your destination
- PORT—An integer specifying the port number

Another form of the constructor requires only the first two arguments. It is designed for local communication when the IP address and port are already known. You will see it in action in the following section, "Receiving a Datagram Packet."

You first build a string (theStringToSend) that contains the string you want to send. Then you create a byte array that is as long as your string. You use the String class's length() method to do this. The PORT constant is used to store the port number, 6969.

The getBytes() instance method of the java.lang.String class converts strings into byte array form. You store this in your byte array theByteArray.

The getByName() method of InetAddress converts a string into an Internet address in the form that the DatagramPacket constructor accepts. In this case the string is a simple one: localhost.

Next, an instance of DatagramSocket is constructed with no arguments, meaning that Java will attempt to use any available port. Finally, the packet is sent using the send() method of the DatagramSocket.

Receiving a Datagram Packet

The packet is on its way, so it is time to receive it. Listing 40.5 shows the receiving program.

Listing 40.5 *DatagramReceive.java*—A Prototype Program to Receive a Datagram Packet

```
import java.net.*;

public class DatagramReceive {
  static final int PORT = 6969;
  public static void main( String args[] ) throws Exception {
    String theReceiveString;
    byte[] theReceiveBuffer = new byte[ 2048 ];

    // Make a packet to receive into...
    DatagramPacket theReceivePacket =
      new DatagramPacket( theReceiveBuffer, theReceiveBuffer.length );

    // Make a socket to listen on...
    DatagramSocket theReceiveSocket = new DatagramSocket( PORT );

    // Receive a packet...
    theReceiveSocket.receive( theReceivePacket );

    // Convert the packet to a string...
    theReceiveString =
      new String( theReceiveBuffer, 0, theReceivePacket.getLength() );
```

continues

Listing 40.5 Continued

```
            // Print out the string...
            System.out.println( theReceiveString );

            //  Close the socket...
            theReceiveSocket.close();
            }
        }
```

The `DatagramReceive` class, like the `DatagramSend` class, uses the `DatagramSocket` and `DatagramPacket` classes from `java.net`. First, make a buffer large enough to hold the message. The buffer in this example (`theReceiveBuffer`) is a 2K byte array. Your buffer size may vary. Just make sure it will hold the largest packet you will receive.

You then make a new datagram packet. Note that the receive program already knows its IP address and port, and so it can use the two-argument form of the constructor. The new `DatagramSocket` is set up to receive data at port 6969.

The `receive()` method of `Datagram` receives the packet as a `byte` array. The `String` (`theReceiveString`) is constructed out of the `byte` array and it is displayed on the user's screen. Finally, the socket is closed—a good practice, freeing memory rather than waiting for Java's garbage collection.

 T I P   To alternatively get the IP address of the host you are running on, call the `getLocalHost()` and `getAddress()` methods of the class `java.net.InetAddress`. First, `getLocalHost()` returns an `InetAddress` object. Then you use the `getAddress()` method, which returns a `byte` array consisting of the four bytes of the IP address. Here's an example:

```
        InetAddress theLocalIPAddress = InetAddress.getLocalHost();

        byte[] theLocalIPAddressDecoded = theLocalIPAddress.getAddress();
```

If the IP address of the machine on which your program is running on is `221.111.112.23`, then

```
            theLocalIPAddressDecoded[0] = 221

            theLocalIPAddressDecoded[1] = 111

            theLocalIPAddressDecoded[2] = 112

            theLocalIPAddressDecoded[3] = 23
```

Customized Network Solutions

The Internet provides no transactional security whatsoever, nor do the socket-oriented communications methods discussed so far verify whether any particular request for reading or writing data is coming from a source that should have such access. To do this, you need a customized network protocol.

These protocols sit as a layer between your network protocol (that is, TCP/IP) and your application. They encrypt outgoing packets and decrypt incoming packets while verifying that you are still talking to whom you think you are talking.

Netscape has proposed the Secure Sockets Layer (SSL) protocol. SSL is a protocol that resides between the services—such as Telnet, FTP, and HTTP—and the TCP/IP connection sessions that are illustrated in this chapter. SSL would check that the client and server networks are valid, provide data encryption, and ensure that the message does not contain any embedded commands or programs. SSL would thus provide for secure transactions to occur across the Internet.

Another proposal is to write a server that provides security from the start. This is the idea behind *Secure Hypertext Transfer Protocol* (S-HTTP), developed by Enterprise Information Technologies (EIT), RSA Labs, and the National Center for Supercomputer Applications (NCSA).

▶ To learn more about security protocols, **see** "Server-Side Security Issues," **p. 937**.

N O T E   The National Center for Supercomputer Applications (NCSA) is the group that developed Mosaic, the first graphical Web browser. Marc Andressen and the Mosaic design team went on to fame and fortune by completely rewriting Mosaic into a new and original Web browser: Netscape Navigator. ▮

In your organization, you might want to provide a firewall between the public and private areas of your networks. Therefore, for a number of reasons, you might need more protection for your network than TCP/IP provides.

Java provides a set of methods called `SocketImpl`, an abstract class, for implementing either of these strategies. To use it, you create a subclass and implement its methods, such as connecting to the server, accepting client requests, getting file information, writing to local files, and so on. Even if you have never written your own server or a custom socket class, it is nice to know it's possible to do in Java.

Part
VII

Ch
40

Will Security Considerations Disable Java Applets?

Imagine a world in which Java applets on any network can set up client/server communications of the type discussed in this chapter. Perhaps an applet on your network can call a method in an applet on someone else's network or run a program on that other network remotely. An applet connects to a quote server, for example, determines that the price of a certain stock has reached the target price, and then connects to a user's machine on a network, displaying a message and requesting permission to buy. Or perhaps the applet can run an Excel spreadsheet macro to update the portfolio every 10 minutes. Many powerful applets could be written.

With this power comes potential danger. How can you prevent the applet from deleting files, downloading unauthorized data, or even being aware of the existence of such files? In this world of distributed objects, a profound tension exists between enabling more capabilities for an applet and fear of unwanted use. This tension is why the debate on object access is fierce. The main stage is a standard called *Common Object Request Broker Architecture*, or CORBA.

ON THE WEB

`http://www.acl.lanl.gov/CORBA/`   You can get an overview of CORBA online and earn more about writing Java programs that can interface with object request brokers.

Currently, untrusted applets loaded from a network cannot run Windows DLLs on the local machine, nor can they run local commands, such as the DOS `dir` command, that would find out the names of files on the client. In addition, network applets cannot make network connections except to the machine from which they were loaded.

N O T E   These limitations apply only to applets loaded from a network. Locally loaded applets have fewer restrictions. See Sun's Security FAQ at `http://java.sun.com/sfaq/` for details. ▧

▶ To learn more about Java security protocols, **see** "Executable Content and Security," **p. 1142**.

The debate between power and security seems to be veering toward the security side. An example is a "bug" that Drew Dean, Ed Felten, and Dan Wallach of Princeton University found in an old version of Netscape Navigator (version 2.0) running a Java applet. They tricked the domain name server (DNS—the program that resolves host names, such as `www.yahoo.com`, into IP addresses) into disguising their origin. They made DNS believe they were actually from another computer, and then they were able to breach security on it. Netscape acknowledged the situation and quickly provided an update (version 2.01) that provided closer control over how an IP address is resolved.

Another security flaw was found in Internet Explorer version 3.0. It allowed a Web site or Webmaster to place a Windows 95 shortcut on your system. This shortcut could be any kind of command to run a program or even format your hard disk.

These situations have caused a stir in the Internet community. Concerns about Internet security are rampant. Many users and developers have also raised concerns about restricting applet access to the point where the usefulness of the applications is diminished.

With JDK 1.2, you can attach a digital signature to your applets before they are distributed. This approach ensures the user that he or she is getting the applet they want.

▶ To learn more about signed applets, **see** "Signing Your JARs," **p. 1166**.

Using Network Communications in Applets

Recall from "Writing Your Own Client and Server" earlier in this chapter that you can write your own server or use a commercial server to communicate with your applets. You'll find a collection of servers written in Java at `http://www.developer.com/directories/pages/dir.java.net.server.html`.

You can review the applets at `http://www.developer.com/directories/pages/dir.java.net.html` to get an idea of what other developers are doing with network programming. You'll find a set of classes, for example, that gives you access to your SMTP (email) server at `http://www.io.com/~maus/JavaPage.html`. Visit `http://www.io.com/~maus/qsmtp/SmtpApplet.html` to see these classes in action.

Sock Bean is an applet that gives you direct access to network sockets (although you're still restricted regarding which servers your applet can contact). Read about Sock Bean at `http://www.iaccess.com/au/customers/detailer/software.html`.

The Gamelan page `http://www.developer.com/directories/pages/dir.java.net.intertools.html` also lists several Telnet clients and an FTP client, all written as applets. ●

Part
VII

Ch
40

Security

by Mike Morgan

Executable Content and Security

Java has changed the face of the Web from a static publishing medium to an interactive application development platform by providing executable "live" content embedded in HTML documents. This is a frightening thought to many system administrators. After all, it's bad enough that people can download software that might contain viruses that could damage their machines. How can the network stay secure with programs coming in and running on the host machines all on their own? What is to keep somebody from reading sensitive data, wiping out hard drives, setting up back doors to the network, or something worse? Fortunately, the folks at Sun gave this matter some thought and designed Java with security in mind from the ground up, starting with the language and continuing on through the compiler, compiled code, and runtime environment.

To understand Java's preventative measures, we'll start by reviewing the special security concerns that apply to interactive content. We'll then cover the types of attacks that unscrupulous programmers attempt and the kinds of security issues that relate to a well-intentioned but poorly written program. After we've covered the issues, we'll discuss the security features of the Java language, the Java compiler, and the Java Virtual Machine. Finally, we'll talk about the remaining open issues related to Java security and what you can (and can't) do about them, as well as the new Security API being implemented in Java 1.2.

In this section, we'll briefly discuss how interactivity on the Web has evolved and how security issues have changed with each new technique. We'll then focus on how live content, executing on host machines, poses the most challenging security issues of all.

We will discuss the general security issues that relate only to executable content on the Web, as opposed to other means of interactivity. From there, we'll outline the issues and illustrate possible attack scenarios.

Interactivity Versus Security

A direct correlation exists between interactivity and security:

> The greater the level of interactivity, the greater the security risk.

The Internet enables information to be spread, but this capability is also what makes it potentially dangerous. This risk is especially high when the information is executable code, such as Java. An image or other non-program file cannot execute instructions on your machine, and so is inherently safer than a Java applet (or ActiveX control). As you will see, this relationship between interactivity and security is true on the server side as well as the client side.

Let's step back to the basic building block of the Web—HTTP. *HTTP*, the *Hypertext Transfer Protocol*, is the protocol of the Web. It is a simple, stateless protocol. When an HTTP server receives a request for a file, it simply hands that file over. No interaction occurs between the server and client beyond the call and response. An HTTP server is similar to a television transmitter, and an HTTP client is similar to a television. A television is a receiver that receives signals from a transmitter. The only real difference between the way television transmitters and

HTTP servers interact with televisions and HTTP clients is that instead of broadcasting, the server is responding to individual requests. The HTTP server is sending out whatever was specifically requested by an HTTP client and not just pumping out information to everyone. HTTP is a fairly secure protocol on both the client and server sides. The server controls what files and information the client has access to by choosing what it serves. The client is open to very little risk, except maybe being overloaded by too much data from the server, but the operating system on the client side usually prevents that. Although this protocol is quite reliable and more interactive than television, it is still a relatively passive medium.

Of course, the basic HTTP protocol leaves much to be desired in the way of interactivity, and people had to really fight it to build compelling, interactive content. Still, interactivity techniques were developed. The most popular of these have been the combination of forms and CGI programs.

The use of forms and CGI is still relatively secure on the client side, but significantly less so for the server. The process works like this. The browser on the client side receives an HTML form document. The form can contain combo boxes, radio buttons, check boxes, and text fields as well as buttons to post the form data. An end user fills out the form and submits its contents to the server. Form contents are submitted by passing them as an argument to a program that executes on the server. Most often, this program is a CGI (Common Gateway Interface) program. It can be written in any language that executes on the server and commonly consists of a UNIX shell script, a C program, or a Perl script. The CGI program parses up the parameter string supplied by the client and utilizes the data. The CGI program can store the data in a local database, email it, and so forth. All access to the server is accomplished by the CGI program. No direct access to the server by the client ever occurs. This arrangement presents a server-side security risk because badly behaved CGI programs can damage a server by depleting system resources, corrupting files, or doing anything else an executable program is capable of doing.

Although Active Server Pages and other non-CGI server-side scripting methods were not mentioned in the preceding discussion, the security issues are much the same.

▶ For more information on CGI programs and security, **see** Chapter 35, "Server-Side Security Issues."

The next logical step in the evolution of interactivity on the Web was client-side executable content. This actually existed before Java in the form of helper apps and plug-ins. Through the use of helper apps—and helper apps that execute right in the browser, called plug-ins—it is possible to view and interact with Web content by using code that executes on your own machine. You simply need to download and install the helper software first (assuming it is available for your platform) and get the content later. The content is not executable but contains information about itself that tells the browser what program to use to interact with it. This is accomplished by use of a MIME (Multipurpose Internet Mail Extensions) type. This model allows a security risk on the client that is worse than the Java model because no limits are imposed on the application running on the client. The person using the helper application must trust that it won't do any harm. The content (images, sounds, and movies) is not executable, and an end user must explicitly install the viewer software. Hence, no more risk exists than in installing any other kind of application.

Part

VII

Ch

41

What about the Java model? It is one big step forward for interactivity, which would typically cause security concerns. If the client can download executable code without knowing exactly what it does, what's to prevent a malicious Java programmer from writing an applet that wipes out the user's hard drive, infects files with viruses, steals private information, or crashes the machine? The remainder of this section describes these risks in more detail and talks about how these security risks have been closed in Java.

The Security Problem

How is network-distributed dynamic executable content any different from software installed and running on a local machine? A piece of software needs to be able to access all of the system resources within the limits of what the operating system allows. It typically needs to save files, read information, and access the system's memory. Although defects exist in software as well as malicious attacks, the person installing the software generally makes a decision to trust the person who wrote the software. This approach is the traditional software model.

An application arriving over a network must also be able to make use of system resources in order to function. The only difference is that executable content arriving in a Web page does not need to be installed first. The user might not even know where it is coming from. If the applet needs access to key system resources, it will contact the browser and ask for special access. Typically, the browser responds by displaying a special dialog box, asking the user if he or she is willing to trust this applet. If the code was written by a malicious programmer who wanted to damage the end user's machine or violate that user's security, and if the end user was willing to grant that live content all the same freedoms a regular local application would have, the user would have no warning and no protection.

How do we allow for a useful applet and maintain a level of trust? It doesn't make sense to completely restrict outside programs from doing anything on the local machine. Such an approach severely limits the functionality of the network application. A better strategy is to develop limitations that hinder the malicious behavior but allow for the freedom to do the things that need to be done. Six steps define this strategy:

1. Determine in advance all potential malicious behavior and attack scenarios.
2. Reduce all potential attack scenarios to a basic set of behaviors.
3. Design a programming language and architecture that does not allow the basic set of behaviors that forms the basis for attack. Hopefully, this disallows the malicious behavior.
4. Prove that the language and architecture are secure against the intended attack scenarios.
5. Allow executable content using only this secure architecture.
6. Design the language and architecture to be extensible so that new attack scenarios can be dealt with as they are discovered and new countermeasures can be retrofitted into the existing security measures.

Java was designed with each of these steps in mind, and it addresses most, if not all, of these points. Before exploring Java's security architecture, we'll discuss the types of potential attack scenarios.

Potential Attack Scenarios

An adversary may try to perpetrate two basic categories of attack. The first of these is the security breach; the second is the nuisance attack. Some examples of nuisance attacks are as follows:

- Application starts a process that hogs all system resources and brings all computer use to a halt.
- Application locks the browser by attacking it internally.
- Application interferes with or reassigns the browser's Domain Name Service (DNS) server. Such an attack can prevent the user from loading documents and possibly cause a security breach if the user were on as the privileged superuser (called root in UNIX and Administrator in Windows NT).
- Application searches and destroys other applications by interfering with some specific process. Someone has written a Java applet, for example, that kills any other Java applets that try to load.
- Application displays obscene pictures or profanity.
- Application deletes or damages files on your computer.

These types of attacks might not necessarily open you up to a security breach because they do not leak private information about your company or yourself to any unauthorized third party. They can, however, make your computing experience unpleasant and even damage your computer's operating system. The goal of these attacks is to wreak havoc of one type or another.

The other, more serious, types of attacks are security breaches, where somebody attempts to gain private or sensitive information about you or your business. More strategies are used to accomplish this than can be covered in a single chapter of a book. You'll find full coverage of the subject in *Internet Security Professional Reference, Second Edition* (New Riders, 1997) and *Maximum Security, Second Edition* (Sams, 1998). A few of the major strategies that people might try include

- Installing a back door into your network for future unauthorized access
- Accessing confidential files on the network and giving them to an unauthorized third party
- Usurping your identity and impersonating you or your computer to carry out attacks on other computers

The Java Approach to Security

Not only is Java a programming language, it also is a cross-platform operating environment—the Java Virtual Machine (JVM). The JVM is separate and independent of Java, the language. The Java Development Kit (JDK) also includes a compiler (javac) for the Java language that produces *bytecodes* for the JVM. The JVM could run bytecodes compiled from any language, not only Java, and the .class files that make up Java objects could be created by any compiler that targeted the Java Virtual Machine. Security needs to be implemented separately on each of these fronts: in the language, the compiler, and the Virtual Machine.

What is special about the Java programming language that makes it more secure than other languages? The Java language was designed to be

- Portable
- Secure
- Object oriented
- Network aware
- Extensible

Many of these requirements affect the way security is implemented in the language, the compiler, and the Virtual Machine. The portability requirement, for example, means that Java cannot rely on any security measures built into an operating system because it needs to run on any system.

Defending Against Attacks from Network Software

If you're going to design a language that makes it easy for programmers to send their work to end users, you have to deal with an unpleasant reality: Not all programmers are as nice as you are. In fact, a few twisted people write programs that are positively malicious.

Trojan horse programs pretend to be useful applications, but when they run they carry out some hidden (and generally malicious) operation. *Viruses* attach themselves to other programs. As part of their function, they copy themselves to still other programs. As these programs are spread around the network, more and more machines are affected. At some point, the virus delivers its payload, which may be anything from a mischievous message on the screen to actually deleting data.

Two lines of defense prevent programs such as trojan horses and viruses from being spread. First, you can enable the developer to "sign" the program with an unforgeable signature. If the signature is valid, the program does not have any viruses or other code that was added after the programmer finished the program. Second, you can design the language in such a way that certain operations, such as reading or writing the local hard drive, are prohibited. Although these operations may be useful to some programs, they are also exploited by malicious programmers.

The only serious competitor to Java applets is Microsoft's ActiveX control. Both Java and ActiveX give the programmer a way to digitally sign the program so the end user can be confident that the code he or she is downloading is actually the program the programmer wrote. Java differs from ActiveX, however, in that Java prevents the programmer from doing things on the client's machine that might be used by a virus or a trojan horse.

If you have a signed program that can do anything it likes to the end user's machine, you have a serious vulnerability. Not every malicious operation is immediately obvious. If a malicious program starts deleting files off your hard drive, you'll probably notice. But will you notice if it goes through your Web browser's disk cache looking up confidential information from your intranet?

Even if you detect a malicious program at work, you may not be able to identify which program is doing the work. In fact, there's no guarantee that the problem-causing program came to you over the Internet. Some security experts have reported that more viruses are loaded from CD-ROMs than from the Internet.

So the best that an electronic signature can guarantee you is that if you detect something going wrong, and if you can determine that the problem was caused by something you downloaded, and if you can determine which downloaded program caused the problem, you now have someone to blame.

Many security experts—not to mention users—would prefer that the problem never occur in the first place. That's the Java approach—deny the malicious programmer any opportunity to write a virus or a trojan horse in the first place.

ON THE WEB

http://java.sun.com/sfaq/   As an applet developer, you should become familiar with the security capabilities offered by Java. Visit the Security Frequently Asked Questions page to get the latest reports on Java security. Visit http://java.sun.com/security/ for an overview of Java security.

To ensure security, Java designers implemented a mechanism called the *sandbox*. The sandbox ensures that untrusted (and possibly malicious) Java applets are allowed access to only a limited set of capabilities on the end user's machine.

N O T E   The comments here about security are directed at applets, not applications. An end user can run an applet simply by downloading a Web page, so applets need tight security. End users must install applications explicitly, so applications are allowed to exercise capabilities that are denied to applets. ▪

This section describes the three major mechanisms that implement a sandbox:

- JVM-level checks
- Language-level safeguards
- The *JavaSecurity* interface

JVM-Level Checks

Suppose you've written a Java applet and have compiled it into a class file. You use this applet on your Web page; when an end user who uses a Java-aware browser downloads this page, he also downloads the applet. In order to ensure that the applet cannot access system-level resources such as the hard drive, the Java Virtual Machine (JVM) that is built into the browser performs several checks.

First, the JVM includes a *class loader*, which is responsible for finding and downloading all the classes used by the applet. Second, before the class file is allowed to execute, the contents of the class file are tested by the *bytecode verifier*. Third, the class runs under the supervision of the JVM *Security Manager*. Figure 41.1 illustrates how these three components work together.

FIGURE 41.1

Before applet code is executed, it must pass security checks by the class loader, the bytecode verifier, and the Security Manager.

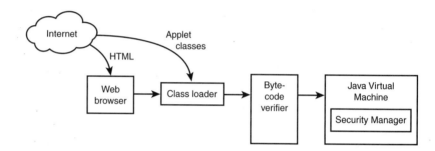

These three mechanisms work together to ensure that

- Only the proper classes are loaded.
- Each class is in the proper format.
- Untrusted classes are not allowed to execute dangerous instructions.
- Untrusted classes are not allowed to access system resources.

Understanding the Class Loader   When a Java-aware browser sees the <APPLET> tag, it invokes the class loader and asks the class loader to load the specified applet. The class loader defines a *namespace* associated with that particular Web page. Classes loaded as part of this applet are not allowed to access other classes (although they can access classes that form part of the standard Java libraries). Figure 41.2 illustrates the class loader's namespaces.

FIGURE 41.2

The Java class loader uses namespaces to isolate one applet from another.

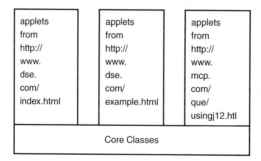

The security provided by a class loader is only as good as the class loader itself. If the class loader was built by Sun or based on Sun's template, it should provide the safeguards described here. Sun's model class loader contains checks to make sure the applet does not install its own class loader, for example, or call methods that are used solely by the class loader. If the browser vendor has not followed Sun's guidelines, the class loader may have security holes.

> **N O T E**   Any application designer can write his or her own class loader. End users should not trust a class loader unless they trust the application developer. ▪

Security Afforded by the Bytecode Verifier   After a class is loaded (by the class loader) it is inspected by the bytecode verifier. The bytecode verifier includes a sophisticated theorem prover that ensures that the applet does not forge pointers, circumvent access restrictions, or convert objects illegally. Just as the class loader's namespace mechanism ensures that one applet cannot interfere with another, the bytecode verifier ensures that an applet cannot wreak havoc within its own namespace. The bytecode verifier also checks for stack overflow or underflow—a traditional way malicious programmers have breached system security. We'll talk more about the bytecode verifier later in this chapter, in the section "The Security of Compiled Code."

Working with the JVM's Security Manager   The final set of checks at the JVM level is made by the JVM's Security Manager. The Security Manager watches out for "dangerous" operations—those that could be exploited by a malicious programmer. The Security Manager must agree any time the applet attempts to access any of the following:

- Network communications
- Protected information (including the hard drive or personal data)
- Operating-system level programs and processes
- The class loader
- Libraries of Java classes (known as *packages*)

The Security Manager is also responsible for preserving thread integrity. That is, code in one group of threads cannot interfere with code in another group of threads, even if the two groups have the same parent applet.

▶ To learn more about threads, **see** "Adding Animation" on **p. 1104**.

Language-Level Safeguards

Many languages, such as SmallTalk, enable the programmer to easily convert objects of one sort to objects of another. This *loose typing* enables programmers to get code up and running quickly, but also opens opportunities for the malicious programmer (in addition to leaving opportunities for software defects).

Strongly typed languages such as Ada are somewhat more difficult to use, but they generally result in programs with fewer defects and tighter compiled code. For this reason loosely typed languages are popular for prototyping, and strongly typed languages are often used for production code.

Part
VII

Ch
41

C and C++ offer a combination of typing methods. The language presents itself as being strongly typed—the compiler needs to be able to determine the type of each object—but the programmer can override a type and coerce an object of one type into a different type. This override mechanism is called *casting*. To cast an object of type Book to be of type Volume, you could write

```
Volume myVolume = (Volume) aBook;
```

Java's approach to typing provides three security benefits:

- Objects cannot be cast to a subclass without an explicit runtime check.
- All references to methods and variables are checked to make sure that the objects are of the correct type.
- Integers cannot be converted into objects, and objects cannot be converted to integers.

In general, much of C and C++'s strength comes from the capabilities of those languages to use *pointers*—variables that hold memory addresses of other data. Although you'll sometimes see descriptions of Java that claim the language has no pointers, the fact is that everything in Java is a pointer—they're just not accessible by the user. The reason pointers are "invisible" is that the Java designers removed the capability to point a pointer to an arbitrary location. This capability, often used by C and C++ programmers, is called *pointer arithmetic*—the capability to modify a pointer so that it points to a new location. Pointer arithmetic enables a malicious C or C++ programmer to access anything within the program's range of allowable addresses (called the *address space*). In some operating systems and on some processors, each program has access to the entire machine's address space. On those systems, a malicious programmer can use pointer arithmetic to wreak havoc in other programs.

N O T E If you're an experienced C or C++ programmer, you may ask, "Won't I miss pointer arithmetic?" Most pointer arithmetic is used to get efficient access to character strings or other arrays. Java supports strings and arrays as explicit classes, with efficient methods to get at their contents. If you use these built-in methods, chances are you'll never miss pointer arithmetic.

Another technique commonly used by malicious programmers is to deliberately overflow an array. Suppose a programmer defines an array of characters named myString to have 128 bytes. The locations myString[0] through myString[127] are reserved for use by the program. By accessing myString[128] and beyond, the program is reading and writing outside its assigned bounds. You can get away with that in C or C++, but in Java array accesses are checked at runtime. The program will not be allowed to access myString[] outside the range 0 to 127. Not only does this bounds-checking close a security hole, it also prevents one common source of program defects.

Strings are also immutable—after you've made a character string, no one can change it (although you can extract substrings and put them together to make new strings). By requiring that strings be immutable, Java's designers closed another security hole and prevented still more common programming errors.

In addition to strong typing and overflow protection, Sun's engineers also took advantage of the object-oriented nature of the language itself to add security. With the exception of the primitive types, everything in Java is a basic object. This strict adherence to object-oriented methodology means that all the theoretical benefits of object-oriented programming (OOP) are realized in Java. These include

- Encapsulation of data within objects
- The capability to inherit from existing secure objects
- Controlled access to data structures via public methods only, so no operator overloading occurs

Every Java object has a unique hash code associated with it. This feature enables the current state of a Java program to be fully inventoried at any time, enabling the Java Virtual Machine to watch for unauthorized objects.

How Java Provides Security over the Internet

Because of the protection of the JVM and the language itself, most users can run most applets and be confident that the applet will "play in its own sandbox" without interfering with system resources on the end user's machine. Sometimes, however, you need to write an applet that accesses those system resources, and the end user is willing to trust that you won't damage his or her system or steal confidential information.

The problem is that an end user downloading your applets over the Internet could be duped into running malicious applets written by someone else. Figure 41.3 illustrates the problem, known as the "man-in-the-middle" attack.

FIGURE 41.3
Bob thinks he's trusting the applet written by Alice, but in reality, he's running an applet written by Charlie.

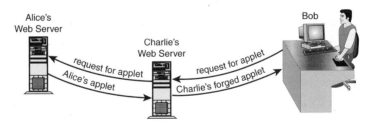

Part
VII

Ch
41

In this example, Bob has connected to Alice's server. His browser downloaded a Web page that included an applet. In reality, Charlie has programmed his server to intercept the applet on its way to Bob and substitute Charlie's version of the applet. While Bob thinks he's trusting Alice's applet, in reality he has opened his system to a malicious applet written by Charlie.

ON THE WEB

`http://www.cs.princeton.edu/sip/pub/spoofing.html` For a technical description of how a man-in-the-middle attack applies to the Web, read this paper on *web spoofing* developed by the Secure Internet Programming team at Princeton University.

The solution to this problem is offered by an applet-level security mechanism called the JavaSecurity API. (An API is an *Application Programming Interface*—a way for a library developer to give the programmer access to a set of features.)

One of the capabilities offered in the JavaSecurity API is *digital signing*. To use this capability, bundle your Java class files and any related files that your applet needs into a *Java archive* (JAR). You then electronically sign the JAR file. When the end user retrieves the JAR from your server, he or she can verify your signature. If a man in the middle attempts to substitute a different applet, the signature will not verify and the end user is warned about the forgery.

ON THE WEB

`http://java.sun.com/products/jdk/1.1/docs/guide/jar/jarGuide.html` Learn more about the Java archive format. Here you'll learn how to reference a JAR in the <APPLET> tag instead of a class file.

Applets Versus ActiveX Controls

The only serious competitor to Java applets is offered by Microsoft and is called ActiveX controls. ActiveX controls are an Internet version of an older standard, called OCX controls. These controls can be written in any language and can do anything that anyone can do in that language. No technical reason prevents an ActiveX programmer from writing a trojan horse that deletes every file on your hard drive or that copies confidential information back to the Internet. Microsoft has tried to address this problem by encouraging ActiveX developers to use their code-signing facility, making ActiveX controls proof against man-in-the-middle attacks.

Sun's approach, with Java, is different, with security checks built into the language itself. As you'll see, Sun also supports signed applets, which the end user may choose to trust.

The Microsoft Way

Microsoft's approach means that every ActiveX control functions like a trusted Java applet. Because most end users will not want to download unsigned ActiveX controls, no equivalent exists to the untrusted applet, in which security is ensured by the Java sandbox.

If an end user chooses to trust all ActiveX controls, sooner or later the end user's machine may fall victim to an attack. With most attacks, it may be difficult to determine which ActiveX control was responsible. An ActiveX control could replace a system file such as move.exe, for example, and then alter itself so the malicious part of the ActiveX control was deleted. The next time the end user attempts to move a file, the trojan horse version of move.exe runs, accomplishing the malicious programmer's objective. Even if the end user detects the problem, it will be difficult to trace the problem back to the specific ActiveX control.

N O T E Microsoft's side of the applet vs. ActiveX argument is that Java represents a "lowest common denominator." Microsoft casts the argument not as "Java vs. ActiveX" but as "PCs vs. Sun." They also point to `http://www.webfayre.com/pendragon/jpr/index.html`, which benchmarks Java performance on a number of different machines. (Windows NT and Windows 95 running on high-speed Pentiums outperform all other platforms.) ▪

Java Browser Restrictions

Sun recommends that browser vendors limit applets by enforcing three rules. These rules are enforced by the Sun code licensed by major browser vendors, such as Netscape Communications and Microsoft, as well as by the Sun Java plug-in:

- Untrusted applets cannot access the local hard drive.
- All standalone windows put up by untrusted applets are labeled as such. Figure 41.4 shows such a window.
- Untrusted applets can establish a network connection only back to the server from which they were loaded.

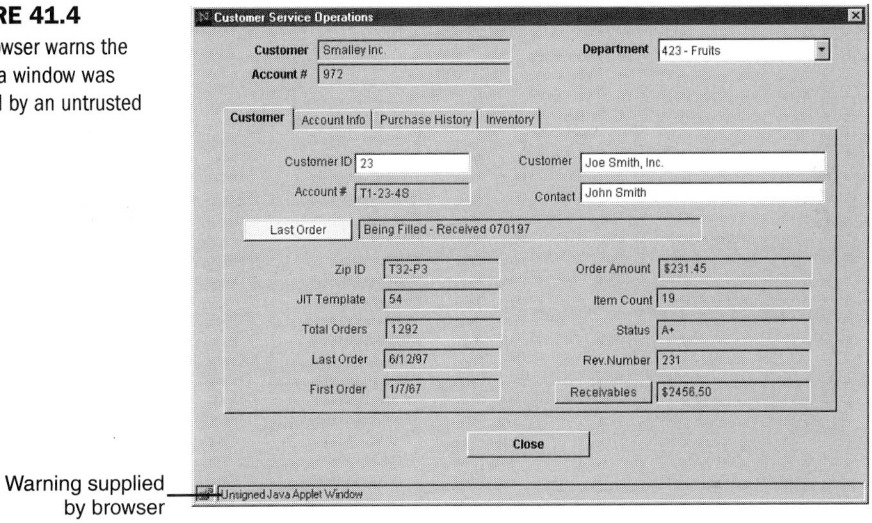

FIGURE 41.4

The browser warns the user if a window was opened by an untrusted applet.

Warning supplied by browser

The first rule closes most security holes. If an applet cannot read the local hard drive, it cannot access most confidential information. If it cannot write the hard drive, it cannot plant viruses or trojan horses.

The second rule makes it less likely that the user will inadvertently enter confidential information (such as a credit card number) into an untrusted applet.

The third rule prevents someone from accessing non-local hard drives, such as those on a local area network or intranet. Like the first rule, this provision closes many opportunities the malicious programmer might have for stealing confidential information or for planting malicious programs.

ON THE WEB

`http://java.sun.com/sfaq/#examples`   Use these Sun examples to test your browser's behavior.

Part

VII

Ch

41

Sun provides sample applets at `http://java.sun.com/sfaq/#examples` to test your browser's security. Your browser should catch security exceptions when you attempt to run these applets from the Internet. You shouldn't get exceptions when you run `http://java.sun.com/sfaq/example/getOpenProperties.html`, which demonstrates the 10 system properties untrusted applets are allowed to read, or `http://java.sun.com/sfaq/example/myWindow.html`, which opens a standalone window (although you should see the "Untrusted Applet" message).

Note that Sun recommends somewhat tighter restrictions for applets downloaded from the Web versus those loaded from the local file system. For full details see `http://java.sun.com/sfaq/`.

Although no one has suggested that it's impossible to build malicious applets—someone is probably working on one right now—Sun has certainly gone to great lengths to make it difficult. If someone wants to attack your system, it's far easier for them to attack through a mechanism such as an ActiveX control than through a Java applet. As long as most users are downloading both, malicious programmers will continue to favor ActiveX controls.

ON THE WEB

`http://www.cert.org/`   If you're responsible for security at your organization, you should get familiar with the services of the Computer Emergency Response Team (CERT) Coordination Center. They'll keep you up to date on known security holes and fixes.

The Security of Compiled Code

The Java compiler checks Java code for security violations. It is a thorough, stringent compiler that enforces the restrictions previously listed. However, it is possible that Java code could be compiled with a "fixed" compiler that allows illegal operations. This is where the Java class loader and bytecode verifier come into play. Various types of security are enforced by the runtime system on compiled code.

Java *.class* File Structure

Java applets and applications are made up of `.class` files that are compiled bytecode. All public classes used in a Java applet or application reside in their own separate `.class` file. They may be transferred over the network a file at a time or bundled into a `.zip` or `.jar` file. The `.class` file is a series of bytes. Longer values are formed by reading two or four of these bytes and joining them together. Each `.class` file contains

- A magic constant
- Major and minor version information
- The constant pool
- Information about the class
- Information about each of the fields and methods in the class
- Debugging information

The *constant pool* is how constant information about the class is stored. It can be any of the following:

- A Unicode string
- A class or interface name
- A reference to a field or method
- A numeric value
- A constant string value

As previously mentioned, all references to variables and classes in the Java language are done through symbolic names, not pointers. This is true in the `.class` file as well. Elsewhere in the `.class` file, references to variables, methods, and objects are accomplished by referring to indices in this constant pool. Security is thus maintained inside the `.class` file.

N O T E Each method can have multiple code attributes. The `CODE` attribute signifies Java bytecode, but other code attributes, such as `SPARC-CODE` and `386-CODE`, allow for a machine code implementation of the method. This technique allows for faster execution, but such native code cannot be verified to be secure. ▓

The class loader of most current Java implementations, including Sun's own HotJava browser, considers any code that comes from a remote source to be potentially hostile and will not use any native code contained in a Java `.class` file unless the user designates the applet as "trusted." Some of these browsers will run native code loaded from local `.class` files, however.

More About Bytecodes

In addition to the actual bytecodes that execute a method, the `CODE` attribute also supplies other information about the method. This information is for the memory manager, the bytecode verifier, and the JVM's exception handling mechanism:

- Maximum stack space used by the method.
- Maximum number of registers used by the method.
- Bytecodes for executing the method.
- Exception handler table. This is a lookup table for the runtime system that provides an offset to where the exception handler is found for code within a starting and ending offset.

Six primitive types are available in the JVM:

- 32-bit integer (integers)
- 64-bit integer (long integers)
- 32-bit floating point numbers (single float)
- 64-bit floating point numbers (double float)
- Pointers to objects and arrays (handles)
- Pointers to the virtual machine code (return addresses)

The Java VM also recognizes several array types:

- Arrays of each of the primitive types (except return addresses)
- Arrays of Booleans, bytes (8-bit integers), shorts (16-bit integers), and Unicode characters

In the case of an array of handles, an additional type field indicates the class of object that the array can store.

Each method has its own expression-evaluation stack and set of local registers. The registers must be 32-bit and hold any of the primitive types other than the double floats and the long integers. These are stored in two consecutive registers, and the JVM instructions, *opcodes,* address them using the index of the lower-numbered register.

The JVM instruction set provides opcodes that operate on various data types and can be divided into several categories:

- Pushing constants onto the stack
- Accessing and modifying the value of a register
- Accessing arrays
- Stack manipulation
- Arithmetic, logical, and conversion instructions
- Control transfer
- Function return
- Manipulating object fields
- Method invocation
- Object creation
- Type casting

The bytecodes consist of a one-byte opcode followed by zero or more bytes of additional operand information. With two exceptions, all instructions are fixed length and based on the opcode.

The Bytecode Verifier

The bytecode verifier is the last line of defense against a bad Java applet. This is where the classes are checked for integrity, where the compiled code is checked for its adherence to the Java rules, and where a misbehaving applet is most likely caught. If the compiled code was created with a "fixed" compiler to get around Java's restrictions, it will still fail the verifier's checks and be stopped. The bytecode verifier is one of the most interesting parts of the Java security mechanism because of the way it is designed to be thorough and general at the same time. The bytecode verifier does not have to work only on code created by a Java compiler, but on any bytecodes created for a JVM, so it needs to be general. However, it also needs to catch all exceptions to the rules laid out for a Java applet or application and must, therefore, be thorough.

All bytecode goes through the bytecode verifier, which makes four passes over the code.

Pass 1 is the most basic pass. The verifier makes sure that the following criteria are met:

- The `.class` file conforms to the format of a `.class` file.
- The magic constant at the beginning is correct.
- All attributes are of the proper length.
- The `.class` file does not have any extra bytes, nor too few.
- The constant pool does not have any unrecognized information.

Pass 1 finds any corrupt `.class` files from a faulty compiler and also catches `.class` files that were damaged in transit. Assuming everything goes well, you get to the second pass.

Pass 2 adds a little more scrutiny. It verifies almost everything without actually looking at the bytecodes themselves. Some of the things that Pass 2 is responsible for are

- Ensuring that final classes are not subclassed and that final methods are not overridden
- Checking that every class (except `Object`) has a superclass
- Ensuring that the constant pool meets certain constraints
- Checking that all field references and methods in the constant pool have legal names, classes, and a type signature

On Pass 2, everything needs to look legal—that is, at face value all the classes appear to refer to classes that really exist, rules of inheritance aren't broken, and so on. It does not check the bytecodes themselves; this task is left up to further passes. Passes 3 and 4 check to see if the fields and methods actually exist in a real class and if the types refer to real classes.

On Pass 3, the actual bytecodes of each method are verified. Each method undergoes dataflow analysis to ensure that the following things are true:

- The stack is always the same size and contains the same types of objects.
- No registers are accessed unless they are known to contain values of a specific type.
- All methods are called with the correct arguments.
- All opcodes have appropriate type arguments on the stack and in the registers.
- Fields are modified with values of the appropriate type.

The verifier ensures that the exception handler offsets point to legitimate starting and ending offsets in the code. It also makes sure the code does not end in the middle of an instruction.

Pass 4 occurs as the code actually runs. During Pass 3, the bytecode verifier does not load any classes unless it must to check its validity. This approach makes the bytecode verifier more efficient. On Pass 4, the final checks are made the first time an instruction referencing a class executes. The verifier then does the following:

- Loads in the definition of the class (if not already loaded)
- Verifies that the currently executing class is allowed to reference the given class

Likewise, the first time an instruction calls a method or accesses or modifies a field, the verifier does the following:

- Ensures that the method or field exists in the given class
- Checks that the method or field has the indicated signature
- Checks that the currently executing method has access to the given method or field

Namespace Encapsulation Using Packages

Java classes are defined within packages that give them unique names. The Java standard for naming packages is the domain the package originates from, but in reverse order with the first part capitalized. If your domain is www.yourdomain.com, your classes should be in the COM.yourdomain.www package.

What is the advantage to using packages? With packages, a class arriving over the network is distinguishable, and therefore, cannot impersonate a trusted local class.

Runtime Linking and Binding

The exact layout of runtime resources is one of the last things done by the JVM. Java uses *dynamic linking*—linking and binding during runtime. This technique prevents an unscrupulous programmer from making assumptions about the allocation of resources or utilizing this information to attack security.

Security in the Java Runtime System

Classes can be treated differently when loaded locally, in contrast to over a network. One of these differences is how the class is loaded into the runtime system. The default way for this to happen is to load the class from a local .class file. Any other way of retrieving a class requires the class to be loaded with an associated ClassLoader. The ClassLoader class is a subtype of a standard Java object that has the methods to implement many of the security mechanisms we have discussed so far. A lot of the attack scenarios that have been used against Java have involved getting around the ClassLoader.

The ClassLoader comes into play after Pass 3 of the bytecode verifier as the classes are actually loaded on Pass 4. The ClassLoader is fairly generic because it does not know for certain that it is loading classes written in Java. It could be loading classes written in C++ and compiled into bytecode.

The ClassLoader, therefore, has to check general rules for consistency within ClassFiles. If a class fails these checks, it isn't loaded and an attack on an end user's system fails. It is an important part of the Java security system.

Automatic Memory Management and Garbage Collection

In C or C++, the programmer is responsible for allocating and deallocating memory and needs to keep track of the pointers to all the objects in memory. This can result in memory leaks, dangling pointers, null pointers, and other defects that are difficult to find and fix. Additionally, leaving memory management up to the programmer can allow for mischief. Manual allocation and deallocation of memory opens the door for unauthorized replication of objects, impersonation of trusted objects, and attacks on data consistency. By having automatic memory management, Java gets around these problems and, at the same time, makes life easier for the programmer. The following example shows how a programmer might go about impersonating a trusted class (for instance, the ClassLoader) if Java did not have automatic deallocation of memory. First, the program would create a legitimate object of class MyFakeClassLoader and make a reference to that object. Now, with a little sleight of hand and knowledge of how allocation and deallocation work, the programmer removes the object from memory but leaves the reference. He or she then instantiates a new instance of ClassLoader, which happens to be the exact same size, in the same memory space, and *voila*! The pointer now refers to the other class, and the programmer has access to methods and variables that are supposed to be private. This scenario is not possible in Java because of the automatic memory management. The Java automatic memory management system doesn't allow manual manipulation of references.

The *SecurityManager* Class

The Java security model is open to extension when new holes are found. A key to this is the SecurityManager class. This class is a generic class for implementing security policies and providing security wrappers around other parts of Java. This class does not get used by itself— it is simply a base for implementing security in other classes. Actual implementation of security in other objects is accomplished through subclassing the SecurityManager class. Although not a comprehensive list, this class contains methods to

- Determine whether a security check is in progress
- Check to prevent the installation of additional ClassLoaders
- Check if a .class file can be read by the Java Virtual Machine
- Check if native code can be linked in
- Check if a file can be written to
- Check if a network connection can be created
- Check if a certain network port can be listened to for connections
- Check if a network connection can be accepted
- Check if a certain package can be accessed
- Check if a new class can be added to a package
- Verify security of a native OS system call
- Prevent a new Security Manager from being created

As you might guess from the preceding list, the names of many of the methods in the java.lang.SecurityManager class begin with check. All but one of these checkXXX methods return if all is well or throw a SecurityException if there was a problem. Only checkTopLevelWindow returns a value—a Boolean.

The following example of the use of the checkXXX methods is based on that in the Java 1.2 API documentation (found at http://java.sun.com/products/jdk/1.2/docs/api/java.lang.SecurityManager.html) for java.lang.SecurityManager:

```
SecurityManager secMgr = System.getSecurityManager();

if (secMgr != null) {

    secMgr.checkXXX(arguments go here,... );

}
```

Everything discussed so far in this section has been about Java as a whole. The language has no pointers whether you are working with applets or applications. The bytecode verifier and class loading mechanisms still apply. Applications in Java function like any other applications in any full-featured language, including direct memory access through use of native code. Some limitations on applets exist, however, that do not apply to applications.

Time-Tested Applet Security

Java would not have made the splash that it did only by being cross platform and object oriented. It was the Internet and applets that put it on the cover of *Time* magazine. The Internet is also where the biggest risks come for Java applets.

Applets are limited Java programs, extended from class Applet, that execute within the user's Web browser. Applets usually load from remote machines and are subject to severe limitations on the client machine.

Untrusted applets arriving on the client machine are subject to the following file system and network restrictions:

- Cannot read or write files on the local file system.
- Cannot create, copy, delete, or rename files or directories on the local file system.
- Can only connect to the machine from which they originally came. This is the URL of the source machine as specified in the APPLET tag in the HTML document or in the CODEBASE parameter of the APPLET tag. This cannot be a numeric IP address.
- Cannot call external programs.
- Cannot manipulate Java threadgroups other than their own.
- Cannot run outside the Java Virtual Machine's memory area.

N O T E This set of restrictions on the applet can vary slightly from one implementation of Java to another. All these apply, for instance, when using Netscape Navigator 2.0 or later, but the JDK appletviewer enables you to designate an explicit list of files that can be accessed by applets. The HotJava browser, Netscape Navigator, Microsoft Internet Explorer, and the JDK appletviewer (to name a few) all have minor differences ranging from handling of certain exceptions to access control lists for applets. If you want to know of detailed limitations for a particular browser, go to the applicable Web site and get the most up-to-date information. For the Microsoft Internet Explorer, check http://www.microsoft.com/ie/security/, and for the Netscape Navigator, check `http://home.netscape.com/comprod/products/communicator/navigator.html`. If you need to have a consistent security model no matter where your applet runs, consider designing your Web pages to load Sun's Java plug-in instead of relying on the browser's JVM. ▓

▶ For more information on the Java plug-in, **see** "Running the Applet" on **p. 992**.

Some system information is available to applets, however. Access to this information depends on the specific Java implementation. A method of the `System` object is called `getProperty`. By calling `System.getProperty(String key)`, an applet can learn about its environment. The information available to the applet is as follows:

- ▓ `java.version`—The version of Java currently running
- ▓ `java.vendor`—The name of the vendor responsible for this specific implementation of Java
- ▓ `java.vendor.URL`—The URL of the vendor listed in `java.vendor`
- ▓ `java.class.version`—The Java class version number
- ▓ `os.name`—The name of the operating system
- ▓ `os.arch`—The architecture of the operating system
- ▓ `file.separator`—The file separator (for example, /)
- ▓ `path.separator`—The path separator (for example, :)
- ▓ `line.separator`—The line separator (for example, `CRLF`)

Other pieces of information that may or may not be available, depending on the implementation, are

- ▓ `java.home`—The Java home directory
- ▓ `java.class.path`—The Java class path
- ▓ `user.name`—The logon name of the current user
- ▓ `user.home`—The location of the user's home directory
- ▓ `user.dir`—The user's current directory

Making and Using Signed Applets

Part

VII

Ch

41

Starting in JDK 1.1, Sun introduced several new APIs to the core set of Java APIs. One of these is Security and Signed Applets, a subset of the Security API. This API provides for digital signatures and message digests (in accordance with the industry standard X.509v3). These signatures are based on `public`/`private` key pairs.

To sign your applets or to prepare your system to use signed applets, you need the *jar, keytool, jarsigner,* and *appletviewer* tools included with JDK 1.2. You make and access Java archives with jar, make keys with keytool, sign archives with jarsigner, and test and develop using the appletviewer mini-browser.

Before getting started, you might want to see what happens when an applet throws a security exception. Sun provides a harmless sample applet that does just that. You can try it by running

```
appletviewer http://java.sun.com/security/signExample/writeFile.html
```

at a command prompt.

Digital Signature Enhancements in JDK 1.2

As you've seen throughout this chapter, tight security is one of Java's distinctives. It's not surprising that JDK 1.2 includes some major improvements in security. These changes include

- Policy-based access control—The capability to grant rights to software is based on an external configuration file.

- Support for X.509v3 certificates—You can use the latest industry-standard encryption technology to sign the Java archives in which you distribute your classes.

- New security tools—These include tools to manage certificates and write your security policy file.

Policy-Based Access Control

If you've used the UNIX operating system, then you're familiar with the concept of permissions. The owner of a file can grant other users (or programs) the right to read, write, or execute a file. Processes take on the rights of the person who started them—although some users will choose to restrict the rights of programs they launch. (Web servers are often started by someone with `root` authority, for example, but run as the nonprivileged user `nobody`.)

Beginning in version 1.2, Java developers have similar choices with their applications and applets—although the level of control is finer grained than that offered by many UNIX implementations.

Computer resources include files, directories, hosts, and ports. The person responsible for a computer that will be running Java can set up a *security policy* that specifies who is allowed to access each resource. Access includes read and write permission (for files and directories) and connect permission (for hosts and ports). The security policy is specified in an external security configuration file.

When a Java class is loaded, the JVM examines the security policy currently in effect. If the code is signed, then permissions may be granted on the basis of the identity of the signer. Permissions may also be granted based on the location of the class file. (A file loaded from the local host might be given more access, for example, than one loaded from the Internet.)

Certificate Interfaces and X.509v3 Implementation

Not so long ago, the only way for a server to identify a client was to ask the user for a username and password. If the username and password matched those stored in the password file, the server granted the user access.

Several problems occur with password-based authentication. First, the password often has to travel over a non-secure network. If an adversary is able to "sniff" the username and password from the Net, he or she will be able to masquerade as a valid user.

Another problem is that most users access more than one system and have more than one username and password. Users find it difficult to keep these names and passwords straight, so they either write down the names and passwords or use the same name and password on every system. Either solution is subject to abuse.

A better solution is for the user to generate a special kind of cryptographic key, called a public/private key pair. These keys work together—if you encrypt something with my public key, only a person with my private key can decrypt it. If I keep my private key secret, you can be sure that I am the only one who can read your message.

In an ideal world, we could all post our public keys on servers somewhere and begin to communicate securely with each other. That practice is subject to abuse, too—an opponent could put a public key on the server with my name on it. If my opponent can trick you into using the bogus key, he or she will be able to read messages intended for me. (This strategy is a variation of the man-in-the-middle attack described earlier in this chapter, in the section entitled "The Java Approach to Security.")

The solution is simple—I generate my public/private key pair, making sure I keep my private key secret. I send my public key to a "public key certifying authority," who requires that I prove my identity. After I've satisfied the certifying authority that I am who I say I am, they sign my key with *their* private key. Now anyone who wants to be sure that a public key with my name on it really belongs to me can check the signature of the certifying authority. If you find that the signature is valid, and you're satisfied with their policy for checking my identity, then you can trust my public key.

The combination of a public key, identifying information, and a certification authority's signature is called a *certificate*. The current generation of the standard for certificates is *X.509v3*. For more information about certificates and public-key encryption, see the section, "Signing Your JARs," later in this chapter.

Version 1.2 of the JDK includes new APIs for parsing certificates and maintaining local databases of X.509v3 certificates.

New Security Tools

Version 1.2 of the JDK also includes tools to help you manage X.509v3 certificates. Within your company, for example, you may decide to issue certificates to any employee. The Java *keytool*, new in version 1.2, enables each user to generate a public/private keypair. The user can also use keytool to generate his or her own certificate (although the certificate is to a slightly older standard—X.509v1).

ON THE WEB

`http://home.netscape.com/comprod/server_central/product/certificate/`
`index.html` If you plan to issue your own certificates, you'll need a Certificate Server. Visit the
Netscape site and learn about Netscape's Certificate Server, part of the SuiteSpot family of servers.

You use *jarsigner* in combination with your certificate to digitally sign Java archives (JARs).

TIP If you've been using javakey from JDK 1.1 or earlier, replace it with keytool and jarsigner. The older tool,
javakey, is now obsolete.

You can write an external security configuration file that specifies your machine's security
policy. The easiest way to write such a file is to use Sun's *policytool*, also new in JDK 1.2.

Making a JAR

In the earliest versions of Java, it was common to write simple applets that had only a single
class file. More sophisticated applets may have dozens of class files as well as supporting files
such as images and sounds. It became common to use the popular DOS archive format, `.zip`,
to bundle class files together. The Java Virtual Machine can read the `.zip` format, so it's not
necessary to unzip these files.

Unfortunately, many users automatically unzip any arriving `.zip` file, breaking the applet. In
JDK 1.2 Sun provides tools for working with the Java archive format, JAR. A JAR file is still a
`.zip` file, but includes a special manifest file to identify its contents. By using a suffix that is
more clearly Java related, Sun has decreased the likelihood that end users will open the
archive.

You can place all the files associated with an applet into a JAR file and write

```
<APPLET CODE="TMyApplet.class"
  ARCHIVE="MyArchive.jar, AnotherArchive.jar"
  WIDTH="200" HEIGHT="200">
</APPLET>
```

This bit of code tells the browser to download the two JARs named. The browser can expect
that the components of TMyApplet will all be found in those two JARs. Furthermore, if the
browser already has a current copy of one or both of those JAR files in its cache, it may be able
to skip the download and display the applet right away. Figure 41.5 illustrates how the class
files for TMyApplet are distributed across the two JAR files.

N O T E If your applet uses files that aren't in the JAR file, the Web browser will go back to the Web
server and look in the current CODEBASE directory for the missing files. ▪

FIGURE 41.5

You can store the files of an applet in one or more JAR files.

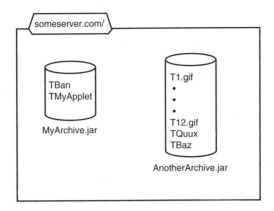

As an applet developer, you get six benefits from JARs:

- Improved download efficiency—You need only one HTTP transfer per JAR instead of one per class file.
- Improved file storage—A JAR stores the class files in one compressed file instead of leaving them "loose" in the directory.
- Improved security—You can sign JAR files digitally, giving the end user a guarantee that the file has not been tampered with since you signed it. If the end user trusts you, he or she may be willing to give your signed applet access to the hard drive or other sensitive resources.
- Platform independence—JAR files are based on PKZIP, a popular DOS compression utility, but they can be built and stored on any computer platform.
- Backwards compatibility—A JAR file doesn't care what kind of files you put into it. You could take a JDK 1.0 applet and store its class files in a JAR file. As long as the user's browser understands how to read JAR files, he or she will be able to download and run the applet.
- Extensibility—Sun acknowledges that Internet technology in general—and Java technology in particular—is still in a state of flux. They've provided some hooks in the JAR specification for future growth, so that future developers can extend it as demands change.

Although you can use PKZIP-based tools to make and change JARs, Sun provides a tool specifically designed for the task. This utility is called *jar*—versions for all supported platforms are offered.

Suppose you have the directory structure shown in Figure 41.6: several `.class` files plus an `images` directory. You could use the jar utility to put all these into a new JAR file. We'll name it `MyApplet.jar`.

The general format for the `jar` command line is

```
jar options filenames
```

Part

VII

Ch

41

FIGURE 41.6

This directory contains a typical set of files for an applet or application.

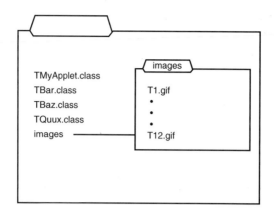

N O T E   The name for Sun's Java archive format is not accidental. Sun's jar utility is consciously modeled on a UNIX utility called "tar" (for tape archiver). The tar utility is used by UNIX users for building a variety of archives (not just those on tape) in much the same way as PKZIP and WinZip are used by MS-DOS and Windows users. ▨

The first file named in the *filenames* list is the name of the archive. The use of any remaining files named in this list is given in the options list:

- ▨ c—Make a new archive.
- ▨ m—Use an external manifest file, named as the second file in the *filenames* list.
- ▨ M—Do not make a manifest file for this archive.
- ▨ t—List the contents of this archive.
- ▨ x—Extract the files named in the *filenames* list; if none, extract all the files in the archive.
- ▨ f—Specifies that the archive is named as the first file in the *filenames* list.
- ▨ v—Specifies that the utility should produce verbose information while it performs the actions described by the other options.
- ▨ 0—Stores files in the archive without using compression.

N O T E   Unlike other utilities you may be familiar with, jar doesn't require that you use / or - in front of the options. ▨

In order to make our new archive, then, we write

```
jar cf MyApplet.jar *.class images/*.gif
```

If you had prepared a manifest file in the text file MyApplet.MF, you would write

```
jar cfm MyApplet.jar MyApplet.MF *.class images/*.gif
```

> **CAUTION**
>
> A package name such as com.mcp.que.platinumHTMLXMLJava.chapter41 means that the class file is located in the com/mcp/que/platinumHTMLXMLJava.chapter41 directory underneath one of the directories named in the CLASSPATH environment variable. Be sure to place these class files into the proper directory before installing them into the JAR, or the JVM won't be able to find the class file.

You can examine a JAR file by using any PKZIP-compatible tool, including the jar utility itself. To get a listing of the files in MyApplet.jar, type

```
jar tf MyApplet.jar
```

Suppose you want to make a copy of a file that's come to you in a JAR file. Use the x option. To read the manifest file out of MyApplet.jar, for example, type

```
jar xf MyApplet.jar MyApplet.MF
```

Signing Your JARs

Regardless of what your JAR file contains, there are times when you want to be able to prove to the person using it that you are, indeed, the originator, and that no one has tampered with the contents after you made the JAR. If your JAR contains an applet, this need is particularly critical because, without such proof, applets are left in an untrusted state and will have no access to the hard drive or operating system services on the machine to which they're downloaded.

You can provide this guarantee by *digitally signing* your JAR. In order to understand how to set up a digital signature, you need to understand a little about cryptography.

Understanding Public Key Encryption

Many years ago encryption was the province of the military and the diplomats. You kept messages secret by combining the message with a secret piece of information called a *key*. The receiver needed a copy of the key. With the key and the proper equipment, anyone could decrypt a message. Figure 41.7 illustrates one of these old systems.

FIGURE 41.7
Old-style encryption systems were based on secret keys.

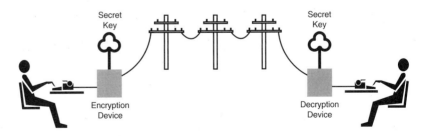

Introducing Public Key Technology In more recent days, cryptographers have invented *public key encryption*. A public key encryption system is based on two pieces of information, or keys. These keys come in pairs—they must be used together. One of these keys is secret and is kept under tight security by the owner. The other is public and may be distributed widely. Figure 41.8 illustrates how a public key encryption system works.

FIGURE 41.8

Public key encryption is based on the fact that no one can read a message that was signed with one key unless he or she has the other key.

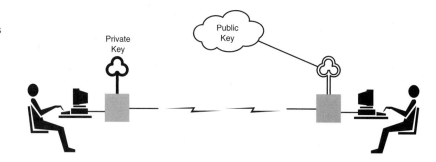

Suppose you want to send a message (which could be a JAR file) and be able to assure the person receiving the message that the message is really from you and hasn't been tampered with. You would start by encrypting the message with your private key. Because only you have your private key—you're being very careful to keep it secret—only you could have produced this encrypted file. Your public key is well known—assume the recipient already has a copy. When the recipient receives your message, he or she attempts to decrypt the message by using your public key. Remember that these keys work together—only one key can successfully decode a message encrypted by your private key. If the recipient is able to decrypt the message with your public key, he or she can safely assume that it was signed by you.

> **CAUTION**
>
> You should never send your private key out over the Internet. Most of the time, it never even needs to leave your computer. When you generate it, choose a good long (multiword) passphrase no one else is likely to guess, but that you're certain to remember.

Why Do You Need a Certificate? A flaw is present in this system—I claimed that your public key was well known and that the recipient already has a copy. That's not true—the recipient doesn't necessarily know you, and he or she probably doesn't have a copy of your public key. You could send one by email, but then how could the recipient know that *that* message didn't come from someone impersonating you?

The solution is to have your public key embedded in a message that is signed by someone whom both you and the recipient trust. Such a message is called a *digital certificate*. The current standard version is X.509 version 3, so these certificates are often called *X.509v3 certificates*. The "someone" whom both parties trust is called a *Certification Authority*, or CA. If both you and the recipient work for the same company, or if the recipient trusts my employer, you might present a certificate signed by my company CA. If the two parties have no other relationship, you might present a certificate signed by a public Certification Authority, such as Verisign (http://www.verisign.com/). If the recipient is the trusting sort, he or she might even accept a certificate you signed yourself—a self-certifying certificate.

N O T E Although Certification Authorities and X.509v3 certificates are emerging as the *de facto* standard, other systems are available. Phil Zimmermann's PGP (Pretty Good Privacy) software, for example, is based on a "web of trust," in which you are invited to trust an unknown person because people whom you know and trust either vouch for the unknown person or they vouch for people who vouch for the unknown person, and so on. Learn more about PGP online at http://www.nai.com/ and http://www.pgpi.com/. ■

Why Do You Need a Message Digest Algorithm?   Another flaw is present in this system. Computationally, it's inefficient to encrypt a large file, such as a JAR file, with a private key. Actual public key encryption systems don't try to do this—instead, they apply an efficient algorithm called a *message digest* algorithm to produce a long number—one that is virtually unique to this message. Then they encrypt only the message digest itself.

One of the most common message digest algorithms is called SHA1; one of the most common public key encryption algorithms is called DSA. The rest of this section shows you how to sign JAR files with an SHA1/DSA-based signature.

The Java Utilities   In addition to the jar utility, you'll need two tools to sign JARs:

- keytool—Used to produce public/private keypairs and certificates. For complete documentation on keytool, see docs/guide/security/spec/security-spec.doc17.html in your JDK directory.

- jarsigner—Used to actually sign the JARs, based on your certificate. For complete documentation on jarsigner, see docs/tooldocs/win32/jarsigner.html in the JDK directory on your hard drive. (If you're a Solaris user, a corresponding file in the solaris directory shows how jarsigner works on your machine.)

T I P   Both keytool and jarsigner are designed to be run from the command line—they're simply wrappers around the Java classes that implement keys, certificates, and signatures. Sun provides a tool for users to use in setting their security policy—called policytool—that has a graphical interface.

Signing a JAR—Step-by-Step   Here's a step-by-step procedure for signing your JAR files. The remainder of this section describes each of these steps in detail.

1. Generate a keypair.
2. Obtain a certificate for your keypair.
3. Distribute your certificate so people will know that you're the person behind the trusted applet.
4. Use your certificate to sign your JAR.

Figure 41.9 illustrates this process.

FIGURE 41.9
Use Sun's tools to
generate a keypair,
request a certificate,
install it, and sign a
JAR file.

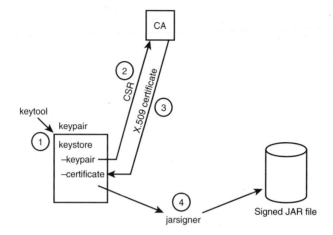

If you've already generated a keypair and obtained a certificate through another means (such as Netscape Navigator and the Netscape Certificate Server or Verisign, Inc.), you can skip the first two steps and go right to jarsigner. In the rest of this section we'll assume you're starting from scratch. In the first step, we'll generate a keypair and a self-signed certificate. In the second step we'll send off a Certificate Signing Request to the CA of your choice.

> **CAUTION**
>
> You could use a self-signed certificate to claim you were anyone. Sophisticated users will often ignore such certificates. For serious work on the Internet, consider having your certificate generated by a reputable firm such as Verisign (`http://www.verisign.com/`).

Generating a Keypair

Sun provides the utility keytool to administer databases of keys and certificates for use by the utility jarsigner. You can get basic usage information by typing

```
keytool -help
```

at the command prompt.

To generate a new key you might type

```
keytool -genkey -alias mike
```

This line tells the keytool to generate a new key to be stored under the name "mike."

N O T E Not enough information is in this line for keytool to generate a new key. It needs a Distinguished Name, a passphrase for the password itself, and a passphrase for the keystore. It will prompt you for any required fields you fail to specify. ■

When you generate a new keypair, you may include the following options:

- ■ -v—Produce verbose information.
- ■ -alias *alias*—A common name to be associated with this key.
- ■ -keyalg *keyalg*—Specifies the algorithm to be used for generating the key.
- ■ -keysize *keysize*—Specifies the size of the key, in bits.
- ■ -sigalg *sigalg*—Specifies the algorithm to be used for preparing a message digest.
- ■ -dname *distinguishedName*—Your personal Distinguished Name, which usually includes your organization and country.

 TIP The X.500 Distinguished Name uses commas to separate the fields. If one of your fields contains a comma, escape it with a \ character.

- ■ -keypass *keypass*—The passphrase for this key. If you don't provide one, you'll be prompted for it. The tool requires that the passphrase be at least six characters long—for better security, make yours much longer than that.
- ■ -keystore *keystore*—The location where the keys will be stored.

N O T E If you allow keytool to put your keys in the default file, it will build a keystore in a file named .keystore in your home directory. On a Windows system your "home directory" is the concatenation of the HOMEDRIVE and HOMEPATH environment variables. If they're not defined or they don't constitute a valid path, the keystore is put in the JDK installation directory. ■

- ■ -storepass *storepass*—The passphrase for the keystore.

The default key size is 1024 bits and uses a key algorithm of DSA. Your Distinguished Name should follow the format

CN=*Common Name* OU=*Organizational Unit* ORG=*Organization* C=*Country*

For example, my Distinguished Name is

CN=Michael L Morgan OU=Software Engineering ORG=DSE Inc C=US

CAUTION

If you default your Distinguished Name, it will prompt you for your state and locality, which are usually unnecessary.

-alias refers to a shorter name by which you will know this Distinguished Name. For example, I might write

```
keytool -genkey -alias Mike Morgan
➥-dname CN=Michael L Morgan OU=Software Engineering
➥ORG=DSE Inc C=US
➥-keypass A password for Platinum Edition
```

Part
VII

Ch
41

> **CAUTION**
>
> Don't enter your passphrases as parameters or embed them in scripts—wait and let the system prompt you for them. When you enter them, keytool will echo the characters. Make sure no one can see you when you type in this information.

By default, keytool wraps the public key into a self-signed X.509v1 certificate (but not the newer X.509v3). The two formats (X.509v1 and X.509v3) are similar—most end users who know the difference won't care whether you're using v1 or v3, but they may hesitate before accepting a self-signed certificate. If you want an X.509v3 certificate, you'll have to go to a public Certification Authority such as Verisign or obtain your own Certificate Server.

N O T E If you've worked with JARs in an earlier release of the JDK, you'll have seen a utility called javakey. That program is now obsolete—stick with keytool and jarsigner. ■

Obtaining a Certificate

After you've generated your keypair, you need to generate a Certificate Signing Request, or CSR, and send that CSR to the Certificate Authority (CA) of your choice—either a public CA or your own organization's CA.

ON THE WEB

http://www.verisign.com/   You can learn how to get your keypair certified by Verisign from their Web site. You'll need to be able to prove to them that you are who you say you are, and you'll pay a small fee.

To learn more about the Netscape Certificate Server, visit http://home.netscape.com/comprod/ server_central/product/certificate/index.html.

To generate a Certificate Signing Request (CSR), type

```
keytool -csr
```

Just as with `-genkey`, the program will prompt you for any required parameters you omit. You may want to use one or more of the following options:

- `-v`—Generate verbose output.
- `-alias alias`—Specifies the alias of the key you want to certify. The default is `mykey`.
- `-sigalg sigalg`—The signing algorithm to be used. The default is DSA with SHA1.
- `-file csr_file`—The file into which the CSR should be written.
- `-keypass keypass`—The passphrase for this key.
- `-keystore keystore`—The file where the keys are stored.
- `-storepass storepass`—The passphrase of the keystore.

After you've generated the CSR, send it to your CA following the instructions they'll give you. (CAs generally accept CSRs by email, although some prefer that you copy the CSR and paste it into an HTML form.) After the CA follows its certificate-signing policy to verify your identify (and, in the case of a commercial CA, after they've received payment), they'll issue you a certificate. This certificate may come by email, or you may be sent to pick it up at a Web page. Either way, get it into a file by itself and type

```
keytool -import
```

 If your certificate comes by email, mail headers and footers may be on the message. The part of the message you want to copy into a file is the part bounded by "––BEGIN CERTIFICATE––" and "––END CERTIFICATE––."

Some other parameters for the import option that you may find useful are

- `-v`—To get a verbose output
- `-alias` *alias*—The common name of the person associated with this certificate
- `-file` *cert_file*—The name of the file where the certificate is stored

CAUTION

Do not use the `-noprompt` option of keytool. Require the keytool to show you the certificate—satisfy yourself that it's not a forgery. You can call the CA and read them the certificate's message digest (it's called the fingerprint) if you want to be sure.

 Your CA will probably send you a copy of *their* certificate so you can verify the signature on *your* certificate. Install their certificate too, but first, doublecheck their fingerprint to make sure no one has forged their certificate.

To learn even more about keysigner, point your Web browser to `/docs/tooldocs/win32/keytool.html` in your JDK directory (on a Windows machine). An analogous directory for Solaris is available should you need to learn about the differences between `keytool` on Windows and keytool on Solaris.

Distributing Your Certificate

Now that you have a signed certificate, let people know it exists so they can get your public key. They'll use this key to verify messages and applets from you. You might type

```
keytool -export -alias mike -file filename
```

You can also specify a filename in the `-file` parameter. The utility will copy your certificate to the designated *filename*. Distribute that certificate to people who might use your signed applet—they should verify your signature on the certificate before they put a strange applet to work on their machines.

Using jarsigner to Sign a JAR File

After you have a public/private keypair and an X.509 certificate that attests to its authenticity, you're able to digitally sign your JAR files. Sun provides the jarsigner utility for this purpose.

> **N O T E** The version of jarsigner that is distributed with JDK 1.2 can only sign JAR files that have been built with Sun's jar utility. ■

In addition to signing JAR files, jarsigner can also verify the integrity of a signed JAR. Just run it with the -verify option.

> **N O T E** If you used to use javakey (the forerunner of keytool), you'll have to get a new keypair and certificate. jarsigner has no backward compatibility with the javakey database. ■

The simplest way to use jarsigner is to type

```
jarsigner MyJarFile.jar
```

In this case jarsigner will use the default keystore (.keystore in your home directory) and will prompt you for the passwords to the keystore and the password. jarsigner will also use the default alias, mykey. The output will be written to the file named MyJarFile.jar, overwriting the original file. You can specify more information on the command line:

```
jarsigner -keystore C:\JDK\projects\.keystore -signedjar
➡MySignedJarFile.jar MyJarFile.jar mike
```

tells jarsigner to sign the file MyJarFile.jar by using the certificate associated with the alias mike. The keystore is located at C:\JDK\projects\.keystore. The output is written to MySignedJarFile.jar, and the original file (MyJarFile.jar) is left unchanged.

> **N O T E** When you run jarsigner, it computes a message digest of the JAR file (using either the MD5 or the SHA-1 algorithm, depending upon your certificate) and then encodes that message digest by using your private key. It writes two new files—a signature file with an .SF suffix and a signature block file (with a .DSA or .RSA suffix)—into the JAR file. The base name used in these two files is based on the alias you used to sign the file. ■

Working with Encryption from Inside Your Program

You can write Java to do everything we've just done from the command line. Look at the documentation in java.security and its subpackages, java.security.cert, java.security.interfaces, and java.security.spec. These packages provide you with such classes as KeyPairGenerator, Signature, and MessageDigest, and the interface Key.

You can read more about the new JDK 1.2 security architecture in your JDK documentation at docs/guide/security/spec/security-spec.doc.html. You can also get detailed information about using the jar and javakey tools in the JDK 1.2 documentation.

ON THE WEB

`http://java.sun.com/products/jdk/1.2/docs/guide/security/index.html`   You can
read more about JDK 1.2 security features, including the Java Security API and new classes, at Sun's
JDK 1.2 security site.

Open Issues on Security

In the case of Java, the security is only as good as its runtime implementation. Holes have been
found and fixed in various implementations, but these same issues may arise again in future
implementations as Java is ported to other platforms. After all, each version of the JVM needs
to be written in a platform-specific programming language, such as C, and can have its own
flaws and weaknesses.

Aside from that, many types of malicious behavior are difficult (if not impossible) to avoid. No
matter what is done to the Java security model, for instance, it will not stop someone from
putting rude or obscene material in an applet or starting long, resource-intensive processes.
Such actions are not defects but will continue to be nuisances.

For links to and discussions of current problems and a chronology of security-related bugs, see
the Java Security FAQ at `http://java.sun.com/sfaq/index.html`. Every implementation of
Java has its own open issues, and Sun's is no exception. The best thing to do is to keep on top
of the issues for the implementation you are using.

Further References on Java and Security

The following references can help you keep up with the changing world of Java security. It is by
no means a comprehensive list, but it should get you started on researching the topic further
and give you some valuable starting places from which to continue your research.

- UseNet:

  `alt.2600`

  `comp.risks`

  `comp.lang.java.*` (especially `comp.lang.java.security`)

  `comp.infosystems.www.*`

- WWW:

  Sun's Java Security site, with a wealth of links about Java security bug chronology, the
  Applet Security FAQ, Security API information, applet and code signing, JDK 1.2
  features, JDK 1.2 security documentation, the Java security model, Java cryptographic
  architecture, the Java Security Q&A archives, the Java Cryptography Extension (JCE) to
  the JDK 1.2, and more. Highly recommended:

  `http://java.sun.com/security/index.html`

Part
VII

Ch
41

Slides from a presentation by Li Gong, Sun's Java security architect, at JavaOne 1997, on the future and direction of Java security:

`http://java.sun.com/javaone/sessions/slides/TT03/TT03.zip`

The Java Security Q&A archives:

`http://java.sun.com/security/hypermail/java-security-archive/index.html`

The Java Security FAQ:

`http://java.sun.com/sfaq/index.html`

Sun's recommendations for security policies:

`http://java.sun.com/security/policy.html`

Sun's *Jar Guide*, about using the new JAR file format and tools:

`http://java.sun.com/products/jdk/1.2/docs/guide/jar/jarGuide.html`

Netscape Navigator Security FAQ:

`http://developer.netscape.com:80/support/faqs/champions/security.html`

"Java Security," the December 1995 classic paper by Joseph A. Bank, MIT:

`http://www-swiss.ai.mit.edu/~jbank/javapaper/javapaper.html`

JavaScript 1.2 Language Reference

How This Reference Is Organized

The first part of this reference is organized by object, with properties and methods listed by the object to which they apply. It covers most of the objects included in the Document Object Model supported by JavaScript 1.2. The second part covers independent functions in JavaScript not connected with a particular object, as well as operators in JavaScript.

A Note About JavaScript 1.2

JavaScript 1.2 is designed to interface seamlessly with Netscape Navigator 4.0. New features have been introduced in various areas of the language model, including but not limited to the following:

- Events
- Objects
- Properties
- Methods

Netscape Navigator 4.0 has been coded to support these new features, but earlier versions of Navigator have not. Backward compatibility is, therefore, an issue.

Finally, note that when developing, you can now clearly identify which version of JavaScript you're using. If you don't, your scripts might not work. You identify the version by using the LANGUAGE attribute in the <SCRIPT> tag. The following are some examples:

```
<SCRIPT LANGUAGE="JavaScript">-—Compatible with 2.0 and above

<SCRIPT LANGUAGE="JavaScript1.1">—Compatible with 3.0 and above

<SCRIPT LANGUAGE="JavaScript1.2">—Compatible with 4.0 and above
```

The following codes are used next to section headings to indicate where objects, methods, properties, and event handlers are implemented:

- 2—Netscape Navigator 2.
- 3—Netscape Navigator 3.
- 4—Netscape Navigator 4 only. (That's not to say Navigator 4 works with these items only; Navigator 4 will handle all implementations.)
- I—Microsoft Internet Explorer 4.

N O T E   All the JavaScript information referenced in this appendix is client-side JavaScript; server-side JavaScript is not covered.

The *anchor* Object [2 | 3 | 4 | I]

The anchor object reflects an HTML anchor.

Properties

■ name—A string value indicating the name of the anchor (not 2|3)

The *applet* Object [3]

The applet object reflects a Java applet included in a Web page with the <APPLET> tag.

Properties

■ name—A string reflecting the NAME attribute of the <APPLET> tag

The *area* Object [3]

The area object reflects a clickable area defined in an imagemap; area objects appear as entries in the links array of the document object.

Properties

■ hash—A string value indicating an anchor name from the URL

■ host—A string value reflecting the host and domain name portion of the URL

■ hostname—A string value indicating the host, domain name, and port number from the URL

■ href—A string value reflecting the entire URL

■ pathname—A string value reflecting the path portion of the URL (excluding the host, domain name, port number, and protocol)

■ port—A string value indicating the port number from the URL

■ protocol—A string value indicating the protocol portion of the URL, including the trailing colon

■ search—A string value specifying the query portion of the URL (after the question mark)

■ target—A string value reflecting the TARGET attribute of the <AREA> tag

Methods

■ getSelection—Gets the current selection and returns this value as a string

Event Handlers

■ onDblClick—Specifies JavaScript code to execute when the user double-clicks the area (not implemented on Macintosh; Netscape Navigator 4.0 only) (4)

■ onMouseOut—Specifies JavaScript code to execute when the mouse moves outside the area specified in the <AREA> tag

New Properties with JavaScript 1.2

type   indicates a `MouseOut` event

target   indicates the object to which the event was sent

layer[n]   where [n] represents x or y, used (with `page[n]` and `screen[n]`) to describe the cursor location when the `MouseOut` event occurred

page[n]   where [n] represents x or y, used (with `layer[n]` and `screen[n]`) to describe the cursor location when the `MouseOut` event occurred

screen[n]   where [n] represents x or y, used (with `layer[n]` and `page[n]`) to describe the cursor location when the `MouseOut` event occurred

■ onMouseOver—Specifies JavaScript code to execute when the mouse enters the area specified in the <AREA> tag

New Properties with JavaScript 1.2

type   indicates a `MouseOver` event

target   indicates the object to which the event was sent

layer[n]   where [n] represents x or y, used (with `page[n]` and `screen[n]`) to describe the cursor location when the `MouseOver` event occurred

page[n]   where [n] represents x or y, used (with `layer[n]` and `screen[n]`) to describe the cursor location when the `MouseOver` event occurred

screen[n]   where [n] represents x or y, used (with `layer[n]` and `page[n]`) to describe the cursor location when the `MouseOver` event occurred

The *array* Object [3|I]

The `array` object provides a mechanism for creating arrays and working with them. New arrays are created with *arrayName* = `new Array()` or *arrayName* = `new Array(`*arrayLength*`)`.

Properties

■ `length`—An integer value reflecting the number of elements in an array

■ `prototype`—Used to add properties to an `array` object.

Methods

■ `concat(`*arrayname*`)`—Combines elements of two arrays and returns a third, one level deep, without altering either of the derivative arrays. (Netscape Navigator 4.0 only)

■ `join(`*string*`)`—Returns a string containing each element of the array, separated by *string*. (not I)

■ `reverse()`—Reverses the order of an array. (not I)

■ `slice(`arrayName, beginSlice, endSlice`)`—Extracts a portion of some array and derives a new array from it. The `beginSlice` and `endSlice` parameters specify the target elements at which to begin and end the slice. (Netscape Navigator 4.0 only)

■ sort(*function*)—Sorts an array based on function, which indicates a *function* defining the sort order. *function* can be omitted, in which case the sort defaults to dictionary order. Note: sort now works on all platforms.

The *button* Object [2|3|I]

The button object reflects a pushbutton from an HTML form in JavaScript.

Properties

■ enabled—A Boolean value indicating whether the button is enabled (not 2|3)

■ form—A reference to the form object containing the button (not 2|3)

■ name—A string value containing the name of the button element

■ type—A string value reflecting the TYPE attribute of the <INPUT> tag (not 2|I)

■ value—A string value containing the value of the button element

Methods

■ click()—Emulates the action of clicking the button

■ focus()—Gives focus to the button (not 2|3)

Event Handlers

■ onMouseDown—Specifies JavaScript code to execute when a user presses a mouse button

■ onMouseUp—Specifies JavaScript code to execute when the user releases a mouse button

■ onClick—Specifies JavaScript code to execute when the button is clicked

■ onFocus—Specifies JavaScript code to execute when the button receives focus (not 2|3)

The *checkbox* Object [2|3|I]

The checkbox object makes a check box in an HTML form available in JavaScript.

Properties

■ checked—A Boolean value indicating whether the check box element is checked

■ defaultChecked—A Boolean value indicating whether the check box element was checked by default (that is, it reflects the CHECKED attribute)

■ enabled—A Boolean value indicating whether the check box is enabled (not 2|3)

■ form—A reference to the form object containing the check box (not 2|3)

■ name—A string value containing the name of the check box element

■ type—A string value reflecting the TYPE attribute of the <INPUT> tag (not 2|I)

■ value—A string value containing the value of the check box element

Methods

- ■ `click()`—Emulates the action of clicking the check box
- ■ `focus()`—Gives focus to the check box (not 2|3)

Event Handlers

- ■ `onClick`—Specifies JavaScript code to execute when the check box is clicked
- ■ `onFocus`—Specifies JavaScript code to execute when the check box receives focus (not 2|3)

The *combo* Object [I]

The `combo` object reflects a combo field in JavaScript.

Properties

- ■ `enabled`—A Boolean value indicating whether the combo box is enabled (not 2|3)
- ■ `form`—A reference to the `form` object containing the combo box (not 2|3)
- ■ `listCount`—An integer reflecting the number of elements in the list
- ■ `listIndex`—An integer reflecting the index of the selected element in the list
- ■ `multiSelect`—A Boolean value indicating whether the combo field is in multiselect mode
- ■ `name`—A string value reflecting the name of the combo field
- ■ `value`—A string containing the value of the combo field

Methods

- ■ `addItem(index)`—Adds an item to the combo field before the item at *index*
- ■ `click()`—Simulates a click on the combo field
- ■ `clear()`—Clears the contents of the combo field
- ■ `focus()`—Gives focus to the combo field
- ■ `removeItem(index)`—Removes the item at *index* from the combo field

Event Handlers

- ■ `onClick`—Specifies JavaScript code to execute when the mouse clicks the combo field
- ■ `onFocus`—Specifies JavaScript code to execute when the combo field receives focus

The *date* Object [2|3|I]

The `date` object provides mechanisms for working with dates and times in JavaScript. Instances of the object can be created with the following syntax:

```
newObjectName = new Date(dateInfo)
```

Here, *dateInfo* is an optional specification of a particular date and can be one of the following:

```
"month day, year hours:minutes:seconds"
```

```
year, month, day
```

```
year, month, day, hours, minutes, seconds
```

The latter two options represent integer values.

If no *dateInfo* is specified, the new object represents the current date and time.

Properties

- ▣ `prototype`—Provides a mechanism for adding properties to a `date` object (not 2)

Methods

- ▣ `getDate()`—Returns the day of the month for the current `date` object as an integer from 1 to 31.

- ▣ `getDay()`—Returns the day of the week for the current `date` object as an integer from 0 to 6 (0 is Sunday, 1 is Monday, and so on).

- ▣ `getHours()`—Returns the hour from the time in the current `date` object as an integer from 0 to 23.

- ▣ `getMinutes()`—Returns the minutes from the time in the current `date` object as an integer from 0 to 59.

- ▣ `getMonth()`—Returns the month for the current `date` object as an integer from 0 to 11 (0 is January, 1 is February, and so on).

- ▣ `getSeconds()`—Returns the seconds from the time in the current `date` object as an integer from 0 to 59.

- ▣ `getTime()`—Returns the time of the current `date` object as an integer representing the number of milliseconds since January 1, 1970 at 00:00:00.

- ▣ `getTimezoneOffset()`—Returns the difference between the local time and GMT as an integer representing the number of minutes.

- ▣ `getYear()`—Returns the year for the current `date` object as a two-digit integer representing the year less 1900.

- ▣ `parse(dateString)`—Returns the number of milliseconds between January 1, 1970 at 00:00:00 and the date specified in *dateString*, which should take the following format: (not I)

  ```
  Day, DD Mon YYYY HH:MM:SS TZN
  ```

  ```
  Mon DD, YYYY
  ```

- ▣ `setDate(dateValue)`—Sets the day of the month for the current `date` object. *dateValue* is an integer from 1 to 31.

■ setHours(*hoursValue*)—Sets the hours for the time for the current date object. *hoursValue* is an integer from 0 to 23.

■ setMinutes(*minutesValue*)—Sets the minutes for the time for the current date object. *minutesValue* is an integer from 0 to 59.

■ setMonth(*monthValue*)—Sets the month for the current date object. *monthValue* is an integer from 0 to 11 (0 is January, 1 is February, and so on).

■ setSeconds(*secondsValue*)—Sets the seconds for the time for the current date object. *secondsValue* is an integer from 0 to 59.

■ setTime(*timeValue*)—Sets the value for the current date object. *timeValue* is an integer representing the number of milliseconds since January 1, 1970 at 00:00:00.

■ setYear(*yearValue*)—Sets the year for the current date object. *yearValue* is an integer greater than 1900.

■ toGMTString()—Returns the value of the current date object in GMT as a string using Internet conventions in the following form:

Day, DD Mon YYYY HH:MM:SS GMT

■ toLocaleString()—Returns the value of the current date object in the local time using local conventions.

■ UTC(*yearValue*, *monthValue*, *dateValue*, *hoursValue*, *minutesValue*, *secondsValue*)—Returns the number of milliseconds since January 1, 1970 at 00:00:00 GMT. *yearValue* is an integer greater than 1900. *monthValue* is an integer from 0 to 11. *dateValue* is an integer from 1 to 31. *hoursValue* is an integer from 0 to 23. *minutesValue* and *secondsValue* are integers from 0 to 59. *hoursValue*, *minutesValue*, and *secondsValue* are optional. (not I)

The *document* Object [2|3|I]

The document object reflects attributes of an HTML document in JavaScript.

Properties

■ alinkColor—The color of active links as a string or a hexadecimal triplet.

■ anchors—Array of anchor objects in the order they appear in the HTML document. Use anchors.length to get the number of anchors in a document.

■ applets—Array of applet objects in the order they appear in the HTML document. Use applets.length to get the number of applets in a document. (not 2)

■ bgColor—The color of the document's background.

■ cookie—A string value containing cookie values for the current document.

■ embeds—Array of plugin objects in the order they appear in the HTML document. Use embeds.length to get the number of plug-ins in a document. (not 2|I)

■ fgColor—The color of the document's foreground.

- forms—Array of form objects in the order the forms appear in the HTML file. Use `forms.length` to get the number of forms in a document.

- images—Array of image objects in the order they appear in the HTML document. Use `images.length` to get the number of images in a document. (not 2|I)

- lastModified—String value containing the last date of the document's modification.

- linkColor—The color of links as a string or a hexadecimal triplet.

- links—Array of link objects in the order the hypertext links appear in the HTML document. Use `links.length` to get the number of links in a document.

- location—A string containing the URL of the current document. Use `document.URL` instead of `document.location`. This property is expected to disappear in a future release.

- referrer—A string value containing the URL of the calling document when the user follows a link.

- title—A string containing the title of the current document.

- URL—A string reflecting the URL of the current document. Use instead of `document.location`. (not I)

- vlinkColor—The color of followed links as a string or a hexadecimal triplet.

Event Handlers

- onMouseDown—Specifies JavaScript code to execute when a user presses a mouse button

- onMouseUp—Specifies JavaScript code to execute when the user releases a mouse button

- onKeyUp—Specifies JavaScript code to execute when the user releases a specific key (Netscape Navigator 4.0 only) (4)

- onKeyPress—Specifies JavaScript code to execute when the user holds down a specific key (Netscape Navigator 4.0 only) (4)

- onKeyDown—Specifies JavaScript code to execute when the user presses a specific key (Netscape Navigator 4.0 only) (4)

- onDblClick—Specifies JavaScript code to execute when the user double-clicks the area (not implemented on Macintosh; Netscape Navigator 4.0 only) (4)

Methods

- captureEvents()—Used in a window with frames (along with `enableExternalCapture`), it specifies that the window will capture all specified events. New in JavaScript 1.2.

- clear()—Clears the document window. (not I)

- close()—Closes the current output stream.

- open(*mimeType*)—Opens a stream that allows `write()` and `writeln()` methods to write to the document window. *mimeType* is an optional string that specifies a document type supported by Navigator or a plug-in (for example, `text/html` or `image/gif`).

- releaseEvents(*eventType*)—Specifies that the current window must release events (as opposed to capture them) so that these events can be passed to other objects, perhaps further on in the event hierarchy. New in JavaScript 1.2.

- ■ `routeEvent(event)`—Sends or routes an event through the normal event hierarchy.
- ■ `write()`—Writes text and HTML to the specified document.
- ■ `writeln()`—Writes text and HTML to the specified document followed by a newline character.

The *fileUpload* Object [3]

Reflects a file upload element in an HTML form.

Properties

- ■ `name`—A string value reflecting the name of the file upload element.
- ■ `value`—A string value reflecting the file upload element's field.

The *form* Object [2|3|I]

The `form` object reflects an HTML form in JavaScript. Each HTML form in a document is reflected by a distinct instance of the `form` object.

Properties

- ■ `action`—A string value specifying the URL to which the form data is submitted
- ■ `elements`—Array of objects for each form element in the order in which they appear in the form
- ■ `encoding`—String containing the MIME encoding of the form as specified in the ENCTYPE attribute
- ■ `method`—A string value containing the method of submission of form data to the server
- ■ `target`—A string value containing the name of the window to which responses to form submissions are directed

Methods

- ■ `reset()`—Resets the form (not 2|I)
- ■ `submit()`—Submits the form

Event Handlers

- ■ `onReset`—Specifies JavaScript code to execute when the form is reset. (Not 2|I)
- ■ `onSubmit`—Specifies JavaScript code to execute when the form is submitted. The code should return a `true` value to allow the form to be submitted. A `false` value prevents the form from being submitted.

The *frame* Object [2|3|I]

The frame object reflects a frame window in JavaScript.

Properties

■ frames—An array of objects for each frame in a window. Frames appear in the array in the order in which they appear in the HTML source code.

■ onblur—A string reflecting the onBlur event handler for the frame. New values can be assigned to this property to change the event handler. (not 2)

■ onfocus—A string reflecting the onFocus event handler for the frame. New values can be assigned to this property to change the event handler. (not 2)

■ parent—A string indicating the name of the window containing the frame set.

■ self—An alternative for the name of the current window.

■ top—An alternative for the name of the topmost window.

■ window—An alternative for the name of the current window.

Methods

■ alert(*message*)—Displays *message* in a dialog box.

■ blur()—Removes focus from the frame. (not 2)

■ clearInterval(intervalID)—Cancels timeouts created with the setInterval method; new in JavaScript 1.2.

■ close()—Closes the window.

■ confirm(*message*)—Displays *message* in a dialog box with OK and Cancel buttons. Returns true or false based on the button clicked by the user.

■ focus()—Gives focus to the frame. (not 2)

■ open(*url*,*name*,*features*)—Opens *url* in a window named *name*. If *name* doesn't exist, a new window is created with that name. *features* is an optional string argument containing a list of features for the new window. The feature list contains any of the following name-value pairs separated by commas and without additional spaces:

toolbar=[yes,no,1,0]	indicates whether the window should have a toolbar
location=[yes,no,1,0]	indicates whether the window should have a location field
directories=[yes,no,1,0]	indicates whether the window should have directory buttons
status=[yes,no,1,0]	indicates whether the window should have a status bar
menubar=[yes,no,1,0]	indicates whether the window should have menus
scrollbars=[yes,no,1,0]	indicates whether the window should have scrollbars

      `resizable=[yes,no,1,0]`   indicates whether the window should be resizable

      `width=pixels`   indicates the width of the window in pixels

      `height=pixels`   indicates the height of the window in pixels

- `print()`—Prints the contents of a frame or window. This is the equivalent of the user clicking the Print button in Netscape Navigator. New in JavaScript 1.2.

- `prompt(message,response)`—Displays *message* in a dialog box with a text entry field with the default value of *response*. The user's response in the text entry field is returned as a string.

- `setInterval(function, msec, [args])`—Repeatedly calls a function after the period specified by the `msec` parameter. New in JavaScript 1.2.

- `setInterval(expression, msec)`—Evaluates *expression* after the period specified by the `msec` parameter. New in JavaScript 1.2.

- `setTimeout(expression,time)`—Evaluates *expression* after *time*; *time* is a value in milliseconds. The timeout can be named with the following structure:

  name = setTimeOut(*expression,time*)

- `clearTimeout(name)`—Cancels the timeout with the name *name*.

Event Handlers

- `onBlur`—Specifies JavaScript code to execute when focus is removed from a frame (Not 2)

- `onFocus`—Specifies JavaScript code to execute when focus is removed from a frame (Not 2)

- `onMove`—Specifies JavaScript code to execute when the user moves a frame (Netscape Navigator 4.0 only)

- `onResize`—Specifies JavaScript code to execute when a user resizes the frame (Netscape Navigator 4.0 only)

The *function* Object [3]

The `function` object provides a mechanism for indicating JavaScript code to compile as a function. This is the syntax to use the `function` object:

```
functionName = new Function(arg1, arg2, arg3, ..., functionCode)
```

This is similar to the following:

```
function functionName(arg1, arg2, arg3, ...) {
    functionCode
}
```

In the former, *functionName* is a variable with a reference to the function, and the function is evaluated each time it's used instead of being compiled once.

Properties

- `arguments`—An integer reflecting the number of arguments in a function
- `prototype`—Provides a mechanism for adding properties to a `function` object

The *hidden* Object [2|3|I]

The `hidden` object reflects a hidden field from an HTML form in JavaScript.

Properties

- `name`—A string value containing the name of the hidden element
- `type`—A string value reflecting the TYPE property of the `<INPUT>` tag (not 2|I)
- `value`—A string value containing the value of the hidden text element

The *history* Object [2|3|I]

The `history` object enables a script to work with the Navigator browser's history list in JavaScript. For security and privacy reasons, the actual content of the list isn't reflected into JavaScript.

Properties

- `length`—An integer representing the number of items on the history list (not I)

Methods

- `back()`—Goes back to the previous document in the history list. (not I)
- `forward()`—Goes forward to the next document in the history list. (not I)
- `go(location)`—Goes to the document in the history list specified by *location*, which can be a string or integer value. If it's a string, it represents all or part of a URL in the history list. If it's an integer, *location* represents the relative position of the document on the history list. As an integer, *location* can be positive or negative. (not I)

The *image* Object [3]

The `image` object reflects an image included in an HTML document.

Properties

- `border`—An integer value reflecting the width of the image's border in pixels
- `complete`—A Boolean value indicating whether the image has finished loading
- `height`—An integer value reflecting the height of an image in pixels

- hspace—An integer value reflecting the HSPACE attribute of the <IMG> tag
- lowsrc—A string value containing the URL of the low-resolution version of the image to load
- name—A string value indicating the name of the image object
- prototype—Provides a mechanism for adding properties as an image object
- src—A string value indicating the URL of the image
- vspace—An integer value reflecting the VSPACE attribute of the <IMG> tag
- width—An integer value indicating the width of an image in pixels

Event Handlers

- onKeyUp—Specifies JavaScript code to execute when the user releases a specific key. (Netscape Navigator 4.0 only) (4)
- onKeyPress—Specifies JavaScript code to execute when the user holds down a specific key. (Netscape Navigator 4.0 only) (4)
- onKeyDown—Specifies JavaScript code to execute when the user presses a specific key. (Netscape Navigator 4.0 only) (4)
- onAbort—Specifies JavaScript code to execute if the attempt to load the image is aborted. (not 2)
- onError—Specifies JavaScript code to execute if an error occurs while loading the image. Setting this event handler to null suppresses error messages if an error occurs while loading. (not 2)
- onLoad—Specifies JavaScript code to execute when the image finishes loading. (not 2)

The *layer* Object [4]

The layer object is used to embed layers of content within a page; they can be hidden or not hidden. Either type is accessible through JavaScript code. The most common use for layers is in developing Dynamic HTML (DHTML). With layers, you can create animation or other dynamic content on a page by cycling through the layers you have defined.

Properties

- above—Places a layer on top of a newly created layer.
- background—Used to specify a tiled background image of the layer.
- below—Places a layer below a newly created layer.
- bgColor—Sets the background color of the layer.
- clip(left, top, right, bottom)—Specifies the visible boundaries of the layer.
- height—Specifies the height of the layer, expressed in pixels (integer) or by a percentage of the instant layer.

- ID—Previously called NAME. Used to name the layer so that it can be referred to by name and accessed by other JavaScript code.

- left—Specifies the horizontal positioning of the top-left corner of the layer; used with the Top property.

- page[n]—Where [n] is x or y. Specifies the horizontal (x) or vertical (y) positioning of the top-left corner of the layer, in relation to the overall enclosing document. (Note: This is different from the Left and Top properties.)

- parentLayer—Specifies the layer object that contains the present layer.

- SRC—Specifies HTML source to be displayed with the target layer. (This source can also include JavaScript.)

- siblingAbove—Specifies the layer object immediately above the present one.

- siblingBelow—Specifies the layer object immediately below the present one.

- top—Specifies the vertical positioning of the top-left corner of the layer. (Used with the Left property.)

- visibility—Specifies the visibility of the layer. Three choices are possible: show (visible), hidden (not visible), and inherit (layer inherits the properties of its parent).

- width—Specifies the width of the layer. Used for wrapping procedures; that is, the width denotes the boundary after which the contents wrap inside the layer.

- z-index—Specifies the Z-order (or stacking order) of the layer. Used to set the layer's position within the overall rotational order of all layers. Expressed as an integer. (Used where there are many layers.)

Events

- onBlur—Specifies JavaScript code to execute when the layer loses focus

- onFocus—Specifies JavaScript code to execute when the layer gains focus

- onLoad—Specifies JavaScript code to execute when a layer is loaded

- onMouseOut—Specifies JavaScript code to execute when the mouse cursor moves off the layer

New Properties

type	indicates a MouseOut event
target	indicates the object to which the event was sent
layer[n]	where [n] represents x or y, used (with page[n] and screen[n]) to describe the cursor location when the MouseOut event occurred
page[n]	where [n] represents x or y, used (with layer[n] and screen[n]) to describe the cursor location when the MouseOut event occurred
screen[n]	where [n] represents x or y, used (with layer[n] and page[n]) to describe the cursor location when the MouseOut event occurred

- onMouseover—Specifies the JavaScript code to execute when the mouse cursor enters the layer

  New Properties with JavaScript 1.2

  type   indicates a MouseOver event

  target   indicates the object to which the event was sent

  layer[n]   where [n] represents x or y, used (with page[n] and screen[n]) to describe the cursor location when the MouseOver event occurred

  page[n]   where [n] represents x or y, used (with layer[n] and screen[n]) to describe the cursor location when the MouseOver event occurred

  screen[n]   where [n] represents x or y, used (with layer[n] and page[n]) to describe the cursor location when the MouseOver event occurred

Methods

- captureEvents()—Used in a window with frames (along with enableExternalCapture), it specifies that the window will capture all specified events. New in JavaScript 1.2.
- load(*source*, *width*)—Alters the source of the layer by replacing it with HTML (or JavaScript) from the file specified in *source*. Using this method, you can also pass a width value (in pixels) to accommodate the new content.
- moveAbove(*layer*)—Places the layer above *layer* in the stack.
- moveBelow(layer)—Places the layer below *layer* in the stack.
- moveBy(x,y)—Alters the position of the layer by the specified values, expressed in pixels.
- moveTo(x,y)—Alters the position of the layer (within the containing layer) to the specified coordinates, expressed in pixels.
- moveToAbsolute(x,y)—Alters the position of the layer (within the page) to the specified coordinates, expressed in pixels.
- releaseEvents(*eventType*)—Specifies that the current window should release events instead of capturing them so that these events can be passed to other objects, perhaps further on in the event hierarchy. New in JavaScript 1.2.
- resizeBy(*width*,*height*)—Resizes the layer by the specified values, expressed in pixels.
- resizeTo(*width*,*height*)—Resizes the layer to the specified height and size, expressed in pixels.
- routeEvent(event)—Sends or routes an event through the normal event hierarchy.

The *link* Object [2|3|I]

The link object reflects a hypertext link in the body of a document.

Properties

- ▥ hash—A string value containing the anchor name in the URL
- ▥ host—A string value containing the host name and port number from the URL
- ▥ hostname—A string value containing the domain name (or numerical IP address) from the URL
- ▥ href—A string value containing the entire URL
- ▥ pathname—A string value specifying the path portion of the URL
- ▥ port—A string value containing the port number from the URL
- ▥ protocol—A string value containing the protocol from the URL (including the colon, but not the slashes)
- ▥ search—A string value containing any information passed to a GET CGI-BIN call (such as any information after the question mark)
- ▥ target—A string value containing the name of the window or frame specified in the TARGET attribute

Event Handlers

- ▥ onMouseDown—Specifies JavaScript code to execute when a user presses a mouse button (JavaScript 1.2 and Netscape Navigator 4.0 only) (4)
- ▥ onMouseOut—Specifies JavaScript code to execute when the user moves the mouse cursor out of an object (JavaScript 1.2 and Netscape Navigator 4.0 only) (4)

New Properties with JavaScript 1.2

type	indicates a MouseOut event
target	indicates the object to which the event was sent
layer[n]	where [n] represents x or y, used (with page[n] and screen[n]) to describe the cursor location when the MouseOut event occurred
page[n]	where [n] represents x or y, used (with layer[n] and screen[n]) to describe the cursor location when the MouseOut event occurred
screen[n]	where [n] represents x or y, used with layer[n] and page[n]) to describe the cursor location when the MouseOut event occurred

- ▥ onMouseUp—Specifies the JavaScript code to execute when the user releases a mouse button
- ▥ onKeyUp—Specifies the JavaScript code to execute when the user releases a specific key (Netscape Navigator 4.0 only) (4)
- ▥ onKeyPress—Specifies the JavaScript code to execute when the user holds down a specific key (Netscape Navigator 4.0 only) (4)
- ▥ onKeyDown—Specifies the JavaScript code to execute when the user presses a specific key (Netscape Navigator 4.0 only) (4)

▓ onDblClick—Specifies the JavaScript code to execute when the user double-clicks the area (not implemented on Macintosh; Netscape Navigator 4.0 only) (4)

▓ moveMouse—Specifies the JavaScript code to execute when the mouse pointer moves over the link (not 2|3)

▓ onClick—Specifies the JavaScript code to execute when the link is clicked

▓ onMouseOver—Specifies the JavaScript code to execute when the mouse pointer moves over the hypertext link

New Properties with JavaScript 1.2

type	indicates a MouseOver event
target	indicates the object to which the event was sent
layer[n]	where [n] represents x or y, used (with page[n] and screen[n]) to describe the cursor location when the MouseOver event occurred
page[n]	where [n] represents x or y, used (with layer[n] and screen[n]) to describe the cursor location when the MouseOver event occurred
screen[n]	where [n] represents x or y, used (with layer[n] and page[n]) to describe the cursor location when the MouseOver event occurred

The *location* Object [2|3|I]

The location object reflects information about the current URL.

Properties

▓ hash—A string value containing the anchor name in the URL

▓ host—A string value containing the host name and port number from the URL

▓ hostname—A string value containing the domain name (or numerical IP address) from the URL

▓ href—A string value containing the entire URL

▓ pathname—A string value specifying the path portion of the URL

▓ port—A string value containing the port number from the URL

▓ protocol—A string value containing the protocol from the URL (including the colon, but not the slashes)

▓ search—A string value containing any information passed to a GET CGI-BIN call (such as information after the question mark)

Methods

▓ reload()—Reloads the current document. (not 2|I)

▓ replace(*url*)—Loads *url* over the current entry in the history list, making it impossible to navigate back to the previous URL with the Back button (not 2|I)

The *math* Object [2|3|I]

The math object provides properties and methods for advanced mathematical calculations.

Properties

- E—The value of Euler's constant (roughly 2.718) used as the base for natural logarithms
- LN10—The value of the natural logarithm of 10 (roughly 2.302)
- LN2—The value of the natural logarithm of 2 (roughly 0.693)
- LOG10E—The value of the base-10 logarithm of e (roughly 0.434)
- LOG2E—The value of the base 2 logarithm of e (roughly 1.442)
- PI—The value of Π; used to calculate the circumference and area of circles (roughly 3.1415)
- SQRT1_2—The value of the square root of one-half (roughly 0.707)
- SQRT2—The value of the square root of two (roughly 1.414)

Methods

- abs(*number*)—Returns the absolute value of *number*. The absolute value is the value of a number with its sign ignored—for example, abs(4) and abs(-4) both return 4.
- acos(*number*)—Returns the arc cosine of *number* in radians.
- asin(*number*)—Returns the arc sine of *number* in radians.
- atan(*number*)—Returns the arc tangent of *number* in radians.
- atan2(*number1*,*number2*)—Returns the angle of the polar coordinate corresponding to the Cartesian coordinate (*number1*,*number2*). (Not I)
- ceil(*number*)—Returns the next integer greater than *number*; in other words, rounds up to the next integer.
- cos(*number*)—Returns the cosine of *number*, which represents an angle in radians.
- exp(*number*)—Returns the value of E to the power of *number*.
- floor(*number*)—Returns the next integer less than *number*; in other words, rounds down to the nearest integer.
- log(*number*)—Returns the natural logarithm of *number*.
- max(*number1*,*number2*)—Returns the greater of *number1* and *number2*.
- min(*number1*,*number2*)—Returns the smaller of *number1* and *number2*.
- pow(*number1*,*number2*)—Returns the value of *number1* to the power of *number2*.
- random()—Returns a random number between zero and 1 (at press time, this method was available only on UNIX versions of Navigator 2.0).
- round(*number*)—Returns the closest integer to *number*; in other words, rounds to the closest integer.
- sin(*number*)—Returns the sine of *number*, which represents an angle in radians.

▓ `sqrt(number)`—Returns the square root of *number*.

▓ `tan(number)`—Returns the tangent of *number*, which represents an angle in radians.

The *mimeType* Object [3]

The `mimeType` object reflects a MIME type supported by the client browser.

Properties

▓ `type`—A string value reflecting the MIME type

▓ `description`—A string containing a description of the MIME type

▓ `enabledPlugin`—A reference to `plugin` object for the plug-in supporting the MIME type

▓ `suffixes`—A string containing a comma-separated list of file suffixes for the MIME type

The *navigator* Object [2 | 3 | I]

The `navigator` object reflects information about the version of browser being used.

Properties

▓ `appCodeName`—A string value containing the code name of the client (for example, "Mozilla" for Netscape Navigator).

▓ `appName`—A string value containing the name of the client (for example, "Netscape" for Netscape Navigator).

▓ `appVersion`—A string value containing the version information for the client in the following form:

`versionNumber (platform; country)`

For example, Navigator 2.0, beta 6 for Windows 95 (international version) would have an `appVersion` property with the value `"2.0b6 (Win32; I)"`.

▓ `language`—Specifies the translation of Navigator (a read-only property). New in JavaScript 1.2.

▓ `mimeTypes`—An array of `mimeType` objects reflecting the MIME types supported by the client browser. (not 2|I)

▓ `platform`—Specifies the platform for which Navigator was compiled (for example, Win32, MacPPC, UNIX). New in JavaScript 1.2.

▓ `plugins`—An array of `plugin` objects reflecting the plug-ins in a document in the order of their appearance in the HTML document. (not 2|I)

▓ `userAgent`—A string containing the complete value of the user-agent header sent in the HTTP request. The following contains all the information in `appCodeName` and `appVersion`:

`Mozilla/2.0b6 (Win32; I)`

Methods

■ javaEnabled()—Returns a Boolean value indicating whether Java is enabled in the browser. (not 2|I)

■ preference(*preference.Name*, setValue)—In signed scripts, this method enables the developer to set certain browser preferences. Preferences available with this method are the following:

general.always_load_images	true/false value that sets whether images are automatically loaded.
security.enable_java	true/false value that sets whether Java is enabled.
javascript.enabled	true/false value that sets whether JavaScript is enabled.
browser.enable_style_sheets	true/false value that sets whether style sheets are enabled.
autoupdate.enabled	true/false value that sets whether autoinstall is enabled.
network.cookie.cookieBehavior	(0,1,2) value that sets the manner in which cookies are handled. There are three parameters. 0 accepts all cookies; 1 accepts only those that are forwarded to the originating server; 2 denies all cookies.
network.cookie.warnAboutCookies	true/false value that sets whether the browser will warn on accepting cookies.

The *option* Object [3]

The option object is used to create entries in a select list by using the following syntax:

optionName = new Option(*optionText*, *optionValue*, *defaultSelected*, *selected*)

Then the following line is used:

selectName.options[index] = *optionName*.

Properties

■ defaultSelected—A Boolean value specifying whether the option is selected by default

■ index—An integer value specifying the option's index in the select list

■ prototype—Provides a mechanism to add properties to an option object

■ selected—A Boolean value indicating whether the option is currently selected

■ text—A string value reflecting the text displayed for the option

■ value—A string value indicating the value submitted to the server when the form is submitted

The *password* Object [2|3|I]

The password object reflects a password text field from an HTML form in JavaScript.

Properties

- defaultValue—A string value containing the default value of the password element (such as the value of the VALUE attribute)
- enabled—A Boolean value indicating whether the password field is enabled (not 2|3)
- form—A reference to the form object containing the password field (not 2|3)
- name—A string value containing the name of the password element
- value—A string value containing the value of the password element

Methods

- focus()—Emulates the action of focusing in the password field
- blur()—Emulates the action of removing focus from the password field
- select()—Emulates the action of selecting the text in the password field

Event Handlers

- onBlur—Specifies JavaScript code to execute when the password field loses focus (not 2|3)
- onFocus—Specifies JavaScript code to execute when the password field receives focus (not 2|3)

The *plugin* Object [2|3|I]

The plugin object reflects a plug-in supported by the browser.

Properties

- name—A string value reflecting the name of the plug-in
- filename—A string value reflecting the filename of the plug-in on the system's disk
- description—A string value containing the description supplied by the plug-in

The *radio* Object [2|3|I]

The radio object reflects a set of radio buttons from an HTML form in JavaScript. To access individual radio buttons, use numeric indexes starting at zero. Individual buttons in a set of radio buttons named testRadio, for example, could be referenced by testRadio[0], testRadio[1], and so on.

Properties

- checked—A Boolean value indicating whether a specific radio button is checked. Can be used to select or deselect a button.
- defaultChecked—A Boolean value indicating whether a specific radio button was checked by default (that is, it reflects the CHECKED attribute). (not I)
- enabled—A Boolean value indicating whether the radio button is enabled. (not 2|3)
- form—A reference to the form object containing the radio button. (not 2|3)
- length—An integer value indicating the number of radio buttons in the set. (not I)
- name—A string value containing the name of the set of radio buttons.
- value—A string value containing the value of a specific radio button in a set (that is, it reflects the VALUE attribute).

Methods

- click()—Emulates the action of clicking a radio button
- focus()—Gives focus to the radio button (not 2|3)

Event Handlers

- onClick—Specifies the JavaScript code to execute when a radio button is clicked
- onFocus—Specifies the JavaScript code to execute when a radio button receives focus (not 2|3)

The *regExp* Object [3 | I]

The regExp object is relevant to searching for regular expressions. Its properties are set before or after a search is performed. They don't generally exercise control over the search itself, but instead articulate a series of values that can be accessed throughout the search.

Properties

- input—The string against which a Regular Expression is matched. New in JavaScript 1.2.
- multiline [true, false]—Sets whether the search continues beyond line breaks on multiple lines (true) or not (false). New in JavaScript 1.2.
- lastMatch—Indicates the characters last matched. New in JavaScript 1.2.
- lastParen—Indicates the last matched string that appeared in parentheses. New in JavaScript 1.2.
- leftContext—Indicates the string just before the most recently matched Regular

Expression. New in JavaScript 1.2.

- rightContext—Indicates the remainder of the string, beyond the most recently matched Regular Expression. New in JavaScript 1.2.

- $1,..$9—Indicates the last nine substrings in a match; those substrings are enclosed in parentheses. New in JavaScript 1.2.

The Regular Expression Object [3|I]

The Regular Expression object contains the pattern of a Regular Expression.

Parameters

- regexp—Specifies the name of the Regular Expression object. New in JavaScript 1.2.
- pattern—Specifies the text of the Regular Expression. New in JavaScript 1.2.

Flags

- i—Specifies that during the Regular Expression search, case is ignored (that is, the search is not case sensitive)
- g—Specifies that during the Regular Expression search, the match (and search) should be global
- gi—Specifies that during the Regular Expression search, case is ignored and during the Regular Expression search, the match (and search) should be global

Properties

- global [true,false]—Sets the g flag value in code, such as whether the search is global (true) or not (false). New in JavaScript 1.2.
- ignoreCase [true,false]—Sets the i flag value in code, such as whether the search is case sensitive (true) or not (false). New in JavaScript 1.2.
- lastIndex—(Integer value) Indicates the index position at which to start the next matching procedure (for example, lastIndex == 2). New in JavaScript 1.2.
- source—(Read-only) Contains the pattern's text. New in JavaScript 1.2.

Methods

- compile—Compiles the Regular Expression. This method is usually invoked at script startup, when the Regular Expression is already known and will remain constant. New in JavaScript 1.2.
- exec(str)—Executes a search for a Regular Expression within the specified string (str). New in JavaScript 1.2. Note: It uses the same properties as the RegExp object.
- test(str)—Executes a search for a Regular Expression and a specified string (str). New in JavaScript 1.2. Note: It uses the same properties as the RegExp object.

The *reset* Object [2|3|I]

The reset object reflects a reset button from an HTML form in JavaScript.

Properties

- enabled—A Boolean value indicating whether the reset button is enabled (not 2|3)
- form—A reference to the form object containing the reset button (not 2|3)
- name—A string value containing the name of the reset element
- value—A string value containing the value of the reset element

Methods

- click()—Emulates the action of clicking the reset button
- focus()—Specifies the JavaScript code to execute when the reset button receives focus (not 2|3)

Event Handlers

- onClick—Specifies the JavaScript code to execute when the reset button is clicked
- onFocus—Specifies the JavaScript code to execute when the reset button receives focus (not 2|3)

The *screen* Object [4|I]

The screen object describes (or specifies) the characteristics of the current screen.

Properties

- availHeight—Specifies the height of the screen in pixels (minus static display constraints set forth by the operating system). New in JavaScript 1.2.
- availWidth—Specifies the width of the current screen in pixels (minus static display constraints set forth by the operating system). New in JavaScript 1.2.
- height—Specifies the height of the current screen in pixels. New in JavaScript 1.2.
- width—Specifies the width of the current screen in pixels. New in JavaScript 1.2.
- pixelDepth—Specifies the number of bits (per pixel) in the current screen. New in JavaScript 1.2.
- colorDepth—Specifies the number of possible colors to display in the current screen. New in JavaScript 1.2.

The *select* Object [2|3]

The select object reflects a selection list from an HTML form in JavaScript.

Properties

- length—An integer value containing the number of options in the selection list.
- name—A string value containing the name of the selection list.
- options—An array reflecting each of the options in the selection list in the order they appear. The options property has its own properties:

defaultSelected	A Boolean value indicating whether an option was selected by default (that is, it reflects the SELECTED attribute).
index	An integer value reflecting the index of an option.
length	An integer value reflecting the number of options in the selection list.
name	A string value containing the name of the selection list.
selected	A Boolean value indicating whether the option is selected. Can be used to select or deselect an option.
selectedIndex	An integer value containing the index of the currently selected option.
text	A string value containing the text displayed in the selection list for a particular option.
value	A string value indicating the value for the specified option (that is, it reflects the VALUE attribute).

- selectedIndex—Reflects the index of the currently selected option in the selection list

Methods

- blur()—Removes focus from the selection list (not 2|3)
- focus()—Gives focus to the selection list (not 2|3)

Event Handlers

- onBlur—Specifies the JavaScript code to execute when the selection list loses focus
- onFocus—Specifies the JavaScript code to execute when focus is given to the selection list
- onChange—Specifies the JavaScript code to execute when the selected option in the list changes

The *string* Object [2|3|I]

The `string` object provides properties and methods for working with string literals and variables.

Properties

- ▓ `length`—An integer value containing the length of the string expressed as the number of characters in the string
- ▓ `prototype`—Provides a mechanism for adding properties to a `string` object (not 2)

Methods

- ▓ `anchor(name)`—Returns a string containing the value of the string object surrounded by an A container tag with the NAME attribute set to *name*.
- ▓ `big()`—Returns a string containing the value of the string object surrounded by a BIG container tag.
- ▓ `blink()`—Returns a string containing the value of the string object surrounded by a BLINK container tag.
- ▓ `bold()`—Returns a string containing the value of the string object surrounded by a B container tag.
- ▓ `charAt(index)`—Returns the character at the location specified by *index*.
- ▓ `charCodeAt(index)`—Returns a number representing an ISO-Latin-1 codeset value at the instant *index*. (Netscape Navigator 4.0 and higher only)
- ▓ `concat(string2)`—Combines two strings and derives a third, new string. (Netscape Navigator 4.0 and higher only.)
- ▓ `fixed()`—Returns a string containing the value of the string object surrounded by a FIXED container tag.
- ▓ `fontColor(color)`—Returns a string containing the value of the string object surrounded by a FONT container tag with the COLOR attribute set to *color*, which is a color name or an RGB triplet. (not I)
- ▓ `fontSize(size)`—Returns a string containing the value of the string object surrounded by a FONTSIZE container tag with the size set to *size*. (not I)
- ▓ `fromCharCode(num1, num2, …)`—Returns a string constructed of ISO-Latin-1 characters. Those characters are specified by their codeset values, which are expressed as *num1*, *num2*, and so on.
- ▓ `indexOf(findString,startingIndex)`—Returns the index of the first occurrence of *findString*, starting the search at *startingIndex*, which is optional; if it's not provided, the search starts at the start of the string.
- ▓ `italics()`—Returns a string containing the value of the string object surrounded by an I container tag.

- lastIndexOf(*findString,startingIndex*)—Returns the index of the last occurrence of *findString*. This is done by searching backward from *startingIndex*. *startingIndex* is optional and is assumed to be the last character in the string if no value is provided.

- link(*href*)—Returns a string containing the value of the string object surrounded by an A container tag with the HREF attribute set to *href*.

- match(*regular_expression*)—Matches a Regular Expression to a string. The parameter *regular_expression* is the name of the Regular Expression, expressed either as a variable or a literal.

- replace(*regular_expression*, newSubStr)—Finds and replaces *regular_expression* with newSubStr.

- search(*regular_expression*)—Finds *regular_expression* and matches it to some string.

- slice(*beginSlice*, [*endSlice*])—Extracts a portion of a given string and derives a new string from that excerpt. *beginSlice* and *endSlice* are both zero-based indexes that can be used to grab the first, second, and third character, and so on.

- small()—Returns a string containing the value of the string object surrounded by a SMALL container tag.

- split(*separator*)—Returns an array of strings created by splitting the string at every occurrence of *separator* (not 2|I). split has additional functionality in JavaScript 1.2 and for Navigator 4.0 and higher. That new functionality includes the following elements:

regex and fixed string splitting	You can now split the string by both Regular Expression argument and fixed string.
limit count	You can now add a limit count to prevent including empty elements within the string.
whitespace splitting	The capability to split on a whitespace (including any whitespace, such as space, tab, newline, and so on).

- strike()—Returns a string containing the value of the string object surrounded by a STRIKE container tag.

- sub()—Returns a string containing the value of the string object surrounded by a SUB container tag.

- substr(start, [length])—Used to extract a set number (length) of characters within a string. Use start to specify the location at which to begin this extraction process. New in JavaScript 1.2.

- substring(*firstIndex,lastIndex*)—Returns a string equivalent to the substring beginning at *firstIndex* and ending at the character before *lastIndex*. If *firstIndex* is greater than *lastIndex*, the string starts at *lastIndex* and ends at the character before *firstIndex*. Note: In JavaScript 1.2, x and y are no longer swapped. To get this result, you must specify JavaScript 1.2 with the language attribute within the <SCRIPT> tag.

- sup()—Returns a string containing the value of the string object surrounded by a SUP container tag.

- ■ toLowerCase()—Returns a string containing the value of the string object with all characters converted to lowercase.
- ■ toUpperCase()—Returns a string containing the value of the string object with all characters converted to uppercase.

The *submit* Object [2|3|I]

The submit object reflects a submit button from an HTML form in JavaScript.

Properties

- ■ enabled—A Boolean value indicating whether the submit button is enabled (not 2|3)
- ■ form—A reference to the form object containing the submit button (not 2|3)
- ■ name—A string value containing the name of the submit button element
- ■ type—A string value reflecting the TYPE attribute of the <INPUT> tag (not 2|I)
- ■ value—A string value containing the value of the submit button element

Methods

- ■ click()—Emulates the action of clicking the submit button
- ■ focus()—Gives focus to the submit button (not 2|3)

Event Handlers

- ■ onClick—Specifies the JavaScript code to execute when the submit button is clicked
- ■ onFocus—Specifies the JavaScript code to execute when the submit button receives focus (not 2|3)

The *text* Object [2|3|I]

The text object reflects a text field from an HTML form in JavaScript.

Properties

- ■ defaultValue—A string value containing the default value of the text element (that is, the value of the VALUE attribute)
- ■ enabled—A Boolean value indicating whether the text field is enabled (not 2|3)
- ■ form—A reference to the form object containing the text field (not 2|3)
- ■ name—A string value containing the name of the text element
- ■ type—A string value reflecting the TYPE attribute of the <INPUT> tag (not 2|I)
- ■ value—A string value containing the value of the text element

Methods

- focus()—Emulates the action of focusing in the text field
- blur()—Emulates the action of removing focus from the text field
- select()—Emulates the action of selecting the text in the text field

Event Handlers

- onBlur—Specifies the JavaScript code to execute when focus is removed from the field
- onChange—Specifies the JavaScript code to execute when the content of the field is changed
- onFocus—Specifies the JavaScript code to execute when focus is given to the field
- onSelect—Specifies the JavaScript code to execute when the user selects some or all of the text in the field

The *textarea* Object [2|3|I]

The textarea object reflects a multiline text field from an HTML form in JavaScript.

Properties

- defaultValue—A string value containing the default value of the textarea element (that is, the value of the VALUE attribute)
- enabled—A Boolean value indicating whether the textarea field is enabled (not 2|3)
- form—A reference to the form object containing the textarea field (not 2|3)
- name—A string value containing the name of the textarea element
- type—A string value reflecting the type of the textarea object (not 2|I)
- value—A string value containing the value of the textarea element

Methods

- focus()—Emulates the action of focusing in the textarea field
- blur()—Emulates the action of removing focus from the textarea field
- select()—Emulates the action of selecting the text in the textarea field

Event Handlers

- onKeyUp—Specifies the JavaScript code to execute when the user releases a specific key (Netscape Navigator 4.0 only) (4)
- onKeyPress—Specifies the JavaScript code to execute when the user holds down a specific key (Netscape Navigator 4.0 only) (4)
- onKeyDown—Specifies the JavaScript code to execute when the user presses a specific key (Netscape Navigator 4.0 only) (4)

- onBlur—Specifies the JavaScript code to execute when focus is removed from the field
- onChange—Specifies the JavaScript code to execute when the content of the field is changed
- onFocus—Specifies the JavaScript code to execute when focus is given to the field
- onSelect—Specifies the JavaScript code to execute when the user selects some or all of the text in the field

The *window* Object [2|3|I]

The window object is the top-level object for each window or frame and the parent object for the document, location, and history objects.

Properties

- defaultStatus—A string value containing the default value displayed in the status bar.
- frames—An array of objects for each frame in a window. Frames appear in the array in the order in which they appear in the HTML source code.
- innerHeight()—Specifies the vertical size of the content area (in pixels). New in JavaScript 1.2.
- innerWidth()—Specifies the horizontal size of the content area (in pixels). New in JavaScript 1.2.
- length—An integer value indicating the number of frames in a parent window. (Not I)
- name—A string value containing the name of the window or frame.
- opener—A reference to the window object containing the open() method used to open the current window. (Not 2|I)
- pageXOffset—Specifies the current x position of the viewable window area (expressed in pixels). New in JavaScript 1.2.
- pageYOffset—Specifies the current y position of the viewable window area (expressed in pixels). New in JavaScript 1.2.
- parent—A string indicating the name of the window containing the frameset.
- personalbar [visible=true,false]—Represents the Directories bar in Netscape Navigator and whether it's visible. New in JavaScript 1.2.
- scrollbars [visible=true,false]—Represents the scrollbars of the instant window and whether they are visible. New in JavaScript 1.2.
- self—An alternative for the name of the current window.
- status—Used to display a message in the status bar; it's done by assigning values to this property.
- statusbar=[true,false,1,0]—Specifies whether the status bar of the target window is visible.

- ▓ toolbar=[true,false,1,0]—Specifies whether the toolbar of the target window is visible.
- ▓ top—An alternative for the name of the topmost window.
- ▓ window—An alternative for the name of the current window.

Methods

- ▓ alert(*message*)—Displays *message* in a dialog box.
- ▓ back()—Sends the user back to the previous URL stored in the history list. (Simulates a user clicking the Back button in Navigator.) New in JavaScript 1.2.
- ▓ blur()—Removes focus from the window. On many systems, it sends the window to the background. (not 2|I)
- ▓ captureEvents()—Used in a window with frames (along with enableExternalCapture), it specifies that the window will capture all specified events.
- ▓ clearInterval(*intervalID*)—Cancels timeouts created with the setInterval method. New in JavaScript 1.2.
- ▓ close()—Closes the window. (not I)
- ▓ confirm(*message*)—Displays *message* in a dialog box with OK and Cancel buttons. Returns true or false based on the button clicked by the user.
- ▓ disableExternalCapture()—Prevents the instant window with frames from capturing events occurring in pages loaded from a different location. New in JavaScript 1.2.
- ▓ enableExternalCapture()—Enables the instant window (with frames) to capture events occurring in pages loaded from a different location. New in JavaScript 1.2.
- ▓ find([string], [true, false], [true, false])—Finds string in the target window. There are two true/false parameters: The first specifies the Boolean state of case sensitivity in the search; the second specifies whether the search is performed backward. New in JavaScript 1.2.
- ▓ focus()—Gives focus to the window. On many systems, it brings the window to the front. (not 2|I)
- ▓ forward()—Sends the user to the next URL in the history list. (Simulates a user clicking the Forward button in Navigator.) New in JavaScript 1.2.
- ▓ home()—Sends the user to the user's Home Page URL. (For example, in a default configuration of Netscape Navigator, it sends the user to http://home.netscape.com.) New in JavaScript 1.2.
- ▓ moveBy(horizontal, vertical)—Moves the window according to the specified values horizontal and vertical. New in JavaScript 1.2.
- ▓ moveTo(*x*, *y*)—Moves the top-left corner of the window to the specified location; *x* and *y* are screen coordinates. New in JavaScript 1.2.
- ▓ navigator(*url*)—Loads *url* in the window. (Not 2|3)

- `open(url,name,features)`—Opens *url* in a window named *name*. If *name* doesn't exist, a new window is created with that name. *features* is an optional string argument containing a list of features for the new window. The feature list contains any of the following name-value pairs separated by commas and without additional spaces—(not I)

`toolbar=[yes,no,1,0]`	Indicates whether the window should have a toolbar.
`location=[yes,no,1,0]`	Indicates whether the window should have a location field.
`directories=[yes,no,1,0]`	Indicates whether the window should have directory buttons.
`status=[yes,no,1,0]`	Indicates whether the window should have a status bar.
`menubar=[yes,no,1,0]`	Indicates whether the window should have menus.
`scrollbars=[yes,no,1,0]`	Indicates whether the window should have scrollbars.
`resizable=[yes,no,1,0]`	Indicates whether the window should be resizable.
`width=pixels`	Indicates the width of the window in pixels.
`alwaysLowered=[yes,no,1,2]`	Indicates (if true) that the window should remain below all other windows. (This feature has varying results on varying window systems.) New in JavaScript 1.2. Note: The script must be signed to use this feature.
`alwaysRaised=[yes,no,1,2]`	Indicates (if true) that the window should always remain the top-level window. (This feature has varying results on varying window systems.) New in JavaScript 1.2. Note: The script must be signed to use this feature.
`dependent[yes,no,1,2]`	Indicates that the current child window will die (or close) when the parent window does. New in JavaScript 1.2.
`hotkeys=[yes,no,1,2]`	Indicates (if true) that most hot keys are disabled within the instant window. New in JavaScript 1.2.
`innerWidth=pixels`	Indicates the width (in pixels) of the instant window's content area. New in JavaScript 1.2.
`innerHeight=pixels`	Indicates the height (in pixels) of the instant window's content area. New in JavaScript 1.2.
`outerWidth=pixels`	Indicates the instant window's horizontal outside width boundary. New in JavaScript 1.2.

`outerHeight=pixels`	Indicates the instant window's horizontal outside height boundary. New in JavaScript 1.2.
`screenX=pixels`	Indicates the distance that the new window is placed from the left side of the screen (horizontally). New in JavaScript 1.2.
`screenY=pixels`	Indicates the distance that the new window is placed from the top of the screen (vertically). New in JavaScript 1.2.
`z-lock=[yes,no,1,2]`	Indicates that the instant window does not move through the cycling of the z-order; that is, it doesn't rise above other windows, even if activated. New in JavaScript 1.2. Note: The script must be signed for this feature to work.
`height=pixels`	Indicates the height of the window in pixels.

- `print()`—Prints the contents of a frame or window. It's the equivalent of the user pressing the Print button in Netscape Navigator. New in JavaScript 1.2.

- `prompt(message,response)`—Displays *message* in a dialog box with a text entry field with the default value of *response*. The user's response in the text entry field is returned as a string.

- `releaseEvents(eventType)`—Specifies that the current window should release events instead of capturing them so that these events can be passed to other objects, perhaps further on in the event hierarchy. New in JavaScript 1.2.

- `resizeBy(horizontal, vertical)`—Resizes the window, moving from the bottom-right corner. New in JavaScript 1.2.

- `resizeTo(outerWidth, outerHeight)`—Resizes the window, using `outerWidth` and `outerHeight` properties. New in JavaScript 1.2.

- `routeEvent(event)`—Sends or routes an event through the normal event hierarchy. New in JavaScript 1.2.

- `scrollBy(horizontal, vertical)`—Scroll the viewing area of the current window by the specified amount. New in JavaScript 1.2.

- `scrollTo(x, y)`—Scrolls the current window to the specified position, calculated in x,y coordinates, starting at the top-left corner of the window. New in JavaScript 1.2.

- `setInterval(function, msec, [args])`—Repeatedly calls a function after the period specified by the `msec` parameter. New in JavaScript 1.2.

- `setInterval(expression, msec)`—Evaluates *expression* after the period specified by the `msec` parameter. New in JavaScript 1.2.

- `setTimeout(expression,time)`—Evaluates *expression* after *time*, which is a value in milliseconds. The timeout can be named with the following structure:

  `name = setTimeOut(expression,time)`

- `scrollTo(x,y)`—Scrolls the window to the coordinate *x,y*. (not 2|I)

- `stop()`—Stops the current download. It's the equivalent of the user pressing the Stop button in Netscape Navigator.

- `clearTimeout(name)`—Cancels the timeout with the name *name*.

Event Handlers

- `onDragDrop`—Specifies the JavaScript code to execute when the user drops an object onto the window. (Netscape Navigator 4.0 and higher only) (4.0)

- `onBlur`—Specifies the JavaScript code to execute when focus is removed from a window. (not 2|I)

- `onError`—Specifies the JavaScript code to execute when a JavaScript error occurs while loading a document. It can be used to intercept JavaScript errors. Setting this event handler to `null` effectively prevents JavaScript errors from being displayed to the user. (not 2|I)

- `onFocus`—Specifies the JavaScript code to execute when the window receives focus. (not 2|I)

- `onLoad`—Specifies the JavaScript code to execute when the window or frame finishes loading.

- `onMove`—Specifies the JavaScript code to execute when the user moves a window. (Netscape Navigator 4.0 only)

- `onResize`—Specifies the JavaScript code to execute when a user resizes the window.

- `onUnload`—Specifies the JavaScript code to execute when the document in the window or frame is exited.

Independent Functions, Operators, Variables, and Literals

The following subsections describe the functions, operators, variables, and literals that are built in to JavaScript, without being attached to a specific JavaScript object.

Independent Functions

- `escape(character)`—Returns a string containing the ASCII encoding of *character* in the form %xx; xx is the numeric encoding of the character. (2|3|I)

- `eval(expression)`—Returns the result of evaluating *expression*, which is an arithmetic expression. (2|3|I)

- `isNaN(value)`—Evaluates *value* to see if it's NaN. Returns a Boolean value. (2|3|I) (On UNIX platforms, not 2)

- `parseFloat(string)`—Converts *string* to a floating-point number and returns the value. It continues to convert until it hits a non-numeric character and then returns the result. If the first character can't be converted to a number, the function returns NaN (zero on Windows platforms). (2|3|I)

- parseInt(*string*,*base*)—Converts *string* to an integer of base *base* and returns the value. It continues to convert until it hits a non-numeric character and then returns the result. If the first character can't be converted to a number, the function returns NaN (zero on Windows platforms). (2|3|I)

- taint(*propertyName*)—Adds tainting to *propertyName*. (3)

- toString()—This is a method of all objects. It returns the object as a string or returns "[object *type*]" if no string representation exists for the object. (2|3) Note: In JavaScript 1.2, it converts objects and strings into literals.

- unescape(*string*)—Returns a character based on the ASCII encoding contained in *string*. The ASCII encoding should take the form "%integer" or "hexadecimalValue". (2|3|I)

- untaint(*propertyName*)—Removes tainting from *propertyName*. (3)

Statements

- break—Terminates a while or for loop and passes program control to the first statement following the loop. (2|3|4) Note: In JavaScript 1.2, break has the added functionality of being able to break out of labeled statements.

- comment—Used to add a comment within the script. This comment is ignored by Navigator. Comments in JavaScript work similarly to those in C. They are enclosed in a /* (start), */ (end) structure. (2|3|4)

- continue—Terminates execution of statements in a while or for loop and continues iteration of the loop. (2|3|4) Note: In JavaScript 1.2, continue has added functionality that enables you to continue within labeled statements.

- do while: Sets up a loop that continues to execute statements and code until the condition evaluates to false. New in JavaScript 1.2.

- export—Used with the import statement. In secure, signed scripts, it enables the developer to export all properties, functions, and variables to another script. New in JavaScript 1.2.

- for([*initial-expression*]; [*condition*]; [*incremental-expression*];))—Specifies the opening of a for loop. The arguments are these: initialize a variable (*initial-expression*), create a condition to test for (*condition*), and specify an incrementation scheme (*incremental-expression*). (2|3|4)

- for...in—Imposes a variable to all properties of an object and executes a block of code for each. (2|3|4)

- function [*name*]()—Declares a function so that it can be referred to or reached by event handlers (or other processes). (2|3|4)

- if...else—A structure used to test whether a certain condition is true. If...else blocks can contain nested statements and functions (and call them) if a condition is either true or false. (2|3|4)

- `import`—Used with the `export` statement. In secure, signed scripts, it enables the developer to import all properties, functions, and variables from another script. New in JavaScript 1.2.

- `label (labeled statements)`—Statement that creates a label or pointer to code elsewhere in the script. By calling this label, you redirect the script to the labeled statement.

- `new`—Creates an instance of a user-defined object. (It can also be used to create an instance of built-in objects, inherent to JavaScript, such as new `Date`.) (2|3|4)

- `return [value]`—Specifies a value to be returned by a given function. For example, `return x` returns the variable value associated with *x*. (2|3|4)

- `switch`—Evaluates an expression and attempts to match it to a `case` pattern or label. If the expression matches the `case`, trailing statements associated with that label are executed. New in JavaScript 1.2. (Operates similarly to the `switch` statement in C shell syntax.)

- `this`—A statement used to refer to a specific object, as shown in this example: [2|3|4]
  `onClick = 'javascript:my_function(this.form)'`

- `var [name]`—Declares a variable by `name`. (2|3|4)

- `while`—Statement that begins a `while` loop. `while` loops specify that as long as (while) a condition is true, execute some code. (2|3|4)

- `with`—Statement that sets the value for the default object; a method that's similar to creating a global variable with a function. (2|3|4)

Operators

- **Assignment Operators:** See Table A.1. (2|3|I)

Table A.1 Assignment Operators in JavaScript

Operator	Description
`=`	assigns the value of the right operand to the left operand
`+=`	adds the left and right operands and assigns the result to the left operand
`-=`	subtracts the right operand from the left operand and assigns the result to the left operand
`*=`	multiplies the two operands and assigns the result to the left operand
`/=`	divides the left operand by the right operand and assigns the value to the left operand
`%=`	divides the left operand by the right operand and assigns the remainder to the left operand

■ **Arithmetic Operators:** See Table A.2. (2|3|I)

Table A.2 Arithmetic Operators in JavaScript

Operator	Description
+	adds the left and right operands
-	subtracts the right operand from the left operand
*	multiplies the two operands
/	divides the left operand by the right operand
%	divides the left operand by the right operand and evaluates to the remainder
++	increments the operand by one (can be used before or after the operand)
- -	decreases the operand by one (can be used before or after the operand)
-	changes the sign of the operand

■ Bitwise Operators—Bitwise operators deal with their operands as binary numbers, but return JavaScript numerical value. (See Table A.3.) (2|3|I)

Table A.3 Bitwise Operators in JavaScript

Operator	Description
AND (or &)	Converts operands to integers with 32 bits, pairs the corresponding bits, and returns one for each pair of ones. Returns zero for any other combination.
OR (or ¦)	Converts operands to integers with 32 bits, pairs the corresponding bits, and returns one for each pair when one of the two bits is one. Returns zero if both bits are zero.
XOR (or ^)	Converts operands to integer with 32 bits, pairs the corresponding bits, and returns one for each pair when only one bit is one. Returns zero for any other combination.
<<	Converts the left operand to an integer with 32 bits and shifts bits to the left the number of bits indicated by the right operand. Bits shifted off to the left are discarded, and zeros are shifted in from the right.
>>>	Converts the left operand to an integer with 32 bits and shifts bits to the right the number of bits indicated by the right operand. Bits shifted off to the right are discarded, and zeros are shifted in from the left.
>>	Converts the left operand to an integer with 32 bits and shifts bits to the right the number of bits indicated by the right operand. Bits shifted off to the right are discarded, and copies of the leftmost bit are shifted in from the left.

■ Logical Operators—See Table A.4. (2|3|I)

Table A.4   Logical Operators in JavaScript

Operator	Description
&&	Logical AND. Returns true when both operands are true; otherwise, it returns false.
||	Logical OR. Returns true if either operand is true. It returns false only when both operands are false.
!	Logical NOT. Returns true if the operand is false and false if the operand is true. This is a unary operator and precedes the operand.

■ Comparison Operators—See Table A.5. [2|3|I]

Table A.5   Logical (Comparison) Operators in JavaScript

Operator	Description
==	returns true if the operands are equal
!=	returns true if the operands are not equal
>	returns true if the left operand is greater than the right operand
<	returns true if the left operand is less than the right operand
>=	returns true if the left operand is greater than or equal to the right operand
<=	returns true if the left operand is less than or equal to the right operand

■ Conditional Operators—Conditional expressions take one form:

```
(condition) ? val1 : val2
```

If condition is true, the expression evaluates to val1; otherwise, it evaluates to val2. (2|3|I)

■ String Operators—The concatenation operator (+) is one of two string operators. It evaluates to a string combining the left and right operands. The concatenation assignment operator (+=) is also available. (2|3|I)

■ The typeof Operator—The typeof operator returns the type of its single operand. Possible types are object, string, number, boolean, function, and undefined. (3|I)

■ The void Operator—The void operator takes an expression as an operand but returns no value. (3)

■ Operator Precedence—JavaScript applies the rules of operator precedence as follows (from lowest to highest precedence):

Comma (,)

Assignment operators (=, +=, -=, *=, /=, %=)

Conditional (? :)

Logical OR (¦¦)

Logical AND (&&)

Bitwise OR (¦)

Bitwise XOR (^)

Bitwise AND (&)

Equality (==, !=)

Relational (<, <=, >, >=)

Shift (<<, >>, >>>)

Addition/subtraction (+, -)

Multiply/divide/modulus (*, /, %)

Negation/increment (!, -, ++, --)

Call, member ((), [])

What's on the CD-ROM

Source Code from the Book

Complete examples and listings from the book are included on the CD-ROM. All examples are organized by chapter for ease of use.

Virtual Reference Library of Books on Related Topics

- *Special Edition Using HTML 4.0, Fifth Edition*
- *Special Edition Using Java 1.2*
- *Special Edition Using FrontPage98*
- *Special Edition Using Active Server Pages*
- *Sams Teach Yourself JBuilder 2 in 21 Days*

Que's Internet Knowledgebase

Valuable information for Web authors that has been compiled into a handy, searchable database containing material from six best-selling Que titles.

Third-Party Software

Audio Utilities

- Syntrillium Cool Edit Pro 1.0 Demo
- Midigate
- Mod4Win 2.3
- WHAM 1.31
- WPLANY 1.2

Multimedia Utilities

- Nettoob Stream 3.5 Duplexx Software
- Macromedia Flash 2
- Microsoft Media Player

Browsers

- Netscape Navigator
- Microsoft Internet Explorer

CGI Perl Tool

- PerlBuilder 30 day trial

What's on the CD-ROM

Compression Utilities

- WinZip 6.3
- Stuffit Expander 4.01

FTP Clients

- Cute FTP 2.5
- WS_FTP Pro 30 day trial

Graphics Applications

- Paint Shop Pro 5.01 30 day trial
- ACDSee 2.3
- WinJPEG 2.8 shareware for Windows 3.x
- Mapedit 2.43 30 day trial

3D Software

- Strata Vision3d Demo
- Caligari Truespace 4 Trial

Webcasting Helpers

- Marimba Castanet Publisher 2
- Marimba Castanet Transmitter 2
- Netscape Netcaster (included with Netscape Communicator 4.5)

Application Development Tool

- Allaire ColdFusion Studio 4 30 day trial

HTML Tools

- Sausage Software Hotdog Pro 5.1
- Brooklyn North HTML Assistant Pro 97 Demo
- BBEdit Lite 4
- Various Microsoft Internet Assistants
- Webber Active 4 Demo
- Freeway 2 60 day trial

XML Tool

- XML<PRO> 1.2 Demo

Java Tools

- JDesigner Pro 3
- JFactory 1.1 Demo
- JTools 2.0 Demo
- JWidgets 2.1 Demo
- KAWA 3
- Snaglet Pack

Plugin

- Shockwave

ISP

- Earthlink Total Access

Graphics Collection

- Button Collection from Andy Evans

Documentation

- HTML 4.0 Specification
- HTML 4.0 Tag Reference (from book)
- RFCs 1865, 1945, and 2068
- CSS Specification
- XML Specification
- XLL Specification
- XSL Specification
- DSSSL Specification
- PNG Specification
- VBScript Tutorial
- VBScript FAQ
- VBScript Language Reference
- JavaScript Language Reference
- JavaScript Guide
- HTTP 1.1 Specification
- Netscape DHTML Guide
- Microsoft DHTML FAQ
- Java FAQ
- JDK API Documentation
- JDK Guide to New Features

Index

C

Other Related Titles

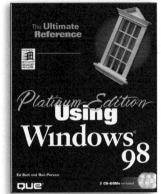

Platinum Edition Using Windows 98
Ron Person
ISBN: **0789714892**
$49.99 US/$71.95 CAN

Special Edition Using Visual InterDev 6
Steve Banick
ISBN: **078971549X**
$39.99 US/$57.95 CAN

Special Edition Using Windows 98
Ed Bott
ISBN: **0789714884**
$39.99 US/$57.95 CAN

Special Edition Using Visual C++ 6
Kate Gregory
ISBN: **0789715392**
$39.99 US/$57.95 CAN

Special Edition Using NetObjects Fusion 3
Mary Gillen
ISBN: **0789716712**
$39.99 US/$57.95 CAN

Special Edition Using Visual Basic 6
Jeff Spotts; Brian Siler
ISBN: **0789715422**
$39.99 US/$57.95 CAN

Special Edition Using Microsoft Office 97 With Windows 98
Ed Bott
ISBN: **0789716615**
$39.99 US/$57.95 CAN

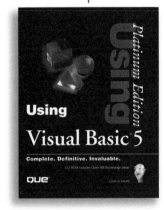

Platinum Edition Using Visual Basic 5
Loren Eidahl
ISBN: **0789714124**
$60.00 US/$85.95 CAN

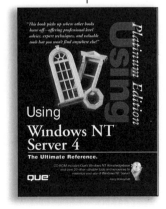

Platinum Edition Using Windows NT Server 4
Jerry Honeycutt
ISBN: **0789714361**
$65.00 US/$93.95 CAN

www.quecorp.com

All prices are subject to change.

What's on the CD-ROM

Source Code from the Book

Complete examples and listings from the book.

Virtual Reference Library of Books on Related Topics

- *Special Edition Using HTML 4.0, Fifth Edition*
- *Special Edition Using Java 1.2*
- *Special Edition Using FrontPage 98*
- *Special Edition Using Active Server Pages*
- *Sams Teach Yourself JBuilder 2 in 21 Days*

Que's Internet Knowledgebase

Valuable information for Web authors that has been compiled into a handy searchable database containing material from six best-selling Que titles.

Third-Party Software

- Audio Utilities
- Multimedia Utility
- Browsers
- CGI Perl
- Compression Utilities
- FTP Clients
- Graphics Applications
- 3D Software
- Webcasting Helpers
- Application Development Tool
- HTML Tools
- Java Tools
- Graphics Collections
- Various Documentation and Specifications

▶ For more detailed information about the CD-ROM, **see** "What's on the CD-ROM," **p. 1217**.

Other Related Titles

HTML Goodies
Joe Burns
ISBN: 0789718235
$19.99 US/$28.95 CAN

Using HTML 4, Fourth Edition
Lee anne Phillips
ISBN: 0789715627
$29.99 US/$42.95 CAN

Complete Idiot's Guide to Java
Michael Morrison
ISBN: 0789718049
$16.99 US/$24.95 CAN

Sams' Teach Yourself JBuilder 2 in 21 Days
Don Doherty
ISBN: 0672313189
$39.99 US/$57.95 CAN

Using Visual J++ 6
Scott Mulloy
ISBN: 0789714000
$29.99 US/$42.95 CAN

Special Edition Using Microsoft FrontPage 98
Neil Randall
ISBN: 0789713438
$49.99 US/$71.95 CAN

Special Edition Using Java 1.2
Joe Weber
ISBN: 0789715295
$39.99 US/$57.95 CAN

Special Edition Using HTML 4, Fifth Edition
Molly Holzschlag
ISBN: 0789718510
$39.99 US/$57.95 CAN

Sams' Teach Yourself Web Publishing with HTML 4 in 21 Days, Professional Reference
Laura Lemay
ISBN: 0672314088
$49.99 US/$71.95 CAN

Sams' Teach Yourself Java 1.2 in 21 Days
Laura Lemay
ISBN: 1575213907
$29.99 US/$42.95 CAN

Sams' Teach Yourself CGI Programming in a Week
Rafe Coburn
ISBN: 1575213818
$29.99 US/$42.95 CAN

www.quecorp.com

All prices are subject to change.